Timeline for Application/Admission

AAMC

This should be considered a general guide for applicants. It is important that an applicant considering medical school consult with his or her pre-health advisor to devise a schedule that works for him or her.

COLLEGE YEAR 1
- **Fall semester**
  - Meet pre-health advisor and investigate pre-health advisory program
  - As applicable, ensure that pre-health advisor receives course directors' evaluations
  - Successfully complete first-semester required premedical coursework and other degree requirements
- **Spring semester**
  - Visit "Considering a Career in Medicine" Web site at *www.aamc.org/students*
  - Identify summer employment/volunteer medically related opportunities
  - Successfully complete second-semester required premedical coursework and other degree requirements
  - Ensure that pre-health advisor receives course directors' evaluations

SUMMER 1
- Complete summer employment/volunteer medically related experience
- Attend summer school, if desired or necessary

COLLEGE YEAR 2
- **Fall semester**
  - Check in with pre-health advisor and participate in pre-health activities
  - Investigate available volunteer/paid medically related clinical or research activities
  - Successfully complete first-semester required premedical coursework and other degree requirements
  - Ensure that pre-health advisor receives course directors' evaluations
- **Spring semester**
  - Check in with pre-health advisor and participate in pre-health activities
  - Participate in volunteer/paid medically related clinical or research activities
  - Identify summer employment/volunteer medically related opportunities
  - Successfully complete second-semester required premedical coursework and other degree requirements
  - Ensure that pre-health advisor receives course directors' evaluations

SUMMER 2
- Complete summer employment/volunteer medically related experience
- Participate in a summer health careers program, if available
- Attend summer school, if desired or necessary

COLLEGE YEAR 3
- **Fall semester**
  - Check in with pre-health advisor and participate in pre-health activities
  - Continue participation in volunteer/paid medically related activities
  - Investigate:
    - Medical education options in MSAR and *www.aamc.org/members/listings/msalphaae.htm*
    - Medical College Admission Test (MCAT®) Web site *www.aamc.org/mcat*
    - Information about the Medical College Admission Test (MCAT®) and American Medical College Application Service (AMCAS) fee assistance on the AAMC Fee Assistance Program Web site *www.aamc.org/fap*, as appropriate
    - AAMC's "Applying to Medical School" Web site *www.aamc.org/students/applying/start.htm*
    - As applicable, information for students from groups underrepresented in medicine on the AAMC Minorities in Medicine Web site *www.aamc.org/students/minorities/start.htm*
  - Begin preparation and register for desired MCAT® administration; visit MCAT® web site *www.aamc.org/mcat* for available test date options
  - Successfully complete first-semester required premedical coursework and other degree requirements
  - Ensure that pre-health advisor receives course directors' evaluations
- **Spring semester**
  - Consult regularly with pre-health advisor regarding:
    - Schedule for completion of school-specific requirements for advisor/committee evaluation
    - Advice about medical education options
  - Continue participation in volunteer/paid medically related activities
  - Prepare for and take desired MCAT® administration; visit MCAT® web site *www.aamc.org/mcat* for available test date options

continued...

COLLEGE YEAR 3	o Continue review of medical education options o Take desired MCAT® administration. Registration opens for summer MCAT® administrations o Investigate information about medical school application services: • the American Medical College Application Service (AMCAS) on the AMCAS Web site *www.aamc.org/amcas* • the Texas Medical and Dental Schools Application Service (TMDSAS) on the TMDSAS Web site *www.utsystem.edu/tmdsas/* • the Ontario Medical School Application Service (OMSAS) on the OMSAS Web site *www.ouac.on.ca/* • the American Association of Colleges of Osteopathic Medicine Application Service (AACOMAS) on the AACOMAS Web site *https://aacomas.aacom.org/* o Investigate as applicable, the AAMC Curriculum Directory Web site *http://services.aamc.org/currdir* for information about medical school curricula and joint, dual, and combined-degree programs o Successfully complete second-semester required premedical coursework and other degree requirements o Ensure that pre-health advisor receives course directors' evaluations
SUMMER 3	• Participate in a summer health careers program, if available • Complete AMCAS application • Take desired MCAT® administration • Attend summer school, if desired or necessary • Become familiar with: o AAMC Recommendations for Medical School Applicants document *www.aamc.org/students/applying/policies* o AAMC Recommendations for Medical School Admission Officers document *www.aamc.org/students/applying/policies*
COLLEGE YEAR 4	• **Fall semester** o Complete supplementary application materials for schools applied to o Consult regularly with pre-health advisor regarding: • Completion of school-specific requirements for advisor/committee evaluation • Status of application/admission process at medical schools applied to o Continue participation in volunteer/paid medically related activities o Interview at medical schools o Continue review of medical education options o Investigate financial aid planning process o Successfully complete first-semester elective science and non-science coursework and other degree requirements o Ensure that pre-health advisor receives course directors' evaluations • **Spring semester** o Make interim and final decisions about medical school choice o Immediately notify medical schools which you will not be attending o Ensure that all IRS forms are submitted as early as possible for financial aid consideration o Successfully complete second-semester elective science and non-science coursework and other degree requirements o Graduate
SUMMER 4	o Prepare for medical school enrollment: purchase books and equipment and make appropriate living arrangements o Relax and prepare for medical school o Attend orientation programs and matriculate at medical school

AAMC
Tomorrow's Doctors, Tomorrow's Cures®

Medical School Admission Requirements (MSAR®)
The Most Authoritative Guide to U.S. and Canadian Medical Schools

Serve the community

Help the underserved

Prevent disease

Stop suffering

Find cures

Includes Newly Accredited Medical Schools

The Commonwealth Medical College
Oakland University William Beaumont School of Medicine
Virginia Tech Carilion School of Medicine

Association of
American Medical Colleges

Medical School Admission
Requirements, 2011–2012,
United States and Canada

AAMC Staff

MSAR® Guide Program Staff
Tami Levin,
Senior Web and Technology Specialist
Academic Affairs

Kim Reed,
Web and MSAR Content Specialist
Academic Affairs

Deborah Finkel,
Senior Writer, Communications

Douglas Ortiz,
Director, Creative Services

Content Specialist
Henry M. Sondheimer, M.D.,
Senior Director,
Student Affairs and Programs
Academic Affairs

Consultants
Kelly Begatto,
Program Director, AMCAS
Mission Support

Susan Gaillard,
Database Specialist
Mission Support

Gwen Garrison, Ph.D.,
Director, Student and Applicant Studies
Mission Support

Lily May Johnson,
Manager, Constituent Diversity Services
Office of the Executive Vice President

Jack Krakower, Ph.D.,
Senior Director, Med School Financial and
Administrative Affairs
Mission Support

Jodi Lubetsky, Ph.D.,
Manager, Science Policy
Scientific Affairs

David A. Matthew, Ph.D.,
Senior Research Analyst,
Student and Applicant Studies
Mission Support

H. Collins Mikesell,
Senior Research Analyst,
Student and Applicant Studies
Mission Support

Karen Mitchell,
Senior Director,
Admissions Testing Services
Mission Support

Nancy-Pat Weaver,
Senior Education Debt Management
Specialist
Academic Affairs

Shelley Yerman,
Senior Specialist, Student Financial Aid
Academic Affairs

**To order additional copies of this
publication, please contact:**
Association of American
Medical Colleges
Publications Department
2450 N Street, NW
Washington, DC 20037
Phone: 202-828-0416
Fax: 202-828-1123
E-mail: *publications@aamc.org*
Web site: *www.aamc.org/publications*

Price: $25.00, plus $8 shipping
(single copy)
*Copyright 2010 by the Association of
American Medical Colleges.*

ISBN 978-1-57754-093-9

Printed in the United States of America
Revised annually; new edition available in
early spring.

Group on Student Affairs (GSA) Steering Committee, 2009–2010

Chair
Michael G. Kavan, Ph.D.
Associate Dean for Student Affairs
Creighton University
School of Medicine

Chair Elect
Maureen Garrity, Ph.D.
Associate Dean for Student Affairs
University of Colorado
School of Medicine

Vice Chair
Patricia A. Barrier, M.D., M.P.H.
Associate Dean for Student Affairs
Mayo Medical School

Immediate Past Chair
Molly Osborne, M.D., Ph.D.
Associate Dean for Student Affairs
Oregon Health & Science University
School of Medicine

Previous Past Chair
Georgette A. Dent, M.D.
Associate Dean for Student Affairs
University of North Carolina
School of Medicine

Chair, Central Region
Kathleen J. Kashima, Ph.D.
Senior Associate Dean, Student Affairs
University of Illinois at Chicago
College of Medicine

Chair, Southern Region
Stacey R. McCorison
Associate Dean, Medical Education
Administration
Duke University School of Medicine

Chair, Northeast Region
Thomas W. Koenig, M.D.
Associate Dean for Student Affairs
Johns Hopkins University
School of Medicine

Chair, Western Region
Eve L. Espey, M.D., M.P.H.
Associate Dean of Students
Assistant Professor Department of OB-GYN
University of New Mexico
School of Medicine

Chair, Committee on Admissions
Steven Case, Ph.D., M.S.
Associate Dean for Admissions
University of Mississippi
School of Medicine

Chair, Committee on Diversity Affairs
Karen A. Lewis
Assistant Vice President for Enrollment
Management Student Services
Meharry Medical College

Chair, Committee on Student Affairs
Samuel K. Parrish, M.D.
Associate Dean for Student Affairs
Drexel University
College of Medicine

Chair, Committee on Student Financial Assistance
Robert D. Coughlin
Director of Financial Aid
Harvard Medical School

Chair, Committee on Student Records
Chris Meiers
Assistant Dean of Students Registrar
University of Kansas
School of Medicine

Council of Deans Liaison
Jay Perman, M.D.
Dean, College of Medicine
Vice President for Clinical Affairs
University of Kentucky
College of Medicine

Chair, Organization of Student Representatives
Catherine Spina
Student
Boston University
School of Medicine

National Association of Advisors for the Health Professions
Jeremiah L. Putnam, Ph.D.
Chief Health Professions Advisor
Davidson College

Association of American Medical Colleges

The Association of American Medical Colleges (AAMC) has as its purpose the advancement of medical education and the nation's health. In pursuing this purpose, the Association works with many national and international organizations, institutions, and individuals interested in strengthening the quality of medical education at all levels, searching for biomedical knowledge, and applying these tools to providing effective health care.

As an educational association representing members with similar purposes, the primary role of the AAMC is to assist those members by providing services at the national level that will facilitate the accomplishment of their missions. Such activities include collecting data and conducting studies on issues of major concern, evaluating the quality of educational programs through the accreditation process, providing consultation and technical assistance to institutions as needs are identified, synthesizing the opinions of an informed membership for consideration at the national level, and improving communication among those concerned with medical education and the nation's health. Other activities of the Association reflect the expressed concerns and priorities of the officers and governing bodies.

The Association of American Medical Colleges is a not-for-profit association representing all 132 accredited U.S. and 17 accredited Canadian medical schools; nearly 400 major teaching hospitals and health systems, including 68 Department of Veterans Affairs medical centers; and nearly 90 academic and scientific societies. Through these institutions and organizations, the AAMC represents 125,000 faculty members, 70,000 medical students, and 104,000 resident physicians.

In addition to the activities listed above, the AAMC is responsible for the Medical College Admission Test (MCAT®) and the American Medical College Application Service (AMCAS®) and provides detailed admissions information to the medical schools and to undergraduate premedical advisors.

Important Notice

The information in this book is based on the most recent data provided by member medical schools prior to publication at the request of the Association of American Medical Colleges (AAMC).

This material has been edited and in some instances condensed to meet space limitations. In compiling this edition, the AAMC made every reasonable effort to assure the accuracy and timeliness of the information, and, except where noted, the information was updated as of January 2009. All information contained herein, however, especially figures on tuition and expenses, is subject to change and is non-binding for medical schools listed or the AAMC. All medical schools listed in this edition, as with other educational institutions, are also subject to federal and state laws prohibiting discrimination on the basis of race, color, religion, sex, age, handicap, or national origin. Such laws include Title VI of the Civil Rights Act of 1964, Title IX of the Education Amendments of 1972, Section 504 of the Rehabilitation Act of 1973, the Americans with Disabilities Act, and the Age Discrimination Act of 1975, as amended. For the most current and complete information regarding costs, official policies, procedures, and other matters, individual schools should be contacted.

In applying to U.S. or Canadian medical schools, applicants need not go through any commercial agencies. The AAMC does not endorse any organization or entity that purports to assist applicants to achieve admission to medical school other than undergraduate pre-medical advisors and medical school admissions officers.

All URLs in this book can be found at *www.aamc.org/msar.*

AAMC Commitment to Diversity

Diversity within medical education and the physician workforce is essential to the health of the nation. The benefits of diversity in medicine will continue to increase as the nation ages, becomes more diverse along many dimensions, and experiences inequities in health care. The AAMC's commitment to diversity in medicine and biomedical research spans more than three decades and is demonstrated by ongoing leadership and engagement in activities that promote diversity through programs, advocacy, and research. This commitment has

been reaffirmed in the publication Learn, Serve, Lead: The Mission, Vision, and Strategic Priorities of the AAMC, which states that the AAMC's mission is to serve and lead the academic medicine community to improve the health of all. To support its mission, AAMC's vision and that of its members is, in part, to establish "…a healthy nation and world in which… [t]he nation's medical students, biomedical graduate students, residents, fellows, faculty, and the health care workforce are diverse and culturally competent…." As a result, leading efforts to increase diversity in medicine is among the AAMC's nine strategic priorities.

To achieve this end, the AAMC works with its members to:

- advance diversity in academic medicine and biomedical research that fully embraces the diversity of the nation;

- generate and coordinate research, collect evidence, and disseminate studies pertinent to diversity in academic medicine and biomedical research;

- lead policy and advocacy efforts for diversity in academic medicine and biomedical research;

- direct pipeline programs and services across the education continuum to increase diversity in academic medicine and biomedical research;

- communicate the relationship of diversity in medicine and biomedical research to ameliorating disparities in health and health access outcomes; and

- supply resources and guidance to educators seeking to maximize the benefits of diversity across the medical education continuum.

Contents

List of Tables and Charts

Alphabetical Listing of Medical Schools

Geographical Listing of Medical Schools

Florida

Maybe it was the great feeling you had from volunteering, or the profound concern stirred by a family member's illness that made you first think seriously about becoming a doctor. Or, perhaps it was the thrill you experienced solving a complex research problem that inspired you to dream about finding the next "big cure." Whatever reason led you to consider a career in medicine, you have come to the right place: the Medical School Admissions Requirements (MSAR®).

Published annually by the AAMC (Association of American Medical Colleges)—the national association representing all 132 accredited U.S. and 17 accredited Canadian medical schools—the MSAR is the only medical school application guide authorized by medical schools themselves. This comprehensive resource will tell you about each school's focus, mission, and curriculum, as well as its entrance requirements and selection factors. It also will explain how, increasingly, medical schools are taking a holistic approach to admissions decisions by evaluating candidates' experiences and personal attributes in addition to their academic credentials and metrics such as the MCAT®.

Here, you will find details about financial aid and costs, and see the degree of diversity represented by 2009–10 matriculants. And, in what I think is one of the MSAR's best features, you will see that diversity reflected in the number of accepted applicants at each school who took certain premed courses, performed community service, or worked in research or other medically related positions. In other words, you will read about students who, only a few years ago, went through the same decision-making process you are undertaking now.

This year, we have made a special effort to further "demystify" the medical school application and acceptance process. For example, the book provides a more detailed description of the American Medical College Application Service® (which you will use to apply to medical school) and includes a new chapter on choosing the right school for you. We also have drawn from a wealth of data gathered by the AAMC and other sources to provide a more in-depth profile of today's medical students. Examples range from at what age these students decided to become a doctor, to the specialties they considered at the time of matriculation, to the ways they prepared for medical school.

Should you decide to apply to medical school, I think you will find it is an extraordinary time to be a doctor. You will be entering medicine at a time when the country needs your services most, given predicted physician shortages in coming years, and when national attention is focused like never before on the need to improve health care delivery. It is also a time when our profession is undergoing an exciting period of transformative change, with clinical care becoming increasingly patient-centered and team-based, biomedical research more technically sophisticated and collaborative, and medical education itself evolving into a continuum of lifelong learning.

Whatever career you decide to pursue, please accept my best wishes for success. And, if being a doctor is the path you choose, please know that the AAMC stands ready to help you. It would be a special pleasure for me if—during your education and training—our paths should cross and we have the opportunity to meet.

Darrell G. Kirch

Darrell G. Kirch, M.D.
President and CEO
Association of American Medical Colleges

Organization of Student Representatives 2009–2010

Dear Medical School Applicant,

Congratulations on your decision to pursue a career in medicine! In so doing, you've committed yourself to a challenging and exciting profession. In becoming a physician, you will learn the skills necessary to become a healer, an advocate, a lifelong learner, and a leader in your community, as you work to improve the health and well-being of your patients.

The process of applying to medical school is daunting. Learning how to navigate this time-consuming, expensive, and difficult process can be extremely frustrating. To help demystify the process and guide you through the steps necessary to successfully complete the application process, the American Association of Medical Colleges (AAMC) has created this book to help you along the way. The Medical School Admission Requirements (MSAR®) guide will provide you with the most up-to-date information about U.S. and Canadian medical schools so that you can make a well-informed decision about how and where to pursue your medical studies.

Don't forget that there is no one path to becoming a physician. Medical schools around the country are interested in applicants with a diverse set of experiences and backgrounds. If your goal is to become a doctor, stay focused, become as informed as possible about the process, and stick with it. The rewards are great.

As Chair of the AAMC Organization of Student Representatives (OSR), and on behalf of the 75,000 medical students and 106,000 resident physicians, we look forward to welcoming you into the profession as a future colleague. It's an exciting time for the health care industry with promise of reform and innovation. We hope you will join us as we commit ourselves to learn, serve and lead, while working towards improving the health of all.

Katie Spina

Katie Spina
Boston University School of Medicine
MD/PhD Candidate
2009-2010 Chair, AAMC Organization of Student Representatives

Chapter 1:
So… You Want to Be a Doctor

Maybe it was the day you won first place in your 7th grade science fair. Maybe it was the time your family physician made a saving call during your little brother's illness. Maybe it was the summer you volunteered with a health care program in an underdeveloped country.

At some point, you just knew. You wanted to be a doctor.

But, as you also undoubtedly know, you now face a major step in the journey: getting into medical school. It involves everything from completing your undergraduate preparation to taking the MCAT exam…from selecting appropriate schools to navigating the application process…from arranging for financing to performing well on the interview. Big challenges do indeed lie ahead.

But so too does the ultimate reward: a career in medicine.

An Exciting and Gratifying Career

It's something that many of you knew from an early age. In fact, a recent AAMC survey shows that almost half of all entering medical students had decided upon a medical career before they even set foot in undergraduate school—and almost one in five had made the decision before they even started high school.

When Did You Decided to Study Medicine?

Most of you knew early on that you wanted to be a doctor. According to an AAMC survey, half of all entering medical students made their decision to study medicine before they even started college:

- 19% before high school
- 28% during high school or before college
- 25% during first two years of college
- 12% during junior year of college
- 4% during senior year of college
- 10% after receiving bachelor's degree
- 2% after receiving advanced degree

Source: AAMC's 2009 Matriculating Student Questionnaire (MSQ)

And small wonder. Nowhere else can you find a career that offers as many opportunities to make a real difference in the lives of thousands of people.

You'll have job security, of course, knowing that your services will always be in demand. You'll earn an excellent living. You'll never experience the tedium of a nine-to-five desk job.

There's so much more than that, of course. As a doctor, you're likely to see new life come into the world, or provide comfort to those about to leave it. Or maybe you'll choose to help build the future of medicine by educating the next generation of physicians. Perhaps you'll dedicate yourself to discovering new cures for diseases that devastate millions of people and their families.

Whichever direction you follow, you will—either directly or indirectly—reduce or eliminate people's pain and suffering, improve their quality of life, and, in general, provide invaluable service to your local community or the country as a whole.

How many careers can even come close?

Dozens of Options from Which to Choose

The fact that you have so many options is yet another benefit of a career in medicine. From clinical practice to biomedical research, from public health to medical education—the choices are almost limitless. Beyond that, you'll also enjoy the flexibility that a medical career provides. If your interests change with time and experience, medicine—because of its emphasis on lifelong learning—will provide you with ample opportunity to refine your skills and reorient your practice. A number of possible career options are listed below:

- The satisfaction of long-term patient relationships is one attraction of **family medicine or internal medicine**, where the bulk of time is spent in direct contact with patients. Physicians in this area—which comes under the umbrella term of "primary care"—often care for entire families and enjoy the challenge that comes from treating a diverse population with varied backgrounds and conditions.

- Other physicians may prefer to pursue detailed knowledge about the intricacies of a single organ or system, such as that required of **cardiologists, ophthalmologists, dermatologists, and oncologists**.

- Interested in **scientific exploration** and the desire to **break new ground in medical knowledge**? Physicians with these traits are found in the nation's private and public laboratories and research institutions.

- Those with a commitment to social justice and an interest in fulfilling the health care needs of the underserved and disadvantaged can meet those challenges in **urban and rural clinics, in public health, or as medical missionaries**.

- Careers in **general surgery** often suit those with a desire to see immediate results of their interventions. **Plastic and reconstructive surgery** draws others with artistic skills and aesthetic interests.

- Those interested in mind-body interactions and the emotional lives of their patients might find a home in **neurology or psychiatry**.

- The fast pace of medicine draw some to work as **emergency room physicians or trauma surgeons**.

- Others motivated in the interest of national defense may use their skills as **flight surgeons or in military medicine**.

- The **economic and public policy aspects of health care** guide some physicians to think-tanks and health-related organizations, as well as to serve in the legislative and executive branches of government.

- For those fascinated by the issues facing groups of patients with age-defined illnesses and problems—from the risks of infancy and early childhood to the challenges of older life—fulfillment can come in careers as **pediatricians and geriatricians**.

- Assisting patients in overcoming complex fertility and gestational problems is the hallmark of the specialists in **reproductive endocrinology and obstetrics and gynecology**.

- Those dedicated to reducing the incidence of birth defects and inherited diseases might find their calling in the field of **medical genetics**.

- The detection, prevention, and eradication of injury and disease draw people to the fields of **preventive medicine and epidemiology**.

Clearly, the possibilities in medicine are almost endless. No matter what your personal interests, skills, or needs may be, medicine encourages you to find your niche.

How to Decide Which Path Is "Best"

Which path is right for you? With the ever-changing world of medicine and a myriad of options and practice settings, figuring out where you belong as a physician can be one of the hardest decisions of your career.

Fortunately, you won't have to make this determination alone.

That's because medical schools realize how daunting this decision can be—and the critical role they play in helping you make it. They therefore have a program in place to help you assess your personal values and interests, identify specialty options, determine personal "fit," and make a well-informed choice about your career path. This program, called Careers in Medicine™ (CiM) was developed by the Association of American Medical Colleges (AAMC) in collaboration with its 132 member medical schools, consists of four phases (described on next page) to guide you through the decision-making process.

The Careers in Medicine program is completely free-of-charge to students attending AAMC-member medical schools. For more information, go to *www.aamc.com/careersinmedicine*.

What About the Future?

As long as we're looking ahead, let's look way ahead. Five years. Ten years. Fifteen years. What will medicine look like then?

Career Intentions: Academic v. Clinical?

A relatively small—but not insignificant—percentage of matriculants plan to work in academia, and a larger percentage are undecided. Students' career intentions at the time they enter medical school are shown below.

Full-time academic faculty **9.0%**
(teaching and research)

Full-time clinical practice **61.3%**

Other **8.7%**

Undecided **21.1%**

Source: AAMC's 2009 Matriculating Student Questionnaire (MSQ)

Specialties Entering Students Are Considering

Entering medical students have a definite preference for the medical practice areas they plan to enter after graduation. The following list shows the percent of students who are considering the specialties listed below.

Specialty	Percent
Internal Medicine	17.0
Pediatrics	13.1
Surgery	10.2
Orthopedic Surgery	8.9
Emergency Medicine	8.6
Family Practice	7.6
Obstetrics and Gynecology	5.1
Neurology	4.6
Radiology	3.4
Dermatology	3.3
Neurological Surgery	3.0
Anesthesiology	2.9
Ophthalmology	2.6

Source: AAMC's 2009 Matriculating Student Questionnaire (MSQ)

Recent Advances and Future Trends

One thing is for certain. This is not your father's (or mother's*) medical career. Take a look back just a single generation, and you'll discover an abundance of fields that weren't even in the embryonic stage 25 years ago.

- An obvious example made its entrance in the early 1980s. Back then, a new—and fatal—illness was taking hold that nobody could identify. Now, though, it has a well-known name—**AIDS**—and infectious disease is currently a large medical subspecialty. As a result, significant advances have been made in extending the lives of those infected with **HIV**.

- Other advances are more recent. **Minimally invasive surgery**, in which surgeons carry out precise procedures with the assistance of a robot, is becoming increasingly more popular. It is currently used for a variety of surgeries, including those involving the lungs, esophagus, prostate, uterus, and kidneys. Through robotic-assisted surgery, patients are likely to benefit from smaller incisions, lower risk of complications, shorter hospital stays, less pain, and a speedier recovery.

* In the 1976–77 academic year, women comprised just 24.7 percent of all medical school matriculants. Compare that to 2008–09, the latest year for which data are available, in which they made up almost half—or 47.9 percent—of the entering class. Source: AAMC Data Book.

- What about the exciting advances in **personalized medicine**? A nonexistent career path for the previous generation, the technology in this field allows physicians to identify mutated genes and alert patients of their predisposition to a specific disease. (The next step—to actually treat disease with genes—is on the horizon. See section below.)

- Then there are more established fields that have evolved to take on new parameters. Take radiology, for example, which is no longer about just reading an X-ray. The radiologist can now do the actual surgery as part of a new field called **interventional radiology**.

Even more exciting, though, is what lies ahead. Genetics therapy. Portable medical records. Distance surgery. Focused medication. And more.

- Right now, physicians can diagnose predisposition to certain illnesses by identifying mutated genes. Currently in the research and development stage is the next step—**gene therapy**—in which physicians will actually kill defective genes by giving patients copies of the correct gene (which, in turn, "overtakes" the mutant gene). Early tests have been especially favorable for cystic fibrosis, in which the correct CFTR gene is transported via a harmless virus or liposome.

- Similarly, research is underway in the field of **pharmogenetics**—in which a patient's treatment is tailored according to the specific genetic code in question. For example, if a patient's genes fit a certain type of cancer code, the physician will prescribe the "matching" pharmaceutical that has been developed to destroy them—and will know, rather than hope, that the treatment is likely to work. Most forms of focused medication care involve oncology, but studies are progressing in areas of cardiology, diabetes, psychiatric disorders, and more.

- Also in development is **focused preventive care**, which, using genetic diagnosis, identifies to a very specific degree how likely a patient is to develop a certain disease or condition—and then usurps that development before it has a chance to begin.

- Other advances will be administrative in nature: The days of hunting down medical records may come to an end. One possibility being explored is a **portable medical records system**, or a national online database of individual health records. Everyone will carry a smart card (or have a microchip inserted under his or her skin!), allowing physicians to access medical records. The benefit? Errors are reduced; files can no longer be lost; delays are minimized; and the experience of having repeated—i.e., unnecessary—tests is eliminated.

- And what about the robotics-assisted surgery we mentioned earlier? It provides the foundation for the next step forward—that of **distance surgery**. One day, surgeons will operate via a computerized system that will be located hundreds, even thousands, of miles away from patients. This, of course, opens up a "world" of possibilities and opportunities, in which specialists in one country can perform surgery on patients located in another.

New Trends in the Past 25 Years	New Trends on the Horizon
Interventional Radiology	Genetics Therapy
Virtual Surgery	Focused Preventive Medicine
HIV Specialty	Pharmogenetics
Genetics Diagnosis	Portable Medical Records
	Distance Surgery

Workforce Issues

Above all, know this: Whatever specialty you choose, your services as a physician will be needed—a need that will only increase as the years move forward.

The United States is expected to face a shortage of between 124,000 and 159,000 physicians by 2025. The population is not only growing, but aging as well, and these two trends foreshadow an escalating call for medical services: First, the U.S. Census Bureau projects that the population will grow by more than 50 million between 2006 and 2025, which alone will lead to a considerable increase in the demand for physicians. Add to that the fact that as the baby boomers age, they are more likely to develop complex conditions that require more extensive medical care. Continued demand for physicians and other medical professionals is obvious.

The graph below depicts the problem the nation faces as our numbers—and our median age—increase. Still, the shortage will be experienced unevenly, and some areas will feel the effect more strongly than others. With that in mind, you may wish to consider the trends as you think about the direction you'd like your career to take.

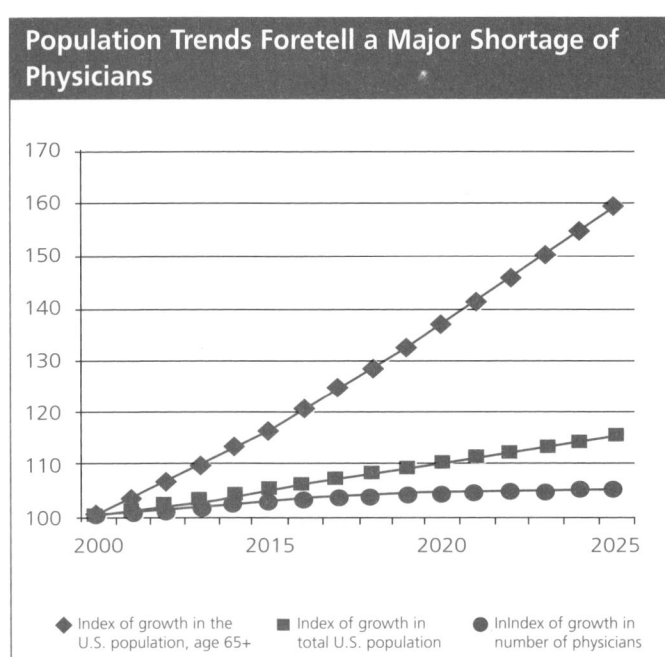

Population Trends Foretell a Major Shortage of Physicians

◆ Index of growth in the U.S. population, age 65+

■ Index of growth in total U.S. population

● InIndex of growth in number of physicians

Sources: U.S. Census Bureau, Population Division; Dill, Michael J. & Edward S. Salsberg. 2008. The Complexities of Physician Supply and Demand: Projections through 2025. AAMC: Washington, D.C.

- *Primary Care:* Although the nation is facing an overall shortage of physicians, many are particularly concerned about the growing deficit of primary care doctors. To encourage more U.S. medical school graduates to pursue a career in primary care, the government is exploring ways to more fairly value primary care efforts and lessen administrative burdens associated with general medicine. You might want to explore the rewards this specialty offers, including the satisfaction that comes from the delivery of comprehensive care and the continuity of patient relationships.

- *Underserved Areas:* In addition, the impact of this shortage is expected to be greatest on underserved areas—the urban and rural areas where health care is already scarce. If you choose to serve in a community designated as a Health Professional Shortage Area, you may be able to take advantage of a federal program—the National Health Services Corps—that offers scholarships and loan repayment. *(Learn more about this program in Chapter 11, How to Finance Your Medical Education.)*

A More Collaborative Approach

As Congress explores various scenarios as it moves toward instituting health care reform, one thing is all but certain: Given the projected shortage of physicians, we'll need to develop new models of health care delivery that make better and more efficient use of all health care professionals—not just doctors. That means you can expect to work within a more collaborative, "shared" environment, in which a team of health care providers—including physician's assistants and nurse practitioners, for example—work more in tandem. Exactly how that will play out is still in the development stages, but the idea is to create a more efficient system, increase patient satisfaction, and, ultimately, improve health incomes.

This collaborative approach to health care delivery is instilled beginning in the early years of medical education. Read more about the use of small group discussions, problem-based learning, and other educational models in Chapter 3, From Here to There: The Medical Education Process.

The Immediate Steps that Lie Ahead

That's the long-range future, or at least what we anticipate it is likely to entail. Right now, though, you're undoubtedly more fixated on the short term—getting into medical school.

So what's the process like? What lies ahead?

First, let's be candid. Getting into medical school isn't easy. (But it's definitely doable, a fact to which the more than 76,000 students currently there can testify!) You'll need to prepare for and do well on the MCAT® exam, select appropriate schools to which to apply, complete the application process, write a personal statement, gather letters of recommendation, and make it through the interview. And then you'll need to wait (…and wait… and wait) for notices of acceptance and make your final decision. On the other hand, if you're not accepted, you will need to evaluate options and determine a course of action.

All this we review in the following chapters.

But first, there are many steps you can take while still in college to make yourself a more attractive candidate to admissions committees. From taking the necessary courses, to working effectively with your pre-health advisor, to participating in extracurricular and volunteer activities that demonstrate your true interest in medicine, there's much you can do.

In the next chapter, we take a look at your undergraduate preparation.

Countdown to Medical School

The Timeline for Application and Admission, included as a tear sheet at the front of this guide, outlines in detail the steps you should take at various stages during your undergraduate years. Major components include:

- Taking the MCAT® exam
- Selecting schools to which to apply
- Investigating medical school application services
- Completing the application process
- Learning about the financial aid system
- Applying for financial aid, if necessary
- Preparing a personal statement
- Participating in interviews
- Waiting for notification(s) of acceptance
- Making a final acceptance decision

Chapter 2:
Building a Strong Foundation: Your Undergraduate Years

Your voyage to that coveted M.D. degree begins well before you set foot on a medical school campus. In reality, it starts during your undergraduate years—a time during which you'll build a foundation that will not only make you a strong candidate to medical school, but ultimately an effective physician, as well.

As a college student planning to pursue the study of medicine, you have much to accomplish. You'll need to master general academic skills, select a major and fulfill its requirements, complete all necessary premedical courses, and, ideally, pursue advanced coursework in areas of special interest. But there's more to your undergraduate years than intellectual development alone. You'll also want to participate in a variety of extracurricular activities, and cultivate the personal traits expected of a physician.

Some Ways Students Prepare for Medical School

College students take advantage of a wide variety of programs to prepare for a career in medicine or science. The following shows the percentage of students who participated in:

Program	Percent
Volunteered or worked in the health care field	93.3
MCAT preparation course	67.9
Laboratory research apprenticeship	57.1
Summer academic enrichment	13.0
Post-baccalaureate program to complete premedical requirements	8.3
Post-baccalaureate program to strengthen academic skills	6.0

Source: AAMC's 2009 Matriculating Student Questionnaire (MSQ)

And finally, you'll want to seek out someone to advise you. Although there are a number of people who can be invaluable—a professor, a current medical student, a physician, your parents—you'll certainly want to establish a relationship with a pre-health advisor.

These areas combined—academic preparation, the nurturing of desirable personal attributes, participation in extracurricular activities, and appropriate guidance—will help ready you for entry to medical school.

Academic Preparation

Much of your preparation for medical school comes in the form of academic groundwork and development, which encompasses your major field of study, the mastery of specific scientific principles, and advanced coursework. Let's take a look at each of these a bit further.

Choice of Major

Unbeknownst to many college students, there is no such thing as the "best" major for those bound for medical school. **In fact, no medical school requires a specific major of its applicants.** That's because admissions committee members know that students develop the essential skills of acquiring and synthesizing information through a wide variety of academic disciplines and therefore should be free to select whichever majors they find interesting and challenging.

Undergraduate Major: Difference in MCAT Scores?

In this phase, students consider what activities they enjoy, the values that underlie their lives and work, and the nature of their relationships with other people.

The Official Guide to the MCAT Exam®, available for purchase at *www.aamc.org/publications*, includes a chart that provides the median MCAT scores of applicants by undergraduate major. There you will see that the total median score for humanities majors, biology majors, and social sciences majors were 28.7, 27.2, and 27.1, respectively). This attests to the fact that students from any major, as long as they have the basic science preparation, are equally prepared for acceptance to medical school.

Source: Official Guide to the MCAT Exam®, 2008

Even so, many premedical students choose to major in a scientific discipline. If that's the direction you're heading, and you're doing so because you are fascinated by science and believe that such a major will be the foundation for a variety of career options, great. If you're doing so because you believe it will enhance your chances for admission, think again. Admissions committee welcome students whose intellectual curiosity leads them to a wide variety of disciplines.

And no…you won't necessarily be at a disadvantage if you choose to major in English, for example, rather than biology. Using just one measure, those of MCAT scores, you may be surprised to learn that there is very little difference in median total scores among those who major in the humanities, social sciences, and biological sciences. (See box, above.)

Scientific Preparation

Still, medical schools recognize the importance of a strong foundation in the natural sciences—biology, chemistry, and physics—and mathematics, and most schools have established minimum course requirements for admission. These courses usually represent about one-third of the credit hours needed for degree completion (hence, leaving room for applicants to pursue a broad spectrum of college majors, as mentioned on the left). In particular, medical schools expect that their entering students will have mastered basic scientific principles by successfully completing one academic year (two semesters or three quarters) of biology and physics and one academic year each of general chemistry and organic chemistry, and including adequate laboratory experiences.

While only a few medical schools require applicants to complete a specific course in mathematics, all schools appreciate that mathematical competence provides a strong foundation for understanding basic sciences. A working knowledge of statistics helps students fully grasp medical literature, and familiarity with computers is valuable, as well. Many medical schools therefore recommend coursework in mathematics, statistics, and computer science in addition to the science courses named above. The table on the next page gives an overview of the most common courses required by medical schools.

AP and CLEP Courses

Students intending to apply college credit earned through **Advanced Placement (AP) and College Level Examination Placement (CLEP)** to meet premedical requirements should be aware that some medical schools have requirements involving the use of such credit. Please review the Web sites and publications of the medical schools in which you're interested for information.

Subjects Required by U.S. Medical Schools

Finally, for those of you reading this in the early years of college (or even in high school), we'd like to draw your attention to the fact that some medical schools may one day define their prerequisites by competencies—rather than courses. This comes about because, as a study undertaken by the Howard Hughes Medical Institute (HHMI) and the AAMC points out, the scientific knowledge medical schools seek in their applicants can be obtained in a variety of courses as opposed to specific ones. (In other words, a student might be able to master chemistry principles in a zoology class.) The box on the next page provides additional information.

Table 2-A
Subjects Required by 10 or More U.S. Medical Schools

Required Subject	# of Schools
Biochemistry	15
Biology	93
Biology/Zoology	37
Calculus	20
College Mathematics	33
English	85
Humanities	15
Inorganic (General) Chemistry	124
Organic Chemistry	124
Physics	123

N = 132. For premedical coursework required by the specific medical schools in which you are interested, please see the school entries later in this guide.

Advanced Coursework

You should also know that upper-level science coursework is not typically required by medical schools. That said, your success in advanced courses is often a way to demonstrate science proficiencies and strengthen your preparation for medical school. Still, taking additional science courses that duplicate basic science content of the first two years of medical school is not recommended.

In fact, practicing physicians often suggest that premedical students take advantage of what might be their final opportunity for study in non-science areas (such as music, art, history, and literature) they find of interest. Beyond that, medical schools

---

Into the Future: Competency-Based Prerequisites

The study undertaken by the HHMI and the AAMC recommends a shift in focus from requiring specific courses to requiring specific competencies and outlines the competencies that entering medical students should demonstrate. In brief, these include:

- both the knowledge of and ability to apply basic principles of mathematics and statistics, physics, chemistry, biochemistry, and biology to human health and disease;
- the ability to demonstrate observational and analytical skills; and
- the ability to apply those skills and principles to biological situations.

You may download a copy of this report, free-of-charge, at www.aamc.org/scientificfoundations.

---

encourage honors courses, independent study, and research work by premedical students. Activities such as these demonstrate in-depth scholarly exploration and the presence of life-long learning skills that are essential to a career in the medicine.

Personal Attributes

As we mentioned in this chapter's introduction, academic and scientific accomplishments alone are not sufficient for a student's entry into medical school. While intellectual capacity is obviously important to success as a physician, so too are other attributes—those that portend the ability to develop and maintain effective relationships with patients, work collaboratively with other team members, act ethically and compassionately, and in many other ways master the "art" of medicine.

An AAMC publication entitled *Learning Objectives for Medical Student Education: Guidelines for Medical Schools* describes the personal attributes required of a physician. While making note of the fact that graduating medical students must, of course, be knowledgeable about medicine and skillful in its application, the publication also emphasizes how vital it is for students to:

- Make ethical decisions;

- Act with compassion, respect, honesty, and integrity;

- Work collaboratively with team members;

- Advocate on behalf of one's patients;

- Be sensitive to potential conflicts of interest;

- Be able to recognize one's own limits;

- Be dedicated to continuously improving one's knowledge and abilities;

- Appreciate the complex nonbiological determinants of poor health;

- Be aware of community and public health issues;

- Be able to identify risk factors for disease;

- Be committed to early identification and treatment of diseases;

- Accept responsibility for making scientifically based medical decisions; and

- Be willing to advocate for the care of the underserved.

A number of these traits are developed not only in medical school, but also may be nurtured throughout the college years, as well (and, as you will see in Chapter 7, are among the attributes that admissions officers seek when deciding whom to admit to their programs). You will have an abundance of opportunities to foster many of these qualities through your interactions with friends, classmates, and faculty…in the classroom, dining hall, and dorm…on sports teams, in school clubs, and during summer or part-time jobs.

Extracurricular Activities Related to Medicine

Your undergraduate years offer wonderful opportunities to become involved in a wide range of extracurricular activities, and certainly at least a few of them should involve the medical field. Experience in a health care setting; caring for an ill or elderly family member; participating in basic or clinical research efforts; working as an emergency medical technician; "shadowing" a physician; providing support to people in a rape crisis center, emergency room, or social service agency—these types of activities are recommended to those considering a career in medicine.

These pursuits provide you with the chance to learn more about the medical profession—and yourself. You will, for example, be able to:

- Explore different interests,

- Test out your natural inclinations to one or more endeavors,

- Come to better understand the nature of medical practice and the daily demands placed upon physicians,

- Assess your ability to communicate and empathize with people from different backgrounds and cultures, and

- Evaluate your willingness to put others' needs before your own.

While this self-analysis can help you decide if a career in medicine is an appropriate choice for you, your involvement with

Dutifulness and Altruism

In the publication referenced on the previous page, the AAMC categorizes these varied traits as they relate to **dutifulness** and **altruism**. Those interested in exploring these concepts further can download the publication, free-of-charge.

Go to www.aamc.org/msop to read more.

clinical or research activities might help admissions committees determine where your interests lie and demonstrate to them that you have explored various aspects of the medical field. We say *might*, though—rather than *will*—because admissions committees evaluate your experiences using at least three different criteria, and a greater value is assigned to certain types of pursuits than others.

Specifically, admissions committees look at the length of time you've invested, the depth of the experience, and lessons learned—in relation to any particular activity—so that a day-long blood drive or one-time-only shadowing experience is less enlightening than semester or year-long commitments. By the same token, active participation in an activity is viewed as more instructive than a passive one (such as observation). Most important, though, admissions committees want to know what students learned from their experiences, and you should therefore be prepared to address these kinds of questions about your community, clinical, or research experiences in your application materials (which we will discuss in Chapter 6).

Be Wary of the Checklist Approach

Do **not** approach your extracurricular activities with the idea of "checking off" a wide range and number of pursuits in order to impress the admissions committee. Three or four in-depth experiences from which you gained invaluable lessons are far more significant—and telling—to admissions officers than dozens of short-term involvements.

Pre-Health Advisors

Fortunately, you're not on your own when it comes to preparing for medical school. You have a valuable resource to which you can turn—a resource very likely available right on your college campus.

We speak of your pre-health advisor.

Depending on the individual school, pre-health advisors function on either a full- or part-time basis, and may be faculty members (often in the science department), staff members in the office of an academic dean or in the career center, directors of an advising office for pre-professional students, or a physician in part-time practice. Advisors belong to organizations such as the National Association of Advisors for the Health Professions (NAAHP, *www.naahp.org*) that assist them in their work—and help them to help you.

Services Provided

The support provided by pre-health advisors varies according to a number of factors. Generally speaking, though, services fall into five categories:

- **Academics.** Advisors are well informed about premedical coursework on their campuses and about developing suitable academic programs for premedical students. They collaborate with campus academic staff in designing study, reading skill, and test preparation workshops, and in offering tutoring programs, as well as inform their students of regional and national programs likely to be of interest.

- **Clinical and research experiences.** In working with advisory groups composed of college and medical school teaching and research faculty and community clinicians, advisors help identify part-time jobs, volunteer positions, and opportunities for independent study credit in local laboratories and offices.

- **Advising and support.** Advisors help students pursue realistic goals and maximize their potential, both meeting with them individually and providing group opportunities for students to meet with one another. Advisors often establish peer advising and mentoring programs, and are particularly sensitive to the needs of students who are members of a group currently underrepresented in medicine or are the first in their family to attend college.

- **Assistance to student organizations.** Advisors coordinate the activities of local and national organizations that serve premed students by planning programs, identifying funding sources, and arranging for campus visits from admissions and financial aid officers.

- **Sharing resources.** Well aware of the need by students for timely and pertinent information, advisors disseminate publications and other resources from relevant organizations, including the AAMC and the NAAHP. In addition, advisors provide computer access to Web-based content on health careers programs and educational financing; distribute information about local regional, national, and international research and service opportunities; and stock a library of publications related to medical school and medical education.

Please contact your school's advisor to discuss the availability of these services.

The Pre-Health Committee Letter of Recommendation

There's another vital service that pre-health advisors offer their students (and often their alumni) that we haven't yet mentioned: the pre-health committee letter of recommendation.

This is usually a composite letter written on behalf of a medical school applicant by the college or university's pre-health committee. It presents an overview of the student's academic strengths, exposures to health care and medical research environments, contributions to the campus and community, and personal attributes such as maturity and altruism. In addition, the letter may address any extenuating circumstances that may have resulted in deficits in the student's performance during a course or semester, provide perspective on challenges the student may have encountered, and explain school-specific courses and programs in which the student has participated.

Some undergraduate institutions do not provide composite letters of recommendation but instead collect individual letters throughout the student's enrollment. Then, at the appropriate time, they distribute the letters to the medical schools where the student has applied.

Pre-Health Advisors Offer a Wide Range of Guidance

There are many instances in which a pre-health advisor may assist you. These include helping you:

- Identify courses that satisfy premedical requirements;
- Determine a sequence for completing those courses;
- Find tutorial assistance, if needed;
- Plan academic schedules to accommodate both premedical coursework and other educational objectives, such as a study program abroad, a dual major, or a senior honors thesis;
- Locate volunteer or paid clinical and research experience;
- Strengthen your medical school application;
- Prepare for interviews and standardized tests;
- Arrange for letters of evaluation and recommendation; and
- Determine the most appropriate career paths based on individual strengths, values, and life goals.

Special Programs

Finally, we'd like to draw your attention to the following two programs that may be of interest (depending on where you fall in the education process):

- *Combined Baccalaureate/M.D. Programs*
  If you're reading this book during the latter stages of high school, you might want to explore a combined B.S./M.D. program, offered at about a quarter of U.S. medical schools. Graduates of these programs, which range in length from six to nine years, receive both a bachelor's degree from the undergraduate institution and an M.D. from the medical school. For more details and a list of participating schools, please see Chapter 12.

- *Post-Baccalaureate Programs*
  Perhaps, though, you're at a different stage along the educational continuum and have already graduated from college. If your major was something other than science, it's quite possible that you'll need to pursue additional coursework before applying to medical school. Post-baccalaureate programs, offered at colleges and universities across the country and ranging from formal one- or two-year programs to information part-time programs, allow those with a college degree to strengthen their knowledge in the sciences or complete certain required premedical courses. A searchable database of these programs can be found at *http://services.aamc.org/postbac*.

Finding a Pre-Health Advisor through the NAAHP

If you can't identify the pre-health advisor on your campus, contact the NAAHP for help. If your school does not have an advisor, you may make use of the services of volunteer advisors at other institutions, as listed on the NAAHP Web site. In addition, the NAAHP offers publications to help student prepare for medical school that may be of interest, as well.

Contact the NAAHP at:
National Association of Advisors for the Health Professions
P.O. Box 1518, Champaign, IL 61824-1518
T (217) 355-0063   F (217) 355-1287
www.naahp.org

Chapter 3:

From Here to There: The Medical Education Process

What lies on the journey between the day you grasp your college diploma, shake the dean's hand, and flash a broad smile for your family and friends—and the day you're licensed as a fully certified physician? What steps must you successfully navigate before you are deemed a competent doctor, ready to function independently in your chosen field?

You probably already know the answer: Four demanding years of medical school, a residency program lasting anywhere from three to eight years (or more, on occasion), and passing scores on the three USLME step exams administered at various stages along the way.

But that's only the short version. There's more to the discussion than that—much more. How has the medical education process changed in recent years—both in terms of teaching methods and the topics you'll be taught? Which technological innovations are being used to train students? How does medical education today differ from that of a generation ago?

Undergraduate Medical Education

↓

Graduate Medical Education (Residency)

↓

Licensure and Certification

↓

Continuing Medical Education

We take a look at these questions, and others, in the material that follows.

Undergraduate Medical Education: An Overview of the Medical School Years

At the core, all U.S. and Canadian medical schools have the same purpose—to educate their students in both the art and science of medicine, provide them with clinical experience, and, ultimately, prepare them to enter a three- to eight-year-long residency program (otherwise referred to as "graduate medical education"). That is why every school follows the same basic program—requiring students to acquire a basic foundation in the medical sciences, apply this knowledge to diseases and treatments, and master clinical skills through a series of "rotations."

That doesn't mean that a medical school...is a medical school...is a medical school. Far from it. Each school establishes its own curriculum and course format, so that, for example, a particular class required by one institution is an elective course in another. Even when medical schools seem to require identical courses, the content within them may differ, so that the some of the material covered in immunology in one school, for instance, is presented in pathology in another. (The sequence in which courses are taken—and the very method by which the content is taught—may differ, as well.) Beyond that, the processes by which students are graded also vary from school to school, with some institutions following a pass/fail system, others an honors/pass/fail system, and still others a letter grading system.

But we're not saying that "anything goes," either, when it comes to medical schools. To the contrary, they must meet very exacting standards to earn (and maintain) accreditation, as established by the **Liaison Committee on Medical Education** (LCME). The LCME, cosponsored by the AAMC and the American Medical Association, is the authority that accredits programs of medical schools that grant the M.D. degree in the United States, and reviews and approves curricula, organization, and student performance.

Beyond that required by the standards of accreditation, there are other strong parallels among medical schools. Speaking in

very simplistic terms—and recognizing there is significant overlap between what has traditionally been referred to as "pre-clinical" and "clinical" years (see box below)—the general structure of the overall programs follow a similar path: Students concentrate their efforts on the scientific underpinnings of medicine during the first two years, and on applying and refining that knowledge during a series of rotations during the second two years.

Let's take a look...

Building a Foundation of Knowledge

In almost all cases, you'll begin your medical school studies by learning how the human body is supposed to work—both in terms of structure and function. The focus will then shift to abnormal conditions and diseases, methods of diagnosis, and treatment options. We follow with a brief summary.

- *Normal Structure and Function*
  How does the healthy body work? That's what you'll be studying right out of the starting gate, and your courses will be many—and varied. Typically, your "basic" classes will include gross and microscopic anatomy, physiology, biochemistry, behavioral sciences, and neurology.

- *Abnormalities, Diagnostics, and Treatment*
  After you've learned what "healthy" looks like (and acts like), the focus of your coursework will shift—again, both in terms of structure and function. You'll study the full range of diseases and atypical conditions, methods by

---

Accreditation by the LCME is required for schools to receive federal grants and to participate in federal loan programs. In addition, eligibility of U.S. students to take the United States Medical Licensing Exam (USMLE)—a discussion of which appears on page 22—requires LCME accreditation of their school. All medical schools listed in this guide are accredited by the LCME.

which diagnoses are made, and therapeutic principles and treatments. It is at this stage that you'll have classes in immunology, pathology, and pharmacology.

- *Other Topics*
You'll also be exposed to a wide variety of other topics, too. These will range from nutrition, to medical ethics, to genetics…from laboratory medicine, to substance abuse, to geriatrics. Health care delivery systems. Human values. Research. Preventive medicine. Human sexuality. Community health. The fact is that the subjects taught at medical schools are as varied, and potentially as numerous, as are the institutions themselves.

And that's just part of the picture. There's much more to "building a foundation" than simply (or not so simply!) mastering the scientific basis of medicine. During this period of your medical education, you will also learn the basics of interviewing and obtaining historical data from patients, conducting physical exams, interpreting laboratory findings, and considering diagnostic treatment and alternatives—in effect, readying yourself for the clinical rotations that follow in the latter half of medical school.

Finally, keep in mind that it's not all science—or even application of science (such as that required to interpret lab results and figure out a course of treatment). Medical schools recognize that physicians practice in a social environment—one in which effec-

tive team-building, collaborative, and communications skills are necessary. As a result, the very way in which students learn, and are taught, has evolved in recent years. *We discuss this in more depth in the section on the next page—the "Changing Face of Medical Education."*

Acquiring "Hands-On" Experience through Clerkships

A major component of your undergraduate medical education, typically occurring in the third and fourth years, will be a series of required clinical clerkships or "rotations." These clerkships usually last from four to 12 weeks each, and provide students with first-hand experience in working with both patients and their families, and in both inpatient and outpatient settings.

While the pattern, length, and number of rotations differ from school to school, core clinical training usually includes clerkships in internal medicine, family medicine, obstetrics/gynecology, pediatrics, psychiatry, and surgery. Beyond that, and depending on your specific school's requirements, your program may also include clerkships in primary care and neurology, for example, or require participation in a community or rural program.

- *What You'll Do*
During a clerkship, you'll be assigned to an outpatient clinic or inpatient hospital unit where you will assume responsibility for "working-up" a number of patients each week—collecting relevant data and information from them—and presenting findings to a faculty member. Beyond that, you'll participate in the ongoing care of patients, either during hospitalizations or through the course of outpatient treatment, and, when appropriate, interact not only with the patients themselves, but with their families, as well.

- *And What You'll Learn*
There's no substitute, as you know, for "hands-on" experience—and plenty of it. During the course of your clerkships, you'll learn to apply basic science knowledge and clinical skills in diagnosing and treating patients' illnesses and injuries and will become adept interacting with patients (and their families) as you provide information, answer questions, and prepare them for the likely outcome. At the same time, you'll become effective working with all members of the health care team, whether at the bedside, during inpatient team discussions ("rounds"), or in case-based lectures and small-group discussions.

What A Typical Curriculum* May Include

Year 1 – Normal structure and function
Biochemistry, cell biology, medical genetics, gross anatomy, structure and function of human organs, behavioral science, and neuroscience

Year 2 – Abnormal structure and function
Abnormalities of structure and function, disease, microbiology, immunology, pathology, and pharmacology

Years 3 and 4 – Clinical clerkships
Generalist core: family and community medicine, general and ambulatory care, internal medicine, obstetrics and gynecology, pediatrics, surgery, and research

Other requirements: neurology, psychiatry, subspecialty segments (anesthesia, dermatology, urology, radiology, etc.), emergency room and intensive care experiences, and electives.

*The curriculum outlined above is a representation only—and not inclusive of all courses/clerkships.

Electives

Medical schools, just like colleges, each have their own requirements—the courses and clerkships you must take to graduate. That's a given.

But, also just like college, you'll enjoy an opportunity to explore special interests by way of electives. Offered in basic, behavioral, and clinical sciences, as well as in basic and clinical research, electives are usually available during your final year of medical school (although you might be able to take them at other times). They may be completed on your own campus, at other medical schools through a "visiting student program," through federal and state agencies, in international settings, and service organizations.

The Changing Face of Medical Education

Some of you may have heard of Abraham Flexner, who wrote a groundbreaking report on medical education 100 years ago. Although the basics of his 1910 model have survived to the present day—mainly, a four-year program affiliated with a university*—he never intended his model to serve for more than a generation. He knew, after all, that he could not predict the future.

Time has certainly proven him correct.

Medical School Activities on Elective/ Volunteer Basis	

The range of activities in which medical students participate is broad. The following are among the most popular:

Activity	% Participating
Experience related to cultural awareness/competence	67.0
Learned proper use of interpreter when needed	69.2
Experience related to health care disparities	65.3
Research project w/faculty member	64.8
Provided health education (e.g., HIV education, Breast cancer awareness, smoking cessation)	56.1
Field experience in community health (e.g., rape hotline, adult/child protective services, family violence program)	44.3
Educating elementary, high school, or college students about health care careers	43.1

Source: AAMC's 2009 Graduation Questionnaire (GQ)

There is no way that Flexner could have anticipated the shifting demographics, technological advances, and evolving teaching techniques of the late 20th century and the first decade of the 21st century. You, on the other hand, will experience first-hand the reforms taking place in medical education—both in terms of what you'll learn, and how you'll learn it. Your courses may range from cultural diversity to health care financing, and you'll benefit from educational developments such as computer-aided instruction, virtual patients, and human patient simulation. It's an exciting (albeit very challenging!) time to be a medical student.

What You'll Learn

You're going to have to wield a scalpel in anatomy class early on in medical school, just as students in your parents' and grandparents' generations did 30 and 60 years ago. Certain things stay the same. That type of effort aside, though, there are many significant changes in medical education content, and schools are continually revising their curricula to reflect advances in science, breakthroughs in medicine, and changes in society. For example:

- Consider the demographic shift we'll experience as the baby boomers age. By 2030, the population of those over age 65 is expected to have doubled, and physicians will spend an increasing amount of time treating age-related problems such as Alzheimer's, heart failure, pulmonary disease, and bone disorders. As a result, most medical schools now include courses on geriatrics, palliative care, pain management, and complementary medicine, and other similar age-based material, in their curricula.

- Issues such as health literacy, nutrition, drug abuse, and family violence are important components of medical education. Because many of these and other health problems are related to culture and lifestyle, medical schools haves increasingly focused efforts on areas such as disease prevention, health promotion, and cultural diversity.

- Medical schools are placing an increasingly important emphasis on helping their students develop effective communications, allowing them to interact successfully with a diverse group of patients. Rather than being "left to chance," you'll be directly taught to assess family, lifestyle, and socioeconomic factors that may influence your patients' behavior, or affect their care.

*At the time of Flexner's report, many medical schools were small trade schools unaffiliated with a university, and a degree was awarded after only two years of study.

Changing Demographics = Changing Education

The U.S. population is expected to be almost 70 million by 2030—accounting for one in every five Americans. Demographics such as that, together with advanced technologies, scientific discoveries, and evolving teaching techniques, all contribute to significant changes in medical education.

Source: Population Projections of the United States by Age, Sex, Race, and Hispanic Origin: 1995 to 2050, U.S. Bureau of the Census

Then, of course, there are the advancements in science and medicine themselves. (As researchers make breakthroughs in genetics diagnoses and treatments, for instance, that new knowledge is incorporated into the medical school program.) There are also expanded courses on medical ethics, examining some of the dilemmas physicians may face amid the advent of new technology; classes on financial decision making, in which students are taught to weigh the likely costs and benefits of various treatments; and sessions on evidence-based medicine and patient quality, providing students with the informational and tools they will need to deliver the best possible care.

The topics described here are only an overview of some possibilities. The specific courses you'll take as a medical student will vary depending on the school. For a listing of curricula by institution, go to the Curriculum Directory at http://services.aamc.org/currdir.

And How You'll Learn It

Do you have an image of sitting in a large lecture hall, surrounded by hundreds of your peers? While you'll certainly experience that aspect of medical school, that method of teaching is being replaced (to a significant degree) by other techniques. Here are a few of the most widespread methods:

• The traditional lecture-based approach is increasingly giving way to student-centered, small-group instruction—similar to the "case study" teaching method so popular in both law and business schools. In your case (pun intended!), you're likely to be assigned to small groups of students—overseen by a faculty member—in which you will focus on specific clinical problems. The aim here is to instill medical knowledge and skill as well as help you build the communications and collaboration skills you'll need as a resident, and, ultimately, as a fully licensed physician.

• Fast-moving technological advances have certainly affected the medical school education program. You'll probably use

a computerized patient mannequin (or "whole body simulator") to apply the basic sciences you've mastered to a clinical context and refine your diagnostic skills. These simulators, which are easily customized to replicate a wide range of situations, are currently part of the curriculum in most medical schools.

• Another way medical schools employ new technology is with computer-aided instruction and "virtual" patients. Here, you'll apply newfound knowledge and skills via interactive Web-based (or software) programs that simulate complex cases.

To learn more about the specific teaching methods of the medical school(s) in which you are interested, please see the applicable school listing in the latter portion of this guide.

Choosing a Specialty and Applying for Residency

Required courses. Clerkships. Electives. There's a lot occupying your time and energy as you advance through medical school. Along with all that, you undoubtedly will give a lot of thought about the career path you'd like to pursue, exploring various options and researching different possibilities.

Examples of "New" Topics in Medical Education

Of 126 medical schools surveyed, the following topics were required at the vast majority of institutions:

Topic area	# of Medical Schools Requiring Topic
Cultural Diversity	125
Substance Abuse	125
Communication Skills	124
Preventive/Health Maintenance	124
Medical Genetics	121
Family/Domestic Violence	121
Culturally-Related Health Behaviors	121
Pain Management	120
Counseling for Health Risk Reduction	120
Health Care Systems	119
Alternative/Complementary Medicine	113
Health Care Financing	111

Source: 2008 LCME Part II Annual Medical School Questionnaire

It is during your final year, though, that some real decisions must be made. It is at this stage that you'll choose a specialty and begin applying to residency programs (the portion of your education that follows graduation from medical school). These training programs are described below, but for now…how will you make your selection, and how will you get in?

Choosing a Specialty

You really should begin exploring specialty options in your second year of medical school, and there's much to think about. You'll want to consider the nature of the work, training and residency requirements, lifestyle and salary factors, characteristics of physicians in the specialty, issues facing professionals in that particular field, and, of course, your own interests, values, and skills.

Where to begin your explorations? You will, of course, seek out the guidance of your advisor as you investigate your options, and your school will likely offer various workshops and presentations to help you with your decision. In addition, and as we mentioned in the first chapter of this guide, you will probably have access to the **Careers in Medicine**® (CiM) program sponsored by the Association of American Medical Colleges (AAMC). This largely Web-based program—which is available free-of-charge to students attending AAMC-member medical schools—contains detailed information and interactive tools to help you work through the specialty choice process. Included in this program are:

- specialty descriptions;

- residency and training requirements;

- Match data;

- workforce statistics;

- compensation; and

- links to more than 1,000 specialty associations, journals, and publications.

Registration and an access code are required for access to the CiM program. For more, go to www.aamc.org/careersinmedicine.

Getting In

Once you've decided on a specialty, there's more to it than simply shooting off an e-mail to the director of a residency program and letting him or her know of your interest (as we're sure you already suspect). Rather, you must compete for a slot. Much like the application process to medical school, you'll complete an application, craft a personal statement, submit letters of recommendation, and go through interviews. This undertaking is usually facilitated through an application service such as the AAMC's **Electronic Residency Application Service** (ERAS®), which transmits all related documentation via the Internet.

Applying is just the half of it, though, you've also got to be accepted by (or "matched" with) a residency program. This pairing comes about through the **National Resident Matching Program** (NRMP®) by which students' preferences for specific residency programs are compared with the preferences of residency program directors for specific applicants. The matching process occurs on a specific day every March—more familiarly known as **"Match Day"**—and is met with a great deal of anticipation as 16,000 medical school seniors learn where they will spend the next several years of their training.*

Graduate Medical Education (GME): The Residency Program

Once you've graduated from medical school, you can claim title to that hard-earned M.D. (or D.O., for graduates of osteopathic schools). But although much of the work is done—and people now call you "doctor"—the journey is far from over. In actuality, you're a "doctor-in-training," and your next phase is that of graduate medical education. The residency program awaits.

Types of Educational Technologies

Most medical schools use a combination of the following technologies in their educational programs:

Computer-aided instruction
- Enables visualizing complex processes
- Allows independent exploration
- Offers easy access
- Relatively low cost

Virtual patients
- Covers multiple aspects of a clinical encounter
- Offers easy access
- Readily customized

Human Patient Simulation
- Offers active experience
- Engages emotional and sensory learning
- Fosters critical thought and communication

Source: AAMC Handbook

These 16,000 students are the graduates of medical schools that grant the M.D. In addition, 15,000 graduates of osteopathic (those granting the D.O.), Canadian, and international medical schools also compete for residency program assignments through the NRMP. To learn more about ERAS and NRMP, go to www.aamc.org/eras and www.nrmp.org.

We won't get into the details of postgraduate work here, as we imagine that right now you're more interested in getting into medical school—and that you plan to worry about your residency program later. In a nutshell, though, the primary purpose of these programs is to provide medical school graduates (such as you, one day) with the skills and knowledge they need to become competent, independent physicians. Ranging in length from three to five years, and sometimes more, their completion is necessary for board certification.

Because of their very nature, residency programs are conducted primarily in clinical settings—hospitals, outpatient clinics, community health centers, and physicians' offices, for example—and require residents (or "house officers" as they're sometimes known) to participate fully in patient diagnoses and treatment. When your time comes, you'll work under the supervision of physician faculty as you develop experience in your chosen specialty, become proficient with both common and uncommon illnesses and conditions, attend conferences, teach less experienced colleagues, and, in general, adjust to the demands of medical practice.

Finally, just as medical schools vary, so too do residency programs. Depending on the area you choose to pursue, you might complete a preliminary year of broad clinical training before focusing on the specialty, as is common in anesthesiology, dermatology, psychiatry, and radiology. In other areas, such

Inter-professional Education

When it comes to caring for patients, remember…you're not in this alone.

Rather, the delivery of medical care is a "team-based" effort that often includes not only doctors, but nurses, pharmacists, physical therapists, and other health care providers, as well. Because of that, it's absolutely vital that practitioners from all disciplines become familiar with one another's roles, perspectives, and even language and communication styles in order to be able to collaborate effectively and efficiently.

And medical educators want to help you develop that knowledge and ability. Your medical education therefore is likely to involve some form of "inter-professional education" in which you will share learning resources, work as a unit, or participate in other activities that encourage interaction among various categories of health care providers. In such a way, you—and they—will become more adept and successful working as a team, and, ultimately, be able to deliver a higher quality of care to patients.

U.S. Residents by Specialty

Specialty	Number
Allergy/Immunology	288
Anesthesiology	5,208
Colon/Rectal Surgery	129
Dermatology	1,069
Emergency Medicine	4,750
Family Medicine	9,353
Internal Medicine	22,132*
Medical Genetics	76
Neurological Surgery	961
Neurology	1,743
Nuclear Medicine	148
OB/GYN	4,815
Ophthalmology	1,220
Orthopedic Surgery	3,303
Otolaryngology	1,372
Pain Medicine	226
Pathology	2,312
Pediatrics	8,089
Physical Medicine/Rehab	1,203
Plastic Surgery	508
Preventive Medicine	241
Psychiatry	4,751
Radiation Oncology	588
Radiology, Diagnostic	4,455
Sleep Medicine	99
Surgery, General	7,712
Thoracic Surgery	230
Urology	1,031

Source: AAMC Data Book, 2010, for the 2008–09 academic year

Breaking it down further, the most popular subspecialties in internal medicine (by number of residents) include cardio-vascular disease (2,434); gastroenterology (1,292); hematology and oncology (1,393); and pulmonary disease and critical care medicine (1,266).

as family medicine and pediatrics, you'll enter the specialty track directly. (Your medical school advisor, and programs such as Careers in Medicine®, will present you with full information as you approach this stage of your medical education.)

Residency will be a demanding time, no doubt, but rewarding as well. Many physicians look back on their residency years as ones providing invaluable lessons that they carry with them to this day.

Note: The standards surrounding residency programs—including educational experiences, duty hours, evaluations, and safety—are established and enforced by the Accreditation Council of Graduate Medical Education (ACGME). You can learn more about the ACGME and its requirements at www.acgme.org.

Examples of Training Requirements for Specialty Board Certification

Specialty	Years Required
Anesthesiology	4
Emergency Medicine	3
Family Practice	3
Internal Medicine	3
OB/GYN	4
Pathology	4
Pediatrics	3
Psychiatry	4
Radiology	5
Surgery	5
Surgical subspecialties	6 or 7

Source: 2008 LCME Part II Annual Medical School Questionnaire

Licensure and Certification: Ready to Function Independently

There's something else you'll need to do before you can be licensed as a physician: You've got to meet the standards of the **National Board of Medical Examiners** (NBME) and the **Federation of State Medical Boards** (FSMB). Together, these two bodies cosponsor the United States Medical Licensing Examination (USMLE), a three-step exam given at various stages of the medical education process.

So, along with documenting that you've completed the necessary educational and training programs for your specialty, you must also get passing scores on the USMLE. It is administered in stages as follows:

- **Step 1:** Usually taken at the end of your second year of medical school, Step 1 tests whether you understand and can apply sciences basic to the practice of medicine. Its focus is on principles and systems of health, disease, and methods of therapy.

- **Step 2:** Many medical schools require you to take (and pass!) Step 2 prior to graduation. It's actually two tests in one—the first evaluating your clinical knowledge (CK) and the second your clinical skills (CS). Basically, Step 2 assesses your ability to provide patient care *under supervision*.

- **Step 3:** After you've completed the first year of your residency program, you're eligible for Step 3—the concluding test that determines your readiness to apply your medical knowledge and clinical skills *without supervision*, with an emphasis on patient management in ambulatory settings. It is the final assessment of your ability to assume independent responsibility for delivering medical care.

Upon completion of the appropriate educational and training programs, and achievement on the USMLE, you've done it. You are ready to apply for licensure in any of the 50 states, 10 provinces, 3 territories or the District of Columbia.

But…there's one additional step: certification. While it's not required for medical practice—as is licensure from a state or provincial medical board—certification in a specialty is strongly encouraged. Physicians apply voluntarily for this additional credential, which is granted by the **American Board of Medical Specialties** (ABMS) and involves a comprehensive examination. (Those who have satisfied all ABMS requirements are certified and are known as "diplomates" of the specialty board.) More than 85 percent of licensed physicians in the United States have been certified, and interest remains high among the current cohort of new doctors. Almost 9 in 10 medical school graduates plan to become certified in a medical specialty.

Continuing Medical Education: The Practice of Lifelong Learning

Finally, medical education is a lifelong process, providing you with the opportunity to learn new skills and stay current with exciting and innovative developments.

The fast pace of change in medicine makes continuing education essential, and most states require participation in accredited continuing medical education (CME) activities. Physicians therefore participate in CME programs throughout their careers, ensuring they stay up-to-date with the rapid advancements in their specialties and maintain their clinical competence. Offered by medical schools, teaching hospitals, and professional organizations, these CME programs are reviewed by the **Accreditation Council for Continuing Medical Education** (ACCME) to ensure that high standards are achieved and upheld.

Continuing medical education reflects a commitment to lifelong learning that is a hallmark of the medical profession. For those of you interested in what your CME efforts will entail, go to *www.accme.org*.

Plans for Certification in a Specialty

When asked if they planned to become certified in a specialty, medical school graduates answered:

Yes	89.7%
No	2.9%
Undecided	7.4%

Source: AAMC's 2009 Graduation Questionnaire (GQ)

Chapter 4:
All About the MCAT® Exam

One of our MCAT staffers overheard a couple of college seniors commiserating with one another about the test that loomed so ominously in their futures. After about 20 minutes of nonstop talk about various review courses, prep books, and practice options, one student stopped mid-sentence, looked at the other, and asked with a mix of exasperation and fear, "Why do they DO this to us?" The other student shook her head and shrugged in empathy, but we know the answer:

Because the MCAT exam does its job.

MCAT Essentials: A Must-Read!

To be sure that you get the most complete and up-to-date information about the MCAT exam, it is crucial that you read **MCAT Essentials** (posted online at *www.aamc.org/mcat*) prior to registration.

The Role of the Exam

Simply put, the MCAT exam helps admissions officers identify which students are likely to succeed in medical school. It does that by spotting those students who not only have a basic knowledge of science—which provides the foundation necessary in the early years of medical school—but also those with strong critical thinking and written communications skills.

Your MCAT Score: One of Many Selection Factors

It's important to recognize that admissions officers consider MCAT results in concert with many other selection factors—including those related to your experience and personal attributes—when making their decisions. See Chapter 7 to learn more about the various ways in which admissions officers evaluate medical school applicants.

One can argue that college grades do essentially the same thing. But because an "A" in one school is not necessarily equivalent to an "A" in another, admissions officers do not have a "standard measure" against which to evaluate students. The MCAT exam fills that void.

It's no surprise, then, that when admissions officers look at MCAT scores in conjunction with grades—as opposed to grades alone—their ability to predict who will be successful in medical school increases by as much as 50 percent (using first- and second-year medical school grades as a benchmark). As a result, virtually every medical school in the United States, and many in Canada, requires applicants to submit recent MCAT scores.

How the Exam Is Structured

It's a pretty sure bet that you're no stranger to the concept of standardized testing. Starting in elementary school, and continuing on through your college admission exam (be it the SAT™ or ACT®), you've had lots of experience with multiple-choice and essay questions taken in a controlled, timed environment.

Exam Structure

Specialty	# of Qs	Time
Physical Sciences	.52	.70 minutes
Verbal Reasoning	.40	.60 minutes
Writing Sample	.2	.60 minutes
Biological Sciences	.52	.70 minutes

There are optional breaks of 10 minutes each between sections.

The MCAT exam follows the same basic format. In this case, it's a computer-based test that lasts just over five hours and consists of three multiple-choice sections—that of Physical Sciences, Biological Sciences, and Verbal Reasoning—and a writing assessment. Let's take a closer look:

- *Physical Sciences (PS)*
  The PS section covers general chemistry and physics via a total of 52 questions—39 of which are based on passages, as well as 13 "free-standing," independent questions. For this section, you will be tested on your capacity to interpret data presented in graphs and tables, your knowledge of basic physical sciences concepts and principles, and your ability to solve problems using that knowledge as a foundation.

- *Verbal Reasoning (VR)*
  The VR section evaluates your ability to understand, evaluate, and apply information and arguments presented in writing. The test consists of seven passages, each of which is about 600 words long, taken from the humanities, social sciences, and natural sciences. Each passage-based set consists of five to seven questions that assess your ability to extrapolate information from the accompanying passage. In total, there are 40 questions in this section.

- *Writing Sample (WS)*
  Consisting of two 30-minute essays, the WS assesses your skill in developing ideas cohesively and logically, and writing clearly and accurately. Your general assignment will be to craft a response to a "prompt"—or statement—that discusses a topic of general interest in areas such as business, politics, or history (as examples). Topics do not pertain to the technical content of biology, chemistry, physics, or math, or to religious or other emotionally charged issues.

- *Biological Sciences (BS)*
  The format of the BS section, which covers biology and organic chemistry, is identical to that of the PS section. It too has 52 questions, 39 passage-based and 13 independent. Like the PS section, it too tests your problem-solving

ability and scientific knowledge (but in this instance based on biological sciences).

There's another reason for the wide range of content you'll find covered on the MCAT exam. Medical school faculty hope to encourage undergraduates with broad educational backgrounds to consider careers in medicine, and, on the flip side, they want to persuade premed majors to explore a wide variety of courses outside of the natural sciences. That explains why the exam tests for such diverse abilities, and why everyone has an equal crack at achieving a high score (assuming they've mastered the entry-level science courses tested on the exam).

MCAT Scores

There are five scores associated with the MCAT exam, one for each of the four sections, and a "composite" (or total) score that presents the results in the aggregate. The following is a quick overview:

- Each of the three multiple-choice sections (PS, VR, and BS) is scored individually from a low of 1 to a high of 15.

- The WS is scored on an alphabetic scale, from a low of J to a high of T.

- In addition to the four scores above, you will also receive a score representing the total of your three multiple-choice sections together with your writing score. If, for example, you received a 9-10-11 and P, your total score would be reported as 30P.

Putting Your Scores in Context

Comparing Your Score to Other Applicants and Acceptees, in General
For more information about how your score compares to others (and how likely you are to be accepted to any medical school based on your score and other selection factors), see Chapter 10 on Applicant and Acceptee Data or *www.aamc.org/facts.*

Comparing Your Score to Those Accepted by a Specific Medical School
You're likely to want to know even more—namely, how your scores compare to those accepted by the specific medical school(s) in which you're interested. For that information, see the applicable page listing in Chapter 14.

If you'd like to learn more about the scoring process itself, including how scores are "equated" across test forms and the myth of the "curve," you'll find a full discussion included in The Official Guide to the MCAT® Exam, available for purchase online.

Preparing for the Exam

There's no real mystery when it comes to preparing for the MCAT exam. Although there are a number of ways to get ready—poring over various review guides, studying your class notes, rereading your textbooks, and/or taking a commercial prep course—it all comes down to the same three steps:

1. *Master the content.* You should complete the usual pre-medical biology, general and organic chemistry, and physics coursework before you take the MCAT exam. (You can learn more about the specific subject matter covered on the exam by reviewing the topic outlines posted on the MCAT Web site.)

2. *Become familiar with the exam.* You'll also want to get comfortable with the passage-based testing format, prepare with "real" questions (i.e., ones that appeared on previous MCAT exams), gain insights as to why specific answers are correct, and become familiar with the pitfalls that sometimes trip up examinees.

3. *Practice effectively.* Finally, you've got to practice as effectively as possible. You'll want to create your own mock testing environment—one that mimics the operational exam—and focus much of your effort on your weak spots. The AAMC's official practice tests (see box at right) can provide that opportunity.

As always, we recommend you speak to your advisor for further guidance in preparing for the exam.

Test Dates, Registration, and Fees

The MCAT exam is administered more than two dozen times from January through September. (Specific dates are listed on the **MCAT Exam Schedule**, posted on the MCAT Web site at *www.aamc.org/mcat.*) While the AAMC selects exam dates to ensure that scores are available to meet most medical school application deadlines, we recommend that you check the specific scheduling requirements of the school(s) of your choice, provided in the "school pages" of this guide. Once you've determined the date you prefer, you can find the registration schedule for that particular exam session on the **MCAT Registration Deadline & Score Release Schedule**, also posted online.

After you have read the MCAT Essentials (*www.aamc.org/mcat*), you can register for the exam—a process available online through the MCAT Web site. There will be a fee of $230 for each exam you take, a payment that covers both the cost of the test itself as well as distribution of your scores. If you register late, make changes to your registration, and/or test at an international site, there will be additional charges.

As a general rule, you should plan on taking the MCAT exam about 12 to 18 months prior to your expected entry into medical school—but not before you've completed basic coursework in general biology, inorganic chemistry, organic chemistry, and general physics. Many medical schools prefer that applicants take the MCAT exam in the spring because of the short time between the availability of late summer scores and school application deadlines. (Taking the exam in the spring also allows time for students to retake the test later in the summer, if necessary). For more guidance, please see your pre-health advisor.

Testing with Accommodations

The AAMC proudly supports the policies of the federal government and will provide accommodations to students whose dis-

MCAT Preparation Resources

Computer-aided instruction.
The Official MCAT Web Site. Your first stop should be the MCAT Web site where you will find a wealth of information. Included there, and available free of charge, are such materials as the MCAT Essentials (required reading), a "Preparing for the Exam" section, and Preparation FAQs.

The Official Guide to the MCAT® Exam.
You can get even more detailed information from this affordable 400-page guidebook, which includes more than 100 practice questions taken from real exams, tips to arrive at the correct answer, thoroughly explained solutions, step-by-step registration instructions, and extensive data on both applicants and acceptees.

Official Practice Tests from the AAMC.
Also available are eight practice tests—updated versions of retired exams—that include solutions for each item, automated scoring and diagnostics, customizable feedback, and test assistance features such as the ability to highlight and search the passage text. *One of the practice tests is available free-of-charge.*

For more information about these preparation resources, go to *www.aamc.org/mcat.*

abilities—or other conditions—necessitate an adjustment to the test or testing environment, pending review and approval by the MCAT Office of Accommodated Testing Services. Information about the process by which accommodations are requested (and the documentation that must accompany the request) is available at *www.aamc.org/mcat*.

Score Reporting

The time between the date of your exam and the day you find out how you did can seem like an eternity. In reality, though, scores will be reported through the MCAT program's computerized Testing History Report System (THx) approximately 30 days after each exam. Through this program, located at *www.aamc.org/mcat*, you can check your scores and print your own official score report.

Of course, you're not the only one who's interested in finding out how you did. The medical schools to which you've applied (or will apply) want to know, as well. How then do admissions committees learn of their applicants' scores?

- *Automatic Score Release to AMCAS:*
  The good news is that, in most cases, it's all automatic—and no action is required on your part. The American Medical College Application Service, or AMCAS (see box at right), automatically releases your scores via the THx for all scores that date from April 2003 (which is probably your situation). For those of you who have scores prior to April 2003, you can use the THx system to make selected scores part of your current AMCAS application.

- *Score Release to Non-AMCAS Schools:* For the 2010 entering classes, all but 8 of the 132 U.S. medical schools

are part of the AMCAS program. In the event you're applying to a non-AMCAS institution, you can use the THx system to select those recipients.

The various options and procedures available through the THx system are explained in detail when you log into the system.

Retaking the Exam

If you're not happy with your performance on the MCAT exam, you have the option to take it again. But it's a tough decision. Many medical schools average the scores from all tests taken—or consider only the last take—so that if you do worse the second time around, you may have actually weakened your position.

There are times when a retake is well worth considering. Perhaps you discovered that your coursework or study didn't cover the topics as thoroughly as you needed. Or there's a large discrepancy between your grade in a subject and your score on a particular section. Or maybe you simply didn't feel well the day of the exam. In all these cases, your pre-health advisor may be of great help, and we recommend you discuss the issue with him or her.

If you decide to retake the exam, please bear in mind that it may be taken a maximum of three times during each calendar year. Registration procedures for retaking the exam are identical to those for initial testing.

The MCAT exam is administered and scored by the MCAT Program Office at the direction of the AAMC. Information about the exam's content, organization, scoring system, accommodations process, and more, is available at www.aamc.org/mcat.

Chapter 5:

Choosing the School That's Right for You

No doubt you have many questions about the medical school application process. What forms will I need to complete? What are the logistics involved? What type of supporting documentation must I get? What's the timing of it all? How much will it cost me?

We address all that in the next chapter. For now, though, you've got an even bigger question to consider, and that's because the initial stage of the application process isn't really a "how" at all. It's a "where." You first need to figure out to which school (or schools) you should apply. It's a question that is answered by looking not only at various medical schools, but at yourself, as well.

Students Weigh a Host of Selection Factors

There's much to take into account when choosing schools. Among the factors medical students consider in making their ultimate selection as to which school to attend are:

- Interviews/meetings with administrators, faculty, and current students
- Advice of parents
- Advice of medical school graduates
- Advice of family physician
- Research reputation and opportunities
- Community-based experience and opportunities
- Geographic location
- School's teaching methods
- Program of elective courses
- Faculty mentorship
- Ability of school to place students in particular residency programs

Source: AAMC Matriculating Student Questionnaire, 2009

Because you're not searching merely for a school you can "get into." You're searching for a match.

The Overall Mission of the School

If you've seen one medical school…you've seen one medical school.

That's a cute way of saying that medical schools differ from one another. And many of these differences are pretty obvious. Some schools are located in the East; some in the West. Some are private; others, public. Some have a large entering class; others, small. And, as we explained in Chapter 3, medical schools vary in the content of their courses, in the way they teach, and even in the way they grade students.

These are all factors you'll want to consider as you narrow your selection, and we touch upon them in the pages that follow. But the differences go even deeper, and at a very core level: Medical schools have diverse missions and priorities. Because of those distinctions, what's significant to one school may be of only moderate importance to another, and these goals naturally carry into the selection process.

To figure out where to apply, then, requires that you become aware not only of the differences among schools, but that you also analyze yourself—your skills, experiences, career goals, and so forth—to identify the most appropriate matches. Take, for instance, an institution that places a strong emphasis on primary care. Is that the career path you intend to follow? If so, and especially if you can demonstrate your interest through extensive experience related to that area, you become a more attractive candidate on that basis alone.

That's one example. Other schools may be actively seeking students from specific geographic or rural areas. Others may be looking for students with a high potential for a research career. Still others may want to increase the number of doctors who plan to practice in their states (this last goal is often found among public institutions). The differing missions among schools will be reflected in their admissions policies and standards.

If you need help with this self-analysis, think back to the various experiences you've had over the years. The ones you found especially rewarding or inspirational are likely to correlate to a specific area of interest, and, by extension, a career goal.

- Did you volunteer two summers for a clinic in a **rural, underserved area**? Perhaps that's the direction you'd like your career to take, and, if so, you'll want to seek out medical schools that place a high priority on that area.

- Were the part-time jobs you had with a research firm particularly gratifying? If you'd like to pursue **a research career**, look for schools that have a strong reputation in that area or are known for graduating a large percentage of medical students going into research careers.

- There are also other ways that speak to your interests and career goals. Did you spend your junior year tutoring freshmen and sophomores in entry-level biology or chemistry? Perhaps you'd like to join a **medical school faculty** and educate the next generation of physicians. If so, look for a medical school with a relatively large percentage of their graduates in teaching positions.

Once again, keep in mind that this is a two-way street. While you're looking for a match, so are the schools. Your experiences will provide good insights for the admissions officers and help them determine if your interests and their missions are congruent.

The Educational Program

As you weigh your decision, you'll also want to consider the differences among the educational programs themselves. We touch on a few of these below.

- There's very likely going to be a relationship between a school's mission and its **curriculum**. You'll therefore be able to further gauge whether a particular institution's objectives and your interests align by analyzing course requirements and electives programs. A medical school with a mission to graduate more primary care doctors may, for example, have a track that provides for additional training in that area. A school that emphasizes research might have their students devote an extended period of time to scholarly pursuits.

- As you do your research, also consider what **teaching methods** you find most effective. Do you tend to do well with self-directed or participatory learning exercises, or do you do better with the more traditional, lecture-based style of learning? While most medical schools use an educational model that combines various methods, there will be a difference as to precisely how this mix has been adapted. You'll want to explore the degree to which you're likely to find small group discussions and problem-based learning exercises (as examples) versus a traditional teaching approach. A good starting point for your exploration is a school's Web site, as well as the AAMC's curriculum directory.

- There are key differences as to **grading intervals** (or systems), also. Some institutions use a pass/fail system; others an honors/pass/fail system; and still others use letter grades. Some students have definite preferences, and if you're one of them, you may wish to consider a school's grading system as you narrow your selection.

There are many other factors connected with the educational program that you might want to think about. How will you be evaluated? At what point must students pass the first two steps of the United States Medical Licensing Examination (USMLE) before advancing in their education? What level of academic support is available? Is there a mentor system, for instance? What about support services or organizations for cultural and other minorities—are they available? Questions such as these will undoubtedly enter into your final decision as you deliberate between offers, and you may wish to consider them now.

"How Do My Grades and MCAT Scores Factor In?"

Don't choose schools based solely on where you think your grades and MCAT scores will be accepted. While there's no question that your educational record is important and that admissions officers seek candidates who are likely to succeed academically in their programs, it's important to realize that **academics alone do not predict who will become an effective physician, and admissions officers know that all too well**.

The very fact that there are so many instances in which a "high scoring" applicant does not receive an acceptance to medical school—and in which an applicant with lower-than-average grades and scores does—tells you that admissions officers must be looking at other factors.

Admissions officers are taking a more "holistic" approach to evaluating their applicants, a method we discuss thoroughly in Chapter 7. Through this practice, admissions officers assess their candidates more broadly, looking not only at their "metrics" (GPA and MCAT scores) but at their experiences and personal attributes, as well.

You can read about the holistic approach to admissions in Chapter 7, "The Admissions Decision."

Attending Medical School in Your "Home" State

State residents enrolled in state-supported medical schools pay lower tuition than nonresidents. In addition to that, though, in-state residents are often given preference for admission (compared to out-of-state residents) for at least some of their places because the school receives state government support. You therefore may want to give strong consideration to the public institution in your state as you decide where to apply.

And many students do just that. Nationally, 62 percent of 2009 matriculants attended schools in their home states.

State Residency Requirements

Requirements are established by state legislatures and are usually available from school officials or the school's (or state's) Web site. We encourage you to clarify your official residency status before applying.

Public or Private?

You also may be deliberating between public and private institutions. If you're considering a public medical school in your state of residence, one aspect of this decision, as we just mentioned, is likely to be cost. (If you're from out of state, the cost differential between a public institution and a private school virtually disappears. See chart in Chapter 11.) But don't automatically assume, even if you are interested in a state school near your home, that the private route will be more expensive under all circumstances. Some private institutions, for example, may have large endowments that allow them to provide significant scholarship aid to qualifying students and thus lower the "effective" tuition rate, permitting those students to graduate with less educational debt than they would have generated if they had attended a public medical school in their "home" state.

But cost is only one consideration. Another element to be aware of when investigating the differences between private and public institutions is the school's mission—and how it might relate to your own aspirations and interests. Although all medical schools—public or private—have different missions, certain public institutions may have specific goals related to their state, such as increasing the supply of physicians there. (If the school is in your home state and you'd like to remain there after graduation, that will be a factor from both your perspective and the school's.) Other public institutions were founded by state legislators with an emphasis on the needs of a particular patient population—such as elder, rural, or underserved groups—which should enter into your evaluation if that objective corresponds to your own.

Additional Factors to Consider

There are many other factors that may be important to you as you search for a good "match." Some of these include:

- *Location*
  Besides the impact of state residency on the costs of a public medical school, there are other aspects to the issue of location and how it factors into your decision where to apply. Perhaps you simply prefer a specific geographic

region. Do you, for example, want to be close to family and friends? Do you prefer a warmer (or cooler) climate? Are you a fan of the East coast…or the South…or the West? These factors play to your comfort level, and are all valid considerations. Beyond that, though, location can also relate to your career goals, as well as to a school's mission. If you hope to specialize in geriatrics, for example, a medical school located in an area with a higher-than-average proportion of older adults may be able to provide you with the experience you seek.

That's looking at it from your perspective. Consider, for a moment, the school's perspective. In some cases, a school may be seeking students from particular geographic regions in order to bolster its diversity, and you'll want to consider the impact—if any—that your own state residence might have on your application to medical schools in other areas.

- *Size and Demographics*
  The size and demographics of the medical school—both in terms of its student body as well as its faculty—may be a consideration for you, as well. The school entries in this guide include data on the prior year's entering class, including the number of students by gender as well as by (self-reported) race and ethnicity.

- *Costs*
  Medical education doesn't come cheap, and the expenses associated with particular institutions will no doubt be a factor in your decision. At this stage, though, you won't know what your actual costs will be (or the degree of assistance you will get) until a school sends you a financial aid package in conjunction with its offer. Still, in looking through the school entries, you can get a general idea as to the relative expenses of various institutions, and you will probably keep that in mind as you narrow your selection.

Special Regional Opportunities

Finally, you should be aware that some states without a public medical school participate in special interstate and regional agreements to provide their residents with access to a medical education. Currently, there are six interstate agreements, listed below:

- The Delaware Institute of Medical Education and Research
  http://dhss.delaware.gov/dhss/dhcc/dimer.html
  1-302-577-3240, 1-800-292-7934

- The Finance Authority of Maine's Access to Medical Education Program
  www.famemaine.com
  1-800-228-3734

- University of Utah School of Medicine Idaho Contract
  http://medicine.utah.edu/admissions/begin/residency.htm
  1-208-282-2475, residency@sa.utah.edu

- Program conducted under the auspices of the Southern Regional Education Board (SREB)
  www.sreb.org
  1-404-875-9211, 1-404-872-1477

- The Western Interstate Commission for Higher Education
  www.wiche.edu/SEP/PSEP/cert-off.asp

- The WWAMI (Washington, Wyoming, Alaska, Montana, and Idaho) Program
  www.uwmedicine.org/education/wwami

You can learn more about each of these regional opportunities by visiting their Web sites or calling their program offices.

Chapter 6:
Applying to Medical School

Ahh…the signs of spring. The robins chirp, the dandelions bloom, and thousands of students embark on the annual application process to medical school. This year, one of those students is likely to be you.

The big question is how to proceed.

Now that you've identified the schools that seem right for you, you're ready to tackle the steps in applying to them. In this chapter, we'll review the AAMC's American Medical College Application Service (AMCAS®), provide an overview of the application and admissions cycle, talk about your personal statement and letters of recommendation, and give you information about application costs and other specifics.

The Responsibilities of the Medical School Applicant

It is vital that you be aware of the responsibilities you have as an applicant to medical school. These are reviewed at length at the end of this chapter, but we'd like to list a few of the most critical below:

- Meet all deadlines
- Complete the AMCAS application accurately
- Know the admission requirements at each school
- Promptly notify AMCAS of any change in contact information
- Respond promptly to interview invitations
- File for financial aid as soon as possible
- Withdraw from the schools you will not attend

Please see "AAMC Recommendations for Medical School and M.D.-Ph.D. Candidates" on page 37 for detail.

American Medical College Application Service (AMCAS®)

You very likely may have heard about AMCAS from your pre-health advisor, career counselor, or even your classmates. In a nutshell, AMCAS is a Web-based application processing service offered by the AAMC and utilized by almost every medical school in the country. (For schools that do not participate in AMCAS, see box on page 33.) This service does not screen applicants, but rather provides admissions officers with an abundance of information they can use to make preliminary assessments.

This service has benefits to applicants, as well. The most obvious one is that AMCAS allows students to apply to as many medical schools as they want with a single application (although many schools require a "secondary application," a topic we will discuss later in this chapter). Beyond that, it provides applicants with a single point of transmission for official transcripts, letters of recommendation, and other supporting documentation.

Even if you're not yet ready to begin the application process, you might want to go to *www.aamc.org/amcas* for a preview. There, you'll find links to key steps involved in starting an application, including an application timeline, tips, and checklists useful in completing the application, answers to frequently asked questions, and a comprehensive instruction booklet.

Sections of the AMCAS Application

The AMCAS application consists of nine basic sections. It might sound like a lot, but remember…you don't have to complete it all in one sitting. (You can save your work and return to your application as many times as you wish until you've finished it.) We thought we'd give you an overview of what to expect:

1. **Identifying Information.** This section asks you to enter your name, identification numbers, birth information, and sex.

2. **Schools Attended.** Here, you'll enter high school and college information. Once this section (and the identifying section above) is completed, you will be able to download a "transcript request form" from AMCAS.

3. **Biographic Information.** You'll use this section to enter basic information about citizenship, legal residence, languages spoken, and other biographic information.

4. **Course Work.** You'll next enter grades and credits for every course that you have enrolled in at any U.S., U.S. territorial, or Canadian postsecondary institution. (It is important that you provide information for all courses.)

5. **Work/Activities.** Here, you'll enter any work and extracurricular activities, awards, honors, or publications that you would like to bring to the attention of the medical school(s). Up to 15 experiences may be listed.

6. **Letters of Evaluation.** You will use this section to provide information about letters of evaluation that will be submitted to schools on your behalf. (We cover this step in a bit more detail later in this chapter.)

7. **Medical Schools.** In this section, you will designate the medical schools to which you want to submit an application. In addition to that, you will have an opportunity to

designate which letters of recommendation you wish to submit to specific schools.

8. **Personal Statement.** Here, you will compose a personal essay. (We discuss this step more thoroughly later in this chapter, as well.)

9. **Standardized Tests.** And finally…your MCAT scores. In this section, you'll review your MCAT scores and enter any additional test information such as GRE scores. Please note: MCAT scores earned in 2003 or later will automatically be released to AMCAS, and no further action will be required on your part.

Bear in mind that the above is a brief overview of the AMCAS application. We suggest you read the instruction book, available online, and explore the various resources on the general AMCAS site at *www.aamc.org/amcas*.

Transcript Requests via AMCAS

In addition to completing your AMCAS application, you must request that an official transcript be forwarded to AMCAS by the registrar of every postsecondary school you've attended. Here again, AMCAS facilitates the application process by providing a "transcript request form." This includes junior college, community college, trade school, or other professional school—regardless of whether credit was earned—within the United States, Canada, or U.S. territories. (This requirement also applies to any college courses you took in high school.) For regular applicants, all official transcripts must be received no later than two weeks following the deadline date for application materials. Please refer to the AMCAS online instruction booklet or help text for detailed information about official transcript requirements.

Limited Changes After Submission

You'll want to check your work carefully before you hit "submit." That's because you're limited in what changes you can make to your application following submission. More specifically, you can make changes to your contact information (such as addresses) and add additional schools or letters of recommendation. Other than these few exceptions, your application will be submitted to schools exactly as you have completed it.

Application Processing and Verification

Once AMCAS has received the service fee and official transcripts from each postsecondary school at which you've been registered, AMCAS verifies the accuracy of your academic record by comparing the information you entered on the application to that contained in your transcripts. Once processing has been completed, AMCAS makes the application available to all medical schools you designated and distributes MCAT scores. (As mentioned earlier, MCAT scores from 2003 and later are automatically included; those from years prior to 2003 are provided to medical schools only if the applicant has released those scores to AMCAS.)

AMCAS Verification

As part of the processing system, AMCAS verifies the accuracy of your academic record by comparing the information you entered on the application to that contained in your official transcripts.

The Application and Admissions Cycle

Now that you have an idea as to what the AMCAS process involves, you're likely wondering when it all takes place. Generally speaking, the AMCAS application process opens to students in early May of each year, and participating schools begin receiving applicant data in late June.

Also generally speaking, the deadlines for receipt of primary applications to medical schools that participate in AMCAS are from mid-October to mid-December. (See page 35 for information on secondary applications.) Speaking in specifics, though, there is no one application timetable, as each school establishes its own deadlines for receipt of required materials. You can find the dates in medical schools' bulletins and Web sites and in the school listings in this guide. It is critical, of course, that you are aware of and adhere to all deadlines.

That's probably obvious.

What is less obvious, though, is that medical schools vary not only in terms of their application deadlines, but also in the timing by which they make their admissions decisions. Most schools use a system of "rolling admissions," selecting students

Non-AMCAS Schools

The U.S. medical schools that will not participate in AMCAS for the 2011 entering class are:

- University of Missouri-Kansas City School of Medicine
- University of North Dakota School of Medicine and Health Sciences
- Texas A&M University System Health Science Center College of Medicine*
- Texas Tech University Health Sciences Center School of Medicine*
- Texas Tech University Health Sciences Center, El Paso, Paul. L. Foster School of Medicine*
- University of Texas Southwestern Medical Center at Dallas Southwestern Medical School*
- University of Texas Medical School at Galveston*
- University of Texas School of Medicine at Houston*
- University of Texas School of Medicine at San Antonio*

If you are interested in schools that do not participate in AMCAS, please contact them directly for application instructions. You should also contact schools directly for application information if you wish to pursue a joint program, such as a B.A./M.D. or M.D./Ph.D.

*The seven public medical schools in Texas listed here participate in the Texas Medical and Dental School Application Service for those pursuing the M.D. degree. You can learn more about this application service at www.utsystem.edu/tmdsas.

for interviews (and sending out acceptance letters!) as the applications are received, rather than waiting until a specific cut-off date before beginning their decision process. In these instances, schools are likely to have offered admission to some students while others have yet to be interviewed—meaning that you run the risk that a medical school you're interested in fills all slots for its entering class before you've even had a turn at bat! (You can find out if a medical school uses a rolling admissions system by checking its Web site.) That's why, when it comes to applying to medical school…the sooner, the better.

As far as interviews go, admissions committees usually meet with candidates from fall through spring, with most interviews held during the winter months. (We discuss this part of the admissions cycle in Chapter 7.) By March 30, medical schools will—by collective agreement—issue a number of acceptances at least equal to the size of their first-year entering class.

Personal Statements and Letters of Recommendation

As you'll learn when you get to Chapter 7, admissions officers want to know more about you than just where you went to college, what courses you took and what grades you got, and how you scored on the MCAT exam. They want to know who you are at a more personal level. That's why an essay and letters of recommendation are integral components of your application to medical school and part of the AMCAS process. We briefly describe both of these on the following page.

Your Personal Statement

Every applicant is required to submit a Personal Comments essay of up to 5,300 characters (or approximately one page) in length. This is your opportunity to distinguish yourself from the others and provide admissions officers with insights as to why you are interested in medicine—and why you would be a dedicated and effective physician.

You should know that many admissions committees place significant weight on this section, so you should take the time and effort to craft an organized, well-written, and compelling statement. Some questions you may want to consider while formulating your essay are:

- Why have you selected the field of medicine?

- What motivates you to learn more about medicine? Were there any special hardships, challenges, or obstacles that may have influenced your decision?

- Or, were there any special hardships or challenges that you overcame in general?

- What do you want medical schools to know about you that hasn't been disclosed in another section of the application? Are there, for example, any significant fluctuations in your academic record that are not explained elsewhere?

- Why are you unique? What sets you apart from the pack?

As you begin to carve out your essay, keep in mind that in order to be unique, you must be specific. Rather than write, for example, that *"challenges in my childhood led me to consider medicine at an early age,"* write that *"the summer I turned eight my 11-year-old sister was diagnosed with Diabetes Type I, and I witnessed firsthand the compassion and understanding with which the doctor dealt with my parents. It was during those first few difficult months that I decided I wanted to be a physician."*

In addition to being specific, you will want to ensure that your essay is persuasive (and interesting!), follows a logical and orderly flow, and relates to your reasons for choosing medicine and/or why you believe you will be successful in medical school and as a physician. Beyond that, of course, your writing must adhere to correct grammar and be free of typographical errors and misspellings.

Letters of Recommendation or Evaluation

Medical schools have various requirements regarding letters of recommendation or evaluation, but they all require them in one form or another. If your college has a pre-health advisor, for example, medical schools will probably require a letter from him or her (or from the pre-med committee, if your school has one) as well as a letter of evaluation from at least one faculty member. In instances where there is no pre-health advisor, many medical schools may ask for additional letters from faculty—often specifying that at least one comes from a science professor. Still, other medical schools do not specify from where the letters come, welcome additional letters beyond

AMCAS Letters of Evaluation/ Recommendation Service

Instead of sending your letters of evaluation to individual medical schools, you can now arrange to have them transmitted to participating schools as part of your AMCAS application. This time-saving service is available at no additional fee (beyond that of your regular AMCAS fee), and the vast majority of medical schools participate.

For a list of these schools and a description of the service, go to www.aamc.org/students/amcas/faq/amcasletters.

those that are required, and/or limit the number they will accept. In all cases, you should review the Web sites of the medical schools in which you are interested to learn of their specific requirements.

In general, though—and as you would expect—medical schools want references from those who are in a position to judge your ability to be successful in medical school. While these individuals are largely in the academic arena, primarily pre-health advisors and science professors, those outside the "college gates" may also be helpful. If the medical school you are considering invites additional letters, you might want to ask your current supervisor, particularly if the position is medically related.

In all cases, letters should be from those who know you well and will speak enthusiastically about your abilities, dedication, and unique traits. Beyond that, though, make sure to seek out those whose opinions will be highly valued. (Admissions committees, for example, are not likely to value the input of your teaching assistant. On the other hand, they will weigh heavily the thoughts of the chair of the biology department who taught your "honors" biology class.) In short, seek out letters from those who know you well…can speak highly of you…and count in the eyes of the admissions committee!

Secondary Applications

Your "primary" application is that associated with AMCAS. In addition, though, about half of all medical schools require school-specific, or "secondary," applications. That's because, while the primary application provides admissions officers with much of the information they need, by its very nature a universal application—such as AMCAS—cannot be "all things to all people" and address issues specific to individual schools. Many

institutions therefore require a secondary application that will be used to assess students' reasons for applying to that particular school. (Medical schools will notify you if such an application is needed.) Secondary applications may call for additional letters of recommendation, supplementary writing samples, and/or updated transcripts. Go to the Web sites of the medical schools in which you are interested to learn more.

Costs of Applying

Finally, and as you probably know, there are fees associated with applying to medical school. These costs fall into four general categories, which we summarize below.

Primary Application

For the 2011 entering class, the fee will be $160 for the first school and $32 for each additional school. (Remember, too, that there are several schools that do not use AMCAS and that you may incur a different fee in those instances.)

Secondary Application

Fees for secondary applications typically range from $25 to $100.

College Service Fees

There is usually a small fee for transmittal of your transcript from your college registrar and occasionally a fee for transmittal of letters of recommendation.

MCAT Exam Fees

Although technically not an "application" fee, the costs associated with the MCAT exam are a necessary component of the overall process. Registration for the MCAT exam is $230 and covers the cost of the exam as well as distribution of your scores. In addition, you may incur fees for late registration, changes to your registration, or testing at international test sites. You can read more about the MCAT exam in Chapter 4 and at the MCAT Web site *(www.aamc.org/mcat)*.

Go to *www.aamc.org/firstfacts* for more information on the costs of applying.

Criminal Background Check

The AAMC has initiated a national background check service through which Certiphi Screening, Inc. (a Vertical Screen® Company) will obtain a background report on all accepted applicants to participating medical schools. This service benefits both medical schools and applicants alike, filling the needs of schools to obtain criminal background checks, while, at the same time, preventing applicants from paying additional fees to each medical school to which they are accepted. For more information, please go to
www.aamc.org/students/amcas/faq/background.

You should be aware that participating medical schools may continue to require applicants to undergo a separate national background check process, if required to do so by their own institutional regulations or by applicable state law.

Special Note About Deferred Entry

In recent years, most medical schools have developed delayed matriculation policies to allow their accepted applicants to defer entry without giving up their medical school places. Deferrals are only granted after acceptance. These programs usually require that the applicant submit a written request, and some schools may also ask for a report at the end of the deferral period. Delays of matriculation are usually granted for one year, although some schools may occasionally defer for longer periods of time. Some institutions may require delayed matriculants to sign an agreement to not apply to other medical schools in the interim, while others permit application to other schools. Interested applicants should seek specific information from schools where they applied.

Fee Assistance Program

The AAMC's Fee Assistance Program (FAP), available to individuals with financial limitations,* assists MCAT examinees and AMCAS applicants by reducing the associated costs. FAP recipients receive:

- Waiver of the application fee for submitting the completed AMCAS application to a maximum of 14 medical schools. (Applicants pay $32 for each school beyond the 14 free applications.)
- Reduction of the MCAT registration fee from $230 to $85.
- One complimentary copy of the both the *Official Guide to the MCAT Exam*® and the *Medical School Admissions Requirements (MSAR®)*.

Go to *www.aamc.org/fap* for details on this program.

FAP eligibility decisions are tied directly to the U.S. Department of Health and Human Services' poverty-level guidelines. For the 2010 calendar year, applicants whose total family income is 300 percent or less of the poverty level for their family size are eligible for fee assistance.

AAMC Recommendations for Medical School and M.D.-Ph.D. Candidates

To help ensure that all M.D. and M.D.-Ph.D. candidates are provided timely notification of the outcome of their application and timely access to available first-year positions, and that schools and programs are protected from having unfilled positions in their entering classes, the Association of American Medical Colleges has distributed the following recommendations. They are provided for the information of prospective students, their advisors, and personnel at the medical schools and programs to which they apply. The AAMC recommends that:

1. Each applicant be familiar with, understand, and comply with the application, acceptance, and admission procedures at each school or program to which the applicant has applied, as well as with these Recommendations.

2. Each applicant provide accurate and truthful information in all aspects of the application, acceptance, and admission processes for each school or program to which the applicant has applied.

3. Each applicant submit all application documents (e.g., primary and secondary application forms, transcript[s], letters of evaluation/recommendation, fees) to each school in a timely manner and no later than the school's or program's published deadline date.

4. Each applicant promptly notify all relevant medical school application services and all medical schools or programs with independent application processes of any change, permanent or temporary, in contact information (e.g., mailing address, telephone number, e-mail address).

5. Any applicant who will be unavailable for an extended period of time (e.g., during foreign travel, vacation, holidays) during the application/admission process:

a. Provide instructions regarding his or her application and the authority to respond to offers of acceptance to a parent or other responsible individual in the applicant's absence.

b. Inform all schools or programs at which the applicant remains under consideration of this individual's name and contact information.

6. Each applicant respond promptly to a school's or program's invitation for interview. Any applicant who cannot appear for a previously scheduled interview should notify the school or program immediately of the cancellation of the appointment in the manner requested by the school or program.

7. Each applicant in need of financial aid initiate, as early as possible, the steps necessary to determine eligibility, including the early filing of appropriate need analysis forms and the encouragement of parents, when necessary, to file required income tax forms.

8. In fairness to other applicants, when an applicant has made a decision, prior to May 15, April 30 for M.D.-Ph.D. applicants, not to attend a medical school or program that has made an offer of acceptance, the applicant promptly withdraw his or her application from that (those) other school(s) or program(s) by written correspondence delivered by regular or electronic methods.

9. By May 15 of the matriculation year (April 15 for schools whose first day of class is on or before July 30), April 30 for M.D.-Ph.D. programs, each applicant who has received an offer of acceptance from more than one school or program choose the specific school or program at which the applicant prefers to enroll and withdraw his or her application, by written correspondence delivered by regular or electronic methods, from all other schools or programs from which acceptance offers have been received. (See additional explanation in box below.)

10. Immediately upon enrollment in, or initiation of an orientation program immediately prior to enrollment at, a U.S. or Canadian school or program, each applicant withdraw his or her application from consideration at all other schools or programs at which he or she remains under consideration.

Approved: Council of Deans Administrative Board, February 17, 2009

Chapter 7:
The Admissions Decision

Your heart pounds as you tear open the envelope or click on the e-mail. Will the answer be yea—or nay?

So much seems to come down to this moment. The years of college study and extracurricular activities, the MCAT exam and application process, the campus tours and interviews—all culminate as you learn whether the admissions committee at the medical school(s) of your choice has offered you a slot in its entering class.

You know how you chose to which schools to apply. How do schools choose which applicants to accept?

AAMC Recommends a Holistic Approach...

In its *Handbook for Admissions Officers*, the AAMC clearly states that admissions committees have a responsibility to **"Create the process that identifies applicants whose personal characteristics, level of educational achievement, and professional and career goals conform to those of the institution and who are most likely to contribute to and benefit from the school's learning climate."**

Source: AAMC Handbook for Admissions Officers

The Holistic Approach to Medical School Admissions

Holistic. What does that mean, and how does it enter into the admissions decision?

The term comes from the Greek word holos—meaning all, entire, or total—and it's far from a new idea. In fact, Aristotle himself is credited with having recognized that "the whole is greater than the sum of its parts" in his philosophical work Metaphysics more than two millennia ago. Fast forward 2,000 years and you'll find that medical school admissions committees are making use of this very concept.

How so? In brief, admissions officers carefully review a multitude of criteria—rather than emphasize just one or two facets—in order to gain an appreciation of the "whole" person. Take, for example, the erroneous belief among many applicants that admissions officers weigh high GPAs and MCAT scores above all else. While these metrics are important components of the admissions decision, they are only one part of the overall package. That explains why there are so many instances in which a high-scoring student with a near-perfect GPA does not get into medical school, and why many of those with scores and grades below the average do.

Obviously, something more than metrics alone enters into the admissions decision.

In fact, according to a survey of medical schools conducted by the AAMC, the #1 factor that determines your acceptance to medical school is…the interview. It all ties back to the fact that schools have different missions, and that it is during the interview that admissions officers can really get a sense of who you are and how well your interests and aspirations align with their own goals and purpose. If that sounds familiar, it should. It's the flip side to the analysis you did while you were searching for the "right" schools, analyzing the goals and philosophies of individual schools to determine where you would best fit. Now, it's the medical school's turn to do the same thing from its perspective.

Experiences

Your experiences convey a lot about your interests, your capabilities, and your knowledge. As a result, medical schools take a hard look at what you've done—and where you've been—up to this stage in your life. It helps them gauge not only how likely you are to be successful in their programs, but to what degree you will support their mission and contribute as a physician.

We mentioned in the chapter on undergraduate preparation how important your extracurricular activities may be to an admissions committee, and we don't mean just those clubs and organizations within your college. We mean outside of school, as well. Your experience—particularly that related to medical or clinical work—is an important component of your appeal as a candidate to medical school.

Beyond that, the degree to which you contributed in these activities is vital, too. (See box below.) Medicals schools value a demonstration of true commitment, so if you have been an officer of an organization or a long-term member, for example, you'll want to make that clear to the admissions committee.

Here again, the mission of each school will play a large part in how it evaluates your experiences. Institutions with a stated goal

Depth...not Breadth!

As we mentioned in Chapter 2, a series of short-term involvements (volunteering a day here, spending an afternoon there, and so forth) does not really convey a true interest in the area, and this underlying motivation is actually transparent to admissions officers. Rather, admissions officers are looking for deep, committed participation in areas that are truly of importance to you. Only then are they able to gain some insights as to your real interests and judge how well your goals and their missions align.

of increasing the number of physicians practicing in underserved areas will look with great interest on the summer you spent volunteering in a clinic in a rural location or inner city. In general, though, medical schools especially value community or volunteer experience related to the medical or clinical field.

Concept of "Distance Traveled"

There's another element we'd like to draw to your attention. We mention in the box below that admissions officers are likely to place significance on any obstacles or hardships you've overcome to get to this point in your education. This is a concept known as "distance traveled," and medical schools view life challenges you've faced and conquered as admirable experience—and indicative of some very positive traits.

Examples of Experiences Likely to Be Important to Admissions Committees

- Serving as the primary caregiver for an ill family member
- Special obstacles or hardships overcome
- Employment history (if medically related)
- Research experience
- Experience in a health care setting
- Membership in community-based or volunteer organizations

Source: Roadmap to Diversity: Integrating Holistic Review into Medical School Admissions Processes, AAMC 2010.

Attributes

Admissions committees want to know if you have what it takes to become a good doctor. You've got to have the ability to master the science and medicine behind it all, of course, but you also must have some key personal attributes.

Are you empathetic? Do you have integrity? Can you communicate effectively? Traits such as these are necessary to develop into an effective physician, and admissions committees will use a number of means to determine if you possess them. While your experiences can help demonstrate your appeal in these areas (volunteering for three consecutive summers at a medical clinic certainly conveys dedication, for instance), admissions committees will look to your personal statement, letters of recommendation, and interview(s) to gauge whether you have the desired qualities.

Academic History

Your academic history helps admission committees establish whether your study skills, persistence, course of study, and grades predict success in (their) medical school. Committee members are able to make this determination, to a significant degree, by reviewing your college transcript. More specifically, committee members consider:

- Grades earned in each course and laboratory

- Number of credit hours carried in each academic period

- Distribution of coursework among the biological, physical, and social sciences and the humanities

- Need for remediation of unsatifactory academic work

- Number of incomplete grades and course withdrawals

- Number of years taken to complete the degree program

MCAT Scores

The ability of admission committees to predict success is heightened when they add MCAT scores into the mix. That's because, as you probably already know, there can be significant differences in grading scales and standards from college to college, and MCAT scores provide admissions officers with a standardized measure by which to compare applicants. In fact, the ability of admissions officers to predict who will be successful in their programs increases by as much as 50 percent (gauging by first- and second-year medical school grades) when they look at MCAT scores in conjunction with undergraduate GPAs as opposed to grades alone.

As a result, the better your grades and higher your scores, the more likely you are to be accepted. It is important to remember, though, that there is still a wide range of MCAT scores and GPAs found among accepted applicants, and that scores and grades are used in conjunction with other factors as discussed earlier in this chapter.

Making the Evaluation

Admission committees gauge all three of these areas—experience, attributes, and metrics—in several ways.

First, areas connected with the application process speak to your experience and attributes. Your personal statement, as

---

Examples of Attributes Likely to Be Important to Admissions Committees

- Adaptability
- Critical thinking
- Integrity
- Logical reasoning
- Oral communication skills
- Personal maturity
- Reliability
- Self-discipline
- Work habits
- Compassion
- Cultural competence
- Intellectual curiosity
- Motivation for medicine
- Persistence
- Professionalism
- Resilience
- Teamwork

Source: Survey conducted by the AAMC's Medical College Admission Test, 2008

Medical schools analyze a broad range of attributes, including those related to the applicant's skills and abilities, personal and professional characteristics, and demographic factors. Examples follow.

- **Skills and abilities** could include active listing, critical thinking, and multilingual ability

- **Personal and professional characteristics** could include resilience, intellectual curiosity, and empathy

- **Demographic factors** could include socioeconomic status, race, and gender

We've listed many of the attributes that admissions committees consider in evaluating their application. In addition to these general qualities, though, remember that medical schools give weight to specific characteristics in alignment with their missions. Examples could include research experience and potential, commitment to caring for the underserved, volunteer and community service experience, and knowledge about health care delivery systems.

Metrics

Admissions committees also need to determine (of course!) if you have the academic skills and knowledge necessary to successfully complete the medical school program. To a large extent, committee members will look to your academic record and MCAT scores to answer those questions. Taken together, these two measures provide objective information about your knowledge and ability (compared to other applicants).

What Do Committee Members Generally Prefer?

Although each medical school establishes its own criteria, schools usually prefer applicants who balanced science and humanities coursework, carried respectable course loads, and, generally speaking, earned 3.0–4.0 grades (on a 4.0 scale).

See Chapter 10 for information on the range of GPA averages of all applicants for the 2009 entering class. Or, for the range of GPAs of accepted applicants to a particular medical school, see that institution's entry in the school listings section of this guide.

mentioned in Chapter 6, provides the opportunity for you to tell committee members of your extracurricular activities, "distance traveled" (if applicable; see page 40), volunteer efforts, and medical-related work experience—and, by inference, the personal attributes that go along with that. A role as the officer in a school club conveys leadership skills. Working in a medical clinic summer after summer demonstrates motivation for medicine. A long history of volunteering with fundraisers for cancer research certainly suggests teamwork and compassion.

Your letters of recommendation, also described in Chapter 6, attest to your personal attributes, as well. You'll certainly want your professors and advisor (and other evaluators) to address your persistence, strong work habits, and self-discipline. (The faculty and administrative staff at your undergraduate school will know how to craft a letter, but for others, you might want to suggest a few key concepts.)

Then there are the metrics. As you know, your academic record is part of your AMCAS application and includes both your college transcript(s) and MCAT scores. From there, committee members can determine whether you have the grades, range of coursework, and foundation of knowledge they seek in their successful applicants.

Wondering Where YOUR Metrics Place You?

You can gain some insights by reviewing the chart on page 60, which shows what percentage of applicants were accepted to medical school based on combinations of specific grades and scores. In addition, the individual school entries in this guide include the range of MCAT scores generally deemed acceptable for admission, along with the median overall GPA and science GPA of their accepted students.

The Interview Is Key

And then…there is the interview.

If you've been invited to an interview, you've made it through the preliminary trials by virtue of an impressive personal statement, an appealing background of experiences, strong letters of recommendation, and a superior academic history. But now, you've really got to "shine." Medical schools usually interview three, four, even five times as many applicants as their class size, and that is why the interview is likely to be the #1 determining factor at this phase in the assessment as to whether or not you receive an acceptance.

The very fact that interviews are given at all, by the way, is a significant distinction of medical schools, since some professional schools do not necessarily require them. This alone attests to the degree to which admissions officers seek—and medical schools value—qualities and characteristics such as empathy, self-awareness, communications ability, and interpersonal skills that can best be judged in a direct interview situation. You can take a number of steps to ensure you're prepared for it:

- *Know the Basics*
  Whether it's for a new job or for a slot in a medical school's entering class, certain similarities exist in all interviewing situations. A good start would be to pick up one of any of the dozens of books on interviewing skills and familiarize yourself with the basics.

- *Know What Type of Interview to Expect*
  It will also be helpful to be ready for any number of different interview formats. At some schools, interviews are held with individual admission committee members; at others, group interviews are the norm. In addition, while most interviews are typically held on the medical school campus, some schools have designated interviewers in different geographic regions to minimize time and expense for applicants. (Information about a school's interview policies and procedures is usually provided to applicants in the initial stages of the selection process.)

- *Be Comfortable with Different Interviewing Styles*
  You've probably had some experience interviewing for summer and part-time jobs (and possibly for your undergraduate school), so it won't surprise you that interviewers have their own styles and follow different formats. Some follow a structured design, asking questions from a predetermined list and assigning numeric scores to each answer.

Some Interview-related Data

- The median number of applicants interviewed per school was 528, with a range of 122 to 1,550.
- 60% of applicants participate in two interviews, lasting between 30 and 60 minutes.
- 80% of interviewers have access to personal statements, 59% have access to GPA data, and 57% to MCAT data.
- 65% of interviewers formulate questions from a list of topics.
- 51% of interviewers make overall numeric rating of performance.

Source: Survey conducted by the AAMC's Medical College Admission Test, 2008

Others prefer a more free-flowing arrangement and provide the applicant with a greater degree of open input. Still others fall somewhat in the middle. Again, be ready for any approach.

- *Do Your Research*

  Investigate the school thoroughly by reviewing its entry in this guidebook, its Web site, the information packet sent to you, and any articles you can get your hands on. (Hint: Do an Internet search.) You'll want to impress your interviewer with not only your potential for success but also your interest in his or her specific institution. You can demonstrate these qualities through the answers to the interviewer's questions as well as by the questions you ask (see box at below).

When It's Your Turn to Ask the Questions...

There will come a point in your interview when you will be asked if you have any questions, and it's an opportunity you don't want to pass up. Not only can you clarify any remaining issues, but you'll have another means by which you can demonstrate your commitment, astuteness, and interest in that particular school. With that in mind, you'll want to prepare two or three questions specific to that very school.

Need a way to generate ideas? Check out the AAMC's "Thirty-Five Questions I Wish I Had Asked" at *www.aamc.org/students/applying/about/35questions.htm.*

- *Practice*

  Since most admission committee members are experienced interviewers who want to learn about the "real" person, you should be forthright and open in your meeting and not try to "game" the interviewer. If you're apprehensive about the process, find a trusted advisor or friend with whom you can conduct mock interviews to help build your confidence.

Remember, the interview provides applicants with opportunities to discuss their personal histories and motivation for a medical career and to draw attention to any aspects of their application that merit emphasis or explanation. Make certain you present yourself in the best possible light by preparing thoroughly for your meeting.

AAMC Podcast on Interviewing Basics!

What Are the Basics About Interviewing for Medical School?

Sunny Gibson, director of the Office of Minority and Cultural Affairs at the Feinberg School of Medicine at Northwestern University, goes into careful detail on how to prepare for and increase your chances of success in the interview process while applying to medical school.

Go to www.aamc.org/podcasts for podcasts provided by the AAMC and AspiringDocs.org. You can subscribe at no charge at the iTunes store.

Know Your Interview Rights and Responsibilities

Although interviewers are instructed by admissions officers and guided by federal statutes on what are unfair or discriminatory pre-admission inquiries, there may be an occasion when an interviewer asks an inappropriate question. (See examples in box at right.)

You have the right not to answer what you sense is an inappropriate question. If such a question is asked, try to relax and provide a thoughtful and articulate response (two essential characteristics of a good physician). You may also respectfully decline to answer the question and explain that you were advised not to answer questions that you sensed were inappropriate.

You have the responsibility to report being asked an inappropriate question to help prevent further occurrences. Medical schools have the responsibility to establish procedures that enable applicants to report such incidents in a confidential manner. Medical schools should inform applicants of these procedures prior to interviews and assure them that reporting an incident will not bias the applicant's evaluation.

If a medical school did not inform you of its procedure and an incident occurs, use these guidelines. If possible, report in confidence the interviewer's name and the interview question(s) that was asked to an admissions officer during the interview day. Otherwise, e-mail this informaton to an admissions officer within 24 hours of the interview noting the date and time of the incident. Furthermore, you have the right to ask if another interview is deemed necessary to ensure an unbiased evaluation of your application to that medical school.

Some interviewers use the interview to assess how well you function under stress and may purposely ask challenging questions to observe how you respond under pressure. How you communicate will be a critical part of the encounter; however, this does not give an interviewer the right to ask you inappropriate questions in their attempt to challenge you during the interview.

Examples of inappropriate questions:

- What is your race, ethnicity, religion, sexual orientation, political affiliation, marital status, opinion on abortion and/or euthanasia, income, value of your home, credit score, etc.?
- Are you planning on having children during medical school?
- Do you have any disabilities?
- Will you require special accommodations?
- Have you ever been arrested?
- Have you ever done drugs?
- How old are you?

Sample response to an inappropriate questions:

Q. *What are your plans for expanding your family during medical school?*

A. Can you please clarify your question? I want to make sure that I'm providing information that is most relevant to my candidacy.

Q. *Have you ever done drugs?*

A. I am uncomfortable discussing my medical history and possible use of prescription medications during this interview.

Chapter 8:
Building Toward Greater Diversity

Why is diversity in medical education important?

The very process of education itself is enhanced when the student body includes those from varying cultures and backgrounds—and research bears it out. Over the past 30 years, many studies on undergraduate campuses have attested to the value of diversity in the classroom and the overall school environment. It generates a wealth of ideas, helps students challenge their assumptions, and broadens their perspectives. Diversity in group settings has even been linked to greater cognitive results, ultimately leading to better learning outcomes.*

Benefits of Diversity Extend Beyond Education*

Increased diversity brings with it benefits that extend beyond the classroom. For example, a greater degree of diversity:

- **Increases access to health care.**
  Research has shown that diversity in the physician workforce contributes to increased access to health care.
- **Accelerates advances in research.**
  Diversity among clinician-scientists has been linked to an increase in research dedicated to diseases that disproportionately affect racial and ethnic minorities.
- **Makes good business sense.**
  Given the growth in racial ethnic minority populations in the country and the increasing purchasing power these groups represent, achieving greater diversity within physician networks can be seen as a way for health plans to attract "customers" from these communities.

It is for all these reasons that the AAMC strives to increase diversity among medical school applicants and therefore offers students a wide range of programs and resources to help meet that goal. Similarly, medical schools themselves almost always have programs—and staff— to ensure that all candidates to their institutions have an equal opportunity for admittance. We review these resources in the pages that follow.

The Diversity of Diversity, and Where We Now Stand

But first…what exactly do we mean by "diversity"?

When you mention that word, many people automatically think in terms of race and ethnicity. And while it is certainly true that it is important to attract more racial and ethnic minority populations to medicine, the concept of diversity is much more expansive. The AAMC recognizes that diversity encompasses a variety of factors that also include gender, socioeconomic status, life experiences, age, sexual orientation, and other personal characteristics.

So, what's our current situation? Let's look at it from a few different perspectives.

*See list of suggested readings and resources at the end of this chapter to learn more about diversity in educational settings.

- First, consider **race and ethnicity**. While diversity extends beyond this particular measure, as just mentioned, it nevertheless remains a critical component. With that in mind, you can see from the chart below that racial ethnic minority groups are underrepresented in medicine. The data show, for example, that only 8.2 percent of matriculating students are black or African American, 7.2 percent are Hispanic or Latino, and slightly less than 1 percent are American Indian or Alaska Native.

- What about **family income**? This is another area of great imbalance—and inequity. Parental income of students entering medical school skews heavily to the upper range, with average income of $164,483. (That's almost double the estimated U.S. median income of $70,000 for 4-person families reported by the U.S. Department of Health and Human Services.) Looking at it from another angle, we see that almost one in five students come from homes in which their parents earn $250,000 or more a year.

- Let's look at the situation from yet a third perspective— **gender**. On the surface, it appears that male and female applicants are fairly equal in number, but there are instances

...As Are Those from Low-Income Households

Parental Income of Entering Medical Students, 2009

Income	Percent
Less than $10,000	2.6
$10,000 - $19,999	2.3
$20,000 - $29,999	3.0
$30,000 - $39,999	3.9
$40,000 - $49,999	4.3
$50,000 - $74,999	12.9
$75,000 - $99,999	11.3
$100,000 - $249,999	43.9
$250,000 - $499,999	12.7
$500,000 or more	3.1
Average income of parents:	$164,485*

Source: AAMC's 2009 Matriculating Student Questionnaire (MSQ)

*from 2008 survey

where that is not the case. You'll see, for example, from the chart below left, that there is a relative shortage of male applicants within the black or African American demographic. Within this specific group, males comprise barely one-third of those who apply to medical school.

These examples barely scratch the surface when it comes to the issue of diversity, but they should be sufficient to demonstrate our point.

For information about the AAMC's definition of those "underrepresented in medicine," go to www.aamc.org/urm.

AAMC Programs and Resources

With the benefits that diversity offers, it's no wonder that the AAMC is strongly committed to improving the situation. To that end, the AAMC's Diversity Policy and Programs is engaged in a number of programs and initiatives to help increase diversity and open the campus gates to capable and promising students from a broad range of backgrounds. (It's important to note that while these programs are open to all, they are sensitive to the challenges and needs of those from groups underrepresented in medicine.) Examples of these initiatives are described below.

Applicants to U.S. Medical Schools by Race, Ethnicity, and Sex, 2009

Women | Men

	Women	Men
White (n=23,493)	43.9%	56.1%
Asian (n=8,501)	49.1%	50.9%
Black or African American (n=3,106)	67.5%	32.5%
Native Hawaiian or Other Pacific Islander (n=115)	46.8%	56.8%
American Indian or Alaska Native (n=111)	54.1%	45.9%
Hispanic or Latino* (n=3,061)	54.1%	45.9%
Multiple Race (n=1,038)	54.1%	45.9%
Other Race or No Race Repsonse (n=1,038)	51.5%	48.5%
Foreign/Unkown Citizenship (n=1,639)	46.5%	53.5%

Note: Since 2002, following U.S. federal guidelines, AMCAS has asked applicants who are U.S. citizens or permanent residents to self-identify using two separate questions: the first question ("Ethnicity") asks applicants whether they are "Spanish/Hispanic/Latino/Latina" or "Not Spanish/Hispanic/Latino/Latina"; the second question ("Race") asks applicants to self-identify using non-Hispanic or Latino race categories, and applicants are asked to "check all that apply." The ethnicity category and several race categories permit further self-identification by sub-categories. Prior to 2002, AMCAS applicants were not able to select more than one race. Three applicants in 2009, who declined to report gender, are not reflected. Source: AAMC: Data Warehouse: Applicant Matriculant File as of November 16, 2009.

Racial Ethnic Minorities Are Underrepresented...

Demographics of Entering Medical Students*, 2009

Demographic	Percent
American Indian or Alaska Native	0.9
Hispanic/Latino	7.2
Black or African American	8.2
Asian	22.0
White	62.3

*self-identified
Source: AAMC Data Warehouse, 2009

Career Fairs and Enrichment Programs

Medical schools throughout the country provide all sorts of programs and resources designed to recruit students and prepare them for medical education. Some of these programs are held during the school year; others in the summer. Some are designed for high school students; others, for college students; and still others, for those who have completed undergraduate study. The AAMC is affiliated with two such programs:

- *Minority Student Medical Career Awareness Workshops and Recruitment Fair*
  This event, held each fall at the AAMC's annual meeting, is a wonderful opportunity for high school and college students to explore medical careers. Representatives from all 132 AAMC-member medical schools are invited, and students have the chance to talk with them about preparing for medical school, enrichment programs, admission policies and procedures, financial aid, and more. There are interactive medical and health activities, as well, and workshops are also sponsored for family members. You can find out the date and location of the next annual fair at *www.aamc.org/careerfair*.

- *Summer Medical and Dental Education Program (SMDEP)*
  The Summer Medical and Dental Education Program is a free six-week summer academic enrichment program for college freshmen and sophomores interested in careers in medicine or dentistry. Components of the program include science and mathematics-based courses, learning and study skills seminars, career development activities, clinical experiences, and a financial planning workshop. Funded by the Robert

Wood Johnson Foundation and offered at 12 U.S. medical and 9 dental schools across the nation, the program includes tuition, housing, and meals. For additional information, visit *www.smdep.org*, or call toll-free at 1-866-58SMDEP.

AspiringDocs.org

The AAMC has developed a campaign designed to encourage students who aspire to medical school—especially those from groups underrepresented in medicine—by providing a broad range of information and support. The centerpiece of the campaign is a rich Web site at *www.aspiringdocs.org* that allows "aspiring doctors" to get the information they need to prepare for application to medical school. Through a variety of online features, such as Ask the Experts, Hot Topics, and Inspiring Stories, and podcasts, students are provided with easy-to-understand information about applying to medical school and financing a medical education.

Other AAMC Resources

And that's just the start. The AAMC also offers a wide variety of publications, online tools, and other information in the "Minorities in Medicine" section of the AAMC's Web site at *www.aamc.org/students/minorities* and the AAMC's Diversity Web site at *www.aamc.org/diversity*. Among the resources you will find there are:

- *Minority Student Opportunities in United States Medical Schools (MSOUSMS)*
  Everything you wanted to know—and then some! This publication is packed full of information on all sorts of diversity-related programs and data, which are provided on a school-by-school basis. Here, you can learn about an individual institution's recruitment efforts, admission policies,

Benefits of Diversity from the Student View...

Students themselves recognize the benefits of diversity on their medical education. The data below show to what extent they agree with the following statement:

"I expect the racial and ethnic diversity of my school's study body to positively influence my professional growth and development."

Strongly Agree	Agree	No Opinion	Disagree	Strongly Disagree
48.9%	38.3%	10.7%	1.6%	0.5%

Source: AAMC's 2009 Matriculating Student Questionnaire (MSQ)

academic support initiatives, enrichment programs, student financial assistance, and more. Intended for use in conjunction with the Medical School Admissions Requirements, all content for MSOUSMS is supplied directly from the schools themselves in response to a questionnaire from the AAMC's Diversity Policy and Programs. You can read a complete description of this publication and order a copy at *www.aamc.org/msousms*.

- *Enrichment programs online*
  This site includes a free database to help undergraduate students locate summer enrichment programs on medical school campuses. You can search by school, state, region, area of focus, and length of program. Go to *www.services.aamc.org/summerprograms* to explore programs of interest.

- *Medical Minority Applicant Registry*
  Students applying to medical school who identify themselves as members of groups that are underrepresented in medicine, or who are economically or educationally disadvantaged, can register for Med-MAR at the time they take the MCAT exam. This Web-based program circulates basic biographical information and MCAT scores of registered examinees to all U.S. medical schools, thereby providing institutions with opportunities to enhance their diversity efforts. Go to *www.aamc.org/students/minorities/resources/medmar* for more information.

- *Medical School Career Fairs and Events Calendar*
  With this online calendar, students can search for recruitment events at schools in their state or within a specific date range. Information is available at *www.aamc.org/calendar/careerfairs*.

- *Fee Assistance Program (FAP)*
  The AAMC is pleased to offer its Fee Assistance Program to students whose financial limitations would otherwise prevent them from taking the MCAT exam or applying to medical school. Details about the FAP can be found at *www.aamc.org/fap* and in Chapter 6 of this book.

- *Data about race and ethnicity*
  The AAMC also collects and presents detailed data about medical students from an array of racial and ethnic groups, most of which are available online free-of-charge on the AAMC Web site (and a good deal of which is included in this guide). Several resources likely to be of interest are highlighted below.

o AAMC information about recent matriculant data for each medical school is presented in this chapter in Table 8-A, Matriculants by *Medical School and Race and Ethnicity*, 2009.

o Chapter 10 includes a table showing the self-reported racial and ethnic identification of medical school applicants and accepted applicants for the 2009 entering class.

o A large collection of data about medical school applicants, matriculants, and graduates are available on the AAMC Web site at *www.aamc.org/facts*.

o The AAMC publication, *Diversity in Medical Education, Facts & Figures* 2008, provides race and ethnicity data on medical school applicants, accepted applicants, matriculants, enrollment, graduates, and faculty. You can access the full text without charge at *www.aamc.org/students/minorities*.

o Data on medical school faculty, including information by race and ethnicity, can be found at *www.aamc.org/data/facultyroster/reports*.

School Programs and Resources

It's not just the AAMC that's interested in the issue of diversity. As you would expect, colleges and medical schools are also committed to making medical education accessible to individuals from all segments of society—and you'll certainly want to take advantage of these resources as well. Among them are:

- *Pre-medical school programs at undergraduate colleges*
  Pre-health advisors have an abundance of pertinent information at their fingertips. Not only can they help you with the application process and refer you to appropriate contacts, they also know about programs that students from underrepresented groups and disadvantaged backgrounds are likely to find useful. If your college has a pre-health advisor (and the majority of them do), make sure you take advantage of this valuable resource.

- *Medical School Web sites*
  You'll also want to explore the medical school Web sites for information on their diversity programs and resources. Go to *www.aamc.org/medicalschools* for a listing of all U.S. and Canadian M.D.-granting medical schools and links to their Web sites.

- *Medical school diversity affairs officers*

  Another invaluable resource will be the medical school diversity affairs officers. These individuals are dedicated to increasing diversity among medical schools at their institutions and are an excellent source of information for applicants (or potential applicants). You can get the name of the diversity affairs contacts at any U.S. medical school through a searchable database (see box at right) provided by the AAMC.

- *Financial assistance for medical school*

  Don't let the cost of medical school deter you from your dreams. As you'll learn in Chapter 11 of this publication, more than four-fifths of medical students across the country receive some form of financial assistance. Medical schools—both public and private—work hard to offer a variety of financial aid plans to ensure that capable students are not denied access to their institutions as a result of financial limitations. In addition to discussing possibilities for assistance with the financial aid officer at the medical schools that interest you, you should familiarize yourself with general information about financing a medical education by reading the relevant material in this book, reviewing the wealth of information about loans (and other programs) at *www.aamc.org/students/financing*, and learning about scholarships at *www.aamc.org/students/minorities/scholarships.htm*.

- *Programs at medical schools*

  Once you've enrolled in medical school, you'll find that a variety of academic and personal support programs are available to you. These programs assist students from various backgrounds to successfully complete their medical studies, with the ultimate goal of increasing diversity among physicians entering careers in patient care, teaching, and research, and of eliminating racial and ethnic disparities in health care. The staff members at each medical school who are responsible for these programs are identified in the school-by-school entries in Chapters 14 and 15 of this publication.

Directory of Diversity Affairs Officers

The Directory of Diversity Affairs Officers is a searchable database of diversity affairs representatives at all U.S. medical schools. It is searchable by name, location, and institution, and is available at *www.aamc.org/coda*.

For those who wish to explore the benefits of diversity, may we suggest the following readings:

Antonio AL, Chang MJ, Hakuta K, Kenny DA, Levin S, Milem JF. *Effects of racial diversity on complex thinking in college students.* Psychological Science. 2004:15;507-10.

Astin AW. *What matters in college? Four critical years revisited.* San Francisco, CA:Jossey-Bass, 1993.

Gurin P. *The compelling need for diversity in higher education: Expert testimony in Gratz,* et al. v. Bollinger, et al. Michigan J of Race & Law. 1999:5; 363–425.

Nemeth CJ, Wachtler J. *Creative problem solving as a result of majority vs. minority influence.* European J of Social Psychology, 1983:13; 45–55.

Saha Guiton G; Wimmers PF.; Wilkerson L. *Student Body Racial and Ethnic Composition and Diversity-Related Outcomes in US Medical Schools.* Journal of the American Medical Association, JAMA, 2008. 300: 1135–1145.

Smith DG & Associates. *Diversity works: The emerging picture of how students benefit.* Washington, DC: Association of American Colleges and Universities, 1997.

No Advisor? Contact the NAAHP for Help

If your institution does not have a pre-health advisor, you can contact the National Association of Advisors for the Health Professions (NAAHP). There, you will find a list of NAAHP members who have volunteered to help students without access to a pre-health advisor. Learn more about what pre-health advisors do and how to locate one at *www.naahp.org/advisors.htm*.

Table 8-A Matriculants by Medical School and Race and Ethnicity 2009*

School State	School Name	Mexican American	Cuban	Puerto Rican	Other Hispanic or Latino	Total Hispanic or Latino	Chinese	Asian Indian	Pakistani	Filipino	Japanese	Korean	Vietnamese	Other Asian	Total Asian	Native American (incl AK)	Black	Native Hawaiian/O PI	White	Unduplicated Total
AL	Alabama	0	0	0	3	3	7	12	1	1	0	1	5	2	28	3	10	0	133	175
	South Alabama	0	0	1	0	1	1	4	1	0	1	0	1	2	10	0	3	0	60	74
AR	Arkansas	1	1	0	4	5	3	5	3	1	0	0	3	1	15	0	10	1	136	165
AZ	Arizona	8	0	1	3	12	11	10	0	9	2	4	2	4	32	2	4	1	121	163
CA	Loma Linda	1	0	0	8	8	14	4	1	9	6	23	2	2	56	1	5	3	98	159
	Southern Cal-Keck	14	0	2	8	23	14	9	1	2	4	4	5	5	41	1	8	1	95	166
	Stanford	4	0	0	5	9	15	10	0	2	1	4	5	3	34	1	8	0	34	86
	UC Berkeley/SF Joint Prog	0	0	0	2	2	0	0	0	0	1	1	0	1	2	0	1	0	13	16
	UC Davis	6	0	0	6	12	9	5	3	4	2	3	6	1	30	0	4	2	54	93
	UC Irvine	10	0	1	2	13	18	7	0	2	2	4	6	7	40	1	2	1	49	104
	UC San Diego	6	0	0	3	11	22	12	0	2	1	5	11	3	54	4	5	0	58	125
	UC San Francisco	19	0	0	7	25	24	8	2	9	3	0	2	3	47	3	10	3	80	149
	UCLA-Drew	5	0	2	3	8	3	1	0	4	0	0	0	2	10	0	10	0	3	24
	UCLA-Geffen	17	0	1	1	20	24	10	2	2	4	7	11	2	63	1	10	0	79	162
CO	Colorado	3	0	1	6	9	6	4	0	2	0	3	1	4	18	3	2	1	132	160
CT	Connecticut	1	0	2	1	4	5	3	0	1	0	2	0	4	16	3	12	0	49	85
	Yale	2	0	2	5	9	18	11	0	1	0	1	1	5	33	1	6	0	49	99
DC	George Washington	1	2	1	3	6	3	28	6	3	4	2	2	1	48	0	22	0	104	177
	Georgetown	2	2	0	2	4	15	12	2	1	5	4	2	6	43	0	10	1	139	197
	Howard	0	2	0	5	5	2	8	2	0	0	1	3	1	19	1	66	1	8	105
FL	Central Florida	0	3	1	1	5	2	1	0	0	0	1	0	2	6	2	4	0	28	41
	FIU-Wertheim	0	9	0	6	15	1	5	0	1	0	0	0	2	9	0	3	0	25	43
	Florida	0	4	0	6	10	9	11	3	1	2	2	3	2	31	0	2	0	86	128
	Florida State	1	3	1	11	16	3	4	0	2	0	1	0	3	13	2	12	0	88	118
	Miami-Miller	0	13	2	13	25	8	29	2	5	3	9	0	6	50	1	14	1	123	194
	South Florida	4	4	5	8	19	6	16	4	5	1	3	3	1	34	1	6	0	77	120
GA	Emory	0	3	1	3	5	9	10	2	0	1	1	1	1	24	0	14	0	90	136
	MC Georgia	1	1	0	1	3	11	22	4	1	0	10	5	4	55	3	15	0	117	190
	Mercer	0	0	0	1	1	1	5	1	1	0	0	0	0	10	1	3	0	79	92
	Morehouse	0	0	0	1	3	1	1	0	1	0	0	0	0	3	1	51	2	4	56
HI	Hawaii-Burns	0	0	1	2	6	24	0	0	7	21	0	0	0	52	1	1	2	18	62
IA	Iowa-Carver	4	0	0	0	6	3	4	0	3	3	1	3	1	15	2	8	0	119	148
IL	Chicago Med-Franklin	4	0	0	1	5	10	28	3	3	3	6	3	11	64	0	5	0	106	190
	Chicago-Pritzker	3	0	1	0	4	6	7	0	0	0	2	2	2	16	3	11	3	56	88
	Illinois	19	3	3	19	41	19	39	3	3	2	19	2	7	89	4	38	0	169	313
	Loyola-Stritch	5	0	2	1	10	2	7	2	0	1	2	1	4	16	2	11	1	118	145
	Northwestern-Feinberg	6	1	1	3	10	19	19	1	2	2	9	1	8	58	3	11	1	86	164
	Rush	1	1	1	8	11	7	14	3	3	4	5	3	3	37	0	6	0	93	144
	Southern Illinois	2	0	1	1	4	0	6	1	0	0	0	0	0	7	0	9	0	51	72
IN	Indiana	7	1	0	5	13	8	14	2	0	3	6	2	8	42	2	12	1	259	322
KS	Kansas	5	0	0	1	7	1	3	1	1	1	2	3	5	17	1	12	0	144	175
KY	Kentucky	0	0	1	0	1	3	4	0	0	0	0	1	2	13	0	4	0	92	115
	Louisville	0	0	1	1	2	4	7	1	1	0	4	0	1	18	1	11	0	132	160
LA	LSU New Orleans	2	0	0	5	7	7	7	0	4	0	0	4	2	19	1	20	0	154	193
	LSU Shreveport	0	0	0	2	2	3	6	0	0	0	0	1	1	12	0	6	0	99	117
	Tulane	1	0	2	2	5	14	11	1	3	2	8	1	3	38	1	2	0	130	177
MA	Boston	8	3	2	7	19	20	23	4	3	1	7	2	6	60	0	12	1	92	176
	Harvard	6	1	5	5	17	26	20	2	1	3	4	1	7	61	0	18	0	68	165
	Massachusetts	0	0	1	3	3	10	8	1	1	0	0	2	6	25	1	5	0	100	125
	Tufts	4	1	1	2	7	22	12	0	1	3	6	0	3	48	1	5	0	148	200
MD	Johns Hopkins	2	1	0	3	4	16	17	3	0	1	7	1	5	41	0	11	0	58	120
	Maryland	1	0	0	2	6	8	11	1	1	1	7	1	4	35	1	20	2	105	160
	Uniformed Services-Hebert	4	1	0	2	6	8	3	1	3	2	8	0	3	28	1	5	2	134	172
MI	Michigan	1	1	1	4	7	19	19	2	1	1	3	1	2	51	2	6	1	99	170
	Michigan State	4	0	1	4	10	6	15	9	2	0	4	3	2	31	2	14	0	106	155
	Wayne State	2	1	0	0	3	16	32	9	5	1	4	3	10	77	0	18	1	168	290
MN	Mayo	0	0	1	7	3	4	3	1	1	1	0	0	1	9	0	4	2	32	49
	Minnesota	1	1	1	8	5	5	4	0	1	0	4	0	1	17	1	3	1	138	169
	Minnesota Duluth	0	0	0	0	0	0	0	0	0	0	0	0	0	0	7	0	0	54	60
MO	Missouri Columbia	1	0	0	3	4	5	0	0	0	0	2	0	3	11	1	6	0	80	95
	Missouri Kansas City	1	0	0	0	0	0	0	0	0	0	0	0	49	49	0	2	0	28	104
	St Louis	0	0	2	0	5	15	29	1	1	1	6	3	5	59	1	10	1	107	175
	Washington U St Louis	3	0	2	0	5	23	8	1	1	1	3	1	4	42	2	15	0	67	121
MS	Mississippi	0	0	0	0	0	1	3	1	0	1	1	1	0	8	2	15	0	97	120
NC	Duke	1	2	4	2	7	11	11	1	0	0	1	1	0	25	1	16	0	62	100

Source: AAMC Data Warehouse: Applicant Matriculant File as of 10/19/2009. *Hispanic Ethnicities are alone or in combination with some other Hispanic Ethnicity and include any Race. Ethnicity Counts include U.S. Citizens and Permanent Residents only. Race Counts include U.S. Citizens and Permanent Residents only, are alone or in combination with some other Race, and include both Hispanic and Non-Hispanic Ethnicity. The total represents an unduplicated count and also includes matriculants for whom we have no race data or who are foreign.

Table 8-A Matriculants by Medical School and Race and Ethnicity 2009*

Matriculants 2009		Mexican American	Cuban	Puerto Rican	Other Hispanic or Latino	Total Hispanic or Latino	Chinese	Asian Indian	Pakistani	Filipino	Japanese	Korean	Vietnamese	Other Asian	Total Asian	Native American (Incl AK)	Black	Native Hawaiian/O PI	White	Total Unduplicated
NE	Creighton	3	2	1	1	7	6	7	0	1	1	1	6	1	21	2	5	0	95	126
	Nebraska	2	0	0	0	2	2	3	1	1	0	1	1	2	10	1	3	0	111	124
NH	Dartmouth	0	1	0	1	2	7	3	0	0	0	1	0	0	11	2	1	0	61	84
NJ	UMDNJ New Jersey	1	4	3	9	16	16	42	4	1	0	9	1	2	73	0	15	0	71	171
	UMDNJ-RW Johnson	0	0	3	1	4	16	24	3	2	1	4	0	2	50	0	11	0	88	163
NM	New Mexico	16	0	1	6	23	4	0	0	0	1	2	0	0	6	9	1	0	52	77
NV	Nevada	1	1	0	2	4	4	3	1	4	1	2	0	0	14	0	2	1	47	62
NY	Albany	1	0	1	2	3	5	19	2	2	1	4	2	1	34	1	3	1	79	133
	Buffalo	0	0	1	0	1	16	9	0	2	1	5	1	5	40	2	5	1	96	144
	Columbia	5	2	3	2	11	11	6	1	1	1	5	2	1	28	0	13	0	100	153
	Cornell-Weill	5	1	1	4	11	10	6	1	0	2	2	1	0	21	2	16	2	55	101
	Einstein	3	0	0	8	11	23	16	1	1	1	4	1	9	51	1	13	0	112	183
	Mount Sinai	3	2	1	12	17	21	11	1	0	1	2	0	3	37	2	7	0	82	140
	New York Medical	2	1	1	10	13	23	12	3	0	3	4	3	12	56	0	8	0	119	194
	New York University	0	3	3	6	14	20	13	1	0	1	7	0	2	44	1	3	2	107	164
	Rochester	0	0	2	5	7	5	10	1	0	1	0	1	3	21	0	15	0	67	104
	SUNY Downstate	0	1	4	12	17	28	19	3	8	0	6	1	14	74	0	18	0	89	190
	SUNY Upstate	3	0	0	2	5	8	7	2	0	0	3	0	2	21	1	23	3	87	151
	Stony Brook	1	1	1	4	6	10	8	3	0	0	4	1	4	30	1	9	0	75	124
OH	Case Western	1	0	1	5	7	36	15	3	1	3	8	2	3	67	1	20	0	101	199
	Cincinnati	3	0	0	1	4	21	19	3	0	1	8	1	3	54	0	8	0	104	166
	Northeastern Ohio	1	2	1	2	5	5	26	3	1	0	2	0	4	39	0	1	0	64	107
	Ohio State	14	4	5	3	21	7	17	4	1	1	7	2	1	36	0	21	2	155	220
	Toledo	2	0	5	3	4	7	14	4	1	1	3	2	2	33	0	7	2	132	175
	Wright State-Boonshoft	0	0	2	0	2	0	11	2	2	0	3	0	5	22	0	6	0	69	100
OK	Oklahoma	1	0	0	1	1	5	6	4	0	2	3	10	2	29	9	2	0	126	162
OR	Oregon	1	0	0	3	3	7	4	0	0	2	4	7	3	26	3	0	0	85	120
PA	Commonwealth	1	1	0	1	2	3	2	1	1	0	1	0	3	11	0	1	0	53	65
	Drexel	2	1	0	7	10	19	37	4	5	2	12	3	5	85	0	15	2	148	260
	Jefferson	2	0	4	14	20	14	23	1	0	1	6	10	2	53	1	4	0	170	255
	Penn State	0	0	1	8	5	7	13	2	2	0	4	2	2	32	1	6	0	101	144
	Pennsylvania	1	2	0	8	11	20	10	2	0	3	1	0	2	35	1	10	0	116	161
	Pittsburgh	3	2	0	5	9	23	12	0	2	4	3	0	4	43	1	11	1	92	148
	Temple	3	4	2	4	13	13	13	1	2	4	3	1	4	39	1	15	3	131	196
PR	Caribe	1	7	52	6	62	0	0	0	0	0	0	0	0	0	2	5	0	50	65
	Ponce	2	8	54	1	62	1	0	3	0	0	0	0	0	1	1	2	0	53	66
	Puerto Rico	1	6	102	8	103	1	0	0	0	0	0	0	0	3	0	11	0	68	105
	San Juan Bautista	1	6	38	2	52	1	2	0	0	0	0	0	0	3	0	4	0	55	63
RI	Brown-Alpert	4	2	3	2	9	5	5	0	0	0	5	1	0	18	0	10	0	54	94
SC	MU South Carolina	2	2	0	6	10	2	9	2	0	1	0	1	3	18	2	22	0	121	164
	South Carolina	0	2	0	5	7	1	3	1	0	0	1	2	3	9	0	1	0	69	79
SD	South Dakota-Sanford	0	0	0	1	1	1	0	0	0	0	1	0	0	2	1	0	0	51	54
TN	East Tennessee-Quillen	0	1	1	0	0	1	4	0	0	0	1	0	0	6	0	4	0	57	66
	Meharry	1	1	0	3	5	2	3	2	0	1	0	1	2	9	1	85	1	10	105
	Tennessee	1	0	1	2	4	4	10	3	0	1	3	0	5	23	2	12	0	126	165
	Vanderbilt	2	0	0	2	4	8	12	1	0	1	1	2	3	25	0	11	0	59	111
TX	Baylor	21	1	0	7	29	24	24	2	2	1	6	7	6	69	0	11	1	100	186
	Texas A & M	15	0	0	5	20	6	10	3	1	0	2	3	22	47	1	4	0	90	150
	Texas Tech	10	0	0	1	11	5	9	1	1	0	2	2	16	36	0	3	0	94	140
	Texas Tech-Foster	6	0	0	1	7	4	0	1	0	0	0	1	6	12	0	0	0	24	40
	UT Galveston	30	2	0	5	37	8	9	2	2	0	2	3	21	44	1	21	0	139	230
	UT Houston	15	0	0	15	32	7	13	1	1	1	2	2	10	36	1	12	1	170	230
	UT San Antonio	38	0	2	8	47	6	14	1	0	1	3	2	7	33	2	13	1	148	221
	UT Southwestern	19	1	0	2	22	28	20	2	0	1	3	8	25	87	1	9	1	112	227
UT	Utah	1	0	0	2	4	5	1	0	0	1	0	1	1	9	1	2	1	66	82
VA	Eastern Virginia	0	1	0	8	9	2	8	3	0	1	8	2	4	29	1	10	0	72	118
	Virginia	4	3	1	4	15	5	10	1	0	0	2	2	5	23	2	11	0	103	143
	Virginia Commonwealth	0	1	0	4	7	14	25	6	2	1	6	10	5	68	5	9	2	116	200
VT	Vermont	2	4	1	9	15	6	4	0	2	1	2	0	1	12	0	3	0	93	115
WA	U Washington	2	1	1	5	8	16	4	2	2	0	3	5	5	40	2	8	1	163	216
WI	MC Wisconsin	6	2	2	2	9	12	13	1	1	1	7	4	4	48	2	8	1	150	204
	Wisconsin	0	0	2	2	4	10	5	0	0	0	0	0	4	26	2	9	0	137	168
WV	Marshall-Edwards	0	0	0	0	0	1	3	1	0	0	0	0	1	1	1	2	0	65	74
	West Virginia	0	0	0	2	2	2	7	2	4	2	2	2	1	22	0	0	1	87	110
	Totals	473	141	370	488	1,412	1,230	1,343	191	187	159	423	263	525	4,114	153	1,312	67	12,045	18,390

Chapter 9:

Be in the Know: AAMC Recommendations for Medical School Admission Officers

This chapter is a little different from the ones that have come before it—and the ones that will come after it. That's because it does not talk to you about the application process, or about financing your medical education, or about the MCAT exam.

In fact, it doesn't contain any information directed specifically at you at all.

What follows are a set of recommendations for medical school application, acceptance, and admission procedures that all 132 of our members have agreed to follow. We share them with you here because it is important you be aware of these procedures as they relate to your own application, ensuring that these processes are timely and fair for all concerned.

These recommendations correspond directly to the AAMC Recommendations for Applicants in Chapter 6.

The AAMC recommends that:

1. Each school:
   a. Publish annually, amend publicly, and adhere to its application, acceptance, and admission procedures.

   b. Utilizing an application service, abide by all conditions of its participation agreement with that application service.

2. Each school:
   a. Between August 1 and March 15, notify the AAMC Section for Medical School Application Services of all admission actions within four weeks of those actions being taken.

   b. Between March 16 and the first day of class, notify the AAMC Section for Medical School Application Services of all admission actions within seven days of those actions being taken.

3. Each school notify all applicants—other than Combined College/M.D., Early Decision Program (EDP), and deferred matriculation applicants—of acceptance to medical school only after October 15 of each admission cycle. It may be appropriate to communicate notifications of decisions other than acceptance to medical school to applicants prior to October 15.

4. By March 30 of the matriculation year, March 15 for M.D.-Ph.D. programs, each school or program have issued a number of offers of acceptance at least equal to the expected number of students in its first-year entering class and have reported those acceptance actions to the AAMC Section for Medical School Application Services.

5. Prior to May 15 of the matriculation year (April 15 for schools whose first day of class is on or before July 30), April 30 for M.D.-Ph.D. programs, each school or program permit ALL applicants (except for EDP applicants)—including those to whom merit or other special scholarships have been awarded:
    a. A minimum two-week time period for their response to the acceptance offer.

    b. To hold acceptance offers from any other schools or programs without penalty.

6. After May 15 of the matriculation year (April 15 for schools whose first day of class is on or before July 30), April 30 for M.D.-Ph.D. programs, each school or program implement school-specific procedures for accepted applicants who, without adequate explanation, continue to hold one or more places at other schools or programs. These procedures:
    a. May require applicants to:
        i.   Respond to acceptance offers in less than two weeks.
        ii. Submit a statement of intent, a deposit, or both.

    b. Should recognize the problems of applicants with multiple acceptance offers, applicants who have not yet received an acceptance offer, and applicants who have not yet been informed about financial aid opportunities at schools to which they have been accepted.

    c. Should permit accepted applicants to remain on other schools' or programs' waiting lists and to withdraw if they later receive an acceptance offer from a preferred school or program.

7. Each school's acceptance deposit not exceed $100 and (except for EDP applicants) be refundable until May 15, April 30 for M.D.-Ph.D. applicants. If the applicant enrolls at the school, the school is encouraged to credit the deposit toward tuition.

8. After June 1, May 15 for M.D.-Ph.D. programs, any school that plans to make an acceptance offer to an applicant already known to have been accepted by another school or program for that entering class ensure that the other school or program is advised of this offer at the time that the offer is made. This notification should be made immediately by telephone and promptly thereafter by written correspondence delivered by regular or electronic methods. Schools and programs should communicate fully with each other with respect to anticipated late roster changes in order to minimize inter-school miscommunication and misunderstanding, as well as the possibility of unintended vacant positions in a school's first-year entering class.

9. No school make an acceptance offer, either verbal or written, to any individual who has enrolled in, or begun an orientation program immediately prior to enrollment at, a U.S. or Canadian school. Enrollment is defined as being officially matriculated as a member of the school's first-year class.

10 Each school treats all letters of recommendation submitted in support of an application as confidential, except in those states with applicable laws to the contrary. The contents of a letter of recommendation should not be revealed to an applicant at any time.

Approved: AAMC Council of Deans Administrative Board, February 17, 2009.

Chapter 10:

Applicant and Acceptee Data

Up until this point, we've touched upon a wide range of topics related to acceptance to medical school—including undergraduate preparation, the MCAT exam, choosing a school, the application process, and the factors that enter into the admissions decision. We now turn to two additional questions that are likely at the very top of your mind:

A Quick Look at the 2009 Entering Class

- In 2008–09, 42,269 people applied to the 2009 entering class at all M.D.-granting medical schools in the United States.
- By the fall of 2009, 19,332 applicants had been offered an acceptance to at least one medical school, and 18,390 accepted applicants had matriculated.

These accepted applicants possessed a broad range of MCAT® scores and undergraduate grade point averages, and a wide variety of personal characteristics and life experiences. Both male and female applicants were distributed across numerous racial and ethnic groups. A small number applied through the Early Decision Program, but the majority used the regular application process. A small number of accepted applicants chose not to matriculate in 2009.

Who applies to medical school…and who gets in?

We realize, of course, that the question you're really asking is "based on my numbers, will I get in?" We can't tell you. What we can do, however, is provide you with data related to last year's applicants—both those who were accepted and those who were not—so that you can determine your relative standing on a variety of admissions-related factors. Together with the school-specific data in Chapter 14 and your advisor's help, this information will enable you to make appropriate decisions related to your application to medical school. Extensive information about medical school applicants and matriculants can also be found at www.aamc.org/facts.

This chapter contains graphic representations of relevant data for the entire applicant pool, as well as for accepted and nonaccepted applicants, for the 2009 entering class. All data presented in this chapter are accurate as of October 14, 2009 [Source: AAMC Data Warehouse; Applicant Matriculant File]. In the following charts:

- "All applicants" refers to all applicants to the 2009 entering class
- "Accepted applicants" refers to those applicants accepted to at least one medical school
- "Not accepted applicants" refers to those applicants not accepted to any medical school

In the following pages, we provide data related to performance on the MCAT, undergraduate grade point average, MCAT and undergraduate GPA combined, undergraduate major, gender, age, type of application, and race and ethnicity.

Chart 10-A

MCAT Verbal Reasoning Score Distribution, Year 2009 Applicants

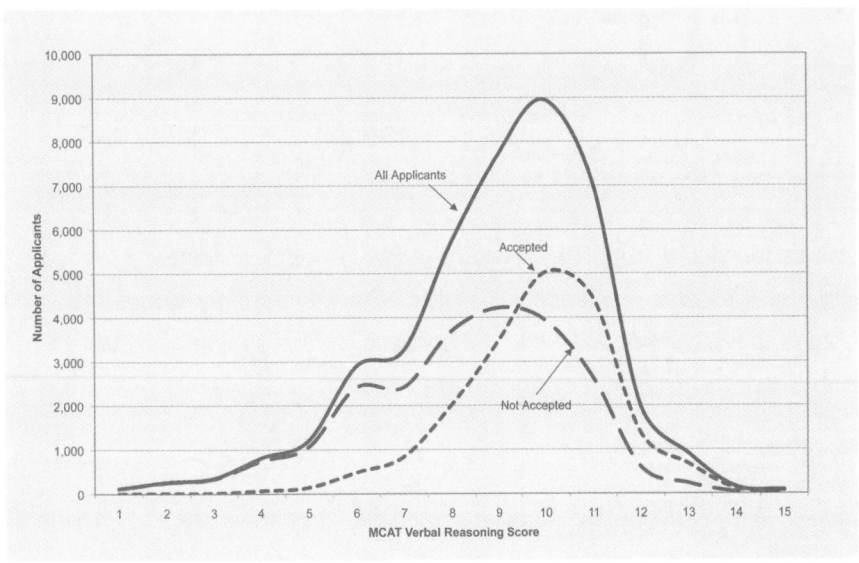

Source: AAMC Data Warehouse: Applicant Matriculant File   As of October 14, 2009

*The new medical schools accredited in 2009 and 2010 will enroll their first matriculants in 2010.

Chart 10-B

Physical Sciences Score Distribution, Year 2009 Applicants

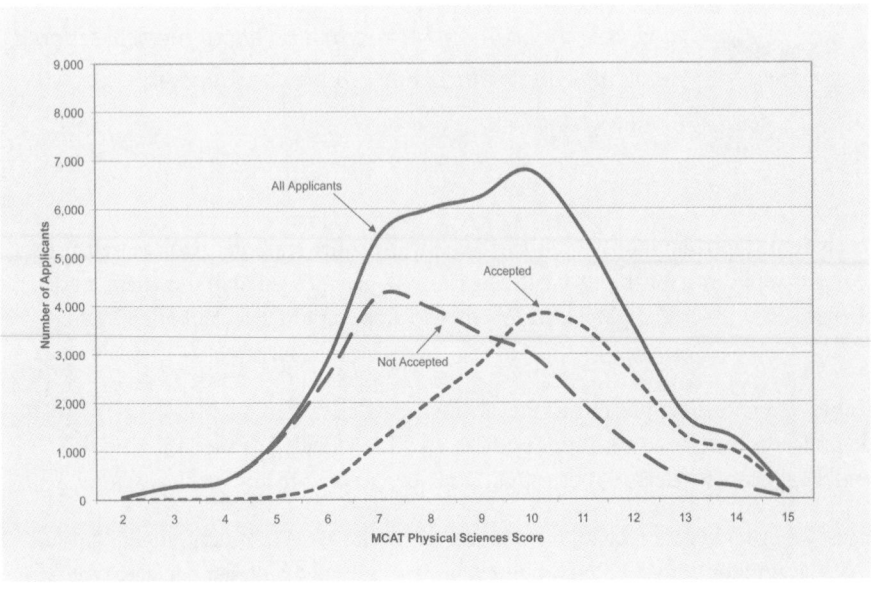

Source: AAMC Data Warehouse: Applicant Matriculant File   As of October 14, 2009

Performance on the MCAT

Charts 10-A—10-E present information about the performance of applicants on the MCAT:

- **Chart 10-A** shows that applicants achieved Verbal Reasoning (VR) scores at each score from 1 to 15; the largest number achieved a VR score of 10. Accepted applicants' scores ranged from 1 to 15, although very few had VR scores below 5 (just under 100). At a VR score of 10, the number of accepted applicants exceeded the number not accepted.

- **Chart 10-B** shows that applicants achieved Physical Sciences (PS) scores at each score from 2 to 15; the largest number achieved a PS score of 10. Accepted applicants' scores ranged from 2 to 15; fewer than 90 accepted applicants achieved a score of 5 or below. Accepted applicants exceeded not accepted applicants at a PS score of 10.

- **Chart 10-C** shows that applicants achieved Writing Sample (WS) scores at each score from J to T; the largest number achieved a WS score of Q. Accepted applicants' scores ranged from J to T; the number with scores of K and below was about 160. Accepted applicants exceeded not accepted applicants at a score of Q.

- **Chart 10-D** shows that applicants achieved Biological Sciences (BS) scores at each score from 1 to 15; the largest number achieved a BS score of 10. Accepted applicants' scores ranged from 3 to 15; about 25 scored 5 or below. Accepted applicants exceeded not accepted applicants at a score of 11.

Chart 10-C

MCAT Writing Sample Score Distribution, Year 2009 Applicants

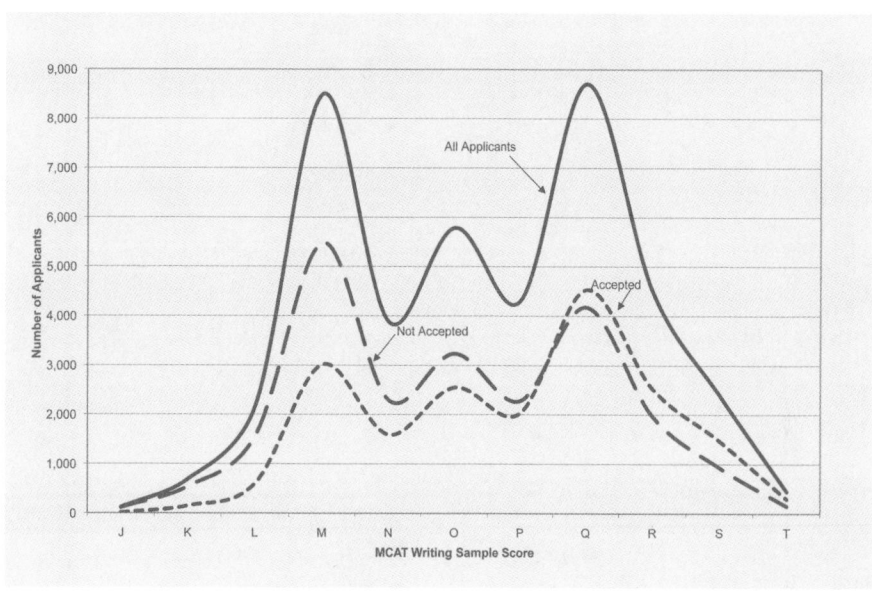

Source: AAMC Data Warehouse: Applicant Matriculant File   As of October 14, 2009

Chart 10-D

MCAT Biological Sciences Score Distribution, Year 2009 Applicants

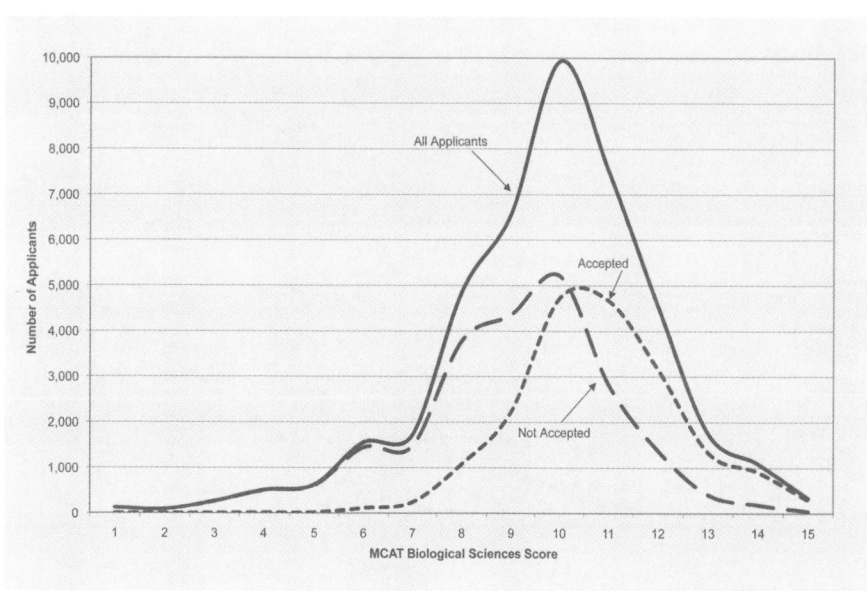

Source: AAMC Data Warehouse: Applicant Matriculant File   As of October 14, 2009

Chart 10-E
MCAT Total Numeric Score Distribution, Year 2009 Applicants

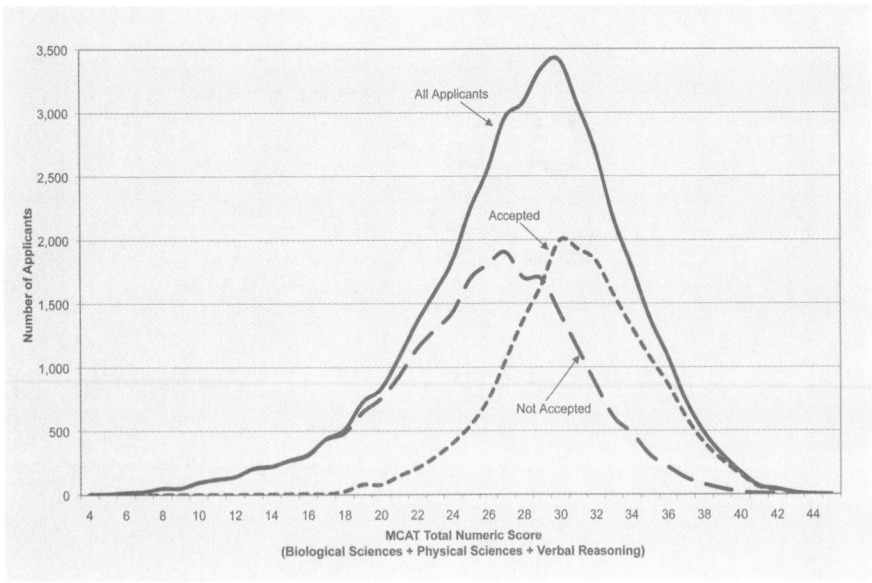

Source: AAMC Data Warehouse: Applicant Matriculant File   As of October 14, 2009

Chart 10-F
Science GPA Distribution, Year 2009 Applicants

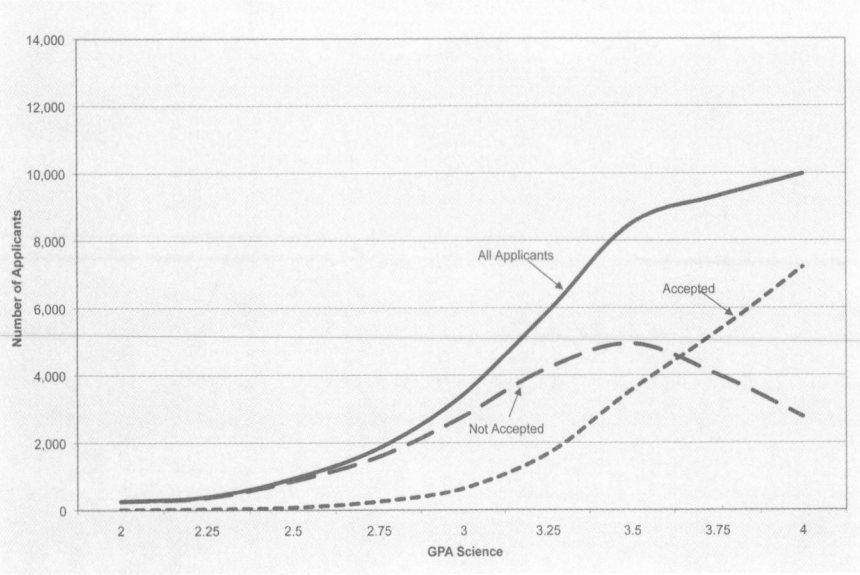

Source: AAMC Data Warehouse: Applicant Matriculant File   As of October 14, 2009

- Chart 10-E—which shows total scores on the numerically scored sections of Verbal Reasoning, Physical Sciences, and Biological Sciences—reveals that applicants achieved total scores from 4 to 45; the largest number achieved a total score of 30. Accepted applicants achieved total scores from 11 to 45; the number of accepted applicants with total scores of 17 and below (an average of almost 6 on each section) was about 20. Accepted applicants exceeded not accepted applicants at a total score of 30.

No score on a single MCAT section and no total MCAT score "guarantees" admission to medical school. Charts 10-A, 10-B, and 10-D reveal that, while applicants with VR, PS, and BS scores of 10 and above had a higher probability of being accepted to medical school, a significant number of applicants with such scores were not accepted. The same holds true for the Writing Sample section; a score of Q and above is a likely, though not definite, barometer for acceptance. Finally, Chart 10-E shows that a substantial number of applicants with total MCAT scores of 29 and above were not accepted. These findings reveal the importance of factors other than MCAT performance—including undergraduate academic performance and a variety of personal characteristics and experiential variables—in the medical student selection process.

Undergraduate Grade Point Average (GPA)

Charts 10-F—10-H present information about the undergraduate academic performance of applicants:

- **Chart 10-F:** undergraduate science GPA (biology, chemistry, physics, and mathematics)

- **Chart 10-G:** undergraduate non-science GPA

- **Chart 10-H:** undergraduate total GPA

Chart 10-F shows that the undergraduate science GPAs of all applicants were on a continuum from 2.0 to 4.0, on a 4.0 scale; most were between 3.75 and 4.0. Accepted applicants also had undergraduate science GPAs across the entire range, but few had GPAs of 2.50 or below (just over 100). The undergraduate science GPA at which accepted applicants exceeded those not accepted was between 3.50 and 3.75.

Chart 10-G shows applicants' undergraduate non-science GPAs along the continuum from 2.0 to 4.0, with most between 3.75 and 4.0. Accepted applicants' undergraduate non-science GPAs also ranged from 2.0 to 4.0, but only about 80 had a GPA of 2.75 or below. At 3.75 to 4.0, accepted applicants exceeded not accepted applicants.

As shown in Chart 10-H, all applicants had total undergraduate GPAs from 2.0 to 4.0, and most were in the range of 3.50 to 3.75. Accepted applicants' total undergraduate GPAs ranged from 2.25 to 4.0, but only about 100 possessed undergraduate total GPAs of 2.75 or below. Accepted applicants exceeded not accepted applicants at an undergraduate total GPA of between 3.50 and 3.75.

As is the case with MCAT data, GPA data in Charts 10-F–10-H show that no undergraduate GPA assures admission to medical school. While applicants with undergraduate science, nonscience, and total GPAs in the range of 3.50 to 3.75, 3.75 to 4.0, and 3.50 to 3.75, respectively, were more likely to be accepted to medical school, a significant number of such applicants were not accepted. Again, these findings underscore the importance of a wide variety of personal characteristics and experiential variables in the medical student selection process.

Chart 10-G
Non-Science GPA Distribution, Year 2009 Applicants

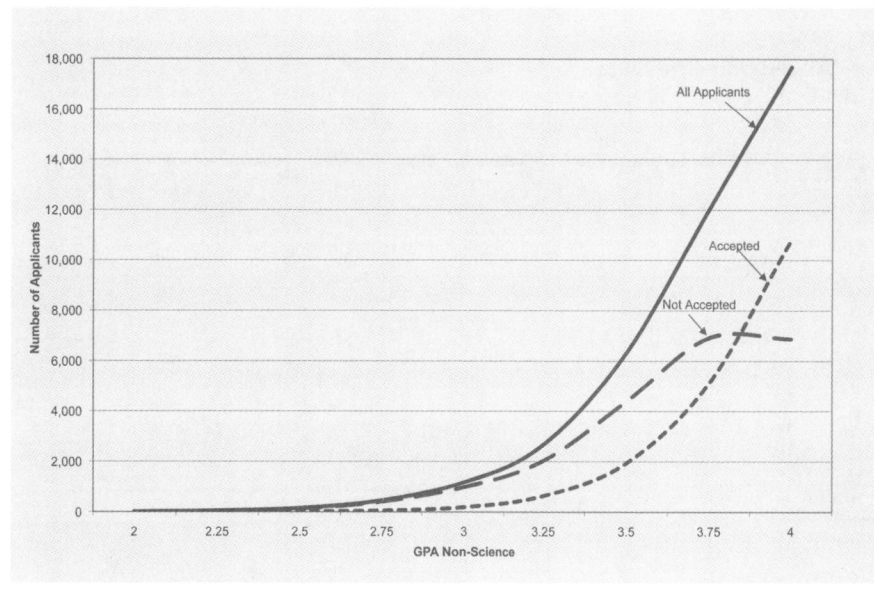

Source: AAMC Data Warehouse: Applicant Matriculant File

As of October 14, 2009

Chart 10-H
Total GPA Distribution, Year 2009 Applicants

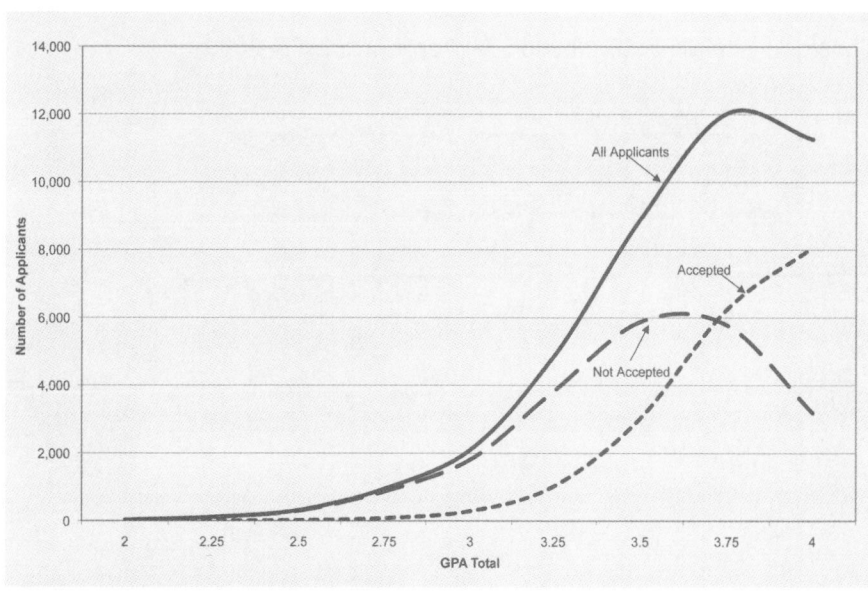

Source: AAMC Data Warehouse: Applicant Matriculant File

As of October 14, 2009

Chart 10-I
MCAT and Undergraduate GPA Combined

MCAT and Undergraduate GPA

Chart 10-I combines MCAT scores and undergraduate GPA for all applicants to medical school from 2007 to 2009. The data may not reflect your particular circumstances. As a result, we recommend that you go to *www.aamc.org/facts* to see acceptance rates for particular demographic groups. Note that these results are presented without regard to any of the other selection factors.

Chart 10-J presents information about the undergraduate majors of all medical school applicants to the 2005–2009 entering classes. Over the past five years, more than half of all applicants reported undergraduate biological science majors, while the remainder reported a variety of majors, including the humanities, mathematics and statistics, physical sciences, social sciences, other health sciences, and a broad "other" category. The proportion of these majors has remained relatively constant over time, despite annual fluctuations in the applicant pool.

Chart 5-I
MCAT and Undergraduate GPA Combined

Percent accepted — **87%**
Number accepted — 4,584/5,272 — Number of applicants

GPA Total	5-14	15-17	18-20	21-23	24-26	27-29	30-32	33-35	36-38	39-45
3.80 – 4.00	6% 5/79	5% 9/177	17% 91/523	27% 357/1,345	43% 1,374/3,230	68% 3,830/5,606	83% 5,640/6,825	87% 4,584/5,272	90% 2,777/3,073	93% 1,116/1,205
3.60 – 3.79	2% 3/204	4% 14/367	13% 135/1,011	19% 426/2,275	31% 1,387/4,498	53% 3,707/6,985	73% 5,256/7,178	81% 3,545/4,399	85% 1,605/1,891	85% 380/445
3.40 – 3.59	3% 9/354	3% 14/538	10% 126/1,234	17% 422/2,557	24% 1,081/4,537	39% 2,547/6,599	57% 3,443/6,049	68% 2,106/3,083	74% 840/1,142	77% 175/226
3.20 – 3.39	1% 3/412	2% 11/616	9% 102/1,181	13% 302/2,265	18% 627/3,473	27% 1,204/4,428	40% 1,511/3,807	51% 892/1,739	60% 333/551	67% 62/93
3.00 – 3.19	1% 3/491	3% 15/609	6% 57/957	11% 177/1,619	17% 358/2,139	22% 541/2,468	31% 550/1,804	37% 320/863	49% 125/256	41% 18/44
2.80 – 2.99	0% 0/429	1% 6/425	5% 36/667	11% 101/935	14% 163/1,132	17% 180/1,051	23% 167/742	30% 102/336	26% 23/89	56% 10/18
2.60 – 2.79	0% 0/356	1% 3/235	6% 22/393	8% 41/523	11% 56/532	13% 61/469	19% 55/287	20% 28/142	18% 7/40	13% 1/8
2.40 – 2.59	0% 0/232	1% 1/156	2% 3/189	5% 13/251	8% 19/228	11% 21/192	18% 25/137	27% 13/48	9% 1/11	--
2.20 – 2.39	0% 0/165	0% 0/92	2% 2/103	6% 5/86	4% 3/85	5% 3/67	13% 5/39	6% 1/17	17% 1/6	--
2.00 – 2.19	0% 0/78	3% 1/40	0% 0/40	4% 1/27	4% 1/26	0% 0/25	0% 0/10	43% 3/7	0% 0/1	--
1.47 – 1.99	0% 0/28	4% 1/25	0% 0/18	0% 0/14	13% 1/8	0% 0/4	33% 1/3	0% 0/3		

75 – 100%
50% – 74%
25% – 49%

Note: – – Signifies cells with fewer than 10 applicants.

Source: AAMC Data Warehouse: Applicant Matriculant File

As of November 18, 2009

Chart 10-J
Undergraduate Major Distribution, All Applicants, 2005–2009

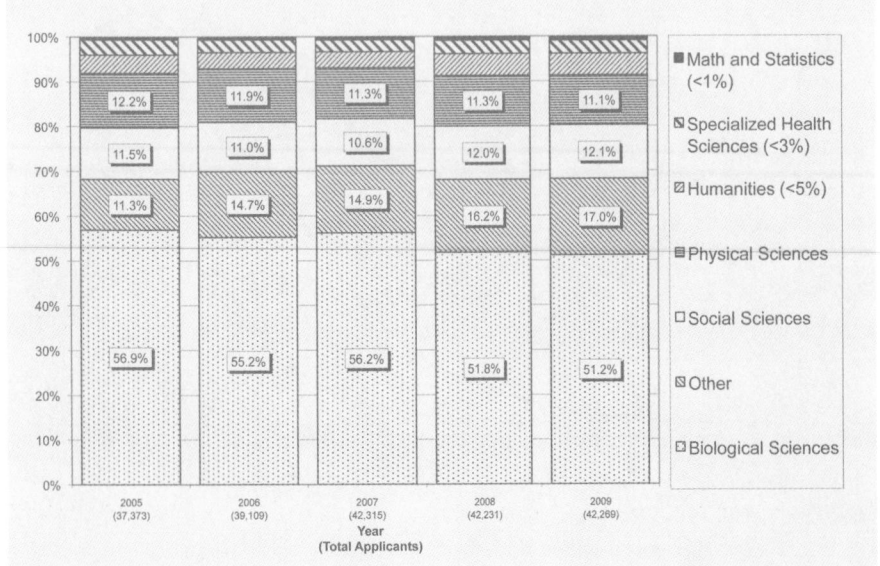

Source: AAMC Data Warehouse: Applicant Matriculant File

As of October 14, 2009

Chart **10-K** presents similar information about the undergraduate majors of applicants accepted to the 2005–2009 entering classes. Comparisons of the majors of the total applicant pool with those of accepted applicants reveal acceptance rates, for various science-related majors, ranging from 38.5 percent for applicants with specialized health science majors, to 44.3 percent for biological science majors, to 52.8 percent for physical science majors, the highest rate of acceptance for science-related majors.

Gender

Chart **10-L** presents information about the number and gender of the entire applicant pool and of accepted applicants for the 1992–2009 entering classes. The largest annual applicant pool during the past decade was for the 1996 entering class; since that year, the pool gradually declined until 2003, when there was a slight increase (3.5 percent) in applicants. The applicant pool increased again by 2.7 percent in 2004, by 4.6 percent in 2005, by another 4.6 percent in 2006, and by 8.2 percent in 2007. In 2008 and 2009, the applicant pool held relatively steady, with a slight decrease of 0.2 percent from 2007 to 2008 and a slight increase of 0.1 percent from 2008 to 2009. The number of male applicants to the 2009 entering class increased by about 140 from the number of male applicants to the previous year's entering class, but that number was still smaller than it had been for any other entering class from 1993 through 1998. The number of female applicants to the 2009 class decreased by about 110 over the number of female applicants to the previous year's entering class, the year prior to that being the largest number of female applicants on record. While the number of accepted applicants remained fairly constant for 10 years, it has started to increase in recent years, from a low of 17,312 in 1997 to a high of 19,332 in

Chart 10-K

Undergraduate Major Distribution, Accepted Applicants, 2005–2009

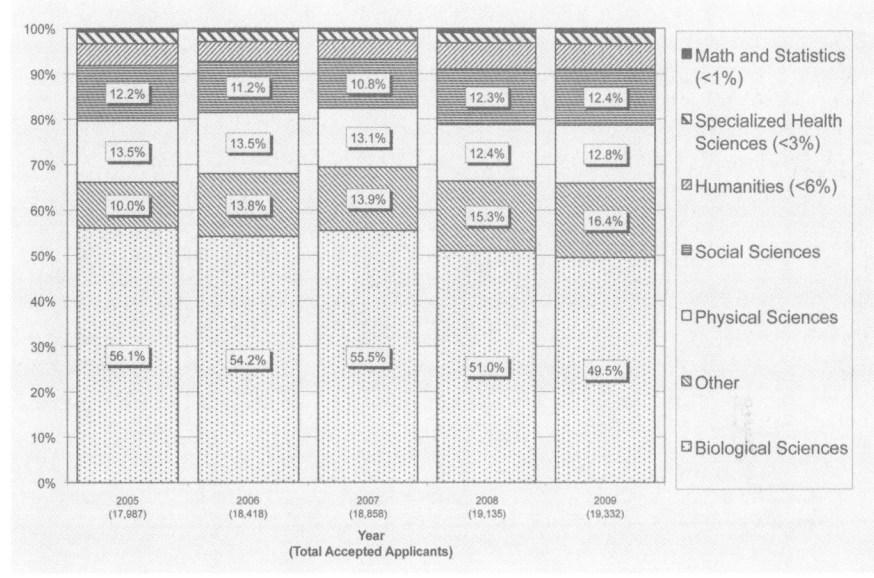

Source: AAMC Data Warehouse: Applicant Matriculant File   As of October 14, 2009

Chart 10-L

Applicants by Gender and Acceptance Status, 1992–2009

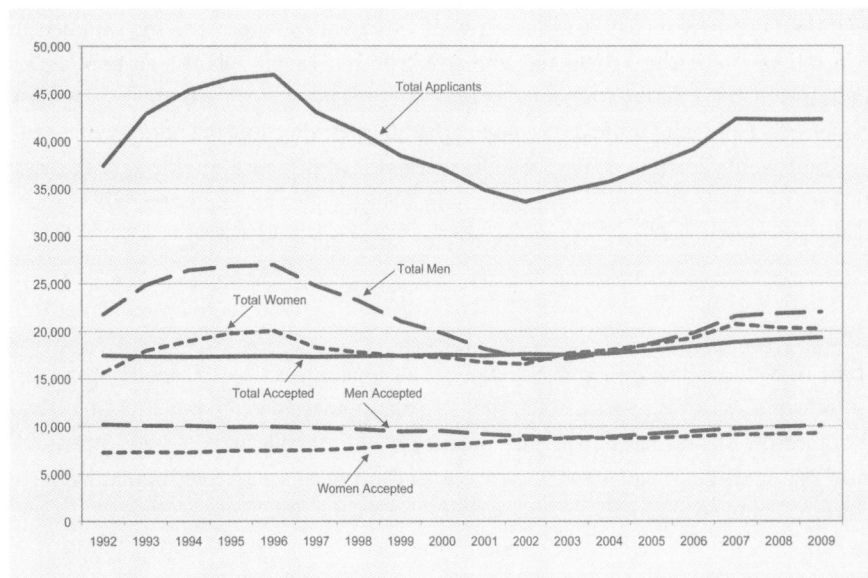

Source: AAMC Data Warehouse: Applicant Matriculant File   As of October 14, 2009

Chart 10-M

Age Distribution, Year 2009 Applicants

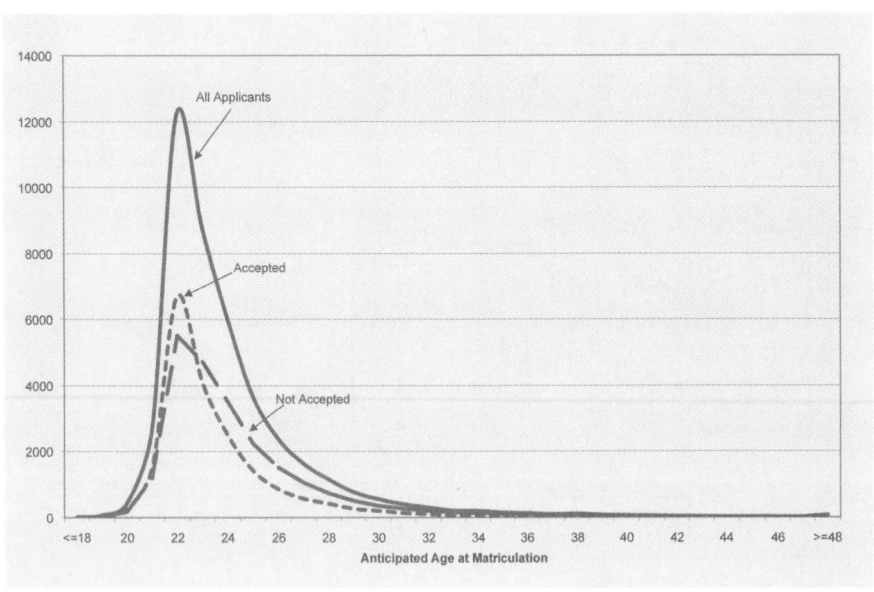

Source: AAMC Data Warehouse: Applicant Matriculant File   As of October 14, 2009

2009. The number of accepted male applicants has fluctuated from a high of 10,208 in 1992 to a low of 8,810 in 2003 and is back up to 10,068 in 2009. The number of accepted female applicants has increased, with small fluctuations, from a low of 7,255 in the 1994 entering class to a high of 9,264 in 2009. The significant gaps between male and female applicants for the 1992 entering class (6,166) and the 1993 entering class (6,892) have disappeared; 553 and 301 more women than men applied to the 2003 and 2004 entering classes, respectively. In 2005, only 121 more men than women applied. In 2009, 1,762 more men than women applied to medical school. During the same time span, the gaps between accepted male and accepted female applicants also dropped. Accepted male applicants outnumbered accepted female applicants by 2,951 for the 1992 entering class, but only by 756 for the 2009 entering class. The national ratio of male to female applicants was 49.2: 50.8 percent for the 2003 entering class, the first time that the number of female applicants was greater than the number of male applicants to medical school. For the 2004 entering class, this trend continued, with a ratio of male to female applicants of 49.6 : 50.4. For the 2005 entering class, there were once again more male than female applicants, with a ratio of male to female applicants of 50.2 : 49.8. This trend continued in 2009, with a ratio of male to female applicants of 52.1 : 47.9.

Age

Chart 10-M shows that the age distribution for all applicants to the 2009 entering class was broad, with 11 applicants under the age of 19 at the time of anticipated matriculation, and 76 applicants aged 48 and over. The largest contingent of applicants, 38,449, was between 21 and 28 at the time of anticipated matriculation; the rest of the applicant pool were either under 21 (511) or over 28 (3,309) at the time of antici-pated matriculation. Chart 10-M illustrates a similar finding for accepted applicants. Accepted applicants for the 2009 entering class were between 18 and 56 years of age at the time of expected matriculation.

Chart 10-N

Percentage of Applicants and Accepted Applicants Reporting Selected Experiences

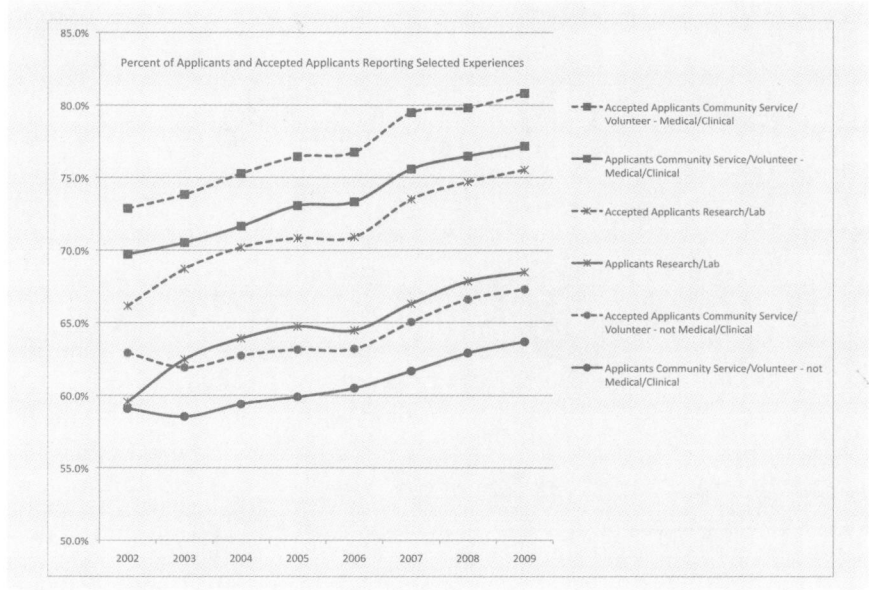

Source: AAMC Data Warehouse: Applicant Matriculant File   As of October 14, 2009

Applicant and Accepted Applicant Experiences

Chart 10-N presents information regarding the volunteer, paid, and lab experiences of applicants and accepted applicants to the 2009 entering class. The chart clearly shows the steady increase in both applicants and accepted applicants reporting volunteer medical, community service, and research experience since 2002:

- 81% of accepted applicants reported medical/clinical community service/volunteer clinical experience, an increase of about 8% since 2002

- 77% of applicants reported medical/clinical community service/volunteer clinical experience, an increase of about 7% since 2002

- 76% of accepted applicants reported research/lab experience, an increase of about 9% since 2002

- 68% of applicants reported research/lab experience, an increase of about 9% since 2002

- 67% of accepted applicants reported non-medical/non-clinical community service/volunteer clinical experience, an increase of about 4% since 2002

- 64% of applicants reported non-medical/non-clinical community service/volunteer clinical experience, an increased of about 5% since 2002

The rising trend in reported experiences among applicants and accepted applicants is expected to continue in the coming years.

Chart 10-O
Distribution of Self-Reported Ethnicity and Race: All Applicants, 2005–2009

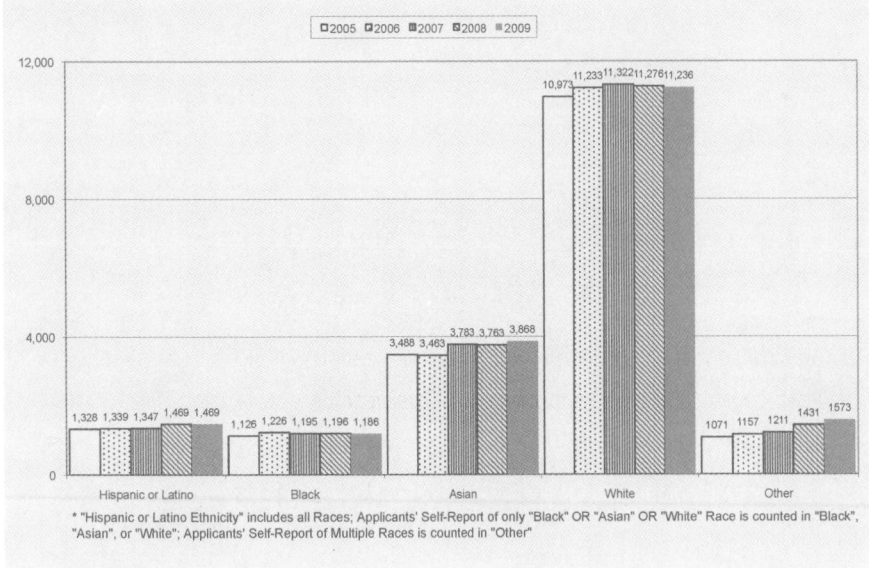

Source: AAMC Data Warehouse: Applicant Matriculant File   As of October 14, 2009

Race and Ethnicity

Chart 10-O shows applicant self-reported race and ethnicity data for all applicants to the 2005 through 2009 entering classes. The following changes occurred in the self-reported racial and ethnic make-up of the applicant pool from 2008 to 2009:

- The number of self-described white applicants in 2008 was 23,816; the number of white applicants in 2009 was 23,493, a decrease of 1.4 percent.

- The number of self-described Asian applicants in 2008 was 8,280; the number of Asian applicants in 2009 was 8,501, an increase of 2.7 percent.

- The number of self-described black applicants in 2008 was 3,024; the number of black applicants in 2009 was 3,106, an increase of 2.7 percent.

- The number of self-described Hispanic applicants in 2008 was 3,086; the number of Hispanic applicants in 2009 was 3,061, a decrease of 0.8 percent.

- The number of applicants in 2008 whose self-description of their race or ethnicity was in some other category was 4,025; the number of applicants in this cohort in 2009 was 4,108, an increase of 2.1 percent from 2008.

Simultaneously, the following changes occurred among those applicants accepted to the 2008 and 2009 entering classes:

- The number of self-described white accepted applicants in 2008 was 11,276; the number of white accepted applicants in 2009 was 11,236, a decrease of 0.4 percent.

- The number of self-described Asian accepted applicants in 2008 was 3,763; the number of accepted Asian applicants in 2009 was 3,868, an increase of 2.8 percent.

- The number of self-described black accepted applicants in 2008 was 1,196; the number of accepted black applicants in 2009 was 1,186, a decrease of 0.8 percent.

- The number of self-described Hispanic accepted applicants in 2008 was 1,469; the number of Hispanic accepted applicants in 2009 was also 1,469.

- The number of accepted applicants in 2008 whose self-description of their race or ethnicity was in some other category was 1,431; the number of accepted applicants in this cohort in 2009 was 1,573, an increase of 9.9 percent from 2008.

Additional information of interest to applicants from groups under-represented in medicine is available in Chapter 8.

Chapter 11:
Financing Your Medical Education

The very thought of medical school undoubtedly conjures up feelings of excitement and anticipation. You're about to embark on the journey to a medical degree, a road filled with new discoveries, challenging professors, and wide-open opportunities.

But on the other hand, you've got to figure out how to pay for it.

There's no doubt that medical school is an expensive undertaking, and you'll soon face a myriad of expenses. Beyond the tuition itself, you'll also have fees, books, equipment, living expenses, medical insurance, and transportation to consider.

Fortunately, there's help. In this chapter, we review the various ways you can finance your medical education—from grants and scholarships, to federal student loans with attractive terms, to service commitment programs that provide financial support—as well as the resources available to help you through the process.

Distribution of Total Financial Aid

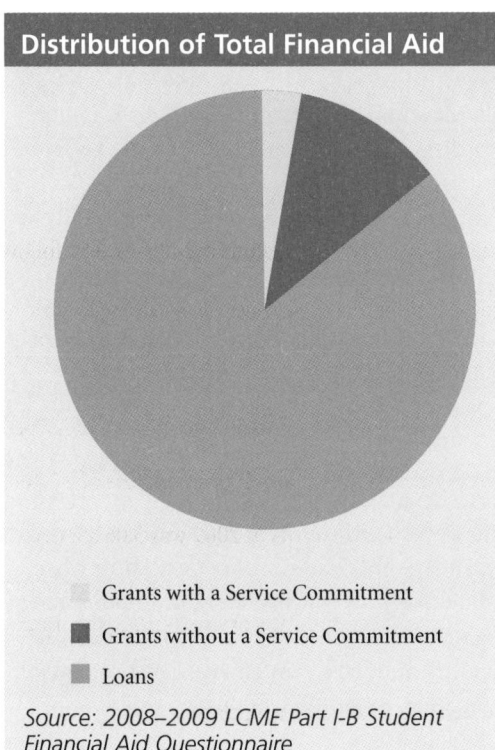

   Grants with a Service Commitment

■ Grants without a Service Commitment

   Loans

Source: 2008–2009 LCME Part I-B Student Financial Aid Questionnaire

Building a Strong Financial Plan

You'll need to develop a strategy to cover the significant costs associated with your education. Tuition and fees top the list, of course, but you'll also need to buy books and equipment, purchase insurance, cover the costs of transportation, and, quite likely, pay for housing and food.

When you look at the figures in the table on the following page, we understand how the financial challenges that face you might seem overwhelming. Annual tuition and fees at state medical schools in 2009–2010 average approximately $23,000 for state residents and $44,000 for nonresidents; at private schools, the averages were $41,000 for residents and $42,000 for nonresidents.

But don't let these numbers discourage you. There's help available—and lots of it.

And you certainly won't be the only one taking advantage of that assistance. According to recent surveys conducted by the AAMC, 84.7 percent of newly graduated M.D.'s have medical school education loans, while 59.2 percent reported receiving some degree of help through scholarships, stipends, and/or grants (which you don't have to repay). So, it can be done, and it is…by tens of thousands of medical students, every single year.

But first… you'll need a plan.

Table 11-A

Tuition and Fees for 2009–2010
First-Year Students in U.S. Medical Schools* (in Dollars)

PRIVATE SCHOOLS

Student Category	Range	Median	Average
Resident	$14,828 – $50,968	$42,974	$40,797
Nonresident	$21,920 – $51,102	$43,980	$42,156

PUBLIC SCHOOLS

Student Category	Range	Median	Average
Resident	$10,344 – $36,086	$24,812	$23,627
Nonresident	$20,309 – $74,670	$44,478	$44,314

*Analysis excludes Arizona, Massachusetts, Mercer, and Mississippi. These schools do not accept nonresident medical students, and therefore, they do not report nonresident tuition and fees.

Source: 2009–10 AAMC Tuition and Student Fees Questionnaire

And by "plan," we mean more than simply learning about the assistance available to you and securing the necessary financing. Before you can get to that admittedly vital step, it's important that you understand—and adhere to—the basic principles of successful money management. With that in mind, the two basic recommendations that follow should help you build a strong financial foundation.

Overview: The Financial "Basics"

1. Live Within Your Means

Let's face it. Money will be tight during your medical school years, and a realistic budget will be critical to your financial well-being. A well-crafted plan will help you maintain better control of your spending, ensure you cover your essential expenses before making an optional purchase, and prepare for an unexpected expense by building an emergency fund.

The steps involved in creating a budget are actually quite simple. You just add up your monthly income, determine your monthly expenses, and calculate the difference. One helpful tip is to categorize your expenses as either "fixed" (ones that stay the same each month, such as rent and insurance premiums) and "variable" expenses (such as groceries and clothing).

From that point, you can identify areas in which you can scale back (if necessary) to assure that your income and outgo

remain in balance. Obvious cost-savings steps include sharing housing costs with a roommate, buying generic products rather than brand names, preparing more of your meals at home, and taking public transportation or carpooling when possible.

Need a hand? Check out the interactive budget worksheet available from the AAMC's FIRST program (see box on next page) at *www.aamc.org/first/facts/budget_worksheet.pdf*

2. Manage Your Debt Wisely

Given the costs of medical school, it's understandable that the vast majority of medical students borrow money to fund their education—and graduate with an average medical school debt of $140,000. And although the ability to manage debt wisely is important regardless of one's situation, it becomes even more critical for you—a prospective medical student—when you consider the degree to which you're likely to rely on loans to help pay for your education.

- Your first step is to be fully cognizant of the amount you plan to borrow and be comfortable that your future income will allow you to cover your debt payments.

- You will, of course, need to learn about, apply for, and secure the most cost-effective financing available.

- You'll need to understand your responsibilities as a borrower. Your primary obligation is, of course, know what loans you hold (and from which lender), the amount of each, and the repayment schedule, but beyond that, you must keep lenders notified of any changes in your name, contact information, or enrollment status.

Get Your Financial House in Order

Before you apply for student loans, make sure your "financial house" is in order by:

- Creating a budget
- Paying down debt to the extent possible
- Making sure you are current on all outstanding credit obligations

Students with a history of credit problems may not qualify for the loans that are based on credit, whether federal or private.

* The entries in school and combined undergraduate program pages provide information about individual schools' tuition and fee schedules and other financial data.

- You must maintain accurate records, including promissory notes (your legal promise to pay back the loans), copies of application forms, and any related disclosure statements.

- You need to build and maintain a good credit score by meeting your financial obligations. In doing so, you'll strengthen your ability to qualify for and obtain attractive interest rates for credit-based loans, land a job, or even rent an apartment. For more information, go to *www.aamc.org/first/facts/creditscore.pdf.*

Fortunately, you have an abundance of resources to assist you through this process—including that provided by your pre-health advisor, the pages that follow in this very book, and the FIRST program (see box below) offered by the AAMC.

FIRST *for Medical Education*

FIRST *for Medical Education* is an AAMC program that provides a wide range of **F**inancial **I**nformation, **R**esources, **S**ervices, and **T**ools to help medical school applicants and students make smart decisions about students loans, effectively manage their education debt, and expand their financial literacy.

Please see *www.aamc.org/first* for more information.

Types of Financial Aid

Now we're ready for specifics. How will you pay for medical school?

First, we'd like to remind you that you're not on your own here. While the ultimate financial responsibility for your medical education rests with you and your family, there are many resources and tools available to help. The financial aid office at the medical school to which you've been accepted will be of great assistance, of course, but you'll also want to talk to your pre-health advisor and familiarize yourself with the informational "fact sheets" you'll find on the AAMC FIRST Web site.

That said, there are two* general types of financial aid available to medical students: loans and grants or scholarships. We discuss both of these funding sources below.

You Can Help Your Credit Score By...

- Paying your bills on time
- Having no more than three credit cards
- Keeping balances less than 50% of the assigned credit limit
- Checking your credit report for errors at *www.annualcreditreport.com*

Loans

Most of your funding will come from loans—which, in the case of federal loans, are a form of financial aid. Fortunately, there are a variety of loan programs available to help you finance your education. Within this category, there are both subsidized and unsubsidized loans, each of which is described briefly below.

- *Subsidized Loans (Based on Financial Need)*
  Subsidized loans carry no interest cost to borrowers during the time they are in school, in grace (a period following graduation during which no payments are due), or in deferment (a temporary suspension of payments granted to qualifying borrowers). It is only during the active period of repayment that these loans incur any interest.

- *Unsubsidized Loans (Not Based on Financial Need)*
  Unsubsidized loans, on the other hand, accrue interest from the date they are disbursed. While borrowers are not required to pay interest that is accruing on unsubsidized loans while they are in school, in grace, or in deferment, any unpaid accrued interest costs on these loans will be capitalized (adding to the loan principal) and must be repaid.

Available Sources of Financing Include...

Grants, Scholarships and Loan Repayment Programs
- Service Commitment Programs
- Scholarships for Disadvantaged Students
- Loan Repayment/Forgiveness Programs

Loans
- Stafford Loans
- Grad PLUS Loans
- Federal Perkins Loans
- Primary Care Loans
- Loans for Disadvantaged Students

Information on these programs is provided on the following pages and in the table on page 69.

Federal work-study programs are a third type of financial aid. Most medical students, however, are unable to supplement their funds with employment due to educational demands.

In both cases, however—subsidized or unsubsidized—interest charges and repayment options for federal loans are quite attractive, and students are advised to apply for these loans before considering private options. The table on the next page provides specific information about four popular federal student loan programs.

Finally, we want to say a word about the amount of the debt itself. We know it sounds like a lot—and it is. Bear in mind, though, that your income as a physician is likely to be excellent. (Starting salaries for doctors in family practice, for example, are projected to average $165,000 by 2012,* with many other specialties averaging even higher.) An investment in medical education is likely to be returned to you many times over.

Students With Medical School Loans

Nearly 85 percent of graduating medical students owe money on medical school education loans, with an average debt of $139,739.

Source: 2008–09 LCME Student Financial Aid Questionnaire

Grants and Scholarships

Naturally, when it comes to financing your medical education, the most desirable way is through "free" money—sometimes referred to as "gift aid"—which you don't have to repay.

While grants and scholarships are likely to cover only a portion of your overall educational costs, it's worth noting that many students get some degree of funding from these sources. The source of gift aid can be the federal government, the state government, and/or your medical school itself. Your medical school financial aid office is the best source of information as to which grants and scholarships may be available to you.

The Financial Aid Application Process

Because the specific process by which you'll apply for financial aid varies by medical school, you'll need to check with the financial aid office for exact instructions. Still, regardless of the medical school, there's an overall process which every prospective student should take. We review these steps below.

- **Step 1: Complete the FAFSA**
  Complete and submit the FAFSA form in January—preferably after you've filed your income taxes—filling in both

Make Sure You Are "Credit Ready"

Some medical schools require a credit history as part of the financial aid application and require that the applicant resolve any credit problems before the process gets underway. Many medical schools will grant a delay of matriculation to an accepted applicant who must address credit problems. Applicants are advised to contact financial aid offices at medical schools of interest to them to discuss financial aid eligibility and, if necessary, resolve any outstanding credit problems.

the student and parent*information. The resulting Institutional Student Information Report (ISIR) is sent to your school and determines your financial need. Remember to list your medical school's federal ID code to ensure the results of your FAFSA are sent to your medical school's financial aid office.

Although the FAFSA does not ask for parental information for students working toward a graduate degree, many medical schools require that information for purposes of awarding institutional aid (funds given by the school itself).

- **Step 2: Investigate Sources of Aid**
  Contact the financial aid office at your medical school to investigate sources of institutional aid as well as to learn about various student loan programs in detail. (You'll need to complete a separate application from the FAFSA when applying for a student loan.)

- **Step 3: Apply Early**
  Complete and return applications as soon as possible. In many cases, programs have limited funds and students who apply early have a better chance of receiving aid. You'd hate to miss out on an offer of financial aid simply because you were late in submitting applications.

- **Step 4: Receive and Reply to the Award Letter**
  Once your FAFSA results are received and processed by your medical school's financial aid office, you'll receive an award letter indicating the types and amounts of financial aid for which you qualify—along with directions for accepting or declining the aid.

The table on the next page outlines the parameters of four major federal loan programs—Primary Care Loans, Federal Perkins Loans, Federal Stafford Loans, and Graduate PLUS loans. For eligibility and other information, we suggest you talk with the financial aid office at the medical school you plan to attend.

From AAMC's The Economics of Becoming a Doctor (www.aamc.org/first/training/mdeconomics.htm). For other compensation studies, see www.aamc.org/first/compensation.pdf.

Federal Loan Programs for Students

Characteristic	Primary Care Loan	Federal Perkins	Federal Subsidized/ Unsubsidized Stafford	Graduate PLUS Loan
Lender	Medical school financial aid office on behalf of the Department of HHS	Medical school financial aid office on behalf of the federal government	Bank or other lending institution, the federal government, or an eligible institution	Bank or other lending institution, the federal government, or an eligible institution
Based on Need	Note[1]	Yes	Subsidized–Yes Unsubsidized–No	No
Citizenship Requirement	U.S. citizen, U.S. national, U.S. permanent resident, or asylum status	U.S. citizen, U.S. national, U.S. permanent resident, or asylum status	U.S. citizen, U.S. national, U.S. permanent resident, or asylum status	U.S. citizen, U.S. national, U.S. permanent resident, or asylum status
Borrowing Limits	Up to cost of attendance (Third- and fourth-year students may receive additional funds to repay previous educational loans received while attending medical school)	$6,000/year $40,000 aggregate undergraduate and graduate	$40,500 including subsidized Stafford $8,500, annual maximum; $224,000 including $65,000 subsidized Stafford, cumulative maximum, for premed and medical borrowing[2]	Annual cost of attendance minus other financial aid
Interest Rate	Note[3]	5%	For loans first disbursed since July 1, 2006, 6.8% for life of loan	For loans first disbursed since July 1, 2006, 8.5% from bank or other lending institution or 7.9% from the federal government, for life of loan
Borrower is responsible for interest during:				
• School	No	No	Subsidized: No Unsubsidized: Yes	Yes
• Deferments	No	No	Subsidized: No Unsubsidized: Yes	Yes
• Grace Period	No	No	Subsidized: No Unsubsidized: Yes	N/A
Grace Period	1 year after graduation	9 months after graduation	6 months after graduation	None
Deferments	During school and primary care residency (check your promissory note or ask your financial aid officer)	During school and other deferment periods based on eligibility (check your promissory note or ask your financial aid office)	During school and other deferment periods based on eligibility (check your promissory note or ask your financial aid office)	During school and other deferment periods based on eligibility (check your promissory note or ask your financial aid office)
Repayment Requirements	Minimum: $40/month; 10 to 25 years to repay; Not eligible for loan consolidation	Minimum: $40/month, including interest; maximum 10 years to repay; eligible for loan consolidation	Minimum: $50/month; level, graduated, income-sensitive, income-based, and extended repayment options available; eligible for loan consolidation	Minimum: $50/month; level, graduated, income-sensitive, income-based, and extended repayment options available; eligible for loan consolidation
Prepayment Penalties	None			
Allowable Cancellations	Death or total and permanent disability			

[1] Yes; in addition, borrower must agree upon signing loan agreement to enter and complete a primary care residency and practice in a primary care field until the loan is repaid in full. Family resource information is required for consideration.

[2] Both annual and aggregate maximums are subject to change, pending congressional action.

[3] Five percent; however, rate is recomputed at 18% from the date of noncompliance should borrower fail to meet primary care requirements (for primary care loans made on or after November 13, 1998).

How Medical Schools Determine Eligibility for Financial Aid

Medical schools are well aware that their programs are expensive, and that most students will need at least some degree of financial aid. Financial aid offices will determine the amount of aid for which you are eligible by answering the following three questions:

1. *How much does it cost?*

   For purposes of determining financial need, the cost of medical education is comprised of three components: tuition and fees; books, supplies, and equipment; and living expenses. The total dollar amount of these three –which varies not only by school but also by the specific year in school—is frequently referred to as the COA ("cost of attendance") or the "student financial aid budget."

   The COA for each medical school is included in that institution's entry in the latter section of this book.

2. *What are your resources?*

   The next area to be considered is the degree to which you can contribute to the overall costs (see "the financial aid philosophy" box on next page). This amount, called the "Expected Family Contribution (EFC)," is determined

through a need-analysis formula to ensure that all students are treated equitably. Both income and assets are considered.

A word about the "family" in the EFC: Even though you are considered to be independent for purposes of federal loans, some institutions require financial information about parents or other family members to determine eligibility for institutional grants, scholarships, and school-based loans. School officials use this information to assess ability—rather than willingness—to pay, thus helping ensure that certain types of aid are awarded to students with the greatest need.

3. *What additional resources are needed?*

   Finally, the financial aid office will subtract your EFC from the institution's total cost of attendance. The remainder determines how much need-based financial assistance you will require for the upcoming academic year.

   The medical school will then send you an "award letter," detailing the amount and type of financial aid it can provide. You will then be asked to accept or decline the offer—or a portion of it—and return the letter to the school. (The amount of financial aid an institution offers is, of course, an

important factor in choosing which school to attend. See Chapter 5 for additional information and guidance on making your selection.)

Service Commitment and Loan Forgiveness Programs

Were you aware of ways to minimize or almost negate your debt? Either may be possible through a service commitment or loan forgiveness program.

Service commitment programs provide financial assistance to enrolled medical students in return for services after completion of medical training. (Most programs require one year of service for each year of funding, and sometimes offer monthly stipends

The Financial Aid Philosophy

The philosophy of financial aid is that a student and his or her family bear primary responsibility of paying educational expenses to the extent possible. That is why eligibility for financial aid is determined by comparing the cost of attendance to a student's available resources.

in addition to payments for educational expenses.) The other possibility—a loan forgiveness program—cancels a portion of a borrower's student loan debt, assuming eligibility requirements are met, while he or she is working in a qualifying public service job. Students must apply for these competitive programs,
examples of which are described below.

•   The U.S. Army, Navy, and Air Force have programs that offer full support to students enrolled in civilian medical schools in exchange for service in the branch that provided the funding. On the civilian side, the federal government provides both service commitment and loan repayment benefits to medical students interested in pursuing careers in primary care for the underserved.

•   State programs are frequently available to students and graduates in return for a commitment to serve in the state's areas of need.

•   The College Cost Reduction and Access Act of 2007 passed by Congress brings you yet another possible means of loan

Service Commitment and Loan Forgiveness Programs

Learn more about these programs at the applicable web site(s) listed below:

Army: *www.goarmy.com/amedd/hpsp.jsp*

Navy: *www.navy.com/careers/healthcare/physicians/#students*

Air Force: *www.airforce.com/opportunities/healthcare/education*

Federal Government: *www.nhsc.hrsa.gov/index.htm*

State Programs: *www.aamc.org/stloan*

Public Service Programs: *www.studentaid.ed.gov/students/ attachments/siteresources/LoanForgivenessv4.pdf*

General Eligibility Criteria

Financial aid programs usually require that the applicant or student is:

• A U.S. citizen, a permanent resident, or permitted to reside indefinitely in the U.S. by the U.S. Citizenship and Immigration Services.
• Making satisfactory academic progress
• In compliance with Selective Service registration requirements

repayment assistance—a program that forgives some federal student loans under certain circumstances.

For additional details on service commitment and loan forgiveness, please see the AAMC's First Fact sheets (listed in the "Repayment" section) at www.aamc.org/firstfacts.

Education Tax Credits and Deductions

Do you know that the IRS can help you put some of the cost of medical school back in your pocket? It does so through (a) a student loan interest deduction of up to $2,500 for qualified individuals, and (b) the Lifetime Learning Tax Credit of up to $2,000 for eligible borrowers

Want to learn more? Read an overview of these programs—and learn the difference between a tax deduction and a tax credit!—by clicking on "Education Tax Credits" at *www.aamc.org/firstfacts.*

A Word About Repayment

There are, no doubt, a number of benefits to the federal student loans—whether subsidized or unsubsidized. You don't have to begin repaying the loan until after medical school and residency. There are often interest rate deductions for electronic payment and/or making your payments on time.

And…there is an array of options available to you when it comes time to repaying your loans. Beyond standard repayment, which involves a fixed payment that remains the same during the repayment period, you may choose a graduated repayment schedule, in which your payments are smaller in the early years and increase in the later years, an income-sensitive (or income-contingent) program, in which payments are based on the borrower's income and other data, or even an income-based repayment plan that caps loans payments at a particular percentage of income.

Your financial aid office will provide you with complete information as the time nears for repayment as part of your "Exit Counseling" program. For those of you interested in learning more now, please check out the First Fact sheets on loan repayment choices at www.aamc.org/firstfacts.

A Final Word About Financing Your Medical Education

This chapter is intended to provide you with an overview of the types of available financial aid, the various student loan programs, the financial aid process, and how eligibility for aid is determined. Please bear in mind that once you have been accepted to medical school, you will work closely with that institution's (or institutions') financial aid office(s) to determine the requirements for and specifics of your own education financing plan.

Chapter 12:
Information on Combined Undergraduate/ M.D. Programs

About one-quarter of U.S. medical schools offer combined college/M.D. programs for graduating high school students. These programs range in length from six to nine years. The first two to four years of the curriculum consist of undergraduate courses, including required premedical courses; the remaining years are devoted to the medical school curriculum. Graduates receive both a bachelor's degree from the undergraduate institution and an M.D. degree from the medical school.

The purposes of these programs vary by institution:

- to permit highly qualified students to plan and complete a broad liberal arts education before initiating their medical studies

- to attract highly capable students to the sponsoring medical school

- to enhance diversity in the educational environment

- to reduce the total number of years required to complete the M.D. degree

- to educate physicians likely to practice in particular geographic areas or to work with medically underserved populations

- to reduce the costs of a medical education

- to prepare physician-scientists and future leaders in health policy.

Potential applicants should familiarize themselves with the mission and goals statement of each combined degree program in which they have an interest to ensure a match between their educational and professional goals and those of the program.

These programs typically represent relationships between a medical school and one or more undergraduate colleges located in the same geographic region. They are sometimes part of the same university system, or they can be independent institutions.

Admission is open to highly qualified, mature high school students who are committed to a future career in medicine. State-supported schools generally admit few out-of-state applicants to their combined college/M.D. programs; private schools tend to have greater flexibility regarding state of residency.

While academic requirements vary among the schools sponsoring these programs, they typically include biology, chemistry, physics, English, mathematics, and social science courses. Calculus and foreign-language courses are also frequently required; a computer science course is sometimes recommended. Admission to the medical curriculum may occur immediately or after a student completes a prescribed number of semesters with a minimum grade point average (GPA). In some programs, students are not required to take the MCAT®; in other programs, a minimum MCAT score must be attained for progression through the program.

Progressing through the program from the undergraduate to the medical curriculum is usually contingent on a student's achieving specific criteria in terms of standardized test scores and GPAs and meeting the school's expectations regarding personal and professional behavior.

High school students interested in a combined undergraduate/M.D. program should consult their high school guidance counselor to ensure that they are enrolled in a challenging college preparatory curriculum, one that incorporates the specific courses required for admission to the program. The program descriptions that follow were compiled from responses to a survey sent to all medical schools sponsoring programs of interest to high school students. For additional information, contact each school directly.

The following abbreviations are used in the school entries in this chapter:

ACT
American College Testing Program

AP
Advanced Placement

BCPM
Biology, Chemistry, Physics, and Mathematics

CEEB
College Entrance Examination Board

FAFSA
Free Application for Federal Student Aid

GPA
Grade Point Average

MCAT
Medical College Admission Test

SAT
Scholastic Aptitude Test

USMLE
United States Medical Licensing Examination

List of Medical Schools Offering Combined Undergraduate/M.D. Programs, 2011–12

Alabama
University of Alabama School of Medicine

University of South Alabama College of Medicine

California
University of California, San Diego, School of Medicine

University of Southern California College of Letters, Arts, and Sciences and Keck School of Medicine

Connecticut
University of Connecticut and University of Connecticut School of Medicine

District of Columbia
The George Washington University School of Medicine and Health Sciences and The Columbian School of Arts and Sciences

Howard University College of Medicine

Florida
University of Florida College of Medicine

University of Miami

Illinois
Northwestern University Feinberg School of Medicine

University of Illinois at Chicago College of Medicine

Massachusetts
Boston University School of Medicine

Michigan
Wayne State University School of Medicine

Missouri
Saint Louis University School of Medicine

University of Missouri—Kansas City School of Medicine

New Jersey
Rutgers University and Drexel University College of Medicine

Rutgers University and UMDNJ—New Jersey Medical School

Rutgers University and UMDNJ—Robert Wood Johnson Medical School

University of Medicine and Dentistry of New Jersey—New Jersey Medical School

New Mexico
University of New Mexico School of Medicine

New York
Brooklyn College and SUNY Downstate Medical Center

Hobart and William Smith Colleges/SUNY Upstate Medical University

Rensselaer Polytechnic Institute and Albany Medical College

St. Bonaventure University/The George Washington University School of Medicine and Health Sciences

Siena College and Albany Medical College

Sophie Davis School of Biomedical Education at the City College of New York

Stony Brook University and Stony Brook University School of Medicine

Union College and Albany Medical College

University of Rochester School of Medicine and Dentistry

Ohio
Case Western Reserve University School of Medicine

Northeastern Ohio Universities College of Medicine

The Ohio State University College of Medicine Early Admissiion Pathway

University of Cincinnati College of Medicine

Pennsylvania
Drexel University and Drexel University College of Medicine

Lehigh University and Drexel University College of Medicine

Pennsylvania State University and Jefferson Medical College

Temple University School of Medicine

Villanova University and Drexel University College of Medicine

Wilkes University/SUNY-Upstate Medical University

Rhode Island
Warren Alpert Medical School of Brown University

Tennessee
Fisk University and Meharry Medical College

Texas
Rice University and Baylor College of Medicine

University of Texas School of Medicine at San Antonio

Virginia
Eastern Virginia Medical School

Virginia Commonwealth University School of Medicine

List of Medical Schools Offering Combined Undergraduate/M.D. Programs, 2011–12

6 Years
University of Missouri—Kansas City School of Medicine

6-7 Years
University of Miami

Northeastern Ohio Universities College of Medicine

Pennsylvania State University and Jefferson Medical College

7 Years
The George Washington University School of Medicine and Health Sciences and The Columbian School of Arts and Sciences

University of Florida College of Medicine

Northwestern University Feinberg School of Medicine

University of Illinois at Chicago College of Medicine

Boston University School of Medicine (8-year option available)

University of Medicine and Dentistry of New Jersey—New Jersey Medical School

Rensselaer Polytechnic Institute and Albany Medical College

Sophie Davis School of Biomedical Education/City College of New York

The Ohio State University College of Medicine Early Admission Pathway

Drexel University and Drexel University College of Medicine

Lehigh University and Drexel University College of Medicine

Villanova University and Drexel University College of Medicine

Fisk University and Meharry Medical College

University of Texas School of Medicine at San Antonio

8 Years
University of Alabama School of Medicine

University of South Alabama College of Medicine

University of California, San Diego School of Medicine

University of Southern California College of Letters, Arts, and Sciences and Keck School of Medicine

University of Connecticut and University of Connecticut School of Medicine

Howard University College of Medicine

University of New Mexico School of Medicine Combined BA/MD Degree Program

Wayne State University School of Medicine

Saint Louis University School of Medicine

Rutgers University and Drexel University College of Medicine

Rutgers University and UMDNJ—New Jersey Medical School

Rutgers University and University of Medicine and Dentistry of New Jersey—Robert Wood Johnson Medical School

Brooklyn College and SUNY Downstate Medical Center

Hobart and William Smith Colleges/SUNY Upstate Medical University

St. Bonaventure University/The George Washington University School of Medicine and Health Sciences

Siena College and Albany Medical College

Stony Brook and Stony Brook University School of Medicine

Union College and Albany Medical College

University of Rochester School of Medicine and Dentistry

Case Western Reserve University School of Medicine

University of Cincinnati College of Medicine

Temple University School of Medicine

Wilkes University/SUNY-Upstate Medical University

Warren Alpert Medical School of Brown University

Rice University and Baylor College of Medicine

Eastern Virginia Medical School

Virginia Commonwealth University School of Medicine

9 Years
University of Cincinnati College of Medicine (College of Engineering—undergraduate)

University of Alabama
School of Medicine

Birmingham, Alabama

Address Inquiries To:
Amelia Johnson
Program Administrator
UAB Honors Academy, HUC 531
University of Alabama at Birmingham
1530 3rd Avenue, South, Birmingham, Alabama 35294-1150
T (205) 996-9842 F (205) 996-9838
honorsacademy@uab.edu
www.uab.edu/emsap

Purpose

The UAB Early Medical School Acceptance Program (EMSAP) is designed to give exceptional high school graduates an opportunity to take advantage of the best resources of the undergraduate and medical programs through a mentored relationship with medical school faculty. A medical school professor advises students from high school graduation until the second year of the medical program, establishing a unique relationship. This is not an accelerated program, rather a program to allow gifted students to explore a broad range of educational, research and community service opportunities beyond the typical premedical experiences.

Requirements for Entrance

Students are selected in their senior year of high school. Both residents and non-residents of Alabama are eligible to apply to the program. Applicants must submit the following documents: (1) a UAB application; (2) a completed EMSAP application; (3) two letters of recommendation from high school administrators, counselors, or teachers describing their suitability for a career in medicine; (4) a brief essay incorporating information about themselves and their career objectives and expectations for contributing to society; and (5) a resume listing their academic achievements, honors received, activities, employment, health-related experience, etc. Applicants must meet the requirements for freshman admission to the university and be admitted to the University by the EMSAP application deadline, December 15, 2010.

Selection Factors

Required high school courses include: four years of English, four years of mathematics, one year of chemistry or physics, and one year of biology. Minimum GPA: 3.5 overall GPA (on a 4.0 scale). Test scores: at least 30 ACT or a minimum 1320 SAT (critical reading + math). Selected applicants are invited for a required interview.

Curriculum

This eight-year program leads to a baccalaureate degree awarded by the University of Alabama at Birmingham (UAB), and to the M.D. degree granted by the University of Alabama School of Medicine. Students must meet the regular undergraduate course requirements for the University of Alabama at Birmingham, complete two required EMSAP (Early Medical School Acceptance Program) seminars and live on campus during their first two years. Applicants may apply to one of three other Honors programs in the Honors Academy. The deadline to apply for both programs is December 15. In order to matriculate to the medical school phase of the program, students must: (1) take the MCAT and receive a minimal total score of 28; (2) maintain an overall GPA of 3.6 and a math and science GPA of 3.5; (3) receive their baccalaureate degree; and (4) meet all requirements

and conditions to remain in good standing for their acceptance into the University of Alabama School of Medicine. After the second year of medical school, students must pass the USMLE Step 1 in order to be promoted and graduate. Passing the USMLE Step 2 Clinical Knowledge (CK) examination and sitting for the Step 2 Clinical Skills (CS) examination are required in order to graduate from the medical school. Passing an Observed Structured Clinical Examination (OSCE) is also required for graduation from medical school.

Expenses

Expenses	Resident Tuition and Fees	Non-resident Tuition and Fees
Undergraduate	$5,144	$11,480
U.S. Medical School	$19,921	$53,175

Financial Aid

UAB awards comprehensive federal, state, institutional, and private financial aid on the basis of merit, financial need, or both. Each year, the university offers more than 1,500 scholarships, including approximately $1.5 million in merit-based awards. Applicants are automatically considered for all academic scholarships when accepted to the university. As academic scholarships are awarded on a first come-first served basis, applicants are encouraged to apply no later than December 1 (prior to EMSAP application deadline) of the senior year of high school.

Application and Acceptance Policies

Filing of application:
    Earliest date: September 1, 2010
    Latest date: December 15, 2010
Application fee: $30   Fee Waiver Available: Yes
Acceptance notice:
    Earliest date: Mid-February 2011
    Latest date: Late February 2011
Applicant's response to acceptance offer:
    Latest date: May 1, 2011
Deposit to hold place in class: None
Starting date: Mid-August 2011

Information on 2009–2010 Entering Class

Number of	In-State	Out-of-State	Total
Applicants	85	55	140
Applicants Interviewed	18	10	28
New Entrants	5	5	10
Total number of students enrolled in program: 39			

University of South Alabama
College of Medicine

Mobile, Alabama

Address Inquiries To:
Donna Pigg, Assistant Director of Admissons
University of South Alabama Meisler Hall, Room 2500
Mobile, Alabama, 36688-0022
T (251) 460-6141 F (251) 460-7876
dpigg@usouthal.edu
www.southalabama.edu/com/

Purpose

Candidates selected for the program will receive early acceptance from the University of South Alabama and its College of Medicine. Students participating in the program are expected to enter the University of South Alabama College of Medicine in the fall after completion of the baccalaureate degree.

Requirements for Entrance

Students in the senior year of high school or recently graduated individuals who have not yet entered college are eligible to apply for the program. Both residents and non-residents of Alabama may apply.

Selection Factors

Candidates must have a minimum high school GPA of 3.5, as computed by the University of South Alabama, and must present a minimum enhanced composite ACT score of 30 (or comparable SAT score). Candidates must also have demonstrated evidence of leadership qualities, community service, communication skills, and motivation for the study of medicine.

Curriculum

The curriculum will include core requirements for the selected baccalaureate program and prerequisites for matriculation in medical school. Students in the program must maintain a minimum overall GPA of 3.5 and a minimum GPA of 3.4 in the sciences (biology, chemistry, physics) and mathematics. All required courses must be taken at the University of South Alabama unless otherwise approved in advance by the student's undergraduate program director and the Director of Admissions for the College of Medicine. Students will be required to participate in CP-200 (Career Planning; Clinical Observation) for a minimum of four quarters. Students will be given the opportunity to participate in a special summer premedical clerkship. These activities will be planned to give participants a broad exposure to medical education. Students will be required to take the MCAT for admission to the College of Medicine and will be required to achieve a composite score of 27. A formal assessment, including an interview, will be conducted after the student has completed 96 quarter hours of academic work. At this time, students' academic performance and continued interest in a medical career will be assessed.

Expenses

Expenses	Resident Tuition and Fees	Non-resident Tuition and Fees
Undergraduate	$6,500	$13,000
U.S. Medical School	$19,643	$36,251

Financial Aid

Information can be obtained from the Office of Financial Aid, Meisler Hall, Room 1200, University of South Alabama, Mobile, Alabama 36688-0002; by phone at (251) 460-6231; or on the school Web site at *www.finaid2.usouthal.edu*.

Application and Acceptance Policies

Filing of application:
 Earliest date: December 15, 2010
 Latest date: June 11, 2011
Application fee: $35   Fee Waiver Available: No
Acceptance notice:
 Earliest date: March 1, 2011
 Latest date: Until program is filled
Applicant's response to acceptance offer:
 Maximum time: Two weeks
Deposit to hold place in class: None
Starting date: August 18, 2011

Information on 2009–2010 Entering Class

Number of	In-State	Out-of-State	Total
Applicants	93	38	131
Applicants Interviewed	31	14	45
New Entrants	11	4	15
Total number of students enrolled in program: 60			

University of California, San Diego School of Medicine

La Jolla, California

Address Inquiries To:
Yvonne Coleman, Director of Medical Scholars Program
University of California, San Diego School of Medicine
Office of Admissions, 0621
9500 Gilman Drive, La Jolla, California 92093-0621
T (858) 534-3880 F (858) 534-5282
somadmissions@ucsd.edu
http://meded.ucsd.edu/groups/med-scholars/

Purpose

The Medical Scholars Program was established to encourage the recruitment of unusually talented high school students, who would then be attracted to both the University of California, San Diego, (UCSD) undergraduate and medical schools, and to promote the goal of increasing diversity on both campuses.

Requirements for Entrance

Students are selected for this program during their senior year of high school. The program is open to California residents only. Applicants must meet course requirements for UCSD undergraduate admission. They must take either the SAT or ACT and achieve a minimum score of 2250 on the SAT or 34 on the ACT.

Selection Factors

To be eligible for consideration, applicants must have a minimum high school GPA of 4.0 and 2250 on the SAT or 34 on the ACT. The average high school grade-point average for the 2009 entering class was 4.29. Applicants must also demonstrate strong extracurricular involvement, particularly in community service and leadership. Letters of recommendation and an essay are additional considerations. An interview is required. The MCAT is not required.

Curriculum

This program leads to a baccalaureate degree granted by the University of California, San Diego, and to the M.D. degree granted by the UCSD School of Medicine. It takes eight years to fulfill the requirements for both degrees. The specific course requirements for the baccalaureate degree include a minimum of 6 quarters in either humanities or social sciences and 15 quarters in the natural and physical sciences. Students must take Step 1 of the USMLE after the second year of medical school. Passing Steps 1 and 2 of the USMLE is required in order to be promoted and to graduate.

Financial Aid

Sources of financial aid include scholarships, grants, loans, and work-study. Additional information is available from the undergraduate financial aid office: Building 201, University Center, La Jolla, California 92093-0013, or at *http://ucsd.edu/prospective-students/finances/financial-aid.html*.

Expenses	Resident Tuition and Fees	Non-resident Tuition and Fees
Undergraduate	$8,906	$29,813
U.S. Medical School	$25,313	$37,558

Application and Acceptance Policies

Filing of application:
   Earliest date: February 14, 2011
   Latest date: March 14, 2011
Application fee: None   Fee Waiver Available: n/a
Acceptance notice:
   Earliest date: April 19, 2011
   Latest date: April 29, 2011
Applicant's response to acceptance offer:
   Maximum time: 1 week
Deposit to hold place in class: None
Starting date: September 2011

Information on 2009–2010 Entering Class

Number of	In-State	Out-of-State	Total
Applicants	312	n/a	312
Applicants Interviewed	30	n/a	30
New Entrants	11	n/a	11
Total number of students enrolled in program: 42			

University of Southern California
College of Letters, Arts, and Sciences
and Keck School of Medicine
Los Angeles, California

Address Inquiries To:
Karen Rowan-Badger, Director of Admission
College of Letters, Arts, and Sciences
University of Southern California
Los Angeles, California 90089-0152
T (213) 740-5930 F (213) 740-1338
admission@college.usc.edu
www.usc.edu/schools/college/admission/baccalaureatemd/

Purpose

The goal of this program is to encourage bright and motivated students to expand the breadth of their education through a diverse liberal arts education. Students accepted into this program have the opportunity to study a wide variety of disciplines beyond the course of the standard premedical curriculum. It is the hope of the university to graduate physicians who are educated in medical science, the arts, and the humanities.

Requirements for Entrance

Students are selected for this program in the senior year of high school. Both residents and non-residents of California and international students are eligible to apply. Although there are no specific high school course requirements, applicants are required to take either the SAT or ACT.

Selection Factors

Academic factors considered include grades and standardized test scores. Participation in extracurricular activities and demonstrated leadership and community service are valued. Students who enrolled in 2008 had a mean high school GPA of 4.34 (weighted) and a mean SAT score of 2190. An interview is required and is granted by invitation following careful evaluation of an applicant's file.

Curriculum

This program leads to a baccalaureate degree awarded by the University of Southern California, and to the M.D. degree granted by the University of Southern California Keck School of Medicine. This is not an accelerated program; all students must complete four years of undergraduate education and four years of medical school. Students must complete requirements for the bachelor's degree and may pursue any major offered in the university that is compatible with the requirements of the program. There are specific requirements for the bachelor's degree, which include the humanities and social, natural, and physical sciences. Advancement to the medical school phase of the program is based on acceptable academic performance and MCAT scores as defined by the program. The MCAT is required and must be taken by the spring of the junior year. Students must take USMLE Steps 1 and 2, and pass Step 1 of the USMLE in order to graduate from the School of Medicine.

Expenses

	Resident Tuition and Fees	Non-resident Tuition and Fees
Undergraduate	$38,570	$38,570
U.S. Medical School	$45,482	$45,482

Financial Aid

Sources of aid include scholarships, grants, work-study programs, and loans. For additional information, contact the Office of Financial Aid, University of Southern California, Los Angeles, California 90089-0912; call (213) 740-1111; or visit *www.usc.edu/admission/fa/*.

Application and Acceptance Policies

Filing of application:
    Earliest date: August 1, 2010
    Latest date: December 1, 2010
Application fee: $65   Fee Waiver Available: Yes
Acceptance notice:
    Earliest date: April 1, 2011
    Latest date: April 1, 2011
Applicant's response to acceptance offer:
    Maximum time: 1 month
Deposit to hold place in class: $300; nonrefundable
Starting date: August 2011

Information on 2009–2010 Entering Class

Number of	In-State	Out-of-State	Total
Applicants	637	308	945
Applicants Interviewed	67	35	102
New Entrants	15	6	21

Total number of students enrolled in program: 103

University of Connecticut and University of Connecticut School of Medincine

Storrs, Connecticut

Address Inquiries To:
Special Programs in Medicine & Dental Medicine
University of Connecticut, 2131 Hillside Road, U-88
Storrs, Connecticut 06269-3088
T (860) 486-3137 F (860) 486-1476
http://medicine.uchc.edu/prospective/admissions/babs_md/index.html
Medical School Contact: Richard Zeff, Ph.D.,
Assistant Dean for Admissions

Purpose

This program offers gifted and talented high school students, who are focused on a career in medicine, the opportunity to combine a broad-based liberal arts program with a medical education. This program links undergraduate preparation with four years of medical education, resulting in dual degrees: a B.A. or B.S. degree and the M.D. degree.

Requirements for Entrance

Students are selected for this program during the senior year of high school. Both residents and non-residents of Connecticut are eligible to apply. Applicants must take either the SAT I or ACT.

Selection Factors

To be considered for this program, the student should have the following: a high school class ranking in the top five percent; an overall high school grade-point average of 3.5 (4.0 scale); an SAT combined score of 1300 or an ACT composite score of 30; a completed regular undergraduate admission application and a supplemental application for the program in medicine by the January 1 postmark deadline; and, an interview at the School of Medicine. In addition, recommendations from teachers/advisors, as well as evidence maturity, extracurricular activities, and a commitment to the health profession, are considered. To matriculate in the School of Medicine upon completion of under-graduate preparation, the student must meet additional criteria that include: maintaining a college 3.5 cumulative grade-point average (4.0 scale); ordinarily obtaining an MCAT score of 30+ (with a minimum score of 28), with section scores of 7 or greater; participation in clinical, research, and community service activities; and favorable interviews during the senior undergraduate year.

Curriculum

Students must complete requirements for a baccalaureate degree from the University of Connecticut. Requirements include courses in the humanities and social sciences. The curriculum typically takes eight years to complete: Years 1 through 4 in the liberal arts and sciences and Years 5 through 8 in the School of Medicine. The MCAT is required for admission to the medical school phase of the program. Students are required to pass Step 1 of the USMLE for promotion and Step 2 of the USMLE in order to graduate.

Expenses

Expenses	Resident Tuition and Fees	Non-resident Tuition and Fees
Undergraduate	$7,632	$22,232
U.S. Medical School	$26,956	$50,001

Financial Aid

All enrolled candidates will be automatically considered for merit scholarships. A full range of financial aid options based on student financial need is available, as well. Candidates for need-based aid must submit the Free Application for Federal Student Aid (FAFSA) by March 1. For more information about student aid programs, contact the University of Connecticut's Office of Student Financial Aid Services at (860) 486-2819; write to U-4116, Storrs, Connecticut 06269; or visit the UConn homepage at *www.uconn.edu*.

Additional Information

Students are provided with enrichment experiences while completing the undergraduate program. Programming includes: courses offered at the main University campus by faculty from the School of Medicine (these have included Mini-Medical School and The Patient and the Healer.); a summer research fellowship opportunity at the School of Medicine; placements to obtain clinical experience; placements to obtain community service experience; and assigned advisory commit-tees for each student including faculty from the School of Medicine.

Application and Acceptance Policies

Filing of application:
  Earliest date: September 1, 2010
  Latest date: January 1, 2011
Application fee: $70   Fee Waiver Available: Yes
Acceptance notice:
  Earliest date: March 1, 2011
  Latest date: Until full
Applicant's response to acceptance offer:
  Latest date: May 1, 2011
Deposit to hold place in class: $150; nonrefundable
Starting date: August 2011

Information on 2009–2011 Entering Class

Number of	In-State	Out-of-State	Total
Applicants	93	139	232
Applicants Interviewed	26	16	42
New Entrants	12	3	15
Total number of students enrolled in program: 56			

The George Washington University School of Medicine and The Columbian College of Arts and Sciences

Washington, D.C.

Address Inquiries To:
Office of Undergraduate Admissions
The George Washington University
2121 I Street N.W., Suite 201
Washington, D.C. 20052
T (202) 994-6040
gwadm@gwu.edu
http://gwired.gwu.edu/adm/apply/honors.html

Purpose

A joint program of The George Washington (GW) University Columbian College of Arts and Sciences and the School of Medicine and Health Sciences, the seven-year B.A.–M.D. program is designed for the high school senior who exhibits academic excellence, leadership in activities, and community service and healthcare experience, and who has confirmed the goal to become a physician. The purpose of the program is to encourage a liberal arts focus in preparation for medical school. Students typically choose majors in a wide variety of fields ranging from economics and psychology to religion and biology. The new, state-of-the-art GW Hospital opened in 2002. Housed on the 6th floor of the new GW Hospital is the GW Clinical Skills Center. Dedicated to education and research, this floor of the hospital features cutting-edge technology in a setting that is among the most innovative in the nation. Through the use of the Surgical Simulation and Demonstration Area and the Standardized Patient Examining Area, medical students gain the comprehensive clinical exposure, feedback, and evaluation they need to become both technically adept and humane caregivers for their patients.

Requirements for Entrance

Students are selected in their senior year of high school. Applicants must be a U.S. citizen, U.S. permanent resident, or Canadian citizen in order to apply. Applicants are expected to complete the SAT or ACT, as well as the SAT Subject Tests in Mathematics, Science, and English. Competitive SAT scores for the program are (equivalent) 2100 and above.

Selection Factors

Academic factors considered in selecting applicants include the strength of the academic program, grades in high school, class rank, and standardized test scores. In addition to academic factors, extra-curricular and health-related activities, community service, essays, and letters of recommendation are reviewed. Competitive applicants are those who rank in the top ten percent of their high school class, have shown leadership ability through participation in extracurricular activities, have demonstrated interest in the medical field through experience, and have taken advantage of advanced course offerings. An interview is required and is by invitation only.

Curriculum

A special faculty committee reviews each student's progress throughout the program annually. To continue each year in the program, students must maintain a minimum of a "B" in courses required for admission to the medical school and an overall 3.6 average. Students do not take the MCAT. Students participate in seminars of interest and are involved in community service and health care experiences throughout the undergraduate portion of the curriculum. The review committee will make a final recommendation concerning promotion to the medical school curriculum at the end of the third year. In the fourth year,

students enroll in the School of Medicine and Health Sciences and begin their formal medical training. The baccalaureate degree is received before entrance to the M.D. program. The integration of clinical skills begins in the first and second years of medical school, as students spend time with physicians, learning the art and skill of patient interviewing and physical diagnosis. The sixth and seventh years are devoted to developing clinical expertise in a wide variety of hospitals in the D.C. metropolitan area. At the end of the seventh year, students are awarded the M.D. degree.

Expenses

	Resident Tuition and Fees	Non-resident Tuition and Fees
Undergraduate	$56,329	$56,329
U.S. Medical School	$47,644	$47,644

Financial Aid

Information may be obtained from The George Washington University, Office of Student Financial Assistance, 2121 "I" Street, N.W., #310, Washington, D.C. 20052. The Office of Student Financial Assistance may be reached by phone at 1-800-222-6242.

Additional Information

Students accepted to the 2010 seven-year B.A.–M.D. program receive a $15,000 award yearly, resulting in combined tuition and fees of $41,329. Tuition and fees remain the same for each year of the seven-year program.

Application and Acceptance Policies

Filing of application:
    Earliest date: September 1, 2010
    Latest date: December 1, 2010
Application fee: $70   Fee Waiver Available: Yes
Acceptance notice:
    Earliest date: April 2011
    Latest date: April 2011
Applicant's response to acceptance offer:
    Maximum time: May 1, 2011
Deposit to hold place in class: $800; nonrefundable
Starting date: August 2011

Information on 2009–2010 Entering Class

Number of	In-State	Out-of-State	Total
Applicants	n/a	700	700
Applicants Interviewed	n/a	45	45
New Entrants	n/a	11	11

Total number of students enrolled in program: 105

Howard University College of Medicine

Washington, D.C.

Address Inquiries To:
Julie Chang Andrist, M.Ed., Asst. Coordinator/Preprofessional Advisor
Center for Preprofessional Education
College of Arts and Sciences, 2225 Georgia Avenue N.W., Room 518,
Howard University
Washington, D.C. 20059
T (202) 238-2363 F (202) 588-9828
preprofessional@howard.edu,
www.coas.howard.edu/preprofessionaleducation

Purpose

The goal of this combined-degree program is to encourage talented undergraduate students to choose medicine as a career and to retain these excellent students in the Howard University College of Medicine.

Requirements for Entrance

Students can be selected for this program during the senior year of high school or during the first year of college. There are no state residence requirements. Applicants are expected to have completed the following courses by the time they graduate from high school: at least two years of a foreign language; at least one year each of biology, chemistry, and physics; two years of mathematics; and, four years of English, including literature. They must take either the SAT or the ACT Assessment.

Selection Factors

The academic factors considered in offering admission to an applicant are rank in high school class, GPA, and test scores. Applicants are expected to be in the top five percent of their high school class. In the 2009–2010 entering class, the average GPA was 3.7, and the average SAT combined score was 2200. ACT Assessment cumulative scores ranged from 28 to 30. Personal qualities considered are: superior writing skills, maturity, positive self-confidence, realistic self-appraisal, a realistic assessment of the medical profession, good leadership skills, and sustained demonstration of service to people who are less fortunate. An interview is required.

Curriculum

This program leads to a bachelor's degree awarded by the College of Arts and Sciences at Howard University and to the M.D. degree granted by the Howard University College of Medicine. Students must complete work for a baccalaureate degree. They are expected to complete at least 40 semester hours of humanities and social sciences courses to fulfill general education requirements and at least 46 semester hours of natural and physical sciences courses. Students meet with the director (the advisor) of the Center for Preprofessional Education to design a curriculum tailored to their individual needs. The specific course selection must have the advisor's approval. Students are encouraged to select a major of personal interest. The curricula for both degrees are completed in six years. In the first two years, the curriculum focuses on work toward the bachelor's degree and premedical requirements, and in the last four years the focus is on studies related to medicine. Students in this program must take the MCAT in April of the second year. The results of the MCAT, the GPA, the demonstration of a high level of maturity, and a strong commitment to service in areas where there is a shortage of health professionals are factors in gaining admission to the medical school phase of the combined degree program. Students are also expected to take Steps 1 and 2 of the USMLE while at Howard University College of Medicine; they must pass these examinations prior to promotion and graduation.

Expenses

	Resident Tuition and Fees	Non-resident Tuition and Fees
Undergraduate	$16,075	$16,075
U.S. Medical School	$36,781	$36,781

Financial Aid

Information can be obtained from The Office of Financial Aid, Scholarships and Student Employment at Room 205, Johnson Administration Building, 2400 6th Street, N.W., Washington, D.C. 20059. Contact Information: Tel 202-806-2820 Fax 202-806-2818 *www.howard.edu/financialaid/contacts/*

Application and Acceptance Policies

Filing of application:
Earliest date: March 1, 2011
Latest date: n/a
Application fee: $45   Fee Waiver Available: No
Acceptance notice:
Earliest date: varies
Latest date: varies
Applicant's response to acceptance offer:
Maximum time: June 15, 2011
Deposit to hold place in class: $300; nonrefundable
Starting date: August 2011

Information on 2009–2010 Entering Class

Number of	In-State	Out-of-State	Total
Applicants	5	60	65
Applicants Interviewed	3	15	18
New Entrants	2	10	12
Total number of students enrolled in program: 12			

University of Florida
College of Medicine

Gainesville, Florida

Address Inquiries To:
Denise Chichester
Medical Selection Committee
University of Florida College of Medicine P.O. Box 100216
Gainesville, Florida 32610
T (352) 273-7990 F (352) 392-1307
med-admissions@ufl.edu

Purpose

The Junior Honors Medical Program is for undergraduate students who have chosen a career in the medical profession and who have demonstrated superior scholastic ability and personal development during their first two academic years of college enrollment. Experience in health care, community service, and research are extracurricular activities that are considered valuable for these applicants.

Requirements for Entrance

Students are selected for this program during the sophomore year of college enrollment. Admission is open to all possible candidates who are United States citizens or permanent residents, with preference given to Florida residents. There are no specific high school course requirements. However, admission tests such as the SAT and/or ACT achievement tests are required. The minimum GPA required for application is 3.7 on college coursework; the minimum required SAT score is a 1200. The courses listed must be completed by the spring semester of the applicant's sophomore year: General Chemistry I & II (both with labs), Organic Chemistry I & II (both with labs), General Biology I & II (both with labs) and Calculus I & II. The following courses may be completed in the junior year: General Physics I & II (both with labs) and Biochemistry.

Selection Factors

The academic factors considered in offering admission to an applicant include sophomore standing (two years of college classroom enrollment), competitive SAT or ACT scores, competitive GPA, and completion of prerequisite courses. Involvement in research prior to application is considered positively as well as consistent health care experience and community service. The MCAT is currently not required. Selected applicants are invited for a required interview held in April. Acceptance decisions are not made until grades for the Spring semester are posted and an official transcript is received in the UF COM Admissions Office, usually in May.

Curriculum

The most frequent major for the baccalaureate degree is the B.S. in interdisciplinary biological and medical sciences through the College of Liberal Arts and Sciences. Some students choose nutrition as a major through the College of Agricultural and Life Sciences; this option requires approval. The junior year in the program includes undergraduate college required courses and seminars with College of Medicine faculty. During the junior year, JHMP students must complete an Honors Thesis prior to entering medical school. Completion of the thesis earns the designation of honors or high honors in research at graduation for the MD degree. The bachelor's degree is awarded after the fourth year of college enrollment, which is concurrently the first year of medical school. The University of Florida College of Medicine awards the Doctor of Medicine degree. It takes seven years to complete the requirements for both the Bachelor of Science and Doctor of Medicine degrees. All courses in the first two years are completed from the various undergraduate colleges in the majors prospective students have declared. After acceptance into the Junior Honors Medical Program, the Junior Honors students complete courses from the College of Medicine in the third year, and any remaining requirements for the Liberal Arts and Sciences or Agricultural and Life Sciences. In years 4 through 7, all courses are in medicine.

Expenses

Expenses	Resident Tuition and Fees	Non-resident Tuition and Fees
Undergraduate	$2,186	$11,872
U.S. Medical School	$28,727	$57,967

Additional Information

For the research requirement, the Junior Honors student chooses a faculty member in a department of interest to the student. The faculty member supervising the research is a mentor to the student. Continued interest in the research area can be achieved during the medical school years either through the Medical Student Research Program or the M.D./Ph.D. Program.

Application and Acceptance Policies

Filing of application:
    Earliest date: January 14, 2011
    Latest date: January 28, 2011
Application fee: None   Fee Waiver Available: n/a
Acceptance notice:
    Earliest date: May 16, 2011
    Latest date: August 15, 2011
Applicant's response to acceptance offer:
    Maximum time: 2 weeks
Deposit to hold place in class: None
Starting date: August 2011

Information on 2009–2010 Entering Class

Number of	In-State	Out-of-State	Total
Applicants	63	0	63
Applicants Interviewed	27	0	27
New Entrants	13	0	13

Total number of students enrolled in program: 60

84   *Medical School Admission Requirements, 2011–2012*

University of Miami

Coral Gables, Florida

Address Inquiries To:
Yamilet Medina-Lopez, Sr. Assistant Director of Admission Office of Admissions,
University of Miami
P.O. Box 248025
Coral Gables, Florida 33124
T (305) 284-4323
webrequest.admission@miami.edu
http://www6.miami.edu/UMH/CDA/UMH_Main/0,1770,2613-1;14415-3,00.html

Purpose

The Honors Program in Medicine (HPM) offers exceptionally motivated and talented high school students, who have reached a mature and independent decision to study medicine, an opportunity to earn the B.S. and M.D. degrees in seven or eight years.

Requirements for Entrance

Applicants must be U.S. citizens or permanent residents. Both residents and non-residents of Florida are considered for admission. Applicants must be in their last year of high school at the time of application. Applicants must have a minimum combined score of 1400 on the SAT (Math and Verbal) or a composite score of 32 on the ACT, an unweighted GPA of at least 3.75, and take the SAT II Subject Tests in Mathematics, and one science (a minimum score of 600 is required in each). All applicants must have completed eight semesters of mathematics and English and two semesters each of biology and chemistry by the time of graduation from high school.

Selection Factors

Academic factors taken into account include scores on standardized tests, the quality of the high school curriculum (including the number and nature of Advanced Placement courses and/or International Baccalaureate coursework), and the amount of university-level work already completed. Of equal importance to academic achievements are personal factors such as maturity of thought and action, common sense, empathy, interpersonal skills, appropriate freedom from parental influence, and social cognizance. Most important, the applicant must have made a practical decision to study medicine based on self-initiated patient-contact experiences.

Curriculum

The first three years are spent on the Coral Gables campus taking required science and humanities courses and focusing almost exclusively on work related to the bachelor's degree. The undergraduate portion of the curriculum may be extended to four years if the student is in good academic standing and has established a clear plan of academic and personal growth. All HPM students must have a 3.7 science GPA and a 3.7 cumulative GPA and an MCAT composite score of 30 to be promoted to the School of Medicine after three or four years. All students must develop a continuous history of involvement at the undergraduate level in a variety of experiences that must include patient contact, and some combination of research, campus or community service, study abroad, or employment, consistent with a sincere desire to study and practice medicine. HPM students may attend either the parent medical campus in Miami or the regional medical campus located in Boca Raton, Florida, on the campus of Florida Atlantic University. The missions of the educational programs at both campuses are identical but the regional medical campus emphasizes continuity of care and community medicine. Students at the Miami campus receive their clinical training at Jackson Memorial Hospital and other hospitals affiliated with the Miller School of Medicine, while students at the regional campus will receive their clinical training at John F. Kennedy Community Hospital.

Expenses

Expenses	Resident Tuition and Fees	Non-resident Tuition and Fees
Undergraduate	$34,834	$34,834
U.S. Medical School	$30,188	$39,394

Financial Aid

Scholarships, work-study, loans, and state tuition grants are sources of financial assistance. Information on undergraduate financial aid is available from the Office of Admissions on the Coral Gables campus.

Application and Acceptance Policies

Filing of application:
  Earliest date: October 1, 2010
  Latest date: November 1, 2010
Application fee: $55   Fee Waiver Available: No
Acceptance notice:
  Earliest date: April 1, 2011
  Latest date: April 1, 2011
Applicant's response to acceptance offer:
  Maximum time: May 1, 2011
Deposit to hold place in class: $300; nonrefundable
Starting date: August 2011

Information on 2009–2010 Entering Class

Number of	In-State	Out-of-State	Total
Applicants	64	119	183
Applicants Interviewed	31	65	96
New Entrants	10	11	21

Total number of students enrolled in program: 55

Northwestern University Feinberg School of Medicine

Evanston, Illinois

Address Inquiries To:
Dr. Marianne Green, Associate Dean for Medical Education
Office of Admission and Financial Aid Northwestern University
1801 Hinman Avenue
Evanston, Illinois 60204-3060
T (312) 503-8915 F (312) 503-0840
ug-ad@northwestern.edu
www.medschool.northwestern.edu/hpme

Purpose

The Honors Program in Medical Education (HPME), one of the oldest in the nation, offers a unique opportunity for gifted and highly motivated students who seek careers in medicine or medical science. The HPME provides a broad, flexible and challenging undergraduate education free from many of the pressures related to gaining acceptance to medical school.

Requirements for Entrance

Students are selected for this program during their senior year of high school. Both residents and non-residents of Illinois are eligible to apply. Applicants must meet the following high school course requirements: English, eight semesters; mathematics, including differential and integral calculus, eight semesters; chemistry, two semesters; physics, two semesters; biology, two semesters; and, foreign language, four semesters. They must take either the SAT Reasoning Test or the ACT Assessment with Writing, plus the SAT Subject Tests (in mathematics level 2 and chemistry).

Selection Factors

Academic factors considered in selecting applicants include class rank, grades in high school, and scores on college entrance tests. Average test scores of students in the 2008–2009 entering class were: SAT Critical Reading, 732; SAT Mathematics, 775; SAT Writing 750; CEEB Subject Tests – Chemistry, 764; Mathematics II, 788; ACT plus Writing, 34. Non-academic factors considered are motivation for a career in medicine, concern for others, maturity, team work, and leadership. An interview is required.

Curriculum

The degrees offered in the honors program are a baccalaureate degree (B.A., B.S. in medicine, B.S. in biomedical engineering, or B.S. in communication) and the M.D., all from Northwestern University. Students must complete requirements for a baccalaureate degree in addition to the required science courses (inorganic and organic chemistry, calculus-based physics, biological science sequence). The majority of students in the Feinberg College of Arts & Science major in biological sciences but have many other options within the college. Students in the McCormick School of Engineering & Applied Sciences major in biomedical engineering and take the basic and advanced engineering courses, in addition to non-science courses. The program in the School of Communication includes special courses in communication sciences and disorders. The curriculum usually takes seven or eight years to complete, and students are encouraged to develop a unique curricular path. During the undergraduate years, the curriculum consists of courses in the liberal arts and sciences, engineering, or speech. After matriculation to Feinberg School of Medicine, the curriculum focuses on medicine. The MCAT is not required. Students must take Steps 1 and 2 of the USMLE and record passing grades in order to graduate from the medical school.

Expenses

Expenses	Resident Tuition and Fees	Non-resident Tuition and Fees
Undergraduate	$38,088	$38,088
U.S. Medical School	$42,974	$42,974

Financial Aid

Sources of aid include Northwestern University and federal, state, and private programs. Undergraduate applicants can receive more information from the Office of Admission and Financial Aid, 1801 Hinman Avenue, Evanston, Illinois 60204-3060; or phone (847) 491-7271. Information about medical school financial aid can be obtained from Financial Aid Professional Schools, Abbott Hall, 710 Superior Street, Chicago, Illinois 60611.

Additional Information

Students are encouraged to explore focused areas of concentration during their undergraduate years that may prepare them personally and professionally for their careers in medicine. Students spend their undergraduate years on the Evanston Northwestern Campus; the medical school curriculum is conducted at the Feinberg School of Medicine Chicago Campus. Tours of the Evanston Campus are given on a regular basis, however, tours are not generally offered for the Chicago Campus. For more detailed information about the program, please see our Web site: *www.medschool.northwestern.edu/hpme*.

Application and Acceptance Policies

Filing of application:
  Earliest date: n/a
  Latest date: January 1, 2011
Application fee: $65   Fee Waiver Available: Yes
Acceptance notice:
  Earliest date: April 1, 2011
  Latest date: n/a
Applicant's response to acceptance offer:
  Latest Date: May 1, 2011
Deposit to hold place in class: $400; nonrefundable
Starting date: September 15, 2011

Information on 2009–2010 Entering Class

Number of	In-State	Out-of-State	Total
Applicants	96	500	596
Applicants Interviewed	6	104	110
New Entrants	4	13	17
Total number of students enrolled in program: 68			

University of Illinois at Chicago
College of Medicine

Chicago, Illinois

Address Inquiries To:
Josephine Volpe, Assistant Director Academic Affairs/Special Scholarship Programs
University of Illinois at Chicago, 2506 University Hall, M/C 115
601 S. Morgan Street
Chicago, Illinois 60607
T (312) 355-2477 F (312) 355-1233
gppauic@uic.edu
www.uic.edu/depts/oaa/spec_prog/gppa/

Purpose

The Guaranteed Professional Program Admissions (GPPA) initiative is a combined effort of the University of Illinois at Chicago (UIC) Honors College on the undergraduate campus and the College of Medicine. This program is offered only to high school seniors from Illinois. The GPPA guarantees incoming freshmen a seat in the College of Medicine at one of the four locations provided they qualify upon completion of their undergraduate studies at UIC.

Requirements for Entrance

This program is limited to Illinois residents. Students are selected for this program during the senior year of high school. There are no specific high school course requirements.

Selection Factors

The academic factors considered are rank in high school class, grade-point average, and test scores. Applicants must be in the top 15 percent of their high school class. Applicants must have a minimum ACT composite score of 28, or its SAT equivalent score. In addition to academic factors, extracurricular health-related activities and letters of recommendations are required. All applicants are invited for a required interview. A selected number of applicants are invited to return for a second interview.

Curriculum

The GPPA-Medicine program is designed to be completed in four years of undergraduate education at the University of Illinois at Chicago. Students are free to choose any of UIC's majors in eight undergraduate colleges. Throughout their undergraduate education, students participate in a number of required seminars and courses that will introduce them to various aspects of the medical profession. The final course is the Independent Study Seminar, which is a "capstone" project and presentation. Students must maintain at least 3.5 cumulative grade-point average throughout their undergraduate education. During the year proceeding expected entry into medical school, students must take the Medical College Admissions Test (MCAT). Students must earn a MCAT score of at least the mean of the matriculating students into the College of Medicine in the year prior to expected entry, with no score below 9 in any segment of the exam. Students successfully completing the GPPA requirements are guaranteed a seat in one of the four University of Illinois College of Medicine campuses. However, students are not required to attend the University of Illinois College of Medicine. Once enrolled in the College of Medicine, students in the program are bound by the policies in force at the time of their matriculation.

Expenses

Expenses	Resident Tuition and Fees	Non-resident Tuition and Fees
Undergraduate	$12,034	N/A
U.S. Medical School	$32,348	$65,724

Additional Information

Interested students should consult the GPPA-Medicine Conditions of Acceptance for more detailed information. All students are assigned a faculty mentor from the College of Medicine for their undergraduate years. All undergraduate classes take place in Chicago. University of Illinois College of Medicine has four campuses, Chicago, Urbana/Champaign, Peoria and Rockford.

Application and Acceptance Policies

Filing of application:
    Earliest date: September 15, 2010
    Latest date: December 1, 2010
Application fee: $0   Fee Waiver Available: n/a
Acceptance notice:
    Earliest date: March 15, 2011
    Latest date: April 1, 2011
Applicant's response to acceptance offer:
    Maximum time: May 1, 2011
Deposit to hold place in class: None
Starting date: August 2011

Information on 2009–2010 Entering Class

Number of	In-State	Out-of-State	Total
Applicants	289	n/a	289
Applicants Interviewed	75	n/a	75
New Entrants	32	n/a	32
Total number of students enrolled in program: 100			

Boston University
School of Medicine
Boston, Massachusetts

Address Inquiries To:
Jon Korhonen
Assistant Director of Undergraduate Admissions
Boston University
Office of Undergraduate Admissions, 121 Bay State Road
Boston, Massachusetts 02215
T (617) 353-2300 **F** (617) 353-9695
admissions@bu.edu; www.bu.edu/bulletins/und/item14.html

Purpose

This combined degree program, one of the oldest in the nation, provides an undergraduate premedical preparation that also emphasizes the humanities and social sciences and affords a quality medical education even though the overall period of study is shortened.

Requirements for Entrance

Students are selected for the program at Boston University during the senior year of high school (or after high school if they have not been enrolled in any other degree-granting program). There are no state residence requirements. Students who are completing their high school graduation requirements in three years in order to graduate early are not eligible for this program. Applicants are expected to have completed the following courses by the time they graduate from high school: four years each of English and mathematics (one year of calculus is required); three years each of social sciences and a foreign language; and one year each of biology, chemistry (AP chemistry is strongly recommended), and physics. Applicants must take the SAT or the ACT with Writing. They must take SAT Subject Tests in Mathematics Level 2 and Chemistry. An SAT Subject Test in a foreign language is recommended.

Selection Factors

The academic factors taken into account in offering admission to an applicant include the following: the high school GPA, the SAT or the ACT with Writing score, scores on the SAT Subject Tests, rank in high school class, and the nature of the applicant's high school curriculum. In the 2009–2010 entering class, the average high school GPA was an unweighted 3.9 on a 4.0 scale, and rank in class was in the top two percent. The average combined Critical Reading and Math SAT score was 1504. The average SAT Writing score was 741. SAT Subject Test scores in Chemistry averaged 755. SAT Subject Tests in Mathematics Level 2 averaged 767. Personal characteristics sought in applicants are compassion, integrity, maturity, motivation and an understanding of a career in medicine. An interview with College of Arts and Sciences and School of Medicine faculty is required.

Curriculum

This program leads to a baccalaureate degree granted by the College of Arts and Sciences at Boston University and to the M.D. degree awarded by Boston University School of Medicine. Students must complete work for the baccalaureate degree in three years with a major in medical science and a minor concentration in a division of the College of Arts and Sciences. Students must also satisfy the course distribution and language requirements of the college. Requirements for this degree include nine one-semester

courses in the natural and physical sciences and two one-semester courses in the humanities, mathematics and computer science, and social sciences. The program is seven years in length, with an eight-year option. Students must meet GPA and MCAT requirements of the program. They are also required to take Step 1 of the USMLE during the medical school portion of the program. Taking Step 2 of the USMLE is not a requirement for graduation, but is strongly recommended.

Expenses

Expenses	Resident Tuition and Fees	Non-resident Tuition and Fees
Undergraduate	$37,910	$37,910
U.S. Medical School	$47,088	$47,088

Financial Aid

The usual sources of financial aid are available to students during the undergraduate portion of this program. Once in the medical school, students can qualify for need-based, low-interest, and government-sponsored loans. More information about aid can be obtained from the Office of Financial Assistance, Boston University, 881 Commonwealth Avenue, Boston, Massachusetts 02215, or by phone (617) 353-2965.

Application and Acceptance Policies

Filing of application:
  Earliest date: September 1, 2010
  Latest date: December 1, 2010
Application fee: $75   Fee Waiver Available: Yes
Acceptance notice:
  Earliest date: April 1, 2011
  Latest date: April 15, 2011
Applicant's response to acceptance offer:
  Maximum time: May 1, 2011
Deposit to hold place in class: $650; non-refundable
Starting date: September 2011

Information on 2009–2010 Entering Class

Number of	In-State	Out-of-State	Total
Applicants	46	469	515
Applicants Interviewed	9	84	93
New Entrants	2	23	25
Total number of students enrolled in program: 73			

Wayne State University School of Medicine

Detroit, Michigan

Address Inquiries To:
Nancy Galster, Program Coordinator,
Irvin D. Reid Honors College
Wayne State University
2100 Undergraduate Library
Detroit, Michigan 48202
T (313) 577-8523 F (313) 577-6425
honors@wayne.edu
www.honors.wayne.edu/medstart.php

Purpose

The MedStart Program is intended to train medical innovators and creative thinkers. As undergraduates, students are treated as part of the medical community, with an emphasis on mentoring and research.

Requirements for Entrance

Students are selected for this program during their senior year of high school. Applicants must be citizens or permanent residents of the United States or citizens of Canada. Although there are no specific high school course requirements, applicants are required to take the ACT.

Selection Factors

To be considered for this program, applicants must have a minimum ACT score of 25 and a high school GPA of at least 3.5. Community service, team activities, leadership, extracurricular activities, and experience in health care are among the personal attributes and experiential factors sought in applicants. An interview is also required. Once admitted into the program, students are expected to maintain a 3.50 GPA in the sciences and overall during their undergraduate studies. For subsequent admission to Wayne State University School of Medicine, students in this program must complete all prerequisite courses, take the MCAT (with a minimum total score of 27, and no less than a nine in any individual section), and submit an AMCAS application.

Curriculum

The program, eight years in duration, allows students to obtain a baccalaureate degree from Wayne State University and the M.D. degree from Wayne State University School of Medicine. During the four years of their undergraduate studies, 100 percent of their coursework will be related to the bachelor's degree. The coursework in the four years of medical school will be spent in achieving the medical degree. Students must meet university requirements for the Irvin D. Reid Honors College and degree completion. Throughout the eight-year baccalaureate-medical program, monthly seminars are held which are relevant to medical fields and topics in medicine. Students may apply for a ten-week paid clinical research experience in the summer following the junior undergraduate year.

Expenses

Expenses	Resident Tuition and Fees	Non-resident Tuition and Fees
Undergraduate	$8,050	$16,848
U.S. Medical School	$29,298	$59,275

Financial Aid

Information about financial aid can be obtained from the Office of Scholarships and Financial Aid, Welcome Center, P.O. Box 4230, Detroit, MI 48202; by telephone (313) 577-3378; or visit *www.financialaid.wayne.edu*.

Application and Acceptance Policies

Filing of application:
    Earliest date: November 1, 2010
    Latest date: January 15, 2011
Application fee: $30   Fee Waiver Available: No
Acceptance notice:
    Earliest date: April 1, 2011
    Latest date: varies
Applicant's response to acceptance offer:
    Maximum time: May 1, 2011
Deposit to hold place in class: None
Starting date: September 2011

Information on 2009–2010 Entering Class

Number of	In-State	Out-of-State	Total
Applicants	205	66	271
Applicants Interviewed	26	4	30
New Entrants	15	0	15

Total number of students enrolled in program: 55

Saint Louis University
School of Medicine

St Louis, Missouri

Address Inquiries To:
Monica Kempland, Ph.D., Interim Director, Preprofessional Health Studies
Preprofessional Health Studies, Verhaegen Hall Room 314
3634 Lindell Blvd.
St. Louis, Missouri 63108-3302
T (314) 977-2840 F (314) 977-3660
prehealth@slu.edu
www.slu.edu/prehealth.xml

Purpose

This combined-degree program awards special recognition to exceptional first-year (freshmen) premedical students. It is intended to enhance the educational experience and reduce the stress associated with premedical-medical education.

Requirements for Entrance

Students apply to this program when they apply to Saint Louis University for undergraduate admission. Both residents and non-residents of Missouri are eligible to apply to the program. Applicants are required to complete the following courses prior to graduation from high school: one year of biology, one year of chemistry, and three years of mathematics. In addition to meeting these requirements, applicants must take either the ACT (minimum score of 30) or SAT (minimum score of 1330).

Selection Factors

Outstanding academic achievement in high school is a favorable factor in qualifying for the combined-degree program at Saint Louis University. Selected applicants usually rank in the top ten percent of their high school class. It is required that all candidates achieve a minimum ACT score of 30 or SAT score of 1330. An interview is not required. Students are required to take the MCAT in April of the junior year (no minimum score required). MCAT scores are not a factor for promotion or admission to the medical school phase of the program.

Curriculum

This eight-year program leads to a baccalaureate degree awarded by Saint Louis University and to the M.D. degree granted by the Saint Louis University School of Medicine. Students have much flexibility in choosing a major and are encouraged to study in an area of their choice. During the first four years of the curriculum, students will spend 100 percent of their time in coursework related to the bachelor's degree, which includes 42 to 46 semester hours of natural and physical science, 3 to 4 semester hours of mathematics, and 12 semester hours of humanities. There are strict GPA requirements to remain in the program. The remaining four years focus on achieving the M.D. degree.

Financial Aid

Information can be obtained from the Office of Financial Aid/Scholarships, DuBourg Hall 121, Saint Louis University, 221 North Grand Boulevard, St. Louis, MO 63103.

Expenses	Resident Tuition and Fees	Non-resident Tuition and Fees
Undergraduate	$30,940	$30,940
U.S. Medical School	$45,315	$45,315

Application and Acceptance Policies

Filing of application:
  Earliest date: October 1, 2010
  Latest date: December 1, 2010
Application fee: None   Fee Waiver Available: n/a
Acceptance notice:
  Earliest date: March 1, 2011
  Latest date: n/a
Applicant's response to acceptance offer:
  Maximum time: May 1, 2011
Deposit to hold place in class: $200; non-refundable
Starting date: Mid-August 2011

Information on 2009–2010 Entering Class

Number of	In-State	Out-of-State	Total
Applicants	103	361	464
Applicants Interviewed	0	0	0
New Entrants	39	100	139

Total number of students enrolled in program: 312

University of Missouri-Kansas City School of Medicine

Kansas City, Missouri

Address Inquiries To:
Alice Arredondo, Assistant Dean for Admissions & Recruitment
Council on Selection
University of Missouri – Kansas City School of Medicine
2411 Holmes, Kansas City, Missouri 64108-2792
T (816) 235-1870 F (816) 235-6579
medicine@umkc.edu
www.med.umkc.edu

Purpose

The combined baccalaureate-M.D. degree program integrates the humanities, social sciences, basic sciences, and clinical medicine throughout the curriculum so that graduates will develop nine core competencies: effective communication; clinical skills; using basic science in medicine; diagnosis, management, continuing care and prevention; lifelong learning in medicine, basic sciences, the social sciences and humanities; self-awareness, self-care, personal growth and professional behavior; diversity and the social context of health care; moral reasoning and ethical judgment; problem solving skills.

Requirements for Entrance

Designed for high school graduates who are entering college, both residents and non-residents of Missouri may apply. All applicants must meet the minimum academic standards for the College of Arts and Sciences at UMKC. An applicant's core high school curriculum must include, at a minimum, the following: eight semesters of English; eight semesters of mathematics; six semesters of science, including two semesters of biology and two semesters of chemistry; six semesters of social studies; two semesters of fine arts; and four semesters of a foreign language. Applicants must also submit all required application materials in order to be considered for admission. This includes the UMKC application for admission, the School of Medicine supplemental application, standardized test score, high school transcript, an essay, list of high school activities and health experience, and a minimum of three references.

Selection Factors

Cognitive and non-cognitive characteristics are utilized in evaluating applications. Applicants' academic potential is evaluated by the strength of high school courses, core grade point average, and scores on the ACT/SAT. In the 2009-2010 entering class, the average test score for MO residents was in the 95th percentile, and the average GPA was 3.81. For residents of other states, the average test score was at the 97th percentile, and the average GPA was 3.85. Non-cognitive characteristics, such as maturity, leadership, motivation for medicine, interpersonal skills, and compassion are assessed by the essay, high school activities, health experience, and references. Qualified applicants are invited for a required interview, which is designed to also assess non-cognitive characteristics.

Curriculum

The six-year curriculum leads to a baccalaureate degree granted by the UMKC College of Arts and Sciences or the UMKC School of Biological Sciences and the doctor of medicine degree granted by the UMKC School of Medicine. Students must complete requirements for the bachelor's degree. Students have a choice of majors, but most select liberal arts or psychology. Course requirements for the bachelor's degree in liberal arts include 21 semester hours of humanities, 21 semester hours of social sciences, and 50 semester hours of natural and physical sciences. During the first two years of the curriculum, students spend 75 percent of their time in coursework related to the bachelor's degree. Conversely, in the last four years, students spend 75 percent of their time in courses, clerkships, and electives related to the M.D. degree. Thus, the study of liberal arts, basic sciences, and clinical medicine is integrated throughout the entire curriculum. Students are assigned a faculty advisor (docent), and younger students are paired with older students in a mentoring relationship. During the last four years of the curriculum, students attend a general medicine outpatient clinic for a half-day each week. Students in this program do not take the MCAT. They must pass Steps 1 and 2 of the USMLE for graduation. An alternate path is available for extended study.

Expenses

	Resident Tuition and Fees	Non-resident Tuition and Fees
Undergraduate	N/A	N/A
U.S. Medical School	$30,150	$57,619

Financial Aid

Contact the UMKC Financial Aid Office at the AC 101, 5115 Oak, Kansas City, Missouri 64110, (816) 235-1154.

Application and Acceptance Policies

Filing of application:
  Earliest date: August 1, 2010
  Latest date: November 1, 2010
Application fee: $35   Fee Waiver Available: No
Acceptance notice:
  Earliest date: April 1, 2011
  Latest date: varies
Applicant's response to acceptance offer:
  Latest date: May 1, 2011
Deposit to hold place in class: $100; refundable by May 14, 2010
Starting date: August 2011

Information on 2009–2010 Entering Class

Number of	In-State	Out-of-State	Total
Applicants	291	449	740
Applicants Interviewed	131	147	278
New Entrants	61	48	109
Total number of students enrolled in program: 634			

Rutgers University and Drexel University College of Medicine

Piscataway, New Jersey

Address Inquiries To:
Tracey Hasse, Administrative Assistant
Rutgers, The State University of New Jersey Bachelor/Medical
Degree Program Nelson Biological Laboratory, Room A207, 604
Allison Road Piscataway, New Jersey 08854-8082
T (732) 445-5667 F (732) 445-6341
hpo@biology.rutgers.edu

Purpose

The program is designed to attract highly motivated students of superior ability and accomplishments. The program permits the early identification of these students and their making of an early decision regarding admission to Drexel University College of Medicine (DUCOM).

Requirements for Entrance

Qualified students who are in their fourth term (semester) at one of the Rutgers-New Brunswick undergraduate schools may apply for admission into the program. Applicants are required to have completed at least 40 college credits of which 30 credits are earned at Rutgers, and they must have been in attendance in Rutgers a minimum of one year. Students are required to have a minimum GPA of 3.5 by the end of their third semester and sustain this GPA through the fourth semester at Rutgers University. Applicants should have completed, or be in the process of completing by the end of their fourth semester, one semester of English, one semester of college-level Mathematics, two semesters of Biology with lab, two semesters of General Chemistry, General Chemistry lab, and two semesters of Organic Chemistry.

Selection Factors

Applicants are screened on the basis of academic credentials, letters of recommendation, a personal statement, official high school and college transcripts and SAT scores. Selected applicants will be invited for two separate interviews; one with Rutgers University and one with Drexel University College of Medicine. The Rutgers/Drexel Review Committee will then make the final recommendation of students to be admitted to the DUCOM Admissions Committee. The DUCOM Admissions Committee makes the final decision on acceptance into the program.

Curriculum

The program consists of four years at a Rutgers-New Brunswick/Piscataway undergraduate school followed by a four-year medical program. Students in the program are required to maintain a minimum cumulative GPA of 3.5 and a minimum cumulative GPA of 3.5 in all BCPM courses (all biological sciences, chemistry, physics and mathematics courses) with no individual grade of less than a "C" in any course. No repeated courses are allowed. The MCAT must be taken no later than April 30 of the third year and students must receive in a single examination a minimum MCAT score of "9" or better in the verbal section and "10's" in the physical and biological sciences section, or a total minimum score of 31 (with no individual sub-section score less than "8"), a letter score of "P" or higher on the MCAT writing section. Students are not allowed to take the MCAT more than three (3)

times to achieve the required scores. In New Jersey, DUCOM is affiliated with Saint Peter's University Hospital, and accepted BAMD students have the unique opportunity to conduct a required clinical and/or research project at Saint Peter's University Hospital for which they will earn two credits each for their last four (4) semesters at Rutgers. Furthermore, students will complete a preceptorship with staff physicians. The credits awarded will fulfill elective credits towards the Rutgers BA degree. Students cannot apply to any other medical school other than DUCOM and must matriculate into the College of Medicine in the year stipulated in their offer letter from the College of Medicine. Once matriculated, students take a minimum of one of DUCOM's clinical experiences at Saint Peter's University Hospital and, during their senior year, enroll in at least one clinical rotation experience at the hospital.

Expenses

	Resident Tuition and Fees	Non-resident Tuition and Fees
Undergraduate	$11,886	$22,796
U.S. Medical School	$45,540	$45,540

Financial Aid

Undergraduates should contact the Office of Financial Aid, Rutgers University, 620 George Street, New Brunswick, New Jersey 08901-1175; call (732) 932-7057; or visit the Website at http://studentaid.rutgers.edu. For DUCOM, visit the Website at *http://www.drexel.edu/financialaid/com_students.asp*

Application and Acceptance Policies

Filing of application:
  Earliest date: April 1, 2011
  Latest date: May 25, 2011
Application fee: None   Fee Waiver Available: n/a
Acceptance notice:
  Earliest date: July 15, 2011
  Latest date: n/a
Applicant's response to acceptance offer:
  Maximum time: 2 weeks
Deposit to hold place in class: None
Starting date: August 1, 2011

Information on 2009–2010 Entering Class

Number of	In-State	Out-of-State	Total
Applicants			
Applicants Interviewed			
New Entrants	**Data Not Available**		
Total number of students			

Rutgers University and UMDNJ-New Jersey Medical School

Piscataway, New Jersey

Address Inquiries To:
Loretta Stepka, Administrative Assistant
Rutgers, The State University of New Jersey Bachelor/Medical
Degree Program Nelson Biological Laboratory, Room A207,
604 Allison Road, Piscataway, New Jersey 08854-8082
T (732) 445-5667 F (732) 445-6341
hpo@biology.rutgers.edu

Purpose

Designed for high-achieving premedical students on the Rutgers-New Brunswick campus, the BA/MD program permits students to begin their medical education after their third year or at least 94 degree credits at Rutgers. Specially selected students will obtain bachelors and medical degrees in a seven-year program of study.

Requirements for Entrance

The program is open to all students enrolled at Rutgers University-New Brunswick who are United States citizens or permanent residents of the United States. It is not directly associated with any one college within the Univeristy. Applicants must have completed a minimum of 40 credits, of which 30 credits must be at Rutgers, and they must have been in attendance at Rutgers a minimum of 1 year. Additionally, applicants must have a minimum cumulative GPA of 3.5.

Selection Factors

The applicants must provide the Executive Committee with official high school and college transcripts. A minimum of five letters of recommendation from Rutgers University faculty must also be submitted. The academic and personal criteria to be evaluated are, in many ways, the same as those used to evaluate regular candidates for admission to medical school. Successful applicants should be those who have demonstrated interests that they have pursued in depth. The Executive Committee will take into account how the applicant has used his or her free time in the past. Because the program hopes to graduate broadly educated students who will assume leadership roles in medicine and their communities, the Executive Committee will look for evidence of positive peer recognition and leadership potential. In the 2008-2009 entering class, matriculants had achieved an average GPA of 3.756 at the end of the first two years of college. An interview is required. The MCAT is required but it is not a determining factor in the aceptance or retention of the student.

Curriculum

This program leads to the baccalaureate degree awarded by Rutgers University and to the M.D. degree granted by the University of Medicine and Dentistry of New Jersey-New Jersey Medical School. Students may choose either a seven-or eight-year program with year one being the first undergraduate year. Students will be admitted at the end of the spring term of year two and be formal members of the joint program beginning with year three. In the seven-year program students will spend one year at Rutgers University after admission to the program and prior to matriculation at NJMS. In the eight-year rpogram, students will spend two years at Rutgers after admission to the program and before moving to NJMS. Prior to leaving Rutgers, students must satisfy all college and major requirements, except for the 26 credits which they will receive from NJMS. Fifteen of the latter credits from NJMS will be applied towards a Biological Sciences major. The most popular major is Biological Sciences.

Expenses

Expenses	Resident Tuition and Fees	Non-resident Tuition and Fees
Undergraduate	$11,886	$22,796
U.S. Medical School	$27,347	$42,159

Financial Aid

Undergraduates should contact the Office of Financial Aid, Rutgers University, 620 George Street, New Brunswick, New Jersey 08901-1175; or visit the Web site at *http://studentaid.rutgers.edu*. For NJMS, visit the Web site at *www.umdnj.edu/studentfinancialaid*.

Application and Acceptance Policies

Filing of application:
 Earliest date: April 1, 2011
 Latest date: June 1, 2011
Application fee: None   Fee Waiver Available: n/a
Acceptance notice:
 Earliest date: July 15, 2011
 Latest date: n/a
Applicant's response to acceptance offer:
 Maximum time: 2 weeks
Deposit to hold place in class: None
Starting date: August 1, 2011

Information on 2009–2010 Entering Class

Number of	In-State	Out-of-State	Total
Applicants	7	1	8
Applicants Interviewed	6	0	6
New Entrants	6	0	6

Total number of students enrolled in program: 7

Rutgers University and UMDNJ
Robert Wood Johnson Medical School
Piscataway, New Jersey

Address Inquiries To:
Betsi Platt, Administrative Assistant
Rutgers, The State University of New Jersey Bachelor/Medical
Degree Program Nelson Biological Laboratory, Room A207, 604
Allison Road Piscataway, New Jersey 08854-8082
T (732) 445-5667 F (732) 445-6341
hpo@biology.rutgers.edu
http://hpo.rutgers.edu

Purpose

The program permits the early identification and admission of quality medical students. It also integrates medical studies with liberal arts study.

Requirements for Entrance

This program is open to all students enrolled at Rutgers University who are citizens or permanent residents of the United States. Students are selected for this program at the end of their sophomore year. Students must have a 3.50 overall GPA by the end of their third semester and sustain this GPA through the fourth semester at Rutgers University. Residents and non-residents of New Jersey are considered.

Selection Factors

An applicant's high school and college transcripts and faculty recommendations are taken into account in offering admission. In the 2009–2010 entering class, matriculants had achieved an average GPA of 3.9 at the end of the first two years of college. They had average scores of 620 on the Critical Reading section, 750 on the Mathematics section, and 650 on the Writing section. Maturity, motivation, and broad interests are personal characteristics sought in applicants. An interview is required. The MCAT is not used.

Curriculum

This program leads to the baccalaureate degree awarded by Rutgers University and to the M.D. degree granted by the University of Medicine and Dentistry of New Jersey–Robert Wood Johnson Medical School. Students must complete requirements for a baccalaureate degree. The most frequent majors for that degree are biological sciences, followed by biochemistry. The program is eight years in duration and has the possibility of completing the program in seven years. The basic sciences and the liberal arts are studied together during a four-year period. While in medical school, students must take and pass Steps 1 and 2 of the USMLE.

Financial Aid

Undergraduates should contact the Office of Financial Aid, Rutgers University, 620 George Street, New Brunswick, New Jersey 08901-1175; call (732) 932-7057; or visit the Web site at *http://studentaid.rutgers.edu*.

Expenses

Expenses	Resident Tuition and Fees	Non-resident Tuition and Fees
Undergraduate	$11,886	$22,262
U.S. Medical School	$27,670	$42,482

Application and Acceptance Policies

Filing of application:
   Earliest date: April 1, 2011
   Latest date: May 25, 2011
Application fee: None   Fee Waiver Available: n/a
Acceptance notice:
   Earliest date: July 1, 2011
   Latest date: n/a
Applicant's response to acceptance offer:
   Maximum time: 2 weeks
Deposit to hold place in class: None
Starting date: August 2, 2011

Information on 2009–2010 Entering Class

Number of	In-State	Out-of-State	Total
Applicants	36	0	36
Applicants Interviewed	29	0	29
New Entrants	7	0	7

Total number of students enrolled in program: 16

University of Medicine and Dentistry of New Jersey-New Jersey Medical School

Newark, New Jersey

Address Inquiries To:
Lisa Houston, Admissions Coordinator
Office of Admissions
UMDNJ – New Jersey Medical School
P.O. Box 1709
Newark, New Jersey 07101-1709
T (973) 972-4631 F (973) 973-7986
njmsadmiss@umdnj.edu
http://njms.umdnj.edu/education/admissions/seven_year_ba_md.cfm

Purpose

The New Jersey Medical School (NJMS) currently has baccalaureate/M.D. degree programs in collaboration with eight undergraduate institutions. The goal of these programs is to give highly qualified students the best opportunity to broaden their premedical preparation, while establishing their career path.

Requirements for Entrance

Applicants must be high school seniors who are in the top ten percent of their class and have a combined SAT Critical Reading and Math test score of 1400. Please note that we only consider the Critical Reading and Math sections and not the Essay section of the SAT. Applicants must be either U.S. citizens or permanent residents of the U.S. The most qualified and dedicated applicants will receive the highest consideration.

Selection Factors

Applicants are screened on the basis of academic credentials, letters of recommendation, and an essay. Those meeting the criteria are invited for an interview at the undergraduate school. The undergraduate schools then forward credentials of qualified applicants to NJMS for review and selection for a NJMS interview. The application deadline to the undergraduate institution is January 5, 2011.

Curriculum

The program consists of three years at an undergraduate school followed by a four-year medical program. Although not used to determine admission, the MCAT must be taken prior to medical school matriculation. Promotion to the medical school is contingent upon achieving grades of "B" or better in all premedical courses and maintaining an overall grade point average of at least 3.5 each semester. The baccalaureate degree is awarded by the undergraduate institution upon completion of the first year of medical school. The M.D. degree is awarded by NJMS upon successful completion of all NJMS degree requirements. Students are required to pass Step 1 of the USMLE for promotion to the third year. Passing Step 2 of the USMLE is required for graduation. Eight programs are currently available: Caldwell College provides a well-rounded program that incorporates course work in the humanities, liberal arts and social behavioral sciences, as well as the premedical sciences. For additional information contact: squinn@caldwell.edu. Drew University offers premedical preparation in all sciences and liberal arts subjects. For more information contact: ksmall@drew.edu. Montclair State University offers premedical preparation in biology, chemistry, biochemistry, molecular biology, computer science, mathematics, psychology, and anthropology. For more information contact: vegaq @mail.montclair.edu. New Jersey Institute of Technology offers undergraduate study in the Honors Premedical Curriculum within the Engineering Science Program. For more information contact: kristol@adm.njit.edu . Rutgers University-Newark Campus offers premedical preparation in the sciences. For more infor-

mation contact: nyeste@ugadm.rutgers.edu. Stevens Institute of Technology offers premedical preparation in chemical biology. For more information contact: mhadidi@stevens.edu. The College of New Jersey offers preparation in biology, chemistry, history, philosophy, and psychology. For more information contact: shevlin@tcnj.edu. The Richard Stockton College of New Jersey offers preparation in chemistry, biology, physics, and liberal arts. For more information contact: admissions@stockton.edu. NJMS also offers Articulated Programs, which allow students in their second year of college to apply to matriculate at NJMS after completion of their third year of college through programs with: St. Peter's College (contact lsciorra@spc.edu), Rutgers University-Newark (contact jmaiello@andromeda.rutgers.edu) and Rutgers University - New Brunswick (contact hpo@biology.rutgers.edu).

Expenses

	Resident Tuition and Fees	Non-resident Tuition and Fees
Undergraduate	$25,218	$39,461
U.S. Medical School	$27,347	$42,159

Financial Aid

Financial aid packages for the undergraduate years are determined by the undergraduate schools.

Application and Acceptance Policies

Filing of application:
    Earliest date: Varies by school
    Latest date: January 5, 2011
Application fee: Varies   Fee Waiver Available: n/a
Acceptance notice:
    Earliest date: Varies by school
    Latest date: April 14, 2011
Applicant's response to acceptance offer:
    Maximum time: Varies by undergraduate school.
Deposit to hold place in class: No
Starting date: Varies

Information on 2009–2010 Entering Class

Number of	In-State	Out-of-State	Total
Applicants	341	n/a	341
Applicants Interviewed	187	n/a	187
New Entrants	26	n/a	26
Total number of students enrolled in program: 169			

University of New Mexico
School of Medicine
Albuquerque, New Mexico

Address Inquiries To:
Dr. Valerie Romero-Leggot, SOM Director, Combined BA/MD Program
1 University of New Mexico, MSC 09 5065
Albuquerque, New Mexico 87131
T (505) 925-4500 **F** (505) 925-4004
combinedbamd@salud.unm.edu
http://hsc.unm.edu/som/combinedbamd/

Purpose
The Combined BA/MD Degree Program is designed to help address the physician shortage in New Mexico by assembling a class of diverse students who are committed to serving New Mexico communities with the greatest need.

Requirements for Entrance
Application eligibility for the Combined BA/MD Degree Program requires that a student must be: 1) a New Mexico resident (at time of application); 2) a current New Mexico high school senior (high school seniors outside NM who are enrolled members of the Navajo Tribe and live in the Navajo Nation are also eligible); 3) have an ACT math sub-score of 22 or better or a SAT math sub-score of 510 or better; and 4) have a personal commitment to pursue a medical career in New Mexico's rural or underserved areas.

Selection Factors
The Combined BA/MD Degree Program considers all aspects of an applicants background, experience and academic progress including: Academic excellence (ACT, GPA, honors courses, Advanced Placement courses); community connection and involvement & volunteer service; commitment to practice medicine in New Mexico; honors and awards; extracurricular activities; letters of recommendation; personal statement; medically related experience (where feasible/available). Applicants with a Math ACT subscore of a 22 or a Math SAT subscore of a 510 will automatically be invited for two individual interviews with members of the Admissions Committee. Application deadline: November 15th (of the applicant's senior year).

Curricular Highlights
All BA/MD students are required to apply for any and all scholarships for which they are qualified. The BA/MD Undergraduate Scholarship, which all BA/MD students are eligible to receive, meets basic educational costs that are not covered by other scholarships. The amount of BA/MD scholarship awarded varies from student to student. Student loans and workstudy awards are included in the award package and BA/MD scholarship will be adjusted accordingly. Awards are totaled for the academic year and cannot exceed UNM's cost of attendance. UNM's "cost of attendance" includes basic educational costs (below) plus personal and transportation costs. The BA/MD Program considers basic educational costs to include tuition, student fees, housing, meals, and books. Housing cost is based on Redondo apartment rates; meal plan is based on an average cost of available plans; book allowance is set at $460 per semester. Course fees over $210 per semester will be the student's responsibility. Any choices made by a student that produce extra cost, will be the student's responsibility.

Expenses

Expenses	Resident Tuition and Fees	Non-resident Tuition and Fees
Undergraduate	$5,101	n/a
U.S. Medical School	$18,252	$46,993

Financial Aid
All BA/MD students are required to apply for any and all scholarships for which they are qualified. The BA/MD Undergraduate Scholarship, which all BA/MD students are eligible to receive, meets basic educational costs that are not covered by other scholarships. The amount of BA/MD scholarship awarded varies from student to student. Student loans and workstudy awards are included in the award package and BA/MD scholarship will be adjusted accordingly. Awards are totaled for the academic year and cannot exceed UNM's cost of attendance. UNM's "cost of attendance" includes basic educational costs (below) plus personal and transportation costs. The BA/MD Program considers basic educational costs to include tuition, student fees, housing, meals, and books. Housing cost is based on Redondo apartment rates; meal plan is based on an average cost of available plans; book allowance is set at $460 per semester. Course fees over $210 per semester will be the student's responsibility. Any choices made by a student that produce extra cost, will be the student's responsibility. The BA/MD scholarship covers only undergraduate costs.

Application and Acceptance Policies
Filing of application:
    Earliest date: n/a
    Latest date: November 15, 2010
Application fee: None   Fee Waiver Available: n/a
Acceptance notice:
    Earliest date: n/a
    Latest date: April 1, 2011
Applicant's response to acceptance offer:
    Maximum time: May 1, 2011
Deposit to hold place in class: None
Starting date: August 22, 2011

Information on 2009–2010 Entering Class

Number of	In-State	Out-of-State	Total
Applicants	201	0	201
Applicants Interviewed	163	0	163
New Entrants	28	0	28
Total number of students enrolled in program: 108			

Brooklyn College and SUNY Downstate Medical Center

Brooklyn, New York

Address Inquiries To:
Dr. Steven B. Silbering, Director, B.A.–M.D. Program
2231 Boylan Hall, Brooklyn College
2900 Bedford Avenue
Brooklyn, New York 11210-2889
T (718) 951-4706 F (718) 951-4559
silbering@brooklyn.cuny.edu
http://bamd.brooklyn.cuny.edu/bamdmain.html

Purpose

The undergraduate portion of this program is designed to expose students to a broad range of disciplines, which includes not only the sciences but the humanities and social sciences as well. The students then enter medical school better prepared to become skilled and knowledgeable physicians who are also sensitive to cultural differences and the emotional needs of their patient population.

Requirements for Entrance

Students are selected in their senior year of high school. Admission is limited to residents of the states of New York, New Jersey, and Connecticut, with preference given to New York State residents. Applicants are recommended to have at least a 90 percent CAA (College Admission Average, academic subjects only) and a combined score of at least 1200 on the Mathematics and Critical Reading sections of the SAT Reasoning Test.

Selection Factors

The academic factors taken into account in offering admission to applicants include the high school GPA, SAT scores, New York State Regents Examination scores, and scores on Advanced Placement tests. In the 2008 entering class, most students had a high school average above 90, and the sum of the SAT Mathematics and Critical Reading scores was between 1300 and 1450. Non-academic factors include community service, participation in scientific research projects and other extracurricular activities. These should preferably be described in a separate resume. Maturity and motivation are qualities highly sought after among the applicants. An interview is required.

Curriculum

This program leads to a baccalaureate degree from Brooklyn College and an M.D. degree from SUNY Downstate Medical Center College of Medicine. Students in the baccalaureate portion of the B.A.–M.D. program are encouraged to choose a non-science major; however, if a science major is chosen, the student must choose a non-science minor. While in Brooklyn College, B.A.–M.D. students must fulfill not only the requirements for the major and minor, but must also complete a liberal arts (Core) curriculum consisting of six lower-tier and two upper-tier core classes. Three of the lower-tier classes must be Honors sections. In addition, students must complete the pre-med requirement, which includes various biology, chemistry and physics courses. No student is permitted to remain in the B.A.–M.D. program if either the overall or science GPA's fall below 3.5 in any semester after the freshman year. The MCAT examination must be taken no later than the summer following the junior year. If a score on any of the three sections of the MCAT examination is less than 9, the MCAT must be repeated. Students are permitted to take the

MCAT three times in order to achieve a 9 on each section of the same examination. Aside from the academic requirements, undergraduate BA-MD students must complete 320 hours of a clinical internship during any of the summers except that following the senior year. Also, during each semester after the freshman year, BA-MD students must perform 60 hours of non-clinical community service. After four years at Brooklyn College, students matriculate into the four-year medical school program at SUNY Downstate.

Expenses

	Resident Tuition and Fees	Non-resident Tuition and Fees
Undergraduate	$4,600	$12,450
U.S. Medical School	$23,363	$41,203

Financial Aid

All students admitted to the BA-MD program are provided with a $4000 scholarship. If any student receives TAP financial aid, the amount of this aid is subtracted from the scholarship.

Additional Information

A supplementary application must be filed with the BA-MD office, in addition to the filing of an on-line application for admission to Brooklyn College itself. This supplementary application can be downloaded from the BA-MD website. A letter of recommendation from a science teacher, a math teacher and either a humanities or social science teacher are required to be submitted on behalf of an applicant.

Application and Acceptance Policies

Filing of application:
  Earliest date: September 1, 2010
  Latest date: December 31, 2010
Application fee: None   Fee Waiver Available: No
Acceptance notice:
  Earliest date: April 1, 2011
  Latest date: April 1, 2011
Applicant's response to acceptance offer:
  Latest date: April 30, 2011
Deposit to hold place in class: None
Starting date: August 26, 2011

Information on 2009–2010 Entering Class

Number of	In-State	Out-of-State	Total
Applicants	292	6	298
Applicants Interviewed	90	0	90
New Entrants	15	0	15

Total number of students enrolled in program: 51

Hobart and William Smith Colleges/ SUNY Upstate Medical University

Geneva, New York

Address Inquiries To:
Renee Nearpass, Pre-Health Advisor
Elizabeth Blackwell Medical Scholars Program
Hobart & William Smith Colleges
Office of Admissions, 629 South Main Street
Geneva, New York 14456
T (800) 852-2256 F (315) 781-3914
admissions@hws.edu; http://www.hws.edu/admissions/pdf/blackwell_scholars.pdf

Purpose

The Elizabeth Blackwell Medical Scholars program is designed for exceptional high school seniors who wish to attend medical school. Applicants to this program must be from a rural community, a group underrepresented in medicine, or be a first generation college student.

Requirements for Entrance

Students apply to the program in their senior year of high school. They must have a minimum SAT I score of 1250 (Mathematics and Critical Reading only) or a 28 ACT score and a high school grade point average of 90 or higher, as well as have demonstrated a commitment to a career in medicine. Students accepted into this program will complete their undergraduate degree at Hobart and William Smith Colleges and are guaranteed admission to Upstate Medical University's College of Medicine, pending all program standards are met.

Selection Factors

This program is for high school students who are from rural areas, from groups underrepresented in medicine, or who are among the first generation in their families to attend college. The following factors are taken into consideration in assessing applicants for admission into this program: grades, rank in class, SAT (ACT) scores, and extracurricular activities. Selected applicants are invited for a required interview.

Curriculum

This eight-year program leads to a baccalaureate degree awarded by Hobart and William Smith Colleges, and to the medical degree awarded by SUNY Upstate Medical University. Students in this program are not required to take the MCAT for promotion or for admission to the medical school.

Financial Aid

Blackwell Scholars are awarded a full-tuition scholarship to attend Hobart and William Smith Colleges. To retain the full-tuition scholarship, awardees must maintain a GPA of at least 3.0 during each semester while at Hobart and William Smith Colleges. More information about financial aid at Hobart and William Smith Colleges can be found at: *www.hws.edu/admissions/fin_edu.aspx* or *www.upstate.edu/prospective/tuition.php*.

Expenses	Resident Tuition and Fees	Non-resident Tuition and Fees
Undergraduate	$40,221	$40,221
U.S. Medical School	$24,112	$41,952

Application and Acceptance Policies

Filing of application:
  Earliest date: August 2010
  Latest date: January 15, 2011
Application fee: $45   Fee Waiver Available: Yes
Acceptance notice:
  Earliest date: Within two weeks of interview
  Latest date: n/a
Applicant's response to acceptance offer:
  Maximum time: 2 weeks after offer is sent
Deposit to hold place in class: $100;
refundable by May 15 of year of entry
Starting date: The fall following graduation from Hobart and William Smith Colleges

Information on 2009–2010 Entering Class

Number of	In-State	Out-of-State	Total
Applicants	28	4	32
Applicants Interviewed	6	0	6
New Entrants	3	0	3
Total number of students enrolled in program: 11			

Rensselaer Polytechnic Institute and Albany Medical College

Troy, New York

Address Inquiries To:
Dean of Undergraduate Admissions
Rensselaer Polytechnic Institute
110 Eighth Street
Troy, New York 12180-3590
T (518) 276-6216 F (518) 276-4072
admissions@rpi.edu
www.rpi.edu/dept/admissions/resources/Physician-ScientistProgramAccelerated.pdf

Purpose

The Accelerated Physician-Scientist Program offers qualified individuals the opportunity to become physicians who are intensively trained in medical research. This innovative approach provides a well-rounded perspective that prepares future practitioners and physician-scientists to perform with confidence and care in a technologically changing environment.

Requirements for Entrance

Students are selected for this program during the senior year of high school. Residents of New York, as well as non-residents of the state, are eligible to apply. Applicants are expected to have completed the following courses by the time they graduate from high school: four years of English; one year each of biology, chemistry, and physics; and four years of mathematics (through pre-calculus). They must take the SAT Reasoning Test and two SAT Subject Area Tests: one mathematics and one science. In lieu of these tests, American College Testing (ACT) Assessment program scores, including the Writing Test, may be submitted. All tests must be completed by the December testing date prior to the proposed September matriculation.

Selection Factors

Academic factors considered in offering admission to an applicant include the quality and nature of coursework in high school, performance in those courses, rank in high school class, and test scores. The 2009–2010 entering class had an average score of 737 on the SAT Critical Reading, 734 on the SAT Mathematics, and 721 on the SAT Writing. Personal qualities sought in applicants are motivation, maturity, and intellectual capacity necessary to pursue the accelerated course of study. An interview is required.

Curriculum

The program leads to a B.S. degree awarded by Rensselaer Polytechnic Institute and the M.D. degree granted by Albany Medical College (AMC). The curriculum for the B.S. and M.D. degrees usually requires seven years to complete. During the first three years of the program spent at Rensselaer, the curriculum involves 70 percent premedical science courses and 30 percent liberal arts courses. Students take 18 courses in the natural and physical sciences and 8 elective courses in the humanities and social sciences. The cornerstone of the program is a mentored research project. During the sixth semester, students split their time between Rensselaer and AMC and begin research that extends over the third and final year at Rensselaer and into the summer preceding the first year of medical school. The research continues throughout the freshman year at AMC and into the following summer. Training in making oral and written scientific presentations is also included. At the medical college, basic and clinical sciences are integrated into themes (primarily organ systems) stressing normal function in Year 1 and pathological processes in Year 2. There are also five longitudinal themes that are integrated throughout the curriculum: clinical skills, ethical and health systems issues, evidence-based medicine, nutrition and informatics. In every theme, student learning is focused on clinical resentations. Basic science seminars reinforce the importance of the basic sciences in Years 3 and 4. Emphasis is placed on primary care throughout the four years, with an increased emphasis on care in ambulatory settings in the clinical rotations of Year 3. Year 4 emphasizes specialty care in various required rotations. Additional electives are available in Year 4. Students admitted to the program are not required to take the MCAT for admission to Albany Medical College. Students are expected to pass Steps 1 and 2 of the USMLE while at Albany Medical College.

Expenses

Expenses	Resident Tuition and Fees	Non-resident Tuition and Fees
Undergraduate	$52,160	$52,160
U.S. Medical School	$46,407	$46,407

Financial Aid

Sources of financial aid are restricted and include endowed scholarships based on need, merit scholarships, work-study, and student loans through federal and institutional programs. Applicants can receive more information by contacting the Financial Aid Office of Rensselaer Polytechnic Institute at (518) 276-6813 or Albany Medical College at (518) 262-5435.

Application and Acceptance Policies

Filing of application:
  Earliest date: September 1, 2010
  Latest date: November 1, 2010
Application fee: $70   Fee Waiver Available: Yes
Acceptance notice:
  Earliest date: March 2011
  Latest date: Until class is filled
Applicant's response to acceptance offer:
  Latest date: May 1, 2011
Deposit to hold place in class: $500; nonrefundable
Starting date: August 2011

Information on 2009–2010 Entering Class

Number of	In-State	Out-of-State	Total
Applicants	115	204	319
Applicants Interviewed	26	39	65
New Entrants	9	5	14
Total number of students enrolled in program: 32			

St. Bonaventure University/George Washington University School of Medicine Dual Degree (BS/BA/MD) Program

St. Bonaventure, New York

Address Inquiries To:
Dr. Allen Knowles, III, Director
Franciscan Health Care Professions Programs
Biology Department
De La Roche Hall, Room 219
St. Bonaventure, New York 14778
T (716) 375-2656
prehealth@sbu.edu; aknowles@sbu.edu
www.sbu.edu

Purpose

A joint program of St. Bonaventure University (SBU) and the George Washington University School of Medicine and Health Sciences in Washington, DC (GW), the eight-year program is designed for the high school senior who exhibits academic excellence, leadership in activities, and community service and health-care experience, all of which have resulted in a passion for a career as a physician. The goal is to prepare the student with a strong background in the natural sciences in preparation for the rigors of medical school. SBU opened its new science facilities that will coordinate with the educational processes at GW, utilizing the state-of-the-art GW hospital. The GW Clinical Skills Center is dedicated to education and research with cutting-edge technology. Through the Surgical Simulation and Demonstration Area, medical students gain comprehensive and clinical exposure and feedback and skill improvement to enable them to become technically adept and humane caregivers. More information on the GW M.D. program can be found at *http://www.gwumc.edu/smhs*.

Requirements for Entrance

Students are selected in their senior year of high school. Applicants must be U.S. or Canadian citizens or Permanent Residents of the U.S. Applicants must complete the SAT (Verbal/Mathematics of at least 1300) or ACT (minimal score of 29), as well as the SAT Subject Test in Biology (preferably M).

Selection Factors

Academic factors considered in selecting applicants include high school grades, class rank, and standardized test scores. In addition, extracurricular and health-related activities, community service, volunteerism, research, medical field exposure, personal essays, and letters of recommendation are reviewed. Rank must be in the top 10% of the class, with a GPA of greater than 90 percent. Qualities demonstrating leadership, interest in the medical field through experiences, and AP and Honors courses are considered. An interview is required at SBU and GW and is by invitation only.

Curriculum

The student's progress is reviewed on a regular basis. Students must maintain a minimum of a "B" in courses required for admission to the medical school and an overall 3.6 average. The recommended major is biology, with interests outside of the sciences being encouraged. Students do not take the MCAT. Students are required to remain active in community service, volunteer programs, research components, and internships established through SBU. Students attend presentations and interact with GW M.D. students on the Medical Center campus. At the end of four years, the student is granted the baccalaureate degree from SBU. In the first and second years at GW, the integration of clinical skills begins, as students spend time with physicians, developing patient interviewing skills, conducting physical examinations, and assisting in diagnosis. The third and fourth years at GW are used to develop clinical expertise in a variety of hospitals in the greater D.C. metropolitan area. Upon completion of all requirements, the M.D. degree is awarded by GW.

Expenses

	Resident Tuition and Fees	Non-resident Tuition and Fees
Undergraduate	$25,885	$25,885
U.S. Medical School	$47,644	$47,644

Financial Aid

For information on financial aid, fees, and expenses, please refer to the Web sites for each institution (*www.sbu.edu* and *www.gwumc.edu*) or contact the Financial Aid Offices.

Application and Acceptance Policies

Filing of application:
 Earliest date: September 1, 2010
 Latest date: December 15, 2010
Application fee: $30   Fee Waiver Available: Yes
Acceptance notice:
 Earliest date: March 15, 2011
 Latest date: n/a
Applicant's response to acceptance offer:
 Latest date: May 1, 2011
Deposit to hold place in class: $500; nonrefundable
Starting date: Late August 2011

Information on 2009–2010 Entering Class

Number of	In-State	Out-of-State	Total
Applicants	n/c	52	52
Applicants Interviewed	n/c	42	42
New Entrants	n/c	8	8
Total number of students enrolled in program: 46			

Siena College and Albany Medical College
Loudonville, New York

Address Inquiries To:
Office of Admissions
Siena College
515 Loudon Road
Loudonville, New York 12211-1462
T (518) 783-2423
admit@siena.edu
www.siena.edu/amc

Purpose
The Science, Humanities, and Medicine Program offers an eight-year continuum of education that has a special emphasis on the humanities and on community service to the medically underserved, while providing a sound understanding of both the natural and social sciences.

Requirements for Entrance
Students are selected for this program during the senior year of high school. Both residents and non-residents of New York are eligible to apply. Candidates for admission to the Siena/Albany Medical College program must have completed: four years of laboratory science (including biology, chemistry, and physics) and four years of mathematics (including a minimum of pre-calculus [calculus preferred]). Typically, successful candidates will have enrolled in, or completed, advanced-level courses by the end of their senior year in high school. A well-rounded background and demonstrated leadership experience are also important. Of equal significance is the student's proven concern for others and for the community. Applicants must take either the SAT Reasoning Test or ACT Assessment, including the optional Writing test. Tests must be completed by the November testing date prior to the proposed September matriculation.

Selection Factors
Academic factors considered in offering admission to an applicant include: required and elective courses taken, grades earned, class standing, SAT Reasoning Test or ACT scores, including the Writing test, honors received, letters of recommendation, and unique academic experiences. Of great importance to the admission committee are such factors as extracurricular activities, evidence of intellectual curiosity, and interest in the humanities and in the sciences. Students generally rank among the top ten percent of their high school class. The 2009–2010 entering class had an average score of 677 on the SAT Critical Reading section and 706 on the SAT Mathematics section. An interview is required.

Curriculum
This program offers a coordinated eight-year curriculum of premedical and medical education. The undergraduate phase offers an equal distribution of science and non-science courses. Students graduate in four years with a bachelor of arts degree in biology with a minor in the humanities. The undergraduate phase of the program also includes a required summer of human service in a health-related agency, usually in an urban setting or developing nation. Passage from the undergraduate college to the medical school requires achievement of a 3.40 GPA and a continued interest in the human service dimension of the program. At the medical college, basic and clinical sciences are integrated into themes (primarily organ systems) stressing normal function in Year 1 and pathological processes in Year 2. There are also five longitudinal themes integrated throughout the curriculum: clinical skills, ethical and health systems issues, evidence-based medicine, nutrition, and informatics. In every theme, student learning is focused on clinical presentations. The summer between the sophomore and junior years is dedicated to medically related volunteer service, usually in a rural or inner city clinic. Seminars reinforce the importance of the basic sciences in Years 3 and 4. Emphasis is placed on primary care throughout the four years, with an increased emphasis on care in ambulatory settings in Year 3 clinical rotations. Year 4 emphasizes specialty care in various required rotations. Additional electives are available in Year 4. Students admitted to the program are not required to take the MCAT for admission to AMC. Students must pass Steps 1 and 2 of the USMLE while at AMC.

Expenses

	Resident Tuition and Fees	Non-resident Tuition and Fees
Undergraduate	$35,280	$35,280
U.S. Medical School	$46,407	$46,407

Financial Aid
Applicants can receive more information by contacting the Siena College Financial Aid Office at (518) 783-2427 or the Albany Medical College Financial Aid Office at (518) 262-5435.

Application and Acceptance Policies
Filing of application:
    Earliest date: September 1, 2010
    Latest date: December 1, 2010
Application fee: $50   Fee Waiver Available: Yes
Acceptance notice:
    Earliest date: March 2011
    Latest date: Until classes are filled
Applicant's response to acceptance offer:
    Latest date: May 1, 2011
Deposit to hold place in class: $350; nonrefundable
Starting date: September 2011

Information on 2009–2010 Entering Class

Number of	In-State	Out-of-State	Total
Applicants	225	137	362
Applicants Interviewed	21	20	41
New Entrants	6	9	15

Total number of students enrolled in program: 52

Chapter 12: Information on Combined Undergraduate/M.D. Programs   101

Sophie Davis School of Biomedical Education at the City College of New York

New York, New York

Address Inquiries To:
Chris Wanyonyi, Director of Admissions
Sophie Davis School of Biomedical Education at the City College of New York
Office of Admission, Harris Hall, 160 Convent Avenue
New York, New York 10031
T (212) 650-7718 F (212) 650-7708
cwanyonyi@med.cuny.edu
http://www1.ccny.cuny.edu/prospective/med/admissions/bsmd_program.cfm

Purpose

The purposes of this combined-degree program are to train primary care physicians who will work in medically underserved urban areas, to increase the number of physicians from groups underrepresented in medicine, to intervene in the disparity of access to high quality pre-college science education, and create a medical school pipeline.

Requirements for Entrance

Students are selected for this program in the senior year of high school. Only residents of New York State are eligible to apply. Applicants are expected to have completed the following courses by the time they graduate from high school: two semesters each of chemistry and biology and six to eight semesters of mathematics. They must take the ACT Assessment and SAT tests.

Selection Factors

Academic factors taken into account in offering admission to an applicant are: high school GPA, SAT I scores, ACT Assessment scores, and scores on the New York State Regents Examinations. In the 2009 entering class, high school grades averaged 95 and the subscore on the Mathematics ACT Assessment averaged 29. The SAT Mathematics average was 655, and the SAT Verbal average was 623. Personal qualities sought in applicants include interest in people, concern for others, initiative, and leadership. An interview is required.

Curriculum

This seven-year program leads to a baccalaureate degree granted by The City College of New York (CCNY) and to the M.D. degree awarded by one of six participating medical schools (Albany Medical College, Dartmouth Medical College, New York Medical College, New York University, SUNY Brooklyn, or SUNY Stony Brook University). During the first five years of the program, students fulfill all requirements for the B.S. degree and study the preclinical portion of the medical school curriculum. After successfully completing the five-year sequence and passing Step 1 of the USMLE, students transfer to one of the participating medical schools for their final two years of clinical training. Students are expected to pass Step 1 of the USMLE to proceed to Years 3 and 4 of medical school. Additionally, students are expected to pass Step 2 of the USMLE to graduate. Students complete the core liberal arts curriculum of CCNY during the first two years. At this time, they also take courses emphasizing the importance of understanding cultural differences for good medical practice and, through community medicine courses, do field work at various community agencies, including many family practice clinics. The final years of the five-year sequence at CCNY include courses necessary in the first two years of medical school, including basic science courses and several community medicine courses. Students also benefit from counseling and academic support services.

Expenses

Expenses	Resident Tuition and Fees	Non-resident Tuition and Fees
Undergraduate	$4,600	N/A
U.S. Medical School	Varies	Varies

Financial Aid

Pell grants, New York State Tuition Assistance Program Awards, and NYC Merit Awards are all sources of financial aid. The school generally awards several scholarships to incoming students, including the CCNY New Era Scholarship, the Bronx High School of Science/CCNY Scholarship, the Stuyvesant High School/CCNY Scholarship, The Lois Pope L.I.F.E. Scholarships and the William R. Hearst Endowed Scholarship. Scholarships available later in the program include those from the Alan Seelig Memorial Fund, the Aranow Fund, and the Sophie and Leonard Davis Scholarships.

Application and Acceptance Policies

Filing of application:
  Earliest date: September 2010
  Latest date: January 8, 2011
Application fee: None   Fee Waiver Available: n/a
Acceptance notice:
  Earliest date: March 26, 2011
  Latest date: April 1, 2011
Applicant's response to acceptance offer:
  Maximum time: May 1, 2011
Deposit to hold place in class: None
Starting date: Late August 2011

Information on 2009–2010 Entering Class

Number of	In-State	Out-of-State	Total
Applicants	755	n/a	755
Applicants Interviewed	262	n/a	262
New Entrants	75	n/a	75
Total number of students enrolled in program: 373			

Stony Brook University and Stony Brook University School of Medicine

Stony Brook, New York

Address Inquiries To:
Undergraduate Admissions, Honors Programs
118 Administration Building
Stony Brook University
Stony Brook, New York 11794-1901
T (631) 632-6868 F (631) 632-9898
www.stonybrook.edu/ugadmissions/newhonors/
scholarsmed.shtml

Purpose

The Scholars for Medicine Program offers conditional acceptance to the Stony Brook University School of Medicine to a select number of outstanding and highly motivated students through one of three programs: The Honors College, WISE (Women in Science and Engineering) and the Engineering Program of Stony Brook University. In addition to acquiring a solid background in the sciences, accepted students have access to a wide array of liberal arts courses through the university. Students also have access to medical school programs in research and a series of health-related seminars.

Requirements for Entrance

Students are selected for this program only during the senior year of high school. There are no state residency requirements. No specific courses are required. Applicants must take the SAT. For non-U.S. citizens, documentation of permanent residency status will be required of accepted students prior to matriculation.

Selection Factors

To be considered for this program, applicants must have a minimum SAT score of 1350 (Critical Reading and Mathematics) and an unweighted high school GPA of 95. The applicant's high school academic record, standardized test reports, essay, history of interests and activities, and required interview at the School of Medicine are factors taken into account in offering admission.

Curriculum

This eight-year program leads to the baccalaureate and M.D. degrees granted by Stony Brook University. Students are expected to complete the requirements for any of the baccalaureate degrees awarded by the university as well as the requirements for either the Honors College, WISE Program or Engineering Program. Undergraduate work taken must include courses required by the School of Medicine, including one year each of biology, physics, inorganic chemistry, organic chemistry (all with lab), and English. No specific major is required for the premedical undergraduate phase. The program provides a seminar series of health-related lectures given by nationally and internationally recognized individuals in health care delivery. In addition, students have an opportunity to engage in cutting-edge research. Admission to the School of Medicine is contingent upon maintaining a minimum specified GPA during the first three undergraduate years. All scholars are required to take the MCAT no later than spring of their junior year in college and must attain a specified minimum MCAT score. USMLE Steps 1 and 2 are required for promotion and graduation from the School of Medicine.

Expenses	Resident Tuition and Fees	Non-resident Tuition and Fees
Undergraduate	$7,355	$15,255
U.S. Medical School	$24,049	$41,889

Financial Aid

Financial aid available to enrolled students includes federal Perkins loans, Equal Opportunity Program, federal work-study, federal Pell Grants, Federal Supplemental Educational Opportunity, NY State Tuition Assistance Program (TAP), and NY State Aid for Part-Time Students. Applicants can receive more information by contacting the Office of Financial Aid and Student Employment at Stony Brook University at (631) 632-6840 or visiting the Web site at *www.stonybrook.edu/ugadmissions/financial/*. Please contact the programs directly concerning scholarship opportunities.

Application and Acceptance Policies

Filing of application:
  Earliest date: September 1, 2010
  Latest date: December 31, 2010
Application fee: n/a   Fee Waiver Available: n/a
Acceptance notice:
  Earliest date: March 1, 2011
  Latest date: April 4, 2011
Applicant's response to acceptance offer:
  Latest date: May 1, 2011
Deposit to hold place in class: $100; refundable
Starting date: August 2011

Information on 2009–2010 Entering Class

Number of	In-State	Out-of-State	Total
Applicants	1361	268	1629
Applicants Interviewed	23	0	23
New Entrants	6	0	6

Total number of students enrolled in program: 23

Union College and Albany Medical College

Schenectady, New York

Address Inquiries To:
Associate Dean of Admissions
Union College
Schenectady, New York 12308
T (518) 388-6112 **F** (518) 388-8034
admissions@union.edu
www.union.edu/Admissions/Applying/TypesOfAdmission/Medical.php

Purpose

The Leadership in Medicine Program is specifically designed for students who want to prepare for the challenge of medical leadership by taking advantage of additional educational opportunities as part of their undergraduate education. In addition to offering the standard coursework required for attaining the degrees of B.S., M.S. or M.B.A., and M.D., the integrated program focuses on three areas essential for future leaders in medicine: the economic and financial problems facing medicine, including health policy and health management; the increasing complexity of biomedical ethics; and the need to maintain a global perspective.

Requirements for Entrance

Students are selected for this program during the senior year of high school. Residents of New York, as well as non-residents of the state, are eligible to apply. Applicants are expected to have completed a challenging curriculum in high school, which must include biology, chemistry, and physics. They must take either the ACT Assessment or the SAT Reasoning Test and two SAT Subject Area Tests (one mathematics and one science). Tests must be completed by the December testing date prior to the proposed September matriculation.

Selection Factors

Academic factors considered in offering admission to an applicant include the quality and nature of coursework in high school, performance in those courses, rank in high school class, and standardized test scores. In the 2009–2010 entering class, the average score was 683 for SAT Critical Reading, 741 for SAT Mathematics, and 710 for SAT Writing. Personal qualities sought in applicants include motivation, maturity, and personal development. Interviews at Union College and Albany Medical College are required.

Curriculum

This program leads to B.S. and M.S. or M.B.A. degrees awarded by Union College and the M.D. degree granted by Albany Medical College. At Union College, students take 30 courses (15 science and 15 non-science) and complete an interdepartmental major in the humanities or social sciences. A special bioethics program supplemented by a health services practicum, a term abroad, and a program in health care management at the Union College Graduate Management Institute are also integral parts of the educational experience. The curriculum for the B.S., M.S., or M.B.A. and M.D. degrees requires eight years to complete. At the medical college, basic and clinical sciences are integrated into themes (primarily organ systems) stressing normal function in Year 1 and pathological processes in Year 2. Five longitudinal themes are inte-

grated throughout the curriculum: clinical skills, ethical and health systems issues, evidence-based medicine, nutrition, and informatics. In every theme, student learning is focused on clinical presentations. Basic science seminars reinforce the importance of the basic sciences in Years 3 and 4. Emphasis is placed on primary care throughout the four years, with an increased emphasis on care in ambulatory settings in Year 3 clinical rotations. Year 4 emphasizes specialty care in various required rotations. Additional electives are available in Year 4. Students admitted to the program are not required to take the MCAT for admission to Albany Medical College. Students are expected to pass Steps 1 and 2 of the USMLE while at Albany Medical College.

Expenses

Expenses	Resident Tuition and Fees	Non-resident Tuition and Fees
Undergraduate	$50,439	$50,439
U.S. Medical School	$46,407	$46,407

Financial Aid

Sources of financial aid include various programs based on need, student loans through federal and state assistance, work-study, and merit scholarships. For more information, contact the Financial Aid Office of Union College at (518) 388-6123 or at Albany Medical College at (518) 262-5435.

Application and Acceptance Policies

Filing of application:
  Earliest date: September 1, 2010
  Latest date: December 1, 2010
Application fee: $50   Fee Waiver Available: Yes
Acceptance notice:
  Earliest date: March 2011
  Latest date: Until class is filled
Applicant's response to acceptance offer:
  Latest date: May 1, 2011
Deposit to hold place in class: $500; nonrefundable
Starting date: September 2011

Information on 2009–2010 Entering Class

Number of	In-State	Out-of-State	Total
Applicants	171	194	365
Applicants Interviewed	43	41	84
New Entrants	7	11	18
Total number of students enrolled in program: 60			

University of Rochester
School of Medicine and Dentistry
Rochester, New York

Address Inquiries To:
Rochester Early Medical Scholars Coordinator
University of Rochester
Undergraduate Admissions, Box 270251
Rochester, New York 14627-0251
T (585) 275-3221 F (585) 461-4595
http://enrollment.rochester.edu/admissions/
admit@admissions.rochester.edu

Purpose
The Rochester Early Medical Scholars Program (REMS) provides both acceptance to the University of Rochester College of Arts, Sciences, and Engineering and conditional acceptance to the School of Medicine and Dentistry to a group of exceptionally talented and motivated students. REMS highly encourages the utmost flexibility in degree programs, focuses on mentoring relationships with medical school staff, and promotes early exposure to the medical school curriculum through a series of lectures and seminars.

Requirements for Entrance
Students are selected for this program during their senior year of high school from a large pool. A recommended high school curriculum includes at least three years of foreign language and social studies, four years each of English, mathematics, and science. A transcript that includes honors, AP and/or IB courses is strongly recommended. Applicants are expected to take the SAT or ACT Assessment. SAT Subject Tests are highly recommended, especially, Mathematics Level 1C or Mathematics Level 2C, and Biology or Chemistry.

Selection Factors
Outstanding achievement in a challenging high school curriculum, character, interests, maturity, experience in health care or research settings, and motivation necessary for a career in medicine are required for consideration for entry into the REMS program. Fifty finalists will be invited to interview for REMS, and those interviews are required. In the 2009–2010 entering class, REMS students had an average SAT Verbal (Critical Reading) score of 712, an average Mathematics score of 723 and average Writing score of 722. In order to take their place in the first-year medical school class, REMS students must carry at least a 3.3 overall GPA and a 3.3 biology-chemistry-physics-math GPA by the end of the freshman year, a 3.4 for the sophomore year, and 3.5 thereafter by the time of undergraduate graduation. In order to matriculate into medical school, all students must have an overall GPA of 3.5 and a biology-chemistry-physics-math overall GPA of 3.5. REMS students do not have to take the MCAT examination.

Curriculum
The eight-year program leads to a baccalaureate degree and the M.D. degree, both granted by the University of Rochester. Students must complete the baccalaureate degree in order to matriculate into medical school. The most popular major is biology, followed by chemistry, and health and society. However, an undergraduate science major is not required nor encouraged in order to matriculate into medical school. A Social Service project is also required in order to matriculate to the medical school, this project is highly individual. The University of Rochester School of Medicine and Dentistry's particularly innovative Double-Helix Curriculum (DHC) focuses on a fully integrated basic and clinical science curriculum across all four years of medical school. Students begin their clinical clerkships in January of their first year and learn in an environment that fosters critical thinking, problem-solving and active learning in small group Problem-Based Learning sessions, lectures, laboratories and clinical skills workshops. See *www.urmc.rochester.edu/education/md* for details. As home of the "biopsychosocial model," Rochester values the art and science of medicine as a continuum, and fosters an educational model that is humanistic and patient-centered. REMS students also may apply for any of our combined degree programs; M.D./Ph.D., M.D./M.B.A., M.D./M.P.H., M.D./M.S. A "Take 5" program, offering a tuition-free, fifth undergraduate year, is available to selected REMS students. Summer research programs and extensive international experiences are available at both the undergraduate and medical school levels.

Expenses

	Resident Tuition and Fees	Non-resident Tuition and Fees
Undergraduate	$38,975	$38,975
U.S. Medical School	$41,483	$41,483

Financial Aid
University of Rochester scholarships and loans, plus governmental loans, are available. For more information, write the Financial Aid Office, University of Rochester, Box 270261, Rochester, New York 14627-0261, or phone (585) 275-3226 or (800) 881-8234. Web site: *http://enrollment.rochester.edu/financial.*

Application and Acceptance Policies
Filing of application:
    Earliest date: July 1, 2010
    Latest date: December 1, 2010
Application fee: $30   Fee Waiver Available: Yes
Acceptance notice:
    Earliest date: March 10, 2011
    Latest date: May 2011
Applicant's response to acceptance offer:
    Maximum time: May 1, 2011
Deposit to hold place in class: $600; nonrefundable
Starting date: Early September 2011

Information on 2009–2010 Entering Class

Number of	In-State	Out-of-State	Total
Applicants	319	732	1051
Applicants Interviewed	15	34	49
New Entrants	2	9	11

Total number of students enrolled in program: 67

Case Western Reserve University
School of Medicine
Cleveland, Ohio

Address Inquiries To:
Christine DeSalvo Miller, Senior Assistant Director
Office of Undergraduate Admission
Wolstein Hall, Case Western Reserve University
10900 Euclid Avenue; Cleveland, Ohio 44106-7055
T (216) 368-4450 **F** (216) 368-5111
admission@case.edu
http://admission.case.edu

Purpose
This program is intended to provide college students with a greater sense of freedom and choice in the pursuit of a premedical baccalaureate degree.

Requirements for Entrance
Students are selected for this program during the senior year of high school. Both residents and non-residents of Ohio are considered for admission. Applicants are expected to have completed the following courses by the time they graduate from high school: one year each of biology, chemistry, and physics and four years of mathematics. They must take either the ACT Assessment with the Writing Test or the SAT Reasoning Test.

Selection Factors
The applicant's high school academic record, standardized test reports, history of interests and activities, and a required interview are factors taken into account in offering admission. Evidence of strong interpersonal and leadership skills is also sought. While there is no minimum requirement for standardized test scores, in the Fall 2009 entering class, SAT scores ranged from approximately 650–710 on the Critical Reading section and 710–800 on the Math section and 710–800 on the Writing section. The average composite ACT score ranged from 31-34.

Curriculum
This eight-year program leads to the baccalaureate and M.D. degrees granted by Case Western Reserve University. Students are expected to complete the requirements for any of the baccalaureate degrees awarded by the colleges of the university. They are expected to satisfy all requirements of, and earn a baccalaureate prior to matriculating in, the School of Medicine. The work taken for the baccalaureate must include the studies specifically required of applicants by the School of Medicine, including one year of biology, two years of chemistry (including organic chemistry), one year of physics, one year of calculus, and first-year (freshman) seminar. One year of biochemistry is strongly recommended. No specific major concentration is required for the premedical undergraduate phase. To date, the majors most commonly taken have been biology and biochemistry. Psychology, anthropology, chemistry, and biomedical engineering are also popular majors. The first four years of the program are devoted to study for the baccalaureate and the last four years to the curriculum in medicine. Students in the medical phase are required to pass Step 1 of the USMLE for promotion within the program and to pass Step 2 of the USMLE in order to graduate.

Expenses

	Resident Tuition and Fees	Non-resident Tuition and Fees
Undergraduate	$35,900	$35,900
U.S. Medical School	$45,970	$45,970

Financial Aid
Sources of aid for the undergraduate phase include merit and need-based aid, college work-study, and university grants and scholarships. For information about aid, contact the Office of University Financial Aid at (216) 368-4530.

Additional Information
The PPSP is intended to include a four-year undergraduate program of study and is not designed as an accelerated program. Matriculation at the School of Medicine will occur no earlier than four years after matriculation into the bachelor's degree program at Case Western Reserve University. Students who complete degree requirements in fewer than four years are required to pursue other significant experiences intended to enhance their professional and/or personal development during the terms following the receipt of their bachelor's degree and until study at the School of Medicine begins. Examples of this experience may include, but are not limited to: research, study abroad, community service and/or additional undergraduate or graduate coursework. This interim experience must be approved in advance by the Case Western Reserve University School of Medicine Admissions Committee.

Application and Acceptance Policies
Filing of application:
    Earliest date: n/a
    Latest date: December 1, 2010
Application fee: $35   Fee Waiver Available: Yes
Acceptance notice:
    Earliest date: n/a
    Latest date: Approximately April 1, 2011
Applicant's response to acceptance offer:
    Maximum date: May 1, 2011
Deposit to hold place in class: $500; nonrefundable
Starting date: August 29, 2011

Information on 2009–2010 Entering Class

Number of	In-State	Out-of-State	Total
Applicants	199	453	652
Applicants Interviewed	12	28	40
New Entrants	0	5	5
Total number of students enrolled in program: 30-35			

Northeastern Ohio Universities College of Medicine

Rootstown, Ohio

Address Inquiries To:
Michelle Cassetty Collins, M.S.Ed., Director, Admissions and Student Services
Northeastern Ohio Universities College of Medicine
4209 State Route 44, P.O. Box 95
Rootstown, Ohio 44272-0095
T (330) 325-6270 F (330) 325-8372
admission@neoucom.edu
www.neoucom.edu/audience/applicants

Purpose

The mission of the Northeastern Ohio Universities College of Medicine (NEOUCOM) is to graduate qualified physicians oriented to the practice of medicine at the community level, with an emphasis on primary care (family medicine, internal medicine, pediatrics, and obstetrics-gynecology). NEOUCOM strives to improve the quality of health care in northeast Ohio. All graduates, regardless of specialty, are provided with a strong background in community and public health.

Requirements for Entrance

Students are selected for the BS/MD program during their senior year of high school. During high school, applicants should pursue a college preparatory curriculum, including 4 years of math and science; and take either the ACT or SAT; and be citizens or permanent residents of the U.S. Strong preference given to in-state applicants.

Selection Factors

Factors considered in admission include standardized test scores, high school overall and science/math GPAs, extracurricular involvement, medical exposure, coursework, and interview outcome. The past year, the mean high school unweighted GPA of matriculants was 3.87; average ACT test score was 31; average SAT was 1350 (verbal and math only). An interview is required and is offered by invitation only.

Curriculum

Students accepted into the combined B.S./M.D. program pursue the baccalaureate degree at The University of Akron, Kent State University, or Youngstown State University. The accelerated B.S./M.D. program may be completed in six or seven years. The M.D. degree is granted by NEOUCOM. The integrated curriculum is offered in five steps during the four years of medical school. The four-year longitudinal curriculum includes the biomedical, behavioral, social, community and population health, clinical sciences, and humanities. Step 1: Curriculum focuses on professionalism, doctor-patient relationships, clinical skills, human anatomy, biochemistry, molecular pathology, and genetics. Step 2: Curriculum establishes physiological concepts in the body while introducing the medical impact of pathologies; includes anatomy, physiology, and chemistry of the nervous system; and integrates the microbiology, immunology, and pharmacology of infectious diseases. Step 3: Curriculum is centered on organ systems pathophysiology. Step 4: Curriculum is core clinical clerkships in family medicine, internal medicine, obstetrics/gynecology, pediatrics, psychiatry, and surgery, and a four-week exploratory experience. Step 5: Curriculum is clinical electives and Clinical Epilogue and Capstone, which focus on professionalism and social science disciplines, and provides vital skills needed as residents.

Financial Aid

Financial aid at the B.S. phase of the program is administered by the undergraduate universities. During medical school, students apply for aid by completing the FAFSA, the NEOUCOM financial aid application, and submitting copies of federal tax returns. A limited number of need-based grants are available, as well as other limited scholarship funds for disadvantaged students and students from groups underrepresented in medicine. Federal educational loans are a major part of the aid program. About 80 percent of enrolled students receive some form of financial aid. Financial need is not a factor in admission considerations.

Expenses	Resident Tuition and Fees	Non-resident Tuition and Fees
Undergraduate	Varies	Varies
U.S. Medical School	$30,599	$59,212

Additional Information

Starting in the fall of 2007, the first class of pharmacy students enrolled for study in an interdisciplinary curriculum with the Northeastern Ohio Universities College of Medicine students.

Application and Acceptance Policies

Filing of application:
  Earliest date: August 1, 2010
  Latest date: December 15, 2010
Application fee: $195*   Fee Waiver Available: Yes
Acceptance notice:
  Earliest date: December 18, 2010
  Latest date: March 19, 2011
Applicant's response to acceptance offer:
  Maximum time: May 1, 2011
Deposit to hold place in class: None
Starting date: June 2011

Information on 2009–2010 Entering Class

Number of	In-State	Out-of-State	Total
Applicants	331	224	555
Applicants Interviewed	198	25	223
New Entrants	109	5	114

Total number of students enrolled in program: 258

*The one fee is for application to NEOUCOM, The University of Akron, Kent State University and Youngstown State University.

The Ohio State University
College of Medicine
Early Admission Pathway
Columbus, Ohio

Address Inquiries To:
Lorna Kenyon, Director, Admissions Office
College of Medicine, The Ohio State University
155D Meiling Hall, 370 West 9th Avenue
Columbus, Ohio 43210
T (614) 292-7137 F (614) 247-7959
medicine@osu.edu
http://medicine.osu.edu/students/admissions/medicaladmissions
pathway/Pages/index.aspx

Purpose
The Medical Admissions Pathway provides conditional acceptance into the College of Medicine after four years of undergraduate study for a select group of students accepted into Honors who have checked the "pre-med" box on their freshman application entering The Ohio State University in Autumn Quarter.

Requirements for Entrance
Students are selected in their senior year of high school. Both residents and non-residents of Ohio are eligible to apply to the program. In addition to meeting the requirements for freshman admission, applicants are required to submit the results of the ACT Assessment or the SAT I.

Selection Factors
The following factors are taken into consideration in assessing applicants for admission: approval for University Honors affiliation; ; grade-point average; high school activities; leadership roles; clinical experiences, exposure to research and extracurricular activities. In the 2008 entering class, the average high school GPA was 4.47. The average SAT score was 1615 and the average ACT Assessment score was 33.9.

Curriculum
This eight-year program leads to a baccalaureate degree awarded by The Ohio State University and to the M.D. degree granted by The Ohio State University College of Medicine. The most frequent major for the baccalaureate degree is biology. Regardless of major, students must complete the prerequisites including one year of: biological sciences, general chemistry, organic chemistry with lab, physics with lab, one course in biochemistry and one course in Anatomy (any area). Eligible MAP participants have the option to petition for entry into the College of Medicine after three years of undergraduate coursework and will be able to earn a Bachelor of Science degree in absentia after successful completion of the first year of medical school. Students with a cumulative grade point average of 3.50 or above in all coursework and in all courses in biological sciences, chemistry, physical sciences, and mathematics (BCPM) are not required to take the MCAT. The MCAT is required for students who have not met the above requirements by the end of Spring Quarter of the third year. They must: complete the baccalaureate degree prior to entry into medical school; register for and take the MCAT by October 1 of the fourth year and present a composite MCAT score of at least 32, with no subscore less than 9 in order to continue in good standing; work with the MAP academic advisor to determine appropriate course work for the remainder of their undergraduate program; and regain undergraduate college Honors affiliation by the end of Spring Quarter of the third year and maintain it through the completion of their undergraduate degree program. Students who lose and do not regain college Honors affiliation are no longer eligible for conditional acceptance into the College of Medicine. Students are held to the College of Medicine's standards of honor and professional conduct.

Expenses

	Resident Tuition and Fees	Non-resident Tuition and Fees
Undergraduate	$8,679	$21,918
U.S. Medical School	$29,403	$44,913

Financial Aid
For information on sources of financial aid available, contact the Office of Student Financial Aid, The Ohio State University, 517 Lincoln Tower, 1800 Cannon Drive, Columbus, Ohio 43210; (614) 292-0300.

Additional Information
MAP students have unique opportunities to meet and talk with distinguished College of Medicine faculty and students engaged in clinical and graduate education and research. Faculty and staff meet with MAP students to discuss opportunities for practical experience and the development of desired non-cognitive traits. Mentoring and medical career counseling are also provided. MAP students are expected to take full advantage of the opportunities to gain clinical exposure, participate in research activities, become involved in community and volunteer service, leadership and extracurricular activities. They are also encouraged to participate in enrichment activities sponsored by Alpha Epsilon Delta (AED), the premedical honor society at The Ohio State University.

Application and Acceptance Policies

Filing of application:
    Earliest date: October 1, 2010
    Latest date: March 1, 2011
Application fee: $40   Fee Waiver Available: No
Acceptance notice:
    Earliest date: April 15, 2011
    Latest date: May 2, 2011
Applicant's response to acceptance offer:
    Latest date: May 1, 2011
Deposit to hold place in class: None
Starting date: September 2011

Information on 2009–2010 Entering Class

Number of	In-State	Out-of-State	Total
Applicants	48	30	78
Applicants Interviewed	23	14	37
New Entrants	8	1	9

Total number of students enrolled in program: 46

University of Cincinnati College of Medicine

Cincinnati, Ohio

Address Inquiries To:
Nikki Bibler, M.Ed., Assistant Director of Dual Admissions
University of Cincinnati College of Medicine
P.O. Box 670668
Cincinnati, Ohio 45267-0668
T (513) 558-5581 F (513) 558-6259
DualAdmissionsProgram@uc.edu
www.med.uc.edu/HS2MD

Purpose

The University of Cincinnati College of Medicine's Connections Dual Admissions Program accepts high school seniors into our undergraduate college and into the College of Medicine. Once accepted into this special program, students will receive an outstanding education while preparing for medical school and developing the qualities and characteristics to become excellent physicians.

Requirements for Entrance

Students are selected in their senior year of high school. Both residents and non-residents of Ohio are eligible to apply. Priority will be given to Ohio residents. Students must achieve a minimum composite ACT score of 29 or a minimum composite SAT score of 1300 in order to be considered for admissions.

Selection Factors

In making admissions decisions, the College of Medicine works in conjunction with the University of Cincinnati undergraduate institution to review an applicant's academic record, standardized test performance, examples of leadership, interpersonal skills, and interest in and motivation for medicine. Mature and independent-thinking students who have good decision-making and coping skills are very desirable. Only students who have applied to and been accepted by the undergraduate college will be considered for the Connections Dual Admissions Program. Thus, students are encouraged to apply first to the undergraduate institution and then complete the Connections Dual Admissions Application.

Curriculum

The course of study consists of four years at the undergraduate college, followed by four years in the College of Medicine. Connections Dual Admissions Program students are required to satisfactorily fulfill graduation requirements at the undergraduate college. Students must earn a 3.4 cumulative GPA and a 3.45 BCPM GPA by the beginning of the senior undergraduate year. At this time, they must also earn a composite score of 27 on the MCAT, with no less than a 9 in Biological Sciences and no less than an 8 in Verbal Reasoning or Physical Sciences. The student must pass Steps 1 and 2 of the USMLE in order to graduate from the College of Medicine. The USMLE Step 1 is administered at the completion of Year 2.

Financial Aid

Opportunities for Financial Aid are made available by the University of Cincinnati undergraduate college.

Expenses	Resident Tuition and Fees	Non-resident Tuition and Fees
Undergraduate	18,909	33,432
U.S. Medical School	$29,385	$45,135

Application and Acceptance Policies

Filing of application:
  Earliest date: November 1, 2010
  Latest date: February 1, 2011
Application fee: $25   Fee Waiver Available: Yes
Acceptance notice:
  Earliest date: April 1, 2011
  Latest date: May 1, 2011
Applicant's response to acceptance offer:
  Maximum time: May 1, 2011
Deposit to hold place in class: None
Starting date: September, 2011

Information on 2009–2010 Entering Class

Number of	In-State	Out-of-State	Total
Applicants	147	96	243
Applicants Interviewed	37	14	51
New Entrants	13	1	14

Total number of students enrolled in program: 88

Drexel University and
Drexel University College of Medicine

Philadelphia, Pennsylvania

Address Inquiries To:
Matthew Biester, Assistant Director
Drexel University
3141 Chestnut Street
Philadelphia, Pennsylvania 19104
T (215) 895-2400 F (215) 895-5939
enroll@drexel.edu
www.drexel.edu/em/undergrad/academic-programs/accelerated-degrees/

Purpose

This combined-degree program provides outstanding high school seniors, who are highly motivated toward the medical profession, an opportunity to combine a strong liberal arts undergraduate program in a highly technological environment with a medical education in seven years.

Requirements for Entrance

Students are selected for this program during their senior year of high school. Both residents and non-residents of Pennsylvania are eligible to apply. Students must be U.S. citizens or permanent residents and graduate from a U.S. high school. Prior to graduating from high school, applicants are required to complete one semester of biology, one semester of chemistry, one semester of physics, four years of English, and four years of mathematics. They must take either the SAT or the ACT Assessment.

Selection Factors

The academic factors taken into consideration for admission into the combined-degree program include SAT/ACT scores, high school GPA, and AP and honors courses. The average high school GPA for the 2009-2010 entering class was 3.9, with a mean score of 1472 on the Math and Critical Resoning sections of the SAT and a 33 Composite on the ACT. Medically related volunteer activities, leadership qualities, and community service are among the personal attributes sought in applicants. An interview at the college of medicine is also required. Once admitted into the program, students are expected to maintain an overall GPA of 3.5 in undergraduate studies; complete all prerequisite courses; and receive no grade less than a C in any course. Additionally, applicants must receive, in a single examination, a minimum MCAT score of "9" or better in the verbal section and "10's" or better in the physical or biological science section, or a total minimum score of 31 (with no individual subsection score less than an 8), and a letter score of "P" or higher in the MCAT written section. Students apply through AMCAS in the second year. The MCAT is a factor in admittance and promotion to the medical school phase of the program.

Curriculum

This seven-year program leads to a baccalaureate degree awarded by Drexel University and to the M.D. degree granted by the Drexel University College of Medicine. The most frequent major is biology, followed by chemistry. Students may also choose from a variety of humanities majors. During the first three years of the undergraduate phase, students spend 100 percent of their time in coursework related to the bachelor's degree, which includes 3 semester hours of natural and physical science.

Expenses

Expenses	Resident Tuition and Fees	Non-resident Tuition and Fees
Undergraduate	$38,735	$38,735
U.S. Medical School	$45,540	$45,540

Financial Aid

All Students are automatically considered for academic scholarships when applying for admission. Students should complete the FAFSA form by March 1st to be considered for need based financial aid.

Application and Acceptance Policies

Filing of application:
  Earliest date: Rolling
  Latest date: December 1, 2010
Application fee: $75   Fee Waiver Available: Yes
Acceptance notice:
  Earliest date: March 31, 2011
  Latest date: April 15, 2011
Applicant's response to acceptance offer:
  Latest date: May 1, 2011
Deposit to hold place in class: $300; nonrefundable
Starting date: September 20, 2011

Information on 2009–2010 Entering Class

Number of	In-State	Out-of-State	Total
Applicants	195	1254	1449
Applicants Interviewed	29	131	160
New Entrants	6	20	26
Total number of students enrolled in program: 75			

Lehigh University and Drexel University College of Medicine

Bethlehem, Pennsylvania

Address Inquiries To:
Majed Dergham, Assistant Director
Office of Admissions
Lehigh University
27 Memorial Drive West
Bethlehem, Pennsylvania 18015
T (610) 758-3100 F (610) 758-4361
http://cas.lehigh.edu/casweb/content/default.aspx?pageid=129

Purpose

This program is designed to give gifted high school students, who are highly motivated for a career in medicine, the opportunity to combine a liberal arts program with a medical education. The baccalaureate degree is awarded after Year 4 (the first year of medical school).

Requirements for Entrance

Applicants are expected to take the SAT Reasoning Test. SAT Subject tests are highly recommended in Mathematics Level 1 or Mathematics Level 2 and Chemistry. Applicants must be U.S. citizens or permanent residents.

Selection Factors

Generally, a combined SAT score of 1360 (or minimum 31 ACT), a class rank in the top 5 percent of the high school class, and a strong motivation for science are necessary for entrance into this program. Most recent matriculants had a high school GPA of 3.7, an SAT Verbal score of 720, and an SAT Mathematics score of 780. Maturity, stability, scholarship, flexibility, independence, and service to others are personal characteristics sought among applicants. An interview is required. Once admitted to the program, students are expected to maintain an overall grade point average of 3.5 or better and a science and math GPA of 3.5 or better with no grade less than a "C" in any courses. All program requirements must be completed at Lehigh University. Candidates are required to take the MCAT. Scores of either 9 or better on the verbal section of the MCAT and 10 or better on the science sections or a total minimum score of 31 (with no individual section score less than 8) are required.

Curriculum

This program, seven years in duration, allows students to obtain a bachelor's degree from Lehigh University and the M.D. degree from Drexel University College of Medicine. The Lehigh bachelor's degree is awarded after completion of the first year of study at Drexel. Students have the flexibility to pursue additional coursework or study abroad during the undergraduate portion of the program. However, specific course requirements for the degree include two semesters of English, three semesters of mathematics, eight semesters of natural and physical sciences, three semesters each of humanities and social sciences, a first year seminar, a writing intensive, and four elective courses. All students must pass USMLE Steps 1 and 2 in order to graduate from the medical school.

Expenses	Resident Tuition and Fees	Non-resident Tuition and Fees
Undergraduate	$48,830	$48,830
U.S. Medical School	$45,540	$45,540

Financial Aid

Institutional scholarships and loans are available, as well as federal loan programs and armed services scholarships. More financial aid information can be obtained from the Financial Aid Office, Lehigh University, 218 W. Packer Avenue, Bethlehem, Pennsylvania 18015.

Application and Acceptance Policies

Filing of application:
    Earliest date: September 1, 2010
    Latest date: November 15, 2010
Application fee: $70   Fee Waiver Available: No
Acceptance notice:
    Earliest date: April 1, 2011
    Latest date: n/a
Applicant's response to acceptance offer:
    Latest date: May 1, 2011
Deposit to hold place in class: $500; nonrefundable
Starting date: August 2011

Information on 2009–2010 Entering Class

Number of	In-State	Out-of-State	Total
Applicants	33	177	210
Applicants Interviewed	9	51	60
New Entrants	0	4	4

Total number of students enrolled in program: 13

Pennsylvania State University and Jefferson Medical College

University Park, Pennsylvania

Address Inquiries To:
Director of Admissions
Undergraduate Admissions Office
Pennsylvania State University, 201 Shields Building
University Park, Pennsylvania 16802
T (814) 865-5471 F (814) 863-7590
www.science.psu.edu/premedmed

Purpose

This accelerated, B.S.–M.D. premedical-medical program, which began in 1963 and has graduated over 900 students, is a cooperative effort between Pennsylvania State University, University Park, and Jefferson Medical College of Thomas Jefferson University in Philadelphia. Accepted students can select either a six- or seven-year schedule, which gives them either two years (with summers) or three years at Penn State before proceeding to four years at Jefferson Medical College. All students selecting the six-year option must begin their studies at the University Park campus in the summer session. Students selecting the seven-year option begin their studies at the University Park campus in the fall semester.

Requirements for Entrance

Students are selected for this program only during the senior year of high school. Both residents and non-residents of Pennsylvania are considered for admission, but preference is given to qualified applicants from Pennsylvania. Applicants are expected to have completed the following courses by the time they graduate from high school: four units of English, 1 1/2 units of algebra, one unit of plane geometry, one-half unit of trigonometry, three units of science, and five units of social studies, humanities, and/or the arts.

Selection Factors

To be considered for this program, applicants must be in the top ten percent of their high school class and offer a minimum combined score of 2100 on the critical reading and mathematics section of the SAT I or ACT score of 32. In the 2009–2010 entering class, the average combined score on the SAT was 2270. Motivation, compassion, integrity, dedication, and performance in nonacademic areas are among the personal characteristics sought in applicants. An interview is required. Special attention is given to the student's progress during each semester while at Pennsylvania State University. Students must take a full course load and maintain a minimum GPA of 3.5 in both science and non-science courses. For subsequent admission to Jefferson Medical College, students in this combined-degree program must achieve an average score of 9 (average) or better on each section of the MCAT prior to matriculation in medical school.

Curriculum

This six-year program leads to a baccalaureate degree granted by Pennsylvania State University and to the M.D. degree awarded by Jefferson Medical College. Students begin this program in June immediately after high school graduation. They spend two full years on the Pennsylvania State, University Park, campus; they then proceed to Jefferson Medical College for the regular four-year curriculum. The B.S. degree from Pennsylvania State University is awarded after successful completion of the second year at Jefferson Medical College, and the M.D. degree is awarded after successful completion of the senior year at Jefferson Medical College. Students in the seven-year schedule spend three years at Pennsylvania State, but do not attend summer sessions. Their B.S. degree is awarded after Year 1 at Jefferson Medical College.

Expenses

Expenses	Resident Tuition and Fees	Non-resident Tuition and Fees
Undergraduate	$14,426	$26,020
U.S. Medical School	$44,547	$44,547

Financial Aid

At Penn State, scholarships, loans, and grants are the sources of financial assistance available. For more information, write the Office of Student Financial Aid, Pennsylvania State University, University Park, Pennsylvania 16802; or call (814) 865-5471. At Jefferson Medical College, financial aid application materials are mailed in January of the year of medical school matriculation. Students are encouraged to contact the University Office of Student Financial Aid to discuss all financial aid matters.

Application and Acceptance Policies

Filing of application:
    Earliest date: August 1, 2010
    Latest date: November 30, 2010
Application fee: $50   Fee Waiver Available: Yes
Acceptance notice:
    Earliest date: March 15, 2011
    Latest date: March 30, 2011
Applicant's response to acceptance offer:
    Latest date: May 1, 2011
Deposit to hold place in class: $300; nonrefundable
Starting date: Late June 2011

Information on 2009–2010 Entering Class

Number of	In-State	Out-of-State	Total
Applicants	92	384	476
Applicants Interviewed	12	77	89
New Entrants	5	22	27
Total number of students enrolled in program: 60			

Temple University School of Medicine

Philadelphia, Pennsylvania

Address Inquiries To:
Office of Admissions
Temple University School of Medicine
3500 North Broad Street, Suite 124
Philadelphia, Pennsylvania 19140
T (215) 707-3656 **F** (215) 707-6932
medadmissions@temple.edu
www.temple.edu/medicine/admissions/special_admissions.htm

Purpose

The Medical Scholars Program, in conjunction with three under-graduate institutions in Pennsylvania, provides an opportunity for outstanding high school seniors to gain a provisional acceptance to Temple University School of Medicine at the same time that they are accepted into their undergraduate school.

Requirements for Entrance

Students are selected for this program during their senior year of high school. Both residents and non-residents of Pennsylvania are eligible to apply. Although there are no specific high school course requirements, applicants are expected to have a substantial back-ground in science and mathematics. AP coursework is viewed favorably, and students are required to take the SAT or ACT.

Selection Factors

In conjunction with the School of Medicine, each undergraduate institution considers an applicant's GPA, standardized test perform-ance, extracurricular activities (including leadership roles), and interpersonal skills in making admission decisions. Substantial maturity and strong motivation are among the important personal qualities considered by the Admission Committee. The minimum SAT score required is 1350 in the combined Critical Reading and Mathematics sections, with no individual section less than 600 (including the Writing section). The minimum composite ACT score required is 31. Students are expected to be in the top one to five percent of their high school graduating class. Academic ability should be demonstrated across a wide variety of courses, including AP science coursework. Selected applicants are required to inter-view with a representative of the undergraduate institution and a medical school admissions officer. Contact the partnering under-graduate institutions directly to obtain additional information about the Medical Scholars Program: Duquesne University, (412) 396-6335; Washington and Jefferson College, tklitz@washjeff.edu; and Widener University, (610) 499-4030.

Curriculum

Students in this combined-degree program will complete their bac-calaureate degree at one of the three partnering universities listed above. The medical degree is granted by Temple University School of Medicine. Students may choose to be a science major, but are free to explore all available options as long as they complete the premedical science requirements. Matriculation to Temple University School of Medicine is conditional upon successful com-pletion of all GPA and MCAT requirements as outlined by each institution's agreement. Educational innovations are unique at each undergraduate institution. All students are required to complete

the M.D. program without deviation from the standard curriculum, including passing USMLE Steps 1, 2CS (Clinical Skills), and 2CK (Clinical Knowledge).

Expenses	Resident Tuition and Fees	Non-resident Tuition and Fees
Undergraduate	Varies	Varies
U.S. Medical School	$41,936	$51,202

Financial Aid

For information about financial aid, contact the Financial Aid Office of the specific partnering undergraduate institution listed above. Financial aid available to medical students includes grants, scholar-ships, and student loans. For additional information, visit the School of Medicine Web site at: *www.temple.edu/sfs/med/*.

Application and Acceptance Policies

Filing of application:
    Earliest date: Varies by program
    Latest date: n/a
Application fee: $0   Fee Waiver Available: n/a
Acceptance notice:
    Earliest date: March 15, 2011
    Latest date: April 15, 2011
Applicant's response to acceptance offer:
    Latest date: May 1, 2011
Deposit to hold place in class: None
Starting date: Varies by undergraduate program

Information on 2009–2010 Entering Class

Number of	In-State	Out-of-State	Total
Applicants	n/a	n/a	20
Applicants Interviewed	n/a	n/a	15
New Entrants	n/a	n/a	5

Total number of students enrolled in program: 20

Villanova University and
Drexel University College of Medicine

Villanova, Pennsylvania

Address Inquiries To:
John D. Friede, Ph.D., Health Professions Advisor
Office of University Admission
Villanova University
800 Lancaster Avenue, Villanova, Pennsylvania 19085
T (610) 519-4833 F (610) 519-8042
admission@villanova.edu
www.villanova.edu/artsci/healthprofessions/affiliates/
medicine/index.htm

Purpose

This combined-degree program provides outstanding high school seniors, who are highly motivated toward the medical profession, an opportunity to combine a strong liberal arts undergraduate program with a medical education in seven years.

Requirements for Entrance

Students are selected for this program in their senior year of high school. Both residents and non-residents of Pennsylvania are eligible to apply to the program; applicants must be U.S. citizens or permanent residents. Applicants are required to complete the following courses prior to graduation from high school: one year of biology, one year of chemistry, one year of physics, four years of English, and four years of mathematics. In addition to meeting these academic requirements, applicants are also required to submit the results of the ACT or SAT. An ACT score of at least 31 or an SAT score of 1360 (Critical Reading and Mathematics) is required. SAT II scores are recommended.

Selection Factors

The academic factors taken into consideration for admission into the combined-degree program include: SAT scores, high school GPA and class rank, and letters of recommendation. The average high school GPA for the 2009–2010 entering class was 3.80, unweighted. Extracurricular activities and community service are among the personal attributes sought in applicants; exposure to medicine is expected. An interview is required. Once admitted into the program, students are expected to maintain an overall GPA of 3.50 and a science GPA of 3.50, and they are required to achieve scores of either a 9 on the Verbal Reasoning and a 10 on the Physical Sciences and Biological Sciences sections or a combined score of 31 or better (with no score less than 8 on any section of the MCAT). A "P" or greater on the Writing Sample is required.

Curriculum

Students are required to complete a baccalaureate degree within the first year of medical school. The most frequent major is biology, followed by comprehensive science. This seven-year program leads to a baccalaureate degree awarded by Villanova University and to the M.D. degree granted by the Drexel University College of Medicine. During the undergraduate phase of the program, students will spend 100 percent of their time in coursework related to the bachelor's degree, which includes 41 semester hours of natural and physical science, six semester hours of mathematics, and 51 semester hours of humanities.

Expenses

Expenses	Resident Tuition and Fees	Non-resident Tuition and Fees
Undergraduate	$38,820	$38,820
U.S. Medical School	$45,540	$45,540

Financial Aid

For information on financial aid, visit *www.finaid.villanova.edu* and *http://webcampus.drexelmed.edu/admissions/financialaid.asp*.

Application and Acceptance Policies

Filing of application:
  Earliest date: September 1, 2011
  Latest date: November 1, 2011
Application fee: $75   Fee Waiver Available: Yes
Acceptance notice:
  Earliest date: March 15, 2011
  Latest date: March 30, 2011
Applicant's response to acceptance offer:
  Maximum time: May 1, 2011
Deposit to hold place in class: $700; nonrefundable
Starting date: August 24, 2011

Information on 2009–2010 Entering Class

Number of	In-State	Out-of-State	Total
Applicants	36	141	177
Applicants Interviewed	15	47	62
New Entrants	4	7	11
Total number of students enrolled in program: 21			

Wilkes University/SUNY-Upstate Medical University

Wilkes-Barre, Pennsylvania

Address Inquiries To:
Eileen Sharp
Coordinator for Health Science Professional Programs
Wilkes University, 84 West South Street
Wilkes-Barre, Pennsylvania 18766
T (570) 408-7812 F (570) 408-7812
eileen.sharp@wilkes.edu
www.wilkes.edu/pages/102.asp

Purpose

This cooperative program is motivated by the need for physicians interested in serving in rural and semi-rural health care delivery systems, as well as the interest of each institution in attracting students of superior ability and accomplishment.

Requirements for Entrance

Students apply to the program in their senior year of high school; applicants must be New York State residents. Candidates for admission must have completed the following high school course requirements: four years each of mathematics, English, science, and social science. Applicants must take the ACT or SAT examination.

Selection Factors

The following factors are taken into consideration in assessing the applicant for admission: grades, rank in class, SAT (ACT) scores, and extracurricular activities. Selected applicants are invited for a required interview.

Curriculum

This eight-year program leads to a baccalaureate degree awarded by Wilkes University and to the M.D. degree granted by SUNY Upstate Medical University. The most frequent major for the baccalaureate degree is biology, followed by chemistry and biochemistry. The M.D. portion of the curriculum does not depart from the "traditional" design. Upstate accepts a special responsibility to provide physicians to New York's underserved rural communities. A student from a rural setting or one subsequently trained there is more likely to practice there. This B.S.–M.D. program attracts students from rural areas who are not likely to otherwise find their way to medical school. Upstate also provides many special opportunities during medical school (Rural Medicine Program, Clinical Campus) to train students in community and rural settings. Students in this program are not required to take the MCAT for promotion or admission to the medical school. The USMLE Step 1 is required; it must be passed, prior to beginning clinical rotations, to be promoted and in order to graduate. Students must record a score on USMLE Step 2, but passing USMLE Step 2 is not a factor in graduation from the medical school.

Financial Aid

The sources of available financial aid are grants, scholarships, and student loans. For more information about financial aid, visit *www.wilkes.edu/pages/573.asp*, or contact the Financial Aid Office at SUNY Upstate Medical University by emailing FinAid@upstate.edu.

Expenses

Expenses	Resident Tuition and Fees	Non-resident Tuition and Fees
Undergraduate	$26,010	$26,010
U.S. Medical School	$24,112	$41,952

Application and Acceptance Policies

Filing of application:
  Earliest date: August 1, 2010
  Latest date: November 10, 2010
Application fee: $40   Fee Waiver Available: Yes
Acceptance notice:
  Earliest date: Within two weeks of medical school interview
  Latest date: Two weeks after medical school interview
Applicant's response to acceptance offer:
  Maximum time: Two weeks from receiving acceptance offer
Deposit to hold place in class: $100; refundable
Starting date: The Fall following graduation from Wilkes

Information on 2009–2010 Entering Class

Number of	In-State	Out-of-State	Total
Applicants	7	n/a	7
Applicants Interviewed	6	n/a	6
New Entrants	1	n/a	1
Total number of students enrolled in program: 5			

The Warren Alpert Medical School of Brown University

Providence, Rhode Island

Address Inquiries To:
College Admission Office
Brown University, Box 1876
Providence, Rhode Island 02912
T (401) 863-2378
Admissions@Brown.edu
http://med.brown.edu/plme

Purpose

The Program in Liberal Medical Education (PLME) seeks to graduate physicians who are broadly and liberally educated and who will view medicine as a socially responsible human service profession. Designed as an eight-year program, the PLME combines liberal arts and professional education. Great flexibility is built into the program. Working with PLME advising deans who are physicians, each student develops an individualized educational plan consistent with his or her particular interests. The PLME is a primary route of admission to The Warren Alpert Medical School.

Requirements for Entrance

Students are selected for the PLME in the senior year of high school. The Brown Admission Office recommends that applicants should have completed the following courses: four years of English, with significant emphasis on writing; three years of college preparatory mathematics; three years of a foreign language; two years of laboratory science above the freshman level; two years of history, including American history; at least one year of coursework in the arts; and at least one year of elective academic subjects. Prospective science or engineering majors should have taken physics, chemistry, and advanced mathematics. Applicants must take the SAT Reasoning Test and any two SAT Subject Tests (except for the SAT II Writing Test), or the ACT. (PLME applicants are encouraged to include a science SAT Subject Test.)

Selection Factors

Students are selected on the basis of scholastic accomplishment and promise, intellectual curiosity, emotional maturity, character, motivation, sensitivity, caring, and particularly the degree to which they seem adapted to the special features of the program. In the 2009-2010 entering class, the average SAT Reasoning Test scores were 735 Critical Reading, 747 Math, and 749 Writing. Of the students whose schools rank, 85% were in the top one percent of their high school class. An interview is not required.

Curriculum

The PLME leads to a baccalaureate degree and to the M.D. degree granted by The Warren Alpert Medical School. Students must complete a baccalaureate degree in the field of their choice. Each student's educational plan is highly individualized. The PLME combines the flexibility and opportunities of an undergraduate education at Brown University with effective preparation for participation in an equally innovative medical education program.

Expenses

Expenses	Resident Tuition and Fees	Non-resident Tuition and Fees
Undergraduate	$49,128	$39,448
U.S. Medical School	$41,706	$41,706

Financial Aid

For undergraduates in the first four years of the PLME, financial aid is awarded by the Financial Aid Office at Brown University as a package. Students are awarded monies via scholarships, work-study, and loans. During the last four years of the PLME, financial aid is administered by the The Warren Alpert Medical School Office of Financial Aid. Both loans and scholarships are available, although loans are the most common form of assistance.

Additional Information

The MCAT exam is not required for PLME students to continue into the medical school. Effective for Students Applying to the PLME Class of 2015 and Future PLME Classes: PLME students have the option to apply to other medical schools. In doing so, they will be withdrawn from the position being held for them in the Alpert Medical School (AMS). However, they will have the option of applying to AMS via the standard (AMCAS) route in which case their application will be considered alongside other standard route applicants.

Application and Acceptance Policies

Filing of application:
  Earliest date: November 1, 2010
  Latest date: January 1, 2011
Application fee: $75   Fee Waiver Available: No
Acceptance notice:
  Earliest date: December 15, 2010
  Latest date: Early April 2011
Applicant's response to acceptance offer:
  Latest date: May 1, 2011
Deposit to hold place in class: None
Starting date: September 2011

Information on 2009–2010 Entering Class

Number of	In-State	Out-of-State	Total
Applicants	46	1812	1858
Applicants Interviewed	n/a	n/a	n/a
New Entrants	3	52	55

Total number of students enrolled in program: 203

Fisk University and Meharry Medical College

Nashville, Tennessee

Address Inquiries To:
Office of Admissions
1000 17th Avenue North
Nashville, Tennessee 37208
T (615) 329-8666 F (615) 329-8774
Kchandler@fisk.edu
www.mmc.edu

Purpose

The Joint Program in Biomedical Sciences is designed to address America's need to train bright young students from groups under-represented in medicine who are dedicated to finding solutions to biomedical problems through research and who will be future health care providers.

Requirements for Entrance

Students are selected at the end of their first semester of under-graduate coursework on the Fisk University campus. There are no specific high school course requirements. Applicants must have competitive scores on the ACT and/or the SAT. They must have completed at least one semester at Fisk University. Participants must submit an application with a personal statement which details their career goals and letters of recommendation from two college science or mathematics professors to the Office of Admissions.

Selection Factors

The courses taken and grades earned at Fisk University, plus ACT and/or SAT scores, are considerations for eligibility for this program. Applicants must rank in the top 20 percent of their high school class. Students must maintain an undergraduate GPA of 3.50 in Fisk coursework. Students must take the MCAT prior to admission and earn a minimum score of 24.

Curriculum

The Joint Program in Biomedical Sciences, seven years in duration, allows students to obtain a baccalaureate degree from Fisk University and the M.D. degree from Meharry Medical College. Course requirements for the baccalaureate degree include 8 semesters of natural and physical sciences and 12 semesters each in the humanities and social sciences. Students are required to spend two summers in a structured academic enrichment program. Students must take Steps 1 and 2 of the USMLE during the medical school portion of the program. Passing these examinations is a factor in promotion and graduation from medical school. The most frequent major chosen by students is biology, followed by chemistry.

Expenses	Resident Tuition and Fees	Non-resident Tuition and Fees
Undergraduate	$25,170	$25,170
U.S. Medical School	$37,002	$37,002

Financial Aid

Applicants and students can apply for institutional scholarships and grants, U.S. Department of Education Title IV Federal Student Aid (work-study and loans), U.S. Department of Health and Human Services Student Aid Programs (loans and scholarships), Southern Regional Education Board Grants, and Tennessee Black Conditional Grants. Meharry's Office of Student Financial Aid makes available most federal, regional, and state financial aid applications and brochures on numerous funding opportunities. Visit *www.mmc.edu /students/studentfinancialaid.html* for sources of financial aid. The Meharry Medical College Library and local public libraries have publications on most sources of student financial aid. Applicants can receive more information from the Office of Student Financial Aid, Meharry Medical College, 1005 D.B. Todd Boulevard, Nashville, Tennessee 37208.

Additional Information

All students who are selected for the program are on scholarship while enrolled at Fisk University.

Application and Acceptance Policies

Filing of application:
    Earliest date: September 15, 2010
    Latest date: February 1, 2011
Application fee: None   Fee Waiver Available: n/a
Acceptance notice:
    Earliest date: February 15, 2011
    Latest date: March 15, 2011
Applicant's response to acceptance offer:
    Maximum time: 1 week
Deposit to hold place in class: None
Starting date: Retroactive second semester, undergraduate year one

Information on 2009–2010 Entering Class

Number of	In-State	Out-of-State	Total
Applicants	3	2	5
Applicants Interviewed	2	2	4
New Entrants	1	1	2

Total number of students enrolled in program: 7

Rice University and
Baylor College of Medicine

Houston, Texas

Address Inquiries To:
Rice University, Office of Admissions—MS-17
P.O. Box 1892
Houston, Texas 77251-1892
T (713) 348-7423 F (713) 348-5323
admi@rice.edu
www.bcm.edu/medschool/baccmd.htm

Purpose

To promote the education of future physicians who are scientifically competent, compassionate, and socially conscious in order to apply insight from the extensive study of liberal arts and other disciplines to the study of modern medical science.

Requirements for Entrance

Students are selected for this program during their senior year of high school. Both residents and non-residents of Texas are considered for admission. Applicants are expected to have had a varied and rigorous high school program with high academic achievement. They must take the SAT Reasoning Test or ACT, plus three SAT Subject tests.

Selection Factors

The high school academic record, standardized test scores, course selection, extracurricular activities, and letters of recommendation are some of the factors taken into account in offering admission to an applicant. In the most recent entering class, students averaged above the top five percent in their high school class.

Curriculum

This is not an accelerated program; all students are expected to complete four years of undergraduate education and four years of medical school. Students earn a baccalaureate degree from Rice University, and are awarded the M.D. degree by Baylor College of Medicine. Minimum course requirements for this program include at least two semesters each in the humanities and social sciences and eight semesters in the natural and physical sciences. The medical part of the curriculum devotes approximately 1 ½ years to the basic sciences with clinical experience, and 2 ½ years to clinical science with some basic science coursework. The MCAT is not required for promotion or admission to the medical school. Students are required to take Step 1 of the USMLE in their second or third years. They are also required to take Step 2 of the USMLE, but passing these examinations is not a graduation requirement.

Financial Aid

Sources of financial aid include academic, athletic, and need-based scholarships. Applicants can receive more information from the Rice University Admission Office, M.S. 17, 6100 Main Street, Houston, Texas 77035.

Expenses

	Resident Tuition and Fees	Non-resident Tuition and Fees
Undergraduate	$31,430	$31,430
U.S. Medical School	$14,828	$27,928

Application and Acceptance Policies

Filing of application:
    Earliest date: August 1, 2010
    Latest date: December 1, 2010
Application fee: $65   Fee Waiver Available: Yes
Acceptance notice:
    Earliest date: n/a
    Latest date: Mid-April 2011
Applicant's response to acceptance offer:
    Latest date: May 1, 2011
Deposit to hold place in class: $300; refundable by May 2011
Starting date: August 2011

Information on 2009–2010 Entering Class

Number of	In-State	Out-of-State	Total
Applicants	118	220	338
Applicants Interviewed	16	31	47
New Entrants	4	9	13

Total number of students enrolled in program: 50

University of Texas
School of Medicine at San Antonio
San Antonio, Texas

Address Inquiries To:
David Jones, Ph.D.
University of Texas School of Medicine at San Antonio
7703 Floyd Curl Drive, Mail Code 7790
San Antonio, Texas 78229
T (210) 567-6080 F (210) 567-6962
medadmissions@uthscsa.edu
http://som.uthscsa.edu/admissions/index.asp

Purpose
In partnership with the University of Texas-Pan American this program offers the opportunity to achieve conditional acceptance to medical school as early as the junior year at UT Pan American. Participants are provided mentorship by medical school faculty and educational enrichment and clinical experiences in the Summer Premedical Academy. Frequent meetings with medical school faculty during the year provide encouragement and support toward matriculation into medical school. Acceptance to medical school after three years of undergraduate school is possible.

Requirements for Entrance
Students are selected during their senior year of high school. The program is only open to residents of Texas who are citizens or permanent residents of the United States. While there are no specific high school course requirements, applicants are required to take the SAT and/or ACT. Concurrent or AP coursework is encouraged.

Selection Factors
Academic factors considered in selecting applicants include SAT/ACT scores and strength in science and mathematics coursework. In addition to an impressive academic portfolio, applicants must also demonstrate a sincere interest in medicine and present letters of recommendation from their high school counselors or teachers. An interview by members of the School of Medicine Admissions Committee is also required. Students are admitted to medical school based on a sliding scale of the ratio of MCAT scores and science GPA, a succesful interview with the Admissions Committee as well as a demonstrated continued commitment to study medicine.

Curriculum
Students must maintain a science and overall GPA of 3.25 or better and are required to complete all medical school prerequisite coursework with a grade of "C" or better. Students also participate in six-week Summer Premedical Academies for which scholarships are provided. During each summer starting after their freshman year, students come to the medical school campus in San Antonio to participate in academic enrichment programs, as well as twice weekly clinical preceptorships. The program is designed to increase the students' academic preparedness for the next year's coursework and for an MCAT review course during the summer between their junior and senior years. The clinical preceptorships are designed to increase students' awareness of issues in clinical medicine and to develop a clear understanding of performance expectations while in medical school.

Expenses

Expenses	Resident Tuition and Fees	Non-resident Tuition and Fees
Undergraduate	$11,898	$26,361
U.S. Medical School	$15,170	$28,270

Additional Information
The Summer Premedical Academy provides academic enrichment coursework along with clinical preceptorships. Students are also mentored by faculty and students of the medical school. There is also an opportunity to meet with education specialists to assist with learning disabilities.

Application and Acceptance Policies
Filing of application:
    Earliest date: December 1, 2010
    Latest date: February 1, 2011
Application fee: None   Fee Waiver Available: Yes
Acceptance notice:
    Earliest date: April 1, 2011
    Latest date: April 1, 2011
Applicant's response to acceptance offer:
    Maximum time: Two weeks
Deposit to hold place in class: None
Starting date: May 20, 2011

Information on 2009–2010 Entering Class

Number of	In-State	Out-of-State	Total
Applicants	24	n/a	24
Applicants Interviewed	12	n/a	12
New Entrants	3	n/a	3
Total number of students enrolled in program: 20			

Eastern Virginia Medical School
Norfolk, Virginia

Address Inquiries To:
Office of Admissions, Mail Code 3
Eastern Virginia Medical School
700 W. Olney Road
Norfolk, Virginia 23507-1607
T (757) 446-5812 F (757) 446-5896
www.evms.edu/md-programs/md-programs-home.html

Purpose

Eastern Virginia Medical School currently has combined programs with ten colleges and universities: Christopher Newport University, The College of William and Mary, Old Dominion University, Hampton University, Norfolk State University, Hampden-Sydney College, Saint Paul's College, Virginia State University, Virginia Union University and Virginia Wesleyan College. The purpose of these programs is to enlist outstanding undergraduate students into a track that provides great freedom and choice in the pursuit of a baccalaureate degree.

Requirements for Entrance

Students are selected during their sophomore year of college. Both residents and non-residents of Virginia are eligible to apply. There are no specific high school course requirements, but students must take the SAT.

Selection Factors

Applicants will be evaluated on their academic performance during their freshman year of college and the first semester of their sophomore year of college. An emphasis is placed on leadership skills and extracurricular activities, including medical volunteering. Selected applicants are invited for an interview.

Curriculum

The eight-year curriculum leads to a baccalaureate degree awarded by Christopher Newport University, The College of William and Mary, Old Dominion University, Hampton University, Norfolk State University, Hampden-Sydney College, Saint Paul's College, Virginia State University, Virginia Union University or Virginia Wesleyan College. The M.D. degree is granted by Eastern Virginia Medical School. Course requirements for the baccalaureate degree vary at each undergraduate institution. The most frequent major is biology. This early assurance program does, however, permit the student the opportunity for academic diversity. Students selected who have combined SAT scores greater than 1250 (math and verbal) will not be required to take the MCAT. Step 1 of the USMLE must be taken at the completion of the second year of medical school. Students must pass Steps 1 and 2 of the USMLE to complete the program and receive the M.D. degree.

Expenses

	Resident Tuition and Fees	Non-resident Tuition and Fees
Undergraduate	Varies	Varies
U.S. Medical School	$27,620	$50,380

Financial Aid

For information about financial aid during the undergraduate phase, contact the Office of Financial Aid at the undergraduate institutions identified. Ten programs are available: Christopher Newport University, Harold Grau, Ph.D., (757) 594-7946; The College of William and Mary, Beverley T. Sher, Ph.D., (757) 221-2852; Old Dominion University, Terri Mathews, (757) 683-5201; Hampton University, Michael Druitt, (757) 728-6757; Norfolk State University, Alicia McClain, Ph.D., (757) 823-8991; Hampden-Sydney College, H.O. Thurman, Ph.D., (434) 223-6177; Saint Paul's College, Sunday Adesuyi, Ph.D., (434) 848-6484; Virginia State University, Pamela Leigh-Mack, Ph.D., (804) 524-5285, Virginia Union University, Phillip W. Archer, Ph.D., (804) 257-5692 and Virginia Wesleyan College, Deirdre Gonsalves-Jackson, Ph.D., (757) 455-3265. For information about financial aid during the medical school phase, contact the Office of Financial Aid at Eastern Virginia Medical School at (757) 446-5804.

Application and Acceptance Policies

Filing of application:
  Earliest date: Varies
  Latest date: Varies
Application fee: $35   Fee Waiver Available: No
Acceptance notice:
  Earliest date: Varies
  Latest date: Varies
Applicant's response to acceptance offer:
  Maximum time: Varies
Deposit to hold place in class: $100; refundable by May 15, 2011
Starting date: August 2011

Information on 2009–2010 Entering Class

Number of	In-State	Out-of-State	Total
Applicants	18	8	26
Applicants Interviewed	14	7	21
New Entrants	8	2	10
Total number of students enrolled in program: n/a			

Virginia Commonwealth University School of Medicine

Richmond, Virginia

Address Inquiries To:
Dr. Anne L. Chandler, Senior Associate Dean
The Honors College
Virginia Commonwealth University
P.O. Box 843010, Richmond, Virginia 23284-3010
T (804) 828-1803 F (804) 827-1669
achandle@vcu.edu
www.pubapps.vcu.edu/honors/guaranteed/medicine/index.aspx

Purpose

The Guaranteed Admission Program of the Honors College offers academically capable, highly focused students an opportunity to pursue diverse, intellectually challenging programs of study. Students who successfully complete the Guaranteed Admission Program will be able to enter the medical school without the pressure of further competition. Close contact with the School of Medicine throughout the undergraduate program aids students in testing their career choice and in preparing for a lifelong commitment to learning in the profession.

Requirements for Entrance

Students are selected during their senior year of high school, and there are no state residency restrictions. All candidates are considered. The specific minimum high school course requirements are as follows: four units in English; three units in mathematics (to include algebra I and either geometry or algebra II); two units in science (at least one a laboratory science); and three units of history or social sciences or government. Students are strongly encouraged to present at least two units in a modern or ancient foreign language. Also required are standardized test scores on the ACT or SAT. The ACT composite score must be at or above 29. The combined SAT1 score must be at or above 1910 and obtained in a single sitting, with no score below 530. An unweighted GPA of 3.5 (on a 4.0 scale) is also required.

Selection Factors

Factors considered in offering admission to an applicant include: GPA, letters of reference, test scores, well-rounded and rigorous academic preparation, health care-related experience, and written and oral communication skills. The average GPA for students accepted for the 2009–2010 class was 3.85 (unweighted scale of 4.0), and the average SAT score was 2150. Selected applicants are invited for a required interview.

Curriculum

Students are required to complete a baccalaureate degree. The most frequent major is biology; the next most frequent major is chemistry. The undergraduate degree is awarded by Virginia Commonwealth University. Specific course requirements vary, depending upon the major. During the medical school program, there is a longitudinal clinical experience (Foundations of Clinical Medicine) in a community primary care practice that meets weekly for both of the first two years. Students are required to take Step 1 of the USMLE at the end of their second year. They must also take USMLE Step 2, but passing these examinations is not a promotion or graduation requirement. The doctor of medicine degree is also awarded by Virginia Commonwealth University. It takes eight years to fulfill the requirements for both degrees.

Expenses

Expenses	Resident Tuition and Fees	Non-resident Tuition and Fees
Undergraduate	$7,117	$20,749
U.S. Medical School	$28,416	$42,870

Financial Aid

There are several sources of financial aid available to students, including scholarships, loans, grants, and work-study. For more information, contact the Virginia Commonwealth University Financial Aid Office, P.O. Box 842506, Richmond, Virginia 23284-2506; (804) VCU-MONY.

Application and Acceptance Policies

Filing of application:
  Earliest date: September 1, 2010
  Latest date: November 15, 2010
Application fee: $40   Fee Waiver Available: Yes
Acceptance notice:
  Earliest date: April 1, 2011
  Latest date: n/a
Applicant's response to acceptance offer:
  Maximum time: May 1, 2011
Deposit to hold place in class: $100; nonrefundable
Starting date: August 2011

Information on 2009–2010 Entering Class

Number of	In-State	Out-of-State	Total
Applicants	67	119	186
Applicants Interviewed	22	38	60
New Entrants	5	11	16
Total number of students enrolled in program: 90			

Chapter 13:
M.D.-Ph.D. Dual Degree Programs

Almost all medical students will ultimately become practicing clinicians. The specialties they select will differ, and so will the settings. But regardless of the variation, these students share one major similarity: They plan to devote themselves completely to the direct care and treatment of patients.

Perhaps you envision something different. You look forward to a future in which you help advance medical knowledge. In addition to—or maybe even in lieu of—clinical work, you want to develop innovative techniques and study new treatments. You want to engage in scientific research to promote health, solve medical problems, combat disease, and improve medical care. You want to bridge the gap between the laboratory and a patient's bedside.

You want a career in medical research.

The Education of a Physician-Scientist

Physician-scientists—those who are trained in both medicine and research—are greatly needed in today's world. There is a synergy that results when experimental and clinical thinking are joined, and that combination is found among those who have completed both M.D. and Ph.D. degrees. These individuals help translate the achievements of basic research into active clinical practice, and, in doing so, strengthen the link between medical knowledge and prevent, diagnose, and treat disease. If this is the path you prefer, you will enjoy a busy, challenging, and rewarding career.

Advantages of the M.D.-Ph.D. Dual Degree

One route to a career as a physician-scientist is enrollment in a combined M.D.-Ph.D. program. Although you can complete a Ph.D. program after receiving your M.D. degree, there are several advantages to pursuing joint M.D.-Ph.D. training:

- The greatest advantage of the dual-degree program is the integration of research and clinical training. This integrated approach may include seminars that cross departments and interactions with teams composed of both basic science and clinical investigators.

- In addition, you can save a significant amount of time. The combined program can be completed in a total of seven or eight years, compared to the nine or ten it would take to earn both degrees independently.

- Beyond that, M.D.-Ph.D. students enjoy opportunities for research and faculty mentoring frequently unavailable to M.D.-only students. As a result, these students are often able to enhance their mastery of the basic science background underlying patients' clinical problems, and, ultimately, use that information to develop improvements in diagnosis and treatment.

Research Specialities

Just as with an M.D.-only career, students with a combined degree can pursue any one of many scientific specialties. Most students earn their Ph.D. degrees in biomedical laboratory disciplines such as biochemistry, biomedical engineering, biophysics, cell biology, genetics, immunology, microbiology, neuroscience, and pharmacology.

It is important to realize that not every research specialty is offered at every medical school, and that curricula can vary from institution to institution. In some schools, for example, M.D.-Ph.D. trainees also can complete their graduate work outside of laboratory disciplines in fields such as anthropology, computational biology, economics, health care policy, mathematics, physics, and sociology.

The Typical Program

Almost all U.S. and Canadian medical schools have M.D.-Ph.D. programs in one or more areas of specialization. Some are relatively small in size (one or two new students each year, with a dozen or so total students), while others are much larger (up to 20 new students annually and a total enrollment of around 150).

Although, as we mentioned, there are differences among programs, core elements are common to almost all. The typical program is completed in a total of seven to nine years and includes:

- Completion of the first two years of combined medical and graduate school coursework, followed by

- Three to five years of doctoral research, including the completion of a thesis project, and

- A return to medical school for core clinical training and electives during the final years of the medical curriculum.

At most schools, integrated approaches to graduate and medical education have been introduced throughout the curricula. In addition, most programs engage students in a wide range of other activities to enrich their training experience. The median time for completion of a M.D.-Ph.D. program is eight years.

Application and Admission

Nearly all M.D.-Ph.D. programs participate in the AMCAS application process described in Chapter 6.

If you choose to pursue the dual-degree program, you will designate yourself as a Combined M.D.-Ph.D. Training Applicant and complete two additional essays—one related to why you are interested in the joint training program, and the other describing your research experience. There are, however, specifics in the application process—and the prerequisites required for admission—that vary from school to school. (Some institutions, for example, require GRE scores.) For complete information, make certain to review the description of the dual-degree program at the Web site of each medical school in which you are interested.

Factors Considered by the Admission Committee

Admission committee members will review the application material for the usual experiences, attributes, and metrics that are important for admission of students to M.D.-only programs (see Chapter 7). But because M.D.-Ph.D. applicants plan to become both physicians and scientists, committee members will also look for evidence of an applicant's passion and aptitude for research. They accomplish this largely through review of an applicant's statement of career goals and in letters of recommendation from faculty or researchers with whom the applicant has previously worked. In particular, committee members seek confirmation of:

- Relevant and substantive research experience during or after college;

- An appreciation for and understanding of the work of physician-scientists; and

- Intellectual drive, research ability, and perseverance.

If you hope to pursue the M.D.-Ph.D. joint degree, you will be expected to have clinical experience—be it through volunteer work, shadowing a physician-scientist, or specific training. Other experiences that admission committee members generally look favorably upon are similar to those of the M.D.-only candidate, such as leadership positions, community service activities, and teaching roles.

Finally, it's important to be aware that while significant weight is placed upon an applicant's interest and experience in research activities, he or she is also expected to demonstrate a degree of academic excellence similar to those accepted in the M.D.-only program. For students entering M.D.-Ph.D. programs in 2009, for example, the median GPA for students was 3.7 and total MCAT scores was 34* as reported by the American Medical College Application Service (AMCAS).

Keep in mind that the range of GPAs and MCAT scores for accepted applicants is quite broad, and considered in conjunction with other selection factors.

A Significant Factor in Selection

An important factor in selecting M.D.-Ph.D. applicants is evidence of their passion and aptitude for research.

AAMC Podcast on Dual Degree Program!

How Does a Joint M.D.-Ph.D. Degree Combine the Best of Science and Medicine?

In this podcast, David Engman, M.D., Ph.D., director of the Medical Scientist Training Program at Northwestern University School of Medicine, and M. Kerry O'Banion, M.D., Ph.D., director of the Medical Scientist Training Program at the University of Rochester, discuss how pursuing a joint M.D.-Ph.D. can enable motivated students to follow their passions.

Go to *www.aamc.org/podcasts/* for this and other AAMC podcasts. You can subscribe at no charge at the iTunes store.

Acceptance Policies

Just as application requirements vary from school to school, so too do their acceptance policies. Some institutions permit an applicant who is not accepted to the M.D.-Ph.D. dual degree program to pursue admission to the M.D.-only curriculum. Other medical schools will accept applications from M.D.-Ph.D. candidates only for both degree programs, and failure to gain admittance to one program precludes consideration from another. Since school policies differ, applicants should clarify these matters at each school prior to application, and let admission office staff know of their interest in pursuing an M.D.-only program (if that is the case) should they not be admitted to the dual-degree program.

Lisiting of Policies by M.D.-Ph.D. Program

Review policies of M.D.-Ph.D. programs at *www.aamc.org/mdphd/faqtable.pdf.*

Financing M.D.-Ph.D. Programs

The sources of funding for M.D.-Ph.D. programs vary from school to school. Many schools offer full support for both the M.D. and Ph.D. components of their education, including tuition waivers, a stipend, and health insurance. At other institutions, varying degrees of support are available, sometimes only for the Ph.D. component of the program. Before you apply to an M.D.-Ph.D. dual-degree program, you should determine the level of financial assistance available.

A significant amount of funding comes from institutional sources and both individual and institutional grants. The latter includes the Medical Scientist Training Program (MSTP) sponsored by the National Institutes of Health (NIH), as well as other NIH grants. While you will undoubtedly want to review the list of medical schools participating in the MSTP (*www.nigms.nih.gov/Training/InstPredoc/PredocInst-MSTP.htm*), you will also want to contact the program officials at the institutions of interest and review their Web sites for full information.

Bear in mind that although most M.D.-Ph.D. programs offer support for their students, additional resources are available. Most take the form of competitive applications submitted by the trainee and their research mentor. These include fellowships from both private sources and a number of NIH institutes. You can review the list of these opportunities at *www.aamc.org/mdphd/fundingformdphd.pdf*.

Medical Scientist Training Program (MSTP)

During the award period from July 1, 2008 through June 30, 2009, the NIH supported 43 M.D.-Ph.D. programs through the MSTP.

For additional information and guidance about application to and enrollment in a combined M.D.-Ph.D. program, please visit the AAMC's Web site on the dual-degree program at www.aamc.org/mdphd or contact your pre-health advisor and the M.D.-Ph.D. program director at the medical schools of interest.

Chapter 14:

Information About U.S. Medical Schools Accredited by the LCME

Information about individual U.S. medical schools is given in the following two-page entries for the 132 schools (128 in the 50 states, four in Puerto Rico) that will be considering applications for the summer 2011 entering class. The schools presented here are accredited as of February 2010 by the Liaison Committee on Medical Education (LCME), which is sponsored by the Association of American Medical Colleges (AAMC) and the American Medical Association (AMA).

Individual school entries are each two pages, one devoted to narrative information and the other devoted to data and tabular information:

Page one: Narrative Information

- Contact Information—Admissions office staff, mail and e-mail addresses, phone and fax numbers, and Web site addresses for the medical school, admissions office, and financial aid office.

- General Information—Background and basic information about the medical school and its program.

- Curricular Highlights—Information about the medical education curriculum and educational philosophy and methodologies.

- USMLE Step 1 and Step 2 Clinical Knowledge (CK) and Clinical Skills (CS) Policies—United States Medical Licensing Examination (USMLE) policies and requirements for promotion and/or graduation. For the most current policies, see the AAMC Curriculum Directory Web site at *http://services.aamc.org/currdir*.

- Selection Factors—Basic information regarding coursework, personal characteristics and experiences, and general requirements for applicants to be considered for acceptance and matriculation.

- Financial Aid—General information about the financial aid programs provided by the school, as well as additional contact information.

- Information about Diversity Programs—Information about the school's diversity initiatives and programs for students from groups underrepresented in medicine, as well as additional contact information.

- Campus Information—Information about total enrollment figures, campus setting, housing, special features, and satellite and/or regional campuses.

Page two: Data and Tabular Information

- **Application Process and Requirements**

  Primary Application Service—Notation of which type of application the school utilizes for primary applications (the American Medical College Application Service [AMCAS], the Texas Medical and Dental School Application Service [TMDSAS], or a school-specific application) and information about the earliest and latest filing dates for the primary application.

  Secondary Application—This section notes if a secondary application is required, to whom the secondary application is to be submitted, required fees, the potential availability of a fee waiver, and the earliest and latest filing dates for secondary application materials.

  Latest MCAT® Considered—The most recent MCAT administration from which an MCAT score can be submitted in support of an application.

  Oldest MCAT® Considered—The earliest MCAT administration from which an MCAT score can be submitted in support of an application.

  Early Decision Program—This section notes if the school participates in an Early Decision Program (EDP), when EDP applicants are notified about acceptance decisions, and if the Early Decision Program is available only to state residents or to both state residents and nonresidents.

  Regular Acceptance Notice—The earliest and latest dates on which acceptance notices are sent to applicants. These dates do not refer to those applicants who have applied to special programs.

  Applicant's Response to Acceptance Notice—Maximum Time—The maximum period of time applicants are provided to respond to an acceptance offer.

  Requests for Deferred Entrance Considered—Information about deferred entrance opportunities at the school.

  Deposit—Information on the amount of the deposit required to hold a place in the next entering class, when the deposit is due, if the deposit is applied to tuition, if the deposit is refundable, and final date for requesting a deposit refund.

  Estimated Number of New Entrants—The number of regular, EDP, and special program applicants expected to matriculate in the next year's entering class.

  Start Month/Year—The anticipated starting date in 2011 for the program.

  Interview Format—General information on how interviews are conducted and about the availability of regional interviews.

- **Other Programs**—Information regarding the availability of postbaccalaureate premedical, summer, and combined degree programs. Web sites and contact information are provided, as available.

- **Premedical Coursework**—Coursework and laboratories that applicants are either required or recommended to complete prior to matriculation. Schools have also noted their policy regarding acceptance of online course work.

- **MCAT® Information for Accepted Applicants**—This chart displays, for each section of the MCAT, the median total numeric score for all 2009 accepted applicants, the Median Total Numeric MCAT score for all 2009 accepted applicants to all U.S. medical schools (the number in the shaded circle), the individual school's median MCAT scores for all 2009 applicants accepted to the school (the number in the white circle), and the range of scores on each MCAT section for all 2009 applicants accepted to the school (the gradient line behind the circled numbers). Where applicable, schools have noted if it is their policy to average an applicant's MCAT scores from various MCAT administrations. Note: Chart 10-E (Chapter 10) presents information about the likelihood of acceptance for applicants whose scores on all MCAT sections are at the lower end of the score range. Additionally, schools have noted whether the MCAT is required for admission and the percentage of accepted applicants who took the MCAT. Note: Several schools have special programs that do not require applicants to provide MCAT scores. Therefore, although the MCAT may be required for admission to the regular M.D. program, the percentage of accepted applicants who took the MCAT may be less than 100 percent.

The national median scores for each MCAT section published in this chapter represent median scores for the entire pool of accepted applicants to all medical schools. Thus, based on the fact that each acceptance of an applicant reflects an independent decision by each medical school, when an applicant has been accepted by more than one medical school, that applicant's MCAT scores are included in the calculation of the national median more than once.

- **Overall GPA Median and Science GPA Median**—These data are for all applicants accepted to the medical school's 2009–2010 entering class.

- **Selection Factors**—Proportion of Accepted Applicants with Relevant Experience—These percentages were derived from applicant self-reports on the 2009 AMCAS application. They represent the percentage of accepted applicants who reported experiences in the categories of Community Service/Volunteer Work, Medically-Related Work, and Research Experience. Data provided from schools that participate in the TMDSAS application or that use a school-specific primary application were calculated in the same manner as those derived from the AMCAS application.

- **Acceptance & Matriculation Data for 2009–10**—Data in this chart reflect verified applications, not initiated applications. The top half of the chart notes the number of applicants (resident, nonresident, international, and total) who applied, were interviewed, and/or deferred entrance.

The lower portion of the chart displays information about the number of resident, nonresident, international, and total matriculants who were accepted through any Early Assurance Program (EAP), the Early Decision Program (EDP), and any college/M.D. or M.D./Ph.D. program, as well as the total number of matriculants from any application process in the school's 2009–2010 entering class. Information is also noted regarding the school's ability to accept applications from international applicants.

- **Matriculant Demographics**—Information about the number of men and women who matriculated in the 2009 first-year class for the first time.

- **Matriculants' Self-Reported Race/Ethnicity**—This information reflects data that were self-reported by applicants on their applications. Note: The sum of the columns may not reflect the actual number of matriculants. Applicants are permitted to select, in their racial and ethnic self-descriptions, more than one race and/or ethnicity. Each selection is counted. Therefore, if a given matriculant selects three races and/or ethnicities, that matriculant will be counted in three different columns. The total number of matriculants is presented in the row labeled "unduplicated."

- **Matriculants Who Were Science and Math Majors**—In this calculation, "Science and Math Majors" include: Aerospace Engineering, Agriculture, Anatomy, Astronomy, Biochemistry, Biology, Biomathematics, Biomedical Engineering, Biomedical Science,

Bio-physics, Botany, Chemical Engineering, Chemistry, Chemistry and Biology, Civil Engineering, Computer Science, Double Major Science, Electrical Engineering, Engineering, Environmental Studies, Forestry, Genetics, Geology, Geophysics, Human Biology, Mathematics, Mechanical Engineering, Meteorology, Microbiology, Molecular Biology, Natural Science, Neuroscience, Oceanography, Pathology, Pharmacology, Physics, Physiology, Premedicine, Psychobiology, Science General, Science–Other, Biology, Science–Other Physics, Statistics, and Zoology. These definitions reflect applicants' self-report on their AMCAS application; assistance was also provided by members of the National Association of Advisors for the Health Professions (NAAHP).

- **Matriculants with Baccalaureate and/or Graduate Degrees**—Information about the percentage of matriculants with baccalaureate and/or graduate degrees at the time of matriculation.

- **Specialty Choice**—Information in this chart was derived from program directors' reports to the National Graduate Medical Education (GME) Census in GME Track™ for 2005, 2006, and 2007 graduates of each medical school.

- **Financial Information**—Cost of Attendance, Tuition and Fees, Other Expenses, and Health Insurance information is derived from the 2009–2010 AAMC Tuition and Student Fees Questionnaire. Regarding health insurance, "can be waived" means that this fee may be waived for any student with existing and comparable health insurance coverage (e.g., through a parent or a spouse).

Data about Percentage of Enrolled Students Receiving Financial Aid and For 2010, Total Indebtedness Are Derived from the 2008–2009 Liaison Committee on Medical Education (LCME) 1B Survey. Note: Scholarship and Grant amounts include funding from programs with a service commitment.

Abbreviations

Listed below are the abbreviations used in the school entries in this chapter.

AMCAS®—American Medical College Application Service

CACMS—Committee on Accreditation of Canadian Medical Schools

CLEP—College-Level Examination Program

EAP—Early Assurance Program

EDP—Early Decision Program

FAF—Financial Aid Form

FAFSA—Free Application for Federal Student Aid

FAP—AAMC Fee Assistance Program

GPA—Grade Point Average

LCME—Liaison Committee on Medical Education

LCME 1B—Liaison Committee on Medical Education 1B Survey

MCAT—Medical College Admission Test

NA—Not Applicable

NC—Not Collected

NR—Not Reported

REC—Recommended

REQ—Required

TMDSAS—Texas Medical and Dental School Application Service

TSF—Tuition and Student Fees Questionnaire

USMLE—United States Medical Licensing Examination

WICHE—Western Interstate Commission for Higher Education

WWAMI—WWAMI is an enduring partnership between the University of Washington School of Medicine and the states of Wyoming, Alaska, Montana, and Idaho. Its purpose is to provide access to publicly supported medical education across the five-state region. "WWAMI" is derived from the first letter of each of the five cooperating states.

University of Alabama School of Medicine
Birmingham, Alabama

Medical Student Services/Admissions
University of Alabama School of Medicine
VH 100, 1530 3rd Ave. S.
Birmingham, Alabama 35294-0019
T 205 934 2433   **F** 205 934 8740

Admissions www.medicine.uab.edu/admissions
Main www.medicine.uab.edu
Financial www.medicine.uab.edu/financial
E-mail medschool@uab.edu

Public Institution

Dr. Robert R. Rich, Dean

Dr. Nathan B. Smith, Assistant Dean for Admissions

Dr. Anjanetta L. Foster, Assistant Dean for Diversity and Multicultural Affairs

Ann Little, Financial Aid Specialist

General Information

The School of Medicine was founded in Mobile in 1859 and has been located in Birmingham since 1945. The main campus is in Birmingham, with branch campuses, created in 1969, in Huntsville and Tuscaloosa.

Mission Statement

The School of Medicine is dedicated to the education of physicians and scientists in all of the disciplines of medicine and biomedical investigation for careers in practice, teaching, and research. Necessary to this educational mission are the provision of outstanding medical care and services and the enhancement of new knowledge through clinical and basic biomedical research.

Curricular Highlights

Community Service Requirement: Optional.
Research/Thesis Requirement: Optional.

The four-year program emphasizes the fundamentals underlying clinical medical practice, with attention to the emotional, cultural, and social characteristics of patients and to the importance of adapting care to meet their needs. The Preclinical curriculum integrates basic and clinical sciences around organ system modules co-directed by basic scientists and clinicians. The objective of the curriculum is for students to learn basic sciences in a clinically relevant context, teaching them to think comprehensively about organ function and disease rather than to memorize mountains of facts. The first two years also provide training in medical professionalism, interviewing, and physical examination. The third and fourth years consist of required rotations and electives, with clinical experiences in both hospital and ambulatory settings. There are structured opportunities for research.

USMLE

Step 1: Required. Students must record a passing score for promotion.
Step 2: Clinical Skills (CS): Required. Students must only record a score.
Step 2: Clinical Knowledge (CK): Required. Students must record a passing total score to graduate.

Selection Factors

The Admissions Committee is committed to admitting those applicants who possess the intelligence, skills, attitudes, and other personal attributes to become excellent physicians and to meet the health care needs of the state of Alabama. Desirable attributes include: solid academic performance, effective communication and interpersonal skills, evidence of service to others, empathy, emotional maturity, personal resilience, honesty, leadership ability, sense of purpose, and experiences to promote an understanding of what it means to be a physician (shadowing). Particular attention is directed to individuals with commitment and ability to meet the school's missions including: meeting healthcare needs of Alabama's underserved populations (urban and rural), careers in biomedical research/academics and primary care. There is a special acceptance program for state residents committed to rural practice in Alabama. AP or CLEP coursework appearing on the AMCAS application will be accepted to meet a premedical requirement, although further coursework in biology and chemistry are desirable and may be necessary to be a competitive applicant. To meet our English coursework requirement, we accept composition and literature courses or intensive interdisciplinary reading and writing courses that expand knowledge beyond science. Other requirements: minimal total MCAT of 24 on the most recent exam, minimum grade of "C" on all required coursework, and completion of 90 hours of undergraduate credit from an accredited US college or university. With rare exceptions, completion of an undergraduate degree is required; all work toward current degrees must be completed prior to matriculation to the medical school.

Financial Aid

There are financial resources to fund an entire medical education. Resources include scholarships and low and higher interest loans. State merit scholarships are available in limited numbers to Alabama residents with exceptional academic records. State residents committed to rural practice in Alabama may qualify for aid.

Information about Diversity Programs

With the Office for Diversity Programs, the Admissions Committee attempts to identify and provide career counseling to students from groups under-represented in medicine.

Campus Information

Setting

The Birmingham campus is part of the UAB Medical Center, a world-renowned academic medical center with more than 70 research centers across 82 city blocks. All students complete the Pre-Clerkship Phase in Birmingham. For required clinical rotations, students are assigned to Birmingham or one of two branch campuses.

Enrollment

For 2009, total enrollment was: 747

Special Features

Students are encouraged to participate in mentored research opportunities, ranging from one-month projects to degree programs (MPH and MS). Students are required to complete a two month Scholarly Activity in the third year.

Housing

Housing is available on campus. Most medical students live off-campus and find affordable housing within a 15-minute commute to the campus.

Satellite Campuses/Facilities

Both the Huntsville and Tuscaloosa campuses offer students opportunities for community-based education, as well as rotations in regional medical centers offering a full range of medical specialties. Both campuses have new clinical education facilities.

Application Process and Requirements 2011–2012

Primary Application Service: AMCAS
Earliest filing date: June 1, 2010
Latest filing date: November 1, 2010

Secondary Application Required?: Yes
Sent to: Screened applicants
URL: Provided to invited applicants
E-mail: medschool@uab.edu
Fee: Yes, $30   **Waiver available:** Yes
Earliest filing date: August 1, 2010
Latest filing date: November 15, 2010

MCAT® required?: Yes
Latest MCAT® considered: September 2010
Oldest MCAT® considered: September 2008

Early Decision Program: School does have EDP
Applicants notified: October 1, 2010
EDP available for: Residents only

Regular Acceptance Notice
Earliest date: October 15, 2010
Latest date: Until class is full
Applicant's Response to Acceptance Offer – Maximum Time: Two weeks

Requests for Deferred Entrance Considered: Yes

Deposit to Hold Place in Class: Yes
Deposit (Resident): $50   **(Non-resident):** $100
Deposit due: With acceptance offer
Applied to tuition: Yes   **Refundable:** Yes
Refundable by: May 15, 2011

Estimated number of new entrants: 176
EDP: 10, special program: 55

Start Month/Year: July 2011

Interview Format: Individual interviews are held only on most Thursdays, September through March. Regional interviews are not available. Video interviews are not available.

Other Programs

PREPARATORY PROGRAMS

Postbaccalaureate Program: No
Summer Program: Yes, www.uasom.uab.edu/shep
Rural Medical Programs: Yes, http://medicine.uab.edu/education/prospectie/66902
Summer Health Enrichment Program: Yes, www.uasom.uab.edu/shep

COMBINED DEGREE PROGRAMS

Baccalaureate/M.D.: Yes, www.uab.edu/emsap
M.D./M.P.H.: Yes, www.soph.uab.edu/prospective/academicprograms
M.D./M.B.A.: No
M.D./J.D.: No
M.D./Ph.D.: Yes, www.uab.edu/uasom/mstp/

Premedical Coursework

On-line courses accepted in fulfillment of prerequisites: No

Course	Req.	Rec.	Lab.	Hrs.
Inorganic Chemistry	•		•	8
Behavioral Sciences				
Biochemistry		•		
Biology	•		•	8
Biology/Zoology				
Calculus				
College English	•			6
College Mathematics	•			6

Course	Req.	Rec.	Lab.	Hrs.
Computer Science				
Genetics				
Humanities				
Organic Chemistry	•		•	8
Physics	•		•	8
Psychology				
Social Sciences				
Other				

Selection Factors: 2009 Accepted Applicants

Proportion of Accepted Applicants with Relevant Experience (Data Self-Reported to AMCAS®)		
Community Service/Volunteer		77%
Medically-Related Work		84%
Research		81%

Shaded bar represents school's accepted scores ranging from the 10th percentile to the 90th percentile ▬   **School Median** ● **National Median** ◉

Overall GPA	2.0	2.1	2.2	2.3	2.4	2.5	2.6	2.7	2.8	2.9	3.0	3.1	3.2	3.3	3.4	3.5	3.6	3.7	(3.8)	3.9	4.0
Science GPA	2.0	2.1	2.2	2.3	2.4	2.5	2.6	2.7	2.8	2.9	3.0	3.1	3.2	3.3	3.4	3.5	3.6	3.7	(3.8)	3.9	4.0

MCAT® Total Numeric Score 9 10 11 12 13 14 15 16 17 18 19 20 21 22 23 24 25 26 27 28 29 30 (31) (32) 33 34 35 36 37 38 39 40 41 42 43

Writing Sample			J	K	L	M	N	O	(P)	(Q)	R	S	T
Verbal Reasoning	3	4	5	6	7	8	9	(10)	11	12	13	14	15
Biological Sciences	3	4	5	6	7	8	9	10	(11)	12	13	14	15
Physical Sciences	3	4	5	6	7	8	9	(10)	(11)	12	13	14	15

Acceptance & Matriculation Data for 2009–2010 First Year Class

	Resident	Non-resident	International	Total
Applications	430	1764	30	2224
Interviewed	252	153	0	405
Deferred	5	0	0	5
Matriculants				
Early Assurance Program	0	0	0	0
Early Decision Program	7	0	0	7
Baccalaureate/M.D.	5	0	0	5
M.D./Ph.D.	0	6	0	6
Matriculated	152	23	0	**175**

Applications accepted from International Applicants: No

Specialty Choice

2005, 2006, 2007 Graduates, Specialty Choice (As reported by program directors to GME Track™)	
Anesthesiology	5%
Emergency Medicine	6%
Family Practice	10%
Internal Medicine	16%
Obstetrics/Gynecology	6%
Orthopaedic Surgery	5%
Pediatrics	11%
Psychiatry	3%
Radiology	5%
Surgery	8%

Matriculant Demographics: 2009–2010 First Year Class

Men: 94   **Women:** 81

Matriculants' Self-Reported Race/Ethnicity

Mexican American	0	**Korean**	1
Cuban	0	**Vietnamese**	5
Puerto Rican	0	**Other Asian**	2
Other Hispanic	3	**Total Asian**	28
Total Hispanic	3	**Native American**	3
Chinese	7	**Black**	10
Asian Indian	12	**Native Hawaiian**	0
Pakistani	1	**White**	133
Filipino	1	**Unduplicated Number**	
Japanese	0	**of Matriculants**	175

Science and Math Majors: 75%
Matriculants with:
   Baccalaureate degree: 100%
   Graduate degree(s): 10%

Financial Information

Source: 2008–2009 LCME I-B survey and 2009–2010 AAMC TSF questionnaire

	Residents	Non-residents
Total Cost of Attendance	$38,743	$71,997
Tuition and Fees	$19,921	$53,175
Other (includes living expenses)	$17,120	$17,120
Health Insurance (can be waived)	$1,702	$1,702

Average 2009 Graduate Indebtedness: $111,710
% of Enrolled Students Receiving Aid: 79%

Criminal Background Check

This medical school requires a criminal background check prior to matriculation.

University of South Alabama
College of Medicine
Mobile, Alabama

Office of Admissions, MSB 241
University of South Alabama
College of Medicine
Mobile, Alabama 36688-0002
T 251 460 7176   **F** 251 460 6278

Admissions www.southalabama.edu/
com/admissions.shtml
Main www.southalabama.edu/com/
Financial www.finaid2.usouthal.edu/
E-mail mscott@usouthal.edu

Public Institution

Dr. Samuel J. Strada, Dean

Mark Scott, Director for Admissions

Sharon Bull, Director of Financial Aid

Dr. Margaret O'Brien, Associate Dean, Student Affairs

Dr. Hattie M. Myles, Assistant Dean, Special Programs and Student Affairs

General Information
The College of Medicine of the University of South Alabama was approved by the Board of Trustees of the university in 1967; the Alabama state legislature passed a resolution authorizing the college on August 19, 1967. The college admitted a charter class in January 1973. The basic medical sciences are housed on the university campus. The University of South Alabama Medical Center, operating continuously since 1831, has provided clinical medical education for more than a century. It is the major physician-staffed emergency facility in South Alabama and has been named a Level I trauma center by the Alabama Committee on Trauma. Other clinical training facilities include the USA Children's and Women's Hospital, Infirmary West Hospital and the USA Mitchell Cancer Institute.

Mission Statement
To prepare talented, highly qualified students to become physicians, providing them the opportunity to develop basic science and clinical skills that will carry them successfully through residency and their career in medicine.

Curricular Highlights
Community Service Requirement: Optional.
Research/Thesis Requirement: Optional.

The first year is devoted to the basic sciences of anatomy, physiology, biochemistry, neuroanatomy, and embryology. Early introduction to clinical problems is also offered in courses through Clinical Correlation Conferences and Medical Practice and Society. The second year includes pathology, physical diagnosis, microbiology-immunology, pharmacology, and behavioral science. Public

health/epidemiology and medical genetics round out the second-year curriculum. The third year has six clinical clerkships: medicine, surgery, pediatrics, psychiatry/neurology, obstetrics-gynecology, and family practice. The fourth year is composed of nine rotations of four weeks each. Students are required to select one rotation each in clinical neuroscience, surgical subspecialties, ambulatory care, primary care, subspecialty in medicine, pediatrics or obstetrics-gynecology, an acting internship, and an in-house elective. Three of the rotations may be used for approved extramural experiences. Letter grades are given until the fourth year, where a pass/fail/honors system is used.

USMLE
Step 1: Required. Students must record a passing score for promotion.
Step 2: Clinical Skills (CS): Required. Students must record a passing total score to graduate.
Step 2: Clinical Knowledge (CK): Required. Students must record a passing total score to graduate.

Selection Factors
The Committee on Admissions will consider candidates whose undergraduate grades and scores on the MCAT indicate that they can handle the rigorous curriculum of the College of Medicine. However, admission is based on more than scholastic achievement. Applicants will be considered on their potential to become conscientious and capable physicians. The University of South Alabama provides equal educational opportunities and is open to all qualified students without regard to race, creed, national origin, sex, or handicap with respect to all of its programs and activities. Because the college is state-supported, preference is given to Alabama residents. However, highly qualified out-of-state applicants are seriously considered. Disadvantaged, rural, and minority residents are strongly encouraged to apply. Fee waivers, based solely on economic need, are granted, when documented.

Financial Aid
The Office of Financial Aid coordinates the programs of assistance available to medical students demonstrating financial need. Scholarships are also available for entering

freshmen and medical students who have demonstrated academic excellence and/or financial need.

Information about Diversity Programs
The school is committed to the enrollment and education of individuals from all disadvantaged groups. For information, contact Dr. Hattie M. Myles, Assistant Dean of Special Programs and Student Affairs.

Campus Information

Setting
The medical school is located in a suburban setting with easy access to restaurants, shopping, and the city's largest park system, which has affordable golf and tennis facilities. Gulf Shores and Dauphin Island are less than an hour away, where students can enjoy some of the finest beaches in the United States. The hospitals and clinics are located throughout Mobile County and serve the health care needs of the community. These facilities include the only Level I trauma center in the region, as well as the latest in cancer treatments offered through the USA Mitchell Cancer Institute.

Enrollment
For 2009, total enrollment was: 296

Special Features
With only 74 students in each class and a large research-based clinical system consisting of four hospitals, students are exposed to significant procedural opportunities.

Housing
Very few, if any, students choose to live on campus due to the many safe and affordable housing options within a 5-mile radius of the campus. With the relative low cost of home ownership in the Mobile area, many students have found buying a house or condo more cost-effective than leasing.

Satellite Campuses/Facilities
Students do their hospital training in any one of four hospitals, depending on the rotation. The College of Medicine also has clinic-based training with preceptors in facilities located throughout Alabama.

Application Process and Requirements 2011–2012

Primary Application Service: AMCAS
Earliest filing date: June 1, 2010
Latest filing date: November 15, 2010

Secondary Application Required?: Yes
Sent to: Screened applicants
URL: www.usouthal.edu
Contact: D. Mark Scott, (251) 460-7176
mscott@usouthal.edu
Fee: Yes, $75
Fee waiver available: Yes
Earliest filing date: June 15, 2010
Latest filing date: December 31, 2010

MCAT® required?: Yes
Latest MCAT® considered: September 2010
Oldest MCAT® considered: 2007

Early Decision Program: School does have EDP
Applicants notified: October 1, 2010
EDP available for: Both residents and non-residents

Regular Acceptance Notice
Earliest date: November 15, 2010
Latest date: Until class is full
Applicant's Response to Acceptance
Offer – Maximum Time: Two weeks

Requests for Deferred
Entrance Considered: Yes

Deposit to Hold Place in Class: Yes
Deposit (Resident): $50
Deposit (Non-resident): $50
Deposit due: With response to acceptance offer
Applied to tuition: Yes
Deposit refundable: Yes
Refundable by: May 15, 2011

Estimated number of new entrants: 74

EDP: 15, special program: 5

Start Month/Year: August 2011

Interview Format: Students meet one-on-one with three interviewers. Regional interviews are not available. Video interviews are not available.

Other Programs

PREPARATORY PROGRAMS

Postbaccalaureate Program: Yes, Dr. Cindy Stanfield, (251) 380-2686, cthursto@usouthal.edu
Summer Program: Yes, Dr. Hattie Myles, (251) 460-7313, hmyles@usouthal.edu

COMBINED DEGREE PROGRAMS

Baccalaureate/M.D.: Yes, www.usouthal.edu
Chris Lynch, (251) 460-6141, admiss@usouthal.edu
M.D./M.P.H.: No
M.D./M.B.A.: No
M.D./J.D.: No
M.D./Ph.D.: Yes,
www.southalabama.edu/com/programs.shtml,
D. Mark Scott, (251) 460-7176, mscott@usouthal.edu

Premedical Coursework

On-line courses accepted in fulfillment of prerequisites: On a case-by-case basis

Course	Req.	Rec.	Lab.	Hrs.
Inorganic Chemistry	•		•	8
Behavioral Sciences				
Biochemistry		•		
Biology	•		•	8
Biology/Zoology				
Calculus		•		
College English	•			6
College Mathematics	•			6

Course	Req.	Rec.	Lab.	Hrs.
Computer Science				
Genetics		•		
Humanities	•			6
Organic Chemistry	•		•	8
Physics	•		•	8
Psychology				
Social Sciences				
Other				

Selection Factors: 2009 Accepted Applicants

Proportion of Accepted Applicants with Relevant Experience (Data Self-Reported to AMCAS®)		
Community Service/Volunteer		76%
Medically-Related Work		78%
Research		72%

Shaded bar represents school's accepted scores ranging from the 10th percentile to the 90th percentile ▨   School Median ● National Median ○

Overall GPA	2.0	2.1	2.2	2.3	2.4	2.5	2.6	2.7	2.8	2.9	3.0	3.1	3.2	3.3	3.4	3.5	3.6	(3.7)	3.8	3.9	4.0
Science GPA	2.0	2.1	2.2	2.3	2.4	2.5	2.6	2.7	2.8	2.9	3.0	3.1	3.2	3.3	3.4	3.5	3.6	(3.7)	3.8	3.9	4.0

MCAT® Total Numeric Score 9 10 11 12 13 14 15 16 17 18 19 20 21 22 23 24 25 26 27 28 (29) 30 31 (32) 33 34 35 36 37 38 39 40 41 42 43

Writing Sample				J		K		L		M		N	(O)		P		(Q)		R		S		T
Verbal Reasoning	3		4		5		6		7		8		9	(10)		11		12		13		14		15
Biological Sciences	3		4		5		6		7		8		9	(10)		(11)		12		13		14		15
Physical Sciences	3		4		5		6		7		8		9	(10)		(11)		12		13		14		15

Acceptance & Matriculation Data for 2009–2010 First Year Class

	Resident	Non-resident	International	Total
Applications	411	825	62	1298
Interviewed	181	11	1	193
Deferred	1	1	0	2
Matriculants				
Early Assurance Program	n/a	n/a	n/a	n/a
Early Decision Program	12	0	1	13
Baccalaureate/M.D.	4	0	0	4
M.D./Ph.D.	0	0	0	0
Matriculated	69	4	1	**74**

Applications accepted from International Applicants: Yes

Specialty Choice

2005, 2006, 2007 Graduates, Specialty Choice (As reported by program directors to GME Track™)	
Anesthesiology	2%
Emergency Medicine	4%
Family Practice	3%
Internal Medicine	23%
Obstetrics/Gynecology	9%
Orthopaedic Surgery	0%
Pediatrics	12%
Psychiatry	1%
Radiology	6%
Surgery	11%

Matriculant Demographics: 2009–2010 First Year Class

Men: 41   **Women:** 33

Matriculants' Self-Reported Race/Ethnicity

Mexican American	0	**Korean**	0
Cuban	0	**Vietnamese**	1
Puerto Rican	1	**Other Asian**	2
Other Hispanic	0	**Total Asian**	10
Total Hispanic	1	**Native American**	0
Chinese	1	**Black**	3
Asian Indian	4	**Native Hawaiian**	0
Pakistani	1	**White**	60
Filipino	0	**Unduplicated Number**	
Japanese	1	**of Matriculants**	74

Science and Math Majors: 81%
Matriculants with:
  Baccalaureate degree: 100%
  Graduate degree(s): 4%

Financial Information

Source: 2008–2009 LCME I-B survey and 2009–2010 AAMC TSF questionnaire

	Residents	Non-residents
Total Cost of Attendance	$44,336	$60,944
Tuition and Fees	$19,643	$36,251
Other (includes living expenses)	$21,673	$21,673
Health Insurance (can be waived)	$3,020	$3,020

Average 2009 Graduate Indebtedness: $130,890
% of Enrolled Students Receiving Aid: 91%

Criminal Background Check

This medical school does not require a criminal background check prior to matriculation.

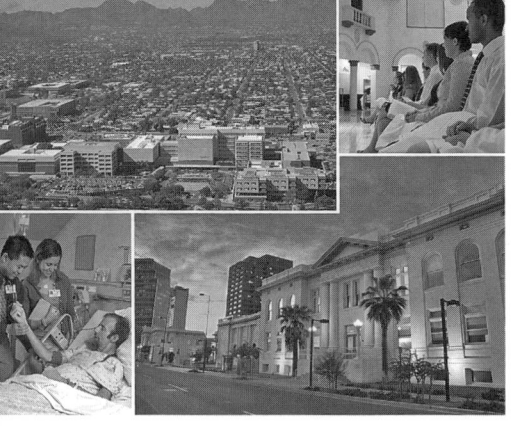

University of Arizona College of Medicine

Tucson, Arizona

Admissions Office - Tucson
P.O. Box 245075, Tucson, Arizona 85724-5075
Office of Admissions and Student Affairs - Phoenix
550 E Van Buren Street, Phoenix, Arizona 85043
T 520 626 6214 (Tucson), 602 827 2005 (Phoenix)
F 520 626 3777 (Tucson), 602 827 2212 (Phoenix)

Admissions www.admissions.medicine.arizona.edu
Main www.medicine.arizona.edu/
Financial www.medicine.arizona.edu/financial-aid
E-mail medapp@email.arizona.edu (Tucson)
phxmed@email.arizona.edu (Phoenix)

Public Institution

Dr. Steven Goldschmid, Dean - Tucson

Dr. Stuart D. Flynn, Dean - Phoenix

Dr. Jacqueline A. Chadwick, Vice Dean for Academic Affairs - Phoenix

Dr. Lee Jones, Associate Dean, Student Affairs & Admissions - Tucson

Dr. Ana Maria Lopez, Associate Dean, Office of Outreach & Multicultural Affairs - Tucson

Maggie Gumble, Associate Director, Financial Aid - Tucson

General Information

The University of Arizona College of Medicine provides education and training for the MD and PhD degrees through two separate four-year campuses: Tucson and Phoenix. The Tucson campus enrolled its first class of medical students in 1967 and is located adjacent to the main UA campus. Located in downtown Phoenix and run in partnership with Arizona State University, Phoenix started in 1992 as a clinical campus and became a four-year campus in 2006.

Mission Statement

The Tucson and Phoenix campuses offer distinct, but related four-year educational programs leading to the M.D. degree. Both are designed for student achievement in the following six core competencies: (1) Medical Knowledge; (2) Patient Care; (3) Interpersonal and Communication skills; (4) Professionalism; (5) Practice-based Learning and Improvement; and (6) Systems-based Practice & Population Health.

Curricular Highlights

Community Service Requirement: Extensive community service opportunities.
Research/Thesis Requirement: Scholarly Project required in Phoenix.

The educational track at each campus utilizes a similar core structure, while each also offers distinct elements. The first two years of curricula at each campus are structured in integrated blocks that focus on organs systems. The second two years consist of required clinical clerkships in key disciplines and significant time for elective work. Basic and clinical science are inter-woven with threads: behavioral science and humanism, health and society, and interprofessional education. Both curricula emphasize active learning, guided independent learning, working in teams, and early clinical experience. Nearly all students take part in our robust co-curricular activities, including medical student research, rural health and service learning programs.

USMLE

Step 1: Required. Students must record a passing score for graduation, but not promotion.
Step 2: Clinical Skills (CS): Required. Students must only record a score.
Step 2: Clinical Knowledge (CK): Required. Students must record a passing total score to graduate.

Selection Factors

Each campus gives strong preference to residents of Arizona, Native Americans who reside on reservations contiguous with the State of Arizona, and WICHE applicants from Montana and Wyoming. Highly qualified non-resident applicants will be considered for up to 25% of the student body.

Many factors are considered when evaluating applicants, including the entire academic record, performance on the MCAT, personal statement, interviews, and letters of recommendation. Applicants are chosen on the basis of their career goals, motivation, academic ability, integrity, maturity, altruism, communication skills, and leadership abilities. Clinical, research, and community service experience are viewed favorably. Each campus strives to accept a student body representative of the diverse Arizona population and who are determined to best meet the medical needs of our state. Students who are conversant in Spanish are highly encouraged to apply.

Financial Aid

Each campus is staffed with financial aid officer(s) to serve the respective student body.

Information about Diversity Programs

Each campus believes in the educational benefits of a diverse student body, and provides ample opportunities and activities that enhance the educational experience.

Campus Information

Setting

The Tucson campus is located on the campus of the University of Arizona, with all the facilities and services expected of a major university and is contiguous to the University Medical Center and faculty clinics. It is adjacent to the Colleges of Nursing, Pharmacy, and Public Health and to the interdisciplinary Bio5 Research Institute. The University of Arizona College of Medicine has numerous affiliated hospitals and clinical sites and many research affiliations throughout Arizona.

The Phoenix campus, named the University of Arizona College of Medicine-Phoenix in partnership with Arizona State University, is located on the Phoenix Biomedical Campus, also home to the UA College of Pharmacy, Arizona State University Department of Biomedical Informatics, Northern Arizona University Allied Health programs and the Translational Genomics Research Institute. The Phoenix Biomedical Campus is near the ASU Downtown Campus, which includes the ASU College of Nursing and Healthcare Innovation and School of Social Work. Multiple clinical affiliates throughout the greater Phoenix area serve as training sites for the Phoenix students.

Enrollment

For 2009, total enrollment was: 577

Application Process and Requirements 2011–2012

Primary Application Service: AMCAS
Earliest filing date: June 1, 2010
Latest filing date: November 1, 2010

Secondary Application Required?: Yes
Sent to: Selected Applicants
URL: n/a
Fee: Yes, $100
Fee waiver available: Yes
Earliest filing date: July 1, 2010
Latest filing date: January 15, 2011

MCAT® required?: Yes
Latest MCAT® considered: September 2010
Oldest MCAT® considered: 2007

Early Decision Program: School does not have EDP
Applicants notified: N/A
EDP available for: N/A

Regular Acceptance Notice
Earliest date: December 2010
Latest date: Until class is full
Applicant's Response to Acceptance Offer – Maximum Time: Two weeks

Requests for Deferred Entrance Considered: Yes

Deposit to Hold Place in Class: No
Deposit (Resident): N/A
Deposit (Non-resident): N/A
Deposit due: N/A
Applied to tuition: N/A
Deposit refundable: N/A
Refundable by: N/A

Estimated number of new entrants: 163

EDP: N/A, special program: n/a

Start Month/Year: July (Phoenix), August (Tucson) 2011

Interview Format: One-to-two on-site interviews. Regional interviews are not available. Video interviews are not available.

Other Programs

PREPARATORY PROGRAMS
Postbaccalaureate Program: No
Summer Program: No

COMBINED DEGREE PROGRAMS
Baccalaureate/M.D.: No
M.D./M.P.H.: Yes, www.admissions.medicine.arizona.edu
M.D./M.B.A.: Yes, www.admissions.medicine.arizona.edu
M.D./J.D.: No
M.D./Ph.D.: Yes, www.admissions.medicine.arizona.edu

Premedical Coursework

On-line courses accepted in fulfillment of prerequisites: Yes

Course	Req.	Rec.	Lab.	Sems.
Inorganic Chemistry	•			2
Behavioral Sciences				
Biochemistry				
Biology				
Biology/Zoology	•			2
Calculus				
College English	•			2
College Mathematics				

Course	Req.	Rec.	Lab.	Sems.
Computer Science				
Genetics				
Humanities				
Organic Chemistry	•			2
Physics	•			2
Psychology				
Social Sciences				
Other				

Selection Factors: 2009 Accepted Applicants

Proportion of Accepted Applicants with Relevant Experience (Data Self-Reported to AMCAS®)	
Community Service/Volunteer	73%
Medically-Related Work	93%
Research	80%

Shaded bar represents school's accepted scores ranging from the 10th percentile to the 90th percentile   School Median ●   National Median ◐

Overall GPA	2.0	2.1	2.2	2.3	2.4	2.5	2.6	2.7	2.8	2.9	3.0	3.1	3.2	3.3	3.4	3.5	3.6	3.7	(3.8)	3.9	4.0
Science GPA	2.0	2.1	2.2	2.3	2.4	2.5	2.6	2.7	2.8	2.9	3.0	3.1	3.2	3.3	3.4	3.5	3.6	(3.7)	3.8	3.9	4.0

MCAT® Total Numeric Score 9 10 11 12 13 14 15 16 17 18 19 20 21 22 23 24 25 26 27 28 29 (30) 31 (32) 33 34 35 36 37 38 39 40 41 42 43

Writing Sample			J	K	L	M	N	O	P	(Q)	R	S	T
Verbal Reasoning	3	4	5	6	7	8	9	(10)	11	12	13	14	15
Biological Sciences	3	4	5	6	7	8	9	(10)	(11)	12	13	14	15
Physical Sciences	3	4	5	6	7	8	9	(10)	(11)	12	13	14	15

Acceptance & Matriculation Data for 2009–2010 First Year Class

	Resident	Non-resident	International	Total
Applications	598	228	6	832
Interviewed	476	18	0	494
Deferred	2	0	0	2
Matriculants				
Early Assurance Program	n/a	n/a	n/a	n/a
Early Decision Program	0	0	0	0
Baccalaureate/M.D.	n/a	n/a	n/a	n/a
M.D./Ph.D.	0	0	0	0
Matriculated	160	3	0	**163**

Applications accepted from International Applicants: No

Matriculant Demographics: 2009–2010 First Year Class

Men: 75   **Women:** 88

Matriculants' Self-Reported Race/Ethnicity

Mexican American	8	Korean	4
Cuban	0	Vietnamese	2
Puerto Rican	1	Other Asian	4
Other Hispanic	3	Total Asian	32
Total Hispanic	12	Native American	2
Chinese	11	Black	4
Asian Indian	10	Native Hawaiian	1
Pakistani	0	White	121
Filipino	3	Unduplicated Number	
Japanese	2	of Matriculants	163

Science and Math Majors: 61%
Matriculants with:
Baccalaureate degree: 100%
Graduate degree(s): 13%

Specialty Choice

2005, 2006, 2007 Graduates, Specialty Choice (As reported by program directors to GME Track™)	
Anesthesiology	5%
Emergency Medicine	9%
Family Practice	13%
Internal Medicine	12%
Obstetrics/Gynecology	4%
Orthopaedic Surgery	2%
Pediatrics	16%
Psychiatry	4%
Radiology	5%
Surgery	9%

Financial Information

Source: 2008–2009 LCME I-B survey and 2009–2010 AAMC TSF questionnaire

	Residents	Non-residents*
Total Cost of Attendance	$44,500	$44,500
Tuition and Fees	$22,699	$22,699
Other (includes living expenses)	$20,104	$20,104
Health Insurance (not applicable)	$1,697	$1,697

*Non-resident tuition rates TBD. See School's Web site.

Average 2009 Graduate Indebtedness: $114,829
% of Enrolled Students Receiving Aid: 95%

Criminal Background Check

This medical school does not require a criminal background check prior to matriculation.

University of Arkansas College of Medicine

Little Rock, Arkansas

Office of the Dean, University of Arkansas for
Medical Sciences College of Medicine
4301 West Markham Street, Slot 551
Little Rock, Arkansas 72205-7199
T 501 686 5354 **F** 501 686 5873

Admissions www.uams.edu/com/applicants/
Main www.uams.edu/com/
Financial www.uams.edu/com/fin-aid/default.asp
E-mail southtomg@uams.edu

Public Institution

Dr. Debra Fiser, Vice Chancellor and Dean

Dr. Richard P. Wheeler, Executive Associate Dean, Academic Affairs

Tom G. South, Assistant Dean, Admissions and Financial Aid

Dr. Billy R. Thomas, Associate Dean, Office of Diversity

Gina Daulton, Director, Student Financial Aid

Linda DuPuy, Director of Admissions and Recruitment

General Information

In 1879, eight visionary physicians had the foresight to each invest $625 to secure a charter from the Arkansas Industrial University. On October 7, 1879, the medical school opened its doors to 22 eager students. From these humble beginnings grew the excellence and prestige now embodied in the College of Medicine. Today, the College of Medicine has over 1000 full-time and part-time faculty, over 600 residents, and almost 600 medical students. UAMS is Arkansas' only institution of professional and graduate education devoted solely to the health and biological sciences. In fulfilling its educational mission, the College of Medicine, in conjunction with the UAMS Medical Center, provides the environment and opportunities for students and practitioners alike to learn and maintain the knowledge and skills required in the 21st century. Comprehensive services are delivered in an interdisciplinary environment to all Arkansans, regardless of their ability to pay. The school is in the planning phase for a major expansion initiative: a replacement hospital, new student housing, new psychiatry center, an addition to both the Jones Eye Institute and the Outpatient Center, and a new affiliated state psychiatric hospital. The university's commitment is to facilitate discovery through applied research and to teach the best science and compassionate care to tomorrow's caregivers. As much as the school is proud of its past achievements, it believes that its best still lies ahead.

Mission Statement

"In relentless pursuit of excellence, every day" summarizes the essence of the school's fourfold mission to teach, to heal, to search, and to serve.

Curricular Highlights

Community Service Requirement: Optional.
Research/Thesis Requirement: Optional.

Along with the standard courses in anatomy, biochemistry, and physiology, the first year includes a program to introduce the student to clinical contacts and concepts. This is accomplished with formal lectures in medico-socioeconomic topics, small-group discussions, faculty-supervised interviews with patients, and the extensive use of standardized patients. The third year is a full 48 weeks with rotation through the major clinical services. This expanded clinical year provides substantial preparation for the predominantly elective fourth year, which consists of a minimum of 36 weeks to a maximum of 48 weeks of courses selected with the assistance of a faculty advisor. On- and off-campus electives are available to round out preparation for each student's career goals. Opportunities are provided for students to engage in research activities and to pursue graduate courses leading to the M.D./Ph.D. and M.D./M.P.H. degrees. The number of M.D./Ph.D. scholarships has increased significantly in recent years. Students are also provided with expanded opportunities through the M.D./M.B.A. and M.D./J.D. degree programs.

USMLE

Step 1: Required. Students must record a passing score for promotion.
Step 2: Clinical Skills (CS): Required. Students must record a passing total score to graduate.
Step 2: Clinical Knowledge (CK): Required. Students must record a passing total score to graduate.

Selection Factors

Selection is based on scholastic attainment, performance on the MCAT, personal interviews with members of the faculty, and recommendations, particularly evaluations by college pre-professional advisory committees. Applicants

should also demonstrate time and effort devoted to volunteerism and community service. Selection is made without regard to race, sex, creed, national origin, age, or handicap. Unsuccessful applicants may reapply without prejudice. Non-Arkansas residents who have strong ties to Arkansas are encouraged to apply.

Financial Aid

An applicant's financial status is not a factor in selection for admission. The Rural Practice Programs allow students who commit to practice primary care medicine in rural communities in Arkansas to receive loans during medical school. The student is obligated to return to a rural community following residency training and to practice full time for the same number of years the student was assisted during medical school. For each year of service, one year of loans is forgiven until the debt is retired. A unique feature of the Rural Practice Programs allows Arkansas residents on the Alternate List, who are willing to practice full-time in a rural community in Arkansas, to interview with the Arkansas Rural Medical Practice Student Loan and Scholarship Board. If the Board approves the alternate's Rural Practice Program application, the applicant is advanced to the top of the alternate list. For additional details, contact the Financial Aid Office.

Information about Diversity Programs

Students from groups underrepresented in medicine are encouraged to apply. The Office of Diversity has developed an active recruitment and retention program. The five-week Summer Science Program offers an introduction to the medical school curriculum, along with reading and study skill enrichment sessions designed to strengthen students' mastery of these areas. A pre-matriculation program is available to all students accepted for admission.

Campus Information

Enrollment

For 2009, total enrollment was: 618

Application Process and Requirements 2011–2012

Primary Application Service: AMCAS
Earliest filing date: July 1, 2010
Latest filing date: November 1, 2010

Secondary Application Required?: Yes
Sent to: All applicants
URL: www.uams.edu
Contact: Tom South, (501) 686-5354
SouthTomG@uams.edu
Fee: Yes, $100
Fee waiver available: Yes
Earliest filing date: July 1, 2010
Latest filing date: November 1, 2010

MCAT® required?: Yes
Latest MCAT® considered: September 2010
Oldest MCAT® considered: April 2008

Early Decision Program: School does not have EDP
Applicants notified: n/a
EDP available for: n/a

Regular Acceptance Notice
Earliest date: December 15, 2010
Latest date: Until class is full
Applicant's Response to Acceptance
Offer – Maximum Time: Two weeks

Requests for Deferred
Entrance Considered: Yes

Deposit to Hold Place in Class: No
Deposit (Resident): n/a
Deposit (Non-resident): n/a
Deposit due: n/a
Applied to tuition: n/a
Deposit refundable: n/a
Refundable by: n/a

Estimated number of new entrants: 174
EDP: 160, special program: n/a

Start Month/Year: August 2011

Interview Format: Blind team interviews on scheduled interview dates. All interviews are conducted on campus. Video interviews are not available.

Other Programs

PREPARATORY PROGRAMS
Postbaccalaureate Program: No
Summer Program: Yes, www.uams.edu/physiology/eduadv/main.htm
Dr. James Pasley, (501) 686-5128

COMBINED DEGREE PROGRAMS
Baccalaureate/M.D.: No
M.D./M.P.H.: Yes, www.uams.edu
M.D./M.B.A.: Yes, www.uams.edu
M.D./J.D.: Yes, www.uams.edu
M.D./Ph.D.: Yes, www.uams.edu
William D. Wessinger, PhD

Premedical Coursework

On-line courses accepted in fulfillment of prerequisites: No

Course	Req.	Rec.	Lab.	Sems.
Inorganic Chemistry	•			2
Behavioral Sciences		•		
Biochemistry		•		
Biology	•			2
Biology/Zoology		•		
Calculus		•		
College English	•			2
College Mathematics	•			2

Course	Req.	Rec.	Lab.	Sems.
Computer Science		•		
Genetics		•		
Humanities		•		
Organic Chemistry	•			2
Physics	•			2
Psychology		•		
Social Sciences	•			
Spanish & Speech Comm.		•		

Selection Factors: 2009 Accepted Applicants

Proportion of Accepted Applicants with Relevant Experience (Data Self-Reported to AMCAS®)	
Community Service/Volunteer	80%
Medically-Related Work	74%
Research	71%

Shaded bar represents school's accepted scores ranging from the 10th percentile to the 90th percentile   School Median ●   National Median ○

Overall GPA 2.0 2.1 2.2 2.3 2.4 2.5 2.6 2.7 2.8 2.9 3.0 3.1 3.2 3.3 3.4 3.5 3.6 (3.7) 3.8 3.9 4.0
Science GPA 2.0 2.1 2.2 2.3 2.4 2.5 2.6 2.7 2.8 2.9 3.0 3.1 3.2 3.3 3.4 3.5 (3.6) 3.7 3.8 3.9 4.0

MCAT® Total Numeric Score 9 10 11 12 13 14 15 16 17 18 19 20 21 22 23 24 25 26 27 28 (29) 30 31 (32) 33 34 35 36 37 38 39 40 41 42 43

Writing Sample			J	K	L	M	N	(O)	P	(Q)	R	S	T	
Verbal Reasoning	3	4	5	6	7	8	9	(10)	11	12	13	14	15	
Biological Sciences	3	4	5	6	7	8	9	(10)	(11)	12	13	14	15	
Physical Sciences	3	4	5	6	7	8	(9)	10	(11)	12	13	14	15	

Acceptance & Matriculation Data for 2009–2010 First Year Class

	Resident	Non-resident	International	Total
Applications	294	1397	10	1701
Interviewed	269	110	0	379
Deferred	6	0	0	6
Matriculants				
Early Assurance Program	0	0	0	0
Early Decision Program	0	0	0	0
Baccalaureate/M.D.	n/a	n/a	n/a	n/a
M.D./Ph.D.	2	1	0	3
Matriculated	143	22	0	**165**

Applications accepted from International Applicants: No

Specialty Choice

2005, 2006, 2007 Graduates, Specialty Choice (As reported by program directors to GME Track™)	
Anesthesiology	6%
Emergency Medicine	4%
Family Practice	17%
Internal Medicine	14%
Obstetrics/Gynecology	8%
Orthopaedic Surgery	4%
Pediatrics	9%
Psychiatry	8%
Radiology	5%
Surgery	4%

Matriculant Demographics: 2009–2010 First Year Class

Men: 86   **Women:** 79

Matriculants' Self-Reported Race/Ethnicity

Mexican American	0	Korean	0
Cuban	1	Vietnamese	3
Puerto Rican	0	Other Asian	1
Other Hispanic	4	Total Asian	15
Total Hispanic	5	Native American	0
Chinese	3	Black	14
Asian Indian	5	Native Hawaiian	1
Pakistani	3	White	136
Filipino	1	Unduplicated Number	
Japanese	0	of Matriculants	165

Science and Math Majors: 82%
Matriculants with:
      Baccalaureate degree: 100%
      Graduate degree(s): 8%

Financial Information

Source: 2008–2009 LCME I-B survey and 2009–2010 AAMC TSF questionnaire

	Residents	Non-residents
Total Cost of Attendance	$36,780	$53,904
Tuition and Fees	$18,032	$35,156
Other (includes living expenses)	$16,850	$16,850
Health Insurance (can be waived)	$1,898	$1,898

Average 2009 Graduate Indebtedness: $129,886
% of Enrolled Students Receiving Aid: 91%

Criminal Background Check

This medical school requires a criminal background check prior to matriculation.

Keck School of Medicine of the University of Southern California

Los Angeles, California

University of Southern California
Keck School of Medicine, Office of Admissions
1975 Zonal Avenue, KAM 100-C
Los Angeles, California 90089-9021
T 323 442 2552   F 323 442 2433

Admissions www.usc.edu/schools/medicine/
education/admissions
Main www.usc.edu/schools/medicine
Financial www.usc.edu/schools/medicine/
education/financial_aid
E-mail medadmit@usc.edu

Private Institution

Dr. Carmen A. Puliafito, Dean

*Dr. Erin A. Quinn, Associate Dean
for Admissions*

*Althea Alexander, Assistant Dean
for Minority Student Affairs*

Gina Camello, Director of Admissions

*Alicia M. Rugley, Scholarships and
Grants Coordinator*

General Information

The Keck School of Medicine of the University of Southern California was established in 1885 as the region's first medical school. All Keck students train at the Los Angeles County+USC Medical Center, one of the largest medical teaching centers in the United States. Through affiliations with over a dozen other private and public hospitals, Keck students have a highly diverse clinical training experience.

Mission Statement

The mission of the Keck School of Medicine is to improve the quality of life for individuals and society by promoting health, preventing and curing disease, advancing biomedical research, and educating tomorrow's physicians and scientists.

Curricular Highlights

Community Service Requirement: Optional.
Research/Thesis Requirement: Optional.

Students are progressively involved with regular patient contact beginning the first week of medical school. An important feature in the curriculum is the Introduction to Clinical Medicine course. The doctor-patient relationship and interviewing are presented during the first year, and physical diagnosis and history-taking are taught in the second. Groups of six to seven students are led by a faculty member who serves as a clinical tutor for their first two years. The curriculum is designed to enhance students' understanding of the basic sciences and their relevance to clinical medicine. Curricular themes are guided by select Pathways and delivered in a case-centered format with the integration of small-group learning

sessions, directed-independent study, and innovative instructional technologies. The first year of the Year I-II continuum begins with 18 weeks of Core Principles of Health and Disease, followed by 49 weeks of organ system review, ending with a 10-week Integrated Case Study section. Each week of the academic year is composed of approximately 20 hours of lecture and small-group sessions, with an additional 20 hours of directed-independent study or Introduction to Clinical Medicine. Examinations in all systems throughout the first two years are graded pass/fail. Dean's Recognition is awarded on the basis of year-end comprehensive examinations and special projects. The final two years are designed as a continuum of two academic calendar years. Each student's program is individually designed to include 50 weeks of required clerkships, 16 weeks of selective clerkships, 16 weeks of elective clerkships, and required senior seminars. Grading for the final two years is on an honors, high pass, pass, and fail basis.

USMLE

Step 1: Required. Students must record a passing score for promotion.
Step 2: Clinical Skills (CS): Required. Students must only record a score.
Step 2: Clinical Knowledge (CK): Required. Students must only record a score.

Selection Factors

The Admissions Committee seriously considers candidates whose academic achievement and MCAT performance indicate the ability to satisfactorily complete the rigorous demands of the medical school curriculum. Also, the committee evaluates various non-academic factors, including personal motivations, evidence of qualities deemed desirable for the study and practice of medicine, significant achievements in extracurricular pursuits, and demonstrated commitment to service and community.

Financial Aid

A variety of university scholarships and loans are available to supplement federal and state programs. Awards are based on need as demonstrated through a financial statement. Merit based awards are also available.

Information about Diversity Programs

The Office of Diversity at the Keck School of Medicine strives to recruit, enroll, and retain students of all socioeconomic, cultural, and ethnic backgrounds. For additional information and opportunities, please visit *www.usc.edu/schools/medicine/school/offices/diversity.html*.

Campus Information

Setting

Located on USC's Health Sciences Campus, the 31-acre medical campus is part of an ethnically diverse community in northeast Los Angeles. The campus is a short drive away from many of the recreational, cultural, and entertainment activities that Los Angeles has to offer.

Enrollment

For 2009, total enrollment was: 670

Special Features

The Keck School of Medicine ranks in the top 25 U.S. medical schools in terms of federal research support. Its affiliations with Los Angeles County Hospital, one of the nation's largest teaching hospitals, and a number of state-of-the-art private hospitals and centers, provide students with an unparalleled hands-on clinical education in a broad range of diseases and settings.

Housing

The majority of students live off-campus in nearby communities, many of which are within five miles of campus. During the summer months, the Student Services Office compiles and posts listings of available housing and roommate announcements to assist students in finding housing.

Satellite Campuses/Facilities

Supervised by Keck School faculty, medical students play a key role in patient care in more than a dozen affiliated hospitals, including the adjacent LAC+USC Medical Center.

Application Process and Requirements 2011–2012

Primary Application Service: AMCAS
Earliest filing date: July 1, 2010
Latest filing date: November 1, 2010

Secondary Application Required?: Yes
Sent to: All AMCAS-certified applicants
URL: www.usc.edu/schools/medicine/ksomnfl.html
Fee: Yes, $90
Fee waiver available: Yes
Earliest filing date: July 1, 2010
Latest filing date: December 1, 2010

MCAT® required?: Yes
Latest MCAT® considered: September 2010
Oldest MCAT® considered: 2008

Early Decision Program: School does have EDP
Applicants notified: September 15, 2010
EDP available for: Both Residents and Non-residents

Regular Acceptance Notice
Earliest date: November 1, 2010
Latest date: Until class is full
Applicant's Response to Acceptance Offer – Maximum Time: Ten Days

Requests for Deferred Entrance Considered: Yes

Deposit to Hold Place in Class: Yes
Deposit (Resident): $100
Deposit (Non-resident): $100
Deposit due: Within ten days after notification of acceptance
Applied to tuition: Yes
Deposit refundable: No
Refundable by: n/a

Estimated number of new entrants: 168
EDP: 10, special program: n/a

Start Month/Year: August 2011

Interview Format: On-campus interviews only, closed-file. Regional interviews are not available. Video interviews are not available.

Other Programs

PREPARATORY PROGRAMS

Postbaccalaureate Program: Yes, http://chem.usc.edu/undergraduate/premed.html
Summer Program: No

COMBINED DEGREE PROGRAMS

Baccalaureate/M.D.: Yes, www.usc.edu/schools/medicine/ksomnfl.html
M.D./M.P.H.: Yes, www.usc.edu/schools/medicine/ksomnfl.html
M.D./M.B.A.: Yes, www.usc.edu/schools/medicine/ksomnfl.html
M.D./J.D.: No
M.D./Ph.D.: Yes, www.usc.edu/schools/medicine/ksomnfl.html
Master of Science in Clinical & Biomedical Investigations: Yes, www.usc.edu/schools/medicine/ksomnfl.html
Additional: Master of Science in Clinical & Biomedical Investigations: ww.usc.edu/schools/medicine/ksomnfl.html

Premedical Coursework

On-line courses accepted in fulfillment of prerequisites: No

Course	Req.	Rec.	Lab.	Sems.	Course	Req.	Rec.	Lab.	Sems.
Inorganic Chemistry	•		•	2	Computer Science		•		
Behavioral Sciences					Genetics				
Biochemistry	•			1	Humanities	•			
Biology	•		•	2	Organic Chemistry	•		•	1
Biology/Zoology					Physics	•		•	2
Calculus		•			Psychology				
College English	•				Social Sciences	•			
College Mathematics		•			Molecular Biology	•			1

Selection Factors: 2009 Accepted Applicants

Proportion of Accepted Applicants with Relevant Experience (Data Self-Reported to AMCAS®)		
Community Service/Volunteer		70%
Medically-Related Work		92%
Research		88%

Shaded bar represents school's accepted scores ranging from the 10th percentile to the 90th percentile   School Median ◐   National Median ◒

Overall GPA	2.0	2.1	2.2	2.3	2.4	2.5	2.6	2.7	2.8	2.9	3.0	3.1	3.2	3.3	3.4	3.5	3.6	(3.7)	3.8	3.9	4.0
Science GPA	2.0	2.1	2.2	2.3	2.4	2.5	2.6	2.7	2.8	2.9	3.0	3.1	3.2	3.3	3.4	3.5	3.6	(3.7)	3.8	3.9	4.0

MCAT® Total Numeric Score 9 10 11 12 13 14 15 16 17 18 19 20 21 22 23 24 25 26 27 28 29 30 31 (32) 33 (34) 35 36 37 38 39 40 41 42 43

Writing Sample				J	K	L	M	N	O	P	(Q)	R	S	T
Verbal Reasoning	3		4	5	6	7	8	9	(10)	11	12	13	14	15
Biological Sciences	3		4	5	6	7	8	9	10	(11)	(12)	13	14	15
Physical Sciences	3		4	5	6	7	8	9	10	(11)	12	13	14	15

Acceptance & Matriculation Data for 2009–2010 First Year Class

	Resident	Non-resident	International	Total
Applications	3406	2627	276	6309
Interviewed	349	194	2	545
Deferred	3	2	1	6
Matriculants				
Early Assurance Program	n/a	n/a	n/a	n/a
Early Decision Program	1	0	0	1
Baccalaureate/M.D.	6	2	0	8
M.D./Ph.D.	4	2	0	6
Matriculated	118	46	2	**166**
Applications accepted from International Applicants: Yes				

Specialty Choice

2005, 2006, 2007 Graduates, Specialty Choice (As reported by program directors to GME Track™)	
Anesthesiology	4%
Emergency Medicine	7%
Family Practice	6%
Internal Medicine	16%
Obstetrics/Gynecology	6%
Orthopaedic Surgery	5%
Pediatrics	8%
Psychiatry	6%
Radiology Diagnostic	7%
Surgery General	7%

Matriculant Demographics: 2009–2010 First Year Class

Men: 82   **Women:** 84

Matriculants' Self-Reported Race/Ethnicity

Mexican American	14	**Korean**	4
Cuban	0	**Vietnamese**	5
Puerto Rican	2	**Other Asian**	5
Other Hispanic	8	**Total Asian**	41
Total Hispanic	23	**Native American**	0
Chinese	14	**Black**	8
Asian Indian	9	**Native Hawaiian**	1
Pakistani	1	**White**	95
Filipino	2	**Unduplicated Number**	
Japanese	4	**of Matriculants**	166

Science and Math Majors: 66%
Matriculants with:
     Baccalaureate degree: 100%
     Graduate degree(s): 10%

Financial Information

Source: 2008–2009 LCME I-B survey and 2009–2010 AAMC TSF questionnaire

	Residents	Non-residents
Total Cost of Attendance	$72,406	$72,406
Tuition and Fees	$45,482	$45,482
Other (includes living expenses)	$25,938	$25,938
Health Insurance (can be waived)	$986	$986

Average 2009 Graduate Indebtedness: $175,475
% of Enrolled Students Receiving Aid: 91%

Criminal Background Check

This medical school does not require a criminal background check prior to matriculation.

Loma Linda University School of Medicine

Loma Linda, California

Associate Dean for Admissions
Loma Linda University
School of Medicine
Loma Linda, California 92350
T 909 558 4467   F 909 558 0359

Admissions www.llu.edu/medicine/admissions.page
Main www.llu.edu/medicine
Financial www.llu.edu/ssweb/finaid
E-mail admissions.sm@llu.edu

Private Institution

Dr. H. Roger Hadley, Dean

*Dr. Stephen A. Nyirady,
Associate Dean for Admissions*

*Dr. Daisy Deleon, Assistant
to the Dean for Diversity*

Verdell Schaefer, MBA, Financial Aid Director

*Lenoa Edwards, MA, MPH, Assistant Dean for
Admissions*

General Information

The School of Medicine was established in 1909. It consists of basic science facilities and the Loma Linda University Medical Center. Also used for clinical instruction are local, regional, county, community, and Veterans Affairs hospitals. The School of Medicine's objectives include providing the student with a solid foundation of medical knowledge, assisting the student to attain professional skills, motivating investigative curiosity, and instilling a desire to participate in the advancement of knowledge. The school reinforces interest in the practical application of Christian principles through service to humanity.

Mission Statement

The school's overriding purpose is the formation of Christian physicians, educated to serve as generalists or specialists and providing whole-person care to individuals, families, and communities.

Curricular Highlights

Community Service Requirement: Optional.
Research/Thesis Requirement: Optional.
Numerous opportunities available

The School of Medicine seeks to prepare students who will be well grounded in the science and art of medicine. The first two years involve an organ systems-based approach to the study of the biomedical sciences, including their application to clinical medicine. The last two years provide clinical rotations in the major areas of medical practice: surgery, internal medicine, pediatrics, obstetrics-gynecology, family medicine, emergency medicine, ambulatory care, psychiatry, and preventive medicine. Elective time is available for additional experi-

ence in clinical or research areas. Qualified students interested in a career in academic medicine may earn an M.S. or Ph.D. degree along with the M.D. degree in a total of six to eight years. Student performance is evaluated by standard or scaled scores. The grading system is on a pass/fail basis.

USMLE

Step 1: Required. Students must record a passing score for promotion.
Step 2: Clinical Skills (CS): Required. Students must record a passing total score to graduate.
Step 2: Clinical Knowledge (CK): Required. Students must record a passing total score to graduate.

Selection Factors

The MCAT and a minimum of three years (90 semester hours or 135 quarter hours) of collegiate preparation in an accredited college or university in the U.S. or Canada are required. Preference is given to applicants who will have completed the baccalaureate degree prior to matriculation. No specific major is preferred. Demonstrated ability in the sciences is important. CLEP and pass/fail credits are not acceptable for required courses. Applicants are urged to take the MCAT by the spring of the application year. The Admissions Committee seeks candidates who have demonstrated the greatest potential for becoming capable physicians. A strong academic background is needed in preparation for medical studies. While special attention is given to performance in science courses, candidates should also have a solid foundation in the humanities, social sciences, and human behavior. The Admissions Committee seeks applicants who demonstrate problem-solving skills, critical judgment, and the ability to pursue independent study and thinking. For nonacademic qualifications, the committee looks for a commitment to medicine, sound judgment, a positive attitude, the ability to make decisions, participation in meaningful extracurricular activities, emotional stability, and integrity. The School of Medicine is owned and operated by the Seventh-day Adventist Church. While, therefore, preference for admission is given to members of this church, it is a firm policy of the Admissions Committee to admit a number of applicants from other faith

traditions who have demonstrated a strong commitment to Christian principles. No candidate is accepted on the basis of religious affiliation alone. The school does not discriminate on the basis of race, sex, age, or handicap. After receipt of the AMCAS application, each applicant is requested to submit a supplementary form and supply preprofessional faculty evaluations and/or personal letters of recommendation. Invitations for an interview are extended to selected applicants. Applicants with an outstanding academic record and with a particular interest in Loma Linda University School of Medicine are encouraged to apply through the Early Decision Program (EDP). Final selections are made by the Admissions Committee on the basis of overall scholastic record, personal qualities, promise of success as a physician, and commitment to the school's mission.

Financial Aid

The School of Medicine has loan funds available through the Student Finance Office. All aid is awarded on the basis of a uniform needs analysis. Financial aid information is provided to all accepted students. In view of the costs of a medical education, students are urged to plan their financial programs carefully.

Information about Diversity Programs

The School of Medicine encourages applications from persons from groups underrepresented in medicine. The Assistant to the Dean for Diversity works closely with the Office of Admissions to facilitate the admissions process for these applicants.

Campus Information

Enrollment
For 2009, total enrollment was: 696

Application Process and Requirements 2011–2012

Primary Application Service: AMCAS
Earliest filing date: June 1, 2010
Latest filing date: November 1, 2010

Secondary Application Required?: Yes
Sent to: All applicants
URL: Made available upon receipt of verified AMCAS application
Contact: Office of Admissions, (909) 558-4467, admissions.sm@llu.edu
Fee: Yes, $75
Fee waiver available: Yes
Earliest filing date: July 1, 2010
Latest filing date: November 15, 2010

MCAT® required?: Yes
Latest MCAT® considered: September 2010
Oldest MCAT® considered: 2008

Early Decision Program: School does have EDP
Applicants notified: October 1, 2010
EDP available for: Both Residents and Non-residents

**Regular Acceptance Notice
Earliest date:** December 16, 2010
Latest date: Until class is full
Applicant's Response to Acceptance Offer – Maximum Time: 30 days

Requests for Deferred Entrance Considered: Yes

Deposit to Hold Place in Class: Yes
Deposit (Resident): $100
Deposit (Non-resident): $100
Deposit due: With acceptance offer
Applied to tuition: Yes
Deposit refundable: Yes
Refundable by: May 15, 2011

Estimated number of new entrants: 165
EDP: 10, special program: n/a

Start Month/Year: August 2011

Interview Format: Regional interviews are not available. Video interviews are not available.

Other Programs

**PREPARATORY PROGRAMS
Postbaccalaureate Program:** No
Summer Program: No

**Combined Degree Programs
Baccalaureate/M.D.:** No
M.D./M.P.H.: No
M.D./M.B.A.: No
M.D./J.D.: No
M.D./Ph.D.: Yes, www.llu.edu/llu/medicine/basicsciences/msp.html
Lawrence Sowers, PhD, (909) 558-4480, lsowers@llu.edu

Premedical Coursework

On-line courses accepted in fulfillment of prerequisites: No

Course	Req.	Rec.	Lab.	Hrs.	Course	Req.	Rec.	Lab.	Hrs.
Inorganic Chemistry	•		•	8	Computer Science		•		
Behavioral Sciences					Genetics				
Biochemistry		•			Humanities				
Biology					Organic Chemistry	•		•	8
Biology/Zoology	•		•	8	Physics	•		•	8
Calculus					Psychology				
College English	•				Social Sciences				
College Mathematics					Intro to Basic Statistics		•		

Selection Factors: 2009 Accepted Applicants

Proportion of Accepted Applicants with Relevant Experience (Data Self-Reported to AMCAS®)		Community Service/Volunteer	76%
		Medically-Related Work	66%
		Research	64%

Shaded bar represents school's accepted scores ranging from the 10th percentile to the 90th percentile   School Median ●   National Median ○

Overall GPA	2.0	2.1	2.2	2.3	2.4	2.5	2.6	2.7	2.8	2.9	3.0	3.1	3.2	3.3	3.4	3.5	3.6	3.7	(3.8)	3.9	4.0
Science GPA	2.0	2.1	2.2	2.3	2.4	2.5	2.6	2.7	2.8	2.9	3.0	3.1	3.2	3.3	3.4	3.5	3.6	3.7	(3.8)	3.9	4.0

MCAT® Total Numeric Score 9 10 11 12 13 14 15 16 17 18 19 20 21 22 23 24 25 26 27 28 29 30 (31) (32) 33 34 35 36 37 38 39 40 41 42 43

Writing Sample			J	K	L	M	N	O	(P)	(Q)	R	S	T
Verbal Reasoning	3	4	5	6	7	8	9	(10)	11	12	13	14	15
Biological Sciences	3	4	5	6	7	8	9	10	(11)	12	13	14	15
Physical Sciences	3	4	5	6	7	8	9	(10)	(11)	12	13	14	15

Acceptance & Matriculation Data for 2009–2010 First Year Class

	Resident	Non-resident	International	Total
Applications	2019	2498	271	4788
Interviewed	193	184	21	398
Deferred	3	5	0	8
Matriculants				
Early Assurance Program	0	0	0	0
Early Decision Program	2	5	0	7
Baccalaureate/M.D.	n/a	n/a	n/a	n/a
M.D./Ph.D.	0	0	0	0
Matriculated	74	78	7	**159**

Applications accepted from International Applicants: Yes

Matriculant Demographics: 2009–2010 First Year Class

Men: 99   **Women:** 60

Matriculants' Self-Reported Race/Ethnicity

Mexican American	1	**Korean**	23
Cuban	0	**Vietnamese**	2
Puerto Rican	0	**Other Asian**	2
Other Hispanic	8	**Total Asian**	56
Total Hispanic	8	**Native American**	1
Chinese	14	**Black**	5
Asian Indian	4	**Native Hawaiian**	3
Pakistani	1	**White**	98
Filipino	9	**Unduplicated Number**	
Japanese	6	**of Matriculants**	159

Science and Math Majors: 77%
Matriculants with:
      Baccalaureate degree: 99%
      Graduate degree(s): 5%

Specialty Choice

2005, 2006, 2007 Graduates, Specialty Choice (As reported by program directors to GME Track™)	
Anesthesiology	9%
Emergency Medicine	6%
Family Practice	15%
Internal Medicine	12%
Obstetrics/Gynecology	3%
Orthopaedic Surgery	2%
Pediatrics	7%
Psychiatry	6%
Radiology	4%
Surgery	5%

Financial Information

Source: 2008–2009 LCME I-B survey and 2009–2010 AAMC TSF questionnaire

	Residents	Non-residents
Total Cost of Attendance	$62,570	$62,570
Tuition and Fees	$39,408	$39,408
Other (includes living expenses)	$21,570	$21,570
Health Insurance (cannot be waived)	$1,592	$1,592

Average 2009 Graduate Indebtedness: $162,005
% of Enrolled Students Receiving Aid: 89%

Criminal Background Check

This medical school requires a criminal background check prior to matriculation.

Stanford University School of Medicine

Stanford, California

Office of M.D. Admissions
Stanford University School of Medicine
251 Campus Drive, MSOB X301
Stanford, California 94305-5404
T 650 723 6861   F 650 725 7855

Admissions http://med.stanford.edu/md/admissions
Main http://med.stanford.edu
Financial http://med.stanford.edu/md/financial_aid
E-mail mdadmissions@stanford.edu

Private Institution

Dr. Philip A. Pizzo, Dean

Dr. Gabriel Garcia, Associate Dean of Medical School Admissions

Dr. Ronald D. Garcia, Assistant Dean of Minority Affairs

Martha Trujillo, Director of Financial Aid

Charlene Hamada, Assistant Dean of Student Affairs

Greg Vaughn, Assistant Director of Medical School Admissions

General Information

The School of Medicine is an integral part of Stanford University. The history of Stanford Medical School begins in 1858 with the founding in San Francisco by Dr. Elias Samuel Cooper of the first medical school on the Pacific Coast. Stanford's School of Medicine is the lineal descendent of this pioneer medical school. In 1908, Stanford University adopted the Cooper Medical College in San Francisco as its medical school and moved it to the university campus in 1959. The Stanford School of Medicine is consistently ranked in the top ten of all research university medical centers in the country.

Mission Statement

Stanford is committed to being a premier research-intensive medical school that improves health through leadership, collaborative discoveries, and innovation in patient care, education, and research. In particular, Stanford seeks individuals whose leadership will result in significant advances in the ability to care for patients. We strive to admit a diverse body of students who are interested in the intellectual substance of medicine and are committed to advancing the field of medicine, broadly defined (i.e. clinical medicine, biomedical sciences, health policy, medical education, and community health).

Curricular Highlights

Community Service Requirement: Optional. Opportunities available and encouraged.
Research/Thesis Requirement: Optional. Opportunities available and encouraged.

Stanford is committed to ensuring that each graduate has fully explored his/her potential as a student and as a scholar. Key goals of the curriculum are the melding of 21st century laboratory and medical sciences, and helping each student build in-depth expertise in an area of personal interest through our Scholarly Concentrations program. While traditional courses and clerkships are required for graduation, the duration of study leading to the M.D. degree may vary from four to six years. All M.D. candidates must satisfactorily complete at least 13 quarters of academic work. Fees for additional quarters are nominal. Courses are graded pass/fail.

USMLE

Step 1: Required. Students must record a passing score for promotion.
Step 2: Clinical Skills (CS): Required. Students must only record a score.
Step 2: Clinical Knowledge (CK): Required. Students must record a passing total score to graduate.

Selection Factors

Stanford does not discriminate on the basis of race, religion, national origin, sex, marital status, age, or disability. The applicant's state of residence is not relevant in the selection process. Applicants whose MCAT scores are below the national mean are highly unlikely to be admitted to the medical school. Transfer Students: For information on the transfer policy, see the Stanford Web site.

Financial Aid

Available grant and loan funds are awarded to students on the basis of demonstrated need. Our generous financial aid program allows our students to graduate with one of the lowest educational debts for any medical school, private or public. For federal aid, students are considered to be independent. For university-based aid, students are considered to be dependent up until the age of 30, and the school will consider the student's parents' ability to contribute to the cost of financing the student's education in determining eligibility for institutional loans and grants. Foreign students must complete a certification of finances reflecting an account of funds to cover the cost of education for the M.D. degree.

Information about Diversity Programs

Stanford takes pride in its highly diverse and exceptionally qualified student body and is committed to increasing the representation of members of groups underrepresented in medicine. A year long program in Leadership in Health Disparities provides all Stanford medical students with the skills, attitudes and knowledge to address the social determinants of health and understand the urgency to provide access to high quality care to all communities.

Campus Information

Setting
The school is located on the 8,800 acre campus of Stanford University (second largest university complex in the world) and is situated in Northern California, approximately 35 miles south of San Francisco and 25 miles north of San Jose.

Enrollment
For 2009, total enrollment was: 470

Special Features
The combination of scientists who pursue basic science research questions and clinicians closely involved in patient care leads to innovative, fruitful collaboration. An example is Bio-X, a unique program designed to promote interdepartmental bioscience research. The program fosters the convergence of leading-edge research in basic, applied and clinical sciences across the spectrum from molecules to organisms. The program involves the schools of Humanities and Sciences, Engineering, and Medicine and is housed in the James H. Clark Center for Biomedical and Engineering Sciences.

Housing
On-campus housing is guaranteed for the first year.

Satellite Campuses/Facilities
Student rotations take place in the major clinical teaching facilities: Stanford Hospital (663 beds), Lucile Packard Children's Hospital (152 beds), Santa Clara County Valley Medical Center (791 beds), the Palo Alto Veterans Affairs Hospital (1,000 beds), and Kaiser Santa Clara Medical Center (327 beds).

Application Process and Requirements 2011–2012

Primary Application Service: AMCAS
Earliest filing date: June 1, 2010
Latest filing date: October 15, 2010

Secondary Application Required?: Yes
Sent to: All applicants
URL: https://med.stanford.edu/aes/
Fee: Yes, $80
Fee waiver available: Yes
Earliest filing date: July 1, 2010
Latest filing date: November 15, 2010

MCAT® required?: Yes
Latest MCAT® considered: September 2010
Oldest MCAT® considered: August 2007

Early Decision Program: School does have EDP
Applicants notified: October 1, 2010
EDP available for: Both Residents and Non-residents

Regular Acceptance Notice
Earliest date: December 2010
Latest date: Until class is full
Applicant's Response to Acceptance Offer – Maximum Time: Two weeks

Requests for Deferred Entrance Considered: Yes

Deposit to Hold Place in Class: Yes
Deposit (Resident): $100
Deposit (Non-resident): $100
Deposit due: May 15, 2010
Applied to tuition: Yes
Deposit refundable: Yes
Refundable by: May 15, 2011

Estimated number of new entrants: 86
EDP: 1, special program: n/a

Start Month/Year: August 2011

Interview Format: One faculty and one student interview. Regional interviews are not available. Video interviews are not available.

Other Programs

PREPARATORY PROGRAMS
Postbaccalaureate Program: No
Summer Program: Yes, http://coe.stanford.edu/

COMBINED DEGREE PROGRAMS
Baccalaureate/M.D.: No
M.D./M.P.H.: Yes, http://med.stanford.edu/md-mph/
M.D./M.B.A.: No
M.D./J.D.: No
M.D./Ph.D.: Yes, http://mstp.stanford.edu

Premedical Coursework

On-line courses accepted in fulfillment of prerequisites: Case-by-case basis

Course	Req.	Rec.	Lab.	Sems.	Course	Req.	Rec.	Lab.	Sems.
Inorganic Chemistry	•		•	2	Computer Science				
Behavioral Sciences		•			Genetics		•		
Biochemistry		•			Humanities		•		
Biology	•		•	2	Organic Chemistry	•		•	2
Biology/Zoology					Physics	•		•	2
Calculus		•			Psychology				
College English		•			Social Sciences		•		
College Mathematics									

Selection Factors: 2009 Accepted Applicants

Proportion of Accepted Applicants with Relevant Experience (Data Self-Reported to AMCAS®)		
Community Service/Volunteer		74%
Medically-Related Work		87%
Research		96%

Shaded bar represents school's accepted scores ranging from the 10th percentile to the 90th percentile   School Median ●   National Median ○

Overall GPA	2.0	2.1	2.2	2.3	2.4	2.5	2.6	2.7	2.8	2.9	3.0	3.1	3.2	3.3	3.4	3.5	3.6	3.7	3.8	(3.9)	4.0
Science GPA	2.0	2.1	2.2	2.3	2.4	2.5	2.6	2.7	2.8	2.9	3.0	3.1	3.2	3.3	3.4	3.5	3.6	3.7	(3.8)	3.9	4.0

MCAT® Total Numeric Score 9 10 11 12 13 14 15 16 17 18 19 20 21 22 23 24 25 26 27 28 29 30 31 (32) 33 34 (35) 36 37 38 39 40 41 42 43

Writing Sample			J	K	L	M	N	O	P	(Q)	R	S	T
Verbal Reasoning	3	4	5	6	7	8	9	(10)	(11)	12	13	14	15
Biological Sciences	3	4	5	6	7	8	9	10	(11)	(12)	13	14	15
Physical Sciences	3	4	5	6	7	8	9	10	(11)	(12)	13	14	15

Acceptance & Matriculation Data for 2009–2010 First Year Class

	Resident	Non-resident	International	Total
Applications	2293	3231	296	5820
Interviewed	157	273	20	450
Deferred	3	2	1	6
Matriculants				
Early Assurance Program	n/a	n/a	n/a	n/a
Early Decision Program	0	0	0	0
Baccalaureate/M.D.	n/a	n/a	n/a	n/a
M.D./Ph.D.	1	4	0	5
Matriculated	36	44	6	**86**

Applications accepted from International Applicants: Yes

Matriculant Demographics: 2009–2010 First Year Class

Men: 40   **Women:** 46

Matriculants' Self-Reported Race/Ethnicity

Mexican American	4	Korean	3
Cuban	0	Vietnamese	2
Puerto Rican	0	Other Asian	3
Other Hispanic	5	Total Asian	34
Total Hispanic	9	Native American	1
Chinese	15	Black	5
Asian Indian	10	Native Hawaiian	0
Pakistani	1	White	34
Filipino	1	Unduplicated Number	
Japanese	1	of Matriculants	86

Science and Math Majors: 73%
Matriculants with:
   Baccalaureate degree: 100%
   Graduate degree(s): 24%

Specialty Choice

2005, 2006, 2007 Graduates, Specialty Choice (As reported by program directors to GME Track™)	
Anesthesiology	5%
Emergency Medicine	7%
Family Practice	5%
Internal Medicine	13%
Obstetrics/Gynecology	2%
Orthopaedic Surgery	4%
Pediatrics	11%
Psychiatry	6%
Radiology	5%
Surgery	8%

Financial Information

Source: 2008–2009 LCME I-B survey and 2009–2010 AAMC TSF questionnaire

	Residents	Non-residents
Total Cost of Attendance	$73,856	$73,856
Tuition and Fees	$45,909	$45,909
Other (includes living expenses)	$25,547	$25,547
Health Insurance (can be waived)	$2,400	$2,400

Average 2009 Graduate Indebtedness: $90,006
% of Enrolled Students Receiving Aid: 80%

Criminal Background Check

This medical school does not require a criminal background check prior to matriculation.

University of California, Davis, School of Medicine

Sacramento, California

Office of Admissions
UC Davis School of Medicine
4610 X Street, Suite 1202
Sacramento California 95817
T 916 734 4800

Admissions www.ucdmc.ucdavis.edu/mdprogram/
admissions/
Main www.ucdmc.ucdavis.edu/medschool/
Financial www.ucdmc.ucdavis.edu/mdprogram/
/financialaid/
E-mail medadmsinfo@ucdavis.edu

Public Institution

Dr. Claire Pomeroy, Dean

Edward D. Dagang, Sr., Director of Admissions

Dr. Mark Henderson, Associate Dean, Admissions

Lauren Snow, Financial Aid Director

*Dr. Darin Latimore, Director,
Medical Student Diversity*

General Information

With a new, state-of-the-art home on the Sacramento campus, the UC Davis School of medicine prides itself in offering a rich and diverse academic environment. The school grooms students for leadership roles in medicine, research, health policy, medical education and management/administration. Distinctions include: ranking in the top 50 schools for research and primary care, strong, dual-degree programs (M.P.H., M.B.A., Ph.D.), and a new five-year program for students interested in telecommunications-enhanced rural medicine. The school admitted its first class in 1968.

Mission Statement

With a mantra of, "Learn. Discover. Share.", the school's educational mission is to create a supportive and collaborative environment which empowers students to develop skills, knowledge and attitudes to become tomorrow's leaders in patient care, public service, research and education. The mission of the larger UC Davis Health System is "discovering and sharing knowledge to advance health."

Curricular Highlights

Community Service Requirement: Optional.
Research/Thesis Requirement: Optional.

UC Davis believes that acquiring and perfecting the skills needed to become a compassionate, culturally-competent and knowledgeable physician requires a combination of hands-on experiences, didactic instruction and problem-based challenges. With an emphasis on self-directed and small group learning, our curriculum is designed to encourage students to evaluate, think and formulate decisions to provide the highest level of patient care. Basic and clinical science courses are designed to illuminate situations that arise in the clinical setting as well as to spark interest in biomedical research, public health and other areas. A cutting-edge Clinical Skills Center in our new medical education building maximizes technology's role in learning from standardized patients. Finally, our students gain valuable experience through their leadership roles in the community, including our seven student-run free health clinics which benefit various underserved populations in the diverse Sacramento area.

USMLE

Step 1: Required. Students must record a passing score for promotion.
Step 2: Clinical Skills (CS): Required. Students must record a passing total score to graduate.
Step 2: Clinical Knowledge (CK): Required. Students must record a passing total score to graduate.

Selection Factors

Academic strengths in both physical/biological sciences and humanities are valued, as are experiences in both research and clinical care. We look for a broad array of life experiences which align with our institutional values of diversity, equality, community engagement and accessible healthcare.

Financial Aid

Most financial aid is based on demonstrated need, and a wide range of scholarships, fellowships, grants and loans are available. All students are considered for university-awarded, merit and need-based scholarships.

Information about Diversity Programs

Our curriculum's emphasis on cultural competency aligns well with our diverse medical student body, which reflects the diversity of California. The health system often hosts and/or sponsors local, state and regional meetings of medical student organizations including the Latino Medical Student Association and the Student National Medical Association. The UC Davis Health System's Office of Diversity is committed to fostering a supportive environment that maximizes the learning and working experiences for all medical students, residents, faculty and staff.

Campus Information

Setting

The new Medical Education building is located on UC Davis' growing Sacramento campus. The 140-acre campus is adjacent to downtown Sacramento and is home to our level-one trauma teaching hospital (UC Davis Medical Center), our Children's Hospital, our NCI-designate Cancer Center, a leading national autism facility called the MIND Institute, our outpatient clinics, and a variety of research labs. The Sacramento campus will also soon be home to the UC Davis Institute for Regenerative Cures, the UC Davis Betty Irene Moore School of Nursing and the California Telemedicine Resource Center.

Enrollment

For 2009, total enrollment was: 430

Special Features

The school continues to rise quickly in NIH rankings and was awarded one of the first twelve prestigious NIH Clinical and Translational Science Awards in 2006. In 2005, the school won the AAMC's Outstanding Community Service Award.

Housing

Most students reside in communities surrounding the Sacramento campus, including the thriving urban Midtown area. Sacramento residents benefit from a variety of recreational, cultural, political and nightlife activities while living in one of California's more manageable and navigable cities.

Satellite Campuses/Facilities

Most clinical rotations take place at the UC Davis Medical Center in Sacramento and other facilities in the UC Davis Health System. Others take place at Sacramento's Kaiser, Sutter and Methodist hospitals as well as David Grant Medical Center at Travis Air Force Base and San Joaquin General Hospital in Stockton. Students enrolled in our new Rural-PRIME program have opportunities to rotate through our rural hospital network sites and some students gain credit at hospitals and clinics abroad.

Application Process and Requirements 2010–2011

Primary Application Service: AMCAS
Earliest filing date: June 1, 2010
Latest filing date: October 1, 2010

Secondary Application Required?: Yes
Sent to: Screened applicants
Contact: Terri Hall
(916)734-4800, terri.hall@ucdmc.ucdavis.edu
Fee: Yes, $60
Fee waiver available: Yes
Earliest filing date: June 29, 2010
Latest filing date: December 18, 2010

MCAT® required?: Yes
Latest MCAT® considered: September 2010
Oldest MCAT® considered: September 2007

Early Decision Program: School does not have EDP
Applicants notified: n/a
EDP available for: n/a

Regular Acceptance Notice
Earliest date: October 15, 2010
Latest date: Until class is full
Applicant's Response to Acceptance
Offer – Maximum Time: Two weeks

Requests for Deferred
Entrance Considered: Yes

Deposit to Hold Place in Class: No
Deposit (Resident): n/a
Deposit (Non-resident): n/a
Deposit due: n/a
Applied to tuition: n/a
Deposit refundable: n/a
Refundable by: n/a

Estimated number of new entrants: 93
EDP: n/a, special program: n/a

Start Month/Year: End of July 2011

Interview Format: Open file, two interviews. Regional interviews are not available. Video interviews are not available.

Other Programs

PREPARATORY PROGRAMS
Postbaccalaureate Program: Yes,
www.ucdmc.ucdavis.edu/ome/postbacc/index.html
Summer Program: No

COMBINED DEGREE PROGRAMS
Baccalaureate/M.D.: No
M.D./M.P.H.: Yes, http://mph.ucdavis.edu
Stephen McCurdy, M.D.
(530) 752-8051, samccurdy@ucdavis.edu
M.D./M.B.A.: Yes, www.gsm.ucdavis.edu/students
David L. Woodruff, (530) 752-0515
dlwoodruff@ucdavis.edu
M.D./J.D.: No
M.D./Ph.D.: Yes, http://mdphd.ucdavis.edu
Mark Henderson, M.D., (916) 734-4800,
mark.henderson@ucdavis.edu

Additional Program: www.ucdmc.ucdavis.edu/
medschool/rural_prime/
Rebecca Miller, (916) 734-4105, rebecca.miller@ucdmc.ucdavis.edu

Premedical Coursework

On-line courses accepted in fulfillment of prerequisites: No

Course	Req.	Rec.	Lab.	Qtrs.
Inorganic Chemistry	•		•	3
Behavioral Sciences		•		
Biochemistry		•		1
Biology	•		•	3
Biology/Zoology				
Calculus	•			2
College English	•			3
College Mathematics				
Computer Science				

Course	Req.	Rec.	Lab.	Qtrs.
Genetics		•		1
Humanities		•		
Organic Chemistry	•		•	3
Physics	•		•	3
Psychology				
Social Sciences		•		
College Statistics	•			1
Advanced Biology	•			2
Other				

Selection Factors: 2009 Accepted Applicants

Proportion of Accepted Applicants with Relevant Experience (Data Self-Reported to AMCAS®)		
Community Service/Volunteer		68%
Medically-Related Work		93%
Research		92%

Shaded bar represents school's accepted scores ranging from the 10th percentile to the 90th percentile.   School Median ● National Median ○

Overall GPA	2.0	2.1	2.2	2.3	2.4	2.5	2.6	2.7	2.8	2.9	3.0	3.1	3.2	3.3	3.4	3.5	(3.6)	3.7	3.8	3.9	4.0
Science GPA	2.0	2.1	2.2	2.3	2.4	2.5	2.6	2.7	2.8	2.9	3.0	3.1	3.2	3.3	3.4	3.5	(3.6)	3.7	3.8	3.9	4.0

MCAT® Total Numeric Score 9 10 11 12 13 14 15 16 17 18 19 20 21 22 23 24 25 26 27 28 29 30 31 (32) 33 34 35 36 37 38 39 40 41 42 43

Writing Sample			J	K	L	M	N	O	P	(Q)	R	S	T	
Verbal Reasoning	3	4	5	6	7	8	9	(10)	11	12	13	14	15	
Biological Sciences	3	4	5	6	7	8	9	10	(11)	12	13	14	15	
Physical Sciences	3	4	5	6	7	8	9	10	(11)	12	13	14	15	

Acceptance & Matriculation Data for 2009–2010 First Year Class

	Resident	Non-resident	International	Total
Applications	3565	965	106	4636
Interviewed	572	32	0	604
Deferred	0	0	0	0
Matriculants				
Early Assurance Program	n/a	n/a	n/a	n/a
Early Decision Program	0	0	0	0
Baccalaureate/M.D.	n/a	n/a	n/a	n/a
M.D./Ph.D.	2	1	0	3
Matriculated	91	2	0	**93**

Applications accepted from International Applicants: Yes

Matriculant Demographics: 2009–2010 First Year Class

Men: 38   **Women:** 55

Matriculants' Self-Reported Race/Ethnicity

Mexican American	6	Korean	3
Cuban	0	Vietnamese	6
Puerto Rican	0	Other Asian	1
Other Hispanic	6	Total Asian	30
Total Hispanic	12	Native American	0
Chinese	9	Black	4
Asian Indian	5	Native Hawaiian	2
Pakistani	3	White	54
Filipino	4	Unduplicated Number	
Japanese	2	of Matriculants	93

Science and Math Majors: 61%
Matriculants with:
Baccalaureate degree: 100%
Graduate degree(s): 17%

Specialty Choice

2005, 2006, 2007 Graduates, Specialty Choice (As reported by program directors to GME Track™)	
Anesthesiology	5%
Emergency Medicine	12%
Family Practice	10%
Internal Medicine	14%
Obstetrics/Gynecology	2%
Orthopaedic Surgery	4%
Pediatrics	15%
Psychiatry	9%
Radiology	4%
Surgery	7%

Financial Information

Source: 2008–2009 LCME I-B survey
and 2009–2010 AAMC TSF questionnaire

	Residents	Non-residents
Total Cost of Attendance	$48,662	$60,907
Tuition and Fees	$28,081	$40,326
Other (includes living expenses)	$18,984	$18,984
Health Insurance (can be waived)	$1,597	$1,597

Average 2009 Graduate Indebtedness: $119,700
% of Enrolled Students Receiving Aid: 93%

Criminal Background Check

This medical school does not require a criminal background check prior to matriculation.

University of California, Irvine, School of Medicine

Irvine, California

University of California Irvine School of Medicine
Office of Admissions and Outreach
836 Medical Sciences Court
Irvine, California 92697-4089
T 800 824 5388   **F** 949 824 2485

Admissions www.meded.uci.edu/Admissions
Main www.som.uci.edu/
Financial www.ofas.uci.edu/content/Medical.aspx
E-mail medadmit@uci.edu

Public Institution

Dr. Ralph V. Clayman, Dean, School of Medicine

Dr. Ellena M. Peterson, Associate Dean, Admissions and Outreach

Dr. Charles Vega, Director, Diversity and Community Engagement

Luis Medina, Director, School of Medicine Financial Aid

Gayle Pierce, Director, Admissions and Outreach

General Information

The UC Irvine School of Medicine is in Southern California. Academic and clinical training facilities are located on the UC Irvine main campus, the UC Irvine Douglas Hospital in the City of Orange and its community clinics and affiliates. The School of Medicine has an enrollment of 450 medical students, 650 full-time faculty and 1,500 voluntary members in 25 academic departments. Areas of research and clinical emphasis include: neurosciences, oncology, urology, cardiovascular and pulmonary diseases, infectious diseases, and stem cell research. Special programs within the medical school include MD/MBA and MD/PhD (MSTP) programs and the Program in Medical Education for the Latino Community (PRIME-LC) that incorporates a MD and Master's degree emphasizing Latino heath care issues.

Mission Statement

The UC Irvine School of Medicine is dedicated to advancing the knowledge and practice of medicine for the benefit of society. This mission will be achieved through programs of excellence in education, research, clinical care, and service to the public.

Curricular Highlights

Community Service Requirement: Optional.
Research/Thesis Requirement: Optional.

The curriculum has been designed to provide training in the technical skills necessary to be a competent physician and to foster the humanistic qualities essential to be a well-rounded, caring and compassionate clinician. In addition to the basic science courses in the first two years, substantial clinical material has been integrated

into the curriculum through the Clinical Foundations series which spans the four years of medical school. In the first year, students work with standardized patients to develop interview and physical examination skills. These clinical skills are further strengthened in the second year through a community preceptorship program. In addition, clinically oriented courses are designed to complement the material covered in basic science courses. During the clinical years, students rotate through the core clinical services of internal medicine, family medicine, surgery, obstetrics and gynecology, psychiatry, pediatrics, emergency medicine, radiology and neurology. In addition, students assume advanced clinical responsibilities through intensive care unit experience and a sub internship. Clinical advisors guide students in the selection of 20 weeks of electives tailored to the students' career goals and educational needs.

USMLE

Step 1: Required. Students must record a passing score for promotion.
Step 2: Clinical Skills (CS): Required. Students must record a passing total score to graduate.
Step 2: Clinical Knowledge (CK): Required. Students must record a passing total score to graduate.

Selection Factors

The Admissions Committee screens for applicants whose academic records indicate that they will be able to handle the medical school curriculum. In addition to scholastic achievement, attributes deemed desirable in prospective students include leadership and participation in extracurricular activities, including exposure to clinical medicine, research, and community service. Consideration is given to applicants from disadvantaged backgrounds. Preference is given to California residents and applicants who are either U.S. citizens or Permanent Residents. The School of Medicine does not accept transfer students.

Financial Aid

The Financial Aid Office coordinates financial aid application materials; reviews and evaluates information provided by applicants; secures, manages, and provides funds in the form of scholarships, grants, and loans to assist in

meeting students' educational expenses; and provides debt management counseling.

Information about Diversity Programs

UC Irvine is a multicultural community composed of individuals from diverse backgrounds. The Office of Diversity and Community Engagement and the Office of Admissions and Outreach work together to encourage and support applicants from disadvantaged backgrounds. Post baccalaureate programs provide students from disadvantaged backgrounds the academic platform and support they may need to gain acceptance to medical school. In addition, workshops and conferences are held that are focused on increasing diversity in the Health Sciences.

Campus Information

Enrollment
For 2009, total enrollment was: 450

Special Features
The first two years of medical school are conducted on the UC Irvine campus. A new Medical Education Building opened in 2010 on the Irvine campus. Included in this facility are simulation and clinical skills suites, lecture halls and small group teaching rooms, all with telemedicine and video conferencing capability. The UC Irvine Douglas Hospital is the main university teaching hospital. Also located in the University Hospital complex are a Neuropsychiatric Center, the Chao Family Comprehensive Cancer Center and a Clinical Research Facility. As part of its focus on family and preventive health, UC Irvine has five neighborhood health centers located throughout Orange County.

Housing
On-campus apartment communities are available to single students as well as married students and their families. Services are also available to assist students looking for off-campus housing.

Application Process and Requirements 2011–2012

Primary Application Service: AMCAS
Earliest filing date: June 1, 2010
Latest filing date: November 1, 2010

Secondary Application Required?: Yes
Sent to: Screened applicants
URL: n/a
Fee: Yes, $70
Fee waiver available: Yes
Earliest filing date: July 15, 2010
Latest filing date: January 15, 2011

MCAT® required?: Yes
Latest MCAT® considered: September 2010
Oldest MCAT® considered: September 2008

Early Decision Program: School does not have EDP
Applicants notified: n/a
EDP available for: n/a

Regular Acceptance Notice
Earliest date: November 15, 2010
Latest date: Until class is full

Applicant's Response to Acceptance Offer – Maximum Time: Two weeks

Requests for Deferred Entrance Considered: Yes

Deposit to Hold Place in Class: No
Deposit (Resident): n/a
Deposit (Non-resident): n/a
Deposit due: n/a
Applied to tuition: n/a
Deposit refundable: n/a
Refundable by: n/a

Estimated number of new entrants: 104

EDP: n/a, special program: n/a

Start Month/Year: August 2011

Interview Format: Selected applicants are interviewed by both a faculty member and a student. Regional interviews are not available. Video interviews are not available.

Other Programs

PREPARATORY PROGRAMS
Postbaccalaureate Program: Yes, outreach@uci.edu, www.meded.uci.edu/Admissions/PostBac.html
Summer Program: No

COMBINED DEGREE PROGRAMS
Baccalaureate/M.D.: No
M.D./M.P.H.: No
M.D./M.B.A.: Yes, mchandle@uci.edu, www.healthaffairs.uci.edu/som/meded/Students/MD_MBA/index.html
M.D./J.D.: No
M.D./Ph.D.: Yes, mstp@uci.edu, http://mstp.uci.edu
Additional Program: Yes, primelc@uci.edu, www.meded.uci.edu/PrimeLC/index.html

Premedical Coursework

On-line courses accepted in fulfillment of prerequisites: Case-by-case basis

Course	Req.	Rec.	Lab.	Sems.
Inorganic Chemistry	•		•	2
Behavioral Sciences		•		
Biochemistry	•			1
Biology	•		•	2
Biology/Zoology				
Calculus	•			1
College English	•			1
College Mathematics				

Course	Req.	Rec.	Lab.	Sems.
Genetics		•		
Humanities				
Organic Chemistry	•		•	2
Physics	•			2
Psychology		•		
Social Sciences		•		
Upper Division Biology	•			1
Statistics	•			1

Selection Factors: 2009 Accepted Applicants

Proportion of Accepted Applicants with Relevant Experience (Data Self-Reported to AMCAS®)		
Community Service/Volunteer		71%
Medically-Related Work		95%
Research		93%

Shaded bar represents school's accepted scores ranging from the 10th percentile to the 90th percentile. School Median ● National Median ○

Overall GPA	2.0	2.1	2.2	2.3	2.4	2.5	2.6	2.7	2.8	2.9	3.0	3.1	3.2	3.3	3.4	3.5	3.6	(3.7)	3.8	3.9	4.0
Science GPA	2.0	2.1	2.2	2.3	2.4	2.5	2.6	2.7	2.8	2.9	3.0	3.1	3.2	3.3	3.4	3.5	3.6	(3.7)	3.8	3.9	4.0

MCAT® Total Numeric Score 9 10 11 12 13 14 15 16 17 18 19 20 21 22 23 24 25 26 27 28 29 30 31 (32) 33 34 35 36 37 38 39 40 41 42 43

Writing Sample			J	K	L	M	N	O	P	(Q)	R	S	T	
Verbal Reasoning	3	4	5	6	7	8	9	(10)	11	12	13	14	15	
Biological Sciences	3	4	5	6	7	8	9	10	(11)	12	13	14	15	
Physical Sciences	3	4	5	6	7	8	9	10	(11)	12	13	14	15	

Acceptance & Matriculation Data for 2009–2010 First Year Class

	Resident	Non-resident	International	Total
Applications	3716	832	56	4604
Interviewed	494	17	0	511
Deferred	3	0	0	3
Matriculants				
Early Assurance Program	0	0	0	0
Early Decision Program	0	0	0	0
Baccalaureate/M.D.	n/a	n/a	n/a	n/a
M.D./Ph.D.	4	1	0	5
Matriculated	103	1	0	**104**

Applications accepted from International Applicants: No

Matriculant Demographics: 2009–2010 First Year Class

Men: 48   **Women:** 56

Matriculants' Self-Reported Race/Ethnicity

Mexican American	10	Korean	4
Cuban	0	Vietnamese	6
Puerto Rican	1	Other Asian	7
Other Hispanic	2	Total Asian	40
Total Hispanic	13	Native American	1
Chinese	18	Black	2
Asian Indian	7	Native Hawaiian	1
Pakistani	1	White	49
Filipino	1	Unduplicated Number	
Japanese	2	of Matriculants	104

Science and Math Majors: 75%
Matriculants with:
Baccalaureate degree: 100%
Graduate degree(s): 5%

Specialty Choice

2005, 2006, 2007 Graduates, Specialty Choice (As reported by program directors to GME Track™)	
Anesthesiology	5%
Emergency Medicine	12%
Family Practice	8%
Internal Medicine	17%
Obstetrics/Gynecology	6%
Orthopaedic Surgery	4%
Pediatrics	12%
Psychiatry	10%
Radiology	3%
Surgery	5%

Financial Information

Source: 2008-2009 LCME I-B survey and 2009-2010 AAMC TSF questionnaire

	Residents	Non-residents
Total Cost of Attendance	$50,005	$62,250
Tuition and Fees	$25,571	$37,816
Other (includes living expenses)	$22,090	$22,090
Health Insurance (can be waived)	$2,344	$2,344

Average 2009 Graduate Indebtedness: $117,010
% of Enrolled Students Receiving Aid: 92%

Criminal Background Check

This medical school requires a criminal background check prior to matriculation.

University of California, Los Angeles
David Geffen School of Medicine at UCLA

Los Angeles, California

David Geffen School of Medicine at UCLA
Office of Admissions
10833 Le Conte Avenue
Los Angeles, California 90095-7035
T 310 825 6081

Admissions www.medstudent.ucla.edu/ prospective/
Main http://dgsom.healthsciences.ucla.edu/ms-resources
Financial www.medstudent.ucla.edu/current/fao/
?pgID=210
E-mail somadmiss@mednet.ucla.edu

Public Institution

Dr. Eugene Washington, Dean

Lili Fobert, Director of Admissions

Elizabeth Yzquierdo, Director of Outreach

Gloria Pinedo, Director of Financial Aid

*Dr. Neil Parker, Dean for
Admissions and Students*

General Information

The David Geffen School of Medicine at UCLA is on the UCLA campus. Ronald Reagan Medical Center, Mattel Children's, Neuropsychiatric Hospital, and Jules Stein Eye Institute are all located in the Westwood Campus. These institutions, together with the School of Dentistry, Nursing, and Public Health, are integral parts of the environment. Major affiliations include LA County Harbor and Oliveview Medical Centers, Veterans Affairs Medical Centers West LA and Sepulveda, Cedars-Sinai Medical Center and Kaiser Permanente. The decision of which medical school to attend is extremely important. We provide applicants with critical information on-line. Applicants may check their status on the Admission Web site. Students invited for interviews participate in student tours, meet faculty, students, staff, and members of the Admissions Committee.

Mission Statement

The school seeks students who will be future leaders, have distinguished careers in clinical practice, teaching, research, and public service. The school strives to create an environment in which students prepare for a future where scientific knowledge, societal values and human needs are ever-changing.

Curricular Highlights

Community Service Requirement: Optional. Student-run Clinics are numerous; 80% do service.
Research/Thesis Requirement: Optional. Over 75% participate in research.

The first two years present a thorough grounding in the science basic to medicine. An integrated approach to basic & clinical sciences is enhanced through problem-based learning in small groups. Students are introduced to a holistic approach to patient care from the beginning through the nationally recognized Doctoring course. The first two years center on processes of disease, with emphasis on organ system-oriented instruction. The third year core clerkships encompass internal medicine, surgery, obstetrics and gynecology, pediatrics, psychiatry, family practice, radiology, and neurology. The senior year, through a set of Colleges, provide a unique mentoring and educational experience bringing together student and faculty with similar interests. Senior electives are designed to provide students with a foundation to develop and fulfill personal interests, broaden clinical knowledge, and provide an advantage in securing desired residencies. UCLA has a pass/fail grading system, allowing students to actively participate in school and student-organized activities. There are student run clinics at the Salvation Army Homeless Center, Mobile Clinic, Health Fairs, and activities teaching high school students preventive health, and work with the underserved. Student use summers for research, community work, and international work. The MSTP programs leads to M.D.–Ph.D. degrees for those interested in research. This program requires 3–5 additional years to the M.D. study. Stipends are provided for this program. The school also offers joint M.D.–M.B.A. and M.D.–M.P.H. programs chosen in the junior year. The program is designed for students interested in organization leadership roles. Our Drew program is for those interested in the underserved. Our UCR/UCLA Program is a cooperative venture with the University of California, Riverside. Students spend their first two years at UCR with the same curriculum as UCLA, followed by their final two clinical years at the UCLA School of Medicine.

USMLE

Step 1: Required. Students must record a passing score for promotion.
Step 2: Clinical Skills (CS): Required. Students must record a passing total score to graduate.
Step 2: Clinical Knowledge (CK): Required. Students must record a passing total score to graduate.

Selection Factors

Preference is given to those showing evidence of broad training and high achievement in college education and those who possess those traits of personality and character essential to the success in medicine and the provision of quality, professional and humane medical care. We look for through coursework, school activities, community service and research for evidence of maturity, intellect, scholarship, and service to their communities and to those who are underprivileged and disadvantaged, are culturally aware and are able to speak a second language, especially Spanish. Final selections are made on the basis of individual qualifications and not on the basis of race, ethnicity, sex, age, sexual orientation, national origin or disability.

Financial Aid

Scholarships and loan are available to US citizens and are awarded on the basis of financial need and academics. Every effort is made to provide as much aid as needed.

Information about Diversity Programs

We pride ourselves on the diversity of our student body. Multiple programs to celebrate our diversity are part of student life and are integral to the learning environment.

Campus Information

Setting

We are located on the main UCLA campus offering numerous opportunities for theatre, recreation, athletics and cultural events.

Enrollment

For 2009, total enrollment was: 760

Special Features

A new state of the art medical center opened this year.

Housing

Graduate housing in walking distance is available for the first two years.

Application Process and Requirements 2011–2012

Primary Application Service: AMCAS
Earliest filing date: June 1, 2010
Latest filing date: November 1, 2010

Secondary Application Required?: Yes
Sent to: Screened applicants
URL: Supplied after screening
Fee: Yes, $70
Fee waiver available: Yes
Earliest filing date: n/a
Latest filing date: within 45 days of request

MCAT® required?: Yes
Latest MCAT® considered: September 2010
Oldest MCAT® considered: 2008

Early Decision Program: School does not have EDP
Applicants notified: n/a
EDP available for: n/a

Regular Acceptance Notice
Earliest date: December 15, 2010
Latest date: Until class is full
Applicant's Response to Acceptance Offer – Maximum Time: Two weeks

Requests for Deferred Entrance Considered: Yes

Deposit to Hold Place in Class: No
Deposit (Resident): n/a
Deposit (Non-resident): n/a
Deposit due: n/a
Applied to tuition: n/a
Deposit refundable: n/a
Refundable by: n/a

Estimated number of new entrants: 187
EDP: n/a, special program: n/a

Start Month/Year: August 2011

Interview Format: One-on-one with faculty. Regional interviews are not available. Video interviews are not available.

Other Programs

PREPARATORY PROGRAMS
Postbaccalaureate Program: Yes, www.medstudent.ucla.edu/prospective
Summer Program: Yes, Elizabeth Yzquierdo (310) 825-3575

Combined Degree Programs
Baccalaureate/M.D.: No
M.D./M.P.H.: Yes, www.medstudent.ucla.edu/prospective
M.D./M.B.A.: Yes, www.medstudent.ucla.edu/prospective
M.D./J.D.: No
M.D./Ph.D.: Yes, www.medstudent.ucla.edu/prospective
Additional Program: Yes, www.medsch.ucla.edu/uclaprime/program.htm

Premedical Coursework

On-line courses accepted in fulfillment of prerequisites: No

Course	Req.	Rec.	Lab.	Sems.	Course	Req.	Rec.	Lab.	Sems.
Inorganic Chemistry	•		•	2	Computer Science		•		
Behavioral Sciences					Genetics				
Biochemistry					Humanities		•		
Biology	•		•	2	Organic Chemistry	•		•	2
Biology/Zoology					Physics	•		•	2
Calculus	•			1	Psychology				
College English	•			2	Social Sciences				
College Mathematics	•			2	Other 1 & 2		•		

Selection Factors: 2009 Accepted Applicants

Proportion of Accepted Applicants with Relevant Experience (Data Self-Reported to AMCAS®)		
Community Service/Volunteer		71%
Medically-Related Work		89%
Research		94%

Shaded bar represents school's accepted scores ranging from the 10th percentile to the 90th percentile ▨   School Median ● National Median ●

Overall GPA 2.0 2.1 2.2 2.3 2.4 2.5 2.6 2.7 2.8 2.9 3.0 3.1 3.2 3.3 3.4 3.5 3.6 3.7 (3.8) 3.9 4.0
Science GPA 2.0 2.1 2.2 2.3 2.4 2.5 2.6 2.7 2.8 2.9 3.0 3.1 3.2 3.3 3.4 3.5 3.6 3.7 (3.8) 3.9 4.0

MCAT® Total Numeric Score 9 10 11 12 13 14 15 16 17 18 19 20 21 22 23 24 25 26 27 28 29 30 31 (32) 33 (34) 35 36 37 38 39 40 41 42 43

			J	K	L	M	N	O	P	(Q)	R	S	T
Writing Sample			J	K	L	M	N	O	P	(Q)	R	S	T
Verbal Reasoning	3	4	5	6	7		8	9	(10)	11	12	13	14	15
Biological Sciences	3	4	5	6	7		8	9	10	(11)	(12)	13	14	15
Physical Sciences	3	4	5	6	7		8	9	10	(11)	(12)	13	14	15

Acceptance & Matriculation Data for 2009–2010 First Year Class

	Resident	Non-resident	International	Total
Applications	5383	2635	241	8259
Interviewed	645	176	0	821
Deferred	1	2	0	3
Matriculants				
Early Assurance Program	0	0	0	0
Early Decision Program	0	0	0	0
Baccalaureate/M.D.	n/a	n/a	n/a	n/a
M.D./Ph.D.	7	5	0	12
Matriculated	167	19	0	**186**

Applications accepted from International Applicants: Yes

Matriculant Demographics: 2009–2010 First Year Class

Men: 91   **Women:** 95

Matriculants' Self-Reported Race/Ethnicity

Mexican American	22	**Korean**	8
Cuban	0	**Vietnamese**	12
Puerto Rican	4	**Other Asian**	4
Other Hispanic	4	**Total Asian**	73
Total Hispanic	28	**Native American**	1
Chinese	27	**Black**	20
Asian Indian	11	**Native Hawaiian**	0
Pakistani	2	**White**	82
Filipino	8	**Unduplicated Number**	
Japanese	4	**of Matriculants**	186

Science and Math Majors: 74%
Matriculants with:
   Baccalaureate degree: 100%
   Graduate degree(s): 10%

Specialty Choice

2005, 2006, 2007 Graduates, Specialty Choice (As reported by program directors to GME Track™)	
Anesthesiology	8%
Emergency Medicine	7%
Family Practice	9%
Internal Medicine	11%
Obstetrics/Gynecology	5%
Orthopaedic Surgery	4%
Pediatrics	10%
Psychiatry	5%
Radiology	5%
Surgery	6%

Financial Information

Source: 2008–2009 LCME I-B survey and 2009–2010 AAMC TSF questionnaire

	Residents	Non-residents
Total Cost of Attendance	$52,004	$64,249
Tuition and Fees	$24,550	$36,795
Other (includes living expenses)	$25,890	$25,890
Health Insurance (can be waived)	$1,564	$1,564

Average 2009 Graduate Indebtedness: $107,081
% of Enrolled Students Receiving Aid: 92%

Criminal Background Check

This medical school requires a criminal background check prior to matriculation.

University of California, San Diego, School of Medicine
La Jolla, California

Office of Admissions, 0621, Medical Teaching Facility
UC San Diego School of Medicine
9500 Gilman Drive
La Jolla, California 92093-0621
T 858 534 3880   **F** 858 534 5282

Admissions http://meded.ucsd.edu/admissions
Main http://meded-portal.ucsd.edu
Financial http://meded.ucsd.edu/hsfao
E-mail somadmissions@ucsd.edu

Public Institution

Dr. David A. Brenner, Vice Chancellor and Dean

Dr. Carolyn Kelly, Associate Dean for Admissions and Student Affairs

Dr. Lindia Willies-Jacobo, Assistant Dean for Diversity & Community Partnerships

Carol Hartupee, Director of Financial Aid

Brian Zeglen, Director of Admissions

General Information
Students at the University of California, San Diego (UCSD) benefit from a diverse faculty and access to a wide variety of research and clinical opportunities.

Mission Statement
The overall objective of the medical school curriculum is to instill graduates with the knowledge, skills, and attributes that will lead to their becoming capable and compassionate physicians. Our educational philosophy is to give students an opportunity to go beyond the core curriculum and pursue electives and independent study that take full advantage of the resources available at UCSD and in the surrounding region, helping them to become expert clinicians and scientists who are aware of, and responsive to, community needs.

Curricular Highlights
Community Service Requirement: Optional. Many community service activities are available.
Research/Thesis Requirement: Optional. Independent Study Project is required.

The goal of the medical curriculum and faculty-student interactions is to develop critical, objective, conscientious physicians prepared for changing conditions of medical practice and continuing self-education. The new integrated scientific curriculum will utilize a systems based approach to provide a solid foundation in the various scientific disciplines basic to medicine. Students are introduced to patient care in the outpatient setting from the beginning of their first year. The core curriculum of the last two years is composed of the major clinical specialties taught in hospital and outpatient settings, and relevant extended-care

facilities. Elective opportunities are pursued during both the pre-clinical and clinical years. Several combined M.D.-Master's degree programs are available. A Program in Medical Education in Health Equity (PRIME-HEq) has been recently developed. The Medical Scientist Training Program provides the opportunity to earn both the M.D. and Ph.D. degrees over a seven to eight-year period of study. A Medical Scholars Program at UCSD (B.S.-M.D.) is available for outstanding California high school seniors planning careers in medicine. A second B.S.-M.D. program is available between UCSD School of Medicine and California Institute of Technology.

USMLE
Step 1: Required. Students must record a passing score for promotion.
Step 2: Clinical Skills (CS): Required. Students must record a passing total score to graduate.
Step 2: Clinical Knowledge (CK): Required. Students must record a passing total score to graduate.

Selection Factors
The Admissions Committee selects applicants who have demonstrated intelligence, maturity, integrity, and dedication to the ideal of service to society. The school is seeking a student body with a broad diversity of backgrounds and interests. The Admissions Committee seeks students with broad training and in-depth achievement in a particular area of knowledge, whether in the humanities, social sciences, or natural sciences. Other evaluation factors include evidence of meaningful involvement in extracurricular activities, performance on the MCAT, letters of recommendation, and personal interviews. The Admissions Committee interview evaluates the applicant's abilities and skills necessary to satisfy the non-academic or technical standards established by the faculty and the personal characteristics necessary to become an effective physician. Preference is afforded to California residents, and applicants who are U.S. citizens or permanent residents. The UCSD School of Medicine participates in the WICHE Professional Student Exchange Program. The School of Medicine does not accept transfer students.

Financial Aid
Financial aid in the form of scholarships, grants, loans, and work opportunities is offered to help students in need of financial assistance. Medical Scientist Training Program participants may receive full tuition and stipend support during their combined degree training.

Information about Diversity Programs
The UCSD School of Medicine is committed to expanding the educational opportunities for applicants coming from disadvantaged educational or economic backgrounds. This institutional commitment is expressed through a pre-matriculation summer program, a conditional acceptance program, tutorial support programs, and financial aid assistance.

Campus Information

Setting
UCSD School of Medicine is located in La Jolla, California.

Enrollment
For 2009, total enrollment was: 498

Special Features
UCSD is a hub both for outstanding clinical programs and cutting-edge research. Recognized regional clinical programs include a Level 1 trauma center, an innovative Stroke Center, a leading AIDS/HIV treatment program, and a Regional Burn Center. Other specialized resources include the UCSD Cancer Center, the functional MRI facility, the Institute for Molecular Medicine, and the Stein Institute for Research on Aging. Both the prestigious Ludwig Institute for Cancer Research and the Howard Hughes Medical Institute have significant presences on campus.

Housing
Medical students at UCSD live both in on- and off-campus housing.

Satellite Campuses/Facilities
Clinical rotations are conducted at the UCSD Medical Centers, VA San Diego Healthcare System, Rady Children's Hospital, Scripps-Mercy Hospital, Balboa Naval Medical Center, and a variety of ambulatory care sites throughout San Diego.

Application Process and Requirements 2011–2012

Primary Application Service: AMCAS
Earliest filing date: June 1, 2010
Latest filing date: November 1, 2010

Secondary Application Required?: Yes
Sent to: Screened applicants,
(858) 534-3880, somadmissions@ucsd.edu
Fee: Yes, $70
Fee waiver available: Yes
Earliest filing date: July 1, 2010
Latest filing date: One month after receiving Secondary Application invitation

MCAT® required?: Yes
Latest MCAT® considered: September 2010
Oldest MCAT® considered: January 2008

Early Decision Program: School does not have EDP
Applicants notified: n/a
EDP available for: n/a

Regular Acceptance Notice
Earliest date: October 15, 2010
Latest date: Until class is full
Applicant's Response to Acceptance Offer – Maximum Time: Two weeks

Requests for Deferred Entrance Considered: Yes

Deposit to Hold Place in Class: No
Deposit (Resident): n/a
Deposit (Non-resident): n/a
Deposit due: n/a
Applied to tuition: n/a
Deposit refundable: n/a
Refundable by: n/a

Estimated number of new entrants: 125
EDP: n/a, special program: 18

Start Month/Year: August 2011

Interview Format: Two one-hour open-file interviews. Regional interviews are not available. Video interviews are not available.

Other Programs

PREPARATORY PROGRAMS
Postbaccalaureate Program: Yes, http://meded. ucsd.edu/asa/dcp/postbac/, Saundra Kirk, (858) 534-4171, sjkirk@ucsd.edu
Summer Program: Yes, http://meded.ucsd .edu/ugme/oess/summer_program/, Carrie Owen, (858) 534-1519, cnowen@ucsd.edu

COMBINED DEGREE PROGRAMS
Baccalaureate/M.D.: Yes, http://meded.ucsd.edu/ groups/med-scholars/, Yvonne Coleman, (858) 534-3880, somadmissions@ucsd.edu
M.D./M.P.H.: Yes, http://meded.ucsd.edu/ ugme/goddp/
M.D./M.B.A.: No
M.D./J.D.: No
M.D./Ph.D.: Yes, http://mstp.ucsd.edu/
Additional Program: Yes, http://meded.ucsd.edu/ ugme/goddp/

Premedical Coursework

On-line courses accepted in fulfillment of prerequisites: No

Course	Req.	Rec.	Lab.	Hrs.
Inorganic Chemistry	•			8
Behavioral Sciences		•		
Biochemistry		•		
Biology	•			8
Biology/Zoology		•		
Calculus		•		
College English		•		
College Mathematics	•			8

Course	Req.	Rec.	Lab.	Hrs.
Computer Science		•		
Genetics		•		
Humanities		•		
Organic Chemistry	•			8
Physics	•			8
Psychology		•		
Social Sciences		•		
Other				

Selection Factors: 2009 Accepted Applicants

Proportion of Accepted Applicants with Relevant Experience (Data Self-Reported to AMCAS®)		
Community Service/Volunteer		65%
Medically-Related Work		90%
Research		95%

Shaded bar represents school's accepted scores ranging from the 10th percentile to the 90th percentile | School Median ● | National Median ○

Overall GPA	2.0	2.1	2.2	2.3	2.4	2.5	2.6	2.7	2.8	2.9	3.0	3.1	3.2	3.3	3.4	3.5	3.6	3.7	(3.8)	3.9	4.0
Science GPA	2.0	2.1	2.2	2.3	2.4	2.5	2.6	2.7	2.8	2.9	3.0	3.1	3.2	3.3	3.4	3.5	3.6	3.7	3.8	(3.9)	4.0

MCAT® Total Numeric Score 9 10 11 12 13 14 15 16 17 18 19 20 21 22 23 24 25 26 27 28 29 30 31 (32) 33 34 (35) 36 37 38 39 40 41 42 43

	J	K	L	M	N	O	P	Q	R	S	T
Writing Sample	J	K	L	M	N	O	P	(Q)	(R)	S	T

Verbal Reasoning	3	4	5	6	7	8	9	(10)	(11)	12	13	14	15
Biological Sciences	3	4	5	6	7	8	9	10	(11)	(12)	13	14	15
Physical Sciences	3	4	5	6	7	8	9	10	(11)	(12)	13	14	15

Acceptance & Matriculation Data for 2009–2010 First Year Class

	Resident	Non-resident	International	Total
Applications	3440	1642	10	5092
Interviewed	580	114	0	694
Deferred	4	0	0	4
Matriculants				
Early Assurance Program	0	0	0	0
Early Decision Program	0	0	0	0
Baccalaureate/M.D.	10	0	0	10
M.D./Ph.D.	6	2	0	8
Matriculated	113	12	0	**125**

Applications accepted from International Applicants: No

Matriculant Demographics: 2009–2010 First Year Class

Men: 62   **Women:** 63

Matriculants' Self-Reported Race/Ethnicity

Mexican American	6	Korean	5
Cuban	0	Vietnamese	11
Puerto Rican	2	Other Asian	3
Other Hispanic	3	Total Asian	54
Total Hispanic	11	Native American	4
Chinese	22	Black	5
Asian Indian	12	Native Hawaiian	0
Pakistani	0	White	58
Filipino	2	Unduplicated Number	
Japanese	1	of Matriculants	125

Science and Math Majors: 72%
Matriculants with:
Baccalaureate degree: 100%
Graduate degree(s): 10%

Specialty Choice

2005, 2006, 2007 Graduates, Specialty Choice (As reported by program directors to GME Track™)	
Anesthesiology	6%
Emergency Medicine	10%
Family Practice	6%
Internal Medicine	19%
Obstetrics/Gynecology	5%
Orthopaedic Surgery	4%
Pediatrics	12%
Psychiatry	6%
Radiology	5%
Surgery	4%

Financial Information
Source: 2008–2009 LCME I-B survey and 2009–2010 AAMC TSF questionnaire

	Residents	Non-residents
Total Cost of Attendance	$48,319	$60,564
Tuition and Fees	$25,313	$37,558
Other (includes living expenses)	$21,350	$21,350
Health Insurance (can be waived)	$1,656	$1,656

Average 2009 Graduate Indebtedness: $100,015
% of Enrolled Students Receiving Aid: 89%

Criminal Background Check

This medical school requires a criminal background check prior to matriculation.

University of California, San Francisco, School of Medicine

San Francisco, California

School of Medicine, Admissions
C-200, Box 0408
University of California, San Francisco
San Francisco, California 94143
T 415 476 4044

Admissions http://medschool.ucsf.edu/admissions
Main http://medschool.ucsf.edu
Financial http://finaid.ucsf.edu
E-mail admissions@medsch.ucsf.edu

Public Institution

Dr. Sam Hawgood, Dean

Carrie Steere-Salazar, Director, Student Financial Services

Hallen Chung, Director of Admissions

Dr. David Wofsy, Associate Dean for Admissions

Kathleen Ryan, Admissions Officer

General Information

The UCSF School of Medicine is dedicated to excellence in education, research, and patient care. Woven throughout all of these pursuits is a strong commitment to public service. The UCSF School of Medicine earns its greatest distinction from the quality of its students and its outstanding faculty — including three Nobel laureates, 36 National Academy of Sciences members, 53 American Academy of Arts and Sciences members, 69 Institute of Medicine members, and 17 Howard Hughes Medical Institute investigators.

Mission Statement

The UCSF School of Medicine strives to advance human health through a four-fold mission of education, research, patient care, and public service.

Curricular Highlights

Community Service Requirement: Optional.
Research/Thesis Requirement: Optional.

The first two years consist of integrated core instruction in the basic, behavioral, social, and clinical sciences; clinical experience is introduced within the first week of classes and continues as a longitudinal patient care experience through the Foundations of Patient Care Course. Emphasis is placed on small-group teaching. In the last two years, the various clinical departments provide 54 weeks of Clinical Core, which teach students the basic skills of clinical medicine. The fourth year includes Advanced Studies, which encompass elective rotations, research, and specific fields of inquiry that prepare students for post-graduate training. For more detailed information, visit the School of Medicine Web site at *www.med school.ucsf.edu/curriculum/overview/index.aspx.*

The UCB-UCSF Joint Medical Program is a five-year M.S./M.D. program with the first three years spent at UC Berkeley completing a case-based core medical curriculum, elective coursework and research in support of a health related MS. JMP students then transition to UCSF for their last two years of clinical work. For detailed information, please visit *http://jmp.berkeley.edu.*

USMLE

Step 1: Required. Students must record a passing score for promotion.
Step 2: Clinical Skills (CS): Required. Students must record a passing total score to graduate.
Step 2: Clinical Knowledge (CK): Required. Students must record a passing total score to graduate.

Selection Factors

UCSF students must have demonstrated the ability to perform at a very high level in their prior academic pursuits. Among the many applicants who meet this essential criterion, the school seeks to create a student community that is characterized by diversity in background, extra-curricular talents, academic interests, and career aspirations. There is no single mold that defines a UCSF student. UCSF wants some students who aspire to become terrific doctors, some who will become great scientists, some who will be leaders in health policy, and so on. The goal is to create the most stimulating and enjoyable possible environment in which to live and learn. For further details regarding the admissions process, please visit the School of Medicine's Web site at *www.medschool.ucsf.edu/ admissions/apply/index.aspx.*

Financial Aid

Scholarships are awarded to entering students on the basis of scholarship and/or need. General financial support is awarded through the Student Financial Services Office. Aid packages consist of a combination of loans, grants-in-aid, and scholarships. Financial aid is only available to U.S. citizens or permanent residents. For detailed information, please visit *http://finaid.ucsf.edu.*

Information about Diversity Programs

The School of Medicine welcomes applicants from all ethnic, economic, and cultural backgrounds without discrimination, and has a long-standing commitment to increasing the number of physicians who come from communities that are underserved and/or underrepresented in medicine. As a result, over the last 30 years, UCSF has had one of the highest minority enrollment and graduation rates of any continental U.S. medical school. The curriculum includes both coursework and practical opportunities focused on narrowing health care disparities.

Campus Information

Setting

The main UCSF campus is located in the center of San Francisco, a short walk from Golden Gate Park and no more than 10 minutes from the Pacific Ocean. Downtown San Francisco, easily accessible by car or public transportation, is located approximately two miles from the main campus. Other major UCSF teaching sites include San Francisco General Hospital, the VA Medical Center, the Cancer Center, and the new Mission Bay campus. The surrounding area of northern California provides a natural backdrop and opportunities for recreation that are hard to match.

Enrollment

For 2009, total enrollment was: 595

Special Features

Please visit the UCSF Web site for the latest facts and figures unique to the campus: *http://medschool2.ucsf.edu/facts-figures.*

Housing

For detailed information about housing, please visit the UCSF Housing Services Web site at *www.campuslifeservices.ucsf.edu/housing.*

Satellite Campuses/Facilities

Student rotations may be conducted at the UCSF Parnassus Campus, San Francisco General Hospital, UCSF/Mt Zion, SF VA Medical Center, and the UCSF Fresno Medical Education Program, as well as at several other Bay Area affiliated hospitals and clinics.

Application Process and Requirements 2011–2012

Primary Application Service: AMCAS
Earliest filing date: June 1, 2010
Latest filing date: October 15, 2010

Secondary Application Required?: Yes
Sent to: Screened applicants after preliminary review
Contact: UCSF School of Medicine Admissions
(415) 476-4044, admissions@medsch.ucsf.edu
Fee: Yes, $60
Fee waiver available: Yes
Earliest filing date: August 1, 2010
Latest filing date: January 12, 2011

MCAT® required?: Yes
Latest MCAT® considered: September 2010
Oldest MCAT® considered: September 2008

Early Decision Program: School does not have EDP
Applicants notified: n/a
EDP available for: n/a

Regular Acceptance Notice
Earliest date: December 15, 2010
Latest date: Until class is full
Applicant's Response to Acceptance
Offer – Maximum Time: Two weeks

Requests for Deferred
Entrance Considered: Yes

Deposit to Hold Place in Class: No
Deposit (Resident): n/a
Deposit (Non-resident): n/a
Deposit due: n/a
Applied to tuition: n/a
Deposit refundable: n/a
Refundable by: n/a

Estimated number of new entrants: 150
EDP: n/a, special program: n/a

Start Month/Year: June 2011 (UCB/UCSF Joint Medical Program); September 2011 (UCSF)

Interview Format: Required to interview at UCSF, if invited. Two interviews, 40 minutes to one hour each. Regional interviews are not available. Video interviews are not available.

Other Programs

PREPARATORY PROGRAMS
Postbaccalaureate Program: Yes, www.medschool.ucsf.edu/outreach
Summer Program: No

COMBINED DEGREE PROGRAMS
Baccalaureate/M.D.: No
M.D./M.P.H.: Yes, www.medschool.ucsf.edu/admissions/degrees/Curriculum.aspx
M.D./M.B.A.: No
M.D./J.D.: No
M.D./Ph.D.: Yes, http://medschool.ucsf.edu/mstp
Joint Medical Program: Yes, http://jmp.berkeley.edu/

Premedical Coursework

On-line courses accepted in fulfillment of prerequisites: No

Course	Req.	Rec.	Lab.	Hrs.	Course	Req.	Rec.	Lab.	Hrs.
Inorganic Chemistry	•		•	12	Computer Science				
Behavioral Sciences					Genetics				
Biochemistry					Humanities				
Biology					Organic Chemistry	•			8
Biology/Zoology	•		•	12	Physics	•		•	12
Calculus					Psychology				
College English					Social Sciences				
College Mathematics					Other				

Selection Factors: 2009 Accepted Applicants

Proportion of Accepted Applicants with Relevant Experience (Data Self-Reported to AMCAS®)		Community Service/Volunteer	75%
		Medically-Related Work	91%
		Research	91%

Shaded bar represents school's accepted scores ranging from the 10th percentile to the 90th percentile   School Median ●   National Median ◐

Overall GPA	2.0	2.1	2.2	2.3	2.4	2.5	2.6	2.7	2.8	2.9	3.0	3.1	3.2	3.3	3.4	3.5	3.6	3.7	(3.8)	3.9	4.0
Science GPA	2.0	2.1	2.2	2.3	2.4	2.5	2.6	2.7	2.8	2.9	3.0	3.1	3.2	3.3	3.4	3.5	3.6	3.7	(3.8)	3.9	4.0

MCAT® Total Numeric Score 9 10 11 12 13 14 15 16 17 18 19 20 21 22 23 24 25 26 27 28 29 30 31 (32) 33 (34) 35 36 37 38 39 40 41 42 43

Writing Sample				J	K	L	M	N	O	P	(Q)	R	S	T
Verbal Reasoning	3	4	5	6	7	8	9	(10)	11	12	13	14	15
Biological Sciences	3	4	5	6	7	8	9	10	(11)	(12)	13	14	15
Physical Sciences	3	4	5	6	7	8	9	10	(11)	(12)	13	14	15

Acceptance & Matriculation Data for 2009–2010 First Year Class

	Resident	Non-resident	International	Total
Applications	3159	2754	149	6062
Interviewed	320	181	1	502
Deferred	4	1	0	5
Matriculants				
Early Assurance Program	n/a	n/a	n/a	n/a
Early Decision Program	0	0	0	0
Baccalaureate/M.D.	n/a	n/a	n/a	n/a
M.D./Ph.D.	4	6	0	10
Matriculated	131	34	0	**165**

Applications accepted from International Applicants: Yes

Specialty Choice

2005, 2006, 2007 Graduates, Specialty Choice (As reported by program directors to GME Track™)	
Anesthesiology	9%
Emergency Medicine	8%
Family Practice	6%
Internal Medicine	17%
Obstetrics/Gynecology	6%
Orthopaedic Surgery	2%
Pediatrics	11%
Psychiatry	6%
Radiology	3%
Surgery	6%

Matriculant Demographics: 2009–2010 First Year Class

Men: 73   **Women:** 92

Matriculants' Self-Reported Race/Ethnicity

Mexican American	19	Korean	1
Cuban	0	Vietnamese	2
Puerto Rican	0	Other Asian	4
Other Hispanic	9	Total Asian	49
Total Hispanic	27	Native American	3
Chinese	24	Black	11
Asian Indian	8	Native Hawaiian	3
Pakistani	0	White	93
Filipino	9	**Unduplicated Number**	
Japanese	4	**of Matriculants**	165

Science and Math Majors: 63%
Matriculants with:
   Baccalaureate degree: 100%
   Graduate degree(s): 12%

Financial Information

Source: 2008–2009 LCME I-B survey and 2009–2010 AAMC TSF questionnaire

	Residents	Non-residents
Total Cost of Attendance	$49,075	$61,320
Tuition and Fees	$24,393	$36,638
Other (includes living expenses)	$21,946	$21,946
Health Insurance (cannot be waived)	$2,736	$2,736

Average 2009 Graduate Indebtedness: $101,333
% of Enrolled Students Receiving Aid: 90%

Criminal Background Check

This medical school requires a criminal background check prior to matriculation.

University of Colorado Denver School of Medicine

Denver, Colorado

Medical School Admissions
University of Colorado Denver School of Medicine
Anschutz Medical Campus, Mail Stop 297
13001 East 17th Place
Aurora, Colorado 80045
T 303 724 8025   F 303 724 8028

Admissions www.uchsc.edu/som/admissions/
Main www.uchsc.edu/som
Financial www.uchsc.edu/finaid/
E-mail SOMadmin@uchsc.edu

Public Institution

Dr. Richard D. Krugman, Dean

Dr. Robert A. Winn, Associate Dean for Admissions

Dominic Martinez, Director Office of Diversity and Inclusion

Deedra A. Colussy, Financial Aid Advisor

General Information

The University of Colorado Denver School of Medicine (UCDSOM) is a part of the University of Colorado Denver located in Denver and Aurora, Colorado. The Anshutz Medical Campus in Aurora includes the schools of dentistry, nursing, and pharmacy and the graduate school as well as the SOM. Clinical opportunities for medical students are located throughout the Denver metropolitan area and Colorado. The UCDSOM is home to 1,927 full-time and 2,956 volunteer faculty. In addition to educating students and participating in research, the faculty assumes considerable responsibility for patient care. Student research opportunities and a variety of extracurricular activities are available. The UCDSOM moved to the new 217-acre Anschutz Medical Campus in Aurora in January 2008.

Mission Statement

The mission of the University of Colorado School of Medicine is to provide Colorado, the nation, and the world with programs of excellence in: Education – through the provision of educational programs to medical students, allied health students, graduate students and house staff, practicing health professionals, and the public at large; Research – through the development of new knowledge in the basic and clinical sciences, as well as in health policy and health care education; Clinical Care – through state-of-the-art clinical programs, which reflect the unique educational environment of the university, as well as the needs of the patients it serves; and Community Service – through sharing the School's expertise and knowledge to enhance the broader community, including our affiliated institutions, other health care professionals, alumni and other colleagues, and citizens of the state.

Curricular Highlights

Community Service Requirement: Optional. Many community service electives are available.
Research/Thesis Requirement: Required. A scholarly project is required for graduation.

The curriculum is designed to provide the scientific and clinical background to prepare graduates for the practice of medicine. A systems-based curriculum was introduced in 2005. The Essentials block runs for 18 months. The core clinical year runs through April of year 3. The elective year allows students time to do sub-internships, critical care rotations and other courses essential to their career choices. A capstone presentation and course occurs in the spring of year 4. The Foundations of Doctoring curriculum begins after the first block of year one and continues through year 3. Standardized patients are widely used in Foundations.

USMLE

Step 1: Required. Students must record a passing score for promotion.
Step 2: Clinical Skills (CS): Required. Students must record a passing total score to graduate.
Step 2: Clinical Knowledge (CK): Required. Students must record a passing total score to graduate.

Selection Factors

Places are offered to the applicants who are most highly qualified in terms of intelligence, achievement, character, motivation, and maturity. Grades, MCAT scores, recommendations, and personal interviews are assessed. Humanistic qualities, indications of peer collaboration, and professionalism are characteristics of our students. Approximately 75 percent of the class is comprised of Colorado residents. Applicants from rural areas and from groups underrepresented in medicine are encouraged to apply. Wyoming and Montana (WICHE) applicants are treated as in-state. All undergraduate majors are considered acceptable. Excellent performance in the required science courses is essential. The medical school has an active Medical Scientist Training Program (MSTP) for those who wish to combine medical school with intensive laboratory research. The UCDSOM does not discriminate on the basis of race, sex, creed, national origin, age, or disability. Financial status is not a factor in the selection of applicants.

Financial Aid

The UCSOM participates in federal aid programs and has a number of scholarships which are diversity and merit-based. Colorado student grant funds are available for Colorado residents. Financial aid questions should be directed to (303) 556-2886.

Information about Diversity Programs

The UCSOM encourages applications from qualified students from groups underrepresented in American medicine. Detailed information may be obtained from the Office of Diversity at (303) 724-8005.

Campus Information

Setting

The UCDSOM is an urban campus in Aurora, Colorado. In addition to the schools on the campus, the University of Colorado Hospital, The Children's Hospital, the Barbara Davis Center for Childhood Diabetes, and the Ben Nighthorse Campbell Center for Native American Studies are on the Anschutz Medical Campus.

Enrollment

For 2009, total enrollment was: 614

Special Features

The 2009 total NIH research awards to the SOM and affiliated hospitals were $362,745,000.

Housing

Rental property and roommate information are available in the Student Assistance Office. Call (303) 724-7684 or visit *www.uchsc.edu/ studentassistance*.

Satellite Campuses/Facilities

Besides the hospitals on the Anschutz campus, students rotate through Denver Health Medical Center, National Jewish Hospital, and multiple hospitals throughout Denver and Colorado.

Application Process and Requirements 2011–2012

Primary Application Service: AMCAS
Earliest filing date: June 7, 2010
Latest filing date: November 1, 2010

Secondary Application Required?: Yes
Sent to: All applicants
Ashley Ehlers, (303) 724-8025,
ashley.ehlers@ucdenver.edu
URL: n/a
Fee: Yes, $100
Fee waiver available: Yes
Earliest filing date: August 1, 2010
Latest filing date: December 31, 2010

MCAT® required?: Yes
Latest MCAT® considered: September 2010
Oldest MCAT® considered: September 2008

Early Decision Program: School does not have EDP
Applicants notified: n/a
EDP available for: n/a

Regular Acceptance Notice
Earliest date: October 16, 2010
Latest date: Until class is full
Applicant's Response to Acceptance
Offer – Maximum Time: Two weeks

Requests for Deferred
Entrance Considered: Yes

Deposit to Hold Place in Class: Yes
Deposit (Resident): $200
Deposit (Non-resident): $200
Deposit due: Upon acceptance
Applied to tuition: Yes
Deposit refundable: Yes
Refundable by: July 1, 2011

Estimated number of new entrants: 160
EDP: n/a, special program: n/a

Start Month/Year: August 2011

Interview Format: Two one-on-one academically blind interviews. Regional interviews are not available. Video interviews are not available.

Other Programs

PREPARATORY PROGRAMS
Postbaccalaureate Program: Yes,
By invitation only. Ashley Ehlers, (303) 724-8025,
ashley.ehlers@ucdenver.edu
Summer Program: No

COMBINED DEGREE PROGRAMS
Baccalaureate/M.D.: No
M.D./M.P.H.: No
M.D./M.B.A.: No, www.uchsc.edu/sm/sm/mdmbadegree.htm
M.D./J.D.: No
M.D./Ph.D.: Yes, www.uchsc.edu/sm/mstp/

Premedical Coursework

On-line courses accepted in fulfillment of prerequisites: Case-by-case basis

Course	Req.	Rec.	Lab.	Hrs.	Course	Req.	Rec.	Lab.	Hrs.
Inorganic Chemistry	•		•	8	Computer Science		•		
Behavioral Sciences					Genetics		•		
Biochemistry		•			Humanities		•		
Biology	•		•	8	Organic Chemistry	•		•	8
Biology/Zoology					Physics	•		•	8
Calculus					Psychology		•		
College English	•			6	Social Sciences		•		
College Mathematics	•			6	Other		•		

Selection Factors: 2009 Accepted Applicants

Proportion of Accepted Applicants with Relevant Experience (Data Self-Reported to AMCAS®)		
Community Service/Volunteer		71%
Medically-Related Work		86%
Research		83%

Shaded bar represents school's accepted scores ranging from the 10th percentile to the 90th percentile   School Median ●   National Median ○

Overall GPA	2.0	2.1	2.2	2.3	2.4	2.5	2.6	2.7	2.8	2.9	3.0	3.1	3.2	3.3	3.4	3.5	3.6	3.7	(3.8)	3.9	4.0
Science GPA	2.0	2.1	2.2	2.3	2.4	2.5	2.6	2.7	2.8	2.9	3.0	3.1	3.2	3.3	3.4	3.5	3.6	(3.7)	3.8	3.9	4.0

MCAT® Total Numeric Score 9 10 11 12 13 14 15 16 17 18 19 20 21 22 23 24 25 26 27 28 29 30 31 (32) 33 34 35 36 37 38 39 40 41 42 43

Writing Sample			J	K	L	M	N	O	P	(Q)	R	S	T
Verbal Reasoning	3	4	5	6	7	8	9	(10)	(11)	12	13	14	15
Biological Sciences	3	4	5	6	7	8	9	10	(11)	12	13	14	15
Physical Sciences	3	4	5	6	7	8	9	10	(11)	12	13	14	15

Acceptance & Matriculation Data for 2009–2010 First Year Class

	Resident	Non-resident	International	Total
Applications	584	3017	59	3660
Interviewed	298	273	2	573
Deferred	9	4	1	14
Matriculants				
Early Assurance Program	0	0	0	0
Early Decision Program	0	0	0	0
Baccalaureate/M.D.	n/a	n/a	n/a	n/a
M.D./Ph.D.	3	7	0	10
Matriculated	120	40	0	**160**

Applications accepted from International Applicants: Yes

Specialty Choice

2005, 2006, 2007 Graduates, Specialty Choice (As reported by program directors to GME Track™)	
Anesthesiology	7%
Emergency Medicine	7%
Family Practice	12%
Internal Medicine	20%
Obstetrics/Gynecology	5%
Orthopaedic Surgery	4%
Pediatrics	12%
Psychiatry	6%
Radiology	4%
Surgery	4%

Matriculant Demographics: 2009–2010 First Year Class

Men: 89   **Women:** 71

Matriculants' Self-Reported Race/Ethnicity

Mexican American	3	Korean	3
Cuban	0	Vietnamese	1
Puerto Rican	1	Other Asian	4
Other Hispanic	6	Total Asian	18
Total Hispanic	9	Native American	3
Chinese	6	Black	2
Asian Indian	4	Native Hawaiian	1
Pakistani	0	White	132
Filipino	2	Unduplicated Number	
Japanese	0	of Matriculants	160

Science and Math Majors: 63%
Matriculants with:
     Baccalaureate degree: 100%
     Graduate degree(s): 16%

Financial Information

Source: 2008–2009 LCME I-B survey
and 2009–2010 AAMC TSF questionnaire

	Residents	Non-residents
Total Cost of Attendance	$50,230	$75,056
Tuition and Fees	$28,151	$52,977
Other (includes living expenses)	$19,235	$19,235
Health Insurance (can be waived)	$2,844	$2,844

Average 2009 Graduate Indebtedness: $138,666
% of Enrolled Students Receiving Aid: 93%

Criminal Background Check

This medical school requires a criminal background check prior to matriculation.

University of Connecticut School of Medicine

Farmington, Connecticut

Medical Student Affairs
University of Connecticut
School of Medicine
263 Farmington Avenue, Rm. AG-062
Farmington, Connecticut 06030-1906
T 860 679 4713   F 860 679 6763

Admissions http://medicine.uchc.edu/prospective/admissions/
Main http://medicine.uchc.edu
Financial http://studentservices.uchc.edu/financial/index.html
E-mail fox@nso1.uchc.edu, zeff@neuron.uchc.edu

Public Institution

Dr. Cato Laurencin, Dean

Dr. Richard Zeff, Assistant Dean of Admissions

Dr. Marja Hurley, Associate Dean of Minority Affairs

Andrea Devereux, Director of Financial Assistance

Lynda Fox, Administrative Coordinator

Tracy Dieli, Administrative Coordinator

General Information

The School of Medicine occupies the University of Connecticut Health Center complex in Farmington. The Health Center also includes the School of Dental Medicine, graduate programs in Biomedical Sciences and Public Health, the University Hospital and Ambulatory Unit, Research buildings, and Stowe Library. Students receive clinical training in Hartford area-affiliated hospitals.

Mission Statement

The School of Medicine's curriculum is designed to prepare professional men and women to practice medicine in a health care system that is evolving at an accelerated rate. The curriculum will equip students to formulate creative and courageous solutions to health care problems and issues. The primary goal is to develop in all students a fund of knowledge, skills, and attitudes that will enable them to pursue the postgraduate training necessary for their chosen career.

Curricular Highlights

Community Service Requirement: Required. Numerous opportunities available.
Research/Thesis Requirement: Optional. Numerous opportunities available.

The curriculum is based on a multi-departmental, organ-system approach. Normal structure/ function is presented first, followed by pathophysiology and therapeutic approaches. Students learn medical history-taking, physical diagnosis, and other aspects of the physician-patient relationship. They participate in longitudinal ambulatory clinical experience all four years. Students rotate through major clinical disciplines in the third year. Students complete a sub-internship, courses in emergent and urgent care, a selective experience, and five elective months in the fourth year. The grading system is pass/fail; grading in year three is honors and pass/fail; no class rank or class standing scales are used.

USMLE

Step 1: Required. Students must record a passing score to for graduation, but not promotion.
Step 2: Clinical Skills (CS): Required. Students must record a passing total score to graduate.
Step 2: Clinical Knowledge (CK): Required. Students must record a passing total score to graduate.

Selection Factors

The University of Connecticut accepts highly qualified Connecticut residents, with special effort to include those who are disadvantaged. Highly qualified out-of-state residents are considered to achieve a diverse class. The Admissions Committee considers the applicant's interests, achievements, abilities, motivation, and character. GPA and MCAT scores are considered, along with academic program difficulty, academic achievement beyond regular coursework, intellectual growth and development, nonacademic activities, and recommendations. UCSOM policy prohibits discrimination in education, in employment, and in the provision of services on account of race, religion, sex, age, marital status, national origin, ancestry, sexual orientation, disabled veteran status, physical or mental disability, mental retardation, other specifically covered mental disabilities, and criminal records that are not job-related, in accordance with provisions of the Civil Rights Act of 1964, Title IX Education Amendments of 1972, the Rehabilitation Act of 1973, the Americans with Disabilities Act, and other existing federal and state laws and executive orders pertaining to equal rights.

Financial Aid

Educational costs are modest and the financial assistance program is strong. Financial need is not considered relevant to the admissions process. Every effort is made to meet each student's financial requirements through scholarships and loans. Entrance, exit, and debt counseling are provided.

Information about Diversity Programs

The UCSOM recruits disadvantaged applicants and applicants from groups underrepresented in medicine through the Admissions Office and the Department of Health Careers Opportunity Programs (HCOP). The Admissions Committee reviews applications from these candidates in the same manner as those of all other candidates. Candidates receive a full and sensitive review and are selected on a competitive basis. Candidates invited for an interview meet with HCOP staff. Summer enrichment programs are available for high school and college students from groups traditionally underrepresented in American medicine. The HCOP Department's telephone number is (860) 679-3483.

Campus Information

Setting

The 162 acre Health Science Complex is seven miles west of Hartford, with panoramic views of rural hills and the Hartford skyline. The John Dempsey University Hospital is onsite. A major research university, extensive research facilities are an integral part of the Health Center's lifeblood.

Enrollment

For 2009, total enrollment was: 346

Special Features

Signature programs include The Pat and Jim Calhoun Cardiology Center, The Carole and Ray Neag Comprehensive Cancer Center, and The Musculoskeletal Institute. Research centers include: International Community Health Studies, Microbial Pathogenesis, Molecular Medicine, Immunotherapy of Cancer and Infectious Diseases, and Women's Health Research.

Housing

The School of Medicine helps students identify housing in the local community.

Satellite Campuses/Facilities

Students rotate through clinical sites to insure a mix of inpatient and ambulatory experiences. Students complete a Continuity Practice experience with a physician in the community.

Application Process and Requirements 2011–2012

Primary Application Service: AMCAS
Earliest filing date: June 1, 2010
Latest filing date: December 15, 2010

Secondary Application Required?: Yes
Sent to: All applicants
Contact: Lynda Fox, (860) 679-4306, fox@nso1.uchc.edu
Fee: Yes, $85
Fee waiver available: Yes
Earliest filing date: June 1, 2010
Latest filing date: January 30, 2011

MCAT® required?: Yes
Latest MCAT® considered: September 2010
Oldest MCAT® considered: 2007

Early Decision Program: School does have EDP
Applicants notified: October 1, 2010
EDP available for: Both Residents and Non-residents

**Regular Acceptance Notice
Earliest date:** October 15, 2010
Latest date: Until class is full
**Applicant's Response to Acceptance
Offer – Maximum Time:** Two weeks

**Requests for Deferred
Entrance Considered:** Yes

Deposit to Hold Place in Class: Yes
Deposit (Resident): $100
Deposit (Non-resident): $100
Deposit due: with response to acceptance offer
Applied to tuition: Yes
Deposit refundable: Yes
Refundable by: May 15, 2011

Estimated number of new entrants: 85
EDP: 8, special program: n/a

Start Month/Year: August 2011

Interview Format: One-on-one and group interview session. Some regional interviews are done. Video interviews are not available.

Other Programs

PREPARATORY PROGRAMS
Postbaccalaureate Program: Yes, Dr. Richard Zeff
http://medicine.uchc.edu/prospective/postbac
Summer Research Fellowships Program: Yes, Dr. Richard Zeff
Medical/Dental Preparatory Program: Yes, http://medicine.uchc.edu/prospective/enrichment/collegefellow

COMBINED DEGREE PROGRAMS
Baccalaureate/M.D.: Yes, Dr. Richard Zeff
http://medicine.uchc.edu/prospective/admissions/babs_md/index.html
M.D./M.P.H.: Yes, Dr. Richard Zeff
http://publichealth.uconn.edu/acprgms_mph_combined.php
M.D./M.B.A.: Yes, Dr. Richard Zeff
http://medicine.uchc.edu/prospective/admissions/mba_md/index.html
M.D./J.D.: No
M.D./Ph.D.: Yes, http://medicine.uchc.edu/prospective/admissions/md_phd/index.html, Dr. Barbara Kream, (860) 679-3849, kream@nso1.uchc.edu

Premedical Coursework

On-line courses accepted in fulfillment of prerequisites: On a case-by-case basis

Course	Req.	Rec.	Lab.	Hrs.
Inorganic Chemistry	•		•	8
Behavioral Sciences				
Biochemistry		•		
Biology		•		
Biology/Zoology	•		•	8
Calculus		•		
College English		•		
College Mathematics		•		

Course	Req.	Rec.	Lab.	Hrs.
Computer Science				
Genetics		•		
Humanities		•		
Organic Chemistry	•		•	8
Physics	•		•	8
Psychology		•		
Social Sciences				
Physiology		•		

Selection Factors: 2009 Accepted Applicants

Proportion of Accepted Applicants with Relevant Experience (Data Self-Reported to AMCAS®)		
Community Service/Volunteer		70%
Medically-Related Work		84%
Research		88%

Shaded bar represents school's accepted scores ranging from the 10th percentile to the 90th percentile   School Median ● National Median ◯

Overall GPA	2.0	2.1	2.2	2.3	2.4	2.5	2.6	2.7	2.8	2.9	3.0	3.1	3.2	3.3	3.4	3.5	3.6	3.7	(3.8)	3.9	4.0
Science GPA	2.0	2.1	2.2	2.3	2.4	2.5	2.6	2.7	2.8	2.9	3.0	3.1	3.2	3.3	3.4	3.5	3.6	3.7	(3.8)	3.9	4.0

MCAT® Total Numeric Score 9 10 11 12 13 14 15 16 17 18 19 20 21 22 23 24 25 26 27 28 29 30 31 (32) 33 34 35 36 37 38 39 40 41 42 43

Writing Sample			J	K	L	M	N	O	P	(Q)	R	S	T
Verbal Reasoning	3	4	5	6	7	8	9	(10)	11	12	13	14	15
Biological Sciences	3	4	5	6	7	8	9	10	(11)	12	13	14	15
Physical Sciences	3	4	5	6	7	8	9	10	(11)	12	13	14	15

Acceptance & Matriculation Data for 2009–2010 First Year Class

	Resident	Non-resident	International	Total
Applications	418	2050	244	2712
Interviewed	239	147	6	392
Deferred	4	0	0	4
Matriculants	2	1	0	3
Early Assurance Program	1	0	0	1
Early Decision Program	0	0	0	0
Baccalaureate/M.D.	0	0	0	0
M.D./Ph.D.	1	4	0	5
Matriculated	69	15	1	**85**

Applications accepted from International Applicants: Yes

Matriculant Demographics: 2009–2010 First Year Class

Men: 39   **Women:** 46

Matriculants' Self-Reported Race/Ethnicity

Mexican American	1	Korean	2
Cuban	0	Vietnamese	0
Puerto Rican	2	Other Asian	4
Other Hispanic	1	Total Asian	16
Total Hispanic	4	Native American	3
Chinese	5	Black	12
Asian Indian	3	Native Hawaiian	0
Pakistani	1	White	49
Filipino	1	**Unduplicated Number**	
Japanese	0	**of Matriculants**	85

Science and Math Majors: 66%
Matriculants with:
  Baccalaureate degree: 99%
  Graduate degree(s): 4%

Specialty Choice

2005, 2006, 2007 Graduates, Specialty Choice (As reported by program directors to GME Track™)	
Anesthesiology	6%
Emergency Medicine	9%
Family Practice	6%
Internal Medicine	21%
Obstetrics/Gynecology	4%
Orthopaedic Surgery	2%
Pediatrics	17%
Psychiatry	4%
Radiology	5%
Surgery	7%

Financial Information

Source: 2008-2009 LCME I-B survey and 2009-2010 AAMC TSF questionnaire

	Residents	Non-residents
Total Cost of Attendance	$53,951	$76,996
Tuition and Fees	$26,956	$50,001
Other (includes living expenses)	$24,375	$24,375
Health Insurance (can not be waived)	$2,620	$2,620

Average 2009 Graduate Indebtedness: $114,429
% of Enrolled Students Receiving Aid: 91%

Criminal Background Check

This medical school requires a criminal background check prior to matriculation.

Yale University School of Medicine

New Haven, Connecticut

Richard A. Silverman, Director of Admissions
Yale University School of Medicine
Edward S. Harkness Hall, 367 Cedar Street
New Haven, Connecticut 06510
T 203 785 2696 F 203 785 3234

Admissions http://info.med.yale.edu/education/admissions/
Main http://info.med.yale.edu/ysm/
Financial www.med.yale.edu/education/finaid/index.html
E-mail medical.admissions@yale.edu

Private Institution

Dr. Robert J. Alpern, Dean

Dr. Laura R. Ment, Associate Dean for Admissions

Dr. Forrester A. Lee, Assistant Dean for Multicultural Affairs

Susan H. Gerber, Director of Financial Aid

Dr. Richard Belitsky, Deputy Dean for Education

Dr. Nancy R. Angoff, Associate Dean for Student Affairs

General Information

The Yale University School of Medicine was established in 1810 as the Medical Institution of Yale College. The present-day Yale-New Haven Medical Center includes the School of Medicine, the School of Nursing, and Yale-New Haven Hospital.

Mission Statement

The mission of the Yale University School of Medicine is to educate and inspire scholars and future leaders who will advance the practice of medicine and the biomedical sciences.

Curricular Highlights

Community Service Requirement: Optional. Extensive community service opportunities.
Research/Thesis Requirement: Required. Original thesis required since 1839.

The Yale System of Medical Education is founded on a belief in the maturity and responsibility of students. Highlights of the program are anonymous examinations, the absence of competitive grades, and a required thesis. The ideal Yale physician is schooled in the current state of knowledge of both medical biology and patient care, with a lifelong commitment to learning. The first two years of the curriculum focus on the basic and clinical sciences. The first year emphasizes normal biological form and function, the second year the study of disease. Throughout both years, a pre-clinical clerkship course provides instruction in history, physical examination, and the art of communicating with patients. The third year is largely devoted to clinical clerkships. In the fourth year, students take electives and a primary care clerkship, and complete their thesis.

Required since 1839, the thesis is designed to develop critical thinking, habits of self-education, and application of the scientific method to medicine. Thesis work also gives students an opportunity to work closely with Yale faculty members.

USMLE

Step 1: Required. Students must record a passing score for graduation, but not promotion.
Step 2: Clinical Skills (CS): Required. Students must record a passing total score to graduate.
Step 2: Clinical Knowledge (CK): Required. Students must record a passing total score to graduate.

Selection Factors

The Admissions Committee seeks exceptional students who best suit the educational philosophy of the school. Because of the importance of diversity, applications are encouraged from women and persons from groups underrepresented in medicine. The committee considers each applicant's academic record, MCAT scores, premedical committee evaluations, letters of recommendation, extracurricular and community activities, and personal qualities. In general, the school strives to admit students with the ability to make significant contributions in medicine and a demonstrated capacity for leadership. Interviews are arranged only by invitation of the Admissions Committee. The class that enrolled in 2009 includes graduates of 46 undergraduate colleges. The diversity of the student body is also reflected in a wide variety of academic interests, professional goals, and personal backgrounds. The Yale School of Medicine does not discriminate on the basis of sex, race, color, religion, age, disability, national or ethnic origin, sexual orientation, or gender identity or expression.

Financial Aid

Financial aid is based primarily on need and is intended to enable any accepted student to attend without unreasonable hardship. All financial aid applicants must submit the FAFSA and the Yale financial aid application, which will be available (online only) on January 1. In addition, those applying for Yale scholarship funds must submit a supplemental needs analysis, which requires student, spouse, and family financial statements.

Information about Diversity Programs

Diversity is important in Yale's collaborative learning environment, and applications are encouraged from individuals from groups underrepresented in medicine. Several student organizations sponsor a range of activities throughout the year, all supported by the Office of Multicultural Affairs.

Campus Information

Setting

The School of Medicine is near the heart of the Yale University campus, and medical students benefit from academic and extracurricular opportunities provided by other Yale schools and by the city of New Haven, a culturally diverse city located 75 miles east of New York.

Enrollment

For 2009, total enrollment was: 414

Special Features

The Anlyan Center is an immense structure for disease-based research and teaching. The Smilow Cancer Hospital, opened in 2009, consolidates the Yale Comprehensive Cancer Center's services into a single world-class cancer hospital. The incorporation of a new "West Campus" provides vast facilities for research and clinical care. Yale was recently honored with a Clinical and Translational Science Award from NIH, reflecting the school's deep commitment to clinical research. A Master of Health Science degree is available for MD students who choose to take a tuition-free fifth year. These and other new facilities and programs are part of an unprecedented period of growth at Yale.

Housing

On-campus housing is available for single and married students, as well as a variety of off-campus apartments.

Satellite Campuses/Facilities

Satellite Campuses/Facilities: Clinical training occurs at Yale-New Haven Hospital and 11 other affiliated hospitals in the region. In addition, there are training sites elsewhere in the United States and abroad. International research and community service opportunities are also available.

Application Process and Requirements 2011–2012

Primary Application Service: AMCAS
Earliest filing date: June 1, 2010
Latest filing date: October 15, 2010

Secondary Application Required?: Yes
Sent to: All applicants
URL: http://info.med.yale.edu/education/admissions/
Fee: Yes, $85
Fee waiver available: Yes
Earliest filing date: June 1, 2010
Latest filing date: November 15, 2010

MCAT® required?: Yes
Latest MCAT® considered: September 2010
Oldest MCAT® considered: April 2007

Early Decision Program: School does have EDP
Applicants notified: October 1, 2010
EDP available for: Both Residents and Non-residents

Regular Acceptance Notice
Earliest date: March 15, 2011
Latest date: Until class is full
Applicant's Response to Acceptance
Offer – Maximum Time: Three weeks

Requests for Deferred
Entrance Considered: Yes

Deposit to Hold Place in Class: Yes
Deposit (Resident): $100
Deposit (Non-resident): $100
Deposit due: With response to acceptance offer
Applied to tuition: Yes
Deposit refundable: Yes
Refundable by: May 15, 2011

Estimated number of new entrants: 100
EDP: 1, special program: n/a

Start Month/Year: August 2011

Interview Format: One-on-one, open-file interviews. Regional interviews only available if applicant is unable to come to campus. Video interviews are not available.

Other Programs

PREPARATORY PROGRAMS
Postbaccalaureate Program: No
Summer Program: Yes, http://info.med.yale.edu/omca/programs/mmep.htm
Yale Summer Medical and Dental Education Program: http://info.med.yale.edu/omca/programs/mmep.htm
Biomedical Science Training & Enrichment Program: http://info.med.yale.edu/omca/programs/biostep.htm

COMBINED DEGREE PROGRAMS
Baccalaureate/M.D.: No
M.D./M.P.H.: Yes, http://info.med.yale.edu/ysm/admissions/index.html
M.D./M.B.A.: Yes, http://mba.yale.edu/mba/curriculum/md_mba/index.shtml
M.D./J.D.: Yes, www.law.yale.edu/academics/jointdegrees.asp
M.D./Ph.D.: Yes, http://info.med.yale.edu/mdphd/
Additional Program: Yes, http://info.med.yale.edu/ysm/admissions/index.html

Premedical Coursework

On-line courses accepted in fulfillment of prerequisites: No

Course	Req.	Rec.	Lab.	Hrs.	Course	Req.	Rec.	Lab.	Hrs.
Inorganic Chemistry	•		•	6-8	Computer Science				
Behavioral Sciences					Genetics				
Biochemistry					Humanities				
Biology					Organic Chemistry	•		•	6-8
Biology/Zoology	•		•	6-8	Physics	•		•	6-8
Calculus					Psychology				
College English					Social Sciences				
College Mathematics					Other				

Selection Factors: 2009 Accepted Applicants

Proportion of Accepted Applicants with Relevant Experience (Data Self-Reported to AMCAS®)		
Community Service/Volunteer		72%
Medically-Related Work		91%
Research		97%

Shaded bar represents school's accepted scores ranging from the 10th percentile to the 90th percentile.   School Median ●   National Median ○

Overall GPA	2.0	2.1	2.2	2.3	2.4	2.5	2.6	2.7	2.8	2.9	3.0	3.1	3.2	3.3	3.4	3.5	3.6	3.7	3.8	(3.9) 4.0
Science GPA	2.0	2.1	2.2	2.3	2.4	2.5	2.6	2.7	2.8	2.9	3.0	3.1	3.2	3.3	3.4	3.5	3.6	3.7	(3.8)	3.9 4.0

MCAT® Total Numeric Score 9 10 11 12 13 14 15 16 17 18 19 20 21 22 23 24 25 26 27 28 29 30 31 (32) 33 34 35 (36) 37 38 39 40 41 42 43

Writing Sample			J	K	L	M	N	O	P	(Q)	(R)	S	T
Verbal Reasoning	3	4	5	6	7	8	9	(10)	(11)	12	13	14	15
Biological Sciences	3	4	5	6	7	8	9	10	(11)	12	(13)	14	15
Physical Sciences	3	4	5	6	7	8	9	10	(11)	(12)	13	14	15

Acceptance & Matriculation Data for 2009–2010 First Year Class

	Resident	Non-resident	International	Total
Applications	194	4476	424	5094
Interviewed	52	708	46	806
Deferred	0	4	0	4
Matriculants				
Early Assurance Program	n/a	n/a	n/a	n/a
Early Decision Program	0	0	0	0
Baccalaureate/M.D.	n/a	n/a	n/a	n/a
M.D./Ph.D.	1	11	0	12
Matriculated	11	81	7	**99**

Applications accepted from International Applicants: Yes

Matriculant Demographics: 2009–2010 First Year Class

Men: 52   **Women:** 47

Matriculants' Self-Reported Race/Ethnicity

Mexican American	2	Korean	1
Cuban	0	Vietnamese	1
Puerto Rican	2	Other Asian	5
Other Hispanic	5	Total Asian	33
Total Hispanic	9	Native American	1
Chinese	18	Black	6
Asian Indian	11	Native Hawaiian	0
Pakistani	0	White	49
Filipino	0	Unduplicated Number	
Japanese	0	of Matriculants	99

Science and Math Majors: 77%
Matriculants with:
Baccalaureate degree: 100%
Graduate degree(s): 8%

Specialty Choice

2005, 2006, 2007 Graduates, Specialty Choice (As reported by program directors to GME Track™)	
Anesthesiology	5%
Emergency Medicine	3%
Family Practice	2%
Internal Medicine	23%
Obstetrics/Gynecology	4%
Orthopaedic Surgery	3%
Pediatrics	5%
Psychiatry	4%
Radiology	5%
Surgery	4%

Financial Information

Source: 2008-2009 LCME I-B survey and 2009-2010 AAMC TSF questionnaire

	Residents	Non-residents
Total Cost of Attendance	$64,300	$64,300
Tuition and Fees	$44,350	$44,350
Other (includes living expenses)	$18,098	$18,098
Health Insurance (can be waived)	$1,852	$1,852

Average 2009 Graduate Indebtedness: $122,247
% of Enrolled Students Receiving Aid: 92%

Criminal Background Check

This medical school does not require a criminal background check prior to matriculation.

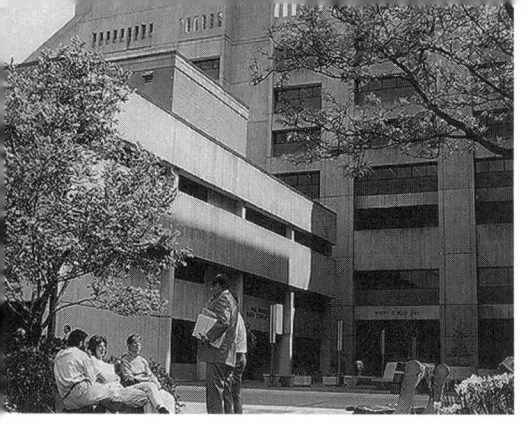

The George Washington University School of Medicine and Health Sciences
Washington, District of Columbia

The George Washington University
School of Medicine and Health Sciences
Office of M.D. Admissions
2300 I Street, N.W., Ross Hall 716
Washington, District of Columbia 20037
T 202 994 3506 **F** 202 994 1753

Admissions www.gwumc.edu/edu/admis
Main www.gwumc.edu/smhs
Financial www.gwumc.edu/smhs/Fin-Aid
E-mail medadmit@gwu.edu

Private Institution

Dr. John F. Williams, Provost and Vice President for Health Affairs

Dr. James L. Scott, Dean, School of Medicine and Health Sciences

Diane P. McQuail, Assistant Dean of Admissions

Charles W. Carpenter, Director of Financial Aid

General Information
Founded in 1825, the School of Medicine and Health Sciences is the 11th oldest medical school in the country. The school is housed in Ross Hall, a research, educational and administrative facility located in the nation's capital. Located adjacent to Ross Hall, the new, state-of-the-art GW Hospital opened in August 2002. The facility boasts an Educational Center consisting of a clinical simulation facility, a standardized patient examination facility, a computer resource center, and lounge/conference areas.

Mission Statement
With a vision to be a pre-eminent health institution in the Washington area, GW is committed to providing the highest quality of care and health services to the public; excellence and innovation in education; and research that expands the frontiers of science and knowledge.

Curricular Highlights
Community Service Requirement: Required.
Research/Thesis Requirement: Optional.

The curriculum contains a course entitled "The Practice of Medicine" (POM). This course spans all four years, allowing students to immediately begin clinical training during the first two years while studying the basic sciences. Each first-year student has a physician mentor. Clinical clerkships begin in the third year, and opportunities for international clinical experiences are available during the fourth year. An Honors/Pass/Conditional/Fail system is used for grading. Early Selection Programs are available to sophomores in the spring semester at GW, the University of Maryland-College Park, St. Bonaventure, and George Mason Universities, and Franklin & Marshall, Claremont McKenna, Scripps, Rowan, Knox, Colgate, Lyon, Rhodes, and Hampden-Sydney Colleges. In addition, linkage agreements exist with postbaccalaureate programs at Goucher College, the University of Pennsylvania, Brandeis University, New York University, Scripps College, Johns Hopkins University, and Bryn Mawr College. Transfer information for the second- and third-year classes is available at *www.gwumc.edu/edu/admis/html/admissions/transfer.html*.

USMLE
Step 1: Required. Students must record a passing score for promotion.
Step 2: Clinical Skills (CS): Required. Students must record a passing total score to graduate.
Step 2: Clinical Knowledge (CK): Required. Students must record a passing total score to graduate.

Selection Factors
The initial evaluation is based on data in the AMCAS and GW applications. This evaluation reviews academic performance; MCAT scores; extracurricular, health-related, research, and work experiences; and evidence of non-scholastic accomplishments. The next phase of the selection procedure is based on examination of personal comments and letters of recommendation. The most promising applicants are invited for interview. The last phase includes the review by the Committee on Admissions of the entire dossier. This phase selects academically prepared students with motivational and personal characteristics the Committee considers important in future physicians.

Financial Aid
Information is available at *www.gwumc.edu/mhs/Fin-Aid/*. Merit-based admissions scholarships are available.

Information about Diversity Programs
The School of Medicine is committed to providing an education to students from groups underrepresented in medicine. Applicants are encouraged to meet with students and faculty from groups underrepresented in medicine. There are focused student organizations such as NBLHO and SNMA.

Campus Information

Setting
The Medical Center is on the Foggy Bottom campus of The George Washington University in Washington, DC. A subway stop sits immediately outside the medical school. The campus is within walking distance of the White House and the National Mall.

Enrollment
For 2009, total enrollment was: 718

Special Features
Students study histology and pathology in a state-of-the-art laboratory, reviewing digital slides on computer monitors. The newly created Office of Student Opportunities serves as a clearinghouse for various research, scholarships, awards, conferences, and study abroad opportunities. The Track Program offers students an opportunity to choose a program of study outside the standard curriculum, *www.gwumc.edu/smhs/students/opportunities*. Electives in first and second years include humanities and ethics. GW operates a Mobile Mammography Program (GW Mammovan), which provides screening mammograms to women in the DC area. The Interdisciplinary Student Community-Oriented Prevention Enhancement Service (ISCOPES) is an interdisciplinary team service-learning experience providing a wide range of health-related services. The student-run Healing Clinic also provides health care to DC's underserved.

Housing
Some graduate student housing is available. The Washington, DC area has abundant off-campus housing options. For information, visit *www.gwumc.edu/edu/admis/html/student/housing.html*.

Satellite Campuses/Facilities
In addition to the GW Hospital, the teaching services of the Children's National Medical Center, Inova Fairfax Hospital, Holy Cross Hospital, National Naval Medical Center, St. Elizabeth's Hospital, Veterans Administration Hospital, and Washington Hospital Center are also available to students. A variety of ambulatory sites in the DC area are also utilized, including neighborhood clinics that serve indigent patients.

Application Process and Requirements 2011–2012

Primary Application Service: AMCAS
Earliest filing date: June 1, 2010
Latest filing date: December 1, 2010

Secondary Application Required?: Yes
Sent to: All applicants
URL: n/a
Fee: Yes, $125
Fee waiver available: Yes
Earliest filing date: June 1, 2010
Latest filing date: January 1, 2011

MCAT® required?: Yes
Latest MCAT® considered: September 2010
Oldest MCAT® considered: April 2008

Early Decision Program: School does have EDP
Applicants notified: October 1, 2010
EDP available for: Both Residents and Non-residents

Regular Acceptance Notice
Earliest date: October 15, 2010
Latest date: Until class is full
Applicant's Response to Acceptance Offer – Maximum Time: Three weeks

Requests for Deferred Entrance Considered: Yes

Deposit to Hold Place in Class: Yes
Deposit (Resident): $100
Deposit (Non-resident): $100
Deposit due: May 15, 2011
Applied to tuition: Yes
Deposit refundable: Yes
Refundable by: May 15, 2011

Estimated number of new entrants: 177
EDP: 3, special program: 39

Start Month/Year: August 2011

Interview Format: Two blind interviews with a faculty member and a student. All interviews take place at GW. Video interviews are not available.

Other Programs

PREPARATORY PROGRAMS
Postbaccalaureate Program: No
Summer Program: yes, http://www.gwumc.edu/dchapp/dchapp.html

COMBINED DEGREE PROGRAMS
Baccalaureate/M.D.: Yes, 7 year program with George Washington University, www.gwumc.edu/edu/admis/html/academics/bamd.html, 8 year program with St. Bonaventure University, www.sbu.edu and www.gwumc.edu
M.D./M.P.H.: Yes, www.gwumc.edu/edu/admis/html/academics/mdmph.html
M.D./M.B.A.: No
M.D./J.D.: No
M.D./Ph.D.: Yes, www.gwumc.edu/edu/admis/html/academics/mdphd.html

Premedical Coursework

On-line courses accepted in fulfillment of prerequisites: No

Course	Req.	Rec.	Lab.	Hrs.
Inorganic Chemistry	•		•	8
Behavioral Sciences				
Biochemistry				
Biology				
Biology/Zoology	•		•	8
Calculus				
College English	•			6
College Mathematics				

Course	Req.	Rec.	Lab.	Hrs.
Computer Science				
Genetics				
Humanities				
Organic Chemistry	•		•	8
Physics	•		•	8
Psychology				
Social Sciences				
Other				

Selection Factors: 2009 Accepted Applicants

Proportion of Accepted Applicants with Relevant Experience (Data Self-Reported to AMCAS®)		
Community Service/Volunteer		65%
Medically-Related Work		89%
Research		81%

Shaded bar represents school's accepted scores ranging from the 10th percentile to the 90th percentile   School Median ● National Median ○

Overall GPA	2.0	2.1	2.2	2.3	2.4	2.5	2.6	2.7	2.8	2.9	3.0	3.1	3.2	3.3	3.4	3.5	3.6	(3.7)	3.8	3.9	4.0
Science GPA	2.0	2.1	2.2	2.3	2.4	2.5	2.6	2.7	2.8	2.9	3.0	3.1	3.2	3.3	3.4	3.5	(3.6)	3.7	3.8	3.9	4.0

MCAT® Total Numeric Score 9 10 11 12 13 14 15 16 17 18 19 20 21 22 23 24 25 26 27 28 29 (30) 31 (32) 33 34 35 36 37 38 39 40 41 42 43

Writing Sample			J	K	L	M	N	O	P	(Q)	R	S	T
Verbal Reasoning	3	4	5	6	7	8	9	(10)	11	12	13	14	15
Biological Sciences	3	4	5	6	7	8	9	(10)	(11)	12	13	14	15
Physical Sciences	3	4	5	6	7	8	9	(10)	(11)	12	13	14	15

Acceptance & Matriculation Data for 2009–2010 First Year Class

	Resident	Non-resident	International	Total
Applications	63	13161	485	13709
Interviewed	17	1044	7	1068
Deferred	0	4	0	4
Matriculants				
Early Assurance Program	1	21	0	22
Early Decision Program	1	2	0	3
Baccalaureate/M.D.	0	14	0	14
M.D./Ph.D.	0	0	0	0
Matriculated	3	170	4	**177**
Applications accepted from International Applicants: Yes				

Matriculant Demographics: 2009–2010 First Year Class

Men: 74   **Women:** 103

Matriculants' Self-Reported Race/Ethnicity

Mexican American	1	Korean	2
Cuban	2	Vietnamese	2
Puerto Rican	1	Other Asian	1
Other Hispanic	3	Total Asian	48
Total Hispanic	6	Native American	0
Chinese	3	Black	22
Asian Indian	28	Native Hawaiian	0
Pakistani	6	White	104
Filipino	3	Unduplicated Number	
Japanese	4	of Matriculants	177

Science and Math Majors: 52%
Matriculants with:
    Baccalaureate degree: 100%
    Graduate degree(s): 16%

Specialty Choice

2005, 2006, 2007 Graduates, Specialty Choice (As reported by program directors to GME Track™)	
Anesthesiology	8%
Emergency Medicine	6%
Family Practice	4%
Internal Medicine	24%
Obstetrics/Gynecology	4%
Orthopaedic Surgery	3%
Pediatrics	13%
Psychiatry	6%
Radiology	4%
Surgery	8%

Financial Information

Source: 2008–2009 LCME I-B survey and 2009–2010 AAMC TSF questionnaire

	Residents	Non-residents
Total Cost of Attendance	$70,020	$70,020
Tuition and Fees	$47,644	$47,644
Other (includes living expenses)	$22,376	$22,376
Health Insurance (can be waived)	$0	$0

Average 2009 Graduate Indebtedness: $179,616
% of Enrolled Students Receiving Aid: 84%

Criminal Background Check

This medical school currently requires a criminal background check prior to matriculation.

Georgetown University School of Medicine
Washington, District of Columbia

Office of Admissions
Georgetown University School of Medicine
Box 571421
Washington, District of Columbia 20057-1421
T 202 687 1154   F 202 687 3079

Admissions http://som.georgetown.edu/
prospectivestudents
Main http://som.georgetown.edu
Financial http://som.georgetown.edu/
prospectivestudents/financialaid/
E-mail medicaladmissions@georgetown.edu

Private Institution

Dr. S. Ray Mitchell, Dean for Medical Education

*Brandon C. Schneider,
Assistant Dean for Admissions*

*Joy P. Williams, Associate Dean for
Students and Special Programs*

*David J. Pollock, Assistant Dean for
Student Financial Planning*

*Dr. Russell T. Wall III, Associate Dean for
Admissions and Student Services*

General Information

The School of Medicine works in association
with the 609-bed Georgetown University
Hospital, part of the MedStar not-for-profit
health care system. The school has affiliations
with eight federal and community hospitals in
the Washington, DC area. The campus contains
a health science library and an integrated learning center with 10 clinical examination rooms.
Adjacent to the hospital is the Lombardi Cancer
Research, which provides both research and
clinical care. The School is near the NIH and
other internationally prominent health care and
research facilities. The Yates Field House offers
swimming, jogging tracks, and other athletic
programs. The Leavey Center hosts dining
establishments and guest quarters.

Mission Statement

Guided by the University's Jesuit tradition of
'cura personalis,' caring for the whole person,
Georgetown University School of Medicine
will educate, in an integrated way, knowledgeable, skillful, ethical, and compassionate physicians and biomedical scientists, dedicated to
the care of others and the health needs of our
society. Our educational approach involves the
integration of the basic sciences, clinical experiences, and the humanistic disciplines in each
systems-based module, reinforcing the learning
experience with clinical care skills and patient
interactions.

Curricular Highlights

Community Service Requirement: Required.
Research/Thesis Requirement: Research
project required.

Georgetown's curriculum is systems based,
emphasizing the body's normal and altered
structure and functions reinforced with clinically oriented educational experiences, early
introduction to patients, the art of advocacy,
and the ethical/cultural dimensions of medicine. Small-group teaching in labs, seminars,
and at the bedside begins early in the first year.
The third year provides comprehensive clinical
training in the care of patients through clerkships in the major medical specialties. The
fourth year gives each student substantial
responsibility for the management of patient
care through acting internships, elective study,
and research. The grading system is Honors,
High Pass, Pass, and Fail.

USMLE

Step 1: Required. Students must record a passing
score for promotion.
Step 2: Clinical Skills (CS): Required. Students
must record a passing total score to graduate.
Step 2: Clinical Knowledge (CK): Required.
Students must record a passing total score to
graduate.

Selection Factors

The Committee on Admissions selects students
on the basis of academic achievement, character, maturity, and motivation. The committee
evaluates the applicant's entire academic record,
performance on the MCAT, college premedical
committee evaluations or letters of recommendation, personal essays, and personal interview.
A secondary application and essay are required
of all applicants. An applicant may be invited to
interview once all credentials have been
reviewed by the committee. The personal interview is required and conducted on the medical
center campus. Applicants are urged to submit
their applications and supporting credentials
early. The School of Medicine does not discriminate on the basis of race, sex, creed, age, disability, sexual orientation, or national or ethnic
origin. The School of Medicine has an Early
Assurance Program with its undergraduate
institution. Applicants for transfer are only considered from LCME-accredited medical schools.

Financial Aid

The school participates in federal financial aid
programs and awards school-administered

scholarships and low-interest loans to students
on the basis of financial need. Parents' financial
information is required for students seeking
school-administered aid. Loan indebtedness
counseling is an important function of the Office
of Student Financial Planning, as a majority of
students incur substantial educational debt.
Candidates for admission are strongly encouraged to contact the office with questions.

Information about Diversity Programs

The School of Medicine has a diverse student
body, with students from groups underrepresented in medicine. Inquiries can be addressed
to the Director of the Office of Minority
Student Development. The Georgetown
Experimental Medical Studies (GEMS) postbaccalaureate program is for qualified disadvantaged students and students from groups
underrepresented in medicine. For information visit *http://gems.georgetown.edu*.

Campus Information

Setting
Located on the undergraduate campus in the
heart of Georgetown, Our School of Medicine
is next to Georgetown University Hospital.

Enrollment
For 2009, total enrollment was: 804

Special Features
Special features include Georgetown's state-
of-the-art Clinical Skills Center, the Lombardi
Cancer Center, opportunities for international
clerkships following the first year and in the
fourth year, community outreach programs,
mind-body electives, and the Health Justice
Scholars Program. Students also serve on educational and student affairs committees.

Housing
No on-campus housing is available. The Office
of Admissions attempts to assist students in
finding housing.

Satellite Campuses/Facilities
Rotations are divided among the University
Hospital, MedStar Hospital Network, and
other hospitals in the metro area. Ambulatory
care experiences are within the area.

Application Process and Requirements 2011–2012

Primary Application Service: AMCAS
Earliest filing date: June 1, 2010
Latest filing date: November 1, 2010

Secondary Application Required?: Yes
Sent To: All applicants
URL: http://som.georgetown.edu/prospectivestudents
Fee: $130
Fee Waiver Available: Yes
Earliest filing date: June 15, 2010
Latest filing date: January 5, 2011

MCAT® required?: Yes
Latest MCAT® considered: September 2010
Oldest MCAT® considered: January 2008

Early Decision Program: School does not have EDP
Applicants notified: n/a
EDP available for: n/a

Regular Acceptance Notice
Earliest date: October 15, 2010
Latest date: Until class is full
Applicant's Response to Acceptance Offer – Maximum Time: Three weeks

Requests for Deferred Entrance Considered: Yes

Deposit to Hold Place in Class: Yes
Deposit (Resident): $100
Deposit (Non-resident): $100
Deposit due: March 15, 2011. Partial tuition pre-payment due June 1, 2011
Applied to tuition: Yes
Deposit refundable: Yes
Refundable by: May 15, 2011

Estimated number of new entrants: 196
EDP: n/a, special program: n/a

Start Month/Year: August 2011

Interview Format: Interviews are one-on-one, in-person and on-campus only. Regional interviews are not available. Video interviews are not available.

Other Programs

PREPARATORY PROGRAMS
Postbaccalaureate Program: Yes, http://gems.georgetown.edu
Summer Program: Yes, http://gsmi.georgetown.edu

COMBINED DEGREE PROGRAMS
Baccalaureate/M.D.: No
M.D./M.P.H.: No

M.D./M.B.A.: Yes, http://msb.georgetown.edu/prospective/graduate/mba/curriculum/enrichment/joint_degree/
M.D./J.D.: No
M.D./Ph.D.: Yes, http://biomedgrad.georgetown.edu/MDPhD/index.html

Premedical Coursework

On-line courses accepted in fulfillment of prerequisites: On a case-by-case basis

Course	Req.	Rec.	Lab.	Sems.	Course	Req.	Rec.	Lab.	Sems.
Inorganic Chemistry	•		•	2	Computer Science		•		
Behavioral Sciences					Genetics		•		
Biochemistry		•			Humanities		•		
Biology	•		•	2	Organic Chemistry	•		•	2
Biology/Zoology					Physics	•		•	2
Calculus					Psychology				
College English	•			2	Social Sciences		•		
College Mathematics	•			1	Other				

Selection Factors: 2009 Accepted Applicants

Proportion of Accepted Applicants with Relevant Experience (Data Self-Reported to AMCAS®)		
Community Service/Volunteer		72%
Medically-Related Work		88%
Research		82%

Shaded bar represents school's accepted scores ranging from the 10th percentile to the 90th percentile. School Median ● National Median ○

Overall GPA 2.0 2.1 2.2 2.3 2.4 2.5 2.6 2.7 2.8 2.9 3.0 3.1 3.2 3.3 3.4 3.5 3.6 3.7 (3.8) 3.9 4.0
Science GPA 2.0 2.1 2.2 2.3 2.4 2.5 2.6 2.7 2.8 2.9 3.0 3.1 3.2 3.3 3.4 3.5 3.6 (3.7) 3.8 3.9 4.0

MCAT® Total Numeric Score 9 10 11 12 13 14 15 16 17 18 19 20 21 22 23 24 25 26 27 28 29 30 31 (32) 33 34 35 36 37 38 39 40 41 42 43

Writing Sample			J	K	L	M	N	O	P	(Q)	R	S	T	
Verbal Reasoning	3	4	5	6	7	8	9	(10)	11	12	13	14	15	
Biological Sciences	3	4	5	6	7	8	9	10	(11)	12	13	14	15	
Physical Sciences	3	4	5	6	7	8	9	10	(11)	12	13	14	15	

Acceptance & Matriculation Data for 2009–2010 First Year Class

	Resident	Non-resident	International	Total
Applications	51	10334	412	10797
Interviewed	10	1125	23	1158
Deferred	0	11	0	11
Matriculants				
Early Assurance Program	0	4	0	4
Early Decision Program	0	0	0	0
Baccalaureate/M.D.	n/a	n/a	n/a	n/a
M.D./Ph.D.	0	1	0	1
Matriculated	4	193	0	**197**
Applications accepted from International Applicants: Yes				

Specialty Choice

2005, 2006, 2007 Graduates, Specialty Choice (As reported by program directors to GME Track™)	
Anesthesiology	9%
Emergency Medicine	7%
Family Practice	5%
Internal Medicine	19%
Obstetrics/Gynecology	5%
Orthopaedic Surgery	9%
Pediatrics	7%
Psychiatry	2%
Radiology	5%
Surgery	7%

Matriculant Demographics: 2009–2010 First Year Class

Men: 99 　　　　**Women:** 98

Matriculants' Self-Reported Race/Ethnicity

Mexican American	2	Korean	4
Cuban	0	Vietnamese	2
Puerto Rican	0	Other Asian	6
Other Hispanic	2	Total Asian	43
Total Hispanic	4	Native American	0
Chinese	15	Black	10
Asian Indian	12	Native Hawaiian	1
Pakistani	2	White	139
Filipino	1	Unduplicated Number	
Japanese	5	of Matriculants	197

Science and Math Majors: 59%
Matriculants with:
　　Baccalaureate degree: 100%
　　Graduate degree(s): 17%

Financial Information
Source: 2008–2009 LCME I-B survey and 2009–2010 AAMC TSF questionnaire

	Residents	Non-residents
Total Cost of Attendance	$70,800	$70,800
Tuition and Fees	$46,177	$46,177
Other (includes living expenses)	$22,123	$22,123
Health Insurance (can be waived)	$2,500	$2,500

Average 2009 Graduate Indebtedness: $183,586
% of Enrolled Students Receiving Aid: 88%

Criminal Background Check

This medical school requires a criminal background check prior to matriculation.

Howard University College of Medicine

Washington, District of Columbia

Office of Admissions, Office of the Dean
Howard University College of Medicine,
520 W Street, N.W., Room 2310
Washington, District of Columbia 20059
T 202 806 6270   **F** 202 265 0048

Admissions http://medicine.howard.edu/students/
prospective/admissions
Main www.medicine.howard.edu
Financial http://medicine.howard.edu/finance/
overview.htm
E-mail hucmadmissions@howard.edu

Private Institution

Dr. Robert E. Taylor, Dean

Dr. Walter P. Bland, Associate Dean for Student Affairs and Admissions

Judith M. Walk, Director of Admissions

Sharmon Jones, Admissions Officer

General Information

The Howard University College of Medicine is the oldest and largest historically black medical school in the United States and the 36th oldest of all 132 medical schools in this country. The medical department's primary goal at inception remains the college's goal today: to train students to become competent, compassionate physicians who will provide care in medically underserved communities. The college has more than 4,000 living alumni, including approximately 25 percent of all black practicing physicians in this country. Until 1950, the college contributed nearly half of the black physicians in the United States. The 321-bed Howard University Hospital is the college's primary teaching hospital for medical students and is used for postgraduate training in the various specialties of medicine. Medical students also serve clerkships at the Children's National Medical Center, INOVA Fairfax Hospital, St. Elizabeth's Hospital, the Washington Veterans Affairs Medical Center, Providence Hospital, the Washington Hospital Center, and Prince George's Hospital Center.

Mission Statement

Howard University College of Medicine provides students of high academic potential with a medical education of exceptional quality and prepares physicians and other health care professionals to serve the underserved. Particular focus is on the education of disadvantaged students for careers in medicine. Special attention is directed to teaching and research activities that address health care disparities.

Curricular Highlights

Community Service Requirement: Optional.
Research/Thesis Requirement: Optional.

An integrated curriculum was implemented in August 2001. Students in the first year complete curriculum blocks in Molecules and Cells, Structure and Function, and Medicine and Society. In year two, pathophysiology, pathology and pharmacology are integrated according to organ systems, and the Medicine and Society block is continued. Blocks in Physical Diagnosis and Introduction to Clinical Medicine are also included in year two. The third and fourth years consist of blocks of instruction in a continuum of clerkships and examinations in core clinical disciplines. During the fourth year, opportunity is available for additional clinical or research experience through 24 or 28 weeks of required electives. Pedagogical approaches include learning in small group settings and opportunities for practical application.

USMLE

Step 1: Required. Students must record a passing score for promotion.
Step 2: Clinical Skills (CS): Required. Students must record a passing total score to graduate.
Step 2: Clinical Knowledge (CK): Required. Students must record a passing total score to graduate.

Selection Factors

There are four major criteria used in the selection of applicants for admission to the College of Medicine: (1) character and discernible motivation for a career in medicine, (2) academic record, (3) results of the MCAT, and (4) letters of recommendation from pre-professional advisors and faculty. Candidates for admission and alternates are selected from among those applicants who satisfy the criteria and who are most likely to serve in communities needing physician services. An invitation for an interview may be extended to an applicant after the Committee on Admissions has made a preliminary examination of the applicant's credentials and has decided that an interview is desirable. Although the total student is evaluated, the Committee on Admissions gives strongest consideration to those who have GPAs of 3.0 and above. There are no residence restrictions. All applicants will be evaluated regardless of the applicants sex, race, religion, national or ethnic origin, age, marital status, or disability. A $100 (refundable) deposit and a $300 (non-refundable) enrollment fee (due with response to acceptance) is required of accepted applicants who have never previously enrolled at Howard University.

Financial Aid

Nearly all of the students enrolled in the College of Medicine receive some sort of financial assistance. Financial aid applicants must submit the FAFSA. Students with demonstrated need may receive school-based scholarships and loans, and those who qualify are recommended for federally guaranteed and private educational loans. Some merit awards are offered to outstanding entering first-year students and for exceptional academic performance in the medical curriculum. Some students receive scholarships funded by the National Health Service Corps or by the military.

Campus Information

Setting

The location of the campus in Washington, D.C., provides a cosmopolitan setting with a diversity of population and activities. The campus is Metrorail and Metrobus-accessible, and within walking distance of the hospital.

Enrollment

For 2009, total enrollment was: 477

Housing

Limited on-campus housing is available for graduate and professional students. Most medical students live off-campus within a short commute to the university.

Satellite Campuses/Facilities

Student rotations are divided between Howard University Hospital and several hospitals, ambulatory centers, and private physicians' offices in the metropolitan area.

Application Process and Requirements 2011–2012

Primary Application Service: AMCAS
Earliest filing date: June 1, 2010
Latest filing date: December 15, 2010

Secondary Application Required?: Yes,
http://medicine.howard.edu/students/prospective/admissions/process.htm
Sent to: All applicants
Contact: Ms. Judith Walk
(202) 806-6279, jwalk@howard.edu
Fee: Yes, $75
Fee waiver available: No
Earliest filing date: August 15, 2010
Latest filing date: Thrity days after receipt of secondary email. Latest date to mail secondary is January 15, 2011.

MCAT® required?: Yes
Latest MCAT® considered: January 2011
Oldest MCAT® considered: August 2008

Early Decision Program: School does not have EDP
Applicants notified: n/a
EDP available for: n/a

Regular Acceptance Notice
Earliest date: October 15, 2010
Latest date: Until class is full
Applicant's Response to Acceptance
Offer – Maximum Time: 30 days, until April 15, 2011

Requests for Deferred
Entrance Considered: Yes

Deposit to Hold Place in Class: Yes
Deposit (Resident): $100
Deposit (Non-resident): $100
Deposit due: With acceptance offer, accompanied by non-refundable enrollment fee
Applied to tuition: Yes
Deposit refundable: Yes
Refundable by: April 15, 2011

Estimated number of new entrants: 115
EDP: n/a, special program: 10

Start Month/Year: July 2011

Interview Format: One-on-one interview with admissions committee member. Regional interviews are not available. Video interviews are not available.

Other Programs

PREPARATORY PROGRAMS
Postbaccalaureate Program: No
Summer Program: Yes, www.smdep.org/progsites/howard.htm
Summer Medical and Dental Education Program (SMDEP): www.smdep.org/progsites/howard.htm

COMBINED DEGREE PROGRAMS
Baccalaureate/M.D.: Yes, www.founders.howard.edu/preprof/BSMD-Brochure.pdf
M.D./M.P.H.: No
M.D./M.B.A.: Yes, Dr. Sheik N. Hassan, (202) 806-9494, shassan@howard.edu
M.D./J.D.: No
M.D./Ph.D.: Yes, Dr. Verle Headings, (202) 806-6100, vheadings@howard.edu

Premedical Coursework

On-line courses accepted in fulfillment of prerequisites: No

Course	Req.	Rec.	Lab.	Hrs.
Inorganic Chemistry	•		•	8
Behavioral Sciences				
Biochemistry		•		4
Biology	•		•	8
Biology/Zoology				
Calculus				
College English	•			6
College Mathematics	•			6

Course	Req.	Rec.	Lab.	Hrs.
Computer Science				
Genetics		•		4
Humanities	•			6
Organic Chemistry	•		•	8
Physics	•		•	8
Psychology				
Social Sciences				
Other				

Selection Factors: 2009 Accepted Applicants

Proportion of Accepted Applicants with Relevant Experience (Data Self-Reported to AMCAS®)	
Community Service/Volunteer	67%
Medically-Related Work	74%
Research	75%

Shaded bar represents school's accepted scores ranging from the 10th percentile to the 90th percentile. School Median ● National Median ○

Overall GPA 2.0 2.1 2.2 2.3 2.4 2.5 2.6 2.7 2.8 2.9 3.0 3.1 3.2 3.3 3.4 ③.5 3.6 3.7 3.8 3.9 4.0
Science GPA 2.0 2.1 2.2 2.3 2.4 2.5 2.6 2.7 2.8 2.9 3.0 3.1 3.2 ③.3 3.4 3.5 3.6 3.7 3.8 3.9 4.0

MCAT® Total Numeric Score 9 10 11 12 13 14 15 16 17 18 19 20 21 22 23 24 ㉕ 26 27 28 29 30 31 ㉜ 33 34 35 36 37 38 39 40 41 42 43

			J	K	L	M	N	O	P	Q	R	S	T
Writing Sample								○		●			
Verbal Reasoning	3	4	5	6	7	⑧	9	⑩	11	12	13	14	15
Biological Sciences	3	4	5	6	7	8	⑨	10	⑪	12	13	14	15
Physical Sciences	3	4	5	6	7	⑧	9	10	⑪	12	13	14	15

Acceptance & Matriculation Data for 2009–2010 First Year Class

	Resident	Non-resident	International	Total
Applications	30	5499	477	6006
Interviewed	5	323	16	344
Deferred	0	4	1	5
Matriculants				
Early Assurance Program	0	0	0	0
Early Decision Program	0	0	0	0
Baccalaureate/M.D.	0	2	1	3
M.D./Ph.D.	0	1	0	1
Matriculated	1	94	11	**106**

Applications accepted from International Applicants: Yes

Matriculant Demographics: 2009–2010 First Year Class

Men: 47 **Women:** 59

Matriculants' Self-Reported Race/Ethnicity

Mexican American	0	Korean	1
Cuban	2	Vietnamese	3
Puerto Rican	1	Other Asian	1
Other Hispanic	2	Total Asian	19
Total Hispanic	5	Native American	1
Chinese	2	Black	67
Asian Indian	8	Native Hawaiian	1
Pakistani	2	White	8
Filipino	2	Unduplicated Number	
Japanese	0	of Matriculants	106

Science and Math Majors: 73%
Matriculants with:
    Baccalaureate degree: 100%
    Graduate degree(s): 17%

Specialty Choice

2005, 2006, 2007 Graduates, Specialty Choice (As reported by program directors to GME Track™)	
Anesthesiology	5%
Emergency Medicine	3%
Family Practice	9%
Internal Medicine	19%
Obstetrics/Gynecology	6%
Orthopaedic Surgery	3%
Pediatrics	10%
Psychiatry	6%
Radiology	3%
Surgery	10%

Financial Information

Source: 2008-2009 LCME I-B survey and 2009-2010 AAMC TSF questionnaire

	Residents	Non-residents
Total Cost of Attendance	$56,797	$56,797
Tuition and Fees	$36,781	$36,781
Other (includes living expenses)	$20,016	$20,016
Health Insurance	$0	$0

Average 2009 Graduate Indebtedness: $154,216
% of Enrolled Students Receiving Aid: 95%

Criminal Background Check

This medical school requires a criminal background check prior to matriculation.

Florida International University
Herbert Wertheim College of Medicine
Miami, Florida

Office of Admissions
Florida International University
Herbert Wertheim College of Medicine
11200 S.W 8th Street – HLSII 660 W2
Miami, Florida 33199
T 305 348 0644   **F** 305 348 0650

Admissions http://medicine.fiu.edu
Main http://medicine.fiu.edu
Financial: http://medicine.fiu.edu
E-mail med.admissions@fiu.edu

Public Institution

Dr. Sanford Markham, Executive Associate Dean for Student Affairs

Dr. Robert Dollinger, Assistant Dean, Student Affairs (Counseling and Communities)

Dr. Barbra Roller, Assistant Dean, Student Affairs (Admissions and Records)

Betty L. Monfort, MPH, Director, Admissions and Records

Charlotte Rhine, MEd, Associate Director, Admissions and Records

Pemra Cetin, MBA, Director, Financial Aid

General Information
In August 2009, the College of Medicine welcomed the inaugural class. The four year program, leading to the MD degree, involves in-depth exposure and training in all areas of medical education with specific focus on family and community medicine. Unique to the College is the hands-on experience each student receives in observing and caring for families who have little or no access to medical care. Key in the medical training is the focus on the importance of the doctor-patient relationship in diverse patient populations.

Mission Statement
The mission of the Florida International University Herbert Wertheim College of Medicine is to lead the next generation of medical education and continually improve the quality of healthcare available to the South Florida community. The College of Medicine will accomplish its mission by training physicians to serve South Florida's diverse population through a patient-centered curriculum instilling cultural competence, providing Florida students greater access to medical education, and fostering research to discover and advance medically relevant knowledge.

General Information

Curricular Highlights
Community Service Requirement: Integral part of admission and curriculum.
Research/Thesis Requirement: Required.

The College has created a new curriculum that is community based and emphasizes patient-centered learning with a focus on developing an understanding of personal, cultural, and social factors in healthcare. Students will develop competencies in a full range of medical specialties. Organized as a four year integration of studies, the curriculum has five strands: Clinical Medicine, Disease, Illness and Injury (pathological approaches), Human Biology (basic medical sciences), Medicine and Society, and Professional Development (statistical and evidence based medicine). Curricular innovations include the Medicine and Society strand, the goal of which is to enable students to gain an understanding of factors that affect personal and community health care. As part of our signature program NeighborhoodHELP, students work with individuals, families and communities in interdisciplinary student teams from Public Health, Nursing and Social Work. This strand integrates ethics, public health, cultural competency and sustained community experiences. Cases are used throughout the curriculum as a context for learning. Small class sizes provide individualized attention. Small group learning and independent study are emphasized; research is part of the curriculum. The faculty has been selected for their excellence in teaching; the learning format is focused on individual student achievement.

USMLE
Step 1: Required. Students must record a passing score for promotion.
Step 2: Clinical Skills (CS): Required. Students must only record a score.
Step 2: Clinical Knowledge (CK): Required. Students must only record a score.

Selection Factors
The Admissions Committee uses AMCAS, a secondary application, letters of recommendation and interview feedback to select applicants who have demonstrated a well-rounded, rigorous academic preparation, character and maturity and who best suit our mission. Applicants must show a strong interest in medicine, a record of personal experiences suggesting medical care exposure, research, altruism, integrity, community service, and leadership with the ability and desire to pursue lifelong learning. Most important are the personal attributes necessary to be a competent compassionate physician. Presently, only US Citizens, Permanent Residents and Canadian citizens are considered.

Financial Aid
Financial Aid is awarded on the basis of merit and demonstrated financial need. Scholarships, institutional grants, federal and private student loans are available for eligible students.

Information about Diversity Programs
FIU takes pride in its commitment to diversity as exemplified among our students, faculty and staff.

Campus Information

Setting
Located in Miami, a major international and cultural center, FIU is an urban, research university serving South Florida, the state, the nation and the international community. The 344-acre main campus, where the College of Medicine is housed, offers a wealth of services and access to living and learning communities and is only minutes from Miami International Airport, the Port of Miami, cultural centers, outdoor recreation, sporting events, schools, shopping and beautiful beaches.

Enrollment
For 2009, total enrollment was 43.

Special Features
Clinical training is integrated throughout the South Florida medical community. Students rotate through a vast array of excellent hospitals and clinics including Jackson and Baptist Health Systems, Mt. Sinai, Mercy and Miami Children's Hospitals.

Housing
The Department of Housing and Residential Life provides state-of-the-art, on-campus housing complemented by a supportive Residential Life program. Off-campus housing is also available.

Application Process and Requirements 2011–2012

Primary Application Service: AMCAS
Earliest filing date: June 1, 2010
Latest filing date: December 15, 2010

Secondary Application Required?: Yes
URL: n/a
Name: Betty L. Monfort, (305) 348-0644
med.admissions@fiu.edu
Sent to: All AMCAS verified applicants
Fee: Yes, $30.00
Fee Waiver Available: Yes (if waived by AMCAS)
Earliest filing date: June 2010
Latest filing date: January 1, 2011

MCAT® required?: Yes
Latest MCAT® considered: September 2010
Oldest MCAT® considered: January 2008

Early Decision Program: School does have EDP
Applicants notified: October 1, 2010
EDP available for: See Website

Regular Acceptance Notice
Earliest date: October 15, 2010
Latest date: Varies
Applicant's Response to Acceptance
Offer – Maximum Time: 3 weeks from date of offer

Requests for deferred entrance considered: No

Deposit to Hold Place in Class: Yes
Deposit (Resident): $100
Deposit (Non-resident): $100
Deposit due: with offer acceptance
Applied to tuition: Yes
Deposit refundable: No
Refundable by: n/a

Estimated number of new entrants: 80
EDP: n/a, **special program:** n/a

Start month/year: August 2011

Interview format: Two committee members will interview invited applicants. Regional interviews are not available. Video interviews are not available.

Other Programs

PREPARATORY PROGRAMS
Postbaccalaureate Program: No
Summer Program: No

COMBINED DEGREE PROGRAMS
Baccalaureate/M.D.: No
M.D./M.P.H.: No
M.D./M.B.A.: No
M.D./J.D.: No
M.D./Ph.D.: No

Premedical Coursework

On-line courses accepted in fulfillment of prerequisites: On a case-by-case basis

Course	Req.	Rec.	Lab.	Sems.
Inorganic Chemistry	•		•	2
Behavioral Sciences		•		
Biochemistry		•		
Biology	•		•	2
Biology/Zoology				
Calculus and/or Statistics	•			2
College English	•			2
College Mathematics		•		

Course	Req.	Rec.	Lab.	Sems.
Computer Science		•		
Genetics		•		
Humanities		•		
Organic Chemistry	•		•	2
Physics	•		•	2
Psychology		•		
Social Sciences		•		
Cell Biology		•		

Selection Factors: 2009 Accepted Applicants

Proportion of Accepted Applicants with Relevant Experience (Data Self-Reported to AMCAS®)		
Community Service/Volunteer		77%
Medically-Related Work		96%
Research		80%

Shaded bar represents school's accepted scores ranging from the 10th percentile to the 90th percentile ▓   School Median ● National Median ○

Overall GPA	2.0	2.1	2.2	2.3	2.4	2.5	2.6	2.7	2.8	2.9	3.0	3.1	3.2	3.3	3.4	3.5	(3.6)	3.7	3.8	3.9	4.0
Science GPA	2.0	2.1	2.2	2.3	2.4	2.5	2.6	2.7	2.8	2.9	3.0	3.1	3.2	3.3	3.4	3.5	(3.6)	3.7	3.8	3.9	4.0

MCAT® Total Numeric Score 9 10 11 12 13 14 15 16 17 18 19 20 21 22 23 24 25 26 27 28 29 30 (31) (32) 33 34 35 36 37 38 39 40 41 42 43

Writing Sample			J	K	L	M	N	O	(P)	(Q)	R	S	T
Verbal Reasoning	3	4	5	6	7	8	9	(10)	11	12	13	14	15
Biological Sciences	3	4	5	6	7	8	9	10	(11)	12	13	14	15
Physical Sciences	3	4	5	6	7	8	9	10	(11)	12	13	14	15

Acceptance & Matriculation Data for 2009–2010 First Year Class

	Resident	Non-resident	International	Total
Applications	1485	1727	53	3265
Interviewed	221	148	0	369
Deferred	0	0	0	0
Matriculants				
Early Assurance Program	0	0	0	0
Early Decision Program	0	0	0	0
Baccalaureate/M.D.	0	0	0	0
M.D./Ph.D.	0	0	0	0
Matriculated	34	9	0	**43**

Applications accepted from International Applicants: Yes

Specialty Choice

2005, 2006, 2007 Graduates, Specialty Choice
(As reported by program directors to GME Track™)

Anesthesiology
Emergency Medicine
Family Practice
Internal Medicine
Obstetrics/Gynecology   **DATA NOT**
Orthopaedic Surgery   **AVAILABLE**
Pediatrics
Psychiatry
Radiology
Surgery

Matriculant Demographics: 2009–2010 First Year Class

Men: 27   **Women:** 16

Matriculants' Self-Reported Race/Ethnicity

Mexican American	0	**Korean**	0
Cuban	9	**Vietnamese**	0
Puerto Rican	0	**Other Asian**	0
Other Hispanic	6	**Total Asian**	9
Total Hispanic	15	**Native American**	0
Chinese	1	**Black**	3
Asian Indian	5	**Native Hawaiian**	0
Pakistani	1	**White**	25
Filipino	1	**Unduplicated Number**	
Japanese	1	**of Matriculants**	43

Science and Math Majors: 60%
Matriculants with:
   Baccalaureate degree: 100%
   Graduate degree(s): 14%

Financial Information

Source: 2008-2009 LCME I-B survey and 2009-2010 AAMC TSF questionnaire

	Residents	Non-residents
Total Cost of Attendance	$ 52,796	$ 84,296
Tuition and Fees	$ 23,997	$ 55,497
Other (includes living expenses)	$ 27,077	$ 27,077
Health Insurance (can be waived)	$ 1,722	$ 1,722

Average 2009 Graduate Indebtedness: n/r
% of Enrolled Students Receiving Aid: n/r

Criminal Background Check

This medical school requires a criminal background check prior to matriculation.

Florida State University College of Medicine

Tallahassee, Florida

Division of Student Affairs and Admissions
Florida State University College of Medicine
1115 West Call Street
P.O. Box 3064300
Tallahassee, Florida 32306-4300
T 850 644 7904   **F** 850 645 2846

Admissions www.med.fsu.edu/admission/md
Main www.med.fsu.edu
Financial www.med.fsu.edu/StudentAffairs/finaid
E-mail medadmissions@med.fsu.edu

Public Institution

Dr. John P. Fogarty, Dean

Dr. Graham A. Patrick, Assistant Dean for Admissions

Dr. Helen Livingston, Assistant Dean for Undergraduate and Graduate Programs

TBA, Student Financial Specialist

Dana Urrutia, Admissions Coordinator

Melinda McDaniel, Enrollment Services Coordinator

General Information

The Florida State University College of Medicine was created in July 2000 by a legislative act to train physicians with a focus on serving medically underserved populations in rural and inner-city areas and the growing geriatric population in the state. The FSU College of Medicine is located in Tallahassee, with regional medical campuses, where students complete third and fourth-year clerkships, in Pensacola, Orlando, Sarasota, Tallahassee, Daytona Beach, and Fort Pierce.

Mission Statement

The mission of the FSU College of Medicine is to educate and develop exemplary physicians who practice patient-centered health care, discover and advance knowledge, and respond to community needs, especially through service to elder, rural, and other medically underserved populations.

Curricular Highlights

Community Service Requirement: Optional.
Research/Thesis Requirement: Optional.

The academic program includes instruction in the biopsychosocial sciences and community-based health care. The first and second-year integrated curriculum uses a combination of lecture and case-based and problem-based learning in small-group discussions and simulated standardized-patient interviews. A three-year doctoring course, composed of lecture, small-group discussion, patient encounters, clinical skills instruction, and preceptorships, provides application models to complement

years 1, 2, and 3. The third year and part of the fourth year consist of required rotations in internal medicine, surgery, pediatrics, obstetrics-gynecology, family medicine/rural medicine, geriatrics, emergency medicine, advanced medicine (critical care unit), advanced family practice, and psychiatry. Students may spend up to 24 weeks in electives designed to provide a foundation on which to develop and fulfill personal interests, broaden clinical knowledge, and prepare for postgraduate medical training.

USMLE

Step 1: Required. Students must record a passing score for promotion.
Step 2: Clinical Skills (CS): Required. Students must record a passing total score to graduate.
Step 2: Clinical Knowledge (CK): Required. Students must record a passing total score to graduate.

Selection Factors

Although scholastic aptitude is necessary to complete studies in medical school, neither high GPAs nor high MCAT scores alone or in combination are adequate to obtain admission. International applicants must have a permanent resident visa. Applicants who have grades and test scores predictive of success in medical school, have demonstrated through their experiences a high degree of motivation for medicine and a strong commitment to the service of others, and have a likelihood of practicing medicine with medically underserved populations will be invited to interview. The committee evaluates all aspects of the applicant's academic record, including trends in scholastic performance.

Financial Aid

Scholarships and loan funds from private, state, and federal sources are available to qualified students and are awarded on the basis of need and/or scholarship.

Information about Diversity Programs

Because of the mission of the FSU College of Medicine and the educational value of admitting a diverse class, we developed a Master's Bridge Program to provide opportunities for applicants from groups underrepresented in medicine. Applicants from these groups who embody the characteristics valued by the col-

lege are selected for the Bridge year, which is used to develop and enhance study, time management, and test-taking skills; psychosocial and basic science backgrounds; and clinical experiences. If these students meet all requirements established for the year, they are admitted to the next year's medical school class. Students may contact the Office of Outreach and Advising at (850) 644-7678 for more information.

Campus Information

Setting

The main medical school campus is located on the Florida State University campus in a newly constructed $65 million dollar medical school complex. Each regional campus is located near affiliated hospitals in its respective community and includes study and resource areas. Applicants are invited to take a virtual tour of the campus at *www.med.fsu.edu*.

Enrollment

For 2009, total enrollment was: 453

Special Features

The FSU College of Medicine utilizes a state of the art Clinical Learning Center on the main campus and community resources to ensure that students receive a significant amount of one-on-one training with physician preceptors. The College of Medicine has affiliation agreements with over 20 hospitals across the state of Florida, as well as affiliations with nearby rural community hospitals. A wide range of elective opportunities is available in the fourth year at each of the regional sites, as well as at other accredited institutions both nationally and internationally.

Housing

On-campus housing is available. A list of affordable housing within Tallahassee and at each of the regional campuses is maintained.

Satellite Campuses/Facilities

Student rotations in the third year occur at one of the regional campuses. Rural learning opportunities are also available within driving distance of each site.

Application Process and Requirements 2011–2012

Primary Application Service: AMCAS
Earliest filing date: June 1, 2010
Latest filing date: December 1, 2010

Secondary Application Required?: Yes
Sent to: Screened applicants
Contact: (850) 644-7904,
medadmissions@med.fsu.edu
Fee: No
Fee waiver available: No
Earliest filing date: June 1, 2010
Latest filing date: December 31, 2010

MCAT® required?: Yes
Latest MCAT® considered: September 2010
Oldest MCAT® considered: May 2008

Early Decision Program: School does have EDP
Applicants notified: October 1, 2010
EDP available for: Both Residents
and Non-residents

**Regular Acceptance Notice
Earliest date:** October 15, 2010
Latest date: Until Class is Full
**Applicant's Response to Acceptance
Offer – Maximum Time:** Two weeks

**Requests for Deferred
Entrance Considered:** Yes

Deposit to Hold Place in Class: Yes
Deposit (Resident): $30
Deposit (Non-resident): $30
Deposit due: Within two weeks of receipt
of letter of acceptance
Applied to tuition: No
Deposit refundable: No
Refundable by: n/a

Estimated number of new entrants: 120
EDP: 20, special program: 10

Start Month/Year: May 2011

Interview Format: Two committee
members interview invited applicants.
Regional interviews are not available.
Video interviews are not available.

Other Programs

PREPARATORY PROGRAMS
Postbaccalaureate Program: Yes, www.med.fsu.
edu/StudentAffairs/outreach/bridge.asp

COMBINED DEGREE PROGRAMS
Baccalaureate/M.D.: No
M.D./M.P.H.: No
M.D./M.B.A.: No
M.D./J.D.: No
M.D./Ph.D.: No

Additional Program: Yes, http://med.fsu.edu/
admission/MedicalScholars.pdf

Premedical Coursework

On-line courses accepted in fulfillment of prerequisites: Case-by-case basis

Course	Req.	Rec.	Lab.	Hrs.
Inorganic Chemistry	•		•	8
Behavioral Sciences		•		
Biochemistry	•			3
Biology	•		•	8
Biology/Zoology				
Calculus				
College English	•			6
College Mathematics	•			6

Course	Req.	Rec.	Lab.	Hrs.
Computer Science				
Genetics		•		3
Humanities				
Organic Chemistry	•		•	8
Physics	•		•	8
Psychology		•		3
Social Sciences				
Spanish		•		6

Selection Factors: 2009 Accepted Applicants

Proportion of Accepted Applicants with Relevant Experience (Data Self-Reported to AMCAS®)		
Community Service/Volunteer	73%
Medically-Related Work	89%
Research	72%

Shaded bar represents school's accepted scores ranging from the 10th percentile to the 90th percentile.   School Median ●   National Median ○

Overall GPA	2.0	2.1	2.2	2.3	2.4	2.5	2.6	2.7	2.8	2.9	3.0	3.1	3.2	3.3	3.4	3.5	3.6	(3.7)	3.8	3.9	4.0
Science GPA	2.0	2.1	2.2	2.3	2.4	2.5	2.6	2.7	2.8	2.9	3.0	3.1	3.2	3.3	3.4	3.5	3.6	(3.7)	3.8	3.9	4.0

MCAT® Total Numeric Score 9 10 11 12 13 14 15 16 17 18 19 20 21 22 23 24 25 26 27 28 (29) 30 31 (32) 33 34 35 36 37 38 39 40 41 42 43

Writing Sample			J	K	L	M	N	(O)	P	(Q)	R	S	T
Verbal Reasoning	3	4	5	6	7	8	(9)	(10)	11	12	13	14	15
Biological Sciences	3	4	5	6	7	8	9	(10)	(11)	12	13	14	15
Physical Sciences	3	4	5	6	7	8	9	(10)	(11)	12	13	14	15

Acceptance & Matriculation Data for 2009–2010 First Year Class

	Resident	Non-resident	International	Total
Applications	1834	1412	34	3280
Interviewed	360	5	0	365
Deferred	4	0	0	4
Matriculants				
Early Assurance Program	0	0	0	0
Early Decision Program	6	0	0	6
Baccalaureate/M.D.	n/a	n/a	n/a	0
M.D./Ph.D.	n/a	n/a	n/a	0
Matriculated	114	4	0	**118**

Applications accepted from International Applicants: No

Specialty Choice

2005, 2006, 2007 Graduates, Specialty Choice (As reported by program directors to GME Track™)	
Anesthesiology	3%
Emergency Medicine	10%
Family Practice	18%
Internal Medicine	15%
Obstetrics/Gynecology	11%
Orthopaedic Surgery	5%
Pediatrics	9%
Psychiatry	1%
Radiology	4%
Surgery	10%

Matriculant Demographics: 2009–2010 First Year Class

Men: 51   **Women:** 67

Matriculants' Self-Reported Race/Ethnicity

Mexican American	1	Korean	1
Cuban	3	Vietnamese	0
Puerto Rican	1	Other Asian	3
Other Hispanic	11	Total Asian	13
Total Hispanic	16	Native American	2
Chinese	3	Black	12
Asian Indian	4	Native Hawaiian	0
Pakistani	0	White	88
Filipino	2	Unduplicated Number	
Japanese	0	of Matriculants	118

Science and Math Majors: 71%
Matriculants with:
Baccalaureate degree: 100%
Graduate degree(s): 7%

Financial Information

Source: 2008–2009 LCME I-B survey
and 2009–2010 AAMC TSF questionnaire

	Residents	Non-residents
Total Cost of Attendance	$49,116	$83,667
Tuition and Fees	$18,231	$52,782
Other (includes living expenses)	$30,885	$30,885
Health Insurance (cannot be waived)	$0	$0

Average 2009 Graduate Indebtedness: $150,277
% of Enrolled Students Receiving Aid: 85%

Criminal Background Check

This medical school requires a criminal background
check prior to matriculation.

University of Central Florida College of Medicine

Orlando, Florida

MD Program Admissions Office
6850 Lake Nona Blvd
Orlando, FL, 32827
T 407 266 1350 F 407 266 1399

Admissions www.med.ucf.edu/admissions
Main www.med.ucf.edu
Financial www.med.ucf.edu/academics/financial_aid/index.asp
E-mail mdadmissions@mail.ucf.edu

Public Institution

Dr. Deborah C. German, Dean

REL Larkin, Director of Admissions

Dr. Marcy Verduin, Assistant Dean for Student Affairs

Ruthanne Madsen, Director of Student Financial Services

Teresa Lyons-Oten, Registrar

Dr. Randy Manning, Associate Dean for Student Affairs

General Information

UCFs College of Medicine enrolled its charter class of 41 students in 2009. The colleges vision is to be the nation's premier 21st century college of medicine. Fully integrated into the Central Florida communitys health care and medical research infrastructure, the college partners with Orlando Health and Florida Hospital systems, Orlando VA Medical Center and Nemours Children's Hospital to provide students clinical opportunities at more than 17 major facilities. Capitalizing on UCFs strengths in biomedical sciences, modeling and simulation, and optics and photonics, faculty in the college's Burnett School of Biomedical Sciences conduct groundbreaking research in cancer, cardiovascular diseases, neurological diseases and infectious diseases. The Central Florida community has embraced UCF COMs future physicians with their financial contributions and with more than 900 local doctors serving as volunteer faculty.

Mission Statement

The University of Central Florida College of Medicine educates and inspires individuals to be exemplary physicians and scientists, leaders in medicine, scholars in discovery, and adopters of innovative technology to improve the health and well-being of all. Our patient-centered mission is achieved by outstanding medical care and services, groundbreaking research, and leading edge medical and biomedical education in an environment enriched by diversity.

Curricular Highlights

Community Service Requirement: Required.
Research/Thesis Requirement: Required.

The curriculum is a unique and exciting blend of state-of-the-art technology, virtual patients, clinical and laboratory experiences, research, directed small group sessions, and interactive didactic lectures. The first two years of the curriculum are structured into instructional modules. The first year focuses on how basic science relates to the human body and disease; the second year is an organ system-based approach, applying first-year knowledge to the study of clinical disease, pathological processes, diagnosis, and treatment. Numerous clinical experiences occur throughout the first two years that also includes a Focused Individualized Research Experience module. Third and fourth year curriculum is devoted to clinical experience through core clerkships and electives in our affiliated hospital facilities.

USMLE

Step 1: Required. Students must record a passing score for graduation, but not promotion.
Step 2: Clinical Skills (CS): Required. Students must only record a score.
Step 2: Clinical Knowledge (CK): Required. Students must only record a score.

Selection Factors

Supplemental applications are available to all qualified U.S. citizens, permanent residents, and asylees upon verification of an AMCAS application providing that the applicant meets the minimum GPA/MCAT requirements. Applicants chosen for an interview are highly motivated, capable, passionate, academically proven, and possess diverse skills, talents, and life experiences that will benefit the program, community, and fellow classmates.

Financial Aid

The financial status of the applicant is not considered in the admissions process. Student Financial Services staff assist M.D. students in obtaining funding resources and also provide counseling for many financial and debt management topics.

Information about Diversity Programs

Increasing diversity and inclusiveness is one of the central goals of UCF. Minorities account for nearly 20 percent of UCF faculty, and an aggressive minority recruitment plan continues to be a priority for the university.

Campus Information

Setting

The college occupied a new state-of-the-art Medical Education Building in Lake Nona in the summer of 2010. The Medical Education Building incorporates the latest educational technology to support the lecture halls, small group rooms, health sciences, library, anatomy and microscopy labs, clinical skills center and simulation laboratories. The UCF Health Sciences Campus, that currently includes the COM Medical Education and Burnett Biosciences buidlings, is at the center of a new medical citybeing developed at Lake Nona on the southeast edge of Orlando, only a short ride to the Space Coast and Daytona Beach. The medical city at Lake Nona also includes the completed Burnham Institute for Medical Research, the Orlando VA Medical Center, Nemours Childrens Hospital, the M.D. Anderson Cancer Center Orlando Cancer Research Institute, and a University of Florida research center, among others. The rapidly growing area also includes single and multi-family housing, retail areas, schools, and spacious parks.

Enrollment

For 2009, total enrollment was: 41

Special Features

All facilities from the classrooms to the numerous study areas are equipped with the latest communication and teaching technologies. Students enjoy the latest developments in medical simulation and clinical cases. Clinical experiences are fully integrated into all four years of the program and into the community allowing participation in rural or urban medicine at multiple hospitals and clinics in the Central Florida area.

Housing

On-campus housing is not available. A list of affordable housing near the UCF campus in Orlando as well as in the Lake Nona area is available.

Application Process and Requirements 2011–2012

Primary Application Service: AMCAS
Earliest filing date: June 1, 2010
Latest filing date: December 1, 2010

Secondary Application required?
URL: Provided to qualified applicants via e-mail
Sent to: Screened Applicants
Fee: Yes, $30
Fee Waiver Available: Yes
Earliest filing date: July 1, 2010
Latest filing date: January 15, 2011

MCAT® required?: Yes
Latest MCAT® considered: September 2010
Oldest MCAT® considered: January 2008

Early Decision Program: School does have EDP
Applicants notified: October 1, 2010
EDP available for: Both Residents and Non-residents

Regular Acceptance Notice
Earliest date: October 15, 2010
Latest date: Until Class is Full
Applicant's Response to Acceptance Offer – Maximum Time: 2 weeks

Requests for deferred entrance considered: Yes

Deposit to Hold Place in Class: No
Deposit (Resident): n/a
Deposit (Non-resident): n/a
Deposit due: n/a
Applied to tuition: n/a
Deposit refundable: n/a
Refundable by: n/a

Estimated number of new entrants: 60
EDP: 0, special program: n/a

Start month/year: August 2011

Interview format: Two partially closed faculty interviews. Regional interviews are not available. Video interviews are not available.

Other Programs

PREPARATORY PROGRAMS
Postbaccalaureate Program: No
Summer Program: No

COMBINED DEGREE PROGRAMS
Baccalaureate/M.D.: No
M.D./M.P.H.: No
M.D./M.B.A.: No
M.D./J.D.: No
M.D./Ph.D.: No

Premedical Coursework

On-line courses accepted in fulfillment of prerequisites: No

Course	Req.	Rec.	Lab.	Hrs.
Inorganic Chemistry	•		•	8
Behavioral Sciences				
Biochemistry		•		
Biology	•		•	8
Biology/Zoology				
Calculus/Statistics		•		
College English	•			6
College Mathematics	•			6
Computer Science				

Course	Req.	Rec.	Lab.	Hrs.
Genetics		•		
Humanities		•		
Organic Chemistry	•		•	8
Physics	•		•	8
Psychology				
Social Sciences				
Molecular Biology		•		
Statistics		•		
Cell Biology		•		

Selection Factors: 2009 Accepted Applicants

Proportion of Accepted Applicants with Relevant Experience (Data Self-Reported to AMCAS®)		
Community Service/Volunteer		67%
Medically-Related Work		98%
Research		81%

Shaded bar represents school's accepted scores ranging from the 10th percentile to the 90th percentile. School Median ● National Median ○

Overall GPA 2.0 2.1 2.2 2.3 2.4 2.5 2.6 2.7 2.8 2.9 3.0 3.1 3.2 3.3 3.4 3.5 3.6 3.7 3.8 (3.9) 4.0
Science GPA 2.0 2.1 2.2 2.3 2.4 2.5 2.6 2.7 2.8 2.9 3.0 3.1 3.2 3.3 3.4 3.5 3.6 3.7 3.8 (3.9) 4.0

MCAT® Total Numeric Score 9 10 11 12 13 14 15 16 17 18 19 20 21 22 23 24 25 26 27 28 29 30 31 (32) 33 34 35 36 37 38 39 40 41 42 43

Writing Sample			J	K	L	M	N	O	P	(Q)	R	S	T	
Verbal Reasoning	3	4	5	6	7	8	9	(10)	11	12	13	14	15	
Biological Sciences	3	4	5	6	7	8	9	10	(11)	12	13	14	15	
Physical Sciences	3	4	5	6	7	8	9	10	(11)	12	13	14	15	

Acceptance & Matriculation Data for 2009–2010 First Year Class

	Resident	Non-resident	International	Total
Applications	1782	2501	24	4307
Interviewed	185	48	0	233
Deferred	0	0	0	0
Matriculants				
Early Assurance Program	0	0	0	0
Early Decision Program	1	1	0	2
Baccalaureate/M.D. Program	0	0	0	0
M.D./Ph.D. Program	0	0	0	0
Matriculated	31	10	0	**41**

Applications accepted from International Applicants: Cannot be accepted.

Specialty Choice

2005, 2006, 2007 Graduates, Specialty Choice (As reported by program directors to GME Track™)

Anesthesiology
Emergency Medicine
Family P
Internal
Obstetr
Orthop: **DATA NOT AVAILABLE**
Pediatri
Psychiat
Radiolo
Surgery

Matriculant Demographics: 2009–2010 First Year Class

Men: 19 **Women:** 22

Matriculants' Self-Reported Race/Ethnicity

Mexican American	0	Korean	1
Cuban	3	Vietnamese	0
Puerto Rican	1	Other Asian	2
Other Hispanic	1	Total Asian	6
Total Hispanic	5	Native American	2
Chinese	2	Black	4
Asian Indian	1	Native Hawaiian	0
Pakistani	0	White	28
Filipino	0	Unduplicated Number	
Japanese	0	of Matriculants	41

Science Majors: 61%
Matriculants with:
Baccalaureate Degree: 100%
Graduate Degree(s): 10%

Financial Information (Estimated)

Source: 2008–2009 LCME I-B survey and 2009–2010 AAMC TSF questionnaire

	Residents	Non-residents
Total Cost of Attendance	$48,425	$75,625
Tuition and Fees	$23,800	$51,000
Other (includes living expenses)	$22,625	$23,125
Health Insurance (can be waived)	$1,800	$2,000

Average 2009 Graduate Indebtedness: n/a
% of Enrolled Students Receiving Aid: n/a

Criminal Background Check

This medical school requires a criminal background check prior to matriculation.

University of Florida
College of Medicine
Gainesville, Florida

Director, Office of Admissions
PO Box 100216, UF Health Sciences Center
Univ. of Florida College of Medicine
Gainesville, Florida 32610-0216
T 352 273 7990   **F** 352 392 1307

Admissions http://admissions.med.ufl.edu
Main www.med.ufl.edu/
Financial www.med.ufl.edu/oea/finaid/
E-mail med-admissions@ufl.edu

Public Institution

Dr. Michael L. Good, Dean

Denise Chichester, Director of Admissions

Dr. Donna M. Parker, Assistant Dean for Minority Affairs

Eileen M. Parris, Coordinator of Financial Aid

Dr. Ira H. Gessner, Chair, Medical Selection Committee

General Information
The University of Florida College of Medicine admitted its first class in September 1956. Located in the Health Science Center on the 2,000-acre University of Florida campus, the College of Medicine enjoys strong ties with HSC colleges and other university programs. The UF Health Science Center includes the Shands at UF Hospital including the Cancer Hospital and Critical Care Center that opened in 2009; Stetson Medical Science Building; Communicore; Academic Research Building; Health Professions, Nursing and Pharmacy Building; Cancer and Genetics Research Building; McKnight Brain Institute; Veterans Administration Medical Center; Nanotechnology Center and the Emerging Pathogens Center.

Mission Statement
The College of Medicine strives to improve health care through consistently excellent leadership in education, clinical care, discovery, and service. We aspire to the following goals: to develop medical professionals who are committed to the highest ideals and standards of the profession and who model an exceptional standard of care for those they treat, lead, and serve; to educate and inspire the next generation of leaders; to provide comprehensive, patient-centered, culturally sensitive, compassionate, and innovative health care of the highest quality to all; to develop and utilize innovative models of interdisciplinary health care delivery; to provide leadership in efforts to promote health, to predict and prevent disease, and to deliver care; to improve our understanding of human health and disease and to translate these discoveries into new solutions;

to recruit, develop, and nurture a diverse and academically outstanding community of faculty, students, trainees, and staff; to promote sustained, robust professional and personal growth, productivity, accountability, integrity, and synergy of faculty, students, and staff.

Curricular Highlights
Community Service Requirement: Required. Consistent health care experience preferred.
Research/Thesis Requirement: Optional.

The four years are divided into three blocks of time - Preclinical Coursework (2 years), Clinical Clerkships (1 year), and Post-clerkship Electives and Required Courses (1 year). Preclinical coursework provides students with essential basic science and substantial clinical training and experience. The third year is devoted to clinical clerkships. Required clerkships include family medicine, medicine, neurology, pediatrics, psychiatry, obstetrics/gynecology, and surgery. Students spend 10-12 weeks participating in clerkships at UF Health Science Center Jacksonville. During clerkships, students become integral members of the medical team and have direct responsibility for assigned patients. The fourth year includes seven elective periods and three required courses: anesthesiology, emergency medicine, and either senior medicine, community medicine, or pediatrics. An eleventh period is available for accomplishing residency interviews. For students who have already chosen a specialty, fourth-year programs may be designed to provide career choice-related experiences.

USMLE
Step 1: Required. Students must record a passing score for promotion.
Step 2: Clinical Skills (CS): Required. Students must only record a score.
Step 2: Clinical Knowledge (CK): Required. Students must only record a score.

Selection Factors
We appraise applicants on personal attributes, academic record, activities, MCAT, and recommendations. A personal interview is required and is granted at the discretion of the Medical Selection Committee. We do not discriminate on the basis of race, sex, age, disability, creed, or

national origin. Florida residents are given preference. Exceptionally well qualifed non-residents are considered. We welcome applicants from groups underrepresented in medicine.

Financial Aid
Financial assistance is available to all students who show need. Scholarships and low interest loans are available, as well as research fellowships.

Information about Diversity Programs
The Office of Minority Affairs offers summer research programs.

Campus Information
Setting
The Gainesville campus lies midway between the Atlantic Ocean and the Gulf of Mexico in the lush beauty of north central Florida. The surrounding area includes fresh water springs, wild prairies, and many parks exhibiting a great diversity of wildlife. Arts and culture abound in Gainesville. The Phillips Center for the Performing Arts features world-class entertainers from all genres. Museums include The Harn Museum of Art and the Florida Museum of Natural History, featuring the McGuire Butterfly Rainforest. Gainesville's many professional Performing Arts groups include the Hippodrome Theatre, Dance Alive National Ballet and The Gainesville Chamber Orchestra, each performing regularly throughout the year.

Enrollment
For 2009, total enrollment was: 522

Housing
On-campus housing is not available.

Satellite Campuses/Facilities
The UF Health Science Center in Jacksonville is our urban campus and includes one of the few Proton Beam facilities in the country. Formal educational affiliations have also been established in Ft. Lauderdale, Miami, Orlando, and Pensacola.

Application Process and Requirements 2011–2012

Primary Application Service: AMCAS
Earliest filing date: June 1, 2010
Latest filing date: December 1, 2010

Secondary Application Required?: Yes
Sent to: Applicants of interest
URL: n/a
Contact: Denise Chichester, (352) 273-7990, med-admissions@ufl.edu
Fee: Yes, $30 **Waiver available:** No
Earliest filing date: July 15, 2010
Latest filing date: January 15, 2011

MCAT® required?: Yes
Latest MCAT® considered: September 2010
Oldest MCAT® considered: January 2008

Early Decision Program: School does not have EDP
Applicants notified: n/a
EDP available for: n/a

Regular Acceptance Notice
Earliest date: October 16, 2010
Latest date: Until class is full
Applicant's Response to Acceptance Offer – Maximum Time: Two weeks

Requests for Deferred Entrance Considered: Yes

Deposit to Hold Place in Class: Yes
Deposit (Resident): $200 **(Non-resident):** $200
Deposit due: Two weeks after notice of acceptance
Applied to tuition: Yes **Refundable:** Yes
Refundable by: May 15, 2011

Estimated number of new entrants: 135
EDP: n/a, special program: 12

Start Month/Year: August 2011

Interview Format: Two open-file interviews at COM. Regional interviews are not available. Video interview possible under extraordinary circumstances.

Other Programs

PREPARATORY PROGRAMS
Postbaccalaureate Program: No
Summer Program: Yes, http://oma.med.ufl.edu/8/summer-research-program/ Office of Minority Affairs, (352) 273-6656

COMBINED DEGREE PROGRAMS
Baccalaureate/M.D.: Yes, http://jhmp.sites.medinfo.ufl.edu/
M.D./M.P.H.: Yes, www.mph.ufl.edu/programs/collaborative/md.htm
M.D./M.B.A.: Yes, www.med.ufl.edu/oea/osa/cat-research_option.shtml
M.D./J.D.: Yes, www.med.ufl.edu/oea/osa/cat-research_option.shtml
M.D./Ph.D.: Yes, http://mdphd.med.ufl.edu/
Additional Program: Yes, http://msrp.med.ufl.edu/

Premedical Coursework

On-line courses accepted in fulfillment of prerequisites: No

Course	Req.	Rec.	Lab.	Hrs.
Inorganic Chemistry	•		•	8
Behavioral Sciences				
Biochemistry	•		•	4
Biology				
Biology/Zoology	•		•	8
Calculus				
College English				
College Mathematics				

Course	Req.	Rec.	Lab.	Hrs.
Computer Science				
Genetics				
Humanities				
Organic Chemistry	•		•	4
Physics	•		•	8
Psychology				
Social Sciences				
Other				

Selection Factors: 2009 Accepted Applicants

Proportion of Accepted Applicants with Relevant Experience (Data Self-Reported to AMCAS®)		
Community Service/Volunteer	67%
Medically-Related Work	84%
Research	83%

Shaded bar represents school's accepted scores ranging from the 10th percentile to the 90th percentile   School Median ● National Median ◐

Overall GPA 2.0 2.1 2.2 2.3 2.4 2.5 2.6 2.7 2.8 2.9 3.0 3.1 3.2 3.3 3.4 3.5 3.6 3.7 (3.8) 3.9 4.0
Science GPA 2.0 2.1 2.2 2.3 2.4 2.5 2.6 2.7 2.8 2.9 3.0 3.1 3.2 3.3 3.4 3.5 3.6 3.7 (3.8) 3.9 4.0

MCAT® Total Numeric Score 9 10 11 12 13 14 15 16 17 18 19 20 21 22 23 24 25 26 27 28 29 30 31 (32)(33) 34 35 36 37 38 39 40 41 42 43

Writing Sample			J	K	L	M	N	O	P	(Q)	R	S	T
Verbal Reasoning	3	4	5	6	7	8	9	(10)	11	12	13	14	15
Biological Sciences	3	4	5	6	7	8	9	10	(11)	12	13	14	15
Physical Sciences	3	4	5	6	7	8	9	10	(11)	12	13	14	15

Acceptance & Matriculation Data for 2009–2010 First Year Class

	Resident	Non-resident	International	Total
Applications	1601	946	26	2573
Interviewed	328	19	0	347
Deferred	2	0	0	2
Matriculants				
Early Assurance Program	0	0	0	0
Early Decision Program	0	0	0	0
Baccalaureate/M.D.	10	1	0	11
M.D./Ph.D.	4	1	0	5
Matriculated	123	5	0	**128**

Applications accepted from International Applicants: No

Matriculant Demographics: 2009–2010 First Year Class

Men: 70   **Women:** 58

Matriculants' Self-Reported Race/Ethnicity

Mexican American	0	Korean	4
Cuban	4	Vietnamese	3
Puerto Rican	0	Other Asian	2
Other Hispanic	6	Total Asian	31
Total Hispanic	10	Native American	0
Chinese	9	Black	2
Asian Indian	11	Native Hawaiian	0
Pakistani	3	White	86
Filipino	0	Unduplicated Number	
Japanese	2	of Matriculants	128

Science and Math Majors: 57%
Matriculants with:
 Baccalaureate degree: 100%
 Graduate degree(s): 4%

Specialty Choice

2005, 2006, 2007 Graduates, Specialty Choice (As reported by program directors to GME Track™)	
Anesthesiology	9%
Emergency Medicine	7%
Family Practice	4%
Internal Medicine	15%
Obstetrics/Gynecology	6%
Orthopaedic Surgery	3%
Pediatrics	12%
Psychiatry	8%
Radiology	7%
Surgery	5%

Financial Information
Source: 2008-2009 LCME I-B survey and 2009-2010 AAMC TSF questionnaire

	Residents	Non-residents
Total Cost of Attendance	$ 45,658	$ 74,898
Tuition and Fees	$ 28,727	$ 57,967
Other (includes living expenses)	$ 16,931	$ 16,931
Health Insurance (can be waived)	$ 0	$ 0

Average 2009 Graduate Indebtedness: $116,746
% of Enrolled Students Receiving Aid: 88%

Criminal Background Check

This medical school does not require a criminal background check prior to matriculation.

University of Miami
Miller School of Medicine
Miami, Florida

Office of Admissions
University of Miami Miller School of Medicine
P.O. Box 016159
Miami, Florida 33101
T 305 243 3234   F 305 243 6548

Admissions www.miami.edu/medical-admissions
Main www.med.miami.edu
Financial www.mededu.miami.edu/OSFA
E-mail med.admissions@miami.edu

Private Institution

Dr. Pascal Goldschmidt, Dean

Dr. Richard S. Weisman, Associate Dean for Admissions

Dr. Robert L. Hernandez, Senior, Associate Dean for Minority Affairs

Laura L. Kasperski, Assistant Dean for Student Financial Assistance

General Information
The University of Miami Miller School of Medicine is the largest and oldest medical school in the state of Florida. Six hospitals containing nearly 3,000 beds are located on the medical campus and provide a complete spectrum of clinical experiences. Specialty centers at the Miller School of Medicine include The Bascom Palmer Eye Institute and Anne Bates Leach Eye Hospital, the Ambulatory Care Center, the Diabetes Research Institute, the Lois Pope Life Center (which houses The Miami Project to Cure Spinal Cord Paralysis), the Bachelor Children's Research Institute, the Ryder Trauma Center, and the Sylvester Comprehensive Cancer Center.

Mission Statement
The Miller School of Medicine has four interrelated missions: patient care, teaching, research, and community service.

Curricular Highlights
Community Service Requirement: Optional.
Research/Thesis Requirement: Optional.

The curriculum is an integrated program that requires students to be active and responsible learners. It emphasizes faculty and student-led small-group experiences wherein basic science concepts are introduced and assimilated in light of common disease states and clinical relevance. It also includes material not traditionally emphasized: professionalism, humanism and ethics, population medicine, prevention and screening, quality and outcome assessment, medical informatics, geriatrics, alternative medicine, nutrition, medical economics, and end-of-life care. An over-arching theme throughout all four years is the continuous acquisition and refinement of clinical skills

through expert teaching and patient encounters, starting in the first weeks of the first year of the curriculum.

USMLE
Step 1: Required. Students must record a passing score for promotion.
Step 2: Clinical Skills (CS): Required. Students must only record a score.
Step 2: Clinical Knowledge (CK): Required. Students must only record a score.

Selection Factors
Secondary applications are sent to all U.S. citizens and permanent residents who submit a verified AMCAS application. In deciding whether to return secondary materials, applicants are reminded that the last entering class had an average undergraduate cumulative GPA of 3.7 and an average composite MCAT score of 31. Factors assessed by the committee to rate all completed applications include: preparedness to study medicine, diversity of life experiences, meaningfulness of direct patient contact experiences, and quality of letters of recommendation. Applicants with the highest ratings are invited for an interview. Applicants' files are reviewed without regard to race, creed, sex, national origin, age, or handicap.

Financial Aid
In 2009-2010, the amount of financial aid awarded totaled about $22 million. The school participates in all major federal and state programs. A number of scholarships are awarded each year for merit and for life diversity and financial need. Information concerning financial assistance and student budgets may be obtained on the Office of Financial Assistance web site at *www.mededu.miami.edu/OSFA* or by calling 305-243-6211.

Information about Diversity Programs
The school sponsors a special seven-week summer program that provides pre-medical undergraduates with opportunities to gain first-hand knowledge of the requirements of a medical education. Applications and information may be obtained by calling 305-243-5998.

Campus Information

Setting
The School of Medicine is at the heart of the Miami Health District, located in the Civic Center area of Miami, about midway between Miami International Airport and downtown Miami. The regional medical campus is located in Boca Raton, Florida, on the campus of Florida Atlantic University, about 50 miles north of the parent campus.

Enrollment
For 2009, total enrollment was: 740

Special Features
The entire medical campus is completely "wireless," and lectures are now podcasted, both in audio and in video formats. Numerous opportunities exist for students to participate in community medicine, outreach programs, and international medicine to study the root causes of medical inequalities at multiple sites in the Caribbean, Russia, Central America, and Africa.

Housing
Many medical students live in two apartment buildings adjacent to campus. The Medical Campus is served by Metro Rail, an elevated light railway, which has made large areas of Miami accessible to medical students.

Satellite Campuses/Facilities
The School of Medicine has a regional medical campus in Boca Raton on the campus of Florida Atlantic University. Up to 56 students each year will start and complete their medical educations at the regional campus. While the Medical Campus and regional campus curricula are identical in their missions, they have different emphases. Students at the regional campus gain their clinical training at John F. Kennedy (JFK) Community Hospital and other local hospitals and clinics in a patient-centered environment.

Application Process and Requirements 2011–2012

Primary Application Service: AMCAS
Earliest filing date: June 1, 2010
Latest filing date: December 1, 2010

Secondary Application Required?: Yes
Sent to: All U.S. citizens and permanent residents
Contact: Richard S. Weisman, (305) 243-3234, med.admissions@miami.edu
Fee: Yes, $75 **Waiver available:** Yes
Earliest filing date: June 15, 2010
Latest filing date: January 31, 2011

MCAT® required?: Yes
Latest MCAT® considered: September 2010
Oldest MCAT® considered: January 2008

Early Decision Program: School does not have EDP
Applicants notified: n/a
EDP available for: n/a

Regular Acceptance Notice
Earliest date: October 15, 2010
Latest date: Until class is full
Applicant's Response to Acceptance Offer – Maximum Time: Two weeks

Requests for Deferred Entrance Considered: Yes

Deposit to Hold Place in Class: Yes
Deposit (Resident): $100 **(Non-resident):** $100
Deposit due: response to acceptance letter
Applied to tuition: Yes **Refundable:** No
Refundable by: May 15, 2011

Estimated number of new entrants: 206
EDP: 0, special program: 30

Start Month/Year: August 2011

Interview Format: Open file, structured, one hour interviews. Regional interviews are not available. Video interviews are not available.

Other Programs

PREPARATORY PROGRAMS
Postbaccalaureate Program: No
Summer Program: Yes, www.miami.edu/medical-admissions
Robert Hernandez, MD, (305) 284-5998

COMBINED DEGREE PROGRAMS
Baccalaureate/M.D.: Yes
www.miami.edu/medical-admissions
M.D./M.P.H.: Yes, http://spider.med.miami.edu/grad/phd.html
Dr. Jay Wilkinson, (305) 243-2209
M.D./M.B.A.: Yes, Dr. Lori Pryor, (305) 284-2510
M.D./J.D.: No
M.D./Ph.D.: Yes, http://chroma.med.miami.edu/mdphd. Dr. Sandra Lemmon, (305) 243-1094

Premedical Coursework

On-line courses accepted in fulfillment of prerequisites: No

Course	Req.	Rec.	Lab.	Hrs.	Course	Req.	Rec.	Lab.	Hrs.
Inorganic Chemistry	•		•	8	Computer Science				
Behavioral Sciences					Genetics		•		
Biochemistry		•			Humanities				
Biology					Organic Chemistry	•		•	8
Biology/Zoology	•		•	6	Physics	•		•	8
Calculus					Psychology				
College English	•			6	Social Sciences				
College Mathematics					Additional Sciences		•		6

Selection Factors: 2009 Accepted Applicants

Proportion of Accepted Applicants with Relevant Experience (Data Self-Reported to AMCAS®)		
Community Service/Volunteer	67%
Medically-Related Work	89%
Research	82%

Shaded bar represents school's accepted scores ranging from the 10th percentile to the 90th percentile **School Median** ○ **National Median** ○

Overall GPA 2.0 2.1 2.2 2.3 2.4 2.5 2.6 2.7 2.8 2.9 3.0 3.1 3.2 3.3 3.4 3.5 3.6 3.7 (3.8) 3.9 4.0

Science GPA 2.0 2.1 2.2 2.3 2.4 2.5 2.6 2.7 2.8 2.9 3.0 3.1 3.2 3.3 3.4 3.5 3.6 (3.7) 3.8 3.9 4.0

MCAT® Total Numeric Score 9 10 11 12 13 14 15 16 17 18 19 20 21 22 23 24 25 26 27 28 29 30 31 (32) 33 34 35 36 37 38 39 40 41 42 43

Writing Sample				J	K	L	M	N	O	P	(Q)	R	S	T
Verbal Reasoning	3	4	5	6	7	8	9	(10)	11	12	13	14	15	
Biological Sciences	3	4	5	6	7	8	9	10	(11)	12	13	14	15	
Physical Sciences	3	4	5	6	7	8	9	10	(11)	12	13	14	15	

Acceptance & Matriculation Data for 2009–2010 First Year Class

	Resident	Non-resident	International	Total
Applications	1642	3249	31	4922
Interviewed	283	166	0	449
Deferred	2	3	0	5
Matriculants				
Early Assurance Program	0	0	0	0
Early Decision Program	0	0	0	0
Baccalaureate/M.D.	24	9	0	33
M.D./Ph.D.	1	4	0	5
Matriculated	143	51	0	**194**

Applications accepted from International Applicants: No

Matriculant Demographics: 2009–2010 First Year Class

Men: 104   **Women:** 90

Matriculants' Self-Reported Race/Ethnicity

Mexican American	0	Korean	1
Cuban	13	Vietnamese	1
Puerto Rican	2	Other Asian	6
Other Hispanic	13	Total Asian	50
Total Hispanic	25	Native American	1
Chinese	8	Black	14
Asian Indian	29	Native Hawaiian	0
Pakistani	2	White	123
Filipino	1	Unduplicated Number	
Japanese	3	of Matriculants	194

Science and Math Majors: 64%
Matriculants with:
    Baccalaureate degree: 99%
    Graduate degree(s): 12%

Specialty Choice

2005, 2006, 2007 Graduates, Specialty Choice (As reported by program directors to GME Track™)	
Anesthesiology	9%
Emergency Medicine	4%
Family Practice	4%
Internal Medicine	23%
Obstetrics/Gynecology	7%
Orthopaedic Surgery	2%
Pediatrics	7%
Psychiatry	4%
Radiology	8%
Surgery	5%

Financial Information

Source: 2008-2009 LCME I-B survey and 2009-2010 AAMC TSF questionnaire

	Residents	Non-residents
Total Cost of Attendance	$ 54,711	$ 64,417
Tuition and Fees	$ 30,188	$ 39,394
Other (includes living expenses)	$ 22,775	$ 23,275
Health Insurance (can be waived)	$ 1,748	$ 1,748

Average 2009 Graduate Indebtedness: n/r
% of Enrolled Students Receiving Aid: 77%

Criminal Background Check

This medical school does not require a criminal background check prior to matriculation.

University of South Florida College of Medicine

Tampa, Florida

Office of Admissions/MDC-3
University of South Florida College of Medicine
12901 Bruce B. Downs Boulevard
Tampa, Florida 33612-4799
T 813 974 2229   F 813 974 4990

Admissions www.hsc.usf.edu/nocms/medicine/
mdadmissions
Main http://health.usf.edu/medicine/home.html
Financial http://hsc.usf.edu/medicine/studentaffairs/
financial_aid/index.htm
E-mail md-admissions@health.usf.edu

Public Institution

Dr. Stephen K. Klasko, Dean College of Medicine and VP for USF Health

Dr. Alicia D.H. Monroe, Vice Dean of for Educational Affairs

Jonathan Perez, Director of MD Admissions

Suzanne Jackson, Director of Student Diversity and Enrichment

Michelle Williamson, Director of Financial Aid

General Information

USF Health is composed of the College of Medicine (COM), Colleges of Public Health and Nursing and the School of Physical Therapy. All offer immersive experiences to interact with diverse patient populations, building inter-professional relationships at nationally ranked clinical facilities. In our four-year SELECT program, students have the opportunity to complete two years at Tampa and complete their clinical years at Lehigh Valley Health Network (LVHN), one of the most progressive, technologically advanced and highest ranked medical learning facilities in the country.

Mission Statement

The College of Medicine educates students and professionals of the health and biomedical sciences within a scholarly environment, fostering excellence in the lifelong goals of education, research and compassionate care and providing a training ground for those who harbor a deeply rooted desire to selflessly serve in the medical profession to become medical leaders.

Curricular Highlights

Community Service Requirement: Required. International, national and local opportunities. **Research/Thesis Requirement:** Optional.

Areas of study include the sciences basic to medicine, the major clinical disciplines, behavioral science, medical ethics, human services and many more. We promote customized, diverse experiences, allowing students the opportunity to be a part of a scholarly concentration in one of nine areas in education, research, public health, health disparities, law and medicine, medical humanities, business and entrepreneur-

ship, health systems engineering or international medicine. The preclinical curriculum years utilize an integrated, systems-based approach and emphasize early clinical experiences from day one. Required clerkships emphasize a patient-centered interdisciplinary approach, and students are given increasing responsibility leading up to graduation. The SELECT program curriculum emphasizes scholarly excellence, leadership experiences, and collaborative training. Students complete their clinical years at LVHN for an expanded network of inter-professional educational experiences.

USMLE

Step 1: Required. Students must record a passing score for promotion.
Step 2: Clinical Skills (CS): Required. Students must record a passing total score to graduate.
Step 2: Clinical Knowledge (CK): Required. Students must record a passing total score to graduate.

Selection Factors

Applicants are selected for interview based on academic achievement, demonstrated motivation to practice medicine, humanism, and leadership. The Admissions Committee reviews all materials including interview evaluations, letters of recommendations, and course load and types of courses taken. The majority of the matriculating class are Florida residents. Highly qualified non-Florida residents are also considered particularly for the SELECT program.
Applicants are encouraged to apply and complete their applications as soon as possible

Financial Aid

The financial status of applicants does not affect their acceptance. Limited funds are available for loans and scholarships. First-year students are not permitted to engage in outside employment. There are employment opportunities in Tampa and the surrounding area for spouses. Contact our Office of Financial Aid at (813) 974-2068.

Information about Diversity Programs

The Office of Student Diversity and Enrichment (OSDE) collaborates with Admissions and USF Health to recruit/support a diverse student body. USF Health embraces diversity and fosters academic success. OSDE provides assistance to

minority organizations such as the APAMSA, IHSC, LAMSA, and SNMA. Visit *http://health.usf.edu/medicine/osde/index.htm*.

Campus Information

Setting

The COM program is located in Tampa, the nation's fifth most diverse city, with a widely diverse patient population and medical training facilities. The COM's community training partners include Tampa General Hospital, All Children's Hospital, Moffitt Cancer Center, two large Veterans Affairs hospitals, and various rural clinics. The SELECT program's clinical campus is located in the Lehigh Valley of Pennsylvania. The Lehigh Valley is located about 60 miles north of Philadelphia and 90 miles west of New York City.

Enrollment

For 2009, total enrollment was: 482

Special Features

In the Scholarly Concentration program students pursue one of nine fields of study. Early clinical experience is offered in many clinical settings. Interdisciplinary clerkships are organized around patient experience. The Center for Advance Clinical Learning and Simulation provides skills training working with standardized patients and high-fidelity simulators. The SELECT program provides training in emotionally competent leadership, patient quality and safety, and the business of medicine using immersion experiences in a technology-rich environment at LVHN.

Housing

Relocation information is provided to assist with housing for students. Student centered complexes are in close proximity to campus and medical facilities.

Satellite Campuses/Facilities

The SELECT program was developed in partnership with LVHN, one of the 100 Most Wired U.S. hospitals that use technology to promote quality and safety. LVHN has a Level I tertiary care referral center for trauma, burns and transplants; a cancer center; primary stroke center; a behavioral health science center; a community hospital; and inner city health centers

Application Process and Requirements 2011–2012

Primary Application Service: AMCAS
Earliest filing date: June 1, 2010
Latest filing date: November 15, 2010

Secondary Application Required?: Yes
Sent to: All applicants
URL: Office of MD Admissions, 813-974-2229, md-admissions@health.usf.edu
Contact: Office of MD Admissions, (813) 974-2229, md-admissions@health.usf.edu
Fee: Yes, $30   **Waiver available:** Yes
Earliest filing date: June 1, 2010
Latest filing date: January 5, 2011

MCAT® required?: Yes
Latest MCAT® considered: October 2010
Oldest MCAT® considered: September 2007

Early Decision Program: School does have EDP
Applicants notified: October 1, 2010
EDP available for: Both Residents and Non-residents

Regular Acceptance Notice
Earliest date: October 15, 2010
Latest date: Until class is full
Applicant's Response to Acceptance Offer – Maximum Time: Two weeks

Requests for Deferred Entrance Considered: Yes

Deposit to Hold Place in Class: No
Deposit (Resident): n/a   **(Non-resident):** n/a
Deposit due: n/a
Applied to tuition: n/a   **Refundable:** n/a
Refundable by: n/a

Estimated number of new entrants: 144
EDP: 4, special program: 0

Start Month/Year: August 2011

Interview Format: Open file. Regional interviews are not available. Video interviews are not available.

Other Programs

PREPARATORY PROGRAMS
Postbaccalaureate Program: No
Summer Program: Yes, http://health.usf.edu/medicine/osde/programs.htm
Pre-Matriculation Program: Yes, USF COM encourages and promotes an environment that welcomes and embraces diversity in the student body. http://health.usf.edu/medicine/osde

COMBINED DEGREE PROGRAMS
Baccalaureate/M.D.: Yes, www.hsc.usf.edu/medicine/mdadmissions/special_programs.htm
M.D./M.P.H.: Yes, www.hsc.usf.edu/medicine/mdadmissions/special_programs.htm
M.D./M.B.A.: Yes, www.hsc.usf.edu/medicine/mdadmissions/special_programs.htm
M.D./J.D.: Yes, www.hsc.usf.edu/medicine/mdadmissions/special_programs.htm
M.D./Ph.D.: Yes, www.hsc.usf.edu/medicine/mdadmissions/special_programs.htm

Premedical Coursework

On-line courses accepted in fulfillment of prerequisites: No

Course	Req.	Rec.	Lab.	Sems.
Inorganic Chemistry	•		•	2
Behavioral Sciences				
Biochemistry		•		2
Biology	•		•	2
Biology/Zoology				
Calculus				
College English	•			2
College Mathematics	•			2

Course	Req.	Rec.	Lab.	Sems.
Computer Science				
Genetics				
Humanities		•		
Organic Chemistry	•		•	2
Physics	•		•	2
Psychology		•		
Social Sciences		•		
Other				

Selection Factors: 2009 Accepted Applicants

Proportion of Accepted Applicants with Relevant Experience (Data Self-Reported to AMCAS®)		
Community Service/Volunteer		79%
Medically-Related Work		90%
Research		81%

Shaded bar represents school's accepted scores ranging from the 10th percentile to the 90th percentile   School Median ● National Median ○

Overall GPA 2.0 2.1 2.2 2.3 2.4 2.5 2.6 2.7 2.8 2.9 3.0 3.1 3.2 3.3 3.4 3.5 3.6 3.7 (3.8) 3.9 4.0
Science GPA 2.0 2.1 2.2 2.3 2.4 2.5 2.6 2.7 2.8 2.9 3.0 3.1 3.2 3.3 3.4 3.5 3.6 3.7 (3.8) 3.9 4.0

MCAT® Total Numeric Score 9 10 11 12 13 14 15 16 17 18 19 20 21 22 23 24 25 26 27 28 29 30 (31)(32) 33 34 35 36 37 38 39 40 41 42 43

Writing Sample		J	K	L	M	N	O	(P)	Q	R	S	T
Verbal Reasoning	3	4	5	6	7	8	9	(10)	11	12	13	14	15
Biological Sciences	3	4	5	6	7	8	9	10	(11)	12	13	14	15
Physical Sciences	3	4	5	6	7	8	9	(10)	(11)	12	13	14	15

Acceptance & Matriculation Data for 2009–2010 First Year Class

	Resident	Non-resident	International	Total
Applications	1854	1116	21	2991
Interviewed	332	68	0	400
Deferred	1	0	0	1
Matriculants				
Early Assurance Program	0	0	0	0
Early Decision Program	3	0	0	3
Baccalaureate/M.D.	16	0	0	16
M.D./Ph.D.	0	0	0	0
Matriculated	111	9	0	**120**

Applications accepted from International Applicants: No

Matriculant Demographics: 2009–2010 First Year Class

Men: 58   **Women:** 62

Matriculants' Self-Reported Race/Ethnicity

Mexican American	4	Korean	3
Cuban	4	Vietnamese	3
Puerto Rican	5	Other Asian	1
Other Hispanic	8	Total Asian	34
Total Hispanic	19	Native American	1
Chinese	6	Black	6
Asian Indian	16	Native Hawaiian	0
Pakistani	4	White	77
Filipino	5	Unduplicated Number	
Japanese	1	of Matriculants	120

Science and Math Majors: 74%
Matriculants with:
    Baccalaureate degree: 100%
    Graduate degree(s): 24%

Specialty Choice

2005, 2006, 2007 Graduates, Specialty Choice (As reported by program directors to GME Track™)	
Anesthesiology	6%
Emergency Medicine	7%
Family Practice	8%
Internal Medicine	18%
Obstetrics/Gynecology	5%
Orthopaedic Surgery	2%
Pediatrics	8%
Psychiatry	7%
Radiology	8%
Surgery	6%

Financial Information

Source: 2008-2009 LCME I-B survey and 2009-2010 AAMC TSF questionnaire

	Residents	Non-residents
Total Cost of Attendance	$ 48,815	$ 76,026
Tuition and Fees	$ 26,833	$ 54,044
Other (includes living expenses)	$ 21,982	$ 21,982
Health Insurance (can be waived)	$ 0	$ 0

Average 2009 Graduate Indebtedness: $141,223
% of Enrolled Students Receiving Aid: 88%

Criminal Background Check

This medical school requires a criminal background check prior to matriculation.

Emory University School of Medicine

Atlanta, Georgia

Emory University School of Medicine
Office of Admissions
1648 Pierce Drive NE, Suite 231
Atlanta, Georgia 30322-4510
T 404 727 5660   **F** 404 727 5456

Admissions www.med.emory.edu/admissions
Main www.med.emory.edu
Financial www.emory.edu/FINANCIAL_AID
E-mail medadmiss@emory.edu

Private Institution

Dr. Thomas J. Lawley, Dean

Dr. Ira K. Schwartz, Associate Dean for Medical Education/Student Affairs

Dr. Robert Lee, Associate Dean and Director, Multicultural Medical Student Affairs

Michael Behler, Associate Director of Financial Aid and Scholarships

Dr. J. William Eley, Executive Associate Dean for Medical Education/Student Affairs

June Eddingfield, Associate Director of Admissions

General Information

The Emory University School of Medicine was founded in 1915, resulting from several reorganizations dating from 1854 when the Atlanta Medical College was founded. Student clinical experiences are in numerous teaching hospitals, which provide more than 3,000 beds and large outpatient clinics. The university has close ties with Grady Memorial Hospital, the Atlanta VA Medical Center, the Centers for Disease Control and Prevention, the Carter Center of Emory University, and other local institutions.

Mission Statement

We are committed to recruiting and developing a diverse group of students and innovative leaders in biomedical science, public health, medical education, and clinical care. We foster a culture that integrates leading edge basic, translational, and clinical research to further the ability to deliver quality health care, to predict illness and treat the sick, and to promote health of our patients and community.

Curricular Highlights

Community Service Requirement: Optional. Encouraged.
Research/Thesis Requirement: Optional.

The new curriculum features a hybrid of lectures, small groups, and enhanced clinical exposure throughout the first 18 months of training. Students begin 12 months of clinical rotations midway through the second year, followed by a 5 month Discovery Phase which allows time for clinical or bench research, international experience, or other academic inquiry. The fourth year is highlighted by a capstone experience which helps further prepare students for entering residency.

USMLE

Step 1: Required. Students must record a passing score for promotion.
Step 2: Clinical Skills (CS): Required. Students must only record a score.
Step 2: Clinical Knowledge (CK): Required. Students must record a passing total score to graduate.

Selection Factors

Students are selected without regard to race, color, sex, sexual orientation, gender or gender identity, age, religion, disability, creed, ethnic or national origin, or veteran status. In addition to the AMCAS application, all applicants must: (a) present a very high level of scholarship and leadership; (b) demonstrate a strong motivation to practice medicine; (c) have experience in a clinical setting; (d) take the MCAT within four years of the matriculating year; (e) complete the Emory supplemental application, including an application fee; (f) submit the required letter(s) of recommendation; and, (g) appear for a personal interview, if invited. Students from foreign schools must complete all science course requirements at a regionally accredited U.S. or Canadian institution.

Financial Aid

The financial aid status of an applicant is not a determining factor in the admissions process. Those who establish documented financial need are eligible to receive funding in the form of scholarships and loans. Parental financial information is necessary to determine institutional need-based funding. Each year, Emory awards 4 entering students merit-based Woodruff Fellowships, which provide full tuition and stipend for all four years. International students are expected to secure their own funding for tuition and living expenses, and they are not eligible for federal or institutional financial aid, including loans.

Information about Diversity Programs

Emory University School of Medicine welcomes applications from students representing minority groups from all areas of the country. Emory is strongly committed to increasing opportunities for minority students, including thorough and individual consideration of each applicant during the admissions process. The Office of Multicultural Medical Student Affairs works in conjunction with the Admissions Committee and the Office of Medical Education and Student Affairs in the recruitment, selection, and retention of qualified minority students

Campus Information

Setting

EUSM is located on the main university campus, situated on 631 acres in the historic neighborhood of Druid Hills, 6 miles from downtown Atlanta. Emory is positioned along the Clifton Corridor, which also includes the U.S. Centers for Disease Control and Prevention. Clinical facilities are located on the main campus and at numerous sites around the metro Atlanta area.

Enrollment

For 2009, total enrollment was: 519

Special Features

Emory's clinical facilities provide for an extraordinary variety of training opportunities with diverse patient populations. Students are trained at the Emory University Hospital, Emory University Hospital Midtown, Wesley Woods Geriatric Center, Children's Healthcare of Atlanta at Egleston and at Hughes Spalding, The Emory Clinic, Winship Cancer Institute, Atlanta VA Medical Center, Grady Memorial Hospital (one of the largest hospitals in the U.S.), and numerous community out-patient clinical sites.

Housing

Most students live in close proximity to the main campus. Nearby off-campus apartments and houses are plentiful and affordable. A new Emory graduate housing facility, Campus Crossings at Briarcliff, opened in August 2009. A Housing Weekend, hosted by current medical students, is held each summer to assist incoming students in their housing/roommate search.

Application Process and Requirements 2011–2012

Primary Application Service: AMCAS
Earliest filing date: June 1, 2010
Latest filing date: October 15, 2010

Secondary Application Required?: Yes
Sent to: All verified applicants
Contact: Medical School Admissions, (404) 727-5660, medadmiss@emory.edu
Fee: Yes, $100   **Waiver available:** Yes
Earliest filing date: August 1, 2010
Latest filing date: December 1, 2010

MCAT® required?: Yes
Latest MCAT® considered: September 2010
Oldest MCAT® considered: January 2007

Early Decision Program: School does not have EDP
Applicants notified: n/a
EDP available for: n/a

Regular Acceptance Notice
Earliest date: November 2010
Latest date: Until class is full
Applicant's Response to Acceptance Offer – Maximum Time: Two weeks

Requests for Deferred Entrance Considered: Yes

Deposit to Hold Place in Class: No
Deposit (Resident): n/a   **(Non-resident):** n/a
Deposit due: n/a
Applied to tuition: n/a   **Refundable:** n/a
Refundable by: n/a

Estimated number of new entrants: 138
EDP: n/a, special program: n/a

Start Month/Year: July 2011

Interview Format: Group interview and individual interview. Regional interviews are not available. Video interviews are not available.

Other Programs

PREPARATORY PROGRAMS
Postbaccalaureate Program: No
Summer Program: No

COMBINED DEGREE PROGRAMS
Baccalaureate/M.D.: No
M.D./M.P.H.: Yes, www.med.emory.edu
John E. McGowan, Jr., M.D.
jmcgowa@sph.emory.edu
M.D./M.B.A.: No
M.D./J.D.: No
M.D./Ph.D.: Yes, http://med.emory.edu/education/MDPHD
Mary Horton, MPH, MA
(404) 727-6977, mdphd@emory.edu
Additional Program: Yes, actsi.org/areas/retcd/mscr1/mscr_emory/index.html
Cheryl Sroka, MD/MSCR Program,
csroka@emory.edu

Premedical Coursework

On-line courses accepted in fulfillment of prerequisites: No

Course	Req.	Rec.	Lab.	Hrs.
Inorganic Chemistry	•		•	8
Behavioral Sciences				
Biochemistry		•		
Biology	•		•	8
Biology/Zoology				
Calculus				
College English	•			6
College Mathematics				

Course	Req.	Rec.	Lab.	Hrs.
Computer Science				
Genetics				
Humanities	•			18
Organic Chemistry	•		•	8
Physics	•		•	8
Psychology				
Social Sciences	•			
Other				

Selection Factors: 2009 Accepted Applicants

Proportion of Accepted Applicants with Relevant Experience (Data Self-Reported to AMCAS®)		
Community Service/Volunteer		75%
Medically-Related Work		88%
Research		90%

Shaded bar represents school's accepted scores ranging from the 10th percentile to the 90th percentile.   School Median ● National Median ◐

Overall GPA 2.0 2.1 2.2 2.3 2.4 2.5 2.6 2.7 2.8 2.9 3.0 3.1 3.2 3.3 3.4 3.5 3.6 3.7 (3.8) 3.9 4.0
Science GPA 2.0 2.1 2.2 2.3 2.4 2.5 2.6 2.7 2.8 2.9 3.0 3.1 3.2 3.3 3.4 3.5 3.6 (3.7) 3.8 3.9 4.0

MCAT® Total Numeric Score 9 10 11 12 13 14 15 16 17 18 19 20 21 22 23 24 25 26 27 28 29 30 31 (32) 33 (34) 35 36 37 38 39 40 41 42 43

Writing Sample			J	K	L	M	N	O	P	(Q)	R	S	T
Verbal Reasoning	3	4	5	6	7	8	9	(10)	(11)	12	13	14	15
Biological Sciences	3	4	5	6	7	8	9	10	(11)	(12)	13	14	15
Physical Sciences	3	4	5	6	7	8	9	10	(11)	(12)	13	14	15

Acceptance & Matriculation Data for 2009–2010 First Year Class

	Resident	Non-resident	International	Total
Applications	603	4860	289	5752
Interviewed	124	511	24	659
Deferred	3	1	0	4
Matriculants				
Early Assurance Program	0	0	0	0
Early Decision Program	0	0	0	0
Baccalaureate/M.D.	0	0	0	0
M.D./Ph.D.	1	6	2	9
Matriculated	42	88	6	**136**

Applications accepted from International Applicants: Yes

Specialty Choice

2005, 2006, 2007 Graduates, Specialty Choice (As reported by program directors to GME Track™)	
Anesthesiology	7%
Emergency Medicine	5%
Family Practice	4%
Internal Medicine	20%
Obstetrics/Gynecology	2%
Orthopaedic Surgery	5%
Pediatrics	9%
Psychiatry	3%
Radiology	6%
Surgery	8%

Matriculant Demographics: 2009–2010 First Year Class

Men: 59   **Women:** 77

Matriculants' Self-Reported Race/Ethnicity

Mexican American	0	Korean	1
Cuban	3	Vietnamese	1
Puerto Rican	1	Other Asian	1
Other Hispanic	3	Total Asian	24
Total Hispanic	5	Native American	0
Chinese	9	Black	14
Asian Indian	10	Native Hawaiian	0
Pakistani	2	White	90
Filipino	0	Unduplicated Number	
Japanese	1	of Matriculants	136

Science and Math Majors: 53%
Matriculants with:
Baccalaureate degree: 99%
Graduate degree(s): 8%

Financial Information
Source: 2008-2009 LCME I-B survey and 2009-2010 AAMC TSF questionnaire

	Residents	Non-residents
Total Cost of Attendance	$ 73,272	$ 73,272
Tuition and Fees	$ 42,876	$ 42,876
Other (includes living expenses)	$ 28,238	$ 28,238
Health Insurance (can be waived)	$ 2,158	$ 2,158

Average 2009 Graduate Indebtedness: $134,442
% of Enrolled Students Receiving Aid: 88%

Criminal Background Check

This medical school does not require a criminal background check prior to matriculation.

Medical College of Georgia
School of Medicine
Augusta, Georgia

Dr. Geoffrey H. Young
Associate Dean for Admissions
Medical College of Georgia
School of Medicine
Augusta, Georgia 30912-4760
T 706 721 3186   F 706 721 0959

Admissions www.mcg.edu/careers/medicine.htm
Main www.mcg.edu
Financial www.mcg.edu/students/finaid
E-mail stdadmin@mail.mcg.edu

Public Institution

Dr. D. Douglas Miller, Dean

Dr. Geoffrey H. Young, Associate Dean for Admissions

Wilma A. Sykes-Brown, M.A., Assistant Dean for Educational Outreach and Partnerships

Dr. Beverly Ann Boggs, Director of Student Financial Aid

Linda R. DeVaughn, Director of Admissions

General Information

The School of Medicine of the Medical College of Georgia was founded in 1828 and is the nation's 13th oldest medical school. The institution is a separate university under the University System of Georgia. It consists of five schools: medicine, allied health, dentistry, graduate studies, and nursing.

Mission Statement

The Medical College of Georgia is committed to a supportive campus climate, necessary services, and leadership and development opportunities, all to educate the whole person and meet the needs of students, faculty, and staff; cultural, ethnic, racial, and gender diversity supported by practices that embody the ideals of an open democratic and global society; technology to advance education; collaborative relationships with other System institutions, state agencies, local schools and technical institutes, and industry, sharing physical, human, and information resources to enhance services available to the citizens of Georgia.

Curricular Highlights
Community Service Requirement: Optional.
Research/Thesis Requirement: Optional.

During the pre-clinical years, students acquire the building blocks that underlie medical practice. The modular content of the curriculum is taught in lectures and labs with integrated clinical conferences and small-group activities. The first year of the curriculum is a year long module divided into six systems-based blocks. This module introduces students to Gross Anatomy, Biochemistry, Development, Genetics, Histology, Neuroscience, Physiology,

and Psychiatry. The Essentials of Clinical Medicine (ECM) is a two-year sequence emphasizing patient care skills. In year two, the year-long Cellular and Systems Disease States module exposes students to Microbiology, Pathology, and Pharmacology in the context of clinical medicine. Clinical Training: Patient contact begins in year one in the ECM course that extends through year two. Year three consists of required clerkships in Family Medicine, Internal Medicine, Neurology, OB/Gyn, Pediatrics, Psychiatry, and Surgery. During year four, students complete rotations in Emergency Medicine, Critical Care, Ambulatory Medicine, and an acting internship, with the remainder of the year for electives that can include research.

USMLE
Step 1: Required. Students must record a passing score for promotion.
Step 2: Clinical Skills (CS): Required. Students must record a passing total score to graduate.
Step 2: Clinical Knowledge (CK): Required. Students must record a passing total score to graduate.

Selection Factors
Applicants for admission are evaluated on a competitive basis. Information used includes, but is not limited to, the applicant's responsibilities prior to application; activities; shadowing physicians; ethnic, socioeconomic, and cultural background; region of residence with respect to its health professional needs; commitment to practice in an underserved area; references; motivation and potential for serving as a physician; interviews; MCAT performance; and grades. In addition, students must meet specified technical standards to participate effectively in the medical education program and in the practice of medicine. Preference is given to Georgia residents. See *www.mcg.edu/SOM/admit/* for more information.

Financial Aid
The Office of Financial Aid coordinates programs of assistance available to students. Information may be obtained at *www.mcg.edu/students/finaid.*

Information about Diversity Programs
The Medical College of Georgia seeks to encourage applications from qualified students from groups underrepresented in medicine. A summer program is designed for disadvantaged college students who show academic promise and who desire to practice medicine. Students may apply by writing to: Wilma A. Sykes-Brown, M.A., Assistant Dean for Educational Outreach and Partnerships, CB-1801, Medical College of Georgia, Augusta, GA 30912-1900.

Campus Information

Setting
The medical school is located in Augusta, GA, the second-largest city in Georgia, which is located on the south bank of the Savannah River, midway between the Great Smokey Mountains and the Atlantic Ocean. Augusta is a thriving city and a leading health care center, with nine area hospitals.

Enrollment
For 2009, total enrollment was: 762

Special Features
MCG Children's Medical Center is dedicated to serving the health care needs of children, from newborns to teenagers. The 149-bed modern center recognizes the importance of family involvement in a child's healing process and embraces the philosophy of family-centered care. A new $54 million Cancer Research Center opened in 2006. The campus has a new student Wellness Center.

Housing
A variety of on-campus living environments are available.

Satellite Campuses/Facilities
Core clerkships take place at the MCG Hospitals and Clinics, the Children's Medical Center, and affiliated hospitals and community-based teaching sites throughout Georgia. The Medical College of Georgia in partnership with the University of Georgia will matriculate students to the Medical College of Georgia/University of Georgia Medical Partnership Campus in Athens in 2010. The medical partnership campus would be a four year curriculum campus.

Application Process and Requirements 2011–2012

Primary Application Service: AMCAS
Earliest filing date: June 1, 2010
Latest filing date: November 1, 2010

Secondary Application Required?: Yes
Sent to: All Georgia residents; others are screened
URL: Provided by school
Contact: (706) 721-3186
Fee: No **Waiver available:** n/a
Earliest filing date: June 1, 2010
Latest filing date: Two weeks after receipt and must be in the student file by December 1, 2010

MCAT® required?: Yes
Latest MCAT® considered: September 2010
Oldest MCAT® considered: 2008

Early Decision Program: School does have EDP
Applicants notified: October 1, 2010
EDP available for: Residents only

Regular Acceptance Notice
Earliest date: October 2010
Latest date: Until class is full
Applicant's Response to Acceptance
Offer – Maximum Time: Two weeks

Requests for Deferred
Entrance Considered: Yes

Deposit to Hold Place in Class: Yes
Deposit (Resident): $100 **(Non-resident):** $100
Deposit due: With response to acceptance offer
Applied to tuition: Yes **Refundable:** Yes
Refundable by: May 15, 2011

Estimated number of new entrants: 230
EDP: 60, special program: 6

Start Month/Year: August 2011

Interview Format: One individual interview with committee member. Regional interviews are not available. Video interviews are not available.

Other Programs

PREPARATORY PROGRAMS
Postbaccalaureate Program: No
Summer Program: Yes,
mcg.edu/careers/specop/
Wilma A. Sykes-Brown, MA, 706-721-2522,
wsykes@mail.mcg.edu
Summer Student Training and
Research (STAR) Program: www.mcg.edu/star

COMBINED DEGREE PROGRAMS
Baccalaureate/M.D.: No
M.D./M.P.H.: No
M.D./M.B.A.: No
M.D./J.D.: No
M.D./Ph.D.: Yes, www.mcg.edu/som/mdphd/
geninfo.htm, Edward Inscho, PhD, 706-721-5615,
einscho@mcg.edu

Premedical Coursework

On-line courses accepted in fulfillment of prerequisites: No

Course	Req.	Rec.	Lab.	Sems.
Inorganic Chemistry	•		•	2
Behavioral Sciences				
Biochemistry		•		
Biology				
Biology/Zoology	•		•	2
Calculus				
College English	•			2
College Mathematics				
Computer Science				

Course	Req.	Rec.	Lab.	Sems.
Genetics				
Humanities				
Organic Chemistry	•		•	1
Physics	•		•	2
Psychology				
Social Sciences				
Advanced Chemistry	•			1
Cellular Biology		•		
Statistics		•		

Selection Factors: 2009 Accepted Applicants

Proportion of Accepted Applicants with Relevant Experience (Data Self-Reported to AMCAS®)		
Community Service/Volunteer	75%
Medically-Related Work	86%
Research	79%

Shaded bar represents school's accepted scores ranging from the 10th percentile to the 90th percentile. **School Median** ● **National Median** ○

Overall GPA 2.0 2.1 2.2 2.3 2.4 2.5 2.6 2.7 2.8 2.9 3.0 3.1 3.2 3.3 3.4 3.5 3.6 (3.7) 3.8 3.9 4.0
Science GPA 2.0 2.1 2.2 2.3 2.4 2.5 2.6 2.7 2.8 2.9 3.0 3.1 3.2 3.3 3.4 3.5 3.6 (3.7) 3.8 3.9 4.0

MCAT® Total Numeric Score 9 10 11 12 13 14 15 16 17 18 19 20 21 22 23 24 25 26 27 28 29 30 (31)(32) 33 34 35 36 37 38 39 40 41 42 43

Writing Sample			J	K	L	M	N	O	(P)	(Q)	R	S	T
Verbal Reasoning	3	4	5	6	7	8	9	(10)		11	12	13	14	15
Biological Sciences	3	4	5	6	7	8	9	10	(11)	12	13	14	15
Physical Sciences	3	4	5	6	7	8	9	(10)	(11)	12	13	14	15

Acceptance & Matriculation Data for 2009–2010 First Year Class

	Resident	Non-resident	International	Total
Applications	1011	974	70	2055
Interviewed	511	22	0	533
Deferred	2	0	0	2
Matriculants				
Early Assurance Program	0	0	0	0
Early Decision Program	69	0	0	69
Baccalaureate/M.D.	0	0	0	0
M.D./Ph.D.	3	1	0	4
Matriculated	186	4	0	**190**

Applications accepted from International Applicants: Only Canadian

Matriculant Demographics: 2009–2010 First Year Class

Men: 114 **Women:** 76

Matriculants' Self-Reported Race/Ethnicity

Mexican American	1	Korean	10
Cuban	1	Vietnamese	5
Puerto Rican	0	Other Asian	4
Other Hispanic	1	Total Asian	55
Total Hispanic	3	Native American	3
Chinese	11	Black	15
Asian Indian	22	Native Hawaiian	0
Pakistani	4	White	117
Filipino	1	Unduplicated Number	
Japanese	0	of Matriculants	190

Science and Math Majors: 76%
Matriculants with:
Baccalaureate degree: 99%
Graduate degree(s): 8%

Specialty Choice

2005, 2006, 2007 Graduates, Specialty Choice (As reported by program directors to GME Track™)	
Anesthesiology	7%
Emergency Medicine	6%
Family Practice	7%
Internal Medicine	14%
Obstetrics/Gynecology	6%
Orthopaedic Surgery	5%
Pediatrics	17%
Psychiatry	2%
Radiology	5%
Surgery	7%

Financial Information

Source: 2008-2009 LCME I-B survey and 2009-2010 AAMC TSF questionnaire

	Residents	Non-residents
Total Cost of Attendance	$ 47,700	$ 57,268
Tuition and Fees	$ 22,180	$ 31,748
Other (includes living expenses)	$ 24,269	$ 24,269
Health Insurance (can be waived)	$ 1,251	$ 1,251

Average 2009 Graduate Indebtedness: $106,710
% of Enrolled Students Receiving Aid: 80%

Criminal Background Check

This medical school requires a criminal background check prior to matriculation.

Mercer University School of Medicine
Macon, Georgia

Office of Admissions and Student Affairs
Mercer University School of Medicine
1550 College Street
Macon, Georgia 31207
T 478 301 2524   F 478 301 2547

Admissions http://medicine.mercer.edu/admissions
Main http://medicine.mercer.edu
Financial http://medicine.mercer.edu/Admissions/
admissions_financial
E-mail admissions@med.mercer.edu

Private Institution

Dr. William F. Bina, Dean

Dr. Maurice S. Clifton, Associate Dean for Admissions and Student Affairs

Youvette D. Hudson, Registrar/Director for Financial Aid Planning

Mary G. Scott, Associate Director of Financial Planning

Mary C. Putnam, Assistant Director of Admissions and Student Affairs

General Information
Mercer University School of Medicine was founded in 1982 to improve health care access to the residents of Georgia. A private institution with strong state support, MUSM has been a leader in educating physicians who practice in the state after their training. MUSM also offers multiple graduate degrees including a Masters in Public Health.

Mission Statement
The mission of Mercer University School of Medicine (MUSM) is to educate physicians and health professionals to meet the primary care and health care needs of rural and medically underserved areas of Georgia.

Curricular Highlights
Community Service Requirement: Required. Numerous volunteer opportunities are available
Research/Thesis Requirement: Optional.

One of the first schools to adopt an all Problem-Based-Learning curriculum, there are no lectures and students take responsibility for their own learning. This open-ended nature requires and generates maturity and confidence not seen in traditional curricula. Learning must go well beyond the basic facts in that students are called upon to integrate and demonstrate verbally their basic science knowledge base to explain clinical findings. In addition, students are evaluated in areas related to group and interpersonal, problem-solving, information-gathering and evaluation skills. Students interview and examine actual and standardized patients early in the first year. The Community Medicine program provides a

continuity experience in the clinical aspects of a community-oriented primary care medical practice during the first, second and fourth years. The third year consists of required clinical rotations in internal medicine, surgery, pediatrics, obstetrics-gynecology, family medicine, and psychiatry. The fourth year includes community medicine and two selectives from acute and critical care and geriatrics.

USMLE
Step 1: Required. Students must record a passing score for promotion.
Step 2: Clinical Skills (CS): Required. Students must record a passing total score to graduate.
Step 2: Clinical Knowledge (CK): Required. Students must record a passing total score to graduate.

Selection Factors
The Admissions Committee only accepts applicants who are legal residents of Georgia. Each applicant must show promise of learning effectively in Mercer's curriculum and strong potential for practice in a medical specialty commensurate with the health care needs of rural and other underserved areas of Georgia. Most counties in Georgia have underserved status by the federal government, and the specialties that are needed include the primary care specialties of Internal Medicine, Pediatrics and Family Medicine, but also Surgery, and Obstetrics and Gynecology. Interviews are by invitation only and are held at both the Macon and Savannah campuses. In making the final decisions for acceptance or rejection, the Admissions Committee considers all criteria, but emphasizes strongly an applicant's demonstrated desire to fulfill the mission of the institution. The committee does not discriminate on the basis of race, sex, creed, national origin, age, or handicap.

Financial Aid
Financial aid in the form of loans and scholarships is available to incoming accepted students. Financial need is determined by a federally approved need analysis and awards are made on the basis of need and merit. Most scholarships are based on need and mission compliance. The Office of Student Financial Planning provides easy access to information about all

financial aid programs available and financial planning and debt management thru financial management conferences and workshops.

Information about Diversity Programs
MUSM embraces the position that promoting and supporting diversity among the student body is central to the mission of the school. A diverse student body enriches professional education by providing a multiplicity of views and prospective that enhances learning within this highly interactive, student centered curriculum. For additional information and opportunities, please contact diversity@med.mercer.edu.

Special Features
The assessment system includes oral exams which foster integration of basic science knowledge base to explain clinical findings. Our students participate in a wide variety of leadership and community service programs, and many in international outreach programs throughout the world.

Campus Information

Setting
There are two branch campuses, the Macon campus at Mercer University and at the Medical Center of Central Georgia, and the Savannah campus at the Memorial Health University Medical Center. Clinical teaching is also provided at several rural hospitals and clinics throughout Georgia.

Enrollment
For 2009, total enrollment was: 311

Housing
The Office of Student Affairs maintains a housing list of available apartments/houses and a list of those students who wish to secure roommates.

Satellite Campuses/Facilities
Students may study all four years on either the Macon or Savannah campus with a limited number of spaces for students to complete the first two years in Macon, and the clinical years in Savannah. There are many sites available for the Community Medicine program, and most students are able to return to a location near their home.

Application Process and Requirements 2011–2012

Primary Application Service: AMCAS
Earliest filing date: June 1, 2010
Latest filing date: November 1, 2010

Secondary Application Required?: Yes
Sent to: Screened applicants
Contact: Gail Coleman, (478) 301-2524, admissions@mercer.edu
Fee: Yes, $50   **Waiver available:** Yes
Earliest filing date: June 2010
Latest filing date: January 15, 2011

MCAT® required?: Yes
Latest MCAT® considered: September 2010
Oldest MCAT® considered: January 2008

Early Decision Program: School does have EDP
Applicants notified: October 1, 2010
EDP available for: Residents only

Regular Acceptance Notice
Earliest date: November 2010
Latest date: Until class is full
Applicant's Response to Acceptance Offer – Maximum Time: Two weeks

Requests for Deferred Entrance Considered: Yes

Deposit to Hold Place in Class: Yes
Deposit (Resident): $100   **(Non-resident):** n/a
Deposit due: With response to acceptance offer
Applied to tuition: Yes   **Refundable:** Yes
Refundable by: May 15, 2011

Estimated number of new entrants: 90
EDP: 40, special program: n/a

Start Month/Year: August 2011

Interview Format: Two, one-hour interviews. Regional interviews are not available. Video interviews are not available.

Other Programs

PREPARATORY PROGRAMS
Postbaccalaureate Program: No
Summer Program: No

COMBINED DEGREE PROGRAMS
Baccalaureate/M.D.: No
M.D./M.P.H.: No
M.D./M.B.A.: No
M.D./J.D.: No
M.D./Ph.D.: No

Premedical Coursework

On-line courses accepted in fulfillment of prerequisites: No

Course	Req.	Rec.	Lab.	Sems.
Inorganic Chemistry	•		•	2
Behavioral Sciences				
Biochemistry		•		
Biology	•		•	2
Biology/Zoology				
Calculus				
College English				
College Mathematics				

Course	Req.	Rec.	Lab.	Sems.
Computer Science				
Genetics				
Humanities				
Organic Chemistry	•		•	2
Physics	•		•	2
Psychology				
Social Sciences				
Other				

Selection Factors: 2009 Accepted Applicants

Proportion of Accepted Applicants with Relevant Experience (Data Self-Reported to AMCAS®)		
Community Service/Volunteer		77%
Medically-Related Work		84%
Research		66%

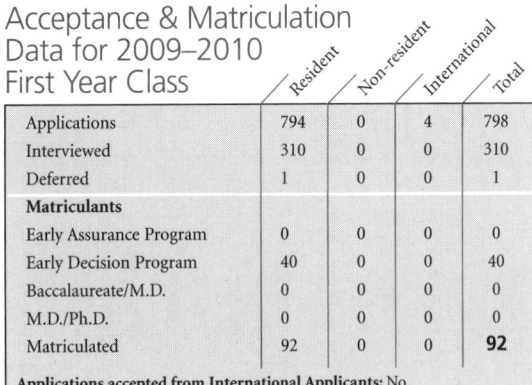

Shaded bar represents school's accepted scores ranging from the 10th percentile to the 90th percentile.   School Median ●   National Median ◐

Overall GPA 2.0 2.1 2.2 2.3 2.4 2.5 2.6 2.7 2.8 2.9 3.0 3.1 3.2 3.3 3.4 3.5 (3.6) 3.7 3.8 3.9 4.0
Science GPA 2.0 2.1 2.2 2.3 2.4 2.5 2.6 2.7 2.8 2.9 3.0 3.1 3.2 3.3 3.4 (3.5) 3.6 3.7 3.8 3.9 4.0

MCAT® Total Numeric Score 9 10 11 12 13 14 15 16 17 18 19 20 21 22 23 24 25 26 27(28)29 30 31(32)33 34 35 36 37 38 39 40 41 42 43

Writing Sample			J	K	L	M	N	(O)	P	(Q)	R	S	T
Verbal Reasoning	3	4	5	6	7	8	(9)	(10)	11	12	13	14	15
Biological Sciences	3	4	5	6	7	8	9	(10)	(11)	12	13	14	15
Physical Sciences	3	4	5	6	7	8	(9)	10	(11)	12	13	14	15

Acceptance & Matriculation Data for 2009–2010 First Year Class

	Resident	Non-resident	International	Total
Applications	794	0	4	798
Interviewed	310	0	0	310
Deferred	1	0	0	1
Matriculants				
Early Assurance Program	0	0	0	0
Early Decision Program	40	0	0	40
Baccalaureate/M.D.	0	0	0	0
M.D./Ph.D.	0	0	0	0
Matriculated	92	0	0	**92**

Applications accepted from International Applicants: No

Specialty Choice

2005, 2006, 2007 Graduates, Specialty Choice (As reported by program directors to GME Track™)	
Anesthesiology	5%
Emergency Medicine	5%
Family Practice	8%
Internal Medicine	18%
Obstetrics/Gynecology	7%
Orthopaedic Surgery	2%
Pediatrics	17%
Psychiatry	2%
Radiology	6%
Surgery	11%

Matriculant Demographics: 2009–2010 First Year Class

Men: 46   **Women:** 46

Matriculants' Self-Reported Race/Ethnicity

Mexican American	0	Korean	1
Cuban	0	Vietnamese	1
Puerto Rican	0	Other Asian	0
Other Hispanic	1	Total Asian	10
Total Hispanic	1	Native American	1
Chinese	1	Black	3
Asian Indian	5	Native Hawaiian	0
Pakistani	1	White	79
Filipino	1	Unduplicated Number	
Japanese	0	of Matriculants	92

Science and Math Majors: 75%
Matriculants with:
        Baccalaureate degree: 100%
        Graduate degree(s): 8%

Financial Information

Source: 2008-2009 LCME I-B survey and 2009-2010 AAMC TSF questionnaire

	Residents	Non-residents
Total Cost of Attendance	$ 63,085	$ 0
Tuition and Fees	$ 39,085	$ 0
Other (includes living expenses)	$ 23,627	$ 0
Health Insurance (can be waived)	$ 373	$ 0

Average 2009 Graduate Indebtedness: $164,548
% of Enrolled Students Receiving Aid: 95%

Criminal Background Check

This medical school requires a criminal background check prior to matriculation.

Morehouse School of Medicine

Atlanta, Georgia

Admissions and Student Affairs
Morehouse School of Medicine
720 Westview Drive, S.W.
Atlanta, Georgia 30310-1495
T 404 752 1650   F 404 752 1512

Admissions www.msm.edu/educational/
mdprogram.htm
Main www.msm.edu/
Financial www.msm.edu/admissions/fa/financial_aid.htm
E-mail mdadmissions@msm.edu

Private Institution

Dr. Ngozi F. Anachebe, Assistant Dean for Admissions & Student Affairs

Dr. Sterling Roaf, Director of Admissions

Cynthia Handy, Director of Student Fiscal Affairs

General Information

Established in 1975 as the School of Medicine at Morehouse College, Morehouse School of Medicine became independent from its founding institution in 1981. MSM is a member of the Atlanta University Center Consortium Inc.- a consortium of five Historically Black Colleges and Universities. Through our affiliations with Atlanta-based Grady Health System, Children's Healthcare of Atlanta at Hughes Spalding, South Fulton Medical Center and the Atlanta Medical Center, our students and residents are able to experience a broad patient population and engage in the opportunity for the best training experience possible.

Mission Statement

Morehouse School of Medicine is dedicated to improving the health and well-being of individuals and communities; increasing the diversity of the health professional and scientific workforce; and addressing primary health-care needs through programs in education, research, and service, with emphasis on people of color and the underserved urban and rural populations in Georgia and the nation.

Curricular Highlights

Community Service Requirement: Optional.
Research/Thesis Requirement: Optional.

The first two years of the curriculum emphasize an understanding of the principles, concepts, and a major factual background of the basic medical sciences. Exposure to clinical medicine begins in the first year through assignment to a preceptor and increases in the second year with introduction to clinical medicine. Clinical education is continued through core clerkships during the third and fourth years, with 20 weeks of electives in the senior year. Student performance is evaluated primarily by letter grades. Learning resources and other support services are available to all students throughout their four years.

USMLE

Step 1: Required. Students must record a passing score for promotion.
Step 2: Clinical Skills (CS): Required. Students must record a passing total score to graduate.
Step 2: Clinical Knowledge (CK): Required. Students must record a passing total score to graduate.

Selection Factors

Selection of students for admission is made after careful consideration of many factors. These include MCAT scores, the academic record, the extent of academic improvement, balance and depth of academic program, difficulty of courses taken, and other indicators of maturation of learning ability. Additional factors considered are extracurricular activities, hobbies, the need to work, research projects and experiences, evidence of activities that indicate concurrence with the school's mission, and evidence of pursuing interests and talents in depth. Finally, the committee looks for evidence of those traits of personality and character essential to succeed in medicine: compassion, integrity, motivation, and perseverance. All information available about each applicant is considered without assigning priority to any single factor. Students are admitted on the basis of individual qualifications regardless of sex, age, race, creed, national origin, or handicap. Preferential consideration is given to qualified applicants who are residents of the state of Georgia. Foreign applicants must have a permanent resident visa. Technical standards have been established as a prerequisite for admission and graduation from the MSM. A candidate for the M.D. degree must have aptitude, abilities, and skills in five areas: observation, communication, motor, conceptual integrative and quantitative, as well as behavioral and social attributes. Applicants are not considered for admission who have been dismissed from another medical school for academic or disciplinary reasons. Transfer applications are considered only from students in good standing at an LCME-accredited U.S. or Canadian medical school; transfers from foreign medical schools or osteopathic, veterinary, or dental schools are not accepted. Transfers are accepted into the second year only on a space-available basis. The transfer application deadline is May 1.

Financial Aid

In addition to federal loan programs, a number of scholarships and grants are available.

Campus Information

Setting

Morehouse School of Medicine is situated five minutes from downtown Atlanta within the Atlanta University Center (AUC) in the historic West End. Atlanta is also home to the Centers for Disease Control and Prevention (CDC), over 20 major medical centers, Jimmy Carter Library & Museum, The Martin Luther King Center, and a plethora of educational, entertainment, and cultural opportunities. Atlanta's sports teams consist of the Atlanta Braves, Atlanta Falcons, Atlanta Thrashers, and the Atlanta Hawks. Home to one of the busiest airports in the world, Hartsfield-Jackson Atlanta International Airport, the city is a major international transportation hub. A premier city for the 21st century, Atlanta is a bustling, progressive metropolis with an energy all its own.

Enrollment

For 2009, total enrollment was: 213

Housing

On-campus housing is not available. Students seeking assistance in their relocation can access the school's very useful Web site at *http://web.msm.edu/relocation_guide/housing.htm.*

Application Process and Requirements 2011–2012

Primary Application Service: AMCAS
Earliest filing date: June 1, 2010
Latest filing date: December 1, 2010

Secondary Application Required?: Yes
Sent to: All eligible applicants after preliminary screening
URL: URL given to invited applicants only
Fee: Yes, $50   **Waiver available:** Yes
Earliest filing date: July 15, 2010
Latest filing date: January 8, 2011

MCAT® required?: Yes
Latest MCAT® considered: December 2010
Oldest MCAT® considered: 2008

Early Decision Program: School does have EDP
Applicants notified: October 1, 2010
EDP available for: Residents only

Regular Acceptance Notice
Earliest date: November 2010
Latest date: Until class is full
**Applicant's Response to Acceptance
Offer – Maximum Time:** 14 days

**Requests for Deferred
Entrance Considered:** Yes

Deposit to Hold Place in Class: Yes
Deposit (Resident): $100   **(Non-resident):** $100
Deposit due: 14 days from acceptance offer
Applied to tuition: Yes   **Refundable:** Yes
Refundable by: May 15, 2011

Estimated number of new entrants: 56
EDP: 2, special program: n/a

Start Month/Year: July 2011

Interview Format: One-on-one interview. Regional interviews are not available. Video interviews are not available.

Other Programs

PREPARATORY PROGRAMS
Postbaccalaureate Program: No
Summer Program: Yes
www.applyweb.com/apply/mhsum/index.html

COMBINED DEGREE PROGRAMS
Baccalaureate/M.D.: No
M.D./M.P.H.: Yes, Sterling Roaf, M.D.
(404) 752-1650, sroaf@msm.edu
M.D./M.B.A.: No
M.D./J.D.: No
M.D./Ph.D.: Yes, Sterling Roaf, M.D.
(404) 752-1650, sroaf@msm.edu

Premedical Coursework

On-line courses accepted in fulfillment of prerequisites: No

Course	Req.	Rec.	Lab.	Sems.
Inorganic Chemistry	•		•	2
Behavioral Sciences		•		1
Biochemistry		•	•	1
Biology	•		•	2
Biology/Zoology				
Calculus				
College English	•			2
College Mathematics	•			2

Course	Req.	Rec.	Lab.	Sems.
Computer Science				
Genetics		•	•	1
Humanities				
Organic Chemistry	•		•	2
Physics	•		•	2
Psychology				
Social Sciences				
Other				

Selection Factors: 2009 Accepted Applicants

Proportion of Accepted Applicants with Relevant Experience (Data Self-Reported to AMCAS®)		
Community Service/Volunteer		69%
Medically-Related Work		79%
Research		73%

Shaded bar represents school's accepted scores ranging from the 10th percentile to the 90th percentile   School Median ● National Median ◯

Overall GPA	2.0 2.1 2.2 2.3 2.4 2.5 2.6 2.7 2.8 2.9 3.0 3.1 3.2 3.3 3.4 (3.5) 3.6 3.7 3.8 3.9 4.0
Science GPA	2.0 2.1 2.2 2.3 2.4 2.5 2.6 2.7 2.8 2.9 3.0 3.1 3.2 (3.3) 3.4 3.5 3.6 3.7 3.8 3.9 4.0

MCAT® Total Numeric Score 9 10 11 12 13 14 15 16 17 18 19 20 21 22 23 24 25 26 (27) 28 29 30 31 (32) 33 34 35 36 37 38 39 40 41 42 43

Writing Sample			J	K	L	M	N	(O)	P	(Q)	R	S	T
Verbal Reasoning	3	4	5	6	7	8	(9)	(10)	11	12	13	14	15
Biological Sciences	3	4	5	6	7	8	9	(10)	(11)	12	13	14	15
Physical Sciences	3	4	5	6	7	8	(9)	10	(11)	12	13	14	15

Acceptance & Matriculation Data for 2009–2010 First Year Class

	Resident	Non-resident	International	Total
Applications	440	3501	46	3987
Interviewed	113	105	0	218
Deferred	0	0	0	0
Matriculants				
Early Assurance Program	0	0	0	0
Early Decision Program	0	0	0	0
Baccalaureate/M.D.	0	0	0	0
M.D./Ph.D.	0	0	0	0
Matriculated	28	28	0	**56**

Applications accepted from International Applicants: No

Specialty Choice

2005, 2006, 2007 Graduates, Specialty Choice (As reported by program directors to GME Track™)	
Anesthesiology	2%
Emergency Medicine	5%
Family Practice	18%
Internal Medicine	24%
Obstetrics/Gynecology	4%
Orthopaedic Surgery	0%
Pediatrics	14%
Psychiatry	8%
Radiology	2%
Surgery	7%

Matriculant Demographics: 2009–2010 First Year Class

Men: 18   **Women:** 38

Matriculants' Self-Reported Race/Ethnicity

Mexican American	0	Korean	0
Cuban	0	Vietnamese	0
Puerto Rican	1	Other Asian	0
Other Hispanic	2	Total Asian	3
Total Hispanic	3	Native American	1
Chinese	1	Black	51
Asian Indian	1	Native Hawaiian	0
Pakistani	0	White	4
Filipino	1	Unduplicated Number	
Japanese	0	of Matriculants	56

Science and Math Majors: 73%
Matriculants with:
    Baccalaureate degree: 100%
    Graduate degree(s): 23%

Financial Information

Source: 2008-2009 LCME I-B survey and 2009-2010 AAMC TSF questionnaire

	Residents	Non-residents
Total Cost of Attendance	$ 62,881	$ 62,881
Tuition and Fees	$ 31,854	$ 31,854
Other (includes living expenses)	$ 28,517	$ 28,517
Health Insurance (can be waived)	$ 2,510	$ 2,510

Average 2009 Graduate Indebtedness: $166,449
% of Enrolled Students Receiving Aid: 97%

Criminal Background Check

This medical school requires a criminal background check prior to matriculation.

University of Hawai'i
John A. Burns School of Medicine

Honolulu, Hawaii

Office of Student Affairs - Admissions
Medical Education Building
University of Hawai'i, John A. Burns
School of Medicine
651 Ilalo Street
Honolulu, Hawai'i 96813-5534
T 808 692 1000   F 808 692 1251

Admissions http://jabsom.hawaii.edu/
Main http://jabsom.hawaii.edu
Financial http://jabsom.hawaii.edu/
E-mail mnishiki@hawaii.edu

Public Institution

Dr. Jerris R. Hedges, Dean

Dr. Satoru Izutsu, Vice Dean and Director of Admissions

Gail C. Koki, Student Liaison, Financial Aid and Scholarships

Marilyn M. Nishiki, Admissions Officer & Registrar

General Information

The University of Hawai'i at Manoa John A. Burns School of Medicine is in the College of Health Sciences and Social Welfare. The School of Medicine is located in Kaka'ako.
It also has teaching facilities in affiliated community hospitals and primary care clinics throughout the state.

Mission Statement

To educate outstanding physicians, scientists, biomedical students, and allied health professionals for Hawai'i and the Pacific, and to conduct both clinical and basic research, education, and community service of specific interest to our region and community. Its student body mirrors the rich diversity of the state's population.

Curricular Highlights

Community Service Requirement: Optional.
Research/Thesis Requirement: Optional.

The school utilizes a problem-based learning curriculum (PBL), in which basic sciences are learned in the context of the study of health care problems and supplemented by selected lecture and laboratory sessions. Clinical skills and community health activities are prominent, and begin in the first year of the curriculum. Special features include an emphasis on PBL as the primary instructional method in the pre-clinical years; early introduction of clinical training, community service, and research experiences; rural health training opportunities; a longitudinal, interdisciplinary clerkship opportunity in the third-year; and opportunities for training experiences in various communities throughout Hawai'i, the Pacific, and Asia.

USMLE

Step 1: Required. Students must record a passing score for promotion.
Step 2: Clinical Skills (CS): Required. Students must record a passing total score to graduate.
Step 2: Clinical Knowledge (CK): Required. Students must record a passing total score to graduate.

Selection Factors

Applicants are considered without discrimination as to age, sex, race, creed, national origin, religion, or handicap. The school admits 64 students to its first-year class. A priority is to admit applicants with strong ties to the State of Hawai'i. Applications go through a screening process. The first screen determines an applicant's ties to the State of Hawai'i: legal residence, birthplace, high school graduated, college attended, parent's legal residence, and legacy. Three of the six categories are required to be a resident for application purposes. Applicants who pass the second academic screen will be invited for interviews and asked to submit letters of recommendation. Applicants are responsible for scheduling three one-on-one interviews to be conducted in Hawai'i. Acceptance, alternate, and rejection letters are e-mailed in late March.

Financial Aid

Financial status is not a factor in considering applicants for acceptance. Efforts are made to assist medical students in obtaining loans and scholarships, wherever possible. Loan funds from federal sources are available only to U.S. citizens and permanent residents. In general, students are discouraged from engaging in outside employment. Applicants are referred to the Student Liaison-Financial Aid and Scholarships, Office of Student Affairs at the John A. Burns School of Medicine or to the University of Hawai'i at Manoa Financial Aid Services Office.

Information about Diversity Programs

The student body and faculty are culturally diverse. The school is actively involved in the recruitment, admission, and retention of students from disadvantaged backgrounds who have potential and are interested in pursuing an M.D. degree. Dr. Mary Ann Antonelli (mantonel@hawaii.edu, or 808- 692-1000), Director of Student Affairs, is the Diversity contact person at the John A. Burns School of Medicine. The Imi Ho'ola Post-Baccalaureate Program is for students from socially, educationally, or economically disadvantaged backgrounds who have demonstrated a strong commitment to serve areas of need in Hawai'i and the U.S.-Affiliated Pacific Islands. For more information, contact Dr. Nanette L.K. Judd, Imi Ho'ola Post-Baccalaureate Program Director (judd@hawaii.edu or 808-692-1030).

Campus Information

Setting

The School of Medicine is located at a 10.5-acre state-owned parcel in Kaka'ako, on the water's edge, between Waikiki and downtown Honolulu. It is an environment conducive to the school's goal of becoming a top-ranked research-intensive medical school with the opportunity to attract world-class research scientists to join the school's faculty.

Enrollment

For 2009, total enrollment was: 254

Special Features

The school's Problem-Based Learning (PBL) curriculum was established in 1989. For the past several years, emphasis has been placed on promoting international partnerships to advance PBL principles. Research in education methodologies have been enhanced by the state of art facilities at the Kaka'ako medical school campus. In addition, recruitment of world-class scientists to modern research labs has resulted in a significant increase in research funding.

Housing

Medical students and candidates for graduate degrees in the medical school are expected to make their own living arrangements. The University of Hawai'i at Manoa campus provides limited dormitory and apartment facilities.

Satellite Campuses/Facilities

Clinical activities of the school's curriculum are conducted in affiliated community hospitals and clinics. There is no university hospital connected to the school of medicine.

Application Process and Requirements 2011–2012

Primary Application Service: AMCAS
Earliest filing date: June 1, 2010
Latest filing date: November 1, 2010

Secondary Application Required?: Yes
Sent to: Screened applicants who minimally achieve the required cut-off scores.
Contact: Marilyn Nishiki,
(808) 692-1000, mnishiki@hawaii.edu
Fee: Yes, $50   **Waiver available:** No
Earliest filing date: School-specific deadlines
Latest filing date: School-specific deadlines

MCAT® required?: Yes
Latest MCAT® considered: September 2010
Oldest MCAT® considered: January 2008

Early Decision Program: School does have EDP
Applicants notified: October 1, 2010
EDP available for: Residents only

Regular Acceptance Notice
Earliest date: October 15, 2010
Latest date: Until class is full
Applicant's Response to Acceptance Offer – Maximum Time: Two weeks

Requests for Deferred Entrance Considered: Yes

Deposit to Hold Place in Class: Yes
Deposit (Resident): $250   **(Non-resident):** $250
Deposit due: Advanced tuition deposit required after acceptance-date to be specified.
Applied to tuition: Yes   **Refundable:** No
Refundable by: Nonrefundable advanced tuition deposit to be requested in May 2011.

Estimated number of new entrants: 64

EDP: 1, special program: 10

Start Month/Year: July 2011

Interview Format: One-on-one interviews. Regional interviews are not available. Video interviews are not available.

Other Programs

PREPARATORY PROGRAMS
Postbaccalaureate Program: Yes,
http://jabsom.hawaii.edu
Nanette K. Judd, PhD, MPH, RN
(808) 692-1030, judd@hawaii.edu
Summer Program: No

COMBINED DEGREE PROGRAMS
Baccalaureate/M.D.: No
M.D./M.P.H.: No
M.D./M.B.A.: No
M.D./J.D.: No
M.D./Ph.D.: No

Premedical Coursework

On-line courses accepted in fulfillment of prerequisites: Case-by-case basis

Course	Req.	Rec.	Lab.	Sems.
Inorganic Chemistry	•		•	8
Behavioral Sciences		•		
Biochemistry	•			3
Biology	•		•	8
Biology/Zoology		•		
Calculus				
College English		•		
College Mathematics		•		

Course	Req.	Rec.	Lab.	Sems.
Computer Science				
Genetics		•		
Humanities		•		
Organic Chemistry	•		•	8
Physics	•		•	8
Psychology				
Social Sciences		•		
Cell and Molecular Bio	•			3

Selection Factors: 2009 Accepted Applicants

Proportion of Accepted Applicants with Relevant Experience (Data Self-Reported to AMCAS®)		Community Service/Volunteer	62%
		Medically-Related Work	91%
		Research	88%

Shaded bar represents school's accepted scores ranging from the 10th percentile to the 90th percentile   School Median ●   National Median ◐

Overall GPA	2.0	2.1	2.2	2.3	2.4	2.5	2.6	2.7	2.8	2.9	3.0	3.1	3.2	3.3	3.4	3.5	3.6	3.7	(3.8)	3.9	4.0
Science GPA	2.0	2.1	2.2	2.3	2.4	2.5	2.6	2.7	2.8	2.9	3.0	3.1	3.2	3.3	3.4	3.5	3.6	3.7	(3.8)	3.9	4.0

MCAT® Total Numeric Score 9 10 11 12 13 14 15 16 17 18 19 20 21 22 23 24 25 26 27 28 29 30 (31)(32) 33 34 35 36 37 38 39 40 41 42 43

Writing Sample			J	K	L	M	N	O	(P)	(Q)	R	S	T
Verbal Reasoning	3	4	5	6	7	8	9	(10)	11	12	13	14	15
Biological Sciences	3	4	5	6	7	8	9	10	(11)	12	13	14	15
Physical Sciences	3	4	5	6	7	8	9	10	(11)	12	13	14	15

Acceptance & Matriculation Data for 2009–2010 First Year Class

	Resident	Non-resident	International	Total
Applications	206	1398	96	1700
Interviewed	151	60	4	215
Deferred	0	0	1	1
Matriculants				
Early Assurance Program	0	0	0	0
Early Decision Program	0	0	0	0
Baccalaureate/M.D.	0	0	0	0
M.D./Ph.D.	0	0	0	0
Matriculated	55	7	0	**62**

Applications accepted from International Applicants: Yes

Matriculant Demographics: 2009–2010 First Year Class

Men: 33   **Women:** 29

Matriculants' Self-Reported Race/Ethnicity

Mexican American	0	Korean	5
Cuban	0	Vietnamese	2
Puerto Rican	0	Other Asian	5
Other Hispanic	0	Total Asian	52
Total Hispanic	0	Native American	1
Chinese	24	Black	1
Asian Indian	0	Native Hawaiian	2
Pakistani	0	White	18
Filipino	7	Unduplicated Number	
Japanese	21	of Matriculants	62

Science and Math Majors: 77%
Matriculants with:
  Baccalaureate degree: 98%
  Graduate degree(s): 18%

Specialty Choice

2005, 2006, 2007 Graduates, Specialty Choice
(As reported by program directors to GME Track™)

Anesthesiology	7%
Emergency Medicine	6%
Family Practice	6%
Internal Medicine	22%
Obstetrics/Gynecology	8%
Orthopaedic Surgery	2%
Pediatrics	9%
Psychiatry	4%
Radiology	4%
Surgery	3%

Financial Information

Source: 2008-2009 LCME I-B survey and 2009-2010 AAMC TSF questionnaire

	Residents	Non-residents
Total Cost of Attendance	$ 52,969	$ 79,057
Tuition and Fees	$ 25,205	$ 51,293
Other (includes living expenses)	$ 25,336	$ 25,336
Health Insurance (can be waived)	$ 2,428	$ 2,428

Average 2009 Graduate Indebtedness: $71,042
% of Enrolled Students Receiving Aid: 82%

Criminal Background Check

This medical school requires a criminal background check prior to matriculation.

Loyola University Chicago Stritch School of Medicine

Maywood, Illinois

Loyola University Chicago Stritch School of Medicine
Office of Admissions
2160 South First Avenue
Maywood, Illinois 60153
T 708 216 3229

Admissions www.stritch.luc.edu/admissions
Main www.stritch.luc.edu
Financial www.stritch.luc.edu/financialaid
E-mail SSOM-admissions@lumc.edu

Private Institution

Dr. Richard Gamelli, Dean

Adrian Jones, J.D., Assistant Dean for Admissions & Recruitment

Donna J. Sobie, M.ED., Director, Financial Aid

General Information

Loyola University Chicago, founded in 1870 by the Jesuits, is one of the largest Catholic universities in the United States. By 1909, the university had organized several small medical colleges into a new medical school and, in 1948, the school was named in honor of Samuel Cardinal Stritch, Archbishop of Chicago. In 1969 the university opened the Loyola University Medical Center, built on land given by the Veterans Administration, in Maywood, a suburban community located 12 miles west of downtown Chicago. The medical center is home to the Stritch School of Medicine, Loyola University Hospital, Cardinal Bernardin Cancer Center, and Loyola Outpatient Center. Students receive their clinical training at the 801-bed Loyola University Hospital, 483-bed Hines Veterans Affairs Hospital, and other affiliated hospitals in the Chicago area.

Curricular Highlights

Community Service Requirement: Optional. Highly desirable.
Research/Thesis Requirement: Optional.

Stritch's primary purpose is to train physicians who will care for their patients with skill, respect, and compassion. The personal and intellectual development of each student is promoted through close contact with faculty members and the administration. Students are exposed to a large academic medical center, as well as to VA and community offices and hospitals, where they learn in an atmosphere of cooperation and mutual assistance. The first year of the curriculum concentrates on the basic principles and processes related to the normal structure, function, and regulation of the human body. In addition, the first year includes instruction in health promotion/disease prevention, and communication skills, medical ethics, and the doctor/patient relationship. The second year focuses on basic

science principles related to the mechanisms of human disease, neuroscience, and the therapeutic approach to disease. Additionally, students continue to develop their knowledge about human behavioral science, physical examination skills, basic clinical skills, evidence-based clinical decision-making, and professionalism, medical ethics and the social and community context of healthcare. Students have early clinical experiences through a physician mentor program in ambulatory settings and the peer mentor program. The third and fourth years are organized into clinical clerkships which include up to 34 weeks of elective time during the fourth year as well as exposure to learning seminars offering topics such as business, professional and justice in health care, disaster preparedness, end of life, global health, and religion and healthcare. Special curricular features include an emphasis on bioethics and professionalism and intensive training in patient history-taking, physical examination, and communication skills using the Clinical Skills and Human Simulation Centers, which combine the latest in educational technology.

USMLE

Step 1: Required. Students must record a passing score for graduation, but not promotion.
Step 2: Clinical Skills (CS): Required. Students must record a passing total score to graduate.
Step 2: Clinical Knowledge (CK): Required. Students must record a passing total score to graduate.

Selection Factors

A bachelor's degree and the MCAT taken no later than September of the year of application, are required. Any undergraduate major is acceptable. Applicants must be U.S. citizens or hold a permanent resident visa at the time of application. As a rule, applicants are limited to applying no more than twice. Applicants enrolled in advanced degree programs must expect to complete their degrees prior to matriculation. Applicants who present academic credentials that indicate they are capable of succeeding in the rigorous medical education program will be evaluated for evidence of the personal qualifications they can bring to the medical profession. Essential characteristics

include an interest in learning, integrity, compassion, and the ability to assume responsibility. Of particular concern will be an applicant's exploration of the field of medicine and the nature of the motivation to enter this profession. Early submission of the AMCAS application and prompt return of all supporting material will enhance an applicant's chance of being offered a place in the class. Loyola University does not discriminate on the basis of race, religion, national origin, sex, age, or disability.

Financial Aid

Financial aid is primarily in the form of loans, but limited scholarship and grant money is also available. Applicants should receive a preliminary financial aid award prior to May 15.

Information about Diversity Programs

The Summer Enrichment Program (SEP) at Loyola University Chicago Stritch School of Medicine is a six-week experience for pre-medical students. The program's mission is to offer students a variety of educational experiences and service activities to enhance their preparation for a career in medicine. The program targets students who have the potential to enrich the diversity of the medical student community.

Campus Information

Enrollment

For 2009, total enrollment was: 574

Application Process and Requirements 2011–2012

Primary Application Service: AMCAS
Earliest filing date: June 1, 2010
Latest filing date: November 15, 2010

Secondary Application Required?: Yes
Sent to: Screened applicants
URL: n/a
Fee: Yes, $75   **Waiver available:** Yes
Earliest filing date: June 2010
Latest filing date: February 2011

MCAT® required?: Yes
Latest MCAT® considered: September 2010
Oldest MCAT® considered: 2007

Early Decision Program: School does not have EDP
EDP available for: n/a
Applicants notified: n/a

Regular Acceptance Notice
Earliest date: October 15, 2010
Latest date: Until class is full
Applicant's Response to Acceptance Offer – Maximum Time: Two weeks

Requests for Deferred Entrance Considered: Yes

Deposit to Hold Place in Class: No
Deposit (Resident): n/a   **(Non-resident):** n/a
Deposit due: n/a
Applied to tuition: n/a   **Refundable:** n/a
Refundable by: n/a

Estimated number of new entrants: 150
EDP: n/a, special program: n/a

Start Month/Year: July 2011

Interview Format: Semi-open file with admission committee members. Regional interviews are not available. Video interviews are not available.

Other Programs

PREPARATORY PROGRAMS
Postbaccalaureate Program: No
Summer Program: Yes, Office of Student Affairs, (708) 216-3220, kcalhoun@lumc.edu

COMBINED DEGREE PROGRAMS
Baccalaureate/M.D.: No
M.D./M.P.H.: No
M.D./M.B.A.: No
M.D./J.D.: No
M.D./Ph.D.: Yes, http://www.stritch.luc.edu/node/83 Charles S. Hemenway, M.D., Ph.D, chemenway@lumc.edu
Additional Program: Yes, http://bioethics.lumc.edu/education/MD_MA_Program.html

Premedical Coursework

On-line courses accepted in fulfillment of prerequisites: No

Course	Req.	Rec.	Lab.	Sems.
Inorganic Chemistry	•		•	2
Behavioral Sciences				
Biochemistry		•		
Biology				
Biology/Zoology	•		•	2
Calculus				
College English				
College Mathematics				

Course	Req.	Rec.	Lab.	Sems.
Computer Science				
Genetics		•		
Humanities		•		
Organic Chemistry	•		•	2
Physics	•		•	2
Psychology				
Social Sciences				
Molecular Biology		•		

Selection Factors: 2009 Accepted Applicants

Proportion of Accepted Applicants with Relevant Experience (Data Self-Reported to AMCAS®)		
Community Service/Volunteer		77%
Medically-Related Work		92%
Research		83%

Shaded bar represents school's accepted scores ranging from the 10th percentile to the 90th percentile. School Median ● National Median ○

Overall GPA 2.0 2.1 2.2 2.3 2.4 2.5 2.6 2.7 2.8 2.9 3.0 3.1 3.2 3.3 3.4 3.5 3.6 ⓷.7 3.8 3.9 4.0
Science GPA 2.0 2.1 2.2 2.3 2.4 2.5 2.6 2.7 2.8 2.9 3.0 3.1 3.2 3.3 3.4 3.5 ⓷.6 3.7 3.8 3.9 4.0

MCAT® Total Numeric Score 9 10 11 12 13 14 15 16 17 18 19 20 21 22 23 24 25 26 27 28 29 30 31 ⓷2 33 34 35 36 37 38 39 40 41 42 43

		J	K	L	M	N	O	P	Q	R	S	T
Writing Sample		J	K	L	M	N	O	P	Ⓠ	R	S	T
Verbal Reasoning	3	4	5	6	7	8	9	⑩	11	12	13	14	15
Biological Sciences	3	4	5	6	7	8	9	10	⑪	12	13	14	15
Physical Sciences	3	4	5	6	7	8	9	10	⑪	12	13	14	15

Acceptance & Matriculation Data for 2009–2010 First Year Class

	Resident	Non-resident	International	Total
Applications	1430	8716	27	10173
Interviewed	188	327	0	515
Deferred	0	0	0	0
Matriculants				
Early Assurance Program	0	0	0	0
Early Decision Program	0	0	0	0
Baccalaureate/M.D.	0	0	0	0
M.D./Ph.D.	0	0	0	0
Matriculated	65	80	0	**145**

Applications accepted from International Applicants: No

Matriculant Demographics: 2009–2010 First Year Class

Men: 60   **Women:** 85

Matriculants' Self-Reported Race/Ethnicity

Mexican American	5	Korean	2
Cuban	0	Vietnamese	1
Puerto Rican	2	Other Asian	4
Other Hispanic	1	Total Asian	16
Total Hispanic	8	Native American	2
Chinese	2	Black	11
Asian Indian	7	Native Hawaiian	2
Pakistani	2	White	118
Filipino	0	Unduplicated Number	
Japanese	1	of Matriculants	145

Science and Math Majors: 59%
Matriculants with:
  Baccalaureate degree: 100%
  Graduate degree(s): 14%

Specialty Choice

2005, 2006, 2007 Graduates, Specialty Choice (As reported by program directors to GME Track™)

Anesthesiology	4%
Emergency Medicine	9%
Family Practice	12%
Internal Medicine	24%
Obstetrics/Gynecology	4%
Orthopaedic Surgery	5%
Pediatrics	12%
Psychiatry	2%
Radiology	2%
Surgery	6%

Financial Information

Source: 2008-2009 LCME I-B survey and 2009-2010 AAMC TSF questionnaire

	Residents	Non-residents
Total Cost of Attendance	$60,734	$61,234
Tuition and Fees	$40,238	$40,238
Other (includes living expenses)	$18,886	$19,386
Health Insurance (can be waived)	$1,610	$1,610

Average 2009 Graduate Indebtedness: $158,702
% of Enrolled Students Receiving Aid: 89%

Criminal Background Check

This medical school requires a criminal background check prior to matriculation.

Northwestern University
Feinberg School of Medicine

Chicago, Illinois

Office of Admissions
Northwestern University
Feinberg School of Medicine
303 East Chicago Avenue, Morton I-606
Chicago, Illinois 60611-3008
T 312 503 8206   F 312 503 0550

Admissions www.feinberg.northwestern.edu/
admissions/md/index.html
Main www.feinberg.northwestern.edu
Financial http://chicagofinancialaid.
northwestern.edu
E-mail med-admissions@northwestern.edu

Private Institution

Dr. J. Larry Jameson, Dean

Dr. Warren H. Wallace, Associate Dean for Admissions

Dr. John E. Franklin, Associate Dean for Minority and Cultural Affairs

General Information

Northwestern University's Feinberg School of Medicine (FSM), founded in 1859, continues to educate today's students at a premier medical school and in outstanding hospitals: Northwestern Memorial, Children's Memorial, Prentice Women's, the Rehabilitation Institute of Chicago, and the Jesse Brown VA Medical Center. Students have translational and clinical research options as well as the opportunitiy to engage the cultural life of Chicago and work with its diverse population.

Mission Statement

The mission of the Feinberg School of Medicine is to educate physicians and physician-scientists who will excel both scientifically and clinically. We expect our students to take leadership roles in medicine and to serve the people of our increasingly diverse communities.

Curricular Highlights

Community Service Requirement: Optional. Multiple free clinics are available.
Research/Thesis Requirement: Optional. This option includes summer and senior selectives.

We strive to provide a student centered environment where adult learners employ their own questions as the starting point for inquiry. The first two years of the curriculum feature an integrated, organ-system based approach to the essential basic sciences. Small group "Problem Based Learning" sessions augment the concepts developed in lectures and laboratory sessions. The psychosocial foundations of medicine are emphasized in "Patient, Physician and Society (PPS)": students develop clinical skills and study the many ways in which medicine interacts with the larger society. Three short blocks are devoted to medical decision-making where students hone their ability to analyze and to manage the information

required for effective clinical decision-making. During the third year clerkships, students continue the PPS curriculum by returning to the medical school each month for discussion of topics common to all clerkships. A sub-internship, ICU and ER rotations, and several electives round out the curriculum in the fourth year.

USMLE

Step 1: Required. Students must record a passing score for graduation, but not promotion.
Step 2: Clinical Skills (CS): Required. Students must record a passing score in each section to graduate.
Step 2: Clinical Knowledge (CK): Required. Students must record a passing score in each section to graduate.

Selection Factors

The Committee on Admissions looks for evidence of academic excellence, mature motivation for a career in medicine, altruism, and character. A premium is placed on the breadth and depth of academic and life experiences, as well as clinical and research exposure. Applicants should be liberally educated men and women whose studies have gone beyond the conventional premedical courses. We seek a diverse class and do not discriminate on the basis of race, religion, national origin, gender, sexual orientation, age, or disability. The Illinois Medical School Matriculant Criminal History Records Act requires each entering medical student to submit to a criminal history records check prior to matriculation.

Financial Aid

Financial considerations do not influence admissions decisions. We make every effort to ensure that accepted students receive a competitive financial aid package, including support through national and university loan programs, scholarships, and grants. Students receive financial management counseling, and we offer a loan program to international students who have a credit-worthy U.S. loan co-signer.

Information about Diversity Programs

FSM strives to admit a student body whose diversity mirrors that of our society. The Office of Minority and Cultural Affairs supports the

broad array of student groups involved in community outreach and offers programming in the formal curriculum, lunchtime speakers, dialogue groups and a film series on health disparities and social justice.

Campus Information

Setting

Located in the Streeterville neighborhood of downtown Chicago, the medical school is adjacent to beautiful Lake Michigan and within easy walking distance of apartments, museums, restaurants, athletic facilities, and retailers. Public and university transportation makes Chicago's diverse neighborhoods and cultural opportunities readily accessible.

Enrollment

For 2009, total enrollment was: 680

Special Features

The Medical School offers numerous research centers, institutes and programs including Lurie Comprehensive Cancer Center, Feinberg Cardiovascular Research Center, Institute for Genetic Medicine, Northwestern University Clinical and Translationl Sciences Institute, and Institute for Women's Health among many others (please see *www.feinberg.northwestern. edu/directory/centers.html*). New clinical facilities include the recently completed Prentice Women's Hospital. The new Children's Memorial Hospital building is currently under construction on the downtown campus. The Jesse Brown Medical Center has recently completed a new in-patient bed tower.

Housing

Most students live in high-rise apartments near the medical center although excellent public transportation makes commuting from city neighborhoods or Chicago's suburbs feasible.

Satellite Campuses/Facilities

Students do required clinical rotations in Chicago at Northwestern Hospitals and the Jesse Brown VA. Senior away rotations are available at affiliated institutions in Latin America, Africa, Europe, and Asia.

Application Process and Requirements 2011–2012

Primary Application Service: AMCAS
Earliest filing date: July 1, 2010
Latest filing date: October 15, 2010

Secondary Application Required?: Yes
Sent to: AMCAS
URL: https://medicalapp.northwestern.edu
Fee: Yes, $75 **Waiver available:** Yes
Earliest filing date: July 1, 2010
Latest filing date: Varies

MCAT® required?: Yes
Latest MCAT® considered: September 2010
Oldest MCAT® considered: 2007

Early Decision Program: School does have EDP
Applicants notified: Winter 2011
EDP available for: Both residents and non-residents

Regular Acceptance Notice
Earliest date: November 2010
Latest date: Until class is full
Applicant's Response to Acceptance Offer – Maximum Time: Two weeks

Requests for Deferred Entrance Considered: Yes

Deposit to Hold Place in Class: No
Deposit (Resident): n/a **(Non-resident):** n/a
Deposit due: n/a
Applied to tuition: n/a **Refundable:** n/a
Refundable by: n/a

Estimated number of new entrants: 170
EDP: 5, special program: 20

Start Month/Year: August 2011

Interview Format: Individual and panel interview. Regional interviews are not available. Video interviews are not available.

Other Programs

PREPARATORY PROGRAMS
Postbaccalaureate Program: No
Summer Program: No

COMBINED DEGREE PROGRAMS
Baccalaureate/M.D.: Yes, www.feinberg.northwestern.edu/hpme/index.html
M.D./M.P.H.: Yes, www.publichealth. northwestern.edu/admissions_mdmph.htm
M.D./M.B.A.: No
M.D./J.D.: No
M.D./Ph.D.: Yes, www.mstp.northwestern.edu
MD/MA-Medical Humanities & Bioethics: Yes, www.bioethics.northwestern.edu/masters/feinbergma.html

Premedical Coursework

On-line courses accepted in fulfillment of prerequisites: No

Course	Req.	Rec.	Lab.	Sems.
Inorganic Chemistry	•		•	2
Behavioral Sciences				
Biochemistry				
Biology	•		•	2
Biology/Zoology				
Calculus				
College English		•		
College Mathematics				

Course	Req.	Rec.	Lab.	Sems.
Computer Science				
Genetics		•		
Humanities		•		2
Organic Chemistry	•		•	2
Physics	•		•	2
Psychology		•		
Social Sciences		•		
Statistics		•		2

Selection Factors: 2009 Accepted Applicants

Proportion of Accepted Applicants with Relevant Experience (Data Self-Reported to AMCAS®)		
Community Service/Volunteer		71%
Medically-Related Work		85%
Research		91%

Shaded bar represents school's accepted scores ranging from the 10th percentile to the 90th percentile   **School Median** ○ **National Median** ○

Overall GPA	2.0	2.1	2.2	2.3	2.4	2.5	2.6	2.7	2.8	2.9	3.0	3.1	3.2	3.3	3.4	3.5	3.6	3.7	3.8	(3.9)	4.0
Science GPA	2.0	2.1	2.2	2.3	2.4	2.5	2.6	2.7	2.8	2.9	3.0	3.1	3.2	3.3	3.4	3.5	3.6	3.7	3.8	(3.9)	4.0

MCAT® Total Numeric Score 9 10 11 12 13 14 15 16 17 18 19 20 21 22 23 24 25 26 27 28 29 30 31 (32) 33 34 35 (36) 37 38 39 40 41 42 43

			J	K	L	M	N	O	P	(Q)	R	S	T
Writing Sample			J	K	L	M	N	O	P	(Q)	R	S	T
Verbal Reasoning	3	4	5	6	7	8	9	(10)	(11)	12	13	14	15
Biological Sciences	3	4	5	6	7	8	9	10	(11)	(12)	13	14	15
Physical Sciences	3	4	5	6	7	8	9	10	(11)	(12)	13	14	15

Acceptance & Matriculation Data for 2009–2010 First Year Class

	Resident	Non-resident	International	Total
Applications	910	5457	383	6750
Interviewed	79	560	42	681
Deferred	0	6	0	6
Matriculants				
Early Assurance Program	4	1	0	5
Early Decision Program	0	0	0	0
Baccalaureate/M.D.	4	26	0	30
M.D./Ph.D.	1	9	1	11
Matriculated	35	123	6	**164**

Applications accepted from International Applicants: Yes

Specialty Choice

2005, 2006, 2007 Graduates, Specialty Choice (As reported by program directors to GME Track™)	
Anesthesiology	5%
Emergency Medicine	8%
Family Practice	3%
Internal Medicine	23%
Obstetrics/Gynecology	6%
Orthopaedic Surgery	5%
Pediatrics	11%
Psychiatry	4%
Radiology	5%
Surgery	7%

Matriculant Demographics: 2009–2010 First Year Class

Men: 91 **Women:** 73

Matriculants' Self-Reported Race/Ethnicity

Mexican American	6	Korean	9
Cuban	1	Vietnamese	1
Puerto Rican	1	Other Asian	8
Other Hispanic	3	Total Asian	58
Total Hispanic	10	Native American	3
Chinese	19	Black	11
Asian Indian	19	Native Hawaiian	1
Pakistani	1	White	86
Filipino	2	Unduplicated Number	
Japanese	2	of Matriculants	164

Science and Math Majors: 61%
Matriculants with:
Baccalaureate degree: 99%
Graduate degree(s): 4%

Financial Information

Source: 2008-2009 LCME I-B survey and 2009-2010 AAMC TSF questionnaire

	Residents	Non-residents
Total Cost of Attendance	$ 70,228	$ 70,228
Tuition and Fees	$ 42,974	$ 42,974
Other (includes living expenses)	$ 24,894	$ 24,894
Health Insurance (can be waived)	$ 2,360	$ 2,360

Average 2009 Graduate Indebtedness: $156,186
% of Enrolled Students Receiving Aid: 78%

Criminal Background Check

This medical school requires a criminal background check prior to matriculation.

Rosalind Franklin University of Medicine and Science Chicago Medical School

North Chicago, Illinois

Rosalind Franklin University of Medicine and Science
Office of Medical School Admissions
3333 Green Bay Road
North Chicago, Illinois 60064
T 847 578 3204

Admissions www.rosalindfranklin.edu/tabid/1629/default.aspx
Main www.rosalindfranklin.edu/tabid/363/default.aspx
Financial www.rosalindfranklin.edu/tabid/1942/default.aspx
E-mail cms.admissions@rosalindfranklin.edu

Private Institution

Dr. Arthur J. Ross, III, MD, MBA, Dean

Rebecca Durkin, Associate Vice President, Division of Student Affairs and Enrollment Management

Dr. Cathy Lazarus, MD, Senior Associate Dean for Student Affairs and Medical Education

Maryanne DeCaire, Associate Vice President of Institutional Research, Director of Financial Aid

General Information

Founded in 1912, The Chicago Medical School has been dedicated to excellence in medical education for nearly a century. The Chicago Medical School has educated thousands of professionals with recognized innovation in health education, excellence in the creation of knowledge and scientific discovery focused on prediction and prevention of disease, outstanding clinical programs, and compassionate community service. Major hospital affiliates include Advocate Christ Medical Center, Advocate Condell Medical Center, Advocate Illinois Masonic, Advocate Lutheran General Hospital, John H. Stroger, Jr., Hospital of Cook County, Mount Sinai Hospital and Medical Center, and the North Chicago Veterans Affairs Medical Center (NCVAMC).

Mission Statement

The Chicago Medical School educates physicians and scientists dedicated to providing exemplary, compassionate patient care and excellence in scientific discovery within an inter-professional environment.

Curricular Highlights

Community Service Requirement: Optional.
Research/Thesis Requirement: Optional.

The Chicago Medical School's curriculum offers a strong grounding in the sciences basic to medicine along with assuring competency in skills necessary for the practice of medicine. The CMS curriculum features a unique inter-professional approach, with interaction among a broad range of health professional students and practitioners. The curriculum is a mix of lectures, labs, small-group discussions, team-based learning, and opportunities for peer-to-

peer learning. The educational information system, Desire to Learn (D2L), provides 24-hour-a-day access to learning materials. Students have early clinical experiences in the state-of-the-art evaluation and education center, as well as opportunities to connect with physician preceptors. The required junior clinical clerkships include medicine, ambulatory care, surgery, family medicine, obstetrics/gynecology, psychiatry, medCore, pediatrics, neurology, and emergency medicine. The senior requirements include four weeks in a medicine or pediatrics subinternship, plus 32 weeks of approved electives (14 of which must be completed at one of the school's primary affiliated sites). The elective period gives students an opportunity, through both intramural and extramural experiences, to explore and strengthen their personal career interests.

USMLE

Step 1: Required. Students must record a passing score for promotion.
Step 2: Clinical Skills (CS): Required. Students must record a passing total score to graduate.
Step 2: Clinical Knowledge (CK): Required. Students must record a passing total score to graduate.

Selection Factors

Students are selected on the basis of various criteria, including scholarship, character, motivation, and educational background. A student's potential for the study and practice of medicine will be evaluated on the basis of academic achievement, MCAT results, appraisals by a preprofessional advisory committee or individual instructors, and a personal interview, if requested by the Student Admissions Committee. To fulfill the mission of The Chicago Medical School, admissions policies are designed to ensure that the selection process matriculates a class made up of individuals capable of meeting the needs of current and future patients. Applicants will be evaluated not only for educational potential, but with the aim of providing diverse educational experience for other members of the class.

Financial Aid

The Financial Aid Office is committed to helping students secure the funding needed to pursue their educational endeavors. Financial Aid is available in the form of loans, scholarships, and work-study. For more information, contact the Financial Aid Office at (847) 578-3217.

Information about Diversity Programs

The school maintains an extensive recruitment and retention program for students from groups underrepresented in medicine.

Campus Information

Setting

Rosalind Franklin University of Medicine and Science is situated in the northern suburbs of Chicago, with easy access to downtown Chicago and the surrounding areas by car or public transportation. State-of-the-art facilities include a recently completed $10 million research wing expansion; multimedia classrooms and gross anatomy laboratory; and an Education and Evaluation Center for physical examination skills training. Recreational facilities include an exercise room, game room, and the Student Union (home to the University Bookstore, Union Café, and dedicated e-mail stations).

Enrollment

For 2009, total enrollment was: 763

Housing

On-campus housing is available at Rosalind Franklin University. Each of the University's three apartment buildings has one and two-bedroom apartments. Individual apartments feature a variety of amenities, such as kitchen appliances (range, refrigerator, dishwasher, and microwave), University networked Internet access, and washer/dryer hookups. Each apartment building also includes study and lounge areas, shared laundry facilities on every floor, and individual storage units. For more information about student housing, contact the Office of Student Housing at (847) 578-8350 or campus.housing@rosalindfranklin.edu.

Application Process and Requirements 2011–2012

Primary Application Service: AMCAS
Earliest filing date: June 1, 2010
Latest filing date: November 1, 2010

Secondary Application Required?: Yes
Sent to: All applicants
URL: n/a
Fee: Yes, $100   **Waiver available:** Yes
Earliest filing date: July 1, 2010
Latest filing date: December 15, 2010

MCAT® required?: Yes
Latest MCAT® considered: September 2010
Oldest MCAT® considered: 2008

Early Decision Program: School does have EDP
Applicants notified: October 1, 2010
EDP available for: Both Residents and Non-residents

Regular Acceptance Notice
Earliest date: October 15, 2010
Latest date: Until class is full
Applicant's Response to Acceptance
Offer – Maximum Time: Two weeks

Requests for Deferred
Entrance Considered: Yes

Deposit to Hold Place in Class: Yes
Deposit (Resident): $100   **(Non-resident):** $100
Deposit due: With response to acceptance offer.
Applied to tuition: Yes   **Refundable:** Yes
Refundable by: May 15, 2011

Estimated number of new entrants: 185

EDP: 3, special program: n/a

Start Month/Year: August 2011

Interview Format: Two on-campus interviews with committee members, faculty, staff, and/or fourth-year students. Regional interviews are not available. Video interviews are not available.

Other Programs

PREPARATORY PROGRAMS
Postbaccalaureate Program: No
Summer Program: No

COMBINED DEGREE PROGRAMS
Baccalaureate/M.D.: No
M.D./M.P.H.: No
M.D./M.B.A.: No
M.D./J.D.: No
M.D./Ph.D.: Yes, www.rosalindfranklin.edu/tabid/710/default.aspx

Premedical Coursework

On-line courses accepted in fulfillment of prerequisites: No

Course	Req.	Rec.	Lab.	Sems.	Course	Req.	Rec.	Lab.	Sems.
Inorganic Chemistry	•		•	2	Computer Science				
Behavioral Sciences					Genetics				
Biochemistry					Humanities				
Biology					Organic Chemistry	•		•	2
Biology/Zoology	•		•	2	Physics	•		•	2
Calculus					Psychology				
College English					Social Sciences				
College Mathematics					Other				

Selection Factors: 2009 Accepted Applicants

Proportion of Accepted Applicants with Relevant Experience (Data Self-Reported to AMCAS®)		
Community Service/Volunteer		74%
Medically-Related Work		91%
Research		83%

Shaded bar represents school's accepted scores ranging from the 10th percentile to the 90th percentile.   School Median ●   National Median ○

Overall GPA	2.0	2.1	2.2	2.3	2.4	2.5	2.6	2.7	2.8	2.9	3.0	3.1	3.2	3.3	3.4	3.5	3.6	3.7	(3.8)	3.9	4.0
Science GPA	2.0	2.1	2.2	2.3	2.4	2.5	2.6	2.7	2.8	2.9	3.0	3.1	3.2	3.3	3.4	3.5	3.6	(3.7)	3.8	3.9	4.0

MCAT® Total Numeric Score 9 10 11 12 13 14 15 16 17 18 19 20 21 22 23 24 25 26 27 28 29 30 (31) (32) 33 34 35 36 37 38 39 40 41 42 43

Writing Sample				J	K	L	M	N	O	(P)	(Q)	R	S	T
Verbal Reasoning	3	4	5	6	7	8	9	(10)	11	12	13	14	15
Biological Sciences	3	4	5	6	7	8	9	10	(11)	12	13	14	15
Physical Sciences	3	4	5	6	7	8	9	(10)	(11)	12	13	14	15

Acceptance & Matriculation Data for 2009–2010 First Year Class

	Resident	Non-resident	International	Total
Applications	1173	8596	642	10411
Interviewed	240	379	37	656
Deferred	1	1	0	2
Matriculants				
Early Assurance Program	0	0	0	0
Early Decision Program	0	1	0	1
Baccalaureate/M.D.	0	0	0	0
M.D./Ph.D.	0	0	0	0
Matriculated	78	101	11	**190**

Applications accepted from International Applicants: Yes

Matriculant Demographics: 2009–2010 First Year Class

Men: 107   **Women:** 83

Matriculants' Self-Reported Race/Ethnicity

Mexican American	4	Korean	6
Cuban	0	Vietnamese	3
Puerto Rican	0	Other Asian	11
Other Hispanic	1	Total Asian	64
Total Hispanic	5	Native American	0
Chinese	10	Black	5
Asian Indian	28	Native Hawaiian	0
Pakistani	3	White	106
Filipino	3	Unduplicated Number	
Japanese	3	of Matriculants	190

Science and Math Majors: 66%
Matriculants with:
    Baccalaureate degree: 99%
    Graduate degree(s): 32%

Specialty Choice

2005, 2006, 2007 Graduates, Specialty Choice (As reported by program directors to GME Track™)	
Anesthesiology	5%
Emergency Medicine	10%
Family Practice	7%
Internal Medicine	20%
Obstetrics/Gynecology	5%
Orthopaedic Surgery	3%
Pediatrics	10%
Psychiatry	3%
Radiology	6%
Surgery	7%

Financial Information

Source: 2008-2009 LCME I-B survey and 2009-2010 AAMC TSF questionnaire

	Residents	Non-residents
Total Cost of Attendance	$ 63,597	$ 63,597
Tuition and Fees	$ 43,841	$ 43,841
Other (includes living expenses)	$ 17,956	$ 17,956
Health Insurance (can be waived)	$ 1,800	$ 1,800

Average 2009 Graduate Indebtedness: $189,640
% of Enrolled Students Receiving Aid: 93%

Criminal Background Check

This medical school requires a criminal background check prior to matriculation.

Rush Medical College of Rush University

Chicago, Illinois

Rush Medical College of Rush University
Office of Admissions, Suite 524
600 South Paulina Street
Chicago, Illinois 60612
T 312 942 6915   **F** 312 942 6840

Admissions www.rushu.rush.edu/
medcol/admissions.html
Main www.rushu.rush.edu/medcol
Financial www.rushu.rush.edu/finaid
E-mail RMC_Admissions@rush.edu

Private Institution

Dr. Thomas A. Deutsch, Dean

*Dr. Cynthia Boyd, Recruitment
Team Leader*

David Nelson, Director of Student Financial Aid

Dr. Susan K. Jacob, Associate Dean

*Jill M. Volk, Director of Recruitment
and Special Programs*

General Information

Rush Medical College, founded in 1837, is the oldest component of Rush University. Through an academic and healthcare network of more than a dozen affiliated hospitals and a neighborhood health center, Rush University Medical Center serves 1.5 to 2 million people annually. Thus, students train in urban and suburban areas in a variety of socioeconomic and ethnic settings.

Mission Statement

Rush educates students as practitioners, scientists and teachers who will become leaders in advancing health care and furthering the advancement of knowledge through research. The university integrates patient care, education and research through the practitioner-teacher model. Rush encourages the growth of its students by committing itself to the pursuit of excellence, dedication to community service, free inquiry and the highest intellectual and ethical standards.

Curricular Highlights

Community Service Requirement: Optional.
Research/Thesis Requirement: Optional.

Rush provides a firm background in the science of medicine and a balanced introduction to the practice of clinical medicine in a four-year curriculum designed to provide educational flexibility. The faculty have created an environment that fosters a commitment to competent and compassionate patient care and to attitudes of inquiry and life-long learning. PRECLINICAL CURRICULUM - The primary objective of the first year (M1) is to provide students with exposure to the vocabulary and fundamental concepts upon which clinical medicine is based.

The courses utilize lecture, laboratory, small group and workshop formats. The second-year (M2) curriculum centers on the causes and effects of disease and therapeutics. Courses utilize a case-based approach integrating basic sciences into the context of clinical medicine. The Physicianship Program is an integrated, multi-disciplinary program that spans the M1 and M2 years and is designed to provide students with a foundation of clinical knowledge, skills, attitudes and behaviors so students are prepared for clinical experiences where physician skills are practiced in the context of patient care. CLINICAL CURRICULUM - The third and fourth years provide students with training in clinical skills, diagnosis and patient management in a variety of clinical settings. The third year is comprised of required core clerkships, while the fourth year provides students with the opportunity to pursue areas of special interest. Students complete the majority of their required clinical rotations at Rush University Medical Center

USMLE

Step 1: Required. Students must record a passing score for promotion.
Step 2: Clinical Skills (CS): Required. Students must record a passing total score to graduate.
Step 2: Clinical Knowledge (CK): Required. Students must record a passing total score to graduate.

Selection Factors

All applicants are invited to complete the supplemental application and submit letters of recommendation. The Committee on Admissions considers both academic and non-academic qualifications of applicants in making decisions. The Committee looks for objective evidence that the applicant will be able to handle the academic demands of the curriculum. In addition, the Committee places strong emphasis on the applicant's humanistic concerns, unique experiences and demonstrated motivation for a career in medicine, including healthcare experience. Academic achievement, letters of recommendation, MCAT performance, healthcare experience and interviews are considered in the final evaluation of all applicants. Only U.S. citizens or permanent residents are considered for admission.

Financial Aid

Rush University grant eligibility is based on both student and parent resources, regardless of the student's age or status. After acceptances are offered, students are awarded financial aid packages--grants, scholarships and loans--to meet 100 percent of the demonstrated financial need during each year of their medical education.

Information about Diversity Programs

Rush seeks to attract a diverse student body that is representative of the national population and informed about multicultural determinants of health and the socioeconomic problems affecting the delivery of care.

Campus Information

Setting

Rush Medical College is located on the near west side of Chicago; the John H. Stroger, Jr. Hospital of Cook County, a major teaching affiliate, is two blocks away. The community is thriving and culturally diverse, with easy access by public transportation.

Enrollment

For 2009, total enrollment was: 547

Special Features

The Rush Community Service Initiatives Program creates a network of community programs that matches students' interest and initiative with the social and healthcare needs of Chicago's underserved population. Students have the opportunity to participate in clinical and non-clinical programs.

Housing

Student housing is available in the Center Court Garden Apartments, located one block from campus.

Application Process and Requirements 2011–2012

Primary Application Service: AMCAS
Earliest filing date: June 1, 2010
Latest filing date: November 1, 2010

Secondary Application Required?: Yes
Sent to: All applicants
URL: www.rushsupp.com
Contact: RMC_Admissions@rush.edu
Fee: Yes, $75   **Waiver available:** Yes
Earliest filing date: July 1, 2010
Latest filing date: December 15, 2010

MCAT® required?: Yes
Latest MCAT® considered: October 2010
Oldest MCAT® considered: January 2008

Early Decision Program: School does not have EDP
Applicants notified: n/a
EDP available for: n/a

Regular Acceptance Notice
Earliest date: November 2010
Latest date: Varies
Applicant's Response to Acceptance Offer – Maximum Time: Two weeks after acceptance offer

Requests for Deferred Entrance Considered: Yes

Deposit to Hold Place in Class: Yes
Deposit (Resident): $100   **(Non-resident):** $100
Deposit due: Two weeks after acceptance offer
Applied to tuition: Yes   **Refundable:** Yes
Refundable by: May 15, 2011

Estimated number of new entrants: 128
EDP: n/a, special program: n/a

Start Month/Year: August/September 2011

Interview Format: Two individual interviews with faculty. Regional interviews are not available. Video interviews are not available.

Other Programs

PREPARATORY PROGRAMS
Postbaccalaureate Program: No
Summer Program: No

COMBINED DEGREE PROGRAMS
Baccalaureate/M.D.: No
M.D./M.P.H.: No
M.D./M.B.A.: No
M.D./J.D.: No
M.D./Ph.D.: Yes,
RMC_Admissions@rush.edu

Premedical Coursework

On-line courses accepted in fulfillment of prerequisites: Yes

Course	Req.	Rec.	Lab.	Hrs.	Course	Req.	Rec.	Lab.	Hrs.
Inorganic Chemistry	•			8	Computer Science				
Behavioral Sciences					Genetics				
Biochemistry					Humanities				
Biology	•			8	Organic Chemistry	•			8
Biology/Zoology					Physics	•			8
Calculus					Psychology				
College English					Social Sciences				
College Mathematics					Other				

Selection Factors: 2009 Accepted Applicants

Proportion of Accepted Applicants with Relevant Experience (Data Self-Reported to AMCAS®)		
Community Service/Volunteer		74%
Medically-Related Work		90%
Research		86%

Shaded bar represents school's accepted scores ranging from the 10th percentile to the 90th percentile   School Median ● National Median ●

Overall GPA	2.0	2.1	2.2	2.3	2.4	2.5	2.6	2.7	2.8	2.9	3.0	3.1	3.2	3.3	3.4	3.5	(3.6)	3.7	3.8	3.9	4.0
Science GPA	2.0	2.1	2.2	2.3	2.4	2.5	2.6	2.7	2.8	2.9	3.0	3.1	3.2	3.3	3.4	(3.5)	3.6	3.7	3.8	3.9	4.0

MCAT® Total Numeric Score 9 10 11 12 13 14 15 16 17 18 19 20 21 22 23 24 25 26 27 28 29 (30) 31 (32) 33 34 35 36 37 38 39 40 41 42 43

Writing Sample			J	K	L	M	N	O	P	(Q)	R	S	T
Verbal Reasoning	3	4	5	6	7	8	9	(10)	11	12	13	14	15
Biological Sciences	3	4	5	6	7	8	9	(10)	(11)	12	13	14	15
Physical Sciences	3	4	5	6	7	8	9	(10)	(11)	12	13	14	15

Acceptance & Matriculation Data for 2009–2010 First Year Class

	Resident	Non-resident	International	Total
Applications	1401	5048	36	6485
Interviewed	268	96	0	364
Deferred	2	0	0	2
Matriculants				
Early Assurance Program	0	0	0	0
Early Decision Program	0	0	0	0
Baccalaureate/M.D.	0	0	0	0
M.D./Ph.D.	0	0	0	0
Matriculated	116	28	0	**144**

Applications accepted from International Applicants: No

Matriculant Demographics: 2009–2010 First Year Class

Men: 76   **Women:** 68

Matriculants' Self-Reported Race/Ethnicity

Mexican American	1	Korean	5
Cuban	1	Vietnamese	1
Puerto Rican	1	Other Asian	3
Other Hispanic	8	Total Asian	37
Total Hispanic	11	Native American	0
Chinese	7	Black	5
Asian Indian	14	Native Hawaiian	4
Pakistani	3	White	93
Filipino	3	Unduplicated Number	
Japanese	4	of Matriculants	144

Science and Math Majors: 63%
Matriculants with:
  Baccalaureate degree: 99%
  Graduate degree(s): 10%

Specialty Choice

2005, 2006, 2007 Graduates, Specialty Choice (As reported by program directors to GME Track™)	
Anesthesiology	5%
Emergency Medicine	7%
Family Practice	8%
Internal Medicine	22%
Obstetrics/Gynecology	3%
Orthopaedic Surgery	4%
Pediatrics	10%
Psychiatry	3%
Radiology	5%
Surgery	7%

Financial Information

Source: 2008-2009 LCME I-B survey and 2009-2010 AAMC TSF questionnaire

	Residents	Non-residents
Total Cost of Attendance	$ 66,335	$ 66,335
Tuition and Fees	$ 46,272	$ 46,272
Other (includes living expenses)	$ 20,063	$ 20,063
Health Insurance (can be waived)	$ 0	$ 0

Average 2009 Graduate Indebtedness: $163,752
% of Enrolled Students Receiving Aid: 88%

Criminal Background Check

This medical school requires a criminal background check prior to matriculation.

Southern Illinois University School of Medicine

Springfield, Illinois

Office of Admissions
Southern Illinois University
School of Medicine, P.O. Box 19624
Springfield, Illinois 62794-9624
T 217 545 6013   F 217 545 5538

Admissions www.siumed.edu/studentaffairs/admissions
Main www.siumed.edu
Financial www.siumed.edu/studentaffairs
E-mail admissions@siumed.edu

Public Institution

Dr. J. Kevin Dorsey, Dean and Provost

Dr. Erik J. Constance, Associate Dean for Student Affairs

Dr. Wesley Robinson-McNeese, Executive Assistant to the Dean for Diversity

Leslie Fry, Director of Financial Aid

Evan Wilson, Director of Admissions

General Information

Southern Illinois University School of Medicine was established in 1969 and graduated its first class in 1975. Students spend the first 12 months of the program at the medical education facilities on the Carbondale campus and the remaining three years at the Medical Center in Springfield.

Mission Statement

The mission of the SIU School of Medicine is to assist the people of central and southern Illinois in meeting their health care needs through education, patient care, research and service to the community.

Curricular Highlights

Community Service Requirement: Optional. Highly recommended.
Research/Thesis Requirement: Optional.

The overall focus of the first two years of the curriculum is on case-based, student-directed learning in a small-group setting supported by lectures/resource sessions. Close integration of basic science and clinical information takes place throughout the four-year course of study. Clinical training begins in the first year with real and simulated patients. An increased emphasis on issues such as community health care and the psychosocial issues of medicine continues SIU School of Medicine's emphasis on caring while curing and treating patients as people rather than medical conditions. The third year consists of a series of multidisciplinary clinical rotations, with emphasis on both hospital-based and ambulatory practice. The fourth year comprises a series of electives designed to help students with final preparations for residency and offers opportunities for off-campus training. The grading system is honors/pass/fail. The school also offers a six-year M.D.-J.D. program.

USMLE

Step 1: Required. Students must record a passing score for graduation, but not promotion.
Step 2: Clinical Skills (CS): Required. Students must only record a score.
Step 2: Clinical Knowledge (CK): Required. Students must only record a score.

Selection Factors

Applications for the M.D. program are accepted from Illinois residents who are U.S. citizens or possess a permanent resident visa. Completion of a minimum of 90 semester hours of undergraduate work in an accredited degree-granting college or university is required. Foreign students are advised to have completed at least 60 semester hours of coursework in the United States. The M.D.–J.D. program is open to non-Illinois residents. All applicants are expected to have a strong foundation in the natural sciences, social sciences, and humanities; they must demonstrate facility in writing and speaking the English language, as well as achieve competitive MCAT scores. Preference is given to those with sufficient recent academic activity to demonstrate the potential for successful completion of the rigorous educational program and to those who demonstrate the necessary noncognitive characteristics of a successful medical student and physician. Applicants are invited for interviews according to their strengths in academics, extracurricular activities, employment and volunteer experiences, and area of residence, with preference given to central and southern Illinois residents. The School of Medicine does not discriminate on the basis of race, religion, age, sex, handicap, or national or ethnic origin in administration of its education policies, admissions policies, scholarship and loan programs, or other school-administered programs.

Financial Aid

The School participates in all major federal student aid programs. Students receive aid on the basis of need as calculated on the FAFSA. Scholarship and grant aid are generally limited to students who demonstrate exceptional need.

Information about Diversity Programs

An effort is made to recruit qualified applicants from groups that have been underrepresented in the medical profession. The school has several active minority student organizations. For more information, contact the Office of Diversity at 217-545-7334. The School of Medicine also sponsors the Medical/Dental Education Preparatory Program (MEDPREP), a non-degree granting program in Carbondale for disadvantaged undergraduate or postbaccalaureate students, as well as underrepresented, rural, or low-income students (*www.siumed.edu/medprep/*).

Campus Information

Setting

SIU School of Medicine holds the first year of medical school in a small-town, collegiate environment on the main quad at SIU-Carbondale, an institution serving over 20,000 undergraduate, graduate, and professional students. The remaining three years take place at the SIU medical campus in the north central residential/commercial region of Springfield (pop. 115,000), the state capital. The facilities in Springfield are located in one of downstate Illinois' largest and fastest growing medical districts. The main medical instructional buildings are adjacent to Memorial Medical Center. A second affiliated hospital, St. John's, and additional clinics are situated within blocks of the main campus.

Enrollment

For 2009, total enrollment was: 292

Housing

Carbondale and Springfield: off-campus housing. Monthly rates for apartments in both locations: $450 to $600 per month.

Satellite Campuses/Facilities

Students receive training in affiliated clinical locations throughout central and southern Illinois.

Application Process and Requirements 2011–2012

Primary Application Service: AMCAS
Earliest filing date: June 2010
Latest filing date: November 15, 2010

Secondary Application Required?: Yes
Sent to: Selected applicants
Contact: Evan Wilson, (217)-545-6013, admissions@siumed.edu
Fee: Yes, $50   **Waiver available:** Yes
Earliest filing date: July 2010
Latest filing date: February 1, 2011

MCAT® required?: Yes
Latest MCAT® considered: September 2010
Oldest MCAT® considered: January 2008

Early Decision Program: School does not have EDP
Applicants notified: n/a
EDP available for: n/a

Regular Acceptance Notice
Earliest date: October 15, 2010
Latest date: Until class is full
Applicant's Response to Acceptance Offer – Maximum Time: Two weeks

Requests for Deferred Entrance Considered: Yes

Deposit to Hold Place in Class: Yes
Deposit (Resident): $100   **(Non-resident):** $100
Deposit due: With receipt of acceptance offer
Applied to tuition: Yes   **Refundable:** Yes
Refundable by: May 15, 2011

Estimated number of new entrants: 72
EDP: n/a, special program: 2

Start Month/Year: August 2011

Interview Format: M.D. two one-on-one interviews; M.D./J.D. three one-on-one. Regional interviews are not available. Video interviews are not available.

Other Programs

PREPARATORY PROGRAMS
Postbaccalaureate Program: Yes, www.siumed.edu/medprep/
Summer Program: No

COMBINED DEGREE PROGRAMS
Baccalaureate/M.D.: No
M.D./M.P.H.: No
M.D./M.B.A.: No
M.D./J.D.: Yes, www.siumed.edu/medhum/mdjdprog.htm
M.D./Ph.D.: No

Premedical Coursework

On-line courses accepted in fulfillment of prerequisites: Yes

Course	Req.	Rec.	Lab.	Sems.
Inorganic Chemistry	•	•		2
Behavioral Sciences				
Biochemistry	•			1
Biology	•	•		2
Biology/Zoology				
Calculus				
College English	•			2
College Mathematics	•			2
Computer Science				

Course	Req.	Rec.	Lab.	Sems.
Genetics		•		
Humanities		•		
Organic Chemistry	•	•		2
Physics	•	•		2
Psychology		•		
Social Sciences		•		
Advanced Level Biology		•		1
Other2				
Other3				

Selection Factors: 2009 Accepted Applicants

Proportion of Accepted Applicants with Relevant Experience (Data Self-Reported to AMCAS)		
Community Service/Volunteer		72%
Medically-Related Work		81%
Research		72%

Shaded bar represents school's accepted scores ranging from the 10th percentile to the 90th percentile   **School Median** ● **National Median** ○

Overall GPA	2.0	2.1	2.2	2.3	2.4	2.5	2.6	2.7	2.8	2.9	3.0	3.1	3.2	3.3	3.4	3.5	(3.6)	3.7	3.8	3.9	4.0
Science GPA	2.0	2.1	2.2	2.3	2.4	2.5	2.6	2.7	2.8	2.9	3.0	3.1	3.2	3.3	3.4	3.5	(3.6)	3.7	3.8	3.9	4.0

MCAT® Total Numeric Score 9 10 11 12 13 14 15 16 17 18 19 20 21 22 23 24 25 26 27 28 (29) 30 31 (32) 33 34 35 36 37 38 39 40 41 42 43

Writing Sample			J	K	L	M	N	(O)	P	(Q)	R	S	T
Verbal Reasoning	3	4	5	6	7	8	9	(10)	11	12	13	14	15
Biological Sciences	3	4	5	6	7	8	9	(10)	(11)	12	13	14	15
Physical Sciences	3	4	5	6	7	8	(9)	10	(11)	12	13	14	15

Acceptance & Matriculation Data for 2009–2010 First Year Class

	Resident	Non-resident	International	Total
Applications	1093	97	1	1191
Interviewed	303	1	0	304
Deferred	4	1	0	5
Matriculants				
Early Assurance Program	0	0	0	0
Early Decision Program	0	0	0	0
Baccalaureate/M.D.	0	0	0	0
M.D./Ph.D.	0	0	0	0
Matriculated	72	0	0	**72**

Applications accepted from International Applicants: No

Specialty Choice

2005, 2006, 2007 Graduates, Specialty Choice (As reported by program directors to GME Track™)	
Anesthesiology	4%
Emergency Medicine	12%
Family Practice	18%
Internal Medicine	10%
Obstetrics/Gynecology	7%
Orthopaedic Surgery	6%
Pediatrics	14%
Psychiatry	1%
Radiology Diagnostic	5%
Surgery General	6%

Matriculant Demographics: 2009–2010 First Year Class

Men: 39   **Women:** 33

Matriculants' Self-Reported Race/Ethnicity

Mexican American	2	Korean	0
Cuban	0	Vietnamese	0
Puerto Rican	1	Other Asian	0
Other Hispanic	1	Total Asian	7
Total Hispanic	4	Native American	0
Chinese	0	Black	9
Asian Indian	6	Native Hawaiian	0
Pakistani	1	White	51
Filipino	0	Unduplicated Number	
Japanese	0	of Matriculants	72

Science and Math Majors: 76%
Matriculants with:
  Baccalaureate degree: 99%
  Graduate degree(s): 14%

Financial Information

Source: 2008-2009 LCME I-B survey and 2009-2010 AAMC TSF questionnaire

	Residents	Non-residents
Total Cost of Attendance	$ 42,660	$ 90,636
Tuition and Fees	$ 26,694	$ 74,670
Other (includes living expenses)	$ 15,398	$ 15,398
Health Insurance (can be waived)	$ 568	$ 568

Average 2009 Graduate Indebtedness: $134,125
% of Enrolled Students Receiving Aid: 91%

Criminal Background Check

This medical school requires a criminal background check prior to matriculation.

University of Chicago Division of the Biological Sciences, The Pritzker School of Medicine

Chicago, Illinois

Office of Admissions, University of Chicago
Pritzker School of Medicine
924 E. 57th Street, BSLC 104W
Chicago, Illinois 60637-5416
T 773 702 1937   **F** 773 834 5412

Admissions http://pritzker.bsd.uchicago.edu
Main http://pritzker.bsd.uchicago.edu
Financial http://pritzker.bsd.uchicago.edu
E-mail pritzkeradmissions@bsd.uchicago.edu

Private Institution

Dr. Holly J. Humphrey,
Dean for Medical Education

Sylvia Robertson, Assistant Dean
for Admissions and Financial Aid

Dr. William McDade, Associate Dean
for Multicultural Affairs

Dr. Herbert T. Abelson, Sr. Assoc. Dean
for Admissions and Student Life

General Information

The Pritzker School of Medicine is unique among medical schools in that it is a part of the academic Division of the Biological Sciences. As an integral part of a world-class university, it offers medical students opportunities for interdisciplinary learning, clinical training, and research in a setting where recognized experts from all disciplines contribute to the development of physicians-in-training.

Mission Statement

At the University of Chicago, in an atmosphere of interdisciplinary scholarship and discovery, the Pritzker School of Medicine is dedicated to inspiring diverse students of exceptional promise to become leaders and innovators in science and medicine for the betterment of humanity.

Curricular Highlights

Community Service Requirement: Optional. Students have an impressive record of service.
Research/Thesis Requirement: Optional. Research is encouraged and supported.

The basic competencies which underlie the curriculum at Pritzker are grouped into four areas: the scientific basis of medicine; the scientific basis of diagnosis, prevention, and treatment of disease; interpersonal communication and teaching; and professional growth and development. Significant programs are devoted to helping students excel in these educational objectives. The library provides a comprehensive set of on-line medical and scientific materials with off-site access by students and faculty. This complements a Web-based curriculum that includes multimedia presentations and searchable text. A Clinical Performance Center uses standardized patients

and videotaped performance to educate students in taking a history, performing a physical examination, and clinical decision-making. The scientific foundation of medicine is achieved through lectures, labs, case-based problem-solving, and computer-based guided self-study and assessment. The clinical biennium consists of eight clinical clerkships and electives taught entirely by full-time clinical faculty and by selected residents who are trained in the humanistic teaching of medical students.

USMLE

Step 1: Required. Students must only record a score.
Step 2: Clinical Skills (CS): Required. Students must only record a score.
Step 2: Clinical Knowledge (CK): Required. Students must only record a score.

Selection Factors

A supplementary application is made available to everyone who submits an AMCAS application to the Pritzker School of Medicine. The Committee on Admissions reviews an application once the supplementary application is returned and the required letters of evaluation are received. About 600 applicants are invited to interview on the university campus from August through January. Offers of admission are extended on a rolling basis from October through April. Offers of admission are made solely on the basis of ability, achievement, motivation, and humanistic qualities. Outstanding personal characteristics and a strong career commitment are as important as excellence in academics.

Financial Aid

Scholarships and low-interest loans are made available to all students who have demonstrated need. There are both federally subsidized loans and low-interest loans from the university. Merit scholarships are available for a limited number of exceptionally well-qualified students. Individual counseling and debt management programs are available to all students. Financial aid packets are mailed to all accepted applicants after January 1. Financial aid resources for international applicants are extremely limited.

Information about Diversity Programs

Pritzker is particularly interested in providing a diverse educational experience for its students. Medical students from groups underrepresented in medicine who have attended Pritzker often assume strong leadership roles, both within their class and at the national level.

Campus Information

Setting

The University of Chicago is located on the south side of Chicago in the ethnically diverse community of Hyde Park, just minutes by train from downtown Chicago. The resources of this world-class city and its extraordinary lake-front are at the campus doorstep. The University of Chicago Medical Center campus, including its 21 buildings with 22 acres of space for research, teaching, and patient care, are within easy walking distance of Pritzker's libraries, classrooms, and labs.

Enrollment

For 2009, total enrollment was: 436

Special Features

The University of Chicago is made up predominantly of graduate and professional students participating in four major academic divisions and six professional schools, all sharing one campus. In this environment, graduates acquire superb skills in medical reasoning, problem-solving, team-building, and life-long learning, which help them assume leadership roles in residency training programs and as faculty in academic medicine. Pritzker students engage in some form of scholarly activity prior to completing their M.D. degree, and approximately 20 percent pursue combined degrees.

Housing

As a part of an extensive orientation program, students are guided in their housing search. Rents average $800/month.

Application Process and Requirements 2011–2012

Primary Application Service: AMCAS
Earliest filing date: June 1, 2010
Latest filing date: October 15, 2010

Secondary Application Required?: Yes
Sent to: All applicants
Contact: Sylvia Robertson, (773) 702-1937, pritzkeradmissions@bsd.uchicago.edu
Fee: Yes, $75   **Waiver available:** Yes
Earliest filing date: July 1, 2010
Latest filing date: December 1, 2010

MCAT® required?: Yes
Latest MCAT® considered: September 2010
Oldest MCAT® considered: 2008

Early Decision Program: School does have EDP
Applicants notified: October 1, 2010
EDP available for: Both Residents and Non-residents

Regular Acceptance Notice
Earliest date: October 15, 2010
Latest date: Until class is full
Applicant's Response to Acceptance
Offer – Maximum Time: On or before May 15, 2011

Requests for Deferred
Entrance Considered: Yes

Deposit to Hold Place in Class: No
Deposit (Resident): n/a   **(Non-resident):** n/a
Deposit due: n/a
Applied to tuition: n/a   **Refundable:** n/a
Refundable by: n/a

Estimated number of new entrants: 88
EDP: 2, special program: n/a

Start Month/Year: August 2011

Interview Format: Three individual interviews. On-campus interviews strongly recommended. Video interviews are available in extremely unusual situations.

Other Programs

PREPARATORY PROGRAMS
Postbaccalaureate Program: No
Summer Program: Yes, http://pritzker.bsd.uchicago.edu/about/diversity/pipeline/psomer.shtml

COMBINED DEGREE PROGRAMS
Baccalaureate/M.D.: No
M.D./M.P.H.: No
M.D./M.B.A.: Yes, http://pritzker.bsd.uchicago.edu/jointdegrees/
M.D./J.D.: Yes, http://pritzker.bsd.uchicago.edu/jointdegrees/
M.D./Ph.D.: Yes, http://pritzker.bsd.uchicago.edu/jointdegrees/

Premedical Coursework

On-line courses accepted in fulfillment of prerequisites:

Course	Req.	Rec.	Lab.	Sems.
Inorganic Chemistry	•		•	2
Behavioral Sciences				
Biochemistry		•	•	
Biology	•		•	2
Biology/Zoology				
Calculus		•		
College English				
College Mathematics				

Course	Req.	Rec.	Lab.	Sems.
Computer Science				
Genetics		•		
Humanities		•		
Organic Chemistry	•		•	2
Physics	•		•	2
Psychology				
Social Sciences		•		
Other				

Selection Factors: 2009 Accepted Applicants

Proportion of Accepted Applicants with Relevant Experience (Data Self-Reported to AMCAS®)		
Community Service/Volunteer		72%
Medically-Related Work		90%
Research		92%

Shaded bar represents school's accepted scores ranging from the 10th percentile to the 90th percentile □   School Median ● National Median ◐

Overall GPA 2.0 2.1 2.2 2.3 2.4 2.5 2.6 2.7 2.8 2.9 3.0 3.1 3.2 3.3 3.4 3.5 **3.6 3.7 3.8 (3.9) 4.0**

Science GPA 2.0 2.1 2.2 2.3 2.4 2.5 2.6 2.7 2.8 2.9 3.0 3.1 3.2 3.3 3.4 3.5 **3.6 3.7 3.8 (3.9) 4.0**

MCAT® Total Numeric Score 9 10 11 12 13 14 15 16 17 18 19 20 21 22 23 24 25 26 27 28 29 30 31 (32) 33 34 35 36 (37) 38 39 40 41 42 43

Writing Sample			J	K	L	M	N	O	P	(Q)	R	S	T
Verbal Reasoning	3	4	5	6	7	8	9	(10)	(11)	12	13	14	15
Biological Sciences	3	4	5	6	7	8	9	10	(11)	(12)	13	14	15
Physical Sciences	3	4	5	6	7	8	9	10	(11)	12	(13)	14	15

Acceptance & Matriculation Data for 2009–2010 First Year Class

	Resident	Non-resident	International	Total
Applications	834	5176	352	6362
Interviewed	91	416	10	517
Deferred	1	4	0	5
Matriculants				
Early Assurance Program	0	0	0	0
Early Decision Program	0	0	0	0
Baccalaureate/M.D.	0	0	0	0
M.D./Ph.D.	2	7	0	9
Matriculated	29	58	1	**88**

Applications accepted from International Applicants: Yes

Specialty Choice

2005, 2006, 2007 Graduates, Specialty Choice (As reported by program directors to GME Track™)	
Anesthesiology	5%
Emergency Medicine	5%
Family Practice	3%
Internal Medicine	22%
Obstetrics/Gynecology	3%
Orthopaedic Surgery	4%
Pediatrics	12%
Psychiatry	5%
Radiology	4%
Surgery	8%

Matriculant Demographics: 2009–2010 First Year Class

Men: 48   **Women:** 40

Matriculants' Self-Reported Race/Ethnicity

Mexican American	3	Korean	2
Cuban	0	Vietnamese	0
Puerto Rican	1	Other Asian	2
Other Hispanic	0	Total Asian	16
Total Hispanic	4	Native American	0
Chinese	6	Black	11
Asian Indian	7	Native Hawaiian	0
Pakistani	0	White	56
Filipino	0	Unduplicated Number	
Japanese	0	of Matriculants	88

Science and Math Majors: 63%
Matriculants with:
    Baccalaureate degree: 100%
    Graduate degree(s): 9%

Financial Information

Source: 2008-2009 LCME I-B survey and 2009-2010 AAMC TSF questionnaire

	Residents	Non-residents
Total Cost of Attendance	$ 66,440	$ 66,440
Tuition and Fees	$ 39,972	$ 39,972
Other (includes living expenses)	$ 24,091	$ 24,091
Health Insurance (can be waived)	$ 2,377	$ 2,377

Average 2009 Graduate Indebtedness: $175,809
% of Enrolled Students Receiving Aid: 93%

Criminal Background Check

This medical school requires a criminal background check prior to matriculation.

University of Illinois at Chicago College of Medicine

Chicago, Peoria, Rockford, and Urbana, Illinois

Medical College Admissions
University of Illinois College of Medicine
808 South Wood St., Room 165 CME M/C 783
Chicago, Illinois 60612-7302
T 312 996 5635   **F** 312 996 6693

Admissions www.medicine.uic.edu/admissions
Main www.medicine.uic.edu
Financial www.medicine.uic.edu/finaid
E-mail medadmit@uic.edu

Public Institution

Dr. Joseph A. Flaherty, Dean

Dr. Jorge A. Girotti, Associate Dean and Director

Dr. Javette Orgain, Assistant Dean Urban Health Program

Peter Aiello, Assistant Director of Financial Aid

Linda Singleton, Associate Director of Admissions

General Information

Opened in 1882 as a private institution and joined the University of Illinois in 1913. Since 1982, the programs leading to the M.D. degree are conducted at four geographic sites. The Chicago site is located in the Medical Center of the university. The Urbana-Champaign site offers a four-year curriculum integrated with the programs of a comprehensive campus. The Peoria site includes facilities in each of the hospitals in that community and a modern downtown campus. The Rockford site has a centrally located campus and conducts programs in each of the Rockford hospitals and in several nearby smaller communities.

Mission Statement

To enhance the health of the citizens of Illinois through the education of physicians and biomedical scientists, the advancement of our understanding and knowledge of health and disease, and the provision of health care in a setting of education and research. In pursuit of this mission, the college is committed to the goal of achieving excellence in teaching, research, and service in the science, art, and practice of medicine. This goal is best attained by applying valid educational principles, demonstrating high-quality patient care, and establishing a spirit of inquiry leading to scholarly achievement in basic and clinical research.

Curricular Highlights

Community Service Requirement: Highly Desirable.
Research/Thesis Requirement: Desirable.

Offers a generalist curriculum whose goal is to graduate physicians who are well grounded in basic and clinical sciences, oriented and competent as beginning general physicians, capable of entering graduate training in either generalist specialties or subspecialties, and able to function in an ever changing health care environment. We offer several special programs that allow students to combine medicine with doctoral degrees, business, clinical and translational science and public health, and independent study options to carry out in-depth studies of topics of their choosing.

USMLE

Step 1: Required. Students must record a passing score for promotion.
Step 2: Clinical Skills (CS): Required. Students must record a passing total score to graduate.
Step 2: Clinical Knowledge (CK): Required. Students must record a passing total score to graduate.

Selection Factors

Selected applicants have the best combination of academic and extracurricular achievement, maturity, integrity, and motivation. Selection of students is based on an individualized evaluation of all available data and a personal interview. We consider the quality of work in all subject areas, breadth of education, and experiences that demonstrate initiative and creativity. The college gives preference to Illinois residents and does not discriminate on the basis of race, creed, sex, religion, national origin, age, disability, or status as a disabled veteran.

Financial Aid

Encouraged to apply early for loans and scholarships. Financial aid information is available by calling (312) 413-0127.

Information about Diversity Programs

The College has programs to encourage applicants from medically underserved areas of Illinois, a program for candidates interested in practicing in an urban area, and has staff to provide guidance to students from groups underrepresented in medicine.

Campus Information

Setting

UIC offers high-quality education to medical and graduate students at four sites across Illinois. Chicago is the largest of the college's four programs, and is located in the heart of the Illinois Medical District, about two miles west of downtown Chicago. The Urbana/Champaign campus is a complete four-year program leading to the M.D.. The first-year basic science program at Urbana also serves students who will complete their last three years of medical school at Peoria or Rockford. Peoria has a greater metropolitan population of over 356,000, Peoria offers the best of both urban and country living. Rockford is the third largest city in Illinois, and offers the appeal of a small town with the advantages of a large city.

Enrollment

For 2009, total enrollment was: 1,425

Special Features

We offer first-rate research facilities and resources. University of Illinois is one of only 88 institutions of higher education nationally to receive the prestigious Research I designation from the Carnegie Foundation for the Advancement of Teaching. Attracting more than $250 million in research funding each year, the College of Medicine faculty and professional staff provide a wealth of expertise. The Molecular Biology Research Building (MBRB), which opened in 1995, is a 230,000 square feet state-of-the-art research facility. The building houses 56 Principal Investigators and 108 laboratories. Researchers from both basic and clinical science departments conduct individual and collaborative research at the MBRB. The campus houses a 9.4 Tesla magnet, which is the world's strongest magnetic field for human imaging. Finally, a new 300,000 square feet Research Building opened in summer 2005. The building is one of the most modern, architecturally innovative facilities in the country, with laboratory space for over 100 investigators.

Housing

On-campus housing is available at Chicago and Urbana. All campuses have private housing available nearby.

Application Process and Requirements 2011–2012

Primary Application Service: AMCAS
Earliest filing date: June 1, 2010
Latest filing date: November 15, 2010

Secondary Application Required?: Yes
Sent to: University of Illinois College of Medicine – Admissions
Contact: Admissions Office, (312) 996-5635, nedadmit@uic.edu
Fee: Yes, $70   **Waiver available:** Yes
Earliest filing date: June 15, 2010
Latest filing date: January 15, 2011

MCAT® required?: Yes
Latest MCAT® considered: September 2010
Oldest MCAT® considered: 2008

Early Decision Program: School does have EDP
Applicants notified: October 1, 2010
EDP available for: Both Residents and Non-resident

Regular Acceptance Notice
Earliest date: October 14, 2010
Latest date: Until class is full
**Applicant's Response to Acceptance
Offer – Maximum Time:** Two weeks

**Requests for Deferred
Entrance Considered:** Yes

Deposit to Hold Place in Class: Yes
Deposit (Resident): $100   **(Non-resident):** $100
Deposit due: With response to acceptance offer
Applied to tuition: Yes   **Refundable:** Yes
Refundable by: May 15, 2011

Estimated number of new entrants: 300
EDP: 5, special program: 25

Start Month/Year: August 2011

Interview Format: Individual or panel. Regional interviews are offered at the regional locations. Video interviews are not available.

Other Programs

PREPARATORY PROGRAMS
Postbaccalaureate Program: www.uic.edu/depts/mcam/uhp/, Dr. Javette Orgain, (312)996-6491, uhpcom@uic.edu
Summer Program: www.uic.edu/depts/mcam/uhp/, Dr. Javette Orgain, (312)996-6491, uhpcom@uic.edu

COMBINED DEGREE PROGRAMS
Baccalaureate/M.D.: www.iuic.edu/depts/oaa/spec_prog/gppa
Josephine Volpe, (312) 355-2477, gppa@uic.edu
M.D./M.P.H.: http://chicago.medicine.uic.edu/departments_programs
Dr. Jorge Girotti, (312) 996-4493, jorgeg@uic.edu
M.D./M.B.A.: http://chicago.medicine.uic.edu/departments_programs
Dr. Jorge Girotti, (312) 996-4493, jorgeg@uic.edu
M.D./J.D.: www.med.uiuc.edu/msp/mdjd.asp
Otoniel Jimenez, (217) 333-8146, mspo@uiuc.edu
M.D./Ph.D.: www.chicago.medicine.uic.edu/mstp
Roberta Bernstein, (312) 996-7473, roberta@uic.edu
Verbal Reasoning Program: www.uic.edu/depts/mcam/uhp/
Dr. Javette Orgain, (312) 996-6491, uhpcom@uic.edu
Additional Program: www.crtp.uic.edu
Dr. Jorge Girotti, (312) 996-4493, jorgeg@uic.edu

Premedical Coursework

On-line courses accepted in fulfillment of prerequisites:

Course	Req.	Rec.	Lab.	Sems.
Inorganic Chemistry	•		•	2
Behavioral Sciences				
Biochemistry				
Biology	•		•	2
Biology/Zoology				
Calculus				
College English				
College Mathematics				

Course	Req.	Rec.	Lab.	Sems.
Computer Science				
Genetics		•		
Humanities				
Organic Chemistry	•		•	2
Physics	•		•	2
Psychology	•			2
Social Sciences				
Anthropology or Sociology	•			1
Advanced Level Biology	•			1

Selection Factors: 2009 Accepted Applicants

Proportion of Accepted Applicants with Relevant Experience (Data Self-Reported to AMCAS®)		
Community Service/Volunteer		72%
Medically-Related Work		87%
Research		85%

Shaded bar represents school's accepted scores ranging from the 10th percentile to the 90th percentile   School Median ● National Median ◐

Overall GPA 2.0 2.1 2.2 2.3 2.4 2.5 2.6 2.7 2.8 2.9 3.0 3.1 3.2 3.3 3.4 3.5 3.6 (3.7) 3.8 3.9 4.0
Science GPA 2.0 2.1 2.2 2.3 2.4 2.5 2.6 2.7 2.8 2.9 3.0 3.1 3.2 3.3 3.4 3.5 (3.6) 3.7 3.8 3.9 4.0

MCAT® Total Numeric Score 9 10 11 12 13 14 15 16 17 18 19 20 21 22 23 24 25 26 27 28 29 30 (31)(32)33 34 35 36 37 38 39 40 41 42 43

Writing Sample			J	K	L	M	N	O	P	(Q)	R	S	T
Verbal Reasoning	3	4	5	6	7	8	9	(10)	11	12	13	14	15
Biological Sciences	3	4	5	6	7	8	9	10	(11)	12	13	14	15
Physical Sciences	3	4	5	6	7	8	9	(10)	(11)	12	13	14	15

Acceptance & Matriculation Data for 2009–2010 First Year Class

	Resident	Non-resident	International	Total
Applications	1649	5004	87	6740
Interviewed	469	434	0	903
Deferred	2	1	0	3
Matriculants				
Early Assurance Program	0	0	0	0
Early Decision Program	1	0	0	1
Baccalaureate/M.D.	0	0	0	0
M.D./Ph.D.	11	21	0	32
Matriculated	230	83	0	**313**

Applications accepted from International Applicants: No

Matriculant Demographics: 2009–2010 First Year Class

Men: 167   **Women:** 146

Matriculants' Self-Reported Race/Ethnicity

Mexican American	19	**Korean**	19
Cuban	3	**Vietnamese**	2
Puerto Rican	3	**Other Asian**	7
Other Hispanic	19	**Total Asian**	89
Total Hispanic	41	**Native American**	4
Chinese	19	**Black**	38
Asian Indian	39	**Native Hawaiian**	3
Pakistani	3	**White**	169
Filipino	3	**Unduplicated Number**	
Japanese	2	**of Matriculants**	313

Science and Math Majors: 65%
Matriculants with:
  Baccalaureate degree: 100%
  Graduate degree(s): 14%

Specialty Choice

2005, 2006, 2007 Graduates, Specialty Choice (As reported by program directors to GME Track™)	
Anesthesiology	9%
Emergency Medicine	8%
Family Practice	9%
Internal Medicine	18%
Obstetrics/Gynecology	4%
Orthopaedic Surgery	3%
Pediatrics	9%
Psychiatry	4%
Radiology	5%
Surgery	7%

Financial Information

Source: 2008-2009 LCME I-B survey and 2009-2010 AAMC TSF questionnaire

	Residents	Non-residents
Total Cost of Attendance	$ 52,449	$ 85,825
Tuition and Fees	$ 32,348	$ 65,724
Other (includes living expenses)	$ 19,299	$ 19,299
Health Insurance (can be waived)	$ 802	$ 802

Average 2009 Graduate Indebtedness: $161,746
% of Enrolled Students Receiving Aid: 92%

Criminal Background Check

This medical school requires a criminal background check prior to matriculation.

Indiana University School of Medicine

Indianapolis, Indiana

Medical School Admissions Office,
Indiana University School of Medicine
1120 South Drive, Fesler Hall 213
Indianapolis, Indiana 46202-5113
T 317 274 3772

Admissions www.medicine.iu.edu/body.cfm?id=166
Main www.medicine.iu.edu
Financial http://msaa.iusm.iu.edu/FinancialAid/
finaidtxt.html
E-mail inmedadm@iupui.edu

Public Institution

Dr. D. Craig Brater, Dean

Karen A. Smartt, Director of Admissions

Dr. George Rausch, Associate Dean for Diversity Affairs

Jose Espada, Director, Student Financial Services

Renee Akins, Associate Director of Admissions

Dr. James J. Brokaw, Associate Dean of Admissions, Co-Chair, Admissions Committee

General Information

Indiana University School of Medicine, founded in 1903, is the sole institution responsible for providing medical education in the state of Indiana and operates the Indiana Statewide Medical Education System. In addition to its responsibilities in teaching, patient care, and service, Indiana University School of Medicine is a major academic research center. In conducting its medical educational programs, Indiana University School of Medicine utilizes six teaching hospitals on or near the medical center campus, as well as other affiliated hospitals in Indianapolis and throughout the state.

Mission Statement

The goal of the Indiana University School of Medicine is the education of physicians, scientists, and other health professionals in an intellectually rich environment with research as its scientific base. In education, we are committed to imparting a fundamental understanding of both clinical practice and the basic scientific knowledge upon which it rests, to provide a firm foundation for lifelong learning. In research, we are committed to the advancement of knowledge. In patient care, we are committed to the highest standards of medical practice in an atmosphere of respect and empathy for our patients. Education, research, and delivery of health care are inseparable components of our mission. Excellence can only be achieved when all components are of highest quality, well integrated, and mutually supportive.

Curricular Highlights

Community Service Requirement: Optional, but expected.

Research/Thesis Requirement: Optional.

The School of Medicine's faculty have adopted a competency-based curriculum which equips students with excellent clinical skills balanced by the development of interpersonal and professional skills. The basic medical sciences are presented in the first two years. In addition, an intensive multidisciplinary course, Introduction to Clinical Medicine, spans both years. The faculty utilizes small problem-based learning groups throughout the first two years. A 12-month clinical clerkship program at the Indianapolis medical center and thoughout the state occupies the third year. In the fourth year, students complete three clerkships and select seven one-month electives. Arrangements can be made for elective experiences around the country and abroad. Students pursuing the M.D. degree may simultaneously pursue graduate degrees in a variety of disciplines, or elect to participate in the five-year Physician Scholar Program, which incorporates a year of research into the M.D. degree program.

USMLE

Step 1: Required. Students must record a passing score for graduation, but not promotion.
Step 2: Clinical Skills (CS): Required. Students must record a passing total score to graduate.
Step 2: Clinical Knowledge (CK): Required. Students must record a passing total score to graduate.

Selection Factors

Students are offered places in the class on the basis of scholarship, character, personality, references, residence, interview, and performance on the MCAT. In addition, the medical school faculty has specified non-academic criteria (technical standards), which all applicants must meet in order to participate effectively in the medical education program and the practice of medicine. The School of Medicine is state-assisted, and the Admissions Committee shows preference to Indiana residents. Nevertheless, a number of nonresidents are offered acceptances each year (179 for 2008). The applications of nonresidents who have significant ties to the state of Indiana may be given greater consideration. The School of Medicine does not discriminate on the basis of age, color, disability, ethnicity, gen-

der, marital status, national origin, race, religion, sexual orientation, or veteran status.

Financial Aid

Both merit and need-based scholarships are available, as are need-based loans. There are scholarships for Indiana residents who commit to practicing primary care medicine in a medically underserved location in Indiana.

Information about Diversity Programs

Information about diversity programs may be found at *www.postdoc.medicine.iu.edu/ body.cfm?id=7697&oTopID=7696*.

Campus Information

Setting

The Indiana University Medical Center campus covers some 85 acres within one mile of the center of Indianapolis and is part of the 30,000 student Indiana University-Purdue University at Indianapolis. The medical center is also host to outstanding schools of dentistry and nursing.

Enrollment

For 2009, total enrollment was: 1,204

Special Features

A Physician Scholars Program permits students to take up to a year off to pursue research or other medically-related interests. The Kenya Program allows students to work with IU faculty at Moi University to provide medical care for Kenyans. Similar programs in Latin America are under development.

Housing

On-campus housing is limited, but there is an abundance of available housing within 5-20 minutes of campus.

Satellite Campuses/Facilities

First- and second-year students may be enrolled at host higher education campuses in Bloomington, Evansville, Fort Wayne, Gary, Lafayette, Muncie, South Bend, and Terre Haute, in addition to Indianapolis. The Terre Haute campus offers a four-year Rural Medicine program which was implemented in 2008.

Application Process and Requirements 2011–2012

Primary Application Service: AMCAS
Earliest filing date: June 1, 2010
Latest filing date: December 15, 2010

Secondary Application Required?: No
Contact: Admissions Office, (317) 274-3772, inmedadm@iupui.edu
URL: n/a
Fee: Yes, $50   **Waiver available:** No
Earliest filing date: n/a
Latest filing date: n/a

MCAT® required?: Yes
Latest MCAT® considered: September 2010
Oldest MCAT® considered: August 2007

Early Decision Program: School does have EDP
Applicants notified: October 1, 2010
EDP available for: Both Residents and Non-residents

Regular Acceptance Notice
Earliest date: October 15, 2010
Latest date: Until class is full
Applicant's Response to Acceptance Offer – Maximum Time: Three weeks

Requests for Deferred Entrance Considered: Yes

Deposit to Hold Place in Class: No
Deposit (Resident): n/a   **(Non-resident):** n/a
Deposit due: n/a
Applied to tuition: n/a   **Refundable:** n/a
Refundable by: n/a

Estimated number of new entrants: 280
EDP: 30, special program: n/a

Start Month/Year: August 2011

Interview Format: Individual interviews. Regional interviews are not available. Video interviews are not available.

Other Programs

PREPARATORY PROGRAMS
Postbaccalaureate Program: Yes, www.msms.iu.edu
Summer Program: No
Additional Program: Master of Science in Medical Science, www.msms.iu.edu

COMBINED DEGREE PROGRAMS
Baccalaureate/M.D.: No
M.D./M.P.H.: Yes, http://grad.medicine.iu.edu/body.cfm?id=1853
M.D./M.B.A.: Yes, http://grad.medicine.iu.edu/body.cfm?id=1852
M.D./J.D.: No
M.D./Ph.D.: Yes, http://grad.medicine.iu.edu/body.cfm?id=1851
Additional Program: Yes, http://grad.medicine.iu.edu/body.cfm?id=1854

Premedical Coursework

On-line courses accepted in fulfillment of prerequisites: On a case-by-case basis

Course	Req.	Rec.	Lab.	Sems.
Inorganic Chemistry				
Behavioral Sciences				
Biochemistry				
Biology	•		•	2
Biology/Zoology				
Calculus				
College English				
College Mathematics				

Course	Req.	Rec.	Lab.	Sems.
Computer Science				
Genetics				
Humanities				
Organic Chemistry	•		•	2
Physics	•		•	2
Psychology				
Social Sciences				
General Chemistry	•			2

Selection Factors: 2009 Accepted Applicants

Proportion of Accepted Applicants with Relevant Experience (Data Self-Reported to AMCAS®)		
Community Service/Volunteer		78%
Medically-Related Work		80%
Research		76%

Shaded bar represents school's accepted scores ranging from the 10th percentile to the 90th percentile   School Median ○   National Median ◔

Overall GPA	2.0	2.1	2.2	2.3	2.4	2.5	2.6	2.7	2.8	2.9	3.0	3.1	3.2	3.3	3.4	3.5	3.6	3.7	(3.8)	3.9	4.0
Science GPA	2.0	2.1	2.2	2.3	2.4	2.5	2.6	2.7	2.8	2.9	3.0	3.1	3.2	3.3	3.4	3.5	3.6	(3.7)	3.8	3.9	4.0

MCAT® Total Numeric Score 9 10 11 12 13 14 15 16 17 18 19 20 21 22 23 24 25 26 27 28 29 30 31 (32) 33 34 35 36 37 38 39 40 41 42 43

Writing Sample				J		K		L	M	N	O	(P)	Q	R	S	T
Verbal Reasoning	3		4		5		6	7	8	9	(10)	11	12	13	14	15
Biological Sciences	3		4		5		6	7	8	9	10	(11)	12	13	14	15
Physical Sciences	3		4		5		6	7	8	9	10	(11)	12	13	14	15

Acceptance & Matriculation Data for 2009–2010 First Year Class

	Resident	Non-resident	International	Total
Applications	695	2653	250	3598
Interviewed	580	341	17	938
Deferred	4	0	1	5
Matriculants				
Early Assurance Program	0	0	0	0
Early Decision Program	26	0	0	26
Baccalaureate/M.D.	0	0	0	0
M.D./Ph.D.	1	4	0	5
Matriculated	266	49	7	**322**

Applications accepted from International Applicants: Yes

Matriculant Demographics: 2009–2010 First Year Class

Men: 181   **Women:** 141

Matriculants' Self-Reported Race/Ethnicity

Mexican American	7	Korean	6
Cuban	1	Vietnamese	2
Puerto Rican	0	Other Asian	8
Other Hispanic	5	Total Asian	42
Total Hispanic	13	Native American	2
Chinese	8	Black	12
Asian Indian	14	Native Hawaiian	1
Pakistani	2	White	259
Filipino	0	Unduplicated Number	
Japanese	3	of Matriculants	322

Science and Math Majors: 70%
Matriculants with:
  Baccalaureate degree: 100%
  Graduate degree(s): 15%

Specialty Choice

2005, 2006, 2007 Graduates, Specialty Choice (As reported by program directors to GME Track™)	
Anesthesiology	11%
Emergency Medicine	6%
Family Practice	11%
Internal Medicine	13%
Obstetrics/Gynecology	4%
Orthopaedic Surgery	4%
Pediatrics	11%
Psychiatry	3%
Radiology	6%
Surgery	7%

Financial Information

Source: 2008-2009 LCME I-B survey and 2009-2010 AAMC TSF questionnaire

	Residents	Non-residents
Total Cost of Attendance	$ 55,509	$ 69,945
Tuition and Fees	$ 28,639	$ 43,075
Other (includes living expenses)	$ 24,156	$ 24,156
Health Insurance (can be waived)	$ 2,714	$ 2,714

Average 2009 Graduate Indebtedness: $163,262
% of Enrolled Students Receiving Aid: 82%

Criminal Background Check

This medical school requires a criminal background check prior to matriculation.

University of Iowa Roy J. and Lucille A. Carver College of Medicine

Iowa City, Iowa

Medical Student Admissions, University of Iowa
Roy J. & Lucille A. Carver College of Medicine
1213 Medical Education and Research Facility
Iowa City, Iowa 52242
T 319 335 8052   **F** 319 335 8049

Admissions www.medicine.uiowa.edu/osac/admissions
Main www.medicine.uiowa.edu
Financial www.medicine.uiowa.edu/osac/
financial/index.html
E-mail medical-admissions@uiowa.edu

Public Institution

Dr. Paul Rothman, Dean

Kathi Huebner, Director of Admissions

Barbara E. Barlow, Recruitment Coordinator

Linda G. Bissell, Director of Financial Services

*Judith D. Lehman, Admissions
Process Coordinator*

General Information

The college is part of a major health center serving the state and region. The health sciences campus includes the University of Iowa Hospitals and Clinics; Veterans Affairs Hospital; Hardin Health Sciences Library; Medical Education and Research Facility and basic sciences, dental, nursing, and pharmacy buildings.

Mission Statement

The Carver College of Medicine has three inextricably linked missions: education, research, and service. The college aspires to be responsive to the needs of society, and in particular the citizens of Iowa, through the excellence of its educational programs in the health professions and biomedical sciences, by the outstanding quality of its research, and through the provision of innovative and comprehensive health care and other services.

Curricular Highlights
Community Service Requirement: Optional.
Research/Thesis Requirement: Optional.

Case-based and self-directed learning, clinical correlation, computer-based learning, small-group activities, and vertical integration of material are emphasized in the curriculum. Year 1: investigation of the normal structure and function of the human body. Year 2: investigation of abnormal structure and function. Patient contact, introduction to medical history-taking and physical diagnosis, and coverage of emerging topic areas are presented in Foundations of Clinical Practice, a course that runs the first two years of the curriculum. In the fourth semester, this course provides students with a foundation in clinical medicine that will prepare them to perform in the clini-

cal arena. The two clinical years of the curriculum afford a broad base of training to provide the student with the essential skills and knowledge required to enter residency training. A generalist core is a feature of the clinical years. Ample time for electives is provided.

USMLE
Step 1: Required. Students must record a passing score for promotion.
Step 2: Clinical Skills (CS): Required. Students must record a passing score in each section to graduate.
Step 2: Clinical Knowledge (CK): Required. Students must record a passing score in each section to graduate.

Selection Factors
The Admissions Committee selects applicants best qualified for the study and practice of medicine. To be eligible for admission, the applicant must attain at least a 2.5 GPA (based on a 4.0 scale) for all college work undertaken. Factors considered: 1. Overall undergraduate academic record. 2. Science GPA. 3. MCAT Scores. 4. Residence: Preference given to Iowa residents with high scholastic standing. Consideration also given to outstanding non-residents. 5. Personal characteristics: Evaluated through letters of recommendation, information on the AMCAS application, interview and information on the supplemental form. 6. On-site personal interview. Applications for transfer are not considered.

Financial Aid
Applicants are selected without consideration of their ability to meet the cost of medical school. Students receive financial aid on the basis of need as calculated using the FAFSA. Scholarship and grant assistance are available. Students are responsible for their own financial support, but the college provides information on locating funding sources. Loan and grant funds from private, state, collegiate, and federal sources are available.

Information about Diversity Programs
The college is committed to the recruitment, selection, and retention of a diverse student body. Financial and academic assistance is provided to disadvantaged students and those

from groups underrepresented in American medicine. Financial aid packages are designed on the basis of need, and grant and scholarship assistance are available. The application fee and admission deposit may be waived for financially disadvantaged students upon request.

Campus Information
Setting
The college is on the 1,900-acre campus of a major research institution, the University of Iowa, and includes UI Hospitals and Clinics, one of the largest university-owned teaching hospitals. Iowa City is a community of 60,000 with local public transportation to the college. Cultural activities, Big 10 sports, shopping, and nearby parks provide outlets for recreation and services.

Enrollment
For 2009, total enrollment was: 576

Special Features
Opportunities in international and domestic cross-cultural sites; courses in global health, U.S. health policy issues and community health outreach; international exchange programs; summer research fellowships; research, service and teaching distinction tracks enhance the medical school experience. A writing program provides advice on CV's and scholarship applications and coordinates activities in literature, music, visual and performing arts as well as a yearly writing conference.

Housing
On-campus housing is generally not available. The university offers a clearinghouse to help students find housing. Rents average range from $350-700/month. There are two coed medical fraternities with rents ranging from $295-475/month.

Satellite Campuses/Facilities
The major satellite campus is the Des Moines Medical Education Consortium, a cooperative venture of several Des Moines hospitals, where some students complete required clerkships. Some ambulatory care clerkships are completed with adjunct faculty across the state.

Application Process and Requirements 2011–2012

Primary Application Service: AMCAS
Earliest filing date: June 1, 2010
Latest filing date: November 1, 2010

Secondary Application Required?: Yes
Sent to: Screened applicants
URL: www.medicine.uiowa.edu/osac/admissions
Fee: Yes, $60   **Waiver available:** Yes
Earliest filing date: July 1, 2010
Latest filing date: December 15, 2010

MCAT® required?: Yes
Latest MCAT® considered: September 2010
Oldest MCAT® considered: April 2005

Early Decision Program: School does not have EDP
Applicants notified: n/a
EDP available for: n/a

Regular Acceptance Notice
Earliest date: October 15, 2010
Latest date: Until class is full
Applicant's Response to Acceptance
Offer – Maximum Time: Two weeks from date of letter

Requests for Deferred
Entrance Considered: Yes

Deposit to Hold Place in Class: Yes
Deposit (Resident): $50   **(Non-resident):** $50
Deposit due: March 1, 2011, or within 3 weeks after acceptance offer if after March 1, 2011
Applied to tuition: Yes   **Refundable:** Yes
Refundable by: June 15, 2011

Estimated number of new entrants: 148
EDP: 0, special program: n/a

Start Month/Year: August 15, 2011
(first day of orientation)

Interview Format: Candidates interviewed by two faculty members in one room. Regional interviews are not available. Video interviews are not available.

Other Programs

PREPARATORY PROGRAMS
Postbaccalaureate Program: No
Summer Program: No
Prematriculation Summer Program (for admitted candidates): Yes, www.medicine.uiowa.edu/osac/medical_education/index.html

COMBINED DEGREE PROGRAMS
Baccalaureate/M.D.: No
M.D./M.P.H.: Yes, www.public-health.uiowa.edu/mph/about/combined_degrees/md_mph.html
M.D./M.B.A.: Yes, http://tippie.uiowa.edu/fulltimemba/academics/joint-degrees.cfm
M.D./J.D.: Yes, www.medicine.uiowa.edu/Osac/registrar/combined_degrees.html
M.D./Ph.D.: Yes, www.healthcare.uiowa.edu/mstp/

Premedical Coursework

On-line courses accepted in fulfillment of prerequisites: On a case-by-case basis

Course	Req.	Rec.	Lab.	Sems.
Inorganic Chemistry	•		•	2
Behavioral Sciences				
Biochemistry		•		
Biology	•		•	2
Biology/Zoology				
Calculus				
College English	•			2
College Mathematics	•			1
Computer Science				

Course	Req.	Rec.	Lab.	Sems.
Genetics		•		
Humanities				
Organic Chemistry	•		•	2
Physics	•		•	2
Psychology				
Social Sciences				
Advanced Biology	•			1
Social, Behavioral Sciences/Humanities	•			4

Selection Factors: 2009 Accepted Applicants

Proportion of Accepted Applicants with Relevant Experience (Data Self-Reported to AMCAS)	
Community Service/Volunteer	79%
Medically-Related Work	88%
Research	88%

Shaded bar represents school's accepted scores ranging from the 10th percentile to the 90th percentile   School Median ● National Median ○

Overall GPA	2.0	2.1	2.2	2.3	2.4	2.5	2.6	2.7	2.8	2.9	3.0	3.1	3.2	3.3	3.4	3.5	3.6	3.7	(3.8)	3.9 4.0
Science GPA	2.0	2.1	2.2	2.3	2.4	2.5	2.6	2.7	2.8	2.9	3.0	3.1	3.2	3.3	3.4	3.5	3.6	3.7	(3.8)	3.9 4.0

MCAT® Total Numeric Score 9 10 11 12 13 14 15 16 17 18 19 20 21 22 23 24 25 26 27 28 29 30 31 (32) 33 34 35 36 37 38 39 40 41 42 43

Writing Sample				J	K	L	M	N	O	(P)	Q	R	S	T
Verbal Reasoning	3	4	5	6	7	8	9	(10)	11	12	13	14	15	
Biological Sciences	3	4	5	6	7	8	9	10	(11)	12	13	14	15	
Physical Sciences	3	4	5	6	7	8	9	10	(11)	12	13	14	15	

Acceptance & Matriculation Data for 2009–2010 First Year Class

	Resident	Non-resident	International	Total
Applications	321	2439	3	2763
Interviewed	265	408	0	673
Deferred	6	0	0	6
Matriculants				
Early Assurance Program	0	0	0	0
Early Decision Program	6	0	0	6
Baccalaureate/M.D.	0	0	0	0
M.D./Ph.D.	1	8	0	9
Matriculated	97	51	0	**148**

Applications accepted from International Applicants: No

Matriculant Demographics: 2009–2010 First Year Class

Men: 75   **Women:** 73

Matriculants' Self-Reported Race/Ethnicity

Mexican American	4	Korean	3
Cuban	0	Vietnamese	3
Puerto Rican	0	Other Asian	1
Other Hispanic	2	Total Asian	15
Total Hispanic	6	Native American	2
Chinese	3	Black	8
Asian Indian	4	Native Hawaiian	0
Pakistani	0	White	119
Filipino	0	Unduplicated Number	
Japanese	1	of Matriculants	148

Science and Math Majors: 64%
Matriculants with:
Baccalaureate degree: 100%
Graduate degree(s): 9%

Specialty Choice

2005, 2006, 2007 Graduates, Specialty Choice (As reported by program directors to GME Track™)	
Anesthesiology	9%
Emergency Medicine	9%
Family Practice	11%
Internal Medicine	15%
Obstetrics/Gynecology	5%
Orthopaedic Surgery	4%
Pediatrics	11%
Psychiatry	2%
Radiology	7%
Surgery	5%

Financial Information

Source: 2008-2009 LCME I-B survey and 2009-2010 AAMC TSF questionnaire

	Residents	Non-residents
Total Cost of Attendance	$ 45,809	$ 61,623
Tuition and Fees	$ 28,248	$ 44,062
Other (includes living expenses)	$ 16,391	$ 16,391
Health Insurance (can be waived)	$ 1,170	$ 1,170

Average 2009 Graduate Indebtedness: $129,365
% of Enrolled Students Receiving Aid: 93%

Criminal Background Check

This medical school requires a criminal background check prior to matriculation.

University of Kansas School of Medicine
Kansas City, Kansas

Associate Dean for Admissions
University of Kansas School of Medicine
Mail Stop 1049, 3901 Rainbow Boulevard
Kansas City, Kansas 66160
T 913 588 5245 F 913 588 5259

Admissions www.kumc.edu/som/prospective
students.html
Main www.kumc.edu/som/
Financial www.kumc.edu/studentcenter/
financialaid.html
E-mail premedinfo@kumc.edu

Public Institution

Dr. Barbara F. Atkinson, Executive Vice Chancellor and Executive Dean

Sandra J. McCurdy, Associate Dean for Admissions

Dr. Patricia A. Thomas, Associate Dean for Cultural Enhancement and Diversity

Sara Honeck, Director of Student Financial Aid

General Information

Since the establishment of the University of Kansas School of Medicine in 1905, its students and faculty have built upon a tradition of excellence. Through exceptional medical education, patient care, service, and research, the medical faculty and staff are dedicated to preparing students for the future of medicine by providing the innovative education and training needed to practice in today's ever-changing health care delivery system.

Mission Statement

The School of Medicine commits to enhance the quality of life and to serve our community through the discovery of knowledge, the education of health professionals, and improving the health of the public.

Curricular Highlights

Community Service Requirement: Optional.
Research/Thesis Requirement: Optional.

The interdisciplinary curriculum promotes self-directed, active learning to facilitate students' mastery of the knowledge, skills, attitudes, and behaviors required to become highly competent and compassionate healers. In preparation for lifelong acquisition and synthesis of new discoveries and knowledge, students become critical thinkers who can analyze difficult problems, formulate effective action plans, and provide optimal clinical care. Years one and two consist of 13 sequential modules organized around central themes or organ systems, with didactic instruction and self-directed learning balanced between lectures and small-group activities. Each student uses a tablet computer to access course management, learning, and research systems. Beginning in the first semester, each student is paired with a mentoring physician in a longitudinal ambulatory clinical experience. Several summer programs are offered for clinical credit to students who have completed their first year. For core clinical rotations, students rotate through hospitals and community-based clinics located in Kansas City, Wichita, Salina, and select sites throughout the state. Students may also choose the Rural Track, a multidisciplinary clinical training program. Clinical electives may be taken locally, across the country, or at more than 20 approved international locations.

USMLE

Step 1: Required. Students must record a passing score for promotion.
Step 2: Clinical Skills (CS): Required. Students must record a passing total score to graduate.
Step 2: Clinical Knowledge (CK): Required. Students must record a passing total score to graduate.

Selection Factors

Applicants are encouraged to submit their AMCAS applications by September 1. Qualified Kansas residents receive strong first preference for interview and admission; successful nonresident applicants will have significant Kansas ties and/or add breadth to the class. Academic performance, MCAT scores, application materials, letters of recommendation, impressions gained from interviews, and nonacademic activities are assessed throughout the admissions process. Transfer applications are considered only if a position is available in the third-year class; Kansas residents with a compelling need to transfer receive priority.

Financial Aid

Loans and scholarships are available, with the FAFSA used to determine recipients of need-based aid. A major source of assistance for selected students is the Kansas Medical Loan Program, which provides payment of tuition and a stipend of up to $2,000 per month. Recipients receive loan forgiveness by practicing primary care or emergency medicine in an underserved county in Kansas.

Information about Diversity Programs

The University of Kansas and the School of Medicine believe the intentional creation of a diverse learning environment is essential to achieving their educational missions. Diversity and quality in medical education and health care delivery are ensured through programs that recruit, enroll, and graduate a diverse population of students; train culturally competent physicians; recruit a diverse faculty; institutionalize measures that develop and retain minority academic physicians; and expand research on health care issues affecting disadvantaged and underserved populations.

Campus Information

Setting

The School of Medicine is located at the tip of the popular 39th Street West district and just north of historic Westport and the Country Club Plaza. The metropolitan area is well-known for its award-winning parks system and an abundance of venues for athletic events and the visual and performance arts.

Enrollment

For 2009, total enrollment was: 709

Special Features

Student educational resources include a high-tech clinical skills teaching laboratory, a computer testing center, and a newly renovated medical library. A new heart hospital and biomedical research center opened in 2006. Medical students provide medical care to uninsured patients through student-operated JayDoc Clinics in Kansas City and Wichita.

Housing

All housing is off-campus, with affordable housing readily available.

Satellite Campuses/Facilities

Approximately one-third of each class completes clinical training on the KU School of Medicine-Wichita campus. This premier community-based program of medical education, patient care, and research is centered upon a partnership with four hospitals that offer a total capacity of more than 3,000 licensed beds.

Application Process and Requirements 2011–2012

Primary Application Service: AMCAS
Earliest filing date: June 1, 2010
Latest filing date: October 15, 2010

Secondary Application Required?: Yes
Sent to: All applicants
URL: https://www2.kumc.edu/som/meds/login.aspx
Fee: Yes, $50   **Waiver available:** Yes
Earliest filing date: July 1, 2010
Latest filing date: November 15, 2010

MCAT® required?: Yes
Latest MCAT® considered: September 2010
Oldest MCAT® considered: January 2008

Early Decision Program: School does have EDP
Applicants notified: October 1, 2010
EDP available for: Both Residents and Non-residents

Regular Acceptance Notice
Earliest date: November 15, 2010
Latest date: Varies
Applicant's Response to Acceptance
Offer – Maximum Time: Two weeks

Requests for Deferred
Entrance Considered: Yes

Deposit to Hold Place in Class: Yes
Deposit (Resident): $50   **(Non-resident):** $50
Deposit due: With response to acceptance offer
Applied to tuition: Yes   **Refundable:** Yes
Refundable by: May 15, 2011

Estimated number of new entrants: 175
EDP: 45, special program: 25

Start Month/Year: July 2011

Interview Format: Two individual interviews, one open-file with a committee member. Regional interviews are not available. Video interviews are not available.

Other Programs

PREPARATORY PROGRAMS
Postbaccalaureate Program: Yes, www2.kumc.edu/oced/hcpp.htm
Summer Program: Yes, www2.kumc.edu/oced/hcpp.htm
Primary Care Workshops: www.kumc.edu/som/primarycareworkshop.html
Premedical Student Conference: www.kumc.edu/som/psc.html

COMBINED DEGREE PROGRAMS
Baccalaureate/M.D.: No
M.D./M.P.H.: Yes, http://mph.kumc.edu/
M.D./M.B.A.: No
M.D./J.D.: No
M.D./Ph.D.: Yes, www3.kumc.edu/mdphd/
Additional Program: Yes, www.kumc.edu/hpm

Premedical Coursework

On-line courses accepted in fulfillment of prerequisites: On a case-by-case basis

Course	Req.	Rec.	Lab.	Sems.
Inorganic Chemistry	•		•	2
Behavioral Sciences		•		
Biochemistry		•		
Biology	•		•	2
Biology/Zoology				
Calculus				
College English	•			2
College Mathematics	•			1

Course	Req.	Rec.	Lab.	Sems.
Computer Science				
Genetics		•		
Humanities				
Organic Chemistry	•		•	2
Physics	•		•	2
Psychology		•		
Social Sciences		•		
Other				

Selection Factors: 2009 Accepted Applicants

Proportion of Accepted Applicants with Relevant Experience (Data Self-Reported to AMCAS®)	
Community Service/Volunteer	77%
Medically-Related Work	79%
Research	59%

Shaded bar represents school's accepted scores ranging from the 10th percentile to the 90th percentile. School Median ● National Median ◐

Overall GPA 2.0 2.1 2.2 2.3 2.4 2.5 2.6 2.7 2.8 2.9 3.0 3.1 3.2 3.3 3.4 3.5 3.6 ③⑦ 3.8 3.9 4.0
Science GPA 2.0 2.1 2.2 2.3 2.4 2.5 2.6 2.7 2.8 2.9 3.0 3.1 3.2 3.3 3.4 3.5 3.6 ③⑦ 3.8 3.9 4.0

MCAT® Total Numeric Score 9 10 11 12 13 14 15 16 17 18 19 20 21 22 23 24 25 26 27 28 ㉙ 30 31 ㉜ 33 34 35 36 37 38 39 40 41 42 43

	J	K	L	M	N	O	P	Q	R	S	T
Writing Sample							Ⓟ	Ⓠ			
Verbal Reasoning	3	4	5	6	7	8	9	⑩	11	12	13	14	15
Biological Sciences	3	4	5	6	7	8	9	⑩	⑪	12	13	14	15
Physical Sciences	3	4	5	6	7	8	⑨	10	⑪	12	13	14	15

Acceptance & Matriculation Data for 2009–2010 First Year Class

	Resident	Non-resident	International	Total
Applications	433	1769	21	2223
Interviewed	333	107	0	440
Deferred	2	0	0	2
Matriculants				
Early Assurance Program	8	0	0	8
Early Decision Program	47	1	0	48
Baccalaureate/M.D.	0	0	0	0
M.D./Ph.D.	1	3	0	4
Matriculated	153	22	0	**175**

Applications accepted from International Applicants: No

Matriculant Demographics: 2009–2010 First Year Class

Men: 87   **Women:** 88

Matriculants' Self-Reported Race/Ethnicity

Mexican American	5	Korean	0
Cuban	0	Vietnamese	3
Puerto Rican	1	Other Asian	5
Other Hispanic	1	Total Asian	17
Total Hispanic	7	Native American	1
Chinese	1	Black	12
Asian Indian	3	Native Hawaiian	0
Pakistani	3	White	144
Filipino	1	Unduplicated Number	
Japanese	2	of Matriculants	175

Science and Math Majors: 61%
Matriculants with:
Baccalaureate degree: 100%
Graduate degree(s): 4%

Specialty Choice

2005, 2006, 2007 Graduates, Specialty Choice (As reported by program directors to GME Track™)	
Anesthesiology	7%
Emergency Medicine	5%
Family Practice	19%
Internal Medicine	14%
Obstetrics/Gynecology	8%
Orthopaedic Surgery	3%
Pediatrics	9%
Psychiatry	2%
Radiology	6%
Surgery	7%

Financial Information
Source: 2008-2009 LCME I-B survey and 2009-2010 AAMC TSF questionnaire

	Residents	Non-residents
Total Cost of Attendance	$ 49,740	$ 69,188
Tuition and Fees	$ 25,678	$ 45,126
Other (includes living expenses)	$ 23,147	$ 23,147
Health Insurance (can be waived)	$ 915	$ 915

Average 2009 Graduate Indebtedness: $131,860
% of Enrolled Students Receiving Aid: 96%

Criminal Background Check

This medical school requires a criminal background check prior to matriculation.

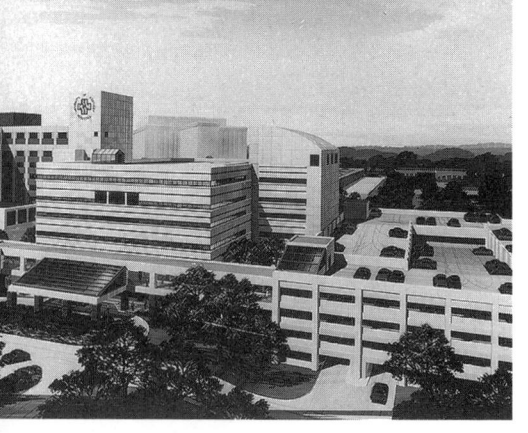

University of Kentucky College of Medicine

Lexington, Kentucky

University of Kentucky College of Medicine
Office of Admissions
138 Leader Avenue, Room 118
Lexington, Kentucky 40506-9983
T 859 323 6161   F 859 323 2076

Admissions www.mc.uky.edu/meded/admissions/
index.asp
Main www.mc.uky.edu/medicine
Financial www.mc.uky.edu/meded/financialaid/
index.asp
E-mail kymedap@uky.edu

Public Institution
Dr. Jay Perman, Dean

*Dr. Carol L. Elam,
Assistant Dean for Admissions
and Institutional Advancement*

*Kairise Conwell, Director, Health Center
Student Diversity Services*

Julie McDaniel, Financial Aid Director

General Information
The University of Kentucky College of Medicine admitted its first class in 1960. The College of Medicine is part of the UK Academic Medical Center located on the university campus in Lexington. The medical center comprises six colleges: medicine, nursing, pharmacy, dentistry, health sciences, and public health. The majority of on-site clinical teaching occurs at the University of Kentucky Chandler Hospital, the Veterans Affairs Medical Center, and the Kentucky Clinic. Hospitals in Lexington and across the state hold affiliation agreements with the college for clinical teaching and patient service. Basic science teaching areas for lecture, laboratory, and small-group instruction, and the Medical Center Library, are located in the Willard Medical Sciences Building.

Mission Statement
Our mission is to assume a leadership role in addressing the health care needs of the Commonwealth of Kentucky and to be preeminent among medical schools in selected areas of education, research, and service.

Curricular Highlights
Community Service Requirement: Required. Interprofessional & underserved exposure required.
Research/Thesis Requirement: Optional.

The curriculum integrates basic and clinical sciences. Students are taught fundamental problems of human biology, how to recognize causes of these problems, and how to prevent disease and treat patients. Year 1 focuses on normal function of the human body (human structure, cellular structure and function, neurosciences, and human function). First-year

students receive early exposure and experience in patient care through the study of interviewing, history-taking, physical exam skills, and clinical decision-making using both standardized and real patients in longitudinal care experiences. In the first two years, students explore principles of prevention and assess the impact of social, ethical, legal, economic, and psychological factors using case study discussions. Year 2 exposes students to abnormal functions of the human body. Coursework is designed to integrate studies of infectious disease, immunology, pathology, pharmacology, and psychiatry. Computer-based instruction and simulation reinforce basic science studies and provide linkages to clinical applications. Clinical students work in both inpatient and outpatient settings and are required to take medical histories, perform physical exams, and monitor laboratory tests. Year 3 includes integrated internal medicine and emergency care clerkships, along with pediatrics, OB/GYN, psychiatry, neurology, family and community medicine, and surgery. Year 4 includes clinical pharmacology, rural medicine experiences, 2 acting internships, and a 4-month elective period. A specialized Rural Track provides clinical education at rural sites.

USMLE
Step 1: Required. Students must record a passing score for promotion.
Step 2: Clinical Skills (CS): Required. Students must record a passing total score to graduate.
Step 2: Clinical Knowledge (CK): Required. Students must record a passing total score to graduate.

Selection Factors
The UKCOM gives preference to qualified applicants who are Kentucky residents. Determination of state residence is made by the registrar's office. Secondary applications are sent to all Kentucky residents and to nonresidents with competitive undergraduate GPAs and MCAT scores. Selected candidates are invited for interviews conducted at the UKCOM. Necessary personal attributes of applicants include time management abilities, interpersonal skills, leadership, and demonstrated service to others. Admission decisions are based upon review of academic and

nonacademic factors, including scholastic excellence, MCAT performance, personal attributes, exposure to the profession, premedical recommendations, and admission interviews. Transfers from LCME-accredited schools are considered on a space-available basis. The University of Kentucky is an equal opportunity university. We encourage applications from all academically qualified people interested in educational opportunities.

Financial Aid
A limited number of scholarships are awarded to selected students with exceptional achievement. Institutional loan/scholarship assistance is available for eligible resident and nonresident students. The Financial Aid Office provides counseling and assists students in applying for aid. A guaranteed tuition plan locks tuition and fees for each entering class.

Information about Diversity Programs
The UKCOM is committed to the recruitment and retention of disadvantaged students and students from groups underrepresented in medicine. Interested applicants are encouraged to contact the admissions office.

Campus Information

Setting
The UKCOM is located on the University campus in Lexington.

Enrollment
For 2009, total enrollment was: 439

Special Features
Adjacent to UKCOM are Chandler Medical Center, UK Children's Hospital, VA Hospital, Markey Cancer Center, Sanders-Brown Center on Aging, University Health Service, the Gill Heart Institute and biomedical research centers. A new bed tower is under construction.

Housing
Housing is available close to campus. Rents average $600 to $800 per month.

Satellite Campuses/Facilities
Students participate in rural health electives throughout Kentucky at Area Health Education Centers.

Application Process and Requirements 2011–2012

Primary Application Service: AMCAS
Earliest filing date: June 1, 2010
Latest filing date: November 1, 2010

Secondary Application Required?: Yes
Sent to: Screened applicants
Contact: Kim Scott, (859) 323-6161, kstahlma@email.uky.edu
Fee: Yes, $50   **Waiver available:** Yes
Earliest filing date: July 1, 2010
Latest filing date: January 15, 2011

MCAT® required?: Yes
Latest MCAT® Considered: September 2010
Oldest MCAT® considered: January 2008

Early Decision Program: School does have EDP
Applicants notified: October 1, 2010
EDP available for: Both Residents and Non-residents

Regular Acceptance Notice
Earliest date: October 15, 2010
Latest date: Until class is full
Applicant's Response to Acceptance Offer – Maximum Time: Two weeks

Requests for Deferred Entrance Considered: Yes

Deposit to Hold Place in Class: Yes
Deposit (Resident): $100   **(Non-resident):** $100
Deposit due: With response to acceptance offer
Applied to tuition: Yes   **Refundable:** Yes
Refundable by: May 15, 2011

Estimated number of new entrants: 113
EDP: 20, special program: 10

Start Month/Year: August 2011

Interview Format: Two individual interviews. Regional interviews are not available. Video interviews are not available.

Other Programs

PREPARATORY PROGRAMS
Postbaccalaureate Program: No
Summer Program: No

COMBINED DEGREE PROGRAMS
Baccalaureate/M.D.: Yes, www.mc.uky.edu/meded/bsmd/index.asp
Marlene Sauer, (859) 323-6437, msauer1@email.uky.edu
M.D./M.P.H.: Yes, Kim Scott, (859) 323-6161, kstahlma@email.uky.edu
M.D./M.B.A.: Yes, Kim Scott, (859) 323-6161, kstahlma@email.uky.edu
M.D./J.D.: No
M.D./Ph.D.: Yes, www.mc.uky.edu/mdphd/
Dr. Susan Smyth, (859) 323-2274, ssmyt2@email.uky.edu

Premedical Coursework

On-line courses accepted in fulfillment of prerequisites: No

Course	Req.	Rec.	Lab.	Sems.	Course	Req.	Rec.	Lab.	Sems.
Inorganic Chemistry	•		•	2	Computer Science				
Behavioral Sciences					Genetics				
Biochemistry		•			Humanities		•		
Biology	•		•	2	Organic Chemistry	•		•	2
Biology/Zoology					Physics	•		•	2
Calculus					Psychology				
College English	•			2	Social Sciences			•	
College Mathematics					Other				

Selection Factors: 2009 Accepted Applicants

Proportion of Accepted Applicants with Relevant Experience (Data Self-Reported to AMCAS®)		Community Service/Volunteer	73%
		Medically-Related Work	80%
		Research	79%

Shaded bar represents school's accepted scores ranging from the 10th percentile to the 90th percentile   School Median ● National Median ○

Overall GPA 2.0 2.1 2.2 2.3 2.4 2.5 2.6 2.7 2.8 2.9 3.0 3.1 3.2 3.3 3.4 3.5 3.6 3.7 (3.8) 3.9 4.0
Science GPA 2.0 2.1 2.2 2.3 2.4 2.5 2.6 2.7 2.8 2.9 3.0 3.1 3.2 3.3 3.4 3.5 3.6 (3.7) 3.8 3.9 4.0

MCAT® Total Numeric Score 9 10 11 12 13 14 15 16 17 18 19 20 21 22 23 24 25 26 27 28 29 30 (31)(32) 33 34 35 36 37 38 39 40 41 42 43

Writing Sample			J	K	L	M	N	O	(P)	(Q)	R	S	T	
Verbal Reasoning	3	4	5	6	7	8	9	(10)	11	12	13	14	15	
Biological Sciences	3	4	5	6	7	8	9	10	(11)	12	13	14	15	
Physical Sciences	3	4	5	6	7	8	9	(10)	(11)	12	13	14	15	

Acceptance & Matriculation Data for 2009–2010 First Year Class

	Resident	Non-resident	International	Total
Applications	406	1528	137	2071
Interviewed	226	137	15	378
Deferred	2	1	0	3
Matriculants				
Early Assurance Program	0	0	0	0
Early Decision Program	19	1	0	20
Baccalaureate/M.D.	0	0	0	0
M.D./Ph.D.	1	2	0	3
Matriculated	77	34	4	**115**

Applications accepted from International Applicants: Yes

Specialty Choice

2005, 2006, 2007 Graduates, Specialty Choice
(As reported by program directors to GME Track™)

Anesthesiology	4%
Emergency Medicine	4%
Family Practice	11%
Internal Medicine	16%
Obstetrics/Gynecology	6%
Orthopaedic Surgery	2%
Pediatrics	9%
Psychiatry	4%
Radiology	5%
Surgery	5%

Matriculant Demographics: 2009–2010 First Year Class

Men: 67   **Women:** 48

Matriculants' Self-Reported Race/Ethnicity

Mexican American	0	Korean	0
Cuban	0	Vietnamese	1
Puerto Rican	1	Other Asian	2
Other Hispanic	0	Total Asian	13
Total Hispanic	1	Native American	0
Chinese	3	Black	4
Asian Indian	4	Native Hawaiian	0
Pakistani	2	White	92
Filipino	0	Unduplicated Number	
Japanese	1	of Matriculants	115

Science and Math Majors: 76%
Matriculants with:
Baccalaureate degree: 99%
Graduate degree(s): 4%

Financial Information

Source: 2008-2009 LCME I-B survey and 2009-2010 AAMC TSF questionnaire

	Residents	Non-residents
Total Cost of Attendance	$ 54,528	$ 78,934
Tuition and Fees	$ 29,233	$ 53,639
Other (includes living expenses)	$ 25,295	$ 25,295
Health Insurance (can be waived)	$ 0	$ 0

Average 2009 Graduate Indebtedness: $141,593
% of Enrolled Students Receiving Aid: 89%

Criminal Background Check

This medical school requires a criminal background check prior to matriculation.

University of Louisville
School of Medicine

Louisville, Kentucky

Office of Admissions, School of Medicine
Abell Administration Center
323 East Chestnut, University of Louisville
Louisville, Kentucky 40202-3866
T 502 852 5193   F 502 852 0302

Admissions www.louisville.edu/medschool/admissions
Main www.louisville.edu/medschool
Financial www.louisville.edu/medschool/finaid
E-mail medadm@louisville.edu

Public Institution

Dr. Edward C. Halperin, Dean

Pamela D. Osborne, Director, Medical School Admissions

Mary Joshua, Associate Director, Office of Minority and Rural Affairs

Leslie Kaelin, Director, Financial Aid

Dr. Stephen F. Wheeler, Associate Dean, Medical School Admissions

Dr. V. Faye Jones, Associate Dean for Academic Affairs, Office of Minority and Rural Affairs

General Information

The School of Medicine was established at the Louisville Medical Institute in 1833 and became affiliated with the University of Louisville in 1846. In 1970 the university became a member of the state system of higher education.

Mission Statement

The University of Louisville School of Medicine's mission is to excel in the education of physicians and scientists for careers in teaching, research, patient care and service, to bring our fundamental discoveries to the bedside, and to be a vital component in the University's quest to become a premier, nationally recognized metropolitan research university.

Curricular Highlights

Community Service Requirement: Optional.
Research/Thesis Requirement: Optional.

The University of Louisville School of Medicine is committed to training physicians who are humanistically oriented and patient-centered and who will meet the diverse health care needs of Kentucky's citizens. The curriculum is focused on providing comprehensive exposure to the fundamental aspects of medicine while retaining sufficient flexibility for effective development of an individual student's abilities and interests. It emphasizes a learning environment that enables students to maximize their success and prepares them to achieve their professional goals. Four goals drive the design, development, implementation and evaluation of our curriculum: Integration of basic and clinical sciences, within courses and clinical rotations; Expanded use of non-lecture teaching and learning modalities such as directed self-learning, small-group activities, and case-based learning; Expanded use of technology to support teaching and learning such as course and clerkship Web sites and patient simulations; and Development of course and clerkship learning objectives that support the overall goals and Educational Objectives for the Undergraduate Medical Education Program.

USMLE

Step 1: Required. Students must record a passing score for promotion.
Step 2: Clinical Skills (CS): Required. Students must record a passing total score to graduate.
Step 2: Clinical Knowledge (CK): Required. Students must record a passing total score to graduate.

Selection Factors

The ULSOM is a state institution which gives preference to residents of Kentucky. International applicants are only considered if they have both strong Kentucky ties and a pending permanent residency application. Applicants are selected on the basis of their individual merits without bias concerning sex, race, creed, national origin, age, or handicap. Applicants are chosen on the basis of intellect, integrity, maturity, and interpersonal sensitivity. Consideration is given to the past academic record, college pre-professional committee evaluations/faculty letters of recommendations, extracurricular activities, and personal interviews held at the medical school and the Trover Campus.

Financial Aid

Financial needs of the applicant are not a consideration in the selection process. Scholarships are available on a limited basis and are granted according to demonstrated financial need, and scholastic and professional promise.

Information about Diversity Programs

Applications from disadvantaged individuals and members of groups underrepresented in medicine are encouraged. Applicants are reviewed by the full Admissions Committee, which accepts students on an individual basis.

Selected matriculants have the option to participate in a summer pre-matriculation program offered through the Office of Minority & Rural Affairs.

Campus Information

Setting

The ULSOM is located in the heart of downtown Louisville's medical center. The main acute and trauma care clinical teaching activities take place in the 404-bed University Hospital. Within two blocks are three formally affiliated hospitals: Kosair Children's Hospital, the only full-service children's hospital in the state of Kentucky; Jewish Hospital; and Norton Hospital. Other facilities include the world-renowned Kentucky Lions Eye Research Institute; James Graham Brown Cancer Center; the Veterans Affairs Medical Center; the Child Evaluation Center; Frazier Rehab Institute; and the ULSOM Trover Campus, located in Madisonville, Kentucky.

Enrollment

For 2009, total enrollment was: 617

Special Features

The ULSOM patient simulation center provides students hands-on, risk free learning, realistic patient encounters and interactive self-directed learning. All of the educational campus is WI-FI. Additionally, we offer students the opportunity to complete clinical training in a rural setting at the ULSOM Trover Campus in Madisonville, Kentucky.

Housing

The U of L medical-dental dormitory/apartment building is on campus. Non-university housing listings are available from the Office of Faculty and Student Advocacy, (502) 852-6185. Beginning in 2010-2011, a new apartment complex bordering the medical school campus will grant priority rental to our students.

Satellite Campuses/Facilities

Students rotate at five primary hospital sites; four sites are within walking distance of the Health Science Center campus. Interested candidates may apply for dedicated admission to complete clinical training at the ULSOM Trover Campus in Madisonville, Kentucky.

Application Process and Requirements 2011–2012

Primary Application Service: AMCAS
Earliest filing date: June 1, 2010
Latest filing date: October 15, 2010

Secondary Application Required?: Yes
Sent to: Screened applicants
Contact: medadm@louisville.edu
Fee: Yes, $75   **Waiver available:** Yes
Earliest filing date: July 1, 2010
Latest filing date: December 31, 2010

MCAT® required?: Yes
Latest MCAT® considered: September 2010
Oldest MCAT® considered: January 2008

Early Decision Program: School does have EDP
Applicants notified: October 1, 2010
EDP available for: Both Residents and Non-residents

Regular Acceptance Notice
Earliest date: October 16, 2010
Latest date: Varies
Applicant's Response to Acceptance Offer – Maximum Time: Two weeks

Requests for Deferred Entrance Considered: Yes

Deposit to Hold Place in Class: Yes
Deposit (Resident): $100   **(Non-resident):** $100
Deposit due: With acceptance letter
Applied to tuition: Yes   **Refundable:** Yes
Refundable by: May 15, 2011

Estimated number of new entrants: 160
EDP: 4, special program: 10

Start Month/Year: August 2011

Interview Format: Academically blind interviews with two committee members. Regional interviews are not available. Video interviews are not available.

Other Programs

PREPARATORY PROGRAMS
Postbaccalaureate Program: Yes, (502) 852-2712, pbpmed@louisville.edu
Summer Program: Yes, www.louisville.edu/medschool/ahec/special.programs/ Mary Joshua, (502) 852-7159, specprog@louisville.edu

COMBINED DEGREE PROGRAMS
Baccalaureate/M.D.: No
M.D./M.P.H.: Yes, http://louisville.edu/medschool/dualdegree
M.D./M.B.A.: Yes, http://louisville.edu/medschool/dualdegree, Toni Ganzel, M.D., M.B.A., (502) 852-5192, medstuaf@gwise.louisville.edu
M.D./J.D.: No
M.D./Ph.D.: Yes, http://louisville.edu/medschool/dualdegree
Additional Program: Yes, www.louisville.edu/bioethicsma, (502) 852-6501, bioethicsma@louisville.edu

Premedical Coursework

On-line courses accepted in fulfillment of prerequisites: No

Course	Req.	Rec.	Lab.	Sems.
Inorganic Chemistry	•		•	2
Behavioral Sciences				
Biochemistry		•		1
Biology	•		•	2
Biology/Zoology				
Calculus				1
College English	•			2
College Mathematics		•		2

Course	Req.	Rec.	Lab.	Sems.
Computer Science				
Genetics		•		1
Humanities				
Organic Chemistry	•		•	2
Physics	•		•	2
Psychology				
Social Sciences				
Physiology		•		1
Statistics		•		1

Selection Factors: 2009 Accepted Applicants

Proportion of Accepted Applicants with Relevant Experience (Data Self-Reported to AMCAS®)		
Community Service/Volunteer		77%
Medically-Related Work		73%
Research		74%

Shaded bar represents school's accepted scores ranging from the 10th percentile to the 90th percentile.   School Median ●   National Median ◐

Overall GPA	2.0	2.1	2.2	2.3	2.4	2.5	2.6	2.7	2.8	2.9	3.0	3.1	3.2	3.3	3.4	3.5	3.6	(3.7)	3.8	3.9	4.0
Science GPA	2.0	2.1	2.2	2.3	2.4	2.5	2.6	2.7	2.8	2.9	3.0	3.1	3.2	3.3	3.4	3.5	(3.6)	3.7	3.8	3.9	4.0

MCAT® Total Numeric Score 9 10 11 12 13 14 15 16 17 18 19 20 21 22 23 24 25 26 27 28 29 (30) 31 (32) 33 34 35 36 37 38 39 40 41 42 43

Writing Sample			J		K		L	M	N	O	(P)	Q	R	S	T
Verbal Reasoning	3		4		5	6	7	8	9	(10)	11	12	13	14	15
Biological Sciences	3		4		5	6	7	8	9	(10)	(11)	12	13	14	15
Physical Sciences	3		4		5	6	7	8	9	(10)	(11)	12	13	14	15

Acceptance & Matriculation Data for 2009–2010 First Year Class

	Resident	Non-resident	International	Total
Applications	392	2086	14	2492
Interviewed	250	132	2	384
Deferred	1	0	0	1
Matriculants				
Early Assurance Program	4	0	0	4
Early Decision Program	5	0	0	5
Baccalaureate/M.D.	0	0	0	0
M.D./Ph.D.	1	1	0	2
Matriculated	120	40	0	**160**

Applications accepted from International Applicants: Yes

Matriculant Demographics: 2009–2010 First Year Class

Men: 89   **Women:** 71

Matriculants' Self-Reported Race/Ethnicity

Mexican American	0	Korean	4
Cuban	0	Vietnamese	0
Puerto Rican	1	Other Asian	1
Other Hispanic	1	Total Asian	18
Total Hispanic	2	Native American	0
Chinese	4	Black	11
Asian Indian	7	Native Hawaiian	0
Pakistani	1	White	132
Filipino	1	Unduplicated Number	
Japanese	0	of Matriculants	160

Science and Math Majors: 73%
Matriculants with:
   Baccalaureate degree: 99%
   Graduate degree(s): 10%

Specialty Choice

2005, 2006, 2007 Graduates, Specialty Choice (As reported by program directors to GME Track™)	
Anesthesiology	7%
Emergency Medicine	6%
Family Practice	8%
Internal Medicine	17%
Obstetrics/Gynecology	3%
Orthopaedic Surgery	5%
Pediatrics	14%
Psychiatry	5%
Radiology	7%
Surgery	5%

Financial Information

Source: 2008-2009 LCME I-B survey and 2009-2010 AAMC TSF questionnaire

	Residents	Non-residents
Total Cost of Attendance	$ 44,458	$ 61,554
Tuition and Fees	$ 26,329	$ 43,425
Other (includes living expenses)	$ 16,395	$ 16,395
Health Insurance (can be waived)	$ 1,734	$ 1,734

Average 2009 Graduate Indebtedness: $144,399
% of Enrolled Students Receiving Aid: 94%

Criminal Background Check

This medical school requires a criminal background check prior to matriculation.

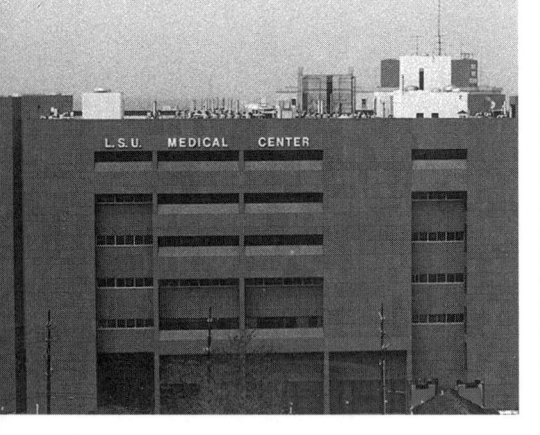

Louisiana State University School of Medicine in New Orleans
New Orleans, Louisiana

Admissions Office, Louisiana State University
School of Medicine in New Orleans
1901 Perdido Street, Box P3-4
New Orleans, Louisiana 70112-1393
T 504 568 6262   F 504 568 7701

Admissions www.medschool.lsuhsc.edu/admissions
Main www.medschool.lsuhsc.edu
Financial www.lsuhsc.edu/no/students/financialaid/
E-mail ms-admissions@lsuhsc.edu

Public Institution

Dr. Steve Nelson, Dean

*Dr. Sam G. McClugage Jr.,
Associate Dean for Admissions*

*Dr. Edward Helm, Associate Dean, Office of
Community and Minority Health Education*

*Patrick Gorman, Director of
Student Financial Aid*

General Information
LSU School of Medicine in New Orleans was established in 1931 in downtown New Orleans. During the past two decades, several new buildings have been erected, including a state-of-the-art Student Learning Center which includes procedural and simulation labs, a computer lounge, and large and small-group meeting rooms. A new residence facility, Stanislaus Hall, containing a comprehensive fitness center, is among the more recent additions to the campus.

Mission Statement
The LSUSOM is dedicated to providing the opportunity for an excellent medical education to all Louisiana applicants who are prepared to benefit from its curriculum and instruction. To this end, the Admissions Committee will strive to recruit and admit residents from Louisiana from every geographic, economic, social, and cultural dimension of the state of Louisiana.

Curricular Highlights
Community Service Requirement: Required.
Research/Thesis Requirement: Optional.

The first two years of the medical school curriculum emphasize several basic sciences and their relevance to clinical medicine. Clinical experiences begin in the first year in courses such as Science and Practice of Medicine. The second year of medical school utilizes an integrated approach to the teaching of basic science and pre-clinical courses within an environment that fosters an early exposure to patient care. Clerkships begin in the third year where students rotate through the various clinical disciplines. In the fourth year, students are given several months for electives in addition to required rotations in Ambulatory Medicine,

Acting Internships, etc. Some of these rotations can be completed at the institutions associated with the LSU School of Medicine throughout the state or at other approved institutions outside the state or country. Computer-assisted instruction is an important component of the curriculum. Entering students are required to purchase laptop computers.

USMLE
Step 1: Required. Students must record a passing score for promotion.
Step 2: Clinical Skills (CS): Required. Students must record a passing total score to graduate.
Step 2: Clinical Knowledge (CK): Required. Students must record a passing total score to graduate.

Selection Factors
Candidates are encouraged to contact the Office of Admissions for a brochure which summarizes the selection process for LSU School of Medicine in New Orleans.

Financial Aid
Financial assistance is available for students through several different methods. There are direct scholarship programs, scholarships for disadvantaged students, state and federal loan programs, work-study programs, and employment opportunities in the New Orleans area for students in their third and fourth years. Financial assistance information is available from the Student Financial Aid Office at (504) 568-4820.

Information about Diversity Programs
Members of groups underrepresented in medicine are encouraged to apply. The School of Medicine's Office of Community and Minority Health Education actively recruits students from groups underrepresented in medicine and provides counseling for high school and college students. Further information may be obtained by contacting Dr. Edward Helm, Associate Dean for Community and Minority Health Education, at (504) 568-8501.

Campus Information

Setting
LSU School of Medicine is located in downtown New Orleans in a medical corridor which is within walking distance of the historic

French Quarter, museums, shopping districts, and two sports arenas for professional football and basketball teams.

Enrollment
For 2009, total enrollment was: 742

Special Features
The interdisciplinary Science and Practice of Medicine course and the Isidore Cohn Learning Center were both created to provide a more innovative way for the clinical teaching of students beginning in the first year. The Learning Center includes over 14,000 square feet of space, small-group teaching rooms, simulation laboratories, a computer center, and meeting rooms. More information is available at *www.medschool.lsuhsc.edu/learning_center/*.

Housing
Two recently renovated student housing facilities are available. Furnished and unfurnished apartments are available for married (with or without children) and single students. Many students choose to rent apartments in New Orleans or the surrounding metropolitan area. Lists of available apartments are supplied upon request.

Satellite Campuses/Facilities
LSU School of Medicine rotates its students among one of several public hospitals, mainly in New Orleans, Baton Rouge, or Lafayette, LA, as well as several private hospitals such as Children's Hospital in the city of New Orleans. The LSU Health Care Services Division has oversight for eight public teaching hospitals in the State of Louisiana in which many LSUSOM medical students, residents and fellows receive training. Several clinics in the metropolitan area and around the state are also similarly used for the training of health care professionals.

Application Process and Requirements 2011–2012

Primary Application Service: AMCAS
Earliest filing date: June 1, 2010
Latest filing date: November 30, 2010

Secondary Application Required?: Yes
Sent to: All applicants
URL: www.medschool.lsuhsc.edu/admissions/secondary_application
Fee: Yes, $50   **Waiver available:** Yes
Earliest filing date: June 15, 2010
Latest filing date: January 1, 2011

MCAT® required?: Yes
Latest MCAT® considered: September 2010
Oldest MCAT® considered: September 2007

Early Decision Program: School does have EDP
Applicants notified: October 1, 2010
EDP available for: Both Residents and Non-residents

Regular Acceptance Notice
Earliest date: October 15, 2010
Latest date: Varies
Applicant's Response to Acceptance Offer – Maximum Time: Two weeks

Requests for Deferred Entrance Considered: Yes

Deposit to Hold Place in Class: Yes
Deposit (Resident): $100   **(Non-resident):** $100
Deposit due: Due with acceptance offer
Applied to tuition: Yes   **Refundable:** Yes
Refundable by: May 15, 2011

Estimated number of new entrants: 200
EDP: 15, special program: 8

Start Month/Year: August 2011

Interview Format: Three one-on-one interviews. Regional interviews are not available. Video interviews are not available.

Other Programs

PREPARATORY PROGRAMS
Postbaccalaureate Program: No
Summer Program: Yes, Dr. Edward Helm, (504) 568-8501, jparke@lsuhsc.edu

COMBINED DEGREE PROGRAMS
Baccalaureate/M.D.: No
M.D./M.P.H.: Yes, http://publichealth.lsuhsc.edu/
M.D./M.B.A.: No
M.D./J.D.: No
M.D./Ph.D.: Yes, http://graduatestudies.lsuhsc.edu/
Additional Program: Yes, Rural Scholars' Track Cathie Stuckey, (504) 568-6262, ms-admissions@lsuhsc.edu

Premedical Coursework

On-line courses accepted in fulfillment of prerequisites: No

Course	Req.	Rec.	Lab.	Hrs.	Course	Req.	Rec.	Lab.	Hrs.
Inorganic Chemistry	•		•	8	Computer Science		•		
Behavioral Sciences		•			Genetics		•		
Biochemistry		•			Humanities		•		
Biology		•			Organic Chemistry	•		•	8
Biology/Zoology	•		•	8	Physics	•		•	8
Calculus		•			Psychology		•		
College English	•			6	Social Sciences		•		
College Mathematics		•			Other				

Selection Factors: 2009 Accepted Applicants

Proportion of Accepted Applicants with Relevant Experience (Data Self-Reported to AMCAS®)		
Community Service/Volunteer		73%
Medically-Related Work		80%
Research		64%

Shaded bar represents school's accepted scores ranging from the 10th percentile to the 90th percentile   ● School Median   ○ National Median

Overall GPA 2.0 2.1 2.2 2.3 2.4 2.5 2.6 2.7 2.8 2.9 3.0 3.1 3.2 3.3 3.4 3.5 3.6 3.7 (3.8) 3.9 4.0
Science GPA 2.0 2.1 2.2 2.3 2.4 2.5 2.6 2.7 2.8 2.9 3.0 3.1 3.2 3.3 3.4 3.5 3.6 (3.7) 3.8 3.9 4.0

MCAT® Total Numeric Score 9 10 11 12 13 14 15 16 17 18 19 20 21 22 23 24 25 26 27 28 (29) 30 31 (32) 33 34 35 36 37 38 39 40 41 42 43

Writing Sample			J	K	L	M	N	(O)	P	(Q)	R	S	T
Verbal Reasoning	3	4	5	6	7	8	9	(10)	11	12	13	14	15
Biological Sciences	3	4	5	6	7	8	9	(10)	(11)	12	13	14	15
Physical Sciences	3	4	5	6	7	8	(9)	10	(11)	12	13	14	15

Acceptance & Matriculation Data for 2009–2010 First Year Class

	Resident	Non-resident	International	Total
Applications	673	423	21	1117
Interviewed	411	20	0	431
Deferred	1	0	0	1
Matriculants				
Early Assurance Program	0	0	0	0
Early Decision Program	15	0	0	15
Baccalaureate/M.D.	0	0	0	0
M.D./Ph.D.	2	4	0	6
Matriculated	182	11	0	**193**

Applications accepted from International Applicants: No

Specialty Choice

2005, 2006, 2007 Graduates, Specialty Choice
(As reported by program directors to GME Track™)

Anesthesiology	6%
Emergency Medicine	9%
Family Practice	7%
Internal Medicine	17%
Obstetrics/Gynecology	6%
Orthopaedic Surgery	4%
Pediatrics	10%
Psychiatry	3%
Radiology	5%
Surgery	8%

Matriculant Demographics: 2009–2010 First Year Class

Men: 103   **Women:** 90

Matriculants' Self-Reported Race/Ethnicity

Mexican American	2	Korean	0
Cuban	1	Vietnamese	2
Puerto Rican	0	Other Asian	1
Other Hispanic	5	Total Asian	19
Total Hispanic	7	Native American	1
Chinese	7	Black	20
Asian Indian	7	Native Hawaiian	1
Pakistani	0	White	154
Filipino	4	Unduplicated Number	
Japanese	0	of Matriculants	193

Science and Math Majors: 72%
Matriculants with:
  Baccalaureate degree: 100%
  Graduate degree(s): 19%

Financial Information

Source: 2008-2009 LCME I-B survey and 2009-2010 AAMC TSF questionnaire

	Residents	Non-residents
Total Cost of Attendance	$ 37,615	$ 53,211
Tuition and Fees	$ 14,175	$ 29,771
Other (includes living expenses)	$ 21,717	$ 21,717
Health Insurance (can be waived)	$ 1,723	$ 1,723

Average 2009 Graduate Indebtedness: $121,406
% of Enrolled Students Receiving Aid: 88%

Criminal Background Check

This medical school requires a criminal background check prior to matriculation.

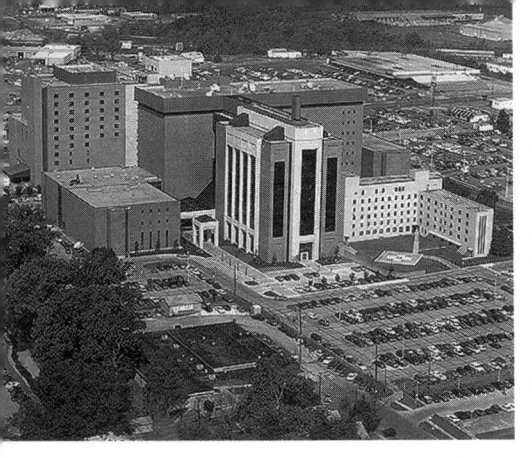

Louisiana State University Health Sciences Center School of Medicine in Shreveport

Shreveport, Louisiana

Office of Student Admissions
Louisiana State University Health Sciences Center
School of Medicine in Shreveport,
1501 Kings Highway
Shreveport, Louisiana 71130
T 318 675 5190 F 318 675 8690

Admissions www.admissions.lsuhsc.edu
Main http://www.lsuhscshreveport.edu/
Financial http://sh-aux.lsuhsc.edu/financialaid/
E-mail shvadm@lsuhsc.edu

Public Institution

Dr. Andrew Chesson, Dean

*Dr. F. Scott Kennedy, Assistant Dean
for Student Admissions*

*Shirley Roberson, Director for
Multicultural Affairs*

*Sherry Gladney, Director of
Student Financial Aid*

Warren E. Cockerham, Registrar

*Jacquline Hatcher, Coordinator of
Student Admissions*

General Information

The LSU Health Sciences Center in Shreveport (LSUHSC-S) provides education, research, patient care services, and community outreach. Educating health professionals and scientists at all levels, its major responsibility includes the advancement and dissemination of knowledge in medicine and the basic sciences. It also provides vital public service through its hospital and clinics.

Mission Statement

LSUHSC-S has a dual mission: to assure the availability of acute and primary health care services to the uninsured, to the underinsured, and to others with problems of access to medical care, and to serve as the principal site for the clinical education of future doctors and other health care professionals.

Curricular Highlights

Community Service Requirement: Optional. Community service is highly desirable.
Research/Thesis Requirement: Optional. Desirable, but not required.

The modern curriculum thoroughly integrates medical issues and applications in the first two years, during which the basic sciences are emphasized. Recently, didactic lecture hours were cut dramatically, and small-group, active-learning experiences were dramatically increased. The overall effect was decreased contact hours and increased self-directed learning. All essential basic-science concepts traditionally taught in the first two years are now integrated with clinical examples, clinical cases and standardized patient experiences. The required clerkships occur in the third year, and the fourth year is devoted to electives.

USMLE

Step 1: Required. Students must record a passing score for promotion.
Step 2: Clinical Skills (CS): Required. Students must only record a score.
Step 2: Clinical Knowledge (CK): Required. Students must only record a score.

Selection Factors

Admission is based upon character, motivation, intellectual ability, and achievement as judged by recommendations of premedical advisors, personal interviews with members of the faculty at the School of Medicine, college grades, and MCAT scores. In recent years, the number of applications filed by well-qualified residents of Louisiana has exceeded the number of places available. For this reason, places have not been offered to nonresidents. Determination of state residence is determined by LSU system regulations. Thirty colleges are represented in the 2009 entering class. The School of Medicine in Shreveport does not discriminate in applicant selection on the basis of race, sex, creed, national origin, age, or handicap.

Financial Aid

Scholarships and long-term, low-interest loan funds are available to students with financial need. In the past, no accepted students have been unable to meet their financial needs. Scholarships and loans are available to students in all four years and are based on applicants' showing verified need. Certain awards are given in recognition primarily of academic accomplishment and promise. The school offers summer employment to many students, but does not advise employment during school sessions, which would interfere with academic performance. Financial need has no bearing on an applicant's acceptance. Applications for financial assistance are furnished by the Financial Aid Office after applicants have been accepted.

Information about Diversity Programs

Applications from students from groups underrepresented in medicine are encouraged and will be given every consideration. All students are encouraged to take advantage of the services provided by the Office of Multicultural Affairs. They include a pre-matriculation program, an MCAT preparation course, and a summer research program for high school students, as well as informal counseling for medical students and applicants.

Campus Information

Setting

The medical school is located near the intersection of I-49 and I-20, in a peaceful neighborhood near the geographic center of Shreveport. Thus, affordable housing is available within a short commute.

Enrollment

For 2009, total enrollment was: 463

Special Features

The hospital includes an ACS-verified Adult Level-One Trauma Center, a Level-One Pediatric Trauma Center and a Pediatric ICU, as well as all features of a tertiary care hospital.

Housing

On-campus housing is not offered; however, safe affordable housing is abundantly available within a short commuting distance.

Satellite Campuses/Facilities

The school is affiliated with other local and regional hospitals.

Application Process and Requirements 2011–2012

Primary Application Service: AMCAS
Earliest filing date: June 1, 2010
Latest filing date: November 1, 2010

Secondary Application Required?: Yes
Sent to: All Louisiana applicants
URL: Provided by school
Student Admissions, (318) 675-5190,
shvadm@lsuhsc.edu
Fee: Yes, $50   **Waiver available:** Yes
Earliest filing date: June 1, 2010
Latest filing date: December 15, 2010

MCAT® required?: Yes
Latest MCAT® considered: September 2010
Oldest MCAT® considered: August 2007

Early Decision Program: School does have EDP
Applicants notified: October 1, 2010
EDP available for: Residents only

Regular Acceptance Notice
Earliest date: October 15, 2010
Latest date: Until class is full
Applicant's Response to Acceptance Offer – Maximum Time: Two weeks

Requests for Deferred Entrance Considered: Yes

Deposit to Hold Place in Class: Yes
Deposit (Resident): $250   **(Non-resident):** $250
Deposit due: May 15, 2011
Applied to tuition: Yes   **Refundable:** Yes
Refundable by: May 15, 2011

Estimated number of new entrants: 118
EDP: 15, special program: n/a

Start Month/Year: July 29, 2011

Interview Format: Two closed file and one open file, non-stress interviews. Regional interviews are not available. Video interviews are not available.

Other Programs

PREPARATORY PROGRAMS
Postbaccalaureate Program: No
Summer Program: Yes, www.sh.lsuhsc.edu/multicultural/front.htm
Shirley Roberson, (318) 675-5049,
srober1@lsuhsc.edu

COMBINED DEGREE PROGRAMS
Baccalaureate/M.D.: No
M.D./M.P.H.: No
M.D./M.B.A.: No
M.D./J.D.: No
M.D./Ph.D.: Yes, www.admissions.lsuhsc.edu

Premedical Coursework

On-line courses accepted in fulfillment of prerequisites: No

Course	Req.	Rec.	Lab.	Hrs.	Course	Req.	Rec.	Lab.	Hrs.
Inorganic Chemistry	•		•	8	Computer Science				
Behavioral Sciences					Genetics		•		6
Biochemistry		•		6	Humanities				
Biology					Organic Chemistry	•		•	8
Biology/Zoology	•		•	8	Physics	•		•	8
Calculus					Psychology				
College English	•			6	Social Sciences				
College Mathematics					Other Science	•		•	6

Selection Factors: 2009 Accepted Applicants

Proportion of Accepted Applicants with Relevant Experience (Data Self-Reported to AMCAS®)		
Community Service/Volunteer	73%
Medically-Related Work	79%
Research	58%

Shaded bar represents school's accepted scores ranging from the 10th percentile to the 90th percentile   School Median ●   National Median ◯

Overall GPA	2.0	2.1	2.2	2.3	2.4	2.5	2.6	2.7	2.8	2.9	3.0	3.1	3.2	3.3	3.4	3.5	3.6	3.7	(3.8)	3.9	4.0
Science GPA	2.0	2.1	2.2	2.3	2.4	2.5	2.6	2.7	2.8	2.9	3.0	3.1	3.2	3.3	3.4	3.5	3.6	(3.7)	3.8	3.9	4.0

MCAT® Total Numeric Score 9 10 11 12 13 14 15 16 17 18 19 20 21 22 23 24 25 26 27 (28) 29 30 31 (32) 33 34 35 36 37 38 39 40 41 42 43

Writing Sample				J	K	L	M	N	(O)	P	(Q)	R	S	T
Verbal Reasoning	3	4	5	6	7	8	(9)	(10)	11	12	13	14	15
Biological Sciences	3	4	5	6	7	8	9	(10)	(11)	12	13	14	15
Physical Sciences	3	4	5	6	7	8	(9)	10	(11)	12	13	14	15

Acceptance & Matriculation Data for 2009–2010 First Year Class

	Resident	Non-resident	International	Total
Applications	569	106	6	681
Interviewed	234	2	0	236
Deferred	5	0	0	5
Matriculants				
Early Assurance Program	0	0	0	0
Early Decision Program	10	0	0	10
Baccalaureate/M.D.	0	0	0	0
M.D./Ph.D.	0	0	0	0
Matriculated	117	0	0	**117**

Applications accepted from International Applicants: No

Specialty Choice

2005, 2006, 2007 Graduates, Specialty Choice (As reported by program directors to GME Track™)	
Anesthesiology	4%
Emergency Medicine	8%
Family Practice	11%
Internal Medicine	12%
Obstetrics/Gynecology	8%
Orthopaedic Surgery	3%
Pediatrics	8%
Psychiatry	3%
Radiology	6%
Surgery	10%

Matriculant Demographics: 2009–2010 First Year Class

Men: 68   **Women:** 49

Matriculants' Self-Reported Race/Ethnicity

Mexican American	0	Korean	0
Cuban	0	Vietnamese	1
Puerto Rican	0	Other Asian	1
Other Hispanic	2	Total Asian	12
Total Hispanic	2	Native American	0
Chinese	3	Black	6
Asian Indian	6	Native Hawaiian	0
Pakistani	1	White	99
Filipino	0	Unduplicated Number	
Japanese	0	of Matriculants	117

Science and Math Majors: 86%
Matriculants with:
   Baccalaureate degree: 100%
   Graduate degree(s): 9%

Financial Information

Source: 2008-2009 LCME I-B survey and 2009-2010 AAMC TSF questionnaire

	Residents	Non-residents
Total Cost of Attendance	$ 37,665	$ 53,262
Tuition and Fees	$ 12,033	$ 27,630
Other (includes living expenses)	$ 24,050	$ 24,050
Health Insurance (can be waived)	$ 1,582	$ 1,582

Average 2009 Graduate Indebtedness: $120,625
% of Enrolled Students Receiving Aid: 84%

Criminal Background Check

This medical school requires a criminal background check prior to matriculation.

Tulane University
School of Medicine

New Orleans, Louisiana

Office of Admissions and Student Affairs
Tulane University School of Medicine
1430 Tulane Avenue, SL67
New Orleans, Louisiana 70112-2699
T 504 988 5187   **F** 504 988 6462

Admissions www.mcl.tulane.edu/admissions
Main www.mcl.tulane.edu
Financial www.finaidhsc.tulane.edu
E-mail medsch@tulane.edu

Private Institution

Dr. Benjamin Sachs, Dean

Dr. Marc J. Kahn, Senior Associate Dean for Admissions and Student Affairs

Dr. Ernest Sneed, Assistant Dean for Student Affairs

Dr. Barbara S. Beckman, Associate Dean for Admissions

Michael T. Goodman, Director of Financial Aid

General Information

Tulane University School of Medicine, a private, nonsectarian institution, was founded in 1834. Today it is one of the eleven colleges comprising Tulane University and is the 15th oldest medical school in the United States.

Mission Statement

Tulane has a rich tradition of education characterized by an environment that is both supportive and enriching in every sense. It strives to present the ideal environment for preparing students to be expert and compassionate clinicians.

Curricular Highlights

Community Service Requirement: Required.
Research/Thesis Requirement: Optional.

Tulane School of Medicine offers a four-year program leading to the M.D. degree. While the emphasis in the first two years is on the principles of the basic medical sciences, the goal of the first two years is helping students develop clinical problem-solving skills instead of emphasizing the transmission of facts devoid of clinical context. The program in Foundations in Medicine, which spans the first two years, is responsible for instructing students in the complex art and science of the patient-doctor interaction. This objective is accomplished through lectures, small-group discussions, clinical demonstrations, visits to community health facilities, and interactions with both real patients and individuals trained as patient instructors. The third and fourth years provide experience in clinical settings where the emphasis is on patient care and community health. Flexibility is attained throughout the four years by designating approximately one-

third of scheduled curriculum time for elective courses and selected advanced studies. The curriculum is under constant review by faculty and students. Tulane offers a wide variety of support systems for medical students, including test-taking skills workshops.

USMLE

Step 1: Required. Students must record a passing score for promotion.
Step 2: Clinical Skills (CS): Required. Students must record a passing total score to graduate.
Step 2: Clinical Knowledge (CK): Required. Students must record a passing total score to graduate.

Selection Factors

In evaluating applicants, the Committee on Admissions relies on such criteria as grade point averages, MCAT scores, faculty appraisals from the applicant's college, special accomplishments and talents, and the substance and level of courses taken in a particular college. Tulane has not established mandatory minimal MCAT or GPA scores, as all components of the application, cognitive and non-cognitive, are taken into account.

Financial Aid

Scholarships and loans (federal, private, and Tulane programs) are available to students based on an analysis of the individual's financial needs. Additionally, each year approximately 30 students are awarded scholarships, which are based exclusively upon academic merit.

Information about Diversity Programs

Tulane encourages qualified disadvantaged students and students from groups underrepresented in medicine to apply. Special activities available for, but not limited to, students from groups underrepresented in medicine include tutorial and counseling services for students in medical school. The diversity in composition of the members of the Committee on Admissions is reflected in the composition of the medical student body.

Campus Information

Setting
Tulane University School of Medicine is located in downtown New Orleans, a few blocks from the New Orleans Superdome and the French Quarter.

Enrollment
For 2009, total enrollment was: 707

Special Features
The School of Medicine and the Tulane University Hospital and Clinic are two components of the Tulane University Health Sciences Center. Other components of the Center include: the School of Public Health and Tropical Medicine, the Tulane/Xavier Center for Bioenvironmental Research, the Tulane National Primate Research Center, and the F. Edward Hebert Research Center. Twelve Centers of Excellence include the Depaul-Tulane Behavioral Health Center, Tulane Cancer Center, Tulane Center for Abdominal Transplant, Tulane Institute of Sports Medicine, Tulane-Xavier National Women's Center, Tulane Center for Gene Therapy, and Tulane Cardio-Vascular Center of Excellence.

Housing
Reasonably priced housing of all kinds is widely available, including the Deming Pavilion student residence, which is adjacent to the Tulane University Hospital and Clinic and across the street from the medical school.

Satellite Campuses/Facilities
Tulane School of Medicine has affiliation agreements with more than 10 hospitals and clinics in New Orleans and other communities; three of its principal clinical teaching facilities are in close proximity to the School of Medicine: University Hospital (a Charity Hospital), Veterans Affairs Medical Center, and the Tulane University Hospital and Clinic.

Application Process and Requirements 2011–2012

Primary Application Service: AMCAS
Earliest filing date: June 1, 2010
Latest filing date: December 15, 2010

Secondary Application Required?: Yes
Sent to: All applicants
URL: www.som.tulane.edu/departments/admissions/
Fee: Yes, $100   **Waiver available:** No
Earliest filing date: June 1, 2010
Latest filing date: January 15, 2011

MCAT® required?: Yes
Latest MCAT® considered: August 2010
Oldest MCAT® considered: August 2007

Early Decision Program: School does have EDP
Applicants notified: October 1, 2010
EDP available for: Both Residents and Non-residents

Regular Acceptance Notice
Earliest date: October 15, 2010
Latest date: Until class is full
Applicant's Response to Acceptance Offer – Maximum Time: Two weeks

Requests for Deferred Entrance Considered: Yes

Deposit to Hold Place in Class: Yes
Deposit (Resident): $500   **(Non-resident):** $500
Deposit due: May 15, 2011
Applied to tuition: Yes   **Refundable:** Yes
Refundable by: May 15, 2011

Estimated number of new entrants: 200
EDP: 10, special program: n/a

Start Month/Year: August 2011

Interview Format: Selected applicants are invited for interviews. Regional interviews are not available. Video interviews are not available.

Other Programs

PREPARATORY PROGRAMS
Postbaccalaureate Program: Yes,
www.som.tulane.edu/departments/scb
Summer Program: No
Master of Science in Pharmacology:
www.pharmacology.tulane.edu
Master of Science in Genetics:
www.som.tulane.edu/human_genetics/masters.html

COMBINED DEGREE PROGRAMS
Baccalaureate/M.D.: Yes, http://tulane.edu/som/admissions/faqs.cfm
M.D./M.P.H.: Yes, http://sph.tulane.edu/mdmph
M.D./M.B.A.: Yes, : http://tulane.edu/som/admissions/special-programs.cfm
M.D./J.D.: Yes, http://tulane.edu/som/admissions/special-programs.cfm
M.D./Ph.D.: Yes, www.som.tulane.edu/psp
James E. Robinson, M.D., (504) 988-5422, jrobinso@tulane.edu

Premedical Coursework

On-line courses accepted in fulfillment of prerequisites: No

Course	Req.	Rec.	Lab.	Hrs.
Inorganic Chemistry	•		•	6
Behavioral Sciences				
Biochemistry				
Biology				
Biology/Zoology	•		•	6
Calculus				
College English	•			6
College Mathematics				

Course	Req.	Rec.	Lab.	Hrs.
Computer Science				
Genetics				
Humanities				
Organic Chemistry	•		•	6
Physics	•		•	6
Psychology				
Social Sciences				
Other				

Selection Factors: 2009 Accepted Applicants

Proportion of Accepted Applicants with Relevant Experience (Data Self-Reported to AMCAS)		
Community Service/Volunteer		73%
Medically-Related Work		85%
Research		80%

Shaded bar represents school's accepted scores ranging from the 10th percentile to the 90th percentile   School Median ● National Median ○

Overall GPA 2.0 2.1 2.2 2.3 2.4 2.5 2.6 2.7 2.8 2.9 3.0 3.1 3.2 3.3 3.4 3.5 ⟨3.6⟩ 3.7 3.8 3.9 4.0
Science GPA 2.0 2.1 2.2 2.3 2.4 2.5 2.6 2.7 2.8 2.9 3.0 3.1 3.2 3.3 3.4 ⟨3.5⟩ 3.6 3.7 3.8 3.9 4.0

MCAT® Total Numeric Score 9 10 11 12 13 14 15 16 17 18 19 20 21 22 23 24 25 26 27 28 29 30 ㉛㉜ 33 34 35 36 37 38 39 40 41 42 43

		J	K	L	M	N	O	P	Q	R	S	T
Writing Sample									⟨Q⟩			
Verbal Reasoning	3	4	5	6	7	8	9	⑩	11	12	13	14	15
Biological Sciences	3	4	5	6	7	8	9	10	⑪	12	13	14	15
Physical Sciences	3	4	5	6	7	8	9	⑩	⑪	12	13	14	15

Acceptance & Matriculation Data for 2009–2010 First Year Class

	Resident	Non-resident	International	Total
Applications	502	8636	293	9431
Interviewed	76	443	12	531
Deferred	0	3	1	4
Matriculants				
Early Assurance Program	0	1	0	1
Early Decision Program	6	24	0	30
Baccalaureate/M.D.	0	0	0	0
M.D./Ph.D.	0	0	0	0
Matriculated	27	147	3	**177**

Applications accepted from International Applicants: Yes

Specialty Choice

2005, 2006, 2007 Graduates, Specialty Choice (As reported by program directors to GME Track™)	
Anesthesiology	5%
Emergency Medicine	7%
Family Practice	7%
Internal Medicine	15%
Obstetrics/Gynecology	5%
Orthopaedic Surgery	4%
Pediatrics	9%
Psychiatry	4%
Radiology	6%
Surgery	6%

Matriculant Demographics: 2009–2010 First Year Class

Men: 101   **Women:** 76

Matriculants' Self-Reported Race/Ethnicity

Mexican American	1	Korean	8
Cuban	0	Vietnamese	1
Puerto Rican	2	Other Asian	3
Other Hispanic	2	Total Asian	38
Total Hispanic	5	Native American	1
Chinese	14	Black	2
Asian Indian	11	Native Hawaiian	0
Pakistani	1	White	130
Filipino	0	Unduplicated Number	
Japanese	2	of Matriculants	177

Science and Math Majors: 56%
Matriculants with:
        Baccalaureate degree: 100%
        Graduate degree(s): 27%

Financial Information
Source: 2008-2009 LCME I-B survey and 2009-2010 AAMC TSF questionnaire

	Residents	Non-residents
Total Cost of Attendance	$ 70,677	$ 70,677
Tuition and Fees	$ 49,666	$ 49,666
Other (includes living expenses)	$ 19,257	$ 19,257
Health Insurance (can be waived)	$ 1,754	$ 1,754

Average 2009 Graduate Indebtedness: $190,364
% of Enrolled Students Receiving Aid: 86%

Criminal Background Check

This medical school does not require a criminal background check prior to matriculation.

Johns Hopkins University School of Medicine

Baltimore, Maryland

Committee on Admissions
Johns Hopkins University School of Medicine
733 North Broadway, Suite G-49
Baltimore, Maryland 21205
T 410 955 3182   **F** 410 955 7494

Admissions www.hopkinsmedicine.org/admissions
Main www.hopkinsmedicine.org/som
Financial www.hopkinsmedicine.org/ admissions/financialaid
E-mail somadmiss@jhmi.edu

Private Institution

Dr. Edward D. Miller, Dean and Chief Executive Officer

Dr. James L. Weiss, Associate Dean for Admissions

Dr. Thomas Koenig, Associate Dean for Student Affairs

Dr. Daniel H. Teraguchi, Assistant Dean for Student Affairs

Hermione M. Hicks, Assistant Dean for Admissions

Terra Jones, Director, Student Financial Aid Services

General Information

Johns Hopkins University School of Medicine, founded in 1893, is a private, nondenominational institution which fosters the training of medical practitioners, teachers, and biomedical scientists. The medical center provides library facilities, the Reed Residence Hall, off-campus housing assistance, cafeterias, recreational sports in the Cooley Center, and performing arts programs. Preclinical courses are given in the adjacent basic science complex. Medical care facilities such as the Johns Hopkins Hospital and the Outpatient Center provide an extensive and diverse patient base for the teaching of all clinical subjects. Students also attend educational programs conducted at community hospitals in Baltimore and pursue elective experiences at other medical schools in the U.S. and foreign countries.

Mission Statement

The Johns Hopkins University School of Medicine is dedicated to preparing students to practice compassionate medicine of the highest standards and to contributing to the advancement of medical knowledge.

Curricular Highlights

Community Service Requirement: Optional.
Research/Thesis Requirement: Encouraged. Exceptional research opportunities are available.

The curriculum provides sound foundations in basic sciences and clinical medicine while retaining the flexibility required for students to identify and develop diverse career interests. In lieu of letter grades, the grading system the first two years is pass/fail. Third and fourth year students' grades are honors, high pass, pass or fail. The M.D. program includes the integration of basic sciences and clinical experiences and the expanded use of case-based, small-group learning sessions. Students learn the medical interview and basic physical examination in the first months of medical school, and working with community physicians practices through years 1 and 2. For more information, see www.hopkinsmedicine.org. First-year includes integrated coverage of introductory basic sciences, neuroscience, epidemiology, and introduction to clinical medicine. Second-year includes the study of advanced basic sciences, behavioral sciences, clinical skills, and beginning clerkships. In the third and fourth-years, with the assistance of faculty advisors, students develop individualized programs incorporating required clerkships in major clinical areas and electives. Students may use electives for specialized clerkships, research, and public health experiences.

USMLE

Step 1: Required. Students must only record a score.
Step 2: Clinical Skills (CS): Required. Students must only record a score.
Step 2: Clinical Knowledge (CK): Required. Students must only record a score.

Selection Factors

A Bachelor's degree is required in addition to proven academic competence, previous achievements and activities help the Committee on Admissions to evaluate applicants' suitability for medicine. Applicants who have unusual talents, strong humanistic qualities, demonstrated leadership, and creative abilities are sought. There are no residency requirements and international students are encouraged to apply. Students matriculating at Hopkins are required to undergo a criminal background check. Due to space limitations, Hopkins does not admit transfer students. JHU complies with federal and state laws prohibiting discrimination.

Financial Aid

Financial aid in the form of federal and institutional grants and loans is awarded solely on the basis of need. Financial considerations do not influence admission decisions. Parents' financial information is required of all students requesting institutional aid. Students' awards fully meet their demonstrated financial need. The cost for living expenses is based on a 12-month budget. Student fellowship stipends are frequently available for projects carried out in summers. Non-U.S. citizens without permanent resident or immigrant visa status are not eligible to receive financial aid. International students must establish an escrow account currently in the amount of $270,000 and subject to change.

Information about Diversity Programs

Johns Hopkins is committed to enrolling a diverse student population with a passion for improving health locally and on a global scale. Hopkins has an excellect record of enrolling high quality students from disadvantaged backgrounds and/or are underrepresented in medicine. Contact the assistant dean for student affairs for more information.

Campus Information

Setting

The School of Medicine is located in east Baltimore, 20 minutes by car from the undergraduate campus and a short walk from the Inner Harbor. The medical campus includes the Schools of Public Health, Nursing, and Johns Hopkins Hospital. The 44-acre campus is accessible by subway and a free Hopkins'shuttle provided to students and faculty.

Enrollment

For 2009, total enrollment was: 480

Housing

Students may live in Reed Hall, the primary residence for the School of Medicine. Students also live throughout Baltimore, where rental costs can be relatively low.

Regional/Satellite Campuses

In addition to the Johns Hopkins Hospital, students may also serve their clinical rotations at the Bayview Medical Center, located three miles from the main medical campus.

Application Process and Requirements 2011–2012

Primary Application Service: AMCAS
Earliest filing date: June 1, 2010
Latest filing date: October 15, 2010

Secondary Application Required?: Yes
Sent to: All applicants
URL: www.hopkinsmedicine.org/admissions
Fee: Yes, $80   **Waiver available:** Yes
Earliest filing date: June 1, 2010
Latest filing date: December 1, 2010

MCAT® required?: Yes
Latest MCAT® considered: September 2010
Oldest MCAT® considered: 2007

Early Decision Program: School does not have EDP
Applicants notified: n/a
EDP available for: n/a

Regular Acceptance Notice
Earliest date: October 15, 2010
Latest date: Varies
Applicant's Response to Acceptance Offer – Maximum Time: Three weeks

Requests for Deferred Entrance Considered: Yes

Deposit to Hold Place in Class: No
Deposit (Resident): n/a   **(Non-resident):** n/a
Deposit due: n/a
Applied to tuition: n/a   **Refundable:** n/a
Refundable by: n/a

Estimated number of new entrants: 120

EDP: 0, special program: n/a

Start Month/Year: August 2011

Interview Format: Interviews are one-one-one. Regional interview available in limited areas. Video interviews are not available.

Other Programs

PREPARATORY PROGRAMS
Postbaccalaureate Program: Yes, www.jhu.edu/postbac/
Summer Program: No

COMBINED DEGREE PROGRAMS
Baccalaureate/M.D.: No
M.D./M.P.H.: No
M.D./M.B.A.: No
M.D./J.D.: No
M.D./Ph.D.: Yes, www.hopkinsmedicine.org/admissions/dualdegree.html, Sharon Welling, (410) 955-8543, swellin1@jhmi.edu

Premedical Coursework

On-line courses accepted in fulfillment of prerequisites: No

Course	Req.	Rec.	Lab.	Hrs.
Inorganic Chemistry	•		•	8
Behavioral Sciences				
Biochemistry				
Biology	•		•	8
Biology/Zoology				
Calculus	•			3-4
College English				
College Mathematics				
Computer Science		•		

Course	Req.	Rec.	Lab.	Hrs.
Genetics				
Humanities				
Organic Chemistry	•		•	4
Physics	•		•	8
Psychology				
Social Sciences				
Humanities, Social & Behavioral Sciences	•			24
Calculus/Statistics	•			6-8
Organic/Bio Chemistry	•		•	4

Selection Factors: 2009 Accepted Applicants

Proportion of Accepted Applicants with Relevant Experience (Data Self-Reported to AMCAS)		
Community Service/Volunteer		78%
Medically-Related Work		91%
Research		94%

Shaded bar represents school's accepted scores ranging from the 10th percentile to the 90th percentile   **School Median** ●   **National Median** ○

Overall GPA	2.0	2.1	2.2	2.3	2.4	2.5	2.6	2.7	2.8	2.9	3.0	3.1	3.2	3.3	3.4	3.5	3.6	3.7	3.8	(3.9) 4.0
Science GPA	2.0	2.1	2.2	2.3	2.4	2.5	2.6	2.7	2.8	2.9	3.0	3.1	3.2	3.3	3.4	3.5	3.6	3.7	3.8	(3.9) 4.0

MCAT® Total Numeric Score 9 10 11 12 13 14 15 16 17 18 19 20 21 22 23 24 25 26 27 28 29 30 31 (32) 33 34 35 (36) 37 38 39 40 41 42 43

Writing Sample			J	K	L	M	N	O	P	(Q) (R) S T
Verbal Reasoning	3	4	5	6	7	8	9	(10)	(11)	12 13 14 15
Biological Sciences	3	4	5	6	7	8	9	10	(11)	12 (13) 14 15
Physical Sciences	3	4	5	6	7	8	9	10	(11)	(12) 13 14 15

Acceptance & Matriculation Data for 2009–2010 First Year Class

	Resident	Non-resident	International	Total
Applications	389	4973	299	5661
Interviewed	97	632	30	759
Deferred	2	5	0	7
Matriculants				
Early Assurance Program	0	0	0	0
Early Decision Program	0	0	0	0
Baccalaureate/M.D.	0	0	0	0
M.D./Ph.D.	1	15	1	17
Matriculated	23	93	4	**120**

Applications accepted from International Applicants: Yes

Matriculant Demographics: 2009–2010 First Year Class

Men: 63   **Women:** 57

Matriculants' Self-Reported Race/Ethnicity

Mexican American	2	Korean	2
Cuban	1	Vietnamese	0
Puerto Rican	1	Other Asian	5
Other Hispanic	3	Total Asian	41
Total Hispanic	7	Native American	0
Chinese	16	Black	11
Asian Indian	17	Native Hawaiian	0
Pakistani	0	White	58
Filipino	2	Unduplicated Number	
Japanese	0	of Matriculants	120

Science and Math Majors: 66%
Matriculants with:
     Baccalaureate degree: 100%
     Graduate degree(s): 10%

Specialty Choice

2005, 2006, 2007 Graduates, Specialty Choice (As reported by program directors to GME Track™)	
Anesthesiology	5%
Emergency Medicine	9%
Family Practice	2%
Internal Medicine	19%
Obstetrics/Gynecology	1%
Orthopaedic Surgery	4%
Pediatrics	10%
Psychiatry	4%
Radiology	7%
Surgery	4%

Financial Information

Source: 2008-2009 LCME I-B survey and 2009-2010 AAMC TSF questionnaire

	Residents	Non-residents
Total Cost of Attendance	$ 61,356	$ 61,356
Tuition and Fees	$ 40,608	$ 40,608
Other (includes living expenses)	$ 17,736	$ 17,736
Health Insurance (can be waived)	$ 3,012	$ 3,012

Average 2009 Graduate Indebtedness: $94,717
% of Enrolled Students Receiving Aid: 79%

Criminal Background Check

This medical school requires a criminal background check prior to matriculation.

Uniformed Services University of the Health Sciences F. Edward Hébert School of Medicine

Bethesda, Maryland

Admissions Office, Room A-1041
Uniformed Services University of the Health
Sciences F. Edward Hébert School of Medicine
4301 Jones Bridge Road
Bethesda, Maryland 20814-4799
T 301 295 3101 **F** 301 295 3545

Admissions www.usuhs.mil/admissions.html
Main www.usuhs.mil
Financial n/a
E-mail admissions@usuhs.mil

Public Institution

Dr. Larry W. Laughlin, M.D., Ph.D., Dean

Dr. Margaret Calloway, M.D., CAPT, MC, USN, Associate Dean for Recruitment and Admissions

Joan C. Stearman, M.S.W., Director, Office of Admissions

General Information

Created by public law in 1972, the Uniformed Services University of the Health Sciences (USUHS) was founded to prepare young men and women for careers as health care professionals in the uniformed services. The school's charter is to provide a comprehensive education in medicine and to select individuals who demonstrate potential for and commitment to careers as medical officers in the uniformed services.

Mission Statement

USUHS is the nation's federal health sciences university and is committed to excellence in military medicine and public health during peace and war. Our mission is to provide the nation with health professionals dedicated to career service in the Department of Defense and the United States Public Health Service and with scientists who serve the common good.

Curricular Highlights

Community Service Requirement: Optional.
Research/Thesis Requirement: Optional.

The school has a four-year program culminating in the doctor of medicine degree. Basic science instruction predominates the initial two academic years, with the final two years devoted to clinical education. Basic science instruction is correlated both interdisciplinarily and clinically. The integration between the clinical and basic sciences is progressive and proceeds with involvement in patient care activities early in the curriculum, starting with the first semester of the first year. The overall program is designed to educate students to serve as providers of primary health care. The curriculum also includes basic military orientation and concentration on unique aspects of military medicine. A conventional letter grading system is used.

USMLE

Step 1: Required. Students must record a passing score for graduation, but not promotion.
Step 2: Clinical Skills (CS): Required. Students must record a passing total score to graduate.
Step 2: Clinical Knowledge (CK): Required. Students must record a passing total score to graduate.

Selection Factors

The school employs a three-stage, progressive screening process for selecting entrants. The first stage consists of the submission of an AMCAS application; the second, the submission of supplementary materials; and the third, personal interviews, which are conducted on campus. Advancement in the process is competitive, based on candidates' personal and intellectual characteristics. The Admissions Committee does not discriminate on the basis of sex, race, religion, marital status, or national origin.

Financial Aid

Upon entering the first-year class of the School of Medicine, a student is commissioned and serves on active duty in the grade of Second Lieutenant in the Army or Air Force or an Ensign in the Navy or Public Health Service, receiving the pay and benefits of that grade. The time spent in medical school is not creditable toward retirement until retirement eligibility has been established. At graduation, students are promoted to Captain in the Air Force or Army or Lieutenant in the Navy and PHS upon receipt of the M.D. degree. Graduates are obligated to serve as active duty medical officers for not less than seven years, as well as six years inactive ready reserve. The period of time spent in internship or residency training is not acceptable toward satisfying the seven-year obligation. If a student is dropped from the program for any reason may be required to perform active duty for a period of time equal to the time spent in the program. A disenrolled student may be required to reimburse the government for tuition and fees. However, one year will be the minimum required active duty for persons separated from the school, regardless of the time spent in the program.

Information about Diversity Programs

The Office of Recruitment and Admissions is instrumental in the recruitment and retention of a student body that mirrors the diversity of our nation. We provide a welcoming environment to all students by encouraging expression of their diverse ethnic, cultural, economic, and experiential backgrounds. Competitive applicants from groups underrepresented in medicine are encouraged to apply. The application/admissions processes are the same for all students. The staff supports all students during the four years of medical school, recognizing that each student's unique circumstances may require various levels of support and encouragement. The learning environment is enhanced by four key student-sponsored groups: Women in Medicine and Science, the Asian Pacific American Medical Student Association, the Latino Medical Student Association, and the Student National Medical Association. Faculty support is provided by the Office of Recruitment and Admissions to advance the community outreach efforts of these student groups.

Campus Information

Setting

Our university is located outside the Nation's Capital, close to the NIH and the National Library of Medicine. We are located near public transportation, shopping, dining, and recreational facilities.

Enrollment

For 2009, total enrollment was: 681

Special Features

The University's nationally ranked military and civilian faculty conduct cutting edge research in the biomedical sciences, combat casualty care and infectious diseases.

Housing

As on-campus housing is not available, students are provided a non-taxable housing allowance.

Application Process and Requirements 2011–2012

Primary Application Service: AMCAS
Earliest filing date: June 1, 2010
Latest filing date: November 15, 2010

Secondary Application Required?: Yes
Sent to: All applicants
Contact: (301) 295-3101, admissions@usuhs.mil
Fee: No   **Waiver available:** n/a
Earliest filing date: June 1, 2010
Latest filing date: December 15, 2010

MCAT® required?: Yes
Latest MCAT® considered: September 2010
Oldest MCAT® considered: April 2008

Early Decision Program: School does not have EDP
Applicants notified: n/a
EDP available for: n/a

Regular Acceptance Notice
Earliest date: October 16, 2010
Latest date: Until class is full
Applicant's Response to Acceptance
Offer – Maximum Time: Two weeks

Requests for Deferred
Entrance Considered: Yes

Deposit to Hold Place in Class: No
Deposit (Resident): n/a   **(Non-resident):** n/a
Deposit due: n/a
Applied to tuition: n/a   **Refundable:** n/a
Refundable by: n/a

Estimated number of new entrants: 171
EDP: 0, special program: n/a

Start Month/Year: June 2011

Interview Format: Two thirty-minute interviews with medical corps officers. Regional interviews are not available. Video interviews are not available.

Other Programs

PREPARATORY PROGRAMS
Postbaccalaureate Program: No
Summer Program: No

COMBINED DEGREE PROGRAMS
Baccalaureate/M.D.: No
M.D./M.P.H.: No
M.D./M.B.A.: No
M.D./J.D.: No
M.D./Ph.D.: Yes, Dr. Eleanor Metcalf, (301) 295-3913, emetcalf@usuhs.mil, http://cim.usuhs.mil/geo/mdphd.htm

Premedical Coursework

On-line courses accepted in fulfillment of prerequisites: No

Course	Req.	Rec.	Lab.	Hrs.	Course	Req.	Rec.	Lab.	Hrs.
Inorganic Chemistry	•		•	8	Computer Science				
Behavioral Sciences					Genetics				
Biochemistry					Humanities				
Biology	•		•	8	Organic Chemistry	•		•	8
Biology/Zoology					Physics	•		•	8
Calculus	•			3	Psychology				
College English	•			6	Social Sciences				
College Mathematics					Other				

Selection Factors: 2009 Accepted Applicants

Proportion of Accepted Applicants with Relevant Experience (Data Self-Reported to AMCAS®)		Community Service/Volunteer	65%
		Medically-Related Work	84%
		Research	68%

Shaded bar represents school's accepted scores ranging from the 10th percentile to the 90th percentile. School Median ⬤   National Median ◯

Overall GPA	2.0	2.1	2.2	2.3	2.4	2.5	2.6	2.7	2.8	2.9	3.0	3.1	3.2	3.3	3.4	3.5	(3.6)	3.7	3.8	3.9	4.0
Science GPA	2.0	2.1	2.2	2.3	2.4	2.5	2.6	2.7	2.8	2.9	3.0	3.1	3.2	3.3	3.4	(3.5)	3.6	3.7	3.8	3.9	4.0

MCAT® Total Numeric Score 9 10 11 12 13 14 15 16 17 18 19 20 21 22 23 24 25 26 27 28 29 ㉚ 31 ㉜ 33 34 35 36 37 38 39 40 41 42 43

	J	K	L	M	N	O	Ⓟ	Ⓠ	R	S	T
Writing Sample							Ⓟ	Ⓠ			
Verbal Reasoning	3	4	5	6	7	8	9	⑩	11	12	13	14	15
Biological Sciences	3	4	5	6	7	8	9	⑩	⑪	12	13	14	15
Physical Sciences	3	4	5	6	7	8	9	⑩	⑪	12	13	14	15

Acceptance & Matriculation Data for 2009–2010 First Year Class

	Resident	Non-resident	International	Total
Applications	126	2212	5	2343
Interviewed	47	519	0	566
Deferred	0	2	0	2
Matriculants				
Early Assurance Program	0	0	0	0
Early Decision Program	0	0	0	0
Baccalaureate/M.D.	0	0	0	0
M.D./Ph.D.	0	2	0	2
Matriculated	12	160	0	**172**

Applications accepted from International Applicants: No

Matriculant Demographics: 2009–2010 First Year Class

Men: 126   **Women:** 46

Matriculants' Self-Reported Race/Ethnicity

Mexican American	4	Korean	7
Cuban	0	Vietnamese	3
Puerto Rican	0	Other Asian	2
Other Hispanic	2	Total Asian	28
Total Hispanic	6	Native American	1
Chinese	8	Black	5
Asian Indian	3	Native Hawaiian	0
Pakistani	0	White	127
Filipino	3	Unduplicated Number	
Japanese	2	of Matriculants	172

Science and Math Majors: 67%
Matriculants with:
Baccalaureate degree: 100%
Graduate degree(s): 16%

Specialty Choice

2005, 2006, 2007 Graduates, Specialty Choice
(As reported by program directors to GME Track™)

Anesthesiology	3%
Emergency Medicine	3%
Family Practice	10%
Internal Medicine	6%
Obstetrics/Gynecology	3%
Orthopaedic Surgery	3%
Pediatrics	7%
Psychiatry	4%
Radiology	3%
Surgery	5%

Financial Information

Source: 2008-2009 LCME I-B survey and 2009-2010 AAMC TSF questionnaire

	Residents	Non-residents
Total Cost of Attendance	$ 0	$ 0
Tuition and Fees	$ 0	$ 0
Other (includes living expenses)	$ 0	$ 0
Health Insurance (can be waived)	$ 0	$ 0

Average 2009 Graduate Indebtedness: $0
% of Enrolled Students Receiving Aid: 0%

Criminal Background Check

This medical school requires a criminal background check prior to matriculation.

University of Maryland School of Medicine

Baltimore, Maryland

Committee on Admissions, Suite 190
University of Maryland School of Medicine
685 West Baltimore Street
Baltimore, Maryland 21201-1559
T 410 706 7478 **F** 410 706 0467

Admissions www.medschool.umaryland.edu/admissions
Main www.medschool.umaryland.edu
Financial www.umaryland.edu/fin
E-mail admissions@som.umaryland.edu

Public Institution

Dr. E. Albert Reece, Dean

Dr. Milford M. Foxwell Jr.,
Associate Dean for Admissions

Patricia Scott, Director of Financial Aid

Dr. Donna L. Parker, Associate Dean
for Student Affairs

General Information

Organized in 1807, The University of Maryland School of Medicine is the nation's oldest public medical college. The first class was graduated in 1810. Among the first to erect its own hospital for clinical instruction, the university also established the first intramural residency for senior students.

Mission Statement

The University of Maryland School of Medicine is dedicated to providing excellence in biomedical education, basic and clinical research, quality patient care, and service to improve the health of the citizens of Maryland and beyond. The School is committed to the education and training of M.D., M.D/M.P.H., M.D./Ph.D., M.D./MBA, M.D./M.S. in BioEngineering, graduate, physical therapy, and medical research technology students. The school will recruit and develop faculty to serve as exemplary role models for our students.

Curricular Highlights

Community Service Requirement: Optional.
Research/Thesis Requirement: Optional.

During the first two years of medical school the basic sciences are integrated and taught as systems, using interdisciplinary teaching by both basic and clinical science faculty. Mornings include lecture and small group sessions; afternoons are devoted to independent study. Curricular materials are available online and laptop computers are required. "Introduction to Clinical Medicine" begins early in the first year and continues through year two, offering instruction in clinical diagnosis, intimate human behavior, problem-based learning, biomedical ethics and dynamics of ambulatory care. Clinical clerkships during the last two years include a month in family medicine and an emphasis on ambulatory teaching in other disciplines and two months of subinternship.

USMLE

Step 1: Required. Students must record a passing score for promotion.
Step 2: Clinical Skills (CS): Required. Students must only record a score.
Step 2: Clinical Knowledge (CK): Required. Students must only record a score.

Selection Factors

Applications are accepted from citizens and permanent residents of the U.S. and citizens of Canada. All AMCAS applicants are invited to submit a Stage II application. Selection of students is based on careful appraisal of character, motivation for medicine, academic achievement, MCAT scores, letters of reference, extracurricular activities and interviews. The University does not discriminate on the basis of race, creed, sex, national origin, age or handicap.

Financial Aid

Scholarships and loans are available for students with demonstrable need. The amount of the award may vary according to need and the level of funding available.

Information about Diversity Programs

The School of Medicine values diversity very highly in the educational process and is committed to the recruitment and retention of talented students from underrepresented and disadvantaged backgrounds. A major focus of our recruitment efforts is to provide information on admissions requirements and preparation for medical school, the selection process, and educational and research opportunities at the School of Medicine. There are no fixed quotas for any group and the admissions procedures are the same for all applicants. The Office of Admissions will make a special effort to provide information that is relevant to prospective applicants in these groups. Information can be obtained from Ms. Raushanah Kareem, in the Office of Admissions.

Campus Information

Setting

The professional campus is located in downtown Baltimore within easy walking distance of the new Hippodrome Theatre, Inner Harbor, Maryland Science Center, National Aquarium and Pier 6 Pavilion. Oriole Park at Camden Yards and M&T Bank Stadium sit adjacent to campus.

Enrollment

For 2009, total enrollment was: 645

Special Features

Built in 1812, the meticulously restored Davidge Hall is the oldest building in North America in continuous use for medical education. The Health Sciences and Human Services Library is the second largest medical library building on the East Coast. Adjacent to the medical center's new Weinberg and Gudelsky clinical towers are the world-renowned Shock Trauma Center, the Baltimore Veterans Administration Medical Center, the University of Maryland Biotechnology Institute and the new UMB Biopark.

Housing

On-campus housing is available at a cost of about $700-1600/month. The new University Suites features furnished apartments plus study lounges, 24-hour security and on-site garage parking. The surrounding neighborhood provides even more choices for students, with both apartments and individual homes (townhomes) available for rent (average $800-1200/month) or purchase. The majority of our students live within walking distance of the campus, particularly during the first two years of medical school.

Satellite Campuses/Facilities

Students complete most of their junior year clinical clerkships at the University of Maryland Medical System and Baltimore Veterans Affairs Medical Center, but do rotate through several of our affiliated community hospitals for selected rotations. During the fourth year of medical school our students will see patients during their ambulatory months at physician's offices in underserved areas of Baltimore City, Western and Southern Maryland and the Eastern Shore.

Application Process and Requirements 2011–2012

Primary Application Service: AMCAS
Earliest filing date: June 1, 2010
Latest filing date: November 1, 2010

Secondary Application Required?: Yes
Sent to: All applicants
Contact: Ms. Towanda Sykes, (410) 706-7478, tsykes@som.umaryland.edu
Fee: Yes, $70 **Waiver available:** No
Earliest filing date: July 15, 2010
Latest filing date: December 15, 2010

MCAT® required?: Yes
Latest MCAT® considered: September 2010
Oldest MCAT® considered: January 2007

Early Decision Program: School does have EDP
Applicants notified: October 1, 2010
EDP available for: Both Residents and Non-residents

Regular Acceptance Notice
Earliest date: October 15, 2010
Latest date: Until class is full
Applicant's Response to Acceptance Offer – Maximum Time: Three weeks

Requests for Deferred Entrance Considered: Yes

Deposit to Hold Place in Class: No
Deposit (Resident): n/a **(Non-resident):** n/a
Deposit due: n/a
Applied to tuition: n/a **Refundable:** n/a
Refundable by: n/a

Estimated number of new entrants: 160
EDP: 5, special program: n/a

Start Month/Year: August 2011

Interview Format: Two, one-on-one interviews with faculty or student. Regional interviews are not available. Video interviews are not available.

Other Programs

PREPARATORY PROGRAMS
Postbaccalaureate Program: No
Summer Program: Yes, Dr. Sandra Dolan, (410) 706-7669, sdolan@clc.umaryland.edu

COMBINED DEGREE PROGRAMS
Baccalaureate/M.D.: No
M.D./M.P.H.: Yes, www.medschool.umaryland.edu/MD_MPH/
Dr. Jordan Warnick, (410) 706-3026, jwarnick@som.umaryland.edu
M.D./M.B.A.: Yes, Dr. Jordan Warnick, (410) 706-3026, jwarnick@som.umaryland.edu
M.D./J.D.: No
M.D./Ph.D.: Yes, Dr. Terry Rogers, (410) 706-3990, trogers@som.umaryland.edu
MD/MS BioEngineering and, MD/MPP, and MD/MBA:
Yes, Dr. Jordan Warnick, (410) 706-3026, jwarnick@som.umaryland.edu

Premedical Coursework

On-line courses accepted in fulfillment of prerequisites: No

Course	Req.	Rec.	Lab.	Hrs.
Inorganic Chemistry	•		•	8
Behavioral Sciences				
Biochemistry		•		
Biology				
Biology/Zoology	•		•	8
Calculus				
College English	•			6
College Mathematics				

Course	Req.	Rec.	Lab.	Hrs.
Computer Science		•		
Genetics		•		
Humanities		•		
Organic Chemistry	•		•	8
Physics	•		•	8
Psychology				
Social Sciences		•		
Other				

Selection Factors: 2009 Accepted Applicants

Proportion of Accepted Applicants with Relevant Experience (Data Self-Reported to AMCAS®)		
Community Service/Volunteer		72%
Medically-Related Work		87%
Research		90%

Shaded bar represents school's accepted scores ranging from the 10th percentile to the 90th percentile ▬ **School Median** ● **National Median** ○

Overall GPA	2.0	2.1	2.2	2.3	2.4	2.5	2.6	2.7	2.8	2.9	3.0	3.1	3.2	3.3	3.4	3.5	3.6	3.7	(3.8)	3.9	4.0
Science GPA	2.0	2.1	2.2	2.3	2.4	2.5	2.6	2.7	2.8	2.9	3.0	3.1	3.2	3.3	3.4	3.5	3.6	(3.7)	3.8	3.9	4.0

MCAT® Total Numeric Score 9 10 11 12 13 14 15 16 17 18 19 20 21 22 23 24 25 26 27 28 29 30 31 (32) 33 34 35 36 37 38 39 40 41 42 43

				J	K	L	M	N	O	P	(Q)	R	S	T
Writing Sample				J	K	L	M	N	O	P	(Q)	R	S	T
Verbal Reasoning	3	4	5	6	7	8	9	(10)	11	12	13	14	15
Biological Sciences	3	4	5	6	7	8	9	10	(11)	12	13	14	15
Physical Sciences	3	4	5	6	7	8	9	10	(11)	12	13	14	15

Acceptance & Matriculation Data for 2009–2010 First Year Class

	Resident	Non-resident	International	Total
Applications	823	3562	183	4568
Interviewed	310	269	15	594
Deferred	0	0	0	0
Matriculants				
Early Assurance Program	0	0	0	0
Early Decision Program	3	1	0	4
Baccalaureate/M.D.	0	0	0	0
M.D./Ph.D.	1	2	0	3
Matriculated	122	37	1	**160**

Applications accepted from International Applicants: Only Canadian

Specialty Choice

2004, 2005, 2006 Graduates Specialty Choices (As reported by program directors to GME Track™)	
Anesthesiology	5%
Emergency Medicine	9%
Family Practice	6%
Internal Medicine	22%
Obstetrics/Gynecology	4%
Orthopaedic Surgery	3%
Pediatrics	12%
Psychiatry	4%
Radiology	4%
Surgery	8%

Matriculant Demographics: 2009–2010 First Year Class

Men: 70 **Women:** 90

Matriculants' Self-Reported Race/Ethnicity

Mexican American	1	Korean	7
Cuban	0	Vietnamese	1
Puerto Rican	0	Other Asian	4
Other Hispanic	3	Total Asian	35
Total Hispanic	4	Native American	1
Chinese	8	Black	20
Asian Indian	11	Native Hawaiian	2
Pakistani	3	White	105
Filipino	1	Unduplicated Number	
Japanese	1	of Matriculants	160

Science and Math Majors: 68%
Matriculants with:
Baccalaureate degree: 100%
Graduate degree(s): 9%

Financial Information

Source: 2008-2009 LCME I-B survey and 2009-2010 AAMC TSF questionnaire

	Residents	Non-residents
Total Cost of Attendance	$ 54,759	$ 76,003
Tuition and Fees	$ 25,719	$ 45,763
Other (includes living expenses)	$ 26,736	$ 27,936
Health Insurance (can be waived)	$ 2,304	$ 2,304

Average 2009 Graduate Indebtedness: $142,795
% of Enrolled Students Receiving Aid: 82%

Criminal Background Check

This medical school does not require a criminal background check prior to matriculation.

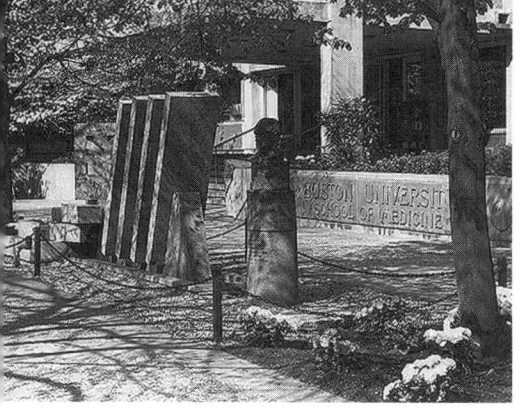

Boston University School of Medicine
Boston, Massachusetts

Admissions Office, Building L, Rm. 124
Boston University School of Medicine
72 East Concord Street
Boston, Massachusetts 02118
T 617 638 4630   **F** 617 638 4718

Admissions www.bumc.bu.edu/admissions/
Main www.bumc.bu.edu/busm/
Financial www.bumc.bu.edu/osfs
E-mail medadms@bu.edu

Private Institution

Dr. Karen Antman, Dean

Dr. Robert A. Witzburg, Associate Dean and Director of Admissions

Dr. Jonathan Woodson, Associate Dean for Diversity and Multicultural Affairs

Kathy Stavropoulos, Executive Director for Student Financial Services

Dr. Phyllis L. Carr, Associate Dean for Student Affairs

Ellen Difiore, Registrar

General Information

The New England Female Medical College, founded in 1848, was the first medical college for women in the world. In 1873 the college became the Boston University School of Medicine, the first coeducational medical school in the U.S. The current health sciences campus includes the Schools of Medicine, Dental Medicine, and Public Health, as well as the hospital, Boston Medical Center, the Division of Graduate Medical Sciences, and extensive research facilities.

Mission Statement

Boston University School of Medicine is dedicated to the educational, intellectual, professional, and personal development of a diverse group of exceptional students, trainees, and faculty who are deeply committed to the study and to the practice of medicine, to biomedical research, and to the health of the public. We, as a community, place great value on excellence, integrity, service, social justice, collegiality, equality of opportunity, and interdisciplinary collaboration.

Curricular Highlights

Community Service Requirement: Optional. Many students and faculty participate.
Research/Thesis Requirement: Optional. Thesis may be required for dual degree programs.

BUSM offers a flexible program of critical inquiry and rigorous study in the biological, social, and behavioral sciences. The early focus is on normal structure and function, unified by Integrated Problems, a clinically focused seminar.

Introduction to Clinical Medicine has students interviewing and evaluating patients from the first week. The basic sciences are linked with applications in clinical practice, emphasizing multidisciplinary, team-based learning. The second-year focus shifts to pathophysiology, with an integrated, multidisciplinary format led by preclinical and clinical faculty. The core clinical training of the third year includes clerkships in all major disciplines, with ambulatory and inpatient experience in generalist and subspecialty venues. There are also clinical electives. The fourth year includes advanced clerkships and is largely elective. Research opportunities are available in basic science and clinical disciplines, and many students choose electives in international health. Any academic year may be spread over two calendar years and students may switch into several dual degree programs.

USMLE

Step 1: Required. Students must record a passing score for promotion.
Step 2: Clinical Skills (CS): Required. Students must only record a score.
Step 2: Clinical Knowledge (CK): Required. Students must only record a score.

Selection Factors

Applicants are selected not only on the basis of academic record, recommendations, research experience, and involvement in community service, but also by qualities of personality, character, resilience, and life experience. Personal interviews are required and are offered at the discretion of the Committee on Admissions.

Financial Aid

BUSM is committed to ensuring that all accepted students can secure adequate financial resources; need-based aid is available in all years. The Office of Student Financial Services administers its portfolio of scholarships and loans, assists students in securing aid from outside sources, conducts debt management seminars, offers entrance and exit counseling, and provides student financial management information. Financial need is not considered in the admissions process. There are no special institutional financial funds disbursed for international students. Unless an international student has an I-551 or I-151 resident alien card,

federally insured loans are not available. Students may secure private educational loans with a co-applicant who is a creditworthy U.S. citizen or resident alien.

Information about Diversity Programs

BUSM is committed to diversity among faculty and students. Programs for the recruitment and support of students from groups underrepresented in medicine are managed by the Office of Admissions and the Office of Diversity and Multicultural Affairs. All applications are submitted to the Office of Admissions.

Campus Information

Setting
BU Medical Center is a beautiful urban campus, shared by clinical, educational, and research institutions. The four-square-block campus, located in the heart of Boston, is accessible by public transportation and is within walking distance of residential areas, shops, and cultural institutions.

Enrollment
For 2009, total enrollment was: 709

Special Features
Most clinical training is done at Boston Medical Center Hospital (BMC), a diverse institution with the busiest emergency department in the Northeast and large programs in ambulatory and inpatient care. BMC hosts residency programs in most disciplines. BUSM graduates pursue careers in all specialties, in full-time clinical practice and in academic centers, in rural and urban settings, all over the U.S., and in international health.

Housing
On-campus housing is limited; most students choose to live off-campus. Rents range from $650 and up, depending on location and number of roommates.

Satellite Campuses/Facilities
Basic science programs are all on-campus. Clinical training is largely on-campus, but each student has some off-campus rotations, ensuring that all students experience different venues and styles of practice. All clinical training is directly supervised by BUSM faculty.

Application Process and Requirements 2011–2012

Primary Application Service: AMCAS
Earliest filing date: June 1, 2010
Latest filing date: November 1, 2010

Secondary Application Required?: Yes
Sent to: All applicants
URL: Provided after receipt of initial application
Contact: Office of Admissions, (617) 638-4630, medadms@bu.edu
Fee: Yes, $110   **Waiver available:** Yes
Earliest filing date: June 1, 2010
Latest filing date: January 3, 2011

MCAT® required?: Yes
Latest MCAT® considered: September 2010
Oldest MCAT® considered: 2007

Early Decision Program: School does have EDP
Applicants notified: October 1, 2010
EDP available for: Both Residents and Non-residents

Regular Acceptance Notice
Earliest date: Early January 2011
Latest date: Until class is full
Applicant's Response to Acceptance Offer – Maximum Time: Two weeks

Requests for Deferred Entrance Considered: No

Deposit to Hold Place in Class: Yes
Deposit (Resident): $500   **(Non-resident):** $500
Deposit due: May 16, 2011
Applied to tuition: Yes   **Refundable:** Yes
Refundable prior to: May 15, 2010

Estimated number of new entrants: 125
EDP: 2, special program: 48

Start Month/Year: August 2011

Interview Format: On-campus interview required. Regional interviews are not available. Video interviews are not available.

Other Programs

PREPARATORY PROGRAMS
Postbaccalaureate Program: Yes, www.bu.edu/met/adult_college_programs/boston_university_metropolitan_college_undergraduate_programs/college_certificate_program/postbaccalaureate_certificate/index.html
Summer Program: No
Early Medical School Selection Program: www.bumc.bu.edu/Dept/Content.aspx?DepartmentID=45&PageID=1295, Jonathan Woodson, M.D., (617) 638-4163, Jonathan.Woodson@bmc.org
Master of Arts in Medical Sciences: Yes, http://cobalt.bumc.bu.edu/current/Catalog/medsci/intro.htm

COMBINED DEGREE PROGRAMS
Baccalaureate/M.D.: Yes, www.bu.edu/cas/forms/accelerated.pdf
M.D./M.P.H.: Yes, www.bumc.bu.edu/sph
M.D./M.B.A.: Yes, http://management.bu.edu/gpo/dual/mdmba/index.html
M.D./Ph.D.: Yes, www.bumc.bu.edu/gms

Premedical Coursework

On-line courses accepted in fulfillment of prerequisites: No

Course	Req.	Rec.	Lab.	Sems.
Inorganic Chemistry	•		•	2
Behavioral Sciences		•		2
Biochemistry		•		1
Biology	•		•	2
Biology/Zoology				
Calculus				
College English	•			2
College Mathematics		•		2
Computer Science				

Course	Req.	Rec.	Lab.	Sems.
Genetics		•		1
Humanities	•			2
Organic Chemistry	•		•	2
Physics	•			2
Psychology				
Social Sciences		•		2
Molecular Biology		•		1
Biostatistics & Epidemiology		•		1

Selection Factors: 2009 Accepted Applicants

Proportion of Accepted Applicants with Relevant Experience (Data Self-Reported to AMCAS®)		
Community Service/Volunteer		73%
Medically-Related Work		85%
Research		88%

Shaded bar represents school's accepted scores ranging from the 10th percentile to the 90th percentile   School Median ● National Median ○

Overall GPA 2.0 2.1 2.2 2.3 2.4 2.5 2.6 2.7 2.8 2.9 3.0 3.1 3.2 3.3 3.4 3.5 3.6 3.7 ⟨3.8⟩ 3.9 4.0

Science GPA 2.0 2.1 2.2 2.3 2.4 2.5 2.6 2.7 2.8 2.9 3.0 3.1 3.2 3.3 3.4 3.5 3.6 ⟨3.7⟩ 3.8 3.9 4.0

MCAT® Total Numeric Score 9 10 11 12 13 14 15 16 17 18 19 20 21 22 23 24 25 26 27 28 29 30 31 ⟨32⟩⟨33⟩ 34 35 36 37 38 39 40 41 42 43

Writing Sample				J	K	L	M	N	O	P	⟨Q⟩	R	S	T
Verbal Reasoning	3	4	5	6	7	8	9	⟨10⟩	11	12	13	14	15	
Biological Sciences	3	4	5	6	7	8	9	10	⟨11⟩	12	13	14	15	
Physical Sciences	3	4	5	6	7	8	9	10	⟨11⟩	12	13	14	15	

Acceptance & Matriculation Data for 2009–2010 First Year Class

	Resident	Non-resident	International	Total
Applications	721	9417	567	10705
Interviewed	145	933	46	1124
Deferred	0	3	0	3
Matriculants				
Early Assurance Program	7	18	0	25
Early Decision Program	1	1	0	2
Baccalaureate/M.D.	3	20	0	23
M.D./Ph.D.	1	6	0	7
Matriculated	34	136	6	**176**

Applications accepted from International Applicants: Yes

Matriculant Demographics: 2009–2010 First Year Class

Men: 80   **Women:** 96

Matriculants' Self-Reported Race/Ethnicity

Mexican American	8	Korean	7
Cuban	3	Vietnamese	2
Puerto Rican	2	Other Asian	6
Other Hispanic	7	Total Asian	60
Total Hispanic	19	Native American	0
Chinese	20	Black	12
Asian Indian	23	Native Hawaiian	1
Pakistani	4	White	92
Filipino	1	Unduplicated Number	
Japanese	1	of Matriculants	176

Science and Math Majors: 55%
Matriculants with:
  Baccalaureate degree: 100%
  Graduate degree(s): 26%

Specialty Choice

2005, 2006, 2007 Graduates, Specialty Choice (As reported by program directors to GME Track™)	
Anesthesiology	4%
Emergency Medicine	6%
Family Practice	4%
Internal Medicine	21%
Obstetrics/Gynecology	7%
Orthopaedic Surgery	3%
Pediatrics	9%
Psychiatry	2%
Radiology	7%
Surgery	8%

Financial Information

Source: 2008-2009 LCME I-B survey and 2009-2010 AAMC TSF questionnaire

	Residents	Non-residents
Total Cost of Attendance	$ 69,924	$ 69,924
Tuition and Fees	$ 47,088	$ 47,088
Other (includes living expenses)	$ 20,703	$ 20,703
Health Insurance (can be waived)	$ 2,133	$ 2,133

Average 2009 Graduate Indebtedness: $181,223
% of Enrolled Students Receiving Aid: 81%

Criminal Background Check

This medical school requires a criminal background check prior to matriculation.

Harvard Medical School
Boston, Massachusetts

Office of the Committee on Admissions
Harvard Medical School
25 Shattuck Street
306 Gordon Hall
Boston, Massachusetts 02115-6092
T 617 432 1550   **F** 617 432 3307

Admissions http://hms.harvard.edu/admissions/
Main http://hms.harvard.edu
Financial www.hms.harvard.edu/finaid/
E-mail admissions_office@hms.harvard.edu

Private Institution

Dr. Jeffrey S. Flier, Dean
of the Faculty of Medicine

Dr. Robert J. Mayer, Faculty Associate
Dean for Admissions

Dr. Alvin F. Poussaint, Associate Dean
for Student Affairs

Robert D. Coughlin, Director of Financial Aid

Joanne M. McEvoy, Director of Admissions

General Information

A leader in medical education since its inception in 1782, the Harvard Medical School forms the center of one of the nation's premier locations for medical training, research and practice. Clinical teaching is carried out in several hospitals, including Massachusetts General, Brigham and Women's, Children's Boston, Beth Israel Deaconess, Mount Auburn, and Cambridge Hospitals. The Massachusetts Mental Health Center and the McLean Hospital are psychiatric facilities. Massachusetts Eye and Ear Infirmary, the Schepens Eye Institute, and several community-based health centers provide additional opportunities for patient care, teaching, and research. Other affiliated institutions include the West Roxbury and Brockton VA Medical Centers, the Forsythe Institute, and the Spaulding Rehabilitation Hospital. The school has seven basic and two social science departments and over 10,000 affiliated faculty, including more than 6,000 full and part-time faculty instructors. Harvard Medical School has been home to 13 Nobel Laureates and many nationally and internationally recognized researchers and medical scholars.

Mission Statement

The mission of Harvard Medical School is to create and nurture a diverse community of the best people committed to leadership in alleviating human suffering caused by disease.

Curricular Highlights

Community Service Requirement: Optional.
Research/Thesis Requirement: Encouraged for NP; required for HST.

The New Pathway Program (NP) is a problem-based curriculum that emphasizes small-group tutorials and self-directed learning, complemented by laboratories and lectures. Students are expected to analyze problems, locate relevant material in library and computer-based resources, and develop habits of lifelong learning and independent study. The NP Program enrolls 135 students each year. A second M.D. pathway is the Harvard-M.I.T. Division of Health Sciences and Technology Program (HST). This collaboration between the Harvard Medical School and the Massachusetts Institute of Technology is designed for students with a strong interest and background in quantitative science. Courses in the first two years are taught at both HMS and MIT by faculty drawn from both institutions. HST students are expected to become conversant with the underlying quantitative and molecular aspects of medicine and biomedical science, achieved through a deep understanding of the physical and biological sciences, complemented with hands-on experience in the clinic. HST enrolls 30 students per year. Basic science and clinical content are interwoven throughout the four years in both programs.

USMLE

Step 1: Required. Students must record a passing score for graduation, but not promotion.
Step 2: Clinical Skills (CS): Required. Students must record a passing total score to graduate.
Step 2: Clinical Knowledge (CK): Required. Students must record a passing total score to graduate.

Selection Factors

Academic excellence is expected. Committee members consider the entire application, including the essay, extracurricular activities, life experiences, research, community work, and the comments contained in letters of recommendation. Harvard Medical School looks for evidence of integrity, maturity, humanitarian concerns, leadership potential, and an aptitude for working with people. The 2009 entering class came from 59 different undergraduate institutions, including representatives from 32 U.S. States and 11 foreign countries. The Harvard Medical School does not accept applications for advanced standing or transfer.

Financial Aid

HMS is deeply committed to helping students manage the expense of medical school, and each year awards millions of dollars in need-based institutional scholarship funds to qualifying students. Altogether, HMS administers over 30 million in scholarship and loan funding from various federal and private sources to approximately 82% of the student body. HMS also offers substantial loan forgiveness programs for graduates who pursue careers in medical fields where starting salaries may be lower than average.

Information about Diversity Programs

Harvard Medical School is committed to the enrollment of a diverse body of talented students who will reflect the character of the people whose health needs the medical profession must serve. HMS's commitment to a diverse student population is reflected not only in the variety of institutions from which students are accepted, but also in the ethnic and economic backgrounds of the student body. For over 30 years, HMS has had one of the highest minority student enrollment and graduation rates of any United States medical school. The HMS Office of Recruitment and Multicultural Affairs provides support services to individuals from groups under-represented in medicine.

Campus Information

Setting

The Harvard Medical School campus is an integral part of the Longwood Medical and Academic Area (LMA), a community of health and educational institutions located adjacent to Fenway Park in the city of Boston, Massachusetts.

Enrollment

For 2009, total enrollment was: 705

Housing

On-campus housing for students is available in Vanderbilt Hall. Alternatively, students may choose to live in one of the residential communities neighboring the Longwood Medical Area.

Application Process and Requirements 2011–2012

Primary Application Service: AMCAS
Earliest filing date: June 1, 2010
Latest filing date: October 15, 2010

Secondary Application Required?: Yes
Sent to: All applicants
URL: Sent via e-mail after verification of AMCAS application.
Contact: Admissions Office, (617) 432-1550, admissions_office@hms.harvard.edu
Fee: Yes, $85   **Waiver available:** Yes
Earliest filing date: July 1, 2010
Latest filing date: November 1, 2010

MCAT® required?: Yes
Latest MCAT® considered: September 2010
Oldest MCAT® considered: 2007

Early Decision Program: School does not have EDP
Applicants notified: n/a
EDP available for: n/a

Regular Acceptance Notice
Earliest date: March 12, 2010
Latest date: Varies
Applicant's Response to Acceptance Offer – Maximum Time: Three weeks

Requests for Deferred Entrance Considered: Yes

Deposit to Hold Place in Class: No
Deposit (Resident): n/a   **(Non-resident):** n/a
Deposit due: n/a
Applied to tuition: n/a   **Refundable:** n/a
Refundable by: n/a

Estimated number of new entrants: 165
EDP: n/a, special program: n/a

Start Month/Year: August 2011

Interview Format: On-campus only; scheduled selectively. Regional interviews are not available. Video interviews are not available.

Other Programs

PREPARATORY PROGRAMS
Postbaccalaureate Program: No
Summer Program: No

COMBINED DEGREE PROGRAMS
Baccalaureate/M.D.: No
M.D./M.P.H.: Yes, www.hms.harvard.edu/dualdegrees/index.html, Admissions Office, (617) 432-1550, admissions_office@hms.harvard.edu
M.D./M.B.A.: Yes www.hbs.edu/mba/academics/mdmba.html
(617) 432-1550, admissions_office@hms.harvard.edu
M.D./J.D.: No
M.D./Ph.D.: Yes, www.hms.harvard.edu/md_phd/ (617) 432-0991, mdphd@hms.harvard.edu
Additional Program: Yes, www.hms.harvard.edu/dualdegrees/index.html
(617) 432-1550, admissions_office@hms.harvard.edu

Premedical Coursework

On-line courses accepted in fulfillment of prerequisites: No

Course	Req.	Rec.	Lab.	Sems.
Inorganic Chemistry	•		•	2
Behavioral Sciences				
Biochemistry		•		1
Biology	•		•	2
Biology/Zoology				
Calculus	•			2
College English				
College Mathematics				

Course	Req.	Rec.	Lab.	Sems.
Computer Science				
Genetics				
Humanities				
Organic Chemistry	•		•	2
Physics	•			2
Psychology				
Social Sciences				
Writing	•			2

Selection Factors: 2009 Accepted Applicants

Proportion of Accepted Applicants with Relevant Experience (Data Self-Reported to AMCAS*)		Community Service/Volunteer	76%
		Medically-Related Work	89%
		Research	97%

Shaded bar represents school's accepted scores ranging from the 10th percentile to the 90th percentile   School Median ● National Median ◉

Overall GPA	2.0	2.1	2.2	2.3	2.4	2.5	2.6	2.7	2.8	2.9	3.0	3.1	3.2	3.3	3.4	3.5	3.6	3.7	3.8	(3.9)	4.0
Science GPA	2.0	2.1	2.2	2.3	2.4	2.5	2.6	2.7	2.8	2.9	3.0	3.1	3.2	3.3	3.4	3.5	3.6	3.7	3.8	(3.9)	4.0

MCAT® Total Numeric Score 9 10 11 12 13 14 15 16 17 18 19 20 21 22 23 24 25 26 27 28 29 30 31 (32) 33 34 35 (36) 37 38 39 40 41 42 43

Writing Sample			J	K	L	M	N	O	P	(Q)	(R)	S	T
Verbal Reasoning	3	4	5	6	7	8	9	(10)	(11)	12	13	14	15
Biological Sciences	3	4	5	6	7	8	9	10	(11)	(12)	13	14	15
Physical Sciences	3	4	5	6	7	8	9	10	(11)	(12)	13	14	15

Acceptance & Matriculation Data for 2009–2010 First Year Class

	Resident	Non-resident	International	Total
Applications	412	5163	391	5966
Interviewed	85	695	50	830
Deferred	1	10	1	12
Matriculants				
Early Assurance Program	0	0	0	0
Early Decision Program	0	0	0	0
Baccalaureate/M.D.	0	0	0	0
M.D./Ph.D.	0	13	0	13
Matriculated	20	136	9	**165**

Applications accepted from International Applicants: Yes

Matriculant Demographics: 2009–2010 First Year Class

Men: 85   **Women:** 80

Matriculants' Self-Reported Race/Ethnicity

Mexican American	6	Korean	4
Cuban	1	Vietnamese	1
Puerto Rican	5	Other Asian	7
Other Hispanic	5	Total Asian	61
Total Hispanic	17	Native American	0
Chinese	26	Black	18
Asian Indian	20	Native Hawaiian	0
Pakistani	2	White	68
Filipino	3	Unduplicated Number	
Japanese	2	of Matriculants	165

Science and Math Majors: 68%
Matriculants with:
Baccalaureate degree: 100%
Graduate degree(s): 6%

Specialty Choice

2005, 2006, 2007 Graduates, Specialty Choice (As reported by program directors to GME Track™)

Anesthesiology	4%
Emergency Medicine	7%
Family Practice	2%
Internal Medicine	23%
Obstetrics/Gynecology	3%
Orthopaedic Surgery	5%
Pediatrics	7%
Psychiatry	4%
Radiology	5%
Surgery	5%

Financial Information

Source: 2008-2009 LCME I-B survey and 2009-2010 AAMC TSF questionnaire

	Residents	Non-residents
Total Cost of Attendance	$ 66,600	$ 66,600
Tuition and Fees	$ 44,119	$ 44,119
Other (includes living expenses)	$ 20,767	$ 20,767
Health Insurance (can be waived)	$ 1,714	$ 1,714

Average 2009 Graduate Indebtedness: $97,925
% of Enrolled Students Receiving Aid: 83%

Criminal Background Check

This medical school does not require a criminal background check prior to matriculation.

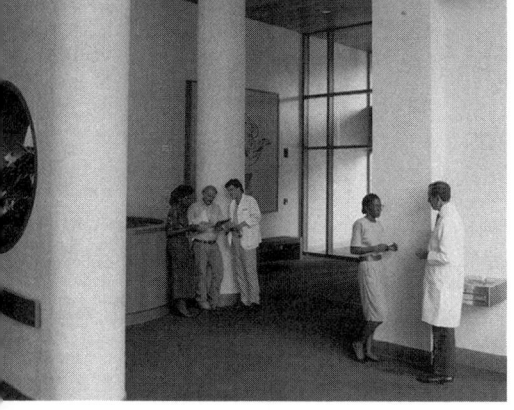

Tufts University School of Medicine

Boston, Massachusetts

Office of Admissions
Tufts University School of Medicine
136 Harrison Avenue
Boston, Massachusetts 02111
T 617 636 6571 **F** unpublished

Admissions www.tufts.edu/med/admissions
Main www.tufts.edu/med
Financial www.tufts.edu/med/about/offices/finaid/index.html
E-mail med-admissions@tufts.edu

Private Institution

Dr. Harris Berman, Interim Dean

Dr. David Neumeyer, Dean for Admissions

Dr. Joyce Sackey, Dean for Multicultural Affairs

Tara Olsen, Director of Financial Aid

Thomas M. Slavin, Director of Admissions

John Matias, Associate Dean of Admissions

General Information

Tufts University School of Medicine was established in 1893. The close association of the School with 30-plus hospitals affords diversified facilities for outstanding clinical experiences.

Mission Statement

The mission of Tufts University School of Medicine is to promote human health. We will fulfill our mission by emphasizing rigorous fundamentals while stimulating innovation as we: educate, in a dynamic learning environment, physicians, scientists, and public health professionals to become leaders in their fields; contribute to the advancement of the sciences basic to medicine through discovery, research, scholarship, and communication, and join with our partner institutions to provide the best care to our patients and communities.

Curricular Highlights

Community Service Requirement: Required.
Research/Thesis Requirement: Optional.

We combine a rigorous academic foundation with innovative teaching in a spirit of collegiality and cooperation. We have an integrated program that blends basic science with clinical practice that is divided amongst traditional lectures and small classroom settings, often in a Problem-based Learning format. The curriculum emphasizes the basic skills needed by a generalist physician and includes expanded topics such as evidence-based medicine, information mastery, team building skills and cultural competency, in addition to integrated topics such as nutrition, gerontology, health care economics, and ethics.

USMLE

Step 1: Required. Students must record a passing score for promotion.
Step 2: Clinical Skills (CS): Required. Students must only record a score.
Step 2: Clinical Knowledge (CK): Required. Students must only record a score.

Selection Factors

The selection of candidates for admission to the first year is based not only on performance in the required premedical courses, but also on the applicant's entire academic record and extracurricular experiences. Letters of recommendation and additional information supplied by the applicant are reviewed for indications of promise and fitness for a medical career. Personal interviews are a prerequisite for admission and are granted only by invitation of the Admissions Committee. Preference is given to U.S. citizens and permanent residents who will receive a bachelor's degree from an U.S. college or university prior to matriculation. Tufts accepts transfers from other U.S. LCME-accredited medical schools into the second- and third-year classes in years when vacancies have been created by attrition. The number of seats available has traditionally been extremely limited. In some years, no transfer openings are available.

Financial Aid

Up to 80 percent of students participate in the federal government student loan programs at some time during their four years of study. Additionally, scholarship and loan assistance is available directly from Tufts for students who qualify on the basis of need or individuals who would enhance the mission of the school. Approximately 25 percent of our students receive student loans or scholarships directly from Tufts during their four years of study.

Information about Diversity Programs

Diversity and inclusion are central to the educational mission of Tufts University. We foster excellence in our research, teaching and scholarship and encourage and support engaged and active citizenship that underscores a desire to make the world a better place. To do this we value a learning community of women and men of different races, ethnicities, religions, geo-graphic origins, socioeconomic backgrounds, sexual orientations, gender identity and expression, ages, personal characteristics, and interests where differences are understood and respected.

Campus Information

Setting

The School of Medicine is located within a health sciences campus that includes the School of Dental Medicine, the Sackler School of Graduate Biomedical Sciences, the Friedman School of Nutrition Science and Policy, the Sackler Center for Health Communications, the Jaharis Center for Biomedical and Nutrition Sciences, the Jean Mayer Nutrition Research Center, and the Tufts Medical Center/Boston Floating Hospital for Children.

Enrollment

For 2009, total enrollment was: 748

Special Features

TUSM has created a unique cadre of combined-degree programs by which students can attain an MD/PhD, MD/MPH, MD/MBA in Health Management at the Heller School at Brandeis and MD/MA in International Relations at the Fletcher School of Tufts. TUSM also offers a Maine Track, with clinical training focused at Maine Medical Center.

Housing

A limited amount of on-campus housing is available in Posner Hall, the Health Sciences Campus dormitory although most TUSM students live off-campus. The Student Affairs Office provides assistance to students at the Boston Health Sciences Campus in finding off-campus housing. They provide access to listings of available housing opportunities and general information about the Greater Boston housing market.

Satellite Campuses/Facilities

Most of the school's clinical affiliates are located in the metropolitan Boston area. Many students participate in rotations that are located outside of Boston, including Baystate Medical Center (the western campus of TUSM) in Springfield, Massachusetts, and Maine Medical Center in Portland.

Application Process and Requirements 2011–2012

Primary Application Service: AMCAS
Earliest filing date: June 1, 2010
Latest filing date: November 1, 2010

Secondary Application Required?: Yes
Sent to: All applicants
URL: www.tufts.edu/med/admissions/
md/howtoapply/secondary.html
Fee: Yes, $105 **Waiver available:** Yes
Earliest filing date: June 1, 2010
Latest filing date: January 15, 2011

MCAT® required?: Yes
Latest MCAT® considered: September 2010
Oldest MCAT® considered: January 2006

Early Decision Program: School does have EDP
Applicants notified: October 1, 2010
EDP available for: Both Residents
and Non-residents

Regular Acceptance Notice
Earliest date: October 15, 2010
Latest date: Until class is full
Applicant's Response to Acceptance
Offer – Maximum Time: Two weeks

Requests for Deferred
Entrance Considered: Yes

Deposit to Hold Place in Class: Yes
Deposit (Resident): $100 **(Non-resident):** $100
Deposit due: With response to acceptance offer
Applied to tuition: Yes **Refundable:** Yes
Refundable by: May 15, 2011

Estimated number of new entrants: 200
EDP: 2, special program: 20

Start Month/Year: August 2011

Interview Format: On-campus interviews
conducted September–March. Regional interviews
are not available. Video interviews are not available.

Other Programs

PREPARATORY PROGRAMS
Postbaccalaureate Program: Yes,
www.tufts.edu/med/education/mbs/index.html
Summer Program: Yes, Colleen Romain,
(617) 636-6534, colleen.romain@tufts.edu

COMBINED DEGREE PROGRAMS
Baccalaureate/M.D.: No
M.D./M.P.H.: Yes, www.tufts.edu/med/education/
phpd/mph/pathways/mdmph_dvmmph/index.html
M.D./M.B.A.: Yes, www.tufts.edu/med/education/
combinedmd/mdmba/index.html
M.D./J.D.: No
M.D./Ph.D.: Yes, www.tufts.edu/sackler/programs/
combined.html
Additional Program: Yes, http://www.tufts.edu/
med/education/combinedmd/mdmafletcher.html

Premedical Coursework

On-line courses accepted in fulfillment of prerequisites: No

Course	Req.	Rec.	Lab.	Sems.	Course	Req.	Rec.	Lab.	Sems.
Inorganic Chemistry	•		•	2	Computer Science				
Behavioral Sciences					Genetics				
Biochemistry					Humanities				
Biology	•		•	2	Organic Chemistry	•		•	2
Biology/Zoology					Physics	•		•	2
Calculus					Psychology				
College English					Social Sciences				
College Mathematics					Other				

Selection Factors: 2009 Accepted Applicants

Proportion of Accepted Applicants with Relevant Experience (Data Self-Reported to AMCAS®)		
Community Service/Volunteer		69%
Medically-Related Work		85%
Research		85%

Shaded bar represents school's accepted scores ranging from the 10th percentile to the 90th percentile **School Median** ● **National Median** ◐

Overall GPA	2.0	2.1	2.2	2.3	2.4	2.5	2.6	2.7	2.8	2.9	3.0	3.1	3.2	3.3	3.4	3.5	3.6	(3.7)	3.8	3.9	4.0
Science GPA	2.0	2.1	2.2	2.3	2.4	2.5	2.6	2.7	2.8	2.9	3.0	3.1	3.2	3.3	3.4	3.5	3.6	(3.7)	3.8	3.9	4.0

MCAT® Total Numeric Score 9 10 11 12 13 14 15 16 17 18 19 20 21 22 23 24 25 26 27 28 29 30 31 (32) 33 (34) 35 36 37 38 39 40 41 42 43

Writing Sample			J	K	L	M	N	O	P	(Q)	R	S	T
Verbal Reasoning	3	4	5	6	7	8	9	(10)	(11)	12	13	14	15
Biological Sciences	3	4	5	6	7	8	9	10	(11)	(12)	13	14	15
Physical Sciences	3	4	5	6	7	8	9	10	(11)	12	13	14	15

Acceptance & Matriculation Data for 2009–2010 First Year Class

	Resident	Non-resident	International	Total
Applications	739	7893	314	8946
Interviewed	188	725	4	917
Deferred	1	3	0	4
Matriculants				
Early Assurance Program	0	0	0	0
Early Decision Program	0	1	0	1
Baccalaureate/M.D.	6	14	0	20
M.D./Ph.D.	0	4	0	4
Matriculated	55	145	0	**200**

Applications accepted from International Applicants: Yes

Specialty Choice

2005, 2006, 2007 Graduates, Specialty Choice (As reported by program directors to GME Track™)	
Anesthesiology	8%
Emergency Medicine	8%
Family Practice	8%
Internal Medicine	23%
Obstetrics/Gynecology	3%
Orthopaedic Surgery	4%
Pediatrics	10%
Psychiatry	2%
Radiology	6%
Surgery	9%

Matriculant Demographics: 2009–2010 First Year Class

Men: 97   **Women:** 81

Matriculants' Self-Reported Race/Ethnicity

Mexican American	5	Korean	5
Cuban	2	Vietnamese	0
Puerto Rican	0	Other Asian	1
Other Hispanic	4	Total Asian	43
Total Hispanic	11	Native American	0
Chinese	22	Black	10
Asian Indian	12	Native Hawaiian	1
Pakistani	3	White	124
Filipino	0	Unduplicated Number	
Japanese	1	of Matriculants	178

Science and Math Majors: 57%
Matriculants with:
       Baccalaureate degree: 99%
       Graduate degree(s): 20%

Financial Information

Source: 2008-2009 LCME I-B survey
and 2009-2010 AAMC TSF questionnaire

	Residents	Non-residents
Total Cost of Attendance	$ 73,336	$ 73,336
Tuition and Fees	$ 50,968	$ 50,968
Other (includes living expenses)	$ 19,092	$ 19,092
Health Insurance (can be waived)	$ 3,276	$ 3,276

Average 2009 Graduate Indebtedness: $193,698
% of Enrolled Students Receiving Aid: 77%

Criminal Background Check

This medical school requires a criminal background check prior to matriculation.

University of Massachusetts Medical School
Worcester, Massachusetts

University of Massachusetts Medical School
Office of Admissions
55 Lake Avenue, North, Room S1-112
Worcester, Massachusetts 01655
T 508 856 2323   **F** 508 856 3629

Admissions www.umassmed.edu/som/admissions
Main www.umassmed.edu/index.aspx
Financial www.umass.edu/financialaid/index.aspx
E-mail admissions@umassmed.edu

Public Institution

Dr. Terence Flotte, Executive Deputy Chancellor/ Provost/Dean

Dr. John Paraskos, Associate Dean for Admissions

Dr. Danna B. Peterson, Assistant Dean of Student Affairs/Diversity and Minority Affairs

Betsy Groves, Director of Financial Aid

Karen Lawton, Director of Admissions

General Information
Established in 1962, the University of Massachusetts Medical School accepted its first class in 1970. UMMS is committed to training physicians in a wide range of medical disciplines and emphasizes training for practice in general medicine and the primary care specialties in the public sector and in underserved areas of Massachusetts. This mission has since been expanded to include graduate education in the biomedical sciences and nursing, graduate medical education, and continuing medical education for health professionals. The school's clinical partner is UMass Memorial Medical Center, consisting of two acute care hospitals with a total of 761 beds. Clinical education is also conducted at a number of affiliated community hospitals and health centers in the region. UMMS Worcester is adjacent to the Massachusetts Biotechnology Research Park, which houses a number of UMass research programs including the Program in Molecular Medicine, the Cancer Center, and the Worcester Foundation for Biomedical Research.

Mission Statement
The mission of the University of Massachusetts Medical School is to serve the people of the Commonwealth through excellence in health sciences education, clinical care, research, and public service.

Curricular Highlights
Community Service Requirement: Optional.
Research/Thesis Requirement: Optional.

The UMMS curriculum encourages interdisciplinary learning and integration of the basic and clinical sciences, with special attention to clinical correlation of subject matter in the pre-clinical years. Emphasis in the first year is on normal structure and function with a balance of small-group learning and large-group function. Emphasis in the second year is on the etiology of disease, pathophysiology, pharmacology, and clinical diagnosis. The third and fourth years are a continuum of required clerkships and both clinical and research electives with emphasis on integration. UMMS encourages students to participate in research programs in advanced biomedical studies.

USMLE
Step 1: Required. Students must record a passing score for graduation, but not promotion.
Step 2: Clinical Skills (CS): Required. Students must only record a score.
Step 2: Clinical Knowledge (CK): Required. Students must only record a score.

Selection Factors
Current policy limits admission to the M.D. program to students who are Massachusetts residents. Residents and non-residents of Massachusetts are eligible for admission to the joint M.D./Ph.D. program through the Graduate School of Biomedical Sciences and the Medical School. All applicants must be U.S. citizens or have permanent resident status. The admissions committee bases its evaluation of applicants on academic ability and achievement, MCAT scores, and such factors as extracurricular achievement, maturity, motivation, and character as these are reflected in letters of recommendation from preprofessional advisory committees and other persons. Interviews are arranged by invitation only. Applicants are selected on the basis of their individual merits without regard to race, sex, creed, national origin, age, or disability. UMMS has a set of technical standards for admission and promotion, which are available upon request. Two semesters of biology or zoology are required.

Financial Aid
Please refer to the UMMS Financial Aid Web page.

Information about Diversity Programs
For additional information, please contact the Vice Provost for School Services at 508-856-2444.

Campus Information

Setting
UMMS is in Worcester, MA and thus conveniently located in central Massachusetts. UMass Memorial Health Care is the clinical partner of UMMS and the largest health care system serving central and western Massachusetts. The medical school and clinical affiliate share adjoining buildings. There are numerous institutions of higher learning in the area offering culturally diverse activities. The campus is accessible by local bus and taxicab services.

Enrollment
For 2009, total enrollment was: 469

Special Features
The UMMS clinical affiliate, UMass Memorial Health Care, houses a regional trauma center and provides specialized education in primary, secondary, tertiary, and quaternary health care. A recently expanded research facility in close proximity to the biotech park has made the campus a focus for biotechnology research in Massachusetts. Students are given the opportunity for international rotations.

Housing
On-campus housing is not available. There are many affordable apartments within fifteen minutes of the medical school. Rents average $800-$1,000 per month.

Satellite Campuses/Facilities
Student rotations are divided among multiple campuses of UMass Memorial Health Care: University, Memorial, and Hahnemann Campuses and Clinton, Marlborough, Wing Memorial, and HealthAlliance Hospitals. The school is also affiliated with other suburban medical centers, such as the Berkshire Medical Center, Milford-Whitinsville Regional Hospital, St. Elizabeth's Hospital in Brighton, St. Vincent Hospital at Worcester Medical Center, and the Day Kimball Hospital in Connecticut. Students are required to have their own transportation.

Application Process and Requirements 2011–2012

Primary Application Service: AMCAS
Earliest filing date: June 1, 2010
Latest filing date: November 1, 2010

Secondary Application Required?: Yes
Sent to: All verified applicants
Contact: Admissions Office, 508-856-2323, admissions@umassmed.edu
Fee: Yes, $75   **Waiver available:** Yes
Earliest filing date: After verified application received
Latest filing date: Must be completed by December 15, 2010

MCAT® required?: Yes
Latest MCAT® considered: September 2010
Oldest MCAT® considered: 2007

Early Decision Program: School does have EDP
Applicants notified: October 1, 2010
EDP available for: Residents only

Regular Acceptance Notice
Earliest date: October 15, 2010
Latest date: Until Class is Full
Applicant's Response to Acceptance Offer – Maximum Time: Two weeks

Requests for Deferred Entrance Considered: Yes

Deposit to Hold Place in Class: Yes
Deposit (Resident): $100   **(Non-resident):** $100
Deposit due: With response to acceptance offer
Applied to tuition: Yes   **Refundable:** Yes
Refundable by: May 15, 2011

Estimated number of new entrants: 125
EDP: 10, special program: n/a

Start Month/Year: August 2011

Interview Format: Students meet one-on-one with two interviewers. Off campus interviews are available. Video interviews are not available.

Other Programs

PREPARATORY PROGRAMS
Postbaccalaureate Program: No
Summer Program: Yes, www.umassmed.edu/summer
Summer Enrichment Program: www.umassmed.edu/outreach/sep.aspx

COMBINED DEGREE PROGRAMS
Baccalaureate/M.D.: No
M.D./M.P.H.: No
M.D./M.B.A.: No
M.D./J.D.: No
M.D./Ph.D.: Yes, www.umassmed.edu/MDPhD/index.aspx

Premedical Coursework

On-line courses accepted in fulfillment of prerequisites: No

Course	Req.	Rec.	Lab.	Sems.
Inorganic Chemistry	•		•	2
Behavioral Sciences				
Biochemistry		•		
Biology	•		•	2
Biology/Zoology	•		•	2
Calculus		•		
College English	•			2
College Mathematics				

Course	Req.	Rec.	Lab.	Sems.
Computer Science		•		2
Genetics				
Organic Chemistry	•		•	2
Physics	•		•	2
Psychology		•		
Social Sciences		•		
Statistics		•		2
Other				

Selection Factors: 2009 Accepted Applicants

Proportion of Accepted Applicants with Relevant Experience (Data Self-Reported to AMCAS®)		
Community Service/Volunteer		68%
Medically-Related Work		85%
Research		84%

Shaded bar represents school's accepted scores ranging from the 10th percentile to the 90th percentile   **School Median** ◯   **National Median** ◯

Overall GPA	2.0	2.1	2.2	2.3	2.4	2.5	2.6	2.7	2.8	2.9	3.0	3.1	3.2	3.3	3.4	3.5	3.6	(3.7)	3.8	3.9	4.0
Science GPA	2.0	2.1	2.2	2.3	2.4	2.5	2.6	2.7	2.8	2.9	3.0	3.1	3.2	3.3	3.4	3.5	3.6	(3.7)	3.8	3.9	4.0

MCAT® Total Numeric Score 9 10 11 12 13 14 15 16 17 18 19 20 21 22 23 24 25 26 27 28 29 30 31 ③②③③ 34 35 36 37 38 39 40 41 42 43

Writing Sample			J	K	L	M	N	O	P	Q	R	S	T
Verbal Reasoning	3	4	5	6	7	8	9	⑩	11	12	13	14	15
Biological Sciences	3	4	5	6	7	8	9	10	⑪	12	13	14	15
Physical Sciences	3	4	5	6	7	8	9	10	⑪	12	13	14	15

Acceptance & Matriculation Data for 2009–2010 First Year Class

	Resident	Non-resident	International	Total
Applications	776	87	3	866
Interviewed	486	26	0	512
Deferred	1	0	0	1
Matriculants				
Early Assurance Program	0	0	0	0
Early Decision Program	4	0	0	4
Baccalaureate/M.D.	0	0	0	0
M.D./Ph.D.	8	3	0	11
Matriculated	122	3	0	**125**

Applications accepted from International Applicants: No

Matriculant Demographics: 2009–2010 First Year Class

Men: 62   **Women:** 63

Matriculants' Self-Reported Race/Ethnicity

Mexican American	0	Korean	0
Cuban	0	Vietnamese	2
Puerto Rican	1	Other Asian	6
Other Hispanic	3	Total Asian	25
Total Hispanic	3	Native American	1
Chinese	10	Black	5
Asian Indian	8	Native Hawaiian	0
Pakistani	1	White	100
Filipino	1	Unduplicated Number	
Japanese	0	of Matriculants	125

Science and Math Majors: 57%
Matriculants with:
    Baccalaureate degree: 100%
    Graduate degree(s): 11%

Specialty Choice

2005, 2006, 2007 Graduates, Specialty Choice (As reported by program directors to GME Track™)

Anesthesiology	5%
Emergency Medicine	11%
Family Practice	10%
Internal Medicine	19%
Obstetrics/Gynecology	7%
Orthopaedic Surgery	3%
Pediatrics	13%
Psychiatry	4%
Radiology	3%
Surgery	5%

Financial Information

Source: 2008-2009 LCME I-B survey and 2009-2010 AAMC TSF questionnaire

	Residents	Non-residents
Total Cost of Attendance	$ 42,646	$ 0
Tuition and Fees	$ 15,738	$ 0
Other (includes living expenses)	$ 22,902	$ 0
Health Insurance (can be waived)	$ 4,006	$ 0

Average 2009 Graduate Indebtedness: $106,847
% of Enrolled Students Receiving Aid: 94%

Criminal Background Check

This medical school requires a criminal background check prior to matriculation.

Michigan State University College of Human Medicine

East Lansing, Michigan

College of Human Medicine, Office of Admissions
A239 Life Science
Michigan State University
East Lansing, Michigan 48824-1317
T 517 353 9620   **F** 517 432 0021

Admissions http://MDadmissions.msu.edu
Main http://chm.msu.edu
Financial http://finaid.msu.edu/med
E-mail MDadmissions@msu.edu

Public Institution

Dr. Marsha Rappley, Dean

Dr. Wanda Lipscomb, Associate Dean for Student Affairs, Diversity and Outreach

Dr. Christine Shafer, Assistant Dean for Admissions

Jay Bryde, Admissions Officer

Letitia Fowler, Admissions Senior Counselor

Diane Batten, Coordinator of Medical Student Financial Aid

General Information

The College of Human Medicine (CHM), founded in response to Michigan's need for primary care physicians, has expanded in mission and size to meet growing needs. Students begin at either the MSU campus in East Lansing or at the Grand Rapids location. After two preclinical years of basic science and clinical skills, students enter clinical years at a community campus.

Mission Statement

The College of Human Medicine at Michigan State University is committed to educating exemplary physicians and scholars, discovering and disseminating new knowledge, and providing service at home and abroad. We enhance our communities by providing outstanding primary and specialty care, promoting the dignity and inclusion of all people, and responding to the needs of the medically underserved.

Curricular Highlights

Community Service Requirement: Required.
Community Service: Numerous service opportunities available.
Research/Thesis Requirement: Optional.
Research Thesis: Research available.

The curriculum integrates basic biological, behavioral, and social sciences using a developmental approach to learning; early teaching of clinical skills, and clinical training utilizing a community-integrated approach. Grading is on a modified pass/no pass system; clinical honors performance is recognized. Block I is a 2½ semester experience in which fundamental medical science is presented in a structured, discipline-based format. It also comprises basic clinical skills, mentor groups, longitudinal patient exposure, opportunities for independent and supplementary learning experiences, and a clinical correlations course that integrates basic science and medicine. Block II presents a clinical problem-based format with emphasis on small-group learning and use of a clinical context for basic science concepts, clinical skills training, and special topics seminars over two semesters. Block III includes 60 weeks of required clerkships, including family medicine, and 20 weeks of elective clerkships. Students may complete elective clerkships in other locations, including third world countries. The Leadership in Medicine for the Underserved/Vulnerable Program, with an international component, and the Rural Physician Program are offered.

USMLE

Step 1: Required. Students must record a passing score for promotion.
Step 2: Clinical Skills (CS): Required. Students must record a passing total score to graduate.
Step 2: Clinical Knowledge (CK): Required. Students must record a passing total score to graduate.

Selection Factors

CHM seeks a class that is academically competent, reflective of the rural and urban character of Michigan, and representative of a wide spectrum of personalities, backgrounds, and talents. Disadvantaged and minority students are encouraged to apply. Ability to pay is not a factor. Selection criteria is multifactorial and includes year-to-year and cumulative GPA (including postbac and graduate); best MCAT performance; fit with the school's mission; relevant clinical and community service; assessment of motivation; ability to communicate and problem solve; maturity and suitability for the MSU program; state of residence, and potential to contribute to the overall quality of the entering class. CHM considers U.S. and Canadian residents and applicants with U.S. permanent resident status.

Financial Aid

Information about specific scholarships and financial aid can be obtained from the Office of Financial Aid at *http://finaid.msu.edu/med*.

Information about Diversity Programs

The Advanced Baccalaureate Learning Experience (ABLE) is a 13-month, enriched academic experience offered to an invited group of disadvantaged students who have applied for admission to CHM. Students who successfully complete the ABLE program are offered regular admission to CHM's entering class.

Campus Information

Setting

The East Lansing preclinical campus, located at the MSU Big Ten park-like setting, is home to 10,311 graduate and professional students, including law, osteopathic, and veterinary students. The Grand Rapids preclinical campus is in the rapidly expanding "Medical Mile" area of downtown Grand Rapids. Clinical training occurs in one of the seven fully supported community campuses in Michigan: Flint, Grand Rapids, Kalamazoo, Lansing, Saginaw, Traverse City, and the Upper Peninsula (Marquette).

Enrollment

For 2009, total enrollment was: 610

Special Features

Students enjoy a cooperative experience where interests and needs are supported by the ABLE program, an extended curriculum option, research opportunities, the Rural Physician Program, the Leadership in Medicine for the Underserved/Vulnerable Program, international opportunities, and the resources of MSU and seven communities in Michigan.

Housing

Affordable housing is readily available at all sites. MSU operates two large apartment complexes and one dormitory for graduate and professional students on campus.

Satellite Campuses/Facilities

Clinical campuses (Flint, Grand Rapids, Kalamazoo, Lansing, Saginaw, Traverse City and the Upper Peninsula) comprise full-time, part-time, and volunteer faculty in the clinical disciplines. Students are connected to a wide array of health care resources in the community that allow for hands-on learning, exposure to diverse patient problems, research, and experience in varied medical practice settings.

Application Process and Requirements 2011–2012

Primary Application Service: AMCAS
Earliest filing date: June 1, 2010
Latest filing date: November 15, 2010

Secondary Application Required?: Yes
Sent to: All applicants with fee paid.
URL: URL provided upon receipt of $80 Secondary Application fee.
Fee: Yes, $80   **Waiver available:** Yes
Earliest filing date: August 2010
Latest filing date: November 30, 2010 or within two weeks of paying fee after November 15.

MCAT® required?: Yes
Latest MCAT® considered: September 2010
Oldest MCAT® considered: April 2007

Early Decision Program: School does have EDP
Applicants notified: October 1, 2010
EDP available for: Both Residents and Non-residents

Regular Acceptance Notice
Earliest date: October 15, 2010
Latest date: Varies
Applicant's Response to Acceptance Offer – Maximum Time: Two weeks

Requests for Deferred Entrance Considered: Yes

Deposit to Hold Place in Class: Yes
Deposit (Resident): $100   **(Non-resident):** $100
Deposit due: With response to acceptance offer
Applied to tuition: Yes   **Refundable:** Yes
Refundable by: May 15, 2011

Estimated number of new entrants: 200
EDP: 5, special program: 25

Start Month/Year: August 2011

Interview Format: Individual 30-minute interviews with one faculty and one student. Regional interviews are being considered. Video interviews are not available.

Other Programs

PREPARATORY PROGRAMS
Postbaccalaureate Program: No
Summer Program: No

COMBINED DEGREE PROGRAMS
Baccalaureate/M.D.: No
M.D./M.P.H.: Yes, http://publichealth.msu.edu
M.D./M.B.A.: No
M.D./J.D.: No
M.D./Ph.D.: Yes,
http://MDadmissions.msu.edu/main/mdphd.htm

Premedical Coursework

On-line courses accepted in fulfillment of prerequisites: No

Course	Req.	Rec.	Lab.	Sems.
Inorganic Chemistry	•		•	2
Behavioral Sciences		•		
Biochemistry		•		
Biology	•		•	2
Biology/Zoology				
Calculus				
College English	•			2
College Mathematics	•			1

Course	Req.	Rec.	Lab.	Sems.
Computer Science		•		
Genetics		•		
Humanities	•			2
Organic Chemistry	•		•	2
Physics		•		
Psychology		•		
Social Sciences	•			
2 Upper-Level Biology	•			2

Selection Factors: 2009 Accepted Applicants

Proportion of Accepted Applicants with Relevant Experience (Data Self-Reported to AMCAS®)		
Community Service/Volunteer		78%
Medically-Related Work		90%
Research		80%

Shaded bar represents school's accepted scores ranging from the 10th percentile to the 90th percentile.   School Median ●   National Median ●

Overall GPA 2.0 2.1 2.2 2.3 2.4 2.5 2.6 2.7 2.8 2.9 3.0 3.1 3.2 3.3 3.4 3.5 (3.6) 3.7 3.8 3.9 4.0
Science GPA 2.0 2.1 2.2 2.3 2.4 2.5 2.6 2.7 2.8 2.9 3.0 3.1 3.2 3.3 3.4 (3.5) 3.6 3.7 3.8 3.9 4.0

MCAT® Total Numeric Score 9 10 11 12 13 14 15 16 17 18 19 20 21 22 23 24 25 26 27 28 29(30)31(32)33 34 35 36 37 38 39 40 41 42 43

Writing Sample			J	K	L	M	N	O	(P)	Q	R	S	T	
Verbal Reasoning	3	4	5	6	7	8	9	(10)	11	12	13	14	15	
Biological Sciences	3	4	5	6	7	8	9	(10)	11	12	13	14	15	
Physical Sciences	3	4	5	6	7	8	9	(10)	11	12	13	14	15	

Acceptance & Matriculation Data for 2009–2010 First Year Class

	Resident	Non-resident	International	Total
Applications	1303	3896	298	5497
Interviewed	310	165	11	486
Deferred	9	4	0	13
Matriculants				
Early Assurance Program	0	0	0	0
Early Decision Program	2	0	0	2
Baccalaureate/M.D.	10	0	0	10
M.D./Ph.D.	1	2	0	3
Matriculated	114	40	1	**155**

Applications accepted from International Applicants: Only Canadian

Matriculant Demographics: 2009–2010 First Year Class

Men: 79   **Women:** 76

Matriculants' Self-Reported Race/Ethnicity

Mexican American	4	Korean	3
Cuban	1	Vietnamese	4
Puerto Rican	1	Other Asian	2
Other Hispanic	4	Total Asian	31
Total Hispanic	10	Native American	2
Chinese	6	Black	14
Asian Indian	15	Native Hawaiian	1
Pakistani	1	White	106
Filipino	2	Unduplicated Number	
Japanese	0	of Matriculants	155

Science and Math Majors: 68%
Matriculants with:
       Baccalaureate degree: 100%
       Graduate degree(s): 17%

Specialty Choice

2005, 2006, 2007 Graduates, Specialty Choice (As reported by program directors to GME Track™)	
Anesthesiology	5%
Emergency Medicine	9%
Family Practice	13%
Internal Medicine	16%
Obstetrics/Gynecology	7%
Orthopaedic Surgery	5%
Pediatrics	13%
Psychiatry	5%
Radiology	4%
Surgery	5%

Financial Information

Source: 2008-2009 LCME I-B survey and 2009-2010 AAMC TSF questionnaire

	Residents	Non-residents
Total Cost of Attendance	$ 55,206	$ 86,428
Tuition and Fees	$ 26,954	$ 58,176
Other (includes living expenses)	$ 26,862	$ 26,862
Health Insurance (can be waived)	$ 1,390	$ 1,390

Average 2009 Graduate Indebtedness: $163,261
% of Enrolled Students Receiving Aid: 93%

Criminal Background Check

This medical school requires a criminal background check prior to matriculation.

Oakland University William Beaumont School of Medicine

Rochester, Michigan

216 O'Dowd Hall
2200 North Squirrel Road
Rochester, Michigan 48309
T 248 370 2769   **F** 248 370 2771

Admissions www.oakland.edu/medicine/admissions
Main www.oakland.edu/medicine
Financial www.oakland.edu/medicine/financial
E-mail medadmit@oakland.edu

Public Institution

Robert Folberg, M.D., Dean

Linda Gillum, Ph.D., Associate Dean for Academic Affairs, Faculty Development and Diversity

Angela Nuzzarello, M.D., M.H.P.E. Associate Dean for Student Affairs

Christina Grabowski, Assistant Dean for Medical School Admissions

General Information

Oakland University and Beaumont Hospitals have partnered to form the Oakland University William Beaumont School of Medicine (OUWB). Oakland, a vibrant research university, has a longstanding commitment to strong biomedical and health education programs. Beaumont's three hospital system includes the Royal Oak campus, which is a major academic referral center with Level 1 trauma status. The hospital is one of the busiest in the country for inpatient admissions and number of surgeries, and is home to a unique simulation center located within the hospital. Ninety-one medical and surgical specialties are represented on the Beaumont medical staff of more than 3,100 physicians.

Mission Statement

The Oakland University William Beaumont School of Medicine is a collaborative, diverse, inclusive, and technologically advanced learning community, dedicated to enabling students to become skillful, ethical, and compassionate physicians, inquisitive scientists who are invested in the scholarship of discovery, and dynamic and effective medical educators.

Curricular Highlights

Community Service Requirement: Optional.
Community Service: Numerous service opportunities available.
Research/Thesis Requirement: Required.
Research Thesis: Time is set aside in each year of instruction to work on the Capstone project.

The School of Medicine curriculum offers a fresh approach to an organ system-based, highly integrated program using a combination of educational strategies including large and small groups, team-based learning, and simulation. A strong biomedical sciences foundation, focusing on the acquisition of scientific competencies that can be applied in clinical settings, is delivered by master educators. Dedicated courses in Medical Humanities—Bioethics, Promotion and Maintenance of Health, and the Art and Practice of Medicine include patient experiences and are synchronized with organ-based modules throughout the first two years. The third year focuses on concentrated experiences in clinical medicine. Monthly class-wide assemblies during the third year allow students to reinforce basic science concepts, refine history and physical examination skills, integrate multidisciplinary knowledge, and engage in professionalism and bioethics discussions in the context of their clinical experiences. In the fourth year, students continue to build clinical competencies as well as participate in electives. Throughout the four years, students will participate in small, faculty-guided mentoring teams, emphasizing communication, reflection, and academic and career guidance.

USMLE

Step 1: Required. Students must record a passing score for promotion.
Step 2: Clinical Skills (CS): Required. Students must record a passing score to graduate.
Step 2: Clinical Knowledge (CK): Required. Students must record a passing total score to graduate.

Selection Factors

Students seeking admission must demonstrate that they have acquired a broad education that extends beyond the basic sciences to include the social sciences, history, and the arts. The school seeks to admit applicants with personal and professional integrity, the potential for professional medical competence, the ability to deliver compassionate care, a passion for lifelong learning, intellectual curiosity, educational excellence, ethical conduct, open-mindedness and tolerance, a service orientation to others, and an understanding that medicine is both art and science.

Financial Aid

The Associate Director of Financial Services is dedicated to assisting medical school students with financial planning. Group financial counseling services, as well as personalized meetings, will be provided to all students. Scholarships, grants, and loans will be available on a need and/or merit basis.

Information about Diversity Programs

The School of Medicine is committed to supporting diversity among applicants for medical school admissions. Both the Associate Dean for Academic Affairs, Faculty Development and Diversity and the Assistant Dean for Diversity and Multi-Cultural Affairs will support student initiatives and activities that promote diversity.

Campus Information

Setting

Oakland University is located on a picturesque 1,441 acre campus of wooded hills and rolling meadows in Southeastern Michigan. At the center of main campus, the OUWB enjoys close access to the Kresge Library, the Oakland Center (student union) and the Recreation Center. The school features wireless access throughout, a new medical student lounge and locker facilities, and technologically advanced breakout rooms – all designed to complement our innovative curriculum and in close proximity to medical student services.

Enrollment

For 2009, total enrollment was: N/A

Special Features

The OUWB is a distinctive learning community integrated into a large, vibrant research university. Master educators who specialize in medical student instruction teach the basic sciences. One of the largest private teaching hospitals in the country is the setting for clinical instruction. The unique Capstone allows students to develop projects with significant scientific or social impact.

Housing

Oakland University offers a selection of on-campus housing options including student apartments, student townhomes and family housing. Affordable, off-campus apartments are located close to campus.

Application Process and Requirements 2011–2012

Primary Application Service: AMCAS
Earliest filing date: June 1, 2010
Latest filing date: November 15, 2010

Secondary Application Required?: Yes
Sent to: All applicants
URL: www.oakland.edu/medicine/admissions
Fee: Yes, $75   **Waiver available:** Yes
Earliest filing date: July 1, 2010
Latest filing date: December 31, 2010

MCAT® required?: Yes
Latest MCAT® considered: September 2010
Oldest MCAT® considered: September 2007

Early Decision Program: School does not have EDP
Applicants notified: n/a
EDP available for: n/a

Regular Acceptance Notice
Earliest date: October 15, 2010
Latest date: until class is full
Applicant's Response to Acceptance Offer – Maximum Time: Two weeks

Requests for Deferred Entrance Considered: Yes

Deposit to Hold Place in Class: Yes
Deposit (Resident): $100   **(Non-resident):** $100
Deposit due: With response to acceptance offer
Applied to tuition: Yes   **Refundable:** Yes
Refundable by: May 15, 2011

Estimated number of new entrants: 50
EDP: 0

Start Month/Year: August 2011

Interview Format: Individual on-campus interviews. Regional interviews are not available. Video interviews are not available.

Other Programs

PREPARATORY PROGRAMS
Postbaccalaureate Program: No
Summer Program: No

COMBINED DEGREE PROGRAMS
Baccalaureate/M.D.: No
M.D./M.P.H.: No
M.D./M.B.A.: No
M.D./J.D.: No
M.D./Ph.D.: No

Premedical Coursework

On-line courses accepted in fulfillment of prerequisites: No

Course	Req.	Rec.	Lab.	Sems.	Course	Req.	Rec.	Lab.	Sems.
Inorganic Chemistry	•		•	2	Computer Science				
Behavioral Sciences		•			Genetics				
Biochemistry		•			Humanities		•		
Biology	•		•	2	Organic Chemistry	•		•	1
Biology/Zoology		•			Physics	•		•	2
Calculus					Psychology		•		
College English		•			Social Sciences		•		
College Mathematics	•			2	Other				

Selection Factors: 2009 Accepted Applicants

Proportion of Accepted Applicants with Relevant Experience (Data Self-Reported to AMCAS®)		
Community Service/Volunteer		n/r
Medically-Related Work		n/r
Research		n/r

Shaded bar represents school's accepted scores ranging from the 10th percentile to the 90th percentile   School Median ◯   National Median ◯

NON-APPLICABLE

(chart axes: Overall GPA, Science, MCAT, Writing, Verbal, Biology, Physical Sciences)

Acceptance & Matriculation Data for 2009–2010 First Year Class

NON-APPLICABLE

(columns: Resident, Non-resident, International, Total; rows: Applications, Interviewed, Deferred, Matriculants, Early..., Early..., Baccalaureate..., M.D...., Ma...)

Applications accepted from International Applicants: No

Specialty Choice

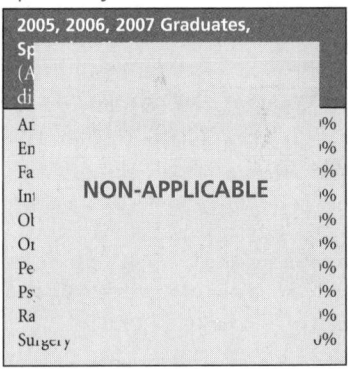

2005, 2006, 2007 Graduates,

NON-APPLICABLE

Matriculant Demographics: 2009–2010 First Year Class

Men: n/r   **Women:** n/r

Matriculants' Self-Reported Race/Ethnicity

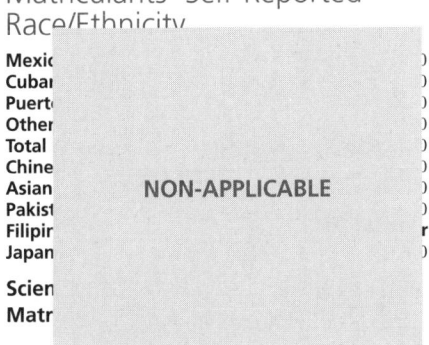

NON-APPLICABLE

(rows: Mexican, Cuban, Puerto..., Other, Total, Chinese, Asian, Pakistani, Filipino, Japanese, Science, Matriculants)

Graduate degree(s): n/r

Financial Information

Source: 2008-2009 LCME I-B survey and 2009-2010 AAMC TSF questionnaire

	Residents	Non-residents
Total Cost of Attendance	$67,065	$67,065
Tuition and Fees	$42,760	$42,760
Other (includes living expenses)	$24,305	$24,305
Health Insurance (can be waived)	$0	$0

Average 2009 Graduate Indebtedness: n/a
% of Enrolled Students Receiving Aid: n/a

Criminal Background Check

This medical school requires a criminal background check prior to matriculation.

University of Michigan Medical School

Ann Arbor, Michigan

Office of Admissions
4303 Medical Science Building I
1301 Catherine Street
University of Michigan Medical School
Ann Arbor, Michigan 48109-5624
T 734 764 6317   F 734 763 0453

Admissions www.med.umich.edu/medschool/admissions
Main www.med.umich.edu/medschool
Financial www.med.umich.edu/medschool/financialaid
E-mail umichmedadmiss@umich.edu

Public Institution

Dr. James Woolliscroft, Dean

Dr. Steven Gay, Assistant Dean for Admissions

Dr. David Gordon, Assistant Dean for Diversity and Career Development

Robert F. Ruiz, Director of Admissions

Carmen Colby, Director of Financial Aid

General Information

The University of Michigan Medical School enjoys a long, distinguished history as part of the world-renowned University of Michigan, which includes many other highly ranked schools in Law, Business, Public Health, Nursing, Dentistry, Social Work and Pharmacy. The University of Michigan has the largest single-site Health System in the world, providing unique opportunities for innovation and collaboration.

Mission Statement

The University of Michigan Medical School seeks to educate students, physicians and biomedical scholars and to provide a spectrum of comprehensive knowledge, research, patient care and service of the highest quality to the people of the state of Michigan and beyond.

Curricular Highlights

Community Service Requirement: Optional.
Research/Thesis Requirement: Optional.

The first year Patients and Populations course acquaints medical students with genetics, principles of disease, epidemiology, and evidence-based medicine. The material is structured within Normal Organ Systems sequences and Microbiology, Infectious Disease and Anatomy courses. Clinical skills are taught in focused 1 & 2 week modules throughout the first and second years. Training begins with the medical interview, history-taking and physical examination skills. In the two-year Family Centered Experience, pairs of first-year students are assigned to a family in the community. These families will serve as resources to help medical students understand how health changes, chronic conditions, and serious illnesses affect patients and their families. The second year

curriculum features Abnormal Organ Systems sequences. Clinical skills modules will continue with expectations for mastery of more advanced physical examination, history-taking, and communication skills. Clinical training in the third year includes 7 required rotations and opportunities for career exploratory electives. Fourth-year requirements include a subinternship, an ICU experience and Advanced Medical Therapeutics. In the subinternship, students are assigned their own patient case-load with nearly the same level of responsibility as a resident. The fourth year includes eight weeks of vacation and interviewing time as well as 12 weeks of electives. This provides opportunities for off-campus and international rotations which are components of the medical school's Global Reach program. All courses in the first & second years are graded pass/fail. In the subsequent years, grades of honors, high pass, pass, or fail are awarded.

USMLE

Step 1: Required. Students must record a passing score for promotion.
Step 2: Clinical Skills (CS): Required. Students must record a passing total score to graduate.
Step 2: Clinical Knowledge (CK): Required. Students must record a passing total score to graduate.

Selection Factors

The Admissions Committee is dedicated to matriculating those individuals with the skills, intelligence, and personal attributes to become leaders in medicine. Although admitted students all have demonstrated the ability to succeed academically, other attributes such as compassion, empathy, altruism, leadership, honesty, communication and interpersonal skills are viewed as being critical to future excellence. The committee considers that all information pertaining to the ability, personality, and character of the applicant is relevant.

Financial Aid

Application for financial aid may be initiated following acceptance to the medical school. In addition, all admitted students will be considered for scholarships.

Information about Diversity Programs

The University of Michigan is committed to training a diverse cohort of physicians who are capable of caring for an increasingly diverse patient population. Medical students are very active in organizations such as LANAMA (Latino/a American/Native American Medical Association) and BMA (Black Medical Association). These students are actively involved in diversity and cultural competency programs and in the Health System's Multi-Cultural Community Health Alliance.

Campus Information

Setting

The Medical School is situated within a large patient care/research complex and is within walking distance of the University's main campuses, as well as Ann Arbor's thriving downtown. Located along the banks of the Huron River, the city offers a compact urban experience and plenty of recreational opportunities that appeal to students, professionals, singles and families. It is a diverse and culturally rich Midwestern community that attracts visitors and residents from all over the world.

Special Features

The new University of Michigan C.S. Mott Children's and Women's Hospitals will open in 2012 and will include a 9-story tower for clinic space and a 12-story tower devoted to inpatient care.

Enrollment

For 2009, total enrollment was: 670

Housing

Ann Arbor offers a wide range of safe and affordable housing for students. Most medical students chose to live in apartments within walking distance of the medical campus but great public transportation opens up many more options, including on- and off-campus housing and medical fraternities.

Application Process and Requirements 2011–2012

Primary Application Service: AMCAS
Earliest filing date: June 1, 2010
Latest filing date: October 15, 2010

Secondary Application Required?: Yes
Sent to: All applicants
URL: Sent electronically upon receipt of AMCAS application.
Fee: Yes, $85   **Waiver available:** Yes
Earliest filing date: July 1, 2010
Latest filing date: November 30, 2010

MCAT® required?: Yes
Latest MCAT® considered: August 2010
Oldest MCAT® considered: August 2008

Early Decision Program: School does not have EDP
Applicants notified: n/a
EDP available for: n/a

Regular Acceptance Notice
Earliest date: October 15, 2010
Latest date: Until class is full
Applicant's Response to Acceptance Offer – Maximum Time: May 15, 2011

Requests for Deferred Entrance Considered: Yes

Deposit to Hold Place in Class: Yes
Deposit (Resident): $200   **(Non-resident):** $200
Deposit due: May 15, 2011
Applied to tuition: Yes   **Refundable:** n/a
Refundable by: n/a

Estimated number of new entrants: 170
EDP: n/a, special program: n/a

Start Month/Year: August 2011

Interview Format: Three open file one-on-one interviews. Regional interviews are not available. Video interviews are not available.

Other Programs

PREPARATORY PROGRAMS
Postbaccalaureate Program: No
Summer Program: No
Additional: Global Reach, http://www.med.umich.edu/lrc/medcurriculum/global-reach.html

COMBINED DEGREE PROGRAMS
Baccalaureate/M.D.: No
M.D./M.P.H.: Yes, http://med.umich.edu/lrc/medcurriculum/highlights/dual-degrees.html
M.D./M.B.A.: Yes, http://med.umich.edu/lrc/medcurriculum/highlights/dual-degrees.html
M.D./J.D.: Yes, http://med.umich.edu/lrc/medcurriculum/highlights/dual-degrees.html
M.D./Ph.D.: Yes, www.med.umich.edu/medschool/mstp/
Additional: Yes, http://med.umich.edu/lrc/medcurriculum/highlights/dual-degrees.html

Premedical Coursework

On-line courses accepted in fulfillment of prerequisites: Yes

Course	Req.	Rec.	Lab.	Sems.
Inorganic Chemistry	•		•	2
Behavioral Sciences				
Biochemistry	•			1
Biology	•		•	2
Biology/Zoology				
Calculus				
College English				
College Mathematics				
Computer Science				

Course	Req.	Rec.	Lab.	Sems.
Genetics				
Humanities				
Organic Chemistry	•		•	2
Physics	•		•	2
Psychology				
Social Sciences				
Non-Science Courses	•			6
Intensive Writing Course	•			2
Other				

Selection Factors: 2009 Accepted Applicants

Proportion of Accepted Applicants with Relevant Experience (Data Self-Reported to AMCAS)	
Community Service/Volunteer	74%
Medically-Related Work	89%
Research	94%

Shaded bar represents school's accepted scores ranging from the 10th percentile to the 90th percentile

School Median ● National Median ○

Overall GPA 2.0 2.1 2.2 2.3 2.4 2.5 2.6 2.7 2.8 2.9 3.0 3.1 3.2 3.3 3.4 3.5 3.6 3.7 (3.8) 3.9 4.0
Science GPA 2.0 2.1 2.2 2.3 2.4 2.5 2.6 2.7 2.8 2.9 3.0 3.1 3.2 3.3 3.4 3.5 3.6 3.7 (3.8) 3.9 4.0

MCAT® Total Numeric Score 9 10 11 12 13 14 15 16 17 18 19 20 21 22 23 24 25 26 27 28 29 30 31 (32) 33 34 35 (36) 37 38 39 40 41 42 43

Writing Sample			J	K	L	M	N	O	P	(Q)	R	S	T	
Verbal Reasoning	3	4	5	6	7	8	9	(10)	(11)	12	13	14	15	
Biological Sciences	3	4	5	6	7	8	9	10	(11)	12	(13)	14	15	
Physical Sciences	3	4	5	6	7	8	9	10	(11)	(12)	13	14	15	

Acceptance & Matriculation Data for 2009–2010 First Year Class

	Resident	Non-resident	International	Total
Applications	1005	4046	83	5134
Interviewed	179	516	0	695
Deferred	4	12	0	16
Matriculants				
Early Assurance Program	0	0	0	0
Early Decision Program	0	0	0	0
Baccalaureate/M.D.	0	0	0	0
M.D./Ph.D.	2	11	0	13
Matriculated	81	89	0	**170**

Applications accepted from International Applicants: No

Matriculant Demographics: 2009–2010 First Year Class

Men: 90   **Women:** 80

Matriculants' Self-Reported Race/Ethnicity

Mexican American	1	Korean	8
Cuban	1	Vietnamese	0
Puerto Rican	1	Other Asian	3
Other Hispanic	4	Total Asian	51
Total Hispanic	7	Native American	1
Chinese	19	Black	6
Asian Indian	19	Native Hawaiian	1
Pakistani	2	White	103
Filipino	2	Unduplicated Number	
Japanese	1	of Matriculants	170

Science and Math Majors: 62%
Matriculants with:
    Baccalaureate degree: 100%
    Graduate degree(s): 11%

Specialty Choice

2005, 2006, 2007 Graduates, Specialty Choice (As reported by program directors to GME Track™)	
Anesthesiology	10%
Emergency Medicine	9%
Family Practice	7%
Internal Medicine	13%
Obstetrics/Gynecology	4%
Orthopaedic Surgery	4%
Pediatrics	9%
Psychiatry	2%
Radiology	5%
Surgery	6%

Financial Information

Source: 2008-2009 LCME I-B survey and 2009-2010 AAMC TSF questionnaire

	Residents	Non-residents
Total Cost of Attendance	$ 50,601	$ 67,655
Tuition and Fees	$ 27,474	$ 43,828
Other (includes living expenses)	$ 21,127	$ 21,827
Health Insurance (can be waived)	$ 2,000	$ 2,000

Average 2009 Graduate Indebtedness: $128,526
% of Enrolled Students Receiving Aid: 90%

Criminal Background Check

This medical school requires a criminal background check prior to matriculation.

Wayne State University School of Medicine

Detroit, Michigan

Richard J. Mazurek M.D.
Medical Education Commons
Office of Admissions
320 E. Canfield, Suite 322
Detroit, Michigan 48201
T 313 577 1466   **F** 313 577 9420

Admissions www.med.wayne.edu/admissions
Main www.med.wayne.edu
Financial www.med.wayne.edu/student_affairs/
financial_aid
E-mail admissions@med.wayne.edu

Public Institution

Dr. Valerie Parisi, Interim Dean

Dr. Silas Norman Jr., Assistant Dean for Admissions

Julia Simmons, Director, Diversity and Integrated Student Services Office

Deirdre Moore, Assistant Director, Financial Aid

Dr. Robert R. Frank, Executive Vice Dean

General Information

The School of Medicine, which originated in 1868, is the oldest component of Wayne State University.

Mission Statement

The mission of the Wayne State University School of Medicine is to provide the Michigan community with medical and biotechnical resources, in the form of scientific knowledge and trained professionals, so as to improve the overall health of the community.

Curricular Highlights

Community Service Requirement: Optional. A co-curricular program is available.
Research/Thesis Requirement: Optional.

The curriculum employs a combination of traditional and newer approaches to the teaching of medical students. Year 1 begins with an introductory Clinical Medicine course which runs through all four years including: human sexuality, medical interviewing, physical diagnosis, public health and prevention, and evidence-based medicine. Year 1 is organized around the disciplines of structure (anatomy, histology, and embryology) and function (biochemistry, physiology, genetics, and nutrition), and ends with an integrated neuroscience course. Second year is a completely integrated year focusing on pathophysiology, including immunology/micro-biology and pharmacology. Year 3 is a series of clinical clerkships including medicine, surgery, pediatrics, family medicine, psychiatry, neurology, and obstetrics/gynecology. During Year 3 all students have a six-month Continuity clerkship. Year 4 is predominately an elective year with only three required one month rotations: emer-

gency medicine, a sub-internship, and an ambulatory block month. The School of Medicine uses traditional lectures, small-group and panel discussions, computer-assisted instruction, and multimedia in its teaching program. Standardized patients are used for student practice and assessment in the new Richard J. Mazurek, M.D. Medical Education Commons.

USMLE

Step 1: Required. Students must record a passing score for promotion.
Step 2: Clinical Skills (CS): Required. Students must only record a score.
Step 2: Clinical Knowledge (CK): Required. Students must record a passing total score to graduate.

Selection Factors

Consideration is given to the entire record, GPA, MCAT scores, recommendations, and interview results, as these reflect the applicant's personality, maturity, character, and suitability for medicine. Additionally, the committee regards health care experience as desirable. Following an initial screening process, individuals with competitive applications are selected to complete a secondary application. As a state-supported school, the institution must give preference to Michigan residents; however, out-of-state applicants are encouraged to apply. Applicants whose educational backgrounds include academic work outside the United States must have completed two years of coursework at a U.S. or Canadian college, including the prerequisite courses. Interviews are required, but scheduled only with those applicants who are given serious consideration. Students are urged to apply by November 1.

Financial Aid

Financial aid awards administered by the School of Medicine are made by the financial aid officer based on federal guidelines and those established by the Committee on Financial Aid and Scholarships, which includes student representation. The College Work-Study Program and other medically oriented jobs are generally available to eligible students for the summer break. Financial aid seminars are held for incoming students and their families. Additional information is available by calling the Office of

Financial Aid at (313) 577-1039 or visiting its Web site.

Information about Diversity Programs

The Diversity Office sponsors programs for students at the high school, undergraduate, and post-baccalaureate educational levels. The programs are designed to develop and support interest in medical careers for students from diverse backgrounds. A one-year post-baccalaureate program for Michigan residents from disadvantaged backgrounds is offered for qualified medical school applicants. The program offers enrichment in the areas of science knowledge, academic skills, and personal and professional development. Students who complete the post-baccalaureate program successfully are admitted to medical school. For additional information, call (313) 577-1598

Campus Information

Setting

WSUSOM is located in the 236 acre Detroit Medical Center in Detroit, and consists of Scott Hall; Richard J. Mazurek, M.D. Medical Education Commons; Shiffman Medical Library; Lande Medical Research Building; Elliman Clinical Research Building; and the C.S. Mott Building.

Enrollment

For 2009, total enrollment was: 1200

Special Features

Harper University Hospital, Hutzel Women's Hospital, the Children's Hospital of Michigan, Detroit Receiving Hospital, University Health Center, the Rehabilitation Institute of Michigan, and the John Dingell V.A. Medical Center make up the Detroit Medical Center (DMC). In addition, the SEMCME (SE Michigan Center for Medical Education) brings together Wayne State University, the DMC, and community-based teaching hospitals in the Southeastern Michigan metropolitan area.

Housing

The Office of Student Organizations maintains a list of affordable apartments located near the medical school.

Application Process and Requirements 2011–2012

Primary Application Service: AMCAS
Earliest filing date: June 1, 2010
Latest filing date: December 15, 2010

Secondary Application Required?: Yes
Sent to: Screened applicants
Contact: Dawn Yargeau
(313) 577-1466, admissions@med.wayne.edu
Fee: Yes, $50 **Waiver available:** Yes
Earliest filing date: July 15, 2010
Latest filing date: March 15, 2011

MCAT® required?: Yes
Latest MCAT® considered: September 2010
Oldest MCAT® considered: September 2007

Early Decision Program: School does have EDP
Applicants notified: October 1, 2010
EDP available for: Both Residents and Non-residents

Regular Acceptance Notice
Earliest date: October 20, 2010
Latest date: Varies
Applicant's Response to Acceptance Offer – Maximum Time: Three weeks
Requests for Deferred Entrance Considered: Yes

Deposit to Hold Place in Class: Yes
Deposit (Resident): $50 **(Non-resident):** $50
Deposit due: With response to acceptance offer
Applied to tuition: Yes **Refundable:** No
Refundable by: n/a

Estimated number of new entrants: 290
EDP: 2, special program: 19

Start Month/Year: August 2011

Interview Format: One-on-one with an Admission Committee member. Regional interviews are not available. Video interviews are not available.

Other Programs

PREPARATORY PROGRAMS
Postbaccalaureate Program: Yes,
Julia Simmons, (313) 577-1598
jsimmons@med.wayne.edu
Summer Program: Yes, Julia Simmons,
(313) 577-1598, jsimmons@med.wayne.edu

COMBINED DEGREE PROGRAMS
Baccalaureate/M.D.: Yes, http://honors.wayne.edu/medstart.php
Nancy Galster, (313) 577-3030, ad4469@wayne.edu
M.D./M.P.H.: Yes, http://www.med.wayne.edu/fam/mph/index.asp
Dr. Richard Severson, (313) 577-6852,
rseverson@med.wayne.edu
M.D./M.B.A.: No
M.D./J.D.: No
M.D./Ph.D.: Yes, www.mdphdprogram.med.wayne.edu/
Ambika Mathur, Ph.D., (313) 577-1455
amathur@med.wayne.edu

Premedical Coursework

On-line courses accepted in fulfillment of prerequisites: No

Course	Req.	Rec.	Lab.	Sems.	Course	Req.	Rec.	Lab.	Sems.
Inorganic Chemistry	•		•	2	Computer Science				
Behavioral Sciences					Genetics				
Biochemistry					Humanities				
Biology					Organic Chemistry	•		•	2
Biology/Zoology	•		•	2	Physics	•		•	2
Calculus					Psychology				
College English	•			2	Social Sciences				
College Mathematics					Other				

Selection Factors: 2009 Accepted Applicants

Proportion of Accepted Applicants with Relevant Experience (Data Self-Reported to AMCAS®)		
Community Service/Volunteer		71%
Medically-Related Work		90%
Research		83%

Shaded bar represents school's accepted scores ranging from the 10th percentile to the 90th percentile ▓ School Median ● National Median ○

Overall GPA	2.0	2.1	2.2	2.3	2.4	2.5	2.6	2.7	2.8	2.9	3.0	3.1	3.2	3.3	3.4	3.5	3.6	(3.7)	3.8	3.9	4.0
Science GPA	2.0	2.1	2.2	2.3	2.4	2.5	2.6	2.7	2.8	2.9	3.0	3.1	3.2	3.3	3.4	3.5	3.6	(3.7)	3.8	3.9	4.0

MCAT® Total Numeric Score 9 10 11 12 13 14 15 16 17 18 19 20 21 22 23 24 25 26 27 28 29 30 (31)(32) 33 34 35 36 37 38 39 40 41 42 43

Writing Sample			J	K	L	M	N	O	P	(Q)	R	S	T
Verbal Reasoning	3	4	5	6	7	8	9	(10)	11	12	13	14	15
Biological Sciences	3	4	5	6	7	8	9	10	(11)	12	13	14	15
Physical Sciences	3	4	5	6	7	8	9	10	(11)	12	13	14	15

Acceptance & Matriculation Data for 2009–2010 First Year Class

	Resident	Non-resident	International	Total
Applications	1394	2022	393	3809
Interviewed	558	327	122	1007
Deferred	4	1	5	10
Matriculants				
Early Assurance Program	0	0	0	0
Early Decision Program	1	0	0	1
Baccalaureate/M.D.	9	0	0	9
M.D./Ph.D.	2	1	0	3
Matriculated	222	50	18	**290**

Applications accepted from International Applicants: Only Canadian

Matriculant Demographics: 2009–2010 First Year Class

Men: 165 **Women:** 125

Matriculants' Self-Reported Race/Ethnicity

Mexican American	2	Korean	4
Cuban	1	Vietnamese	2
Puerto Rican	0	Other Asian	10
Other Hispanic	0	Total Asian	77
Total Hispanic	3	Native American	2
Chinese	16	Black	18
Asian Indian	32	Native Hawaiian	0
Pakistani	9	White	168
Filipino	5	Unduplicated Number	
Japanese	0	of Matriculants	290

Science and Math Majors: 65%
Matriculants with:
Baccalaureate degree: 100%
Graduate degree(s): 13%

Specialty Choice

2005, 2006, 2007 Graduates, Specialty Choice (As reported by program directors to GME Track™)	
Anesthesiology	5%
Emergency Medicine	13%
Family Practice	9%
Internal Medicine	17%
Obstetrics/Gynecology	5%
Orthopaedic Surgery	4%
Pediatrics	7%
Psychiatry	5%
Radiology	7%
Surgery	5%

Financial Information

Source: 2008-2009 LCME I-B survey and 2009-2010 AAMC TSF questionnaire

	Residents	Non-residents
Total Cost of Attendance	$ 52,138	$ 82,422
Tuition and Fees	$ 29,298	$ 59,275
Other (includes living expenses)	$ 20,653	$ 20,960
Health Insurance (can be waived)	$ 2,187	$ 2,187

Average 2009 Graduate Indebtedness: $154,197
% of Enrolled Students Receiving Aid: 89%

Criminal Background Check

This medical school does not require a criminal background check prior to matriculation.

Mayo Clinic College of Medicine
Mayo Medical School
Rochester, Minnesota

Mayo Medical School
200 First Street, SW
Rochester, Minnesota 55905
T 507 284 2316   F 507 284 2634

Admissions www.mayo.edu/mms/md-admissions.htm
Main www.mayo.edu/mms
Financial www.mayo.edu/mms/md-tuition.html
E-mail medschoolAdmissions@mayo.edu

Private Institution

Dr. Keith D. Lindor, Dean

Dr. Patricia A. Barrier, Associate Dean for Student Affairs

Dr. Eddie L. Greene, Director for Diversity

Barbara L. Porter, Assistant Dean for Student Affairs

David L. Dahlen, Director of Financial Aid and Registrar

General Information
Mayo Medical School is an integral part of Mayo Clinic, the world's largest group practice of medicine. Resources of MMS include a diverse patient population of more than 500,000 registrants annually, four affiliated hospitals with facilities for clinical and basic research, primary care facilities including several rural health centers, and affiliations with physicians who practice in surrounding communities and states.

Mission Statement
Mayo Medical School will use the patient-centered focus and strengths of Mayo Clinic to educate physicians to serve society by assuming leadership roles in medical practice, education, and research.

Curricular Highlights
Community Service Requirement: Required. Community outreach free clinic.
Research/Thesis Requirement: Required.

The innovative patient-based curriculum is characterized by extensive early patient interaction and creative integration of sciences in all segments of the curriculum. In the first two years, courses occur in integrated blocks and contain a clinical component with experiences related to topics covered in the classroom. Themes of basic science, clinical experiences, leadership, improving the public's health, principles of pharmacology, and basic and advanced doctoring are represented throughout the curriculum. First and second year selectives engage students in career exploration, shadowing, and volunteer work. Year three is devoted to developing skills in all of the basic clinical clerkships, moving beyond

acquiring information to the level of synthesis and diagnosis. One quarter of the third year is an opportunity to explore the realm of scientific investigation, as every student completes a research endeavor under the mentorship of an experienced Mayo investigator. Over 80 percent of students publish and/or present their research while in medical school. Year three also includes a didactic block to revisit basic science principles. Year four requirements include a sub-internship and rotations in pediatrics, surgery, and emergency medicine. A social medicine rotation is offered to understand the role of community in the mission of medicine. Integrated into the fourth-year curriculum is a three week didactic experience in which students explore preventive medicine, biomedical ethics, palliative medicine and clinical pharmacology. The remainder of the fourth year is fully elective which allows students to customize their learning.

USMLE
Step 1: Required. Students must record a passing score for promotion.
Step 2: Clinical Skills (CS): Required. Students must record a passing total score to graduate.
Step 2: Clinical Knowledge (CK): Required. Students must record a passing total score to graduate.

Selection Factors
Mayo Medical School is dedicated to enrolling students with superior academic credentials who possess leadership characteristics and have a profound desire to commit their lives to service. An evaluation of the entire AMCAS application, including the academic record, MCAT scores, research, healthcare exploration, and service experiences, is considered in the initial review. For selected candidates three letters of recommendation will be requested. If the applicant qualifies, an onsite interview is granted. Appointment notification occurs approximately every four weeks throughout the admissions cycle. Appointments continue to be offered to fill the class up to the time of matriculation. All matriculates must have completed prerequisite courses and must possess a baccalaureate degree granted from an accredited United States or Canadian college or uni-

versity; the final two years of coursework must be completed at this school. Mayo Medical School actively seeks to recruit and matriculate a diverse class of students. Mayo does not discriminate on the basis of race, sex, creed, national origin, age, or disability in its educational programs or activities. Mayo Medical School does not accept transfer students.

Financial Aid
A generous scholarship program provides every student significant financial support. Financial aid in the form of loans and need-based grants are also available.

Campus Information
Setting
Mayo Medical School is located in Rochester, Minnesota, a vibrant, friendly city of over 100,000 that provides a highly livable environment for Mayo Clinic staff and students.

Enrollment
For 2009, total enrollment was: 179

Special Features
Mayo Clinic's three practices and regional health system comprise the largest integrated private group practice in the world. Thus, the clinical resources experienced as a Mayo medical student are unparalleled.

Housing
On-campus housing is not available. A list of affordable housing options in areas adjacent to the campus can be provided to new students.

Satellite Campuses/Facilities
In addition to the Mayo Clinic in Rochester, Minnesota, rotations can be completed at Mayo Clinic's group practice sites in Arizona and Florida.

Application Process and Requirements 2011–2012

Primary Application Service: AMCAS
Earliest filing date: June 1, 2010
Latest filing date: October 15, 2010

Secondary Application Required?: No
Sent to: n/a
URL: n/a
Fee: Yes, $100   **Waiver available:** Yes
Earliest filing date: n/a
Latest filing date: n/a

MCAT® required?: Yes
Latest MCAT® considered: September 2010
Oldest MCAT® considered: 2008

Early Decision Program: School does not have EDP
Applicants notified: n/a
EDP available for: n/a

Regular Acceptance Notice
Earliest date: October 15, 2010
Latest date: Until class is full
Applicant's Response to Acceptance Offer – Maximum Time: Two weeks

Requests for Deferred Entrance Considered: Yes

Deposit to Hold Place in Class: Yes

Deposit (Resident): $100   **(Non-resident):** $100
Deposit due: With response to acceptance offer
Applied to tuition: No   **Refundable:** Yes, Refundable upon matriculation

Estimated number of new entrants: 50
EDP: n/a, special program: n/a

Start Month/Year: July 2011

Interview Format: Two one-on-one interviews with Admissions Committee members. Regional interviews are not available. Video interviews are not available.

Other Programs

PREPARATORY PROGRAMS
Postbaccalaureate Program: No
Summer Program: Yes, www.mayo.edu/mms/prospective-students.html, Marcy Landswerk, (507) 284-2316, landswerk.marcy@mayo.edu

COMBINED DEGREE PROGRAMS
Baccalaureate/M.D.: No
M.D./M.P.H.: Yes, www.mayo.edu/mms/academic-enrichment.html
M.D./M.B.A.: No
M.D./J.D.: Yes, www.mayo.edu/mms/academic-enrichment.html
M.D./Ph.D.: Yes, www.mayo.edu/mms/md-phd.html

Premedical Coursework

On-line courses accepted in fulfillment of prerequisites: No

Course	Req.	Rec.	Lab.	Sems.
Inorganic Chemistry	•		•	2
Behavioral Sciences				
Biochemistry	•			1
Biology	•		•	2
Biology/Zoology				
Calculus				
College English				
College Mathematics				

Course	Req.	Rec.	Lab.	Sems.
Computer Science				
Genetics				
Humanities				
Organic Chemistry	•		•	2
Physics	•		•	2
Psychology				
Social Sciences				
Other				

Selection Factors: 2009 Accepted Applicants

Proportion of Accepted Applicants with Relevant Experience (Data Self-Reported to AMCAS)		
Community Service/Volunteer		86%
Medically-Related Work		90%
Research		95%

Shaded bar represents school's accepted scores ranging from the 10th percentile to the 90th percentile.   School Median ●   National Median ○

Overall GPA	2.0	2.1	2.2	2.3	2.4	2.5	2.6	2.7	2.8	2.9	3.0	3.1	3.2	3.3	3.4	3.5	3.6	3.7	3.8	(3.9)	4.0
Science GPA	2.0	2.1	2.2	2.3	2.4	2.5	2.6	2.7	2.8	2.9	3.0	3.1	3.2	3.3	3.4	3.5	3.6	3.7	3.8	(3.9)	4.0

MCAT® Total Numeric Score 9 10 11 12 13 14 15 16 17 18 19 20 21 22 23 24 25 26 27 28 29 30 31 (32) 33 (34) 35 36 37 38 39 40 41 42 43

Writing Sample			J		K		L		M		N		O	P	(Q)	R	S	T
Verbal Reasoning	3	4	5	6	7	8	9	(10)	(11)	12	13	14	15
Biological Sciences	3	4	5	6	7	8	9	10	(11)	(12)	13	14	15
Physical Sciences	3	4	5	6	7	8	9	10	(11)	12	13	14	15

Acceptance & Matriculation Data for 2009–2010 First Year Class

	Resident	Non-resident	International	Total
Applications	375	3175	156	3706
Interviewed	43	225	13	281
Deferred	0	1	0	1
Matriculants				
Early Assurance Program	0	0	0	0
Early Decision Program	0	0	0	0
Baccalaureate/M.D.	0	0	0	0
M.D./Ph.D.	0	5	0	5
Matriculated	13	34	2	**49**

Applications accepted from International Applicants: Yes

Matriculant Demographics: 2009–2010 First Year Class

Men: 25   **Women:** 24

Matriculants' Self-Reported Race/Ethnicity

Mexican American	0	**Korean**	0
Cuban	0	**Vietnamese**	0
Puerto Rican	1	**Other Asian**	2
Other Hispanic	0	**Total Asian**	9
Total Hispanic	1	**Native American**	0
Chinese	4	**Black**	4
Asian Indian	3	**Native Hawaiian**	2
Pakistani	0	**White**	32
Filipino	0	**Unduplicated Number**	
Japanese	0	**of Matriculants**	49

Science and Math Majors: 69%
Matriculants with:
Baccalaureate degree: 100%
Graduate degree(s): 6%

Specialty Choice

2005, 2006, 2007 Graduates, Specialty Choice (As reported by program directors to GME Track™)	
Anesthesiology	8%
Emergency Medicine	5%
Family Practice	12%
Internal Medicine	16%
Obstetrics/Gynecology	3%
Orthopaedic Surgery	4%
Pediatrics	14%
Psychiatry	3%
Radiology	10%
Surgery	3%

Financial Information

Source: 2008-2009 LCME I-B survey and 2009-2010 AAMC TSF questionnaire

	Residents	Non-residents
Total Cost of Attendance	$ 61,488	$ 61,488
Tuition and Fees	$ 31,060	$ 31,060
Other (includes living expenses)	$ 30,428	$ 30,428
Health Insurance (not applicable)	$ 0	$ 0

Average 2009 Graduate Indebtedness: $65,208
% of Enrolled Students Receiving Aid: 100%

Criminal Background Check

This medical school requires a criminal background check prior to matriculation.

University of Minnesota Medical School

Minneapolis, Minnesota

University of Minnesota
Medical School
MMC 293, 420 Delaware St SE
G254 Mayo Memorial Building
Minneapolis, Minnesota 55455
T 612 625 7977   F 612 625 8228

Admissions www.meded.umn.edu/admissions (TC),
www.med.umn.edu/duluth/admissions (DU)
Main www.med.umn.edu/
Financial www.meded.umn.edu/financial (TC),
www.med.umn.edu/duluth/admissions/tuition/home.
html (DU)
E-mail meded@umn.edu (Twin Cities),
medadmis@d.umn.edu (Duluth)

Public Institution

Dr. Frank B. Cerra, Dean

*Dr. Gary L. Davis, Senior Associate Dean,
Duluth Campus*

*Dr. Lillian A. Repesh, Associate Dean for
Admissions and Student Affairs, Duluth*

*Paul T. White, J.D., Associate Dean of
Admissions, Twin Cities*

*Dr. Joycelyn Dorscher, Director of Center of
American Indian and Minority Health*

*Mary Tate, Director of Minority Affairs
and Diversity, Twin Cities*

General Information

Founded in 1888, the University of Minnesota Medical School is located on the Twin Cities campus of the University. A two-year rural track is located on the Duluth campus. The medical school is a unit of the U of M Academic Health Center.

Mission Statement

Committed to innovation and diversity, the Medical School educates physicians, scientists, and health professionals; generates knowledge and treatments; and cares for patients and communities with compassion and respect. We value excellence, inclusiveness, collaboration and discovery.

Curricular Highlights

Community Service Requirement: Optional.
Research/Thesis Requirement: Optional.

In the Medical School curricula, progress is based on competency achievement, not time. This innovative program offers integrated instruction in scientific foundations of medicine and clinical sciences. An emphasis on critical thinking and self-directed learning is built into courses, reinforced by Foundations of Critical Thinking cases that span the curriculum. Early clinical exposure includes direct patient care focusing on understanding health care processes. Significant flexibility in the structure and scheduling of the 3rd year and beyond allows students to pursue a wide range of clinical/academic interests. Each student has an advisor throughout medical school to ensure mastery

of required competencies. The Twin Cities campus offers a Medical Scientist Training Program and other combined degrees, while Duluth has a mission focused on preparing students for family practice in rural Minnesota and Native American communities.

USMLE

Step 1: Required. Students must record a passing score for promotion.
Step 2: Clinical Skills (CS): Required. Students must record a passing total score to graduate.
Step 2: Clinical Knowledge (CK): Required. Students must record a passing total score to graduate.

Selection Factors

Legal residents of Minnesota are given preference for admission, but qualified out-of-state applicants are also encouraged to apply. Commitment to improving the human condition, unassailable professional conduct, outstanding interpersonal skills, dedication to lifelong learning and cultural sensitivity are evaluated. The medical school seeks to matriculate a diverse student body *(www.meded.umn.edu/admissions/index.cfm).* Applicant qualifications are evaluated through recommendation letters, post-secondary experiences, undergraduate education, responses to the supplemental application, and on-site interviews. In addition, the medical school's Duluth campus seeks persons with traits that indicate a high potential for becoming a family physician in rural Minnesota or American Indian communities. Transfer students are rarely accepted into Year 3 on the Twin Cities campus. Students accepted to the Twin Cities and Duluth campuses enter a class of 170 and 60 students, respectively. The University of Minnesota Medical School does not discriminate on the basis of race, gender, creed, sexual orientation, disability, or national origin.

Financial Aid

Financial aid applicants must file the FAFSA. Loans and scholarship aid are available. Tuition rates for new matriculates are fixed through a cost-of-degree tuition policy. For information, contact B.J. Gibson *[TC]*(612/625-4998,

www. meded.umn.edu/financial) or Dina Flaherty *[DU]* (218/726-6548, *www.med.umn.edu/duluth/admissions/tuition/home.html).*

Information about Diversity Programs

Minnesota is committed to the recruitment and education of students from groups underrepresented in medicine. For more information, contact the Office of Minority Affairs and Diversity (Twin Cities, 612/625-1494), or the Center of American Indian and Minority Health. CAIMH is headquartered in Duluth (218/726-7235) and also has a Twin Cities office (612/624-0465).

Campus Information

Setting

The Twin Cities campus is located on the second largest university campus in the United States. Most major hospitals in the Minneapolis-St. Paul area are affiliated with the Medical School. The Duluth program is located on the U of MN Duluth campus in northeastern Minnesota and has affiliations with Duluth hospitals.

Enrollment

For 2009, total enrollment was: 985

Special Features

The Medical School provides a wide range of clinical and research opportunities *(www.meded. umn.edu/clerkships/index.cfm; www.med.umn. edu/RPAP/; www.med.umn.edu/imer/; www.ahc. umn.edu/; www.meded.umn.edu/resopps/).*

Housing

Medical student fraternities *[TC]* and private housing are available in the campus neighborhoods; both campuses maintain a list of resources for affordable off-campus housing.

Satellite Campuses/Facilities

The two-year program at the Medical School's Duluth campus was established to increase the number of family practice physicians with a commitment to serve in rural Minnesota or American Indian communities. Students transition to the Twin Cities for years 3 and 4 with the opportunity to complete some rotations in Duluth as well as participate in RPAP. For more information: Susan Christensen (218/726-8511; medadmis@d.umn.edu).

Application Process and Requirements 2011–2012

Primary Application Service: AMCAS
Earliest filing date: June 1, 2010
Latest filing date: November 15, 2010

Secondary Application Required?: Yes
Sent to: All qualified applicants
URL: n/a
Fee: Yes, $75   **Waiver available:** Yes
Earliest filing date: June 1, 2010
Latest filing date: January 31, 2011

MCAT® required?: Yes
Latest MCAT® considered: September 2010
Oldest MCAT® considered: 2007

Early Decision Program: School does have EDP
Applicants notified: October 1, 2010
EDP available for: Both Residents and Non-residents

Regular Acceptance Notice
Earliest date: October 15, 2010
Latest date: Until class is full
Applicant's Response to Acceptance Offer – Maximum Time: Two weeks

Requests for Deferred Entrance Considered: Yes

Deposit to Hold Place in Class: Yes
Deposit (Resident): $100   **(Non-resident):** $100
Deposit due: With response to acceptance offer
Applied to tuition: Yes   **Refundable:** Yes
Refundable by: May 15, 2011

Estimated number of new entrants: 230
EDP: 20, special program: 5

Start Month/Year: August 2011

Interview Format: Individual interviews are conducted. Regional interviews are not available. Video interviews are not available.

Other Programs

PREPARATORY PROGRAMS
Postbaccalaureate Program: No
Summer Program: Yes, www.caimh.org
Pre-matriculation Program: Yes, www.caimh.org

COMBINED DEGREE PROGRAMS
Baccalaureate/M.D.: Yes, www.med.umn.edu/duluth/admissions/home.html, Susan Christensen (218) 726-8511, medadmis@d.umn.edu
M.D./M.P.H.: Yes, www.sph.umn.edu/education/degrees/home.html, Sarah Harper, (612) 626-3740; (800) 774-8636, harpe014@umn.edu
M.D./M.B.A.: Yes, www.meded.umn.edu/admissions/MD-MBA.cfm, Tracy Keeling, (612) 625-5555, tkeeling@umn.edu
M.D./J.D.: Yes, www.meded.umn.edu/admissions/JD-MD.cfm, Carol Rachac, (612) 625-3356, crachac@umn.edu
M.D./Ph.D.: Yes, www.med.umn.edu/mdphd/home.html Susan Shurson, (612) 625-3680, shurs002@umn.edu
Additional: Yes, M.D./M.H.I., www.hinfgrad.umn.edu/mhi/MD-MHI.html Stewart Speedie, (612) 624-4657, speed002@umn.edu

Premedical Coursework

On-line courses accepted in fulfillment of prerequisites: On a case-by-case basis

Course	Req.	Rec.	Lab.	Sem.
Inorganic Chemistry	•		•	1
Behavioral Sciences				
Biochemistry		•		1
Biology	•		•	1
Biology/Zoology				
Calculus				
College English				
College Mathematics				
Computer Science				

Course	Req.	Rec.	Lab.	Sem.
Genetics		•		
Humanities		•		1
Organic Chemistry	•		•	2
Physics		•	•	2
Psychology				1
Social Sciences		•		1
Statistics		•		
Ethics		•		
Foreign Language		•		

Selection Factors: 2009 Accepted Applicants

Proportion of Accepted Applicants with Relevant Experience (Data Self-Reported to AMCAS)		
Community Service/Volunteer		77%
Medically-Related Work		87%
Research		81%

Shaded bar represents school's accepted scores ranging from the 10th percentile to the 90th percentile. School Median ● National Median ●

	2.0	2.1	2.2	2.3	2.4	2.5	2.6	2.7	2.8	2.9	3.0	3.1	3.2	3.3	3.4	3.5	3.6	3.7	3.8	3.9	4.0
Overall GPA	2.0	2.1	2.2	2.3	2.4	2.5	2.6	2.7	2.8	2.9	3.0	3.1	3.2	3.3	3.4	3.5	3.6	3.7	(3.8)	3.9	4.0
Science GPA	2.0	2.1	2.2	2.3	2.4	2.5	2.6	2.7	2.8	2.9	3.0	3.1	3.2	3.3	3.4	3.5	3.6	3.7	(3.8)	3.9	4.0

MCAT® Total Numeric Score 9 10 11 12 13 14 15 16 17 18 19 20 21 22 23 24 25 26 27 28 29 30 31 (32) 33 34 35 36 37 38 39 40 41 42 43

Writing Sample				J	K	L	M	N	O	(P)	(Q)	R	S	T
Verbal Reasoning	3	4	5	6	7	8	9	(10)	11	12	13	14	15
Biological Sciences	3	4	5	6	7	8	9	10	(11)	12	13	14	15
Physical Sciences	3	4	5	6	7	8	9	10	(11)	12	13	14	15

Acceptance & Matriculation Data for 2009–2010 First Year Class

	Resident	Non-resident	International	Total
Applications	1152	3155	248	4555
Interviewed	366	216	14	596
Deferred	5	1	0	6
Matriculants				
Early Assurance Program	0	0	0	0
Early Decision Program	10	1	0	11
Baccalaureate/M.D.	1	0	0	1
M.D./Ph.D.	1	4	1	6
Matriculated	175	48	6	**229**

Applications accepted from International Applicants: Yes

Matriculant Demographics: 2009–2010 First Year Class

Men: 121   **Women:** 108

Matriculants' Self-Reported Race/Ethnicity

Mexican American	1	Korean	4
Cuban	1	Vietnamese	1
Puerto Rican	2	Other Asian	1
Other Hispanic	5	Total Asian	17
Total Hispanic	8	Native American	8
Chinese	5	Black	3
Asian Indian	4	Native Hawaiian	1
Pakistani	1	White	192
Filipino	1	Unduplicated Number	
Japanese	0	of Matriculants	229

Science and Math Majors: 72%
Matriculants with:
  Baccalaureate degree: 99%
  Graduate degree(s): 13%

Specialty Choice

2005, 2006, 2007 Graduates, Specialty Choice (As reported by program directors to GME Track™)	
Anesthesiology	5%
Emergency Medicine	7%
Family Practice	17%
Internal Medicine	17%
Obstetrics/Gynecology	5%
Orthopaedic Surgery	4%
Pediatrics	8%
Psychiatry	2%
Radiology	4%
Surgery	6%

Financial Information

Source: 2008-2009 LCME I-B survey and 2009-2010 AAMC TSF questionnaire

	Residents	Non-residents
Total Cost of Attendance	$ 55,719	$ 63,627
Tuition and Fees	$ 34,036	$ 41,944
Other (includes living expenses)	$ 19,275	$ 19,275
Health Insurance (can be waived)	$ 2,408	$ 2,408

Average 2009 Graduate Indebtedness: $151,444
% of Enrolled Students Receiving Aid: 92%

Criminal Background Check

This medical school requires a criminal background check prior to matriculation.

University of Mississippi School of Medicine

Jackson, Mississippi

Associate Dean for Admissions
University of Mississippi School of Medicine
2500 North State Street
Jackson, Mississippi 39216-4505
T 601 984 5010   F 601 984 5008

Admissions http://som.umc.edu/admissions.html
Main http://som.umc.edu
Financial http://som.umc.edu/
acceptedAppl.html#FinanAssist
E-mail AdmitMD@som.umsmed.edu

Public Institution

Dr. LouAnn Woodward, Interim Dean

Dr. Steven T. Case, Associate Dean for Admissions

Dr. Jasmine P. Taylor, Associate Dean for Multicultural Affairs

Stacey Mathews, Director of Student Financial Aid

Dr. Peggy M. Davis, Director of Admissions

Barbara M. Westerfield, Registrar

General Information

The School of Medicine, created by a special act of the Board of Trustees in June 1903, operated as a two-year school in Oxford until 1955, when it expanded to four years and moved to the new University of Mississippi Medical Center in Jackson. The Medical Center now houses the Schools of Medicine, Nursing, Health Related Professions, Dentistry, Graduate Studies in Health Sciences, and the 722-bed University Hospitals and Health System.

Mission Statement

The primary mission of the University of Mississippi School of Medicine is to offer an accredited program of medical education that will provide well-trained physicians and certain supporting health care professionals, in numbers consistent with the health care needs of the state, who are responsive to the health problems of the people and committed to medical education as a continuum, that must prevail throughout professional life.

Curricular Highlights

Community Service Requirement: Optional. Medical students staff the Jackson Free Clinic
Research/Thesis Requirement: Optional.

During the two preclinical years, students learn the sciences basic to the study of medicine and participate in laboratory exercises, small-group discussion, computer-assisted learning, and independent study. The preclinical curriculum was revised to increase integration and improve the sequencing of course content and provide earlier clinical experience for students.

The third year involves full-time clinical study as students rotate through the major clinical disciplines and participate in the team care of patients in the University Hospitals and Clinics, Veterans Affairs Medical Center, and various community settings. The fourth year consists of eight required calendar month blocks that may be taken at any time during the eleven months available from July through May. Fourth-year clinical clerkships provide greater depth of study in core areas of medicine, as well as in a student's anticipated medical specialty. Opportunities exist for advanced study and research in basic science departments and for electives at other institutions in this country or abroad.

USMLE

Step 1: Required. Students must record a passing score for promotion.
Step 2: Clinical Skills (CS): Required. Students must record a passing total score to graduate.
Step 2: Clinical Knowledge (CK): Required. Students must record a passing total score to graduate.

Selection Factors

The Admissions Committee selects applicants on a competitive basis without regard to age, sex, sexual orientation, race, creed, national origin, marital status, handicap, or veteran status. Strong preference is given to legal residents of Mississippi; in recent years, non-residents have not been admitted. Interviews are arranged at the discretion of the Admissions Committee; major considerations are undergraduate BCPM GPA and MCAT scores. Interviews are used to assess non-cognitive variables and communication skills. Experiences listed on an AMCAS application document nonacademic and professional attributes, and premedical faculty evaluations reveal an applicant's approach to academic study and professionalism. For details, see *http://som.umc.edu/admissions.html#EvalApps*. Mississippi residents enrolled in other medical schools accredited by the Liaison Committee on Medical Education may be considered for advanced standing transfer.

Financial Aid

Accepted students may apply for financial aid. The school participates in federal scholarship

and loan programs (such as Perkins and Stafford) and state-funded Mississippi Rural Physician Scholarship and State Medical Education Loan/Scholarship programs. Eligible students may qualify for limited scholarship funds provided by private donors. For details, see *http://som.umc.edu/acceptedappl.html# FinanAssist.*

Information about Diversity Programs

The Admissions Committee encourages students from groups underrepresented in medicine to apply for admission. Information about pipeline programs and support provided by the Division of Multicultural Affairs can be obtained at: *http://mca.umc.edu/.*

Campus Information

Setting

The Medical Center is located on a 164 acre campus in Jackson. The state capital and Mississippi's largest city, Jackson offers a wide array of professional arts attractions. Recreational facilities include a 30,000-acre reservoir, just 15 minutes from the campus.

Enrollment

For 2009, total enrollment was: 466

Special Features

The opening of a new adult medical and surgical hospital in 2006 marked the completion of a project to replace the original teaching hospital with four new state-of-the-art hospitals. The Medical Center opened a 57,000 square foot student union – with a state-of-the-art fitness center and gymnasium – in 1999. Medical students sponsor the Jackson Free Clinic that provides medical care to homeless and uninsured patients on Saturdays.

Housing

Rent averages from $450-$750 a month for area apartments.

Satellite Campuses/Facilities

The Jackson Medical Mall, one mile from the campus, houses the hospital's clinics, offices for the Jackson Heart Study and the Medical Center's Cancer Institute. Originally the city's first shopping mall, the Jackson Medical Mall is recognized as a national model of urban revitalization.

Application Process and Requirements 2011–2012

Primary Application Service: AMCAS
Earliest filing date: June 1, 2010
Latest filing date: October 15, 2010

Secondary Application Required?: Yes
Sent to: URL and password provided after receipt of AMCAS application.
URL: http://som.umc.edu/Amcas/Menu.ctrl?action=Display
Fee: Yes, $50   **Waiver available:** Yes
Earliest filing date: June 1, 2010
Latest filing date: December 1, 2010

MCAT® required?: Yes
Latest MCAT® considered: September 2010
Oldest MCAT® considered: April 2007

Early Decision Program: School does have EDP
Applicants notified: Not later than October 1, 2010
EDP available for: Residents only

**Regular Acceptance Notice
Earliest date:** October 16, 2010
Latest date: Until class is full
**Applicant's Response to Acceptance
Offer – Maximum Time:** Two weeks

**Requests for Deferred
Entrance Considered:** Yes

Deposit to Hold Place in Class: No
Deposit (Resident): n/a   **(Non-resident):** n/a
Deposit due: n/a/
Applied to tuition: n/a   **Refundable:** n/a
Refundable by: n/a

Estimated number of new entrants: 130
EDP: 10, special program: n/a

Start Month/Year: August 2, 2011

Interview Format: Three semi-structured, one-on-one interviews. Regional interviews are not available. Video interviews are not available.

Other Programs

PREPARATORY PROGRAMS

Postbaccalaureate Program: Yes, http://som.umc.edu/admissions.html#PPT
Summer Program: Yes, http://mca.umc.edu/
Pre-matriculation Program: Yes, http://mca.umc.edu/programs/pre_mat.html
MedCorp Program: Yes, http://mca.umc.edu/programs/medcorp.html

COMBINED DEGREE PROGRAMS

Baccalaureate/M.D.: No
M.D./M.P.H.: No
M.D./M.B.A.: No
M.D./J.D.: No
M.D./Ph.D.: Yes, http://som.umc.edu/admissions.html#MDPhD

Premedical Coursework

On-line courses accepted in fulfillment of prerequisites: No

Course	Req.	Rec.	Lab.	Hrs.
Inorganic Chemistry	•		•	8
Behavioral Sciences		•		
Biochemistry		•		
Biology				
Biology/Zoology	•		•	8
Calculus		•		3
College English	•			6
College Mathematics	•			6
Computer Science				

Course	Req.	Rec.	Lab.	Hrs.
Genetics		•		3
Humanities		•		
Organic Chemistry	•		•	8
Physics	•		•	8
Psychology		•		
Social Sciences		•		
Vertebrate Anatomy		•		3
Histology		•		3
Physiology		•		3

Selection Factors: 2009 Accepted Applicants

Proportion of Accepted Applicants with Relevant Experience (Data Self-Reported to AMCAS®)		
Community Service/Volunteer		78%
Medically-Related Work		78%
Research		52%

Shaded bar represents school's accepted scores ranging from the 10th percentile to the 90th percentile. **School Median** ● **National Median** ◐

Overall GPA	2.0	2.1	2.2	2.3	2.4	2.5	2.6	2.7	2.8	2.9	3.0	3.1	3.2	3.3	3.4	3.5	3.6	(3.7)	3.8	3.9	4.0
Science GPA	2.0	2.1	2.2	2.3	2.4	2.5	2.6	2.7	2.8	2.9	3.0	3.1	3.2	3.3	3.4	3.5	3.6	(3.7)	3.8	3.9	4.0

MCAT® Total Numeric Score 9 10 11 12 13 14 15 16 17 18 19 20 21 22 23 24 25 26 27 (28) 29 30 31 (32) 33 34 35 36 37 38 39 40 41 42 43

Writing Sample		J	K	L	M	(N)	O	P	(Q)	R	S	T
Verbal Reasoning	3	4	5	6	7	8	(9)	(10)	11	12	13	14	15
Biological Sciences	3	4	5	6	7	8	9	(10)	(11)	12	13	14	15
Physical Sciences	3	4	5	6	7	8	(9)	10	(11)	12	13	14	15

Acceptance & Matriculation Data for 2009–2010 First Year Class

	Resident	Non-resident	International	Total
Applications	270	1	1	272
Interviewed	201	0	0	201
Deferred	0	0	0	0
Matriculants				
Early Assurance Program	0	0	0	0
Early Decision Program	8	0	0	8
Baccalaureate/M.D.	0	0	0	0
M.D./Ph.D.	2	0	0	2
Matriculated	120	0	0	**120**

Applications accepted from International Applicants: No

Specialty Choice

2005, 2006, 2007 Graduates, Specialty Choice (As reported by program directors to GME Track™)	
Anesthesiology	6%
Emergency Medicine	7%
Family Practice	8%
Internal Medicine	23%
Obstetrics/Gynecology	7%
Orthopaedic Surgery	5%
Pediatrics	11%
Psychiatry	2%
Radiology	5%
Surgery	6%

Matriculant Demographics: 2009–2010 First Year Class

Men: 63   **Women:** 57

Matriculants' Self-Reported Race/Ethnicity

Mexican American	0	**Korean**	1
Cuban	0	**Vietnamese**	1
Puerto Rican	0	**Other Asian**	0
Other Hispanic	2	**Total Asian**	8
Total Hispanic	2	**Native American**	2
Chinese	1	**Black**	15
Asian Indian	3	**Native Hawaiian**	0
Pakistani	1	**White**	97
Filipino	0	**Unduplicated Number**	
Japanese	1	**of Matriculants**	120

Science and Math Majors: 70%
Matriculants with:
   Baccalaureate degree: 100%
   Graduate degree(s): 19%

Financial Information

Source: 2008-2009 LCME I-B survey and 2009-2010 AAMC TSF questionnaire

	Residents	Non-residents
Total Cost of Attendance	$ 41,749	$ 0
Tuition and Fees	$ 13,649	$ 0
Other (includes living expenses)	$ 26,243	$ 0
Health Insurance (can be waived)	$ 1,857	$ 0

Average 2009 Graduate Indebtedness: $109,857
% of Enrolled Students Receiving Aid: 88%

Criminal Background Check

This medical school requires a criminal background check prior to matriculation.

Saint Louis University School of Medicine

St. Louis, Missouri

Saint Louis University School of Medicine
Office of Admissions
1402 S. Grand Blvd. M226
St. Louis, Missouri 63104
T 314 977 9870 **F** 314 977 9825

Admissions http://medschool.slu.edu/admissions
Main www.slu.edu
Financial http://medschool.slu.edu/sfs
E-mail slumd@slu.edu

Private Institution

Dr. Philip O. Alderson, Vice President and Dean

*Dr. L. James Willmore,
Associate Dean, Admissions*

*Dr. Michael T. Railey, Associate Dean,
Multicultural Affairs*

Sandra Pritt, Student Financial Services

Nancy Wilson, Program Coordinator

General Information

Established in 1836, Saint Louis University School of Medicine has the distinction of awarding the first M.D. degree west of the Mississippi River. The school is recognized as a pioneer in geriatric medicine, organ transplantation, chronic disease prevention, cardiovascular disease, neurosciences, and immunology and vaccine research, among others. The School of Medicine trains physicians and biomedical scientists, conducts medical research, and provides health services on a local, national, and international level.

Mission Statement

Beyond the important objective of training physicians who are scholars of human biology, the School of Medicine strives to graduate physicians who manifest in their personal and professional lives an appreciation of humanistic medicine. We regard humanistic medicine as a constellation of ethical and professional attitudes, which affect the physician's interactions with patients, colleagues, and society. Among these attitudes are concern for the sanctity of human life; commitment to dignity and respect in the provision of medical care to all patients; devotion to social justice, especially regarding inequities in the availability of health care; humility and awareness of medicine's limitations in the care of the sick; appreciation of the role of non-medical factors in a patient's state of well-being or illness; and mature, well-balanced professional behavior that derives from comfortable relationships with members of the human family and one's Creator.

Curricular Highlights

Community Service Requirement: Optional. Distinction in Community Service

Research/Thesis Requirement: Optional. Distinction in Research

The M.D. curriculum provides coordination and integration of the basic and clinical sciences across all four years. Additionally, it follows established principles of adult learning, and so is a hybrid of lectures, small-group activities, early clinical activities, self-directed learning, and problem-solving exercises. The first two years of the curriculum are devoted to the study of the fundamental sciences basic to medicine. In year two, a series of integrated modules that are organ-based are coupled with the acquisition of fundamental clinical skills required to begin the clinical clerkships that are taught in the Applied Clinical Skills and Patient, Physician, and Society and Bedside Diagnosis course series. The last two years concentrate on the further development and refinement of essential clinical skills, while also providing ongoing integration of the basic sciences into clinical practice. The grading system is pass/fail for years one and two. The grading system for the next two years consists of the following levels: honors, near honors, pass, and fail.

USMLE

Step 1: Required. Students must record a passing score for promotion.
Step 2: Clinical Skills (CS): Required. Students must record a passing total score to graduate.
Step 2: Clinical Knowledge (CK): Required. Students must record a passing total score to graduate.

Selection Factors

Saint Louis University School of Medicine encourages applications from persons who have demonstrated a high level of academic achievement and who manifest in their personal lives those human qualities that are required for a career of service to society.

Financial Aid

Our mission is to assist you in identifying and providing resources to meet the costs associated with our standard student budget. Students who file the Free Application for Federal Student Aid (FAFSA) with student (and spouse if applicable) and parental data and demonstrate financial need will be considered for scholarships up to $10,000 annually. Students who file the FAFSA with student (and spouse if applicable) data and demonstrate financial need will be considered for scholarships up to $5,000 annually.

Information about Diversity Programs

The School of Medicine is committed to promoting diversity in the classroom and in the clinics so that all students understand and learn from each other about the practice of medicine in a diverse environment. The Office of Multicultural Affairs assists students from diverse backgrounds to be successful as they pursue a career as a physician.

Campus Information

Setting
The medical school is located in the city's arts district five minutes from the Gateway Arch or the Mississippi Riverfront.

Enrollment
For 2009, total enrollment was: 717

Special Features
A Simulation Laboratory and a Clinical Skills Center provide the latest methodology for instruction and evaluation using standardized patients and high end devices to learn clinical skills, in addition to the regular training sites. The new research building provides state-of-the-art facilities for health sciences research that touches lives and provides service to the community.

Housing
St. Louis and the surrounding area offer plenty of affordable housing.

Satellite Campuses/Facilities
Major teaching affiliations include The University Hospital, Cardinal Glennon Children's Medical Center, St. Elizabeth's Hospital, St. John's Mercy Medical Center, St. Mary's Hospital, DesPeres Hospital, Forest Park Hospital, and St. Louis Veterans Affairs Hospitals.

Application Process and Requirements 2011–2012

Primary Application Service: AMCAS
Earliest filing date: June 1, 2010
Latest filing date: December 15, 2010

Secondary Application Required?: Yes
Sent to: All applicants
URL: www.oasprod3.com/schools/slusom
Fee: Yes, $100   **Waiver available:** Yes
Earliest filing date: June 1, 2010
Latest filing date: February 15, 2011

MCAT® required?: Yes
Latest MCAT® considered: September 2010
Oldest MCAT® considered: April 2007

Early Decision Program: School does have EDP
Applicants notified: October 1, 2010
EDP available for: Both Residents and Non-residents

**Regular Acceptance Notice
Earliest date:** October 15, 2010
Latest date: Until class is full
Applicant's Response to Acceptance Offer – Maximum Time: Two weeks

Requests for Deferred Entrance Considered: Yes

Deposit to Hold Place in Class: Yes
Deposit (Resident): $100   **(Non-resident):** $100
Deposit due: With response to acceptance offer
Applied to tuition: Yes   **Refundable:** Yes
Refundable by: May 15, 2011

Estimated number of new entrants: 175
EDP: 2, special program: 30

Start Month/Year: August 2011

Interview Format: A single one-on-one interview. Some regional interviews may be offered. Video interviews are not available.

Other Programs

PREPARATORY PROGRAMS
Postbaccalaureate Program: Yes,
http://medschool.slu.edu/anatomy/caps/
Summer Program: No

COMBINED DEGREE PROGRAMS
Baccalaureate/M.D.: Yes,
www.slu.edu/colleges/AS/phs/medScholars.html
M.D./M.P.H.: Yes, http://publichealth.slu.edu/programs/mph/mdmph.html, Bernard Backer, (314) 977-8144, backerb@slu.edu
M.D./M.B.A.: Yes, www.slu.edu/x16691.xml
M.D./J.D.: No
M.D./Ph.D.: Yes, http://medschool.slu.edu/admissions/index.php?page=mdphd-program, Andrew Lechner, Ph.D., (314) 977-9877, lechnera@slu.edu

Premedical Coursework

On-line courses accepted in fulfillment of prerequisites: No

Course	Req.	Rec.	Lab.	Hrs.	Course	Req.	Rec.	Lab.	Hrs.
Inorganic Chemistry	•		•	8	Computer Science				
Behavioral Sciences					Genetics				
Biochemistry		•			Humanities	•			12
Biology					Organic Chemistry	•		•	8
Biology/Zoology	•		•	8	Physics	•		•	8
Calculus					Psychology				
College English	•			6	Social Sciences				
College Mathematics					Other				

Selection Factors: 2009 Accepted Applicants

Proportion of Accepted Applicants with Relevant Experience (Data Self-Reported to AMCAS®)		
Community Service/Volunteer		70%
Medically-Related Work		85%
Research		81%

Shaded bar represents school's accepted scores ranging from the 10th percentile to the 90th percentile   School Median ●   National Median ●

Overall GPA	2.0	2.1	2.2	2.3	2.4	2.5	2.6	2.7	2.8	2.9	3.0	3.1	3.2	3.3	3.4	3.5	3.6	3.7	(3.8)	3.9	4.0
Science GPA	2.0	2.1	2.2	2.3	2.4	2.5	2.6	2.7	2.8	2.9	3.0	3.1	3.2	3.3	3.4	3.5	3.6	(3.8)	3.9	4.0

MCAT® Total Numeric Score 9 10 11 12 13 14 15 16 17 18 19 20 21 22 23 24 25 26 27 28 29 30 31 (32)(33) 34 35 36 37 38 39 40 41 42 43

Writing Sample				J	K	L	M	N	O	P	(Q)	R	S	T
Verbal Reasoning	3	4	5	6	7	8	9	(10)	11	12	13	14	15
Biological Sciences	3	4	5	6	7	8	9	10	(11)	12	13	14	15
Physical Sciences	3	4	5	6	7	8	9	10	(11)	12	13	14	15

Acceptance & Matriculation Data for 2009–2010 First Year Class

	Resident	Non-resident	International	Total
Applications	390	5614	244	6248
Interviewed	122	789	40	951
Deferred	1	2	5	8
Matriculants				
Early Assurance Program	0	0	0	0
Early Decision Program	1	0	0	1
Baccalaureate/M.D.	0	0	0	0
M.D./Ph.D.	0	1	0	1
Matriculated	49	122	4	**175**

Applications accepted from International Applicants: Yes

Matriculant Demographics: 2009–2010 First Year Class

Men: 112   **Women:** 63

Matriculants' Self-Reported Race/Ethnicity

Mexican American	0	**Korean**	6
Cuban	0	**Vietnamese**	3
Puerto Rican	0	**Other Asian**	5
Other Hispanic	0	**Total Asian**	59
Total Hispanic	0	**Native American**	1
Chinese	15	**Black**	2
Asian Indian	29	**Native Hawaiian**	0
Pakistani	1	**White**	107
Filipino	1	**Unduplicated Number**	
Japanese	1	**of Matriculants**	175

Science and Math Majors: 65%
Matriculants with:
   Baccalaureate degree: 99%
   Graduate degree(s): 7%

Specialty Choice

2005, 2006, 2007 Graduates, Specialty Choice (As reported by program directors to GME Track™)	
Anesthesiology	6%
Emergency Medicine	5%
Family Practice	9%
Internal Medicine	18%
Obstetrics/Gynecology	6%
Orthopaedic Surgery	2%
Pediatrics	14%
Psychiatry	6%
Radiology	4%
Surgery	6%

Financial Information

Source: 2008-2009 LCME I-B survey and 2009-2010 AAMC TSF questionnaire

	Residents	Non-residents
Total Cost of Attendance	$ 67,239	$ 67,239
Tuition and Fees	$ 45,315	$ 45,315
Other (includes living expenses)	$ 19,764	$ 19,764
Health Insurance (can be waived)	$ 2,160	$ 2,160

Average 2009 Graduate Indebtedness: $179,113
% of Enrolled Students Receiving Aid: 87%

Criminal Background Check

This medical school requires a criminal background check prior to matriculation.

University of Missouri School of Medicine

Columbia, Missouri

Alison Martin, M.Ed., Director of Admissions
Office of Med. Education, MA215 Med. Sci. Bldg
Univ. of Missouri School of Medicine
One Hospital Drive, Columbia, Missouri 65212
T 573 882 9219   F 573 884 2988

Admissions http://som.missouri.edu/admit.shtml/
Main http://som.missouri.edu/
Financial http://som.missouri.edu/financial/
E-mail MizzouMed@missouri.edu

Public Institution

Dr. Robert Churchill, Sr. Dean

Alison Martin, Director of Admissions, Recruitment & Career Advising

Traci Wilson-Kleekamp, Diversity Outreach Coordinator

Cheri Marks, Coordinator of Financial Aid

Dr. Rachel Brown, Associate Dean for Student Programs

Dr. Linda Headrick, Senior Associate Dean for Education & Faculty Development

General Information

The University of Missouri School of Medicine was established in 1872. The MU Health Sciences Center includes the University Hospital, and multiple specialized and community clinics, both inpatient and outpatient. The MU School of Medicine has additional affiliations with other hospitals and clinics across the state.

Mission Statement

The mission of MU School of Medicine is to educate physicians to provide effective patient-centered care for the people of Missouri and beyond. Patient-centered care reflects a respect for individual patient's values, preferences, and expressed needs. This care is grounded in the best available evidence and conserves limited resources, and it depends on shared decision-making and active patient participation. Our graduates' care will be marked by compassion, empathy, and patient advocacy. Our graduates also will be: honest, with high ethical standards; knowledgeable in biomedical sciences, evidence-based practice, and societal and cultural issues; critical-thinkers and problem-solvers; able to communicate with patients and other health-care team members; committed to improving quality and safety; and committed to lifelong learning and mastering information.

Curricular Highlights

Community Service Requirement: Optional.
Research/Thesis Requirement: Optional.

In 1993, The University of Missouri School of Medicine implemented a curriculum that substantially reduced lectures in favor of problem-based learning. The curriculum emphasizes problem solving, self-directed learning and early clinical experiences rather than memorization. The first and second years each consist of four 10-week blocks. The third year is made up of seven core clerkships. The fourth year consists of advanced clinical selectives, advanced biomedical selectives and general electives.

USMLE

Step 1: Required. Students must record a passing score for promotion.
Step 2: Clinical Skills (CS): Required. Students must record a passing total score to graduate.
Step 2: Clinical Knowledge (CK): Required. Students must record a passing total score to graduate.

Selection Factors

The Admissions Committee conducts required on-campus personal interviews. Strong preference is given to Missouri residents. Exceptional residents of other states may also be admitted. Non-Missouri residents are evaluated on an individual basis, and may be asked to provide evidence of Missouri ties, diversity, and/or exceptional academics. Selection for interview is based upon academic performance; personal qualities such as motivation, social concern, and integrity; and tested motivation for medicine. Early Decision Program applicants must be Missouri residents with 3.75 cum GPA and MCAT sum of 30 with no individual section score below 9. The School of Medicine does not discriminate on the basis of race, sex, creed, national origin, age, handicap, religion, or status as a Vietnam-era veteran in admission or access to or treatment or employment in its programs and activities.

Financial Aid

Students are admitted to the School of Medicine without regard to financial circumstances. MU participates in federal scholarship and loan programs. The institutional scholarship program is primarily need-based. Institutional long-term loans are available and MU also operates an emergency short-term loan program.

Information about Diversity Programs

The University of Missouri is committed to the recruitment and education of disadvantaged and nontraditional applicants and applicants from groups underrepresented in medicine. The School of Medicine sponsors summer programs targeting rural and disadvantaged high school students, although students from across Missouri may participate.

Campus Information

Setting

The University of Missouri School of Medicine is located in the heart of the University of Missouri's main campus, allowing students to use its programs and facilities. MU has affiliations with all five hospitals in the city and a number of satellite and specialty clinics in the mid-Missouri area.

Enrollment

For 2009, total enrollment was: 387

Housing

Most medical students live in privately-owned apartments, condominiums, and townhouses; some purchase their own homes.

Satellite Campuses/Facilities

Students may choose to complete elective clinical rotations in and around Columbia, or off-site in Missouri or across the country. Students may participate in the Rural Track Program, which offers rural sites for both clerkship and elective experiences.

Application Process and Requirements 2011–2012

Primary Application Service: AMCAS
Earliest filing date: June 1, 2010
Latest filing date: November 1, 2010

Secondary Application Required?: Yes
Sent to: All Missouri residents
and screened out-of-state applicants
Alison Martin, M.Ed., (573) 882-9219
MizzouMed@health.missouri.edu
URL: n/a   **Waiver available:** Yes
Earliest filing date: July 1, 2010
Latest filing date: January 15, 2011

MCAT® required?: Yes
Latest MCAT® considered: September 2010
Oldest MCAT® considered: 2007

Early Decision Program: School does have EDP
Applicants notified: October 1, 2010
EDP available for: Residents only

Regular Acceptance Notice
Earliest date: October 15, 2010
Latest date: Until class is full
Applicant's Response to Acceptance
Offer – Maximum Time: 30 days

Requests for Deferred
Entrance Considered: Yes

Deposit to Hold Place in Class: Yes
Deposit (Resident): $100   **(Non-resident):** $100
Deposit due: Within 30 days of acceptance offer
until July, after which less time is given.
Applied to tuition: Yes   **Refundable:** Yes
Refundable by: May 15, 2011

Estimated number of new entrants: 96
EDP: 4, special program: 15

Start Month/Year: July 2011

Interview Format: Two open file, one-on-one
interviews by Admissions Committee members are
required. Regional interviews are not available. Video
interviews are not available.

Other Programs

PREPARATORY PROGRAMS
Postbaccalaureate Program: No
Summer Program: No

COMBINED DEGREE PROGRAMS
Baccalaureate/M.D.: No
M.D./M.P.H.: No
M.D./M.B.A.: No
M.D./J.D.: No
M.D./Ph.D.: Yes, http://som.missouri.edu/
Research/Training/Combined.aspx
Douglas Anthony, M.D., Ph.D., (573) 884-4079,
mdphd@missouri.edu

Premedical Coursework

On-line courses accepted in fulfillment of prerequisites: No

Course	Req.	Rec.	Lab.	Hrs.	Course	Req.	Rec.	Lab.	Hrs.
Inorganic Chemistry					Computer Science				
Behavioral Sciences					Genetics				
Biochemistry		•			Humanities		•		
Biology	•		•	8	Organic Chemistry	•		•	8
Biology/Zoology					Physics	•		•	8
Calculus					Psychology				
College English					Social Sciences	•			
College Mathematics	•			3	English Composition				6

Selection Factors: 2009 Accepted Applicants

Proportion of Accepted Applicants with Relevant Experience (Data Self-Reported to AMCAS®)		
Community Service/Volunteer		69%
Medically-Related Work		71%
Research		69%

Shaded bar represents school's accepted scores ranging from the 10th percentile to the 90th percentile   School Median ● National Median ◉

Overall GPA	2.0	2.1	2.2	2.3	2.4	2.5	2.6	2.7	2.8	2.9	3.0	3.1	3.2	3.3	3.4	3.5	3.6	3.7	3.8	(3.9)	4.0
Science GPA	2.0	2.1	2.2	2.3	2.4	2.5	2.6	2.7	2.8	2.9	3.0	3.1	3.2	3.3	3.4	3.5	3.6	3.7	(3.8)	3.9	4.0

MCAT® Total Numeric Score 9 10 11 12 13 14 15 16 17 18 19 20 21 22 23 24 25 26 27 28 29 30 (31) (32) 33 34 35 36 37 38 39 40 41 42 43

Writing Sample				J	K	L	M	N	O	P	(Q)	R	S	T
Verbal Reasoning	3	4	5	6	7	8	9	(10)		11	12	13	14	15
Biological Sciences	3	4	5	6	7	8	9	(10)	(11)	12	13	14	15
Physical Sciences	3	4	5	6	7	8	9	(10)	(11)	12	13	14	15

Acceptance & Matriculation Data for 2009–2010 First Year Class

	Resident	Non-resident	International	Total
Applications	453	787	14	1254
Interviewed	237	66	0	303
Deferred	1	0	0	1
Matriculants				
Early Assurance Program	0	0	0	0
Early Decision Program	2	0	0	2
Baccalaureate/M.D.	0	0	0	0
M.D./Ph.D.	0	0	0	0
Matriculated	84	11	0	**95**

Applications accepted from International Applicants: No

Specialty Choice

2005, 2006, 2007 Graduates, Specialty Choice (As reported by program directors to GME Track™)	
Anesthesiology	4%
Emergency Medicine	8%
Family Practice	10%
Internal Medicine	14%
Obstetrics/Gynecology	6%
Orthopaedic Surgery	3%
Pediatrics	14%
Psychiatry	2%
Radiology	5%
Surgery	6%

Matriculant Demographics: 2009–2010 First Year Class

Men: 42   **Women:** 53

Matriculants' Self-Reported Race/Ethnicity

Mexican American	1	Korean	2
Cuban	0	Vietnamese	0
Puerto Rican	0	Other Asian	2
Other Hispanic	0	Total Asian	11
Total Hispanic	1	Native American	1
Chinese	5	Black	3
Asian Indian	2	Native Hawaiian	0
Pakistani	0	White	80
Filipino	1	**Unduplicated Number**	
Japanese	0	**of Matriculants**	95

Science and Math Majors: 76%
Matriculants with:
  Baccalaureate degree: 100%
  Graduate degree(s): 11%

Financial Information

Source: 2008-2009 LCME I-B survey
and 2009-2010 AAMC TSF questionnaire

	Residents	Non-residents
Total Cost of Attendance	$ 45,422	$ 68,934
Tuition and Fees	$ 24,889	$ 48,401
Other (includes living expenses)	$ 18,460	$ 18,460
Health Insurance (can be waived)	$ 2,073	$ 2,073

Average 2009 Graduate Indebtedness: $126,986
% of Enrolled Students Receiving Aid: 96%

Criminal Background Check

This medical school does not require a criminal background check prior to matriculation.

University of Missouri — Kansas City School of Medicine

Kansas City, Missouri

Council on Selection
University of Missouri — Kansas City
School of Medicine
2411 Holmes
Kansas City, Missouri 64108-2792
T 816 235 1870   **F** 816 235 6579

Admissions www.umkc.edu/admissions
Main www.med.umkc.edu
Financial www.sfa.umkc.edu
E-mail medicine@umkc.edu

Public Institution

Dr. Betty M. Drees, Dean

Dr. R. Stephen Griffith, Chair,
Council on Selection

Dr. Susan B. Wilson, Associate Dean,
Cultural Enhancement and Diversity

Jan Brandow, Director of Student Financial Aid

Alice Arredondo, Assistant Dean for
Admissions & Recruitment

General Information

The Board of Curators of the University of Missouri authorized the establishment of a medical school at the University of Missouri-Kansas City in 1969. Located on a 135-acre Hospital Hill campus, the medical school is near both the schools and colleges of the university and affiliated community hospitals.

Mission Statement

The mission of the University of Missouri-Kansas City School of Medicine is to prepare graduates so that they are able to enter and complete graduate programs in medical education, qualify for medical licensure, provide competent medical care, and have the educational background necessary for lifelong learning in order to address the health care needs of our state and nation.

Curricular Highlights

Community Service Requirement: Optional.
Research/Thesis Requirement: Optional.

The School of Medicine, with the College of Arts and Sciences and the School of Biological Sciences, offers a year-round program leading to baccalaureate and M.D. degrees in six calendar years. The student is required to complete both degrees and has the freedom to major in any department of the School of Biological Sciences or the College of Arts and Sciences. The program is designed primarily for high school seniors entering college. To receive the baccalaureate degree, the student must complete 120 semester hours of credit. Under the guidance of a clinician-scholar, called a docent, small groups of first and second-year students are introduced to medicine in community hospitals where they can observe patients and

their care. During the first two years of the program, the student is occupied predominantly with arts and sciences coursework, with about one-fourth of the time being devoted to introduction to medicine courses. After these two years the student advances, with the approval of the Council on Evaluation, to Year 3 of the six-year program. During the last four years of the curriculum, the student, with guidance from a docent and education team coordinator, plans a program for meeting the curricular requirements. Two months of Years 4 through 6 are spent with the docent on an inpatient internal medicine rotation. The remaining months of each year are spent in a number of other required and elective course offerings in the basic and clinical sciences and the humanities and social sciences. Students spend two academic terms in arts and sciences coursework during the last four years of the program. Basic, clinical, and behavioral science information is presented and emphasized throughout the program. Each student is expected to acquire a firm, broad base of information in each of these major content areas. The academic program provides the medical student with a realistic working knowledge of community health problems and resources. There is a strong student support system. An alternative path is available for extended study.

USMLE

Step 1: Required. Students must record a passing score for promotion.
Step 2: Clinical Skills (CS): Required. Students must record a passing total score to graduate.
Step 2: Clinical Knowledge (CK): Required. Students must record a passing total score to graduate.

Selection Factors

Selection criteria include: (1) the applicant's academic potential as evaluated by quality and rigor of high school coursework, high school grade point average, and scores on the ACT/SAT. In the 2009-2010 entering class, the average ACT score fell at the 95th percentile, and the average grade point average was a 3.80; (2) the applicant's individual potential for medicine as evaluated by personal qualities, including maturity, leadership, reliability, motivation for medicine, range of interests, inter-

personal skills, compassion, and job/volunteer experience. After the Council on Selection carefully reviews all applicants, those who appear to be well qualified are invited for interviews. If invited, the applicant is notified by email or phone and is required to be present at the scheduled date and time of the interview. Students are considered on the basis of their individual qualifications without regard to race, creed, sex, or national origin. Interview statistics* for B.A./M.D. are reflected in the Acceptance & Matriculation Chart. The program also accepts a small number of students who have earned, at minimum, a Bachelor's degree. Designated M.D.-Only, they are required to take the MCAT and, if admitted, pursue the last four years of the program. Promoting third-Year B.A./M.D. students and M.D.O. students are listed in the Acceptance & Matriculation Chart as "Matriculants." The school also accepts transfers. The admissions deadlines for B.A./M.D., M.D.-Only and transfer students can be found on the school Web site.

Financial Aid

Financial assistance is available to all medical students. Information for financial aid may be obtained from: Student Financial Aid Office, UMKC, 5115 Oak, Kansas City, Missouri 64110. Priority financial aid application date is February 1.

Information about Diversity Programs

Information for students from groups underrepresented in medicine is available from Dr. Susan B. Wilson, Associate Dean for Cultural Enhancement and Diversity.

Campus Information

Enrollment

For 2009, total enrollment was: 634

Application Process and Requirements 2011–2012

Primary Application Service: School Specific
Earliest filing date: August 1, 2010
Latest filing date: November 1, 2010

Secondary Application Required?: Yes
Sent to: All applicants
URL: n/a
Fee: No   **Waiver available:** n/a
Earliest filing date: n/a
Latest filing date: n/a

MCAT® required?: Yes for M.D. - only
Latest MCAT® considered: June 2010
Oldest MCAT® considered: 2007

Early Decision Program: School does not have EDP
Applicants notified: n/a
EDP available for: n/a

Regular Acceptance Notice
Earliest date: April 1, 2011
Latest date: Varies
Applicant's Response to Acceptance Offer – Maximum Time: 30 days

Requests for Deferred Entrance Considered: No

Deposit to Hold Place in Class: Yes
Deposit (Resident): $100   **(Non-resident):** $100
Deposit due: With response to acceptance offer
Applied to tuition: Yes   **Refundable:** Yes
Refundable by: May 15, 2011

Estimated number of new entrants: 100
EDP: n/a, **special program:** 100

Start Month/Year: August 2011 (B.A./M.D. Only)

Interview Format: Two thirty-minute interviews. Regional interviews are not available. Video interviews are not available.

Other Programs

PREPARATORY PROGRAMS
Postbaccalaureate Program: No
Summer Program: No

COMBINED DEGREE PROGRAMS
Baccalaureate/M.D.: Yes, www.med.umkc.edu
M.D./M.P.H.: No
M.D./M.B.A.: No
M.D./J.D.: No
M.D./Ph.D.: No

Premedical Coursework

On-line courses accepted in fulfillment of prerequisites: No

Course	Req.	Rec.	Lab.	Hrs.	Course	Req.	Rec.	Lab.	Hrs.
Inorganic Chemistry					Computer Science				
Behavioral Sciences					Genetics				
Biochemistry					Humanities				
Biology					Organic Chemistry				
Biology/Zoology					Physics				
Calculus					Psychology				
College English					Social Sciences				
College Mathematics					Other				

Selection Factors: 2009 Accepted Applicants

Proportion of Accepted Applicants with Relevant Experience (Data Self-Reported to AMCAS®)		Community Service/Volunteer	50%
		Medically-Related Work	88%
		Research	75%

Shaded bar represents school's accepted scores ranging from the 10th percentile to the 90th percentile   School Median ●   National Median ●

Overall GPA	2.0	2.1	2.2	2.3	2.4	2.5	2.6	2.7	2.8	2.9	3.0	3.1	3.2	(3.3)	3.4	3.5	3.6	3.7	3.8	3.9	4.0
Science GPA	2.0	2.1	2.2	2.3	2.4	2.5	2.6	2.7	2.8	2.9	3.0	3.1	(3.2)	3.3	3.4	3.5	3.6	3.7	3.8	3.9	4.0

MCAT® Total Numeric Score 9 10 11 12 13 14 15 16 17 18 19 20 21 22 23 24 25 26 27 (28) 29 30 31 (32) 33 34 35 36 37 38 39 40 41 42 43

Writing Sample				J	K	L	M	N	(O)	P	(Q)	R	S	T	
Verbal Reasoning	3	4	5	6	7	8	(9)	(10)	11	12	13	14	15		
Biological Sciences	3	4	5	6	7	8	(9)	10	(11)	12	13	14	15		
Physical Sciences	3	4	5	6	7	8	9	(10)	(11)	12	13	14	15		

Acceptance & Matriculation Data for 2009–2010 First Year Class

	Resident	Non-resident	International	Total
Applications	56	48	0	104
Interviewed	131*	147*	0	278
Deferred	0	0	0	0
Matriculants				
Early Assurance Program	0	0	0	0
Early Decision Program	0	0	0	0
Baccalaureate/M.D.	0	0	0	0
M.D./Ph.D.	0	0	0	0
Matriculated	56	48	0	**104**

Applications accepted from International Applicants: No

Specialty Choice

2005, 2006, 2007 Graduates, Specialty Choice (As reported by program directors to GME Track™)	
Anesthesiology	9%
Emergency Medicine	6%
Family Practice	9%
Internal Medicine	20%
Obstetrics/Gynecology	6%
Orthopaedic Surgery	3%
Pediatrics	12%
Psychiatry	2%
Radiology	4%
Surgery	8%

Matriculant Demographics: 2009–2010 First Year Class

Men: 57   **Women:** 47

Matriculants' Self-Reported Race/Ethnicity

Mexican American	1	Korean	0
Cuban	0	Vietnamese	0
Puerto Rican	0	Other Asian	49
Other Hispanic	3	Total Asian	49
Total Hispanic	4	Native American	0
Chinese	0	Black	6
Asian Indian	0	Native Hawaiian	0
Pakistani	0	White	28
Filipino	0	Unduplicated Number	
Japanese	0	of Matriculants	104

Science and Math Majors: 6%
Matriculants with:
        Baccalaureate degree: 8%
        Graduate degree(s): 6%

Financial Information

Source: 2008-2009 LCME I-B survey and 2009-2010 AAMC TSF questionnaire

	Residents	Non-residents
Total Cost of Attendance	$ 56,988	$ 84,457
Tuition and Fees	$ 30,150	$ 57,619
Other (includes living expenses)	$ 26,838	$ 26,838
Health Insurance (can be waived)	$ 0	$ 0

Average 2009 Graduate Indebtedness: $154,007
% of Enrolled Students Receiving Aid: 86%

Criminal Background Check

This medical school requires a criminal background check prior to matriculation.

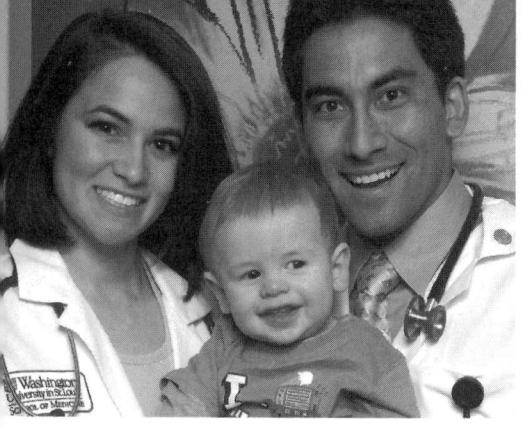

Washington University School of Medicine

St. Louis, Missouri

Office of Admissions
Washington University in St. Louis School of Medicine
660 South Euclid Avenue, #8107
St. Louis, Missouri 63110
T 314 362 6858 **F** 314 362 4658

Admissions medschool.wustl.edu/admissions
Main medschool.wustl.edu
Financial www.wusmfinaid.wustl.edu
E-mail wumscoa@wustl.edu

Private Institution

Dr. Larry J. Shapiro, Dean and Executive Vice Chancellor for Medical Affairs

Dr. W. Edwin Dodson, Associate Vice Chancellor and Associate Dean for Admissions

Dr. Will Ross, Associate Dean, Diversity Programs

Robert McCormack, Assistant Dean and Director of Financial Aid

General Information

Dedicated solely to medical education and located at the heart of the 230-acre Washington University Medical Center, the Farrell Learning and Teaching Center provides a state-of-the-art facility in which to learn the compassionate delivery of scientific medicine. This facility complements the outstanding clinical resources at Barnes-Jewish Hospital, and at St. Louis Children's Hospital, two of the top academic hospitals in the country. Learning among the most talented classmates in the country and in world class facilities, medical students at Washington University enjoy a supportive and non-competitive environment where opportunities for discovery, learning and self-fulfillment abound.

Mission Statement

The mission of Washington University is to promote learning by students and faculty. Teaching, the transmission of knowledge, is central to our mission, as is research, the creation of new knowledge. Our goals are: to foster excellence in our teaching, research, scholarship, and service; to prepare students with attitudes, skills, and habits of lifelong learning and with leadership skills, enabling them to be useful members of a global society; and to be an exemplary institution in our home community, St. Louis, as well as in the nation and the world.

Curricular Highlights
Community Service Requirement: Optional.
Research/Thesis Requirement: Optional.

The curriculum provides a state-of-the-art foundation in the science and the art of medicine. Instruction is by lecture and small-group interactive sessions, and includes problem-

based exercises, self-directed learning using computers, simulation and other resources led by faculty facilitators. Medical humanities and ethics are integrated into all four years of medical training, with emphasis given to the sociological and cultural aspects of adapting medical care to patient's needs. Patient contact begins in the first semester of the first year and the fourth year is all electives. There are abundant opportunities in basic and clinical research. A five-year M.A. and M.D. degree program is available for students desiring one or two years of research training, while a Medical Scientist Training Program leads to both M.D. and Ph.D. degrees. A pass/fail grading system is used in the first year.

USMLE
Step 1: Optional.
Step 2: Clinical Skills (CS): Optional.
Step 2: Clinical Knowledge (CK): Optional.

Selection Factors
A good doctor must be compassionate and understanding, as well as a good scientist. To this end, the School of Medicine selects students who, in addition to possessing keen minds, demonstrate sensitivity and a commitment to serve others. Hence, students are selected on the basis of character, attitude, interest, intellectual ability, motivation, maturity, and achievement as indicated by superior academic and extracurricular accomplishments. Policies and programs are nondiscriminatory, and full consideration is given to all applicants without regard to sex, age, race, handicap, sexual preference, creed, or national or ethnic origin. Students from groups underrepresented in medicine are encouraged to apply. Selected applicants are invited to interview, which is required for acceptance.

Financial Aid
The financial resources of an applicant do not enter into the selection process. Tuition is set at entry and does not increase during the four years of medical school. Students who document finanical need can receive need-based financial aid comprised of both scholarships and loans with need-based medical student borrowing currently capped at $20,000 per year ($80,000 over four years). Merit-based

full-tuition scholarships are awarded to selected students in each entering class and are renewable.

Information about Diversity Programs
Washington University is committed to the recruitment, selection, education, and graduation of students from groups underrepresented in medicine. Students are supported by an active chapter of the Student National Medical Association and a network of faculty from diverse groups.

Campus Information

Setting
The Washington University Medical Center extends over 12 city blocks and is adjacent to the 1,371 acre Forest Park.

Enrollment
For 2009, total enrollment was: 604

Special Features
An education from Washington University School of Medicine prepares graduates for leadership and readies them for rigorous postgraduate clinical training, leading edge research, and rewarding medical careers. Learning takes place at the edge of what is known alongside exceptional colleagues and in state-of-the-art facilities. There are abundant clinical and research opportunities, including one of the largest genome sequencing facilities in the world. Generous need-based financial aid helps limit average indebtedness to among the lowest among graduates of American Medical Schools.

Housing
St. Louis is nationally recognized for its abundant, convenient, safe, and affordable housing. The bus and light rail system are free to students. The on-campus Spencer T. Olin Residence Hall is connected to the medical school buildings.

Application Process and Requirements 2011–2012

Primary Application Service: AMCAS
Earliest filing date: June 1, 2010
Latest filing date: December 1, 2010

Secondary Application Required?: Yes
Sent to: All applicants
URL: http://wumsapply.wustl.edu
Fee: Yes, $65   **Waiver available:** Yes
Earliest filing date: June 15, 2010
Latest filing date: December 31, 2010

MCAT® required?: Yes
Latest MCAT® considered: September 2010
Oldest MCAT® considered: September 2007

Early Decision Program: School does not have EDP
Applicants notified: n/a
EDP available for: n/a

Regular Acceptance Notice
Earliest date: November 1, 2010
Latest date: Until class is full
Applicant's Response to Acceptance Offer – Maximum Time: Two weeks

Requests for Deferred Entrance Considered: Yes

Deposit to Hold Place in Class: Yes
Deposit (Resident): $100   **(Non-resident):** $100
Deposit due: With response to acceptance offer
Applied to tuition: Yes   **Refundable:** Yes
Refundable by: May 15, 2011

Estimated number of new entrants: 120
EDP: n/a, special program: 20

Start Month/Year: August 2011

Interview Format: Open, unstructured, one-on-one. Regional interviews are not available. Video interviews are not available.

Other Programs

PREPARATORY PROGRAMS
Postbaccalaureate Program: Yes, http://ucollege.wustl.edu/programs/special-programs
Elizabeth Fogt, Director of Advising and Student Services, (314) 935-6778, efogt@artsci.wustl.edu
Summer Program: No

COMBINED DEGREE PROGRAMS
Baccalaureate/M.D.: Yes, http://uscholars.wustl.edu
M.D./M.P.H.: No
M.D./M.B.A.: No
M.D./J.D.: No
M.D./Ph.D.: Yes, http://mstp.wustl.edu

Premedical Coursework

On-line courses accepted in fulfillment of prerequisites: No

Course	Req.	Rec.	Lab.	Sems.	Course	Req.	Rec.	Lab.	Sems.
Inorganic Chemistry	•			2	Computer Science				
Behavioral Sciences					Genetics				
Biochemistry					Humanities				
Biology	•			2	Organic Chemistry	•			2
Biology/Zoology					Physics	•			2
Calculus	•			2	Psychology				
College English					Social Sciences				
College Mathematics					Other				

Selection Factors: 2009 Accepted Applicants

Proportion of Accepted Applicants with Relevant Experience (Data Self-Reported to AMCAS®)		Community Service/Volunteer	70%
		Medically-Related Work	85%
		Research	96%

Shaded bar represents school's accepted scores ranging from the 10th percentile to the 90th percentile.   School Median ●   National Median ●

Overall GPA 2.0 2.1 2.2 2.3 2.4 2.5 2.6 2.7 2.8 2.9 3.0 3.1 3.2 3.3 3.4 3.5 3.6 3.7 3.8 (3.9) 4.0
Science GPA 2.0 2.1 2.2 2.3 2.4 2.5 2.6 2.7 2.8 2.9 3.0 3.1 3.2 3.3 3.4 3.5 3.6 3.7 3.8 (3.9) 4.0

MCAT® Total Numeric Score 9 10 11 12 13 14 15 16 17 18 19 20 21 22 23 24 25 26 27 28 29 30 31 (32) 33 34 35 36 (37) 38 39 40 41 42 43

Writing Sample			J	K	L	M	N	O	P	(Q)	R	S	T		
Verbal Reasoning	3	4	5	6	7	8	9	(10)	(11)	12	13	14	15		
Biological Sciences	3	4	5	6	7	8	9	10	(11)	12	(13)	14	15		
Physical Sciences	3	4	5	6	7	8	9	10	(11)	12	(13)	14	15		

Acceptance & Matriculation Data for 2009–2010 First Year Class

	Resident	Non-resident	International	Total
Applications	185	3385	280	3850
Interviewed	54	989	53	1096
Deferred	0	6	0	6
Matriculants				
Early Assurance Program	0	0	0	0
Early Decision Program	0	0	0	0
Baccalaureate/M.D.	0	0	0	0
M.D./Ph.D.	2	17	1	20
Matriculated	10	107	4	**121**

Applications accepted from International Applicants: Yes

Specialty Choice

2005, 2006, 2007 Graduates, Specialty Choice (As reported by program directors to GME Track™)	
Anesthesiology	4%
Emergency Medicine	3%
Family Practice	1%
Internal Medicine	20%
Obstetrics/Gynecology	3%
Orthopaedic Surgery	7%
Pediatrics	17%
Psychiatry	5%
Radiology Diagnostic	6%
Surgery General	7%

Matriculant Demographics: 2009–2010 First Year Class

Men: 60   **Women:** 61

Matriculants' Self-Reported Race/Ethnicity

Mexican American	3	Korean	3
Cuban	0	Vietnamese	3
Puerto Rican	2	Other Asian	4
Other Hispanic	0	Total Asian	42
Total Hispanic	5	Native American	0
Chinese	23	Black	10
Asian Indian	8	Native Hawaiian	0
Pakistani	1	White	67
Filipino	0	Unduplicated Number	
Japanese	1	of Matriculants	121

Science and Math Majors: 69%
Matriculants with:
      Baccalaureate degree: 99%
      Graduate degree(s): 5%

Financial Information

Source: 2008-2009 LCME I-B survey and 2009-2010 AAMC TSF questionnaire

	Residents	Non-residents
Total Cost of Attendance	$ 63,602	$ 63,602
Tuition and Fees	$ 47,150	$ 47,150
Other (includes living expenses)	$ 16,452	$ 16,452
Health Insurance (cannot be waived)	$ 0	$ 0

Average 2009 Graduate Indebtedness: $100,275
% of Enrolled Students Receiving Aid: 87%

Criminal Background Check

This medical school requires a criminal background check prior to matriculation.

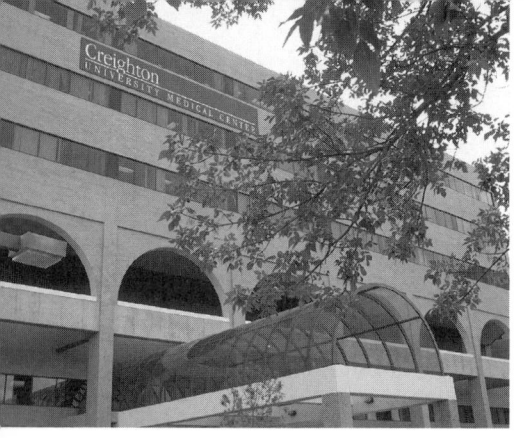

Creighton University School of Medicine

Omaha, Nebraska

Creighton University School of Medicine
Office of Medical Admissions
2500 California Plaza
Omaha, Nebraska 68178
T 402 280 2799   **F** 402 280 1241

Admissions http://www2.creighton.edu/medschool/
medicine.oma/index.php
Main http://www2.creighton.edu/medschool/
Financial http://www2.creighton.edu/financialaid/
E-mail medschadm@creighton.edu

Private Institution

Dr. Rowen K. Zetterman, Dean

Dr. Henry C. Nipper,
Assistant Dean for Admissions

Dr. Sade Kosoko-Lasaki, Associate Vice President
for Multicultural and Community Affairs

Karen Malloy, Financial Aid Coordinator

Garland Jarmon, Jr., Director of Admissions

General Information

Creighton University School of Medicine, a Catholic, Jesuit institution opened in 1892. The School of Medicine expanded in 2010 to meet society's need for caring competent physicians. All 152 students begin at the Omaha campus and after two years of study of basic sciences and clinical skills, continue their hospital-based clinical instruction either in Omaha or at the Phoenix AZ campus where training is centered at Saint Joseph Hospital and Medical Center, a member of Catholic Healthcare West for their last two years of medical school before graduation in Omaha.

Mission Statement

In the Catholic, Jesuit tradition of Creighton University, the mission of the School of Medicine is to improve the human condition through excellence in educating students, physicians and the public, advancing knowledge, and providing comprehensive patient care. Vision Statement: We will be a School of Medicine respected by our peers for excellence in teaching, research, and clinical care. We will be distinguished for preparing graduates who achieve excellence in their chosen fields and who demonstrate extraordinary compassion and commitment to the service of others.

Curricular Highlights

Community Service Requirement: Optional.
Opportunities: ILAC, Magis Clinic, Project CURA.
Research/Thesis Requirement: Optional.

The curriculum integrates basic and clinical science in all four years. Year one combines strong basic science content with the fundamentals of physical diagnosis and interviewing techniques. Year two is organized around a series of organ system-based courses and clinical skills training, including longitudinal clinics. Year three is comprised of core clerkships in a variety of inpatient and ambulatory settings. In year four, clinical training continues in critical care, surgery, and primary care and students explore their interests through electives. Ethical and societal issues are prominent in the curriculum in each year. Research can be planned between years one and two. Instructional methodology uses lectures, case-based small-group sessions and computer-assisted instruction. All lectures are podcast. Students are graded against curriculum standards on an honors/satisfactory/unsatisfactory system, to encourage teamwork.

USMLE

Step 1: Required. Students must record a passing score for promotion.
Step 2: Clinical Skills (CS): Required. Students must only record a score.
Step 2: Clinical Knowledge (CK): Required. Students must only record a score.

Selection Factors

The qualities of intellectual ability and curiosity, emotional maturity, honesty, proper motivation, proven scholastic ability, significant service to humanity, physician shadowing, and documented medical experience are of highest importance. Both the AMCAS and Creighton's secondary applications are required of all applicants. A formal interview on campus is conducted prior to acceptance. No restrictions are placed on applicants due to race, religion, sex, national or ethnic origin, age, disability, veteran status, or state of residence. Creighton values diversity in its medical classes. Applicants who complete their pre-professional education at Creighton are given preference.

Financial Aid

In addition to student loans and other government programs, a limited number of scholarships are available for those who are academically qualified and have strong records of service to others.

Information about Diversity Programs

Qualified candidates from populations underrepresented in medicine are encouraged to apply. Creighton's Office of Health Sciences-Multicultural and Community Affairs has several active programs to increase diversity and provide appropriate support services. The office administers several diversity programs, including pipeline and premedical postbaccalaureate programs.

Campus Information

Setting

Creighton's 108-acre campus is near Omaha's vibrant downtown, the entertainment and business center of the city.

Enrollment

For 2009, total enrollment was: 494

Special Features

"...service is a primary goal of education...our graduates and their mentors should be advocates of justice and crafters of a social order." – Fr. John Schlegel, S.J., President. Student life at the School of Medicine is personified by "balance" between academics and service to others. Activities include the Institute for Latin American Concern in the Dominican Republic, Project CURA, and the student-operated Magis Clinic. Although not required, all students do community service. The school also supports a student Wellness program. The "Vital Signs" mentoring progam provides peer, faculty, and career mentoring opportunities, along with guidance and support throughout all four years of medical education. A variety of sports, music, and recreational activities, are available on campus and in the community nearby.

Housing

Many students find safe and charming apartments in renovated historic buildings close to Creighton and Omaha's "Old Market." Graduate housing is also available on campus.

Satellite Campuses/Facilities

Clinical instruction sites are: Creighton University Medical Center, Omaha VAMC, Childrens Hospital, and Alegent Health. In 2012, the first group of 42 students will begin M3 clinical training on the Phoenix campus.

Application Process and Requirements 2011–2012

Primary Application Service: AMCAS
Earliest filing date: July 1, 2010
Latest filing date: November 1, 2010

Secondary Application Required?: Yes
Sent to: All applicants
URL: www.oasprod3.com/Schools/
CreightonSOM/Login.aspx
Fee: Yes, $95 **Waiver available:** Yes
Earliest filing date: July 1, 2010
Latest filing date: January 15, 2011

MCAT® required?: Yes
Latest MCAT® considered: September 2010
Oldest MCAT® considered: January 2008

Early Decision Program: School does have EDP
Applicants notified: October 1, 2010
EDP available for: Both Residents
and Non-residents

Regular Acceptance Notice
Earliest date: October 15, 2010
Latest date: Until class is full
**Applicant's Response to Acceptance
Offer – Maximum Time:** 14 days

**Requests for Deferred
Entrance Considered:** Yes

Deposit to Hold Place in Class: Yes
Deposit (Resident): $100 **(Non-resident):** $100
Deposit due: With response to acceptance offer
Applied to tuition: Yes **Refundable:** Yes
Refundable by: May 15, 2011

Estimated number of new entrants: 152
EDP: 1, special program: 7

Start Month/Year: August 2011

Interview Format: Two open-file one-on-one interviews with a faculty representative and a medical student. Regional interviews are not available. Video interviews are not available.

Other Programs

PREPARATORY PROGRAMS

Postbaccalaureate Program: Yes,
http://www2.creighton.edu/health/hsmaca/
premedicalpost-bacprogram/index.php,
(402) 280-2799, postbac.appl@creighton.edu
Summer Program: No
Summer Research Institute:
http://medicine.creighton.edu/research/
student_research_opportunities.htm

COMBINED DEGREE PROGRAMS

Baccalaureate/M.D.: No
M.D./M.P.H.: No
M.D./M.B.A.: Yes, Dr. Deborah L. Wells,
(402) 280-2841, dwells@creighton.edu
M.D./J.D.: No
M.D./Ph.D.: No
Additional Program: Yes, MD/MS Healthcare
Ethics Dual Degree Program Manager, (866) 717-6365,
http://www.creighton.edu/gradschool/graduate
programs/health/healthcareethics/in

Premedical Coursework

On-line courses accepted in fulfillment of prerequisites: No

Course	Req.	Rec.	Lab.	Hrs.
Inorganic Chemistry	•		•	8
Behavioral Sciences				
Biochemistry		•		
Biology	•		•	8
Biology/Zoology				
Calculus				
College English	•			6
College Mathematics				
Computer Science				

Course	Req.	Rec.	Lab.	Hrs.
Genetics		•		
Humanities		•		
Organic Chemistry	•		•	8
Physics	•		•	8
Psychology				
Social Sciences				
Spanish		•		
Molecular Biology		•		
Physiology		•		

Selection Factors: 2009 Accepted Applicants

Proportion of Accepted Applicants with Relevant Experience (Data Self-Reported to AMCAS®)		
Community Service/Volunteer	82%
Medically-Related Work	93%
Research	80%

Shaded bar represents school's accepted scores ranging from the 10th percentile to the 90th percentile ●School Median ●National Median

Overall GPA 2.0 2.1 2.2 2.3 2.4 2.5 2.6 2.7 2.8 2.9 3.0 3.1 3.2 3.3 3.4 3.5 3.6 3.7 ⟨3.8⟩ 3.9 4.0
Science GPA 2.0 2.1 2.2 2.3 2.4 2.5 2.6 2.7 2.8 2.9 3.0 3.1 3.2 3.3 3.4 3.5 3.6 3.7 ⟨3.8⟩ 3.9 4.0

MCAT® Total Numeric Score 9 10 11 12 13 14 15 16 17 18 19 20 21 22 23 24 25 26 27 28 29 30 ⟨31⟩⟨32⟩ 33 34 35 36 37 38 39 40 41 42 43

Writing Sample		J	K	L	M	N	O	(P)	(Q)	R	S	T
Verbal Reasoning	3	4	5	6	7	8	9	(10)	11	12	13	14	15
Biological Sciences	3	4	5	6	7	8	9	10	(11)	12	13	14	15
Physical Sciences	3	4	5	6	7	8	9	(10)	(11)	12	13	14	15

Acceptance & Matriculation Data for 2009–2010 First Year Class

	Resident	Non-resident	International	Total
Applications	181	5096	121	5398
Interviewed	52	613	1	666
Deferred	0	3	0	3
Matriculants				
Early Assurance Program	0	0	0	0
Early Decision Program	0	0	0	0
Baccalaureate/M.D.	0	0	0	0
M.D./Ph.D.	0	0	0	0
Matriculated	14	112	0	**126**

Applications accepted from International Applicants: Yes

Matriculant Demographics: 2009–2010 First Year Class

Men: 68   **Women:** 58

Matriculants' Self-Reported Race/Ethnicity

Mexican American	3	**Korean**	1
Cuban	2	**Vietnamese**	6
Puerto Rican	1	**Other Asian**	1
Other Hispanic	1	**Total Asian**	21
Total Hispanic	7	**Native American**	2
Chinese	6	**Black**	5
Asian Indian	7	**Native Hawaiian**	0
Pakistani	0	**White**	95
Filipino	1	**Unduplicated Number**	
Japanese	1	**of Matriculants**	126

Science and Math Majors: 64%
Matriculants with:
   Baccalaureate degree: 100%
   Graduate degree(s): 10%

Specialty Choice

2005, 2006, 2007 Graduates, Specialty Choice (As reported by program directors to GME Track™)	
Anesthesiology	9%
Emergency Medicine	5%
Family Practice	7%
Internal Medicine	19%
Obstetrics/Gynecology	12%
Orthopaedic Surgery	4%
Pediatrics	10%
Psychiatry	6%
Radiology Diagnostic	10%
Surgery General	5%

Financial Information

Source: 2008-2009 LCME I-B survey
and 2009-2010 AAMC TSF questionnaire

	Residents	Non-residents
Total Cost of Attendance	$ 67,526	$ 67,526
Tuition and Fees	$ 46,086	$ 46,086
Other (includes living expenses)	$ 19,520	$ 19,520
Health Insurance (can be waived)	$ 1,920	$ 1,920

Average 2009 Graduate Indebtedness: $194,548
% of Enrolled Students Receiving Aid: 94%

Criminal Background Check

This medical school requires a criminal background check prior to matriculation.

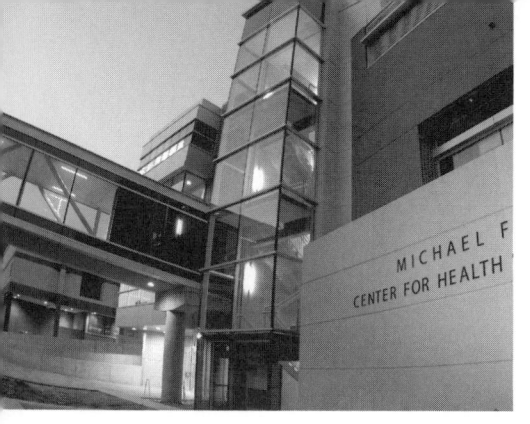

University of Nebraska College of Medicine

Omaha, Nebraska

Office of Admissions and Students
University of Nebraska Medical Center
College of Medicine
985527 Nebraska Medical Center
Omaha, Nebraska 68198-5527
T 402 559 2259   **F** 402 559 6840

Admissions www.unmc.edu/com/admissions.htm
Main www.unmc.edu/com/
Financial www.unmc.edu/financialaid/
E-mail grrogers@unmc.edu

Public Institution

Dr. John L. Gollan, Dean

Dr. Jeffrey W. Hill, Associate Dean, Office of Admissions and Students

Judith Walker, Assistant Director of Financial Aid

Gigi Rogers, Program Coordinator

General Information

Medical education has been continuous in Omaha since students first entered the Omaha Medical College in the fall of 1881. This modern medical center is a major health resource for the State of Nebraska and the surrounding areas. Several integrated units fulfill the mission of the University of Nebraska Medical Center: The Colleges of Medicine, Nursing, Pharmacy, and Dentistry, the Office of Graduate Studies and Research, the Meyer Rehabilitation Institute, the Eppley Institute for Research in Cancer and Allied Diseases, Nebraska Medical Center (Clarkson and University Hospital), and UNMC Physicians. The School of Allied Health Professions is part of the College of Medicine. These facilities are supplemented by direct teaching affiliations with the Veterans Affairs Medical Center and eight community hospitals.

Mission Statement

The mission of the University of Nebraska Medical Center is to improve the health of Nebraska through premier educational programs, innovative research, the highest quality patient care, and outreach to underserved populations.

Curricular Highlights

Community Service Requirement: Required.
Research/Thesis Requirement: Optional.

The College of Medicine enjoys a distinguished record of excellence in medical education. Our goal is for students to acquire the knowledge, skills, experience, and new pattern of behavior that is required in today's rapidly changing health care system, which emphasizes customer satisfaction, practice efficiency, cost management, preventive medicine, teamwork and a spirit of collaboration between health professionals.

USMLE

Step 1: Required. Students must record a passing score for promotion.
Step 2: Clinical Skills (CS): Required. Students must only record a score.
Step 2: Clinical Knowledge (CK): Required. Students must only record a score.

Selection Factors

Selection is based on a total assessment of each candidate's motivation, interests, character, demonstrated intellectual ability, previous academic record and its trends, personal interview, scores on the MCAT, and general fitness and promise for a career in medicine. Admission is based on individual qualifications without regard to age, sex, sexual preference, race, national origin, handicap, or religious or political beliefs. Strong preference is given to residents of Nebraska, but a small number of students from other states may be accepted. The potential for service to underserved communities is taken into consideration during the preadmission evaluation.

Financial Aid

Some scholarships are available each year. Several fellowships and assistantships are available to students who desire to take one or two years of graduate study or research in the basic sciences.

Information about Diversity Programs

The University of Nebraska College of Medicine is committed to increasing the number of physicians from groups currently underrepresented in the medical profession. Information is available through the Office of Student Equity and Multicultural Affairs at (402) 559-4437.

Campus Information

Setting

The University of Nebraska College of Medicine is located in the heart of Omaha. Recreational and cultural activities include the Omaha Symphony Orchestra, the Old Market, the Joslyn Art Museum, the Omaha Community Playhouse, and the nationally recognized Opera Omaha. The Henry Doorly Zoo contains the world's largest indoor tropical rain forest and an IMAX theater. Spectator sports in Omaha include a full range of high school and collegiate sports and minor league teams. Omaha is the home of the College Baseball World Series.

Enrollment

For 2009, total enrollment was: 488

Special Features

The University of Nebraska College of Medicine strives to be a regional and national leader in the education of primary care health professionals, in the application of information technology to health care, and in research and clinical services related to cancer, transplantation, neurosciences, cardiovascular disease, genetics, rural health, and other major areas of healthcare need. UNMC is world-renowned in the treatment of lymphoma and leukemia, and has one of the two most active bone marrow transplant programs in the country. The LifeNet helicopter transport service transfers acutely ill patients from distances up to 200 miles from Omaha to the teaching services of the Nebraska Medical Center. The Clinical Skills Laboratory in the Michael F. Sorrell Center has a 40-seat instructional/preparatory room, 10 large exam rooms, six smaller exam rooms, a hospital suite and two simulation suites. Additionally, the CSL is equipped with high-tech simulation models for interactive instruction.

Housing

Campus housing is available and many affordable apartments are within walking distance.

Satellite Campuses/Facilities

The clinical facilities at the University of Nebraska Medical Center include the Nebraska Medical Center, University Medical Associates, and the Meyer Rehabilitation Institute. The Nebraska Medical Center is the primary teaching hospital for the College of Medicine. The College has affiliations with community hospitals throughout the state. The Omaha Veterans Affairs Medical Center is fully integrated into the educational programs of the College of Medicine.

Application Process and Requirements 2011–2012

Primary Application Service: AMCAS
Earliest filing date: June 1, 2010
Latest filing date: November 1, 2010

Secondary Application Required?: Yes
Sent to: All applicants
URL: http://net.unmc.edu/apply
Contact: Jackie O'Hara, (402) 559-2259
ohara@unmc.edu
Fee: Yes, $70   **Waiver available:** Yes
Earliest filing date: June 1, 2010
Latest filing date: January 15, 2011

MCAT® required?: Yes
Latest MCAT® considered: September 2010
Oldest MCAT® considered: January 2008

Early Decision Program: School does have EDP
Applicants notified: October 1, 2010
EDP available for: Both Residents and Non-residents

**Regular Acceptance Notice
Earliest date:** December 2010
Latest date: Until class is full
**Applicant's Response to Acceptance
Offer – Maximum Time:** Two weeks

**Requests for Deferred
Entrance Considered:** No

Deposit to Hold Place in Class: Yes
Deposit (Resident): $100   **(Non-resident):** $100
Deposit due: With response to acceptance offer
Applied to tuition: Yes   **Refundable:** No
Refundable by: n/a

Estimated number of new entrants: 130
EDP: 35, special program: n/a

Start Month/Year: August 2011

Interview Format: By invitation only. Regional interviews are not available. Video interviews are not available.

Other Programs

PREPARATORY PROGRAMS
Postbaccalaureate Program: No
Summer Program: Yes, www.unmc.edu/smdep/, Carly Crim, (800) 701-9665, smdep@unmc.edu
Summer Undergraduate Research: Yes, www.unmc.edu/students/studentresearch.htm
Rachel Schweitzer, (402) 559-4317, schweitzer@unmc.edu
M.D./Ph.D. Summer Undergraduate Research Program: Yes, http://www.unmc.edu/com/summer/, Sonja Cox, (402) 559-8242, sacox@unmc.edu

COMBINED DEGREE PROGRAMS
Baccalaureate/M.D.: No
M.D./M.P.H.: Yes, www.unmc.edu/mph/default.htm
Jessica B. Tschirren, MPA, (402) 561-7586, tschirren@unmc.edu
M.D./M.B.A.: No
M.D./J.D.: No
M.D./Ph.D.: Yes, www.unmc.edu/mdphd
Sonja Cox, (402) 559-8242, sacox@unmc.edu

Premedical Coursework

On-line courses accepted in fulfillment of prerequisites: Yes

Course	Req.	Rec.	Lab.	Sems.	Course	Req.	Rec.	Lab.	Sems.
Inorganic Chemistry	•		•	8	Computer Science				
Behavioral Sciences		•			Genetics		•		3
Biochemistry	•			3	Humanities		•		12
Biology	•		•	8	Organic Chemistry	•		•	8
Biology/Zoology		•			Physics	•		•	8
Calculus	•			3	Psychology		•		
College English	•			3	Social Sciences		•		
College Mathematics		•			Other				

Selection Factors: 2009 Accepted Applicants

Proportion of Accepted Applicants with Relevant Experience (Data Self-Reported to AMCAS®)		Community Service/Volunteer	75%
		Medically-Related Work	79%
		Research	72%

Shaded bar represents school's accepted scores ranging from the 10th percentile to the 90th percentile ■   School Median ● National Median ●

Overall GPA	2.0	2.1	2.2	2.3	2.4	2.5	2.6	2.7	2.8	2.9	3.0	3.1	3.2	3.3	3.4	3.5	3.6	3.7	(3.8)	3.9	4.0
Science GPA	2.0	2.1	2.2	2.3	2.4	2.5	2.6	2.7	2.8	2.9	3.0	3.1	3.2	3.3	3.4	3.5	3.6	3.7	(3.8)	3.9	4.0

MCAT® Total Numeric Score 9 10 11 12 13 14 15 16 17 18 19 20 21 22 23 24 25 26 27 28 29 (30) 31 (32) 33 34 35 36 37 38 39 40 41 42 43

Writing Sample		J	K	L	M	N	O	(P)	(Q)	R	S	T
Verbal Reasoning	3	4	5	6	7	8	9	(10)	11	12	13	14	15
Biological Sciences	3	4	5	6	7	8	9	10	(11)	12	13	14	15
Physical Sciences	3	4	5	6	7	8	9	(10)	(11)	12	13	14	15

Acceptance & Matriculation Data for 2009–2010 First Year Class

	Resident	Non-resident	International	Total
Applications	288	1097	11	1396
Interviewed	206	137	0	343
Deferred	0	0	0	0
Matriculants				
Early Assurance Program	0	0	0	0
Early Decision Program	25	0	0	25
Baccalaureate/M.D.	0	0	0	0
M.D./Ph.D.	0	5	0	5
Matriculated	103	21	0	**124**

Applications accepted from International Applicants: No

Specialty Choice

2005, 2006, 2007 Graduates, Specialty Choice (As reported by program directors to GME Track™)

Anesthesiology	8%
Emergency Medicine	8%
Family Practice	11%
Internal Medicine	19%
Obstetrics/Gynecology	5%
Orthopaedic Surgery	2%
Pediatrics	10%
Psychiatry	4%
Radiology	4%
Surgery	5%

Matriculant Demographics: 2009–2010 First Year Class

Men: 67   **Women:** 57

Matriculants' Self-Reported Race/Ethnicity

Mexican American	2	Korean	1
Cuban	0	Vietnamese	1
Puerto Rican	0	Other Asian	2
Other Hispanic	0	Total Asian	10
Total Hispanic	2	Native American	1
Chinese	2	Black	3
Asian Indian	3	Native Hawaiian	0
Pakistani	1	White	111
Filipino	1	Unduplicated Number	
Japanese	0	of Matriculants	124

Science and Math Majors: 73%
Matriculants with:
  Baccalaureate degree: 100%
  Graduate degree(s): 11%

Financial Information

Source: 2008-2009 LCME I-B survey and 2009-2010 AAMC TSF questionnaire

	Residents	Non-residents
Total Cost of Attendance	$ 43,305	$ 75,905
Tuition and Fees	$ 26,551	$ 59,151
Other (includes living expenses)	$ 15,790	$ 15,790
Health Insurance (cannot be waived)	$ 964	$ 964

Average 2009 Graduate Indebtedness: $130,199
% of Enrolled Students Receiving Aid: 99%

Criminal Background Check

This medical school requires a criminal background check prior to matriculation.

University of Nevada School of Medicine

Reno, Nevada

Office of Admissions and Student Affairs
University of Nevada School of Medicine
Mail Stop 0357
Reno, Nevada 89557-0357
T 775 784 6063   **F** 775 784 6194

Admissions www.medicine.nevada.edu/dept/asa/
default.asp
Main www.medicine.nevada.edu/
Financial www.medicine.nevada.edu/dept/asa/
students/financial_assistance_home.htm
E-mail asa@med.unr.edu

Public Institution

Dr. Ole Theinhaus, Dean

Dr. Peggy Dupey, Associate Dean for Admissions and Student Affairs

Patricia Romney, Admissions Coordinator

Ann Diggins, Director of Recruitment and Student Services

General Information

The University of Nevada School of Medicine is a state-supported, community based, university-integrated school which relies heavily on community physicians as teachers and community health facilities for the majority of its clinical education. The school is dedicated to selecting individuals with diverse backgrounds to study comprehensive health care delivery while considering the needs of the individual, the family and the community.

Mission Statement

To provide educational opportunities for Nevadans, to improve the quality of healthcare for citizens of Nevada, to create new biomedical knowledge through education, research, patient care and community service, and to provide continuing medical education.

Curricular Highlights

Community Service Requirement: Optional.
Research/Thesis Requirement: Optional.

The first two years of the program are concentrated in classrooms and laboratories on the Reno campus. The curriculum emphasizes the biomedical and behavioral sciences basic to medicine. Basic science disciplines are integrated with each other and with clinical problems to promote the learning of problem-solving skills. Early clinical training is provided for students to learn patient interviewing, doctor-patient relationship skills, and the basics of physical examination and diagnosis. Throughout the first and second years, students spend time with a physician to observe medical practice in office and clinic settings. Opportunities to participate in basic and clinical science research throughout the curriculum are available. The third and fourth years emphasize a balance of ambulatory and inpatient medical education designed to better pre-

pare students for residency. Third and Fourth year students study clinical medicine in Reno, Las Vegas, and rural Nevada.

USMLE

Step 1: Required. Students must record a passing score for promotion.
Step 2: Clinical Skills (CS): Required. Students must record a passing total score to graduate.
Step 2: Clinical Knowledge (CK): Required. Students must record a passing total score to graduate.

Selection Factors

Candidates are evaluated on the basis of academic performance; results of the MCAT; the nature and depth of scholarly, extracurricular, and health care-related activities during college years (excellence and balance of the natural sciences, social sciences, and humanities); academic letters of evaluation; and the personal interview. A small number of non-resident applicants from Alaska, Idaho, Montana, or Wyoming or residents of northern California counties bordering Nevada (medical catchment area) are considered. Applicants from other western states should contact the office of admissions for updated eligibility information. Applicants are required to be U.S. citizens or have a permanent resident visa. Only those students who are currently enrolled and in good academic standing at LCME-accredited medical schools and have a strong residential tie to Nevada are considered for transfer to the second and third years. The number of positions available for transfer is strictly limited by attrition and compatibility to the school's curriculum. Only U.S. citizens are considered. Transfer applications from students attending foreign medical schools are not considered. Completion of a criminal background check is required of all accepted applicants. The fee for this background check is $51.25. Applicants who were denied admission to the School of Medicine during their initial applications are not eligible for transfer from other institutions

Financial Aid

Every attempt is made to assist students and their families in meeting both their financial obligations to the School of Medicine and the student's essential personal needs. Financial

status is not a determinant in selecting qualified applicants. A limited number of loans and scholarships are available on the basis of need and merit. Determination of financial aid awards is made after acceptance.

Information about Diversity Programs

The School of Medicine is committed to the recruitment, selection, and retention of individuals who are members of groups traditionally underrepresented in American medicine. Residents of the state of Nevada and individuals who meet the non-resident criteria and who are from such backgrounds are encouraged to apply. The University of Nevada, Reno, does not discriminate on the basis of race, color, religion, sex, age, creed, national origin, veteran status, physical or mental disability, and in accordance with university policy, sexual orientation, in any program or activity it operates.

Campus Information

Enrollment

For 2009, total enrollment was: 242

Special Features

The Reno campus features state-of-the art research facilities, a new medical education building with the latest wireless technology, and a Human Patient Simulator (S.T.A.N.). Students have opportunities to work in several clinical facilities. The Las Vegas campus features a Level I trauma center.

Housing

Housing is available within short distances of campuses.

Satellite Campuses/Facilities

The University of Nevada School of Medicine is a state-wide institution with varied clinical sites including a Level I trauma center and numerous research and rural clinical opportunities.

Application Process and Requirements 2011–2012

Primary Application Service: AMCAS
Earliest filing date: June 1, 2011
Latest filing date: November 1, 2010

Secondary Application Required?: Yes
Sent to: Screened applicants
Contact: Patricia Romney, (775) 784-6063, promney@medicine.nevada.edu
Fee: Yes, $45   **Waiver available:** Yes
Earliest filing date: September 1, 2010
Latest filing date: December 1, 2010

MCAT® required?: Yes
Latest MCAT® considered: September 2010
Oldest MCAT® considered: 2007

Early Decision Program: School does have EDP
Applicants notified: October 1, 2010
EDP available for: Both Residents and Non-residents

Regular Acceptance Notice
Earliest date: January 15, 2010
Latest date: Varies
Applicant's Response to Acceptance
Offer – Maximum Time: Two weeks

Requests for Deferred
Entrance Considered: Yes

Deposit to Hold Place in Class: No
Deposit (Resident): n/a   **(Non-resident):** n/a
Deposit due: n/a
Applied to tuition: n/a   **Refundable:** n/a
Refundable by: n/a

Estimated number of new entrants: 62
EDP: 5, special program: 7

Start Month/Year: August 2011

Interview Format: Interviews are blind and semi-structured. Applicants are interviewed in Reno and Las Vegas. Video interviews are not available.

Other Programs

PREPARATORY PROGRAMS
Postbaccalaureate Program: No
Summer Program: No

COMBINED DEGREE PROGRAMS
Baccalaureate/M.D.: Yes, www.medicine.nevada.edu /dept/asa/prospective_applicants/programs_md.htm, Gina Sella, (775) 682-8354, gsella@medicine.nevada.edu
M.D./M.P.H.: Yes, www.medicine.nevada.edu/ dept/asa/prospective_applicants.programs_home.htm
M.D./M.B.A.: Yes, www.medicine.nevada.edu/ dept/asa/prospective_applicants/programs_home.htm
M.D./J.D.: No
M.D./Ph.D.: Yes, www.medicine.nevada.edu/dept/asa/ prospective_applicants/programs_graduate.htm, David Lupan, Ph.D., (775) 784-4908, asa@med.unr.edu

Premedical Coursework

On-line courses accepted in fulfillment of prerequisites: No

Course	Req.	Rec.	Lab.	Hrs.
Inorganic Chemistry	•		•	8
Behavioral Sciences	•			6
Biochemistry		•		
Biology	•		•	12
Biology/Zoology				
Calculus		•		
College English		•		
College Mathematics		•		
Computer Science		•		

Course	Req.	Rec.	Lab.	Hrs.
Genetics		•		
Humanities		•		
Organic Chemistry	•		•	8
Physics	•		•	8
Psychology	•			3
Social Sciences		•		
Parasitology		•		
Microbiology/ Immunology		•		

Selection Factors: 2009 Accepted Applicants

Proportion of Accepted Applicants with Relevant Experience (Data Self-Reported to AMCAS®)	
Community Service/Volunteer	72%
Medically-Related Work	89%
Research	84%

Shaded bar represents school's accepted scores ranging from the 10th percentile to the 90th percentile.   School Median ●   National Median ◉

Overall GPA	2.0	2.1	2.2	2.3	2.4	2.5	2.6	2.7	2.8	2.9	3.0	3.1	3.2	3.3	3.4	3.5	3.6	(3.7)	3.8	3.9	4.0
Science GPA	2.0	2.1	2.2	2.3	2.4	2.5	2.6	2.7	2.8	2.9	3.0	3.1	3.2	3.3	3.4	3.5	3.6	(3.7)	3.8	3.9	4.0

MCAT® Total Numeric Score 9 10 11 12 13 14 15 16 17 18 19 20 21 22 23 24 25 26 27 28 29 (30) 31 (32) 33 34 35 36 37 38 39 40 41 42 43

Writing Sample			J	K	L	M	N	(O)	P	(Q)	R	S	T
Verbal Reasoning	3	4	5	6	7	8	9	(10)	11	12	13	14	15
Biological Sciences	3	4	5	6	7	8	9	(10)	(11)	12	13	14	15
Physical Sciences	3	4	5	6	7	8	9	(10)	(11)	12	13	14	15

Acceptance & Matriculation Data for 2009–2010 First Year Class

	Resident	Non-resident	International	Total
Applications	156	1109	12	1277
Interviewed	185	53	0	238
Deferred	0	0	0	0
Matriculants				
Early Assurance Program	0	0	0	0
Early Decision Program	2	0	0	2
Baccalaureate/M.D.	0	0	0	0
M.D./Ph.D.	0	0	0	0
Matriculated	47	15	0	**62**

Applications accepted from International Applicants: No

Specialty Choice

2005, 2006, 2007 Graduates, Specialty Choice (As reported by program directors to GME Track™)	
Anesthesiology	7%
Emergency Medicine	11%
Family Practice	13%
Internal Medicine	15%
Obstetrics/Gynecology	4%
Orthopaedic Surgery	6%
Pediatrics	13%
Psychiatry	3%
Radiology	7%
Surgery	8%

Matriculant Demographics: 2009–2010 First Year Class

Men: 32   **Women:** 30

Matriculants' Self-Reported Race/Ethnicity

Mexican American	1	Korean	2
Cuban	1	Vietnamese	0
Puerto Rican	0	Other Asian	0
Other Hispanic	2	Total Asian	14
Total Hispanic	4	Native American	0
Chinese	4	Black	2
Asian Indian	3	Native Hawaiian	1
Pakistani	1	White	47
Filipino	4	Unduplicated Number	
Japanese	1	of Matriculants	62

Science and Math Majors: 84%
Matriculants with:
Baccalaureate degree: 100%
Graduate degree(s): 2%

Financial Information

Source: 2008-2009 LCME I-B survey and 2009-2010 AAMC TSF questionnaire

	Residents	Non-residents
Total Cost of Attendance	$ 41,611	$ 62,994
Tuition and Fees	$ 14,979	$ 36,362
Other (includes living expenses)	$ 24,344	$ 24,344
Health Insurance (can be waived)	$ 2,288	$ 2,288

Average 2009 Graduate Indebtedness: $111,769
% of Enrolled Students Receiving Aid: 77%

Criminal Background Check

This medical school requires a criminal background check prior to matriculation.

Dartmouth Medical School
Hanover, New Hampshire

Dartmouth Medical School
Office of Admissions
3 Rope Ferry Road
Hanover, New Hampshire 03755-1404
T 603 650 1505 **F** 603 650 1560

Admissions http://dms.dartmouth.edu/admissions/
Main http://dms.dartmouth.edu/
Financial http://dms.dartmouth.edu
admissions/financial_aid/
E-mail dms.admissions@dartmouth.edu

Private Institution

Dr. William Green, Dean

Andrew G. Welch, Director of Admissions

Dr. Susan M. Pepin, Acting Chief Diversity Officer

G. Dino Koff, Director of Financial Aid

Dr. Ann Davis, Chief Medical Student Services Officer

Dr. Jim Yong Kim, President Dartmouth College

General Information

Dartmouth Medical School, the fourth oldest U.S. medical school, is a partner of Dartmouth-Hitchcock Medical Center (DHMC). DHMC serves a patient population of 1.6 million and includes Mary Hitchcock Memorial Hospital, Dartmouth-Hitchcock Clinic, and the Veterans Affairs Hospital in White River Junction, Vermont. Other facilities contributing to the integration of advanced research and quality care within DHMC include the Norris Cotton Cancer Center, Children's Hospital at Dartmouth, and the Borwell Research Building; DHMC is a major force for medical treatment and discovery and is the site of numerous clinical trials. Additional teaching sites span nationally and internationally from the New England states to California to Tanzania. A faculty of approximately 2,000 affords ample opportunity for individual instruction.

Mission Statement

The mission of Dartmouth Medical School is to improve health - locally, nationally, and globally. We do this by educating the leading physicians and scientists of tomorrow, generating new knowledge through research, and empowering all members of our community.

Curricular Highlights

Community Service Requirement: Optional.
Research/Thesis Requirement: Optional.

The DMS curriculum integrates basic and clinical sciences throughout medical school. Its hallmarks are longitudinal experiences in the basic and clinical sciences, early introduction to patient care, small-group instruction, close relationships with faculty, and opportunities for independent learning. DMS uses various pedagogies, including problem-based learning, lectures, and small elective courses. Year One includes On Doctoring, a course that pairs students with faculty practitioners in the clinical environment. The Scientific Basis of Medicine, an interdisciplinary pathophysiology course combined with an introduction to the mechanisms of disease and the principles of clinical medicine, is a feature of Year Two. Six seven-week clerkships, elective time, and opportunities to practice in diverse settings shape the third year. The fourth year includes two required clerkships, a sub-internship, and four short courses, but students largely spend this year refining their interests through electives.

USMLE

Step 1: Required. Students must only record a score.
Step 2: Clinical Skills (CS): Required. Students must only record a score.
Step 2: Clinical Knowledge (CK): Required. Students must only record a score.

Selection Factors

The admissions committee carefully reviews the entire application with attention to personal, scholastic, and scientific qualifications. DMS does not employ numeric cutoffs or inflexible criteria. Selected applicants interview in Hanover from September to March. Dartmouth does not discriminate on the basis of race, color, religion, sex, age, sexual orientation, gender identity or expression, national origin, disability, military or veteran status in access to its programs and activities, and in conditions of admission and employment (hiring, promotion, discharge, pay, fringe benefits).

Financial Aid

DMS practices need-blind admissions. Application fee waivers are granted to individuals who have received an AMCAS fee waiver. All accepted U.S. citizens and permanent residents with documented need are offered financial aid packages. DMS awards scholarships and loans on the basis of need as indicated by the FAFSA, the Need Access form, the DMS financial aid application, and supporting documentation. Financial support for foreign students is limited.

Information about Diversity Programs

DMS seeks to enroll a talented and diverse class of students from various racial, ethnic, cultural, religious, and socio-economic backgrounds. Susan M. Pepin, M.D. is the Acting Chief Diversity Officer.

Campus Information

Setting

DMS is located in the classic New England town of Hanover, NH, on the campus of Dartmouth College. DMS and the surrounding communities provide abundant cultural and recreational opportunities. A sample of venues includes the Hopkins Center, with frequent concerts, films, lectures, and artistic performances, and the Hood Museum, which boasts impressive permanent and temporary exhibits.

Enrollment

For 2009, total enrollment was: 343

Special Features

DMS offers both small classes and one of the nation's top 16 major teaching hospitals. With a patient population of nearly 1.6 million people, Dartmouth medical students gain exposure to a broad spectrum of patients and treatments and are well-prepared for residency training.

Housing

Housing is available on and off-campus.

Satellite Campuses/Facilities

DMS provides a variety of clinical training opportunities; students gain exposure to various patient populations, healthcare delivery systems, and management models. Locations such as Tuba City, AZ; Orange County, CA; San Francisco, CA; Bethel, AK; Dar es Salaam, Tanzania; and every New England state (except Massachusetts) are only some of the possibilities. Students may also study at the internationally known Dartmouth Institute for Health Policy and Clinical Practice.

Application Process and Requirements 2011–2012

Primary Application Service: AMCAS
Earliest filing date: June 1, 2010
Latest filing date: November 1, 2010

Secondary Application Required?: Yes
Sent to: All applicants
URL: http://dms.dartmouth.edu/admissions/instrs_to_applicants.shtml
Contact: Office of Admissions, (603) 650-1505, dms.admissions@dartmouth.edu
Fee: Yes, $130   **Waiver available:** Yes
Earliest filing date: June 1, 2010
Latest filing date: January 3, 2011

MCAT® required?: No
Latest MCAT® considered: September 2010
Oldest MCAT® considered: September 2008

Early Decision Program: School does not have EDP
Applicants notified: n/a
EDP available for: n/a

Regular Acceptance Notice
Earliest date: October 15, 2010
Latest date: Until class is full
Applicant's Response to Acceptance Offer – Maximum Time: Two weeks

Requests for Deferred Entrance Considered: Yes

Deposit to Hold Place in Class: No
Deposit (Resident): n/a   **(Non-resident):** n/a
Deposit due: n/a
Applied to tuition: n/a   **Refundable:** n/a
Refundable by: n/a

Estimated number of new entrants: 90
EDP: 0, special program: n/a

Start Month/Year: August 2011

Interview Format: Two half-hour interviews. Regional interviews are not available. Video interviews are not available.

Other Programs

PREPARATORY PROGRAMS
Postbaccalaureate Program: No
Summer Program: Yes,
Kalindi Trietley, (603) 650-6535
Kalindi.E.Trietley@Dartmouth.edu

COMBINED DEGREE PROGRAMS
Baccalaureate/M.D.: No
M.D./M.P.H.: Yes, http://dms.dartmouth.edu/ed_programs/tdi.shtml
M.D./M.B.A.: Yes, http://dms.dartmouth.edu/ed_programs/md_mbaprog.shtml
M.D./J.D.: No
M.D./Ph.D.: Yes, http://dms.dartmouth.edu/ed_programs/md_phdprog.shtml

Premedical Coursework

On-line courses accepted in fulfillment of prerequisites: Yes

Course	Req.	Rec.	Lab.	Hrs.	Course	Req.	Rec.	Lab.	Hrs.
Inorganic Chemistry	•			8	Computer Science				
Behavioral Sciences					Genetics				
Biochemistry		•		3	Humanities				
Biology	•			8	Organic Chemistry	•			8
Biology/Zoology					Physics	•			8
Calculus	•			3	Psychology				
College English					Social Sciences				
College Mathematics					Other				

Selection Factors: 2009 Accepted Applicants

Proportion of Accepted Applicants with Relevant Experience (Data Self-Reported to AMCAS®)		Community Service/Volunteer	77%
		Medically-Related Work	86%
		Research	90%

Shaded bar represents school's accepted scores ranging from the 10th percentile to the 90th percentile   School Median ● National Median ◉

Overall GPA 2.0 2.1 2.2 2.3 2.4 2.5 2.6 2.7 2.8 2.9 3.0 3.1 3.2 3.3 3.4 3.5 3.6 3.7 (3.8) 3.9 4.0
Science GPA 2.0 2.1 2.2 2.3 2.4 2.5 2.6 2.7 2.8 2.9 3.0 3.1 3.2 3.3 3.4 3.5 3.6 3.7 (3.8) 3.9 4.0

MCAT® Total Numeric Score 9 10 11 12 13 14 15 16 17 18 19 20 21 22 23 24 25 26 27 28 29 30 31 (32) 33 (34) 35 36 37 38 39 40 41 42 43

Writing Sample			J	K	L	M	N	O	P	(Q)	R	S	T
Verbal Reasoning	3	4	5	6	7	8	9	(10)	(11)	12	13	14	15
Biological Sciences	3	4	5	6	7	8	9	10	(11)	(12)	13	14	15
Physical Sciences	3	4	5	6	7	8	9	10	(11)	(12)	13	14	15

Acceptance & Matriculation Data for 2009–2010 First Year Class

	Resident	Non-resident	International	Total
Applications	77	4714	503	5294
Interviewed	31	608	N/A	639
Deferred	0	2	0	2
Matriculants				
Early Assurance Program	0	0	0	0
Early Decision Program	0	0	0	0
Baccalaureate/M.D.	0	0	0	0
M.D./Ph.D.	0	2	3	5
Matriculated	5	71	8	**84**

Applications accepted from International Applicants: Yes

Matriculant Demographics: 2009–2010 First Year Class

Men: 37   **Women:** 47

Matriculants' Self-Reported Race/Ethnicity

Mexican American	0	Korean	1
Cuban	1	Vietnamese	0
Puerto Rican	0	Other Asian	0
Other Hispanic	1	Total Asian	11
Total Hispanic	2	Native American	2
Chinese	7	Black	1
Asian Indian	3	Native Hawaiian	0
Pakistani	0	White	61
Filipino	0	Unduplicated Number	
Japanese	0	of Matriculants	84

Science and Math Majors: 68%
Matriculants with:
Baccalaureate degree: 100%
Graduate degree(s): 7%

Specialty Choice

2005, 2006, 2007 Graduates, Specialty Choice
(As reported by program directors to GME Track™)

Anesthesiology	5%
Emergency Medicine	6%
Family Practice	9%
Internal Medicine	16%
Obstetrics/Gynecology	3%
Orthopaedic Surgery	5%
Pediatrics	11%
Psychiatry	5%
Radiology	7%
Surgery	8%

Financial Information

Source: 2008-2009 LCME I-B survey and 2009-2010 AAMC TSF questionnaire

	Residents	Non-residents
Total Cost of Attendance	$ 62,090	$ 62,090
Tuition and Fees	$ 44,580	$ 44,580
Other (includes living expenses)	$ 15,450	$ 15,450
Health Insurance (can be waived)	$ 2,060	$ 2,060

Average 2009 Graduate Indebtedness: $109,688
% of Enrolled Students Receiving Aid: 85%

Criminal Background Check

This school requires a criminal background check prior to matriculation.

University of Medicine and Dentistry of New Jersey — New Jersey Medical School

Newark, New Jersey

Director of Admissions
UMDNJ — New Jersey Medical School
185 South Orange Avenue C-653
Newark, New Jersey 07103
T 973 972 4631   F 973 972 7986

Admissions http://njms.umdnj.edu/education/admissions
Main http://njms.umdnj.edu
Financial www.umdnj.edu/studentfinancialaid
E-mail njmsadmiss@umdnj.edu

Public Institution

Dr. Robert L. Johnson, Interim Dean

Dr. Maria Soto-Greene, Vice Dean

Dr. George F. Heinrich, Associate Dean for Admissions and Special Programs

Elaine Varas, University Director of Student Financial Aid

Mercedes M. Rivero, Director of Admissions

General Information

New Jersey Medical School (NJMS), formerly Seton Hall College of Medicine and Dentistry, is the state's oldest academic medical institution. More than 600 faculty and 1,300 volunteer faculty in our 20 academic departments play a critical role in transforming our students into qualified clinicians who will meet and exceed the healthcare needs of New Jersey and the nation. Clinical instruction is carried out at the University Hospital, Hackensack University Medical Center, Veterans Affairs Medical Center, St. Barnabus Medical Center, Newark Beth Israel Medical Center, Morristown Memorial Hospital, Overlook Hospital, Mountainside Hospital and Kessler Institute for Rehabilitation.

Mission Statement

To educate students, physicians, and scientists to meet society's current and future healthcare needs through patient-centered education; pioneering research; innovative clinical, rehabilitative and preventive care; and collaborative community outreach.

Curricular Highlights

Community Service Requirement: Optional.
Research/Thesis Requirement: Optional.

Years 1 and 2 are devoted to providing an understanding of the basic sciences integrated with early clinical exposure and a comprehensive introduction to the field of medicine through a course called the "Physician's Core." The basic sciences are taught utilizing a variety of teaching modalities, including lectures, laboratories and small-group sessions. Students receive components of their clinical training in the Clinical Skills Training Center, which features 12 simulated patient examination rooms equipped to monitor mock patient encounters with standardized patients. Years 3 and 4 are devoted to providing in-depth exposure to clinical medicine. In Year 3, students rotate through the major disciplines in medicine (internal medicine, surgery, family medicine, pediatrics, psychiatry and obstetrics-gynecology) and in Year 4, students will assume a higher degree of autonomy and responsibility as they rotate through acting internships and an emergency medicine rotation, and select from a wide range of electives, both at NJMS and throughout the country.

USMLE

Step 1: Required. Students must record a passing score for promotion.
Step 2: Clinical Skills (CS): Required. Students must record a passing total score to graduate.
Step 2: Clinical Knowledge (CK): Required. Students must record a passing total score to graduate.

Selection Factors

Applicants are selected on the basis of academic excellence, leadership qualities, demonstrated compassion for others and broad extracurricular experiences. Related factors such as passion, perseverance, special aptitudes and stamina are also considered. Intense competition tends to favor those with stronger credentials. Although some preference is given to residents of NJ, out-of-state residents are encouraged to apply.

Financial Aid

The student financial aid programs are a centrally managed operation at UMDNJ and not considered in the admissions process. Financial Aid Professionals meet and advise accepted students regarding the financial aspects of their medical education.

Information about Diversity Programs

NJMS is committed to the recruitment of a diverse student body as well as enhancing the cultural competency of all its medical students in order to improve access to care for underserved populations. Several programs have been established to support these goals. Information may be obtained by contacting the Office of Special Programs at (973) 972-3762.

Campus Information

Setting

Located in Newark's University Heights, NJMS is minutes from the Prudential Sports Arena, the Newark Bears Riverfront Stadium, NJ Performing Arts Center, Ironbound district, Weequahic Golf Course and Branch Brook Park. Manhattan is just a 15-minute train ride away. Many buildings on the 65-acre campus are connected, making it convenient to travel from classrooms and labs to the library, University Hospital and student apartments.

Enrollment

For 2009, total enrollment was: 711

Special Features

In recent years, NJMS has received over $104 million in extramural grants supporting basic, clinical and translational research. NJMS is also home to the Global Tuberculosis Institute, The Institute for Ophthalmology and Visual Science, and the Center for Emerging and Reemerging Pathogens. NJMS is a charter member of the New Jersey Stem Cell Research and Education Foundation. Designated Areas of Excellence include: Brain Injury and Stroke, Cancer/Oncology, Cardiovascular Biology, Cellular Signal Transduction, Immunology, Infectious Diseases, Neurosciences, Psychiatry/Behavioral Sciences. NJMS faculty contributions include: the development of the worldwide standard in knee replacement, the New Jersey Knee; a patented method for the early detection of Lyme disease; the identification of pediatric AIDS and the development of drug-therapy to reduce the likelihood of pre-natal transmission; and proof of the connection between smoking and cancer resulting in the warning message printed on cigarette packages.

Housing

On-campus apartments house 465 students in 234 residential apartments. The 14-story building includes a courtyard and a parking garage. For additional information please visit: www.umdnj.edu/fpcweb/housing.

Application Process and Requirements 2011–2012

Primary Application Service: AMCAS
Earliest filing date: June 1, 2010
Latest filing date: December 1, 2010

Secondary Application Required?: Yes
Sent to: All applicants
URL: https://njmsintra.umdnj.edu/nonmbm/
education/admissions/supplementalApp.cfm
Contact: njmsadmiss@umdnj.edu
Fee: Yes, $80   **Waiver available:** Yes
Earliest filing date: July 1, 2010
Latest filing date: December 15, 2010

MCAT® required?: Yes
Latest MCAT® considered: September 2010
Oldest MCAT® considered: n/a

Early Decision Program: School does have EDP
Applicants notified: October 1, 2010
EDP available for: Both Residents
and Non-residents

Regular Acceptance Notice
Earliest date: October 15, 2010
Latest date: Until class is full
Applicant's Response to Acceptance
Offer – Maximum Time: Two weeks

Requests for Deferred
Entrance Considered: Yes

Deposit to Hold Place in Class: Yes
Deposit (Resident): $100   **(Non-resident):** $100
Deposit due: Within two weeks of acceptance
Applied to tuition: Yes   **Refundable:** Yes
Refundable by: May 15, 2011

Estimated number of new entrants: 170
EDP: 20, special program: 25

Start Month/Year: August 2011

Interview Format: One-to-one, non-stress interview with faculty. Video interviews are not available.

Other Programs

PREPARATORY PROGRAMS
Postbaccalaureate Program: No
Summer Program: Yes, http://njms.umdnj.edu/
education/special_programs/index.cfm
(973) 972-3762

Combined Degree Programs

Baccalaureate/M.D.: Yes, http://njms.umdnj.edu/
education/admissions/seven_year_ba_md.cfm,
Lisa Houston, (973) 972-4631,
njmadmiss@umdnj.edu
M.D./M.P.H.: Yes, http://sph.umdnj.edu
M.D./M.B.A.: Yes,
http://njms.umdnj.edu/education/
admissions/md_mba.cfm
M.D./J.D.: No
M.D./Ph.D.: Yes, http://njms.umdnj.edu/
education/admissions/md_phd.cfm

Premedical Coursework

On-line courses accepted in fulfillment of prerequisites: No

Course	Req.	Rec.	Lab.	Hrs.
Inorganic Chemistry	•		•	8
Behavioral Sciences				
Biochemistry		•		
Biology				
Biology/Zoology	•		•	8
Calculus				
College English	•			6
College Mathematics		•		

Course	Req.	Rec.	Lab.	Hrs.
Computer Science				
Genetics		•		
Humanities				
Organic Chemistry	•		•	8
Physics	•		•	8
Psychology				
Social Sciences				
Other				

Selection Factors: 2009 Accepted Applicants

Proportion of Accepted Applicants with Relevant Experience (Data Self-Reported to AMCAS®)		Community Service/Volunteer	61%
		Medically-Related Work	84%
		Research	83%

Shaded bar represents school's accepted scores ranging from the 10th percentile to the 90th percentile.   School Median ● National Median ●

Overall GPA	2.0	2.1	2.2	2.3	2.4	2.5	2.6	2.7	2.8	2.9	3.0	3.1	3.2	3.3	3.4	3.5	3.6	(3.7)	3.8	3.9	4.0
Science GPA	2.0	2.1	2.2	2.3	2.4	2.5	2.6	2.7	2.8	2.9	3.0	3.1	3.2	3.3	3.4	3.5	(3.6)	3.7	3.8	3.9	4.0

MCAT® Total Numeric Score 9 10 11 12 13 14 15 16 17 18 19 20 21 22 23 24 25 26 27 28 29 30 31 (32) 33 34 35 36 37 38 39 40 41 42 43

Writing Sample		J	K	L	M	N	O	P	(Q)	R	S	T
Verbal Reasoning	3	4	5	6	7	8	9	(10)	11	12	13	14	15
Biological Sciences	3	4	5	6	7	8	9	10	(11)	12	13	14	15
Physical Sciences	3	4	5	6	7	8	9	10	(11)	12	13	14	15

Acceptance & Matriculation Data for 2009–2010 First Year Class

	Resident	Non-resident	International	Total
Applications	1187	2609	43	3839
Interviewed	632	23	0	655
Deferred	6	0	0	6
Matriculants				
Early Assurance Program	1	0	0	1
Early Decision Program	12	0	0	12
Baccalaureate/M.D.	29	0	0	29
M.D./Ph.D.	6	1	0	7
Matriculated	163	8	0	**171**

Applications accepted from International Applicants: No

Specialty Choice

2005, 2006, 2007 Graduates, Specialty Choice (As reported by program directors to GME Track™)

Anesthesiology	9%
Emergency Medicine	7%
Family Practice	5%
Internal Medicine	17%
Obstetrics/Gynecology	4%
Orthopaedic Surgery	5%
Pediatrics	10%
Psychiatry	5%
Radiology	6%
Surgery	7%

Matriculant Demographics: 2009–2010 First Year Class

Men: 97   **Women:** 74

Matriculants' Self-Reported Race/Ethnicity

Mexican American	1	Korean	9
Cuban	4	Vietnamese	1
Puerto Rican	3	Other Asian	2
Other Hispanic	9	Total Asian	73
Total Hispanic	16	Native American	0
Chinese	16	Black	15
Asian Indian	42	Native Hawaiian	0
Pakistani	4	White	71
Filipino	1	Unduplicated Number	
Japanese	0	of Matriculants	171

Science and Math Majors: 70%
Matriculants with:
        Baccalaureate degree: 99%
        Graduate degree(s): 13%

Financial Information

Source: 2008-2009 LCME I-B survey
and 2009-2010 AAMC TSF questionnaire

	Residents	Non-residents
Total Cost of Attendance	$ 51,297	$ 66,109
Tuition and Fees	$ 27,347	$ 42,159
Other (includes living expenses)	$ 21,885	$ 21,885
Health Insurance (can be waived)	$ 2,065	$ 2,065

Average 2009 Graduate Indebtedness: $128,250
% of Enrolled Students Receiving Aid: 84%

Criminal Background Check

This medical school requires a criminal background check prior to matriculation.

University of Medicine and Dentistry of New Jersey — Robert Wood Johnson Medical School

Piscataway, New Jersey

Associate Dean for Admissions
University of Medicine and Dentistry of New Jersey
Robert Wood Johnson Medical School
675 Hoes Lane
Piscataway, New Jersey 08854-5635
T 732 235 4576   **F** 732 235 5078

Admissions http://rwjms.umdnj.edu/education/admissions
Main http://rwjms.umdnj.edu
Financial www.umdnj.edu/studentfinancialaid
E-mail rwjapadm@umdnj.edu

Public Institution

Dr. Peter S. Amenta, Dean

Dr. Carol A. Terregino, Associate Dean for Admissions

Dr. Jocelyn Mitchell-Williams, Assistant Dean for Multicultural Affairs

Marshall Anthony, Associate Director of Financial Aid

Meryle Kramer, Admissions Officer

General Information

Robert Wood Johnson Medical School, formerly Rutgers Medical School, has campuses in Piscataway and New Brunswick. A full complement of clinical training facilities including Robert Wood Johnson University Hospital, Bristol Myers Squibb Children's Hospital, and numerous ambulatory sites provide outstanding educational experiences. The medical school encompasses 22 basic science and clinical departments and more than 2,500 full-time and volunteer faculty members.

Mission Statement

The medical school is dedicated to the pursuit of excellence in education, research, health care delivery and the promotion of community health. Excellence is achieved through the work of a scholarly and creative faculty and a high-achieving and diverse student body.

Curricular Highlights

Community Service Requirement: Optional. Distinction in Service to the Community
Research/Thesis Requirement: Optional. Distinction in Research or Distinction in Medical Education

Curriculum 2010 will roll out in August 2010. A systems-based first and second year curriculum will allow integration of relevant content from multiple disciplines and application in the context of real clinical problems. Learner centered teaching strategies will increase the development of skills for life-long study and critical thinking. The preclerkship pass/fail curriculum provides for early introduction to patient care via the learning communities of the Patient Centered Medicine course. There is

ample elective time in the third year. In the fourth year students rotate in emergency medicine and critical care, a sub-internship, outpatient subspecialties and 20 weeks of electives. A longitudinal primary care experience and an independent project round out the clinical curriculum. The Clinical Skills Center runs a summative clinical assessment. Each clerkship has an OSCE, and grading is on a 5-point scale. There are a number of dual degree options including a program in Clinical and Translational research. The MD/PhD is a tri-institutional program with Princeton University and Rutgers University.

USMLE

Step 1: Required. Students must record a passing score for promotion.
Step 2: Clinical Skills (CS): Required. Students must record a passing total score to graduate.
Step 2: Clinical Knowledge (CK): Required. Students must record a passing total score to graduate.

Selection Factors

Preference is given to New Jersey residents. Out-of-state applicants are encouraged to apply. Admission is determined on the basis of academics, MCAT, preprofessional evaluations, character, motivation, and interview. We believe that a diverse student body contributes to the educational program of all students. Selection and recruitment is based on a holistic review of each applicant's experiences, personal qualities and potential to enhance the learning environment. Applications from members of groups underrepresented in medicine are encouraged. Interviews are by invitation. Matriculants must submit to a criminal background check.

Financial Aid

Financial aid is awarded on the basis of evaluated need. All awards consist of a package of loans and grants when funds are available. New funds have been allocated for scholarships. Counseling services are available.

Information about Diversity Programs

Robert Wood Johnson Medical School is committed to the education of physicians from groups underrepresented in medicine. Applications from in-state and out-of-state

candidates are welcome. Numerous support services are available for disadvantaged students, including a pre-matriculation summer program.

Campus Information

Setting

The facilities of the Piscataway campus include the Kessler Teaching Labs/Clinical Skills Center and the Research Tower, University Behavioral Health Care Center, the Center for Advanced Biotechnology and Medicine and the Environmental and Occupational health Sciences Institute,UMDNJ School of Public Health and the Robert Wood Johnson Medical School Research Building. The New Brunswick campus includes the Cancer Hospital, BMS Children's Hospital, Children's Specialized Hospital, the Child Health Institute, and the Cancer Institute of New Jersey.

Enrollment

For 2009, total enrollment was: 700

Special Features

The medical school hosts 85 centers and institutes including the Cancer Institute of New Jersey, the Cardiovascular Institute, the Child Health Institute of New Jersey, the Center for Advanced Biotechnology and Medicine, and the Environmental and Occupational Health Sciences Institute. Students provide continuity care to the community in the Promise Clinic and the Homeless and Indigent Population Health Outreach Project. They tailor their medical school experiences as Student Scholars, researchers, leaders of organizations and non-credit electives and as international travelers. Scholarly and social lives are rich.

Housing

On-campus housing is currently not available. Students are assisted in finding affordable housing through "housing days".

Application Process and Requirements 2011–2012

Primary Application Service: AMCAS
Earliest filing date: June 1, 2010
Latest filing date: December 1, 2010

Secondary Application Required?: No
Sent to: n/a
URL: n/a
Fee: Yes, $75   **Waiver available:** Yes
Earliest filing date: n/a
Latest filing date: n/a

MCAT® required?: Yes
Latest MCAT® considered: September 2010
Oldest MCAT® considered: September 2007

Early Decision Program: School does have EDP
Applicants notified: October 1, 2010
EDP available for: Both Residents and Non-residents

Regular Acceptance Notice
Earliest date: October 15, 2010
Latest date: Until class is full
Applicant's Response to Acceptance Offer – Maximum Time: Two weeks

Requests for Deferred Entrance Considered: Yes

Deposit to Hold Place in Class: Yes
Deposit (Resident): $50   **(Non-resident):** $50
Deposit due: With response to acceptance offer
Applied to tuition: Yes **Refundable:** Yes
Refundable by: May 15, 2011

Estimated number of new entrants: 110
EDP: 5, special program: 15

Start Month/Year: August 2011

Interview Format: One (faculty) or two (faculty and student) interviews. Applicants can interview on any of the campuses. Video interviews are not available.

Other Programs

PREPARATORY PROGRAMS

Postbaccalaureate Program: Yes, Carol Terregino, M.D., (732) 235-4576, terregca@umdnj.edu
Summer Program: Yes, Jocelyn Mitchell-Williams, M.D., (856) 757-7905, jmitchel@umdnj.edu

COMBINED DEGREE PROGRAMS

Baccalaureate/M.D.: Yes, http://lifesci.rutgers.edu/~hpo/
M.D./M.P.H.: Yes, http://sph.umdnj.edu
Tina Greco, (732) 235-4017, grecotm@umdnj.edu
M.D./M.B.A.: Yes, David Seiden, Ph.D.
(732) 235-4577, seiden@umdnj.edu
M.D./J.D.: Yes, Carol A. Terregino, M.D.
(732) 235-4577, terregca@umdnj.edu
M.D./Ph.D.: Yes, http://rwjms.umdnj.edu/research/scientist_training/
Terri Kinzy, Ph.D., (732) 235-5450, kinzytg@umdnj.edu

Premedical Coursework

On-line courses accepted in fulfillment of prerequisites: No

Course	Req.	Rec.	Lab.	Sems.	Course	Req.	Rec.	Lab.	Sems.
Inorganic Chemistry	•		•	2	Genetics		•		
Behavioral Sciences		•			Humanities		•		
Biochemistry		•			Organic Chemistry	•		•	2
Biology					Physics	•		•	2
Biology/Zoology	•		•	2	Psychology		•		
Calculus					Social Sciences		•		
College English	•			2	Molecular Biology		•		
College Mathematics	•			1	Statistics		•		
Computer Science					Cell Biology		•		

Selection Factors: 2009 Accepted Applicants

Proportion of Accepted Applicants with Relevant Experience (Data Self-Reported to AMCAS®)			
Community Service/Volunteer			62%
Medically-Related Work			88%
Research			85%

Shaded bar represents school's accepted scores ranging from the 10th percentile to the 90th percentile   School Median ●   National Median ○

Overall GPA	2.0	2.1	2.2	2.3	2.4	2.5	2.6	2.7	2.8	2.9	3.0	3.1	3.2	3.3	3.4	3.5	3.6	(3.7)	3.8	3.9	4.0
Science GPA	2.0	2.1	2.2	2.3	2.4	2.5	2.6	2.7	2.8	2.9	3.0	3.1	3.2	3.3	3.4	3.5	(3.6)	3.7	3.8	3.9	4.0

MCAT® Total Numeric Score 9 10 11 12 13 14 15 16 17 18 19 20 21 22 23 24 25 26 27 28 29 30 31 (32) 33 34 35 36 37 38 39 40 41 42 43

Writing Sample			J	K	L	M	N	O	P	(Q)	R	S	T
Verbal Reasoning	3	4	5	6	7	8	9	(10)	11	12	13	14	15
Biological Sciences	3	4	5	6	7	8	9	10	(11)	12	13	14	15
Physical Sciences	3	4	5	6	7	8	9	10	(11)	12	13	14	15

Acceptance & Matriculation Data for 2009–2010 First Year Class

	Resident	Non-resident	International	Total
Applications	1175	2136	30	3341
Interviewed	419	81	0	500
Deferred	3	1	0	4
Matriculants				
Early Assurance Program	0	0	0	0
Early Decision Program	2	0	0	2
Baccalaureate/M.D.	7	0	0	7
M.D./Ph.D.	2	2	0	4
Matriculated	156	7	0	**163**

Applications accepted from International Applicants: No

Matriculant Demographics: 2009–2010 First Year Class

Men: 75   **Women:** 88

Matriculants' Self-Reported Race/Ethnicity

Mexican American	0	Korean	4
Cuban	0	Vietnamese	0
Puerto Rican	3	Other Asian	2
Other Hispanic	1	Total Asian	50
Total Hispanic	4	Native American	0
Chinese	16	Black	11
Asian Indian	24	Native Hawaiian	0
Pakistani	3	White	88
Filipino	2	Unduplicated Number	
Japanese	0	of Matriculants	163

Science and Math Majors: 61%
Matriculants with:
   Baccalaureate degree: 99%
   Graduate degree(s): 7%

Specialty Choice

2005, 2006, 2007 Graduates, Specialty Choice (As reported by program directors to GME Track™)	
Anesthesiology	4%
Emergency Medicine	7%
Family Practice	8%
Internal Medicine	23%
Obstetrics/Gynecology	3%
Orthopaedic Surgery	5%
Pediatrics	14%
Psychiatry	4%
Radiology	9%
Surgery	6%

Financial Information

Source: 2008-2009 LCME I-B survey and 2009-2010 AAMC TSF questionnaire

	Residents	Non-residents
Total Cost of Attendance	$ 56,718	$ 71,530
Tuition and Fees	$ 27,670	$ 42,482
Other (includes living expenses)	$ 26,983	$ 26,983
Health Insurance (can be waived)	$ 2,065	$ 2,065

Average 2009 Graduate Indebtedness: $130,243
% of Enrolled Students Receiving Aid: 83%

Criminal Background Check

This medical school requires a criminal background check prior to matriculation.

University of New Mexico School of Medicine
Albuquerque, New Mexico

University of New Mexico Health Sciences Center
School of Medicine, Office of Admissions,
MSC09 5085, Health Sciences Library and
Informatics Center, Room 125
Albuquerque, New Mexico 87131-0001
T 505 272 4766   **F** 505 925 6031

Admissions http://hsc.unm.edu/som/admissions
Main http://hsc.unm.edu/som
Financial http://hsc.unm.edu/som/admissions/aid.shtml
E-mail somadmissions@salud.unm.edu

Public Institution
Dr. Paul B. Roth, Dean

Dr. David G. Bear, Assistant Dean for Admissions

Dr. Valerie Romero-Leggott, Vice President of Diversity

Janell Valdez, Financial Aid Supervisor

Marlene Ballejos, Admissions Director

General Information
The University of New Mexico enrolled its first 24 medical students in September of 1964. The School of Medicine is both a professional and graduate school where students may earn an M.D. degree, a Ph.D. degree, a combined M.D./Ph.D. degree, a combined M.D./M.P.H., or B.S. or M.S. degrees in several allied health science fields. Medical education at the resident and postgraduate levels is offered through the University's teaching hospital and various state-of-the-art facilities.

Mission Statement
The mission of the University of New Mexico is to educate students, scientists, physicians and other health professionals in the art and science of medicine through the transmission of biomedical knowledge acquired from research and patient care. We aspire to improve the health of all New Mexicans by being a model of excellence in education while working to reduce disparities among medically underrepresented populations and communities.

Curricular Highlights
Community Service Requirement: Required. A community research project is required.
Research/Thesis Requirement: Required. A research project and report is required.

The School of Medicine utilizes a hybrid curriculum, which incorporates the integration of basic sciences and clinical medicine with problem-based and student-centered learning techniques. Early clinical skills are coupled with medical education taught from three perspectives: biologic, population, and behavioral, and these perspectives are continued throughout the clinical years. Medical students are exposed to patient care during the first year of education, and finish that year with a 9-week, in-depth Practical Immersion Experience (PIE) in a professional setting in one of New Mexico's communities. The goals of the curriculum are to graduate physicians who are enthusiastic and responsible for their continued learning; have the ability to define problems, formulate questions, and carry out scholarly inquiry; are skilled in self and peer assessment; and have a broad perspective on the importance of human biology, behavior, environment, culture, and social setting in the health of individuals and populations. Student assessment is competency-based and values mastery of knowledge, critical appraisal, interpersonal and clinical skills, and peer and self-assessment.

USMLE
Step 1: Required. Students must record a passing score for promotion.
Step 2: Clinical Skills (CS): Required. Students must record a passing score in each section to graduate.
Step 2: Clinical Knowledge (CK): Required. Students must record a passing score in each section to graduate.

Selection Factors
Upon receipt of the AMCAS application, applicants who pass initial screening will be sent a supplemental application and an invitation to interview. In general, only those applicants with ties to the state of New Mexico or residents of WICHE states (Montana and Wyoming) will receive consideration for admission. Selection is based upon scholastic achievement, performance on the MCAT, personal interviews with members of the Admissions Committee, and recommendations.

Financial Aid
The school makes accessible federal, state and institutional aid in the form of scholarships, grants, and loans. Both need-based and merit-based funding are available to students. The amount of an award varies according to the student's need and the level of funding available. The Office of Financial Aid assists all students in locating necessary funds to support their medical education.

Information about Diversity Programs

Our mission is to promote ethnic, racial, socio-economic, gender, and geographic diversity in the Health Sciences, and to create opportunities to address the health disparities that affect all New Mexicans. Strategies to achieve this mission include creating programs that increase college awareness and identifying, recruiting, and supporting students, residents, and faculty from these diverse backgrounds.

Campus Information

Setting
Albuquerque is home to a unique blend of culture and cuisine, styles and stories, peoples, pursuits, and panoramas.

Enrollment
For 2009, total enrollment was: 323

Special Features
The School of Medicine facilities include a Basic Medical Sciences Building, a Biomedical Research Facility, the Health Sciences Library and Informatics Center, the Mental Health Center, the UNM Children's Hospital, the Children's Psychiatric Center, the Family Practice Center, the Mind Imaging Center, Clinical and Translational Science Center, and the Cancer Research and Treatment Center. Other components include: Addiction and Substance Abuse Programs, Brain Imaging Center, Center for Disease Medicine, Center for Environmental Health Sciences, Center for Telehealth, Center on Aging, Children's Hospital Heart Center, Clinical Trials Center, General Clinical Research Center, Geriatric Education Center, HSC Institute for Ethics, New Mexico AIDS Education and Training Center, New Mexico Immunization Coalition, New Mexico Poison Control Center, Sleep Disorders Center, School of Medicine Center for Community Partnerships and Speech/Language/Swallow Center.

Housing
On-campus housing is not available.

Satellite Campuses/Facilities
Student clinical rotations are divided among University Hospital and several other locations in the Albuquerque area.

Application Process and Requirements 2011–2012

Primary Application Service: AMCAS
Earliest filing date: June 1, 2010
Latest filing date: November 15, 2010

Secondary Application Required?: Yes
Sent to: Screened applicants
URL: http://hsc.unm.edu/som/admissions
Fee: Yes, $75   **Waiver available:** Yes
Earliest filing date: August 1, 2010
Latest filing date: February 1, 2011

MCAT® required?: Yes
Latest MCAT® considered: September 2010
Oldest MCAT® considered: August 2006

Early Decision Program: School does have EDP
Applicants notified: October 1, 2010
EDP available for: Both Residents and Non-residents

Regular Acceptance Notice
Earliest date: March 15, 2011
Latest date: Until class is full
Applicant's Response to Acceptance Offer – Maximum Time: Two weeks

Requests for Deferred Entrance Considered: Yes

Deposit to Hold Place in Class: Yes
Deposit (Resident): $100   **(Non-resident):** $100
Deposit due: May 15, 2011
Applied to tuition: Yes   **Refundable:** Yes
Refundable by: May 15, 2011

Estimated number of new entrants: 100
EDP: 6, special program: 7

Start Month/Year: July 2011

Interview Format: Two one-on-one interviews by committee members. Video interviews are not available.

Other Programs

PREPARATORY PROGRAMS
Postbaccalaureate Program: Yes,
http://ume-oars.health.unm.edu/prep.shtml
Steven Mitchell, (505) 925-4441,
smmitchell@salud.unm.edu
Summer Program: No

COMBINED DEGREE PROGRAMS
Baccalaureate/M.D.: Yes,
http://hsc.unm.edu/som/combinedbamd
Misty Salas, (505) 925-4500
combinedbamd@salud.unm.edu
M.D./M.P.H.: Yes, http://hsc.unm.edu/som/fcm/
mph/mphindex.shtml, Gaylea Garcia, (505) 272-4173, garciag@salud.unm.edu
M.D./M.B.A.: No
M.D./J.D.: No
M.D./Ph.D.: Yes, http://hsc.unm.edu/som/
research/brep/mdphdwelcome.shtm
Fernando Valenzuela,
(505) 272-1887, brep@salud.unm.edu

Premedical Coursework

On-line courses accepted in fulfillment of prerequisites: No

Course	Req.	Rec.	Lab.	Hrs.
Inorganic Chemistry	•		•	8
Behavioral Sciences				
Biochemistry	•			3
Biology				
Biology/Zoology	•		•	8
Calculus				
College English				
College Mathematics				

Course	Req.	Rec.	Lab.	Hrs.
Computer Science				
Genetics				
Humanities				
Organic Chemistry	•		•	8
Physics	•			6
Psychology				
Anatomy & Physiology		•	•	
Microbiology		•		
Immunology		•		

Selection Factors: 2009 Accepted Applicants

Proportion of Accepted Applicants with Relevant Experience (Data Self-Reported to AMCAS)		
Community Service/Volunteer		76%
Medically-Related Work		84%
Research		68%

Shaded bar represents school's accepted scores ranging from the 10th percentile to the 90th percentile   **School Median** ●   **National Median** ○

Overall GPA 2.0 2.1 2.2 2.3 2.4 2.5 2.6 2.7 2.8 2.9 3.0 3.1 3.2 3.3 3.4 3.5 (3.6) 3.7 3.8 3.9 4.0
Science GPA 2.0 2.1 2.2 2.3 2.4 2.5 2.6 2.7 2.8 2.9 3.0 3.1 3.2 3.3 3.4 (3.5) 3.6 3.7 3.8 3.9 4.0

MCAT® Total Numeric Score 9 10 11 12 13 14 15 16 17 18 19 20 21 22 23 24 25 26 27 28 (29) 30 31 (32) 33 34 35 36 37 38 39 40 41 42 43

			J	K	L	M	N	O	P	Q	R	S	T
Writing Sample								(O)		(Q)			
Verbal Reasoning	3	4	5	6	7	8	9	(10)	11	12	13	14	15
Biological Sciences	3	4	5	6	7	8	9	(10)	(11)	12	13	14	15
Physical Sciences	3	4	5	6	7	8	(9)	10	(11)	12	13	14	15

Acceptance & Matriculation Data for 2009–2010 First Year Class

	Resident	Non-resident	International	Total
Applications	206	382	1	589
Interviewed	188	18	0	219
Deferred	4	1	0	5
Matriculants				
Early Assurance Program	0	0	0	0
Early Decision Program	6	0	0	6
Baccalaureate/M.D.	2	0	0	2
M.D./Ph.D.	2	0	0	2
Matriculated	73	4	0	**77**

Applications accepted from International Applicants: No

Matriculant Demographics: 2009–2010 First Year Class

Men: 31   **Women:** 46

Matriculants' Self-Reported Race/Ethnicity

Mexican American	16	Korean	0
Cuban	0	Vietnamese	3
Puerto Rican	1	Other Asian	0
Other Hispanic	6	Total Asian	6
Total Hispanic	23	Native American	9
Chinese	1	Black	1
Asian Indian	0	Native Hawaiian	0
Pakistani	0	White	52
Filipino	1	**Unduplicated Number**	
Japanese	1	**of Matriculants**	77

Science and Math Majors: 69%
Matriculants with:
   Baccalaureate degree: 100%
   Graduate degree(s): 8%

Specialty Choice

2005, 2006, 2007 Graduates, Specialty Choice (As reported by program directors to GME Track™)	
Anesthesiology	5%
Emergency Medicine	6%
Family Practice	13%
Internal Medicine	22%
Obstetrics/Gynecology	10%
Orthopaedic Surgery	3%
Pediatrics	13%
Psychiatry	2%
Radiology	5%
Surgery	5%

Financial Information

Source: 2008-2009 LCME I-B survey and 2009-2010 AAMC TSF questionnaire

	Residents	Non-residents
Total Cost of Attendance	$ 38,867	$ 67,608
Tuition and Fees	$ 18,252	$ 46,993
Other (includes living expenses)	$ 20,452	$ 20,452
Health Insurance (can be waived)	$ 163	$ 163

Average 2009 Graduate Indebtedness: $114,500
% of Enrolled Students Receiving Aid: 94%

Criminal Background Check

This medical school requires a criminal background check prior to matriculation.

Albany Medical College
Albany, New York

Office of Admissions, Mail Code 3
Albany Medical College
47 New Scotland Avenue
Albany, New York 12208
T 518 262 5521   **F** 518 262 5887

Admissions www.amc.edu/academic/Undergraduate_Admissions/
Main www.amc.edu/Academic/
Financial www.amc.edu/academic/Undergraduate/FinancialAid.html
E-mail admissions@mail.amc.edu

Private Institution

Dr. Vincent Verdile, Dean

Joanne H. Nanos, Director, Admissions and Student Records

Dr. Ingrid Allard, Associate Dean, Community Outreach and Medical Education

Ann Loughman, Director of Financial Aid

Dr. Henry Pohl, Vice Dean for Academic Administration

General Information
Founded in 1839, Albany Medical College is one of the oldest medical schools in the country and one of the largest teaching hospitals in New York State. The college is coeducational, nondenominational, and privately supported. The college and the 650-bed Albany Medical Center Hospital comprise Albany Medical Center. Patient care, from primary to tertiary, is provided for over 2.5 million residents of eastern New York and western New England.

Mission Statement
The mission of the Albany Medical College is to: educate medical students, physicians, bio-medical scientists, and other health professionals from demograhically diverse backgrounds to meet future primary and specialty health care needs; foster biomedical research that leads to scientific advances and improvement of public health; and provide a broad range of patient services.

Curricular Highlights
Community Service Requirement: Optional.
Research/Thesis Requirement: Optional.
M.D. with Distinction in Service,
M.D. with Distinction in Research,
M.D. with Distinction in Health Systems Analysis, M.D. with Distinction in Bioethics

Basic and clinical sciences are integrated into themes stressing normal function in Year 1 and pathological processes in Year 2. There are also five longitudinal themes integrated throughout the curriculum: clinical skills, ethical and health systems issues, evidence-based medicine, nutrition, and informatics. In every theme, learning focuses on clinical presentations. Beginning in Year 1, students learn to interview and examine both real and standardized patients. Clinical skills competence is highlighted throughout the four years. Basic science knowledge is reinforced during years 3 and 4. Primary care is emphasized throughout the four years. Year 3 clerkships focus on care in ambulatory settings. Year 4 required rotations concentrate on care in hospital-based settings, preparing students for residency and practice. The remainder of fourth year includes electives chosen by the students and a required course in learning how to teach.

USMLE
Step 1: Required. Students must record a passing score for graduation, but not promotion.
Step 2: Clinical Skills (CS): Required. Students must record a passing total score to graduate.
Step 2: Clinical Knowledge (CK): Required. Students must record a passing total score to graduate.

Selection Factors
In selecting students, emphasis is placed upon integrity, character, academic achievement, motivation, emotional stability, and social and intellectual suitability. The college is committed to the belief that educational opportunities should be available to all eligible persons without regard to race, creed, age, gender, religion, marital status, handicap, national origin, or sexual orientation. Admission is not restricted to state residents. The committee evaluates applications based on a number of factors in addition to MCAT scores and GPAs. Invitations for interview are made at the discretion of the committee. Preapplication inquiries or questions concerning the status of applications are always welcome.

Financial Aid
The mission of the Financial Aid Office is to be the primary source of information and education about financing a degree. Outreach events and media are provided to guide the development of students' immediate and long-range spending plans that secure their financial future. The office awards and certifies need-based aid for 88% of enrolled students and provides lifetime service to graduated students.

Information about Diversity Programs
We believe that Albany Medical College's mission is enriched by a community of people with diverse backgrounds. Recognition and respect of all differences that exist is crucial to the development of core professional attributes in our students, to the continued nurturing of such attributes among our faculty, staff and workforce. To that end we seek to recruit students who will bring a diversity of thought, experience and backgrounds to our community. Please call the Office of Admissions at 518-262-5521 for more information.

Campus Information

Setting
Albany is the capital of New York and a part of the tri-city area which includes Schenectady and Troy. Rich in history, Albany has diverse cultural and recreational opportunities. Fifteen area colleges and universities add to the region's eclectic appeal.

Enrollment
For 2009, total enrollment was: 557

Special Features
Albany Medical Center Hospital provides sophisticated health care to more than 3 million people in 25 counties. A state-of-the-art Patient Safety and Simulation Center is under construction at AMC that will utilize a variety of methods to teach knowledge, skills, behaviors and attitudes necessary to deliver quality health care. The Center's anticipated opening is Fall 2010.

Housing
On-campus housing is not available. The college maintains a list of affordable apartments within a 5-mile radius. Rents average $500–$900 per month.

Satellite Campuses/Facilities
The medical college is affiliated with other hospitals in New York State. Clinical departments utilize a network of community physicians to serve the ambulatory care educational needs of students. The college, which is combined with Albany Medical Center Hospital on its campus, is also affiliated with the Veterans Administration Hospital, community hospitals, and private and community clinics in surrounding counties.

Application Process and Requirements 2011–2012

Primary Application Service: AMCAS
Earliest filing date: June 1, 2010
Latest filing date: November 15, 2010

Secondary Application Required?: Yes
Sent to: All applicants
Contact: Admissions Staff
(518) 262-5521, admissions@mail.amc.edu
Fee: Yes, $105   **Waiver available:** Yes
Earliest filing date: June 2010
Latest filing date: January 15, 2011

MCAT® required?: Yes
Latest MCAT® considered: September 2010
Oldest MCAT® considered: 2007

Early Decision Program: School does not have EDP
Applicants notified: n/a
EDP available for: n/a

Regular Acceptance Notice
Earliest date: November 1, 2011
Latest date: Until class is full
Applicant's Response to Acceptance
Offer – Maximum Time: Two weeks

Requests for Deferred
Entrance Considered: Yes

Deposit to Hold Place in Class: Yes
Deposit (Resident): $100   **(Non-resident):** $100
Deposit due: With response to acceptance offer
Applied to tuition: Yes   **Refundable:** Yes
Refundable by: May 15, 2011

Estimated number of new entrants: 140
EDP: n/a, special program: n/a

Start Month/Year: August 2011

Interview Format: Individual interviews by Admissions Committee. Regional interviews are not available. Video interviews are not available.

Other Programs

PREPARATORY PROGRAMS
Postbaccalaureate Program: No
Summer Program: No

COMBINED DEGREE PROGRAMS
Baccalaureate/M.D.: Yes,
Johanna Comanzo, (518) 262-5529
combineddegreeprograms@mail.amc.edu
M.D./M.P.H.: No
M.D./M.B.A.: No
M.D./J.D.: No
M.D./Ph.D.: No
Additional Program: No

Premedical Coursework

On-line courses accepted in fulfillment of prerequisites: No

Course	Req.	Rec.	Lab.	Hrs.	Course	Req.	Rec.	Lab.	Hrs.
Inorganic Chemistry	•		•	6	Computer Science				
Behavioral Sciences					Genetics				
Biochemistry					Humanities				
Biology	•		•	6	Organic Chemistry	•		•	6
Biology/Zoology	•		•	6	Physics	•		•	6
Calculus					Psychology				
College English					Social Sciences				
College Mathematics					Other				

Selection Factors: 2009 Accepted Applicants

Proportion of Accepted Applicants with Relevant Experience (Data Self-Reported to AMCAS®)		
Community Service/Volunteer		62%
Medically-Related Work		87%
Research		80%

Shaded bar represents school's accepted scores ranging from the 10th percentile to the 90th percentile   **School Median** ● **National Median** ○

Overall GPA	2.0	2.1	2.2	2.3	2.4	2.5	2.6	2.7	2.8	2.9	3.0	3.1	3.2	3.3	3.4	3.5	(3.6)	3.7	3.8	3.9	4.0
Science GPA	2.0	2.1	2.2	2.3	2.4	2.5	2.6	2.7	2.8	2.9	3.0	3.1	3.2	3.3	3.4	3.5	(3.6)	3.7	3.8	3.9	4.0

MCAT® Total Numeric Score 9 10 11 12 13 14 15 16 17 18 19 20 21 22 23 24 25 26 27 28 29 30 31 (32 33) 34 35 36 37 38 39 40 41 42 43

Writing Sample			J	K	L	M	N	O	P	(Q)	R	S	T
Verbal Reasoning	3	4	5	6	7	8	9	(10)	11	12	13	14	15
Biological Sciences	3	4	5	6	7	8	9	10	(11)	12	13	14	15
Physical Sciences	3	4	5	6	7	8	9	10	(11)	12	13	14	15

Acceptance & Matriculation Data for 2009–2010 First Year Class

	Resident	Non-resident	International	Total
Applications	1655	6977	549	9181
Interviewed	167	447	39	614
Deferred	1	0	0	1
Matriculants				
Early Assurance Program	0	0	0	0
Early Decision Program	0	0	0	0
Baccalaureate/M.D.	18	20	1	39
M.D./Ph.D.	0	0	0	0
Matriculated	48	82	3	**133**

Applications accepted from International Applicants: No

Matriculant Demographics: 2009–2010 First Year Class

Men: 72   **Women:** 61

Matriculants' Self-Reported Race/Ethnicity

Mexican American	1	Korean	4
Cuban	0	Vietnamese	2
Puerto Rican	1	Other Asian	1
Other Hispanic	2	Total Asian	34
Total Hispanic	4	Native American	1
Chinese	5	Black	3
Asian Indian	19	Native Hawaiian	1
Pakistani	2	White	79
Filipino	2	Unduplicated Number	
Japanese	1	of Matriculants	133

Science and Math Majors: 65%
Matriculants with:
Baccalaureate degree: 100%
Graduate degree(s): 31%

Specialty Choice

2005, 2006, 2007 Graduates, Specialty Choice (As reported by program directors to GME Track™)	
Anesthesiology	5%
Emergency Medicine	10%
Family Practice	6%
Internal Medicine	15%
Obstetrics/Gynecology	7%
Orthopaedic Surgery	5%
Pediatrics	14%
Psychiatry	4%
Radiology	3%
Surgery	9%

Financial Information

Source: 2008-2009 LCME I-B survey and 2009-2010 AAMC TSF questionnaire

	Residents	Non-residents
Total Cost of Attendance	$ 72,096	$ 72,796
Tuition and Fees	$ 46,407	$ 46,407
Other (includes living expenses)	$ 22,810	$ 23,510
Health Insurance (can be waived)	$ 2,879	$ 2,879

Average 2009 Graduate Indebtedness: $176,498
% of Enrolled Students Receiving Aid: 86%

Criminal Background Check

This medical school requires a criminal background check prior to matriculation.

Albert Einstein College of Medicine of Yeshiva University

Bronx, New York

Office of Admissions, Albert Einstein College of
Medicine of Yeshiva U Jack and Pearl Resnick Campus
1300 Morris Park Avenue
Bronx, New York 10461
T 718 430 2106   F 718 430 8840

Admissions http://www.einstein.yu.edu/admissions/
page.aspx?id=568
Main www.einstein.yu.edu/home/overview.asp
Financial www.einstein.yu.edu/financialaid/page.aspx
E-mail admissions@einstein.yu.edu

Private Institution

Dr. Allen M. Spiegel, Dean

Noreen Kerrigan, Assistant Dean for Student Admissions

Dr. Milton A. Gumbs, Associate Dean for Diversity Enhancement

Damien Jackson, Financial Aid Director

Dr. Martha S. Grayson, Senior Associate Dean for Educational Affairs

Dr. Stephen Baum, Senior Associate Dean for Students

General Information

Clinical education takes place in acute care hospitals, long-term care and skilled nursing facilities, hospices, and neighborhood health centers that serve a diverse population of patients in and around the NY metro area. There are many facilities devoted to biomedical research and teaching, and a new building for genetic and translational research as well as a new Clinical Skills Facility.

Mission Statement

Einstein combines scientific excellence with a social mission to improve health through engagement in local, national, and global communities. Einstein's dynamic curriculum unites the biomedical sciences and hands-on clinical training with the flexibility to pursue research and meet the healthcare needs of underserved populations in the Bronx, the New York metropolitan area, and beyond. Einstein attracts a diverse student body and provides a collegial and collaborative environment that fosters our students' growth as future clinicians, educators, physician scientists, and leaders in the field.

Curricular Highlights

Community Service Requirement: Optional.
Research/Thesis Requirement: Required.

Years 1 and 2 are interdisciplinary courses with self-directed case-based learning in small groups, and the "Introduction to Clinical Medicine" in which students see patients three weeks after matriculation. Year 3 consists of clerkship rotations. Year 4 provides experience in ambulatory care, Neurology and a hospital-based subinternship. Fourth year electives include overseas exchange programs, global health fellowships, and research. Many students do a tuition-free/fellowship supported fifth year, to conduct year-long projects, or to study for the MPH Degree. Performance is Pass/Fail in Years 1 and 2, supplemented by Honors and detailed narrative reports in Years 3 and 4.

USMLE

Step 1: Required. Students must record a passing score for promotion.
Step 2: Clinical Skills (CS): Required. Students must record a passing total score to graduate.
Step 2: Clinical Knowledge (CK): Required. Students must record a passing total score to graduate.

Selection Factors

In addition to the usual selection factors, attention is paid to community service, potential for professional achievement, motivation, and evidence of other personal qualities deemed essential for the study and practice of medicine. Einstein seeks traditional and non-traditional applicants who add diversity to the class and bring various perspectives to the study and practice of medicine. (Non-discrimination statement at: *www.einstein.yu.edu/admissions/page.aspx?id=568&ekmensel=15074e5e_1106*)

Financial Aid

Every attempt is made to assist students in meeting their financial obligations to the college and their essential personal needs. About 50% of students receive institutional loans and/or scholarships; about 80% qualify for outside loans and/or grants.

Information about Diversity Programs

The College of Medicine welcomes applications from students who are from groups underrepresented in medicine and/or who are economically disadvantaged. The College's Office of Diversity Enhancement provides opportunities for students to participate in special programs for high school and college students. Individual counseling is provided to students in need of long-term assistance to assure retention. The Office offers a summer research program to college students. Information on a summer research program can be obtained at (718) 430-3091.

Campus Information

Setting

Located in the northeast Bronx, surrounded by private homes and apartment buildings and near the Westchester County border, the area combines small-town living with easy access to Manhattan. Close by are the Bronx Zoo, Botanical Gardens, Yankee Stadium, City Island (a fishing and sailing community), Orchard Beach, and the sprawling Pelham Bay Park, where there is hiking, swimming, horseback riding, golfing, and bicycling.

Enrollment

For 2009, total enrollment was: 780

Special Features

There are fellowships for projects in basic and clinical research, global health, community and population health, and ethics and humanism. There is an Alternative Pathway to the M.D.-Ph.D. after Year 2, overseas exchange programs, a Clinical Research M.D./M.S. Program, a stipend for the M.P.H. Degree (anywhere in the world), a Medical Spanish Program, and a program for Personal Wellness.

Housing

Apartments are large, rents are low and security is excellent. There are studios, one-and two-bedroom apartments with a/c, fully equipped eat-in-kitchens, and ample closet space. Parking, laundry facilities, children's playground, and a large athletic facility are on the premises. Housing is available to all Einstein students and to their spouses or committed partners.

Satellite Campuses/Facilities

Facilities include: Beth Israel Medical Center, Bronx-Lebanon Hospital, Jacobi Medical Center, North Shore/Long Island Jewish Medical Center, Montefiore and the Jack D. Weiler Hospitals, Bronx Children's Psychiatric Center, Bronx Psychiatric Center, Four Winds Hospital, Beth Abraham Hospital, Hebrew Home for the Aged, Morningside House, the Parker Jewish Geriatric Institute, the Children's Evaluation and Rehabilitation Center, the Division of Substance Abuse, and the Sound View Throgs Neck Community Mental Health Center.

Application Process and Requirements 2011–2012

Primary Application Service: AMCAS
Earliest filing date: June 1, 2010
Latest filing date: November 1, 2010

Secondary Application Required?: Yes
Sent to: All applicants
Contact: Office of Admissions, (718) 430-2106, admissions@einstein.yu.edu
URL: www.aecom.yu.edu/admissions/admission Application.asp
Fee: Yes, $120   **Waiver available:** Yes
Earliest filing date: July 1, 2010
Latest filing date: March 15, 2011

MCAT® required?: Yes
Latest MCAT® considered: September 2010
Oldest MCAT® considered: April 2007

Early Decision Program: School does have EDP
Applicants notified: October 1, 2010
EDP available for: Both Residents and Non-residents

Regular Acceptance Notice
Earliest date: January 15, 2011
Latest date: Until class is full
Applicant's Response to Acceptance Offer
Maximum Time: Two weeks until May 1, 2011; one week thereafter

Requests for Deferred
Entrance Considered: Yes

Deposit to Hold Place in Class: Yes
Deposit (Resident): $100   **(Non-resident):** $100
Deposit due: April 1, 2011
Applied to tuition: Yes   **Refundable:** Yes
Refundable by: June 1, 2011

Estimated number of new entrants: 183
EDP: 2, special program: 5

Start Month/Year: August 2011

Interview Format: One interview with a faculty member only. Regional interviews are not available. Video interviews are not available.

Other Programs

PREPARATORY PROGRAMS
Postbaccalaureate Program: No
Summer Program: Yes, www.einstein.yu.edu/phd/index.asp?surp
Minority Student Summer Research Opportunity Program: www.aecom.yu.edu/admissions/page.aspx?ID=9564, Ms. Nilda Soto, (718) 430-3091, nilda.soto@einstein.yu.edu
Hispanic Center of Excellence Summer Undergraduate Mentorship Program: www.einstein.yu.edu/hcoe/page.aspx?id=16704 , Ms. Hope Spano, (718) 430-2792, hope.spano@einstein.yu.edu

COMBINED DEGREE PROGRAMS
Baccalaureate/M.D.: No
M.D./M.P.H.: Yes, www.aecom.yu.edu/uploadedFiles/IPHS/IPHS_MPH_Brochure.pdf, Paul Marantz, (718) 430-4187, marantz@einstein.yu.edu
M.D./M.B.A.: No
M.D./J.D.: No
M.D./Ph.D.: Yes, mstp.aecom.yu.edu/
Clinical Research Program: Yes, www.einstein.yu.edu/ictr/page.aspx?id=12206&ekmensel=15074e5e_942_1170_12206

Premedical Coursework

On-line courses accepted in fulfillment of prerequisites: No

Course	Req.	Rec.	Lab.	Hrs.	Course	Req.	Rec.	Lab.	Hrs.
Inorganic Chemistry	•		•	8	Computer Science		•		3
Behavioral Sciences					Genetics		•		3
Biochemistry		•	•	4	Humanities				
Biology	•		•	8	Organic Chemistry	•		•	8
Biology/Zoology					Physics	•		•	8
Calculus					Psychology				
College English	•			6	Social Sciences		•		
College Mathematics	•			6	Other				

Selection Factors: 2009 Accepted Applicants

Proportion of Accepted Applicants with Relevant Experience (Data Self-Reported to AMCAS®)		
Community Service/Volunteer		69%
Medically-Related Work		90%
Research		91%

Shaded bar represents school's accepted scores ranging from the 10th percentile to the 90th percentile   School Median ●   National Median ●

Overall GPA	2.0	2.1	2.2	2.3	2.4	2.5	2.6	2.7	2.8	2.9	3.0	3.1	3.2	3.3	3.4	3.5	3.6	3.7	(3.8)	3.9	4.0
Science GPA	2.0	2.1	2.2	2.3	2.4	2.5	2.6	2.7	2.8	2.9	3.0	3.1	3.2	3.3	3.4	3.5	3.6	3.7	(3.8)	3.9	4.0

MCAT® Total Numeric Score 9 10 11 12 13 14 15 16 17 18 19 20 21 22 23 24 25 26 27 28 29 30 31 (32)(33) 34 35 36 37 38 39 40 41 42 43

Writing Sample				J	K	L	M	N	O	P	(Q)	R	S	T
Verbal Reasoning	3	4	5	6	7	8	9	(10)	11	12	13	14	15
Biological Sciences	3	4	5	6	7	8	9	10	(11)	12	13	14	15
Physical Sciences	3	4	5	6	7	8	9	10	(11)	12	13	14	15

Acceptance & Matriculation Data for 2009–2010 First Year Class

	Resident	Non-resident	International	Total
Applications	1545	5143	459	7147
Interviewed	403	967	29	1399
Deferred	3	0	1	4
Matriculants				
Early Assurance Program	0	0	0	0
Early Decision Program	2	2	0	4
Baccalaureate/M.D.	0	0	0	0
M.D./Ph.D.	5	10	0	15
Matriculated	85	95	3	**183**

Applications accepted from International Applicants: Yes

Matriculant Demographics: 2009–2010 First Year Class

Men: 94   **Women:** 89

Matriculants' Self-Reported Race/Ethnicity

Mexican American	3	Korean	4
Cuban	0	Vietnamese	1
Puerto Rican	0	Other Asian	9
Other Hispanic	8	Total Asian	51
Total Hispanic	11	Native American	1
Chinese	23	Black	13
Asian Indian	16	Native Hawaiian	0
Pakistani	1	White	112
Filipino	1	Unduplicated Number	
Japanese	1	of Matriculants	183

Science and Math Majors: 69%
Matriculants with:
      Baccalaureate degree: 100%
      Graduate degree(s): 7%

Specialty Choice

2005, 2006, 2007 Graduates, Specialty Choice (As reported by program directors to GME Track™)	
Anesthesiology	5%
Emergency Medicine	9%
Family Practice	2%
Internal Medicine	27%
Obstetrics/Gynecology	4%
Orthopaedic Surgery	3%
Pediatrics	16%
Psychiatry	5%
Radiology	8%
Surgery	5%

Financial Information

Source: 2008-2009 LCME I-B survey and 2009-2010 AAMC TSF questionnaire

	Residents	Non-residents
Total Cost of Attendance	$ 66,650	$ 66,650
Tuition and Fees	$ 41,626	$ 41,626
Other (includes living expenses)	$ 21,422	$ 21,422
Health Insurance (can be waived)	$ 3,602	$ 3,602

Average 2009 Graduate Indebtedness: $134,012
% of Enrolled Students Receiving Aid: 90%

Criminal Background Check

This medical school does not require a criminal background check prior to matriculation.

Columbia University
College of Physicians and Surgeons
New York, New York

Columbia University
College of Physicians and Surgeons
Admissions Office, Room 1-416
630 West 168th Street
New York, New York 10032
T 212 305 3595   F 212 305 3601

Admissions www.cumc.columbia.edu/dept/
ps/admissions
Main http://cumc.columbia.edu/dept/ps
Financial http://cumc.columbia.edu/student/finaid
E-mail psadmissions@columbia.edu

Private Institution

Dr. Lee Goldman, Dean, Executive Vice President for Health and Biomedical Sciences

Dr. Andrew G. Frantz, Associate Dean for Admissions

Dr. Hilda Y. Hutcherson, Associate Dean, Office of Diversity

Ellen Spilker, Executive Director, Office of Student Financial Planning

General Information

The College of Physicians and Surgeons originated in 1767 as the Medical Faculty of King's College and was the first school to award an earned doctor of medicine degree in the American colonies. The college is part of the Columbia University Medical Center. Clinical teaching is provided at CUMC; Roosevelt-St. Luke's Hospital Center and Harlem Hospital Center in Manhattan; Bassett Hospital in Cooperstown, NY; and Stamford Hospital in Connecticut.

Mission Statement

The mission of Columbia is to produce physicians who excel in both the science and art of medicine, and who will become leaders in their fields. It seeks to do this by providing an atmosphere that is collegial rather than competitive, and by offering students opportunities to express their interests in a wide variety of humanistic as well as scientific activities.

Curricular Highlights

Community Service Requirement: Optional.
Research/Thesis Requirement: Required.

In the fall of 2009, P&S implemented a new curriculum. Hallmarks of the new curriculum include: emphasis on collaboration and teamwork; cultivation of a commitment to life-long inquiry; a self-directed, faculty mentored, in-depth scholarly project in an area of special interest to the student; and a longitudinal approach to content that will teach basic science, professionalism, public health and clinical medicine throughout the four years. The preclinical component of the curriculum is now eighteen months long, integrating basic and clinical sciences with progressive clinical

skills building and patient responsibilities during the first semester. The major clinical year, divided into twelve week long blocks, will offer instruction in all areas of clinical medicine. Between blocks students will return to the campus for inter-sessions focused on topics relevant during clinical training. After the major clinical year students will have an additional fourteen months to explore their individual interests.

USMLE

Step 1: Required. Students must record a passing score for promotion.
Step 2: Clinical Skills (CS): Required. Students must record a passing score in each section to graduate.
Step 2: Clinical Knowledge (CK): Required. Students must record a passing score in each section to graduate.

Selection Factors

We seek applicants who have shown the greatest evidence of excellence and leadership potential in the science and art of medicine. Beyond academic ability, medicine also demands integrity, the ability to relate easily to others, and concern for their welfare. The school evaluates by several means: letters of recommendation, participation in extracurricular and summer activities, breadth of interests and undergraduate education, and the personal interview. Each year, some applicants are accepted who display extraordinary promise with regard to either the science or the art of medicine, even though they do not meet, in optimal measure, all of the criteria described above. CUMC seeks diversity of background among its applicants, geographical and otherwise; no preference is given to state of residence. Admission is possible for all qualified applicants regardless of sex, race, age, religion, sexual orientation, national origin, or handicap.

Financial Aid

Admission is not based on an applicant's ability to pay. We make every effort to help accepted students finance their medical education. More than $9 million in need-based scholarships and low-cost loans have been awarded annually. To be considered for these funds, financial data for student, spouse and parents must be provided.

Need is met first with low-cost loans, then with school scholarships. Federal and private student loan programs are available to cover educational expenses that cannot be met by family resources. Students who do not qualify for need-based funds from the school can access Federal Stafford, Graduate PLUS, and private loans. There is separate grant support for students in Columbia's Bassett track and they can also access federal loans. Please refer to their website.

Information about Diversity Programs

The College has a strong commitment to increase the numbers of medical students from groups underrepresented in medicine. There is a highly diverse student body and faculty. For additional information, call (212) 305-4157.

Campus Information

Setting
Located on the Upper West Side of New York City, the CUMC is on a large multi-acre campus.

Enrollment
For 2009, total enrollment was: 647

Special Features
The New York State Psychiatric Institute building and Morgan Stanley Children's Hospital were recently opened. MS Children's Hospital is ranked among the top five pediatric hospitals in the nation. Faculty members Dr. Eric Kandel and Dr. Richard Axel are our most recent awarded Nobel Prizes in Neural Science.

Housing
On campus housing is available for single students, married couples, and domestic partnerships.

Satellite Campuses/Facilities
Students may train at some–or all–of P&S's affiliated hospitals in rural and urban settings. Columbia's Bassett track provides the first year and a half training in parallel with New York based students, and the next two and a half at a campus located in Cooperstown, NY. This program features education in an integrated health care system serving an extensive rural community.

Application Process and Requirements 2011–2012

Primary Application Service: AMCAS
Earliest filing date: June 1, 2010
Latest filing date: October 15, 2010

Secondary Application Required?: Yes
Sent to: All applicants
URL: https://app.applyyourself.com/?id=COL-MED
Fee: Yes, $85   **Waiver available:** Yes
Earliest filing date: June 15, 2010
Latest filing date: November 15, 2010

MCAT® required?: Yes
Latest MCAT® considered: September 2010
Oldest MCAT® considered: March 2008

Early Decision Program: School does not have EDP
Applicants notified: n/a
EDP available for: n/a

Regular Acceptance Notice
Earliest date: March 1, 2011
Latest date: Varies

Applicant's Response to Acceptance Offer – Maximum Time: Three weeks

Requests for Deferred Entrance Considered: Yes

Deposit to Hold Place in Class: No
Deposit (Resident): n/a   **(Non-resident):** n/a
Deposit due: n/a
Applied to tuition: n/a   **Refundable:** n/a
Refundable by: n/a

Estimated number of new entrants: 163
EDP: n/a, special program: n/a

Start Month/Year: August 2011

Interview Format: Monday-Friday, September through February. Regional interviews are not available. Video interviews are not available.

Other Programs

PREPARATORY PROGRAMS
Postbaccalaureate Program: Yes,
www.columbia.edu/cu/gs/postbacc,
(212) 854-2881, pmaofficers@columbia.edu
Summer Program: Yes,
www.oda-ps.cumc.columbia.edu

COMBINED DEGREE PROGRAMS
Baccalaureate/M.D.: No
M.D./M.P.H.: Yes, www.mailman.hs.columbia.edu,
(212) 305-3927
M.D./M.P.H.: Yes, Betsy Asher, (202) 305-3927,
ba2239@columbia.edu
M.D./M.B.A.: Yes, http://www4.gsb.columbia.edu/mba,
Susan Sullivan, (212) 854-4557, sms12@columbia.edu
M.D./J.D.: No
M.D./Ph.D.: Yes, http://mdphd.columbia.edu,
Patrice Spitalnik, (212) 342-5653,
M.D.-Ph.D.@columbia.edu

Premedical Coursework

On-line courses accepted in fulfillment of prerequisites: No

Course	Req.	Rec.	Lab.	Sems.	Course	Req.	Rec.	Lab.	Sems.
Inorganic Chemistry	•		•	2	Computer Science				
Behavioral Sciences					Genetics				
Biochemistry					Humanities				
Biology	•		•	2	Organic Chemistry	•		•	2
Biology/Zoology					Physics	•			2
Calculus					Psychology				
College English	•			2	Social Sciences				
College Mathematics					Other				

Selection Factors: 2009 Accepted Applicants

Proportion of Accepted Applicants with Relevant Experience (Data Self-Reported to AMCAS®)		
Community Service/Volunteer		67%
Medically-Related Work		87%
Research		89%

Shaded bar represents school's accepted scores ranging from the 10th percentile to the 90th percentile.   School Median ●   National Median ○

Overall GPA	2.0	2.1	2.2	2.3	2.4	2.5	2.6	2.7	2.8	2.9	3.0	3.1	3.2	3.3	3.4	3.5	3.6	3.7	(3.8)	3.9	4.0
Science GPA	2.0	2.1	2.2	2.3	2.4	2.5	2.6	2.7	2.8	2.9	3.0	3.1	3.2	3.3	3.4	3.5	3.6	3.7	(3.8)	3.9	4.0

MCAT® Total Numeric Score 9 10 11 12 13 14 15 16 17 18 19 20 21 22 23 24 25 26 27 28 29 30 31 (32) 33 34 35 (36) 37 38 39 40 41 42 43

Writing Sample		J	K	L	M	N	O	P	(Q)	R	S	T
Verbal Reasoning	3	4	5	6	7	8	9	(10)	(11)	12	13	14	15
Biological Sciences	3	4	5	6	7	8	9	10	(11)	(12)	13	14	15
Physical Sciences	3	4	5	6	7	8	9	10	(11)	(12)	13	14	15

Acceptance & Matriculation Data for 2009–2010 First Year Class

	Resident	Non-resident	International	Total
Applications	1132	5430	419	6981
Interviewed	200	836	60	1096
Deferred	0	2	0	2
Matriculants				
Early Assurance Program	0	0	0	0
Early Decision Program	0	0	0	0
Baccalaureate/M.D.	0	0	0	0
M.D./Ph.D.	2	10	2	14
Matriculated	40	109	5	**154**

Applications accepted from International Applicants: Yes

Matriculant Demographics: 2009–2010 First Year Class

Men: 80   **Women:** 74

Matriculants' Self-Reported Race/Ethnicity

Mexican American	5	Korean	5
Cuban	2	Vietnamese	2
Puerto Rican	3	Other Asian	1
Other Hispanic	2	Total Asian	28
Total Hispanic	11	Native American	0
Chinese	11	Black	13
Asian Indian	9	Native Hawaiian	0
Pakistani	1	White	100
Filipino	1	Unduplicated Number	
Japanese	1	of Matriculants	154

Science and Math Majors: 63%
Matriculants with:
   Baccalaureate degree: 100%
   Graduate degree(s): 4%

Specialty Choice

2005, 2006, 2007 Graduates, Specialty Choice (As reported by program directors to GME Track™)	
Anesthesiology	8%
Emergency Medicine	5%
Family Practice	1%
Internal Medicine	18%
Obstetrics/Gynecology	4%
Orthopaedic Surgery	7%
Pediatrics	10%
Psychiatry	8%
Radiology	4%
Surgery	7%

Financial Information

Source: 2008-2009 LCME I-B survey and 2009-2010 AAMC TSF questionnaire

	Residents	Non-residents
Total Cost of Attendance	$ 69,079	$ 69,079
Tuition and Fees	$ 46,489	$ 46,489
Other (includes living expenses)	$ 19,732	$ 19,732
Health Insurance (can be waived)	$ 2,858	$ 2,858

Average 2009 Graduate Indebtedness: $131,385
% of Enrolled Students Receiving Aid: 80%

Criminal Background Check

This medical school does not require a criminal background check prior to matriculation.

Mount Sinai School of Medicine of New York University

New York, New York

Office of Admissions,
Mount Sinai School of Medicine
Annenberg Building, Room 5-04
One Gustave L. Levy Place – Box 1002
New York, New York 10029-6574
T 212 241 6696   **F** 212 828 4135

Admissions www.mssm.edu/bulletin/admissions/
admissions.htm
Main www.mssm.edu
Financial www.mountsinai.org/Education/School
%20of%20Medicine/Degrees%20and%20Programs/
MD%20Program/Financial%20Aid
E-mail admissions@mssm.edu

Private Institution

Dr. Dennis Charney, Dean

Dr. Valerie Parkas, Associate Dean for Admissions

Dr. Gary C. Butts, Associate Dean for Multicultural and Community Affairs

Dale Fuller, Director of Student Financial Services

General Information

Mount Sinai School of Medicine is privately endowed and affiliated with New York University. The medical center campus includes The Mount Sinai Hospital, research and service laboratories, teaching facilities, and the Graduate School of Biological Sciences. The school recently completed Phase II/IV of the total renovation of its educational space, and will soon start construction that will expand its research space by approximately thirty percent. Additional clinical training sites extend throughout New York City, New Jersey, Westchester County, and Long Island.

Mission Statement

The school is committed to serving science and society through outstanding research, education, patient care, and community service. We strive to develop new approaches to teaching, translate scientific discoveries into improvements in patient care, and identify new ways to enhance the health and educational opportunities of the communities we serve.

Curricular Highlights

Community Service Requirement: Optional.
Research/Thesis Requirement: Optional.

Mount Sinai School of Medicine's curriculum is designed to teach a core knowledge of the biological basis of health and disease, skills in critical thinking, life-long learning skills, professional and humanistic attitudes, a scientific approach to medicine, and an appreciation of the physician's obligations to society and the community. The curriculum emphasizes the interdisciplinary nature of the basic and clinical sciences; it utilizes lectures and small group, case-based seminars and laboratory exercises. Courses are graded pass/fail during the first two years, and honors/high pass/pass/fail in the last two years.

USMLE

Step 1: Required. Students must record a passing score for promotion.
Step 2: Clinical Skills (CS): Required. Students must record a passing total score to graduate.
Step 2: Clinical Knowledge (CK): Required. Students must record a passing total score to graduate.

Selection Factors

Excellence in scholarship, personal maturity, integrity, intellectual creativity, and motivation for medicine are important factors. The interview, recommendations, and MCAT scores are criteria for evaluation. All applicants are considered, regardless of race, sex, color, creed, age, national origin, handicap, veteran status, marital status, or sexual orientation.

Financial Aid

Applications for financial aid are treated confidentially, and awards are made by a faculty committee on financial aid. Each applicant is considered on an individual basis so that the school can provide maximal support for those who most need it. Financial aid may be offered in the form of a scholarship, a loan, or both, in accordance with the requirements of the individual situation and the availability of funds. Students who are not citizens or permanent residents of the United States are not eligible for financial assistance.

Information about Diversity Programs

Strongly motivated students from groups underrepresented in medicine are actively sought and encouraged to apply. A pre-entrance summer enrichment program is available for students who are accepted to the first-year class. Tutorial assistance is available for all students. The school's Center for Multicultural and Community Affairs provides leadership and coordination for minority affairs activities, multicultural diversity program activities, a variety of enrichment programs, and advisory and career counseling services.

Campus Information

Setting

The campus sits on the border between the Upper East Side of Manhattan and the thriving and vibrant community of East Harlem. Student housing is located across the street from the campus, as is Central Park. The Museum Mile, restaurants, shopping, and public transportation are all convenient to the campus.

Enrollment

For 2009, total enrollment was: 533

Special Features

The hospital and the school work together to remain at the cutting-edge of modern medicine, and to maintain regional and national leadership. Mount Sinai was the first U.S. medical school to establish academic Departments of Geriatrics and Environmental and Occupational Medicine, and is one of the few schools of medicine in the United States to have a Department of Health Policy. MD, M.D./Ph.D., M.D./M.P.H. and M.D./M.B.A. degrees are offered. There is extensive online support for the curriculum. Student feedback is highly valued. Special features include: a standardized patient facility, human simulator center, the Global Health Center, the Office of Research Opportunities, and the Center for Multicultural and Community Affairs.

Housing

Single students are guaranteed housing in Aron Hall, located across the street from the school. Couples housing is located within easy walking distance and is on a space available basis.

Satellite Campuses/Facilities

The main teaching site is the Mount Sinai Hospital, located on the main campus. Students also rotate to inpatient and ambulatory sites within a teaching consortium, among the largest in the country, which consists of outstanding public and private institutions in New York City and the suburbs of New Jersey.

Application Process and Requirements 2011–2012

Primary Application Service: AMCAS
Earliest filing date: June 1, 2010
Latest filing date: November 1, 2010

Secondary Application Required?: Yes
Sent to: All applicants
Contact: (212) 241-6996, admissions@mssm.edu
Fee: Yes, $105   **Waiver available:** Yes
Earliest filing date: July 14, 2010
Latest filing date: December 15, 2010

MCAT® required?: Yes
Latest MCAT® considered: September 2010
Oldest MCAT® considered: April 2008

Early Decision Program: School does have EDP
Applicants notified: October 1, 2010
EDP available for: Both Residents
and Non-residents

**Regular Acceptance Notice
Earliest date:** November 1, 2010
Latest date: Until class is full
**Applicant's Response to Acceptance
Offer – Maximum Time:** Two weeks

**Requests for Deferred
Entrance Considered:** Yes

Deposit to Hold Place in Class: No
Deposit (Resident): n/a   **(Non-resident):** n/a
Deposit due: n/a
Applied to tuition: n/a   **Refundable:** n/a
Refundable by: n/a

Estimated number of new entrants: 128
EDP: 1, special program: 12

Start Month/Year: August 17, 2011

Interview Format: Two thirty-minute interviews. Regional interviews are not available. Video interviews are not available.

Other Programs

PREPARATORY PROGRAMS

Postbaccalaureate Program: Yes
(212) 241-6546, www.mountsinai.org/
Education/School%20of%20Medicine/Degrees%20
and%20Programs/Post-Baccalaureate%20Research
%20Education%20Program%20for%20Medicine
Summer Program: Yes
grads@mssm.edu, (212) 241-6546

COMBINED DEGREE PROGRAMS

Baccalaureate/M.D.: No
M.D./M.P.H.: Yes, (212) 241-7941
www.mssm.edu/cpm/mph/
M.D./M.B.A.: Yes, (212) 241-2260
www.mssm.edu/medschool/md_mba/
ray.cornbill@mssm.edu
M.D./J.D.: No
M.D./Ph.D.: Yes, (212) 241-6546
mstp@mssm.edu, www.mssm.edu/gradschool/mstp/

Premedical Coursework

On-line courses accepted in fulfillment of prerequisites: On a case-by-case basis

Course	Req.	Rec.	Lab.	Sems.
Inorganic Chemistry	•		•	2
Behavioral Sciences				
Biochemistry		•		
Biology	•		•	2
Biology/Zoology				
Calculus				
College English	•			2
College Mathematics	•			2

Course	Req.	Rec.	Lab.	Sems.
Computer Science				
Genetics		•		
Humanities				
Organic Chemistry	•		•	2
Physics	•			2
Psychology				
Social Sciences				
Other				

Selection Factors: 2009 Accepted Applicants

Proportion of Accepted Applicants with Relevant Experience (Data Self-Reported to AMCAS®)		
Community Service/Volunteer		64%
Medically-Related Work		88%
Research		87%

Shaded bar represents school's accepted scores ranging from the 10th percentile to the 90th percentile.   School Median ○   National Median ◉

Overall GPA 2.0 2.1 2.2 2.3 2.4 2.5 2.6 2.7 2.8 2.9 3.0 3.1 3.2 3.3 3.4 3.5 3.6 3.7 (3.8) 3.9 4.0
Science GPA 2.0 2.1 2.2 2.3 2.4 2.5 2.6 2.7 2.8 2.9 3.0 3.1 3.2 3.3 3.4 3.5 3.6 3.7 (3.8) 3.9 4.0

MCAT® Total Numeric Score 9 10 11 12 13 14 15 16 17 18 19 20 21 22 23 24 25 26 27 28 29 30 31 (32) 33 34 35 (36) 37 38 39 40 41 42 43

			J	K	L	M	N	O	P	(Q)	R	S	T
Writing Sample			J	K	L	M	N	O	P	(Q)	R	S	T
Verbal Reasoning	3	4	5	6	7	8	9	(10)	(11)	12	13	14	15
Biological Sciences	3	4	5	6	7	8	9	10	(11)	(12)	13	14	15
Physical Sciences	3	4	5	6	7	8	9	10	(11)	(12)	13	14	15

Acceptance & Matriculation Data for 2009–2010 First Year Class

	Resident	Non-resident	International	Total
Applications	1521	4655	396	6572
Interviewed	241	536	70	847
Deferred	0	4	0	4
Matriculants				
Early Assurance Program	12	16	1	29
Early Decision Program	0	0	0	0
Baccalaureate/M.D.	0	0	0	0
M.D./Ph.D.	1	10	0	11
Matriculated	42	91	7	**140**

Applications accepted from International Applicants: Yes

Specialty Choice

2005, 2006, 2007 Graduates, Specialty Choice (As reported by program directors to GME Track™)	
Anesthesiology	10%
Emergency Medicine	4%
Family Practice	2%
Internal Medicine	23%
Obstetrics/Gynecology	4%
Orthopaedic Surgery	2%
Pediatrics	10%
Psychiatry	8%
Radiology	5%
Surgery	8%

Matriculant Demographics: 2009–2010 First Year Class

Men: 66   **Women:** 74

Matriculants' Self-Reported Race/Ethnicity

Mexican American	3	**Korean**	2
Cuban	2	**Vietnamese**	0
Puerto Rican	1	**Other Asian**	3
Other Hispanic	12	**Total Asian**	37
Total Hispanic	17	**Native American**	2
Chinese	21	**Black**	7
Asian Indian	11	**Native Hawaiian**	0
Pakistani	1	**White**	82
Filipino	0	**Unduplicated Number**	
Japanese	1	**of Matriculants**	140

Science and Math Majors: 47%
Matriculants with:
  Baccalaureate degree: 100%
  Graduate degree(s): 6%

Financial Information

Source: 2008-2009 LCME I-B survey
and 2009-2010 AAMC TSF questionnaire

	Residents	Non-residents
Total Cost of Attendance	$ 59,777	$ 59,777
Tuition and Fees	$ 38,260	$ 38,260
Other (includes living expenses)	$ 18,674	$ 18,674
Health Insurance (can be waived)	$ 2,843	$ 2,843

Average 2009 Graduate Indebtedness: $137,591
% of Enrolled Students Receiving Aid: 70%

Criminal Background Check

This medical school requires a criminal background check prior to matriculation.

New York Medical College

Valhalla, New York

Office of Admissions
Administration Building
New York Medical College
Valhalla, New York 10595
T 914 594 4507   F 914 594 4976

Admissions www.nymc.edu/admit/medical/
info/index.asp
Main www.nymc.edu
Financial www.nymc.edu/studentlife/sfs.htm
E-mail mdadmit@nymc.edu

Private Institution

Dr. Ralph A. O'Connell, Provost and Dean

Dr. Fern R. Juster, Senior Associate Dean and Chair, Committee on Admissions

Dr. Gladys M. Ayala, Senior Associate Dean for Student Affairs

Anthony M. Sozzo, Associate Dean and Director of Student Financial Planning

Robin Camhi Baum, Director of Admissions

General Information
Founded in 1860, New York Medical College is located in suburban Westchester County, 25 miles from New York City. The university educates students for careers in medicine, biomedical science, and the health professions through its School of Medicine, Graduate School of Basic Medical Sciences, and School of Public Health.

Mission Statement
New York Medical College is a health sciences university whose purpose is to educate physicians, scientists, public health specialists, and other healthcare professionals, and to conduct biomedical and population-based research. Through its faculty and affiliated clinical partners, the College provides service to its community in an atmosphere of excellence, scholarship and professionalism. New York Medical College believes that the rich diversity of its student body and faculty is important to its mission of educating outstanding health care professionals for the multicultural world of the 21st century.

Curricular Highlights
Community Service Requirement: Optional.
Research/Thesis Requirement: Optional.

NYMC's goal is to provide a general professional education that prepares students for all career options in medicine. There is emphasis on critical thinking, evidence-based decision making, and cultural humility throughout the curriculum. Clinical exposure begins in the first year with a longitudinal assignment to a primary care physician where students focus on communication skills, history-taking, and preventive

medicine. In addition to traditional lectures and laboratory exercises, basic science courses utilize self directed study, small group discussion, computer assisted instruction, and problem-based learning. Clerkships in seven disciplines at a wide variety of hospitals and community-based clinical settings comprise the third year. In the required fourth year sub-internships, students are expected to function at the level of a beginning resident in required rotations and electives at medical institutions around the country and the world. Highlights of the curriculum include an optional Summer Research Fellowship Program between the first and second years; exposure to medical informatics; an integrated curriculum in biomedical ethics; rigorous sub-internships in Medicine or Pediatrics; palliative care components in the medicine clerkship; and a required fourth year rotation in Geriatric Medicine or Chronic Care Pediatrics.

USMLE
Step 1: Required. Students must record a passing score for promotion.
Step 2: Clinical Skills (CS): Required. Students must only record a score.
Step 2: Clinical Knowledge (CK): Required. Students must record a passing total score to graduate.

Selection Factors
The Admissions Committee selects students after considering factors of intellect, character, and personality pointing toward their ability to become informed and caring physicians. A history of academic excellence is essential. Undergraduate major is not a factor in selection. Clear evidence of a strong motivation toward medicine and a sense of dedication to the service of others is encouraged. Qualities of character and personality are evaluated from letters of evaluation, personal statements, and the interview. The school does not deny admission to any applicant on the basis of any legally prohibited discrimination involving, but not limited to, such factors as race, color, creed, religion, national or ethnic origin, age, sex, sexual orientation, or disability.

Financial Aid
Financial aid is awarded on the basis of need; scholarships, based on need, are available to entering students. The college provides debt management and loan counseling services.

Information about Diversity Programs
New York Medical College seeks to admit a diverse class, including diversity of gender, race, ethnicity, cultural and economic background, and life experience. A diverse student body provides a valuable educational experience that prepares medical students for the real world of medical practice in a multicultural society.

Campus Information

Setting
NYMC, Westchester Medical Center, and Maria Fareri Children's Hospital/Regional Trauma Center are located on a 22-acre suburban campus. Affiliated hospitals and clinical sites are located in NYC and lower Hudson Valley.

Enrollment
For 2009, total enrollment was: 790

Special Features
New York Medical College is the only academic biomedical research institution between New York City and Albany, with $41 million in sponsored programs of research, training, and service.

Housing
On-campus housing is available on the main campus in Valhalla. Most first and second year students live on campus. Half of third and fourth year students live in Manhattan. The Housing Office maintains a list of off-campus housing opportunities.

Satellite Campuses/Facilities
New York Medical College's wide range of affiliated hospitals, including large urban medical centers, small suburban hospitals, and technologically advanced regional tertiary care facilities, provide extensive resources and educational opportunities.

Application Process and Requirements 2011–2012

Primary Application Service: AMCAS
Earliest filing date: June 1, 2010
Latest filing date: December 15, 2010

Secondary Application Required?: Yes
Sent to: All applicants
URL: www.nymc.edu/medadmission/Instructions.html
Fee: Yes, $100   **Waiver available:** Yes
Earliest filing date: July 1, 2010
Latest filing date: January 31, 2011

MCAT® required?: Yes
Latest MCAT® considered: September 2010
Oldest MCAT® considered: April 2008

Early Decision Program: School does have EDP
Applicants notified: October 1, 2010
EDP available for: Both Residents and Non-residents

Regular Acceptance Notice
Earliest date: November 15, 2010
Latest date: Until class is full
Applicant's Response to Acceptance Offer – Maximum Time: Two weeks

Requests for Deferred Entrance Considered: Yes

Deposit to Hold Place in Class: Yes
Deposit (Resident): $100   **(Non-resident):** $100
Deposit due: By May 15, 2011
Applied to tuition: Yes   **Refundable:** Yes
Refundable by: May 15, 2011

Estimated number of new entrants: 190
EDP: 2, special program: n/a

Start Month/Year: August 2011

Interview Format: One-on-one blind and minimally structured interviews. Regional interviews are not available. Video interviews are not available.

Other Programs

PREPARATORY PROGRAMS
Postbaccalaureate Program: Yes, www.nymc.edu/gsbms/interdisciplinary.asp
Summer Program: No

COMBINED DEGREE PROGRAMS
Baccalaureate/M.D.: No
M.D./M.P.H.: Yes, www.nymc.edu/hs/department_programs.htm#M.D./M.P.H
M.D./M.B.A.: No
M.D./J.D.: No
M.D./Ph.D.: Yes, www.nymc.edu/gsbms/md-phd-program.asp

Premedical Coursework

On-line courses accepted in fulfillment of prerequisites: No

Course	Req.	Rec.	Lab.	Sems.	Course	Req.	Rec.	Lab.	Sems.
Inorganic Chemistry	•		•	2	Computer Science				
Behavioral Sciences					Genetics		•		1
Biochemistry		•		1	Humanities				
Biology	•		•	2	Organic Chemistry	•		•	2
Biology/Zoology					Physics	•		•	2
Calculus					Psychology				
College English	•			2	Social Sciences				
College Mathematics					Statistics		•		1

Selection Factors: 2009 Accepted Applicants

Proportion of Accepted Applicants with Relevant Experience (Data Self-Reported to AMCAS®)		Community Service/Volunteer	66%
		Medically-Related Work	91%
		Research	88%

Shaded bar represents school's accepted scores ranging from the 10th percentile to the 90th percentile   School Median ● National Median ○

Overall GPA 2.0 2.1 2.2 2.3 2.4 2.5 2.6 2.7 2.8 2.9 3.0 3.1 3.2 3.3 **3.4** 3.5 ⊛3.6 3.7 3.8 3.9 4.0
Science GPA 2.0 2.1 2.2 2.3 2.4 2.5 2.6 2.7 2.8 2.9 3.0 3.1 3.2 **3.3** 3.4 3.5 ⊛3.6 3.7 3.8 3.9 4.0

MCAT® Total Numeric Score 9 10 11 12 13 14 15 16 17 18 19 20 21 22 23 24 25 26 27 28 29 30 ㉛ ㉜ 33 34 35 36 37 38 39 40 41 42 43

Writing Sample			J	K	L	M	N	O	P	Ⓠ	R	S	T
Verbal Reasoning	3	4	5	6	7	8	9	⑩	11	12	13	14	15
Biological Sciences	3	4	5	6	7	8	9	10	⑪	12	13	14	15
Physical Sciences	3	4	5	6	7	8	9	⑩	⑪	12	13	14	15

Acceptance & Matriculation Data for 2009–2010 First Year Class

	Resident	Non-resident	International	Total
Applications	1881	8836	534	11251
Interviewed	350	975	25	1350
Deferred	0	6	2	8
Matriculants				
Early Assurance Program	0	0	0	0
Early Decision Program	0	0	0	0
Baccalaureate/M.D.	0	0	0	0
M.D./Ph.D.	0	0	0	0
Matriculated	63	130	1	**194**

Applications accepted from International Applicants: Only Canadian

Matriculant Demographics: 2009–2010 First Year Class

Men: 100   **Women:** 94

Matriculants' Self-Reported Race/Ethnicity

Mexican American	2	Korean	4
Cuban	1	Vietnamese	3
Puerto Rican	1	Other Asian	12
Other Hispanic	10	Total Asian	56
Total Hispanic	13	Native American	0
Chinese	23	Black	8
Asian Indian	12	Native Hawaiian	0
Pakistani	3	White	119
Filipino	0	Unduplicated Number	
Japanese	3	of Matriculants	194

Science and Math Majors: 66%
Matriculants with:
      Baccalaureate degree: 100%
      Graduate degree(s): 14%

Specialty Choice

2005, 2006, 2007 Graduates, Specialty Choice (As reported by program directors to GME Track™)	
Anesthesiology	9%
Emergency Medicine	5%
Family Practice	3%
Internal Medicine	23%
Obstetrics/Gynecology	5%
Orthopaedic Surgery	3%
Pediatrics	13%
Psychiatry	3%
Radiology	11%
Surgery	6%

Financial Information

Source: 2008-2009 LCME I-B survey and 2009-2010 AAMC TSF questionnaire

	Residents	Non-residents
Total Cost of Attendance	$ 67,274	$ 66,958
Tuition and Fees	$ 44,472	$ 44,156
Other (includes living expenses)	$ 19,484	$ 19,484
Health Insurance (can be waived)	$ 3,318	$ 3,318

Average 2009 Graduate Indebtedness: $181,056
% of Enrolled Students Receiving Aid: 86%

Criminal Background Check

This medical school does not require a criminal background check prior to matriculation.

New York University School of Medicine
New York, New York

New York University School of Medicine
Office of Admissions
550 First Avenue
New York, New York 10016
T 212 263 5290   F 212 263 0720

Admissions www.med.nyu.edu/admissions
Main www.med.nyu.edu
Financial http://admissions.med.nyu.edu/financial-aid/
E-mail admissions@med.nyu.edu

Private Institution

Dr. Robert I. Grossman, Dean

Dr. Nancy B. Genieser,
Associate Dean of Admissions and Financial Aid

Mekbib Gemeda, Assistant Dean of
Diversity Affairs

Phyllis Schulz, Director

Joanne McGrath, Assistant Dean of Admissions

General Information
Founded in 1841, NYU School of Medicine is one of the nation's preeminent academic institutions. For over 150 years, NYU has trained thousands of physician-scientists who have enriched countless lives and helped shape medical history. Through scientific research, medical education, and patient care, NYU continues its deep, abiding commitment to improve the human condition. NYU is among the nation's leaders in consistently producing physician graduates who go on to become full-time members of medical school faculties. Students train at Bellevue, the nation's first hospital. NYU is a "private university in the public service." The School of Medicine combines the best of modern biomedical science with a rich tradition of caring for all populations at the highest level of human achievement.

Mission Statement
NYU has a threefold mission: the education and training of physicians and scientists, the search for new knowledge, and the care of the sick. The three are inseparable. Medicine can be handed on to succeeding generations only by long training in the scientific method of investigation and by the actual care of patients. Progress in medicine, which is medical research, must look constantly to the school for its investigators, and to the patient for its problems, whereas the whole future of medical care rests upon a continuing supply of physicians and upon the promise of new discovery. The purpose, then, can only be achieved by endeavor in all three directions — medical education, research, and patient care — and they must be carried on simultaneously, for they are wholly dependent upon each other,

not only for inspiration, but also for their very means of success.

Curricular Highlights
Community Service Requirement: Optional. Most students participate in community service.
Research/Thesis Requirement: Optional. M.D. with honors given upon completion.

NYU's curriculum innovates basic science teaching and promotes independent, interdisciplinary learning through small-group seminars, problem-solving activities, and computer-assisted instruction. Interdepartmental faculty instruct students in thematic curricular modules during the first two years, providing students with the essential information base, concepts, and skills necessary to understand, apply, and continually build upon the foundation of clinical medicine. Clinical sciences study continues through the four years. Advanced biomedical concepts are brought forward during clerkships through palindromic case studies stressing the translation of molecular biological and molecular genetic knowledge into decision-making and clinical care. Required clerkships and electives throughout the third and fourth years allow students to design specific courses in line with their educational and career goals. Through the honors research program, independent study projects, and the Masters Scholars program, students forge mentored relationships and cultivate their interests including public health, bioethics, human rights, biomedical health sciences, and medical informatics.

USMLE
Step 1: Required. Students must only record a score.
Step 2: Clinical Skills (CS): Required. Students must only record a score.
Step 2: Clinical Knowledge (CK): Required. Students Must only record a score.

Selection Factors
Applicants are considered from several viewpoints: excellence in coursework, trends in college progress, the MCAT, premedical committee evaluation, and the interview. Volunteer activities, independent research, and accomplishments in the humanities and liberal arts

fields are also strongly considered. Only international applicants who hold a permanent resident visa will be considered for admission.

Financial Aid
The Financial Aid Office reviews all applications for financial assistance. Enrolled students and new accepts are eligible to apply for assistance. For more information, see *http://admissions.med.nyu.edu/financial-aid/*.

Information about Diversity Programs
The School of Medicine is committed to admitting a diverse class. The Office of Diversity Affairs and Advisory Council has established programs and services to meet the academic, educational, personal, and cultural needs of students from groups underrepresented in medicine. See: *www.med.nyu.edu/diversity_affairs/index.html*.

Campus Information
Setting
NYUSOM lies at the center of the NYU Langone Medical complex, which includes Tisch Hospital, NYU Cancer Center, Rusk Institute for Rehabilitation Medicine, The Hospital for Joint Diseases and NYU's major hospital affiliates, Bellevue and the VA Hospital.

Enrollment
For 2009, total enrollment was: 747

Special Features
Bellevue is the primary location of clinical instruction and is also a significant research hub. Students complete much of their third-year clinical clerkships there, and many complete their fourth-year subinternships and clinical electives there, as well. Bellevue's Level I Treatment Center is an internationally recognized model for ER development.

Housing
There are three residence halls for students, ranging from single rooms to two bedroom apartments. All buildings are protected by security systems.

Application Process and Requirements 2011–2012

Primary Application Service: AMCAS
Earliest filing date: June 1, 2010
Latest filing date: October 15, 2010

Secondary Application Required?: Yes
Sent to: All applicants
URL: http://admissions.med.nyu.edu/how-apply
Fee: Yes, $100   **Waiver available:** Yes
Earliest filing date: July 1, 2010
Latest filing date: December 1, 2010

MCAT® required?: Yes
Latest MCAT® considered: September 2010
Oldest MCAT® considered: January 2008

Early Decision Program: School does not have EDP
Applicants notified: n/a
EDP available for: n/a

Regular Acceptance Notice
Earliest date: December 15, 2010
Latest date: Until class is full
Applicant's Response to Acceptance Offer – Maximum Time: Two weeks

Requests for Deferred Entrance Considered: Yes

Deposit to Hold Place in Class: Yes
Deposit (Resident): $100   **(Non-resident):** $100
Deposit due: With response to acceptance offer
Applied to tuition: Yes   **Refundable:** Yes
Refundable by: May 15, 2011

Estimated number of new entrants: 166
EDP: 0, special program: n/a

Start Month/Year: August 2011

Interview Format: One-on-one interview with a faculty member. Regional interviews are not available. Video interviews are not available.

Other Programs

PREPARATORY PROGRAMS
Postbaccalaureate Program: Yes
www.nyu.edu/cas/prehealth/postbacc/index.html
Summer Program: Yes, www.med.nyu.edu/sackler/programs/summer.html

COMBINED DEGREE PROGRAMS
Baccalaureate/M.D.: No
M.D./M.P.H.: Yes, www.nyu.edu/mph
M.D./M.B.A.: No
M.D./J.D.: No
M.D./Ph.D.: Yes, http://mdphd.med.nyu.edu/
MD/MPA: Yes, http://wagner.nyu.edu/dualdegrees/dual3.php

Premedical Coursework

On-line courses accepted in fulfillment of prerequisites: No

Course	Req.	Rec.	Lab.	Hrs.	Course	Req.	Rec.	Lab.	Hrs.
Inorganic Chemistry	•		•	6	Computer Science				
Behavioral Sciences					Genetics		•		
Biochemistry		•			Humanities				
Biology	•		•	6	Organic Chemistry	•		•	6
Biology/Zoology					Physics	•		•	6
Calculus					Psychology				
College English	•			6	Social Sciences				
College Mathematics					Other				

Selection Factors: 2009 Accepted Applicants

Proportion of Accepted Applicants with Relevant Experience (Data Self-Reported to AMCAS®)		
Community Service/Volunteer		69%
Medically-Related Work		91%
Research		91%

Shaded bar represents school's accepted scores ranging from the 10th percentile to the 90th percentile   **School Median** ○   **National Median** ◎

Overall GPA	2.0	2.1	2.2	2.3	2.4	2.5	2.6	2.7	2.8	2.9	3.0	3.1	3.2	3.3	3.4	3.5	3.6	3.7	(3.8)	3.9	4.0
Science GPA	2.0	2.1	2.2	2.3	2.4	2.5	2.6	2.7	2.8	2.9	3.0	3.1	3.2	3.3	3.4	3.5	3.6	3.7	(3.8)	3.9	4.0

MCAT® Total Numeric Score 9 10 11 12 13 14 15 16 17 18 19 20 21 22 23 24 25 26 27 28 29 30 31 (32) 33 (34) 35 36 37 38 39 40 41 42 43

Writing Sample				J	K	L	M	N	O	P	(Q)	R	S	T
Verbal Reasoning	3	4	5	6	7	8	9	(10)	(11)	12	13	14	15
Biological Sciences	3	4	5	6	7	8	9	10	(11)	(12)	13	14	15
Physical Sciences	3	4	5	6	7	8	9	10	(11)	(12)	13	14	15

Acceptance & Matriculation Data for 2009–2010 First Year Class

	Resident	Non-resident	International	Total
Applications	1407	5200	203	6810
Interviewed	230	623	19	872
Deferred	1	4	0	5
Matriculants				
Early Assurance Program	0	0	0	0
Early Decision Program	0	0	0	0
Baccalaureate/M.D.	0	0	0	0
M.D./Ph.D.	3	5	0	8
Matriculated	66	98	0	**164**

Applications accepted from International Applicants: Only Canadian

Matriculant Demographics: 2009–2010 First Year Class

Men: 83   **Women:** 81

Matriculants' Self-Reported Race/Ethnicity

Mexican American	2	Korean	7
Cuban	3	Vietnamese	0
Puerto Rican	3	Other Asian	2
Other Hispanic	6	Total Asian	44
Total Hispanic	14	Native American	1
Chinese	20	Black	3
Asian Indian	13	Native Hawaiian	2
Pakistani	1	White	107
Filipino	1	Unduplicated Number	
Japanese	1	of Matriculants	164

Science and Math Majors: 62%
Matriculants with:
        Baccalaureate degree: 100%
        Graduate degree(s): 6%

Specialty Choice

2005, 2006, 2007 Graduates, Specialty Choice (As reported by program directors to GME Track™)	
Anesthesiology	6%
Emergency Medicine	6%
Family Practice	0%
Internal Medicine	23%
Obstetrics/Gynecology	4%
Orthopaedic Surgery	5%
Pediatrics	10%
Psychiatry	5%
Radiology	6%
Surgery	5%

Financial Information

Source: 2008-2009 LCME I-B survey and 2009-2010 AAMC TSF questionnaire

	Residents	Non-residents
Total Cost of Attendance	$ 64,003	$ 64,003
Tuition and Fees	$ 45,353	$ 45,353
Other (includes living expenses)	$ 14,800	$ 14,800
Health Insurance (can be waived)	$ 3,850	$ 3,850

Average 2009 Graduate Indebtedness: $141,127
% of Enrolled Students Receiving Aid: 84%

Criminal Background Check

Please check the School Web site.

State University of New York
Downstate Medical Center College of Medicine

Brooklyn, New York

Admissions Office, State University of New York
Downstate Medical Center
450 Clarkson Avenue — Box 60
Brooklyn, New York 11203-2098
T 718 270 2446   **F** 718 270 4775

Admissions http://sls.downstate.edu/admissions/
medicine/index.html
Main www.downstate.edu/college_of_medicine
Financial http://sls.downstate.edu/financial_aid/costs/
cost_com.html
E-mail admissions@downstate.edu

Public Institution

*Dr. Ian L. Taylor, Dean and Senior
Vice President for Biomedical Education
and Research*

Dr. Marcia Gerber, Dean of Admissions

*Dr. Constance Hill, Associate Dean for
Minority Affairs*

Dr. James Newell, Director

Dr. Lorraine Terracina, VP for Students Affairs

*Dr. Shushawna DeOliveira, Director
of Admissions*

General Information

Current information about the college, curriculum, and admissions is available on the
Web site at *www.downstate.edu.*

Mission Statement

To provide high quality education for the next
generation of health professionals. Integral to
our concept of professional education are both
a commitment to confront the health problems
of urban communities and a responsibility to
advance the state of knowledge and practice in
the health disciplines through basic and
applied clinical research.

Curricular Highlights

Community Service Requirement: Strongly
recommended.
Research/Thesis Requirement: Optional.

In preparing physicians to practice in the
future health care system, the medical education process is under constant evaluation. The
main goals of the curriculum are to improve
the integration of basic and clinical science
throughout the four years of medical school; to
provide earlier exposure to patient care by
introducing clinical experiences in the first and
second years of medical school; to provide for
small-group, self-directed and case-based
learning; and to foster life-long learning skills
through the introduction of new applications
of information science, outcomes studies, and
evidence-based medicine. An organ system
approach is followed. The emphasis is on the
development of clinical reasoning and prob-

lem-solving skills. During the first year, attention is focused on the basic components of
human biology and behavior, as well as on the
essential aspects of the physician-patient relationship. The second year begins the study of
human disease. The third and fourth years
provide integrated clerkships and electives. See
the Web site for more details. All courses are
graded fail, conditional, pass, high pass and
honors.

USMLE

Step 1: Required. Students must record a passing
score for promotion.
Step 2: Clinical Skills (CS): Required. Students
must only record a score.
Step 2: Clinical Knowledge (CK): Required.
Students must only record a score.

Selection Factors

The Committee on Admissions considers the
total qualifications of each applicant without
regard to sex, sexual orientation, race, color,
creed, religion, national origin, age, marital
status, or disability. Decisions are based on
multiple factors, including but not limited to,
prior academic performance; completion of
required courses for admission; the potential
for academic success, including performance
on standardized tests such as the MCAT; communication skills, character, and personal
skills; health-related experiences; and motivation for medicine. The 2009 entering class
attended 75 different colleges and universities.
Matriculants' ages ranged from 20 to 36 years,
with a mean age on matriculation of 23 years.

Financial Aid

The college is committed to help students meet
their educational expenses. Aid is granted on
the basis of need and, for some scholarships,
on academic achievement. The major portion
of assistance is derived from federal and state
allocations: grants, scholarships, loans, and/or
college work-study. Loans are the most common form of assistance. Financial aid application materials are sent to all accepted applicants, and students' financial aid needs are
reviewed annually. Please refer to
*http://sls.downstate.edu/financial_aid/costs/
cost_com.html for current charges.*

Information about Diversity Programs

SUNY Downstate maintains a tradition of commitment to the enrollment of students from
groups underrepresented in medicine. The
Office of Minority Affairs directs several programs targeted to furnish information and support to students from underrepresented and disadvantaged backgrounds. Entering students
from groups underrepresented in medicine are
matched with a faculty mentor. The Daniel Hale
Williams Society also provides peer support for
underrepresented students. Contact the Office of
Minority Affairs at: oma@downstate.edu.

Campus Information

Setting
In NYC, 2.4 million people reside in Brooklyn.
Downstate is located in central Brooklyn on an
urban campus that includes a Basic Science
Building, a Health Science Education Building,
University Hospital, two residence halls, a student center, and a Biotech Center. The school
is across the street from Kings County Hospital
and three blocks from a subway station. More
information is on the Web site.

Enrollment
For 2009, total enrollment was: 770

Special Features
The curriculum includes clinical exposure starting in the first year. Varied clinical settings
throughout the curriculum prepare students
superbly for their residency training (see Web site
for more information). During the fourth year,
20–25 students participate in an international
elective entitled, "Health Care in Developing
Countries." A Clinical Neuroscience Pathway is
available to provide enhanced exposure to neurosciences throughout the four years. Research
opportunities are available throughout the four
years and may lead to graduation honors.
M.D./M.P.H. degrees may be earned concurrently
within four years.

Housing
Two on-campus residence halls offer three different housing accommodations (see Web site
for more information), while being conveniently located across the street from both academic buildings and recreational activities in
the Student Center.

Application Process and Requirements 2011–2012

Primary Application Service: AMCAS
Earliest filing date: June 1, 2010
Latest filing date: December 15, 2010

Secondary Application Required?: Yes
Sent to: All applicants – download from Web site
URL: http://sls.downstate.edu/admissions/medicine/programs/procedures/index.html
Fee: Yes, $80   **Waiver available:** Yes
Earliest filing date: June 1, 2010
Latest filing date: February 1, 2011

MCAT® required?: Yes
Latest MCAT® considered: September 2010
Oldest MCAT® considered: April 2008

Early Decision Program: School does have EDP
Applicants notified: October 1, 2010
EDP available for: Both Residents and Non-residents

Regular Acceptance Notice
Earliest date: October 15, 2010
Latest date: Until class is full
Applicant's Response to Acceptance Offer – Maximum Time: Two weeks

Requests for Deferred Entrance Considered: Yes

Deposit to Hold Place in Class: Yes
Deposit (Resident): $100   **(Non-resident):** $100
Deposit due: Within two weeks of acceptance
Applied to tuition: Yes   **Refundable:** Yes
Refundable by: May 15, 2011

Estimated number of new entrants: 185
EDP: 5, special program: n/a

Start Month/Year: August 2011

Interview Format: One-on-one, about one hour in length. Regional interviews are not available. Video interviews are not available.

Other Programs

PREPARATORY PROGRAMS
Postbaccalaureate Program: No
Summer Program: n/a

COMBINED DEGREE PROGRAMS
Baccalaureate/M.D.: Yes, http://depthome.brooklyn.cuny.edu/bamd/bamdmain.html, Dr. Steven Silbering, (718) 951-5471, silbering@brooklyn.cuny.edu
M.D./M.P.H.: Yes, www.downstate.edu/publichealth/mdmph_about.html, (718) 270-1065, PublicHealth@downstate.edu
M.D./M.B.A.: No
M.D./J.D.: No
M.D./Ph.D.: Yes, http://sls.downstate.edu/admissions/medicine/mdpdh_program.html Dr. Stanley Friedman, (718) 270-1335, sfriedman@downstate.edu

Premedical Coursework

On-line courses accepted in fulfillment of prerequisites: No

Course	Req.	Rec.	Lab.	Sems.	Course	Req.	Rec.	Lab.	Sems.
Inorganic Chemistry	•		•	8	Computer Science				
Behavioral Sciences					Genetics				
Biochemistry		•		4	Humanities				
Biology	•		•	8	Organic Chemistry	•		•	8
Biology/Zoology					Physics	•		•	8
Calculus					Psychology				
College English	•			6	Social Sciences				
College Mathematics					See website for recom.		•		

Selection Factors: 2009 Accepted Applicants

Proportion of Accepted Applicants with Relevant Experience (Data Self-Reported to AMCAS®)		Community Service/Volunteer	63%
		Medically-Related Work	89%
		Research	87%

Shaded bar represents school's accepted scores ranging from the 10th percentile to the 90th percentile   **School Median** ●   **National Median** ○

Overall GPA	2.0	2.1	2.2	2.3	2.4	2.5	2.6	2.7	2.8	2.9	3.0	3.1	3.2	3.3	3.4	3.5	3.6	(3.7)	3.8	3.9	4.0
Science GPA	2.0	2.1	2.2	2.3	2.4	2.5	2.6	2.7	2.8	2.9	3.0	3.1	3.2	3.3	3.4	3.5	3.6	(3.7)	3.8	3.9	4.0

MCAT® Total Numeric Score 9 10 11 12 13 14 15 16 17 18 19 20 21 22 23 24 25 26 27 28 29 30 31 (32)33 34 35 36 37 38 39 40 41 42 43

Writing Sample			J	K	L	M	N	O	P	(Q)	R	S	T
Verbal Reasoning	3	4	5	6	7	8	9	(10)	11	12	13	14	15
Biological Sciences	3	4	5	6	7	8	9	10	(11)	12	13	14	15
Physical Sciences	3	4	5	6	7	8	9	10	(11)	12	13	14	15

Acceptance & Matriculation Data for 2009–2010 First Year Class

	Resident	Non-resident	International	Total
Applications	2212	2966	80	5258
Interviewed	748	427	0	1175
Deferred	1	2	0	3
Matriculants				
Early Assurance Program	0	0	0	0
Early Decision Program	0	0	0	0
Baccalaureate/M.D.	12	0	0	12
M.D./Ph.D.	2	0	0	2
Matriculated	155	35	0	**190**

Applications accepted from International Applicants: No

Matriculant Demographics: 2009–2010 First Year Class

Men: 100   **Women:** 90

Matriculants' Self-Reported Race/Ethnicity

Mexican American	0	Korean	6
Cuban	1	Vietnamese	1
Puerto Rican	4	Other Asian	14
Other Hispanic	12	Total Asian	74
Total Hispanic	17	Native American	0
Chinese	28	Black	18
Asian Indian	19	Native Hawaiian	0
Pakistani	3	White	89
Filipino	8	Unduplicated Number	
Japanese	0	of Matriculants	190

Science and Math Majors: 62%
Matriculants with:
    Baccalaureate degree: 100%
    Graduate degree(s): 7%

Specialty Choice

2005, 2006, 2007 Graduates, Specialty Choice (As reported by program directors to GME Track™)	
Anesthesiology	8%
Emergency Medicine	8%
Family Practice	2%
Internal Medicine	25%
Obstetrics/Gynecology	4%
Orthopaedic Surgery	3%
Pediatrics	12%
Psychiatry	4%
Radiology	7%
Surgery	6%

Financial Information

Source: 2008-2009 LCME I-B survey and 2009-2010 AAMC TSF questionnaire

	Residents	Non-residents
Total Cost of Attendance	$ 48,725	$ 66,565
Tuition and Fees	$ 23,363	$ 41,203
Other (includes living expenses)	$ 21,930	$ 21,930
Health Insurance (can be waived)	$ 3,432	$ 3,432

Average 2009 Graduate Indebtedness: $113,755
% of Enrolled Students Receiving Aid: 85%

Criminal Background Check

This medical school requires a criminal background check prior to matriculation.

State University of New York
Upstate Medical University College of Medicine
Syracuse, New York

Admissions Office
SUNY Upstate Medical University
766 Irving Ave.
Syracuse, New York 13210
T 315 464 4570 **F** 315 464 8867

Admissions www.upstate.edu/com/admissions/
Main www.upstate.edu/com/
Financial www.upstate.edu/com/tuition.php
E-mail admiss@upstate.edu

Public Institution

Dr. Steven J. Scheinman, Dean

Jennifer Welch, Director of Admissions

Nakeia Chambers, Director of Multicultural Affairs

Mike Pede, Director of Financial Aid

Dr. Julie White, Dean, Student Affairs

General Information
The College of Medicine was established in 1834 as the Geneva Medical College. The college was transferred to the State University of New York (SUNY) system in 1950. In 1999, its name changed to SUNY Upstate Medical University to best reflect the college's academic mission in medical care, research, and education.

Mission Statement
The main mission of SUNY Upstate is the education of health professionals and to conduct biomedical research. Upstate's clinical faculty and health care professionals commit themselves to education and patient care, demonstrating excellence and compassion. In pursuing its mission, Upstate provides its faculty, staff, students, and volunteers an environment of mutual trust and respect, with opportunities to grow personally and professionally, and to make a positive difference in the lives of others.

Curricular Highlights
Community Service Requirement: Optional.
Research/Thesis Requirement: Optional.

The curriculum integrates the basic and clinical sciences and provides clinical exposure in the first semester. All courses are aligned by organ systems. The curriculum also addresses the humanistic aspects of medicine, including its ethical, legal, and social implications. During the third year, the students apply the principles of basic science to clinical problem-solving. Clerkships in subspecialty services are required. A research track is available, in which students spend the first two summers and elective time on a research project. Another interesting opportunity is the Rural Medical Education Program, which places students in rural communities for nine consecutive months of clinical

and didactic education during the 3rd and 4th year. A modified pass/fail grading system is used.

USMLE
Step 1: Required. Students must record a passing score for promotion.
Step 2: Clinical Skills (CS): Required. Students must only record a score.
Step 2: Clinical Knowledge (CK): Required. Students must only record a score.

Selection Factors
The Admissions Committee takes an applicant's total qualifications into consideration for the study and practice of medicine. Major factors in the selection of applicants include: review of college records, MCAT scores, letters of recommendation from premedical advisory committees, personal interview, communication skills, character, and motivation.

Financial Aid
Accepted applicants who are U.S. citizens or permanent residents are eligible to apply for financial aid. The Financial Aid Office generally sends out financial aid award letters beginning in March.

Information about Diversity Programs
Upstate is committed to making student enrollment reflective of the diverse New York State population. Disadvantaged students and students from groups underrepresented in medicine are actively sought. A summer Human Anatomy program is available for all students. For more information, please contact the Office of Admissions.

Campus Information

Setting
Located in Syracuse, New York's fourth largest city, SUNY Upstate is a compact, easy-to-navigate campus. We have a new human anatomy lab, an excellent library, and a teaching hospital that is connected to our main academic building. Syracuse is an affordable, medium-sized city with big-city sports, arts, and recreation. Just outside the city, you will find numerous parks, lakes, mountains, golf courses, ski slopes, hiking trails and beaches. University Hospital is a level-one trauma center and tertiary care hospital that services 17 different counties.

Enrollment
For 2009, total enrollment was: 628

Special Features
SUNY Upstate's teaching hospital, University Hospital, is the main clinical site in Syracuse. As the only Level I trauma and burn center in the region, University Hospital treats the most seriously ill and injured patients. University Hospital offers hundreds of specialty services and programs, including the Center for Children's Cancer and Blood Disorders, Clark Burn Center, CNY Gamma Knife Center, and the Joslin Diabetes Center. This year, we will be opening the Gollisano Children's Hospital at University Hospital. It will be the first children's hospital in the region. We also have a clinical campus in the city of Binghamton, which offers clinical training in a community-based setting.

Housing
Clark Tower, SUNY Upstate's residence hall, houses approximately 170 students from all four colleges in fully-furnished standard rooms, studio apartments, and two-bedroom suites. Clark Tower is located next door to the Campus Activities Building, one block from University Hospital and a short walk from the Library and the academic buildings.

Satellite Campuses/Facilities
At the beginning of the third year, one quarter of the class moves from SUNY Upstate's main campus in Syracuse to the Binghamton Campus. The Binghamton Campus is located 70 miles south of Syracuse. There, clinical training occurs in a community-based setting similar to the environment in which most physicians practice.

Application Process and Requirements 2011–2012

Primary Application Service: AMCAS

Earliest filing date: June 1, 2010

Latest filing date: October 15, 2010

Secondary Application Required?: Yes

Sent to: Information on how to access secondary application materials is sent to all verified AMCAS applicants.

URL: n/a

Fee: Yes, $100   **Waiver available:** Yes

Earliest filing date: Upon receipt of verified AMCAS application.

Latest filing date: December 1, 2010

MCAT® required?: Yes

Latest MCAT® considered: September 2010

Oldest MCAT® considered: September 2007

Early Decision Program: School does have EDP

Applicants notified: October 1, 2010

EDP available for: Both Residents and Non-residents

Regular Acceptance Notice

Earliest date: October 15, 2010

Latest date: Until class is full

Applicant's Response to Acceptance Offer – Maximum Time: Two weeks

Requests for Deferred Entrance Considered: Yes

Deposit to Hold Place in Class: Yes

Deposit (Resident): $100   **(Non-resident):** $100

Deposit due: With response to acceptance offer

Applied to tuition: Yes   **Refundable:** Yes

Refundable by: May 15, 2011

Estimated number of new entrants: 160

EDP: 2, special program: 15

Start Month/Year: August 2011

Interview Format: On campus with two individual interviewers. Regional interviews are not available. Video interviews are not available.

Other Programs

PREPARATORY PROGRAMS

Postbaccalaureate Program: No

Summer Program: Yes, Jennifer Welch (315) 464-4570, admiss@upstate.edu

COMBINED DEGREE PROGRAMS

Baccalaureate/M.D.: Yes www.upstate.edu/com/admissions/options/

M.D./M.P.H.: Yes, www.upstate.edu/cnymph/

M.D./M.B.A.: No

M.D./J.D.: No

M.D./Ph.D.: Yes, www.upstate.edu/mdphd/

Premedical Coursework

On-line courses accepted in fulfillment of prerequisites: No

Course	Req.	Rec.	Lab.	Hrs.	Course	Req.	Rec.	Lab.	Hrs.
Inorganic Chemistry	•		•	6-8	Computer Science				
Behavioral Sciences					Genetics		•		
Biochemistry		•			Humanities		•		
Biology					Organic Chemistry	•		•	6-8
Biology/Zoology	•		•	6-8	Physics	•		•	6-8
Calculus		•			Psychology				
College English	•			6	Social Sciences				
College Mathematics					Other				

Selection Factors: 2009 Accepted Applicants

Proportion of Accepted Applicants with Relevant Experience (Data Self-Reported to AMCAS®)		
Community Service/Volunteer		66%
Medically-Related Work		88%
Research		84%

Shaded bar represents school's accepted scores ranging from the 10th percentile to the 90th percentile   School Median ●   National Median ●

Overall GPA	2.0	2.1	2.2	2.3	2.4	2.5	2.6	2.7	2.8	2.9	3.0	3.1	3.2	3.3	3.4	3.5	3.6	(3.7)	3.8	3.9	4.0
Science GPA	2.0	2.1	2.2	2.3	2.4	2.5	2.6	2.7	2.8	2.9	3.0	3.1	3.2	3.3	3.4	3.5	(3.6)	3.7	3.8	3.9	4.0

MCAT® Total Numeric Score 9 10 11 12 13 14 15 16 17 18 19 20 21 22 23 24 25 26 27 28 29 30 (31)(32) 33 34 35 36 37 38 39 40 41 42 43

Writing Sample			J	K	L	M	N	O	(P)	(Q)	R	S	T
Verbal Reasoning	3	4	5	6	7	8	9	(10)	11	12	13	14	15
Biological Sciences	3	4	5	6	7	8	9	10	(11)	12	13	14	15
Physical Sciences	3	4	5	6	7	8	9	(10)	(11)	12	13	14	15

Acceptance & Matriculation Data for 2009–2010 First Year Class

	Resident	Non-resident	International	Total
Applications	1873	2647	413	4933
Interviewed	603	160	37	800
Deferred	3	0	2	5
Matriculants				
Early Assurance Program	17	1	0	18
Early Decision Program	1	0	0	1
Baccalaureate/M.D.	0	0	0	0
M.D./Ph.D.	2	1	0	3
Matriculated	129	13	9	**151**

Applications accepted from International Applicants: Yes

Matriculant Demographics: 2009–2010 First Year Class

Men: 77   **Women:** 74

Matriculants' Self-Reported Race/Ethnicity

Mexican American	3	Korean	3
Cuban	0	Vietnamese	0
Puerto Rican	0	Other Asian	2
Other Hispanic	2	Total Asian	21
Total Hispanic	5	Native American	1
Chinese	8	Black	23
Asian Indian	7	Native Hawaiian	3
Pakistani	2	White	87
Filipino	0	Unduplicated Number	
Japanese	0	of Matriculants	151

Science and Math Majors: 70%

Matriculants with:

Baccalaureate degree: 100%

Graduate degree(s): 22%

Specialty Choice

2005, 2006, 2007 Graduates, Specialty Choice (As reported by program directors to GME Track™)	
Anesthesiology	5%
Emergency Medicine	8%
Family Practice	6%
Internal Medicine	19%
Obstetrics/Gynecology	5%
Orthopaedic Surgery	4%
Pediatrics	11%
Psychiatry	5%
Radiology	7%
Surgery	6%

Financial Information

Source: 2008-2009 LCME I-B survey and 2009-2010 AAMC TSF questionnaire

	Residents	Non-residents
Total Cost of Attendance	$ 45,603	$ 63,443
Tuition and Fees	$ 24,112	$ 41,952
Other (includes living expenses)	$ 18,253	$ 18,253
Health Insurance (can be waived)	$ 3,238	$ 3,238

Average 2009 Graduate Indebtedness: $130,955

% of Enrolled Students Receiving Aid: 84%

Criminal Background Check

This medical school requires a criminal background check prior to matriculation.

Stony Brook University School of Medicine

Stony Brook, New York

Committee on Admissions
Level 4 Health Sciences Center
Stony Brook University School of Medicine
Stony Brook, New York 11794-8434
T 631 444 2113   **F** 631 444 6032

Admissions www.stonybrookmedicalcenter.org/
som/admissions
Main www.stonybrookmedicalcenter.org/
Financial www.stonybrookmedicalcenter.org/som/
financialaid
E-mail somadmissions@stonybrook.edu

Public Institution

Dr. Richard N. Fine, Dean

Dr. Jack Fuhrer, Associate Dean for Admissions

Dr. Aldustus E. Jordan, Associate Dean for Student and Minority Affairs

Mary Jean Allen, Director of Financial Aid

Grace S. Agnetti, Assistant Dean for Admissions

General Information

Stony Brook University's School of Medicine accepted its first class in 1971. It is part of the Stony Brook University Medical Center, which includes the 540-bed University Hospital.

Mission Statement

The School of Medicine strives to improve the quality of health care by demonstrating national leadership in education, research, patient care, and community service. The School of Medicine prepares its students for careers in medical practice or research through its state-of-the-art curriculum and clinical and research opportunities.

Curricular Highlights

Community Service Requirement: Optional.
Research/Thesis Requirement: Optional.

The curriculum of the School of Medicine provides the opportunity for extensive training in the basic medical sciences and teaching in the clinical disciplines of medicine. The curriculum requires the acquisition and utilization of a variety of skills in basic and clinical sciences. The official grading system is honors/pass/fail. The first two years are devoted to basic sciences and the integrated Foundations of Medicine course. The Foundations course teaches medical ethics, patient assessment skills, preventive medicine, human behavior, and nutrition. The second year focuses on an organ system-based pathophysiology and therapeutics course. Third year students complete core clerkships in medicine, pediatrics, family medicine, obstetrics-gynecology, psychiatry, ambulatory medicine and surgery. One month of elective time is available. Fourth year students are offered selectives and electives. Core clerkships are completed at University Hospital or one of three teaching affiliates. Electives can be completed at other sites.

USMLE

Step 1: Required. Students must record a passing score for promotion.
Step 2: Clinical Skills (CS): Required. Students must record a passing total score to graduate.
Step 2: Clinical Knowledge (CK): Required. Students must record a passing total score to graduate.

Selection Factors

Grades, MCAT scores, letters of evaluation, and extracurricular and work experiences are carefully examined. Motivational and personal characteristics as indicated in the application and a personal interview are also a major part of the admissions assessment. There is no discrimination in the admissions process on the basis of race, religion, sex, sexual preference, color, national origin, age, disability, marital status, or status as a disabled or Vietnam-era veteran. The school attempts to enroll a class representative of a variety of backgrounds and academic interests. Stony Brook hopes to attract a significant representation of persons from groups that have historically been underrepresented in medicine. Premedical coursework must be completed at an American college or university. While residents of New York constitute the majority of the applicants and entrants, out-of-state applicants are given due consideration. Required supporting documentation includes official transcripts of all college work and official letters of evaluation. Personal interviews will be arranged at the initiative of the school for candidates who appear to be serious contenders for admission. Stony Brook does not utilize a "cut-off" in grades or MCAT scores in making admission decisions. The school is committed to giving all applicants the individualized attention that they merit.

Financial Aid

Stony Brook participates in all financial aid programs available at the medical schools of the SUNY system. Financial aid and counseling are available through the Office of Student Affairs, as is assistance in securing housing and in meeting other personal needs. On-campus housing is available. Students are advised to have transportation available because there is no public transportation to outlying clinical facilities.

Information about Diversity Programs

Stony Brook is committed to admitting a diverse class each year. The school makes a concerted effort to enroll qualified students from groups underrepresented in medicine.

Campus Information

Setting

Stony Brook University and the School of Medicine are located 60 miles east of NYC on the north shore of Long Island. The campus is surrounded by a picturesque and historic community. The campus provides a wide spectrum of activities ranging from NCAA Division I sporting events to professional theatre and fine arts. Students can participate in a wide range of intramural athletic activities. The clinical campus includes Stony Brook University Hospital and three affiliates.

Enrollment

For 2009, total enrollment was: 492

Special Features

Stony Brook offers excellent research and clinical opportunities and has attracted a faculty of national and international renown. The University enjoys an outstanding research relationship with Cold Spring Harbor and Brookhaven National Laboratories. State-of-the-art Cancer and Heart Centers serve the needs of Long Islanders and a NIH-funded General Clinical Research Center offers cutting-edge clinical research.

Housing

There is limited on-campus housing and most medical students share apartments or houses in the surrounding communities. Housing costs range from $400–$900 per month with a median rent of $600.

Application Process and Requirements 2011–2012

Primary Application Service: AMCAS
Earliest filing date: June 1, 2010
Latest filing date: December 15, 2010

Secondary Application Required?: Yes
Sent to: All applicants.
URL: www.stonybrookmedicalcenter.org/som/admissions
Fee: Yes, $100   **Waiver available:** Yes
Earliest filing date: June 15, 2010
Latest filing date: December 30, 2010

MCAT® required?: Yes
Latest MCAT® considered: September 2010
Oldest MCAT® considered: 2006

Early Decision Program: School does have EDP
Applicants notified: October 1, 2010
EDP available for: Both Residents and Non-residents

Regular Acceptance Notice
Earliest date: October 15, 2010
Latest date: Until class is full
Applicant's Response to Acceptance Offer – Maximum Time: 15 days, unless otherwise specified

Requests for Deferred Entrance Considered: Yes

Deposit to Hold Place in Class: Yes
Deposit (Resident): $100   **(Non-resident):** $100
Deposit due: With response to acceptance offer
Applied to tuition: Yes   **Refundable:** Yes
Refundable by: May 15, 2011

Estimated number of new entrants: 124
EDP: 2, special program: 8

Start Month/Year: August 2011

Interview Format: Two individual interviews with admission committee members. Regional interviews are not available. Video interviews are not available.

Other Programs

PREPARATORY PROGRAMS
Postbaccalaureate Program: Yes
Summer Program: No

COMBINED DEGREE PROGRAMS
Baccalaureate/M.D.: Yes, http://ws.cc.stonybrook.edu/ugadmissions/newhonors/scholarsmed.shtml
M.D./M.P.H.: Yes, www.stonybrookmedical center.org/publichealth/
M.D./M.B.A.: Yes, www.stonybrookcob.com/content/view/88/164/
M.D./J.D.: No
M.D./Ph.D.: www.pharm.stonybrook.edu/mstp/index.html

Premedical Coursework

On-line courses accepted in fulfillment of prerequisites: No

Course	Req.	Rec.	Lab.	Sems.
Inorganic Chemistry	•		•	2
Behavioral Sciences				
Biochemistry		•		1
Biology	•		•	2
Biology/Zoology				
Calculus				
College English	•			2
College Mathematics				

Course	Req.	Rec.	Lab.	Sems.
Computer Science				
Genetics				
Humanities				
Organic Chemistry	•		•	2
Physics	•		•	2
Psychology				
Social Sciences				
Other				

Selection Factors: 2009 Accepted Applicants

Proportion of Accepted Applicants with Relevant Experience (Data Self-Reported to AMCAS®)		
Community Service/Volunteer		61%
Medically-Related Work		87%
Research		91%

Shaded bar represents school's accepted scores ranging from the 10th percentile to the 90th percentile   **School Median** ● **National Median** ◯

Overall GPA	2.0	2.1	2.2	2.3	2.4	2.5	2.6	2.7	2.8	2.9	3.0	3.1	3.2	3.3	3.4	3.5	3.6	(3.7)	3.8	3.9	4.0
Science GPA	2.0	2.1	2.2	2.3	2.4	2.5	2.6	2.7	2.8	2.9	3.0	3.1	3.2	3.3	3.4	3.5	3.6	(3.7)	3.8	3.9	4.0

MCAT® Total Numeric Score 9 10 11 12 13 14 15 16 17 18 19 20 21 22 23 24 25 26 27 28 29 30 31 (32)(33) 34 35 36 37 38 39 40 41 42 43

Writing Sample		J	K	L	M	N	O	P	(Q)	R	S	T
Verbal Reasoning	3	4	5	6	7	8	9	(10)	11	12	13	14	15
Biological Sciences	3	4	5	6	7	8	9	10	(11)	12	13	14	15
Physical Sciences	3	4	5	6	7	8	9	10	(11)	12	13	14	15

Acceptance & Matriculation Data for 2009–2010 First Year Class

	Resident	Non-resident	International	Total
Applications	2089	1570	194	3853
Interviewed	491	139	0	630
Deferred	4	0	0	4
Matriculants				
Early Assurance Program	0	0	0	0
Early Decision Program	0	0	0	0
Baccalaureate/M.D.	5	0	0	5
M.D./Ph.D.	2	3	0	5
Matriculated	105	19	0	**124**

Applications accepted from International Applicants: Yes

Matriculant Demographics: 2009–2010 First Year Class

Men: 68   **Women:** 56

Matriculants' Self-Reported Race/Ethnicity

Mexican American	1	Korean	4
Cuban	1	Vietnamese	1
Puerto Rican	1	Other Asian	4
Other Hispanic	4	Total Asian	30
Total Hispanic	6	Native American	1
Chinese	10	Black	9
Asian Indian	8	Native Hawaiian	0
Pakistani	3	White	75
Filipino	0	Unduplicated Number	
Japanese	1	of Matriculants	124

Science and Math Majors: 65%
Matriculants with:
   Baccalaureate degree: 100%
   Graduate degree(s): 15%

Specialty Choice

2005, 2006, 2007 Graduates, Specialty Choice (As reported by program directors to GME Track™)	
Anesthesiology	10%
Emergency Medicine	9%
Family Practice	4%
Internal Medicine	22%
Obstetrics/Gynecology	4%
Orthopaedic Surgery	2%
Pediatrics	9%
Psychiatry	5%
Radiology	4%
Surgery	9%

Financial Information

Source: 2008-2009 LCME I-B survey and 2009-2010 AAMC TSF questionnaire

	Residents	Non-residents
Total Cost of Attendance	$ 47,604	$ 65,444
Tuition and Fees	$ 24,049	$ 41,889
Other (includes living expenses)	$ 20,765	$ 20,765
Health Insurance (can be waived)	$ 2,790	$ 2,790

Average 2009 Graduate Indebtedness: $128,287
% of Enrolled Students Receiving Aid: 85%

Criminal Background Check

This medical school requires a criminal background check prior to matriculation.

University at Buffalo School of Medicine & Biomedical Sciences

Buffalo, New York

Office of Medical Admissions
University at Buffalo
131 Biomedical Education Building
Buffalo, New York 14214-3013
T 716 829 3466   F 716 829 3849

Admissions www.smbs.buffalo.edu/ome/ome
_admission.htm
Main www.smbs.buffalo.edu
Financial src.buffalo.edu/financialaid
E-mail jjrosso@buffalo.edu

Public Institution

Dr. Michael Cain, Dean

Dr. Charles M. Severin, Associate Dean for Academic Affairs and Admissions

Dr. David A. Milling, Assistant Dean, Multicultural Affairs

Dr. Nancy Nielsen, Senior Associate Dean of Medical Education

General Information

The School of Medicine was founded in 1846 by Millard Fillmore and a group of physicians. In 1962, the University of Buffalo joined the State University of New York (SUNY) system. The University at Buffalo has the most comprehensive campus in the SUNY system and was honored in 1989 with election to the Association of American Universities. The clinical education program is conducted in cooperation with nine area hospitals.

Mission Statement

To provide well-trained physicians and other health care professionals who will attend to the health needs of citizens. To offer a source of continuing education to the community of health care providers. To provide a center of research and scholarship that will advance and promote health-related services. As a public institution, the mission places particular emphasis on diversity, inclusion, and the special needs of New York State, such as minority recruitment and retention, and the underserved urban and rural health populations.

Curricular Highlights

Community Service Requirement: Optional.
Research/Thesis Requirement: Optional.

The curriculum emphasizes the relevance of medical education to the practice of medicine and the relevance of basic science to clinical practice. It introduces patient contact and patient-centered learning in the first year of medical school, and it increases ambulatory care experiences in the clinical years. The first two years contain an integrated curriculum that includes the Introduction to Clinical Medicine course continuum, which prepares students in the knowledge, skills, and attitudes required for

third-year clinical clerkships and provides the foundation for a medical career. Ethics, the doctor-patient relationship, principles of health promotion, disease prevention, and promotion of self-learning and inquiry are emphasized, in addition to extensive education in the skills basic to medical practice and patient care. The clinical years include required clerkships and electives. There is ample time for additional electives during the senior year.

USMLE

Step 1: Required. Students must record a passing score for promotion.
Step 2: Clinical Skills (CS): Required. Students must only record a score.
Step 2: Clinical Knowledge (CK): Required. Students must only record a score.

Selection Factors

The Admissions Committee seeks to identify and select students who display favorable qualities deemed important for the pursuit of a career in medicine. In making its assessments and determinations, the committee relies on information contained in the application and in documents submitted in support of the applicant. Based on careful screening, applicants are invited to appear for an interview. Reapplications are treated no differently than initial applications. Rejected applicants should seek the advice and counsel of their premedical advisor. Students are accepted without regard to race, sex, creed, national origin, age, sexual preference, or handicap. All applicants will receive the "Technical Standards of the Medical School Curriculum" with the secondary application. Some preference is given to qualified residents of New York State. Competitive out-of-state applicants are encouraged to apply.

Financial Aid

The priority due date for receipt of the Free Application for Federal Student Aid (FAFSA) is March 1, 2011. Forms received after the deadline are subject to funds available. Financial aid requests are considered after admission. Awards are made based on need. In most requests, parental income information is required regardless of dependency status. A limited number of scholarships based on academic merit and financial need are provided each year.

Information about Diversity Programs

The Summer Enrichment and Support Program helps facilitate students' retention in medical school. It is designed for admitted first-year educationally and socioeconomically disadvantaged students. Tutorial and counseling services are available throughout the summer and academic year.

Campus Information

Setting

The medical school is located on a recently renovated 33-acre campus on Main Street, in the northeast corner of the city of Buffalo. The world-renowned Shock Trauma Center is located two miles from the main medical school building. There are several public parks, cultural institutions, and shopping areas located in the vicinity. The "Main Street Campus" is accessible by subway to downtown Buffalo and is within walking distance of the VA Medical Center

Enrollment

For 2009, total enrollment was: 570

Special Features

Students receive training in world-renowned clinical centers, including the Children's Hospital Trauma Center and Roswell Park Memorial Cancer Institute. There are also numerous opportunities for clinical and basic science research and varied international clinical experiences.

Housing

While on-campus housing is not available, the University maintains a list of affordable apartments and homes within a 10-mile radius of the campus. Rents average $500–$700 per month.

Satellite Campuses/Facilities

Student rotations are divided among nine teaching hospitals and several clinics in the metro Buffalo area. The medical school is also affiliated with ambulatory care centers in outlying suburban areas.

Application Process and Requirements 2011–2012

Primary Application Service: AMCAS
Earliest filing date: June 1, 2010
Latest filing date: November 15, 2010

Secondary Application Required?: Yes
Sent to: All applicants
Contact: James J. Rosso
(716) 829-3466, jjrosso@buffalo.edu
Fee: Yes, $65 **Waiver available:** Yes
Earliest filing date: June 1, 2010
Latest filing date: December 15, 2010

MCAT® required?: Yes
Latest MCAT® considered: September 2010
Oldest MCAT® considered: April 2007

Early Decision Program: School does have EDP
Applicants notified: October 1, 2010
EDP available for: Both Residents
and Non-residents

Regular Acceptance Notice
Earliest date: October 15, 2010
Latest date: Until class is full
Applicant's Response to Acceptance
Offer – Maximum Time: Two weeks

Requests for Deferred
Entrance Considered: Yes

Deposit to Hold Place in Class: Yes
Deposit (Resident): $100 **(Non-resident):** $100
Deposit due: With response to acceptance offer
Applied to tuition: Yes **Refundable:** Yes
Refundable by: May 15, 2011

Estimated number of new entrants: 140
EDP: 2, special program: 4

Start Month/Year: August 2011

Interview Format: Two, one-on-one interviews.
Regional interviews are not available. Video interviews are not available.

Other Programs

PREPARATORY PROGRAMS
Postbaccalaureate Program: No
Summer Program: No

COMBINED DEGREE PROGRAMS
Baccalaureate/M.D.: No
M.D./M.P.H.: Yes, James J. Rosso
(716) 829-3466, jjrosso@buffalo.edu
M.D./M.B.A.: Yes, James J. Rosso
(716) 829-3466, jjrosso@buffalo.edu
M.D./J.D.: No
M.D./Ph.D.: Yes, Arlene Albrecht
(716) 829-3398, ama7@buffalo.edu

Premedical Coursework

On-line courses accepted in fulfillment of prerequisites: No

Course	Req.	Rec.	Lab.	Sems.
Inorganic Chemistry	•		•	2
Behavioral Sciences				
Biochemistry		•		
Biology	•		•	2
Biology/Zoology				
Calculus				
College English	•			2
College Mathematics				

Course	Req.	Rec.	Lab.	Sems.
Computer Science				
Genetics		•		
Humanities		•		
Organic Chemistry	•		•	2
Physics	•			2
Psychology				
Social Sciences		•		
Other				

Selection Factors: 2009 Accepted Applicants

Proportion of Accepted Applicants with Relevant Experience (Data Self-Reported to AMCAS®)		
Community Service/Volunteer		66%
Medically-Related Work		92%
Research		89%

Shaded bar represents school's accepted scores ranging from the 10th percentile to the 90th percentile ▬   School Median ● National Median ○

Overall GPA 2.0 2.1 2.2 2.3 2.4 2.5 2.6 2.7 2.8 2.9 3.0 3.1 3.2 3.3 3.4 3.5 3.6 (3.7) 3.8 3.9 4.0
Science GPA 2.0 2.1 2.2 2.3 2.4 2.5 2.6 2.7 2.8 2.9 3.0 3.1 3.2 3.3 3.4 3.5 3.6 (3.7) 3.8 3.9 4.0

MCAT® Total Numeric Score 9 10 11 12 13 14 15 16 17 18 19 20 21 22 23 24 25 26 27 28 29 30 (31) (32) 33 34 35 36 37 38 39 40 41 42 43

Writing Sample			J	K	L	M	N	O	P	(Q)	R	S	T
Verbal Reasoning	3	4	5	6	7	8	9	(10)	11	12	13	14	15
Biological Sciences	3	4	5	6	7	8	9	10	(11)	12	13	14	15
Physical Sciences	3	4	5	6	7	8	9	10	(11)	12	13	14	15

Acceptance & Matriculation Data for 2009–2010 First Year Class

	Resident	Non-resident	International	Total
Applications	1760	1996	68	3824
Interviewed	354	235	0	642
Deferred	0	1	0	1
Matriculants				
Early Assurance Program	0	0	0	0
Early Decision Program	0	0	0	0
Baccalaureate/M.D.	0	0	0	0
M.D./Ph.D.	2	2	0	4
Matriculated	102	42	0	**144**

Applications accepted from International Applicants: No

Matriculant Demographics: 2009–2010 First Year Class

Men: 76   **Women:** 68

Matriculants' Self-Reported Race/Ethnicity

Mexican American	0	Korean	5
Cuban	0	Vietnamese	1
Puerto Rican	1	Other Asian	5
Other Hispanic	0	Total Asian	40
Total Hispanic	1	Native American	2
Chinese	16	Black	5
Asian Indian	9	Native Hawaiian	0
Pakistani	0	White	96
Filipino	2	Unduplicated Number	
Japanese	2	of Matriculants	144

Science and Math Majors: 67%
Matriculants with:
    Baccalaureate degree: 99%
    Graduate degree(s): 9%

Specialty Choice

2005, 2006, 2007 Graduates, Specialty Choice (As reported by program directors to GME Track™)	
Anesthesiology	6%
Emergency Medicine	8%
Family Practice	5%
Internal Medicine	15%
Obstetrics/Gynecology	7%
Orthopaedic Surgery	2%
Pediatrics	11%
Psychiatry	7%
Radiology	6%
Surgery	9%

Financial Information

Source: 2008-2009 LCME I-B survey
and 2009-2010 AAMC TSF questionnaire

	Residents	Non-residents
Total Cost of Attendance	$ 48,008	$ 65,848
Tuition and Fees	$ 24,332	$ 42,172
Other (includes living expenses)	$ 21,913	$ 21,913
Health Insurance (can be waived)	$ 1,763	$ 1,763

Average 2009 Graduate Indebtedness: $149,039
% of Enrolled Students Receiving Aid: 98%

Criminal Background Check

This medical school requires a criminal background check prior to matriculation.

University of Rochester School of Medicine and Dentistry
Rochester, New York

Director of Admissions, University of Rochester
School of Medicine and Dentistry
601 Elmwood Avenue, Box 601A
Rochester, New York 14642
T 585 275 4539 F 585 756 5479

Admissions www.urmc.rochester.edu/education/md/admissions
Main www.urmc.rochester.edu/
Financial www.urmc.rochester.edu/education/financial-aid
E-mail mdadmish@urmc.rochester.edu

Private Institution
Dr. Mark Taubman, Dean and Vice Provost

Dr. John T. Hansen, Associate Dean for Admissions

Adrienne Morgan, Senior Director, Center for Advocacy, Community Health, Education and Diversity

B.J. Revill, Director, Financial Aid

Patricia Samuelson, Director of Admissions

General Information
The School of Medicine and Dentistry is an academic division of the University of Rochester, a privately endowed institution founded in 1850. The Medical Center includes the School of Medicine and Dentistry, School of Nursing, Eastman Dental Center, James P. Wilmot Cancer Center, Strong Memorial Hospital, Golisano Children's Hospital at Strong and Highland Hospital.

Mission Statement
As the home of the biopsychosocial model, Rochester offers a student-centered educational program that prepares physicians for the 21st century. The curriculum fosters knowledge, skills, attitudes, and behaviors of the physician/scientist/humanist by combining cutting-edge, evidence-based medical science with the relationship-centered art that is medicine's distinctive trademark.

Curricular Highlights
Community Service Requirement: Required. Community Health Improvement Clerkship.
Research/Thesis Requirement: Optional. Graduate with "Distinction in Research" honors.

Rochester's Double Helix Curriculum captures the integrated strands of basic science and clinical medicine as they are woven throughout the four-year curriculum. The focus of the educational program is not merely the transfer of information, but the transformation of the learner in a culture providing that ingenious combination of support and challenge, which leads to education. Courses are interdisciplinary and clinical exposure begins during the first week of school with an introduction to clinical medicine and the start of the ambulatory care clerkship during the first spring semester. Inpatient clerkships focus on acute care experiences in adult medicine, women's and children's health, mind/brain/behavior, and urgent/emergent care. A formal tutoring system and assistance programs are available. A rich menu of opportunities is available to students, including a strong M.D./Ph.D. program (MSTP), a five-year Academic Research Track, Medical Humanities selectives, and community and international medicine experiences. All courses except required clinical clerkships are graded Pass/Fail. Clerkships are graded Honors/High Pass/Pass/Fail.

USMLE
Step 1: Required. Students must only record a score.
Step 2: Clinical Skills (CS): Required. Students must only record a score.
Step 2: Clinical Knowledge (CK): Required. Students must only record a score.

Selection Factors
Evaluation of applicants includes a careful examination of the entire academic record, letters of recommendation, and the candidate's personal statement. Demonstrated excellence in a demanding academic program, including a high level of achievement in the natural sciences, is a requirement for acceptance. Evidence of intrinsic intellectual drive and curiosity is highly valued since the program at Rochester emphasizes independent learning opportunities for individual students. Particular attention is given to achievements that demonstrate breadth and commitment, especially in areas of research, outreach, and clinical experience. Students interested in academic medicine, outreach to the underserved, and global medicine are especially encouraged to apply.

Financial Aid
The medical school offers scholarships and long-term loans to those students who demonstrate financial need. Entering students applying for institutional financial aid are required to provide a FAFSA, a more detailed financial statement including parent information, and the School of Medicine's financial aid application.

Information about Diversity Programs
The Center for Advocacy, Community Health, Education and Diversity represents a serious commitment on the part of the School of Medicine and Dentistry to meet the urgent need for diverse physicians in all aspects of the medical profession. Rochester believes that a diverse class enriches the educational environment for all of its students. The office also coordinates numerous academic and cultural events for the education of all students.

Campus Information

Setting
The Medical Center is located adjacent to the University of Rochester which enrolls about 4,450 undergraduates and 3,890 graduate students. The Medical Center has new education and research facilities. Three affiliated hospitals, regional Veterans Affairs clinics, and community health centers are in close proximity to the Medical Center. The metropolitan area includes 1.1 million residents and is located in the scenic Finger Lakes region of upstate New York.

Enrollment
For 2009, total enrollment was: 422

Special Features
The University is consistently ranked among the top 30 institutions in federal funding for research and development, and it owns the Strong Memorial Hospital, which is a major referral center for upstate New York.

Housing
Campus housing is available and assigned by lottery; high quality, affordable housing is also located within a short distance of the Medical Center.

Satellite Campuses/Facilities
Students also rotate through three affiliated hospitals and community and private ambulatory clinics within a short distance of the Medical Center. Both inner city and rural clinic/hospital experiences are offered.

Application Process and Requirements 2011–2012

Primary Application Service: AMCAS
Earliest filing date: June 1, 2010
Latest filing date: October 15, 2010

Secondary Application Required?: Yes
Sent to: All applicants
URL: https://admissions.urmc.rochester.edu/StudentLogin.cfm
Fee: Yes, $85   **Waiver available:** Yes, (AMCAS FAP)
Earliest filing date: June 29, 2010
Latest filing date: November 15, 2010

MCAT® required?: Yes
Latest MCAT® considered: September 2010
Oldest MCAT® considered: March 2007

Early Decision Program: School does not have EDP
Applicants notified: n/a
EDP available for: n/a

Regular Acceptance Notice
Earliest date: October 16, 2010
Latest date: Until class is full
Applicant's Response to Acceptance Offer – Maximum Time: Two weeks

Requests for Deferred Entrance Considered: Yes

Deposit to Hold Place in Class: Yes
Deposit (Resident): $100   **(Non-resident):** $100
Deposit due: With response to acceptance offer
Applied to tuition: Yes   **Refundable:** Yes
Refundable by: May 15, 2011

Estimated number of new entrants: 104
EDP: 0, special program: 20

Start Month/Year: August 2011

Interview Format: Two interviews. Regional interviews are not available. Video interviews are not available.

Other Programs

PREPARATORY PROGRAMS

Postbaccalaureate Program: Yes, http://www.rochester.edu/College/premed/
Summer Program: Yes, http://www.urmc.rochester.edu/education/md/cached/surf.cfm
One week pre-matriculation course: Barbara Davis, (585) 273-4862, barbara_davis@urmc.rochester.edu

COMBINED DEGREE PROGRAMS

Baccalaureate/M.D.: Yes, http://enrollment.rochester.edu/admissions/learning/programs.shtm
M.D./M.P.H.: Yes, www.urmc.rochester.edu/education/md/joint-degree.cfm
M.D./M.B.A.: Yes, www.urmc.rochester.edu/education/md/joint-degree.cfm
M.D./J.D.: No
M.D./Ph.D.: Yes, www.urmc.rochester.edu/education/md/joint-degree.cfm

Premedical Coursework

On-line courses accepted in fulfillment of prerequisites: No

Course	Req.	Rec.	Lab.	Sems.
Inorganic Chemistry	•		•	2
Behavioral Sciences				
Biochemistry		•		
Biology				
Biology/Zoology	•		•	2
Calculus				
College English	•			2
College Mathematics				

Course	Req.	Rec.	Lab.	Sems.
Genetics		•		
Humanities	•			2
Organic Chemistry	•		•	2
Physics	•		•	2
Psychology				
Social Sciences	•			2
Anatomy/Physiology		•		
Biostatistics		•		

Selection Factors: 2009 Accepted Applicants

Proportion of Accepted Applicants with Relevant Experience (Data Self-Reported to AMCAS)		
Community Service/Volunteer		77%
Medically-Related Work		86%
Research		88%

Shaded bar represents school's accepted scores ranging from the 10th percentile to the 90th percentile   **School Median ●   National Median ◐**

Overall GPA	2.0	2.1	2.2	2.3	2.4	2.5	2.6	2.7	2.8	2.9	3.0	3.1	3.2	3.3	3.4	3.5	3.6	3.7	(3.8)	3.9	4.0
Science GPA	2.0	2.1	2.2	2.3	2.4	2.5	2.6	2.7	2.8	2.9	3.0	3.1	3.2	3.3	3.4	3.5	3.6	3.7	(3.8)	3.9	4.0

MCAT® Total Numeric Score 9 10 11 12 13 14 15 16 17 18 19 20 21 22 23 24 25 26 27 28 29 30 31 (32)(33) 34 35 36 37 38 39 40 41 42 43

Writing Sample			J	K	L	M	N	O	(Q)	R	S	T
Verbal Reasoning	3	4	5	6	7	8	9	(10)	11	12	13	14	15
Biological Sciences	3	4	5	6	7	8	9	10	(11)	12	13	14	15
Physical Sciences	3	4	5	6	7	8	9	10	(11)	12	13	14	15

Acceptance & Matriculation Data for 2009–2010 First Year Class

	Resident	Non-resident	International	Total
Applications	1223	3501	16	4740
Interviewed	242	433	0	680
Deferred	2	2	0	4
Matriculants				
Early Assurance Program	0	0	0	0
Early Decision Program	0	0	0	0
Baccalaureate/M.D.	8	3	0	11
M.D./Ph.D.	4	2	0	6
Matriculated	50	54	0	**104**

Applications accepted from International Applicants: No

Matriculant Demographics: 2009–2010 First Year Class

Men: 53   **Women:** 51

Matriculants' Self-Reported Race/Ethnicity

Mexican American	0	Korean	2
Cuban	0	Vietnamese	1
Puerto Rican	2	Other Asian	3
Other Hispanic	5	Total Asian	21
Total Hispanic	7	Native American	0
Chinese	5	Black	15
Asian Indian	10	Native Hawaiian	0
Pakistani	1	White	67
Filipino	0	Unduplicated Number	
Japanese	0	of Matriculants	104

Science and Math Majors: 64%
Matriculants with:
Baccalaureate degree: 100%
Graduate degree(s): 12%

Specialty Choice

2005, 2006, 2007 Graduates, Specialty Choice (As reported by program directors to GME Track™)	
Anesthesiology	5%
Emergency Medicine	6%
Family Practice	2%
Internal Medicine	22%
Obstetrics/Gynecology	5%
Orthopaedic Surgery	3%
Pediatrics	12%
Psychiatry	5%
Radiology	5%
Surgery	7%

Financial Information

Source: 2008-2009 LCME I-B survey and 2009-2010 AAMC TSF questionnaire

	Residents	Non-residents
Total Cost of Attendance	$ 59,410	$ 59,410
Tuition and Fees	$ 41,483	$ 41,483
Other (includes living expenses)	$ 16,000	$ 16,000
Health Insurance (can be waived)	$ 1,927	$ 1,927

Average 2009 Graduate Indebtedness: $127,969
% of Enrolled Students Receiving Aid: 89%

Criminal Background Check

This medical school requires a criminal background check prior to matriculation.

Weill Cornell Medical College

New York, New York

Office of Admissions
Weill Cornell Medical College
445 East 69th Street
New York, New York 10021
T 212 746 1067   F 212 746 8052

Admissions www.med.cornell.edu/education/
admissions
Main www.med.cornell.edu
Financial www.med.cornell.edu/education/
admissions/app_fin_aid.html
E-mail wcmc-admissions@med.cornell.edu

Private Institution

Dr. Antonio M. Gotto, Jr., Dean

*Dr. Charles L. Bardes, Associate Dean
and Chair, Committee on Admissions*

*Dr. Carlyle H. Miller, Associate Dean
for Student Affairs*

LaVerne O. Walker, Director of Financial Aid

Liliana Montano, Assistant Dean of Admissions

General Information

Founded in 1898 as Cornell University Medical College, the school is now known as Weill Cornell Medical College. The medical school campus embraces New York-Presbyterian Hospital, Memorial Sloan-Kettering Cancer Center, Rockefeller University, and the Hospital for Special Surgery. In addition, students train in clinical care throughout our affiliated network, including public, private, research, tertiary care, and community hospitals as well as primary care sites.

Mission Statement

WCMC is committed to excellence in research, teaching, patient care, and the advancement of the art and science of medicine. To this end, our mission is to provide the finest education possible for medical students, to provide superior continuing medical education for the life-long education of physicians throughout their careers, to conduct research at the cutting edge of knowledge, to improve the health care of the nation and world both now and for further generations, and to provide the highest level of clinical care for the communities we serve.

Curricular Highlights

Community Service Requirement: Optional.
Special degree program: M.D. with Honors in Service
Research/Thesis Requirement: Optional.
Special degree program: M.D. with Honors in Research

The first two years center on Problem-Based Learning (PBL), in which students learn by actively solving problems with the faculty in small group seminars. Lectures, anatomic dissection, experimental laboratories and journal clubs augment the learning experience. Basic science courses are integrated and multidisciplinary. Students begin to work with patients immediately during the three-year sequence of Medicine, Patients, and Society, which focuses on clinical skills, the doctor-patient relationship, health care systems, ethics and end-of-life care. The core clinical clerkships include Medicine, Neurology, Obstetrics and Gynecology, Pediatrics, Primary Care, Psychiatry, Public Health, and Surgery. Year 4 provides the major time block for electives in clinical medicine, research, and international health experiences, as well as a return to advanced biomedical science.

USMLE
Step 1: Optional.
Step 2: Clinical Skills (CS): Optional.
Step 2: Clinical Knowledge (CK): Optional.

Selection Factors

WCMC considers each applicant on an individual basis and welcomes those with backgrounds in the basic sciences, social sciences, and liberal arts. We encourage applicants to sample a broad range of academic disciplines and to explore one or more areas in depth. Participation in other activities should demonstrate commitment and initiative. We encourage applicants to explore medicine via research, clinical work, and volunteer service. We seek students who demonstrate emotional maturity, personal depth, commitment to others' well-being, and ethical and moral integrity. We seek to build a diverse class and emphasize diversity in all its dimensions, including race, ethnicity, educational background, personal experiences, and fields of interest. Typically a third of our entering students majored in liberal arts, and a quarter are 25 years of age or older.

Financial Aid

Admissions decisions are made without regard to applicants' financial status. All financial aid is based on need. Some 85% of the class receives financial aid, and about 50% receives grants from the College. Housing is guaranteed and subsidized for all students. Financial support for community service, summer research, and international electives is available for all students. The application fee will be waived if it represents a financial hardship to the applicant. Students who are not citizens or permanent residents of the United States are not eligible for Weill Cornell financial aid.

Information about Diversity Programs

Cornell University has been deeply committed to diversity from its very founding, and the Medical College upholds this principle. WMC's educational mission is dedicated to the inclusion of students from diverse ethnic, racial, social, economic, and educational backgrounds. Special summer research programs are available for college undergraduates who have a major interest in the medical problems of the underserved. Further information is available at *www.med. cornell.education/student/min_aff.html.*

Campus Information

Setting
Weill Cornell is located in the heart of New York City in the Upper East Side of Manhattan, a lovely residential neighborhood. Many of the city's cultural resources are a short walk away, including the Metropolitan Museum of Art, The Museum of Modern Art, Carnegie Hall, Central Park, among others.

Enrollment
For 2009, total enrollment was: 406

Special Features
Global Health is a major emphasis. Most students participate in international electives, spanning some eighty countries on six continents, with financial, logistical and curricular support from the College.

Housing
Modern, reduced-cost, housing is guaranteed for all students.

Satellite Campuses/Facilities
Students rotate throughout New York City at public, private, community, research, and tertiary care hospitals, as well as primary care sites. Rural rotations are also available.

Application Process and Requirements 2011–2012

Primary Application Service: AMCAS
Earliest filing date: June 2010
Latest filing date: October 15, 2010

Secondary Application Required?: Yes
Sent to: All applicants
URL: Sent to verified applicants only.
Contact: Office of Admissions
(212) 746-1067, wcmc-admissions@med.cornell.edu
Fee: Yes, $75   **Waiver available:** Yes
Earliest filing date: First transmission of verified AMCAS applications.
Latest filing date: November 15, 2010

MCAT® required?: Yes
Latest MCAT® considered: September 2010
Oldest MCAT® considered: September 2007

Early Decision Program: School does have EDP
Applicants notified: October 1
EDP available for: Both Residents and Non-residents

Regular Acceptance Notice
Earliest date: December 2010
Latest date: Until class is full
Applicant's Response to Acceptance Offer – Maximum Time: Two weeks

Requests for Deferred Entrance Considered: Yes

Deposit to Hold Place in Class: Yes
Deposit (Resident): $100   **(Non-resident):** $100
Deposit due: May 15, 2011
Applied to tuition: Yes   **Refundable:** Yes
Refundable by: May 15, 2011

Estimated number of new entrants: 101
EDP: 1, special program: 3

Start Month/Year: August 2011

Interview Format: Two individual interviews with admissions committee members. No regional interviews. Video interviews are not available.

Other Programs

PREPARATORY PROGRAMS
Postbaccalaureate Program: No
Summer Program: Yes,
www.med.cornell.edu/education/student/
min_sum_pro.html, Elizabeth Wilson-Anstey,
(212) 746-1058, eaanstey@med.cornell.edu

COMBINED DEGREE PROGRAMS
Baccalaureate/M.D.: No
M.D./M.P.H.: No
M.D./M.B.A.: Yes, www.med.cornell.edu/education
M.D./J.D.: No
M.D./Ph.D.: Yes, www.med.cornell.edu/mdphd,
Ruth Gotian, (212) 746-6023,
mdphd@med.cornell.edu
Additional: http://weill.cornell.edu/gradschool/
program/other.html

Premedical Coursework

On-line courses accepted in fulfillment of prerequisites: No

Course	Req.	Rec.	Lab.	Sems.
Inorganic Chemistry	•		•	2
Behavioral Sciences		•		
Biochemistry		•		
Biology	•		•	2
Biology/Zoology				
Calculus		•		1
College English	•			2
College Mathematics				
Computer Science				

Course	Req.	Rec.	Lab.	Sems.
Genetics				
Humanities		•		
Organic Chemistry	•		•	2
Physics	•		•	2
Psychology				
Social Sciences				
Statistics		•		1
Foreign Language		•		
Other				

Selection Factors: 2009 Accepted Applicants

Proportion of Accepted Applicants with Relevant Experience (Data Self-Reported to AMCAS®)		
Community Service/Volunteer		73%
Medically-Related Work		88%
Research		92%

Shaded bar represents school's accepted scores ranging from the 10th percentile to the 90th percentile.   School Median ●   National Median ◐

Overall GPA	2.0	2.1	2.2	2.3	2.4	2.5	2.6	2.7	2.8	2.9	3.0	3.1	3.2	3.3	3.4	3.5	3.6	3.7	(3.8)	3.9	4.0
Science GPA	2.0	2.1	2.2	2.3	2.4	2.5	2.6	2.7	2.8	2.9	3.0	3.1	3.2	3.3	3.4	3.5	3.6	3.7	(3.8)	3.9	4.0

MCAT® Total Numeric Score 9 10 11 12 13 14 15 16 17 18 19 20 21 22 23 24 25 26 27 28 29 30 31 (32) 33 34 35 (36) 37 38 39 40 41 42 43

Writing Sample			J	K	L	M	N	O	P	(Q)	R	S	T
Verbal Reasoning	3	4	5	6	7	8	9	(10)	(11)	12	13	14	15
Biological Sciences	3	4	5	6	7	8	9	10	(11)	(12)	13	14	15
Physical Sciences	3	4	5	6	7	8	9	10	(11)	(12)	13	14	15

Acceptance & Matriculation Data for 2009–2010 First Year Class

	Resident	Non-resident	International	Total
Applications	1138	4157	285	5580
Interviewed	156	561	13	730
Deferred	0	0	0	0
Matriculants				
Early Assurance Program	0	0	0	0
Early Decision Program	0	0	0	0
Baccalaureate/M.D.	0	0	0	0
M.D./Ph.D.	4	10	0	14
Matriculated	33	66	2	**101**

Applications accepted from International Applicants: Yes

Matriculant Demographics: 2009–2010 First Year Class

Men: 55   **Women:** 46

Matriculants' Self-Reported Race/Ethnicity

Mexican American	5	Korean	2
Cuban	1	Vietnamese	1
Puerto Rican	1	Other Asian	0
Other Hispanic	4	**Total Asian**	21
Total Hispanic	11	Native American	2
Chinese	10	Black	16
Asian Indian	6	Native Hawaiian	2
Pakistani	1	White	55
Filipino	0	Unduplicated Number	
Japanese	2	of Matriculants	101

Science and Math Majors: 61%
Matriculants with:
Baccalaureate degree: 100%
Graduate degree(s): 9%

Specialty Choice

2005, 2006, 2007 Graduates, Specialty Choice (As reported by program directors to GME Track™)	
Anesthesiology	8%
Emergency Medicine	7%
Family Practice	0%
Internal Medicine	19%
Obstetrics/Gynecology	4%
Orthopaedic Surgery	3%
Pediatrics	9%
Psychiatry	5%
Radiology	6%
Surgery	9%

Financial Information

Source: 2008-2009 LCME I-B survey and 2009-2010 AAMC TSF questionnaire

	Residents	Non-residents
Total Cost of Attendance	$ 70,280	$ 70,280
Tuition and Fees	$ 47,455	$ 47,455
Other (includes living expenses)	$ 18,733	$ 18,733
Health Insurance (can be waived)	$ 4,092	$ 4,092

Average 2009 Graduate Indebtedness: $120,755
% of Enrolled Students Receiving Aid: 87%

Criminal Background Check

This medical school does not require a criminal background check prior to matriculation.

The Brody School of Medicine at East Carolina University

Greenville, North Carolina

Associate Dean, Office of Admissions
The Brody School of Medicine
at East Carolina University
Greenville, North Carolina 27834
T 252 744 2202   **F** 252 744 1926

Admissions www.ecu.edu/bsomadmissions
Main www.ecu.edu/med
Financial www.ecu.edu/cs-dhs/bsomstudentaffairs/
Brody-School-of-Medicine-Financial-Aid.cfm
E-mail somadmissions@ecu.edu

Public Institution

Dr. Paul R. G. Cunningham, Dean

Dr. James G. Peden Jr.,
Associate Dean for Admissions

Dr. Kathleen Previll, Interim Senior Associate
Dean for Academic Affairs

Kelly Lancaster, Director of
Financial Aid and Student Services

Lynn S. Coward, Director of Admissions

General Information

In 1972, East Carolina University enrolled students in the First-Year Program in Medical Education. The Board of Governors and the State General Assembly authorized the expansion to a degree-granting School of Medicine in 1975, and the first class was enrolled in August 1977. The school's educational facilities are located in the nine-story Brody Medical Sciences Building on the 100-acre Health Sciences Center campus.

Mission Statement

Our mission is threefold: educating primary care physicians, making medical care more readily available to the people of eastern North Carolina, and providing opportunities for disadvantaged students.

Curricular Highlights

Community Service Requirement: Optional.
Research/Thesis Requirement: Optional.

The first year of the four-year curriculum is devoted to the study of the body through courses in anatomy, biochemistry, physiology, microbiology/immunology, nuerosciences, and genetics. Courses in clinical skills, the psychosocial basis of medicine, ethical and social issues in medicine, and a primary care preceptorship are also presented. The second-year curriculum is directed toward clinical medicine, with courses including microbiology, pharmacology, pathology, psychiatry (including human sexuality and lifestyle abuse), ethical and social issues, clinical skills, and a primary care preceptorship. The third year is composed of eight required clerkships in family medicine, internal medicine, obstetrics and gynecology, pediatrics, psychiatry,

surgery, radiology, cardiovascular science, and a two-week clinical elective. The fourth year is composed of 36 weeks of clinical and basic science electives, which must include blocks in primary care, intensive care, and other specific areas. Student performance is evaluated by letter grade, and promotion to the next year's class is recommended to the dean by the Promotions Committee of the respective year.

USMLE

Step 1: Required. Students must record a passing score for promotion.
Step 2: Clinical Skills (CS): Required. Students must record a passing total score to graduate.
Step 2: Clinical Knowledge (CK): Required. Students must record a passing total score to graduate.

Selection Factors

Factors considered in the selection process encompass the social, personal, and intellectual development of each applicant. All available application data are evaluated: MCAT scores; academic performance; comments contained in letters of reference/recommendation; and (for invited applicants) the results of two personal interviews, conducted only at the medical school campus, with two members of the Admissions Committee. The Brody School of Medicine at East Carolina University seeks competent students of diverse personalities and backgrounds, and all applicants are evaluated without discrimination based on race, religion, sex, color, national origin, age, or disability. Very strong preference is given to qualified residents of North Carolina. In conjunction with the undergraduate Office of Admissions, the Brody School of Medicine offers an Early Assurance Program for highly qualified high school seniors. Selected scholars enroll in the University and are assured of a spot in the medical school class after receiving their baccalaureate degree (provided certain academic standards are maintained). Qualified North Carolina residents from schools with similar medical curricula may be considered for transfer into the second- or third-year classes, but advanced standing positions are dependent on the very limited number of seats that become available through attrition. Interested students should send letters describ-

ing their circumstances to the Office of Admissions for further information.

Financial Aid

Many resources are available for loans and scholarships. Information on financial aid is given to every interviewee and accepted students who demonstrate a need for financial aid are given personal assistance in acquiring funds to meet the costs of their educational and living expenses. Awards are based on need as determined by confidential information supplied by the student. Merit awards, such as the Brody Medical Scholars Program, are also available.

Information about Diversity Programs

Persons from groups underrepresented in medicine who hold residence in North Carolina are encouraged to apply. There is diverse membership on the Admissions Committee, and the Academic Support and Enrichment Services Office offers a wide range of services to students desiring assistance or guidance.

Campus Information

Setting

The medical school is located in the 100-acre medical district and is adjacent to the primary clinical training site, Pitt County Memorial Hospital. Greenville is a short drive from several beaches, sounds, and other recreational areas.

Enrollment

For 2009, total enrollment was: 297

Special Features

The medical school houses an international robotic surgery training center and several clinical Centers of Excellence. The $190 million East Carolina Heart Institute was completed in 2009, and a new Family Medicine / Geriatrics center is under construction. The newly-founded dental school is scheduled to begin operation in 2011.

Housing

There are many apartments, duplexes, and houses near the medical school.

Application Process and Requirements 2011–2012

Primary Application Service: AMCAS
Earliest filing date: June 1, 2010
Latest filing date: November 15, 2010

Secondary Application Required?: Yes
Sent to: All NC applicants
Contact: somadmissions@ecu.edu
Fee: Yes, $60 **Waiver available:** Yes
Earliest filing date: July 1, 2010
Latest filing date: November 15, 2010 or 2 weeks after receipt of AMCAS

MCAT® required?: Yes
Latest MCAT® considered: September 2010
Oldest MCAT® considered: April 2007

Early Decision Program: School does have EDP
Applicants notified: October 1, 2010
EDP available for: Residents only

Regular Acceptance Notice
Earliest date: October 15, 2010
Latest date: Varies
Applicant's Response to Acceptance
Offer – Maximum Time: Three weeks

Requests for Deferred
Entrance Considered: No

Deposit to Hold Place in Class: Yes
Deposit (Resident): $100 **(Non-resident):** $100
Deposit due: With response to acceptance offer
Applied to tuition: Yes **Refundable:** Yes
Refundable by: May 15, 2010

Estimated number of new entrants: 78
EDP: 8, special program: n/a

Start Month/Year: August 2011

Interview Format: Two semi-blind interviews by committee members. All interviews are conducted at the medical school. Video interviews are not available.

Other Programs

PREPARATORY PROGRAMS
Postbaccalaureate Program: No
Summer Program: Yes www.ecu.edu/cs-dhs/ascc/SPFD.cfm

COMBINED DEGREE PROGRAMS
Baccalaureate/M.D.: No
M.D./M.P.H.: Yes, www.ecu.edu/mph
M.D./M.B.A.: Yes, www.ecu.edu/cs-dhs/med/MD_MBA.cfm
M.D./J.D.: No
M.D./Ph.D.: Yes, www.ecu.edu/cs-dhs/med/MD_PhD.cfm

Premedical Coursework

On-line courses accepted in fulfillment of prerequisites: On a case-by-case basis

Course	Req.	Rec.	Lab.	Hrs.
Inorganic Chemistry	•		•	8
Behavioral Sciences				
Biochemistry				
Biology				
Biology/Zoology	•		•	8
Calculus				
College English	•			6
College Mathematics				

Course	Req.	Rec.	Lab.	Hrs.
Computer Science				
Genetics		•		
Humanities		•		
Organic Chemistry	•		•	8
Physics	•		•	8
Psychology				
Social Sciences		•		
Biostatistics		•		

Selection Factors: 2009 Accepted Applicants

Proportion of Accepted Applicants with Relevant Experience (Data Self-Reported to AMCAS®)	
Community Service/Volunteer	74%
Medically-Related Work	90%
Research	69%

Shaded bar represents school's accepted scores ranging from the 10th percentile to the 90th percentile. School Median ○ National Median ○

Overall GPA 2.0 2.1 2.2 2.3 2.4 2.5 2.6 2.7 2.8 2.9 3.0 3.1 3.2 3.3 3.4 3.5 3.6 ③.7 3.8 3.9 4.0
Science GPA 2.0 2.1 2.2 2.3 2.4 2.5 2.6 2.7 2.8 2.9 3.0 3.1 3.2 3.3 3.4 3.5 3.6 ③.7 3.8 3.9 4.0

MCAT® Total Numeric Score 9 10 11 12 13 14 15 16 17 18 19 20 21 22 23 24 25 26 27 28 ㉙ 30 31 ㉜ 33 34 35 36 37 38 39 40 41 42 43

	J	K	L	M	N	O	(P)	(Q)	R	S	T
Writing Sample											

Verbal Reasoning	3	4	5	6	7	8	9	⑩	11	12	13	14	15
Biological Sciences	3	4	5	6	7	8	9	⑩	⑪	12	13	14	15
Physical Sciences	3	4	5	6	7	8	9	⑩	⑪	12	13	14	15

Acceptance & Matriculation Data for 2009–2010 First Year Class

	Resident	Non-resident	International	Total
Applications	876	1	2	879
Interviewed	505	0	0	505
Deferred	1	0	0	1
Matriculants				
Early Assurance Program	2	0	0	2
Early Decision Program	3	0	0	3
Baccalaureate/M.D.	0	0	0	0
M.D./Ph.D.	0	0	0	0
Matriculated	78	0	0	**78**

Applications accepted from International Applicants: No

Specialty Choice

2005, 2006, 2007 Graduates, Specialty Choice (As reported by program directors to GME Track™)	
Anesthesiology	2%
Emergency Medicine	7%
Family Practice	18%
Internal Medicine	18%
Obstetrics/Gynecology	9%
Orthopaedic Surgery	1%
Pediatrics	13%
Psychiatry	1%
Radiology	3%
Surgery	4%

Matriculant Demographics: 2009–2010 First Year Class

Men: 39   **Women:** 39

Matriculants' Self-Reported Race/Ethnicity

Mexican American	1	Korean	0
Cuban	0	Vietnamese	1
Puerto Rican	0	Other Asian	1
Other Hispanic	1	Total Asian	7
Total Hispanic	2	Native American	1
Chinese	2	Black	8
Asian Indian	3	Native Hawaiian	0
Pakistani	1	White	59
Filipino	0	Unduplicated Number	
Japanese	0	of Matriculants	78

Science and Math Majors: 69%
Matriculants with:
Baccalaureate degree: 100%
Graduate degree(s): 13%

Financial Information

Source: 2008-2009 LCME I-B survey and 2009-2010 AAMC TSF questionnaire

	Residents	Non-residents
Total Cost of Attendance	$ 28,995	$ 53,985
Tuition and Fees	$ 10,344	$ 35,334
Other (includes living expenses)	$ 17,357	$ 17,357
Health Insurance (can be waived)	$ 1,294	$ 1,294

Average 2009 Graduate Indebtedness: $85,178
% of Enrolled Students Receiving Aid: 90%

Criminal Background Check

This medical school requires a criminal background check prior to matriculation.

Duke University School of Medicine
Durham, North Carolina

Committee on Admissions
Duke University School of Medicine
DUMC 3710
Durham, North Carolina 27710
T 919 684 2985   **F** 919 668 3714

Admissions http://dukemed.duke.edu
Main http://medschool.duke.edu/
Financial http://medschool.duke.edu/modules/
som_finaid/index.php?id=1
E-mail medadm@mc.duke.edu

Private Institution

Dr. Nancy C. Andrews, Dean

Dr. Brenda E. Armstrong, Associate Dean and Director of Admissions

Dr. Delbert R. Wigfall, Associate Dean, Medical Education Director, Multicultural Resource Center

Stacey R. McCorison, Associate Dean of Medical Education, Director of Financial Aid and Registrar

Richard S. Wallace, Associate Director of Admissions

Dr. Colleen O. Grochowski, Associate Dean for Curricular Affairs

General Information

Duke University Health System is a world-class health care network dedicated to outstanding patient care, innovative medical education and biomedical research.

Mission Statement

DukeMed is a community of scholars devoted to understanding the causes, prevention and treatment of human disease. Our missions are to train scholars and leaders across a broad spectrum of careers in medicine. These missions are undertaken by students from diverse communities committed to the highest of academic goals: the generation, conservation, and dissemination of knowledge leading to the prevention and eradication of human disease throughout the world through innovative curricula and broadly-based clinical training, unparalleled resources in education, clinical care, and basic and clinical research.

Curricular Highlights

Community Service Requirement: Optional.
Research/Thesis Requirement: Required. Required to complete the third year of medical school.

The curriculum stimulates rapid expansion of medical knowledge. First-year students study basic science principles alongside the first of two-years' introduction to clinical medicine. The second year is the clinical clerkship year. The third and fourth years are elective including half basic science/half clinical coursework with

opportunities for mentored research. Students also elect from a number of dual-degree programs which begin during the third year. The fourth year is an advanced clinical clerkship year to prepare for postgraduate study. The MST Program provides MD/Ph.D degrees over a six-to-seven-year period. It is expected that candidates for this combined degree plan will have careers in academic medicine.

USMLE

Step 1: Required. Students must only record a score.
Step 2: Clinical Skills (CS): Required. Students must only record a score.
Step 2: Clinical Knowledge (CK): Required. Students must only record a score.

Selection Factors

Selection is based on evidence of outstanding academic and experiential preparation, including but not limited to outstanding curricular/extracurricular achievement, evidence of leadership, participation in volunteer/community service activities, excellent oral and written communications skills, supportive letters of recommendations from teachers/advisors, strong MCAT scores, exposure to and/or participation in scholarly research and the applicant's interview evaluation. Successful students have high GPAs/MCAT scores, demonstrated leadership on campus and in their respective communities. Duke Med does not discriminate on the basis of sex, race, religion, sexual orientation, creed, age, handicap, or national origin.

Financial Aid

The Office of Financial Aid requires the Need Access, the FAFSA, parent and student tax returns. Students applying for only Federal Loans complete the FAFSA. Students are encouraged to submit the applications as soon as possible after acceptance. Prior year tax returns should be submitted. Accepted students receive award notices once all forms are received. 85% of currently enrolled medical students receive some type of financial aid. Admissions is need-blind. Seven Dean's Tuition Scholarships are awarded to excellent students who based on background will contribute to the diversity of the class. Students who enter the Medical Scientist Training Program receive full tuition, fees, and a stipend.

Information about Diversity Programs

The Multicultural Resource Center is a resource-intensive repository providing opportunities for diverse learning experiences for all students and targeted pipeline programs for women, URM/disadvantaged, and students interested in careers in healthcare and biomedical research beginning as early as elementary school through undergraduate and graduate education. MRC integrates cross-cultural issues in medicine to the medical school curriculum and within the entirety of the medical school.

Campus Information

Setting

DukeMed is physically contiguous with the main campus of Duke University. Durham is one of three communities part of the Research Triangle Park, one of the nation's most prolific research centers and one rich in cultural, educational, and recreational opportunities.

Enrollment

For 2009, total enrollment was: 415

Special Features

DukeMed is consistently ranked among the top ten academic health centers in the country and has a national and international reputation for innovation and excellence.

Housing

Students choose from a number of affordable on- and off-campus housing units. Housing costs are extremely affordable and accessible to the School of Medicine, the hospitals and clinical practices to which the students are assigned. Durham boasts a relatively lower cost of living index compared to similar and larger metropolitan areas.

Satellite Campuses/Facilities

Students are based throughout the Duke Health System at Duke University Hospital, the VA Hospital, Durham Regional Hospital, Lennox Baker Children's Hospital, Duke Children's Hospital, and more than 70 outpatient clinics located in Durham, Raleigh, Chapel Hill and surrounding communities.

Application Process and Requirements 2011–2012

Primary Application Service: AMCAS
Earliest filing date: June 1, 2010
Latest filing date: November 1, 2010

Secondary Application Required?: Yes
Sent to: All applicants
URL: http://dukemed.duke.edu
Fee: Yes, $85   **Waiver available:** Yes
Earliest filing date: Once AMCAS has verified application.
Latest filing date: November 15, 2010

MCAT® required?: Yes
Latest MCAT® considered: September 2010
Oldest MCAT® considered: August 2007

Early Decision Program: School does not have EDP
Applicants notified: n/a
EDP available for: n/a

Regular Acceptance Notice
Earliest date: March 1, 2011
Latest date: Until class is full
Applicant's Response to Acceptance Offer – Maximum Time: Two weeks

Requests for Deferred Entrance Considered: Yes

Deposit to Hold Place in Class: Yes
Deposit (Resident): $100   **(Non-resident):** $100
Deposit due: May 15, 2011
Applied to tuition: Yes   **Refundable:** Yes
Refundable by: May 15, 2011

Estimated number of new entrants: 100
EDP: n/a, special program: n/a

Start Month/Year: August 1, 2011

Interview Format: Interviews are held locally at Duke Med School. Regional interviews are available. Virtual interviews are available.

Other Programs

PREPARATORY PROGRAMS
Postbaccalaureate Program: No
Summer Program: Yes, www.smdep.org Maureen Cullins, (919) 684-5882 mcullins@duke.edu
Additional: Yes, Soman Abraham, Ph.D., (919) 681-8018, soman.abraham@duke.edu http://gradschool.duke.edu/gsa/srop/
Duke University Summer Research Opportunity Program (SROP) is a ten-week training program designed to give motivated undergraduate students hands-on experience in graduate-level biomedical research leading to careers at the M.D./Ph.D. and Ph.D. level.

COMBINED DEGREE PROGRAMS
Baccalaureate/M.D.: No
M.D./M.P.H.: Yes, http://dukemed.duke.edu
M.D./M.B.A.: Yes, http://dukemed.duke.edu
M.D./J.D.: Yes, http://dukemed.duke.edu
M.D./Ph.D.: Yes, www.mstp.duke.edu
Additional.: Yes, http://globalhealth.duke.edu/education/graduate-professional/msc-gh

Premedical Coursework

On-line courses accepted in fulfillment of prerequisites: No

Course	Req.	Rec.	Lab.	Sems.	Course	Req.	Rec.	Lab.	Sems.
Inorganic Chemistry	•		•	1	Genetics		•		1
Behavioral Sciences					Humanities				
Biochemistry	•			1	Organic Chemistry	•		•	1
Biology	•		•	2	Physics	•		•	2
Biology/Zoology	•			1	Psychology				
Calculus	•			1	Social Sciences				
College English	•			2	Statistics/Biostatistics		•		1
College Mathematics					Spanish		•		2
Computer Science					Cell Biology		•		1

Selection Factors: 2009 Accepted Applicants

Proportion of Accepted Applicants with Relevant Experience (Data Self-Reported to AMCAS*)		
Community Service/Volunteer		73%
Medically-Related Work		91%
Research		94%

Shaded bar represents school's accepted scores ranging from the 10th percentile to the 90th percentile.   **School Median** ● **National Median** ○

Overall GPA 2.0 2.1 2.2 2.3 2.4 2.5 2.6 2.7 2.8 2.9 3.0 3.1 3.2 3.3 3.4 3.5 3.6 3.7 (3.8) 3.9 4.0
Science GPA 2.0 2.1 2.2 2.3 2.4 2.5 2.6 2.7 2.8 2.9 3.0 3.1 3.2 3.3 3.4 3.5 3.6 3.7 (3.8) 3.9 4.0

MCAT® Total Numeric Score 9 10 11 12 13 14 15 16 17 18 19 20 21 22 23 24 25 26 27 28 29 30 31 (32) 33 34 35 (36) 37 38 39 40 41 42 43

Writing Sample			J	K	L	M	N	O	P	(Q)	R	S	T
Verbal Reasoning	3	4	5	6	7	8	9	(10)	(11)	12	13	14	15
Biological Sciences	3	4	5	6	7	8	9	10	(11)	(12)	13	14	15
Physical Sciences	3	4	5	6	7	8	9	10	(11)	(12)	13	14	15

Acceptance & Matriculation Data for 2009–2010 First Year Class

	Resident	Non-resident	International	Total
Applications	384	4302	281	4967
Interviewed	110	900	37	1047
Deferred	0	3	0	3
Matriculants				
Early Assurance Program	0	0	0	0
Early Decision Program	0	0	0	0
Baccalaureate/M.D.	0	0	0	0
M.D./Ph.D.	0	11	0	11
Matriculated	12	87	1	**100**

Applications accepted from International Applicants: Yes

Matriculant Demographics: 2009–2010 First Year Class

Men: 51   **Women:** 49

Matriculants' Self-Reported Race/Ethnicity

Mexican American	1	Korean	1
Cuban	2	Vietnamese	1
Puerto Rican	4	Other Asian	1
Other Hispanic	2	Total Asian	25
Total Hispanic	7	Native American	1
Chinese	11	Black	20
Asian Indian	11	Native Hawaiian	0
Pakistani	2	White	62
Filipino	0	Unduplicated Number	
Japanese	0	of Matriculants	100

Science and Math Majors: 71%
Matriculants with:
   Baccalaureate degree: 99%
   Graduate degree(s): 9%

Specialty Choice

2005, 2006, 2007 Graduates, Specialty Choice (As reported by program directors to GME Track™)	
Anesthesiology	5%
Emergency Medicine	3%
Family Practice	3%
Internal Medicine	22%
Obstetrics/Gynecology	3%
Orthopaedic Surgery	5%
Pediatrics	10%
Psychiatry	2%
Radiology	8%
Surgery	8%

Financial Information
Source: 2008-2009 LCME I-B survey and 2009-2010 AAMC TSF questionnaire

	Residents	Non-residents
Total Cost of Attendance	$ 70,891	$ 70,891
Tuition and Fees	$ 46,142	$ 46,142
Other (includes living expenses)	$ 23,185	$ 23,185
Health Insurance (can be waived)	$ 1,564	$ 1,564

Average 2009 Graduate Indebtedness: $112,792
% of Enrolled Students Receiving Aid: 91%

Criminal Background Check

This medical school requires a criminal background check prior to matriculation.

University of North Carolina at Chapel Hill School of Medicine

Chapel Hill, North Carolina

Office of Admissions
CB #9500 1001 Bondurant Hall, First Floor
University of North Carolina at Chapel Hill
School of Medicine
Chapel Hill, North Carolina 27599-9500
T 919 962 8331   F 919 966 9930

Admissions www.med.unc.edu/admit
Main www.med.unc.edu
Financial www.med.unc.edu/md/financial-aid
E-mail Admis_UNC-SOM@listserv.med.unc.edu

Public Institution

*Dr. William L. Roper, Dean,
Vice Chancellor for Medical Affairs*

*Dr. Robert A. Bashford,
Associate Dean for Admissions*

*Sheila M. Graham-McDonald,
Financial Aid Officer*

Ms. Randee Reid, Admissions Officer

General Information

The School of Medicine was established in 1879 and expanded to a four-year school in 1952. Other schools of health sciences are adjacent, allowing easy interaction and collaboration. The School of Medicine is continuing a major expansion and renovation of teaching and clinical facilities. Among other projects, three hospitals, Women's, Children's, and Neuroscience recently have been completed, and the North Carolina Cancer Hospital was completed in 2009. Additional educational and clinical facilities are available throughout the State in Area Health Education Centers (AHEC) established in 1972 to provide clinical experiences and educational opportunities in community settings.

Mission Statement

The School of Medicine of the University of North Carolina at Chapel Hill exists to educate students and professionals of the health and biomedical sciences, to conduct scholarly investigation in biomedical, behavioral, and social sciences, and to render service to the people and institutions of the state, the region, the nation, and, as appropriate, throughout the world.

Curricular Highlights

Community Service Requirement: Optional.
Research/Thesis Requirement: Optional.

The curriculum offers an education that reflects our mission. The first year presents courses in basic biomedical science. Presentation is through a compilation of lectures, problem and case based small-group sessions, and electronic resource materials. Introduction to the profession of medicine begins in the first week of the first year through Introduction to Clinical Medicine (ICM). ICM provides a two-year continuum of weekly small-group seminars and experience

with simulated and real patients. A second weekly first-year seminar, Medicine and Society, focuses on health care issues. The second year presents the pathophysiology of disease in organ-based courses. Clinical skills development continues through the second year of ICM, and issues in social aspects of health care are presented through selectives offered by the Department of Social Medicine. The third and fourth year present a 2-year continuum of instruction in clinical medicine. Core clinical rotations, which are primarily completed in the third year, include internal medicine, surgery, family medicine, obstetrics and gynecology, pediatrics, and psychiatry. Some rotations are at AHEC sites. The advanced clinical curriculum of the 4th year builds more independence and increased responsibility into the base of the core. Students are assisted in choosing their interest in post graduate training through counseling and a broad choice of electives. Students conduct research with faculty mentorship support by school or grant funding, or through selection to the Distinguished Medical Scholars or Doris Duke programs (a year of funded study and research). Students pursue interests in rural and community medicine, public policy, or public health through Social Medicine selectives, fourth year Advance Practice Selectives, and Community Health Projects. The grading system is honors/pass/fail.

USMLE

Step 1: Required. Students must record a passing score for promotion.
Step 2: Clinical Skills (CS): Required. Students must only record a score.
Step 2: Clinical Knowledge (CK): Required. Students must record a passing total score to graduate.

Selection Factors

The Committee on Admissions evaluates the qualifications of all applicants to select those with the greatest potential for accomplishment in one of the many careers open to medical graduates. Preference is given to North Carolina residents. UNC does not discriminate on the basis of race, national origin, religion, sex, age, or handicap. In making its final selections from the group of qualified applicants, the committee considers evidence of each candidate's motivation,

maturity, leadership, integrity, and a variety of other personal qualifications and accomplishments in addition to the scholastic record. All information available about each applicant is considered without assigning priority to any single factor. No special admission tracks or quotas are applied among applicants. Undergraduate major is not an important consideration, but excellence in the chosen field is expected. Re-applications are compared to those previously submitted.

Financial Aid

Grants, school-based and Stafford loans are available to students with financial need. Awards are based on information obtained from the Free Application for Federal Student Aid (FAFSA) submitted by the student. A few scholarships are awarded for academic achievement and promise. Economically or environmentally disadvantaged state residents are eligible to apply to the Board of Governors Medical Scholarship-Loan Program. For more information call (919) 962-6118.

Information about Diversity Programs

The Medical Education Development Program acquaints disadvantaged students with the medical school curriculum and faculty. Academic counseling, including tutorial programs, the Learning and Assessment Laboratory, and other resources, are available. Summer review programs are also available.

Campus Information

Enrollment

For 2009, total enrollment was: 732

Application Process and Requirements 2011–2012

Primary Application Service: AMCAS
Earliest filing date: June 1, 2010
Latest filing date: November 15, 2010

Secondary Application Required?: Yes
Sent to: Screened applicants
URL: n/a
Fee: Yes, $68   **Waiver available:** Yes
Earliest filing date: June 1, 2010
Latest filing date: January 1, 2011

MCAT® required?: Yes
Latest MCAT® considered: September 2010
Oldest MCAT® considered: September 2006

Early Decision Program: School does not have EDP
Applicants notified: n/a
EDP available for: n/a

Regular Acceptance Notice
Earliest date: October 15, 2010
Latest date: Until class is full
Applicant's Response to Acceptance Offer – Maximum Time: Three weeks

Requests for Deferred Entrance Considered: Yes

Deposit to Hold Place in Class: Yes
Deposit (Resident): $100   **(Non-resident):** $100
Deposit due: With response to acceptance offer
Applied to tuition: Yes   **Refundable:** Yes
Refundable by: May 15, 2011

Estimated number of new entrants: 160
EDP: 0, special program: 0

Start Month/Year: August 2011

Interview Format: One-on-one, open file. Regional interviews are not available. Video interviews are not available.

Other Programs

PREPARATORY PROGRAMS
Postbaccalaureate Program: No
Summer Program: No

Combined Degree Programs
Baccalaureate/M.D.: No
M.D./M.P.H.: Yes,
Available after completion of first two years.
M.D./M.B.A.: No
M.D./J.D.: No
M.D./Ph.D.: Yes, www.med.unc.edu/mdphd
Alison Regan, (919) 843-6507
aregan@med.unc.edu

Premedical Coursework

On-line courses accepted in fulfillment of prerequisites: No

Course	Req.	Rec.	Lab.	Hrs.	Course	Req.	Rec.	Lab.	Hrs.
Inorganic Chemistry	•		•	8	Computer Science				
Behavioral Sciences					Genetics		•		
Biochemistry		•			Humanities		•		
Biology	•		•	7	Organic Chemistry	•		•	8
Biology/Zoology					Physics	•		•	8
Calculus					Psychology				
College English	•			6	Social Sciences		•		
College Mathematics					Other		•		

Selection Factors: 2009 Accepted Applicants

Proportion of Accepted Applicants with Relevant Experience (Data Self-Reported to AMCAS®)		
Community Service/Volunteer		76%
Medically-Related Work		86%
Research		80%

Shaded bar represents school's accepted scores ranging from the 10th percentile to the 90th percentile   School Median ● National Median ◐

Overall GPA	2.0	2.1	2.2	2.3	2.4	2.5	2.6	2.7	2.8	2.9	3.0	3.1	3.2	3.3	3.4	3.5	3.6	(3.7)	3.8	3.9	4.0
Science GPA	2.0	2.1	2.2	2.3	2.4	2.5	2.6	2.7	2.8	2.9	3.0	3.1	3.2	3.3	3.4	3.5	3.6	(3.7)	3.8	3.9	4.0

MCAT® Total Numeric Score 9 10 11 12 13 14 15 16 17 18 19 20 21 22 23 24 25 26 27 28 29 30 31 (32)(33) 34 35 36 37 38 39 40 41 42 43

Writing Sample			J	K	L	M	N	O	P	(Q)	R	S	T
Verbal Reasoning	3	4	5	6	7	8	9	(10)	(11)	12	13	14	15
Biological Sciences	3	4	5	6	7	8	9	10	(11)	12	13	14	15
Physical Sciences	3	4	5	6	7	8	9	10	(11)	12	13	14	15

Acceptance & Matriculation Data for 2009–2010 First Year Class

	Resident	Non-resident	International	Total
Applications	912	3075	129	4116
Interviewed	470	101		571
Deferred	2	1	0	3
Matriculants				
Early Assurance Program	0	0	0	0
Early Decision Program	5	0	0	5
Baccalaureate/M.D.	0	0	0	0
M.D./Ph.D.	3	5	0	8
Matriculated	138	21	1	**160**

Applications accepted from International Applicants: Yes

Specialty Choice

2005, 2006, 2007 Graduates, Specialty Choice (As reported by program directors to GME Track™)	
Anesthesiology	7%
Emergency Medicine	5%
Family Practice	11%
Internal Medicine	18%
Obstetrics/Gynecology	5%
Orthopaedic Surgery	4%
Pediatrics	13%
Psychiatry	6%
Radiology	3%
Surgery	6%

Matriculant Demographics: 2009–2010 First Year Class

Men: 67   **Women:** 93

Matriculants' Self-Reported Race/Ethnicity

Mexican American	0	Korean	1
Cuban	0	Vietnamese	0
Puerto Rican	2	Other Asian	4
Other Hispanic	4	Total Asian	20
Total Hispanic	6	Native American	2
Chinese	8	Black	20
Asian Indian	5	Native Hawaiian	0
Pakistani	1	White	113
Filipino	1	Unduplicated Number	
Japanese	1	of Matriculants	160

Science and Math Majors: 58%
Matriculants with:
   Baccalaureate degree: 100%
   Graduate degree(s): 12%

Financial Information

Source: 2008-2009 LCME I-B survey and 2009-2010 AAMC TSF questionnaire

	Residents	Non-residents
Total Cost of Attendance	$ 40,834	$ 64,900
Tuition and Fees	$ 13,408	$ 37,474
Other (includes living expenses)	$ 25,536	$ 25,536
Health Insurance (cannot be waived)	$ 1,890	$ 1,890

Average 2009 Graduate Indebtedness: $86,156
% of Enrolled Students Receiving Aid: 85%

Criminal Background Check

This medical school requires a criminal background check prior to matriculation.

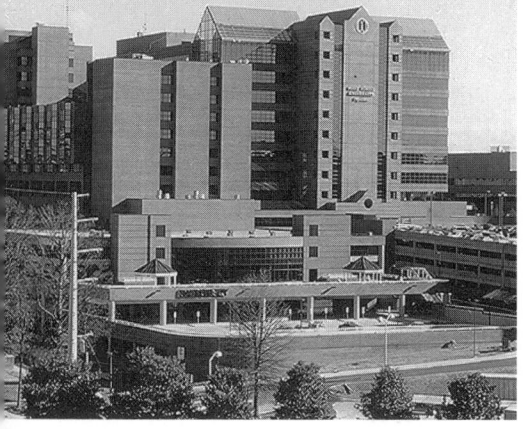

Wake Forest University School of Medicine

Winston-Salem, North Carolina

Office of Medical School Admissions
Wake Forest University School of Medicine
Medical Center Boulevard
Winston-Salem, North Carolina 27157-1090
T 336 716 4264   **F** 336 716 9593

Admissions www.wfubmc.edu/schoolMD
Program/Admissions-General-Homepage.htm
Main www.wfubmc.edu/school
Financial www.wfubmc.edu/school/financialaid/
E-mail medadmit@wfubmc.edu

Private Institution

Dr. William B. Applegate, President and Dean

Dr. Gretchen Wells, Associate Dean for Admissions

Dr. Brenda Latham-Sadler, Assistant Dean, Director Diversity and Development Initiatives

Melissa Stevens, Financial Aid Director

Irene B. Tise, Coordinator, Student Admissions

General Information

The School of Medicine was established in 1902 at Wake Forest, North Carolina, and, of the existing 166 medical schools, it was one of 11 that required college preparation. Patient care, research, education, and community service remain the fourfold mission of the school as part of Wake Forest University. The name of the medical school was changed from The Bowman Gray School of Medicine to Wake Forest University School of Medicine, the Bowman Gray Campus, in 1997. The main teaching hospital of the medical school is the 880-bed North Carolina Baptist Hospital. Affiliated institutions include the 896-bed Forsyth Memorial Hospital, the Downtown Health Plaza of Baptist Hospital, and Northwest Area Health Education Center.

Mission Statement

The Medical Center is committed to serving society by providing a superior education; by rendering exemplary and efficient patient care; by fostering the discovery and application of new knowledge through research; and to improve the health and well-being of the nation.

Curricular Highlights

Community Service Requirement: Optional.
Research/Thesis Requirement: Optional.

WFUSM provides excellence in teaching in a collegial atmosphere. The curriculum is organized to meet the seven goals of the undergraduate medical education program: self-directed learning and life-long learning skills, core biomedical science knowledge, clinical skills, problem-solving/clinical-reasoning skills, interviewing and communication skills, informa-

tion management skills, and professional attitudes and behavior. Students study the basic and clinical sciences in an integrated fashion throughout the four-year curriculum utilizing small-group case centered learning, lectures, and labs which are closely integrated through the computer network. Early community-based clinical experience, as well as a focus on population health, are hallmarks of the curriculum. Professionalism issues are addressed longitudinally across the curriculum in formats designed to provide students with a clear understanding of the role and responsibilities of physicians within society. Information technology is integrated into the curriculum.

USMLE

Step 1: Required. Students must record a passing score for promotion.
Step 2: Clinical Skills (CS): Required. Students must record a passing total score to graduate.
Step 2: Clinical Knowledge (CK): Required. Students must record a passing total score to graduate.

Selection Factors

Candidates are selected on the basis of the quality of their academic records, MCAT scores, and general qualifications. There are no restrictions because of race, creed, sex, religion, age, physical disadvantages, marital status, or national origin. The Committee on Admissions (CoA) and/or the Associate Dean for Admissions evaluate each application. Secondary applications are selectively sent and all other applicants notified of their status. Applicants with completed secondaries are considered for interviews at the medical school. The School of Medicine may be able to accept an application for transfer from a student who is currently enrolled, and in good standing, in a medical school accredited by the Liaison Committee on Medical Education and who meets the prerequisite requirements. Early assurance of a place in medical school is offered to rising juniors who meet certain stringent requirements in an Early Assurance Program (EAP). More detailed information can be found on the Web site or by inquiry to the admissions office.

Financial Aid

Loans and scholarships are awarded to qualified applicants on the basis of financial need and academic standing. Applicants must complete required application forms prior to the April 1 deadline. Students receive a significant amount of their funding from federal student loan programs. Students should not work part-time because of the demands of medical study.

Information about Diversity Programs

The Office of Student Services/Diversity and Development Initiatives actively recruits students from groups underrepresented in medicine and has developed programs for academic enrichment, academic reinforcement, tutorial, and counseling services for enrolled students. Address inquiries to the Office of Diversity and Development Initiatives.

Campus Information

Setting

The school is located in a stable neighborhood near the heart of Winston-Salem, adjacent to hospital and medical facilities.

Enrollment

For 2009, total enrollment was: 475

Special Features

The Wake Forest University Health Sciences and the NC Baptist Hospital-associated medical center has more than 1,000 research studies and clinical trials underway, is home to NC's only Gamma Knife, and is establishing a 200-acre downtown research campus in biotechnology. One of the first tenants on the downtown campus is The Institute for Regenerative Medicine, where staff are working to grow 20 different organs and tissue types. The Anatomical Resource Clinical Training Center is a newly designed multidisciplinary learning center providing computational resources and both CT and MRI data acquired from actual cadavers dissected.

Housing

Available in the community surrounding the medical center. Listings are on Web site.

Application Process and Requirements 2011–2012

Primary Application Service: AMCAS
Earliest filing date: June 1, 2010
Latest filing date: November 1, 2010

Secondary Application Required?: Yes
Sent to: Screened applicants
E-mail: medadmit@wfubmc.edu
Fee: Yes, $55 **Waiver available:** Yes
Earliest filing date: July 15, 2010
Latest filing date: January 15, 2011

MCAT® required?: Yes
Latest MCAT® considered: September 2010
Oldest MCAT® considered: 2007

Early Decision Program: School does have EDP
Applicants notified: October 1, 2010
EDP available for: Both Residents and Non-residents

Regular Acceptance Notice
Earliest date: October 1, 2010
Latest date: Until class is full
Applicant's Response to Acceptance Offer – Maximum Time: Two weeks

Requests for Deferred Entrance Considered: Yes

Deposit to Hold Place in Class: Yes
Deposit (Resident): $100 **(Non-resident):** $100
Deposit due: With response to acceptance offer
Applied to tuition: Yes **Refundable:** Yes
Refundable by: May 1, 2011

Estimated number of new entrants: 120
EDP: 2, special program: 10

Start Month/Year: July 21, 2011

Interview Format: Three individual 20-minute interviews with faculty. Regional interviews are not available. Video interviews are not available.

Other Programs

PREPARATORY PROGRAMS
Postbaccalaureate Program: Yes, www.wfubmc.edu/MDProgram/Student+Services/Diversity/Post+Graduate+Students/PostBacPreMed.htm
Summer Program: No

COMBINED DEGREE PROGRAMS
Baccalaureate/M.D.: No
M.D./M.P.H.: No
M.D./M.B.A.: Yes, http://business.wfu.edu/prospectivestudents
M.D./J.D.: No
M.D./Ph.D.: Yes, www.wfubmc.edu/school/MDProgram/Combined_Degree_Programs.htm
Additional Program: Yes, MD/MA Bioethics, www.wfu.edu/bioethics
MD/MS in Clinical and Population Translational Sciences, www.phs.wfubmc.edu/public/edu.cfm

Premedical Coursework

On-line courses accepted in fulfillment of prerequisites: On a case-by-case basis

Course	Req.	Rec.	Lab.	Hrs.	Course	Req.	Rec.	Lab.	Hrs.
Inorganic Chemistry	•			8	Computer Science				
Behavioral Sciences					Genetics				
Biochemistry					Humanities				
Biology	•			8	Organic Chemistry	•			8
Biology/Zoology					Physics	•			8
Calculus					Psychology				
College English					Social Sciences				
College Mathematics					Other				

Selection Factors: 2009 Accepted Applicants

Proportion of Accepted Applicants with Relevant Experience (Data Self-Reported to AMCAS)		
Community Service/Volunteer		72%
Medically-Related Work		89%
Research		76%

Shaded bar represents school's accepted scores ranging from the 10th percentile to the 90th percentile   School Median ● National Median ◐

Overall GPA	2.0	2.1	2.2	2.3	2.4	2.5	2.6	2.7	2.8	2.9	3.0	3.1	3.2	3.3	3.4	3.5	3.6	3.7	ⓐ 3.8	3.9 4.0
Science GPA	2.0	2.1	2.2	2.3	2.4	2.5	2.6	2.7	2.8	2.9	3.0	3.1	3.2	3.3	3.4	3.5	3.6	ⓐ 3.7	3.8	3.9 4.0

MCAT® Total Numeric Score 9 10 11 12 13 14 15 16 17 18 19 20 21 22 23 24 25 26 27 28 29 30 31 ㉜ 33 34 35 36 37 38 39 40 41 42 43

Writing Sample		J	K	L	M	N	O	Ⓟ	Ⓠ	R	S	T
Verbal Reasoning	3	4	5	6	7	8	9	⑩	11	12	13	14	15
Biological Sciences	3	4	5	6	7	8	9	10	⑪	12	13	14	15
Physical Sciences	3	4	5	6	7	8	9	⑩	⑪	12	13	14	15

Acceptance & Matriculation Data for 2009–2010 First Year Class

	Resident	Non-resident	International	Total
Applications	729	6058	315	7102
Interviewed	150	430	4	584
Deferred	4	6	0	10
Matriculants				
Early Assurance Program	0	0	0	0
Early Decision Program	1	1	0	2
Baccalaureate/M.D.	0	0	0	0
M.D./Ph.D.	0	0	0	0
Matriculated	47	71	2	**120**

Applications accepted from International Applicants: Only Canadian

Matriculant Demographics: 2009–2010 First Year Class

Men: 60   **Women:** 60

Matriculants' Self-Reported Race/Ethnicity

Mexican American	1	Korean	0
Cuban	0	Vietnamese	1
Puerto Rican	1	Other Asian	1
Other Hispanic	1	Total Asian	14
Total Hispanic	3	Native American	2
Chinese	7	Black	15
Asian Indian	3	Native Hawaiian	0
Pakistani	0	White	91
Filipino	1	Unduplicated Number	
Japanese	1	of Matriculants	120

Science and Math Majors: 59%
Matriculants with:
    Baccalaureate degree: 100%
    Graduate degree(s): 6%

Specialty Choice

2005, 2006, 2007 Graduates, Specialty Choice (As reported by program directors to GME Track™)	
Anesthesiology	11%
Emergency Medicine	7%
Family Practice	8%
Internal Medicine	18%
Obstetrics/Gynecology	4%
Orthopaedic Surgery	3%
Pediatrics	13%
Psychiatry	2%
Radiology	6%
Surgery	6%

Financial Information

Source: 2008-2009 LCME I-B survey and 2009-2010 AAMC TSF questionnaire

	Residents	Non-residents
Total Cost of Attendance	$ 60,019	$ 60,019
Tuition and Fees	$ 39,395	$ 39,395
Other (includes living expenses)	$ 18,140	$ 18,140
Health Insurance (can be waived)	$ 2,484	$ 2,484

Average 2009 Graduate Indebtedness: $142,600
% of Enrolled Students Receiving Aid: 88%

Criminal Background Check

This medical school requires a criminal background check prior to matriculation.

University of North Dakota
School of Medicine and Health Sciences
Grand Forks, North Dakota

Secretary, Committee on Admissions
University of North Dakota
School of Medicine and Health Sciences
501 North Columbia Road, Stop 9037
Grand Forks, North Dakota 58202-9037
T 701 777 4221   **F** 701 777 4942

Admissions http://smhs.med.und.nodak.edu/
UNDSMHS/admissions.html
Main www.med.und.nodak.edu
Financial www.med.und.edu/depts/saff/brochure.htm
E-mail jdheit@medicine.nodak.edu

Public Institution

Dr. Joshua Wynne, Dean

*Judy L. DeMers, Associate Dean,
Student Affairs and Admissions*

Eugene DeLorme, Director, INMED Program

Sandra K. Elshaug, Financial Aid Administrator

General Information
The School of Medicine was established in 1905 as a basic science public medical school. In 1973, legislative action created an expanded curriculum and, in 1981, a full four-year medical education program was instituted in the state. The school is university-based and community-integrated.

Mission Statement
The mission of the University of North Dakota School of Medicine and Health Sciences is to educate and prepare physicians, medical scientists, and other health professionals for service to North Dakota and the nation, and to advance medical and biomedical knowledge through research.

Curricular Highlights
Community Service Requirement: Optional. A variety of activities is available.
Research/Thesis Requirement: Required during third year.

The School of Medicine's renewed curriculum was initiated during the 1998-99 academic year. Utilizing a "patient-centered learning" (PCL) approach, the number of lecture hours was reduced significantly, and greater emphasis was placed on small-group teaching and learning, active student participation, and early clinical experience. The curriculum is integrated across disciplines, consisting of four 10-week blocks of instruction during each of the first two years. Students either complete six 8-week clerkships in year 3 or they participate in the ROME (Rural Opportunities in Medical Education) Program, completing 7 months of clinical experience in a rural community. The school emphasizes the training of primary care physicians, but also offers a M.D.-Ph.D. program.

USMLE
Step 1: Required. Students must record a passing score for graduation, but not promotion.
Step 2: Clinical Skills (CS): Required. Students must only record a score.
Step 2: Clinical Knowledge (CK): Required. Students must record a passing total score to graduate.

Selection Factors
A student must maintain a GPA of 3.0 or better to be considered for admission. Selection is based upon the scholastic record, letters of recommendation, MCAT scores, and a personal interview. Interviews are conducted only at the medical school. In addition to high academic achievement, selection is based on a number of factors, including the demonstration of motivation and commitment to a medical career, empathy, compassion in interpersonal relationships, problem-solving, and the ability to work well in small groups. Qualified North Dakota residents are given preference in admission. The only exceptions include a limited number of Minnesota residents or admission through WICHE participation. Only persons who are U.S. citizens or legal permanent residents of the United States are eligible for consideration for admission. The school participates in the Professional Student Exchange Program administered by WICHE, under which legal residents of western states without a medical school may receive preference in admission. WICHE students who are certified and supported by their home state pay resident tuition. The school does not utilize AMCAS. Applications are ranked based on a combination of state of residency, grade-point average, and MCAT scores. The school is unable to accept transfer students from other medical schools except in very unique circumstances.

Financial Aid
The financial resources of applicants are not considered in the selection process. Immediately after acceptance into the School of Medicine, the applicant is sent all available financial aid information and is encouraged to apply. The awarding of financial aid is based on documented need. Loans and a limited number of scholarships and prizes are available. Some awards and scholarships are based on academics as well as need. Students are discouraged from working. The financial aid office may be reached at (701) 777-2849.

Information about Diversity Programs
The INMED (Indians into Medicine) Program is a recruitment and retention program for American Indian students. It is a federally funded program that provides educational opportunities for fully qualified enrolled members of U.S. recognized tribes. State residency is not a consideration for admission through the INMED Program.

Campus Information

Setting
The medical school is located on the UND campus, a state-supported institution located in Grand Forks in the heart of the Red River Valley. The Grand Forks-East Grand Forks (MN) community has a total population of approximately 75,000. UND is classified by the Carnegie Foundation as a high research activity, doctoral/professional and engaged university, and offers a wide diversity of educational programs.

Enrollment
For 2009, total enrollment was: 241

Special Features
The Center for Rural Health is a nationally recognized leader. The Center for Excellence in Neurosciences, the student exchange program with two medical schools in Norway, and elective opportunity in Australia and Peru are other highlights.

Housing
On-campus housing is available in the form of residence halls and apartments for families and single students. A shuttle service runs between the housing area and the main campus. Rental housing also is plentiful in the community.

Satellite Campuses/Facilities
Students are assigned to one of four regional campuses statewide in Bismarck, Fargo, Grand Forks, and Minot for third- and fourth-year clinical experiences.

Application Process and Requirements 2011–2012

Primary Application Service: School specific
Earliest filing date: July 1, 2010
Latest filing date: November 1, 2010

Secondary Application Required?: No
Sent to: All qualified applicants
URL: www.med.und.nodak.edu/
Fee: Yes, $50   **Waiver available:** Yes
Earliest filing date: July 1, 2010
Latest filing date: November 1, 2010

MCAT® required?: Yes
Latest MCAT® considered: September 2010
Oldest MCAT® considered: June 2007

Early Decision Program: School does not have EDP
Applicants notified: n/a
EDP available for: n/a

Regular Acceptance Notice
Earliest date: January 15, 2011
Latest date: Until class is full
Applicant's Response to Acceptance Offer – Maximum Time: Four weeks

Requests for Deferred Entrance Considered: Yes

Deposit to Hold Place in Class: Yes
Deposit (Resident): $100   **(Non-resident):** $100
Deposit due: With response to acceptance offer
Applied to tuition: Yes   **Refundable:** Yes
Refundable by: May 15, 2011

Estimated number of new entrants: 62
EDP: n/a, special program: n/a

Start Month/Year: August 2011

Interview Format: M.D. and Ph.D. faculty members and medical students conduct one-hour interviews. Video interviews are not available.

Other Programs

PREPARATORY PROGRAMS
Postbaccalaureate Program: No
Summer Program: Yes, INMED Program
(701) 777-3039, gdelorme@medicine.nodak.edu

COMBINED DEGREE PROGRAMS
Baccalaureate/M.D.: No
M.D./M.P.H.: Yes, Robert Beattie, M.D.
(701) 777-3264, beattie@medicine.nodak.edu
M.D./M.B.A.: No
M.D./J.D.: No
M.D./Ph.D.: Yes, www.med.und.nodak.edu, John Watt, Ph.D., (701) 777-6225, jwatt@medicine.nodak.edu

Premedical Coursework

On-line courses accepted in fulfillment of prerequisites: On a case-by-case basis

Course	Req.	Rec.	Lab.	Hrs.
Inorganic Chemistry	•		•	8
Behavioral Sciences				
Biochemistry		•		
Biology				
Biology/Zoology	•		•	8
Calculus				
College English	•			6
College Mathematics	•			3

Course	Req.	Rec.	Lab.	Hrs.
Computer Science		•		
Genetics				
Humanities		•		
Organic Chemistry	•		•	8
Physics	•		•	8
Psychology	•			3
Social Sciences				
Other				

Selection Factors: 2009 Accepted Applicants

Proportion of Accepted Applicants with Relevant Experience (Data Self-Reported to AMCAS®)		
Community Service/Volunteer		88%
Medically-Related Work		93%
Research		77%

Shaded bar represents school's accepted scores ranging from the 10th percentile to the 90th percentile   School Median ○   National Median ◯

Overall GPA	2.0	2.1	2.2	2.3	2.4	2.5	2.6	2.7	2.8	2.9	3.0	3.1	3.2	3.3	3.4	3.5	3.6	3.7	(3.8)	3.9	4.0
Science GPA	2.0	2.1	2.2	2.3	2.4	2.5	2.6	2.7	2.8	2.9	3.0	3.1	3.2	3.3	3.4	3.5	3.6	3.7	(3.8)	3.9	4.0

MCAT® Total Numeric Score 9 10 11 12 13 14 15 16 17 18 19 20 21 22 23 24 25 26 27 (28) 29 30 (32) 33 34 35 36 37 38 39 40 41 42 43

Writing Sample			J		K		L	M	N	(O)		P	(Q)	R	S	T
Verbal Reasoning	3	4	5	6	7	8	(9)	(10)	11	12	13	14	15
Biological Sciences	3	4	5	6	7	8	9	(10)	(11)	12	13	14	15
Physical Sciences	3	4	5	6	7	8	(9)	10	(11)	12	13	14	15

Acceptance & Matriculation Data for 2009–2010 First Year Class

	Resident	Non-resident	International	Total
Applications	136	170	0	306
Interviewed	107	44	0	151
Deferred	1	0	0	1
Matriculants				
Early Assurance Program	0	0	0	0
Early Decision Program	0	0	0	0
Baccalaureate/M.D.	0	0	0	0
M.D./Ph.D.	0	0	0	0
Matriculated	43	19	0	**62**

Applications accepted from International Applicants: No

Specialty Choice

2005, 2006, 2007 Graduates, Specialty Choice (As reported by program directors to GME Track™)	
Anesthesiology	1%
Emergency Medicine	10%
Family Practice	17%
Internal Medicine	12%
Obstetrics/Gynecology	12%
Orthopaedic Surgery	6%
Pediatrics	13%
Psychiatry	1%
Radiology	6%
Surgery	7%

Matriculant Demographics: 2009–2010 First Year Class

Men: 22   **Women:** 40

Matriculants' Self-Reported Race/Ethnicity

Mexican American	0	Korean	0
Cuban	0	Vietnamese	0
Puerto Rican	0	Other Asian	0
Other Hispanic	0	Total Asian	2
Total Hispanic	0	Native American	7
Chinese	0	Black	0
Asian Indian	2	Native Hawaiian	0
Pakistani	0	White	53
Filipino	0	Unduplicated Number	
Japanese	0	of Matriculants	62

Science and Math Majors: 72%
Matriculants with:
Baccalaureate degree: 100%
Graduate degree(s): 6%

Financial Information

Source: 2008-2009 LCME I-B survey and 2009-2010 AAMC TSF questionnaire

	Residents	Non-residents
Total Cost of Attendance	$ 44,280	$ 64,205
Tuition and Fees	$ 24,893	$ 44,724
Other (includes living expenses)	$ 19,387	$ 19,481
Health Insurance (can be waived)	$ 0	$ 0

Average 2009 Graduate Indebtedness: $159,376
% of Enrolled Students Receiving Aid: 97%

Criminal Background Check

This medical school requires a criminal background check prior to matriculation.

Case Western Reserve University School of Medicine

Cleveland, Ohio

Office of Admissions, T-308
Case Western Reserve University School of Medicine
10900 Euclid Avenue
Cleveland, Ohio 44106-4920
T 216 368 3450   **F** 216 368 6011

Admissions http://casemed.case.edu/admissions
Main http://casemed.case.edu
Financial http://casemed.case.edu.edu/financial_aid
E-mail casemed-admissions@case.edu

Private Institution

*Dr. Pamela B. Davis, Dean and
Vice President for Medical Affairs*

Dr. Lina Mehta, Associate Dean for Admissions

Christian Essman, Director of Admissions

Wanda L. Rollins, Director of Financial Aid

*Joseph T. Williams, Director of Multicultural
Programs*

General Information

Since 1843, the Case Western Reserve University School of Medicine has been at the forefront of medical education and research. CWRU SOM is one of the nation's leaders in NIH funding. Current educational innovations include curricular reform within the University Track and partnership since 2002 with the Cleveland Clinic in the Cleveland Clinic Lerner College of Medicine (College Track), a distinct program to train physician-investigators.

Mission Statement

To advance the health of humankind through research, service and education.

Curricular Highlights

Community Service Requirement: Optional.
Research/Thesis Requirement: Required.

Case Western School of Medicine offers two types of MD tracks, a Medical Scientist Training program (MSTP), and several dual-degree and masters programs. Applicants may choose one or more tracks through AMCAS by applying to the CWRU School of Medicine, and must interview separately for each. The University track(UT), a 4-year MD program designed to train physician-scholars, is based on four tenets: clinical mastery, research, leadership, and civic professionalism. The innovative curriculum integrates basic sciences, clinical medicine, and population health, focusing on the care of individual patients within social and environmental contexts. Students are introduced to basic sciences in a learner-centered environment which emphasizes small group and team-based learning. Learning is interactive with faculty and students as partners. Independent learning and scholarship are emphasized. Material is organ-

ized in system-based blocks, with basic science and clinical integration throughout the four years. Early clinical experiences include rotating apprenticeships and a longitudinal outpatient preceptorship. A required, mentored research thesis is supported by the Office of Medical Student Research. Advising occurs in small groups by the Office of Student Affairs. The 5-year College Track (CT) admits 32 students, each of whom will graduate with an MD with Special Qualifications in Biomedical Research. A student-centered approach fosters critical thinking and self-directed learning. Basic sciences are taught in small groups using problem-based learning, interactive seminars, journal clubs, and labs; there are no formal lectures. Early clinical experiences include a longitudinal outpatient preceptorship throughout the first two years. A core research curriculum focuses on basic and clinical research and includes hands-on research during the first two summers. A master's level thesis is required. Students document their progress using a portfolio that details skills and expertise they achieve. A physician adviser ensures students' mastery of required competencies. A college level biochemistry course and research experience is required of all applicants to the College Track. Neither program utilizes grades or class rank.

USMLE

Step 1: Required. Students must record a passing score for promotion.
Step 2: Clinical Skills (CS): Required. Students must record a passing total score to graduate.
Step 2: Clinical Knowledge (CK): Required. Students must record a passing total score to graduate.

Selection Factors

The School of Medicine seeks a diverse student body. Students are selected without regard to age, nationality, race, religion, sex, sexual orientation, or state of residence. All candidates must have demonstrated exceptional academic strength and personal achievements. Written statements and letters of recommendation are also important. Transfer students are rarely accepted.

Financial Aid

Financial aid is based on demonstrated need. Merit scholarships may be awarded to some

students with outstanding personal and academic achievement. College Track students do not pay tuition or continuation fees. Accepted students receive financial aid applications in January; awards are made by April.

Information about Diversity Programs

The Office of Multicultural Affairs offers academic and personal support for all underrepresented medical students and recruits students for all programs in the School of Medicine. It sponsors a rigorous, six-week, summer premed/predental program for college freshmen and sophomores and has an NIH-funded summer research program for undergraduate and medical students. The office supports the Case Western Student National Medical Association chapter and the Minority Graduate Student Organization.

Campus Information

Setting
The School of Medicine sits in the heart of the university's 150-acre campus in the city's University Circle area, a cultural and educational hub. Teaching hospitals are adjacent or nearby.

Enrollment
For 2009, total enrollment was: 818

Special Features
Center for Global Health and Diseases offers opportunities for students to study abroad. The Mt. Sinai Skills and Simulation Center offers a state-of-the-art clinical learning laboratory. Center for Reducing Health Disparities offers unique research and community outreach.

Housing
On campus housing is not available, but ample housing exists within walking distance. Rents average $500–$700 month.

Satellite Campuses/Facilities
Teaching hospitals include University Hospitals Case Medical Center (including Rainbow Babies and Children's), Cleveland Clinic, MetroHealth, and the Wade Park VA Hospital.

Application Process and Requirements 2011–2012

Primary Application Service: AMCAS
Earliest filing date: June 1, 2010
Latest filing date: November 1, 2010

Secondary Application Required?: Yes
Sent to: All applicants
URL: Sent when verified AMCAS application is received.
Fee: Yes, $85   **Waiver available:** Yes
Earliest filing date: July 1, 2010
Latest filing date: December 15, 2010

MCAT® required?: Yes
Latest MCAT® considered: September 2010
Oldest MCAT® considered: 2007

Early Decision Program: School does not have EDP
Applicants notified: n/a
EDP available for: n/a

Regular Acceptance Notice
Earliest date: October 15, 2010
Latest date: Until class is full
Applicant's Response to Acceptance Offer – Maximum Time: Four weeks

Requests for Deferred Entrance Considered: Yes

Deposit to Hold Place in Class: No
Deposit (Resident): n/a
Deposit (Non-resident): n/a
Deposit due: n/a
Applied to tuition: n/a   **Refundable:** n/a
Refundable by: n/a

Estimated number of new entrants: 197
EDP: n/a, special program: 5

Start Month/Year: July 2011

Interview Format: UT: one faculty and one student. CT: two faculty and one student interview. Regional interviews are not available. Video interviews are not available.

Other Program

PREPARATORY PROGRAMS
Postbaccalaureate Program: No
Summer Program: Yes, www.smdep.org
Joseph T. Williams, (216) 368-1914
joseph.williams@case.edu

COMBINED DEGREE PROGRAMS
Baccalaureate/M.D.: Yes, http://admission.case.edu/admissions/application/ppsp.asp, Christine DeSalvo (216) 368-5450, christine.desalvo@case.edu
M.D./M.P.H.: Yes, www.casemph.org
Kristina Knight, (216) 368-1967, info@casemph.org
MD/MBA: Yes, http://weatherhead.case.edu/mba/jointDegree/joint_mbaMd.cfm, Deborah Bibb, (216) 368-6702, deborah.bibb@case.edu
M.D./J.D.: Yes, http://law.case.edu/, Alyson Alber, 800-756-0036, alyson.alber@case.edu
M.D./Ph.D.: Yes, http://mstp.cwru.edu
Kathy Schultz, (216) 368-3404, mstp@case.edu
Additional Program: Yes, MD/MS BME, (216) 368-4094, bmedept@case.edu
http://bme.case.edu/

Premedical Coursework

On-line courses accepted in fulfillment of prerequisites: On a case-by-case basis

Course	Req.	Rec.	Lab.	Sems.
Inorganic Chemistry	•		•	2
Behavioral Sciences				
Biochemistry		•		1
Biology	•		•	2
Biology/Zoology				
Calculus				
College English	•			1
College Mathematics				
Computer Science				

Course	Req.	Rec.	Lab.	Sems.
Genetics				
Humanities				
Organic Chemistry	•		•	2
Physics	•		•	2
Psychology				
Social Sciences				
Biochemistry for CT	•			1
Calculus for MSTP	•			2
Epi/biostats			•	1

Selection Factors: 2009 Accepted Applicants

Proportion of Accepted Applicants with Relevant Experience (Data Self-Reported to AMCAS®)			
Community Service/Volunteer			73%
Medically-Related Work			88%
Research			91%

Shaded bar represents school's accepted scores ranging from the 10th percentile to the 90th percentile   School Median ● National Median ◐

Overall GPA	2.0	2.1	2.2	2.3	2.4	2.5	2.6	2.7	2.8	2.9	3.0	3.1	3.2	3.3	3.4	3.5	3.6	3.7	(3.8)	3.9	4.0
Science GPA	2.0	2.1	2.2	2.3	2.4	2.5	2.6	2.7	2.8	2.9	3.0	3.1	3.2	3.3	3.4	3.5	3.6	3.7	(3.8)	3.9	4.0

MCAT® Total Numeric Score 9 10 11 12 13 14 15 16 17 18 19 20 21 22 23 24 25 26 27 28 29 30 31 (32) 33 34 (35) 36 37 38 39 40 41 42 43

Writing Sample			J	K	L	M	N	O	P	(Q)	R	S	T
Verbal Reasoning	3	4	5	6	7	8	9	(10)	(11)	12	13	14	15
Biological Sciences	3	4	5	6	7	8	9	10	(11)	(12)	13	14	15
Physical Sciences	3	4	5	6	7	8	9	10	(11)	(12)	13	14	15

Acceptance & Matriculation Data for 2009–2010 First Year Class

	Resident	Non-resident	International	Total
Applications	737	4457	362	5556
Interviewed	176	1016	104	1296
Deferred	0	2	0	2
Matriculants				
Early Assurance Program	1	5	0	6
Early Decision Program	0	0	0	0
Baccalaureate/M.D.	0	0	0	0
M.D./Ph.D.	4	7	0	11
Matriculated	29	160	10	**199**

Applications accepted from International Applicants: Yes

Matriculant Demographics: 2009–2010 First Year Class

Men: 110   **Women:** 89

Matriculants' Self-Reported Race/Ethnicity

Mexican American	1	Korean	8
Cuban	0	Vietnamese	2
Puerto Rican	1	Other Asian	3
Other Hispanic	5	Total Asian	67
Total Hispanic	7	Native American	0
Chinese	36	Black	20
Asian Indian	15	Native Hawaiian	0
Pakistani	1	White	101
Filipino	1	Unduplicated Number	
Japanese	3	of Matriculants	199

Science and Math Majors: 72%
Matriculants with:
　　Baccalaureate degree: 99%
　　Graduate degree(s): 12%

Specialty Choice

2005, 2006, 2007 Graduates, Specialty Choice (As reported by program directors to GME Track™)	
Anesthesiology	6%
Emergency Medicine	8%
Family Practice	5%
Internal Medicine	14%
Obstetrics/Gynecology	4%
Orthopaedic Surgery	5%
Pediatrics	9%
Psychiatry	7%
Radiology	8%
Surgery	5%

Financial Information

Source: 2008-2009 LCME I-B survey and 2009-2010 AAMC TSF questionnaire

	Residents	Non-residents
Total Cost of Attendance	$ 69,180	$ 69,180
Tuition and Fees	$ 45,970	$ 45,970
Other (includes living expenses)	$ 21,890	$ 21,890
Health Insurance (can be waived)	$ 1,320	$ 1,320

Average 2009 Graduate Indebtedness: $132,811
% of Enrolled Students Receiving Aid: 78%

Criminal Background Check

This medical school requires a criminal background check prior to matriculation.

Northeastern Ohio Universities College of Medicine

Rootstown, Ohio

Office of Admissions and Student Services
Northeastern Ohio Universities College of Medicine
P.O. Box 95
Rootstown, Ohio 44272-0095
T 330 325 6270   F 330 325 8372

Admissions www.neoucom.edu/audience/applicants
Main www.neoucom.edu
Financial www.neoucom.edu/audience/students
E-mail admission@neoucom.edu

Public Institution

Dr. Jay Williamson, Interim Dean

Polly Moss, Assistant Dean, Student Affairs and Admissions

Michelle Cassetty Collins, Director, Admissions and Student Services

General Information

NEOUCOM is a state (public) medical school consisting of a basic medical sciences campus in Rootstown, a consortium of three major public universities and 20 community hospitals with more than 6,500 teaching beds in the greater Akron, Canton, and Youngstown areas. The clinical faculty numbers more than 1,800.

Mission Statement

The mission of the Northeastern Ohio Universities College of Medicine (NEOUCOM) is to graduate qualified physicians oriented to the practice of medicine at the community level, with an emphasis on primary care: family medicine, internal medicine, pediatrics, and obstetrics/gynecology.

Curricular Highlights

Community Service Requirement: Required.
Research/Thesis Requirement: Optional.

The integrated curriculum is offered in five steps. This Longitudinal curriculum includes the biomedical, behavioral, social, community and population health, clinical sciences, and humanities to provide an understanding of the interplay of these in patient care. Step 1: Prologue addresses issues of professionalism, doctor-patient relationships, clinical skills, population health and college orientation; Human Development and Structure emphasizes human anatomy; Molecules to Cells addresses biochemistry, molecular pathology and genetics. Step 2: Physiological Basis of Medicine establishes physiological concepts in the healthy body and the impact of pathologies; Brain, Mind and Behavior includes anatomy, physiology and chemistry of the nervous system; Infection and Immunity integrates the microbiology, immunology and pharmacology of infectious diseases. Step 3: instruction is centered on organ systems pathophysiology, including integrated education in Internal Medicine, Pathology, Pharmacology and

Radiology; with an emphasis on applying knowledge to the clinical settings. Step 4: core clinical clerkships in family medicine, internal medicine, obstetrics/gynecology, pediatrics, psychiatry and surgery and an exploratory experience. Step 5: clinical electives and Clinical Epilogue and Capstone, focusing on professionalism, humanities, social science disciplines and provides vital skills needed as residents and interns.

USMLE

Step 1: Required. Students must record a passing score for promotion.
Step 2: Clinical Skills (CS): Required. Students must only record score.
Step 2: Clinical Knowledge (CK): Required. Students must record a passing total score to graduate.

Selection Factors

Applicants must demonstrate strong academic preparation as measured by GPAs and MCAT scores, and show motivation for the practice of medicine. Interviews are by invitation only. Admission preference is given to Ohio residents. All applicants are considered; no formulas are used for selection. Only those who complete the secondary application are given consideration. Early submission of application material is strongly encouraged, particularly through the Early Decision Program (EDP).

Financial Aid

Loan funds are available through federal sources to all students who qualify. Limited campus-based financial aid in the form of loans and grants are also available and is based on financial need as determined by the FAFSA. Parental information is required for all students seeking campus-based aid consideration. Limited scholarship opportunities are also available for disadvantaged and/or medical students from groups underrepresented in medicine. Application information is provided upon acceptance. Private counseling and debt management programs are offered to all students.

Information about Diversity Programs

NEOUCOM believes that diversity is a value that is central to its educational, research, service and health care missions. The Admissions Committee conducts a holistic review of all

qualified applicants, striving to bring together a diverse student body constituted by academically gifted, highly motivated, resilient students who share a deep committment to the values and goals of our profession and the College.

Campus Information

Setting

Rootstown is 20 minutes from Akron and 50 minutes from Cleveland. The 105-acre NEOUCOM complex, centrally located among the consortium universities (The University of Akron, Kent State University and Youngstown State University) and clinical campuses, houses the College's administrative offices, and the divisions of basic medical sciences and community health sciences.

Enrollment

For 2009, total enrollment was: 474

Special Features

The state-of-the-art facilities on campus include the Wasson Center for Clinical Skills Training, Assessment, and Scholarship; newly renovated lecture halls; multidisciplinary labs; and the Regional Medical Informational Center, which houses more than 110,000 books and more than 725 journals. For relaxation, students can enjoy the workout room, student lounge, and basketball, tennis, and volleyball courts.

Housing

NEOUCOM maintains a listing of local housing options; no on-campus housing is available.

Satellite Campuses/Facilities

Rotations are completed among 20 associated hospitals, eight of which are major teaching facilities.

Application Process and Requirements 2011–2012

Primary Application Service: AMCAS
Earliest filing date: June 1, 2010
Latest filing date: December 15, 2010

Secondary Application Required?: Yes
Sent to: All Applicants
Contact: Luke Gloeckner, (303) 325-6274
URL: www.neoucom.edu/audience/applicants
Fee: Yes, $75   **Waiver available:** Yes
Earliest filing date: June 1, 2010
Latest filing date: December 1, 2010

MCAT® required?: Yes
Latest MCAT® considered: December 2010
Oldest MCAT® considered: June 2008

Early Decision Program: School does have EDP
Applicants notified: October 1, 2010
EDP available for: Both Residents and Non-residents

Regular Acceptance Notice
Earliest date: October 1, 2010
Latest date: Until class is full
Applicant's Response to Acceptance Offer – Maximum Time: Two weeks

Requests for Deferred Entrance Considered: Yes

Deposit to Hold Place in Class: Yes
Deposit (Resident): $100   **(Non-resident):** $100
Deposit due: Two weeks after offer of acceptance
Applied to tuition: Yes   **Refundable:** No
Refundable by: n/a

Estimated number of new entrants: 30
EDP: 5, special program: 80

Start Month/Year: August 2011

Interview Format: 30-minute interview by two faculty. Regional interviews are not available. Video interviews are not available.

Other Programs

PREPARATORY PROGRAMS
Postbaccalaureate Program: No
Summer Program: No

COMBINED DEGREE PROGRAMS
Baccalaureate/M.D.: Yes www.neoucom.edu/audience/applicants
(330) 325-6270, admission@neoucom.edu
M.D./M.P.H.: Yes
MD/MBA: Yes
M.D./J.D.: No
M.D./Ph.D.: Yes
Additional Program: Yes, Pharmacy, M.S.,Ph.D., (330) 325-6270, www.neoucom.edu/PharmD

Premedical Coursework

On-line courses accepted in fulfillment of prerequisites: No

Course	Req.	Rec.	Lab.	Sems.	Course	Req.	Rec.	Lab.	Sems.
Inorganic Chemistry		•			Computer Science				
Behavioral Sciences		•			Genetics		•		
Biochemistry		•			Humanities		•		
Biology	•			1	Organic Chemistry	•			2
Biology/Zoology		•			Physics	•			2
Calculus		•			Psychology		•		
College English		•			Social Sciences		•		
College Mathematics		•			Other				

Selection Factors: 2009 Accepted Applicants

Proportion of Accepted Applicants with Relevant Experience (Data Self-Reported to AMCAS®)		
Community Service/Volunteer		51%
Medically-Related Work		57%
Research		50%

Shaded bar represents school's accepted scores ranging from the 10th percentile to the 90th percentile. School Median ● National Median ○

Overall GPA 2.0 2.1 2.2 2.3 2.4 2.5 2.6 2.7 2.8 2.9 3.0 3.1 3.2 3.3 3.4 3.5 3.6 (3.7) 3.8 3.9 4.0
Science GPA 2.0 2.1 2.2 2.3 2.4 2.5 2.6 2.7 2.8 2.9 3.0 3.1 3.2 3.3 3.4 3.5 (3.6) 3.7 3.8 3.9 4.0

MCAT® Total Numeric Score 9 10 11 12 13 14 15 16 17 18 19 20 21 22 23 24 25 26 27 (28) 29 30 31 (32) 33 34 35 36 37 38 39 40 41 42 43

Writing Sample				J	K	L	M	N	(O)	P	(Q)	R	S	T	
Verbal Reasoning	3	4	5	6	7	8	(9)	(10)	11	12	13	14	15		
Biological Sciences	3	4	5	6	7	8	9	(10)	(11)	12	13	14	15		
Physical Sciences	3	4	5	6	7	8	(9)	10	(11)	12	13	14	15		

Acceptance & Matriculation Data for 2009–2010 First Year Class

	Resident	Non-resident	International	Total
Applications	837	1044	18	1899
Interviewed	122	8	0	130
Deferred	2	1	0	3
Matriculants				
Early Assurance Program	0	0	0	0
Early Decision Program	4	0	0	4
Baccalaureate/M.D.	59	2	0	61
M.D./Ph.D.	0	0	0	0
Matriculated	98	9	0	**107**

Applications accepted from International Applicants: No

Matriculant Demographics: 2009–2010 First Year Class

Men: 55   **Women:** 52

Matriculants' Self-Reported Race/Ethnicity

Mexican American	1	Korean	2
Cuban	2	Vietnamese	0
Puerto Rican	1	Other Asian	4
Other Hispanic	2	Total Asian	39
Total Hispanic	5	Native American	0
Chinese	5	Black	1
Asian Indian	26	Native Hawaiian	0
Pakistani	3	White	64
Filipino	1	Unduplicated Number	
Japanese	0	of Matriculants	107

Science and Math Majors: 64%
Matriculants with:
Baccalaureate degree: 100%
Graduate degree(s): 3%

Specialty Choice

2005, 2006, 2007 Graduates, Specialty Choice (As reported by program directors to GME Track™)	
Anesthesiology	7%
Emergency Medicine	8%
Family Practice	6%
Internal Medicine	23%
Obstetrics/Gynecology	8%
Orthopaedic Surgery	4%
Pediatrics	7%
Psychiatry	2%
Radiology	6%
Surgery	7%

Financial Information

Source: 2008-2009 LCME I-B survey and 2009-2010 AAMC TSF questionnaire

	Residents	Non-residents
Total Cost of Attendance	$ 54,693	$ 83,306
Tuition and Fees	$ 30,599	$ 59,212
Other (includes living expenses)	$ 22,680	$ 22,680
Health Insurance (can be waived)	$ 1,414	$ 1,414

Average 2009 Graduate Indebtedness: $150,375
% of Enrolled Students Receiving Aid: 88%

Criminal Background Check

This medical school requires a criminal background check prior to matriculation.

The Ohio State University College of Medicine
Columbus, Ohio

Admissions Office, The Ohio State University
College of Medicine
155D Meiling Hall, 370 West 9th Avenue
Columbus, Ohio 43210-1238
T 614 292 7137   **F** 614 247 7959

Admissions http://medicine.osu.edu/students/admissions/Pages/index.aspx
Main http://medicine.osu.edu/Pages/default.aspx
Financial http://medicine.osu.edu/students/financial_services/Pages/index.aspx
E-mail medicine@osu.edu

Public Institution

Dr. Wiley Chip Souba, Dean

Dr. Quinn Capers, IV, Associate Dean, Admissions

Dr. Leon McDougle, Assistant Dean, Minority Affairs

Samuel Matheny, Director, Financial Services

Lorna Kenyon, Director, Admissions

General Information

Since 1914 The Ohio State University College of Medicine has blended traditional medical education, innovative learning opportunities, and a strong reputation in the preparation of students for primary care and specialized residencies, encouraging research interests and a strong emphasis on a biopsychosocial approach to patient care.

Mission Statement

The Ohio State University College of Medicine seeks to recruit self-directed learners who are driven to become empathetic physicians providing evidence-based, compassionate medical care. The Admissions Committee will assemble a class that displays diversity in background and thought, strong intellect, and the potential to improve people's lives through innovation in research, education and community service.

Curricular Highlights

Community Service Requirement: Required. Clinical Assessment and Problem Solving component.
Research/Thesis Requirement: Optional.

Initial ten-week gross anatomy and embryology course, followed by choice of two preclinical pathways. Integrated Pathway features body systems-oriented content that fuses basic and clinical sciences using methods of student-centered active learning, small-group case-based discussion, and lectures. Independent Study Pathway students use highly structured objectives, resource guides, Web and computer-based materials to read, review, and learn on their own. Clinical experiences begin in the first year with the Clinical Assessment and Problem Solving course. Additionally, stan-

dardized patients help students build clinical proficiency in the state-of-the-art clinical skills center. Third-year clerkships include family medicine, internal medicine, obstetrics and gynecology, pediatrics, psychiatry, neurology, surgery and one elective. A clinical skills immersion experience ensures all students have an in-depth understanding of a core set of procedurally based clinical skills. Fourth-year selectives focus on caring for patients at various stages of illness and wellness: undifferentiated patient; patient with chronic care needs; and a sub-internship. In the fourth year, students also have 4 months of elective rotations and 3 months of vacation.

USMLE

Step 1: Required. Students must record a passing score for promotion.
Step 2: Clinical Skills (CS): Required. Students must record a passing total score to graduate.
Step 2: Clinical Knowledge (CK): Required. Students must record a passing total score to graduate.

Selection Factors

Completed applications are reviewed to ensure that excellent candidates who do not fit the general profile are not overlooked. Factors considered include clinical experiences, community service and leadership activities, research experience, recommendations, suitability for the study of medicine, and extracurricular activities.

Financial Aid

There is need-based financial aid assistance. Students participate in various scholarship and low-interest loan programs. Accepted candidates are mailed financial aid materials prior to entering to be considered with students already in school. Financial need is not a deterrent to acceptance. Every effort is made to assist each student in securing sufficient resources for continuing their education.

Information about Diversity Programs

The Admissions Committee considers diversity to be a desirable characteristic in the student body. Students whose previous educational and economic deprivation warrants special consideration are carefully evaluated and

offered special help in the acquisition of additional resources. The Medpath Medical Careers Pathway is a postbaccalaureate program aimed at developing the academic knowledge base and skills of students enhancing their preparation for medical school.

Campus Information

Setting

The Ohio State University has the nation's largest single college campus enrollment and the resources that go with it. Columbus offers diversity in the arts, cultural events, festivals, restaurants, sports, and nightlife.

Enrollment

For 2009, total enrollment was: 855

Special Features

The Ohio State Medical Center is at the center of cutting-edge developments in the areas of clinical care, education, and research. ProjectONE, a $1 billion major expansion project, will transform the Medical Center's central campus with a centralized single tower that will house a new cancer hospital and research institute, along with a new critical care building and integrated spaces for research, education and patient care. The OSU Medical Center leads the region with 10 specialties named as among the best in America in the latest U.S. News & World Report magazine. OSU Medical Center is among only 21 hospitals in the country named to the magazines elite Honor Roll, which demonstrates a hospital's excellence in at least six specialties

Housing

The Neil Building and the Gateway Center offer professional student housing. Victorian Village and Grandview Heights are also popular. Rent: $400–2000 monthly.

Satellite Campuses/Facilities

Clinical rotations occur within the Medical Center, at community hospitals within Columbus and Ohio, in rural settings in Ohio, and at locations outside of Ohio. About 35 percent of the fourth-year class gains exposure to international health care with the assistance of the College of Medicine Office of Global Health.

Application Process and Requirements 2011–2012

Primary Application Service: AMCAS
Earliest filing date: June 1, 2010
Latest filing date: December 1, 2010

Secondary Application Required?: Yes
Sent to: All applicants
Contact: Admissions Office
(614) 292-7137, medicine@osu.edu
Fee: Yes, $80 **Waiver available:** Yes
Earliest filing date: July 1, 2010
Latest filing date: December 15, 2010

MCAT® required?: Yes
Latest MCAT® considered: September 2010
Oldest MCAT® considered: 2007

Early Decision Program: School does have EDP
Applicants notified: October 1, 2010
EDP available for: Both Residents and Non-residents

Regular Acceptance Notice
Earliest date: October 16, 2010
Latest date: Varies
Applicant's Response to Acceptance Offer – Maximum Time: Two weeks

Requests for Deferred Entrance Considered: Yes

Deposit to Hold Place in Class: No
Deposit (Resident): n/a **(Non-resident):** n/a
Deposit due: n/a
Applied to tuition: n/a **Refundable:** n/a
Refundable by: n/a

Estimated number of new entrants: 200
EDP: 10, special program: 15

Start Month/Year: August 2011

Interview Format: Open-file conversation; one faculty interview and one student interview. Regional interviews are not available. Video interviews are not available.

Other Programs

PREPARATORY PROGRAMS
Postbaccalaureate Program: Yes, http://medicine.osu.edu/students/diversity/Programs/medpath/Pages/index.aspx, Nikki Radcliffe, (614) 292-3161, nikki.radcliffe@osumc.edu
Summer Program: Yes, Nikki Radcliffe, (614) 292-3161, nikki.radcliffe@osumc.edu

COMBINED DEGREE PROGRAMS
Baccalaureate/M.D.: Yes, http://medicine.osu.edu/students/admissions/medicaladmissionspathway/Pags/index.aspx
Anne Krabacher, (614) 292-3951, krabacher.4@osu.edu
M.D./M.P.H.: Yes, http://cph.osu.edu/academics/dualcombined.cfm, (614) 293-3907, sph@osu.edu
M.D./MBA: Yes, https://fisher.osu.edu/myfisher/login, shergrad@cob.osu.edu
M.D./J.D.: Yes, http://moritzlaw.osu.edu/programs/joint_degree.php
(614) 292-8810, lawadmit@osu.edu
M.D./Ph.D.: Yes, http://biomed.osu.edu/mdphd/
Ashley Bertran, (614) 292-7790

Premedical Coursework

On-line courses accepted in fulfillment of prerequisites: No

Course	Req.	Rec.	Lab.	Sems.
Inorganic Chemistry	•		•	2
Behavioral Sciences		•		
Biochemistry	•			1
Biology	•			2
Biology/Zoology				
Calculus				
College English		•		
College Mathematics				
Computer Science				

Course	Req.	Rec.	Lab.	Sems.
Genetics		•		
Humanities				
Organic Chemistry	•		•	2
Physics	•		•	2
Psychology		•		
Social Sciences		•		
Diversity/Ethics		•		
Anatomy (any area)	•			1
Other				

Selection Factors: 2009 Accepted Applicants

Proportion of Accepted Applicants with Relevant Experience (Data Self-Reported to AMCAS®)		
Community Service/Volunteer		74%
Medically-Related Work		86%
Research		88%

Shaded bar represents school's accepted scores ranging from the 10th percentile to the 90th percentile   School Median ●   National Median ○

Overall GPA 2.0 2.1 2.2 2.3 2.4 2.5 2.6 2.7 2.8 2.9 3.0 3.1 3.2 3.3 3.4 3.5 3.6 3.7 (3.8) 3.9 4.0
Science GPA 2.0 2.1 2.2 2.3 2.4 2.5 2.6 2.7 2.8 2.9 3.0 3.1 3.2 3.3 3.4 3.5 3.6 3.7 (3.8) 3.9 4.0

MCAT® Total Numeric Score 9 10 11 12 13 14 15 16 17 18 19 20 21 22 23 24 25 26 27 28 29 30 31 (32) 33 (34) 35 36 37 38 39 40 41 42 43

Writing Sample			J	K	L	M	N	O	P	(Q)	R	S	T
Verbal Reasoning	3	4	5	6	7	8	9	(10)	(11)	12	13	14	15
Biological Sciences	3	4	5	6	7	8	9	10	(11)	(12)	13	14	15
Physical Sciences	3	4	5	6	7	8	9	10	(11)	12	13	14	15

Acceptance & Matriculation Data for 2009–2010 First Year Class

	Resident	Non-resident	International	Total
Applications	1044	3103	38	4185
Interviewed	279	410	0	689
Deferred	9	6	0	15
Matriculants				
Early Assurance Program	0	0	0	0
Early Decision Program	2	0	0	2
Baccalaureate/M.D.	8	0	0	8
M.D./Ph.D.	2	2	0	4
Matriculated	129	91	0	**220**

Applications accepted from International Applicants: No

Specialty Choice

2005, 2006, 2007 Graduates, Specialty Choice (As reported by program directors to GME Track™)	
Anesthesiology	5%
Emergency Medicine	5%
Family Practice	8%
Internal Medicine	23%
Obstetrics/Gynecology	4%
Orthopaedic Surgery	5%
Pediatrics	8%
Psychiatry	4%
Radiology	4%
Surgery	7%

Matriculant Demographics: 2009–2010 First Year Class

Men: 121   **Women:** 99

Matriculants' Self-Reported Race/Ethnicity

Mexican American	14	Korean	7
Cuban	4	Vietnamese	1
Puerto Rican	5	Other Asian	1
Other Hispanic	2	Total Asian	36
Total Hispanic	21	Native American	2
Chinese	7	Black	21
Asian Indian	17	Native Hawaiian	1
Pakistani	1	White	155
Filipino	1	Unduplicated Number	
Japanese	1	of Matriculants	220

Science and Math Majors: 66%
Matriculants with:
Baccalaureate degree: 100%
Graduate degree(s): 5%

Financial Information

Source: 2008-2009 LCME I-B survey and 2009-2010 AAMC TSF questionnaire

	Residents	Non-residents
Total Cost of Attendance	$ 50,865	$ 66,375
Tuition and Fees	$ 29,403	$ 44,913
Other (includes living expenses)	$ 19,737	$ 19,737
Health Insurance (can be waived)	$ 1,725	$ 1,725

Average 2009 Graduate Indebtedness: $144,271
% of Enrolled Students Receiving Aid: 88%

Criminal Background Check

This medical school requires a criminal background check prior to matriculation.

University of Cincinnati College of Medicine

Cincinnati, Ohio

Office of Student Affairs/Admissions
University of Cincinnati College of Medicine
P.O. Box 670552
Cincinnati, Ohio 45267-0552
T 513 558 7314   **F** 513 558 1165

Admissions www.med.uc.edu/admissions/
Main www.med.uc.edu
Financial http://medonestop.uc.edu
E-mail comadmis@ucmail.uc.edu

Public Institution

Dr. David M. Stern, Dean

Dr. Laura Wexler, Sr. Associate Dean for Student Affairs/Admissions

Dr. Charles W. Collins, Associate Dean for Diversity and Community Affairs

Dr. Daniel Burr, Assistant Dean for Student Financial Planning

Dr. R. Stephen Manuel, Assistant Dean for Admissions

General Information

The UCCOM provides both outstanding research facilities and superb clinical and teaching experiences. Graduates, ranked as highly competitive by national residency program directors, choose careers in a broad range of specialty areas. Extensive research opportunities are available. UCCOM is ranked in the top third among all public medical schools in NIH, research funding.

Mission Statement

The mission of the University of Cincinnati College of Medicine is to improve the health of the public by educating physicians and scientists and by producing new knowledge.

Curricular Highlights

Community Service Requirement: Optional.
Research/Thesis Requirement: Optional.

UCCOM provides a stimulating learning environment, creating the undifferentiated M.D. ready to excel in residency training and provide excellent patient care. Using an integrated curricular approach including lab, small-group discussion, and team-based learning and lectures, the first two years provide students with the scientific, clinical and humanistic principles of medicine. Year 1 focuses on the normal structure, function and development of the human body. Year 2 emphasizes the basis and mechanisms of human disease. During Year 3, students rotate through six core clerkships. Students also begin exploring career options by participating in three specialty clerkships of their choosing. In Year 4, students hone their clinical skills during their Acting Internship

and required Neuroscience selectives. Students can also choose from over 100 elective offerings.

USMLE

Step 1: Required. Students must record a passing score for promotion.
Step 2: Clinical Skills (CS): Required. Students must record a passing total score to graduate.
Step 2: Clinical Knowledge (CK): Required. Students must record a passing total score to graduate.

Selection Factors

After AMCAS, secondary applications and letters of recommendations are received, completed applicants are evaluated for interviews. The UCCOM Web site provides applicants with admissions progress information. The College utilizes the Multiple Mini Interview and the interview day consists of a description of the College and student services and includes: a presentation about the admissions process, curriculum, student services, financial aid, lunch, and tour. Acceptance offers are based on the overall and holistic evaluation of academic and personal qualities. Postbaccalaureate and graduate coursework will be considered. Personal characteristics include demonstrated motivation, maturity, coping skills, interpersonal skills, sensitivity and tolerance toward others and communication and critical-thinking skills. Students are admitted regardless of age, religion, gender, sexual orientation, race, color, or national origin.

Financial Aid

The College provides counseling to help students fund their medical education and make sound financial decisions. Accepted applicants receive a financial aid packet in February. Applicants with complete files are sent estimated award letters by May 15. To be considered for need-based aid, applicants must submit the Need Access application, which includes parental information. Further information at *www.medonestop.uc.edu.*

Information about Diversity Programs

UCCOM Office of Diversity & Community Affairs works to increase diversity of the medical student body, residency training programs and faculty through regional and national

recruitment efforts of underrepresented groups. The Office retention activities include mentoring, connections with community physicians, academic & psychological support and career development. Community partners support the office activities.

Campus Information

Setting

The clinical facilities of University Hospital, VA Medical Center, Cincinnati Children's Hospital Medical Center and Shriners Hospital for Children, along with the Cardiovascular Research Center and Vontz Center for Molecular Studies, are all within walking distance of the college. In 2008, the UCCOM opened the doors of the Care/Crawley Building. Easily accessible by free shuttle service to the main campus are other dining options, a convenience store and top-of-the-line recreation facilities.

Enrollment

For 2009, total enrollment was: 637

Special Features

The Medical Student Scholars Program (MSSP) provides students with extracurricular clinical and didactic experiences throughout their education in topical areas such as Neuroscience; Geriatrics; Child and Adolescent Health; and Nutrition. The Poverty, Justice and Health elective explores international health and includes lectures, discussions and an opportunity to visit Honduras with a medical team. Cincinnati Children's Hospital Medical Center is one of the top pediatric hospitals in the country, providing research and outstanding clinical opportunities. The Center for Surgical Intervention (CSI) bridges new technology in biomedical and surgical care. Using robotics, medical simulation, telecommunications and medical informatics, the CSI uses new technology in surgical procedures.

Housing

While graduate housing is available on campus, most medical school students reside off campus. Housing information is provided, and students are encouraged to look for housing early.

Application Process and Requirements 2011–2012

Primary Application Service: AMCAS
Earliest filing date: June 1, 2010
Latest filing date: November 15, 2010

Secondary Application Required?: Yes
Sent to: All applicants
URL: www.MedOneStop.uc.edu
Fee: Yes, $25   **Waiver available:** Yes
Earliest filing date: July 15, 2010
Latest filing date: December 15, 2010

MCAT® required?: Yes
Latest MCAT® considered: September 2010
Oldest MCAT® considered: April 2008

Early Decision Program: School does have EDP
Applicants notified: October 1, 2010
EDP available for: Both Residents and Non-residents

Regular Acceptance Notice
Earliest date: October 15, 2010
Latest date: Varies
Applicant's Response to Acceptance
Offer – Maximum Time: Two weeks

Requests for Deferred
Entrance Considered: Yes

Deposit to Hold Place in Class: No
Deposit (Resident): n/a   **(Non-resident):** n/a
Deposit due: n/a
Applied to tuition: n/a   **Refundable:** n/a
Refundable by: n/a

Estimated number of new entrants: 165
EDP: 12, special program: 18

Start Month/Year: August 2011

Interview Format: Multiple Mini Interview with a series of six-eight short interviews, one interview at a time, focused on the discussion of common scenarios. Regional interviews are not available. Video interviews are not available.

Other Programs

PREPARATORY PROGRAMS
Postbaccalaureate Program: Yes, www.mcp.uc.edu, Karen Coleman, (513) 558-3104, karen.coleman@uc.edu
Summer Program: Yes, www.med.uc.edu/admissions/summerenrich.cfm
Lathel Bryant, (513) 558-0693, lathel.bryant@uc.edu

COMBINED DEGREE PROGRAMS
Baccalaureate/M.D.: Yes, www.med.uc.edu/HS2MD, Nikki Bibler, (513) 558-5581, DualAdmissionsProgram@uc.edu
M.D./M.P.H.: Yes, http://www.med.uc.edu/PublicHealth/Degree.cfm, William A. Mase, (513) 558-2710 or 558-2737, william.mase@uc.edu
MD/MBA: Yes, www.business.uc.edu, Andrew Vogel, (513) 556-7020, graduate@uc.edu
M.D./Ph.D.: Yes, www.med.uc.edu/pstp, Patrick Tso, (513) 558-2380, patrick.tso@uc.edu

Premedical Coursework

On-line courses accepted in fulfillment of prerequisites: Yes

Course	Req.	Rec.	Lab.	Sems.
Inorganic Chemistry		•		
Behavioral Sciences		•		
Biochemistry		•		
Biology		•		
Biology/Zoology		•		
Calculus		•		
College English		•		
College Mathematics		•		

Course	Req.	Rec.	Lab.	Sems.
Computer Science		•		
Genetics		•		
Humanities		•		
Organic Chemistry		•		
Physics		•		
Psychology		•		
Social Sciences		•		
Other				

Selection Factors: 2009 Accepted Applicants

Proportion of Accepted Applicants with Relevant Experience (Data Self-Reported to AMCAS®)		Community Service/Volunteer	65%
		Medically-Related Work	80%
		Research	80%

Shaded bar represents school's accepted scores ranging from the 10th percentile to the 90th percentile   School Median ●   National Median ●

Overall GPA	2.0	2.1	2.2	2.3	2.4	2.5	2.6	2.7	2.8	2.9	3.0	3.1	3.2	3.3	3.4	3.5	3.6	(3.7)	3.8	3.9	4.0
Science GPA	2.0	2.1	2.2	2.3	2.4	2.5	2.6	2.7	2.8	2.9	3.0	3.1	3.2	3.3	3.4	3.5	3.6	(3.7)	3.8	3.9	4.0

MCAT® Total Numeric Score 9 10 11 12 13 14 15 16 17 18 19 20 21 22 23 24 25 26 27 28 29 30 31 (32 33) 34 35 36 37 38 39 40 41 42 43

	J	K	L	M	N	O	P	(Q)	R	S	T
Writing Sample											
Verbal Reasoning	3	4	5	6	7	8	9	(10)	(11)	12	13	14	15
Biological Sciences	3	4	5	6	7	8	9	10	(11)	12	13	14	15
Physical Sciences	3	4	5	6	7	8	9	10	(11)	12	13	14	15

Acceptance & Matriculation Data for 2009–2010 First Year Class

	Resident	Non-resident	International	Total
Applications	1111	2496	21	3628
Interviewed	366	276	0	642
Deferred	1	1	0	2
Matriculants				
Early Assurance Program	19	1	0	20
Early Decision Program	6	0	0	6
Baccalaureate/M.D.	0	0	0	0
M.D./Ph.D.	3	2	0	5
Matriculated	109	57	0	**166**

Applications accepted from International Applicants: No

Matriculant Demographics: 2009–2010 First Year Class

Men: 89   **Women:** 77

Matriculants' Self-Reported Race/Ethnicity

Mexican American	3	Korean	8
Cuban	0	Vietnamese	1
Puerto Rican	0	Other Asian	3
Other Hispanic	1	Total Asian	54
Total Hispanic	4	Native American	0
Chinese	21	Black	8
Asian Indian	19	Native Hawaiian	0
Pakistani	3	White	104
Filipino	0	Unduplicated Number	
Japanese	1	of Matriculants	166

Science and Math Majors: 75%
Matriculants with:
   Baccalaureate degree: 100%
   Graduate degree(s): 20%

Specialty Choice

2005, 2006, 2007 Graduates, Specialty Choice
(As reported by program directors to GME Track™)

Anesthesiology	6%
Emergency Medicine	7%
Family Practice	9%
Internal Medicine	14%
Obstetrics/Gynecology	5%
Orthopaedic Surgery	5%
Pediatrics	13%
Psychiatry	7%
Radiology	5%
Surgery	9%

Financial Information

Source: 2008-2009 LCME I-B survey and 2009-2010 AAMC TSF questionnaire

	Residents	Non-residents
Total Cost of Attendance	$ 49,914	$ 65,864
Tuition and Fees	$ 29,385	$ 45,135
Other (includes living expenses)	$ 19,188	$ 19,388
Health Insurance (can be waived)	$ 1,341	$ 1,341

Average 2009 Graduate Indebtedness: $146,407
% of Enrolled Students Receiving Aid: 88%

Criminal Background Check

This medical school requires a criminal background check prior to matriculation.

The University of Toledo College of Medicine

(Formerly Medical University of Ohio)

Toledo, Ohio

Admissions Office
3000 Arlington Avenue, Mail Stop 1043
Toledo, Ohio 43614
T 419 383 4229   F 419 383 3322

Admissions www.utoledo.edu/med/md/admissions/index.html
Main www.utoledo.edu/med/md/
Financial www.utoledo.edu/financialaid/hsc/index.html
E-mail medadmissions@utoledo.edu

Public Institution

Dr. Jeffrey P. Gold, Dean

Dr. James F. Kleshinski, Associate Dean for Admissions

Dr. Imran Ali, Associate Dean for Medical Education, Professionalism & Diversity

Carolyn Baumgartner, Director, Student Financial Aid

Dr. Robert S. Crissman, Assistant Dean for Admissions

Dr. Patricia Hogue, Assistant Dean of Diversity

General Information

The Medical University of Ohio and the University of Toledo merged on July 1, 2006, thus creating the third largest university in Ohio, which is now known as The University of Toledo. Four health and research colleges are located on the Health Science Campus: the College of Medicine, the College of Health Science and Human Service, the College of Nursing, and the College of Graduate Studies.

Mission Statement

The mission of The University of Toledo College of Medicine is to improve the human condition. We do this by providing a world-class education for the next generation of physicians and scientists, by creating new knowledge that is translated into cutting-edge clinical practice, and by providing the highest level of professionalism and compassion as we deliver university quality health care.

Curricular Highlights

Community Service Requirement: Optional.
Research/Thesis Requirement: Optional.

The preclinical basic science content is integrated into the following interdisciplinary instructional units: Cellular and Molecular Biology, Human Structure and Development, Neurosciences/ Behaviroal Science, Immunity and Infection and Organ Systems. All students participate in a Clinical Decision Making course, which spans the first two years. This course provide medical students with the fundamental knowledge and skills necessary for clini-

cal decision making. The third year of the curriculum is devoted to mandatory clerkships in internal medicine, surgery, pediatrics, obstetrics and gynecology, psychiatry and family medicine. The fourth year includes a basic science elective requirement as well as a required acting internship. Twenty-four weeks of clinical electives are available. Most components of the curriculum are evaluated on an Honors, High Pass, Pass, Fail System.

USMLE

Step 1: Required. Students must record a passing score for promotion.
Step 2: Clinical Skills (CS): Required. Students must record a passing total score to graduate.
Step 2: Clinical Knowledge (CK): Required. Students must record a passing total score to graduate.

Selection Factors

Interviews are by invitation only. Re-applicants are not penalized. Preference is given to Ohio residents.

Financial Aid

Financial aid is awarded on the basis of demonstrated financial need according to federal methodology. Applicants for financial aid must file the FAFSA. Several full tuition Presidential Scholarships are available, as well as a number of both merit and need-based scholarships. Many students are employed during the academic year in the Federal Work-Study Program. Employment opportunities in research, community health, family practice, and acute care are also provided through the summer preceptorship programs.

Information about Diversity Programs

The University of Toledo is committed to increasing opportunities for individuals traditionally underrepresented groups, as well as those from economically disadvantaged backgrounds. The Admissions Office works in cooperation with the Office of Faculty and Student Diversity, Recruitment and Retention, the Office for Institutional Diversity and the Office of Student Affairs and other campus departments in the recruitment, selection, and retention of qualified students.

Campus Information

Setting

The University of Toledo Health Science Campus is located on 475 acres in suburban south Toledo, approximately three miles south of the Main Campus. Toledo's many cultural attractions include the world famous Toledo Museum of Art, a symphony orchestra, opera company, and a zoological gardens. Recreational activities include metroparks, boating, fishing, hiking, and cross-country skiing.

Enrollment

For 2009, total enrollment was: 666

Special Features

Four schools comprise the University of Toledo Health Science Campus: the College of Medicine, College of Nursing, College of Graduate Studies, and College of Health Science and Human Service. Researchers received more than $21 million in research grants and contracts in the 2009 fiscal year. Major areas of research include cellular and molecular neurobiology, molecular and cellular biology, and the molecular basis of diseases, covering such areas as cancer, diabetes, cardiovascular diseases, molecular and cellular immunology, and vaccine development.

Housing

On-campus housing is available on the main campus.

Satellite Campuses/Facilities

The clinical clerkships are completed at The University of Toledo Medical Center on the Health Science Campus, as well as at several other area teaching hospitals, including St. Vincent Mercy Medical Center, The Toledo Hospital, Mercy Children's Hospital, Toledo Children's Hospital, Flower Hospital, and St. Luke's Hospital. All students complete a minimum of 8 weeks of clerkships in a rural Area Health Education Center. Opportunities are also available for students to do their required clerkships at Riverside Methodist Hospital in Columbus, Ohio, St. Joseph's and St. Mary's Health System in South-ern Michigan and at Henry Ford Health System in Detroit, Michigan. In the fourth-year, students are able to complete up to several months of elective rotations at other approved institutions.

Application Process and Requirements 2011–2012

Primary Application Service: AMCAS
Earliest filing date: June 1, 2010
Latest filing date: November 1, 2010

Secondary Application Required?: Yes
Sent to: Screened applicants
URL: http://hsc.utoledo.edu/med/md/admissions/secondary.html
Fee: Yes, $80 **Waiver available:** Yes
Earliest filing date: June 15, 2010
Latest filing date: January 1, 2011

MCAT® required?: Yes
Latest MCAT® considered: September 2010
Oldest MCAT® considered: September 2008

Early Decision Program: School does have EDP
Applicants notified: October 1, 2010
EDP available for: Residents only

**Regular Acceptance Notice
Earliest date:** October 15, 2010
Latest date: Until class is full
**Applicant's Response to Acceptance
Offer – Maximum Time:** Two weeks

**Requests for Deferred
Entrance Considered:** Yes

Deposit to Hold Place in Class: No
Deposit (Resident): n/a **(Non-resident):** n/a
Deposit due: n/a
Applied to tuition: n/a **Refundable:** n/a
Refundable by: n/a

Estimated number of new entrants: 175
EDP: 2, special program: 15

Start Month/Year: August 2011

Interview Format: Two, one-on-one interviews with faculty. Regional interviews are not available. Video interviews are not available.

Other Programs

**PREPARATORY PROGRAMS
Postbaccalaureate Program:** Yes,
www.utoledo.edu/graduate/prospectivestudents/programs/hsc/medicine/medicalsciences.htm
Summer Program: Yes, www.hsc.utoledo.edu/med/md/admissions/srp.html
Additional Program: Yes, Medstarz. http://utoledo.edu/med/md/admissions.medstarz.html

**COMBINED DEGREE PROGRAMS
Baccalaureate/M.D.:** Yes,
www.bioe.eng.utoledo.edu/undergraduate/programs/bsmd.html
M.D./M.P.H.: Yes, http://mph.bgsu.muo.utoledo.edu
MD/MBA: Yes, www.utoledo.edu/business/MBA/MD-MBA.html
M.D./J.D.: No
M.D./Ph.D.: Yes, http://utoledo.edu/med/mdphd/index.html
Additonal Program: Yes, http://utoledo.edu/med/grad/pdfs/mdms2.pdf

Premedical Coursework

On-line courses accepted in fulfillment of prerequisites: On a case-by-case basis

Course	Req.	Rec.	Lab.	Sems.	Course	Req.	Rec.	Lab.	Sems.
Inorganic Chemistry	•		•	2	Computer Science				
Behavioral Sciences					Genetics				
Biochemistry		•			Humanities		•		
Biology	•			2	Organic Chemistry	•		•	2
Biology/Zoology					Physics	•			2
Calculus					Psychology				
College English	•			2	Social Sciences		•		
College Mathematics	•			2	Other				

Selection Factors: 2009 Accepted Applicants

Proportion of Accepted Applicants with Relevant Experience (Data Self-Reported to AMCAS®)		
Community Service/Volunteer		70%
Medically-Related Work		84%
Research		80%

Shaded bar represents school's accepted scores ranging from the 10th percentile to the 90th percentile   School Median ● National Median ○

Overall GPA	2.0	2.1	2.2	2.3	2.4	2.5	2.6	2.7	2.8	2.9	3.0	3.1	3.2	3.3	3.4	3.5	3.6	(3.7)	3.8	3.9	4.0
Science GPA	2.0	2.1	2.2	2.3	2.4	2.5	2.6	2.7	2.8	2.9	3.0	3.1	3.2	3.3	3.4	3.5	3.6	(3.7)	3.8	3.9	4.0

MCAT® Total Numeric Score 9 10 11 12 13 14 15 16 17 18 19 20 21 22 23 24 25 26 27 28 29 30 (31)(32)33 34 35 36 37 38 39 40 41 42 43

Writing Sample				J	K	L	M	N	O	(P)	(Q)	R	S	T
Verbal Reasoning	3	4	5	6	7	8	9	(10)	11	12	13	14	15
Biological Sciences	3	4	5	6	7	8	9	10	(11)	12	13	14	15
Physical Sciences	3	4	5	6	7	8	9	(10)	(11)	12	13	14	15

Acceptance & Matriculation Data for 2009–2010 First Year Class

	Resident	Non-resident	International	Total
Applications	1045	2885	20	3950
Interviewed	279	224	0	503
Deferred	18	8	0	26
Matriculants				
Early Assurance Program	7	0	0	7
Early Decision Program	7	0	0	7
Baccalaureate/M.D.	0	0	0	0
M.D./Ph.D.	0	2	0	2
Matriculated	115	60	0	**175**

Applications accepted from International Applicants: No

Specialty Choice

2005, 2006, 2007 Graduates, Specialty Choice (As reported by program directors to GME Track™)	
Anesthesiology	6%
Emergency Medicine	9%
Family Practice	9%
Internal Medicine	18%
Obstetrics/Gynecology	6%
Orthopaedic Surgery	3%
Pediatrics	12%
Psychiatry	3%
Radiology	8%
Surgery	5%

Matriculant Demographics: 2009–2010 First Year Class

Men: 92 **Women:** 83

Matriculants' Self-Reported Race/Ethnicity

Mexican American	2	**Korean**	3
Cuban	0	**Vietnamese**	2
Puerto Rican	0	**Other Asian**	2
Other Hispanic	3	**Total Asian**	33
Total Hispanic	4	**Native American**	2
Chinese	7	**Black**	7
Asian Indian	14	**Native Hawaiian**	2
Pakistani	4	**White**	132
Filipino	1	**Unduplicated Number**	
Japanese	1	**of Matriculants**	175

Science and Math Majors: 71%
Matriculants with:
Baccalaureate degree: 100%
Graduate degree(s): 19%

Financial Information

Source: 2008-2009 LCME I-B survey and 2009-2010 AAMC TSF questionnaire

	Residents	Non-residents
Total Cost of Attendance	$ 42,930	$ 71,736
Tuition and Fees	$ 27,956	$ 56,762
Other (includes living expenses)	$ 12,968	$ 12,968
Health Insurance (can be waived)	$ 2,006	$ 2,006

Average 2009 Graduate Indebtedness: $141,250
% of Enrolled Students Receiving Aid: 92%

Criminal Background Check

This medical school requires a criminal background check prior to matriculation.

Wright State University School of Medicine

Dayton, Ohio

Office of Student Affairs/Admissions
Wright State University
Boonshoft School of Medicine
P.O. Box 1751
Dayton, Ohio 45401-1751
T 937 775 2934   F 937 775 3322

Admissions www.med.wright.edu/admiss
Main www.med.wright.edu
Financial www.med.wright.edu/students/
financialaid.html
E-mail som_saa@wright.edu

Public Institution

Dr. Howard Part, Dean

Dr. Gary LeRoy, Associate Dean for Student Affairs and Admissions

Dr. Stephen Peterson, Assistant Dean for Student Affairs and Admissions

Dr. Kevin Watt, Assistant Dean for Diversity and Inclusion

Dr. Gwen Sloas, Director for Financial Aid

Charlotta Taylor, Director for Recruitment

General Information

The Boonshoft School of Medicine is a community-based medical school. Clinical facilities include seven major teaching hospitals with over 3,500 patient beds. A faculty of over 1,200 provides students with opportunities for individualized attention. The educational program emphasizes research, generalist training, community health care, community service, patient focused care, cultural competence, cultural diversity, health promotion, disease prevention, and the provision of care to underserved populations.

Mission Statement

The mission of the School is to educate culturally diverse students to become excellent physicians by focusing on generalist training that is integrated, supported, and strengthened by specialists and researchers. The faculty values patient-focused care, community service, research, and have passion for improving health in our communities. These goals and objectives are achieved through: opportunities to learn in clinical settings beginning in the first month; integration of basic and clinical science throughout four years; instruction in community-based, inpatient and outpatient settings; utilization of diverse learning strategies; interaction with faculty in an atmosphere that fosters teamwork, camaraderie, and collegiality; and diversity in the student body and patient population, reflecting many ethnic, racial, social, age, lifestyle, and gender differences.

Curricular Highlights

Community Service Requirement: Required. Students complete 60 hours.
Research/Thesis Requirement: Optional.

In the first interdisciplinary year, structure, function, cells, tissues, principles of disease, and social and ethical issues are taught. Throughout the first two years, students are instructed in medical history-taking, physical examination, and catastrophic illnesses. Each year includes a two-week clinical elective. In the second organ systems-based year, evidence-based decision making, pathobiology, therapeutics, and eight organ systems are taught. The year concludes with USMLE preparation and time for study. In the third year, students learn through six core clerkships. The fourth year includes two clerkships, six electives (some may be done away), and time for USMLE study and residency interviewing.

USMLE

Step 1: Required. Students must record a passing score for promotion.
Step 2: Clinical Skills (CS): Required. Students must record a passing total score to graduate.
Step 2: Clinical Knowledge (CK): Required. Students must record a passing total score to graduate.

Selection Factors

The school seeks a student body of diverse social, ethnic, and educational backgrounds. Applicants are admitted solely on the basis of individual qualifications without regard to race, religion, gender, sexual orientation, disability, veteran status, national origin, age, or ancestry. Dedication to human concerns, compassion, intellectual capacity, and maturity are of greater importance than specific areas of preprofessional preparation. The School also values evidence of motivation, altruism, leadership, and communication skills. Also considered are one's academic record, MCAT performance, letters of recommendation, history of service, and the results of a personal interview (by invitation). Non-residents of Ohio are encouraged to apply.

Financial Aid

Scholarships and loans are available. The School offers financial counseling services and assists students in obtaining needed support. An emergency loan fund is available. Financial status has no effect on one's acceptance.

Information about Diversity Programs

The School and its faculty have a stated policy of providing educational opportunities to disadvantaged applicants and applicants from groups underrepresented in medicine. The admissions process gives careful consideration to all applicants. A pre-matriculation program, mentoring, big brother/big sister program, tutoring, USMLE preparation, and assistance in critical thinking and learning are available.

Campus Information

Setting

The first two years are spent primarily on the main campus in Fairborn, Ohio, a suburb of Dayton. The bucolic campus occupies 250 acres, with over half devoted to wooded acreage and preserve. Dayton is a mid-sized city within a metropolitan area of nearly one million residents.

Enrollment

For 2009, total enrollment was: 417

Special Features

The School's hallmarks include a focus on wholistic physician training, dynamic partnerships with our community, community service and collaborative research. Our curriculum niche puts us on the cutting edge of medical instruction, but retains the personal touch so important to our students' education.

Housing

Housing is readily available at reasonable costs adjacent to campus and throughout the Dayton area. The School assists students in finding housing and roommates.

Satellite Campuses/Facilities

The School partners with area hospitals, clinics, and other health care providers. Students spend time in federal hospitals, private hospitals, a children's hospital, neighborhood clinics, nursing homes, and private physician offices. Approximately 360 full time clinical faculty are located in affiliated health care institutions. Many of the School's outreach programs have received national recognition.

Application Process and Requirements 2011–2012

Primary Application Service: AMCAS
Earliest filing date: June 1, 2010
Latest filing date: November 1, 2010

Secondary Application Required?: Yes
Sent to: All applicants
URL: www.med.wright.edu/admiss/start.html
Fee: Yes, $50 **Waiver available:** Yes
Earliest filing date: June 15, 2010
Latest filing date: December 31, 2010

MCAT® required?: Yes
Latest MCAT® considered: September 2010
Oldest MCAT® considered: January 2007

Early Decision Program: School does have EDP
Applicants notified: October 1, 2010
EDP available for: Residents only

Regular Acceptance Notice
Earliest date: October 15, 2010
Latest date: Until class is full
Applicant's Response to Acceptance
Offer – Maximum Time: Two weeks for return of Committal Form

Requests for Deferred
Entrance Considered: Yes

Deposit to Hold Place in Class: No
Deposit (Resident): n/a **(Non-resident):** n/a
Deposit due: n/a
Applied to tuition: n/a **Refundable:** n/a
Refundable by: n/a

Estimated number of new entrants: 105
EDP: 5
Special Programs: 12

Start Month/Year: August 2011

Interview Format: Two one-on-one interviews, each lasting 30-40 minutes. Regional interviews are not available. Video interviews are not available.

Other Programs

PREPARATORY PROGRAMS
Postbaccalaureate Program: No
Summer Program: No
Prematriculation Program:
(first three weeks of July) www.med.wright.edu

COMBINED DEGREE PROGRAMS
Baccalaureate/M.D.: No
M.D./M.P.H.: Yes, www.med.wright.edu/md-mph
MD/MBA: Yes, www.med.wright.edu/md-mba
M.D./J.D.: No
M.D./Ph.D.: Yes, www.med.wright.edu/md-phd

Premedical Coursework

On-line courses accepted in fulfillment of prerequisites: On a case-by-case basis

Course	Req.	Rec.	Lab.	Sems.
Inorganic Chemistry	•		•	2
Behavioral Sciences				
Biochemistry		•		
Biology	•		•	2
Biology/Zoology				
Calculus		•		
College English	•			2
College Mathematics	•			2

Course	Req.	Rec.	Lab.	Sems.
Computer Science		•		
Genetics				
Humanities		•		
Organic Chemistry	•		•	2
Physics	•		•	2
Psychology		•		
Social Sciences				
Other				

Selection Factors: 2009 Accepted Applicants

Proportion of Accepted Applicants with Relevant Experience (Data Self-Reported to AMCAS)		
Community Service/Volunteer		69%
Medically-Related Work		87%
Research		78%

Shaded bar represents school's accepted scores ranging from the 10th percentile to the 90th percentile. School Median ● National Median ○

Overall GPA 2.0 2.1 2.2 2.3 2.4 2.5 2.6 2.7 2.8 2.9 3.0 3.1 3.2 3.3 3.4 3.5 3.6 ⬤(3.7) 3.8 3.9 4.0
Science GPA 2.0 2.1 2.2 2.3 2.4 2.5 2.6 2.7 2.8 2.9 3.0 3.1 3.2 3.3 3.4 3.5 (3.6) 3.7 3.8 3.9 4.0

MCAT® Total Numeric Score 9 10 11 12 13 14 15 16 17 18 19 20 21 22 23 24 25 26 27 28 29 (30) 31 (32) 33 34 35 36 37 38 39 40 41 42 43

			J	K	L	M	N	O	(P)	(Q)	R	S	T
Writing Sample													
Verbal Reasoning	3	4	5	6	7	8	9	(10)	11	12	13	14	15
Biological Sciences	3	4	5	6	7	8	9	10	(11)	12	13	14	15
Physical Sciences	3	4	5	6	7	8	9	(10)	(11)	12	13	14	15

Acceptance & Matriculation Data for 2009–2010 First Year Class

	Resident	Non-resident	International	Total
Applications	1009	1738	34	2781
Interviewed	354	89	0	443
Deferred	4	1	0	5
Matriculants				
Early Assurance Program	0	0	0	0
Early Decision Program	8	0	0	8
Baccalaureate/M.D.	0	0	0	0
M.D./Ph.D.	2	0	0	2
Matriculated	91	9	0	**100**

Applications accepted from International Applicants: No

Matriculant Demographics: 2009–2010 First Year Class

Men: 44 **Women:** 56

Matriculants' Self-Reported Race/Ethnicity

Mexican American	0	Korean	3
Cuban	0	Vietnamese	0
Puerto Rican	2	Other Asian	5
Other Hispanic	0	Total Asian	22
Total Hispanic	2	Native American	0
Chinese	0	Black	6
Asian Indian	11	Native Hawaiian	0
Pakistani	2	White	69
Filipino	2	Unduplicated Number	
Japanese	0	of Matriculants	100

Science and Math Majors: 61%
Matriculants with:
    Baccalaureate degree: 100%
    Graduate degree(s): 13%

Specialty Choice

2005, 2006, 2007 Graduates, Specialty Choice (As reported by program directors to GME Track™)	
Anesthesiology	3%
Emergency Medicine	11%
Family Practice	14%
Internal Medicine	13%
Obstetrics/Gynecology	6%
Orthopaedic Surgery	5%
Pediatrics	14%
Psychiatry	4%
Radiology	2%
Surgery	7%

Financial Information

Source: 2008-2009 LCME I-B survey and 2009-2010 AAMC TSF questionnaire

	Residents	Non-residents
Total Cost of Attendance	$ 51,640	$ 66,640
Tuition and Fees	$ 28,790	$ 43,790
Other (includes living expenses)	$ 20,235	$ 20,235
Health Insurance (can be waived)	$ 2,615	$ 2,615

Average 2009 Graduate Indebtedness: $160,750
% of Enrolled Students Receiving Aid: 95%

Criminal Background Check

This medical school requires a criminal background check prior to matriculation.

University of Oklahoma College of Medicine
Oklahoma City, Oklahoma

Dotty Shaw Killam
University of Oklahoma College of Medicine
P.O. Box 26901
Oklahoma City, Oklahoma 73126
T 405 271 2331   F 405 271 8810

Admissions www.oumedicine.com/body.cfm?id=655
Main www.oumedicine.com/medschool
Financial http://w3.ouhsc.edu/sfs/
E-mail AdminMed@ouhsc.edu

Public Institution

Dr. Sherri S. Baker, M.D., Associate Dean for Admissions

Dotty Shaw Killam, Director of Admissions

Pamela Jordan, Director of Financial Aid

Dr. Phebe Tucker, MD, Associate Dean for Student Affairs

Kate Stanton, Executive Director of HSC Student Affairs

General Information

The University of Oklahoma College of Medicine offers students a quality education with added advantages. Access to modern patient care facilities and research are provided at a reasonable cost, with a proven record of choice residency placement. Students gain experience in a variety of clinical settings. The college is part of a modern health sciences complex that serves as the state's principal education and research facility for physicians, dentists, nurses, biomedical scientists, pharmacists, public health administrators, and allied health professionals.

Mission Statement

The University of Oklahoma provides our students the best educational experience through excellence in teaching, research and creative activity, and service to the state and society. New facilities and technology — plus an internationally prominent faculty — will undoubtedly make the University of Oklahoma Health Sciences Center and the College of Medicine one of the next century's regional leaders in education, research, and patient care. OU Medicine believes that caring for our patients with honesty and integrity is essential. We strive for teamwork, effective communication, respect and continual improvement in education and research.

Curricular Highlights

Community Service Requirement: Optional. The Community Health Alliance serves 11 clinics. **Research/Thesis Requirement:** Optional.

Our program focuses on the development of the physician-patient relationship with attendant experiences for acquiring scientific knowledge, problem-solving skills, and professional behaviors. A significant feature of the curriculum is early exposure to clinical skills through a series of courses that integrate the basic and clinical sciences. A new Clinical Skills Education and Testing Center provides students with opportunities to learn and practice a variety of clinical skills. The online Hippocrates system is also a valuable educational tool for students. Several summer research opportunities are available. There is a growing opportunity for students to study abroad through our International Studies Program.

USMLE

Step 1: Required. Students must record a passing score for promotion.
Step 2: Clinical Skills (CS): Required. Students must only record a score.
Step 2: Clinical Knowledge (CK): Required. Students must only record a score.

Selection Factors

Acceptance into the College of Medicine is based on GPA, MCAT scores, letters of recommendation, and personal interviews conducted on campus by members of the Admissions Board. Review of applicants is holistic. Non-residents can represent up to 25% of the student body. The University of Oklahoma College of Medicine does not discriminate on the basis of race, sex, creed, national origin, age, or handicap.

Financial Aid

The College of Medicine offers a number of financial assistance opportunities in addition to the federally sponsored programs. The most prominent scholarships are the Regents' Scholarship Fee Waiver, the Oklahoma Rural Medical Education Loan Scholarship Fund. The loan funds established by the Shepherd Foundation, Inc., and the Lew Wentz Foundation, along with over 50 other scholarships, also aid many students annually. Additional support for students from groups underrepresented in medicine is available through the State Regents for Higher Education, the Ungerman Trust, and the Belknap, Culpeper, Maurer, and Reid-Winnie scholarships. In a need or merit-based application process, the College of Medicine awards up to approximately $590,000.00 in scholarships to 200 medical students.

Information about Diversity Programs

The University of Oklahoma has a strong commitment to identify, recruit, and educate qualified students from groups underrepresented in medicine. Applications are strongly encouraged from these groups, as well as from any candidate with a disadvantaged background.

Campus Information

Setting

The College of Medicine offers programs in Oklahoma City and Tulsa. The Health Sciences Center in Oklahoma City is part of a 200-acre complex of 28 public and private institutions known as the Oklahoma Health Center.

Enrollment

For 2009, total enrollment was: 659

Special Features

The OU College of Medicine and OU Medical Center operate the state's only American College of Surgeons Level-I Trauma Center. The Health Sciences Center also has an Oklahoma Diabetes Center and an Oklahoma Cancer Institute with new facilities being built. The OU College of Medicine also offers an LCME-approved, School of Community Medicine track that provides the 3rd and 4th year of medical school on the Tulsa campus. The mission of the track is to educate and train a new generation of physicians with the skills and desire to improve the health status of all Oklahomans. Students develop multiple competencies through education and training that supplements the traditional medical school curriculum. More information is available on the website at *http://comunity medicine.ou.edu*.

Housing

The University of Oklahoma operates an on-campus apartment complex. Off-campus housing options are also available to students.

Satellite Campuses/Facilities

The College of Medicine's primary campus is in Oklahoma City, with a clinical campus in Tulsa.

Application Process and Requirements 2011–2012

Primary Application Service: AMCAS
Earliest filing date: June 1, 2010
Latest filing date: October 15, 2010

Secondary Application Required?: Yes
Sent to: All applicants and additional information requested as well for applicants to the SCM educational track.
URL: https://app.applyyourself.com/?id=UOK-MED
Fee: Yes, $65   **Waiver available:** No
Earliest filing date: June 1, 2010
Latest filing date: November 1, 2010

MCAT® required?: Yes
Latest MCAT® considered: September 2010
Oldest MCAT® considered: January 2007

Early Decision Program: School does not have EDP
Applicants notified: n/a
EDP available for: n/a

Regular Acceptance Notice
Earliest date: November 1, 2010
Latest date: Until class is full
Applicant's Response to Acceptance Offer – Maximum Time: Two weeks

Requests for Deferred Entrance Considered: Yes

Deposit to Hold Place in Class: Yes
Deposit (Resident): $100   **(Non-resident):** $100
Deposit due: Within two weeks with response to acceptance offer
Applied to tuition: Yes   **Refundable:** Yes
Refundable by: May 15, 2011

Estimated number of new entrants: 165
EDP: n/a, special program: n/a

Start Month/Year: August 2011

Interview Format: Held October through February. Regional interviews are not available. Video interviews are not available.

Other Programs

PREPARATORY PROGRAMS
Postbaccalaureate Program: No
Summer Program: No

COMBINED DEGREE PROGRAMS
Baccalaureate/M.D.: No
M.D./M.P.H.: Yes, www.oumedicine.com/body.cfm?id=702
MD/MBA: No
M.D./J.D.: No
M.D./Ph.D.: Yes, http://mdphd.ouhsc.edu/ Megan Meehan, (405) 271-2503, mdphd-program@ouhsc.edu

Premedical Coursework

On-line courses accepted in fulfillment of prerequisites: No

Course	Req.	Rec.	Lab.	Sems.	Course	Req.	Rec.	Lab.	Sems.
Inorganic Chemistry	•			2	Computer Science				
Behavioral Sciences					Genetics	•			1
Biochemistry					Humanities	•			1
Biology					Organic Chemistry	•			2
Biology/Zoology	•		•	1	Physics	•			2
Calculus					Psychology		•		1
College English	•			3	Social Sciences		•		1
College Mathematics					Other				

Selection Factors: 2009 Accepted Applicants

Proportion of Accepted Applicants with Relevant Experience (Data Self-Reported to AMCAS®)		
Community Service/Volunteer		69%
Medically-Related Work		82%
Research		60%

Shaded bar represents school's accepted scores ranging from the 10th percentile to the 90th percentile   **School Median** ●   **National Median** ●

Overall GPA	2.0	2.1	2.2	2.3	2.4	2.5	2.6	2.7	2.8	2.9	3.0	3.1	3.2	3.3	3.4	3.5	3.6	3.7	(3.8)	3.9	4.0
Science GPA	2.0	2.1	2.2	2.3	2.4	2.5	2.6	2.7	2.8	2.9	3.0	3.1	3.2	3.3	3.4	3.5	3.6	(3.7)	3.8	3.9	4.0

MCAT® Total Numeric Score 9 10 11 12 13 14 15 16 17 18 19 20 21 22 23 24 25 26 27 28 (29) 30 31 (32) 33 34 35 36 37 38 39 40 41 42 43

Writing Sample			J		K		L	M	N	(O)	P	(Q)	R	S	T
Verbal Reasoning	3		4	5	6	7	8	9	(10)	11	12	13	14	15
Biological Sciences	3		4	5	6	7	8	9	(10)	(11)	12	13	14	15
Physical Sciences	3		4	5	6	7	8	9	(10)	(11)	12	13	14	15

Acceptance & Matriculation Data for 2009–2010 First Year Class

	Resident	Non-resident	International	Total
Applications	354	1208	5	1567
Interviewed	243	39	0	282
Deferred	0	3	0	3
Matriculants				
Early Assurance Program	0	0	0	0
Early Decision Program	0	0	0	0
Baccalaureate/M.D.	0	0	0	0
M.D./Ph.D.	3	0	0	3
Matriculated	150	12	0	**162**

Applications accepted from International Applicants: No

Matriculant Demographics: 2009–2010 First Year Class

Men: 100   **Women:** 62

Matriculants' Self-Reported Race/Ethnicity

Mexican American	0	**Korean**	3
Cuban	0	**Vietnamese**	10
Puerto Rican	0	**Other Asian**	2
Other Hispanic	1	**Total Asian**	29
Total Hispanic	1	**Native American**	9
Chinese	5	**Black**	2
Asian Indian	6	**Native Hawaiian**	0
Pakistani	4	**White**	126
Filipino	1	**Unduplicated Number**	
Japanese	0	**of Matriculants**	162

Science and Math Majors: 77%
Matriculants with:
Baccalaureate degree: 100%
Graduate degree(s): 5%

Specialty Choice

2005, 2006, 2007 Graduates, Specialty Choice (As reported by program directors to GME Track™)	
Anesthesiology	8%
Emergency Medicine	4%
Family Practice	13%
Internal Medicine	13%
Obstetrics/Gynecology	4%
Orthopaedic Surgery	4%
Pediatrics	10%
Psychiatry	5%
Radiology	6%
Surgery	9%

Financial Information

Source: 2008-2009 LCME I-B survey and 2009-2010 AAMC TSF questionnaire

	Residents	Non-residents
Total Cost of Attendance	$ 48,368	$ 72,486
Tuition and Fees	$ 20,867	$ 44,985
Other (includes living expenses)	$ 25,801	$ 25,801
Health Insurance (can be waived)	$ 1,700	$ 1,700

Average 2009 Graduate Indebtedness: $137,543
% of Enrolled Students Receiving Aid: 91%

Criminal Background Check

This medical school requires a criminal background check prior to matriculation.

Oregon Health & Science University School of Medicine

Portland, Oregon

Oregon Health & Science University
Office of Education and Student Affairs, L102
3181 S.W. Sam Jackson Park Road
Portland, Oregon 97239-3098
T 503 494 2998   F 503 494 3400

Admissions www.ohsu.edu/xd/education/schools/school-of-medicine/academic-programs/md-program/admissions/index.cfm
Main www.ohsu.edu/xd/education/schools/school-of-medicine/
Financial www.ohsu.edu/finaid

Public Institution

Dr. Mark Richardson, Dean

Dr. Cynthia Morris, Assistant Dean for Admissions

Debbie Melton, Director of Admissions

Leslie Garcia, Assistant Vice Provost, Diversity

Cherie Honnell, Assistant Vice Provost, Student Financial Aid

General Information

Oregon Health & Science University (OHSU) occupies a 101-acre site overlooking the city of Portland. Campus physical facilities include basic science, research, and laboratory buildings, two hospital units with a capacity of 509 beds, and outpatient clinics. The 3rd and 4th year curriculum is regionalized throughout Oregon.

Mission Statement

The mission of the School of Medicine is to enhance human health through programs of excellence in education, research, health care, and public service to the larger community including underserved populations. In achieving these goals, the Oregon Health & Science University School of Medicine seeks to establish an educational environment that challenges students to strive for academic excellence and fosters development of compassion, humanism, professionalism, and cultural competence in the care of patients from their first days in the classroom to their final rotation in the hospitals and clinics. A priority throughout OHSU is to enable each student to fulfill his or her potential as a human being and as a health care professional while effectively meeting the health-related needs of the multiple communities he or she will serve.

Curricular Highlights

Community Service Requirement: Optional. Community service activities are encouraged.
Research/Thesis Requirement: Optional.

The 1st and 2nd year integrated curriculum is devoted to the sciences basic to medicine, focusing on the normal structure and function of the body and continuing with the study of the pathophysiological basis of disease and its treat-ment. An early clinical experience is afforded through the Principles of Clinical Medicine course, which teaches fundamental knowledge and skills in interviewing and physical diagnosis through a continuity clinical preceptorship. Third year clinical clerkships are completed at OHSU Hospital and Clinics and affiliated hospitals in the Portland area. OHSU offers regional clinical experiences throughout Oregon.

USMLE

Step 1: Required. Students must record a passing score for promotion.
Step 2: Clinical Skills (CS): Required. Students must record a passing total score to graduate.
Step 2: Clinical Knowledge (CK): Required. Students must record a passing total score to graduate.

Selection Factors

The Admissions Committee seeks students who have demonstrated academic excellence and readiness for the profession of medicine and who will contribute to the diversity necessary to enhance the medical education of all students. Applicants are selected on the basis of demonstrated motivation for medicine, humanistic attitudes, and a realistic understanding of the role of the physician in providing excellent health care to all communities in need of care. Attention is paid to achievements that demonstrate applicants' breadth of interests and experiences, commitment to others, leadership among their peers, and ability to contribute diverse and innovative perspectives to problem-solving in medicine and health care. Evaluation of applicants includes the academic record as demonstration of scholarship; the MCAT; recommendations from undergraduate or graduate school faculty, employers, and those familiar with applicants' health care, volunteer, and community service experiences; and the personal interview. Preference is given to residents of Oregon, WICHE-certified residents of Montana and Wyoming, MD/PhD and MD/MPH candidates, and non-resident applicants with superior achievements in academics and other related experiences. The School of Medicine Admissions Committee fully recognizes the importance of diversity in its student body and in the physician workforce in the provision of effective health care delivery. Accordingly, the OHSU School of Medicine strongly encourages applications from persons from all socioeconomic, racial, ethnic, religious, and educational backgrounds and persons from groups underrepresented in medicine. The committee adheres to a policy of equal opportunity and non-discrimination on the basis of sex, age, race, ethnic origin, religion, disability, or sexual orientation.

Financial Aid

Financial aid in the form of scholarships, grants, and loans is available based upon the demonstrated need of the student. For more information, please review the Web site at *www.ohsu.edu/finaid*.

Information about Diversity Programs

Information may be obtained by contacting Leslie Garcia, MPA, Asst. Vice Provost, Diversity, Center for Diversity & Multicultural Affairs, (503)494-5657 or email garcial@ohsu.edu. Web site is *www.ohsu.edu/xd/education/student-services/education-diversity/*.

Setting

University Hospital and the School of Medicine are located on a hilltop overlooking the city of Portland, Oregon. Students have easy access to the city center as well as the surrounding communities.

Campus Information

Enrollment

For 2009, total enrollment was: 523

Satellite Campuses/Facilities

Third and fourth year students may participate in required and elective clinical experiences in Eugene and Bend, Oregon. Additionally, third year students have the opportunity to complete a clerkship in a rural Oregon community.

Application Process and Requirements 2011–2012

Primary Application Service: AMCAS
Earliest filing date: June 1, 2010
Latest filing date: October 15, 2010

Secondary Application Required?: Yes
Sent to: All Applicants
URL: Sent via e-mail after verification of AMCAS application.
Fee: Yes, $100   **Waiver available:** Yes
Earliest filing date: July 1, 2010
Latest filing date: February 1, 2011

MCAT® required?: Yes
Latest MCAT® considered: September 2010
Oldest MCAT® considered: 2008

Early Decision Program: School does not have EDP
Applicants notified: n/a
EDP available for: n/a

Regular Acceptance Notice
Earliest date: October 15, 2010
Latest date: Until class is full
Applicant's Response to Acceptance Offer – Maximum Time: Two weeks

Requests for Deferred Entrance Considered: No

Deposit to Hold Place in Class: No
Deposit (Resident): n/a   **(Non-resident):** n/a
Deposit due: n/a
Applied to tuition: n/a   **Refundable:** n/a
Refundable by: n/a

Estimated number of new entrants: 120
EDP: n/a, special program: n/a

Start Month/Year: August 2011

Interview Format: Two, one-on-one 30-45 minute interviews. Regional interviews are not available. Video interviews are not available.

Other Programs

PREPARATORY PROGRAMS
Postbaccalaureate Program: No
Summer Program: No

COMBINED DEGREE PROGRAMS
Baccalaureate/M.D.: No
M.D./M.P.H.: Yes, www.ohsu.edu/public-health
John Stull, M.D., M.P.H., (503) 494-6958, stullj@ohsu.edu
MD/MBA: No
M.D./J.D.: No
M.D./Ph.D.: Yes, www.ohsu.edu/xd/education/schools/school-of-medicine/academic-programs/md-phd/
Laura Dolan, (503) 494-7692, dolanla@ohsu.edu

Premedical Coursework

On-line courses accepted in fulfillment of prerequisites: On a case-by-case basis

Course	Req.	Rec.	Lab.	Qtrs.	Course	Req.	Rec.	Lab.	Qtrs.
Inorganic Chemistry	•		•	1	Computer Science				
Behavioral Sciences					Genetics	•			1
Biochemistry	•		•	1	Humanities				
Biology	•		•	3	Organic Chemistry	•		•	1
Biology/Zoology					Physics	•		•	3
Calculus		•		1	Psychology				
College English	•			1	Statistics		•		1
College Mathematics	•			1	Humanities/Social Sciences	•			6

Selection Factors: 2009 Accepted Applicants

Proportion of Accepted Applicants with Relevant Experience (Data Self-Reported to AMCAS®)		
Community Service/Volunteer		75%
Medically-Related Work		94%
Research		79%

Shaded bar represents school's accepted scores ranging from the 10th percentile to the 90th percentile   **School Median** ● **National Median** ◐

Overall GPA	2.0	2.1	2.2	2.3	2.4	2.5	2.6	2.7	2.8	2.9	3.0	3.1	3.2	3.3	3.4	3.5	3.6	3.7	(3.8)	3.9	4.0
Science GPA	2.0	2.1	2.2	2.3	2.4	2.5	2.6	2.7	2.8	2.9	3.0	3.1	3.2	3.3	3.4	3.5	3.6	(3.7)	3.8	3.9	4.0

MCAT® Total Numeric Score 9 10 11 12 13 14 15 16 17 18 19 20 21 22 23 24 25 26 27 28 29 30 31 (32) 33 34 35 36 37 38 39 40 41 42 43

Writing Sample			J	K	L	M	N	O	P	(Q)	R	S	T
Verbal Reasoning	3	4	5	6	7	8	9	(10)	11	12	13	14	15
Biological Sciences	3	4	5	6	7	8	9	10	(11)	12	13	14	15
Physical Sciences	3	4	5	6	7	8	9	(10)	(11)	12	13	14	15

Acceptance & Matriculation Data for 2009–2010 First Year Class

	Resident	Non-resident	International	Total
Applications	405	4094	22	4521
Interviewed	228	327	0	555
Deferred	0	0	0	0
Matriculants				
Early Assurance Program	0	0	0	0
Early Decision Program	0	0	0	0
Baccalaureate/M.D.	0	0	0	0
M.D./Ph.D.	1	1	0	2
Matriculated	88	32	0	**120**

Applications accepted from International Applicants: No

Matriculant Demographics: 2009–2010 First Year Class

Men: 59   **Women:** 61

Matriculants' Self-Reported Race/Ethnicity

Mexican American	1	Korean	4
Cuban	0	Vietnamese	7
Puerto Rican	0	Other Asian	3
Other Hispanic	3	Total Asian	26
Total Hispanic	3	Native American	3
Chinese	7	Black	0
Asian Indian	4	Native Hawaiian	0
Pakistani	1	White	85
Filipino	0	Unduplicated Number	
Japanese	2	of Matriculants	120

Science and Math Majors: 63%
Matriculants with:
Baccalaureate degree: 100%
Graduate degree(s): 10%

Specialty Choice

2005, 2006, 2007 Graduates, Specialty Choice (As reported by program directors to GME Track™)	
Anesthesiology	5%
Emergency Medicine	9%
Family Practice	15%
Internal Medicine	24%
Obstetrics/Gynecology	5%
Orthopaedic Surgery	1%
Pediatrics	10%
Psychiatry	3%
Radiology	4%
Surgery	7%

Financial Information

Source: 2008-2009 LCME I-B survey and 2009-2010 AAMC TSF questionnaire

	Residents	Non-residents
Total Cost of Attendance	$ 56,343	$ 69,499
Tuition and Fees	$ 34,695	$ 47,851
Other (includes living expenses)	$ 17,659	$ 17,659
Health Insurance (can be waived)	$ 3,989	$ 3,989

Average 2009 Graduate Indebtedness: $172, 433
% of Enrolled Students Receiving Aid: 93%

Criminal Background Check

This medical school requires a criminal background check prior to matriculation.

The Commonwealth Medical College
Scranton, Pennsylvania

The Commonwealth Medical College
P.O. Box 766
Scranton, Pennsylvania 18501
T 570 504 9068   **F** 570 504 2794

Admissions www.thecommonwealthmedical.com
/admissions
Main www.thecommonwealthmedical.com
Financial www.thecommonwealthmedical.com
/financialaid
E-mail admissions@tcmedc.org

Private Institution

Dr. Robert M. D'Alessandri, President and Dean

Dr. David A. Axler, Associate Dean for Student Affairs

Ida Castro, Vice President for Diversity and Social Justice

Ellen McGuire, Director of Financial Aid

Debra E. Stalk, Director of Admissions

General Information

The Commonwealth Medical College (TCMC) is focused on developing practicing physicians for the 21st century skilled in evidence-based medicine, the latest technology and able to care for complex patients in a community setting. TCMC has a distributive model of education with clinical campuses in Scranton, Wilkes-Barre and Williamsport. In these regions, TCMC partners with community hospitals, residency programs and physicians to provide students an exceptional and diverse clinical experience. At the start of the first year curriculum students are assigned a multi-generational family to follow through the end of their medical school career. Working with their physician mentor, the student will experience the health care system through this family-many of whom will have chronic illnesses and challenges with access to care. Students also have the opportunity to work on a community public health project, emphasizing TCMCs commitment to promoting social responsibility and the goal that students will embrace a long term responsibility to community service and health improvement.

Mission Statement

The Commonwealth Medical College will educate aspiring physicians and scientists to serve society using a community-based, patient-centered, interprofessional and evidence-based model of education that is committed to inclusion, promotes discovery and utilizes innovative techniques.

Curricular Highlights

Community Service Requirement: Required.
Research/Thesis Requirement: Optional.

The curriculum was designed around the characteristics designed to make a physician successful the ability to understand new scientific information and adapt practice patterns, the ability to effectively communicate with patients and other members of the health care team, the ability to work as a member of a team, to build long term relationships with patients, and to understand quality improvement, to use technology to enhance patient and physician decision making and patient safety. The curriculum incorporates a variety of learning models but is less than 40% lecture based, relying instead on small group, individual and case based learning. Clinical experiences are integrated into the first two years and the third and fourth year offer a longitudinal clerkship model designed to increase learning and student satisfaction.

USMLE

Step 1: Required. Students must record a passing score for promotion.
Step 2: Clinical Skills (CS): Required. Students must record a passing total score to graduate.
Step 2: Clinical Knowledge (CK): Required. Students must record a passing total score to graduate.

Selection Factors

We are looking for students with a strong sense of social responsibility, who desire a sophisticated community-based practice caring for their patients, while improving the health of the community.

Financial Aid

Information about financial aid at TCMC may be found on the financial aid pages on the TCMC website. TCMC offers need based scholarships and other sources of financial assistance. The College is in the process of applying for Title IV participation for access to Federal student loans and anticipates that this will be available to students for the 2010/2011 year.

Information about Diversity Programs

The Center for Social Justice and Diversity represents The Commonwealth Medical College's commitment to meet the ever-increasing need for diverse physicians. A diverse environment enriches learning and the quality of the student's experience on campus and as they reach out to serve the community. The Center works closely with the Offices of Academic and Student Affairs to develop programs that will support the students experience by imbedding cultural competencies in the curriculum and campus life.

Setting

The College is building a new 186,000 square foot Medical Sciences Building that will house state of the art facilities and be open in 2011. Included in the space will be a Clinical Skills and Simulation Center, Gross Anatomy Center, our 95% digital library, lounge and study space as well as research and educational space. In the interim, the College is located in temporary space. These temporary facilities have had a $5 million investment to create a state of the art Clinical Skills and Simulation Center and Gross Anatomy Lab.

Campus Information

Enrollment

For 2009, total enrollment was: 65

Special Features

Students will receive training in a wide variety of community practice settings-hospitals, private offices, and clinics working with community faculty physicians, residents and other members of the health care team.

Housing

Students will have access to many housing options on the Scranton campus for years 1 & 2 and on the clinical campuses for 3 & 4 years. Student Affairs has prepared housing guides for all campuses.

Satellite Campuses/Facilities

For years 3 & 4 students will select a clinical campus (Scranton, Wilkes-Barre or Williamsport). All campuses are student friendly and experienced with abundant and diverse clinical experiences.

Application Process and Requirements 2011–2012

Primary Application Service: AMCAS
Earliest filing date: June 1, 2010
Latest filing date: December 15, 2011

Secondary Application Required?: Yes
Sent to: Secondary application will be sent to all applicants upon receipt of verified AMCAS application.
Contact: Admissions Office, (570) 504-9068, admissions@tcmedc.org
Fee: Yes, $100 **Waiver available:** Yes
Earliest filing date: August 1, 2010
Latest filing date: January 15, 2011

MCAT® required?: Yes
Latest MCAT® considered: September 2010
Oldest MCAT® considered: 2008

Early Decision Program: School does not have EDP
Applicants notified: n/a
EDP available for: n/a

Regular Acceptance Notice
Earliest date: October 15, 2010
Latest date: Until class is full
Applicant's Response to Acceptance Offer – Maximum Time: Two weeks

Requests for Deferred Entrance Considered: Yes

Deposit to Hold Place in Class: Yes
Deposit (Resident): $100 **(Non-resident):** $100
Deposit due: With response to acceptance offer
Applied to tuition: Yes **Refundable:** Yes
Refundable by: May 15, 2011

Estimated number of new entrants: 60
EDP: n/a, special program: n/a

Start Month/Year: August 2011

Interview Format: Interviews are with both a clinical and basic science faculty member in a conversational format. Regional interviews are not available. Video interviews are not available.

Other Programs

PREPARATORY PROGRAMS
Postbaccalaureate Program: No
Additional Programs: Yes,
Masters in Biomedical Sciences,
www.thecommonwealthmedical.com/mbs

COMBINED DEGREE PROGRAMS
Baccalaureate/M.D.: No
M.D./M.P.H.: No
MD/MBA: No
M.D./J.D.: No
M.D./Ph.D.: No

Premedical Coursework

On-line courses accepted in fulfillment of prerequisites: No

Course	Req.	Rec.	Lab.	Sems.
Inorganic Chemistry	•		•	2
Behavioral Sciences				
Biochemistry		•		
Biology	•		•	2
Biology/Zoology		•		
Calculus		•		
College English	•			1
College Mathematics		•		

Course	Req.	Rec.	Lab.	Sems.
Computer Science				
Genetics		•		
Humanities				
Organic Chemistry	•		•	2
Physics	•		•	2
Psychology				
Social Sciences				
Other1				

Selection Factors: 2009 Accepted Applicants

Proportion of Accepted Applicants with Relevant Experience (Data Self-Reported to AMCAS®)		
Community Service/Volunteer		70%
Medically-Related Work		83%
Research		78%

Shaded bar represents school's accepted scores ranging from the 10th percentile to the 90th percentile   School Median ●   National Median ●

Overall GPA 2.0 2.1 2.2 2.3 2.4 2.5 2.6 2.7 2.8 2.9 3.0 3.1 3.2 3.3 3.4 (3.5) 3.6 3.7 3.8 3.9 4.0
Science GPA 2.0 2.1 2.2 2.3 2.4 2.5 2.6 2.7 2.8 2.9 3.0 3.1 3.2 3.3 (3.4) 3.5 3.6 3.7 3.8 3.9 4.0

MCAT® Total Numeric Score 9 10 11 12 13 14 15 16 17 18 19 20 21 22 23 24 25 26 27 28 29 (30)(31)(32) 33 34 35 36 37 38 39 40 41 42 43

Writing Sample			J	K	L	M	N	O	(P)	(Q)	R	S	T
Verbal Reasoning	3	4	5	6	7	8	9	(10)	11	12	13	14	15
Biological Sciences	3	4	5	6	7	8	9	10	(11)	12	13	14	15
Physical Sciences	3	4	5	6	7	8	9	(10)	(11)	12	13	14	15

Acceptance & Matriculation Data for 2009–2010 First Year Class

	Resident	Non-resident	International	Total
Applications	424	840	27	1291
Interviewed	213	157	0	370
Deferred	0	1	0	1
Matriculants				
Early Assurance Program	0	0	0	0
Early Decision Program	0	0	0	0
Baccalaureate/M.D.	0	0	0	0
M.D./Ph.D.	0	0	0	0
Matriculated	46	19	0	**65**

Applications accepted from International Applicants: Only Canadian

Specialty Choice

2005, 2006, 2007 Graduates, Specialty Choice
(As reported by program directors to GME Track™)

DATA NOT AVAILABLE

Matriculant Demographics: 2009–2010 First Year Class

Men: 42 **Women:** 23

Matriculants' Self-Reported Race/Ethnicity

Mexican American	1	Korean	1
Cuban	0	Vietnamese	0
Puerto Rican	0	Other Asian	3
Other Hispanic	1	Total Asian	11
Total Hispanic	2	Native American	1
Chinese	3	Black	1
Asian Indian	2	Native Hawaiian	0
Pakistani	1	White	53
Filipino	1	Unduplicated Number	
Japanese	0	of Matriculants	65

Science and Math Majors: 75%
Matriculants with:
Baccalaureate degree: 100%
Graduate degree(s): 12%

Financial Information

Source: 2008-2009 LCME I-B survey and 2009-2010 AAMC TSF questionnaire

	Residents	Non-residents
Total Cost of Attendance	$ 61,398	$ 66,398
Tuition and Fees	$ 38,550	$ 43,550
Other (includes living expenses)	$ 19,833	$ 19,833
Health Insurance (can be waived)	$ 3,015	$ 3,015

Average 2009 Graduate Indebtedness: n/r
% of Enrolled Students Receiving Aid: n/r%

Criminal Background Check

This medical school requires a criminal background check prior to matriculation.

Drexel University College of Medicine
Philadelphia, Pennsylvania

Admissions Office
Drexel University College of Medicine
2900 Queen Lane
Philadelphia, Pennsylvania 19129
T 215 991 8202   F 215 843 1766

Admissions www.drexelmed.edu/Home/Admissions/
MDProgram.aspx
Main www.drexelmed.edu
Financial www.drexel.edu/provost/financialaid
E-mail medadmis@drexel.edu

Private Institution

Dr. Richard V. Homan, Dean

Dr. Samuel K. Parrish, Jr., Senior Associate Dean for Student Affairs and Admissions

Dr. Anthony Rodriguez, Associate Dean of Student Affairs and Diversity

Elreo Campbell, Director of Financial Aid

Kelli Kennedy, Director of Admissions

General Information
Drexel University College of Medicine was formed when two historic Philadelphia medical schools joined their rich histories and resources. The Medical College of Pennsylvania (MCP) was founded in 1850 as the first medical school for women. Hahnemann University, a private nondenominational institution, was founded in 1848. Drexel offers a medical education rich in history and diversity, while providing the foundational curriculum and learning environment necessary for the scientific, technological, and ethical decisions required of physicians in the 21st century.

Mission Statement
Drexel is committed to providing our students with the finest possible medical education. Academic instruction in basic and clinical sciences, utilizing state-of-the-art technology, is enriched by an emphasis on compassionate patient care and community service.

Curricular Highlights
Community Service Requirement:
Required. 16 hours required in year one.
Research/Thesis Requirement:
Optional. Though optional, many students conduct research.

Medical students are trained to consider each patient in a comprehensive, integrated manner, taking into account more factors than the presenting physiological condition. The school is dedicated to preparing "physician healers," who practice the art, science, and skill of medicine. Drexel offers a choice between two innovative curricula for the first two years. Interdisciplinary Foundations of Medicine (IFM) integrates basic science courses and

presents them through symptom-based modules. Learning in IFM is faculty-driven; students learn in lectures, labs, and small groups. Learning in the Program for Integrated Learning (PIL), a problem-based curriculum, is student-driven, supervised and facilitated by faculty. Students learn in small groups, labs, and resource sessions by focusing on case studies. Both options stress problem-solving, lifelong learning, and the coordinated training of basic science with clinical medicine. Both include the introduction of clinical skills training very early in the first year. The Pathway Program in the fourth year includes a balance of required and elective clinical experiences selected with the pathway advisors to be consistent with general medical training and the students ultimate career goals.

USMLE
Step 1: Required. Students must record a passing score for promotion.
Step 2: Clinical Skills (CS): Required. Students must record a passing total score to graduate.
Step 2: Clinical Knowledge (CK): Required. Students must record a passing total score to graduate.

Selection Factors
Drexel seeks highly qualified, motivated students who demonstrate the desire, intelligence, integrity, and emotional maturity to become excellent physicians. We encourage nontraditional applicants and are committed to a diverse student body. We seek students who have a firm grasp of the biological and physical sciences as well as broad educational experiences in other areas. Students who demonstrate a commitment to community service are strongly considered. All students must be able to meet the technical standards of the medical school. Applicants must be U.S. citizens or permanent residents. All aspects of an applicant's file are considered, including grades, MCATs, experiences, letters and essay. Interviews with a faculty member and student are important to an applicant's review at committee.

Information about Diversity Programs
Applications are actively encouraged from groups underrepresented in medicine. Applications from women, those who come from Pennsylvania,

and students interested in a career as a generalist physician are also encouraged.

Campus Information
Setting
Located in a largely residential section of Philadelphia, the college is only 15 minutes from Center City. Opened in 1992, this 15-acre site houses the education and research facility which is home for the first and second years of medical education. The campus features wireless internet access.

Enrollment
For 2009, total enrollment was: 1,090

Special Features
The medical school has a supportive environment that fosters a spirit of teamwork and personal interaction. Our state-of-the-art facility includes the CEAC Center with 10 exam rooms where students see standardized patients and our new Independence Blue Cross Medical Simulation Center. Elective enrichment programs include Women's Health and Medical Humanities. Students in their clinical years log patient encounters and procedures in PDAs or web enabled cell phones. The recently added Student Activities Center greatly enhances the learning and living environment of the campus

Housing
On-campus housing is not available. However, the college maintains an on-line list of rentals averaging $750 to $1,500 per month.

Satellite Campuses/Facilities
Students have the opportunity for clinical training in our extensive, integrated network of clinical campuses.

Application Process and Requirements 2011–2012

Primary Application Service: AMCAS
Earliest filing date: June 1, 2010
Latest filing date: December 1, 2010

Secondary Application Required?: Yes
Sent to: All applicants
URL: http://webcampus.drexelmed.edu/admissions/MyApplication
Fee: Yes, $75 **Waiver available:** Yes
Earliest filing date: June 1, 2010
Latest filing date: January 1, 2011

MCAT® required?: Yes
Latest MCAT® considered: September 2010
Oldest MCAT® considered: April 2008

Early Decision Program: School does have EDP
Applicants notified: October 1, 2010
EDP available for: Both Residents and Non-residents

Regular Acceptance Notice
Earliest date: October 15, 2010
Latest date: Until class is full
Applicant's Response to Acceptance Offer – Maximum Time: 21 days

Requests for Deferred Entrance Considered: Yes

Deposit to Hold Place in Class: Yes
Deposit (Resident): $100 **(Non-resident):** $100
Deposit due: 21 days from acceptance offer
Applied to tuition: Yes **Refundable:** Yes
Refundable by: May 15, 2011

Estimated number of new entrants: 260
EDP: n/a, special program: 80

Start Month/Year: August 2011

Interview Format: One faculty open-file, one student closed-file. Regional interviews are not available. Video interviews are not available.

Other Programs

PREPARATORY PROGRAMS
Postbaccalaureate Program: Yes,
www.drexelmed.edu/Home/AcademicPrograms/ProfessionalStudiesintheHealthSciences/Admissions.aspx
Summer Program: No
Drexel links with a number of post-baccalaureate programs: www.drexelmed.edu/Home/Admissions/MDProgram/AcceleratedandEarlyAssuranceLinkagePrograms.aspx

COMBINED DEGREE PROGRAMS
Baccalaureate/M.D.: Yes, www.drexelmed.edu/Home/Admissions/MDProgram/AcceleratedandEarlyAssuranceLinkagePrograms.aspx
M.D./M.P.H.: Yes, http://publichealth.drexel.edu/
MD/MBA: Yes, www.lebow.drexel.edu/Prospects/MBA/MdMBA/index.php
M.D./J.D.: No
M.D./Ph.D.: Yes, www.drexelmed.edu/Home/AcademicPrograms/BiomedicalGraduateStudies/Programs/CombinedMDPhD.aspx
Additional Program: Yes, www.drexelmed.edu/Home/Admissions/MDProgram.aspx

Premedical Coursework

On-line courses accepted in fulfillment of prerequisites: No

Course	Req.	Rec.	Lab.	Sems.	Course	Req.	Rec.	Lab.	Sems.
Inorganic Chemistry	•		•	2	Computer Science				
Behavioral Sciences					Genetics		•		
Biochemistry		•			Humanities		•		
Biology	•		•	2	Organic Chemistry	•		•	2
Biology/Zoology					Physics	•		•	2
Calculus					Psychology				
College English	•			2	Social Sciences				
College Mathematics					Molecular Biology		•		

Selection Factors: 2009 Accepted Applicants

Proportion of Accepted Applicants with Relevant Experience (Data Self-Reported to AMCAS®)		
Community Service/Volunteer	64%
Medically-Related Work	86%
Research	81%

Shaded bar represents school's accepted scores ranging from the 10th percentile to the 90th percentile School Median ● National Median ○

Overall GPA 2.0 2.1 2.2 2.3 2.4 2.5 2.6 2.7 2.8 2.9 3.0 3.1 3.2 3.3 3.4 3.5 3.6 (3.7) 3.8 3.9 4.0
Science GPA 2.0 2.1 2.2 2.3 2.4 2.5 2.6 2.7 2.8 2.9 3.0 3.1 3.2 3.3 3.4 3.5 (3.6) 3.7 3.8 3.9 4.0

MCAT® Total Numeric Score 9 10 11 12 13 14 15 16 17 18 19 20 21 22 23 24 25 26 27 28 29 30 (31)(32) 33 34 35 36 37 38 39 40 41 42 43

Writing Sample				J	K	L	M	N	O	P	(Q)	R	S	T
Verbal Reasoning	3	4	5	6	7	8	9	(10)	11	12	13	14	15
Biological Sciences	3	4	5	6	7	8	9	10	(11)	12	13	14	15
Physical Sciences	3	4	5	6	7	8	9	10	(11)	12	13	14	15

Acceptance & Matriculation Data for 2009–2010 First Year Class

	Resident	Non-resident	International	Total
Applications	1122	10975	54	12151
Interviewed	315	1024	0	1339
Deferred	1	1	0	2
Matriculants				
Early Assurance Program	2	4	0	6
Early Decision Program	0	0	0	0
Baccalaureate/M.D.	5	39	0	44
M.D./Ph.D.	3	2	0	5
Matriculated	76	184	0	**260**

Applications accepted from International Applicants: No

Matriculant Demographics: 2009–2010 First Year Class

Men: 130 **Women:** 130

Matriculants' Self-Reported Race/Ethnicity

Mexican American	2	Korean	12
Cuban	1	Vietnamese	3
Puerto Rican	0	Other Asian	5
Other Hispanic	7	Total Asian	85
Total Hispanic	10	Native American	0
Chinese	19	Black	15
Asian Indian	37	Native Hawaiian	2
Pakistani	4	White	148
Filipino	5	Unduplicated Number	
Japanese	2	of Matriculants	260

Science and Math Majors: 70%
Matriculants with:
Baccalaureate degree: 100%
Graduate degree(s): 22%

Specialty Choice

2005, 2006, 2007 Graduates, Specialty Choice (As reported by program directors to GME Track™)	
Anesthesiology	6%
Emergency Medicine	10%
Family Practice	8%
Internal Medicine	17%
Obstetrics/Gynecology	5%
Orthopaedic Surgery	6%
Pediatrics	10%
Psychiatry	5%
Radiology	6%
Surgery	8%

Financial Information

Source: 2008-2009 LCME I-B survey and 2009-2010 AAMC TSF questionnaire

	Residents	Non-residents
Total Cost of Attendance	$ 70,483	$ 70,483
Tuition and Fees	$ 45,540	$ 45,540
Other (includes living expenses)	$ 21,450	$ 21,450
Health Insurance (can be waived)	$ 3,493	$ 3,493

Average 2009 Graduate Indebtedness: $202,832
% of Enrolled Students Receiving Aid: 89%

Criminal Background Check

This medical school requires a criminal background check prior to matriculation.

Jefferson Medical College of Thomas Jefferson University

Philadelphia, Pennsylvania

Office of Admissions
Jefferson Medical College
of Thomas Jefferson University
1015 Walnut Street, Suite 110
Philadelphia, Pennsylvania 19107-5099
T 215 955 6983   F 215 955 5151

Admissions www.jefferson.edu/jmc/admissions
Main www.jefferson.edu/jmc
Financial www.jefferson.edu/financialaid
E-mail jmc.admissions@jefferson.edu

Private Institution

Dr. Mark L. Tykocinski, Dean

Dr. Clara Callahan, Dean of Students and Admissions

Dr. Edward Christian, Associate Dean for Diversity and Minority Affairs

Susan Batchelor McFadden, Director of Student Financial Aid

Dr. Elizabeth Brooks, Director of Admissions

General Information

As one of the oldest institutions of higher education in the nation, Thomas Jefferson University has, since its founding as the Jefferson Medical College in 1824, emphasized the attainment of clinical excellence in its educational programs. A recent significant expansion of the research programs has created a balanced institutional mission and has enhanced the clinical instruction at Thomas Jefferson University Hospital and its 17 affiliated hospitals.

Mission Statement

Jefferson's teaching mission centers on the education of outstanding individuals in the art and science of medicine. By helping these individuals to develop their medical knowledge, clinical and research skills, and professional values, attitudes, and behaviors, we strive to provide outstanding physicians for the United States and the world.

Curricular Highlights

Community Service Requirement: Required.
Research/Thesis Requirement: Optional.

The curriculum has been developed to enable students to acquire basic knowledge and skills in the biomedical sciences and to develop appropriate professional behaviors. The curriculum also allows students to pursue some of their special interests throughout their medical training. The tradition of providing a clinically balanced medical education, encouraged by the faculty, is that students support and cooperate with each other. In the first year, students focus on the function of human organism in its physical and psychosocial context. Clinical coursework focuses on the doctor-patient rela-tionship, medical interviewing and history-taking, human development, behavioral science principles, and core clinical skills and reasoning. In addition to increasing emphasis on the study of clinical skills, the curriculum shifts in the second year to the study of pathophysioiogy and disease. The curriculum includes small-group sessions focusing on problem-solving, evidence-based medicine, and service-based learning. The clinical program consists of two 42-week phases. Phase I covers required clerkships. Advanced basic science, neurology/rehabilitation medicine, emergency medicine/advanced clinical skills, in- and outpatient subinternships, as well as 16 weeks of elective time, are included in Phase II.

USMLE

Step 1: Required. Students must record a passing score for promotion.
Step 2: Clinical Skills (CS): Required. Students must only record a score.
Step 2: Clinical Knowledge (CK): Required. Students must record a passing total score to graduate.

Selection Factors

Jefferson, in accordance with local, state, and federal law, is committed to providing equal educational and employment opportunities for all persons, without regard to race, color, national and ethnic origin, religion, sexual orientation, age, handicap, or veteran status. Jefferson complies with all relevant ordinances and state and federal statutes in the administration of its educational and employment policies and is an affirmative action employer. The selection of students is made after careful consideration of many factors, including the academic record, letters of recommendation, MCAT scores and interview results regarding the applicant's personal qualities, motivation, interpersonal skills, and achievement in nonacademic areas. Jefferson Medical College traditionally has given special consideration to the offspring of alumni and faculty, groups underrepresented in medicine, and applicants to Jefferson's special programs. International applicants must have a baccalaureate degree from an accredited U.S. or Canadian college or university.

Financial Aid

Financial aid awards are based on need determined by a confidential analysis of information provided by the student and the student's family to the designated needs analysis service. If need is established, the student is directed to obtain a federally subsidized Stafford loan. If need exists beyond this loan program, Jefferson will try to meet a portion of this need from loan and grant funds. Applications for financial aid are available after December from the Office of Student Financial Aid. Completed financial aid applications for the next academic year must be submitted before April 1 or within two weeks of the date of acceptance.

Information about Diversity Programs

Applications from qualified students from groups underrepresented in medicine are encouraged.

Campus Information

Setting

The medical school is proud to be situated near the most historic square mile in America. The campus is 13 square acres in the heart of Center City Philadelphia.

Enrollment

For 2009, total enrollment was: 1018

Special Features

Thomas Jefferson University Hospital is one of the area's largest medical centers and includes both a Level I regional resource trauma center and a Spinal Cord Injury Center (SCI).

Housing

On-campus housing is available.

Application Process and Requirements 2011–2012

Primary Application Service: AMCAS
Earliest filing date: June 1, 2010
Latest filing date: November 15, 2010

Secondary Application Required?: Yes
Sent to: All applicants
URL: www.jefferson.edu/jmc/admissions/appforms.cfm
Fee: Yes, $80 **Waiver available:** Yes
Earliest filing date: June 1, 2010
Latest filing date: January 14, 2011

MCAT® required?: Yes
Latest MCAT® considered: September 2010
Oldest MCAT® considered: 2007

Early Decision Program: School does have EDP
Applicants notified: October 1, 2010
EDP available for: Both Residents and Non-residents

Regular Acceptance Notice
Earliest date: October 15, 2010
Latest date: Until class is full
Applicant's Response to Acceptance Offer – Maximum Time: Two weeks

Requests for Deferred Entrance Considered: Yes

Deposit to Hold Place in Class: Yes
Deposit (Resident): $100 **(Non-resident):** $100
Deposit due: at time of acceptance
Applied to tuition: Yes **Refundable:** Yes
Refundable by: May 15, 2011

Estimated number of new entrants: 255
EDP: 3, special program: 40

Start Month/Year: August 2011

Interview Format: One-on-one, open file (faculty) and closed file (student). Regional interview available on campus only. Video interviews are not available.

Other Programs

PREPARATORY PROGRAMS
Postbaccalaureate Program: No
Summer Program: No

COMBINED DEGREE PROGRAMS
Baccalaureate/M.D.: Yes
www.science.psu.edu/premedmed/
M.D./M.P.H.: Yes, www.jefferson.edu/population_health
M.D./M.B.A.: Yes, www.jefferson.edu/population_health/dual_degrees/md_mba.cfm
M.D./J.D.: No
M.D./Ph.D.: Yes, www.jefferson.edu/jcgs/mdphd

Premedical Coursework

On-line courses accepted in fulfillment of prerequisites: No

Course	Req.	Rec.	Lab.	Sems.
Inorganic Chemistry	•		•	2
Behavioral Sciences				
Biochemistry		•		1
Biology	•		•	2
Biology/Zoology				
Calculus				
College English		•		
College Mathematics		•		

Course	Req.	Rec.	Lab.	Sems.
Computer Science				
Genetics				
Humanities		•		
Organic Chemistry	•		•	2
Physics	•		•	2
Psychology				
Social Sciences		•		
Other				

Selection Factors: 2009 Accepted Applicants

Proportion of Accepted Applicants with Relevant Experience (Data Self-Reported to AMCAS®)		
Community Service/Volunteer		68%
Medically-Related Work		84%
Research		80%

Shaded bar represents school's accepted scores ranging from the 10th percentile to the 90th percentile   School Median ○   National Median ○

Overall GPA	2.0	2.1	2.2	2.3	2.4	2.5	2.6	2.7	2.8	2.9	3.0	3.1	3.2	3.3	3.4	3.5	3.6	(3.7)	3.8	3.9	4.0
Science GPA	2.0	2.1	2.2	2.3	2.4	2.5	2.6	2.7	2.8	2.9	3.0	3.1	3.2	3.3	3.4	3.5	3.6	(3.7)	3.8	3.9	4.0

MCAT® Total Numeric Score 9 10 11 12 13 14 15 16 17 18 19 20 21 22 23 24 25 26 27 28 29 30 31 (32) 33 34 35 36 37 38 39 40 41 42 43

Writing Sample				J	K	L	M	N	O	P	(Q)	R	S	T
Verbal Reasoning	3	4	5	6	7	8	9	(10)	11	12	13	14	15	
Biological Sciences	3	4	5	6	7	8	9	10	(11)	12	13	14	15	
Physical Sciences	3	4	5	6	7	8	9	10	(11)	12	13	14	15	

Acceptance & Matriculation Data for 2009–2010 First Year Class

	Resident	Non-resident	International	Total
Applications	1069	8168	476	9713
Interviewed	234	548	20	802
Deferred	2	4	1	7
Matriculants				
Early Assurance Program	10	15	1	26
Early Decision Program	3	1	0	4
Baccalaureate/M.D.	8	12	0	20
M.D./Ph.D.	2	1	2	5
Matriculated	92	152	11	**255**

Applications accepted from International Applicants: Yes

Matriculant Demographics: 2009–2010 First Year Class

Men: 118   **Women:** 137

Matriculants' Self-Reported Race/Ethnicity

Mexican American	2	Korean	6
Cuban	0	Vietnamese	10
Puerto Rican	4	Other Asian	2
Other Hispanic	14	Total Asian	53
Total Hispanic	20	Native American	1
Chinese	14	Black	4
Asian Indian	23	Native Hawaiian	0
Pakistani	1	White	170
Filipino	0	Unduplicated Number	
Japanese	1	of Matriculants	255

Science and Math Majors: 55%
Matriculants with:
   Baccalaureate degree: 100%
   Graduate degree(s): 7%

Specialty Choice

2005, 2006, 2007 Graduates, Specialty Choice (As reported by program directors to GME Track™)	
Anesthesiology	6%
Emergency Medicine	8%
Family Practice	9%
Internal Medicine	19%
Obstetrics/Gynecology	4%
Orthopaedic Surgery	5%
Pediatrics	8%
Psychiatry	4%
Radiology	5%
Surgery	7%

Financial Information

Source: 2008-2009 LCME I-B survey and 2009-2010 AAMC TSF questionnaire

	Residents	Non-residents
Total Cost of Attendance	$ 68,669	$ 68,669
Tuition and Fees	$ 44,547	$ 44,547
Other (includes living expenses)	$ 20,767	$ 20,767
Health Insurance (can be waived)	$ 3,355	$ 3,355

Average 2009 Graduate Indebtedness: $167,972
% of Enrolled Students Receiving Aid: 83%

Criminal Background Check

This medical school requires a criminal background check prior to matriculation.

Pennsylvania State University College of Medicine

Hershey, Pennsylvania

Pennsylvania State University College of Medicine
Office of Medical Student Affairs, H060
500 University Drive; P.O. Box 850
Hershey, Pennsylvania 17033
T 717 531 8755   **F** 717 531 6225

Admissions www.pennstatehershey.org/college
Main www.pennstatehershey.org
Financial www.pennstatehershey.org/college
E-mail studentadmissions@hmc.psu.edu

Public Institution

Dr. Harold L. Paz, Dean, Senior Vice President for Health Affairs

Dr. Dwight Davis, Associate Dean for Admissions and Student Affairs

Dr. Harjit Singh, Interim Associate Dean for Diversity

Dr. Joetta Bradica, Assistant Director for Financial Aid

Marc Lubbers, Assistant Director for Admissions

General Information

Penn State's Milton S. Hershey Medical Center opened its doors to the first class of medical students in 1967 and became the first medical school in the nation to establish a Department of Humanities, introducing humanistic disciplines into the required medical curriculum. The College of Medicine was also the first to start an independent Department of Family and Community Medicine. From its beginning, medical education and patient care have been guided by the institution's commitment to provide humane, compassionate, and expert care.

Mission Statement

Penn State College of Medicine is dedicated to the education of physicians and scientists in all of the disciplines of medicine and biomedical investigation for careers in practice, teaching, and research. Necessary to this educational mission are the provision of outstanding medical care and services and the enhancement of new knowledge through clinical and basic biomedical research.

Curricular Highlights

Community Service Requirement: Optional. *www.pennstatehershey.org/college*
Research/Thesis Requirement: Required. Full details at: *www.pennstatehershey.org/msr*

A single integrated curriculum for years one and two combines elements of traditional medical teaching and case-based learning. The first-year curriculum and courses are interdisciplinary, combining case-based, student-centered learning with strategic lectures, laboratories, and small-group discussions. The second-year curriculum is more heavily oriented to case-based learning in an organ/organ system approach to human health, pathophysiology, and disease. Year three includes a sequence of required core clinical clerkships in internal medicine, general surgery, pediatrics, obstetrics and gynecology, psychiatry, family and community medicine, and primary care supplemented by available selectives. In addition, there are week-long sessions in Advanced Clinical Diagnostics and Therapeutics, Communications and Professionalism, and Improving Healthcare. Year four consists of four elective rotations and four required advanced experiences. The College of Medicine offers a wide variety of both clinical and research electives. Students may select outpatient clinical rotations at teaching hospitals or in university-affiliated physicians' offices located in a variety of rural and metropolitan communities nationwide and abroad. All students participate in an individualized research program.

USMLE

Step 1: Required. Students must record a passing score for promotion.
Step 2: Clinical Skills (CS): Required. Students must record a passing total score to graduate.
Step 2: Clinical Knowledge (CK): Required. Students must record a passing total score to graduate.

Selection Factors

Applicants must show evidence of superior undergraduate achievement and outstanding personal characteristics. Each application is considered individually. A decision is reached after thorough evaluation of the applicant's academic record, letters of assessment, extracurricular activities, MCAT scores, and personal interviews. Since the practice of medicine requires a lifelong devotion to self-education, emphasis is placed on the excellence of the individual scholar no matter what the student's previous area of study.

Financial Aid

Financial aid is granted based upon need as determined by federal methodology. Parental income information is required for university scholarship and loan consideration, as well as some other financial assistance programs. Additional financial aid information is available on the school's Web site.

Information about Diversity Programs

Diversity is one of the core value statements of the Penn State College of Medicine. Students from groups underrepresented in medicine are strongly encouraged to apply. Faculty, staff and students actively participate in the recruitment of students from underrepresented minorities.

Campus Information

Setting

The 550-acre campus is located in the rolling hills of southeastern Pennsylvania near the state capital, Harrisburg. The main facility houses the College of Medicine, the 500+ bed University Hospital and Children's Hospital, the Rehabilitation Center, the Biomedical Research Building, the Emergency Medical Center, and the Penn State Hershey Cancer Institute. The hospital serves as the only regional Level I Trauma Center for both adult and pediatric cases. Plans for a new, free-standing Penn State Hershey Children's Hospital to be built on the campus have been approved.

Enrollment

For 2009, total enrollment was: 594

Special Features

The College of Medicine has state-of-the art facilities, innovative programs, and an award-winning staff that combines medical expertise with compassionate patient care. Learn more at *www.pennstatehershey.org/college*. A new 8,000-square-foot Clinical Simulation Center recently opened that centralizes clinical training resources.

Housing

University Manor is a safe and affordable housing complex situated on campus with numerous ammenities. Learn more at *www.pennstatehershey.org/housing*

Satellite Campuses/Facilities

The College of Medicine has forged a large number of collaborations that provide extensive opportunities for its medical students. Students rotate at defined institutions that meet the College of Medicine's high standards of educational quality.

Application Process and Requirements 2011–2012

Primary Application Service: AMCAS
Earliest filing date: June 1, 2010
Latest filing date: November 15, 2010

Secondary Application Required?: Yes
Sent to: All applicants
Contact: Office of Medical Student Admissions, (717) 531-8755, studentadmissions@hmc.psu.edu
Fee: Yes, $75   **Waiver available:** Yes
Earliest filing date: Based on e-mail invitation
Latest filing date: January 15, 2011

MCAT® required?: Yes
Latest MCAT® considered: September 2010
Oldest MCAT® considered: 2008

Early Decision Program: School does have EDP
Applicants notified: October 1, 2010
EDP available for: Both Residents and Non-residents

Regular Acceptance Notice
Earliest date: October 16, 2010
Latest date: Until class is full
Applicant's Response to Acceptance Offer – Maximum Time: Two weeks

Requests for Deferred Entrance Considered: Yes

Deposit to Hold Place in Class: Yes
Deposit (Resident): $100   **(Non-resident):** $100
Deposit due: May 15, 2011
Applied to tuition: Yes **Refundable:** Yes
Refundable by: May 15, 2011

Estimated number of new entrants: 145
EDP: n/a, special program: n/a

Start Month/Year: August 2011

Interview Format: Interviews occur on campus by individual invitation. Regional interviews are not available. Video interviews are not available.

Other Programs

PREPARATORY PROGRAMS
Postbaccalaureate Program: No
Summer Program: No
Early Assurance Program: Yes, www.pennstate hershey.org/md/admissions/overview/earlyassurance

COMBINED DEGREE PROGRAMS
Baccalaureate/M.D.: No
M.D./M.P.H.: No
MD/MBA: No
M.D./J.D.: No
M.D./Ph.D.: Yes, www.pennstatehershey.org/mdphd

Premedical Coursework

On-line courses accepted in fulfillment of prerequisites: No

Course	Req.	Rec.	Lab.	Sems.
Inorganic Chemistry	•		•	2
Behavioral Sciences	•			1
Biochemistry		•		
Biology	•		•	2
Biology/Zoology				
Calculus		•		
College English		•		
College Mathematics	•			2

Course	Req.	Rec.	Lab.	Sems.
Computer Science				
Genetics		•		1
Humanities	•			1
Organic Chemistry	•		•	2
Physics	•		•	2
Psychology		•		
Social Sciences		•		
Other				

Selection Factors: 2009 Accepted Applicants

Proportion of Accepted Applicants with Relevant Experience (Data Self-Reported to AMCAS®)		
Community Service/Volunteer		72%
Medically-Related Work		88%
Research		86%

Shaded bar represents school's accepted scores ranging from the 10th percentile to the 90th percentile   **School Median** ●   **National Median** ○

Overall GPA 2.0 2.1 2.2 2.3 2.4 2.5 2.6 2.7 2.8 2.9 3.0 3.1 3.2 3.3 3.4 3.5 3.6 3.7 (3.8) 3.9 4.0
Science GPA 2.0 2.1 2.2 2.3 2.4 2.5 2.6 2.7 2.8 2.9 3.0 3.1 3.2 3.3 3.4 3.5 3.6 (3.7) 3.8 3.9 4.0

MCAT® Total Numeric Score 9 10 11 12 13 14 15 16 17 18 19 20 21 22 23 24 25 26 27 28 29 30 31 (32) 33 34 35 36 37 38 39 40 41 42 43

Writing Sample			J	K	L	M	N	O	P	(Q)	R	S	T	
Verbal Reasoning	3	4	5	6	7	8	9	(10)	11	12	13	14	15	
Biological Sciences	3	4	5	6	7	8	9	10	(11)	12	13	14	15	
Physical Sciences	3	4	5	6	7	8	9	10	(11)	12	13	14	15	

Acceptance & Matriculation Data for 2009–2010 First Year Class

	Resident	Non-resident	International	Total
Applications	1031	5605	449	7085
Interviewed	264	623	21	908
Deferred	0	3	2	5
Matriculants				
Early Assurance Program	1	1	0	2
Early Decision Program	1	0	0	1
Baccalaureate/M.D.	0	0	0	0
M.D./Ph.D.	0	5	1	6
Matriculated	67	73	4	**144**

Applications accepted from International Applicants: Yes

Matriculant Demographics: 2009–2010 First Year Class

Men: 74   **Women:** 70

Matriculants' Self-Reported Race/Ethnicity

Mexican American	0	Korean	4
Cuban	2	Vietnamese	2
Puerto Rican	1	Other Asian	3
Other Hispanic	2	Total Asian	32
Total Hispanic	5	Native American	1
Chinese	7	Black	6
Asian Indian	13	Native Hawaiian	1
Pakistani	2	White	101
Filipino	2	Unduplicated Number	
Japanese	0	of Matriculants	144

Science and Math Majors: 63%
Matriculants with:
  Baccalaureate degree: 100%
  Graduate degree(s): 8%

Specialty Choice

2005, 2006, 2007 Graduates, Specialty Choice (As reported by program directors to GME Track™)	
Anesthesiology	8%
Emergency Medicine	7%
Family Practice	14%
Internal Medicine	15%
Obstetrics/Gynecology	6%
Orthopaedic Surgery	3%
Pediatrics	12%
Psychiatry	3%
Radiology	3%
Surgery	4%

Financial Information

Source: 2008-2009 LCME I-B survey and 2009-2010 AAMC TSF questionnaire

	Residents	Non-residents
Total Cost of Attendance	$ 52,056	$ 63,634
Tuition and Fees	$ 36,086	$ 47,664
Other (includes living expenses)	$ 14,720	$ 14,720
Health Insurance (can be waived)	$ 1,250	$ 1,250

Average 2009 Graduate Indebtedness: $171,822
% of Enrolled Students Receiving Aid: 92%

Criminal Background Check

This medical school requires a criminal background check prior to matriculation.

Temple University
School of Medicine
Philadelphia, Pennsylvania

Office of Admissions
Temple University School of Medicine
3500 N. Broad Street, Suite 124
Philadelphia, Pennsylvania 19140
T 215 707 3656   **F** 215 707 6932

Admissions www.temple.edu/medicine/admissions
Main www.temple.edu/medicine
Financial www.temple.edu/sfs/med
E-mail medadmissions@temple.edu

Private Institution

Dr. John M. Daly, Dean

Dr. Audrey B. Uknis,
Associate Dean for Admissions

Dr. Raul De La Cadena, Assistant Dean for
Recruitment, Admissions, and Retention

General Information

A 480,000 square foot 11-story medical school building opened in 2009. This state of the art teaching and collaborative research space has transformed the medical school campus and allowed its continued growth as one of the nation's premier urban academic medical centers.

Mission Statement

A center of humanistic medicine, Temple University School of Medicine (TUSM) is known for its culture of service, diversity and collaboration. TUSM has three major interrelated missions: 1) provide excellent learner-centered education to a diverse body of medical and graduate students, instilling in them an ethic of human service and lifelong learning; 2) engage in research that advances medical science and clinical care; and 3) provide state-of-the-art health care.

Curricular Highlights

Community Service Requirement: Optional.
Research/Thesis Requirement: Optional.

Temple has an Integrated Curriculum (IC), which provides integration among basic science disciplines and between basic science and clinical disciplines. The IC is competency-based, providing students with the opportunities to learn and practice the basic knowledge, clinical skills, and attitudes/behaviors essential to the medical profession. The curriculum incorporates state-of-the-art teaching technologies, including patient simulation. The IC is divided into a number of interdisciplinary blocks, each organized according to body or organ systems and taught by faculty from several basic science and clinical academic departments. The clerkships in years 3 and 4 will continue to provide exposure to a unique variety of clinical experiences, both inpatient and

ambulatory. The IC facilitates the acquisition of an increasingly large body of biomedical information through the integration of basic science and medical information and places both in relevant clinical contexts.

USMLE

Step 1: Required. Students must record a passing score for promotion.
Step 2: Clinical Skills (CS): Required. Students must only record a score.
Step 2: Clinical Knowledge (CK): Required. Students must record a passing total score to graduate.

Selection Factors

An individualized holistic review of each completed application includes a variety of objective and subjective factors. The academic record, the college attended, MCAT scores, recommendations, extracurricular activities, work experience, medically related experience, and community service activities are all taken into account when selecting candidates for interview. While not required, many students have participated in research activities. Approximately half of the matriculants are Pennsylvania residents, but non-residents with a particular interest in Temple and strong credentials are encouraged to apply. Students in the 2009 entering class attended 100 different colleges and universities.

Financial Aid

Temple offers a variety of both merit and need-based scholarships. Students are encouraged to complete a FAFSA by March 1, including the parental section and submit tax returns to be considered for need-based University funds.

Information about Diversity Programs

The School of Medicine is committed to diversity in the faculty and student body. The Recruitment, Admissions, & Retention (RAR) program provides exceptional resources for professional academic guidance and counseling for applicants and students who are from disadvantaged backgrounds or groups underrepresented in medicine.

Campus Information

Setting

An urban institution, Temple serves a diverse population, drawing patients from the North Philadelphia community and from the greater Philadelphia region for specialized care. The School of Medicine shares a campus with Temple University Hospital and other health-related schools of the University. The campus is easily accessible by public transportation.

Enrollment

For 2009, total enrollment was: 741

Special Features

The William Maul Measey Institute for Clinical Simulation and Patient Safety is an 11,000 sq foot learning laboratory which provides excellence in clinical skills training utilizing a combination of high-tech and traditional methods. The Clinical Simulation Center houses the programmable, anatomically detailed, and physiologically functional mannequins that are used to present a variety of clinical scenarios. The Clinical Skills Center houses the standardized patient program, which helps students learn to take histories, conduct physical examinations, make diagnoses, and communicate in a caring manner.

Housing

Students live about 20 minutes by car, in neighborhoods northwest of the campus or in downtown Philadelphia. The School of Medicine provides local housing information and hosts a blog for the incoming class.

Satellite Campuses/Facilities

Clinical experience and instruction are provided at Temple University Hospital, St. Christopher's Hospital for Children, Crozer-Chester Medical Center, Fox Chase Cancer Center, Abington Memorial Hospital, and other affiliated hospitals located throughout Pennsylvania. Clinical campuses have been established at the Western Pennsylvania Hospital in Pittsburgh, Geisinger Medical Center in Danville, and St. Luke's Hospital in Bethlehem. Students may elect to do all of the third and fourth-year rotations at one of the clinical campuses.

Application Process and Requirements 2011–2012

Primary Application Service: AMCAS
Earliest filing date: June 1, 2010
Latest filing date: December 15, 2010

Secondary Application Required?: Yes
Sent to: U.S. citizens, permanent residents or applicants who have refugee/asylee status.
URL: Sent when verified AMCAS application is received
Fee: Yes, $75   **Waiver available:** Yes
Earliest filing date: July 1, 2010
Latest filing date: January 15, 2011

MCAT® required?: Yes
Latest MCAT® considered: September 2010
Oldest MCAT® considered: January 2008

Early Decision Program: School does have EDP
Applicants notified: October 1, 2010
EDP available for: Both Residents and Non-residents

Regular Acceptance Notice
Earliest date: October 15, 2010
Latest date: Varies
Applicant's Response to Acceptance Offer – Maximum Time: Two weeks

Requests for Deferred Entrance Considered: Yes

Deposit to Hold Place in Class: Yes
Deposit (Resident): $100   **(Non-resident):** $100
Deposit due: Within two weeks of acceptance
Applied to tuition: Yes   **Refundable:** Yes
Refundable by: May 15, 2011

Estimated number of new entrants: 210
EDP: 5, special program: 30

Start Month/Year: August 2011

Interview Format: Applicants have an interview with a faculty member and a student. Regional interviews are not available. Video interviews are not available.

Other Programs

PREPARATORY PROGRAMS

Postbaccalaureate Program: Yes, www.temple.edu/medicine/postbac
Summer Program: Yes, www.temple.edu/medicine/rar
Early Assurance: Yes, www.temple.edu/medicine/admissions/special_admissions.htm

COMBINED DEGREE PROGRAMS

Baccalaureate/M.D.: Yes, www.temple.edu/medicine/admissions/special_admissions.htm
M.D./M.P.H.: Yes, www.temple.edu/medicine/education/dualdegree
MD/MBA: Yes, www.temple.edu/medicine/education/dualdegree
M.D./J.D.: No
M.D./Ph.D.: Yes, www.temple.edu/medicine/education/dualdegree/mdphd.htm

Premedical Coursework

On-line courses accepted in fulfillment of prerequisites: No

Course	Req.	Rec.	Lab.	Hrs.
Inorganic Chemistry	•		•	8
Behavioral Sciences				
Biochemistry				
Biology	•	•		8
Biology/Zoology				
Calculus				
College English				
College Mathematics				

Course	Req.	Rec.	Lab.	Hrs.
Computer Science				
Genetics				
Humanities	•			6
Organic Chemistry	•		•	8
Physics	•		•	8
Psychology				
Social Sciences				
Other				

Selection Factors: 2009 Accepted Applicants

Proportion of Accepted Applicants with Relevant Experience (Data Self-Reported to AMCAS®)		
Community Service/Volunteer		69%
Medically-Related Work		86%
Research		83%

Shaded bar represents school's accepted scores ranging from the 10th percentile to the 90th percentile.   **School Median** ● **National Median** ◐

Overall GPA	2.0	2.1	2.2	2.3	2.4	2.5	2.6	2.7	2.8	2.9	3.0	3.1	3.2	3.3	3.4	3.5	3.6	(3.7)	3.8	3.9	4.0
Science GPA	2.0	2.1	2.2	2.3	2.4	2.5	2.6	2.7	2.8	2.9	3.0	3.1	3.2	3.3	3.4	3.5	(3.6)	3.7	3.8	3.9	4.0

MCAT® Total Numeric Score 9 10 11 12 13 14 15 16 17 18 19 20 21 22 23 24 25 26 27 28 29 30 (31) (32) 33 34 35 36 37 38 39 40 41 42 43

Writing Sample			J	K	L	M	N	O	P	(Q)	R	S	T
Verbal Reasoning	3	4	5	6	7	8	9	(10)	11	12	13	14	15
Biological Sciences	3	4	5	6	7	8	9	10	(11)	12	13	14	15
Physical Sciences	3	4	5	6	7	8	9	(10)	(11)	12	13	14	15

Acceptance & Matriculation Data for 2009–2010 First Year Class

	Resident	Non-resident	International	Total
Applications	1121	7889	62	9072
Interviewed	276	585	0	861
Deferred	0	2	0	2
Matriculants				
Early Assurance Program	1	0	0	1
Early Decision Program	2	0	0	2
Baccalaureate/M.D.	1	2	0	3
M.D./Ph.D.	2	0	0	2
Matriculated	95	101	0	**196**

Applications accepted from International Applicants: No

Matriculant Demographics: 2009–2010 First Year Class

Men: 108   **Women:** 88

Matriculants' Self-Reported Race/Ethnicity

Mexican American	3	Korean	3
Cuban	4	Vietnamese	1
Puerto Rican	2	Other Asian	4
Other Hispanic	4	Total Asian	39
Total Hispanic	13	Native American	1
Chinese	13	Black	15
Asian Indian	13	Native Hawaiian	3
Pakistani	1	White	131
Filipino	2	Unduplicated Number	
Japanese	4	of Matriculants	196

Science and Math Majors: 68%
Matriculants with:
   Baccalaureate degree: 100%
   Graduate degree(s): 4%

Specialty Choice

2005, 2006, 2007 Graduates, Specialty Choice (As reported by program directors to GME Track™)	
Anesthesiology	6%
Emergency Medicine	8%
Family Practice	7%
Internal Medicine	27%
Obstetrics/Gynecology	3%
Orthopaedic Surgery	4%
Pediatrics	8%
Psychiatry	3%
Radiology	6%
Surgery	10%

Financial Information

Source: 2008-2009 LCME I-B survey and 2009-2010 AAMC TSF questionnaire

	Residents	Non-residents
Total Cost of Attendance	$ 64,775	$ 74,275
Tuition and Fees	$ 41,936	$ 51,202
Other (includes living expenses)	$ 19,809	$ 20,043
Health Insurance (can be waived)	$ 3,030	$ 3,030

Average 2009 Graduate Indebtedness: $182,101
% of Enrolled Students Receiving Aid: 89%

Criminal Background Check

This medical school requires a criminal background check prior to matriculation.

University of Pennsylvania School of Medicine
Philadelphia, Pennsylvania

Office of Admissions and Financial Aid
Suite 100, Edward J. Stemmler Hall
University of Pennsylvania School of Medicine
3450 Hamilton Walk
Philadelphia, Pennsylvania 19104-6056
T 215 898 8001   **F** 215 573 6645

Admissions www.med.upenn.edu/admiss
Main www.med.upenn.edu
Financial www.med.upenn.edu/financialaid/
E-mail admiss@mail.med.upenn.edu

Private Institution

Dr. Arthur H. Rubenstein, Dean

Dr. Steve Galetta, Associate Dean for Admissions

Dr. Karen Hamilton, Assistant Dean for Diversity and Community Outreach

Gaye Sheffler, Director of Admissions and Financial Aid

Dr. Gail Morrison, Vice Dean for Education

General Information
The School of Medicine, the first in the United States, was founded in 1765 and is a private, non-denominational school on the urban campus of the University of Pennsylvania. The one university concept enrolls medical students as members of the university as well as the School of Medicine community. Clinical education occurs in the Hospital of the University of Pennsylvania, Children's Hospital of Philadelphia, Veterans Administration Hospital of Philadelphia, Presbyterian Medical Center, and Pennsylvania Hospital.

Mission Statement
Our mission is to create the future of medicine through: Patient Care and Service Excellence, Educational Pre-eminence, New Knowledge and Innovation, and National and International Leadership.

Curricular Highlights
Community Service Requirement: Required. Three-year patient-centered experience.
Research/Thesis Requirement: Required. Three month scholarly pursuit and/or dual degree.

The four-year curriculum has three themes: Science of Medicine, Technology and Practice of Medicine, and Professionalism and Humanism. Module 1 (four months) provides the foundation of basic sciences and is divided into four blocks: Developmental and Molecular Biology; Cell Physiology and Metabolism: Human Body, Structure, and Function; and Host Defenses and Responses. Grades are pass/fail. Module 2 (40 weeks) integrates basic science across organ systems and ends in December of Year 2. Topics are organized by:

Normal Development, Normal Processes, Abnormal Processes, Therapeutics and Disease Management, Epidemiology/Evidenced-based Medicine, Prevention, and Nutrition. Grades are honors/pass/fail. Module 3, Technology and Practice of Medicine, runs concurrent with modules 1 and 2 and promotes competency in epidemiology and biostatistics, decision-making, health care economics, population-based medicine, managed care and quality assurance, and basic clinical medicine. Grades are pass/fail. Module 4, (clinical clerkships), runs from January of Year 2 through December of Year 3 and is composed of 48 weeks of required clinical clerkships divided into four three-month cross-disciplinary experiences. Basic science concepts are reinforced weekly in didactic sessions. Module 5 (16 months) begins in January of Year 3 and continues until graduation. It provides students flexibility in their elective/selective and scholarly pursuit experiences and exposure to upper level electives and mentors prior to residency selection. Grades are honors/high pass/pass/fail. Module 6, Professionalism and Humanism, runs concurrently throughout the curriculum and covers bioethics, multiculturalism, spirituality, research, ethics, and confidentiality. Grades are pass/fail. Detailed curriculum information can be found at *www.med.upenn. edu/admiss/curriculum.*

USMLE
Step 1: Required. Students must only record a score.
Step 2: Clinical Skills (CS): Required. Students must only record a score.
Step 2: Clinical Knowledge (CK): Required. Students must only record a score.

Selection Factors
Selection factors include academic excellence, out-of-classroom activities, and life experience, as well as community service, research, letters of recommendation, and leadership potential. Personal qualities of maturity, integrity, the ability to work with others, and humanistic interests are sought. The entering class of 2009 has representation from 61 undergraduate colleges. Applicants from all states are welcome, but some preference is given to PA residents. Penn does not discriminate on the basis of race, sex, sexual

orientation, age, religion, national or ethnic origin, or physical handicap. There is no transfer admission program.

Financial Aid
Students come from all social, economic, and cultural backgrounds. Financial aid includes: need-based scholarship and loans restricted to U.S. citizens or permanent residents and 11-12 full-tuition merit scholarships awarded annually regardless of citizenship. Approximately 24 students annually are fully funded in the M.D./Ph.D. program.

Information about Diversity Programs
Penn values and encourages diversity of all kinds throughout its student body, housestaff, faculty and health system. The Penn community is one of openness and inclusion while retaining its focus on the recruitment of groups underrepresented in medicine. The cultural competency curriculum, plethora of community outreach programs, and the development of pipeline programs with colleges and high schools are important in meeting our commitment to diversity.

Campus Information

Setting
Penn's urban campus is located in Philadelphia, one of America's most historic and livable cities. The fact that all 12 of Penn's graduate schools are located within walking distance of one another supports and fosters Penn's interdisciplinary approach to education, scholarship, and research. The city is a vibrant cultural center of urban life.

Enrollment
For 2009, total enrollment was: 740

Special Features
Global health experiences throughout the world. Pediatrics at Children's Hospital of Philadelphia, a world-renowned pediatric center.

Housing
Housing is affordable. Campus resources help students find housing. University transit is available within boundaries.

Application Process and Requirements 2011–2012

Primary Application Service: AMCAS
Earliest filing date: June 1, 2010
Latest filing date: October 15, 2010, 12 a.m. EST

Secondary Application Required?: Yes
Sent to: All applicants
URL: n/a
Fee: Yes, $80 **Waiver available:** Yes
Earliest filing date: July 1, 2010
Latest filing date: November 15, 2010, 12 a.m. EST

MCAT® required?: Yes
Latest MCAT® considered: September 2010
Oldest MCAT® considered: September 2007

Early Decision Program: School does have EDP
Applicants notified: October 1, 2010
EDP available for: Both Residents
and Non-residents

Regular Acceptance Notice
Earliest date: March 15, 2011
Latest date: Until class is full
Applicant's Response to Acceptance
Offer – Latest Date: May 15, 2011, 5 p.m., EST

Requests for Deferred
Entrance Considered: Yes

Deposit to Hold Place in Class: Yes
Deposit (Resident): $100 **(Non-resident):** $100
Deposit due: May 15, 2011 5 p.m. EST
Applied to tuition: Yes **Refundable:** Yes
Refundable by: May 15, 2011 5 p.m. EST

Estimated number of new entrants: 160
EDP: 3, special program: 15

Start Month/Year: August 2011

Interview Format: Two individual interviews/
faculty and student. Regional interviews are not
available. Video interviews are not available.

Other Programs

PREPARATORY PROGRAMS
Postbaccalaureate Program: Yes,
www.sas.upenn.edu/lps/postbac/
Summer Program: Yes,
www.med.upenn.edu/bgs/applicants_other.shtml
Clinical Epidemiology Program: Additional
www.med.upenn.edu/educ_combdeg/MDMSCE
Program.shtml
Master's in Translational Research:
www.itmat.upenn.edu/ctsa/mtr/

COMBINED DEGREE PROGRAMS
Baccalaureate/M.D.: No
M.D./M.P.H.: Yes, www.med.upenn.edu/educ_
combdeg/mdmphprogram.shtml
MD/MBA: Yes, www.med.upenn.edu/educ_
combdeg/mdmba.shtml
M.D./J.D.: Yes, www.med.upenn.edu/educ_
combdeg/mdjd.shtml
M.D./Ph.D.: Yes, www.med.upenn.edu/mstp/
M.D./M.S.H.P.: Yes, www.med.upenn.edu/educ_
combdeg/mdmshp.shtml
Additional Program: Yes, www.med.upenn.edu/
educ_combdeg/mdmbioethics.shtml

Premedical Coursework

On-line courses accepted in fulfillment of prerequisites: On a case-by-case basis

Course	Req.	Rec.	Lab.	Hrs.
Inorganic Chemistry		•		
Behavioral Sciences		•		
Biochemistry		•		
Biology		•	•	
Biology/Zoology				
Calculus		•		
College English		•		
College Mathematics		•		

Course	Req.	Rec.	Lab.	Hrs.
Computer Science		•		
Genetics		•		
Humanities		•		
Organic Chemistry		•	•	
Physics		•	•	
Psychology		•		
Social Sciences		•		
Statistics		•		

Selection Factors: 2009 Accepted Applicants

Proportion of Accepted Applicants with Relevant Experience (Data Self-Reported to AMCAS®)		
Community Service/Volunteer		68%
Medically-Related Work		86%
Research		93%

Shaded bar represents school's accepted scores ranging from the 10th percentile to the 90th percentile.   School Median ●   National Median ◐

Overall GPA	2.0	2.1	2.2	2.3	2.4	2.5	2.6	2.7	2.8	2.9	3.0	3.1	3.2	3.3	3.4	3.5	3.6	3.7	3.8	(3.9)	4.0
Science GPA	2.0	2.1	2.2	2.3	2.4	2.5	2.6	2.7	2.8	2.9	3.0	3.1	3.2	3.3	3.4	3.5	3.6	3.7	3.8	(3.9)	4.0

MCAT® Total Numeric Score 9 10 11 12 13 14 15 16 17 18 19 20 21 22 23 24 25 26 27 28 29 30 31 (32) 33 34 35 (36) 37 38 39 40 41 42 43

Writing Sample		J	K	L	M	N	O	P	(Q)	R	S	T
Verbal Reasoning	3	4	5	6	7	8	9	(10)	(11)	12	13	14	15
Biological Sciences	3	4	5	6	7	8	9	10	(11)	(12)	13	14	15
Physical Sciences	3	4	5	6	7	8	9	10	(11)	12	(13)	14	15

Acceptance & Matriculation Data for 2009–2010 First Year Class

	Resident	Non-resident	International	Total
Applications	643	5281	293	6217
Interviewed	120	724	8	852
Deferred	0	6	0	6
Matriculants				
Early Assurance Program	0	0	0	0
Early Decision Program	0	2	0	2
Baccalaureate/M.D.	0	0	0	0
M.D./Ph.D.	2	21	1	24
Matriculated	38	122	1	**161**

Applications accepted from International Applicants: Yes

Specialty Choice

2005, 2006, 2007 Graduates, Specialty Choice (As reported by program directors to GME Track™)	
Anesthesiology	5%
Emergency Medicine	5%
Family Practice	2%
Internal Medicine	19%
Obstetrics/Gynecology	3%
Orthopaedic Surgery	3%
Pediatrics	12%
Psychiatry	4%
Radiology	7%
Surgery	4%

Matriculant Demographics: 2009–2010 First Year Class

Men: 89 **Women:** 72

Matriculants' Self-Reported Race/Ethnicity

Mexican American	1	Korean	1
Cuban	2	Vietnamese	0
Puerto Rican	0	Other Asian	2
Other Hispanic	8	Total Asian	35
Total Hispanic	11	Native American	1
Chinese	20	Black	10
Asian Indian	10	Native Hawaiian	0
Pakistani	2	White	116
Filipino	0	Unduplicated Number	
Japanese	3	of Matriculants	161

Science and Math Majors: 57%
Matriculants with:
   Baccalaureate degree: 100%
   Graduate degree(s): 5%

Financial Information

Source: 2008-2009 LCME I-B survey
and 2009-2010 AAMC TSF questionnaire

	Residents	Non-residents
Total Cost of Attendance	$ 67,324	$ 67,324
Tuition and Fees	$ 45,644	$ 45,644
Other (includes living expenses)	$ 19,080	$ 19,080
Health Insurance (can be waived)	$ 2,600	$ 2,600

Average 2009 Graduate Indebtedness: $121,389
% of Enrolled Students Receiving Aid: 85%

Criminal Background Check

This medical school requires a criminal background
check prior to matriculation.

University of Pittsburgh School of Medicine

Pittsburgh, Pennsylvania

Office of Admissions and Financial Aid
3550 Terrace Street, 518 Scaife Hall
University of Pittsburgh School of Medicine
Pittsburgh, Pennsylvania 15261
T 412 648 9891   **F** 412 648 8768

Admissions www.medadmissions.pitt.edu
Main www.medschool.pitt.edu
Financial www.medadmissions.pitt.edu/financial-aid/
E-mail admissions@medschool.pitt.edu

Private Institution

Dr. Arthur S. Levine, Dean, Senior Vice Chancellor for Health Sciences

Dr. Beth Piraino, Associate Dean for Admissions and Financial Aid

Dr. Chenits Pettigrew, Jr. Assistant Dean for Student Affairs and Diversity Programs

Pamela Rikstad, Director of Financial Aid

Cynthia M. Bonetti, Executive Director of Admissions and Financial Aid

Connie Dobrich, Assistant Director of Admissions

General Information

The University of Pittsburgh School of Medicine is a leader in research, curricular development and clinical care with over 2000 full time faculty and a core group of master educators. The University of Pittsburgh and affiliates are ranked 5th in NIH funding. The students rotate through multiple top hospitals drawing from diverse patient populations.

Mission Statement

The mission of the University of Pittsburgh School of Medicine is to educate physicians who are science-based, skilled, and compassionate clinicians prepared to meet the challenges of practicing medicine in the 21st century and to conduct cutting-edge biomedical research that is focused on bettering the human condition and advancing the fundamental understanding of medical science.

Curricular Highlights

Community Service Requirement: Optional. Participation in multiple activities possible.
Research/Thesis Requirement: Completion of a longitudinal scholarly project.

The focus of the curriculum is on teaching patient centered care that is evidence based. The students are encouraged to develop habits of self-education through problem-based and small group learning, literature review, and computer-assisted education. The curriculum is organized into blocks. By the spring of the first year, study of the organ systems begins with neuroscience, and continues into the second year. Students see

patients in the first week of school. Training in patient interviewing and examination continues throughout the first and second years until the clerkships begin at the end of the second year. All students do rotations in family medicine, internal medicine, obstetrics-gynecology, pediatrics, psychiatry/neurology, surgery, anesthesia, surgical subspecialties and ambulatory care. Students chose from multiple electives during the third and fourth years. All students complete a mentored scholarly project using the scientific method. An honors/pass/fail system is used for grading the first two years.

USMLE

Step 1: Required. Students must record a passing score for graduation, but not promotion.
Step 2: Clinical Skills (CS): Required. Students must record a passing total score to graduate.
Step 2: Clinical Knowledge (CK): Required. Students must record a passing total score to graduate.

Selection Factors

Applicants are chosen on the basis of intellect, integrity, maturity, creativity and strong interpersonal skills. The academic record; MCAT scores; essays; evaluations of college preprofessional committees; letters of recommendation, preferably from faculty members with whom the student has interacted in scholarly pursuits; extracurricular activities, in particular those showing service and medical exposure are all important in the decision to admit. On campus interviews by both a current medical student and faculty member are required and are weighed heavily in the final decision. All applicants are considered without regard to race, color, religion, ethnicity, national origin, age, sex, sexual orientation, marital, veteran, or handicap status.

Financial Aid

Loans and scholarships are awarded on the basis of financial need as documented by information on the FAFSA. Parental income information is required to be considered for University need-based resources. Students are considered for academic scholarships during the admissions process. Additional financial aid information is available on the school's website.

Information about Diversity Programs

The School of Medicine is committed to maintaining a broadly diverse student body/community. We believe such diversity is invaluable in a curriculum heavily based on small group and interactive learning. In the application process, all students are asked how they might contribute to the diversity of the school. The school hosts premedical summer enrichment programs organized by the Diversity Office, as well as a prematriculation program for all those admitted students who might benefit from such a program. Following admission, a broad range of support services are available to ensure retention. Specific information on the services provided to applicants from groups underrepresented in medicine can be obtained by contacting the Office of Student Affairs and Diversity Programs at (412) 648-8987.

Campus Information

Setting
Urban setting on the University of Pittsburgh campus with close proximity to multiple hospitals and the Graduate School of Public Health.

Enrollment
For 2009, total enrollment was: 569

Special Features
The School of Medicine is affiliated with the University of Pittsburgh Medical Center, one of the largest non-profit medical centers in the United States. Medical facilities located close to the medical school include Presbyterian University Hospital, Shadyside Hospital, Magee Womens Hospital, Children's Hospital of Pittsburgh, Eye and Ear Institute, the Starzl Transplantation Center, Benedum Geriatric Center, Western Pennsylvania Psychiatric Center, and the VA Pittsburgh Healthcare System, University Drive Division.

Housing
Housing is available on campus specifically for medical students. See: *www.ocl.pitt.edu/apartments/darragh.html*.

Satellite Campuses/Facilities
UPMC Palermo is a transplant hospital located in Sicily at which students may do a senior elective. Altoona Hospital provides a rural medicine experience.

Application Process and Requirements 2011–2012

Primary Application Service: AMCAS
Earliest filing date: June 1, 2010
Latest filing date: November 1, 2010

Secondary Application Required?: Yes
Sent to: All applicants
URL: https://admissions.medschool.pitt.edu
Fee: Yes, $85   **Waiver available:** Yes
Earliest filing date: July 1, 2010
Latest filing date: December 1, 2010

MCAT® required?: Yes
Latest MCAT® considered: September 2010
Oldest MCAT® considered: 2007

Early Decision Program: School does not have EDP
Applicants notified: n/a
EDP available for: n/a

Regular Acceptance Notice
Earliest date: November 15, 2010
Latest date: Until class is full
Applicant's Response to Acceptance Offer – Maximum Time: Two weeks

Requests for Deferred Entrance Considered: Yes

Deposit to Hold Place in Class: Yes
Deposit (Resident): $100   **(Non-resident):** $100
Deposit due: May 16-20, 2011
Applied to tuition: Yes   **Refundable:** No
Refundable by: n/a

Estimated number of new entrants: 148
EDP: n/a, special program: n/a

Start Month/Year: August 2011

Interview Format: An on-site faculty interview and student interview are required. Regional interviews are not available. Video interviews are not available.

Other Programs

PREPARATORY PROGRAMS
Postbaccalaureate Program: No
Summer Program: Yes, http://www.medschool.pitt.edu/future/future_03_office.asp

COMBINED DEGREE PROGRAMS
Baccalaureate/M.D.: No
M.D./M.P.H.: Yes, www.publichealth.pitt.edu/interior.php?pageID=203
MD/MBA: No
M.D./J.D.: No
M.D./Ph.D.: Yes, www.mdphd.pitt.edu
Additional Program: Yes, www.medadmissions.pitt.edu/admissions-requirements/special-programs.php

Premedical Coursework

On-line courses accepted in fulfillment of prerequisites: No

Course	Req.	Rec.	Lab.	Sems.	Course	Req.	Rec.	Lab.	Sems.
Inorganic Chemistry	•		•	2	Computer Science				
Behavioral Sciences					Genetics				
Biochemistry					Humanities				
Biology	•		•	2	Organic Chemistry	•		•	2
Biology/Zoology					Physics	•		•	2
Calculus		•			Psychology				
College English	•			2	Social Sciences				
College Mathematics		•			Other				

Selection Factors: 2009 Accepted Applicants

Proportion of Accepted Applicants with Relevant Experience (Data Self-Reported to AMCAS®)		
Community Service/Volunteer		71%
Medically-Related Work		87%
Research		91%

Shaded bar represents school's accepted scores ranging from the 10th percentile to the 90th percentile   School Median ● National Median ○

Overall GPA 2.0 2.1 2.2 2.3 2.4 2.5 2.6 2.7 2.8 2.9 3.0 3.1 3.2 3.3 3.4 3.5 3.6 3.7 (3.8) 3.9 4.0
Science GPA 2.0 2.1 2.2 2.3 2.4 2.5 2.6 2.7 2.8 2.9 3.0 3.1 3.2 3.3 3.4 3.5 3.6 3.7 3.8 (3.9) 4.0

MCAT® Total Numeric Score 9 10 11 12 13 14 15 16 17 18 19 20 21 22 23 24 25 26 27 28 29 30 31 (32) 33 34 35 (36) 37 38 39 40 41 42 43

Writing Sample				J	K	L	M	N	O	P	(Q)	R	S	T
Verbal Reasoning	3	4	5	6	7	8	9	(10)	(11)	12	13	14	15	
Biological Sciences	3	4	5	6	7	8	9	10	(11)	(12)	13	14	15	
Physical Sciences	3	4	5	6	7	8	9	10	(11)	(12)	13	14	15	

Acceptance & Matriculation Data for 2009–2010 First Year Class

	Resident	Non-resident	International	Total
Applications	802	4355	45	5202
Interviewed	169	806	0	975
Deferred	0	4	0	4
Matriculants				
Early Assurance Program	3	0	0	3
Early Decision Program	0	0	0	0
Baccalaureate/M.D.	0	0	0	0
M.D./Ph.D.	4	4	0	8
Matriculated	41	107	0	**148**

Applications accepted from International Applicants: No

Matriculant Demographics: 2009–2010 First Year Class

Men: 80   **Women:** 68

Matriculants' Self-Reported Race/Ethnicity

Mexican American	2	Korean	3
Cuban	2	Vietnamese	0
Puerto Rican	0	Other Asian	4
Other Hispanic	5	Total Asian	43
Total Hispanic	9	Native American	1
Chinese	23	Black	11
Asian Indian	12	Native Hawaiian	1
Pakistani	0	White	92
Filipino	2	Unduplicated Number	
Japanese	0	of Matriculants	148

Science and Math Majors: 64%
Matriculants with:
    Baccalaureate degree: 100%
    Graduate degree(s): 9%

Specialty Choice

2005, 2006, 2007 Graduates, Specialty Choice (As reported by program directors to GME Track™)	
Anesthesiology	6%
Emergency Medicine	10%
Family Practice	8%
Internal Medicine	17%
Obstetrics/Gynecology	5%
Orthopaedic Surgery	4%
Pediatrics	10%
Psychiatry	5%
Radiology	4%
Surgery	6%

Financial Information

Source: 2008-2009 LCME I-B survey and 2009-2010 AAMC TSF questionnaire

	Residents	Non-residents
Total Cost of Attendance	$ 58,145	$ 62,165
Tuition and Fees	$ 37,486	$ 41,506
Other (includes living expenses)	$ 17,751	$ 17,751
Health Insurance (can be waived)	$ 2,908	$ 2,908

Average 2009 Graduate Indebtedness: $141,018
% of Enrolled Students Receiving Aid: 88%

Criminal Background Check

This medical school requires a criminal background check prior to matriculation.

Ponce School of Medicine
Ponce, Puerto Rico

Admissions Office
Ponce School of Medicine
P.O. Box 7004
Ponce, Puerto Rico 00732
T 787 840 2575 **F** 787 842 0461

Admissions www.psm.edu/Student_Affairs/
Admissions/about_department.htm
Main www.psm.edu
Financial www.psm.edu/Student_Affairs/
Financial_Aid/fin_aid_about_department.htm
E-mail admissions@psm.edu

Private Institution

Dr. Joxel Garcia, President and Dean

Dr. Wanda Vélez, Admissions Director

Mirriam Gaud, Financial Aid Officer

Dr. Arvin Báez, Assistant Dean for Student Affairs

General Information
The Ponce School of Medicine of the Ponce Medical School Foundation, Inc. (formerly the Catholic University of Puerto Rico School of Medicine) took over the school's operations on July 1, 1980, under the governance of a board of trustees. The school graduated its first class in June 1981. Clinical training is offered at the following facilities in Ponce: Damas Hospital, a private institution with 356 beds; La Playa Diagnostic Center, which serves as the main training area for community and family practice; Dr. Pila Hospital, with 160 beds; and St. Luke's Hospital, with 550 beds. Clinical training is also offered at the Concepcion Hospital, with 188 beds, located in San German, and at Yauco Regional Hospital, with 140 beds.

Mission Statement
Ponce School of Medicine has as its mission the provision of high quality education and graduate training, which shall strengthen students' character, moral fiber, and ethics, and prepare physicians and scientists for a fast-changing world in the area of healthcare delivery and research.

Curricular Highlights
Community Service Requirement: Optional.
Research/Thesis Requirement: Optional.

The medical program's basic objective is to provide the Commonwealth of Puerto Rico, especially the southern region of the island, with ethically motivated, professionally competent physicians. The curriculum provides students with an early experience in family and community health needs. During the first two years, the basic medical sciences are thoroughly emphasized. Clinical experience takes precedence during the third and fourth years. The correlation between the basic and clinical sciences is achieved in a multidisciplinary program. Throughout the four-year program great emphasis is placed on the student's contact with patients and their families as a complement to the student's academic-hospital experience. Every academic semester contains, in addition to the regular curriculum, a series of supplementary seminars dealing with the ethical and social components of medical practice, as well as with additional specific subjects that are incidental and relevant to the profession. A problem-based learning program has been introduced in clinical correlation sessions in the first year of medical studies and in the Pathophysiology course, where it is presented as a student-centered integrative exercise. Subject-oriented small-group discussions are included in basic sciences courses. The program seeks to develop well-balanced, mature general practitioners, equally well qualified in the professional and ethical aspects of medicine. Students' work is graded according to an Honor/Pass/Fail system.

USMLE
Step 1: Required. Students must record a passing score for promotion.
Step 2: Clinical Skills (CS): Required. Students must only record a score.
Step 2: Clinical Knowledge (CK): Required. Students must record a passing total score to graduate.

Selection Factors
Selection of applicants is made by the Adnmissions' Committtee on the basis of academic achivement, MCAT scores, recomendation letters, and personal interviews. Interviews are used to determine the motivation and character of the applicants. Only those who pass a preliminary screening based on MCAT scores and college grades are interviewed. Carefull consideration is give to all applicants regardless of national or ethnic background, religious affiliation, sex or sexual orientation, or handicap (we comply with ADA). Residents of Puerto Rico are given preference, although a limited number of applicants who live in the United States are accepted. Candidates who are not proficiently fluent in both English and Spanish are not encouraged to apply, since teaching is given in both languages. The 2009 entering class composition is of 71% students from Puerto Rico, and 29% from the continental United States.

Financial Aid
Students are admitted to Ponce School of Medicine without regard to financial circumstances. After acceptance, prospective students are informed of the necessary forms they must submit in order to complete the financial aid process.

Campus Information
Setting
The Ponce School of Medicine is located in the city of Ponce, adjacent to Damas Hospital where the majority of our clinical teaching activities take place. Ponce is the major city of the southwestern part of the island. It is seventy miles from San Juan, which is on the northern coast. The city and the surrounding area provide a population base sufficient for medical training.

Enrollment
For 2009, total enrollment was: 66

Housing
On-campus housing is not available. The university does maintain a list of affordable apartments within a 10-mile radius. Rents average $400-$1000 per month.

Application Process and Requirements 2011–2012

Primary Application Service: AMCAS
Earliest filing date: June 1, 2010
Latest filing date: December 15, 2010

Secondary Application Required?: No
Sent to: All applicants
URL: n/a
Fee: Yes, $100   **Waiver available:** No
Earliest filing date: September 1, 2010
Latest filing date: January 15, 2011

MCAT® required?: Yes
Latest MCAT® considered: January 2010
Oldest MCAT® considered: June 2009

Early Decision Program: School does have EDP
Applicants notified: October 1, 2010
EDP available for: Both Residents and Non-residents

Regular Acceptance Notice
Earliest date: November 15, 2010
Latest date: Until class is full
Applicant's Response to Acceptance Offer – Maximum Time: Twenty days

Requests for Deferred Entrance Considered: No

Deposit to Hold Place in Class: Yes
Deposit (Resident): $1,000 **(Non-resident):** $1,000
Deposit due: With response to acceptance offer
Applied to tuition: Yes   **Refundable:** No
Refundable by: n/a

Estimated number of new entrants: 66
EDP: 3, special program: n/a

Start Month/Year: July 2011

Interview Format: Interviews are in groups or individually. Regional interviews are not available. Video interviews are not available.

Other Programs

PREPARATORY PROGRAMS
Postbaccalaureate Program: No
Summer Program: No

COMBINED DEGREE PROGRAMS
Baccalaureate/M.D.: Yes, Haydee Maltés, (787) 841-2000, hmaltes@email.pucpr.edu
M.D./M.P.H.: No
MD/MBA: No
M.D./J.D.: No
M.D./Ph.D.: No

Premedical Coursework

On-line courses accepted in fulfillment of prerequisites: On a case-by-case basis

Course	Req.	Rec.	Lab.	Hrs.	Course	Req.	Rec.	Lab.	Hrs.
Inorganic Chemistry	•		•	8	Computer Science				
Behavioral Sciences	•			12	Genetics				
Biochemistry		•			Humanities				
Biology	•			8	Organic Chemistry	•		•	8
Biology/Zoology			•		Physics	•		•	8
Calculus					Psychology				
College English	•			12	Social Sciences				
College Mathematics	•			6	Spanish	•			6

Selection Factors: 2009 Accepted Applicants

Proportion of Accepted Applicants with Relevant Experience (Data Self-Reported to AMCAS®)		
Community Service/Volunteer		55%
Medically-Related Work		55%
Research		74%

Shaded bar represents school's accepted scores ranging from the 10th percentile to the 90th percentile   School Median ●   National Median ◐

Overall GPA	2.0	2.1	2.2	2.3	2.4	2.5	2.6	2.7	2.8	2.9	3.0	3.1	3.2	3.3	3.4	3.5	(3.6)	3.7	3.8	3.9	4.0
Science GPA	2.0	2.1	2.2	2.3	2.4	2.5	2.6	2.7	2.8	2.9	3.0	3.1	3.2	3.3	(3.4)	3.5	3.6	3.7	3.8	3.9	4.0

MCAT® Total Numeric Score 9 10 11 12 13 14 15 16 17 18 19 20 21 (22) 23 24 25 26 27 28 29 30 31 (32) 33 34 35 36 37 38 39 40 41 42 43

Writing Sample			J	K	L	(M)	N	O	P	(Q)	R	S	T
Verbal Reasoning	3	4	5	6	(7)	8	9	(10)	11	12	13	14	15
Biological Sciences	3	4	5	6	7	(8)	9	10	(11)	12	13	14	15
Physical Sciences	3	4	5	6	(7)	8	9	10	(11)	12	13	14	15

Acceptance & Matriculation Data for 2009–2010 First Year Class

	Resident	Non-resident	International	Total
Applications	371	930	43	1344
Interviewed	176	39	0	215
Deferred	0	0	0	0
Matriculants				
Early Assurance Program	0	0	0	0
Early Decision Program	0	0	0	0
Baccalaureate/M.D.	0	0	0	0
M.D./Ph.D.	0	0	0	0
Matriculated	46	20	0	**66**

Applications accepted from International Applicants: Yes

Specialty Choice

2005, 2006, 2007 Graduates, Specialty Choice (As reported by program directors to GME Track™)	
Anesthesiology	3%
Emergency Medicine	6%
Family Practice	4%
Internal Medicine	17%
Obstetrics/Gynecology	10%
Orthopaedic Surgery	1%
Pediatrics	10%
Psychiatry	7%
Radiology	5%
Surgery	8%

Matriculant Demographics: 2009–2010 First Year Class

Men: 32   **Women:** 34

Matriculants' Self-Reported Race/Ethnicity

Mexican American	2	Korean	0
Cuban	8	Vietnamese	0
Puerto Rican	54	Other Asian	0
Other Hispanic	1	Total Asian	1
Total Hispanic	62	Native American	2
Chinese	1	Black	2
Asian Indian	0	Native Hawaiian	1
Pakistani	0	White	53
Filipino	1	Unduplicated Number	
Japanese	0	of Matriculants	66

Science and Math Majors: 68%
Matriculants with:
  Baccalaureate degree: 100%
  Graduate degree(s): 14%

Financial Information

Source: 2008-2009 LCME I-B survey and 2009-2010 AAMC TSF questionnaire

	Residents	Non-residents
Total Cost of Attendance	$ 45,053	$ 57,283
Tuition and Fees	$ 22,259	$ 32,233
Other (includes living expenses)	$ 21,492	$ 23,748
Health Insurance (can be waived)	$ 1,302	$ 1,302

Average 2009 Graduate Indebtedness: $161,594
% of Enrolled Students Receiving Aid: 87%

Criminal Background Check

This medical school requires a criminal background check prior to matriculation.

San Juan Bautista School of Medicine
Caguas, Puerto Rico

Admissions Office
P.O. Box 4968
Caguas, Puerto Rico 00726-4968
T 787 743 3038 x236   **F** 787 746 3093

Admissions www.sanjuanbautista.edu/
Admissions.aspx
Main www.sanjuanbautista.edu
Financial www.sanjuanbautista.edu/Admissions.aspx
E-mail admissions@sanjuanbautista.edu

Private Institution

Dr. Yocasta Brugal-Mena, President/Dean of Medicine

Dr. Myraida Rivera-Colon, Director of Admissions

Dr. Myraida Rivera-Colon, Minority Affairs Officer

Dr. Beatriz De Leon-Rivera, Financial Aid Officer

Dr. Emilio Dávila, Associate Dean for Student Affairs (interim)

Dr. Jaymi Sanchez-Cruz, Admissions Officer

General Information

The School of Medicine was founded in 1978 in San Juan, Puerto Rico, as a not-for-profit corporation, incorporated under the laws of the Commonwealth of Puerto Rico. It is located in Caguas, Puerto Rico, one of the most important urban centers. It is authorized by the Puerto Rico Council on Higher Education to offer studies leading to the M.D. degree. The MSCHE granted accreditation to the School in 2004. The LCME granted accreditation to the academic program in 2007. As of June 30, 2008, the School of Medicine has graduated a total of 915 medical doctors who have been successfully integrated in their communities as competent and caring health providers, both in Puerto Rico and abroad.

Mission Statement

The Mission of the School is to teach and train students to become primary care physicians that can provide holistic diagnosis and treatment to communities in need of health services in Puerto Rico. The School is committed to provide high quality medical education, service, and research, that will foster student's comprehensive development, so that they can become capable, competent, skilled, and honest professionals.

Curricular Highlights

Community Service Requirement: Required. 155 hrs required during the first three years
Research/Thesis Requirement: n/a

SJBSM had defined its curriculum within a student-centered approach, highlighting the values, attitudes, and social responsibility of the practice of medicine. It facilitates active learning and integration, offering early exposure to clinical scenarios and technological experiences in the learning process and using diverse assessment methodologies. The curriculum is structured in five emphases: medical knowledge, clinical skills, research and information literacy, professionalism and community awareness. These emphases are incorporated throughout the four years. The preclinical courses are offered in a system-based approach during the first two years. The third year is devoted to core clinical clerkships, both inpatient and outpatient scenarios, including a research clerkship. The fourth year reinforces the practice of medicine with core and electives sub-internships. Several curricular innovations strengthen the learning process: multidisciplinary exercises that promote vertical and horizontal integration, development of a research proposal throughout the four years, and different levels/types of community experiences, according to the School's mission.

USMLE

Step 1: Required. Must record a passing score for promotion.
Step 2: Clinical Skills (CS): Required. Students must record a passing total score to graduate.
Step 2: Clinical Knowledge (CK): Required. Students must record a passing total score to graduate.

Selection Factors

The Admissions office evaluates all applications, taking into consideration academic and personal qualifications. The analysis includes academic achievement, premedical studies required for admission to the program, and MCAT scores. The motivations to study medicine, leadership qualities, ability to relate to other people and deal with problems, and participation in community/scientific activities, are also taken into consideration by the Admissions Committee. Qualified applicants are required to appear for an interview.

Financial Aid

The Financial Aid Office counsels students regarding the availability of economic aid and the procedure to file applications. For further information, please refer to: *http://sanjuanbautista.edu/Admissions.aspx.*

Information about Diversity Programs

The School of Medicine is committed to diversity in the faculty and the student body. Its goal is to recruit, admit and graduate students that comply with all the requirements. The office of Diversity Affairs has programs to assist to help meeting the objectives of all student body.

Campus Information

Setting
The School's facilities are located on the grounds of the San Juan Bautista Medical Center. The 52 acre campus is the location for the Hospital and the School, which houses administrative offices, the biomedical sciences faculty, and the Library/ Learning Resources Center, as well as the classrooms and laboratories for teaching and research. Clinical training at the SJBMC brings students into contact with a patient population drawn from many different socio-economic groups. The SJBMC is the principal clinical training facility for third and fourth year students.

Enrollment
For 2009, total enrollment was: 256

Special Features
Our School is a community-based institution, in which community service is a curricular axis. Courses and activities are patient-focused throughout the program.

Housing
The School provides information about available housing facilities in Caguas.

Satellite Campuses/Facilities
The School of Medicine has established several collaborations that provide opportunities for its students. Students rotate at hospitals and ambulatory health care systems that met the School's high standards of educational quality.

Application Process and Requirements 2011–2012

Primary Application Service: AMCAS
Earliest filing date: June 1, 2010
Latest filing date: December 15, 2010

Secondary Application Required: No
URL: www.sanjuanbautista.edu/Admissions.aspx
Jaymi Sanchez-Cruz, (787) 743-3038 x236
admissions@sanjuanbautista.edu
Sent to: n/a
Fee: Yes, $100   **Waiver Available:** No
Earliest filing date: n/a
Latest filing date: n/a

MCAT® required?: Yes
Latest MCAT® considered: December 2010
Oldest MCAT® considered: December 2007

Early Decision Program: School does have EDP
Applicants notified: October 1, 2010
EDP available for: Both residents and non-residents

Regular Acceptance Notice
Earliest date: January 2011
Latest date: Until Class is Full

Applicant's Response to Acceptance
Offer – Maximum Time: Two weeks

Requests for deferred entrance considered: No

Deposit to Hold Place in Class: Yes,
Deposit (Resident): $300   **(Non-resident):** $300
Deposit due: Two weeks
Applied to tuition: Yes   **Refundable:** No
Refundable by: n/a

Estimated number of new entrants: 60
EDP: 3, special program: n/a

Start month/year: July 2011

Interview format: Interviews occur individually or in groups on campus. Regional interviews are not available. Video interviews are not available.

Other Programs

PREPARATORY PROGRAMS
Postbaccalaureate Program: No
Summer Program: No

COMBINED DEGREE PROGRAMS
Baccalaureate/M.D.: No
M.D./M.P.H.: No
MD/MBA: No
M.D./J.D.: No
M.D./Ph.D.: No

Premedical Coursework

On-line courses accepted in fulfillment of prerequisites: Yes

Course	Req.	Rec.	Lab.	Sems.	Course	Req.	Rec.	Lab.	Sems.
Inorganic Chemistry	•			2	Computer Science				
Behavioral Sciences	•			4	Genetics				
Biochemistry		•			Humanities				
Biology	•			2	Organic Chemistry	•			2
Biology/Zoology					Physics	•			2
Calculus					Psychology				
College English	•			4	Social Sciences				
College Mathematics					Spanish	•			2
					Electives	•			6

Selection Factors: 2009 Accepted Applicants

Proportion of Accepted Applicants with Relevant Experience (Data Self-Reported to AMCAS®)		
Community Service/Volunteer		63%
Medically-Related Work		63%
Research		66%

Shaded bar represents school's accepted scores ranging from the 10th percentile to the 90th percentile   School Median ●   National Median ○

Overall GPA	2.0	2.1	2.2	2.3	2.4	2.5	2.6	2.7	2.8	2.9	3.0	3.1	3.2	3.3	(3.4)	3.5	3.6	3.7	3.8	3.9	4.0
Science GPA	2.0	2.1	2.2	2.3	2.4	2.5	2.6	2.7	2.8	2.9	3.0	(3.1)	3.2	3.3	3.4	3.5	3.6	3.7	3.8	3.9	4.0

MCAT® Total Numeric Score 9 10 11 12 13 14 15 16 17 18 19 20 (21) 22 23 24 25 26 27 28 29 30 31 (32) 33 34 35 36 37 38 39 40 41 42 43

Writing Sample			J	K	L	(M)	N	O	P	(Q)	R	S	T
Verbal Reasoning	3	4	5	6	(7)	8	9	(10)	11	12	13	14	15
Biological Sciences	3	4	5	6	7	(8)	9	10	(11)	12	13	14	15
Physical Sciences	3	4	5	6	(7)	8	9	10	(11)	12	13	14	15

Acceptance & Matriculation Data for 2009–2010 First Year Class

	Resident	Non-resident	International	Total
Applications	334	507	19	860
Interviewed	87	51	0	138
Deferred	0	0	0	0
Matriculants				
Early Assurance Program	0	0	0	0
Early Decision Program	0	0	0	0
Baccalaureate/M.D.	0	0	0	0
M.D./Ph.D.	0	0	0	0
Matriculated	35	28	0	**63**

Applications accepted from International Applicants: Yes

Specialty Choice

2005, 2006, 2007 Graduates, Specialty Choice
(As reported by program directors to GME Track™)

Anesthesiology
Emergency Medicine
Family P
Internal
Obstetri
Orthopa   **DATA NOT AVAILABLE**
Pediatric
Psychiat
Radiolog
Surgery

Matriculant Demographics: 2009–2010 First Year Class

Men: 28   **Women:** 35

Matriculants' Self-Reported Race/Ethnicity

Mexican American	1	Korean	0
Cuban	6	Vietnamese	0
Puerto Rican	38	Other Asian	0
Other Hispanic	8	Total Asian	3
Total Hispanic	52	Native American	0
Chinese	1	Black	4
Asian Indian	2	Native Hawaiian	0
Pakistani	0	White	55
Filipino	0	Unduplicated Number	
Japanese	0	of Matriculants	63

Science Majors: 71%
Matriculants with:
  Baccalaureate Degree: 100%
  Graduate Degree(s): 5%

Financial Information

Source: 2008-2009 LCME I-B survey and 2009-2010 AAMC TSF questionnaire

	Residents	Non-residents
Total Cost of Attendance	$ 49,225	$ 52,225
Tuition and Fees	$ 18,920	$ 21,920
Other (includes living expenses)	$ 28,750	$ 28,750
Health Insurance (can be waived)	$ 1,555	$ 1,555

Average 2009 Graduate Indebtedness: $108,561
% of Enrolled Students Receiving Aid: 94%

Criminal Background Check

This medical school requires a criminal background check prior to matriculation.

Universidad Central del Caribe
School of Medicine
Bayamón, Puerto Rico

Office of Admissions
Universidad Central del Caribe
School of Medicine,
P.O. Box 60-327
Bayamon, Puerto Rico 00960-6032
T 787 798 3001   F 787 269 7550

Admissions www.uccaribe.edu
Main www.uccaribe.edu
Financial www.uccaribe.edu
E-mail icordero@uccaribe.edu
edlopez@uccaribe.edu

Private Institution

Dr. Jose Ginel Rodriguez, Dean of Medicine

Irma L. Cordero, Admissions Officer

Dr. Omar Perez, Dean of Admissions & Students Affairs

Nilda Montañez, Registrar

General Information
The Universidad Central del Caribe School of Medicine was founded in 1976 as a nonprofit private institution chartered under the laws of the Commonwealth of Puerto Rico. The new building for the basic sciences, library, animal house, and central administration was inaugurated in 1990 adjacent to Dr. Ramon Ruiz Arnau University Hospital, which serves as the principal teaching hospital. The school facilities are located in a 56-acre academic health center in the city of Bayamon.

Mission Statement
The mission of the School of Medicine is to develop competent physicians with an outstanding academic preparation within a humanistic and holistic framework. A guiding principle of our mission is to ensure that our graduates possess a strong sense of professionalism and commitment to social duties and service to Puerto Rico and Hispanic communities throughout the U.S. mainland.

Curricular Highlights
Community Service Requirement: Optional.
Research/Thesis Requirement: Optional.

The medical curriculum is organized in two years of preclinical and two years of clinical experiences. A longitudinal curriculum in bioethics and humanities in medicine characterizes the medical education program. Clinical correlations are included in the basic science courses. Exposure to real and standardized patients is provided beginning with the first year. Introduction to clinical medicine has as its foundation the biopsychosocial model. A problem-based course is structured around prevalent problems encountered in primary care. The third-year learning experience revolves around required clerkships in internal medicine, pediatrics, obstetrics-gynecology, general surgery, and family medicine. The latter takes place in the ambulatory setting. Also, during the third year, students enroll in the surgical subspecialties and psychiatry clerkships. Eighteen weeks of electives are provided in the fourth year, plus three months in required courses in neurology, ambulatory medicine, selected topics, and bioethics and humanities in medicine. Individual student evaluation in all requisite basic science and clinical science courses is based on letter grade and Pass/Fail systems. Student evaluation in all elective courses is based on an Honors/Pass/Fail system.

USMLE
Step 1: Required. Students must record a passing score for promotion.
Step 2: Clinical Skills (CS): Required. Students must record a passing total score to graduate.
Step 2: Clinical Knowledge (CK): Required. Students must record a passing total score to graduate.

Selection Factors
The selection of candidates for admission is made exclusively by the Admissions Committee. The admission process does not discriminate against any individual on the basis of sex, age, race, religion, economic status, political ideology, or national origin. Applicants must demonstrate proficiency in both Spanish and English. Lectures may be in either language. Spanish is the predominant language of the institution. Major factors considered in the selection of candidates for admission include undergraduate academic record, overall GPA and science GPA, performance in all areas of the MCAT, community services, research and others experiences, results of a personal interview, and letters of recommendation. A personal interview is required prior to consideration for admission. All interviews are arranged by the Office of Admissions and are conducted at the medical school facilities in Bayamon. Rejected applicants are given the opportunity to reapply for admission.

Financial Aid
The Office of the Dean for Student Affairs provides financial aid counseling to all prospective students. Incoming students qualify for application to all pertinent federal and commonwealth scholarship and loan programs. Economic status of the applicant is not a consideration during the selection of candidates for admission.

Campus Information

Enrollment
For 2009, total enrollment was: 266

Housing
On-campus housing is not available. However, the Dean for Student Affairs maintains a list of affordable apartments in the vicinity.

Satellite Campuses/Facilities
Student rotations are divided between the University Hospital and a rich network of clinical settings in the metro area.

Application Process and Requirements 2011–2012

Primary Application Service: AMCAS
Earliest filing date: June 1, 2010
Latest filing date: December 15, 2010

Secondary Application Required?: No
Sent to: Several documents must be submitted.
Irma L. Cordero, (787) 798-3001 x 2403, icordero@uccaribe.edu
Fee: Yes, $100   **Waiver available:** No
Earliest filing date: n/a
Latest filing date: n/a

MCAT® required?: Yes
Latest MCAT® considered: September 2010
Oldest MCAT® considered: January 2007

Early Decision Program: School does not have EDP
Applicants notified: n/a
EDP available for: n/a

Regular Acceptance Notice
Earliest date: January 2011
Latest date: Until class is full
Applicant's Response to Acceptance Offer – Maximum Time: Two weeks

Requests for Deferred Entrance Considered: No

Deposit to Hold Place in Class: Yes
Deposit (Resident): $100   **(Non-resident):** $100
Deposit due: 15 days after notification
Applied to tuition: No   **Refundable:** No
Refundable by: n/a

Estimated number of new entrants: 65
EDP: n/a, special program: n/a

Start Month/Year: August 2011

Interview Format: Group interviews. Video interviews are not available.

Other Programs

PREPARATORY PROGRAMS

Postbaccalaureate Program: Yes, Edllian Lopez, (787) 798-3001 x2404, edlopez@uccaribe.edu
Summer Program: No

COMBINED DEGREE PROGRAMS

Baccalaureate/M.D.: No
M.D./M.P.H.: No
MD/MBA: No
M.D./J.D.: No
M.D./Ph.D.: No

Premedical Coursework

On-line courses accepted in fulfillment of prerequisites: No

Course	Req.	Rec.	Lab.	Hrs.	Course	Req.	Rec.	Lab.	Hrs.
Inorganic Chemistry	•		•	8	Computer Science		•		
Behavioral Sciences		•			Genetics				
Biochemistry		•			Humanities				
Biology		•			Organic Chemistry	•		•	8
Biology/Zoology	•		•	8	Physics	•		•	8
Calculus					Psychology				
College English	•			12	Social Sciences		•		
College Mathematics	•			6	Behavioral/Social Sciences	•			12
					Spanish	•			6

Selection Factors: 2009 Accepted Applicants

Proportion of Accepted Applicants with Relevant Experience (Data Self-Reported to AMCAS®)		
Community Service/Volunteer		56%
Medically-Related Work		58%
Research		72%

Shaded bar represents school's accepted scores ranging from the 10th percentile to the 90th percentile.   School Median ●   National Median ○

Overall GPA 2.0 2.1 2.2 2.3 2.4 2.5 2.6 2.7 2.8 2.9 3.0 3.1 3.2 3.3 3.4 ③.5 3.6 3.7 3.8 3.9 4.0
Science GPA 2.0 2.1 2.2 2.3 2.4 2.5 2.6 2.7 2.8 2.9 3.0 3.1 3.2 ③.3 3.4 3.5 3.6 3.7 3.8 3.9 4.0

MCAT® Total Numeric Score 9 10 11 12 13 14 15 16 17 18 19 20 ㉑ 22 23 24 25 26 27 28 29 30 31 ㉜ 33 34 35 36 37 38 39 40 41 42 43

Writing Sample			J	K	L	Ⓜ	N	O	P	ⓠ	R	S	T
Verbal Reasoning	3	4	5	⑥	7	8	9	⑩	11	12	13	14	15
Biological Sciences	3	4	5	6	7	⑧	9	10	⑪	12	13	14	15
Physical Sciences	3	4	5	6	⑦	8	9	10	⑪	12	13	14	15

Acceptance & Matriculation Data for 2009–2010 First Year Class

	Resident	Non-resident	International	Total
Applications	372	637	32	1041
Interviewed	137	32	0	169
Deferred	0	0	0	0
Matriculants				
Early Assurance Program	0	0	0	0
Early Decision Program	0	0	0	0
Baccalaureate/M.D.	0	0	0	0
M.D./Ph.D.	0	0	0	0
Matriculated	51	14	0	**65**

Applications accepted from International Applicants: Yes

Specialty Choice

2005, 2006, 2007 Graduates, Specialty Choice (As reported by program directors to GME Track™)	
Anesthesiology	2%
Emergency Medicine	4%
Family Practice	2%
Internal Medicine	32%
Obstetrics/Gynecology	4%
Orthopaedic Surgery	1%
Pediatrics	9%
Psychiatry	11%
Radiology	2%
Surgery	5%

Matriculant Demographics: 2009–2010 First Year Class

Men: 29   **Women:** 36

Matriculants' Self-Reported Race/Ethnicity

Mexican American	1	Korean	0
Cuban	7	Vietnamese	0
Puerto Rican	52	Other Asian	0
Other Hispanic	6	Total Asian	0
Total Hispanic	62	Native American	0
Chinese	0	Black	5
Asian Indian	0	Native Hawaiian	0
Pakistani	0	White	50
Filipino	0	Unduplicated Number	
Japanese	0	of Matriculants	65

Science and Math Majors: 86%
Matriculants with:
Baccalaureate degree: 98%
Graduate degree(s): 14%

Financial Information

Source: 2008-2009 LCME I-B survey and 2009-2010 AAMC TSF questionnaire

	Residents	Non-residents
Total Cost of Attendance	$ 49,281	$ 56,631
Tuition and Fees	$ 24,555	$ 31,905
Other (includes living expenses)	$ 23,078	$ 23,078
Health Insurance (can be waived)	$ 1,648	$ 1,648

Average 2009 Graduate Indebtedness: $41,819
% of Enrolled Students Receiving Aid: 95%

Criminal Background Check

This medical school requires a criminal background check prior to matriculation.

University of Puerto Rico School of Medicine

San Juan, Puerto Rico

Central Admissions Office
School of Medicine, Medical Sciences Campus
University of Puerto Rico, P.O. Box 365067
San Juan, Puerto Rico 00936-5067
T 787 758 2525 x5215   **F** 787 282 7117

Admissions www.md.rcm.upr.edu
Main www.md.rcm.upr.edu
Financial www.rcm.upr.edu/estudiantes/Asistencia
conomica/index.htm/
E-mail margarita.rivera4@upr.edu

Public Institution

Dr. Walter Frontera, Dean

Dr. Gladys Gonzalez-Navarrete, Associate Dean for Student Affairs

Margarita Rivera, Director, Admissions Office

Zoraida Cruz, Director, Financial Aid Office

General Information

The UPR-SOM was established in 1949. The affiliated hospitals of the P.R. Medical Center and the Hospital Consortium, which include the main health care facilities in other cities, serve the medical school for teaching purposes. On the Medical Sciences Campus, the School of Medicine works in close relation with the School of Dentistry, the College of Allied Health Professions, the Faculty of Biosocial Sciences and Graduate School of Public Health, the School of Nursing, and the School of Pharmacy in an interdisciplinary team approach. Its location, adjacent to the University District Hospital, permits integration of basic and clinical departments and an improved utilization of all Medical Sciences Campus resources.

Mission Statement

The mission of the UPR-SOM is to transmit, enrich, and increase knowledge in the medical sciences through teaching, research, and clinical service. The school is committed to achieve the ideals of personal and academic excellence through the interdisciplinary model for providing education and health services, especially at the primary level. The school will provide an academic and institutional environment conducive to the personal and professional development of both students and faculty.

Curricular Highlights

Community Service Requirement: Optional.
Research/Thesis Requirement: Optional.

The new curriculum is four academic years in length. The first two years include the fundamentals of biological, behavioral, and clinical sciences and are mostly handled by the basic sciences departments. Part of the sophomore year is dedicated to pathophysiology, physical diagnosis, and basic clerkship, which are offered by a multidisciplinary faculty. Small-group sessions utilizing the problem-based learning approach are introduced at the beginning of the medical studies. Human behavior, environmental factors, and public health concepts are integrated into the curriculum. The third and fourth years are dedicated to required clinical experiences and elective courses. Through the Hispanic Center of Excellence, the curriculum has been focused on community-oriented primary care exposure. Support services, counseling, tutorials, and other services are provided to students to assist in retention. Students are graded on a letter grade system during all four years.

USMLE

Step 1: Required. Students must record a passing score for promotion.
Step 2: Clinical Skills (CS): Optional.
Step 2: Clinical Knowledge (CK): Required. Students must record a passing total score to graduate.

Selection Factors

Since the UPR-SOM is a state-supported institution, preference will be given to qualified applicants who are legal residents of Puerto Rico. Foreign national applicants with an established residence in P.R. will be considered only if, at the time of application, they are either U.S. citizens or have been granted a permanent resident visa in the United States. In selecting students, the Admissions Committee considers the candidate's academic performance, MCAT scores, recommendations of instructors, attitudinal and other personality factors assessed in personal interviews, extracurricular activities, and any other pertinent information. Personal interviews are conducted only by invitation from the Admissions Committee for those students with high numerical ranks according to the admission formula. The admission formula gives equal weight to academic indices and MCAT scores, with somewhat less weight given to ratings derived from evaluations by premedical committees and interviewers. Rejected applicants are given the opportunity to reapply for admission. Applicants, without exception, must submit all application material and supporting documents by December 1 of the year preceding the school year for which they request admission. The UPR-SOM has the policy of giving equal opportunity for education and training in the practice of the health professions without regard to race, creed, sex, national origin, age, or handicap.

Financial Aid

Financial aid is available to students. Awards are made on the basis of confidential applications submitted by students. Financial need is the major criterion. Applicants who require scholarship assistance may make application in conjunction with the application for admission or before April 30. Financial need will not influence the selection process. Forms are available from the Financial Aid Office upon request. We do not offer financial assistance to foreign students.

Campus Information

Enrollment
For 2009, total enrollment was: 445

Application Process and Requirements 2011–2012

Primary Application Service: AMCAS
Earliest filing date: June 1, 2010
Latest filing date: December 1, 2010

Secondary Application Required?: Yes
Sent to: All applicants
URL: www.md.rcm.upr.edu
Fee: Yes, $20   **Waiver available:** No
Earliest filing date: June 1, 2010
Latest filing date: December 1, 2010

MCAT® required?: Yes
Latest MCAT® considered: September 2010
Oldest MCAT® considered: September 2007

Early Decision Program: School does not have EDP
Applicants notified: n/a
EDP available for: n/a

Regular Acceptance Notice
Earliest date: December 2010
Latest date: Varies
Applicant's Response to Acceptance Offer – Maximum Time: Two weeks

Requests for Deferred Entrance Considered: No

Deposit to Hold Place in Class: Yes
Deposit (Resident): $100   **(Non-resident):** $100
Deposit due: With response to acceptance offer
Applied to tuition: Yes   **Refundable:** No
Refundable by: n/a

Estimated number of new entrants: 110
EDP: n/a, special program: n/a

Start Month/Year: August 2011

Interview Format: Regional interviews are not available. Video interviews are not available.

Other Programs

PREPARATORY PROGRAMS
Postbaccalaureate Program: No
Summer Program: No

COMBINED DEGREE PROGRAMS
Baccalaureate/M.D.: No
M.D./M.P.H.: No
MD/MBA: No
M.D./J.D.: Yes, www.md.rcm.upr.edu
M.D./Ph.D.: Yes, www.md.rcm.upr.edu

Premedical Coursework

On-line courses accepted in fulfillment of prerequisites: No

Course	Req.	Rec.	Lab.	Hrs.
Inorganic Chemistry	•		•	8
Behavioral Sciences	•			6
Biochemistry		•		
Biology	•			8
Biology/Zoology				
Calculus				
College English				12
College Mathematics				

Course	Req.	Rec.	Lab.	Hrs.
Computer Science		•		
Genetics				
Humanities		•		
Organic Chemistry	•		•	8
Physics	•		•	8
Psychology				
Social Sciences	•			6
Spanish	•			12

Selection Factors: 2009 Accepted Applicants

Proportion of Accepted Applicants with Relevant Experience (Data Self-Reported to AMCAS°)		
Community Service/Volunteer		47%
Medically-Related Work		43%
Research		78%

Shaded bar represents school's accepted scores ranging from the 10th percentile to the 90th percentile   **School Median** ● **National Median** ●

Overall GPA	2.0	2.1	2.2	2.3	2.4	2.5	2.6	2.7	2.8	2.9	3.0	3.1	3.2	3.3	3.4	3.5	3.6	3.7	(3.8)	3.9	4.0
Science GPA	2.0	2.1	2.2	2.3	2.4	2.5	2.6	2.7	2.8	2.9	3.0	3.1	3.2	3.3	3.4	3.5	3.6	(3.7)	3.8	3.9	4.0

MCAT® Total Numeric Score 9 10 11 12 13 14 15 16 17 18 19 20 21 22 23 (24) 25 26 27 28 29 30 31 (32) 33 34 35 36 37 38 39 40 41 42 43

				J	K	L	M	(N)	O	P	(Q)	R	S	T
Writing Sample														
Verbal Reasoning	3	4	5	6	(7)	8	9	(10)	11	12	13	14	15
Biological Sciences	3	4	5	6	7	8	(9)	10	(11)	12	13	14	15
Physical Sciences	3	4	5	6	(7)	8	9	10	(11)	12	13	14	15

Acceptance & Matriculation Data for 2009–2010 First Year Class

	Resident	Non-resident	International	Total
Applications	320	687	10	1017
Interviewed	150	0	0	150
Deferred	2	0	0	2
Matriculants				
Early Assurance Program	0	0	0	0
Early Decision Program	0	0	0	0
Baccalaureate/M.D.	0	0	0	0
M.D./Ph.D.	0	0	0	0
Matriculated	105	0	0	**105**

Applications accepted from International Applicants: No

Matriculant Demographics: 2009–2010 First Year Class

Men: 37   **Women:** 68

Matriculants' Self-Reported Race/Ethnicity

Mexican American	2	Korean	0
Cuban	1	Vietnamese	0
Puerto Rican	102	Other Asian	0
Other Hispanic	3	Total Asian	0
Total Hispanic	103	Native American	1
Chinese	0	Black	11
Asian Indian	0	Native Hawaiian	0
Pakistani	0	White	68
Filipino	0	Unduplicated Number	
Japanese	0	of Matriculants	105

Science and Math Majors: 78%
Matriculants with:
  Baccalaureate degree: 100%
  Graduate degree(s): 4%

Specialty Choice

2005, 2006, 2007 Graduates, Specialty Choice (As reported by program directors to GME Track™)	
Anesthesiology	2%
Emergency Medicine	2%
Family Practice	3%
Internal Medicine	26%
Obstetrics/Gynecology	4%
Orthopaedic Surgery	3%
Pediatrics	11%
Psychiatry	8%
Radiology	5%
Surgery	7%

Financial Information

Source: 2008-2009 LCME I-B survey and 2009-2010 AAMC TSF questionnaire

	Residents	Non-residents
Total Cost of Attendance	$ 36,030	$ 45,248
Tuition and Fees	$ 11,091	$ 20,309
Other (includes living expenses)	$ 24,939	$ 24,939
Health Insurance (can be waived)	$ 0	$ 0

Average 2009 Graduate Indebtedness: $52,437
% of Enrolled Students Receiving Aid: 74%

Criminal Background Check

This medical school does not require a criminal background check prior to matriculation.

The Warren Alpert Medical School of Brown University

Providence, Rhode Island

Office of Admissions
Alpert Medical School
97 Waterman Street, Box G-A213
Providence, Rhode Island 02912-9706
T 401 863 2149   F 401 863 2660

Admissions http://med.brown.edu/admissions
Main http://med.brown.edu
Financial http://med.brown.edu/financialaid/
E-mail MedSchool_Admissions@brown.edu

Private Institution

Dr. Edward J. Wing, Dean of Medicine and Biological Sciences

Barbara Fuller, Director of Admissions

Dr. Emma Simmons, Assistant Dean for Minority Medical Affairs

Linda A. Gillette, Director of Financial Aid

Dr. Philip Gruppuso, Associate Dean for Medical Education

Lindsay Graham, Executive Dean for Administration

General Information

The projected August 2011 opening of a new medical education building represents a signficant advance in Alpert Medical School's role as a leader in medical education and biomedical research. The new facility will accommodate an increased enrollment and provide for the social, technological and educational needs of the next generation of physician scientists. The medical school and its eight affiliated hospitals receive $220 million annually in research funding. Brown is home to the state's only Master of Public Health degree program and to ten public health research centers. Entry into Alpert Medical School is possible through many admission routes: a combined Bachelor's/Medical degree program; standard AMCAS admission; postbaccalareate linkage program; and an Early Identification Program.

Mission Statement

Our mission is to educate physicians in the scientific, ethical, and humanistic dimensions of medicine and to advance our ability to diagnose, treat, and prevent human illness.

Curricular Highlights

Community Service Requirement: Optional.
Research/Thesis Requirement: Optional.

The medical curriculum is demanding, yet flexible. The first year is devoted to core basic sciences in the form of two semester-length, integrated medical sciences courses and Doctoring, in which students encounter individual, community-based clinical skills teaching with group sessions on ethics, patient interviewing, and professional development topics. The second year consists of organ or system-based pathophysiology with integrated pharmacology, pathology, neurologic pathophysiology, epidemiology, and Doctoring. Students in the third and fourth-years are required to complete 50 weeks of clinical clerkships and 30 weeks of electives. Clinical clerkships include internal medicine, surgery, psychiatry, obstetrics and gynecology, pediatrics, family medicine, and community health. Elective requirements include an advanced clinical clerkship in medicine, surgery, or pediatrics, and an ambulatory longitudinal clerkship.

USMLE

Step 1: Required. Students must record a passing score for graduation, but not promotion.
Step 2: Clinical Skills (CS): Required. Students must only record a score.
Step 2: Clinical Knowledge (CK): Required. Students must only record a score.

Selection Factors

Selection criteria are academic achievement, faculty evaluations, and evidence of maturity, leadership, integrity, and compassion. Eligible candidates generally must present a minimum cumulative grade point average of 3.00 (4.00 scale) in undergraduate courses. Applicants who have attended graduate school must achieve a cumulative grade point average of 3.00 (4.00 scale). Applicants must complete baccalaureate degree requirements before entry into medical school. Brown University adheres to a policy of equal opportunity in medical education and considers applicants without regard to sex, race, religion, age, disability, status as a veteran, national or ethnic origin, sexual orientation, or gender identity. An affirmative action program is maintained in all admission entry routes.

Financial Aid

Alpert Medical School assists students in meeting their educational expenses through a combination of low-interest loans and need-based institutional scholarships. Seventy-six percent of students received financial aid awards in 2009-10. The average award was $44,613, and the average scholarship award was $17,595.

Information about Diversity Programs

Alpert Medical School invites applications from members of ethnic and racial groups underrepresented in medicine. The objective of the Office of Minority Medical Affairs (OMMA) is the recruitment, retention, and graduation of students from groups underrepresented in medicine. The OMMA provides academic and personal counseling, workshops, information on scholarship awards, and a program linking students from groups underrepresented in medicine with alumni/ae from such groups.

Campus Information

Setting

The new medical education building is located in the historic Jewelry District, about a mile from Brown's main campus and within walking distance of several laboratories, research facilities and three affiliated hospitals. Providence's many restaurants, theaters, shopping, and riverwalk are easily accessible on foot.

Enrollment

For 2009, total enrollment was: 414

Special Features

Alpert Medical School is affiliated with eight hospitals within a five-mile radius, including a Level I trauma center, a children's hospital, two community hospitals, separate adult and children's psychiatric hospitals, a Veterans Affairs Medical Center, and a women's hospital with the largest neonatal intensive care unit in the Northeast. Students gain global health experience through clinical electives or exchange programs in Germany, Kenya, Sweden, and Israel.

Housing

Affordable housing options are available in several neighborhoods within walking distance of campus. Students have an on-campus dorm option. The university leases and manages about 150 apartments and homes in the vicinity. Monthly rents range from $760 to $1,150 in Brown-owned housing.

Satellite Campuses/Facilities

Clinical training in all four years occurs in a variety of settings, from the affiliated hospitals to diverse community-based sites.

Application Process and Requirements 2011–2012

Primary Application Service: AMCAS
Earliest filing date: June 1, 2010
Latest filing date: November 1, 2010

Secondary Application Required?: Yes
Sent to: All verified AMCAS applicants
URL: http://bms.brown.edu/admissions/applications
Fee: Yes, $95   **Waiver available:** Yes
Earliest filing date: July 1, 2010
Latest filing date: December 31, 2010

MCAT® required?: Yes
Latest MCAT® considered: September 2010
Oldest MCAT® considered: September 2006

Early Decision Program: School does not have EDP
Applicants notified: n/a
EDP available for: n/a

Regular Acceptance Notice
Earliest date: November 2010
Latest date: Until Class is Full
Applicant's Response to Acceptance Offer – Maximum Time: Three weeks

Requests for Deferred Entrance Considered: Yes

Deposit to Hold Place in Class: No
Deposit (Resident): n/a   **(Non-resident):** n/a
Deposit due: n/a
Applied to tuition: n/a   **Refundable:** n/a
Refundable by: n/a

Estimated number of new entrants: 62
EDP: n/a, special program: 50

Start Month/Year: August 2011

Interview Format: Group session and two individual meetings. All interviews are at Alpert Medical School. Video interviews are not available.

Other Programs

PREPARATORY PROGRAMS
Postbaccalaureate Program: No
Summer Program: No
Scholarly Concentrations Program: Yes, http://med.brown.edu/education/concentrations/index.php
Academic Enhancement Program: Yes, http://med.brown.edu/student_services/enhancement.html

COMBINED DEGREE PROGRAMS
Baccalaureate/M.D.: Yes, http://bms.brown.edu/plme/
M.D./M.P.H.: Yes, http://publichealth.brown.edu/mph/students/prospective/md_mph/
MD/MBA: No
M.D./J.D.: No
M.D./Ph.D.: Yes, http://med.brown.edu/admissions/mdphd.html
Additional Program: Yes, www.brown.edu/Departments/Taubman_Center/minisite/grad/MD_MPP.html

Premedical Coursework

On-line courses accepted in fulfillment of prerequisites: No

Course	Req.	Rec.	Lab.	Sems.
Inorganic Chemistry	•			2
Behavioral Sciences	•			1
Biochemistry		•		
Biology	•			1
Biology/Zoology				
Calculus	•			1
College English		•		
College Mathematics				

Course	Req.	Rec.	Lab.	Sems.
Computer Science				
Genetics		•		
Humanities		•		
Organic Chemistry	•			1
Physics	•			2
Psychology				
Social Sciences	•			1
Other				

Selection Factors: 2009 Accepted Applicants

Proportion of Accepted Applicants with Relevant Experience (Data Self-Reported to AMCAS)	
Community Service/Volunteer	67%
Medically-Related Work	76%
Research	81%

Shaded bar represents school's accepted scores ranging from the 10th percentile to the 90th percentile   **School Median** ●   **National Median** ○

Overall GPA 2.0 2.1 2.2 2.3 2.4 2.5 2.6 2.7 2.8 2.9 3.0 3.1 3.2 3.3 3.4 3.5 3.6 **(3.7)** 3.8 3.9 4.0
Science GPA 2.0 2.1 2.2 2.3 2.4 2.5 2.6 2.7 2.8 2.9 3.0 3.1 3.2 3.3 3.4 3.5 3.6 **(3.7)** 3.8 3.9 4.0

MCAT® Total Numeric Score 9 10 11 12 13 14 15 16 17 18 19 20 21 22 23 24 25 26 27 28 29 30 31 **(32)** 33 34 **(35)** 36 37 38 39 40 41 42 43

			J	K	L	M	N	O	P	Q	R	S	T
Writing Sample			J	K	L	M	N	O	P	**(Q)**	R	S	T
Verbal Reasoning	3	4	5	6	7	8	9	**(10)**	(11)	12	13	14	15
Biological Sciences	3	4	5	6	7	8	9	10	**(11)**	(12)	13	14	15
Physical Sciences	3	4	5	6	7	8	9	10	**(11)**	(12)	13	14	15

Acceptance & Matriculation Data for 2009–2010 First Year Class

	Resident	Non-resident	International	Total
Applications	108	4768	381	5257
Interviewed	17	229	2	248
Deferred	0	0	0	0
Matriculants				
Early Assurance Program	1	3	0	4
Early Decision Program	0	0	0	0
Baccalaureate/M.D.	6	39	0	45
M.D./Ph.D.	0	0	0	0
Matriculated	8	86	0	**94**

Applications accepted from International Applicants: Yes

Matriculant Demographics: 2009–2010 First Year Class

Men: 43   **Women:** 51

Matriculants' Self-Reported Race/Ethnicity

Mexican American	4	Korean	5
Cuban	2	Vietnamese	1
Puerto Rican	3	Other Asian	0
Other Hispanic	2	Total Asian	18
Total Hispanic	9	Native American	0
Chinese	5	Black	10
Asian Indian	5	Native Hawaiian	0
Pakistani	1	White	54
Filipino	1	Unduplicated Number	
Japanese	0	of Matriculants	94

Science and Math Majors: 43%
Matriculants with:
    Baccalaureate degree: 100%
    Graduate degree(s): 9%

Specialty Choice

2005, 2006, 2007 Graduates, Specialty Choice (As reported by program directors to GME Track™)	
Anesthesiology	2%
Emergency Medicine	5%
Family Practice	7%
Internal Medicine	20%
Obstetrics/Gynecology	3%
Orthopaedic Surgery	3%
Pediatrics	9%
Psychiatry	6%
Radiology	5%
Surgery	7%

Financial Information
Source: 2008-2009 LCME I-B survey and 2009-2010 AAMC TSF questionnaire

	Residents	Non-residents
Total Cost of Attendance	$ 61,180	$ 61,180
Tuition and Fees	$ 41,706	$ 41,706
Other (includes living expenses)	$ 17,126	$ 17,126
Health Insurance (can be waived)	$ 2,348	$ 2,348

Average 2009 Graduate Indebtedness: $136,832
% of Enrolled Students Receiving Aid: 76%

Criminal Background Check

This medical school does not require a criminal background check prior to matriculation.

Medical University of South Carolina
College of Medicine
Charleston, South Carolina

College of Medicine Dean's Office
Medical University of South Carolina
96 Jonathan Lucas Street, Suite 601
PO Box 250617, Charleston, South Carolina 29425
T 843 792 3283 F 843 792 0204

Admissions www.musc.edu/es/
Main www.musc.edu/com1
Financial www.musc.edu/financialmanagement/
E-mail taylorwl@musc.edu

Public Institution
Dr. Jerry Reves, Dean

Dr. Paul B. Underwood,
Associate Dean for Admissions

Willette Burnham, Executive Director of
Student Programs

Dr. Deborah Deas,
Associate Dean for Admissions

Wanda Taylor, Director of Admissions

General Information
The College of Medicine at MUSC was found-
ed in Charleston in 1824 and is the South's
oldest medical school. MUSC's Medical Center
is comprised of four separate hospitals (the
University Hospital, Ashley River Tower, the
Institute of Psychiatry, and the Children's
Hospital.) There are centers for specialized care
(Heart Center, Transplantation Center,
Hollings Cancer Center, Digestive Diseases
Center, and Storm Eye Institute). The adjacent
VA Hospital, with consortium/community
hospitals in Greenville, Spartanburg,
Columbia, and Florence, supply additional
facilities for clinical teaching.

Mission Statement
The COM is committed to maintaining an
educational environment for all students which
prepares them for a career of excellence in the
practice of medicine and service. It ensures
optimal opportunities for all students, faculty,
and administration, including all backgrounds
and levels of diversity, to achieve full potential.

Curricular Highlights
Community Service Requirement: Required.
Research/Thesis Requirement: Optional.

The goal of the COM is to produce caring and
competent physicians capable of choosing any
postgrad career. The curriculum in the first 2
years integrates basic science concepts with
problem solving strategies and clinical skills.
Students take histories and physicals and are
introduced to the role of the physician in society. Emphasis is placed on small-group instruction and independent, self-directed learning.
The 3rd year consists of clerkships in medicine,

obstetrics/gynecology, pediatrics, family medicine, surgery, and psychiatry. Selectives in multiple disciplines are also provided for students to
gain exposure to major specialty areas. The
development of clinical, interpersonal, and professional competence is emphasized. In the 4th
year, students are required to have additional
training in surgery and internal medicine, complete an externship, and take up to five elective
rotations in a wide variety of subspecialties.

USMLE
Step 1: Required. Students must record a passing
score for promotion.
Step 2: Clinical Skills (CS): Required.
Students must only record a score.
Step 2: Clinical Knowledge (CK): Required.
Students must record a passing total score to
graduate.

Selection Factors
Selection is based on the total evaluation of a
student. Screening for interviews is based on the
cum GPA and best total MCAT score. Although
SC residency is a primary admission consideration, nonresidents with excellent credentials are
considered, especially those with close SC ties.
Noncognitive traits and accomplishments are
evaluated during interviews. Interpersonal skills,
motivation, judgment, and compassion are
assessed; also, the quality of recommendations,
leadership, and volunteer/clinical/work experiences. Applicants with unique qualities or experiences important for diversity may be considered for added value. Early Decision is offered
for applicants with a GPA of 3.5 or above and
MCAT scores of 27 or higher. Foreign students
must have a permanent resident visa to be considered for the regular MD program.

Financial Aid
Financial need is not a factor in the initial
selection process. Loan programs and scholarships are available for entering students. A
financial aid counselor advises new and current students on loan opportunities and debt
management. Merit scholarships are awarded
by the Scholarship Board and are based on
outstanding academic and personal achievement. Part-time employment while in medical
school is not possible.

Information about Diversity Programs
Students from groups underrepresented in
medicine are encouraged to apply; an active
recruitment program is in place. PREP is an
individually tailored undergraduate course of
study prescribed for a few underprepared, but
promising SC students who seek admission
through AMCAS. The curriculum at the
College of Charleston spans two semesters and
is full time. No separate application is required.
Students considered are those who apply
through AMCAS and are denied admission.
Students are selected annually; stipends are
provided. A Summer Institute, devoted to
underrepresented or rural students, focuses on
MCAT/test-taking skills. The COM and the
Center for Academic Excellence provide counseling and support services for Summer
Institute students.

Campus Information
Setting
MUSC's 67 acre campus is located in historic
Charleston, SC. This city combines the best
that life has to offer: historic homes, art, music,
museums, libraries, restaurants, beaches, and
some of the country's finest golf courses.
Within a short walk from Charleston's main
street are all the hospitals, research centers,
clinical, and basic science buildings that make
up the MUSC complex

Enrollment
For 2009, total enrollment was: 670

Special Features
MUSC has been recognized for its treatment of
gastrointestinal disorders, kidney disease and
rheumatology. Other programs of excellence
are: neuroscience, substance abuse, cardiovascular medicine, perinatal medicine, ophthal-
mology, hearing loss, genetics, & cancer care.

Housing
On-campus housing is not available. The
MUSC Office of Student Programs maintains
an online listing of affordable apartments near
the MUSC campus. Rents average $600-$800
per month.

Application Process and Requirements 2011–2012

Primary Application Service: AMCAS
Earliest filing date: June 1, 2010
Latest filing date: December 1, 2010

Secondary Application Required?: Yes
Sent to: All applicants
URL: www.musc.edu/em/admissions/apply.html
Fee: Yes, $85 **Waiver available:** No
Earliest filing date: July 15, 2010
Latest filing date: January 15, 2011

MCAT® required?: Yes
Latest MCAT® considered: September 2010
Oldest MCAT® considered: August 2008

Early Decision Program: School does have EDP
Applicants notified: October 1, 2010
EDP available for: Residents only

Regular Acceptance Notice
Earliest date: November 1, 2010
Latest date: Until class is full
Applicant's Response to Acceptance
Offer – Maximum Time: Four weeks

Requests for Deferred
Entrance Considered: Yes

Deposit to Hold Place in Class: Yes
Deposit (Resident): $440 **(Non-resident):** $440
Deposit due: Within four weeks of response to acceptance offer
Applied to tuition: No **Refundable:** Yes
Refundable by: May 15, 2011

Estimated number of new entrants: 165
EDP: 31, special program: 3

Start Month/Year: August 2011

Interview Format: Three one-on-one interviews are required. Regional physicians assist with interviews. Video interviews are not available.

Other Programs

PREPARATORY PROGRAMS
Postbaccalaureate Program: No
Summer Program: No
PREP - Postbaccalaureate Reapplication Education Program: Wanda Taylor, (843) 792-2055, taylorwl@musc.edu
MUSC Summer Institute: Wanda Taylor, (843) 792-2055, taylorwl@musc.edu

COMBINED DEGREE PROGRAMS
Baccalaureate/M.D.: No
M.D./M.P.H.: Yes, Wanda Taylor, (843) 792-2055, taylorwl@musc.edu
MD/MBA: Yes, Wanda Taylor, (843) 792-2055, taylorwl@musc.edu
M.D./J.D.: No
M.D./Ph.D.: Yes, www.musc.edu/grad/mstp/ Dr. Perry Halushka, (843) 792-3012, halushpv@musc.edu
Additional Program: Yes, Wanda Taylor, (843) 792-2055, taylorwl@musc.edu

Premedical Coursework

On-line courses accepted in fulfillment of prerequisites: No

Course	Req.	Rec.	Lab.	Sems.
Inorganic Chemistry		•	•	2
Behavioral Sciences				
Biochemistry		•		2
Biology		•	•	2
Biology/Zoology				
Calculus				
College English		•		2
College Mathematics				
Computer Science				
Genetics				

Course	Req.	Rec.	Lab.	Sems.
Humanities				
Organic Chemistry		•	•	2
Physics		•		2
Psychology				
Social Sciences				
Other				
Cell Biology		•		2
Physiology		•		2
Anatomy		•		2

Selection Factors: 2009 Accepted Applicants

Proportion of Accepted Applicants with Relevant Experience (Data Self-Reported to AMCAS®)		
Community Service/Volunteer	77%
Medically-Related Work	83%
Research	74%

Shaded bar represents school's accepted scores ranging from the 10th percentile to the 90th percentile. School Median ● National Median ◐

Overall GPA	2.0	2.1	2.2	2.3	2.4	2.5	2.6	2.7	2.8	2.9	3.0	3.1	3.2	3.3	3.4	3.5	3.6	(3.7)	3.8	3.9	4.0
Science GPA	2.0	2.1	2.2	2.3	2.4	2.5	2.6	2.7	2.8	2.9	3.0	3.1	3.2	3.3	3.4	3.5	3.6	(3.7)	3.8	3.9	4.0

MCAT® Total Numeric Score 9 10 11 12 13 14 15 16 17 18 19 20 21 22 23 24 25 26 27 28 29 (30) 31 (32) 33 34 35 36 37 38 39 40 41 42 43

Writing Sample			J	K	L	M	N	O	(P)	(Q)	R	S	T
Verbal Reasoning	3	4	5	6	7	8	9	(10)	11	12	13	14	15
Biological Sciences	3	4	5	6	7	8	9	(10)	(11)	12	13	14	15
Physical Sciences	3	4	5	6	7	8	9	(10)	(11)	12	13	14	15

Acceptance & Matriculation Data for 2009–2010 First Year Class

	Resident	Non-resident	International	Total
Applications	516	1939	32	2487
Interviewed	350	69	0	419
Deferred	4	1	0	5
Matriculants				
Early Assurance Program	0	0	0	0
Early Decision Program	27	0	0	27
Baccalaureate/M.D.	0	0	0	0
M.D./Ph.D.	2	6	0	8
Matriculated	128	36	0	**164**

Applications accepted from International Applicants: Yes

Specialty Choice

2005, 2006, 2007 Graduates, Specialty Choice (As reported by program directors to GME Track™)	
Anesthesiology	5%
Emergency Medicine	5%
Family Practice	11%
Internal Medicine	17%
Obstetrics/Gynecology	8%
Orthopaedic Surgery	5%
Pediatrics	12%
Psychiatry	4%
Radiology	4%
Surgery	6%

Matriculant Demographics: 2009–2010 First Year Class

Men: 90 **Women:** 74

Matriculants' Self-Reported Race/Ethnicity

Mexican American	2	Korean	0
Cuban	2	Vietnamese	1
Puerto Rican	0	Other Asian	3
Other Hispanic	6	Total Asian	18
Total Hispanic	10	Native American	2
Chinese	2	Black	22
Asian Indian	9	Native Hawaiian	0
Pakistani	2	White	121
Filipino	0	Unduplicated Number	
Japanese	1	of Matriculants	164

Science and Math Majors: 71%
Matriculants with:
Baccalaureate degree: 100%
Graduate degree(s): 9%

Financial Information

Source: 2008-2009 LCME I-B survey and 2009-2010 AAMC TSF questionnaire

	Residents	Non-residents
Total Cost of Attendance	$ 54,220	$ 77,086
Tuition and Fees	$ 30,399	$ 53,265
Other (includes living expenses)	$ 22,752	$ 22,752
Health Insurance (can be waived)	$ 1,069	$ 1,069

Average 2009 Graduate Indebtedness: $161,063
% of Enrolled Students Receiving Aid: 91%

Criminal Background Check

This medical school requires a criminal background check prior to matriculation.

University of South Carolina School of Medicine
Columbia, South Carolina

Associate Dean for Medical Education
and Academic Affairs
University of South Carolina School of Medicine
Columbia, South Carolina 29208
T 803 733 3325   F 803 733 3328

Admissions http://admissions.med.sc.edu
Main www.med.sc.edu
Financial www.sc.edu/financialaid
E-mail jeanette.ford@uscmed.sc.edu

Public Institution

Dr. Richard A. Hoppmann, Dean

Dr. Jeanette H. Ford, Registrar, Administrator, Office of Admissions

Dr. Carol L. McMahon, Assistant Dean for Minority Affairs

Jerel Arceneaux, Assistant Director of Student Services and Financial Aid

Dr. Joshua T. Thornhill, IV Associate Dean for Medical Education and Academic Affairs

Dr. Donald J. Kenney, IV Director, Student Services

General Information
The USC SOM was established in 1977 and is located in the state's capital city. The school offers a wide range of educational and professional opportunities to its students, featuring a small class size, a nationally recognized Senior Mentor Program, and a state-of-the-art ultrasound curriculum. The school works closely with its three major affiliated hospitals to provide students valuable clinical experience.

Mission Statement
The mission of the USC SOM is to improve the health of the people of the state of SC through the development and implementation of programs for medical education, research, and the delivery of health care. Programs will be developed in collaboration with affiliated institutions, and allocation of resources will be based upon the physician manpower and health care needs of SC, the effectiveness and efficiency of specific programs, and the accreditation requirements of all appropriate organizations. Medical education and graduate education at all levels are conducted in a highly personal atmosphere that emphasizes a balance among scientific disciplines, humanistic concerns, and societal needs.

Curricular Highlights
Community Service Requirement: Optional.
Research/Thesis Requirement: Optional.

The SOM offers a program of study designed to provide education and training in the art and science of medicine and to prepare stu-

dents for a wide variety of medical career choices. Each of the first two years consists of two academic semesters of both basic science and clinically relevant coursework in which students are exposed to patients in various inpatient, outpatient, community, and rural settings. The correlation between basic and clinical science information in the first two years is emphasized by means of an interdisciplinary, four-semester Introduction to Clinical Medicine course continuum. The third year consists of required clinical clerkships in medicine, surgery, pediatrics, obstetrics-gynecology, family medicine, neurology, and psychiatry. The fourth year is devoted to advanced clinical work, including 20 weeks each of required and elective rotations, during which students have the opportunity to strengthen their clinical skills and pursue individual academic interests and career goals in preparation for the lifelong study of medicine. An integrated ultrasound curriculum (iUSC) has been introduced in both the basic science and clinical years.

USMLE
Step 1: Required. Students must record a passing score for promotion.
Step 2: Clinical Skills (CS): Required. Students must record a passing total score to graduate.
Step 2: Clinical Knowledge (CK): Required. Students must record a passing total score to graduate.

Selection Factors
The selection process involves the comparative evaluation and review of all available application data, including MCAT scores, undergraduate academic performance, letters of evaluation, and the results of personal interviews with Admissions Committee members. The opportunity for admission is greatest for legal residents of South Carolina. Applications are only accepted from permanent residents or U.S. citizens. The ultimate selection of a student is based upon a total and comparative appraisal of the applicant's suitability for the successful practice of medicine. The AMCAS application is used for preliminary screening. After this initial review, the Admissions Committee may extend an invitation for personal interviews. Each applicant is evaluated on the basis of individual qualifications without regard to age, race,

creed, national origin, sex, or disability.

Financial Aid
The SOM participates in all federally funded loan and scholarship programs. A SOM-sponsored low-interest loan program is available to students with proven need. Every effort is made to provide information and assistance to help students meet their financial obligations. Students seeking part-time employment during medical school should have the prior approval of the director of student services.

Information about Diversity Programs
The SOM actively encourages applications from members of groups underrepresented in the medical profession. There is diverse membership on the Admissions Committee. For additional information, contact the assistant dean for minority affairs at (803) 733-3319.

Campus Information
Setting
The beautiful USC SOM campus, with its spacious lawns and trees, and convenient parking, is located four miles east of the USC Columbia campus and adjacent to the Dorn V.A. Medical Center.

Enrollment
For 2009, total enrollment was: 329

Special Features
Students enjoy 24-hour secure access to USC SOM laboratories and library facilities. They participate in the extensive intramural athletic and recreational sports programs. The fitness center is located on-campus. USC SOM students also have access to all facilities and programs available to USC students.

Housing
The majority of USC SOM students choose housing in the area adjacent to the campus. Housing information can be obtained from the Student Services Office.

Satellite Campuses/Facilities
Students have the option of completing core clinical training in the third and fourth years at the Greenville Hospital System; 30 positions are available.

Application Process and Requirements 2011–2012

Primary Application Service: AMCAS
Earliest filing date: June 1, 2010
Latest filing date: December 1, 2010

Secondary Application Required?: Yes
Sent to: All applicants
URL: n/a
Fee: Yes, $95   **Waiver available:** Yes
Earliest filing date: 2010
Latest filing date: January 15, 2011

MCAT® required?: Yes
Latest MCAT® considered: September 2010
Oldest MCAT® considered: 2005

Early Decision Program: School does have EDP
Applicants notified: October 1, 2010
EDP available for: Residents only

Regular Acceptance Notice
Earliest date: October 15, 2010
Latest date: Until class is full
Applicant's Response to Acceptance
Offer – Maximum Time: Two weeks

Requests for Deferred
Entrance Considered: Yes

Deposit to Hold Place in Class: Yes
Deposit (Resident): $100   **(Non-resident):** $100
Deposit due: With response within two weeks
Applied to tuition: Yes **Refundable:** Yes
Refundable by: May 15, 2011 with written request

Estimated number of new entrants: 90
EDP: 5, special program: n/a

Start Month/Year: August 2011

Interview Format: Two 30-minute interviews. Regional interviews are available in Greenville, South Carolina. Video interviews are not available.

Other Programs

PREPARATORY PROGRAMS
Postbaccalaureate Program: Yes, www.med.sc.edu/Post.Baccalaureate.Certificates.asp
Summer Program: No

COMBINED DEGREE PROGRAMS
Baccalaureate/M.D.: No
M.D./M.P.H.: Yes, www.med.sc.edu/dual.degree.programs.asp
MD/MBA: No
M.D./J.D.: No
M.D./Ph.D.: Yes, www.med.sc.edu/dual.degree.programs.asp

Premedical Coursework

On-line courses accepted in fulfillment of prerequisites: No

Course	Req.	Rec.	Lab.	Sems.	Course	Req.	Rec.	Lab.	Sems.
Inorganic Chemistry	•		•	8	Computer Science				
Behavioral Sciences					Genetics				
Biochemistry		•			Humanities				
Biology					Organic Chemistry	•		•	8
Biology/Zoology	•		•	8	Physics		•		
Calculus					Psychology				
College English	•			6	Social Sciences				
College Mathematics					Other				

Selection Factors: 2009 Accepted Applicants

Proportion of Accepted Applicants with Relevant Experience (Data Self-Reported to AMCAS®)		
Community Service/Volunteer		72%
Medically-Related Work		84%
Research		70%

Shaded bar represents school's accepted scores ranging from the 10th percentile to the 90th percentile   **School Median** ●   **National Median** ○

Overall GPA	2.0	2.1	2.2	2.3	2.4	2.5	2.6	2.7	2.8	2.9	3.0	3.1	3.2	3.3	3.4	3.5	3.6	3.7	(3.8)	3.9	4.0
Science GPA	2.0	2.1	2.2	2.3	2.4	2.5	2.6	2.7	2.8	2.9	3.0	3.1	3.2	3.3	3.4	3.5	3.6	3.7	(3.8)	3.9	4.0

MCAT® Total Numeric Score 9 10 11 12 13 14 15 16 17 18 19 20 21 22 23 24 25 26 27 28 (29) 30 31 (32) 33 34 35 36 37 38 39 40 41 42 43

Writing Sample				J	K	L	M	N	O	(P)	(Q)	R	S	T
Verbal Reasoning	3	4	5	6	7	8	9	(10)	11	12	13	14	15
Biological Sciences	3	4	5	6	7	8	9	(10)	(11)	12	13	14	15
Physical Sciences	3	4	5	6	7	8	(9)	10	(11)	12	13	14	15

Acceptance & Matriculation Data for 2009–2010 First Year Class

	Resident	Non-resident	International	Total
Applications	445	1654	20	2119
Interviewed	281	68	0	349
Deferred	2	1	0	3
Matriculants				
Early Assurance Program	0	0	0	0
Early Decision Program	7	0	0	7
Baccalaureate/M.D.	0	0	0	0
M.D./Ph.D.	0	0	0	0
Matriculated	65	14	0	**79**

Applications accepted from International Applicants: No

Specialty Choice

2005, 2006, 2007 Graduates, Specialty Choice (As reported by program directors to GME Track™)	
Anesthesiology	4%
Emergency Medicine	9%
Family Practice	13%
Internal Medicine	23%
Obstetrics/Gynecology	2%
Orthopaedic Surgery	0%
Pediatrics	12%
Psychiatry	10%
Radiology	3%
Surgery	6%

Matriculant Demographics: 2009–2010 First Year Class

Men: 39   **Women:** 40

Matriculants' Self-Reported Race/Ethnicity

Mexican American	1	Korean	1
Cuban	0	Vietnamese	2
Puerto Rican	0	Other Asian	0
Other Hispanic	1	Total Asian	9
Total Hispanic	1	Native American	0
Chinese	1	Black	1
Asian Indian	3	Native Hawaiian	0
Pakistani	1	White	69
Filipino	1	Unduplicated Number	
Japanese	0	of Matriculants	79

Science and Math Majors: 73%
Matriculants with:
Baccalaureate degree: 99%
Graduate degree(s): 10%

Financial Information
Source: 2008-2009 LCME I-B survey and 2009-2010 AAMC TSF questionnaire

	Residents	Non-residents
Total Cost of Attendance	$ 52,759	$ 86,593
Tuition and Fees	$ 28,278	$ 62,112
Other (includes living expenses)	$ 23,406	$ 23,406
Health Insurance (can be waived)	$ 1,075	$ 1,075

Average 2009 Graduate Indebtedness: $149,098
% of Enrolled Students Receiving Aid: 95%

Criminal Background Check

This medical school requires a criminal background check prior to matriculation.

Sanford School of Medicine of the University of South Dakota

Vermillion, South Dakota

Medical School Admissions
Sanford School of Medicine
University of South Dakota
414 East Clark Street
Vermillion, South Dakota 57069
T 605 677 6886   F 605 677 5109

Admissions www.usd.edu/medical-school/medical-doc-tor-program/admissions.cfm
Main www.usd.edu/medical-school
Financial www.usd.edu/medical-school/medical-doctor-program/tuition-financial-aid.cfm
E-mail md@usd.edu

Public Institution

Dr. Rodney R. Parry, Dean

Dr. Paul C. Bunger, Dean, Medical Student Affairs

Dr. Gerald J. Yutrzenka, Director, Diversity Affairs

Carol Hemmingson, Program Assistant, Financial Aid

Jill Christopherson, Program Assistant – Admissions

General Information

The School of Medicine was established in 1907 as a two-year school for the basic sciences and in 1974 became a four-year, MD degree program with the first class of graduates in 1977. The first two years are located in Vermillion, years three and four are in either Sioux Falls, Yankton or Rapid City. In 2005, the name was changed to Sanford School of Medicine of the University of South Dakota.

Mission Statement

The mission of the Sanford School of Medicine of the University of South Dakota is to provide the opportunity for South Dakota residents to receive a quality, broad-based medical education with an emphasis on family medicine. The curriculum is to be established to encourage graduates to serve people living in medically underserved areas of South Dakota and to require excellence in the basic sciences and in all clinical disciplines. The School of Medicine is to provide to its students and to the people of South Dakota excellence in education, research, and service. (Complete mission statement on Web site.)

Curricular Highlights

Community Service Requirement: Required. A community based, cultural diversity program.
Research/Thesis Requirement: Optional.

The first two years use traditional courses, problem/case-based teaching, and clinical experiences. To cap year two, students spend four weeks with a primary care physician in a South Dakota community. At the Sioux Falls and Rapid City sites, the third year is hospital-based, with clerkships in family medicine, inter-nal medicine, pediatrics, ob/gyn, psychiatry, neurology, and surgery. Students also take clinical colloquium, ambulatory medicine, and radiology. At the Yankton site, the third year is an ambulatory-based program, with students rotating through all six of the clerkships throughout the year. Year four requirements are rural family medicine, emergency medicine, surgical subspecialties and a sub-internship. Students also have 22 weeks of electives; many take 4-8 weeks outside the state. Grading is A-B-C-D-F. Students must pass USMLE Step 1 for promotion, and Step 2-CK and a school OSCE to graduate. They must also take Step 2-CS.

USMLE

Step 1: Required. Students must record a passing score for promotion.
Step 2: Clinical Skills (CS): Required. Students must only record a score.
Step 2: Clinical Knowledge (CK): Required. Students must record a passing total score to graduate.

Selection Factors

Applicants are chosen on the basis of intellect, character, and motivation. The Admissions Committee considers: academic achievement as indicated by scholastic records; recall, reading comprehension, and ability to perform within time constraints as reflected by MCAT scores; intellectual curiosity, work ethic, and fitness for a career in medicine as viewed by the applicant's former instructors; assessments of personal factors of the applicant as determined by interviews conducted by the committee. Applicants invited to interview must meet in person with at least two committee members. Interviews are conducted at the office or clinic of the interviewer or at the Vermillion campus. The school does not discriminate on the basis of race, color, creed, national origin, ancestry, citizenship, gender, sexual orientation, religion, age, or disability. Priority for supplemental applications and interviews is given to legal residents of South Dakota, non-residents with strong ties to South Dakota, and Native Americans affiliated with federally recognized tribes in the region. The School of Medicine does not sponsor an Early Decision Program. An Alumni Student Scholars Program (ASSP) offers a limited number of provisional acceptances to South Dakota high school seniors who meet strict criteria. The School of Medicine will consider applications for transfer only into Year 2 or Year 3 and only from students who are currently in good standing at an LCME-accredited medical school. Transfer opportunities are limited, with priority given to South Dakota residents.

Financial Aid

Financial aid is administered through the office of Medical Student Affairs. Loans are available to matriculated students on the basis of demonstrated financial need.

Information about Diversity Programs

The Sanford School of Medicine is committed to training a diverse group of students to meet the needs of the diverse population of the state. Interested applicants may contact the Director of Diversity Affairs for information about programs for premedical and medical students.

Campus Information

Setting

The first two years are based in Vermillion. The clinical years are based in Sioux Falls (1/2 of the class), Yankton (1/4 of the class), and Rapid City (1/4 of the class).

Enrollment

For 2009, total enrollment was: 214

Special Features

Students have significant one-on-one teaching from clinical faculty, numerous experiences in clinical and surgical procedures, many options for cultural immersion experiences, participation in the Scholarship Pathways program, and research opportunities.

Housing

See USD Web site at *www.usd.edu*.

Satellite Campuses/Facilities

Besides the four major campuses, students have options to rotate through many hospitals/clinics throughout the state.

Application Process and Requirements 2011–2012

Primary Application Service: AMCAS
Earliest filing date: June 1, 2010
Latest filing date: November 15, 2010

Secondary Application Required?: Yes
Sent to: SD residents and selected non-residents with strong ties to SD
Name: Jill Christopherson
Phone: (605) 677-6886
E-mail: Jill.Christopherson@usd.edu
Fee: Yes, $35 **Waiver available:** No
Earliest filing date: July 1, 2010
Latest filing date: Two weeks after invitation to submit Secondary Application

MCAT® required?: Yes
Latest MCAT® considered: September 2010
Oldest MCAT® considered: January 2008

Early Decision Program: School does not have EDP
Applicants notified: n/a
EDP available for: n/a

Regular Acceptance Notice
Earliest date: November 15, 2010
Latest date: Until class is full
Applicant's Response to Acceptance
Offer – Maximum Time: Two weeks after offer

Requests for Deferred
Entrance Considered: Yes

Deposit to Hold Place in Class: Yes
Deposit (Resident): $100 **(Non-resident):** $100
Deposit due: With response to acceptance offer
Applied to tuition: Yes **Refundable:** Yes
Refundable by: June 1, 2011

Estimated number of new entrants: 46
EDP: n/a, special program: 8

Start Month/Year: August 1, 2011

Interview Format: Open file, two individual face-to-face interviews. Regional interviews are not available. Video interviews are not available.

Other Programs

PREPARATORY PROGRAMS
Postbaccalaureate Program: No
Summer Program: No

COMBINED DEGREE PROGRAMS
Baccalaureate/M.D.: No
M.D./M.P.H.: No
MD/MBA: No
M.D./J.D.: No
M.D./Ph.D.: Yes, www.usd.edu/mdphd
Jill Christopherson (605) 677-6886
Jill.Christopherson@usd.edu

Premedical Coursework

On-line courses accepted in fulfillment of prerequisites: No

Course	Req.	Rec.	Lab.	Sems.	Course	Req.	Rec.	Lab.	Sems.
Inorganic Chemistry	•		•	2	Computer Science				
Behavioral Sciences		•			Genetics		•		
Biochemistry		•			Humanities		•		
Biology					Organic Chemistry	•		•	2
Biology/Zoology	•		•	2	Physics	•		•	2
Calculus		•			Psychology				
College English		•			Social Sciences				
College Mathematics	•			2	Statistics		•		

Selection Factors: 2009 Accepted Applicants

Proportion of Accepted Applicants with Relevant Experience (Data Self-Reported to AMCAS*)			Community Service/Volunteer	68%
			Medically-Related Work	72%
			Research	74%

Shaded bar represents school's accepted scores ranging from the 10th percentile to the 90th percentile ▦   **School Median** ● **National Median** ○

| Overall GPA | 2.0 | 2.1 | 2.2 | 2.3 | 2.4 | 2.5 | 2.6 | 2.7 | 2.8 | 2.9 | 3.0 | 3.1 | 3.2 | 3.3 | 3.4 | 3.5 | 3.6 | (3.7) | 3.8 | 3.9 | 4.0 |
| Science GPA | 2.0 | 2.1 | 2.2 | 2.3 | 2.4 | 2.5 | 2.6 | 2.7 | 2.8 | 2.9 | 3.0 | 3.1 | 3.2 | 3.3 | 3.4 | 3.5 | (3.6) | 3.7 | 3.8 | 3.9 | 4.0 |

MCAT® Total Numeric Score 9 10 11 12 13 14 15 16 17 18 19 20 21 22 23 24 25 26 27 28 29 (30) (31) (32) 33 34 35 36 37 38 39 40 41 42 43

Writing Sample				J	K	L	M	N	(O)	P	(Q)	R	S	T
Verbal Reasoning	3	4	5	6	7	8	9	(10)	11	12	13	14	15
Biological Sciences	3	4	5	6	7	8	9	(10)	(11)	12	13	14	15
Physical Sciences	3	4	5	6	7	8	9	(10)	(11)	12	13	14	15

Acceptance & Matriculation Data for 2009–2010 First Year Class

	Resident	Non-resident	International	Total
Applications	121	281	3	405
Interviewed	113	40	0	153
Deferred	0	0	0	0
Matriculants				
Early Assurance Program	0	0	0	0
Early Decision Program	0	0	0	0
Baccalaureate/M.D.	0	0	0	0
M.D./Ph.D.	2	2	0	4
Matriculated	46	8	0	**54**

Applications accepted from International Applicants: Can be accepted from among South Dakota residents only.

Specialty Choice

2005, 2006, 2007 Graduates, Specialty Choice (As reported by program directors to GME Track™)	
Anesthesiology	8%
Emergency Medicine	9%
Family Practice	10%
Internal Medicine	11%
Obstetrics/Gynecology	12%
Orthopaedic Surgery	4%
Pediatrics	7%
Psychiatry	3%
Radiology	3%
Surgery	12%

Matriculant Demographics: 2009–2010 First Year Class

Men: 35   **Women:** 19

Matriculants' Self-Reported Race/Ethnicity

Mexican American	0	Korean	0
Cuban	0	Vietnamese	0
Puerto Rican	0	Other Asian	0
Other Hispanic	1	Total Asian	2
Total Hispanic	1	Native American	1
Chinese	2	Black	1
Asian Indian	0	Native Hawaiian	0
Pakistani	0	White	51
Filipino	0	Unduplicated Number	
Japanese	0	of Matriculants	54

Science and Math Majors: 78%

Matriculants with:
  Baccalaureate degree: 100%
  Graduate degree(s): 15%

Financial Information

Source: 2008-2009 LCME I-B survey and 2009-2010 AAMC TSF questionnaire

	Residents	Non-residents
Total Cost of Attendance	$ 43,039	$ 65,214
Tuition and Fees	$ 21,499	$ 43,674
Other (includes living expenses)	$ 18,306	$ 18,306
Health Insurance (can be waived)	$ 3,234	$ 3,234

Average 2009 Graduate Indebtedness: $127,554
% of Enrolled Students Receiving Aid: 99%

Criminal Background Check

This medical school requires a criminal background check prior to matriculation.

East Tennessee State University
James H. Quillen College of Medicine
Johnson City, Tennessee

Assistant Dean for Admissions and Records
East Tennessee State University
James H. Quillen College of Medicine
P.O. Box 70580, Johnson City, Tennessee 37614-1708
T 423 439 2033   **F** 423 439 2110

Admissions www.etsu.edu/com/sa/admissions/
default.aspx
Main www.etsu.edu/com
Financial www.etsu.edu/com/sa/finaid/
default.aspx
E-mail sacom@etsu.edu

Public Institution

Dr. Philip C. Bagnell, Dean of Medicine

*Edwin D. Taylor, Assistant Dean
for Admissions and Records*

Linda Embree, Director, Financial Services

*Dr. Thomas Kwasigroch, Associate Dean
for Student Affairs*

General Information
Opening in 1978, ETSU's Quillen College of Medicine has established itself as a national leader in primary care and rural medicine. Quillen students enjoy an exceptional success rate in the national residency match, and over 50 percent of graduates choose a career in primary care. Quillen's Community Partnerships Program and the Rural Primary Care Track continues to garner national recognition. A collegial atmosphere is encouraged at all levels and student involvement is encouraged. The medical campus is located on the grounds of the VA Medical Center pictured above and boasts one of the most technologically advanced simulation programs in the nation. The school is located in Tennessee's fourth largest metropolitan area (population 1.2 million) and is part of the state's fourth largest university (enrollment 15,000). It is supported by modern and convenient medical centers and clinics throughout the Tri-Cities area, as well as by hospitals and clinics located in small, rural communities such as Rogersville, Sevierville and Mountain City. The school enrolls one class of 66 new students in August of each year.

Mission Statement
The primary mission of Quillen College of Medicine is to prepare and educate excellent physicians, especially those with an interest in primary care, to practice in underserved rural communities. The college is also committed to excellence in biomedical research and is dedicated to the improvement of health care in Northeast Tennessee and the surrounding Appalachian Region.

Curricular Highlights
Community Service Requirement: Optional.
Research/Thesis Requirement: Optional.

Student input is a key component in curricular change, along with the rapidly changing body of knowledge and the needs of the profession. The curriculum includes a mix of traditional, systems-based, and case-based learning, as well as a wide range of educational experiences, patient populations, and hospitals. The highly diversified faculty considers students as colleagues. Patient contact comes early in the curriculum and continues throughout. Flexibility is allowed for students to decelerate a portion of the curriculum for elective courses, including research and advanced clinical studies. The goals of the curriculum are to prepare students to be well-grounded in the science and art of medicine, capable practitioners of their profession, and self-directed, lifelong learners.

USMLE
Step 1: Required. Students must record a passing score for promotion.
Step 2: Clinical Skills (CS): Required. Students must record a passing total score to graduate.
Step 2: Clinical Knowledge (CK): Required. Students must record a passing total score to graduate.

Selection Factors
To be admitted, an applicant must be a U.S. or Canadian citizen or possess a U.S. permanent resident visa. Admission is based upon a competitive selection process involving those applicants who meet the minimum requirements for admission. The Admissions Committee selects students who give the promise of being not merely satisfactory medical students, but also capable, responsible physicians of high ethical standards. The Admissions Committee screens applicants on the basis of academic achievement, MCAT scores, letters of recommendation, pertinent extracurricular research and work experiences, and evidence of non-scholastic accomplishments. After a general screening, the Admissions Committee may request supplementary information and a personal interview with the applicant. Interviews are held only on the campus and are at the applicant's expense. Admission preferences are for residents of the state of Tennessee who are U.S. citizens, veterans of U.S. military service, and recipients of baccalaureate degrees prior to enrollment. Marginally qualified non-residents should not apply.

Financial Aid
The need for student financial assistance is not a consideration in the selection process. Scholarships, grants, and loans are available for students who demonstrate need as defined by a federal needs analysis and who meet the specific criteria set forth by the various agencies. Additional information may be obtained by writing directly to the medical school Director for Financial Services.

Information about Diversity Programs
The College of Medicine actively seeks applicants of both sexes and members of groups underrepresented in medicine. African-American matriculants may be eligible for financial awards from the state of Tennessee. Support services are available to matriculants to assist in the timely completion of the medical curriculum. ETSU does not discriminate on the basis of race, sex, creed, national origin, age, or disability. The university is an equal opportunity/affirmative action employer.

Campus Information

Enrollment
For 2009, total enrollment was: 253

Application Process and Requirements 2011–2012

Primary Application Service: AMCAS
Earliest filing date: June 1, 2010
Latest filing date: November 15, 2010

Secondary Application Required?: Yes
Sent to: Selected applicants
URL: n/a
Fee: Yes, $50   **Waiver available:** Yes
Earliest filing date: June 1, 2010
Latest filing date: Twenty-one days from request

MCAT® required?: Yes
Latest MCAT® considered: September 2010
Oldest MCAT® considered: January 2008

Early Decision Program: School does have EDP
Applicants notified: October 1, 2010
EDP available for: Both Residents and Non-residents

Regular Acceptance Notice
Earliest date: October 15, 2010
Latest date: Until class is full
Applicant's Response to Acceptance Offer – Maximum Time: Two weeks

Requests for Deferred Entrance Considered: Yes

Deposit to Hold Place in Class: Yes
Deposit (Resident): $100   **(Non-resident):** $100
Deposit due: With response to acceptance offer
Applied to tuition: Yes   **Refundable:** Yes
Refundable by: May 15, 2011

Estimated number of new entrants: 66
EDP: 3, special program: n/a

Start Month/Year: August 2011

Interview Format: Two, one-hour interviews with an admissions committee member. Regional interviews are not available. Video interviews are not available.

Other Programs

PREPARATORY PROGRAMS
Postbaccalaureate Program: No
Summer Program: No

COMBINED DEGREE PROGRAMS
Baccalaureate/M.D.: No
M.D./M.P.H.: Yes
M.D./M.B.A.: No
M.D./J.D.: No
M.D./Ph.D.: No

Premedical Coursework

On-line courses accepted in fulfillment of prerequisites: Yes

Course	Req.	Rec.	Lab.	Hrs.
Inorganic Chemistry	•		•	8
Behavioral Sciences				
Biochemistry		•		
Biology	•		•	8
Biology/Zoology				
Calculus				
College English				
College Mathematics				

Course	Req.	Rec.	Lab.	Hrs.
Computer Science				
Genetics				
Humanities				
Organic Chemistry	•		•	8
Physics	•		•	8
Psychology				
Comm. Skills Courses				9
Electives			•	49

Selection Factors: 2009 Accepted Applicants

Proportion of Accepted Applicants with Relevant Experience (Data Self-Reported to AMCAS)		
Community Service/Volunteer		79%
Medically-Related Work		83%
Research		64%

Shaded bar represents school's accepted scores ranging from the 10th percentile to the 90th percentile   School Median ● National Median ◐

Overall GPA 2.0 2.1 2.2 2.3 2.4 2.5 2.6 2.7 2.8 2.9 3.0 3.1 3.2 3.3 3.4 3.5 3.6 ③.7 3.8 3.9 4.0

Science GPA 2.0 2.1 2.2 2.3 2.4 2.5 2.6 2.7 2.8 2.9 3.0 3.1 3.2 3.3 3.4 3.5 3.6 ③.7 3.8 3.9 4.0

MCAT® Total Numeric Score 9 10 11 12 13 14 15 16 17 18 19 20 21 22 23 24 25 26 27 28 ㉙ 30 31 ㉜ 33 34 35 36 37 38 39 40 41 42 43

Writing Sample			J	K	L	M	N	Ⓞ	P	Ⓠ	R	S	T
Verbal Reasoning	3	4	5	6	7	8	9	⑩	11	12	13	14	15
Biological Sciences	3	4	5	6	7	8	9	⑩	⑪	12	13	14	15
Physical Sciences	3	4	5	6	7	8	⑨	10	⑪	12	13	14	15

Acceptance & Matriculation Data for 2009–2010 First Year Class

	Resident	Non-resident	International	Total
Applications	507	868	70	1445
Interviewed	186	47	0	233
Deferred	1	0	0	1
Matriculants				
Early Assurance Program	0	0	0	0
Early Decision Program	1	1	0	2
Baccalaureate/M.D.	0	0	0	0
M.D./Ph.D.	0	0	0	0
Matriculated	60	6	0	**66**

Applications accepted from International Applicants: Only Canadian

Matriculant Demographics: 2009–2010 First Year Class

Men: 34   **Women:** 32

Matriculants' Self-Reported Race/Ethnicity

Mexican American	0	Korean	1
Cuban	0	Vietnamese	0
Puerto Rican	0	Other Asian	0
Other Hispanic	0	Total Asian	6
Total Hispanic	0	Native American	0
Chinese	1	Black	4
Asian Indian	4	Native Hawaiian	0
Pakistani	0	White	57
Filipino	0	Unduplicated Number	
Japanese	0	of Matriculants	66

Science and Math Majors: 71%
Matriculants with:
    Baccalaureate degree: 100%
    Graduate degree(s): 9%

Specialty Choice

2005, 2006, 2007 Graduates, Specialty Choice (As reported by program directors to GME Track™)	
Anesthesiology	4%
Emergency Medicine	7%
Family Practice	14%
Internal Medicine	13%
Obstetrics/Gynecology	5%
Orthopaedic Surgery	2%
Pediatrics	15%
Psychiatry	6%
Radiology	3%
Surgery	10%

Financial Information

Source: 2008-2009 LCME I-B survey and 2009-2010 AAMC TSF questionnaire

	Residents	Non-residents
Total Cost of Attendance	$ 43,608	$ 67,366
Tuition and Fees	$ 24,457	$ 48,215
Other (includes living expenses)	$ 18,003	$ 18,003
Health Insurance (can be waived)	$ 1,148	$ 1,148

Average 2009 Graduate Indebtedness: $106,539
% of Enrolled Students Receiving Aid: 94%

Criminal Background Check

This medical school requires a criminal background check prior to matriculation.

Meharry Medical College
School of Medicine
Nashville, Tennessee

Director, Admissions and Recruitment
Meharry Medical College
1005 Dr. D. B. Todd Boulevard
Nashville, Tennessee 37208
T 615 327 6223   **F** 615 327 6228

Admissions www.mmc.edu/admissions/index.html
Main www.mmc.edu
Financial www.mmc.edu/students/student
financialaid.html
E-mail admissions@mmc.edu

Private Institution

*Dr. Billy R. Ballard, Acting Dean
and Senior Vice President for Health Affairs*

*Allen D. Mosley, Director,
Admissions and Recruitment*

*Karen A. Lewis, Assistant Vice President -
Student Services & Enrollment Management*

Barbara Tharpe, Director, Student Financial Aid

Dr. Pamela C. Williams, Executive Vice Dean

Deborah Davis, Senior Admissions Manager

General Information
In 1876, Meharry Medical College was founded and established as the Meharry Medical Department of Central Tennessee College by the Freedmen's Aid Society of the Methodist Episcopal Church. Meharry's inception was part of the society's continuing effort to educate freed slaves and to provide health care services for the poor and underserved. Today, the School of Medicine continues to provide excellent educational opportunities to promising students from groups underrepresented in medicine. Clinical teaching facilities include the Metropolitan Nashville General Hospital; Blanchfield Army Hospital; Veterans Affairs Tennessee Valley Health Care System, Nashville Campus and the Alvin C. York Murfreesboro Campus; Vanderbilt's Monroe Carrell Children's Hospital; and a number of affiliated hospitals and clinics. The provision of primary care, particularly in medically underserved areas, is a special emphasis, as is health disparities research.

Mission Statement
Meharry Medical College exists to improve the health and health care of minority and underserved communities by offering excellent education and training programs in the health sciences placing special emphasis on providing opportunities to people of color and individuals from disadvantaged backgrounds, regardless of race or ethnicity; delivering high quality health services; and conducting research that fosters the elimination of health disparities.

Curricular Highlights
Community Service Requirement: Optional.
Research/Thesis Requirement: Required. Encouraged in areas of health disparities.

The school has an integrated curriculum for the freshman year in which instruction is organized into modules that include basic, clinical, and social sciences. The modules include Principles and Practice Of Medicine, Molecular Cell Biology, Genetics, Gross Anatomy, and Embryology; also included are Integrated Neuroscience, Immunology, Principles of Infectious Disease, and Foundations in Human Disease and Treatment. The sophomore year is organized around a series of organ systems. The clinical years consist of the following blocks: family medicine, psychiatry, obstetrics and gynecology, pediatrics, internal medicine, surgery, an ambulatory rotation served in an urban or rural underserved area, internal medicine subinternship, capstone, and radiology, as well as guided electives.

USMLE
Step 1: Required. Students must record a passing score for promotion.
Step 2: Clinical Skills (CS): Required. Students must record a passing total score to graduate.
Step 2: Clinical Knowledge (CK): Required. Students must record a passing total score to graduate.

Selection Factors
Applicants are selected on a competitive basis with regard to cognitive and non-cognitive skills that denote probable success in medical school. Performance in the basic science prerequisite subjects and MCAT scores form the basis for screening for the interview process in which the non-cognitive aspects of the applicant are assessed. While special empathy is held for minority and disadvantaged applicants of all origins, Meharry Medical College seeks to attract a wide demographic, cultural, and educational population to reflect the caliber of social interchange in which the eventual practice of medicine will occur. Meharry Medical College does not discriminate on the basis of race, sex, creed, national origin, age, or handicap.

Financial Aid
Financial aid awards are based on analyses of student needs and academic achievement. The limited financial aid program includes scholarships, grants, and loans. Because of fluctuations in federal and private support for financial aid programs, the types and amounts of awards are revised and adjusted on a continuing basis. Therefore, it is necessary that applicants plan their financial program as carefully as their academic program.

Information about Diversity Programs
For over 130 years, Meharry has produced a large percentage of the minority health professionals in the United States and abroad.

Campus Information

Setting
Its campus in North Nashville places Meharry at the epicenter of Middle Tennessee's most vulnerable citizens. As such, Meharry students, faculty, staff, and residents provide services where they are most needed. Located off Nashville's historic Jefferson Street, nestled between two neighboring historically black universities and near Nashville's thriving downtown, Meharry provides students with a full-range of auxiliary services to make their experience intellectually stimulating and socially comfortable and enjoyable.

Enrollment
For 2009, total enrollment was: 425

Special Features
Through several Centers of Excellence, the college and its faculty are working to unlock the mysteries behind health disparities in a variety of areas, most notably in women's health, cancer, and HIV/AIDS.

Housing
On campus there is the Royal Towers, a 10-story residential complex which contains 156 apartments and Dorothy Brown Hall, which houses 70 students. The college also maintains a list of available off-campus accommodations in the Nashville area.

Application Process and Requirements 2011–2012

Primary Application Service: AMCAS
Earliest filing date: June 1, 2010
Latest filing date: December 15, 2010

Secondary Application Required?: Yes
Sent to: All applicants do not receive the secondary application; they are prescreened.
Contact: Deborah Davis,
(615) 327-6223, ddavis@mmc.edu
Fee: Yes, $65   **Waiver available:** Yes
Earliest filing date: August 1, 2010
Latest filing date: January15, 2011

MCAT® required?: Yes
Latest MCAT® considered: September 2010
Oldest MCAT® considered: April 2008

Early Decision Program: School does have EDP
Applicants notified: October 1, 2010
EDP available for: Both Residents
and Non-residents

Regular Acceptance Notice
Earliest date: November 1, 2010
Latest date: Until class is full
Applicant's Response to Acceptance
Offer – Maximum Time: Three weeks

Requests for Deferred
Entrance Considered: Yes

Deposit to Hold Place in Class: Yes
Deposit (Resident): $300   **(Non-resident):** $300
Deposit due: With response to acceptance offer
Applied to tuition: Yes   **Refundable:** Yes
Refundable by: $200 refundable prior
to April 15, 2011

Estimated number of new entrants: 83
EDP: 2, special program: 20

Start Month/Year: July 2011

Interview Format: One-two 30-minute interviews. Regional interviews are seldom available. Video interviews are not available.

Other Programs

PREPARATORY PROGRAMS
Postbaccalaureate Program: Yes,
By invitation only (20 places)
Summer Program: Yes, Pre-Baccalaureate program, Sharon Turner-Friley, (615) 327-5966, sfriley@mmc.edu

COMBINED DEGREE PROGRAMS
Baccalaureate/M.D.: Yes,
Allen Mosley, (615) 327-6223, amosley@mmc.edu
M.D./M.P.H.: No
M.D./M.B.A.: No
M.D./J.D.: No
M.D./Ph.D.: Yes, Dr. Fatima Lima, (615) 327-6533, admissions@mmc.edu

Premedical Coursework

On-line courses accepted in fulfillment of prerequisites: No

Course	Req.	Rec.	Lab.	Hrs.
Inorganic Chemistry	•		•	8
Behavioral Sciences				
Biochemistry		•		4
Biology				
Biology/Zoology	•		•	8
Calculus		•		
College English	•			6
College Mathematics	•			3

Course	Req.	Rec.	Lab.	Hrs.
Computer Science		•		
Genetics		•		
Humanities				
Organic Chemistry	•		•	8
Physics	•		•	8
Psychology				
Social Sciences				
Other				

Selection Factors: 2009 Accepted Applicants

Proportion of Accepted Applicants with Relevant Experience (Data Self-Reported to AMCAS)		
Community Service/Volunteer		71%
Medically-Related Work		78%
Research		65%

Shaded bar represents school's accepted scores ranging from the 10th percentile to the 90th percentile   **School Median ●   National Median ●**

Overall GPA 2.0 2.1 2.2 2.3 2.4 2.5 2.6 2.7 2.8 2.9 3.0 3.1 3.2 3.3 3.4 ⓷⓹ 3.6 3.7 3.8 3.9 4.0

Science GPA 2.0 2.1 2.2 2.3 2.4 2.5 2.6 2.7 2.8 2.9 3.0 3.1 3.2 ⓷⓷ 3.4 3.5 3.6 3.7 3.8 3.9 4.0

MCAT® Total Numeric Score 9 10 11 12 13 14 15 16 17 18 19 20 21 22 23 24 ㉕ 26 27 28 29 30 31 ㉜ 33 34 35 36 37 38 39 40 41 42 43

			J	K	L	M	Ⓝ	O	P	Ⓠ	R	S	T
Writing Sample													

Verbal Reasoning	3	4	5	6	7	⑧	9	⑩	11	12	13	14	15
Biological Sciences	3	4	5	6	7	8	⑨	10	⑪	12	13	14	15
Physical Sciences	3	4	5	6	7	⑧	9	10	⑪	12	13	14	15

Acceptance & Matriculation Data for 2009–2010 First Year Class

	Resident	Non-resident	International	Total
Applications	225	4175	246	4646
Interviewed	72	410	10	492
Deferred	1	2	0	3
Matriculants				
Early Assurance Program	0	0	0	0
Early Decision Program	0	0	0	0
Baccalaureate/M.D.	0	0	0	0
M.D./Ph.D.	0	0	0	0
Matriculated	14	88	3	**105**

Applications accepted from International Applicants: Only Canadian

Matriculant Demographics: 2009–2010 First Year Class

Men: 47   **Women:** 58

Matriculants' Self-Reported Race/Ethnicity

Mexican American	1	Korean	0
Cuban	1	Vietnamese	1
Puerto Rican	1	Other Asian	0
Other Hispanic	2	Total Asian	9
Total Hispanic	5	Native American	1
Chinese	2	Black	85
Asian Indian	3	Native Hawaiian	0
Pakistani	2	White	10
Filipino	2	**Unduplicated Number**	
Japanese	1	**of Matriculants**	105

Science and Math Majors: 74%
Matriculants with:
Baccalaureate degree: 99%
Graduate degree(s): 15%

Specialty Choice

2005, 2006, 2007 Graduates, Specialty Choice (As reported by program directors to GME Track™)	
Anesthesiology	4%
Emergency Medicine	2%
Family Practice	11%
Internal Medicine	17%
Obstetrics/Gynecology	8%
Orthopaedic Surgery	2%
Pediatrics	10%
Psychiatry	7%
Radiology	3%
Surgery	7%

Financial Information

Source: 2008-2009 LCME I-B survey
and 2009-2010 AAMC TSF questionnaire

	Residents	Non-residents
Total Cost of Attendance	$ 71,518	$ 71,518
Tuition and Fees	$ 37,002	$ 37,002
Other (includes living expenses)	$ 31,918	$ 31,918
Health Insurance (can be waived)	$ 2,598	$ 2,598

Average 2009 Graduate Indebtedness: $175,318
% of Enrolled Students Receiving Aid: 94%

Criminal Background Check

This medical school requires a criminal background check prior to matriculation.

University of Tennessee Health Science Center College of Medicine

Memphis, Tennessee

University of Tennessee,
Health Science Center College of Medicine
910 Madison Avenue, Suite 500
Memphis, Tennessee 38163
T 901 448 5559   **F** 901 448 1740

Admissions www.uthsc.edu/Medicine/Admissions
Main www.uthsc.edu/Medicine
Financial www.uthsc.edu/finaid
E-mail nstrother@uthsc.edu

Public Institution

Dr. Steve J. Schwab, Executive Dean

E. Nelson Strother Jr., Assistant Dean for Admissions and Student Affairs

Dr. Gerald J. Presbury, Representative to Minority Affairs Section

John H. Lewis, IV, Director of Financial Aid

General Information

The UTHSC College of Medicine traces its origin to 1851 as the Medical Department of the University of Nashville. Today, the college utilizes over 20 facilities statewide for its training programs, including the Boston-Baskin Cancer Group, Campbell Orthopaedic Clinic, LeBonheur Children's Medical Center, Methodist University Hospital, Regional Medical Center, Semmes-Murphy Clinic, St. Jude Children's Research Hospital, UT Medical Group, VA Medical Center, Baptist Hospital-Memphis, St. Francis Hospital, UT Knoxville Medical Center, Erlanger Medical Center-Chattanooga, Baptist Hospital-Nashville, and Family Practice Center-Jackson.

Mission Statement

The Faculty of the College of Medicine is committed to educating physicians whose primary responsibilities will be evaluating, treating and preventing disease. The educational program is designed to prepare students to become knowledgeable, skillful, and compassionate physicians. Students are imbued with both the ideal that the study of medicine is a lifelong process and the sense of a physician's deep commitment to high moral and ethical standards regarding patients, colleagues, and society.

Curricular Highlights

Community Service Requirement: Required. Community service project.
Research/Thesis Requirement: Optional.

Year 1 of the curriculum begins in August with Gross Anatomy; Prevention, Community and Culture (PCC); Doctoring: Recognizing Signs and Symptoms (DRS); Molecular Basis of Disease; and Physiology, and runs through March. In April and May of year 1, basic concepts from the Neurosciences, Microbiology, Pathology, and Pharmacology courses are pre-

sented. Year 2 resumes in August with Pharmacology, Microbiology, Pathology, Pathophysiology, Neurosciences, PCC and DRS. Students are introduced to clinical medicine in their first semester through PCC and DRS. These courses expose students to the practice of medicine by placing them in a community physician's office and emphasizing professionalism. The third-year clerkships focus on patient problem-solving with an increasing level of responsibility. The fourth year is composed of six 4-week clerkships and four 4-week electives.

USMLE

Step 1: Required. Students must record a passing score for promotion.
Step 2: Clinical Skills (CS): Required. Students must record a passing total score to graduate.
Step 2: Clinical Knowledge (CK): Required. Students must record a passing total score to graduate.

Selection Factors

The criteria the Committee on Admissions uses in the selection process are the academic record, MCAT scores, preprofessional evaluations, and personal interviews. Personal interviews by members of the committee provide candidates with an opportunity to review their curricular and extracurricular activities. More important, the interviewers gain insight into the character of the applicants, as well as how they have formulated their plans for the study and practice of medicine. Applicants must be citizens or permanent residents of the U.S. at the time of application. Applications are considered from Tennessee and its contiguous states (Mississippi, Arkansas, Missouri, Kentucky, Virginia, North Carolina, Georgia, and Alabama). Children of UT alumni may also be considered, regardless of their state of residence. Since priority is given to qualified Tennesseans, non-residents must possess superior qualifications to be considered by the committee. Only 10 percent of the entering class may be non-residents. Upon initial review of the AMCAS application, a supplemental application will be sent to applicants considered competitive for further review. Advanced standing applications will be considered for year 3 only. Applicants for transfer must be residents of Tennessee, be attending LCME-accredited schools, have successfully completed

the basic science curriculum, and have passed USMLE Step 1. Applicants must also provide evidence of circumstances necessitating a transfer. Deadline for transfer applications is April 1.

Financial Aid

Aid consists of loans, scholarships, and work-study. Merit-based scholarships are available to highly qualified students.

Information about Diversity Programs

The College of Medicine actively encourages applications from members of groups underrepresented in medicine. The Committee on Admissions evaluates both academic and non-academic factors in the selection process, with consideration given to the unique backgrounds and challenges of these applicants. Among American medical schools, the college is a national leader in the admission, matriculation, and graduation of students from groups underrepresented in medicine.

Campus Information

Setting

UTHSC is situated in one of the largest medical centers in the nation and close to vibrant downtown Memphis, home of NBA basketball, AAA baseball, the Symphony, Broadway plays, Beale Street blues and barbecue.

Enrollment

For 2009, total enrollment was: 620

Special Features

Please go to *www.uthsc.edu/Medicine.*

Housing

UTHSC has one dormitory. An abundance of affordable off-campus housing is available. See *www.UTMemOffCampus.com.*

Satellite Campuses/Facilities

Rotations are available at all three UT College of Medicine campuses: Memphis, Knoxville and Chattanooga.

Application Process and Requirements 2011–2012

Primary Application Service: AMCAS
Earliest filing date: June 1, 2010
Latest filing date: November 15, 2010

Secondary Application Required?: Yes
Sent to: Screened applicants
Contact: Nelson Strother
(901) 448-5561, nstrother@uthsc.edu
Fee: Yes, $50 **Waiver available:** Yes
Earliest filing date: July 2010
Latest filing date: February 2011

MCAT® required?: Yes
Latest MCAT® considered: September 2010
Oldest MCAT® considered: August 2005

Early Decision Program: School does not have EDP
Applicants notified: n/a
EDP available for: n/a

Regular Acceptance Notice
Earliest date: October 15, 2010
Latest date: Varies
Applicant's Response to Acceptance Offer – Maximum Time: Two weeks

Requests for Deferred Entrance Considered: Yes

Deposit to Hold Place in Class: No
Deposit (Resident): n/a **(Non-resident):** n/a
Deposit due: n/a
Applied to tuition: n/a **Refundable:** n/a
Refundable by: n/a

Estimated number of new entrants: 165
EDP: 0, special program: n/a

Start Month/Year: August 2011

Interview Format: Two individual interviews with admissions committee members. May have 1 in Memphis and 1 regional. Video interviews are not available.

Other Programs

PREPARATORY PROGRAMS
Postbaccalaureate Program: No
Summer Program: Yes
www.uthsc.edu/TIP

COMBINED DEGREE PROGRAMS
Baccalaureate/M.D. : No
M.D./M.P.H.: No
M.D./M.B.A.: No
M.D./J.D.: No
M.D./Ph.D.: Yes, Dr. Don Thomason,
(901) 448-7224, thomason@physio1.uthsc.edu

Premedical Coursework

On-line courses accepted in fulfillment of prerequisites: On a case-by-case basis

Course	Req.	Rec.	Lab.	Hrs.	Course	Req.	Rec.	Lab.	Hrs.
Inorganic Chemistry	•		•	8	Computer Science				
Behavioral Sciences					Genetics		•		
Biochemistry		•			Humanities				
Biology	•		•	8	Organic Chemistry	•		•	8
Biology/Zoology					Physics	•		•	8
Calculus					Psychology				
College English	•			6	Social Sciences				
College Mathematics									

Selection Factors: 2009 Accepted Applicants

Proportion of Accepted Applicants with Relevant Experience (Data Self-Reported to AMCAS®)		Community Service/Volunteer	76%
		Medically-Related Work	80%
		Research	72%

Shaded bar represents school's accepted scores ranging from the 10th percentile to the 90th percentile   School Median ●   National Median ●

Overall GPA	2.0	2.1	2.2	2.3	2.4	2.5	2.6	2.7	2.8	2.9	3.0	3.1	3.2	3.3	3.4	3.5	3.6	(3.7)	3.8	3.9	4.0
Science GPA	2.0	2.1	2.2	2.3	2.4	2.5	2.6	2.7	2.8	2.9	3.0	3.1	3.2	3.3	3.4	3.5	3.6	(3.7)	3.8	3.9	4.0

MCAT® Total Numeric Score 9 10 11 12 13 14 15 16 17 18 19 20 21 22 23 24 25 26 27 28 29 (30) 31 (32) 33 34 35 36 37 38 39 40 41 42 43

Writing Sample			J	K	L	M	N	(O)	P	(Q)	R	S	T
Verbal Reasoning	3	4	5	6	7	8	9	(10)	11	12	13	14	15
Biological Sciences	3	4	5	6	7	8	9	(10)	(11)	12	13	14	15
Physical Sciences	3	4	5	6	7	8	9	(10)	(11)	12	13	14	15

Acceptance & Matriculation Data for 2009–2010 First Year Class

	Resident	Non-resident	International	Total
Applications	610	733	9	1352
Interviewed	414	54	0	468
Deferred	6	3	0	9
Matriculants				
Early Assurance Program	0	0	0	0
Early Decision Program	0	0	0	0
Baccalaureate/M.D.	0	0	0	0
M.D./Ph.D.	0	0	0	0
Matriculated	157	8	0	**165**

Applications accepted from International Applicants: No

Specialty Choice

2005, 2006, 2007 Graduates, Specialty Choice (As reported by program directors to GME Track™)	
Anesthesiology	6%
Emergency Medicine	4%
Family Practice	10%
Internal Medicine	15%
Obstetrics/Gynecology	8%
Orthopaedic Surgery	5%
Pediatrics	11%
Psychiatry	4%
Radiology	8%
Surgery	6%

Matriculant Demographics: 2009–2010 First Year Class

Men: 106   **Women:** 59

Matriculants' Self-Reported Race/Ethnicity

Mexican American	0	Korean	3
Cuban	0	Vietnamese	0
Puerto Rican	1	Other Asian	5
Other Hispanic	3	Total Asian	23
Total Hispanic	4	Native American	0
Chinese	4	Black	12
Asian Indian	10	Native Hawaiian	0
Pakistani	0	White	126
Filipino	1	Unduplicated Number	
Japanese	0	of Matriculants	165

Science and Math Majors: 70%
Matriculants with:
   Baccalaureate degree: 100%
   Graduate degree(s): 8%

Financial Information

Source: 2008-2009 LCME I-B survey and 2009-2010 AAMC TSF questionnaire

	Residents	Non-residents
Total Cost of Attendance	$ 50,106	$ 71,016
Tuition and Fees	$ 22,789	$ 43,699
Other (includes living expenses)	$ 25,596	$ 25,596
Health Insurance (can be waived)	$ 1,721	$ 1,721

Average 2009 Graduate Indebtedness: $132,190
% of Enrolled Students Receiving Aid: 87%

Criminal Background Check

This medical school requires a criminal background check prior to matriculation.

Vanderbilt University School of Medicine

Nashville, Tennessee

Office of Medical School Admissions
215 Light Hall
Vanderbilt University School of Medicine
Nashville, Tennessee 37232-0685
T 615 322 2145   **F** 615 343 8397

Admissions www.mc.vanderbilt.edu/medschool/admissions
Main www.mc.vanderbilt.edu/medschool
Financial www.mc.vanderbilt.edu/medschool/finaid/finaid1.php
E-mail pat.sagen@vanderbilt.edu

Private Institution

Dr. Jeff Balser, Dean and Associate Vice Chancellor for Health Affairs

Dr. John A. Zic, Associate Dean for Admissions

Dr. George C. Hill, Associate Dean for Diversity in Medical Education

Vicky L. Cagle, Director of Student Financial Services

Dr. Patricia Sagen, Director of Admissions

General Information

VUSM is a private medical school located on the campus of Vanderbilt University. The Vanderbilt University Medical Center and affiliated hospitals provide a total of over 900 beds for diversified, comprehensive clinical experience. These hospitals share common goals of education, research, patient care, and community service.

Mission Statement

VUSM seeks to matriculate a diverse group of academically exceptional students whose attributes and accomplishments suggest that they will be future leaders and/or scholars in medicine to begin the process of lifelong learning in the science and practice of medicine.

Curricular Highlights

Community Service Requirement: Optional.
Research/Thesis Requirement: Optional.

Medical education at Vanderbilt is oriented toward promoting the intellectual development of students and equipping them with the disciplined approach, knowledge, and skills required of both a physician and scientist. The curriculum provides the student with a fundamental knowledge of basic medical principles, but flexibility is stressed. Changes in curriculum content and teaching methods continually evolve from Vanderbilt's focus upon new ways to assist students in their preparation for a lifetime of learning. The curriculum offers a productive blend of required and elective courses throughout all four years of the program. The Emphasis Program, whose primary goal is to develop leadership potential, is scheduled for the first two years of the curriculum, including eight weeks during the intervening summer. Areas of focus include: laboratory-based research, patient-oriented research, healthcare research, community health initiatives, international medicine, biomedical informatics, medical education, law and medicine, and medical humanities.

USMLE

Step 1: Required. Student must record a score.
Step 2: Clinical Skills (CS): Required. Student must record a score.
Step 2: Clinical Knowledge (CK): Required. Student must record a score.

Selection Factors

Applicants are invited without regard to race, sex, religion, national origin, sexual orientation, or state of residence. Applicants must possess sufficient intellectual ability, emotional stability, and sensory and motor functions to meet the academic requirements of the school of medicine without fundamental alteration in the nature of this program. Applications are reviewed in two stages. The initial review is made from material provided through AMCAS. Competitive strength of credentials reflecting preparation for medical studies, motivation, personal qualities, and educational background are evaluated by the Admissions Committee and determine the recipients of secondary applications and invitations to interview. There is a holistic review of academic performance and non-academic factors (patient care experience, research experience, extracurricular involvement, leadership roles, sports activities, relationship to the medical school, and applicants from underserved populations). Interviews are held at Vanderbilt. AP credit, CLEP credit, and PASS/FAIL credit are not accepted for any required courses. In lieu of required courses with AP credit, higher level coursework should be taken. Vanderbilt undergraduates with at least a 3.5 GPA are eligible to apply for the binding Early Acceptance Program during the spring of the sophomore year. Those accepted are encouraged to broaden their curricular experiences. Acceptance for transfer is limited to third year with places made available by attrition only.

Financial Aid

Every effort is made to see that each student who applies has sufficient funds to meet the total estimated cost of attendance by utilizing a variety of loans and scholarships. Thirty-three percent of the class receives full tuition scholarships on merit or through the MST program.

Information about Diversity Programs

Matriculation of a diverse student body is a central goal of VUSM. Diversity is defined in the broadest sense (gender, race, ethnicity, sexual preference, socio-economic background, geographic origin).

Campus Information

Setting

The medical school is part of a 323-acre campus that also serves as a national arboretum.

Enrollment

For 2009, total enrollment was: 453

Special Features

The Monroe Carell, Jr. Children's Hospital at Vanderbilt is a state-of the-art pediatric facility. VUSM has an NIH-sponsored Comprehensive Cancer Center. The Vanderbilt Transplant Center is one of the leaders in the field. The Center for Experiential Learning and Assessment showcases state of the art simulation technologies and standardized patient learning environments to master clinical skills. The new anatomy lab features plasma screen computers to enhance learning.

Housing

There is no on-campus housing. The university does maintain a list of affordable apartments within a 10-mile radius. Rents average $500–$900 per month.

Satellite Campuses/Facilities

Student rotations are divided between Vanderbilt Hospital and the Nashville VA Hospital. Clinical opportunities also exist at Meharry Medical School as part of a formal collaboration.

Application Process and Requirements 2011–2012

Primary Application Service: AMCAS
Earliest filing date: June 1, 2010
Latest filing date: November 15, 2010

Secondary Application Required?: Yes
Sent to: Screened applicants invited to interview
URL: www.mc.vanderbilt.edu/medschool/admissions
Fee: Yes, $50 **Waiver available:** Yes
Earliest filing date: August 1, 2010
Latest filing date: December 31, 2010

MCAT® required?: Yes
Latest MCAT® considered: September 2010
Oldest MCAT® considered: 2007

Early Decision Program: School does not have EDP
Applicants notified: n/a
EDP available for: n/a

Regular Acceptance Notice
Earliest date: October 16, 2010
Latest date: Until class is full
Applicant's Response to Acceptance Offer – Maximum Time: Two weeks

Requests for Deferred Entrance Considered: Yes

Deposit to Hold Place in Class: No
Deposit (Resident): n/a **(Non-resident):** n/a
Deposit due: n/a
Applied to tuition: n/a **Refundable:** n/a
Refundable by: n/a

Estimated number of new entrants: 110
EDP: 2, special program: 10

Start Month/Year: August 2011

Interview Format: Individual interview with faculty member. Regional interviews are not available. Video interviews are not available.

Other Programs

PREPARATORY PROGRAMS
Postbaccalaureate Program: No
Summer Program: Yes, https://medschool.mc.vanderbilt.edu/summer_academy/

COMBINED DEGREE PROGRAMS
Baccalaureate/M.D.: No
M.D./M.P.H.: Yes, Cindy Naron, (615) 322-2017, cindy.naron@vanderbilt.edu
M.D./M.B.A.: Yes, Nancy L. Hyer, (615) 322-2530, nancy.l.hyer.2@vanderbilt.edu
M.D./J.D.: Yes, Nancy J. King, (615) 343-9836, nancy.king@vanderbilt.edu
M.D./Ph.D.: Yes, Michelle S. Grundy, Ph.D., (615) 343-2573, michelle.grundy@vanderbilt.edu
Additional Program: Yes, MD/MDiv., Rev. Angela D. Davis, (615) 343-3963, angela.d.davis@vanderbilt.edu

Premedical Coursework

On-line courses accepted in fulfillment of prerequisites: No

Course	Req.	Rec.	Lab.	Hrs.
Inorganic Chemistry	•		•	8
Behavioral Sciences				
Biochemistry		•		
Biology				
Biology/Zoology	•		•	8
Calculus				
College English	•			6
College Mathematics				

Course	Req.	Rec.	Lab.	Hrs.
Computer Science				
Genetics				
Humanities				
Organic Chemistry	•		•	8
Physics	•		•	8
Psychology				
Social Sciences				
Other				

Selection Factors: 2009 Accepted Applicants

Proportion of Accepted Applicants with Relevant Experience (Data Self-Reported to AMCAS®)		
Community Service/Volunteer		79%
Medically-Related Work		89%
Research		96%

Shaded bar represents school's accepted scores ranging from the 10th percentile to the 90th percentile. School Median ● National Median ◐

Overall GPA	2.0	2.1	2.2	2.3	2.4	2.5	2.6	2.7	2.8	2.9	3.0	3.1	3.2	3.3	3.4	3.5	3.6	3.7	3.8	(3.9) 4.0
Science GPA	2.0	2.1	2.2	2.3	2.4	2.5	2.6	2.7	2.8	2.9	3.0	3.1	3.2	3.3	3.4	3.5	3.6	3.7	3.8	(3.9) 4.0

MCAT® Total Numeric Score 9 10 11 12 13 14 15 16 17 18 19 20 21 22 23 24 25 26 27 28 29 30 31 (32)33 34 (35)36 37 38 39 40 41 42 43

Writing Sample			J	K	L	M	N	O	P	(Q) R S T
Verbal Reasoning	3	4	5	6	7	8	9	(10)	(11)	12 13 14 15
Biological Sciences	3	4	5	6	7	8	9	10	(11)	(12) 13 14 15
Physical Sciences	3	4	5	6	7	8	9	10	(11)	(12) 13 14 15

Acceptance & Matriculation Data for 2009–2010 First Year Class

	Resident	Non-resident	International	Total
Applications	316	4293	283	4892
Interviewed	54	958	75	1087
Deferred	0	5	0	5
Matriculants				
Early Assurance Program	3	8	0	11
Early Decision Program	0	0	0	0
Baccalaureate/M.D.	0	0	0	0
M.D./Ph.D.	1	8	1	10
Matriculated	19	86	6	**111**

Applications accepted from International Applicants: Yes

Matriculant Demographics: 2009–2010 First Year Class

Men: 56 **Women:** 55

Matriculants' Self-Reported Race/Ethnicity

Mexican American	2	Korean	1
Cuban	0	Vietnamese	2
Puerto Rican	0	Other Asian	3
Other Hispanic	2	Total Asian	25
Total Hispanic	4	Native American	0
Chinese	8	Black	11
Asian Indian	12	Native Hawaiian	0
Pakistani	0	White	59
Filipino	0	Unduplicated Number	
Japanese	1	of Matriculants	111

Science and Math Majors: 65%
Matriculants with:
Baccalaureate degree: 100%
Graduate degree(s): 4%

Specialty Choice

2005, 2006, 2007 Graduates, Specialty Choice (As reported by program directors to GME Track™)	
Anesthesiology	4%
Emergency Medicine	7%
Family Practice	1%
Internal Medicine	17%
Obstetrics/Gynecology	4%
Orthopaedic Surgery	6%
Pediatrics	11%
Psychiatry	5%
Radiology	6%
Surgery	9%

Financial Information

Source: 2008-2009 LCME I-B survey and 2009-2010 AAMC TSF questionnaire

	Residents	Non-residents
Total Cost of Attendance	$ 65,010	$ 65,010
Tuition and Fees	$ 40,331	$ 40,331
Other (includes living expenses)	$ 22,658	$ 22,658
Health Insurance (can be waived)	$ 2,021	$ 2,021

Average 2009 Graduate Indebtedness: $125,418
% of Enrolled Students Receiving Aid: 83%

Criminal Background Check

This medical school requires a criminal background check prior to matriculation.

Baylor College of Medicine

Houston, Texas

Office of Admissions
Baylor College of Medicine
One Baylor Plaza, MS BCM 110
Houston, Texas 77030
T 713 798 4842   **F** 713 798 5563

Admissions www.bcm.edu/admissions
Main www.bcm.edu
Financial www.bcm.edu/osa/osa-financial.html
E-mail admissions@bcm.edu

Private Institution

Dr. William T. Butler, Interim President

Dr. Florence Eddins-Folensbee, Sr. Associate Dean, Admissions and Student Affairs

Dr. James L. Phillips, Sr. Associate Dean, Diversity and Community Outreach

Dr. Stephen B. Greenberg, Sr. Vice President and Dean of Medical Education

General Information

Baylor College of Medicine (BCM) is a private, nonsectarian institution governed by an independent Board of Trustees composed of community leaders. BCM is the academic center around which the 1000-acre Texas Medical Center was developed. The Baylor faculty currently is composed of 1,607 full-time members and 1,701 voluntary members. Facilities include teaching and research buildings and seven affiliated teaching hospitals (including private, county, and Veterans Affairs hospitals).

Mission Statement

The mission of BCM is to promote health for all people through education, research, and public service. The college pursues this mission by sustaining excellence in educating medical and graduate students, primary care and specialty physicians, biomedical scientists and allied health professionals; by advancing basic and clinical biomedical research; by fostering public awareness of health and the prevention of disease; and by promoting patient care of the highest standard.

Curricular Highlights

Community Service Requirement: Required.
Research/Thesis Requirement: Optional

The educational program is structured to prepare graduates to pursue careers as primary care physicians, specialists, research scientists, academic physicians, or physicians involved in public health policy. The integration of basic and clinical sciences includes direct patient-care experiences early in the first year and a focus on core basic science topics prior to graduation. This integration also includes special courses featuring integrated problem-solving and clinical skills training that encourages

application of content learned in lectures and labs. The BCM curriculum is unique in that the basic sciences are taught in slightly less than one and a half years, giving students more time to take advantage of a wealth of clinical experiences. During the clinical curriculum, students have flexibility in organizing their schedules to complete 56 weeks of required clinical clerkships, four weeks of selectives, and 20 weeks of elective experiences. All students will be encouraged to develop and execute, with faculty mentorship and a scholarly project of their choice during their medical education. Interested students are given the opportunity to do research or to apply for a combined M.D./Ph.D. program. Students with an interest in ethics, care for the underserved, medical management (business), research, international health, or geriatrics may participate in tracks designed for the specific topic. There are several joint degree programs: a 5 year M.D./M.B.A. program with a health care focus with the Jones School of Management at Rice University; a six year M.D./J.D. program with the University of Houston Law Center and a 5 year M.D./M.P.H. with the University of Texas School of Public Health.

USMLE

Step 1: Required. Students must only record a score.
Step 2: Clinical Skills (CS): Required. Students must only record a score.
Step 2: Clinical Knowledge (CK): Required. Students must only record a score.

Selection Factors

All applicants offered places in the class are interviewed at BCM. All available information is utilized in the selection process. Attention is paid to course selections and the academic challenge imposed by the student's curriculum. Intellectual ability and academic achievement alone are not sufficient to support the development of the ideal physician. To work effectively in a profession dependent upon interpersonal relationships, physicians should possess those traits of personality and character which permit them to communicate effectively with warmth and compassion. Written requests for deferred matriculation from accepted students will be reviewed on an individual basis. BCM does not

discriminate on the basis of race, sex, marital status, creed, national origin, age, or disability.

Financial Aid

Financial need is not a factor in the selection of students. Aid funds are provided by private donors, the Board of Trustees, and various state and federal loan, scholarship, and work-study programs. Financial aid information and application materials are sent to all accepted applicants, and a financial aid officer is available for consultation with students and parents.

Information about Diversity Programs

BCM encourages applications from members of groups underrepresented in medicine. Students from these groups comprise a substantial portion of the student body; they also serve as Admissions Committee members.

Campus Information

Setting

BCM is located at the center of the Texas Medical Center, next door to Hermann Park, the zoo, and a public golf course. To the west are Rice University and the Village Shopping Center. The Museum District is to the north and offers more than 16 art organizations.

Enrollment

For 2009, total enrollment was: 698

Housing

There are many homes, apartments, townhouses, and condominiums for lease or purchase near the Texas Medical Center. Many of these living options are close to a light rail system that provides access to TMC at little or no cost to BCM students.

Application Process and Requirements 2011–2012

Primary Application Service: AMCAS
Earliest filing date: June 1, 2010
Latest filing date: November 1, 2010

Secondary Application Required?: Yes
Sent to: All applicants
URL: www.bcm.edu/admissions/?PMID=1776
Fee: Yes, $100 **Waiver available:** Yes
Earliest filing date: July 1, 2010
Latest filing date: December 1, 2010

MCAT® required?: Yes
Latest MCAT® considered: September 2010
Oldest MCAT® considered: July 2006

Early Decision Program: School does have EDP
Applicants notified: October 1, 2010
EDP available for: Both Residents
and Non-residents

Regular Acceptance Notice
Earliest date: October 15, 2010
Latest date: Until class is full
Applicant's Response to Acceptance
Offer – Maximum Time: n/a

Requests for Deferred
Entrance Considered: Yes

Deposit to Hold Place in Class: Yes
Deposit (Resident): $300 **(Non-resident):** $300
Deposit due: May 15, 2011
Applied to tuition: Yes **Refundable:** No
Refundable by: n/a

Estimated number of new entrants: 190
EDP: 5, special program: 40

Start Month/Year: July 2011

Interview Format: Currently under review.
Regional interviews are not available. Video interviews are not available.

Other Programs

PREPARATORY PROGRAMS
Postbaccalaureate Program: No
Summer Program: No
Additional Programs: Yes,
www.bcm.edu/smart/?PMID=2987

COMBINED DEGREE PROGRAMS
Baccalaureate/M.D.: Yes,
www.bcm.edu/medschool/baccmd.htm
M.D./M.P.H.: Yes, admissions@bcm.tmc.edu,
www.bcm.edu/medschool/dual.html#mph
M.D./M.B.A.: Yes, admissions@bcm.tmc.edu,
www.bcm.edu/medschool/dual.html#mba
M.D./J.D.: Yes, admissions@bcm.tmc.edu,
www.bcm.edu/medschool/dual.html#jd
M.D./Ph.D.: Yes, www.bcm.edu/mstp

Premedical Coursework

On-line courses accepted in fulfillment of prerequisites: On a case-by-case basis

Course	Req.	Rec.	Lab.	Sems.	Course	Req.	Rec.	Lab.	Sems.
Inorganic Chemistry	•		•	2	Computer Science				
Behavioral Sciences					Genetics				
Biochemistry					Humanities				
Biology	•		•	2	Organic Chemistry	•		•	2
Biology/Zoology					Physics				
Calculus					Psychology				
College English	•			2	Social Sciences				
College Mathematics					Other				

Selection Factors: 2009 Accepted Applicants

Proportion of Accepted Applicants with Relevant Experience (Data Self-Reported to AMCAS®)		
Community Service/Volunteer	74%
Medically-Related Work	84%
Research	88%

Shaded bar represents school's accepted scores ranging from the 10th percentile to the 90th percentile. **School Median** ● **National Median** ○

Overall GPA 2.0 2.1 2.2 2.3 2.4 2.5 2.6 2.7 2.8 2.9 3.0 3.1 3.2 3.3 3.4 3.5 3.6 3.7 3.8 (3.9) 4.0
Science GPA 2.0 2.1 2.2 2.3 2.4 2.5 2.6 2.7 2.8 2.9 3.0 3.1 3.2 3.3 3.4 3.5 3.6 3.7 3.8 (3.9) 4.0

MCAT® Total Numeric Score 9 10 11 12 13 14 15 16 17 18 19 20 21 22 23 24 25 26 27 28 29 30 31 (32) 33 34 (35) 36 37 38 39 40 41 42 43

Writing Sample			J	K	L	M	N	O	P	(Q)	R	S	T
Verbal Reasoning	3	4	5	6	7	8	9	(10)	(11)	12	13	14	15
Biological Sciences	3	4	5	6	7	8	9	10	(11)	(12)	13	14	15
Physical Sciences	3	4	5	6	7	8	9	10	(11)	(12)	13	14	15

Acceptance & Matriculation Data for 2009–2010 First Year Class

	Resident	Non-resident	International	Total
Applications	1383	3009	196	4588
Interviewed	408	309	0	717
Deferred	3	1	0	4
Matriculants				
Early Assurance Program	0	0	0	0
Early Decision Program	2	1	0	3
Baccalaureate/M.D.	35	2	0	37
M.D./Ph.D.	3	3	0	6
Matriculated	146	39	1	**186**

Applications accepted from International Applicants: Yes

Matriculant Demographics: 2009–2010 First Year Class

Men: 86 **Women:** 100

Matriculants' Self-Reported Race/Ethnicity

Mexican American	21	Korean	6
Cuban	1	Vietnamese	7
Puerto Rican	0	Other Asian	6
Other Hispanic	7	Total Asian	69
Total Hispanic	29	Native American	0
Chinese	24	Black	11
Asian Indian	24	Native Hawaiian	1
Pakistani	2	White	100
Filipino	2	Unduplicated Number	
Japanese	1	of Matriculants	186

Science and Math Majors: 61%
Matriculants with:
　　　Baccalaureate degree: 99%
　　　Graduate degree(s): 3%

Specialty Choice

2005, 2006, 2007 Graduates, Specialty Choice (As reported by program directors to GME Track™)	
Anesthesiology	8%
Emergency Medicine	3%
Family Practice	3%
Internal Medicine	17%
Obstetrics/Gynecology	4%
Orthopaedic Surgery	5%
Pediatrics	14%
Psychiatry	5%
Radiology	6%
Surgery	5%

Financial Information

Source: 2008-2009 LCME I-B survey
and 2009-2010 AAMC TSF questionnaire

	Residents	Non-residents
Total Cost of Attendance	$ 44,361	$ 57,461
Tuition and Fees	$ 14,828	$ 27,928
Other (includes living expenses)	$ 26,849	$ 26,849
Health Insurance (can be waived)	$ 2,684	$ 2,684

Average 2009 Graduate Indebtedness: $91,402
% of Enrolled Students Receiving Aid: 81%

Criminal Background Check

This medical school requires a criminal background check prior to matriculation.

Paul L. Foster School of Medicine at Texas Tech University Health Sciences Center at El Paso

El Paso, Texas

Paul L. Foster School of Medicine at Texas Tech University Health Sciences Center at El Paso
5001 El Paso Drive
El Paso, Texas 79905
T 915 783 1250 F 915 783 1265

Admissions www.ttuhsc.edu/fostersom/admissions/
Main www.ttuhsc.edu/fostersom/
Financial www.ttuhsc.edu/financialaid/
E-mail fostersom.admissions@ttuhsc.edu

Public Institution

Dr. Jose Manuel de la Rosa, Dean

Dr. Manuel Schydlower, Associate Dean for Admissions

Dr. German R. Nunez, Vice President for Diversity and Multicultural Affairs

E. Marcus Wilson, Director, Financial Aid

John Snelling, Director of Admissions

Lorraine James, M.B.A., Assistant Director of Admissions

General Information

In 1999, then Texas Tech System Chancellor John T. Montford shared with the Board of Regents a vision for a full four-year medical school in El Paso by expanding the existing third and fourth-year clinical program. The addition of the first two years of the medical school would allow students from El Paso and nearby regions to complete their education near home and help retain doctors in the area. On December 9, 2003, the ground breaking for El Paso Medical Science Building I took place and two years later, on January 31, 2006, a ribbon cutting followed. This $38 million, 93,000 sq.-ft. facility houses research on diabetes, cancer, environmental health and infectious diseases, as well as a repository dedicated to data on Hispanic health and a genomic facility to link hereditary diseases in families. The medical classroom building was completed in November 2007. This $48 million 125,000 sq.-ft. building has four floors and a partial penthouse. Included in the building are classrooms, library, small group rooms, a clinical skills area for students, faculty and administrative areas, basic science labs, gross anatomy lab, a student services area, and food services. The School of Medicine's graduates will have seen diseases that only a small fraction of medical students ever come across in their medical school clinical learning experiences. El Paso students may encounter diseases and other ailments that have virtually been wiped out in the United States, but flourish in many emerging nations. The variety and diversity of patients that our students see allow our future doctors to learn so much more than classic "text book" cases.

Mission Statement

The school's mission is to provide exceptional opportunities for students, trainees, and physicians; to advance knowledge through innovative scholarship and research in medicine with a focus on international health and health care disparities; and to provide exemplary patient care and service to the entire El Paso community and beyond.

Curricular Highlights

Community Service Requirement: Required. In Society, Community and the Individual course.
Research/Thesis Requirement: Required. Completion of a research project is required.

Among the goals of the Paul L. Foster School of Medicine is the provision of a medical education that is consistent with modern scientific principles, supportive of strong ethical principles, sensitive to the needs of the community, and committed to excellence. The school offers an integrated curriculum that is permeated with clinical presentations assigned to organ-system based courses. Clinical presentations are the ways in which a patient presents to a physician. Students learn anatomy, biochemistry, physiology and other basic science concepts and content needed to understand specific clinical presentations at the time that the presentation is being addressed. This approach enhances knowledge comprehension and has been shown to improve retention of the basic sciences and to promote the acquisition of diagnostic reasoning skills that are more like those of the expert practicing physician. During the clinical science years students participate in a unique and rich variety of clinical patient-care learning experiences that include not only traditional medicine, but also international, binational, bicultural, and border health medicine.

USMLE

Step 1: Required. Students must record a passing score for promotion.
Step 2: Clinical Skills (CS): Required. Students must record a passing total score to graduate.
Step 2: Clinical Knowledge (CK): Required. Students must record a passing total score to graduate.

Selection Factors

Candidates who are considered to be competitive for admission, based on criteria established by the school, will be invited to interview. These criteria include scores from the MCAT; academic performance as reflected by the science and overall GPA; rigor of the undergraduate curriculum, extracurricular activities (medical and non-medical) and employment and their impact on performance and maturation; recommendations from premedical advisors or faculty; socioeconomic and disadvantaged background; personal statement and its reflection of communication skills, personal qualities, leadership, maturity, determination, and motivation for a career in medicine; and regional origin. The interview evaluates the applicant's interest and knowledge of the health care field and motivation for a medical career; personal characteristics; and problem solving skills.

Financial Aid

Once accepted, financial aid assistance can be obtained from the Office of Student Financial Aid. Employment is discouraged.

Information about Diversity Programs

In an effort to recruit a qualified and diverse student body that reflects the demographics of the West Texas region, ethnicity, as well as socioeconomically disadvantaged background is among the many factors considered in the admissions process.

Campus Information

Setting

The school is located in South Central El Paso just a few hundred yards north of the international border with Mexico.

Enrollment

For 2009, total enrollment was: 39

Housing

No on campus housing. Ample affordable housing available within 20 minute radius.

Application Process and Requirements 2011–2012

Primary Application Service: TMDSAS
Earliest filing date: May 1, 2010
Latest filing date: October 1, 2010

Secondary Application:
URL: n/a
Sent to: n/a
Fee: n/a   **Waiver Available:** n/a
Earliest filing date: n/a
Latest filing date: n/a

MCAT® required?: Yes
Latest MCAT® considered: September 2010
Oldest MCAT® considered: 2006

Early Decision Program: School does not have EDP
Applicants notified: n/a
EDP available for: n/a

Regular Acceptance Notice
Earliest date: November 15, 2010
Latest date: Until class is full
Applicant's Response to Acceptance Offer – Maximum Time: Two weeks

Requests for deferred entrance considered: Yes

Deposit to Hold Place in Class: Yes,
Deposit (Resident): $100   **(Non-resident):** $100
Deposit due: May 15, 2011
Applied to tuition: No   **Refundable:** Yes
Refundable by: May 15, 2011

Estimated number of new entrants: 80
EDP: n/a, special program: n/a

Start month/year: July 2011

Interview format: Two individual 30-minute interviews. Regional interviews are not available. Video interviews are not available.

Other Programs

PREPARATORY PROGRAMS
Postbaccalaureate Program: No
Summer Program: No

COMBINED DEGREE PROGRAMS
Baccalaureate/M.D.: No
M.D./M.P.H.: Yes, Dr. Mary Ann Smith, (713) 500-9236, mary.a.smith@uth.tmc.edu
M.D./M.B.A.: No
M.D./J.D.: No
M.D./Ph.D.: No

Premedical Coursework

On-line courses accepted in fulfillment of prerequisites: On a case-by-case basis

Course	Req.	Rec.	Lab.	Hrs.	Course	Req.	Rec.	Lab.	Hrs.
Inorganic Chemistry	•		•	8	Computer Science				
Behavioral Sciences		•			Genetics				
Biochemistry		•			Humanities		•		
Biology	•		•	14	Organic Chemistry	•		•	8
Biology/Zoology					Physics	•		•	8
Calculus	•			3	Psychology				
College English	•			6	Social Sciences		•		
College Mathematics									

Selection Factors: 2009 Accepted Applicants

Proportion of Accepted Applicants with Relevant Experience (Data Self-Reported to AMCAS®)		
Community Service/Volunteer		87%
Medically-Related Work		83%
Research		77%

Shaded bar represents school's accepted scores ranging from the 10th percentile to the 90th percentile   School Median ● National Median ◐

Overall GPA 2.0 2.1 2.2 2.3 2.4 2.5 2.6 2.7 2.8 2.9 3.0 3.1 3.2 3.3 3.4 3.5 3.6 3.7 (3.8) 3.9 4.0
Science GPA 2.0 2.1 2.2 2.3 2.4 2.5 2.6 2.7 2.8 2.9 3.0 3.1 3.2 3.3 3.4 3.5 3.6 (3.7) 3.8 3.9 4.0

MCAT® Total Numeric Score 9 10 11 12 13 14 15 16 17 18 19 20 21 22 23 24 25 26 27 28 29 (30) 31 (32) 33 34 35 36 37 38 39 40 41 42 43

Writing Sample			J	K	L	M	N	(O)	P	(Q)	R	S	T
Verbal Reasoning	3	4	5	6	7	8	9	(10)	11	12	13	14	15
Biological Sciences	3	4	5	6	7	8	9	(10)	(11)	12	13	14	15
Physical Sciences	3	4	5	6	7	8	9	(10)	(11)	12	13	14	15

Acceptance & Matriculation Data for 2009–2010 First Year Class

	Resident	Non-resident	International	Total
Applications	2151	313	39	2503
Interviewed	367	22	0	389
Deferred	4	0	0	4
Matriculants				
Early Assurance Program	0	0	0	0
Early Decision Program	0	0	0	0
Baccalaureate/M.D.	0	0	0	0
M.D./Ph.D.	0	0	0	0
Matriculated	37	2	1	**40**

Applications accepted from International Applicants: No

Matriculant Demographics: 2009–2010 First Year Class

Men: 16   **Women:** 24

Matriculants' Self-Reported Race/Ethnicity

Mexican American	6	Korean	0
Cuban	0	Vietnamese	3
Puerto Rican	0	Other Asian	6
Other Hispanic	1	Total Asian	12
Total Hispanic	7	Native American	0
Chinese	4	Black	0
Asian Indian	0	Native Hawaiian	0
Pakistani	0	White	24
Filipino	0	Unduplicated Number	
Japanese	0	of Matriculants	40

Science Majors: 23%
Matriculants with:
    Baccalaureate Degree: 98%
    Graduate Degree(s): 12%

Specialty Choice

2005, 2006, 2007 Graduates, Specialty Choice
(As reported by program directors to GME Track™)

Anesthesiology
Emergency Medicine
Family P
Internal
Obstetri
Orthopa   **DATA NOT AVAILABLE**
Pediatric
Psychiatı
Radiolog,
Surgery

Financial Information

Source: 2008-2009 LCME I-B survey and 2009-2010 AAMC TSF questionnaire

	Residents	Non-residents
Total Cost of Attendance	$ 41,864	$ 54,964
Tuition and Fees	$ 14,895	$ 27,995
Other (includes living expenses)	$ 26,069	$ 26,069
Health Insurance (cannot be waived)	$ 900	$ 900

Average 2009 Graduate Indebtedness: n/r
% of Enrolled Students Receiving Aid: n/r

Criminal Background Check

This medical school requires a criminal background check prior to matriculation.

Texas A&M University System Health Science Center College of Medicine

College Station, Texas

Office of Admissions
The Texas A&M Health Science Center
College of Medicine, 159 Joe Reynolds Medical Bldg.
College Station, Texas 77843-1114
T 979 845 7743   F 979 845 5533

Admissions http://medicine.tamhsc.edu/admissions/index.htm
Main http://medicine.tamhsc.edu/
Financial http://tamhsc.edu/academics/finaid
E-mail admissions@medicine.tamhsc.edu

Public Institution

Dr. Edward J. Sherwood, M.D., F.A.C.P., Interim Dean

Filomeno G. Maldonado, Associate Dean for Admissions

Wanda J. Watson, Director of Recruitment and Special Programs

Harold Whitis, Executive Director of Student Financial Aid

Dr. Kathleen F. Fallon, Associate Dean for Student Affairs and Admissions

Leila E. Diaz, Director of Admissions

General Information

Established in 1973, the College of Medicine is part of The Texas A&M Health Science Center, a public health sciences university. The college's first class of 32 began in 1977. In 1999, the College of Medicine joined the newly created Texas A&M Health Science Center and to date, more than 1,400 physicians have received their medical training here. The College of Medicine utilizes approximately 1300 basic and clinical science faculty in instructional programs in Bryan-College Station, Temple, Round Rock, Houston, and Corpus Christi.

Mission Statement

The College of Medicine is dedicated to the education of humane and highly skilled physicians and to the development of knowledge in the biomedical and clinical sciences. In order to improve the quality and efficacy of medical care through its programs of medical education and research, the College of Medicine maintains a personalized educational experience for medical students. The College's overarching goals are building signature research and clinical programs and reaffirming its land grant heritage of community outreach and service.

Curricular Highlights

Community Service Requirement: Optional.
Research/Thesis Requirement: Optional.

The College of Medicine implemented a new integrative curriculum in 2009-2010. The focus of the new medical curriculum is an enhanced level of integration of material that is taught to students in the first two years. Students in the curriculum do not take separate courses in the traditional basic sciences. Rather this material is appropriately organized into integrated blocks of instruction of 3 to 10 weeks in duration depending on the theme of the block and structured into phases of instruction. During the third and fourth years of medical school or Phases III and IV of the curriculum, students receive clinical training in several different patient care venues, ranging from Bryan-College Station, Corpus Christi and Austin, Texas to Houston, Round Rock and Temple, Texas. The curriculum allows for a highly personalized medical education experience from the very onset.

USMLE

Step 1: Required. Students must record a passing score for graduation, but not promotion.
Step 2: Clinical Skills (CS): Required. Students must record a passing total score to graduate.
Step 2: Clinical Knowledge (CK): Required. Students must record a passing total score to graduate.

Selection Factors

Intellectual capacity, record of academic achievement and performance on the MCAT are important selection criteria. Equally important are interpersonal and communication skills, maturity, motivation, and demonstrated compassion. Careful consideration is given to other factors such as community service, disadvantaged circumstances, socioeconomic background, race/ethnicity, support by college faculty, research, primary care interest, and/or service in a rural/underserved area. Knowledge of and experiences in the medical profession are given serious consideration. Admission is open to qualified individuals regardless of race, color, religion, gender, age, national origin, or disability. Applicants are invited for personal interviews based upon their competiveness in the review process.

Financial Aid

Federal and State loan funds are available to students with financial need. Institutional merit and need-based scholarships are awarded on a competitive basis.

Information about Diversity Programs

The college believes that diversity enhances its ability to provide care and to serve communities across a broad range of racial and ethnic groups. As part of its commitment to this effort, the college administers several programs for students who are disadvantaged or from groups underrepresented in medicine. The Joint Admissions Medical Program is open to economically disadvantaged students, and the Partnership for Primary Care Program is open to students from rural/underserved communities in Texas. Also, the adjustment and retention of minority students is facilitated through the college's chapter of the Student National Medical Association (SNMA).

Campus Information

Setting

The college's new campus is located in Bryan, Texas just west of Texas A&M University in College Station, Texas, 100 miles northwest of Houston. Bryan and College Station, its neighboring city to the south, are home to approximately 125,000 people. Bryan-College Station is located in East-Central Texas between the Brazos and Navasota Rivers.

Enrollment

For 2009, total enrollment was: 481

Special Features

The College of Medicine's primary clinical partner, Scott & White Hospital and Clinic, is one of the largest integrated multi-specialty health care systems in the U.S. and is continuously ranked among the 100 Top Hospitals and the 15 Top Teaching Hospitals in the country.

Housing

Although on-campus housing is not available, the Coordinator of Student Services provides access to apartment listings and roommate search options. Rents for unfurnished apartments range from $290 to $1,200 per month.

Satellite Campuses/Facilities

In addition to traditional clerkships and ambulatory care experiences in College Station, Temple, Houston, Corpus Christi, Waco, Austin and Fort Hood, the college recently opened teaching and clinical facilities on new campuses in Round Rock and Bryan.

Application Process and Requirements 2011–2012

Primary Application Service: TMDSAS
Earliest filing date: May 1, 2010
Latest filing date: October 1, 2010

Secondary Application Required?: Yes
Sent to: All applicants
URL: http://medicine.tamhsc.edu/admissions/index.htm
Fee: Yes, $50 **Waiver available:** Yes
Earliest filing date: May 1, 2010
Latest filing date: October 1, 2010

MCAT® required?: Yes
Latest MCAT® considered: September 2010
Oldest MCAT® considered: August 2006

Early Decision Program: School does not have EDP
Applicants notified: n/a
EDP available for: n/a

Regular Acceptance Notice
Earliest date: November 15, 2010 for Texas residents; October 15, 2010 for non-residents
Latest date: Until class is full
Applicant's Response to Acceptance Offer – Maximum Time: Two weeks

Requests for Deferred Entrance Considered: Yes

Deposit to Hold Place in Class: No
Deposit (Resident): n/a **(Non-resident):** n/a
Deposit due: n/a
Applied to tuition: n/a **Refundable:** n/a
Refundable by: n/a

Estimated number of new entrants: 150
EDP: n/a, special program: 12

Start Month/Year: July 2011

Interview Format: Two individual 30-minute interviews. Regional interviews are not available. Video interviews are available.

Other Programs

PREPARATORY PROGRAMS
Postbaccalaureate Program: No
Summer Program: Yes, www.utsystem.edu/jamp/
Partnership for Primary Care: Yes, http://medicine.tamhsc.edu/admissions/ppc/index.html
Summer Research Program: Yes, http://medicine.tamhsc.edu/research/student/index.html

COMBINED DEGREE PROGRAMS
Baccalaureate/M.D.: No
M.D./M.P.H.: Yes, http://medicine.tamhsc.edu/admissions/index.html, Dr. Gary McCord, (979) 845-7743, McCord@medicine.tamhsc.edu
M.D./M.B.A.: Yes, http://medicine.tamhsc.edu/admissions/md-mba.html
Dr. Gary McCord, (979) 845-7743 or (254) 724-0242, McCord@medicine.tamhsc.edu
M.D./J.D.: No
M.D./Ph.D.: Yes, http://medicine.tamhsc.edu/education/md-phd/index.html
Dr. Julian Leibowitz, (979) 845-7288, leibowit@medicine.tamhsc.edu

Premedical Coursework

On-line courses accepted in fulfillment of prerequisites: On a case-by-case basis

Course	Req.	Rec.	Lab.	Hrs.
Inorganic Chemistry	•		•	8
Behavioral Sciences				
Biochemistry		•		3
Biology	•		•	14
Biology/Zoology				
Calculus	•			3
College English	•			6
College Mathematics				

Course	Req.	Rec.	Lab.	Hrs.
Computer Science				
Genetics				
Humanities				
Organic Chemistry	•		•	8
Physics	•		•	8
Psychology				
Social Sciences				
Math-based Statistics	•			3

Selection Factors: 2009 Accepted Applicants

Proportion of Accepted Applicants with Relevant Experience (Data Self-Reported to AMCAS®)	
Community Service/Volunteer	89%
Medically-Related Work	95%
Research	68%

Shaded bar represents school's accepted scores ranging from the 10th percentile to the 90th percentile. School Median ● National Median ◐

Overall GPA 2.0 2.1 2.2 2.3 2.4 2.5 2.6 2.7 2.8 2.9 3.0 3.1 3.2 3.3 3.4 3.5 3.6 3.7 (3.8) 3.9 4.0
Science GPA 2.0 2.1 2.2 2.3 2.4 2.5 2.6 2.7 2.8 2.9 3.0 3.1 3.2 3.3 3.4 3.5 3.6 (3.7) 3.8 3.9 4.0

MCAT® Total Numeric Score 9 10 11 12 13 14 15 16 17 18 19 20 21 22 23 24 25 26 27 28 29 30 (31)(32) 33 34 35 36 37 38 39 40 41 42 43

Writing Sample			J	K	L	M	N	O	(P)	(Q)	R	S	T
Verbal Reasoning	3	4	5	6	7	8	9	(10)	11	12	13	14	15
Biological Sciences	3	4	5	6	7	8	9	10	(11)	12	13	14	15
Physical Sciences	3	4	5	6	7	8	9	(10)	(11)	12	13	14	15

Acceptance & Matriculation Data for 2009–2010 First Year Class

	Resident	Non-resident	International	Total
Applications	2553	465	63	3081
Interviewed	775	20	4	799
Deferred	2	0	0	2
Matriculants				
Early Assurance Program	0	0	0	0
Early Decision Program	0	0	0	0
Baccalaureate/M.D.	0	0	0	0
M.D./Ph.D.	1	2	0	3
Matriculated	134	16	0	**150**

Applications accepted from International Applicants: Yes

Matriculant Demographics: 2009–2010 First Year Class

Men: 92 **Women:** 58

Matriculants' Self-Reported Race/Ethnicity

Mexican American	15	Korean	2
Cuban	0	Vietnamese	3
Puerto Rican	0	Other Asian	22
Other Hispanic	5	Total Asian	47
Total Hispanic	20	Native American	1
Chinese	6	Black	4
Asian Indian	10	Native Hawaiian	1
Pakistani	3	White	90
Filipino	1	Unduplicated Number	
Japanese	1	of Matriculants	150

Science and Math Majors: 62%
Matriculants with:
Baccalaureate degree: 61%
Graduate degree(s): 9%

Specialty Choice

2005, 2006, 2007 Graduates, Specialty Choice (As reported by program directors to GME Track™)	
Anesthesiology	8%
Emergency Medicine	7%
Family Practice	12%
Internal Medicine	15%
Obstetrics/Gynecology	9%
Orthopaedic Surgery	3%
Pediatrics	12%
Psychiatry	5%
Radiology	2%
Surgery	8%

Financial Information

Source: 2008-2009 LCME I-B survey and 2009-2010 AAMC TSF questionnaire

	Residents	Non-residents
Total Cost of Attendance	$ 35,299	$ 48,399
Tuition and Fees	$ 11,394	$ 24,494
Other (includes living expenses)	$ 23,905	$ 23,905
Health Insurance (can be waived)	$ 0	$ 0

Average 2009 Graduate Indebtedness: $105,144
% of Enrolled Students Receiving Aid: 88%

Criminal Background Check

This medical school requires a criminal background check prior to matriculation.

Texas Tech University Health Sciences Center School of Medicine

Lubbock, Texas

Texas Tech University Health Sciences Center
School of Medicine
Office of Admissions, Room 2B116
3601 4th Street
Lubbock, Texas 79430
T 806 743 2297   **F** 806 743 2725

Admissions www.ttuhsc.edu/som/admissions
Main www.ttuhsc.edu
Financial www.ttuhsc.edu/FinancialAid/
E-mail somadm@ttuhsc.edu

Public Institution

Dr. Steven Berk, Dean of the School of Medicine

Dr. Kim Peck, Interim Assistant Dean of Admissions and Minority Affairs

Dr. German Nunez, Vice President for International and Multicultural Affairs

E. Marcus Wilson, Director, Financial Aid

Linda Prado, Director, Office of Admissions

General Information

The TTUHSC School of Medicine was established in 1969. All medical students spend the first two years at the Lubbock campus; third and fourth year students receive their clinical training in Lubbock, Amarillo, or Midland/Odessa (Permian Basin). Affiliations with teaching hospitals provide over 2,900 beds for clinical teaching. The medical school has 399 full-time and 24 part-time faculty members and more than 902 volunteer clinical faculty members. Agreements have been developed with four area universities to provide early acceptance of qualified students into TTUHSC School of Medicine. Applicants must be academically talented. Following satisfactory interview, the Admissions Committee recommends acceptance of the applicant. Applicants who continue to maintain the required GPA are guaranteed admission to Texas Tech School of Medicine in the fall following graduation. The MCAT is waived for these applicants.

Mission Statement

TTUHSC School of Medicine provides the highest standard of excellence in higher education, while pursuing continuous quality improvement. The school is committed to health care delivery for its 135,000 square mile service area. At the same time and as part of improvement of health care, its efforts include support of meaningful academic research for the betterment of future health care.

Curricular Highlights

Community Service Requirement: Optional.
Research/Thesis Requirement: Required. Completion of a research project is required.

The new four-year curriculum provides a broad innovative integration of basic and clinical care, with emphasis on developing the student's analytical problem-solving skills. The first two years blend core concepts of basic sciences with early clinical experience. Introduction to patience care skills begins in the first month. The second year now follows an overall systems approach, again aligned with supervised patient care experiences. Teaching formats include small group discussions, PBL, and team learning. Summer preceptorships are also available. The third and fourth years include clerkships in family medicine, internal medicine, neurology, obstetric-gynecology, pediatrics, psychiatry, and surgery. The fourth year combines required and elective rotations. Research opportunities include summer preceptorships, a Research Honors Program, and an integrated M.D.–Ph.D. program. Joint degree programs in the M.B.A./M.D. and J.D./M.D. are also offered. Students are graded using a categorical grading system: Honors, High Pass, Pass, Marginal Pass and Fail.

USMLE

Step 1: Required. Students must record a passing score for promotion.
Step 2: Clinical Skills (CS): Required. Students must record a passing total score to graduate.
Step 2: Clinical Knowledge (CK): Required. Students must record a passing total score to graduate.

Selection Factors

Applications are invited from qualified Texas residents and service area counties of New Mexico and Oklahoma. Only U.S. citizens or applicants with permanent resident visas are considered. Application forms and procedural information may be obtained from the Texas Medical and Dental Schools Application Service (*www.utsystem.edu/tmdsas*). A secondary application to TTUHSC School of Medicine is also required. The Admissions Committee carefully reviews all applications. Evidence of high intellectual ability and a record of strong academic achievement are essential for success in the study of medicine. Qualities such as compassion, motivation, the ability to communicate with people, maturity, and personal integrity are also important. There is no dis-

crimination on the basis of race, sex, creed, national origin, age, or disability. It is the goal of the institution to recruit a diverse medical class exhibiting the qualities promising academic success and to meet the needs of an increasingly diverse population. Personal interviews are offered to those candidates deemed competitive for admission. Interviews are conducted on the Lubbock campus.

Financial Aid

After an applicant has been accepted, financial aid assistance can be obtained from the Office of Student Financial Aid. Employment is discouraged.

Information about Diversity Programs

In an effort to recruit a highly qualified and diverse student body, which reflects the demographics of the West Texas region, race/ethnicity as well as a socioeconomically disadvantaged background, is among the many factors considered in the admission process.

Campus Information

Setting

The medical school is situated at the north edge of the city of Lubbock. It is adjacent to Texas Tech University, which makes it one of the few medical schools in the country to be on or adjacent to a major undergraduate campus and law school. The Lubbock campus is across the street from a number of apartment complexes and is within easy driving distance of shopping, recreational and cultural areas.

Enrollment

For 2009, total enrollment was: 604

Satellite Campuses/Facilities

All students spend the first two years of medical school on the Lubbock campus. The in-depth clinical training for medical students is divided among three campuses: Lubbock, Amarillo, or Midland/Odessa (Permian Basin).

Application Process and Requirements 2011–2012

Primary Application Service: TMDSAS
Earliest filing date: May 1, 2010
Latest filing date: October 1, 2010

Secondary Application Required?: Yes
Sent to: Required of all applicants
URL: https://www.ttuhsc.edu/som/admissions/ secondaryapp/default.asp
Fee: Yes, $50   **Waiver available:** No
Earliest filing date: May 1, 2010
Latest filing date: October 1, 2010

MCAT® required?: Yes
Latest MCAT® considered: September 2010
Oldest MCAT® considered: September 2005

Early Decision Program: School does have EDP
Applicants notified: October 1, 2010
EDP available for: Residents only

Regular Acceptance Notice
Earliest date: November 15, 2010
Latest date: Until class is full
Applicant's Response to Acceptance
Offer – Maximum Time: Two weeks

Requests for Deferred
Entrance Considered: Yes

Deposit to Hold Place in Class: Yes
Deposit (Resident): $100   **(Non-resident):** $100
Deposit due: May 15, 2011
Applied to tuition: No   **Refundable:** Yes
Refundable by: May 15, 2011

Estimated number of new entrants: 140
EDP: 3, special program: n/a

Start Month/Year: August 2011

Interview Format: Two individual thirty-minute interviews. Regional interviews are not available. Video interviews are not available.

Other Programs

PREPARATORY PROGRAMS
Postbaccalaureate Program: No
Summer Program: Yes
www.ttuhsc.edu/som/admissions
Joint Admission to Medicine Program (JAMP): www.utsystem.edu/jamp

COMBINED DEGREE PROGRAMS
Baccalaureate/M.D.: No
M.D./M.P.H.: No
M.D./M.B.A.: Yes,
www.ttuhsc.edu/som/admissions
M.D./J.D.: Yes, www.ttuhsc.edu/som/admissions,
www.law.ttu.edu/prospective
M.D./Ph.D.: Yes, www.ttuhsc.edu/som/gsbs/ academics/mdphdprogram.aspx

Premedical Coursework

On-line courses accepted in fulfillment of prerequisites: On a case-by-case basis

Course	Req.	Rec.	Lab.	Hrs.	Course	Req.	Rec.	Lab.	Hrs.
Inorganic Chemistry	•		•	8	Computer Science				
Behavioral Sciences					Genetics				
Biochemistry					Humanities				
Biology					Organic Chemistry	•		•	8
Biology/Zoology	•		•	14	Physics	•		•	8
Calculus	•			3	Psychology				
College English	•			6	Social Sciences				
College Mathematics					Statistics	•			3

Selection Factors: 2009 Accepted Applicants

Proportion of Accepted Applicants with Relevant Experience (Data Self-Reported to AMCAS®)		
Community Service/Volunteer	89%
Medically-Related Work	95%
Research	68%

Shaded bar represents school's accepted scores ranging from the 10th percentile to the 90th percentile   School Median ● National Median ○

Overall GPA	2.0	2.1	2.2	2.3	2.4	2.5	2.6	2.7	2.8	2.9	3.0	3.1	3.2	3.3	3.4	3.5	3.6	③.7	3.8	3.9	4.0
Science GPA	2.0	2.1	2.2	2.3	2.4	2.5	2.6	2.7	2.8	2.9	3.0	3.1	3.2	3.3	3.4	3.5	3.6	③.7	3.8	3.9	4.0

MCAT® Total Numeric Score 9 10 11 12 13 14 15 16 17 18 19 20 21 22 23 24 25 26 27 28 29 30 ㉛ ㉜ 33 34 35 36 37 38 39 40 41 42 43

Writing Sample		J	K	L	M	N	O	Ⓟ Ⓠ R S T
Verbal Reasoning	3	4	5	6	7	8	9	⑩ 11 12 13 14 15
Biological Sciences	3	4	5	6	7	8	9	10 ⑪ 12 13 14 15
Physical Sciences	3	4	5	6	7	8	9	⑩ ⑪ 12 13 14 15

Acceptance & Matriculation Data for 2009–2010 First Year Class

	Resident	Non-resident	International	Total
Applications	2511	386	46	2943
Interviewed	615	25	0	640
Deferred	1	1	0	2
Matriculants				
Early Assurance Program	0	0	0	0
Early Decision Program	6	0	0	6
Baccalaureate/M.D.	0	0	0	0
M.D./Ph.D.	2	0	0	2
Matriculated	134	6	0	**140**

Applications accepted from International Applicants: No

Matriculant Demographics: 2009–2010 First Year Class

Men: 72   **Women:** 68

Matriculants' Self-Reported Race/Ethnicity

Mexican American	10	**Korean**	2
Cuban	0	**Vietnamese**	2
Puerto Rican	0	**Other Asian**	16
Other Hispanic	1	**Total Asian**	36
Total Hispanic	11	**Native American**	0
Chinese	5	**Black**	3
Asian Indian	9	**Native Hawaiian**	1
Pakistani	2	**White**	94
Filipino	1	**Unduplicated Number**	
Japanese	0	**of Matriculants**	140

Science and Math Majors: 23%
Matriculants with:
     Baccalaureate degree: 100%
     Graduate degree(s): 12%

Specialty Choice

2005, 2006, 2007 Graduates, Specialty Choice (As reported by program directors to GME Track™)	
Anesthesiology	8%
Emergency Medicine	6%
Family Practice	12%
Internal Medicine	14%
Obstetrics/Gynecology	8%
Orthopaedic Surgery	4%
Pediatrics	13%
Psychiatry	3%
Radiology	3%
Surgery	7%

Financial Information

Source: 2008-2009 LCME I-B survey and 2009-2010 AAMC TSF questionnaire

	Residents	Non-residents
Total Cost of Attendance	$ 38,275	$ 51,375
Tuition and Fees	$ 13,471	$ 26,571
Other (includes living expenses)	$ 23,904	$ 23,904
Health Insurance (can be waived)	$ 900	$ 900

Average 2009 Graduate Indebtedness: $125,883
% of Enrolled Students Receiving Aid: 90%

Criminal Background Check

This medical school requires a criminal background check prior to matriculation.

University of Texas
Medical Branch at Galveston
Galveston, Texas

Office of Student Affairs & Admissions
University of Texas Medical Branch
301 University Boulevard
Galveston, Texas 77555-0817
T 409 772 6958 **F** 409 747 2909

Admissions www.utmb.edu/somstudentaffairs
Main www.som.utmb.edu
Financial www.utmb.edu/enrollmentservices
E-mail tsilva@utmb.edu

Public Institution
Dr. Garland Anderson, IV, Dean and Provost

Dr. Lauree Thomas, Associate Dean for Student Affairs and Admissions

Melvin Williams, Director, Equal Opportunity and Diversity

Vickie Brewer, Director, Enrollment Services and University Financial Aid

Dr. Jeffrey Rabek, Assistant Dean for Student Affairs and Admissions

Theresa Silva, Director of Admissions

General Information
The University of Texas Medical Branch (UTMB), established in 1891, is a state-owned academic health center with 7 hospitals, 797 teaching beds, and 147 specialty and subspecialty clinics directed by UTMB's administration. It is comprised of 4 schools (Medicine, Graduate School of Biomedical Sciences, Nursing, and Allied Health Sciences) and two institutes (Medical Humanities, and Human Infections and Immunity).

Mission Statement
The mission of UTMB is to provide scholarly teaching, innovative scientific investigation, and state-of-the-art patient care in a learning environment to better the health of society. UTMB's education programs enable the state's talented individuals to become outstanding practitioners, teachers, and investigators in the health care sciences. Its comprehensive primary, specialty, and subspecialty clinics support the educational mission of the SOM, which is committed to the health care of all Texans through the delivery of state-of-the-art preventive, diagnostic, and treatment services.

Curricular Highlights
Community Service Requirement: Optional.
Research/Thesis Requirement: Optional.

The Integrated Medical Curriculum (IMC) is a four-year program that emphasizes continuous integration of the basic medical sciences with clinical medicine, early clinical skill, clinical experiences, and professionalism. In this stu-dent-centered curriculum, which utilizes small-group problem-based learning, computer-assisted instruction, lectures, and labs, the basic medical sciences are learned in clinical contexts. Its organ system-based approach and clinical science contexts promote basic science integration across disciplines. The third and fourth years of the IMC are centered on ambulatory and inpatient experiences in emergency medicine, family medicine, internal medicine, neurology, obstetrics and gynecology, pediatrics, psychiatry, and surgery. A unique feature of the third-year curriculum is an elective month, which allows students to expand their experience in a primary care field or explore potential career interests in a medical specialty. The fourth year also includes an acting internship, community-based ambulatory medicine, and a scholarly project in which a basic science or medical humanities topic is explored in depth. UTMB employs a grading system of Honors, High Pass, Pass, and Fail for required core courses and Pass/Fail for elective courses.

USMLE
Step 1: Required. Students must record a passing score for promotion.
Step 2: Clinical Skills (CS): Required. Students must record a passing total score to graduate.
Step 2: Clinical Knowledge (CK): Required. Students must record a passing total score to graduate.

Selection Factors
UTMB includes race and ethnicity to the broad range of criteria considered for student admission and for scholarship awards. All information available is utilized in the selection process such as intellect, achievement, character, interpersonal skills, and motivation. In evaluating candidates, consideration is given to the total academic record, the results of aptitude and achievement tests, college preprofessional committee evaluations, and the personal interview.

Financial Aid
Long-term, low-interest and short-term loans are available to students with financial need. A number of scholarships are also available which are based on need, disadvantaged status and academic merit.

Information about Diversity Programs
UTMB is committed to increasing the number of disadvantaged students in medicine. Each applicant is reviewed holistically and individually by experienced members of the Admissions Committee with particular emphasis on the applicant's potential. Both cognitive and non-cognitive factors are considered. Following admission, a broad range of support services are available to assist students in completing the medical curriculum. UTMB does not discriminate on the basis of race, sex, creed, national origin, age, sexual orientation, religion or handicap.

Campus Information
Setting
UTMB is located on an island in the Gulf of Mexico, 50 miles south of Houston. The 99-acre campus has 77 major modern buildings, including the state-of-the-art Truman Blocker, Jr. Medical Research Building, Trauma Center, and Shriners Burns Hospital. Clinical training takes place in seven teaching hospitals; UTMB owns and operates all of the facilities, and they are physically located on the campus.

Enrollment
For 2009, total enrollment was: 927

Special Features
The Integrated Medical Curriculum (IMC) emphasizes a student-centered, multimodal approach including problem-based learning, lectures, and labs to promote the acquisition of knowledge and skills. The organ system-based approach and clinical science context promote basic science integration across disciplines. The IMC also consists of departmental clerkships, electives, selectives, an internship, and a scholarly project.

Housing
Student housing is available on campus and in the surrounding area.

Satellite Campuses/Facilities
A limited number of clerkship positions are available for third year students to spend their entire year in Austin, Texas. However, all third and fourth year students can choose to do a portion of their clerkships at this additional training site.

Application Process and Requirements 2010–2010

Primary Application Service: TMDSAS
Earliest filing date: May 1, 2010
Latest filing date: October 1, 2010

Secondary Application Required?: No
Sent to: n/a
URL: n/a
Fee: No   **Waiver available:** No
Earliest filing date: n/a
Latest filing date: n/a

MCAT® required?: Yes
Latest MCAT® considered: September 2010
Oldest MCAT® considered: April 2005

Early Decision Program: School does not have EDP
Applicants notified: n/a
EDP available for: n/a

Regular Acceptance Notice
Earliest date: November 15, 2010
Latest date: Until class is full
Applicant's Response to Acceptance Offer – Maximum Time: varies

Requests for Deferred Entrance Considered: Yes

Deposit to Hold Place in Class: No
Deposit (Resident): n/a   **(Non-resident):** n/a
Deposit due: n/a
Applied to tuition: n/a   **Refundable:** n/a
Refundable by: n/a

Estimated number of new entrants: 230
EDP: n/a, special program: 20

Start Month/Year: August 2011

Interview Format: Two interviews, presentation, student panel, and tour. Regional interviews are not available. Video interviews are not available.

Other Programs

PREPARATORY PROGRAMS
Postbaccalaureate Program: No
Summer Program: Yes, www.utmb.edu/somstudentaffairs/specialprograms
Lisa Cain, Ph.D., (409) 772-1212, ldcain@utmb.edu
Early Medical School Acceptance Program (EMSAP): www.utmb.edu/somstudentaffairs/specialprograms
Prematriculation Reinforcement & Enrichment Program:
www.utmb.edu/somstudentaffairs/specialprograms

COMBINED DEGREE PROGRAMS
Baccalaureate/M.D.: No
M.D./M.P.H.: Yes, www.utmb.edu/pmch.mph
Shannon Carroll, (409) 772-6635, smcarrol@utmb.edu
M.D./M.B.A.: Yes, Robert McGlashan, (281) 283-3110, busadvoff@uhcl.edu
M.D./J.D.: No
M.D./Ph.D.: Yes, www.utmb.edu/mdphd
Ana McAfee, (409) 772-5446, abmcafee@utmb.edu
Additional Program: Yes, www.mdphd.utexas.edu
Leslie Walters, (512) 232-0855, mdphd@austin.utexas.edu

Premedical Coursework

On-line courses accepted in fulfillment of prerequisites: No

Course	Req.	Rec.	Lab.	Sems.	Course	Req.	Rec.	Lab.	Sems.
Inorganic Chemistry	•		•	2	Computer Science				
Behavioral Sciences					Genetics		•		
Biochemistry		•		1	Humanities				
Biology	•		•	4	Organic Chemistry	•		•	2
Biology/Zoology					Physics	•		•	2
Calculus				1	Psychology				
College English	•			2	Social Sciences				
College Mathematics					Other				

Selection Factors: 2009 Accepted Applicants

Proportion of Accepted Applicants with Relevant Experience (Data Self-Reported to AMCAS®)		
Community Service/Volunteer	71%
Medically-Related Work	87%
Research	77%

Shaded bar represents school's accepted scores ranging from the 10th percentile to the 90th percentile   School Median ⚪   National Median ⚪

Overall GPA	2.0	2.1	2.2	2.3	2.4	2.5	2.6	2.7	2.8	2.9	3.0	3.1	3.2	3.3	3.4	3.5	3.6	3.7	(3.8)	3.9	4.0
Science GPA	2.0	2.1	2.2	2.3	2.4	2.5	2.6	2.7	2.8	2.9	3.0	3.1	3.2	3.3	3.4	3.5	3.6	3.7	(3.8)	3.9	4.0

MCAT® Total Numeric Score 9 10 11 12 13 14 15 16 17 18 19 20 21 22 23 24 25 26 27 28 29 30 (31) (32) 33 34 35 36 37 38 39 40 41 42 43

Writing Sample			J	K	L	M	N	O	(P)	(Q)	R	S	T
Verbal Reasoning	3	4	5	6	7	8	9	(10)	11	12	13	14	15
Biological Sciences	3	4	5	6	7	8	9	10	(11)	12	13	14	15
Physical Sciences	3	4	5	6	7	8	9	(10)	(11)	12	13	14	15

Acceptance & Matriculation Data for 2009–2010 First Year Class

	Resident	Non-resident	International	Total
Applications	2901	605	73	3579
Interviewed	869	55	5	929
Deferred	6	0	0	6
Matriculants				
Early Assurance Program	0	0	0	0
Early Decision Program	0	0	0	0
Baccalaureate/M.D.	0	0	0	0
M.D./Ph.D.	2	1	2	5
Matriculated	203	19	7	**229**

Applications accepted from International Applicants: Yes

Matriculant Demographics: 2009–2010 First Year Class

Men: 125   **Women:** 104

Matriculants' Self-Reported Race/Ethnicity

Mexican American	30	Korean	2
Cuban	0	Vietnamese	1
Puerto Rican	0	Other Asian	21
Other Hispanic	7	Total Asian	44
Total Hispanic	37	Native American	1
Chinese	8	Black	21
Asian Indian	9	Native Hawaiian	0
Pakistani	2	White	139
Filipino	1	Unduplicated Number	
Japanese	0	of Matriculants	230

Science and Math Majors: 71%
Matriculants with:
   Baccalaureate degree: 99%
   Graduate degree(s): 6%

Specialty Choice

2005, 2006, 2007 Graduates, Specialty Choice (As reported by program directors to GME Track™)

Anesthesiology	10%
Emergency Medicine	7%
Family Practice	7%
Internal Medicine	18%
Obstetrics/Gynecology	3%
Orthopaedic Surgery	3%
Pediatrics	11%
Psychiatry	6%
Radiology	5%
Surgery	7%

Financial Information

Source: 2008-2009 LCME I-B survey and 2009-2010 AAMC TSF questionnaire

	Residents	Non-residents
Total Cost of Attendance	$ 39,920	$ 53,020
Tuition and Fees	$ 14,270	$ 27,370
Other (includes living expenses)	$ 24,904	$ 24,904
Health Insurance (can be waived)	$ 746	$ 746

Average 2009 Graduate Indebtedness: $104,298
% of Enrolled Students Receiving Aid: 81%

Criminal Background Check

This medical school requires a criminal background check prior to matriculation.

University of Texas
Medical School at Houston

Houston, Texas

Office of Admissions—Room G.420
University of Texas Medical School at Houston
6431 Fannin, MSB G.420
Houston, Texas 77030
T 713 500 5116   **F** 713 500 0604

Admissions http://med.uth.tmc.edu/administration/admissions/
Main http://med.uth.tmc.edu
Financial http://sfs.uth.tmc.edu
E-mail ms-uthaskus@uth.tmc.edu

Public Institution

Dr. Giuseppe N. Colasurdo, Dean

Dr. Margaret McNeese, Associate Dean for Admissions and Student Affairs

Dr. Ronald Johnson, D.D.S., Chief Acad. Diversity Officer

Wanda K. Williams, Director, Student Financial Services

Dr. Judianne Kellaway, M.D., Assistant Dean for Admissions

Nancy Murphy, Administrative Coordinator for Admissions

General Information

UT-Houston Medical School is located in the Texas Medical Center in Houston. Memorial Hermann Hosp., a 650-bed general medical and surgical hospital, and Level I trauma center, is the school's primary teaching hospital. Other major teaching hospitals include the U. of Texas M.D. Anderson Cancer Ctr., the LBJ Hosp., the Harris County Psychiatric Center, Texas Heart Inst., St. Luke's Episcopal Hosp., Methodist Hosp. and others.

Mission Statement

The mission of the University of Texas Medical School at Houston is to provide the highest quality of education and training of future physicians for the state of Texas and to conduct the highest caliber of research in the biomedical and health sciences.

Curricular Highlights

Community Service Requirement: Optional.
Community Service: Unlimited opportunities
Research Thesis: Unlimited opportunities
Research/Thesis Requirement: Optional.

The first two academic years are divided into four semesters, with three months of vacation between the first and second years. The initial four semesters are devoted to preparing the student for clerkship experiences in the clinical years. During the first two years the student becomes familiar with the basic and applied biomedical sciences. The student progresses from a study of the morphology of the human body and the fundamentals of molecular and cellular biology to that of the normal and abnormal structure and function of the various organ systems. Taking a history and conducting a physical examination are emphasized. After completion of this sequence, the student progresses through a series of clinical clerkships in the major disciplines for the next 12 months. In the fourth year, there are four required months and five to seven months of electives. Medical jurisprudence and technical skills are taught. In consultation with faculty, each student devises an educational sequence that relates specifically to ultimate career goals and postgraduate educational plans.

USMLE

Step 1: Required. Students must only record a score.
Step 2: Clinical Skills (CS): Required. Students must only record a score.
Step 2: Clinical Knowledge (CK): Required. Students must only record a score.

Selection Factors

Applicants are selected with an emphasis on motivation and potential for service, especially in the state of Texas. Emphasis is given to students who have a broad education as well as academic achievement. A command of the English language with the ability to write and speak well is essential. The applicant's academic record is evaluated with special attention to the subjects taken and the demonstration of a broad-based comprehensive educational experience regardless of undergraduate institution. Significant attention is given to humanitarian endeavors, achievement in a nonacademic field of activity, and the applicant's specific interest in The University of Texas Medical School at Houston. Admission decisions are made in light of the school's mission, with preference given to Texas residents and those who will practice in underserved areas in the state and in needed specialties. Veteran status is also considered. The University of Texas Medical School at Houston does not discriminate on the basis of race, sex, creed, national origin, age, or handicap. For more information, go to *med.uth.tmc.edu.*

Financial Aid

Scholarship and loan funds from federal, state, and local sources are available to students with financial need as determined by the FAFSA.

Information about Diversity Programs

Numerous student organizations create an inclusive and supportive environment at UTH. All are aligned under the broad "Alliance for Diversity and Culture." The primary goal of the Office of Cultural and Institutional Diversity is to enhance success and promote retention of all students through early identification of stress factors and personal challenges, information which is then provided with the student's consent to academic advisors. Workshops and individual consultations are offered to enhance specific skills and time management, and diagnostic testing is available to help identify learning difficulties.

Campus Information

Setting

The Medical School Building (MSB), located in the Texas Medical Center, was built in 1976 and, at 875,365 gross sq. ft., comprises the school's largest facility. A state-of-the-art Surgical and Clinical Skills Center is one of this building's latest additions. Adjoining the MSB, a six-story building dedicated to research was completed in 2007.

Enrollment

For 2009, total enrollment was: 944

Special Features

Our location in the Texas Medical Center and membership in the UT Health Science Ctr. (comprising dentistry, nursing, public health, graduate school, and health informatics) provide many opportunities for students to engage in research, dual-degree programs, and specialty exploration with first-rate physicians and scientists.

Housing

Apartment-living managed by the UTHSC is available to students at two facilities. Various floor plans are available. Many other residential options are located near the Texas Medical Center, convenient shuttle or light rail available.

Satellite Campuses/Facilities

Student rotations are completed at several hospitals and clinics in the Texas Medical Center and nearby.

Application Process and Requirements 2010–2010

Primary Application Service: TMDSAS
Earliest filing date: May 1, 2010
Latest filing date: October 1, 2010

Secondary Application Required?: No
Sent to: n/a
URL: n/a
Fee: No   **Waiver available:** Yes
Earliest filing date: n/a
Latest filing date: n/a

MCAT® required?: Yes
Latest MCAT® considered: September 2010
Oldest MCAT® considered: August 2005

Early Decision Program: School does not have EDP
Applicants notified: October 15, 2010
November 15, 2010
EDP available for: Both Residents and Non-residents

Regular Acceptance Notice
Earliest date: October 15, 2010
Latest date: Until class is full
Applicant's Response to Acceptance Offer – Maximum Time: Two weeks

Requests for Deferred Entrance Considered: No

Deposit to Hold Place in Class: No
Deposit (Resident): n/a   **(Non-resident):** n/a
Deposit due: n/a
Applied to tuition: n/a   **Refundable:** n/a
Refundable by: n/a

Estimated number of new entrants: 230
EDP: n/a, special program: n/a

Start Month/Year: August 2011

Interview Format: Personal interview with two faculty members. Regional interviews are not available. Video interviews are not available.

Other Programs

PREPARATORY PROGRAMS
Postbaccalaureate Program: No
Summer Program: Yes, http://med.uth.tmc.edu/administration/admissions/
Pre-Entry Program: http://med.uth.tmc.edu/administration/edu_programs/ep/summer_programs.htm, Wai-San Johansson, (713) 500-7869, wai-san.johansson@uth.tmc.edu

COMBINED DEGREE PROGRAMS
Baccalaureate/M.D.: No
M.D./M.P.H.: Yes, http://med.uth.tmc.edu/administration/admissions/MDMPH.html
M.D./M.B.A.: No
M.D./J.D.: No
M.D./Ph.D.: Yes, www.uth.tmc.edu/gsbs/programs/mdphd/

Premedical Coursework

On-line courses accepted in fulfillment of prerequisites: No

Course	Req.	Rec.	Lab.	Hrs.	Course	Req.	Rec.	Lab.	Hrs.
Inorganic Chemistry	•		•	8	Computer Science				
Behavioral Sciences					Genetics				
Biochemistry					Humanities		•		
Biology	•		•	14	Organic Chemistry	•		•	8
Biology/Zoology					Physics	•		•	8
Calculus					Psychology				
College English	•			6	Social Sciences				
College Mathematics					Other				

Selection Factors: 2009 Accepted Applicants

Proportion of Accepted Applicants with Relevant Experience (Data Self-Reported to AMCAS®)		
Community Service/Volunteer		74%
Medically-Related Work		82%
Research		77%

Shaded bar represents school's accepted scores ranging from the 10th percentile to the 90th percentile   School Median ●   National Median ◎

Overall GPA	2.0	2.1	2.2	2.3	2.4	2.5	2.6	2.7	2.8	2.9	3.0	3.1	3.2	3.3	3.4	3.5	3.6	3.7	(3.8)	3.9	4.0
Science GPA	2.0	2.1	2.2	2.3	2.4	2.5	2.6	2.7	2.8	2.9	3.0	3.1	3.2	3.3	3.4	3.5	3.6	(3.7)	3.8	3.9	4.0

MCAT® Total Numeric Score 9 10 11 12 13 14 15 16 17 18 19 20 21 22 23 24 25 26 27 28 29 30 31 ③② ㉝ 34 35 36 37 38 39 40 41 42 43

Writing Sample			J	K	L	M	N	O	(P)	Q	R	S	T
Verbal Reasoning	3	4	5	6	7	8	9	(10)	11	12	13	14	15
Biological Sciences	3	4	5	6	7	8	9	10	(11)	12	13	14	15
Physical Sciences	3	4	5	6	7	8	9	10	(11)	12	13	14	15

Acceptance & Matriculation Data for 2009–2010 First Year Class

	Resident	Non-resident	International	Total
Applications	2938	698	72	3708
Interviewed	894	80	7	981
Deferred	0	0	0	0
Matriculants				
Early Assurance Program	0	0	0	0
Early Decision Program	0	0	0	0
Baccalaureate/M.D.	0	0	0	0
M.D./Ph.D.	5	0	0	5
Matriculated	208	21	1	**230**

Applications accepted from International Applicants: Yes

Matriculant Demographics: 2009–2010 First Year Class

Men: 141   **Women:** 89

Matriculants' Self-Reported Race/Ethnicity

Mexican American	15	Korean	2
Cuban	2	Vietnamese	3
Puerto Rican	0	Other Asian	10
Other Hispanic	15	Total Asian	36
Total Hispanic	32	Native American	1
Chinese	7	Black	12
Asian Indian	13	Native Hawaiian	1
Pakistani	1	White	170
Filipino	1	Unduplicated Number	
Japanese	1	of Matriculants	230

Science and Math Majors: 47%
Matriculants with:
   Baccalaureate degree: 74%
   Graduate degree(s): 5%

Specialty Choice

2005, 2006, 2007 Graduates, Specialty Choice (As reported by program directors to GME Track™)	
Anesthesiology	10%
Emergency Medicine	6%
Family Practice	9%
Internal Medicine	14%
Obstetrics/Gynecology	6%
Orthopaedic Surgery	4%
Pediatrics	12%
Psychiatry	7%
Radiology	4%
Surgery	8%

Financial Information

Source: 2008-2009 LCME I-B survey and 2009-2010 AAMC TSF questionnaire

	Residents	Non-residents
Total Cost of Attendance	$ 36,180	$ 49,280
Tuition and Fees	$ 11,040	$ 24,140
Other (includes living expenses)	$ 24,040	$ 24,040
Health Insurance (can be waived)	$ 1,100	$ 1,100

Average 2009 Graduate Indebtedness: $115,796
% of Enrolled Students Receiving Aid: 80%

Criminal Background Check

This medical school requires a criminal background check prior to matriculation.

University of Texas
School of Medicine at San Antonio
San Antonio, Texas

Medical School Admissions, Office of the Dean
Univ. of Texas School of Medicine at San Antonio
7703 Floyd Curl Drive
San Antonio, Texas 78229-3900
T 210 567 6080   F 210 567 6962

Admissions http://som.uthscsa.edu/admissions/index.asp
Main http://som.uthscsa.edu
Financial http:// studentservices.uthscsa.edu/financialaid.aspx
E-mail medadmissions@uthscsa.edu

Public Institution
Dr. Glen A. Halff, Acting Dean

Dr. David J. Jones,
Associate Dean for Admissions

Belinda Chapa, Director of Admissions and Special Programs

General Information
The University of Texas School of Medicine at San Antonio graduated its first class in 1970. The main campus is located at the South Texas Medical Center in NW San Antonio. Clinical instruction is carried out at the University Hospital, University Health Center, Audie Murphy Veterans Hospital, Santa Rosa Children's Hospital, and affiliated hospitals including Wilford Hall USAF Hospital and Brooke Army Hospital.

Mission Statement
The mission of the School of Medicine is to serve the needs of the citizens of Texas by providing medical education and training to medical students and physicians at all career levels and fostering an environment of life-long learning that is flexible and emphasizes professionalism, with special commitment to the preparation of physicians in both the art and science of medical practice; conducting biomedical and other health-related research, with particular attention to translational research; delivering exemplary health care; and providing a responsive resource in health-related affairs for the nation and the state, with particular emphasis on South Texas.

Curricular Highlights
Community Service Requirement: Optional.
Research/Thesis Requirement: Optional.

A four-year curriculum is offered. The first year is devoted to an organ systems-based presentation of anatomy, histology, biochemistry, physiology, and microbiology. The second year is anchored by the pathology course, and it incorporates pharmacology, medicine, pediatrics, obstetrics and gynecology, and surgery coordinated by organ systems. Behavioral sciences and an introduction to psychiatry are also included. Throughout the first two years,

one-half day per week is devoted to clinical integration activities. The third academic year is spent entirely in the clinical setting in eight consecutive assignments of six weeks each in family practice, medicine, the medical specialties, surgery, the surgical specialties, obstetrics and gynecology, psychiatry, and pediatrics. The senior year includes a didactic period of two months, with the rest of the academic year consisting of elective courses. A letter grading system is used.

USMLE
Step 1: Required. Must record a passing score for graduation, but not promotion.
Step 2: Clinical Skills (CS): Required. Students must only record a score.
Step 2: Clinical Knowledge (CK): Required. Students must only record a score.

Selection Factors
Ranking of applicants considers GPA, MCAT section scores, evaluation by premedical advisors, and judgment by the Committee on Admissions of the candidate's nonacademic achievements and personal qualifications, such as responsibility, integrity, maturity, and motivation. In addition, bilingual language ability, hometown or county of residence that has been designated a medically underserved area, socioeconomic history, positions of leadership held, communication skills, and clinical/volunteer experiences are considered. No person shall be excluded from participation in, denied the benefits of, or subject to discrimination under any program or activity sponsored or conducted by the University of Texas System on the basis of age, race, national origin, religion, or sex. Three hundred thirty-five acceptances were offered to obtain a class of 221 first-year students. All procedural information including electronic submission of applications is available through the Texas Medical and Dental Schools Application Service. Questions related to completeness of an application or other information should be directed to the Admissions Office at the medical school (medadmissions@uthscsa.edu). Additional information is available at (210) 567-6080.

Financial Aid
Financial assistance for students in need is available in the form of loans and scholarships. Accepted applicants can obtain complete information regarding financial assistance from the Financial Aid Administrator in the Office of Student Services *http://studentservices.uthscsa.edu/financialinfo/financialaid2.html*.

Information about Diversity Programs
Diversity of the student body is a compelling interest of the University of Texas School of Medicine at San Antonio. With this in mind, race and ethnicity is among the factors considered for acceptance of students.

Campus Information

Setting
The University of Texas School of Medicine at San Antonio is located in the South Texas Medical Center in northwest San Antonio.

Enrollment
For 2009, total enrollment was: 899

Special Features
The HEB Clinical Skills Center offers students 20 state-of-the-art examination rooms to develop patient examination skills.

Housing
On campus housing is not available. Homes, apartments, and condominiums are available within walking distance of the school of medicine and teaching hospitals.

Satellite Campuses/Facilities
The Regional Academic Health Center located in the Rio Grande Valley in Harlingen, Texas, is a second clinical education campus. At the end of their second year, up to 24 students move to Harlingen to complete their third and fourth years of medical school. Third-year clerkships are completed at Valley Baptist Hospital and Su Clinica Familiar. Fourth-year students participate in the same didactic and externship opportunities available at the San Antonio campus.

Application Process and Requirements 2011–2012

Primary Application Service: TMDSAS
Earliest filing date: May 1, 2010
Latest filing date: October 1, 2010

Secondary Application Required?: No
Sent to: n/a
URL: n/a
Fee: n/a   **Waiver available:** n/a
Earliest filing date: n/a
Latest filing date: n/a

MCAT® required?: Yes
Latest MCAT® considered: September 2010
Oldest MCAT® considered: 2007

Early Decision Program: School does not have EDP
Applicants notified: n/a
EDP available for: n/a

Regular Acceptance Notice
Earliest date: October 15, 2010 (non-residents)
November 15, 2010 (residents)
Latest date: Until class is full
Applicant's Response to Acceptance Offer – Maximum Time: Two weeks

Requests for Deferred Entrance Considered: Yes

Deposit to Hold Place in Class: No
Deposit (Resident): n/a   **(Non-resident):** n/a
Deposit due: n/a
Applied to tuition: n/a   **Refundable:** n/a
Refundable by: n/a

Estimated number of new entrants: 220
EDP: 0, special program: 5

Start Month/Year: July 25, 2011

Interview Format: Two 30-minute interviews; interviewers have only personal essays. Regional interviews are not available. Video interviews are not available.

Other Programs

PREPARATORY PROGRAMS
Postbaccalaureate Program: No
Summer Program: No

COMBINED DEGREE PROGRAMS
Baccalaureate/M.D.: Yes, http://som.uthscsa.edu/
Admissions/earlyMatriculationProgram.asp
Belinda Chapa, (210) 567-6080,
chapab@uthscsa.edu
M.D./M.P.H.: Yes, http://som.uthscsa.edu/
AcademicAffairs/mdmph.asp, Dr. Claudia Miller,
(210) 567-7457, millercs@uthscsa.edu
M.D./M.B.A.: No
M.D./J.D.: No
M.D./Ph.D.: Yes, http://som.uthscsa.edu/
Admissions/MDPhD.asp
Dr. Martin Adamo, (210) 567-3742,
adamo@uthscsa.edu

Premedical Coursework

On-line courses accepted in fulfillment of prerequisites: No

Course	Req.	Rec.	Lab.	Hrs.
Inorganic Chemistry	•		•	8
Behavioral Sciences				
Biochemistry	•			3
Biology	•		•	11
Biology/Zoology				
Calculus	•			3
College English	•			6
College Mathematics				

Course	Req.	Rec.	Lab.	Hrs.
Computer Science				
Genetics				
Humanities				
Organic Chemistry	•		•	8
Physics	•		•	8
Psychology				
Social Sciences				
Other				

Selection Factors: 2009 Accepted Applicants

Proportion of Accepted Applicants with Relevant Experience (Data Self-Reported to AMCAS)		
Community Service/Volunteer		79%
Medically-Related Work		89%
Research		81%

Shaded bar represents school's accepted scores ranging from the 10th percentile to the 90th percentile   **School Median** ●   **National Median** ◐

Overall GPA	2.0	2.1	2.2	2.3	2.4	2.5	2.6	2.7	2.8	2.9	3.0	3.1	3.2	3.3	3.4	3.5	3.6	(3.7)	3.8	3.9	4.0
Science GPA	2.0	2.1	2.2	2.3	2.4	2.5	2.6	2.7	2.8	2.9	3.0	3.1	3.2	3.3	3.4	3.5	3.6	(3.7)	3.8	3.9	4.0

| **MCAT® Total Numeric Score** | 9 | 10 | 11 | 12 | 13 | 14 | 15 | 16 | 17 | 18 | 19 | 20 | 21 | 22 | 23 | 24 | 25 | 26 | 27 | 28 | 29 | 30 | 31 | (32) | 33 | 34 | 35 | 36 | 37 | 38 | 39 | 40 | 41 | 42 | 43 |

Writing Sample				J	K	L	M	N	O	(P)	(Q)	R	S	T
Verbal Reasoning	3	4	5	6	7	8	9	(10)	11	12	13	14	15
Biological Sciences	3	4	5	6	7	8	9	10	(11)	12	13	14	15
Physical Sciences	3	4	5	6	7	8	9	10	(11)	12	13	14	15

Acceptance & Matriculation Data for 2009–2010 First Year Class

	Resident	Non-resident	International	Total
Applications	2883	641	47	3571
Interviewed	950	64	0	1014
Deferred	5	0	0	5
Matriculants				
Early Assurance Program	0	0	0	0
Early Decision Program	0	0	0	0
Baccalaureate/M.D.	0	0	0	0
M.D./Ph.D.	0	0	0	0
Matriculated	205	16	0	**221**

Applications accepted from International Applicants: Only Canadian

Matriculant Demographics: 2009–2010 First Year Class

Men: 109   **Women:** 112

Matriculants' Self-Reported Race/Ethnicity

Mexican American	38	Korean	3
Cuban	0	Vietnamese	2
Puerto Rican	2	Other Asian	7
Other Hispanic	8	Total Asian	33
Total Hispanic	47	Native American	2
Chinese	6	Black	13
Asian Indian	14	Native Hawaiian	1
Pakistani	2	White	148
Filipino	0	Unduplicated Number	
Japanese	0	of Matriculants	221

Science and Math Majors: 41%
Matriculants with:
    Baccalaureate degree: 65%
    Graduate degree(s): 7%

Specialty Choice

2005, 2006, 2007 Graduates, Specialty Choice (As reported by program directors to GME Track™)	
Anesthesiology	11%
Emergency Medicine	4%
Family Practice	10%
Internal Medicine	16%
Obstetrics/Gynecology	7%
Orthopedic Surgery	5%
Pediatrics	15%
Psychiatry	4%
Radiology	4%
Surgery	8%

Financial Information

Source: 2008-2009 LCME I-B survey
and 2009-2010 AAMC TSF questionnaire

	Residents	Non-residents
Total Cost of Attendance	$ 40,008	$ 53,108
Tuition and Fees	$ 15,170	$ 28,270
Other (includes living expenses)	$ 24,838	$ 24,838
Health Insurance (can be waived)	$ 0	$ 0

Average 2009 Graduate Indebtedness: $118,321
% of Enrolled Students Receiving Aid: 87%

Criminal Background Check

This medical school requires a criminal background check prior to matriculation.

University of Texas Southwestern Medical Center at Dallas Southwestern Medical School

Dallas, Texas

The University of Texas
Southwestern Medical Center at Dallas
5323 Harry Hines Boulevard
Dallas, Texas 75390-9162
T 214 648 5617   **F** 214 648 3289

Admissions www.utsouthwestern.edu/admissions
Main www.utsouthwestern.edu/home/education/medicalschool
Financial www.utsouthwestern.edu/student
E-mail admissions@utsouthwestern.edu

Public Institution

Dr. J. Gregory Fitz, Dean

Anne P. McLane, Associate Director of Admissions

Dr. Byron Cryer, Associate Dean for Minority Student Affairs

Charles L. Kettlewell, Registrar and Director of Student Financial Aid

Dr. James Wagner, Associate Dean for Student Affairs

Dr. Angela Mihalic, Associate Dean for Student Affairs

General Information

Founded in 1943, UT Southwestern is a multifaceted academic health science center nationally recognized for its excellence in educating physicians, biomedical scientists, and other health care professionals.

Mission Statement

UT Southwestern is dedicated to educating physicians who are thoroughly grounded in the scientific basis of modern medicine, who are inspired to maintain lifelong medical scholarship, and who care for patients in a responsible and compassionate manner. UT Southwestern's mission emphasizes the importance of training primary care physicians, educating doctors who will practice in underserved areas of Texas, and preparing physician-scientists who seek careers in academic medicine and research.

Curricular Highlights

Community Service Requirement: Optional.
Research/Thesis Requirement: Optional.

UT Southwestern offers a four-year curriculum based on departmental as well as interdisciplinary teaching. The purpose of the first two years is to provide a strong background in the basic sciences and an introduction to clinical medicine. The first-year curriculum is designed to begin the study of the normal human body and its processes at the molecular and cellular levels. The second year is an organ system-based curriculum that integrates pharmacology, microbiology, pathology, and clinical medicine. Contact with patients begins early in the first year

with history-taking and physical examination, as well as visits to outpatient clinics. The third and fourth years provide intense clinical experiences involving the student in direct inpatient and outpatient care in a variety of clinical settings. Specific information about the UT Southwestern medical curriculum is available at *http://medschool.swmed.edu/*.

USMLE

Step 1: Required. Students must record a passing score for promotion.
Step 2: Clinical Skills (CS): Required. Students must record a passing total score to graduate.
Step 2: Clinical Knowledge (CK): Required. Students must record a passing total score to graduate.

Selection Factors

The following factors are considered in evaluating each applicant's acceptability: MCAT scores; undergraduate GPA; rigor of the undergraduate curriculum; letters of recommendation; research experience; extracurricular activities; socioeconomic background; time spent in outside employment; personal integrity and compassion for others; race/ethnicity; the ability to communicate in English; other personal qualities and individual factors such as leadership, social/ family support, self-appraisal, maturity/coping skills, and determination; and motivation for a career in medicine. In addition, applicants are evaluated with regard to the mission of Southwestern Medical School. State law requires that at least 90 percent of the class be residents of Texas. Therefore, the minimum credentials for non-residents are more stringent than are those for Texas residents. Early application is strongly advised. A personal on-campus interview is required; interviews are held on Saturdays between early September and early January.

Financial Aid

UT Southwestern works directly with students to obtain funding for their medical education. Most of the financial aid available is obtained through federal and state loan programs. However, a limited number of scholarships from private sources are available. Non-residents are eligible to pay resident tuition on receipt of a competitive academic scholarship. Students rarely discontinue school for financial reasons.

Information about Diversity Programs

The Admissions Committee at UT Southwestern Medical School recognizes the need for increased numbers of physicians from groups underrepresented in medicine and encourages applications from Texas residents who are members of these groups. UT Southwestern uses race/ethnicity as one of the criteria for evaluating applicants in an effort to provide a diverse educational environment.

Campus Information

Setting

Located just north of downtown Dallas, the 150-acre campus includes an extensive medical library, 45,000-square-foot student recreation center, tennis and outdoor basketball courts, jogging paths, and a 6-acre wooded bird sanctuary. Four hospitals are adjacent to the campus: Parkland Hospital, Children's Medical Center Dallas, University Hospital, University Hospital-Zale Lipshy, and UT Southwestern University Hospital.

Enrollment

For 2009, total enrollment was: 896

Special Features

UT Southwestern Medical School offers an M.D. with Research Distinction program to recognize students who distinguish themselves in the conduct of meaningful clinical or basic research activities.

Housing

Ample and affordable housing opportunities are available within 5 to 10 miles of the campus. Additionally, UT Southwestern's Medical Park Apartments is a gated community with one- and two-bedroom units with individually monitored security, clubhouse, study center, exercise room, and pool.

Satellite Campuses/Facilities

Clinical training takes place at university sites and affiliated hospitals and clinics throughout the North Texas area, including Parkland Memorial Hospital, Children's Medical Center Dallas, the Dallas VA Medical Center, University Hospital, and University Hospital-Zale Lipshy.

Application Process and Requirements 2011–2012

Primary Application Service: TMDSAS
Earliest filing date: May 1, 2010
Latest filing date: October 1, 2010

Secondary Application Required?: Yes
Sent to: All applicants
URL: www.utsouthwestern.edu/admissions
Fee: No   **Waiver available:** n/a
Earliest filing date: May 1, 2010
Latest filing date: October 1, 2010

MCAT® required?: Yes
Latest MCAT® considered: September 2010
Oldest MCAT® considered: September 2006

Early Decision Program: School does not have EDP
Applicants notified: n/a
EDP available for: n/a

Regular Acceptance Notice
Earliest date: November 15, 2010
Latest date: Varies
Applicant's Response to Acceptance
Offer – Maximum Time: Three weeks

Requests for Deferred
Entrance Considered: Yes

Deposit to Hold Place in Class: No
Deposit (Resident): n/a   **(Non-resident):** n/a
Deposit due: n/a
Applied to tuition: n/a   **Refundable:** n/a
Refundable by: n/a

Estimated number of new entrants: 230
EDP: n/a, special program: n/a

Start Month/Year: August 2011

Interview Format: Two 25-minute faculty interviews. Regional interviews are not available. Video interviews are not available.

Other Programs

PREPARATORY PROGRAMS
Postbaccalaureate Program: No
Summer Program: No

COMBINED DEGREE PROGRAMS
Baccalaureate/M.D.: No
M.D./M.P.H.: Yes, www.utsouthwestern.edu/utsw/cda/dept20676/files/397484.html#combined
Raul Caetano, M.D., Ph.D., Dean
UTSPH-Dallas@UTSouthwestern.edu
M.D./M.B.A.: Yes,
www.utsouthwestern.edu/md-mba
M.D./J.D.: No
M.D./Ph.D.: Yes,
www.utsouthwestern.edu/md-phd
Dr. Andrew Zinn, (800) 633-6787
MSTP@UTSouthwestern.edu
Additional Program: Yes,
www.utsouthwestern.edu/utsw/cda/dept25793/files/221753.html
Dr. Michael McPhaul, (214) 648-3465
michael.mcphaul@utsouthwestern.edu

Premedical Coursework

On-line courses accepted in fulfillment of prerequisites: On a case-by-case basis

Course	Req.	Rec.	Lab.	Sems.
Inorganic Chemistry	•		•	2
Behavioral Sciences				
Biochemistry		•		1
Biology	•		•	4
Biology/Zoology				
Calculus	•			1
College English	•			2
College Mathematics				

Course	Req.	Rec.	Lab.	Sems.
Computer Science				
Genetics				
Humanities				
Organic Chemistry	•		•	2
Physics	•		•	2
Psychology				
Social Sciences				
Other				

Selection Factors: 2009 Accepted Applicants

Proportion of Accepted Applicants with Relevant Experience (Data Self-Reported to AMCAS®)		
Community Service/Volunteer		70%
Medically-Related Work		87%
Research		87%

Shaded bar represents school's accepted scores ranging from the 10th percentile to the 90th percentile   **School Median** ● **National Median** ◯

Overall GPA	2.0	2.1	2.2	2.3	2.4	2.5	2.6	2.7	2.8	2.9	3.0	3.1	3.2	3.3	3.4	3.5	3.6	3.7	3.8	(3.9) 4.0
Science GPA	2.0	2.1	2.2	2.3	2.4	2.5	2.6	2.7	2.8	2.9	3.0	3.1	3.2	3.3	3.4	3.5	3.6	3.7	(3.8)	3.9 4.0

MCAT® Total Numeric Score 9 10 11 12 13 14 15 16 17 18 19 20 21 22 23 24 25 26 27 28 29 30 31 ㉜ 33 ㉞ 35 36 37 38 39 40 41 42 43

Writing Sample				J	K	L	M	N	O	P	(Q)	R	S	T
Verbal Reasoning	3	4	5	6	7	8	9	⑩	(11)	12	13	14	15	
Biological Sciences	3	4	5	6	7	8	9	10	⑪	(12)	13	14	15	
Physical Sciences	3	4	5	6	7	8	9	10	⑪	(12)	13	14	15	

Acceptance & Matriculation Data for 2009–2010 First Year Class

	Resident	Non-resident	International	Total
Applications	2695	719	106	3520
Interviewed	689	79	6	774
Deferred	4	0	1	5
Matriculants				
Early Assurance Program	0	0	0	0
Early Decision Program	0	0	0	0
Baccalaureate/M.D.	0	0	0	0
M.D./Ph.D.	3	8	3	14
Matriculated	183	37	7	**227**

Applications accepted from International Applicants: Yes

Specialty Choice

2005, 2006, 2007 Graduates, Specialty Choice (As reported by program directors to GME Track™)	
Anesthesiology	6%
Emergency Medicine	4%
Family Practice	7%
Internal Medicine	19%
Obstetrics/Gynecology	6%
Orthopaedic Surgery	3%
Pediatrics	15%
Psychiatry	3%
Radiology	6%
Surgery	8%

Matriculant Demographics: 2009–2010 First Year Class

Men: 120   **Women:** 107

Matriculants' Self-Reported Race/Ethnicity

Mexican American	19	**Korean**	3
Cuban	0	**Vietnamese**	8
Puerto Rican	2	**Other Asian**	25
Other Hispanic	2	**Total Asian**	87
Total Hispanic	22	**Native American**	0
Chinese	28	**Black**	9
Asian Indian	20	**Native Hawaiian**	0
Pakistani	2	**White**	112
Filipino	0	**Unduplicated Number**	
Japanese	1	**of Matriculants**	227

Science and Math Majors: 52%
Matriculants with:
   Baccalaureate degree: 98%
   Graduate degree(s): 6%

Financial Information

Source: 2008-2009 LCME I-B survey and 2009-2010 AAMC TSF questionnaire

	Residents	Non-residents
Total Cost of Attendance	$ 37,846	$ 50,946
Tuition and Fees	$ 14,635	$ 27,735
Other (includes living expenses)	$ 22,011	$ 22,011
Health Insurance (can be waived)	$ 1,200	$ 1,200

Average 2009 Graduate Indebtedness: $96,772
% of Enrolled Students Receiving Aid: 86%

Criminal Background Check

This medical school requires a criminal background check prior to matriculation.

University of Utah
School of Medicine

Salt Lake City, Utah

Office of Admissions
University of Utah School of Medicine
30 North 1900 East Room 1C029
Salt Lake City, Utah 84132-2101
T 801 581 7498   F 801 581 2931

Admissions http://medicine.utah.edu/admissions/
Main http://medicine.utah.edu/
Financial http://medicine.utah.edu/financialaid/
E-mail deans.admissions@hsc.utah.edu

Public Institution

Dr. David J. Bjorkman, Dean

Dr. Wayne M. Samuelson, Associate Dean for Admissions

Dr. Edward Junkins, Assistant Dean for Inclusion & Outreach

Dr. A. Lorris Betz, Senior Vice President for Health Sciences, Executive Dean

General Information

A minimum of 75% of positions are offered to Utah residents. The school contracts with the State of Idaho to accept eight Idaho residents each year. Nonresident applicants must have significant ties to Utah or be specifically recognized as a member of a population group underrepresented in the physician workforce. (Africans and African Americans, American Indians, Alaska Natives, Chamorros, Polynesians including Native Hawaiians, Tongans, Samoans, Filipinos, Tahitians, Maoris, Fijians, Niueans, Palauans; Chicanos/as and Latinos/as including Puerto Ricans, Mexican Americans, Central Americans and South Americans), or apply to the MD/PhD program. MD/PhD applicants must be U.S. citizens or U.S. permanent residents. Application may be made for three consecutive years. Applicants who have been dismissed from, or on probation or under suspension at another medical school will not be considered. Transfers are considered on rare occasions and must meet specific criteria. The school does not discriminate with respect to applicants' age, color, gender, sexual orientation, race, national origin, religion, status as a person with a disability, or status as a veteran or a disabled veteran. The University of Utah provides reasonable accommodation to known disabilities of applicants.

Mission Statement

The School of Medicine has three major missions: education, research, and clinical service. The three missions are closely interrelated. Each supports and, in turn, benefits from the others. All are considered to be of equal importance.

Curricular Highlights

Community Service Requirement: Optional.
Research/Thesis Requirement: Optional.

The curriculum of the University of Utah School of Medicine is designed to produce highly skilled physicians who are technically proficient, caring, compassionate and capable of adapting to the changing health care demands of the 21st century. Active learning approaches, critical thinking skills and information management techniques are all a part of our educational environment. Our curriculum builds upon the strengths of traditional learning methods and explores areas of study opened up by the explosion of biomedical knowledge and the transformation of America's health care delivery system. Medical school students receive basic science instruction and the critical skills of communicating with, examining and diagnosing patients through all 4 years. Instruction integrates Medical Sciences, Medical Arts and Clinical Medicine.

USMLE

Step 1: Required. Students must record a passing score for promotion.
Step 2: Clinical Skills (CS): Required. Students must record a passing total score to graduate.
Step 2: Clinical Knowledge (CK): Required. Students must record a passing total score to graduate.

Selection Factors

Minimum acceptable GPA for science, non-science and overall is 3.0. Average GPA for entering freshmen is 3.6. Minimum acceptable score for each section of the MCAT is 7. The school considers MCATs taken within 3 years of application. The highest scores in each area will be used. The average score for entering freshmen is 30. Letters of Recommendation: 3 Academic letters - Letters must be from professors who taught you in a classroom setting (labs not allowed) and assigned you a grade. At least 1 letter must be from a science professor. 3 Supervisor letters (direct supervisor) Community Service, Clinical Experience, Research-must be in a scholarly or scientific hypothesis investigation. There are specific criteria for each of the following requirements.

Extracurricular, Community/Volunteer Service, Leadership, Research, Physician Shadowing, and Patient Exposure. Please visit our website.

Financial Aid

In addition to Federal subsidized and unsubsidized Stafford Loans and the Federal Perkins Loan, a limited number of institutional loans and scholarships are awarded each year. All awards are based on need. Financial aid supplements the contribution of the student and/or family, who are expected to provide the maximum assistance possible.

Information about Diversity Programs

The Office of Inclusion and Outreach presents a series of pre-college and premedical educational outreach programs throughout the state.

Campus Information

Setting

The medical school is located on the University of Utah campus on the east bench of the Salt Lake Valley with the Wasatch Mountains as a backdrop. Public transportation connects the school with downtown Salt Lake City and surrounding areas.

Enrollment

For 2009, total enrollment was: 396

Special Features

The School of Medicine houses 16 clinical departments and 6 basic science departments. The faculty and staff in each of these departments are dedicated to fulfilling all of the school's missions. Outstanding clinicians, scientists, and educators work together to provide the highest quality medical education in a stimulating, enriching, and enjoyable environment.

Housing

Housing is available on and off campus.

Satellite Campuses/Facilities

Rotations are performed at University, and Intermountain Healthcare hospitals including Primary Children's Medical Center.

Application Process and Requirements 2011–2012

Primary Application Service: AMCAS
Earliest filing date: June 1, 2010
Latest filing date: November 1, 2010

Secondary Application Required?: Yes
Sent to: Screened applicants
E-mail: deans.admissions@hsc.utah.edu
Fee: Yes, $100   **Waiver available:** Yes
Earliest filing date: August 2010
Latest filing date: January 2011

MCAT® required?: Yes
Latest MCAT® considered: September 2010
Oldest MCAT® considered: August 2008

Early Decision Program: School does not have EDP
Applicants notified: n/a
EDP available for: n/a

Regular Acceptance Notice
Earliest date: October 15, 2010
Latest date: Until class is full
Applicant's Response to Acceptance
Offer – Maximum Time: Two weeks

Requests for Deferred
Entrance Considered: Yes

Deposit to Hold Place in Class: Yes
Deposit (Resident): $100   **(Non-resident):** $100
Deposit due: With response to acceptance offer
Applied to tuition: Yes   **Refundable:** Yes
Refundable by: May 15, 2011

Estimated number of new entrants: 82
EDP: 0, special program: n/a

Start Month/Year: August 2011

Interview Format: Each applicant will have two interviews. Regional interviews are not available. Video interviews are not available.

Other Programs

PREPARATORY PROGRAMS
Postbaccalaureate Program: No
Summer Program: No

COMBINED DEGREE PROGRAMS
Baccalaureate/M.D.: No
M.D./M.P.H.: Yes, http://medicine.utah.edu/dfpm/
M.D./M.B.A.: No
M.D./J.D.: No
M.D./Ph.D.: Yes, http://medicine.utah.edu/mdphd
Janet Bassett, (801) 585-6408,
janet.bessett@path.utah.edu

Premedical Coursework

On-line courses accepted in fulfillment of prerequisites: Yes

Course	Req.	Rec.	Lab.	Sems.	Course	Req.	Rec.	Lab.	Sems.
Inorganic Chemistry	•		•	2	Genetics		•		1
Behavioral Sciences		•		1	Humanities	•			1
Biochemistry	•			1	Organic Chemistry	•		•	2
Biology	•			1	Physics	•		•	2
Biology/Zoology		•		1	Psychology		•		1
Calculus		•		1	Social Sciences	•			1
College English	•			2	Diversity	•			1
College Mathematics		•		1	Anatomy		•		1
Computer Science					Cellular Biology	•			1

Selection Factors: 2009 Accepted Applicants

Proportion of Accepted Applicants with Relevant Experience (Data Self-Reported to AMCAS®)		
Community Service/Volunteer		85%
Medically-Related Work		92%
Research		97%

Shaded bar represents school's accepted scores ranging from the 10th percentile to the 90th percentile   **School Median** ● **National Median** ○

Overall GPA 2.0 2.1 2.2 2.3 2.4 2.5 2.6 2.7 2.8 2.9 3.0 3.1 3.2 3.3 3.4 3.5 3.6 3.7 (3.8) 3.9 4.0
Science GPA 2.0 2.1 2.2 2.3 2.4 2.5 2.6 2.7 2.8 2.9 3.0 3.1 3.2 3.3 3.4 3.5 3.6 (3.7) 3.8 3.9 4.0

MCAT® Total Numeric Score 9 10 11 12 13 14 15 16 17 18 19 20 21 22 23 24 25 26 27 28 29 (30) (31) (32) 33 34 35 36 37 38 39 40 41 42 43

Writing Sample				J	K	L	M	N	(O)	P	(Q)	R	S	T
Verbal Reasoning	3	4	5	6	7	8	9	(10)	11	12	13	14	15
Biological Sciences	3	4	5	6	7	8	9	10	(11)	12	13	14	15
Physical Sciences	3	4	5	6	7	8	(9)	10	(11)	12	13	14	15

Acceptance & Matriculation Data for 2009–2010 First Year Class

	Resident	Non-resident	International	Total
Applications	436	780	26	1242
Interviewed	321	182	14	517
Deferred	0	0	0	0
Matriculants				
Early Assurance Program	0	0	0	0
Early Decision Program	0	0	0	0
Baccalaureate/M.D.	0	0	0	0
M.D./Ph.D.	2	1	0	3
Matriculated	61	19	2	**82**

Applications accepted from International Applicants: Yes

Specialty Choice

2005, 2006, 2007 Graduates, Specialty Choice (As reported by program directors to GME Track™)	
Anesthesiology	12%
Emergency Medicine	13%
Family Practice	11%
Internal Medicine	12%
Obstetrics/Gynecology	2%
Orthopaedic Surgery	3%
Pediatrics	11%
Psychiatry	2%
Radiology	4%
Surgery	5%

Matriculant Demographics: 2009–2010 First Year Class

Men: 52   **Women:** 30

Matriculants' Self-Reported Race/Ethnicity

Mexican American	1	Korean	0
Cuban	0	Vietnamese	4
Puerto Rican	0	Other Asian	1
Other Hispanic	3	Total Asian	9
Total Hispanic	4	Native American	1
Chinese	5	Black	2
Asian Indian	1	Native Hawaiian	1
Pakistani	0	White	66
Filipino	2	Unduplicated Number	
Japanese	1	of Matriculants	82

Science and Math Majors: 59%
Matriculants with:
    Baccalaureate degree: 100%
    Graduate degree(s): 11%

Financial Information

Source: 2008-2009 LCME I-B survey and 2009-2010 AAMC TSF questionnaire

	Residents	Non-residents
Total Cost of Attendance	$ 43,572	$ 65,315
Tuition and Fees	$ 25,138	$ 46,881
Other (includes living expenses)	$ 18,434	$ 18,434
Health Insurance (can be waived)	$ 0	$ 0

Average 2009 Graduate Indebtedness: $137,289
% of Enrolled Students Receiving Aid: 95%

Criminal Background Check

This medical school requires a criminal background check prior to matriculation.

University of Vermont College of Medicine
Burlington, Vermont

The University of Vermont College of Medicine
Office of Admissions, The Courtyard at Given
89 Beaumont Avenue
Burlington, Vermont 05405
T 802 656 2154   **F** 802 656 9663

Admissions www.med.uvm.edu/Admissions
Main www.med.uvm.edu
Financial www.uvm.edu/financialaid
E-mail medadmissions@uvm.edu

Public Institution

Dr. Frederick C. Morin III, Dean

Dr. William B. Jeffries, Senior Associate Dean for Medical Education

Dr. Janice M. Gallant, Associate Dean for Admissions

Dr. G. Scott Waterman, Associate Dean for Student Affairs

Dr. Karen Richardson-Nassif, Associate Dean for Faculty & Staff Development & Diversity

Tiffany Delaney, Director of Admissions

General Information

The University of Vermont College of Medicine, located in Burlington, Vermont's largest metropolitan area of 150,000 people, was established in 1822 as the seventh medical school in the U.S. The College is located on the main campus of the University of Vermont and is adjacent to teaching hospital partner Fletcher Allen Health Care, which provides primary, secondary and tertiary health care services to over 1 million people in the region. A spacious new Medical Education Center and Ambulatory Care Center opened in 2005 to support the College's 450 medical students and 275 residents, who also train at over 30 patient care sites and 100 outreach clinics throughout the region.

Mission Statement

The overarching goal of our educational program is to provide our students with a knowledge base that will allow them to practice the science and art of medicine in a framework that offers a foundation for lifelong learning.

Curricular Highlights

Community Service Requirement: Required.
Research/Thesis Requirement: Optional.

The Vermont Integrated Curriculum (VIC) progresses from the study of Foundations of Medicine, both clinical and basic science, to applications in Clinical Clerkship, to senior scholarship and supervised patient management in Advanced Integration. Areas of focus include progressive skill development, health care systems, preventive care, and a greater understanding of applied sciences, particularly genetics, ethics and epidemiology. VIC also places emphasis on professionalism, cultural competency, scholarly research, teaching skills, and community service.

USMLE

Step 1: Required. Students must record a passing score for graduation, but not promotion.
Step 2: Clinical Skills (CS): Required. Students must record a passing total score to graduate.
Step 2: Clinical Knowledge (CK): Required. Students must record a passing total score to graduate.

Selection Factors

The Committee on Admissions seeks a diverse student body. We look for evidence of excellence accompanied by genuine concern for the welfare of others. Effective interpersonal skills are important, and successful applicants often have a history of service to the community. Selection is based upon a past pattern of academic performance plus an assessment of the applicant's fitness for the study and practice of medicine in terms of aptitude, interests, experience, motivation, leadership abilities, and maturity. Letters of recommendation and a personal interview are required and form an important part of the application process. Students from groups underrepresented in medicine are encouraged to apply. The University of Vermont does not discriminate on the basis of race, color, sex, sexual orientation, religion, age, handicap, national origin, or Vietnam veteran status.

Financial Aid

Financial aid funds are distributed according to relative need for both in- and out-of-state students. Entering students are considered for awards on the same basis as those already enrolled. An applicant's financial status has no bearing on the admission determination.

Information about Diversity Programs

The College of Medicine strongly encourages applications from those who have the potential to increase the overall diversity of the class based on a variety of factors such as economic hardship, first generation college graduates, race, and cultural background.

Campus Information

Setting

Located in Burlington, recently named the healthiest city in America, the University of Vermont campus is home to more than 11,000 students, faculty and staff. Burlington is a vibrant community located on the shores of Lake Champlain, between the Adirondack and Green Mountains, and regularly ranks at the top of the best places to live lists. With year-round recreational opportunities, this progressive community is within a half-day's drive of Boston and New York, and Montreal is just 100 miles north of campus. The University of Vermont College of Medicine and teaching partner Fletcher Allen Health Care comprise the only academic medical center in Vermont, which creates opportunities to interact with physicians, educators, and policy-makers at all levels around the state.

Enrollment

For 2009, total enrollment was: 458

Special Features

The University of Vermont College of Medicine is known for innovations in instructional technology and was honored in 2007 by Campus Technology magazine. All of the advances in technology aim to help our students bridge distance and time and to make learning more interactive, engaging, and effective.

Housing

While the college does offer limited campus housing options, most medical students share apartments or houses in the surrounding area. Many housing opportunities are within easy walking or bicycling distance from campus.

Satellite Campuses/Facilities

Students gain clinical experience from the first day of medical school, with our teaching hospital partner Fletcher Allen Health Care, located adjacent to the medical school, and at clinics throughout the region. In addition, new clinical sites for training include Danbury Hospital in Danbury, CT; St. Mary's Medical Center in West Palm Beach, FL; and Eastern Maine Medical Center in Bangor, ME. Students will have the opportunity to complete selected clerkship rotations as well as explore specialty training at these sites beginning in 2010.

Application Process and Requirements 2011–2012

Primary Application Service: AMCAS
Earliest filing date: June 1, 2010
Latest filing date: November 1, 2010

Secondary Application Required?: Yes
Sent to: All Applicants
Contact: Admissions Office,
(802) 656-2154, medadmissions@uvm.edu
Fee: Yes, $85   **Waiver available:** Yes
Earliest filing date: June 15, 2010
Latest filing date: December 30, 2010

MCAT® required?: Yes
Latest MCAT® considered: September 2010
Oldest MCAT® considered: December 2007

Early Decision Program: School does have EDP
Applicants notified: September 30, 2010
EDP available for: Both Residents and Non-residents

Regular Acceptance Notice
Earliest date: October 16, 2010
Latest date: Until class is full
Applicant's Response to Acceptance Offer – Maximum Time: Two weeks

Requests for Deferred Entrance Considered: Yes

Deposit to Hold Place in Class: Yes
Deposit (Resident): $100   **(Non-resident):** $100
Deposit due: With response to acceptance offer
Applied to tuition: Yes   **Refundable:** Yes
Refundable by: May 15, 2011

Estimated number of new entrants: 114
EDP: 5, special program: 4

Start Month/Year: August 2011

Interview Format: Campus interview with admissions committee member. Regional interviews are not available. Video interviews are not available.

Other Programs

PREPARATORY PROGRAMS
Postbaccalaureate Program: Yes
http://learn.uvm.edu/?Page=postbac.html

COMBINED DEGREE PROGRAMS
Baccalaureate/M.D.: No
M.D./M.P.H.: No
M.D./M.B.A.: No
M.D./J.D.: No
M.D./Ph.D.: Yes, www.med.uvm.edu/mdphd

Premedical Coursework

On-line courses accepted in fulfillment of prerequisites: On a case-by-case basis

Course	Req.	Rec.	Lab.	Hrs.	Course	Req.	Rec.	Lab.	Hrs.
Inorganic Chemistry	•		•	8	Computer Science				
Behavioral Sciences		•			Genetics		•		4
Biochemistry				4	Humanities				
Biology	•		•	8	Organic Chemistry	•		•	8
Biology/Zoology					Physics	•		•	8
Calculus					Psychology				
College English		•			Social Sciences				
College Mathematics		•			Other				

Selection Factors: 2009 Accepted Applicants

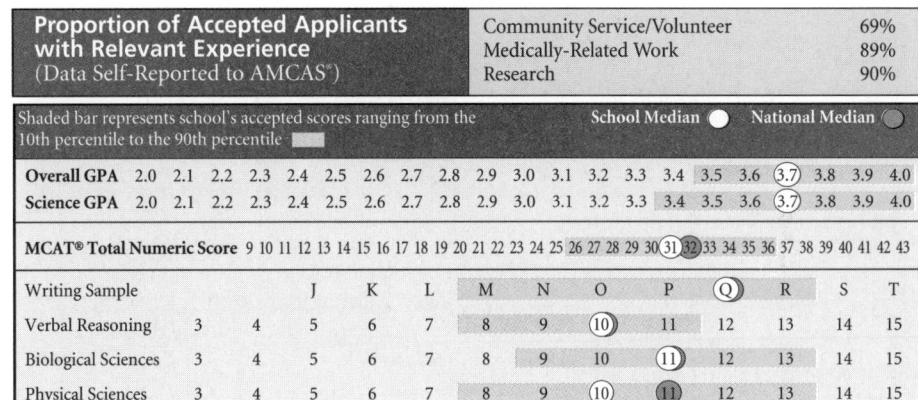

Proportion of Accepted Applicants with Relevant Experience (Data Self-Reported to AMCAS®)	
Community Service/Volunteer	69%
Medically-Related Work	89%
Research	90%

Shaded bar represents school's accepted scores ranging from the 10th percentile to the 90th percentile.   School Median ●   National Median ◐

Overall GPA	2.0	2.1	2.2	2.3	2.4	2.5	2.6	2.7	2.8	2.9	3.0	3.1	3.2	3.3	3.4	3.5	3.6	(3.7)	3.8	3.9	4.0
Science GPA	2.0	2.1	2.2	2.3	2.4	2.5	2.6	2.7	2.8	2.9	3.0	3.1	3.2	3.3	3.4	3.5	3.6	(3.7)	3.8	3.9	4.0

MCAT® Total Numeric Score 9 10 11 12 13 14 15 16 17 18 19 20 21 22 23 24 25 26 27 28 29 30 (31) (32) 33 34 35 36 37 38 39 40 41 42 43

Writing Sample			J	K	L	M	N	O	P	(Q)	R	S	T
Verbal Reasoning	3	4	5	6	7	8	9	(10)	11	12	13	14	15
Biological Sciences	3	4	5	6	7	8	9	10	(11)	12	13	14	15
Physical Sciences	3	4	5	6	7	8	9	(10)	(11)	12	13	14	15

Acceptance & Matriculation Data for 2009–2010 First Year Class

	Resident	Non-resident	International	Total
Applications	85	5347	365	5797
Interviewed	63	556	0	619
Deferred	1	4	0	5
Matriculants				
Early Assurance Program	0	0	0	0
Early Decision Program	3	0	0	3
Baccalaureate/M.D.	0	0	0	0
M.D./Ph.D.	0	2	0	2
Matriculated	27	83	5	**115**

Applications accepted from International Applicants: No

Matriculant Demographics: 2009–2010 First Year Class

Men: 55   **Women:** 60

Matriculants' Self-Reported Race/Ethnicity

Mexican American	2	Korean	0
Cuban	4	Vietnamese	0
Puerto Rican	1	Other Asian	5
Other Hispanic	9	Total Asian	12
Total Hispanic	15	Native American	0
Chinese	2	Black	3
Asian Indian	4	Native Hawaiian	0
Pakistani	0	White	93
Filipino	2	Unduplicated Number	
Japanese	2	of Matriculants	115

Science and Math Majors: 51%
Matriculants with:
  Baccalaureate degree: 100%
  Graduate degree(s): 17%

Specialty Choice

2005, 2006, 2007 Graduates, Specialty Choice (As reported by program directors to GME Track™)	
Anesthesiology	4%
Emergency Medicine	10%
Family Practice	7%
Internal Medicine	19%
Obstetrics/Gynecology	6%
Orthopaedic Surgery	1%
Pediatrics	21%
Psychiatry	4%
Radiology	6%
Surgery	6%

Financial Information

Source: 2008-2009 LCME I-B survey and 2009-2010 AAMC TSF questionnaire

	Residents	Non-residents
Total Cost of Attendance	$ 49,480	$ 70,866
Tuition and Fees	$ 29,583	$ 50,403
Other (includes living expenses)	$ 19,897	$ 20,463
Health Insurance (can be waived)	$ 0	$ 0

Average 2009 Graduate Indebtedness: $158,313
% of Enrolled Students Receiving Aid: 92%

Criminal Background Check

This medical school requires a criminal background check prior to matriculation.

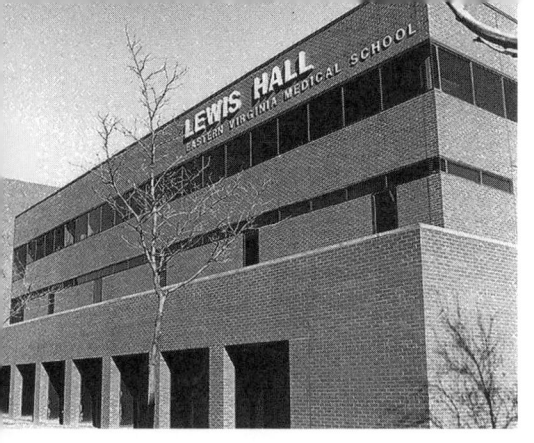

Eastern Virginia Medical School
Norfolk, Virginia

Office of Admissions
Eastern Virginia Medical School
700 W. Olney Road
Norfolk, Virginia 23507-1607
T 757 446 5812   **F** 757 446 5896

Admissions www.evms.edu/md-programs/md-programs-home.html
Main www.evms.edu
Financial www.evms.edu/financial-aid/office-of-financial-aid.html
E-mail mclendm@evms.edu

Public Institution

Dr. Gerald J. Pepe, Dean and Provost

*Dr. Michael J. Solhaug,
Associate Dean for Admissions*

Gail C. Williams, Assistant Dean for Student Affairs and Director of Minority Affairs

Michelle D. Byers, Director of Financial Aid

Susan L. Castora, Director of Admissions

General Information
Established in 1973 to enhance the quality and diversity of health care throughout the Hampton Roads region, the mission of EVMS is deeply rooted in the education and training of primary care physicians, arming them with the requisite scientific, academic, and humanistic skills most relevant to today's practice of medicine. EVMS provides health care for more than one quarter of Virginia's population as well as neighboring regions of North Carolina.

Mission Statement
EVMS is a public institution dedicated to medical and health education, biomedical research, and the enhancement of health care in the Commonwealth of Virginia.

Curricular Highlights
Community Service Requirement: Optional.
Research/Thesis Requirement: Optional.

The first two years focus on clinical medicine through two vehicles: the Theresa A. Thomas Professional Skills Teaching and Assessment Center and a Longitudinal Mentorship with a generalist physician in community practice. Careful coordination between basic sciences and generalist disciplines permits an integrated curriculum. Weekly small-group sessions introduce students to clinical problem-solving. This early introduction to clinical medicine teaches medical history-taking and physical examination along with the application of basic science knowledge to patient care. Third-year clinical clerkships focus on ambulatory care in community-based sites in balance with inpatient care experiences. In addition to the required clerkships are rotations in substance abuse, geriatrics, and surgical subspecialties.

For those interested in generalist medicine, electives are offered in special populations and rural health care, and an elective honors track in generalist medicine. Elective opportunities are available for those interested in research or subspecialty care. Students are graded as Honors, High Pass, Pass, or Fail.

USMLE
Step 1: Required. Students must record a passing score for promotion.
Step 2: Clinical Skills (CS): Required. Students must only record a score.
Step 2: Clinical Knowledge (CK): Required. Students must record a passing total score to graduate.

Selection Factors
EVMS does not discriminate on the basis of sex, race, creed, age, national origin, marital status, or handicap. A supplementary application packet is sent to those applicants receiving a favorable initial screening of their completed AMCAS application. The Admissions Committee considers the entire academic record, including science and overall GPA, MCAT scores, exposure to the medical field, maturity, character, and motivation. The application fee will be waived if a fee waiver is granted by AMCAS. Preference is given to legal residents of Virginia. EVMS seeks persons with personal and background traits that indicate a high potential for becoming a primary care physician. Applicants who have completed one or more years in a medical school accredited by the LCME can be considered for transfer into the second or third year only to fill vacancies that may arise with the withdrawal of previously enrolled students. All transfers must meet the requirements stated for general admission.

Financial Aid
Scholarships are limited. Loans constitute the majority of aid received. Students may fully meet the costs of medical school at EVMS, providing they meet all federal criteria, meet citizenship requirements, are creditworthy, and maintain satisfactory academic progress. Primary care loans are available for those interested in an approved primary care field of study. The Virginia Tuition Assistance Grant Program (VTAG) provides annual grants for state residents. Applicants for financial assistance must file the FAFSA and other additional required forms.

Information about Diversity Programs
EVMS is committed to producing a diverse physician workforce to meet the health care needs of the region. Applicants from rural or other underserved regions and those who have been disadvantaged or underrepresented for economic, racial, or social reasons, and who possess the motivation and aptitude required for the study of medicine are strongly encouraged to apply.

Campus Information
Setting
The EVMS complex includes the Children's Hospital of the King's Daughters and Sentara Norfolk General Hospital. The campus is minutes from downtown shopping areas and cultural attractions.

Enrollment
For 2009, total enrollment was: 448

Special Features
EVMS has numerous Centers of Excellence including the world-renowned Jones Institute for Reproductive Medicine, the Strelitz Diabetes Institute, and the Glennan Center for Geriatric Medicine. The Theresa A. Thomas Professional Skills Teaching and Assessment Center is a leader in the use and training of standardized patients for assessing medical competencies of our students and residents, as well as those from institutes around the world.

Housing
EVMS's Hague Club Apartments offers one- and two-bedroom apartments. Additional housing is located in nearby neighborhoods.

Satellite Campuses/Facilities
EVMS partners with 33 local area hospitals, including Sentara Norfolk General Hospital, the Children's Hospital of the King's Daughters, the U.S. Naval Medical Center in Portsmouth, and the Veterans Affairs Hospital in Hampton.

Application Process and Requirements 2011–2012

Primary Application Service: AMCAS
Earliest filing date: June 1, 2010
Latest filing date: November 15, 2010

Secondary Application Required?: Yes
Sent to: Screened applicants
URL: www.evms.edu/apply-home/md-admissions-application-home.html
Fee: Yes, $100   **Waiver available:** Yes
Earliest filing date: July 2010
Latest filing date: January 2011

MCAT® required?: Yes
Latest MCAT® considered: September 2010
Oldest MCAT® considered: December 2008

Early Decision Program: School does have EDP
Applicants notified: October 1, 2010
EDP available for: Both Residents and Non-residents

Regular Acceptance Notice
Earliest date: October 15, 2010
Latest date: Until class is full
Applicant's Response to Acceptance Offer – Maximum Time: Two weeks

Requests for Deferred Entrance Considered: Yes

Deposit to Hold Place in Class: Yes
Deposit (Resident): $100   **(Non-resident):** $100
Deposit due: With response to acceptance offer
Applied to tuition: Yes   **Refundable:** Yes
Refundable by: May 15, 2011

Estimated number of new entrants: 115
EDP: 2, special program: n/a

Start Month/Year: August 2011

Interview Format: Panel interviews. Regional interviews are not available. Video interviews are not available.

Other Programs

PREPARATORY PROGRAMS
Postbaccalaureate Program: Yes, www.evms.edu/evms-school-of-health-professions/ms-in-biomedical-sciences-medical-masters.html
Summer Program: No

COMBINED DEGREE PROGRAMS
Baccalaureate/M.D.: Yes
M.D./M.P.H.: Yes, www.evms.edu/evms-school-of-health-professions/master-in-public-health.html
M.D./M.B.A.: No
M.D./J.D.: No
M.D./Ph.D.: No

Premedical Coursework

On-line courses accepted in fulfillment of prerequisites: No

Course	Req.	Rec.	Lab.	Sems.	Course	Req.	Rec.	Lab.	Sems.
Inorganic Chemistry	•		•	2	Computer Science				
Behavioral Sciences					Genetics				
Biochemistry					Humanities				
Biology	•		•	2	Organic Chemistry	•		•	2
Biology/Zoology					Physics	•		•	2
Calculus					Psychology				
College English					Social Sciences				
College Mathematics					Other				

Selection Factors: 2009 Accepted Applicants

Proportion of Accepted Applicants with Relevant Experience (Data Self-Reported to AMCAS®)		
Community Service/Volunteer		73%
Medically-Related Work		89%
Research		75%

Shaded bar represents school's accepted scores ranging from the 10th percentile to the 90th percentile.   School Median ●   National Median ◐

Overall GPA	2.0	2.1	2.2	2.3	2.4	2.5	2.6	2.7	2.8	2.9	3.0	3.1	3.2	3.3	3.4	3.5	③.6	3.7	3.8	3.9	4.0
Science GPA	2.0	2.1	2.2	2.3	2.4	2.5	2.6	2.7	2.8	2.9	3.0	3.1	3.2	3.3	3.4	3.5	③.6	3.7	3.8	3.9	4.0

MCAT® Total Numeric Score	9	10	11	12	13	14	15	16	17	18	19	20	21	22	23	24	25	26	27	28	29	30	㉛	㉜	33	34	35	36	37	38	39	40	41	42	43

Writing Sample			J	K	L	M	N	O	Ⓟ	Ⓠ	R	S	T
Verbal Reasoning	3	4	5	6	7	8	9	⑩	11	12	13	14	15
Biological Sciences	3	4	5	6	7	8	9	10	⑪	12	13	14	15
Physical Sciences	3	4	5	6	7	8	9	⑩	⑪	12	13	14	15

Acceptance & Matriculation Data for 2009–2010 First Year Class

	Resident	Non-resident	International	Total
Applications	844	4057	268	5169
Interviewed	371	287	24	682
Deferred	2	1	0	3
Matriculants				
Early Assurance Program	0	0	0	0
Early Decision Program	1	0	0	1
Baccalaureate/M.D.	0	0	0	0
M.D./Ph.D.	0	0	0	0
Matriculated	71	46	1	**118**

Applications accepted from International Applicants: Yes

Specialty Choice

2005, 2006, 2007 Graduates, Specialty Choice (As reported by program directors to GME Track™)	
Anesthesiology	4%
Emergency Medicine	11%
Family Practice	10%
Internal Medicine	18%
Obstetrics/Gynecology	7%
Orthopaedic Surgery	2%
Pediatrics	16%
Psychiatry	3%
Radiology	4%
Surgery	6%

Matriculant Demographics: 2009–2010 First Year Class

Men: 67   **Women:** 51

Matriculants' Self-Reported Race/Ethnicity

Mexican American	0	Korean	8
Cuban	0	Vietnamese	2
Puerto Rican	0	Other Asian	4
Other Hispanic	0	Total Asian	29
Total Hispanic	0	Native American	1
Chinese	2	Black	10
Asian Indian	8	Native Hawaiian	1
Pakistani	3	White	72
Filipino	1	Unduplicated Number	
Japanese	1	of Matriculants	118

Science and Math Majors: 71%
Matriculants with:
Baccalaureate degree: 99%
Graduate degree(s): 32%

Financial Information

Source: 2008-2009 LCME I-B survey and 2009-2010 AAMC TSF questionnaire

	Residents	Non-residents
Total Cost of Attendance	$ 46,969	$ 69,729
Tuition and Fees	$ 27,620	$ 50,380
Other (includes living expenses)	$ 16,972	$ 16,972
Health Insurance (can be waived)	$ 2,377	$ 2,377

Average 2009 Graduate Indebtedness: $168,742
% of Enrolled Students Receiving Aid: 90%

Criminal Background Check

This medical school requires a criminal background check prior to matriculation.

University of Virginia School of Medicine

Charlottesville, Virginia

Medical School Admissions Office
PO Box 800725
University of Virginia School of Medicine
Charlottesville, Virginia 22908
T 434 924 5571   F 434 982 2586

Admissions www.healthsystem.virginia.edu/
internet/admissions
Main www.healthsystem.virginia.edu/internet/som
Financial www.healthsystem.virginia.edu/internet/
financial-aid
E-mail medsch-adm@virginia.edu

Public Institution

Dr. Steven T. DeKosky, Vice President and Dean, School of Medicine

Dr. R.J. Canterbury, Senior Associate Dean for Education

Dr. Norman Oliver, Associate Dean for Diversity

Nancy Zimmer, Director of Financial Aid

Lesley L. Thomas, Assistant Dean for Admissions & Student Affairs

Dr. Gabrielle Marzani-Nissen, Assistant Dean for Admissions

General Information

The University of Virginia School of Medicine was opened for instruction in 1825, making it one of the oldest medical schools in the South. Both the School of Medicine and the University of Virginia Hospital are located on the grounds of the University of Virginia in Charlottesville.

Mission Statement

The mission of the University of Virginia School of Medicine is: to educate students to fulfill the need for practitioners and scientists; to provide cost-effective, high-quality patient care at primary, secondary, and tertiary levels; to produce new knowledge required to advance health by conducting research; and, to provide public service as needed by citizens or by public jurisdictions.

Curricular Highlights

Community Service Requirement: Required. Community service learning activities in Year 1.
Research/Thesis Requirement: Optional. A thesis is required for Generalist Scholars only.

The University of Virginia curriculum integrates scientific knowledge, clinical care, and research throughout the entire four years of medical school. The Claude Moore Medical Education Building, finished in 2010, was created for the "Next Generation" Cells to Society Curriculum. The building integrates small group learning and individual instruction with state of the art educational spaces, including the "Learning Studio" which uses technology to enable active learning. The systems-based curriculum is integrated and

uses clinical cases for problem solving. A Clinical Performance Education Center has 14,000 square feet devoted to 4 mock spaces (an ER, ICU, OR and L&D suite), as well as 20 patient rooms. State of the art stimulators, standardized patients, and other technologies, allow for experiential learning and complement real patient experience. Students have 2-3 afternoons a week for elective activities or productive self study and a largely elective post clerkship period for student directed advanced clinical learning or research. 28 weeks of electives in the fourth year allow students the opportunity to pursue their own interests and needs, including clinical experience, graduate courses, and research activities.

USMLE

Step 1: Required. Students must record a passing score for promotion.
Step 2: Clinical Skills (CS): Required. Students must record a passing total score to graduate.
Step 2: Clinical Knowledge (CK): Required. Students must record a passing total score to graduate.

Selection Factors

All applicants must have completed at least 90 semester hours of course work in a U.S. or Canadian college or university. The Committee on Admissions does not discriminate on the basis of race, gender, sexual preference, creed, national origin, age, or disability. Grades, MCAT scores, work and volunteer experience, letters of recommendation, and the interview influence committee decisions.

Financial Aid

In addition to Federal Stafford Loans, the University of Virginia School of Medicine provides robust school-funded scholarships and loans to students who demonstrate need via the Free Application for Federal Student Aid (FAFSA). Parental financial information is required for all applicants who wish to receive aid from school funds. Student employment is not encouraged. Financial aid applications are available online on January 1 or immediately after acceptance.

Information about Diversity Programs

The University of Virginia encourages applications from qualified applicants from groups that are underrepresented in medicine. Systems

in place to facilitate preparation and success of students include: (1) a six-week summer enrichment program; (2) extensive tutorial and other academic support programs upon admission; and (3) need-based and merit-based financial assistance. For more information, please contact Dr. Norm Oliver, Associate Dean for Diversity, at mno3p@virginia.edu.

Campus Information

Setting
The University of Virginia Health System is one of the nation's 100 Top Hospitals with state-of-the-art emergency, operating, and labor and delivery rooms. The medical center is located in the heart of Charlottesville, with significant historical sites located nearby, including Thomas Jefferson's Monticello.

Enrollment
For 2009, total enrollment was: 571

Special Features
The University of Virginia Health System includes the School of Medicine, the University Hospital, and other special centers of excellence, including the Heart Center, Kidney Center, Digestive Health Center, Cancer Center, Transplant Center, and Primary Care Center. As part of its Global Health Initiative, UVA has twenty-seven sites in developing countries around the world where students are encouraged to participate in direct patient care, public health services, health education and/or research activities.

Housing
Most medical students choose to live in the community close by the medical school and hospital. There are ample housing opportunities in the area, with rents ranging from $300 to $800 per month.

Satellite Campuses/Facilities
During the third-year clinical clerkships, students will spend approximately half their time at the University Health System. They also spend an average of 20 weeks at the Roanoke Memorial Hospital in Roanoke, VA, the Salem Veterans Affairs Hospital, and the Fairfax INOVA Hospital in Fairfax, VA. Housing and meals are provided at offsite clinical locations.

Application Process and Requirements 2011–2012

Primary Application Service: AMCAS
Earliest filing date: June 1, 2010
Latest filing date: November 1, 2010

Secondary Application Required?: Yes
Sent to: All applicants
Contact: Eileen K. Oswald, M.S., (434) 924-5571, eko2v@virginia.edu
Fee: Yes, $80   **Waiver available:** Yes
Earliest filing date: June 1, 2010
Latest filing date: January 1, 2011

MCAT® required?: Yes
Latest MCAT® considered: September 2010
Oldest MCAT® considered: April 2008

Early Decision Program: School does not have EDP
Applicants notified: n/a
EDP available for: n/a

Regular Acceptance Notice
Earliest date: October 16, 2010
Latest date: Until class is full
Applicant's Response to Acceptance Offer – Maximum Time: Three weeks

Requests for Deferred Entrance Considered: Yes

Deposit to Hold Place in Class: No
Deposit (Resident): n/a   **(Non-resident):** n/a
Deposit due: n/a
Applied to tuition: n/a   **Refundable:** n/a
Refundable by: n/a

Estimated number of new entrants: 154
EDP: n/a, special program: n/a

Start Month/Year: August 2011

Interview Format: Two one-on-one, half-hour interviews. Regional interviews are not available. Video interviews are not available.

Other Programs

PREPARATORY PROGRAMS
Postbaccalaureate Program: Yes,
www.uvapostbacpremed.info
postbacpremed@virginia.edu
Summer Program: Yes, www.healthsystem.virginia.edu/internet/academic-support/maap1-A.cfm

COMBINED DEGREE PROGRAMS
Baccalaureate/M.D.: No
M.D./M.P.H.: Yes, www.healthsystem.virginia.edu/internet/phs/mph/jointmdmph.cfm
M.D./M.B.A.: Yes
M.D./J.D.: No
M.D./Ph.D.: Yes, www.healthsystem.virginia.edu/internet/mstp/
Additional Program: Yes, www.med-ed.virginia.edu/handbook/policy/secondDegree.cfm

Premedical Coursework

On-line courses accepted in fulfillment of prerequisites: No

Course	Req.	Rec.	Lab.	Sems.
Inorganic Chemistry	•		•	2
Behavioral Sciences				
Biochemistry		•		
Biology	•		•	2
Biology/Zoology				
Calculus				
College English				
College Mathematics				

Course	Req.	Rec.	Lab.	Sems.
Computer Science				
Genetics				
Humanities				
Organic Chemistry	•		•	2
Physics	•		•	2
Psychology				
Social Sciences				
Other				

Selection Factors: 2009 Accepted Applicants

Proportion of Accepted Applicants with Relevant Experience (Data Self-Reported to AMCAS)		
Community Service/Volunteer		75%
Medically-Related Work		90%
Research		86%

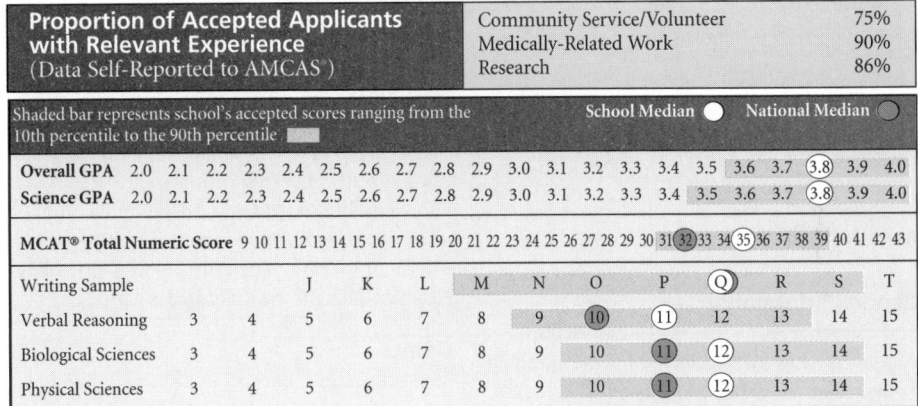

Shaded bar represents school's accepted scores ranging from the 10th percentile to the 90th percentile. School Median ● National Median ○

Overall GPA 2.0 2.1 2.2 2.3 2.4 2.5 2.6 2.7 2.8 2.9 3.0 3.1 3.2 3.3 3.4 3.5 3.6 3.7 (3.8) 3.9 4.0
Science GPA 2.0 2.1 2.2 2.3 2.4 2.5 2.6 2.7 2.8 2.9 3.0 3.1 3.2 3.3 3.4 3.5 3.6 3.7 (3.8) 3.9 4.0

MCAT® Total Numeric Score 9 10 11 12 13 14 15 16 17 18 19 20 21 22 23 24 25 26 27 28 29 30 31(32)33 34(35)36 37 38 39 40 41 42 43

	J	K	L	M	N	O	P	Q	R	S	T
Writing Sample								(Q)			

Verbal Reasoning	3	4	5	6	7	8	9	(10)	(11)	12	13	14	15
Biological Sciences	3	4	5	6	7	8	9	10	(11)	(12)	13	14	15
Physical Sciences	3	4	5	6	7	8	9	10	(11)	(12)	13	14	15

Acceptance & Matriculation Data for 2009–2010 First Year Class

	Resident	Non-resident	International	Total
Applications	762	3253	162	4177
Interviewed	153	377	15	545
Deferred	2	1	0	3
Matriculants				
Early Assurance Program	0	0	0	0
Early Decision Program	0	0	0	0
Baccalaureate/M.D.	0	0	0	0
M.D./Ph.D.	1	5	1	7
Matriculated	81	58	4	**143**

Applications accepted from International Applicants: Yes

Specialty Choice

2005, 2006, 2007 Graduates, Specialty Choice (As reported by program directors to GME Track™)	
Anesthesiology	7%
Emergency Medicine	7%
Family Practice	7%
Internal Medicine	21%
Obstetrics/Gynecology	6%
Orthopaedic Surgery	2%
Pediatrics	12%
Psychiatry	5%
Radiology	5%
Surgery	5%

Matriculant Demographics: 2009–2010 First Year Class

Men: 81   **Women:** 62

Matriculants' Self-Reported Race/Ethnicity

Mexican American	4	Korean	2
Cuban	3	Vietnamese	2
Puerto Rican	1	Other Asian	4
Other Hispanic	8	Total Asian	23
Total Hispanic	15	Native American	2
Chinese	5	Black	11
Asian Indian	7	Native Hawaiian	0
Pakistani	2	White	103
Filipino	1	**Unduplicated Number**	
Japanese	0	**of Matriculants**	143

Science and Math Majors: 63%
Matriculants with:
  Baccalaureate degree: 100%
  Graduate degree(s): 6%

Financial Information

Source: 2008-2009 LCME I-B survey and 2009-2010 AAMC TSF questionnaire

	Residents	Non-residents
Total Cost of Attendance	$ 54,968	$ 64,968
Tuition and Fees	$ 35,150	$ 45,150
Other (includes living expenses)	$ 17,726	$ 17,726
Health Insurance (can be waived)	$ 2,092	$ 2,092

Average 2009 Graduate Indebtedness: $121,729
% of Enrolled Students Receiving Aid: 91%

Criminal Background Check

This medical school requires a criminal background check prior to matriculation.

Virginia Commonwealth University School of Medicine

Richmond, Virginia

Virginia Commonwealth University
School of Medicine
P.O. Box 980565
Richmond, Virginia 23298-0565
T 804 828 9629   F 804 828 1246

Admissions www.medschool.vcu.edu/admissions/md/index.html
Main www.medschool.vcu.edu
Financial www.medschool.vcu.edu/finaid/financial.html
E-mail somume@vcu.edu

Public Institution

Dr. Jerome F. Strauss III, Dean

Dr. Michelle Whitehurst-Cook, Associate Dean for Admissions

Donna Jackson, Director of Student Outreach Programs

Dr. Glenda Palmer, Asst. Dean of Student Affairs/Dir. of Financial Aid

Agnes L. Mack, Director of Admissions

General Information

The School of Medicine, which has been in continuous operation since 1838, is the founding institution of Virginia Commonwealth University. The vitality of VCU's clinical, educational, and research programs is reflected in the caliber of its faculty, the success of its patient care programs, and the level of research funding.

Mission Statement

The mission of the School of Medicine is constant improvement of the quality of health care for citizens of Virginia, using innovative, scholarly activity to create new knowledge, to provide better systems of medical education, and to develop more effective health care methods. The primary aim of the School of Medicine is to provide a diverse academic environment appropriate for the education of its students and continuing education directed toward the needs of practicing physicians.

Curricular Highlights

Community Service Requirement: Optional.
Research/Thesis Requirement: Optional.

The first year is spent studying normal structure and function in a traditional discipline format. The second year emphasizes the pathogenesis of disease and its manifestations and is taught in an organ system manner. Pathogenesis, pathology, pharmacology, and the major manifestations and principles of management are discussed in each of the major body systems. In the longitudinal clinical experience for first- and second-year students, students spend two afternoons per month in a small group learning the fundamentals of clinical medicine. This is supplemented by a clinical experience in the office of a primary care physician two afternoons per month. The clinical experience is integrated with the basic sciences in a way that enhances and enriches students' learning. There is a computer lab with over 40 workstations and a full array of commercial and in-house, faculty-developed educational software. Third-year rotations are at the University and Veterans Affairs Hospitals, with ambulatory care rotations at non-university primary care sites. A select number of students will complete the third and fourth years at the Inova campus in Northern Virginia. The fourth year is primarily elective time with two required rotations.

USMLE

Step 1: Required. Students must record a passing score for promotion.
Step 2: Clinical Skills (CS): Required. Students must record a passing score in each section to graduate.
Step 2: Clinical Knowledge (CK): Required. Students must record a passing score in each section to graduate.

Selection Factors

Applicants are selected on the basis of their potential as prospective physicians as well as students of medicine. Attributes of character, personality factors, academic skills, and exposure to medicine are considered along with academic performance, GPA, MCAT scores, letters of recommendation, and personal interviews at the School of Medicine.

Financial Aid

Assistance to students in meeting the cost of their medical education is available in the form of loans and scholarship. Financial counseling is done through the School of Medicine Financial Aid Office. The FAFSA (Free Application for Federal Student Aid) is required of all students who want aid. For need-based scholarship and grant aid the NeedAccess online form should be completed. This information is used to award grants from the Department of Health and Human Services and institutional need-based aid. Completion of these forms will allow the Financial Aid Office to give students an accurate picture of what their eligibility for aid will be within 48 hours.

Information about Diversity Programs

The office of Student Outreach Programs endeavors to provide support for the school's diverse population. Student Outreach's objectives are to recruit and retain students from disadvantaged or non-traditional backgrounds to an environment conducive for exchange of ideas where students learn from faculty and peers. The main goal of the program is to provide medical school graduates that will best meet the healthcare needs of the state and nation.

Campus Information

Setting
The school is located in downtown Richmond near cultural, historical, and government centers. The medical education buildings are directly across the street from the main hospital.

Enrollment
For 2009, total enrollment was: 760

Special Features
The 779-bed VCU Health Systems Hospital, including our new critical care tower, has both the largest ER and neonatal intensive care units in the state and is one of the largest university-owned medical centers in the U.S. This facility and the full service Veterans and Inova Fairfax Hospitals afford students an unparalleled clinical experience.

Housing
Single student housing is available on campus. Off-campus housing is plentiful, varied in style, and reasonable in cost and ranges from inner city, suburban to rural.

Satellite Campuses/Facilities
There is a regional campus at Inova Hospital, Fairfax, VA, which is used for third- and fourth-year training.

Application Process and Requirements 2011–2012

Primary Application Service: AMCAS
Earliest filing date: June 1, 2010
Latest filing date: October 15, 2010

Secondary Application Required?: Yes
Sent to: Screened applicants
Contact: Shenia Tyler
(804) 828-9629, shenia.tyler@vcu.edu
Fee: Yes, $80 **Waiver available:** Yes
Earliest filing date: June 1, 2010
Latest filing date: January 25, 2011

MCAT® required?: Yes
Latest MCAT® considered: September 2010
Oldest MCAT® considered: January 2008

Early Decision Program: School does have EDP
Applicants notified: October 1, 2010
EDP available for: Both Residents
and Non-residents

Regular Acceptance Notice
Earliest date: October 16, 2010
Latest date: Until class is full
Applicant's Response to Acceptance
Offer – Maximum Time: Two weeks

Requests for Deferred
Entrance Considered: Yes

Deposit to Hold Place in Class: Yes
Deposit (Resident): $100 **(Non-resident):** $100
Deposit due: With response to acceptance offer
Applied to tuition: Yes **Refundable:** Yes
Refundable by: May 15, 2011

Estimated number of new entrants: 200
EDP: 5, special program: n/a

Start Month/Year: August 2011

Interview Format: Single, one-on-one interview
Regional interviews are not available. Video
interviews are not available.

Other Programs

PREPARATORY PROGRAMS
Postbaccalaureate Program: Yes,
www.medschool.vcu.edu/graduate/premed_cert/
index.html
Summer Program: No,
www.healthdisparities.vcu.edu/workforce/
pipeline.html

COMBINED DEGREE PROGRAMS
Baccalaureate/M.D.: Yes, www.honors.vcu.edu/
M.D./M.P.H.: Yes, www.medschool.vcu.edu/
admissions/mdmph.html
M.D./M.B.A.: No
M.D./J.D.: No
M.D./Ph.D.: Yes, www.medschool.vcu.edu/mdphd
Additional Program: Yes, www.had.vcu.edu
Suzanne Havasy, (804) 828-0719, shavasy@hsc.vcu.edu

Premedical Coursework

On-line courses accepted in fulfillment of prerequisites: On a case-by-case basis

Course	Req.	Rec.	Lab.	Sems.	Course	Req.	Rec.	Lab.	Sems.
Inorganic Chemistry	•		•	2	Computer Science				
Behavioral Sciences					Genetics				
Biochemistry					Humanities				
Biology	•		•	2	Organic Chemistry	•		•	2
Biology/Zoology					Physics	•		•	2
Calculus					Psychology				
College English	•			2	Social Sciences				
College Mathematics	•			2	Other				

Selection Factors: 2009 Accepted Applicants

Proportion of Accepted Applicants with Relevant Experience (Data Self-Reported to AMCAS®)		
Community Service/Volunteer		70%
Medically-Related Work		91%
Research		81%

Shaded bar represents school's accepted scores ranging from the 10th percentile to the 90th percentile. **School Median** ● **National Median** ○

Overall GPA	2.0	2.1	2.2	2.3	2.4	2.5	2.6	2.7	2.8	2.9	3.0	3.1	3.2	3.3	3.4	3.5	3.6	(3.7)	3.8	3.9	4.0
Science GPA	2.0	2.1	2.2	2.3	2.4	2.5	2.6	2.7	2.8	2.9	3.0	3.1	3.2	3.3	3.4	3.5	(3.6)	3.7	3.8	3.9	4.0

MCAT® Total Numeric Score 9 10 11 12 13 14 15 16 17 18 19 20 21 22 23 24 25 26 27 28 29 30 (31)(32) 33 34 35 36 37 38 39 40 41 42 43

Writing Sample			J	K	L	M	N	O	P	(Q)	R	S	T
Verbal Reasoning	3	4	5	6	7	8	9	(10)	11	12	13	14	15
Biological Sciences	3	4	5	6	7	8	9	10	(11)	12	13	14	15
Physical Sciences	3	4	5	6	7	8	9	10	(11)	12	13	14	15

Acceptance & Matriculation Data for 2009–2010 First Year Class

	Resident	Non-resident	International	Total
Applications	874	5252	96	6222
Interviewed	431	470	0	901
Deferred	1	3	0	4
Matriculants				
Early Assurance Program	0	0	0	0
Early Decision Program	0	0	0	0
Baccalaureate/M.D.	0	0	0	0
M.D./Ph.D.	4	3	0	7
Matriculated	111	87	2	**200**

Applications accepted from International Applicants: Only Canadian

Matriculant Demographics: 2009–2010 First Year Class

Men: 106 **Women:** 94

Matriculants' Self-Reported Race/Ethnicity

Mexican American	2	Korean	6
Cuban	1	Vietnamese	10
Puerto Rican	0	Other Asian	5
Other Hispanic	4	Total Asian	68
Total Hispanic	7	Native American	5
Chinese	14	Black	9
Asian Indian	25	Native Hawaiian	2
Pakistani	6	White	116
Filipino	2	**Unduplicated Number**	
Japanese	1	**of Matriculants**	200

Science and Math Majors: 64%
Matriculants with:
Baccalaureate degree: 100%
Graduate degree(s): 13%

Specialty Choice

2005, 2006, 2007 Graduates, Specialty Choice (As reported by program directors to GME Track™)	
Anesthesiology	6%
Emergency Medicine	5%
Family Practice	9%
Internal Medicine	23%
Obstetrics/Gynecology	6%
Orthopaedic Surgery	1%
Pediatrics	9%
Psychiatry	3%
Radiology	6%
Surgery	5%

Financial Information

Source: 2008-2009 LCME I-B survey
and 2009-2010 AAMC TSF questionnaire

	Residents	Non-residents
Total Cost of Attendance	$ 55,304	$ 69,758
Tuition and Fees	$ 28,416	$ 42,870
Other (includes living expenses)	$ 24,700	$ 24,700
Health Insurance (can be waived)	$ 2,188	$ 2,188

Average 2009 Graduate Indebtedness: $162,365
% of Enrolled Students Receiving Aid: 84%

Criminal Background Check

This medical school requires a criminal background check
prior to matriculation.

Virginia Tech Carilion School of Medicine

Roanoke, Virginia

1 Riverside Circle
Suite 102
Roanoke, Virginia 24016
T 540 581 0136 **F** 540 985 3951

Admissions http://vtc.vt.edu/education/admissions/index.html
Main www.vtc.vt.edu
Financial www.vtc.vt.edu/education/index.html
E-mail vtc@vt.edu

Public Institution

Dr. Cynda Ann Johnson, M.D., M.B.A., President and Dean

Stephen Workman, Ph.D., Chief Enrollment Management Officer and Director of Admissions

Dr. Dennis Means, M.D., Assistant Dean for Diversity

Terri Workman, J.D., M.B.A., Vice Dean

Richard Vari, Ph.D., Associate Dean for Medical Education and Chair, Department of Interprofessionalism

General Information

The Virginia Tech Carilion School of Medicine and Research Institute (VTC) is a public-private partnership formed by Virginia Tech and Carilion Clinic.Utilizing an innovative patient-centered curriculum, VTC addresses the increasing need for physicians who translate research from the bench to the bedside and into the community. The curriculum provides an exemplary education in basic sciences and clinical sciences and skills, but transcends the traditional medical education model by providing a solid foundation in, and opportunities to explore, the disciplines of research and interprofessionalism. Our small class size of 42 students allows for individualized attention and participation by each student which will in turn foster an intense and rewarding educational experience. We envision that VTC students will be highly sought after by residency programs and will become physician thought leaders in their chosen field of medicine.

Mission Statement

VTC's mission is to develop physician thought leaders through inquiry, research and discovery, using an innovative curriculum based on adult learning methods in a patient-centered context. Our graduates will be physicians with outstanding clinical skills and significantly enhanced research capabilities who will remain life-long learners. The VTC physician will have an understanding of the importance of interprofessionalism to enable them to function more effectively as part of a modern healthcare team.

Curricular Highlights

Community Service Requirement: Required.
Research/Thesis Requirement: Required.

The VTC interprofessionalism program requires students to collaborate with students from other health professions on a required service learning project in the community in the first year. Guided by a mentoring team, each student will be required to complete a hypothesis-driven scholarly project, provide a written document suitable for publication, and present their work in an appropriate venue in order to graduate.

USMLE

Step 1: Required. Students must record a passing score for promotion.
Step 2: Clinical Skills (CS): Required. Students must record a passing total score to graduate.
Step 2: Clinical Knowledge (CK): Required. Students must record a passing total score to graduate.

Selection Factors

VTC offers a four-year M.D. degree and admits both Virginia state and out-of-state residents. Applicants should be U.S. or Canadian citizens or U.S. permanent residents. VTC is committed to attracting a diverse body of learners who will likely achieve academic success in the rigorous academic setting of medical school, while experiencing further growth in other important aspects of professionalism. Our admissions process identifies candidates with evidence of leadership, scholarship, and motivation for a career in medicine as evidenced by superior academic credentials. VTC seeks individuals whose accomplishments reveal originality and a capacity for independent, critical thinking. Those who are interested in a life-long career of inquiry, including the practice of evidence-based medicine, clinical and basic science research, and scholarship are encouraged to apply.

Financial Aid

The financial status of the applicant is not considered in the admissions process. VTC makes every effort to ensure that students receive a competitive financial aid package, including support from national loan programs. Individual counseling and debt management

programs are available. VTC offers merit and need-based scholarships and grants. VTC requires the annual filing of the Free Application for Federal Student Aid (FAFSA). Parental financial information is required to be considered for VTC need-based grants.

Information about Diversity Programs

VTC is committed to matriculating a diverse body of exceptional individuals who reflect the people whose health needs the medical profession must serve. VTC's commitment to diversity will be shown in the ethnic, cultural and socio-economic backgrounds of the student body.

Campus Information

Setting

Along with the VTC Research Institute, the Virginia Tech Carilion School of Medicine is located on a new health sciences campus next to the Carilion Clinic outpatient building and adjacent to Carilion Roanoke Memorial Hospital (CRMH) in Roanoke, Va. The new medical school building is a dedicated learning environment that has been designed around the patient-centered curriculum. Roanoke offers a diverse mix of outdoor, cultural, historical and entertainment activities.

Enrollment

For 2009, total enrollment was: n/r

Special Features

VTC students will spend the majority of their inpatient rotations at CRMH, one of the largest hospitals in the state. CRMH has 825 beds, is a Level I Trauma Center and includes a children's hospital. Carilion Clinic is a healthcare organization with more than 600 physicians in a multi-specialty group practice and eight not-for-profit hospitals. VTC students are viewed as an integral part of a new culture of excellence and innovation at Carilion, where patients come first.

Housing

A range of affordable housing options exist within a short drive, trolley or bicycle ride. Prices range from $600/month for a 1B/1B to $1,200/month for a 2B/2B.

Application Process and Requirements 2011–2012

Primary Application Service: AMCAS
Earliest filing date: June 1, 2010
Latest filing date: December 1, 2010

Secondary Application Required?: Yes
Sent to: Screened applicants
URL: Invitation only
Fee: Yes, $50   **Waiver available:** Yes
Earliest filing date: July 1, 2010
Latest filing date: January 15, 2011

MCAT® required?: Yes
Latest MCAT® considered: September 2010
Oldest MCAT® considered: September 2008

Early Decision Program: School does not have EDP
Applicants notified: n/a
EDP available for: n/a

Regular Acceptance Notice
Earliest date: October 15, 2010
Latest date: Until class is full
Applicant's Response to Acceptance Offer – Maximum Time: Two weeks

Requests for Deferred Entrance Considered: Yes

Deposit to Hold Place in Class: Yes
Deposit (Resident): $100   **(Non-resident):** $100
Deposit due: With response to acceptance offer
Applied to tuition: Yes   **Refundable:** Yes
Refundable by: May 15, 2011

Estimated number of new entrants: 42
EDP: n/a, **Special Programs:** n/a,

Start Month/Year: August 2011

Interview Format: On-campus Multiple Mini-Interview (MMI) with a series of ten raters. Regional interviews are not available. Video interviews are not available.

Other Programs

PREPARATORY PROGRAMS
Postbaccalaureate Program: No
Summer Program: No,

COMBINED DEGREE PROGRAMS
Baccalaureate/M.D.: No
M.D./M.P.H.: Yes, Richard Vari, Ph.D., (540) 581-0130, vtc@vt.edu
M.D./M.B.A.: No
M.D./J.D.: No
M.D./Ph.D.: Yes
Additional Program: Yes, M.D./M.S. Richard Vari, Ph.D., (540) 581-0130, vtc@vt.edu

Premedical Coursework

On-line courses accepted in fulfillment of prerequisites: No

Course	Req.	Rec.	Lab.	Sems.
Inorganic Chemistry	•		•	2
Behavioral Sciences				
Biochemistry		•		
Biology	•		•	2
Biology/Zoology				
Calculus	•			2
College English	•			2
College Mathematics				
Computer Science				

Course	Req.	Rec.	Lab.	Sems.
Genetics				
Humanities				
Organic Chemistry	•		•	2
Physics	•		•	2
Psychology				
Social Sciences				
Cell Biology & Physiology			•	
Comparative Anatomy			•	
Other				

Selection Factors: 2009 Accepted Applicants

Proportion of Accepted Applicants with Relevant Experience (Data Self-Reported to AMCAS)		
Comn		
Medic	DATA NOT AVAILABLE	
Resear		

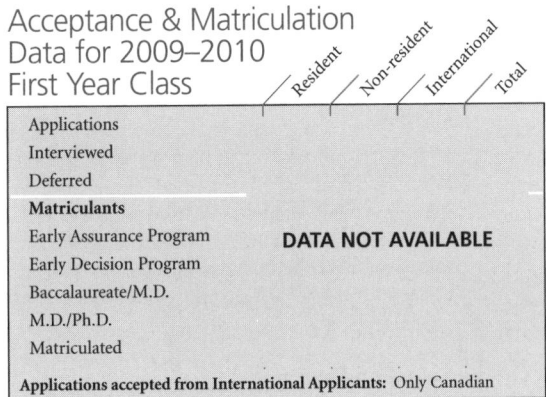

Shaded bar represents school's accepted scores ranging from the 10th percentile to the 90th percentile. School Median ● National Median ○

Overall GPA	2.0 2.1 2.2 2.3 2.4 2.5 2.6 2.7 2.8 2.9 3.0 3.1 3.2 3.3 3.4 3.5 3.6 3.7 3.8 3.9 4.0
Science GPA	4.0
MCAT	43
Writing	T
Verbal Reasoning	15
Biological Sciences	15
Physical Sciences	3 4 5 6 7 8 9 10 11 12 13 14 15

DATA NOT AVAILABLE

Acceptance & Matriculation Data for 2009–2010 First Year Class

	Resident	Non-resident	International	Total
Applications				
Interviewed				
Deferred				
Matriculants				
Early Assurance Program		DATA NOT AVAILABLE		
Early Decision Program				
Baccalaureate/M.D.				
M.D./Ph.D.				
Matriculated				

Applications accepted from International Applicants: Only Canadian

Matriculant Demographics: 2009–2010 First Year Class

Men: n/r   **Women:** n/r

Matriculants' Self-Reported Race/Ethnicity

Mexican American	Korean
Cu	
Pu	
Ot	
Tot	DATA NOT AVAILABLE
Ch	
As	
Pa	
Fili	
Japanese	of Matriculants

Science and Math Majors: n/r
Matriculants with:
          Baccalaureate degree: n/r
          Graduate degree(s): n/r

Specialty Choice

2005, 2006, 2007 Graduates, Specialty Choice (As reported by program directors to GME Track™)

Anesthesiology	%
Eme	%
Fami	%
Inter	%
Obst	%
Orth	DATA NOT AVAILABLE %
Pedi	%
Psycl	%
Radi	%
Surgery	%

Financial Information

Source: 2008-2009 LCME I-B survey and 2009-2010 AAMC TSF questionnaire

	Residents	Non-residents
Total Cost of Attendance	$ 59,936	$ 59,936
Tuition and Fees	$ 42,596	$ 42,596
Other (includes living expenses)	$ 15,000	$ 15,000
Health Insurance (can be waived)	$ 2,340	$ 2,340

Average 2009 Graduate Indebtedness: n/r
% of Enrolled Students Receiving Aid: n/r

Criminal Background Check

This medical school requires a criminal background check prior to matriculation.

University of Washington School of Medicine

Seattle, Washington

Office of Admissions
Health Sciences Center A-300
Box 356340, University of Washington
Seattle, Washington 98195-6340
T 206 543 7212   F 206 616 3341

Admissions www.uwmedicine.org/admissions
Main http://uwmedicine.washington.edu/Pages/
default.aspx
Financial www.uwmedicine.org/financialaid
E-mail askuwsom@u.washington.edu

Public Institution

Dr. Paul G. Ramsey, Dean

Dr. Carol C. Teitz, Associate Dean for Admissions

Dr. David Acosta, Associate Dean for Multicultural Affairs

Diane Noecker, Director of Financial Aid

Dr. Peter Eveland, Associate Dean for Student Affairs

General Information

Ranked as the top medical school training primary care physicians for 16 years, and first among public medical schools in federal research funding, the UWSOM is dedicated to improving the health of the public by advancing medical knowledge, providing outstanding primary and specialty care to people of the region, and preparing tomorrow's physicians and scientists. The top-ranked programs in family medicine and rural health are enhanced by volunteer clinical faculty in the WWAMI region who provide community-based medical education in the states of Washington, Wyoming, Alaska, Montana, and Idaho. The UWSOM is committed to building and sustaining a diverse academic community and to assuring that access to education and training is open to all segments of society.

Mission Statement

The UWSOM has a dual mission: 1) meeting the health care needs of our region, especially by recognizing the importance of primary care and providing service to underserved populations, and 2) advancing knowledge and assuming leadership in the biomedical sciences and academic medicine.

Curricular Highlights

Community Service Requirement: Optional.
Research/Thesis Requirement: Required. Independent Investigative Inquiry is required.

The curriculum in the first two years integrates basic sciences and clinical medicine in both discipline-based and organ-systems courses. Patient contact begins in the first year via community preceptorships and the Introduction to Clinical Medicine course, administered in a

college system. The college groups consist of a faculty mentor who guides 24 students for 4 years in acquiring fundamental clinical skills including physical exam and diagnosis, case presentation and write-up, clinical reasoning, communication with patients and colleagues, and professionalism and ethics. Opportunities range from rural or underserved experiences to bench research. Problem-based learning, observed standardized clinical examinations (OSCE), and special capstone courses provide transitions from 2nd to 3rd year and from 4th year to residency. Required clerkships leave ample time for electives allowing students to identify and develop diverse career interests. Opportunities are provided for a longitudinal interdisciplinary clerkship and for clerkships in communities across the WWAMI region, as well as international electives. Certificate programs include the Indian Health, Global Health, Hispanic Health and Underserved Pathways.

USMLE

Step 1: Required. Students must record a passing score for promotion.
Step 2: Clinical Skills (CS): Required. Students must record a passing total score to graduate.
Step 2: Clinical Knowledge (CK): Required. Students must record a passing total score to graduate.

Selection Factors

Candidates are considered on the basis of motivation, maturity, integrity, and academic performance. Demonstrated humanitarian qualities, community service, ability to communicate with and relate to a diverse group of individuals, as well as knowledge of issues in health care, ability to think analytically, and intellectual curiosity are important considerations. At least 40 hours of M.D. shadowing is expected. Strong preference is given to residents of the WWAMI states; less than 5% of the class is from outside the WWAMI region. Applicants with a demonstrated interest in research may apply for the M.D./Ph.D. program (MSTP) regardless of residency. Only U.S. citizens or permanent residents are considered for either program. Competitive candidates are asked to send additional materials. Matriculation is contingent on the outcome of a criminal background check initiated after acceptance. Candidates

may apply no more than 3 times. Prerequisites have changed for the entering class of 2010.

Financial Aid

Financial status has no bearing on admission. All applicants for aid must submit data for an analysis of need through FAFSA. Applications are available in January. The application deadline of February 28 must be met, regardless of admission status, in order to receive highest priority for aid; applicants should apply on line (*www.fafsa.ed.gov*) by mid-February. Most aid is in the form of loans.

Information about Diversity Programs

UWSOM is committed to creating an inclusive and diverse learning environment for all students and training culturally competent physicians to care for the region's increasingly diverse population. We welcome applicants from groups underrepresented in medicine and those committed to working with underserved groups. The Office of Multicultural Affairs supports student activities that promote inclusion, equity and diversity in all forms.

Campus Information

Setting

Classrooms and hospitals of the UWSOM are located across five states and run the gamut from primary to tertiary care settings including a level I trauma hospital, and renowned research facilities. Cultural and recreational opportunities abound.

Enrollment

For 2009, total enrollment was: 854

Special Features

A unique aspect of the UWSOM is the WWAMI program of decentralized medical education. Students take a portion of their clinical training at sites away from the UW-Seattle campus. Offers of admission are contingent upon agreement to participate in the WWAMI program.

Housing

On-campus housing is available, but the majority of students live off-campus. Average rent $800–$900/month.

Application Process and Requirements 2011–2012

Primary Application Service: AMCAS
Earliest filing date: June 1, 2010
Latest filing date: November 1, 2010

Secondary Application Required?: Yes
Sent to: Screened applicants
URL: www.somas.washington.edu/uwappstatus.htm
Contact: Jennifer Chesnut, (206) 543-7214, jchesnut@u.washington.edu
Fee: Yes, $35 **Waiver available:** Yes
Earliest filing date: July 15, 2010
Latest filing date: January 15, 2011

MCAT® required?: Yes
Latest MCAT® considered: September 2010
Oldest MCAT® considered: January 2008

Early Decision Program: School does not have EDP
Applicants notified: n/a
EDP available for: n/a

Regular Acceptance Notice
Earliest date: November 1, 2010
Latest date: Until Class is Full
Applicant's Response to Acceptance Offer – Maximum Time: Two weeks before May 15, one week thereafter

Requests for Deferred Entrance Considered: Yes

Deposit to Hold Place in Class: No
Deposit (Resident): n/a **(Non-resident):** n/a
Deposit due: n/a
Applied to tuition: n/a **Refundable:** n/a
Refundable by: n/a

Estimated number of new entrants: 216
EDP: n/a, special program: n/a

Start Month/Year: August 2011

Interview Format: A three-member panel interviews each applicant. Limited regional interviews are available. Video interviews are not available.

Other Programs

PREPARATORY PROGRAMS
Postbaccalaureate Program: No
Summer Program: Yes, (206) 685-2489 http://depts.washington.edu/omca/leadership/SMDEP.html
Prematriculation Program: Yes, http://depts.washington.edu/omca/leadership/PREMAT.html, Mary Walls, (206) 616-3047, mwalls@u.washington.edu

COMBINED DEGREE PROGRAMS
Baccalaureate/M.D. : No
M.D./M.P.H.: Yes, http://depts.washington.edu/hserv/mdmph
Kate O'Brien, (206) 685-1762, epi@u.washington.edu
M.D./M.B.A.: No
M.D./J.D.: No
M.D./Ph.D.: Yes, www.mstp.washington.edu/admissions, (206) 685-0762, Maureen Holstad, mstp@u.washington.edu

Premedical Coursework

On-line courses accepted in fulfillment of prerequisites: Yes

Course	Req.	Rec.	Lab.	Sems.
Inorganic Chemistry				
Behavioral Sciences				
Biochemistry		•		1
Biology	•			2-4
Biology/Zoology				
Calculus	•			1
College English		•		1
College Mathematics				
Computer Science				

Course	Req.	Rec.	Lab.	Sems.
Genetics		•		1
Humanities	•			2-4
Organic Chemistry				
Physics	•			1
Psychology				
Social Sciences	•			2-4
Inorgan./Organ. Chem	•			2-4
Biology/Chem/Physics	•			2
Other				

Selection Factors: 2009 Accepted Applicants

Proportion of Accepted Applicants with Relevant Experience (Data Self-Reported to AMCAS®)		
Community Service/Volunteer		75%
Medically-Related Work		86%
Research		81%

Shaded bar represents school's accepted scores ranging from the 10th percentile to the 90th percentile **School Median** ● **National Median** ○

Overall GPA	2.0	2.1	2.2	2.3	2.4	2.5	2.6	2.7	2.8	2.9	3.0	3.1	3.2	3.3	3.4	3.5	3.6	(3.7)	3.8	3.9	4.0
Science GPA	2.0	2.1	2.2	2.3	2.4	2.5	2.6	2.7	2.8	2.9	3.0	3.1	3.2	3.3	3.4	3.5	3.6	(3.7)	3.8	3.9	4.0

MCAT® Total Numeric Score 9 10 11 12 13 14 15 16 17 18 19 20 21 22 23 24 25 26 27 28 29 30 (31)(32)33 34 35 36 37 38 39 40 41 42 43

Writing Sample		J	K	L	M	N	O	P	(Q)	R	S	T
Verbal Reasoning	3	4	5	6	7	8	9	(10)	11	12	13	14	15
Biological Sciences	3	4	5	6	7	8	9	10	(11)	12	13	14	15
Physical Sciences	3	4	5	6	7	8	9	(10)	(11)	12	13	14	15

Acceptance & Matriculation Data for 2009–2010 First Year Class

	Resident	Non-resident	International	Total
Applications	1075	3191	10	4276
Interviewed	604	79	0	683
Deferred	2	0	0	2
Matriculants				
Early Assurance Program	0	0	0	0
Early Decision Program	0	0	0	0
Baccalaureate/M.D.	0	0	0	0
M.D./Ph.D.	2	3	0	5
Matriculated	202	14	0	**216**

Applications accepted from International Applicants: No

Matriculant Demographics: 2009–2010 First Year Class

Men: 94 **Women:** 122

Matriculants' Self-Reported Race/Ethnicity

Mexican American	2	**Korean**	3
Cuban	1	**Vietnamese**	5
Puerto Rican	1	**Other Asian**	5
Other Hispanic	5	**Total Asian**	40
Total Hispanic	8	**Native American**	2
Chinese	16	**Black**	8
Asian Indian	4	**Native Hawaiian**	1
Pakistani	1	**White**	163
Filipino	2	**Unduplicated Number**	
Japanese	7	**of Matriculants**	216

Science and Math Majors: 63%
Matriculants with:
Baccalaureate degree: 100%
Graduate degree(s): 6%

Specialty Choice

2005, 2006, 2007 Graduates, Specialty Choice (As reported by program directors to GME Track™)	
Anesthesiology	8%
Emergency Medicine	10%
Family Practice	14%
Internal Medicine	19%
Obstetrics/Gynecology	5%
Orthopaedic Surgery	3%
Pediatrics	12%
Psychiatry	4%
Radiology	2%
Surgery	6%

Financial Information

Source: 2008-2009 LCME I-B survey and 2009-2010 AAMC TSF questionnaire

	Residents	Non-residents
Total Cost of Attendance	$ 40,435	$ 69,475
Tuition and Fees	$ 20,997	$ 50,037
Other (includes living expenses)	$ 19,438	$ 19,438
Health Insurance (can be waived)	$ 0	$ 0

Average 2009 Graduate Indebtedness: $121,193
% of Enrolled Students Receiving Aid: 91%

Criminal Background Check

This medical school requires a criminal background check prior to matriculation.

Marshall University
Joan C. Edwards School of Medicine
Huntington, West Virginia

Admissions Office, Marshall University
Joan C. Edwards School of Medicine
1600 Medical Center Drive
Huntington, West Virginia 25701-3655
T 800 544 8514   F 304 691 1744

Admissions http://musom.marshall.edu/admissions
Main http://musom.marshall.edu
Financial www.marshall.edu/sfa
E-mail warren@marshall.edu

Public Institution

Dr. Charles H. McKown Jr.,
Vice President and Dean

Cynthia A. Warren, Assistant Dean for
Admissions & Student Affairs

Nadine Hamrick, Associate Director of
Student Financial Aid

Dr. Aaron M. McGuffin, Senior Associate Dean
for Medical Education

Dr. Marie C. Veitia,
Associate Dean for Student Affairs

General Information
The Marshall University School of Medicine was granted full accreditation and graduated its first class in 1981. The School of Medicine is a community-based program which provides learning opportunities in varied settings: a state-of-the-art ambulatory care center, the Veterans Affairs Medical Center, rural clinics, highly specialized tertiary-care hospitals, offices of private physicians and others. Educational opportunities are further enhanced by the Edwards Comprehensive Cancer Center, the Robert C. Byrd Biotechnology Science Center and the Byrd Clinical Center.

Mission Statement
The Marshall University School of Medicine is to respond to the health care needs of West Virginians by emphasizing training primary care specialties and encouraging graduates to practice in the state's underserved rural areas. Marshall ranks third in the nation in the percentage of graduates entering family medicine.

Curricular Highlights
Community Service Requirement: Optional. Can graduation with distinction in Community Service.
Research/Thesis Requirement: Optional.

Students integrate basic science information with clinical medicine the first two years. Year One consists of the traditional foundational disciplines of medicine: Anatomy, Molecular Basis of Medicine, Histology, Physiology and Neuroscience. Year Two is an Integrated Systems Curriculum consisting of: Core Principles,

Infectious Agents & Antimicrobials, Neoplasia & Hematology, Nervous System, Cardiovascular System, Pulmonary System & ENT, Gastro-intestinal System, Renal & Endocrine Systems, Musculoskeletal, Genitourinary, and Derma-tology, Toxicology and Eye. Throughout both years students have direct patient contact through the Mentorship Program giving them a natural framework to integrate their growing knowledge of the traditional sciences basic to medicine. During both years students learn the foundational principles of patient care including the skills of history taking and the physical exam. In addition, topics such as preventative medicine, ethics, professionalism, and biostatistics and epidemiology are woven throughout the curriculum. During the third and fourth years, students rotate through clerkships at participating community hospitals and other locations in the clinical fields of medicine, surgery, pediatrics, psychiatry/neurology, family practice, obstetrics-gynecology and emergency medicine. Two months of rural health care at approved sites are required of all students. Twenty-two weeks are devoted to electives in the senior year. A letter grading system (A,B,C,F) is utilized.

USMLE
Step 1: Required. Students must record a passing score for promotion.
Step 2: Clinical Skills (CS): Required. Students must record a passing total score to graduate.
Step 2: Clinical Knowledge (CK): Required. Students must record a passing total score to graduate.

Selection Factors
There is no discrimination because of race, gender, religion, age, handicap, sexual orientation, or national origin. Qualified members of groups who are underrepresented in medicine are encouraged to apply. Applicants are evaluated on the basis of their academic records, MCAT scores, recommendations from instructors, and personal qualifications as judged through interviews. A minimum MCAT score of 24 is required for an interview. Interviews are arranged only by invitation of the Admissions Committee. As a state-assisted institution, the School of Medicine gives preference in selection of students to West Virginia residents. A limited number of positions will be available to well-qualified nonresidents

from states contiguous to West Virginia or to nonresidents who have strong ties to West Virginia. Other nonresidents are not considered. Only applicants who are U.S. citizens or who have permanent resident visas are eligible for admission.

Financial Aid
The financial needs of the applicant are not a consideration in the admissions process. The supplemental application fee will be waived for individuals who have been granted an AMCAS fee waiver.

Information About Diversity Programs
Hisham Keblawi, M.D., (hkeblawi@marshall.edu), Institutional Diversity Affairs Officer and Marie Veitia, Ph.D., (veitia@marshall.edu), Individual Institutional Diversity Affairs Officer

Campus Information

Enrollment
For 2009, total enrollment was: 300

Special Features
The faculty and administration are committed to meeting the personal, academic and professional needs of students throughout their medical education and work to facilitate a positive learning environment based upon mutual respect between teacher and learner. The Marshall Mentoring Program and the Clinical Skills Laboratory offer students early clinical exposure and skills development beginning in the first semester of the first year. Small class size offers an opportunity to develop close professional relationships with administration, faculty and residents and to participate more fully in supervised direct patient care activities. International Health and Wilderness Medicine represent two of the unique areas in which students can explore their interests.

Housing
The medical school maintains a list of apartments.

Application Process and Requirements 2011–2012

Primary Application Service: AMCAS
Earliest filing date: June 1, 2010
Latest filing date: November 1, 2010

Secondary Application Required?: Yes
Sent to: State residents and those from states bordering West Virginia (NR fee: $100)
Contact: Cynthia A. Warren, (800) 544-8514, warren@marshall.edu
Fee: Yes, $75 **Waiver available:** Yes
Earliest filing date: July 15, 2010
Latest filing date: December 31, 2010

MCAT® required?: Yes
Latest MCAT® considered: September 2010
Oldest MCAT® considered: January 2008

Early Decision Program: School does not have EDP
Applicants notified: n/a
EDP available for: n/a

Regular Acceptance Notice
Earliest date: October 15, 2010
Latest date: Until class is full
Applicant's Response to Acceptance Offer – Maximum Time: Two weeks

Requests for Deferred Entrance Considered: Yes

Deposit to Hold Place in Class: No
Deposit (Resident): n/a **(Non-resident):** n/a
Deposit due: n/a
Applied to tuition: n/a **Refundable:** n/a
Refundable by: n/a

Estimated number of new entrants: 75
EDP: n/a, special program: n/a

Start Month/Year: August 2011

Interview Format: Two one-on-one interviews. Regional interviews are not available. Video interviews are not available.

Other Programs

PREPARATORY PROGRAMS
Postbaccalaureate Program: No
Summer Program: No

COMBINED DEGREE PROGRAMS
Baccalaureate/M.D.: No
M.D./M.P.H.: No
M.D./M.B.A.: No
M.D./J.D.: No
M.D./Ph.D.: Yes, Richard Niles, Ph.D., (304) 696-7323, niles@marshall.edu

Premedical Coursework

On-line courses accepted in fulfillment of prerequisites: Yes

Course	Req.	Rec.	Lab.	Hrs.	Course	Req.	Rec.	Lab.	Hrs.
Inorganic Chemistry	•		•	8	Computer Science				
Behavioral Sciences	•			6	Genetics				
Biochemistry		•			Humanities				
Biology					Organic Chemistry	•		•	8
Biology/Zoology	•		•	8	Physics	•		•	8
Calculus					Social Sciences				6
College English	•			6	Cell & Molecular Biology		•		4
College Mathematics					Anatomy		•		4

Selection Factors: 2009 Accepted Applicants

Proportion of Accepted Applicants with Relevant Experience (Data Self-Reported to AMCAS®)		Community Service/Volunteer	69%
		Medically-Related Work	73%
		Research	65%

Shaded bar represents school's accepted scores ranging from the 10th percentile to the 90th percentile ▨ — School Median ○ National Median ○

Overall GPA 2.0 2.1 2.2 2.3 2.4 2.5 2.6 2.7 2.8 2.9 3.0 3.1 3.2 3.3 3.4 3.5 3.6 ⟨3.7⟩ 3.8 3.9 4.0
Science GPA 2.0 2.1 2.2 2.3 2.4 2.5 2.6 2.7 2.8 2.9 3.0 3.1 3.2 3.3 3.4 3.5 ⟨3.6⟩ 3.7 3.8 3.9 4.0

MCAT® Total Numeric Score 9 10 11 12 13 14 15 16 17 18 19 20 21 22 23 24 25 26 ⟨27⟩ 28 29 30 31 ⟨32⟩ 33 34 35 36 37 38 39 40 41 42 43

				J	K	L	M	N	O	P	Q	R	S	T
Writing Sample									⟨O⟩		⟨Q⟩			
Verbal Reasoning	3	4	5	6	7	8	⟨9⟩	⟨10⟩	11	12	13	14	15
Biological Sciences	3	4	5	6	7	8	⟨9⟩	10	⟨11⟩	12	13	14	15
Physical Sciences	3	4	5	6	7	8	⟨9⟩	10	⟨11⟩	12	13	14	15

Acceptance & Matriculation Data for 2009–2010 First Year Class

	Resident	Non-resident	International	Total
Applications	209	1927	13	2149
Interviewed	145	94	0	239
Deferred	1	0	0	1
Matriculants				
Early Assurance Program	0	0	0	0
Early Decision Program	0	0	0	0
Baccalaureate/M.D.	0	0	0	0
M.D./Ph.D.	0	0	0	0
Matriculated	59	15	0	**74**

Applications accepted from International Applicants: No

Matriculant Demographics: 2009–2010 First Year Class

Men: 40 **Women:** 34

Matriculants' Self-Reported Race/Ethnicity

Mexican American	0	Korean	0
Cuban	0	Vietnamese	0
Puerto Rican	0	Other Asian	1
Other Hispanic	0	Total Asian	6
Total Hispanic	0	Native American	1
Chinese	1	Black	2
Asian Indian	3	Native Hawaiian	0
Pakistani	1	White	65
Filipino	0	Unduplicated Number	
Japanese	0	of Matriculants	74

Science and Math Majors: 80%
Matriculants with:
   Baccalaureate degree: 100%
   Graduate degree(s): 19%

Specialty Choice

2005, 2006, 2007 Graduates, Specialty Choice
(As reported by program directors to GME Track™)

Anesthesiology	5%
Emergency Medicine	9%
Family Practice	14%
Internal Medicine	9%
Obstetrics/Gynecology	9%
Orthopaedic Surgery	2%
Pediatrics	17%
Psychiatry	5%
Radiology	5%
Surgery	4%

Financial Information

Source: 2008-2009 LCME I-B survey and 2009-2010 AAMC TSF questionnaire

	Residents	Non-residents
Total Cost of Attendance	$ 37,886	$ 64,676
Tuition and Fees	$ 17,688	$ 44,478
Other (includes living expenses)	$ 17,618	$ 17,618
Health Insurance (can be waived)	$ 2,580	$ 2,580

Average 2009 Graduate Indebtedness: $138,355
% of Enrolled Students Receiving Aid: 91%

Criminal Background Check

This medical school requires a criminal background check prior to matriculation.

West Virginia University School of Medicine

Morgantown, West Virginia

Office of Student Services
West Virginia University School of Medicine
Health Sciences Center, P.O. Box 9111
Morgantown, West Virginia 26506
T 304 293 2408   **F** 304 293 7814

Admissions www.hsc.wvu.edu/som/students/
aboutSoM/admissionProcess/index.asp
Main www.hsc.wvu.edu/som/
Financial www.hsc.wvu.edu/fin/medbud.htm
E-mail medadmissions@hsc.wvu.edu

Public Institution

Dr. James E. Brick, Interim Dean

*Dr. James Helsley, Chair,
Admissions Committee*

*Dr. G. Anne Cather, Associate Dean
for Student Services*

Candace Frazier, Financial Aid Officer

Beth Ann McCormick, Admissions Associate

General Information

WVU has served for more than 100 years as a public institution of health professions education. The Robert C. Byrd Health Sciences Center has more than 1,900 students in Medicine, Dentistry, Pharmacy, Nursing and Allied Health. The Morgantown campus includes: the Physician Office Center, Ruby Memorial Hospital, Chestnut Ridge Psychiatric Hospital, Health South Regional Rehabilitation Hospital, Mary Babb Randolph Cancer Center, and the WVU Eye Institute. New construction includes the Blanchette Rockefeller Neuro-sciences Institute, research labs and updated Cancer Center. There are three campuses: Morgantown, Charleston, and Eastern Division. Morgantown serves north and central WV with primary and tertiary care. Charleston is the oldest regional medical education campus in the U.S. and serves as a regional referral center for southern WV. Eastern delivers its third year curriculum in an integrated, longitudinal fashion utilizing community based preceptors and learning experiences.

Mission Statement

The mission of the West Virginia University School of Medicine is to improve the health of West Virginians through the education of health professionals, through basic/clinical scientific research and research in rural health care delivery, through the provision of continuing professional education, and through participation in the provision of direct and supportive health care.

Curricular Highlights

Community Service Requirement: Required. 100 hours.
Research/Thesis Requirement: Optional.

WVU's education provides a strong foundation for any medical specialty. The basic medical sciences are covered in the MS1 and MS2 years in lecture and problem-based learning formats with computer-based testing. The Physical Diagnosis course begins in MS1 year and continues through MS2 year. Summer externships are available. The MS2 year has an integrated, organ system-based approach. The foundation MS3 curriculum requires clerkships in medicine, surgery, pediatrics, family medicine, OB-GYN, and psychiatry-neurology. The MS4 year consists of 50% required and 50% elective rotations. Three months of rural rotations are required. International travel scholarships are available.

USMLE

Step 1: Required. Students must record a passing score for promotion.
Step 2: Clinical Skills (CS): Required. Students must record a passing total score to graduate.
Step 2: Clinical Knowledge (CK): Required. Students must record a passing total score to graduate.

Selection Factors

WV residents are given preference for admission. There are available spaces for well-qualified non-residents, especially for those with strong state ties. Admission is based upon scholarship, MCAT scores, personal qualifications noted on interview, recommendations, community service, medical experiences and leadership. We do not discriminate on the basis of race, gender, creed, national origin, age, or disability. Approximately one third of the students are assigned to MS3 and MS4 years at the Charleston Division and a smaller number of students are assigned to the Eastern Division.

Financial Aid

A number of scholarship awards are available based on financial need and merit. Multiple loan funds are also available. Students' significant others with reasonable training and experience often find work near the medical school, at WVU, or in Morgantown. Medical students are discouraged from seeking outside employment while enrolled.

Information about Diversity Programs

The Health Careers Opportunity Program is available for disadvantaged students or those from groups underrepresented in medicine. *www.cahcon.org.*

Campus Information

Setting

There are three clinical campuses. The Morgantown campus (www.morgantown.com) is a vibrant, active community and the medical, cultural, and commercial hub of the region. It has been named "#1 Dreamtown in America," and "Best Small City In The East." Clinical campuses are also located in the Charleston and Eastern Divisions. Charleston is the state capitol and serves as a hub for business and industry. The Charleston Area Medical Center is the largest hospital in the state and serves as the regional referral center. The Eastern Division is located in WV's eastern panhandle and serves a growing population just west of the Baltimore/Washington area. It is associated with two university owned hospitals, the VA system and community and rural health centers.

Enrollment

For 2009, total enrollment was: 432

Special Features

WVU School of Medicine is highly respected for its clinical and rural education. It is a recent recipient of the AAMC Community Service Award, the US News and World Report's Top Ten in Rural Medicine, and the AAFP's Top 10 in students going into Family Medicine. Our computer laptop program provides electronic testing and prepares students well for the USMLE exams. Primary and tertiary care facilities are state-of-the-art. MPH and Global Medicine tracks are available. Community service is required.

Housing

On-campus housing is not available. Affordable housing is available nearby, with average rents of $600–$800/month.

Satellite Campuses/Facilities

Two regional campuses are located at the Charleston (*www.hsc.wvu.edu/charleston*) and Eastern Divisions (*www.hsc.wvu.edu/eastern*) for MS3 and MS4 year clinical rotations.

Application Process and Requirements 2011–2012

Primary Application Service: AMCAS
Earliest filing date: June 1, 2010
Latest filing date: November 1, 2010

Secondary Application Required?: Yes
Sent to: Select applicants by secure e-mail
Contact: Beth Ann McCormick,
1-800-543-5650, medadmissions@hsc.wvu.edu
Fee: Yes, $100   **Waiver available:** Yes
Earliest filing date: July 15, 2010
Latest filing date: January 1, 2011

MCAT® required?: Yes
Latest MCAT® considered: September 2010
Oldest MCAT® considered: January 2009

Early Decision Program: School does have EDP
Applicants notified: October 1, 2010
EDP available for: Both Residents and Non-residents

Regular Acceptance Notice
Earliest date: October 15, 2010
Latest date: Until class is full
Applicant's Response to Acceptance Offer – Maximum Time: Two weeks

Requests for Deferred Entrance Considered: Yes

Deposit to Hold Place in Class: Yes
Deposit (Resident): $100   **(Non-resident):** $100
Deposit due: With response to acceptance offer
Applied to tuition: Yes   **Refundable:** Yes
Refundable by: May 15, 2011

Estimated number of new entrants: 110
EDP: 15, special program: 4

Start Month/Year: August 2011

Interview Format: Medical student led tour of Morgantown campus and interview. Regional tours can be arranged. Video interviews are not available.

Other Programs

PREPARATORY PROGRAMS
Postbaccalaureate Program: No
Summer Program: No

COMBINED DEGREE PROGRAMS
Baccalaureate/M.D.: No
M.D./M.P.H.: Yes, www.hsc.wvu.edu/ResOff/PhDPrograms/MDPhDScholars.aspx
M.D./M.B.A.: No
M.D./J.D.: No
M.D./Ph.D.: Yes, www.hsc.wvu.edu/som/resoff/gradprograms/mdphd_main.asp
Additional Program: Yes, www.hsc.wvu.edu/som/students/aboutSoM/admissionProcess/medStepProgram.asp

Premedical Coursework

On-line courses accepted in fulfillment of prerequisites: No

Course	Req.	Rec.	Lab.	Hrs.
Inorganic Chemistry	•		•	8
Behavioral Sciences				
Biochemistry		•		4-8
Biology				
Biology/Zoology	•		•	8
Calculus				
College English	•			6
College Mathematics				
Computer Science				

Course	Req.	Rec.	Lab.	Hrs.
Genetics				
Humanities				
Organic Chemistry	•		•	8
Physics	•		•	8
Psychology				
Social Sciences				
Adv. Cell & Molecular Biology		•		4-8
Behav/Social Sciences	•			6

Selection Factors: 2009 Accepted Applicants

Proportion of Accepted Applicants with Relevant Experience (Data Self-Reported to AMCAS®)		Community Service/Volunteer	70%
		Medically-Related Work	85%
		Research	73%

Shaded bar represents school's accepted scores ranging from the 10th percentile to the 90th percentile   ● School Median   National Median ◯

Overall GPA	2.0	2.1	2.2	2.3	2.4	2.5	2.6	2.7	2.8	2.9	3.0	3.1	3.2	3.3	3.4	3.5	3.6	3.7	(3.8)	3.9	4.0
Science GPA	2.0	2.1	2.2	2.3	2.4	2.5	2.6	2.7	2.8	2.9	3.0	3.1	3.2	3.3	3.4	3.5	3.6	(3.7)	3.8	3.9	4.0

MCAT® Total Numeric Score 9 10 11 12 13 14 15 16 17 18 19 20 21 22 23 24 25 26 27 28 (29) 30 31 (32) 33 34 35 36 37 38 39 40 41 42 43

Writing Sample				J	K	L	M	N	(O)	P	(Q)	R	S	T
Verbal Reasoning	3	4	5	6	7	8	9	(10)	11	12	13	14	15	
Biological Sciences	3	4	5	6	7	8	9	(10)	(11)	12	13	14	15	
Physical Sciences	3	4	5	6	7	8	9	(10)	(11)	12	13	14	15	

Acceptance & Matriculation Data for 2009–2010 First Year Class

	Resident	Non-resident	International	Total
Applications	211	2371	54	2636
Interviewed	113	256	0	369
Deferred	1	1	0	2
Matriculants				
Early Assurance Program	0	0	0	0
Early Decision Program	11	1	0	12
Baccalaureate/M.D.	0	0	0	0
M.D./Ph.D.	1	3	0	4
Matriculated	71	39	0	**110**

Applications accepted from International Applicants: No

Matriculant Demographics: 2009–2010 First Year Class

Men: 70   **Women:** 40

Matriculants' Self-Reported Race/Ethnicity

Mexican American	0	Korean	2
Cuban	0	Vietnamese	2
Puerto Rican	0	Other Asian	1
Other Hispanic	2	Total Asian	22
Total Hispanic	2	Native American	0
Chinese	2	Black	0
Asian Indian	7	Native Hawaiian	1
Pakistani	2	White	87
Filipino	4	Unduplicated Number	
Japanese	2	of Matriculants	110

Science and Math Majors: 75%
Matriculants with:
    Baccalaureate degree: 100%
    Graduate degree(s): 2%

Specialty Choice

2005, 2006, 2007 Graduates, Specialty Choice (As reported by program directors to GME Track™)	
Anesthesiology	4%
Emergency Medicine	5%
Family Practice	13%
Internal Medicine	15%
Obstetrics/Gynecology	7%
Orthopaedic Surgery	2%
Pediatrics	14%
Psychiatry	4%
Radiology	6%
Surgery	5%

Financial Information

Source: 2008-2009 LCME I-B survey and 2009-2010 AAMC TSF questionnaire

	Residents	Non-residents
Total Cost of Attendance	$ 36,467	$ 61,215
Tuition and Fees	$ 21,270	$ 46,018
Other (includes living expenses)	$ 14,397	$ 14,397
Health Insurance (can be waived)	$ 800	$ 800

Average 2009 Graduate Indebtedness: $154,541
% of Enrolled Students Receiving Aid: 95%

Criminal Background Check

This medical school requires a criminal background check prior to matriculation.

Medical College of Wisconsin
Milwaukee, Wisconsin

Office of Admissions
Medical College of Wisconsin
8701 Watertown Plank Road
Milwaukee, Wisconsin 53226
T 414 955 8246   **F** 414 955 0121

Admissions www.mcw.edu/medicalschool
Main www.mcw.edu
Financial www.mcw.edu/acad/finaid
E-mail medschool@mcw.edu

Private Institution

Dr. Johnathan Ravdin, Dean and Executive Vice President

Michael T. Istwan, Director of Admissions

Dr. Dawn Bragg, Assistant Dean for Student Affairs – Diversity

Linda L. Paschal, Director of Student Financial Services

General Information
The Medical College of Wisconsin became a private, free-standing school of medicine in 1967. Located on the Milwaukee Regional Medical Campus, maintaining strong relationships and educational programs with institutions statewide. Major affiliated teaching hospitals include Froedtert Hospital, Children's Hospital of Wisconsin and the VA Medical Center. Affiliations also include area hospitals and a number of healthcare facilities.

Mission Statement
To be a national leader in the education and development of the next generation of physicians and scientists, to discover and translate new knowledge in the biomedical sciences, to provide "cutting edge" interdisciplinary and compassionate clinical care of the highest quality and to improve the health of the communities we serve.

Curricular Highlights
Community Service Requirement: Optional.
Research/Thesis Requirement: Optional.

The curriculum provides a foundation for a career in any discipline of medicine and is evolving to enhance flexibility, individuality, and early clinical exposure. Currently, students gain exposure to basic science and experience the clinical environment through a mentor course and clinically-related course work in the Clinical Continuum during the first two years. Students rotate through required clinical clerkships and an optional elective experience in the third year. Students are required to take two subinternships, one each in a medically- and surgically-oriented specialty, ambulatory medicine, an Integrated Selective and five one-month electives in the fourth year. Joint degree

programs or an Honors in Research program are available to students with specific research interests. To provide students the opportunity to pursue and strengthen their own interests in medicine, five new Pathways have been implemented that include Master Clinician, Urban and Community Health, Physician Scientist, Clinician Educator and Global Health.

USMLE
Step 1: Required. Students must record a passing score for promotion.
Step 2: Clinical Skills (CS): Required. Students must only record a score.
Step 2: Clinical Knowledge (CK): Required. Students must record a passing total score to graduate.

Selection Factors
Student selection is based on a careful analysis of the suitability for the medical profession. Academic achievement and MCAT scores are carefully evaluated. Subjective factors include the personal statement, experiences, recommendations and interviews. Interviews are integral, done only at the college and required before acceptance. Applications are reviewed on a rolling basis by date of completion. Interviews are conducted and offers are also made on a rolling basis until the class is filled. Candidates are encouraged to complete the application in a timely fashion. The Medical College of Wisconsin does not discriminate on the basis of race, gender, creed, disability, age, national origin or sexual orientation.

Financial Aid
Most financial assistance, including federal and institutional scholarships and loans, is awarded on basis of need. Financial aid award letters are developed using the Federal Methodology formula. Applicants are encouraged to begin the application process as soon as they are interviewed. To matriculate, a student must provide a current clean credit report as defined in the College's credit report policy. A student must be a U.S. citizen or eligible non-citizen to receive aid from federal administered programs. International applicants must file proof of financial support before acceptance.

Information about Diversity Programs
The college encourages applications from students of diverse backgrounds. In addition to academic credentials, letters of recommendation, and personal interviews, a student's motivation and educational background are carefully considered. The Office of Academic Affairs/Diversity offers various programs to assist students, demonstrating the college's commitment to their recruitment, retention and graduation.

Campus Information
Setting
Located on the Milwaukee Regional Medical Center Campus, in a suburb seven miles west of downtown Milwaukee, the College offers a safe comfortable environment to live and study, with easy access to the city and its advantages.

Enrollment
For 2009, total enrollment was: 817

Special Features
Froedtert Hospital and the Medical College of Wisconsin have been selected as one of the top 20 medical centers in the country. Teaching hospitals, Froedtert Hospital and Children's Hospital of Wisconsin are nationally ranked, Level One trauma centers. Children's has been selected as one of the ten best Children's Hospital in the country. With over $145 million in grant funds, the College conducted 3000 studies and had 1500 clinical trials in progress during the past year.

Housing
Student housing is not provided. A list of available housing is maintained and students live within easy driving or walking distance of campus.

Satellite Campuses/Facilities
The Milwaukee Regional Medical Campus provides students with the opportunity to complete all of their clinical clerkships and rotations at this location.

Application Process and Requirements 2011–2012

Primary Application Service: AMCAS
Earliest filing date: June 1, 2010
Latest filing date: November 1, 2010

Secondary Application Required?: Yes
Sent to: All applicants
Contact: Michael Istwan, (414) 456-8246, mistwan@mcw.edu
Fee: Yes, $70 **Waiver available:** Yes
Earliest filing date: July 1, 2010
Latest filing date: January 31, 2011

MCAT® required?: Yes
Latest MCAT® considered: September 2010
Oldest MCAT® considered: September 2008

Early Decision Program: School does have EDP
Applicants notified: October 1, 2010
EDP available for: Both Residents and Non-residents

Regular Acceptance Notice
Earliest date: October 15, 2010
Latest date: Until class is full
Applicant's Response to Acceptance Offer – Maximum Time: One month

Requests for Deferred Entrance Considered: Yes

Deposit to Hold Place in Class: Yes
Deposit (Resident): $100 **(Non-resident):** $100
Deposit due: One month after acceptance
Applied to tuition: Yes **Refundable:** Yes
Refundable by: May 16, 2011

Estimated number of new entrants: 204
EDP: 5, special program: n/a

Start Month/Year: August 2011

Interview Format: Two, thirty-minute interviews. Regional interviews are not available. Video interviews are not available.

Other Programs

PREPARATORY PROGRAMS
Postbaccalaureate Program: No
Summer Program: No

COMBINED DEGREE PROGRAMS
Baccalaureate/M.D.: No
M.D./M.P.H.: No
M.D./M.B.A.: No
M.D./J.D.: No
M.D./Ph.D.: Yes, www.mcw.edu/mstp

Premedical Coursework

On-line courses accepted in fulfillment of prerequisites: Yes

Course	Req.	Rec.	Lab.	Hrs.	Course	Req.	Rec.	Lab.	Hrs.
Inorganic Chemistry	•		•	8	Computer Science				
Behavioral Sciences					Genetics				
Biochemistry		•			Humanities				
Biology	•		•	8	Organic Chemistry	•		•	8
Biology/Zoology					Physics	•			8
Calculus		•			Psychology				
College English	•			6	Social Sciences				
College Mathematics	•			4	Other				

Selection Factors: 2009 Accepted Applicants

Proportion of Accepted Applicants with Relevant Experience (Data Self-Reported to AMCAS)		
Community Service/Volunteer		73%
Medically-Related Work		89%
Research		82%

Shaded bar represents school's accepted scores ranging from the 10th percentile to the 90th percentile. School Median ● National Median ○

Overall GPA 2.0 2.1 2.2 2.3 2.4 2.5 2.6 2.7 2.8 2.9 3.0 3.1 3.2 3.3 3.4 3.5 3.6 3.7 (3.8) 3.9 4.0
Science GPA 2.0 2.1 2.2 2.3 2.4 2.5 2.6 2.7 2.8 2.9 3.0 3.1 3.2 3.3 3.4 3.5 3.6 (3.7) 3.8 3.9 4.0

MCAT® Total Numeric Score 9 10 11 12 13 14 15 16 17 18 19 20 21 22 23 24 25 26 27 28 29 30 (31) (32) 33 34 35 36 37 38 39 40 41 42 43

Writing Sample			J		K		L	M	N	O	(P)	(Q)	R	S	T
Verbal Reasoning	3	4	5	6	7	8	9	(10)	11	12	13	14	15		
Biological Sciences	3	4	5	6	7	8	9	10	(11)	12	13	14	15		
Physical Sciences	3	4	5	6	7	8	9	(10)	(11)	12	13	14	15		

Acceptance & Matriculation Data for 2009–2010 First Year Class

	Resident	Non-resident	International	Total
Applications	612	5587	176	6375
Interviewed	173	474	4	651
Deferred	5	3	0	8
Matriculants				
Early Assurance Program	0	0	0	0
Early Decision Program	9	0	0	9
Baccalaureate/M.D.	0	0	0	0
M.D./Ph.D.	2	2	0	4
Matriculated	89	115	0	**204**

Applications accepted from International Applicants: Yes

Specialty Choice

2005, 2006, 2007 Graduates, Specialty Choice (As reported by program directors to GME Track™)	
Anesthesiology	8%
Emergency Medicine	9%
Family Practice	12%
Internal Medicine	15%
Obstetrics/Gynecology	5%
Orthopaedic Surgery	4%
Pediatrics	9%
Psychiatry	4%
Radiology	7%
Surgery	8%

Matriculant Demographics: 2009–2010 First Year Class

Men: 111 **Women:** 93

Matriculants' Self-Reported Race/Ethnicity

Mexican American	6	Korean	7
Cuban	2	Vietnamese	4
Puerto Rican	2	Other Asian	4
Other Hispanic	2	Total Asian	48
Total Hispanic	9	Native American	2
Chinese	12	Black	8
Asian Indian	13	Native Hawaiian	1
Pakistani	1	White	150
Filipino	6	Unduplicated Number	
Japanese	2	of Matriculants	204

Science and Math Majors: 66%
Matriculants with:
Baccalaureate degree: 100%
Graduate degree(s): 6%

Financial Information

Source: 2008-2009 LCME I-B survey and 2009-2010 AAMC TSF questionnaire

	Residents	Non-residents
Total Cost of Attendance	$ 50,599	$ 56,219
Tuition and Fees	$ 34,558	$ 40,178
Other (includes living expenses)	$ 13,270	$ 13,270
Health Insurance (can be waived)	$ 2,771	$ 2,771

Average 2009 Graduate Indebtedness: $159,426
% of Enrolled Students Receiving Aid: 95%

Criminal Background Check

This medical school requires a criminal background check prior to matriculation.

University of Wisconsin
School of Medicine and Public Health
Madison, Wisconsin

MD Admissions Office
2130 Health Sciences Learning Center
University of Wisconsin School of Medicine
and Public Health
750 Highland Avenue
Madison, Wisconsin 53705-2221
T 608 263 4925   F 608 262 4226

Admissions www.med.wisc.edu/education/md/
admissions/main/102
Main www.med.wisc.edu
Financial www.finaid.wisc.edu/index.php
E-mail medadmissions@mailplus.wisc.edu

Public Institution

Dr. Robert N. Golden, Dean

Lucy J. Wall, Assistant Dean for Admissions

Dr. Gloria V. Hawkins, Assistant Dean for Multicultural Affairs

Amy J. Schrader, Senior Advisor Student Financial Services

General Information
The University of Wisconsin School of Medicine and Public Health has had a four-year program in medicine since 1924 and has the largest research commitment of any school or college on campus, receiving more than $230 million in extramural research support in fiscal 2007. National surveys consistently rank UW Hospital and Clinics among the finest academic medical centers in the United States.

Mission Statement
The University of Wisconsin School of Medicine and Public Health's mission is to advance health without compromise through service, scholarship, science and social responsibility. Our vision is through working together, University of Wisconsin Health will be a national leader in healthcare, advancing the well-being of the people of Wisconsin and beyond. Our values include excellence, innovation, compassion, integrity, respect and accountability.

Curricular Highlights
Community Service Requirement: Optional.
Research/Thesis Requirement: Optional.

The curriculum introduces students to the generalist practice of medicine by exposing them to community-based settings in the first and second years. There is a focus on active learning; case-based problem-solving; interdisciplinary teaching by basic science and clinical faculty throughout the first and second years; a four-year curriculum that prepares students for either a primary care or specialty career; diverse clinical clerkship experiences around the state, including inner-city and rural sites; and a six-week one-on-one preceptorship with an experienced clinician in Year 4. The senior year provides elective opportunities for study

at other institutions and abroad. Opportunities for research are available to medical students in individually arranged programs.

USMLE
Step 1: Required. Students must record a passing score for promotion.
Step 2: Clinical Skills (CS): Required. Students must only record a score.
Step 2: Clinical Knowledge (CK): Required. Students must only record a score.

Selection Factors
The Admissions Committee seeks students with diverse backgrounds and interests. Breadth and depth of academic and nonacademic interests and experiences, ability to communicate with others, motivation for medicine, service personal characteristics, and intellectual ability are some of the factors considered. Preference is given to residents of Wisconsin. Non-resident applicants compete for relatively few places. Secondary applications and interview invitations are sent to selected applicants.

Financial Aid
All financial aid allocated by the University of Wisconsin School of Medicine and Public Health is awarded on the basis of proven need. Need is calculated as the necessary expenses incurred while attending medical school minus the resources provided to the student by outside agencies, personal resources. Priority for financial aid, especially grant awards, will be given to students with the greatest need. The major proportion of total financial aid is available in the form of loans.

Information about Diversity Programs
The University of Wisconsin School of Medicine and Public Health is committed to increasing the number of physicians from groups underrepresented in medicine and those showing evidence of socioeconomically and educationally-disadvantaged backgrounds. Applications are encouraged from persons with socioeconomic disadvantages and from members of groups underrepresented in medicine.

Campus Information

Setting
The University of Wisconsin School of Medicine and Public Health and the Ebling Health Sciences Library are located in the new Health Sciences Learning Center. It is connected to the University of Wisconsin Hospital and Clinics and the School of Pharmacy on the west side of campus. The Learning Center features sophisticated instructional technologies, including advanced digital capabilities throughout its lecture halls, classrooms, clinical training and assessment areas, computing facilities, and distance education centers. The building was designed to enhance individual and small-group learning.

Enrollment
For 2009, total enrollment was: 634

Special Features
The UW medical degree program includes opportunities for global health experiences, a research honors track, rural and urban medicine tracks, the M.P.H. dual degree, and service in the community including free medical clinics. There is a balance between strong primary care and strong cuttng-edge research.

Housing
Housing information is available at *www.housing.wisc.edu.* Additional private housing is widely available within the city of Madison.

Satellite Campuses/Facilities
The typical UW medical student spends at least 16 weeks at clinical sites outside Madison and throughout the state of Wisconsin. Other locations are LaCrosse, Marshfield, Green Bay, and Milwaukee teaching hospitals, and community clinics in other cities.

Application Process and Requirements 2011–2012

Primary Application Service: AMCAS
Earliest filing date: June 1, 2010
Latest filing date: November 1, 2010

Secondary Application Required?: Yes
Sent to: Selected applicants
URL: Invitation only
Fee: Yes, $56 **Waiver available:** Yes
Earliest filing date: July 15, 2010
Latest filing date: December 1, 2010

MCAT® required?: Yes
Latest MCAT® considered: September 2010
Oldest MCAT® considered: April 2007

Early Decision Program: School does have EDP
Applicants notified: October 1, 2010
EDP available for: Residents only

Regular Acceptance Notice
Earliest date: October 15, 2010
Latest date: Until class is full
**Applicant's Response to Acceptance
Offer – Maximum Time:** Two weeks

**Requests for Deferred
Entrance Considered:** Yes

Deposit to Hold Place in Class: No
Deposit (Resident): n/a **(Non-resident):** n/a
Deposit due: n/a
Applied to tuition: n/a **Refundable:** n/a
Refundable by: n/a

Estimated number of new entrants: 208
EDP: 2, special program: 15

Start Month/Year: Mid-August 2011

Interview Format: Selected applicants are invited to interview. Regional interviews are not available. Video interviews are not available.

Other Programs

PREPARATORY PROGRAMS
Postbaccalaureate Program: No
Summer Program: No

COMBINED DEGREE PROGRAMS
Baccalaureate/M.D.: No
M.D./M.P.H.: Yes, http://pophealth.wisc.edu/mph
M.D./M.B.A.: No
M.D./J.D.: No
M.D./Ph.D.: Yes, http://mstp.med.wisc.edu/

Premedical Coursework

On-line courses accepted in fulfillment of prerequisites: On a case-by-case basis

Course	Req.	Rec.	Lab.	Sems.
Inorganic Chemistry	•		•	2
Behavioral Sciences		•		
Biochemistry	•			1
Biology				
Biology/Zoology	•		•	1
Calculus		•		
College English		•		
College Mathematics	•			1

Course	Req.	Rec.	Lab.	Sems.
Computer Science				
Genetics				
Humanities		•		
Organic Chemistry	•			1
Physics	•		•	2
Psychology		•		
Social Sciences				
Statistics	•			1
Advanced level biology	•			1

Selection Factors: 2009 Accepted Applicants

Proportion of Accepted Applicants with Relevant Experience (Data Self-Reported to AMCAS®)	
Community Service/Volunteer	73%
Medically-Related Work	90%
Research	87%

Shaded bar represents school's accepted scores ranging from the 10th percentile to the 90th percentile. School Median ● National Median ○

Overall GPA	2.0	2.1	2.2	2.3	2.4	2.5	2.6	2.7	2.8	2.9	3.0	3.1	3.2	3.3	3.4	3.5	3.6	3.7	(3.8)	3.9	4.0
Science GPA	2.0	2.1	2.2	2.3	2.4	2.5	2.6	2.7	2.8	2.9	3.0	3.1	3.2	3.3	3.4	3.5	3.6	3.7	(3.8)	3.9	4.0

MCAT® Total Numeric Score 9 10 11 12 13 14 15 16 17 18 19 20 21 22 23 24 25 26 27 28 29 30 31 (32) 33 34 35 36 37 38 39 40 41 42 43

Writing Sample			J	K	L	M	N	O	(P)	(Q)	R	S	T		
Verbal Reasoning	3	4	5	6	7	8	9	(10)	11	12	13	14	15		
Biological Sciences	3	4	5	6	7	8	9	10	(11)	12	13	14	15		
Physical Sciences	3	4	5	6	7	8	9	10	(11)	12	13	14	15		

Acceptance & Matriculation Data for 2009–2010 First Year Class

	Resident	Non-resident	International	Total
Applications	624	2504	9	3137
Interviewed	366	130	0	496
Deferred	5	6	0	11
Matriculants				
Early Assurance Program	0	0	0	0
Early Decision Program	2	0	0	2
Baccalaureate/M.D.	12	0	0	12
M.D./Ph.D.	3	6	0	9
Matriculated	127	41	0	**168**

Applications accepted from International Applicants: No

Specialty Choice

2005, 2006, 2007 Graduates, Specialty Choice (As reported by program directors to GME Track™)	
Anesthesiology	8%
Emergency Medicine	8%
Family Practice	12%
Internal Medicine	13%
Obstetrics/Gynecology	6%
Orthopaedic Surgery	4%
Pediatrics	14%
Psychiatry	4%
Radiology	5%
Surgery	4%

Matriculant Demographics: 2009–2010 First Year Class

Men: 78 **Women:** 90

Matriculants' Self-Reported Race/Ethnicity

Mexican American	0	Korean	3
Cuban	1	Vietnamese	3
Puerto Rican	1	Other Asian	4
Other Hispanic	2	Total Asian	26
Total Hispanic	4	Native American	0
Chinese	10	Black	9
Asian Indian	5	Native Hawaiian	0
Pakistani	1	White	137
Filipino	0	Unduplicated Number	
Japanese	1	of Matriculants	168

Science and Math Majors: 67%
Matriculants with:
   Baccalaureate degree: 99%
   Graduate degree(s): 13%

Financial Information

Source: 2008-2009 LCME I-B survey and 2009-2010 AAMC TSF questionnaire

	Residents	Non-residents
Total Cost of Attendance	$ 42,723	$ 53,847
Tuition and Fees	$ 23,598	$ 34,722
Other (includes living expenses)	$ 17,025	$ 17,025
Health Insurance (can be waived)	$ 2,100	$ 2,100

Average 2009 Graduate Indebtedness: $130,857
% of Enrolled Students Receiving Aid: 88%

Criminal Background Check

This medical school requires a criminal background check prior to matriculation.

Chapter 15:

Information About Canadian Medical Schools
Accredited by the LCME and by the CACMS

The 17 medical schools in Canada are members of the Association of Faculties of Medicine of Canada (www.afmc.ca) and affiliate members of the AAMC. They participate in the activities of both associations. Canadian medical schools are accredited jointly by the Liaison Committee on Medical Education (www.lcme.org, LCME) and the Committee on Accreditation of Canadian Medical Schools (www.afmc.ca/index-e.php, CACMS). All are M.D.-degree-granting schools with excellent educational programs.

Admission policies and procedures of Canadian schools are similar in many respects to those followed in U.S. schools; thus, many of the suggestions for applicants in chapters 1 through 9 will also apply. Schools vary with respect to the emphasis placed on selection factors, and applicants are encouraged to refer to the individual school entries for additional details.

Fifteen Canadian medical schools offer four-year educational programs; two, McMaster and Calgary, are three-year programs. Some students at the Université de Montréal are admitted into a one-year preparatory program prior to beginning the M.D. curriculum. McGill University's five-year M.D. program includes an initial year that must be completed by graduates of the province of Quebec's Collège d'en-seignement général et professionnel (CÉGEP).

Selection Criteria

As reflected in the individual school entries in this chapter, Canadian medical schools vary with respect to the number of years of undergraduate instruction required of applicants. Medical schools also vary with respect to recommended content during premedical undergraduate education. Table 15-A shows that physics, inorganic and organic chemistry, biology, biochemistry, humanities, and English are the most common subjects required in undergraduate education by the Canadian medical schools.

Language of Instruction

Three Canadian medical schools—Laval, Montréal, and Sherbrooke, all located in the province of Quebec—require students to be fluent in French as all instruction is in that language. Instruction in the other 14 schools is in English, and the University of Ottawa offers the M.D. curriculum in both French and English.

Table 15-A

Subjects Required by Two or More Canadian Medical Schools, 2010–2011 Entering Class

Required Subject	# of Schools
Biochemistry	6
Biology	7
Calculus	2
College English	4
College Mathematics	3
Humanities	3
Inorganic Chemistry	7
Organic Chemistry	8
Physics	6
Social Sciences	2

NOTE: n=17. Figures based on data provided fall 2009. Three of the 17 medical schools (Northern Ontario, McMaster, and Western Ontario) did not indicate specific course requirements and are not included in the tabulations.

Residency Requirements

In Canada, universities fall under provincial jurisdiction and the majority of places in each faculty of medicine are allocated to permanent residents of the province in which the university is located.

Not all faculties of medicine accept applications from international students. Conversely, some faculties of medicine may reserve positions for international students, possibly as part of agreements with foreign governments and institutions. Statistics compiled by the Association of Faculties of Medicine of Canada (www.afmc.ca) show that most medical schools admit international students. In 2007-08, 234 U.S. students applied to the 15 Canadian medical schools that supplied data and recorded a 4.7 percent success rate. In the same year, 346 non-U.S. international students applied to the 15 Canadian medical schools that supplied data and recorded a 4.7 percent success rate. The success rate for Canadian applicants to the same schools was 22.6 percent. Additional information about Canadian medical schools can be found in the Association of Faculties of Medicine of Canada publication, *Admission Requirements of Canadian Faculties of Medicine* (2009) (www.afmc.ca/publications-admission-2009-e.php).

Positions filled by international students in Canadian medical schools are not necessarily subsidized by provincial/territorial governments. As such, international students, including U.S. students, may pay higher tuition and fees compared to those of Canadian residents.

Academic Record/Suitability

Although an excellent academic record is a very important factor in gaining admission to a Canadian medical school, a great deal of effort is expended in assessing applicants' suitability for a medical career based on other factors. Personal suitability is assessed in a variety of ways by the schools; applicants who can demonstrate that they possess the qualities considered important in the practice of medicine may sometimes be admitted even if their academic record is not outstanding. Alternately, applicants with outstanding records who do not possess these qualities may not gain a place in medical school.

Most applicants to Canadian medical schools are interviewed prior to acceptance, so the interview information in Chapter 7 will be useful.

Medical College Admission Test (MCAT®)

Twelve Canadian medical schools require applicants to take the MCAT: Alberta, British Columbia, Calgary, Dalhousie, Manitoba, McGill, McMaster, Memorial, Queen's, Saskatchewan, Toronto, and Western Ontario.

Other Considerations

Canadian faculties of medicine do not discriminate on the basis of race, religion, or gender in admitting new students. The admission of Aboriginal students (First Nations, Inuit, Métis) is encouraged at several Canadian medical schools, including Laval, Sherbrooke, Montréal, McGill, Ottawa, Queen's, McMaster, Western Ontario, Northern Ontario School of Medicine, Saskatchewan, Alberta, and British Columbia.

The number of female applicants has risen dramatically in recent years, with correspondingly larger proportions of women in schools' entering classes. Women comprised 58 percent of the 2007–08 applicant pool, and the success rate for women was slightly higher than that for men. The 2007 entering classes at the 15 Canadian medical schools reporting data about male and female matriculants included 58 percent women and 42 percent men. Overall, 24 percent of applicants received at least one offer of admission.

Expenses/Financial Aid

Tuition and student fees for Canadian and non-Canadian students in the 2009 entering class are provided in Table 15-B and in individual school entries. Expenses vary from school to school and from student to student. Tuition at several Canadian schools is slightly higher for the first year than for successive years. Tuition and fees at all Canadian universities are expected to increase substantially in the next several years. Some financial aid information is provided in the individual school entries. Eligible Canadian students may apply for a Canadian Student Loan, or they may apply to the Department of Education in their province for a provincial student loan.

Table 15-B

Tuition and Student Fees for 2009–10 First-Year Students at Canadian Medical Schools (In Canadian Dollars)

Categories of Students	Range	Average
In-Province	$3,773–$20,022	$12,212*
Canada, Out-of-Province	$9,308–$20,022	$13,861*
Visa	$21,906–$49,965	$39,719*

NOTE: Figures based on data provided fall 2009

* Average In-Province data were derived from all 17 Canadian schools. Average Out-of-Province data were derived from all 17 Canadian schools reporting. Average visa data were derived from 5 schools that accept foreign students.

Source: Association of Faculties of Medicine of Canada

University of Alberta
Faculty of Medicine and Dentistry
Edmonton, Alberta

2-45 Medical Sciences Building
University of Alberta
Faculty of Medicine and Dentistry
Edmonton, Alberta
Canada, T6G 2H7
T 780 492 6350   **F** 780 492 9531

Contact: Diane Baker, Administrator, MD Admissions
Admissions http://med.ualberta.ca/UME
Main www.med.ualberta.ca
Financial www.registrar.ualberta.ca/ro.cfm?id=287
E-mail admission@med.ualberta.ca

General Information

The Faculty of Medicine & Dentistry at the University of Alberta in Edmonton has a storied history of success in world-class research, education and patient care. Established in 1913, it is now home to 20 departments, nine divisions, and many research groups, centres and institutions. The Medical Sciences Building, Clinical Sciences Building, Walter C Mackenzie Health Sciences Centre, Mazankowski Alberta Heart Institute and the University of Alberta Hospitals are located on the university campus. Clinical instruction is also given at the Royal Alexandra Hospital, Edmonton General Hospital, Misericordia Hospital, Alberta Hospital, Glenrose Hospital, Cross Cancer Institute and Grey Nuns Hospital.

Mission Statement

Dedicated to the optimizations of health through scholarship and leadership in our education programs, in fundamental and applied research, and in the prevention and treatment of illness in conjunction with Alberta Health Services and other partners. Search and service, making important contributions to health. Vision: To be nationally and internationally recognized leaders investing in education, research and service, making important contributions to health.

Curricular Highlights

Community Service Requirement: Required. Rural Family Medicine training.
Research/Thesis Requirement: Optional.

The objectives of our medical education program leading to the M.D. degree are achieved through a four-year program. Years 1 and 2 are the pre-clinical years in which the material is presented in a series of system-based course blocks. Each block presents the material in a reasoned progression from basic information to clinical application. There are two separate, but coordinated courses, dealing with the social /sociological and public/health aspects of medicine, which are scheduled throughout this period. Years 3 and 4 are the clinical years. Third year is 52 weeks duration and includes the Link Course followed by clinical rotations, electives and holidays (4 weeks). A new innovative 34 week Longitudinal Integrated Clerkship is an available option. Fourth year commences immediately after the end of third year and is composed of further clinical studies, rotations and

electives plus holidays (3 weeks). It ends with a Review course and exams. Throughout the program, emphasis is on self-education; much instruction is on a small-group basis. A graduate training program leading to eligibility for specialist qualifications by the Royal College of Physicians and Surgeons of Canada is offered in most clinical specialties.

Selection Factors

The Admissions Committee selects applicants without discrimination to gender, race, religion, or age, and attempts to apply five criteria: undergraduate academic achievement, employment history, extracurricular activities, letters of recommendation, and the MCAT. Final applicants will be required to attend an interview at the University of Alberta at their own expense. Preference is given to Alberta residents. The University of Alberta does not accept applications from international students. Applicants who have been asked to withdraw or who have been suspended or expelled from any medical school will not usually be considered. There are five positions over the regular quota of 172 for the M.D. program to Aboriginal applicants.

Financial Aid

Majority of students obtain financial aid through student loans and lines of credit. The Student Awards Office will provide information to students about student loans, bursaries and awards.

Special Features

Students train in one of Canada's leading clinical, research, and teaching hospitals. The UAH treats more than 700,000 patients annually and is recognized as a national leader in organ and tissue transplant, both in success rates and in transplant volumes. Other major facilities are the Stollery Children's Hospital, Alberta Diabetes Institute, Mazankowski Alberta Heart Institute and the future Lois Hole Women's Pavilion.

Information about Diversity Programs

5 positions above quota for aborginal and 11 positions above quota for rural applicants.

Application & Acceptance Policies

Filing of Application:
Earliest filing date: July 2, 2010
Latest filing date: November 1, 2010
Secondary Application Required?: Yes
Fee: Yes, $115   **Waiver available:** No

MCAT® required?: Yes

Interview Format: Multiple mini-interview (MMI). Regional interviews are not available. Video interviews are not available.

Acceptance Notice:
Earliest date: May 15, 2011
Latest date: Until class is full

Applicant's response to offer:
Maximum time: 10 business days

Deposit to Hold Place in Class: Yes

Start Month/Year: August 2011

International Applicants Accepted: No

Criminal background check: Required

2009–2010 First Year Class

	Residents	Non-residents	International
Applicants	614	570	n/a
Interviewed	407	66	n/a
Matriculated	178	10	n/a

Total Matriculants: 188   **Total Enrollment: 630**

Premedical Coursework

Course	Req.	Rec.	Lab.	Sems.
Inorganic Chemistry	•			6
Behavioral Sciences				
Biochemistry	•			3
Biology	•			6
Biology/Zoology				
Calculus				
College English	•			6
College Mathematics				
Computer Science				
Genetics				
Humanities				
Organic Chemistry	•			6
Physics	•			6
Psychology				
Social Sciences				
Statistics	•			3

Financial Information

	Residents	Non-residents
Total Cost of Attendance	$ 14,421	$14,421
Tuition and Fees	$12,268	$12,268

University of Calgary Faculty of Medicine
Calgary, Alberta

Office of Admissions
University of Calgary, Faculty of Medicine
3330 Hospital Drive, N.W.
Calgary, Alberta
Canada, T2N 4N1
T 403 220 4262   **F** 403 210 8148

Contact: Adele Meyers, Admissions Officer
Admissions www.medicine.ucalgary.ca
Main www.medicine.ucalgary.ca
Financial www.ucalgary.ca/UofC/students/awards
E-mail ucmedapp@ucalgary.ca

General Information
The Faculty of Medicine at the University of Calgary accepted its first students in September 1970. In 1972, the Faculty of Medicine moved into its permanent facilities in the Calgary Health Sciences Centre. The centre has been designed to complement the objectives of the faculty's integrated teaching program.

Mission Statement
We wish to be a medical school which is: responsive to community and societal needs; determined to shape the future of society; rooted in basic research and discovery; committed to excellence and pursuit of excellence and to continuous improvement in all endeavors; and committed to innovation and creativity.

Curricular Highlights
Community Service Requirement: Optional. Strongly recommended.
Research/Thesis Requirement: Optional.

The curriculum is based on clinical presentations of the way patients present to physicians. One hundred twenty clinical presentations have been defined, ranging from simple to complex, and they are grouped by body system and human development. The clinical presentation curriculum teaches the basic science and clinical knowledge pertinent to each clinical presentation and provides an approach to the solution of the clinical problems. The Introductory Clinical Skills of Communication and Physical Examination commence in the first weeks of the curriculum. The curriculum maintains an active learning environment with more than 25 percent of scheduled instructional activities spent in small-group, case-based learning sessions. Students have the opportunity to reinforce in a clinical setting what they have learned in the body systems as they progress through each of the systems. The curriculum also focuses on the relevance of the family and the community in health and disease. The school employs a pass/fail grading system. Each academic year lasts about 11 months. At the end of the three years, students will be granted the M.D. degree. The school's philosophy is to produce generalist physicians who can proceed to further training in specialty, family medicine, or research.

Selection Factors
The Admissions Committee selects applicants without discrimination to gender, race, religion, or age, and attempts to apply five criteria: undergraduate academic achievement, employment history, extracurricular activities, letters of recommendation, and the MCAT. Final applicants will be required to attend an interview at the University of Calgary at their own expense. Final applicants will also be required to write an on-site essay on a topic assigned by the Admissions Committee. Preference is given to Alberta residents. The University of Calgary does not accept applications from individual international students. Presently, seats for international students are limited to those students who come from institutions/countries with whom the Faculty of Medicine has a formal, contractual agreement. Rejected applicants are given the opportunity to reapply for admission. Applicants who have been asked to withdraw or who have been suspended or expelled from any medical school will not usually be considered.

Financial Aid
The majority of students obtain financial aid through student loans and lines of credit. Because students attend school 11 months each year, summer employment is unlikely, and, therefore, financial support must be sufficient to meet their requirements over the subsequent three years. The student awards officer will provide information about student loans, bursaries, and awards. The financial status of the applicant does not affect acceptance into the program. Students receive a total stipend of $3,420 for the third (final) year.

Special Features
The Health Sciences Centre offers students state-of-the-art facilities. Students are encouraged to pursue electives in developing countries.

Satellite Campuses/Facilities
Students have clinical experiences on-site at the Foothills Medical Centre, as well as at two other general hospitals and the children's hospital in Calgary. During the final year, they may rotate through hospitals in smaller centers in the province, in addition to doing electives outside of Alberta.

Application & Acceptance Policies
Filing of Application:
Earliest filing date: July 15, 2010
Latest filing date: October 15, 2010
Secondary Application Required?: No
Fee: No   **Waiver available:** No

MCAT® required?: Yes

Interview Format: A series of short standardized interviews.

Acceptance Notice:
Earliest date: May 15, 2011
Latest date: Varies

Applicant's response to offer:
Two weeks. Less for offers to applicants on the waitlist.

Deposit to Hold Place in Class: Yes

Start Month/Year: August 2011

International Applicants Accepted: No

Criminal background check: Required

2009–2010 First Year Class

	Residents	Non-residents	International
Applicants	950	900	n/a
Interviewed	440	120	n/a
Matriculated	152	28	n/a
Total Matriculants: 180		**Total Enrollment: 465**	

Premedical Coursework

Course	Req.	Rec.	Lab.	Sems.
Inorganic Chemistry		•		2
Behavioral Sciences				
Biochemistry		•		2
Biology		•		2
Biology/Zoology				
Calculus		•		1
College English		•		2
College Mathematics				
Computer Science				
Genetics				
Humanities				
Organic Chemistry		•		2
Physics		•		2
Psychology		•		1
Social Sciences		•		1
Statistics		•		1

Financial Information

	Residents	Non-residents
Total Cost of Attendance	$35,000	$86,000
Tuition and Fees	$14,000	$65,000

University of British Columbia
Faculty of Medicine
Vancouver, British Columbia

MD Undergraduate Program
Faculty of Medicine, Dean's Office
University of British Columbia
317-2194 Health Sciences Mall
Vancouver, British Columbia
Canada, V6T 1Z3
T 604 875 8298   F 604 822 6061

Contact: Denis Hughes, Director, Admissions
Admissions www.med.ubc.ca/admissionsmd
Main www.med.ubc.ca/home.htm
Financial www.med.ubc.ca/education/md_ugrad/
financial_assistance.htm
E-mail admissions.md@ubc.ca

General Information
The expansion and distribution of the UBC Faculty of Medicine undergraduate program began in 2002, creating a partnership in medical education with the University of Northern British Columbia, the University of Victoria, and the regional Health Authorities. In September 2011, UBC Faculty of Medicine undergraduate program will add a fourth site at the University of British Columbia - Okanagan in Kelowna. The expansion provides an education model for other Canadian jurisdictions and advances BC's economic and educational capacity. The photograph above was provided by Bunting Coady Architects.

Mission Statement
The M.D. Undergraduate Program recruits, admits, educates, and supports students who will graduate with defined and demonstrated personal qualities, competencies, knowledge, and behaviors rooted in the vision, missions, and values of UBC and its Faculty of Medicine, and in an ethical context of social responsibility for the health needs of British Columbians.

Curricular Highlights
Community Service Requirement: Required.
Research/Thesis Requirement: Optional.

The program is built on principles of student self-directed learning, integration of biomedical and social sciences, early clinical contact, information management, professional development, and social responsibility. See the UBC Web site for information at *www.med.ubc.ca/education/md_ugrad/Schedule_Courses.htm*.

Selection Factors
The selection of candidates for admission to UBC's medical school is governed by guidelines established by the Senate of UBC, and is the responsibility of the Faculty of Medicine Admissions Selection Committee. See the Web site for selection criteria at *www.med.ubc.ca/education/md_ugrad/MD_Undergraduate_Admissions/Selection.htm*. The UBC Faculty of Medicine's Associate Dean of Admissions oversees the selection process to ensure that all applicants are given careful consideration without regard to age, gender, sexual orientation, race, ancestry, color, place of origin, family status, physical or mental disability, political belief, religion, or marital or economic status.

Special Features
The 40,000 square meter UBC Life Sciences Centre is located on the University of British Columbia campus. It houses basic science departments and teaching and research laboratories. The Northern Health Sciences Centre and the Medical Sciences Building use state-of-the-art technology in the delivery of medical education. The buildings contain labs, lecture halls, classrooms, small seminar rooms, and student common areas.

Financial Aid
UBC and the Faculty of Medicine are committed to ensuring that financial circumstances are not a barrier to qualified domestic students. Graduates who practice in rural areas are eligible for a number of financial incentives. For information regarding financial aid and awards, please contact the Student Financial Assistance Officer Faculty of Medicine, MD Undergraduate Program by telephone at (604) 875-5834, toll free at (1-877) 875-7800, or studentfinances@medd.med.ubc.ca. Additional information is available at *www.med.ubc.ca/education/md_ugrad/financial_assistance.htm*.

Information about Diversity Programs
The UBC Faculty of Medicine is committed to increasing opportunities for Aboriginal (Status or Non-Status Indians, Treaty, First Nations, Metis, or Inuit) applicants through the Aboriginal Admissions Subcommittee. Contact James Andrew, Aboriginal Programs Coordinator, for more information at james.andrew@ubc.ca or 604-875-4111, ext 68946. Applicants with disabilities are considered in accordance with UBC's policy on Academic Accommodation for Students with Disabilities. The Northern Medical Program provides an opportunity to complete undergraduate training in a northern regional centre and may be of particular interest to those applicants who come from, or are interested in, rural, remote, or northern communities.

Application & Acceptance Policies

Filing of Application:
Earliest filing date: June 1, 2010
Latest filing date: September 1, 2010
Secondary Application Required?: Yes
Fee: $105 – $185   **Waiver available:** No

MCAT® required?: Yes

Interview Format: Multiple Mini-Interview. Regional interviews are currently not available.

Acceptance Notice:
Earliest date: Mid-May 2011
Latest date: Until Class is Full

Applicant's response to offer:
Maximum time: Varies

Deposit to Hold Place in Class: Yes

Start Month/Year: August 2011

International Applicants Accepted: No

Criminal background check: Required

2009–2010 First Year Class

	Residents	Non-residents	International
Applicants	1169	469	n/a
Interviewed	615	49	n/a
Matriculated	244	12	n/a
Total Matriculants: 256		**Total Enrollment: 1024**	

Premedical Coursework

Course	Req.	Rec.	Lab.	Sems.
Inorganic Chemistry	•			2
Behavioral Sciences		•		
Biochemistry	•			2
Biology	•			2
Biology/Zoology				
Calculus				
College English	•			2
College Mathematics				
Computer Science				
Genetics		•		
Humanities				
Organic Chemistry	•			2
Physics		•		
Psychology				
Social Sciences				
Other				

Financial Information

	Residents	Non-residents
Total Cost of Attendance	n/c	n/c
Tuition and Fees	$15,154	n/c

University of Manitoba Faculty of Medicine
Winnipeg, Manitoba

Chair, Admissions Committee
Faculty of Medicine
University of Manitoba
260-727 McDermot Avenue
Winnipeg, Manitoba
Canada, R3E 3P5
T 204 789 3499 F 204 789 3929

Contact: Ms. Heather Christensen, Administrator, Admissions and Enrolment Services
Admissions www.umanitoba.ca/medicine/admissions
Main www.umanitoba.ca/medicine
Financial http://umanitoba.ca/admin/financial_services
E-mail registrar_med@umanitoba.ca

General Information
Medical education in Manitoba is designed to provide students with the knowledge and experience they need to practice medicine in a profession where new developments in science and public health policy create an ever-changing environment. In the first two years of the program, the subject matter is divided into blocks which cover core concepts in health and medicine, human development, and body systems. Clinical Skills, Problem-Solving, Medical Humanities, Law, Laboratory and Investigative Medicine, Health Equity and Survival Tactics are integrated into the six blocks. The final two years, called the "clerkship," are spent in direct contact with patients and doctors in a clinical setting in which students gain experience with increasing responsibility for patient care and management. General teaching facilities are located in the medical buildings, and facilities for clinical instruction are provided in the teaching hospitals affiliated with the University of Manitoba and in related institutions. The varied settings in which medicine is practiced in Winnipeg and in rural and northern Manitoba also provide students with the opportunity to study community medicine outside the major teaching institutions. For more information on the institution, please visit the Web site.

Mission Statement
The mission of the Faculty of Medicine is to: develop, deliver, and evaluate high quality educational programs for undergraduate and postgraduate students of medicine and medical rehabilitation, for graduate students and postdoctoral fellows in basic medical sciences and for physicians to practice; to conduct research and other scholarly enquiry into the basic and applied medical sciences; and to provide advice, disseminate information to health professions and plan for the development and delivery of health care services; and to help improve health status and service delivery to the Province of Manitoba and the wider community.

Curricular Highlights
Community Service Requirement: Optional.
Research/Thesis Requirement: Optional.

For information regarding curriculum, scheduling, and enrichment programs, please refer to the links posted at: *www.umanitoba.ca/faculties/medicine/education/undergraduate.html.*

Selection Factors
Selection by the Admissions Committee is made on the basis of (1) adjusted grade-point (GPA is calculated on a 4.5 scale); (2) MCAT; and (3) personal assessment score (PAS). All students must be Canadian citizens or permanent residents of Canada. Preference is given to residents of Manitoba and Aboriginal applicants, although a limited number of Out of Province applicants are accepted. For more information, see the Applicant Information Bulletin: *www.umanitoba.ca/faculties/medicine/admissions.*

Financial Aid
Under the Canadian Students Loan Act, Canadians can obtain interest-free loans during their undergraduate course in medicine. Bursaries from the University, the Manitoba Medical College Foundation, and the provincial government are available to deserving students. Applications for these bursaries are available when classes commence. Students may also obtain assistance from the W. K. Kellogg Student Loan Program. Several entrance scholarships are also offered annually.

Information on Diversity Programs
The Health Careers Access Program: University of Manitoba's Access program provides support to persons who have traditionally not had the opportunity for advanced education because of social, economic, or cultural reasons or lack of formal education. This program is exclusive to Aboriginal (Metis, Status, Non-Status, Inuit) residents of Manitoba with a strong interest in becoming a health professional. Sponsorship includes academic and personal support and may include some financial assistance. These programs are funded by Manitoba Education and Training, Advanced Education and Skills Training Division.

Housing
On-campus housing is not available at the Bannatyne Campus. However affordable apartments are available nearby. See: *http://umanitoba.ca/student/housing.*

Application & Acceptance Policies
Filing of Application:
Earliest filing date: August 16, 2010
Latest filing date: October 8, 2010
Secondary Application Required?: Yes
Fee: Yes, $95   **Waiver available:** No

MCAT® required?: Yes

Interview Format: Multi-Mini Interview (MMI). Regional interviews are not available.

Acceptance Notice:
Earliest date: May 13, 2011
Latest date: Until Class is Full

Applicant's response to offer:
Maximum time: Two weeks or as specified in the offer.

Deposit to Hold Place in Class: Yes

Start Month/Year: August 22, 2011

International Applicants Accepted: No

Criminal background check: Required

2009–2010 First Year Class

	Residents	Non-residents	International
Applicants	311	540	0
Interviewed	279	48	0
Matriculated	104	6	0

Total Matriculants: 110   **Total Enrollment: 421**

Premedical Coursework

Course	Req.	Rec.	Lab.	Hrs.
Inorganic Chemistry				
Behavioral Sciences				
Biochemistry	•			6
Biology		•		
Biology/Zoology		•		
Calculus				
College English				
College Mathematics				
Computer Science				
Genetics		•		
Humanities	•			
Organic Chemistry		•		
Physics		•		
Psychology				
Social Sciences	•			
Cell/Molecular Biology				
Statistics				

Financial Information

	Residents	Non-residents
Total Cost of Attendance	n/r	n/r
Tuition and Fees	$7,774	$7,774

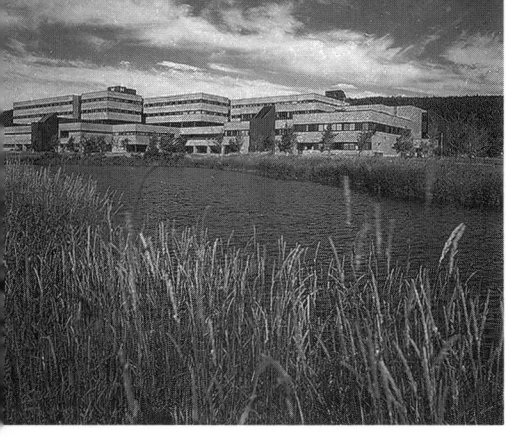

Memorial University of Newfoundland Faculty of Medicine

St. John's, Newfoundland

Memorial University of Newfoundland
Faculty of Medicine
St. John's, Newfoundland/Labrador
Canada, A1B 3V6
T 709 777 6615   **F** 709 777 8422

Contact: Janet McHugh, Admissions Officer
Admissions www.med.mun.ca/admissions
Main www.med.mun.ca/med
Financial www.edu.gov.nf.ca/studentaid
E-mail munmed@mun.ca

General Information

Memorial is the only university in the province of Newfoundland. The university was established as Memorial College in 1925 and incorporated as a university in 1949. In 1959, campus buildings were erected on a 1,000-acre site. There are some 12,000 undergraduates and a faculty of about 1,000 (including visiting professors) working on the campus, which is situated on the periphery of St. John's. The medical school is fully accredited by the Committee on Accreditation of Canadian Medical Schools (CACMS) of the Association of Canadian Medical Colleges and the Canadian Medical Association and the Liaison Committee on Medical Education (LCME) of the Association of American Medical Colleges and the American Medical Association. Thus, the medical school is equivalent in every respect to other medical schools in Canada and the United States. Approved teaching programs for interns and residents are under the direction of the medical school. Research work is being conducted both in the hospitals and in the Health Sciences Centre.

Mission Statement

Our purpose is to enhance the health of people by educating physicians and health scientists, by conducting research in clinical and basic medical sciences and applied health sciences, and by promoting the skills and attitudes of lifelong learning.

Curricular Highlights

Community Service Requirement: Optional.
Research/Thesis Requirement: Optional.

The curriculum, the physical structure, and the administrative organization of the school were planned to allow for maximum cooperation among the various basic science and clinical disciplines. The M.D. degree is granted upon completion of the fourth year. Canadian students take the LMCC (Medical Council of Canada) Examinations and U.S. students take the USMLE (United States Medical Licensing Examination) Step 1 and Step 2. During the first year of the medical program, students take introductory courses in cell structure and functions, biochemistry, physiology, molecular genetics, pharmacology, microbiology, anatomy,

behavioral science, ethics, interviewing skills, and community medicine. In the second half of the first year and the second year, teaching has a systems approach; material from anatomy, physiology, pathology, and clinical medicine is presented in an integrated manner. The third year is a structured clinical clerkship that includes eight weeks of electives, and the fourth year is made up of electives and selectives. Rotations for Rural Medicine take place in the first, third, and fourth years. A pass/fail system is used for grading. Medical students may apply through the Offices of Undergraduate Medical Education and Research/ Graduate Studies for the M.D./Ph.D. program.

Selection Factors

The school admits students on the basis of residency priority as follows: bona fide residents of Newfoundland and Labrador, of New Brunswick, of Prince Edward Island, of other Canadian provinces, and non-Canadians. In every case, a high academic standard is required. Age by itself is not used as a basis for selection or rejection. However, both age and length of time away from full-time academic studies may be taken into consideration. Normally, the medical school does not accept transfer students from other medical schools. In rare circumstances, a transfer applicant may be considered if there is space available.

Financial Aid

Financial assistance is available to medical students through government student loan programs. Information can be obtained by contacting the Student Affairs Office at: Student Affairs Office, Faculty of Medicine, Memorial University of Newfoundland, St. John's, NL, A1B 3VC; by telephone: (709) 777-6690; or by e-mail: mdray@mun.ca.

Information about Diversity Programs

Although there is no formal affirmative action process at this medical school, the Admissions Committee does take into consideration the background of applicants in making its decisions.

Special Features

Health services are open to all students on campus.

Application & Acceptance Policies

Filing of Application:
Earliest filing date: July 1, 2010
Latest filing date: October 15, 2010
Secondary Application Required?: No
Fee: No   **Waiver available:** No

MCAT® required?: Yes

Interview Format: One hour interview with two interviewers. Regional interviews are not available.

Acceptance Notice:
Earliest date: March 1, 2011
Latest date: Until class is full

Applicant's response to offer:
Maximum time: Two weeks

Deposit to Hold Place in Class: Yes, $200

Start Month/Year: Mid-August 2011

International Applicants Accepted: Yes

Criminal background check: Not required

2009–2010 First Year Class

	Residents	Non-residents	International
Applicants	168	467	10
Interviewed	125	83	3
Matriculated	50	15	0

Total Matriculants: 65   **Total Enrollment: 261**

Premedical Coursework

Course	Req.	Rec.	Lab.	Sems.
Inorganic Chemistry		•		
Behavioral Sciences		•		
Biochemistry		•		
Biology		•		
Biology/Zoology				
Calculus		•		
College English	•			2
College Mathematics		•		
Computer Science				
Genetics				
Humanities				
Organic Chemistry		•		
Physics		•		
Psychology				
Social Sciences				
Other				

Financial Information

	Residents	Non-residents
Total Cost of Attendance	$27,500	$51,400
Tuition and Fees	$6,250	$30,000

Dalhousie University Faculty of Medicine
Halifax, Nova Scotia

Admissions and Student Affairs
Room C-124, Lower Level
Clinical Research Centre, Dalhousie University
Halifax, Nova Scotia
Canada, B3H 4H7
T 902 494 1874   F 902 494 6369

Contact: Evelyn Sutton, Assistant Dean, Admissions and Student Affairs
Admissions http://admissions.medicine.dal.ca
Main www.medicine.dal.ca
Financial http://as01.ucis.dal.ca/staccts/2009-2010/MD.pdf
E-mail medicine.admissions@dal.ca

General Information

Dalhousie University, a privately endowed institution founded in 1838, established the Faculty of Medicine in 1868. The main responsibility of the Faculty of Medicine is to the three Maritime Provinces of Canada (Nova Scotia, New Brunswick, and Prince Edward Island), which have a population of 1.7 million. The teaching hospitals located in the immediate vicinity of the medical school have a total of 2,300 beds covering inpatient and outpatient services in all branches of medicine.

Mission Statement

The Faculty of Medicine, Dalhousie University, strives to benefit society through equal commitment to exemplary patient care, education and the discovery and advancement of knowledge. We aim to create and maintain a learning and research environment of national and international stature, enabling our graduates and us to serve the health needs of the Maritime Provinces and Canada.

Curricular Highlights

Community Service Requirement: Optional.
Research/Thesis Requirement: Optional.

Dalhousie aims to provide a basic education that would permit a graduate to enter any branch of postgraduate training. Medicine One and Two begin in early September and extend through May. Medicine Three begins in late August/early September and ends the following September. Medicine Four begins in late September and extends until the following May. In the first year, students have extensive patient contact hours, with great emphasis on the development of clinical skills. During the first two years, students work in small groups with a tutor. The curriculum is organized around clinical problems to provide an integrated context for students to learn both basic and clinical science, and to begin the development of clinical reasoning skills. The third and fourth years are predominantly clinical, with third year comprised of 12-week units in the major disciplines. The fourth year is arranged with initial blocks of elective time. Students finish with a unit in Continuing and Preventive Care. Dalhousie offers post-graduate medical trainees university-arranged and university-supervised clinical training which meets national accreditation

standards. In all provinces with the exception of Quebec, the basis for licensure for the majority of trainees in a postgraduate training program affiliated with a CACMS/LCME medical school is successful completion of the two-part Medical Council of Canada Qualifying Examination (MCCQE), plus certification by either the College of Family Physicians of Canada or the Royal College of Physicians and Surgeons of Canada.

Selection Factors

Sources of information and factors considered by the Admissions Committee include academic requirements, ability as judged on university records and on the MCAT, confidential assessments received from referees of the applicant's choice and from any others the committee may wish to consult, interviews (selected applicants only), and place of residence. Detailed comments and explanations on these selection factors may be obtained in the Faculty of Medicine Calendar. Dalhousie does not discriminate on the basis of race, sex, creed, national origin, age, or handicap.

Setting

Dalhousie Medical School plays a direct and vital role in patient care in the Maritimes. Our students and residents experience "distributed learning" in over 100 teaching sites, including tertiary and community hospitals, continuing care facilities and rural physician offices throughout the Maritimes.

Housing

University housing and a comprehensive Student Health Service are available.

Regional/Satellite Campuses

The New Brunswick-based program will admit thirty students each year and the admission requirements are exactly the same as the Dalhousie MD program in Halifax except that all applicants to the New Brunswick program must meet the residency criteria to be considered a resident of New Brunswick.

Application & Acceptance Policies

Filing of Application:
Earliest filing date: July 1, 2010
Latest filing date: August 15, 2010
Secondary Application Required?: No
Fee: No   **Waiver available:** No

MCAT® required?: Yes

Interview Format: Interview format is Multiple Mini Interview. Regional interviews are not available.

Acceptance Notice:
Earliest date: March 15, 2011
Latest date: Varies

Applicant's response to offer:
Maximum time: Three weeks

Deposit to Hold Place in Class: Yes, $200

Start Month/Year: September 2011

International Applicants Accepted: Yes

Criminal background check: Not required

2009–2010 First Year Class

	Residents	Non-residents	International
Applicants	270	364	n/r
Interviewed	270	80	n/r
Matriculated	n/r	n/r	n/r

Total Matriculants: n/r   **Total Enrollment: 410**

Premedical Coursework

Course	Req.	Rec.	Lab.	Hrs.
Inorganic Chemistry		•		
Behavioral Sciences				
Biochemistry				
Biology		•		
Biology/Zoology				
Calculus				
College English				
College Mathematics				
Computer Science				
Genetics				
Humanities		•		
Organic Chemistry		•		
Physics		•		
Psychology				
Social Sciences		•		
Other				

Financial Information

	Residents	Non-residents
Total Cost of Attendance	n/r	n/r
Tuition and Fees	n/r	n/r

McMaster University, Michael G. DeGroote School of Medicine

Hamilton, Ontario

Michael G. DeGroote School of Medicine
McMaster University
MD Admissions, MDCL 3104
1200 Main Street West
Hamilton, Ontario
Canada, L8N 3Z5
T 905 525 9140 x22235   **F** 905 546 0349

Contact: Harold Reiter, Chair, MD Admissions
Admissions www.fhs.mcmaster.ca/mdprog/
admissions/admissions.htm
Main www.fhs.mcmaster.ca/mdprog
Financial www.sfas.mcmaster.ca
E-mail mdadmit@mcmaster.ca

General Information

The Faculty of Health Sciences at McMaster University offers programs in health sciences education, including undergraduate and post-graduate medical education. The clinical programs use the teaching hospital and extensive ambulatory facilities of the McMaster Division of the Hamilton Health Sciences Corporation, but they also involve clinical teaching units at the major Hamilton hospitals and surrounding community health care centers.

Mission Statement

"Together, Advancing Health Through Learning and Discovery."

Curricular Highlights

Community Service Requirement: Optional.
Research/Thesis Requirement: Optional.

The three-year M.D. program at McMaster uses an approach to learning that will apply throughout a physician's career. The components have been organized in a logical manner, with early exposure to patients. Flexibility is ensured to allow for the variety of backgrounds and career goals. Graduates of McMaster's Medical Program will have developed the knowledge, ability, and attitudes necessary to qualify for further education in any medical career. The goals for students include the following: the development of competency in problem-based learning and problem-solving, the development of personal characteristics and attitudes compatible with effective health care, the development of clinical and communication skills, and the development of the skills to be a lifelong, self-directed learner and self-reflective practitioner. To achieve these objectives, students are introduced to patients within the first Medical Foundation block of the curriculum. They are presented with a series of tutorial cases and questions requiring the understanding of principles and data collection. Much of the students' learning occurs within the small-group tutorial. Faculty members serve as tutors or sources of expert knowledge. The medical program is arranged as a preclerkship sequence of five Medical Foundations followed by clerkship. A Professional Competencies curriculum runs horizontally across the Foundations and into

the clerkship. There are elective opportunities, both in block periods and horizontal electives taken concurrently. The clerkship emphasizes the clinical application of concepts learned in the earlier Foundations and consists of experience in inpatient and ambulatory settings. These include internal medicine, family medicine, emergency medicine, surgery, psychiatry, obstetrics-gynecology, anesthesia, and pediatrics. Students will have the opportunity to work in both teaching hospital and community hospital environments.

Selection Factors

Students and members of the community and faculty are involved in the assessment of applicants. The aim is to select students who not only have the necessary academic standards, but who also display characteristics that are deemed to be important for the study and practice of medicine. These include characteristics that suggest sensitivity to the needs of the community; sensitivity to the emotional, psychological, and physical aspects of patients; the ability to detect and solve problems; the ability to learn independently; the ability to function as a member of a small group; and the ability to plan one's career in a way that reflects the needs of the community. Applicants rating highest in academic achievement and in non-cognitive qualities will be invited to the interview. From these applicants, 203 students will be selected for three campuses.

Financial Aid

The M.D. Program and the University Financial Aid Program offer a bursary program to assist students in financial need. The M.D. Program administers a small loans program for students in further need.

Special Features

McMaster's undergraduate medical program has become internationally known for its small-group, problem-based learning approach to medical education. Most recently, the school has been renamed in honor of the landmark and generous donation from philanthropist Michael G. DeGroote.

Application & Acceptance Policies

Filing of Application:
Earliest filing date: July 1, 2010
Latest filing date: September 15, 2010
Secondary Application Required?: Yes
Fee: Yes, $210   **Waiver available:** No

MCAT® required?: Yes

Interview Format: Multiple mini-interviews. Regional interviews are not available.

Acceptance Notice:
Earliest date: May 15, 2011
Latest date: Until class is full

Applicant's response to offer:
Maximum time: Two weeks

Deposit to Hold Place in Class: Yes, $1,000

Start Month/Year: Late August 2011

International Applicants Accepted: Yes

Criminal background check: Required.

2009–2010 First Year Class

	Residents	Non-residents	International
Applicants	3675	982	69
Interviewed	491	54	1
Matriculated	180	14	0

Total Matriculants: 194   **Total Enrollment: 553**

Premedical Coursework

Course	Req.	Rec.	Lab.	Hrs.
Inorganic Chemistry		•		
Behavioral Sciences		•		
Biochemi				
Biology				
Biology/Z				
Calculus				
College E				
College N		DATA NOT COLLECTED		
Compute				
Genetics				
Humanit				
Organic C				
Physics				
Psycholog				
Social Sciences				
Other				

Financial Information

	Residents	Non-residents
Total Cost of Attendance	$23,023	$106,137
Tuition and Fees	$20,023	$103,137

University of Ottawa
Faculty of Medicine
Ottawa, Ontario

Admissions, University of Ottawa
Faculty of Medicine
451 Smyth Road
Ottawa, Ontario
Canada, K1H 8M5
T 613 562 5409 **F** 613 562 5651

Contact: Chantal Renaud, Admissions Officer
Admissions www.uottawa.ca/prospective
Main www.medicine.uottawa.ca/eng
Financial www.uottawa.ca/student/englishguide/
1section/finance
E-mail admissmd@uottawa.ca

General Information
The University of Ottawa received its charter from the province of Ontario in 1866. It was founded by the Missionary Oblates of Mary Immaculate, who were its administrators until 1965, when important structural reforms were introduced through an act of the legislative assembly of the province of Ontario. The management, discipline, and control of the university are free from the restrictions and control of any outside body, whether lay or religious. The Faculty of Medicine was established in 1945.

Mission Statement
We explore, we learn, we care. We develop society's leaders who improve the health of Canadians and communities worldwide. We do this through the integration of education, research, patient care, and technology in an inclusive environment, in both official languages.

Curricular Highlights
Community Service Requirement: Optional.
Research/Thesis Requirement: Optional.
Students acquire the knowledge, skills and attitudes they need to recognize, understand and apply effective, efficient strategies for the prevention and management of the most common and most severe health problems. Emphasis is placed on self-learning; principles and facts are learned in a multidisciplinary fashion, in the context of clinical problems. Whole-class lectures and seminars are used to discuss basic concepts, explore new developments and provide overviews of the biomedical sciences fundamental to the practice of medicine. Training occurs in ambulatory, primary, secondary and tertiary settings, and the students function as members of the medical team in collaboration with other health professionals. The training fosters trust and compassion, communication skills, ethical professional conduct and patient advocacy. The program is scheduled over four calendar years and is divided into two sections. Pre-clerkship includes 64 weeks of study of essential biomedical principles and consists of six multidisciplinary units. The second section, of two calendar years duration is the clerkships and includes core rotations in, Internal Medicine, Surgery, Pediatrics, Obstetrics &

Gynecology, Psychiatry, Family Medicine, acute care as well as mandatory selective. A period of eighteen weeks is available for elective study in fourth year. All students must also complete a month in a rural setting.

Selection Factors
Academic excellence, the detailed autobiographical sketch, and interview rating are the main selection factors used. Academics are measured by an assessment of marks and by a comparison of the applicant's academic record with those of the other applicants. No preference is given to one academic program over another. The selection is not made by quota. No candidate will be admitted without an interview. It is highly desirable that the candidate who has a broad exposure to biology and physical sciences also have a broad exposure to the arts, humanities, and social sciences. Sex, race, age, religion, and socioeconomic status play no part in the selection process.

Financial Aid
Students may apply to the Student Financial Aid Office of the university and to their respective provincial governments for loan assistance. The Ontario Medical Association Bursaries and Loan Fund, the Kellogg Foundation Loan Fund, and a special bursaries fund are administered by the Awards Committee of the Faculty. The Association of Professors of the University also provides bursaries. Most of these awards are made on the basis of demonstrable financial need and good academic standing.

Information about Diversity Programs
In 2005, the Faculty established a dedicated admissions program for candidates of Aboriginal ancestry as part of its mission to improve access to better health care for Aboriginal peoples and to better serve society's needs.

Special Features
Medical students benefit from a diverse learning environment with a laptop-supported Web-based curriculum and case-based learning (CBL) approach combined with traditional learning methods.

Application & Acceptance Policies

Filing of Application:
Earliest filing date: July 2010
Latest filing date: September 15, 2010
Secondary Application Required?: No
Fee: No   **Waiver available:** No

MCAT® required?: No

Interview Format: Semi-structured, 45-minute interviews. Regional interviews are not available.

Acceptance Notice:
Earliest date: May 13, 2011
Latest date: Until class is full

Applicant's response to offer:
Maximum time: Two weeks

Deposit to Hold Place in Class: Yes, $1,000

Start Month/Year: September 2011

International Applicants Accepted: No

Criminal background check: Required

2009–2010 First Year Class

	Residents	Non-residents	International
Applicants	2804	1037	n/a
Interviewed	553	n/r	n/a
Matriculated	117	27	n/a

Total Matriculants: 144   **Total Enrollment: 616**

Premedical Coursework

Course	Req.	Rec.	Lab.	Sems.
Inorganic Chemistry	•		•	2
Behavioral Sciences				
Biochemistry	•			2
Biology				
Biology/Zoology	•		•	2
Calculus				
College English				
College Mathematics				
Computer Science				
Genetics				
Humanities	•			2
Organic Chemistry	•		•	2
Physics				
Psychology				
Social Sciences				
Other				

Financial Information

	Residents	Non-residents
Total Cost of Attendance	n/r	n/r
Tuition and Fees	$16,775	n/r

Queen's University Faculty of Health Sciences School of Medicine

Kingston, Ontario

Admissions Office, Queen's University
School of Medicine
68 Barrie Street
Kingston, Ontario
Canada, K7L 3N6
T 613 533 3307   F 613 533 3190

Contact: Jennifer Saunders, Admissions Officer
Admissions http://meds.queensu.ca/
undergraduate/prospective_students
Main http://meds.queensu.ca/home
Financial http://meds.queensu.ca/undergrad/
student_information/financial_awards_or_loans
E-mail queensmd@queensu.ca

General Information

The School of Medicine is an integral part of Queen's University. With a legacy of over 150 years of quality teaching and research, the environment and the flexibility of the curriculum complement innovative programs that provide the breadth of training required for practice throughout Canada.

Mission Statement

The mission of Queen's Medicine is to advance our tradition of preparing excellent physicians and leaders in health care. We embrace a spirit of inquiry and innovation in education and research.

Curricular Highlights

Community Service Requirement: Optional.
Research/Thesis Requirement: Optional.

The four-year Undergraduate Medical Program is structured in three sequential phases allowing students to progress from foundational knowledge through specific specialty applications and finally through clinical engagement during an eighteen-month clerkship. Our medical program is well known for the opportunities it provides for close personal interaction between students and faculty members, and for students obtaining relevant extensive hands-on clinical experiences under supervision, particularly in an ambulatory setting. Our medical culture offers opportunities for students to engage in the administration, development and evaluation of our medical curriculum and our governance structures. Our graduates are highly successful in obtaining postgraduate training positions and are known to be committed and enthusiastic professionals within their communities.

Selection Factors

Students are selected on the basis of a strong academic record and assessment of personal characteristics considered to be most appropriate for the study of medicine at Queen's University and for the subsequent practice of medicine. Candidates meeting the academic requirements are then assessed based on confidential letters of reference, the autobiographic sketch, and the personal interview. The Admissions Committee does not give preference to applicants who have studied in any particular university program nor any particu-

lar level of training. Place of residence and location of the university where studies have been undertaken are not criteria in selection. Age, gender, race, and religion are not factors considered in the selection process.

Financial Aid

Student financial assistance at Queen's University is offered through merit-based (scholarships) and need-based (bursaries, awards, and work-study) funding. The Student Awards Web site is located at *www.queensu.ca/registrar/awards.*

Information About Diversity Programs

Queen's University recognizes the critical shortage of aboriginal physicians in Canada and the need to educate more aboriginal physicians to serve as role models and to address the health care needs of Canada's aboriginal people. To meet this need an alternate process for the assessment of aboriginal candidates has been implemented. Candidates interested in this process should review the program's Web site for details.

Setting

The campus is located in Kingston, Ontario, a true university town with the benefits of a small community such as affordable cost-of-living, a peaceful waterfront, and minimal traffic and the cultural richness of an urban centre, including acclaimed restaurants, pubs, theatre and music. Kingston is ideally situated between Toronto, Montreal, and Ottawa.

Special Features

Queen's University School of Medicine produces physicians equipped to handle the complex, ever-changing world of 21st-century health care. Small class sizes, frequent interaction with professors, and a strong mentorship program make for a close-knit community at the school. A regional education model allows students to experience a broad range of health-care settings, while exposure to advanced health sciences research nurtures innovation and critical thinking. Early and extensive hands-on clinical experience is another distinctive feature of the program. Queen's offers all the advantages of one of Canada's leading medical schools—including an international reputation for exceptional graduates—in an intimate, supportive learning environment.

Application & Acceptance Policies

Filing of Application:
Earliest filing date: July 2010
Latest filing date: October 1, 2010
Secondary Application Required?: No
Fee: No   **Waiver available:** No

MCAT® required?: Yes

Interview Format: Panel interviews. Regional interviews are not available.

Acceptance Notice:
Earliest date: May 13, 2011
Latest date: Until class is full

Applicant's response to offer:
Maximum time: Two weeks

Deposit to Hold Place in Class: Yes, $1,000

Start Month/Year: September 2011

International Applicants Accepted: No

Criminal background check: Required

2009–2010 First Year Class

	Residents	Non-residents	International
Applicants	3000	n/a	n/a
Interviewed	725	n/a	n/a
Matriculated	100	n/a	n/a

Total Matriculants: 100   **Total Enrollment: 400**

Premedical Coursework

Course	Req.	Rec.	Lab.	Sems.
Inorganic Chemistry				
Behavioral Sciences				
Biochemistry				
Biology				
Biology/Zoology				
Calculus				
College English				
College Mathematics				
Computer Science				
Humanities				
Organic Chemistry				
Physics				
Psychology				
Social Sciences	•			2
Physical Science	•			2
Biological Science	•			2

Financial Information

	Residents	Non-residents
Total Cost of Attendance	n/r	n/r
Tuition and Fees	$16,878	$16,878

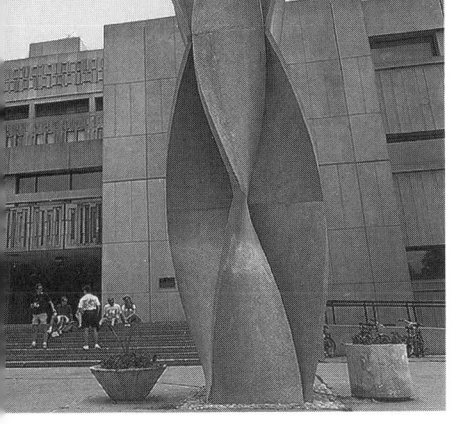

University of Toronto
Faculty of Medicine
Toronto, Ontario

University of Toronto, Faculty of Medicine
Medical Sciences Building, Room 2135
1 King's College Circle
Toronto, Ontario
Canada, M5S 1A8
T 416 978 7928 F 416 971 2163

Contact: Deborah L. Coombs, Coordinator, Admissions and Awards
Admissions www.md.utoronto.ca/admissions.htm
Main www.facmed.utoronto.ca
Financial www.md.utoronto.ca/students/finance.htm
E-mail medicine.admiss@utoronto.ca

General Information

Founded in 1843 as a school of medicine, the University of Toronto's Faculty of Medicine is an integral component of one of North America's largest health science complexes. The Faculty is part of a network of ten fully affiliated and seventeen partially affiliated teaching hospitals and health-care sites, as well as a myriad of community-based health units. With a catchment population of close to five million people, these offer students access to a broad spectrum of educational experience, and an extraordinary environment for clinical care, research, and education.

Mission Statement

We prepare future health leaders, contribute to our communities, and improve the health of individuals and populations through the discovery, application and communication of knowledge.

Curricular Highlights

Community Service Requirement: Required. Community placement during a longitudinal course.

Research/Thesis Requirement: Optional.

Our M.D. program is four years in length, with curriculum provided on two University of Toronto campuses, one in downtown Toronto and one in Mississauga. Placements in all years of the medical program, including core clerkship placements, are not limited to the major teaching hospital sites and will extend into the Greater Toronto Area (GTA), including Peel, York and Durham regions for all students. During the two-year preclerkship phase lectures, seminars and laboratory exercises complement small group, problem-based learning sessions. Additionally, two half-days per week are spent in community and clinical settings. During the clerkship, learning occurs on the wards and in ambulatory care units of the affiliated teaching hospitals in addition to community hospitals and physician offices. Students complete specific core clinical rotations, as well as 12 weeks in elective rotations.

Selection Factors

Applicants are judged upon both their academic and nonacademic records. A maximum of seven places will be offered to applicants with student visas. Applicants must have completed at least

one full-course equivalent in social sciences, humanities, OR a second language, plus at least two full-course equivalents in any life sciences. Successful candidates must be deemed acceptable in all aspects of the admissions process, including cumulative grade point average, MCAT scores, reference letters, nonacademic factors, English proficiency, performance on interview, and any other criteria put forward by the faculty.

Financial Aid

For most students, it will be necessary to incur some debt, through access to government student assistance programs and a private Line of Credit with a financial institution. The Faculty also provides needs-based assistance to eligible students, averaging $6000 per year. Applicants are advised not to plan to earn money in time-consuming work that may jeopardize their standing during the academic year

Information About Diversity Programs

The Faculty of Medicine supports mentorship and role-modeling for students from underrepresented groups through a number of programs. These include summer mentorship programs organized by the Faculty in collaboration with the Association for the Advancement of Blacks in Health Sciences. These programs include both black and Aboriginal students.

Special Features

The University of Toronto's Faculty of Medicine is an integral component of one of North America's largest health science complexes. The Faculty of Medicine provides the only M.D. training program in the Greater Toronto area, providing an extraordinary environment for clinical care, research, and education.

Satellite Campuses

Our M.D. program is centered on two University of Toronto campuses, one in downtown Toronto and one in Mississauga. Placements in all years of the medical program, including core clerkship placements, are not limited to the major teaching hospital sites and will extend into the Greater Toronto Area (GTA), including Peel, York and Durham regions. All students will be required to travel outside of areas served by local transit or hospital and University shuttle services in order to complete their studies.

Application & Acceptance Policies

Filing of Application:
Earliest filing date: July 5, 2010
Latest filing date: September 15, 2010
Secondary Application Required?: No
Fee: No   **Waiver available:** No

MCAT® required?: Yes

Interview Format: 45 minute interview with faculty and student. Regional interviews are not available.

Acceptance Notice:
Earliest date: May 15, 2011
Latest date: Until class is full

Applicant's response to offer:
Maximum time: Two weeks

Deposit to Hold Place in Class: Yes, $1,000

Start Month/Year: August 22, 2011

International Applicants Accepted: Yes

Criminal background check: Required

2009–2010 First Year Class

	Residents	Non-residents	International
Applicants	2880	n/a	39
Interviewed	530	n/a	2
Matriculated	224	n/a	0

Total Matriculants: 224   **Total Enrollment: 890**

Premedical Coursework

Course	Req.	Rec.	Lab.	Sems.
Inorganic Chemistry				
Behavioral Sciences				
Biochemistry				
Biology				
Biology/Zoology				
Calculus				
College English				
College Mathematics				
Computer Science				
Humanities	•			2
Organic Chemistry				
Physics				
Psychology				
Social Sciences	•			2
Life Science	•			4
Language	•			2
Statistics		•		

Financial Information

	Residents	Non-residents
Total Cost of Attendance	$38,332	$67,720
Tuition and Fees	$19,232	$48,620

Northern Ontario School of Medicine
Ontario, Canada

West Campus
955 Oliver Rd
Thunder Bay, ON, P7B 5E1
T 807 766 7300
F 807 766 7370

East Campus
935 Ramsey Lake Rd
Sudbury, ON, P3E 2C6
T 705 675 4883
F 705 675 4858

Contact: Miriam Lappala, Director, Admissions
Admissions www.nosm.ca/education/ume/
general.aspx?id=384
Main www.normed.ca
Financial www.nosm.ca/educatioon/ume/
general.aspx?id=384
E-mail nosmadmit@normed.ca

General Information
The Northern Ontario School of Medicine is the first new medical school in Canada in the 21st century. It is the Faculty of Medicine of Laurentian University, Sudbury, and of Lakehead University, Thunder Bay. With main campuses in Thunder Bay and Sudbury, the school has multiple teaching and research sites distributed across Northern Ontario, including large and small communities.

Mission Statement
The Northern Ontario School of Medicine is a pioneering faculty of medicine working to the highest international standards. Its overall mission is to educate skilled physicians and undertake health research suited to community needs. In fulfilling this mission NOSM will become a cornerstone of community health care in Northern Ontario.

Curricular Highlights
Community Service Requirement: Optional.
Research/Thesis Requirement: Optional.

Grounded in Northern Ontario, our four-year M.D. program provides students with a unique mix of learning opportunities in a diverse range of sites, including Aboriginal and Francophone communities. The curriculum is highly integrated, with students undertaking most learning in small-group, patient-centered Case-Based Learning. The cases present complex real-life scenarios, which present people in their home/family/community context. In addition to small-group learning, students participate in hands-on practical classes, self-directed learning, and clinical education in a range of different health service and community settings. Through the mix of themes and different learning modalities, the program covers core curricula, ensuring that students gain a strong grounding in the basic medical sciences, the humanities, social and behavioral sciences, and clinical medicine.

Selection Factors
Applications that meet the minimum requirement are assigned a score based on the grade point average, the autobiographic sketch and school submission questions, and context. Context is primarily based on place(s) of residence of one year or more. Advantage is given to those applicants from within Northern Ontario, rural and remote areas in the rest of Canada, and Aboriginal and Francophone applicants. Based on the total application score, the top-ranked candidates are invited to participate in the admission interviews. The final selection for admission is based on a combination of the total application and interview scores. Check our Web site for current information.

Financial Aid
Financial assistance is available to medical students through provincial and federal student loan programs. The Northern Ontario School of Medicine also has bursaries and other awards available for students enrolled in the medical program.

Information About Diversity Programs
Aboriginal applicants are given modest advantage. Aboriginal applicants can select either the General or Aboriginal Admission Stream. A minimum of 2 program seats are designated for Aboriginal students.

Special Features
The first medical school in Canada to be opened during the Digital Age, NOSMs four-year Undergraduate Medical Education e-curriculum emphasizes the use of broadband technology to bridge the distance between campuses, and to facilitate an extensive distributed learning model that is unique in modern medical education. NOSM is also the first Canadian medical school established with a social accountability mandate. From its community-based Board of Directors to its extensive reliance on Northern communities to act as hosts for its students, NOSM is committed to engaging Northerners in the education process. By the time the MD program is completed, the average NOSM student will have spent nearly forty per cent of his or her time studying off campus in Aboriginal, small rural and larger urban Northern Ontario communities.

Application & Acceptance Policies

Filing of Application:
Earliest filing date: 2010
Latest filing date: October 1, 2010
Secondary Application Required?: No
Fee: No   **Waiver available:** No

MCAT® required?: No

Interview Format: Multiple mini-interviews which take place at both campuses. Regional interviews are not available.

Acceptance Notice:
Earliest date: May 13, 2010
Latest date: Until class is full

Applicant's response to offer:
Maximum time: Two weeks

Deposit to Hold Place in Class: Yes, $1,000

Start Month/Year: August 2011

International Applicants Accepted: No

Criminal background check: Required

2009–2010 First Year Class

	Residents	Non-residents	International
Applicants	1845	0	n/a
Interviewed	391	0	n/a
Matriculated	56	0	n/a
Total Matriculants: 56		**Total Enrollment: 56**	

Premedical Coursework

Course	Req.	Rec.	Lab.	Hrs.
Inorganic Chemistry				
Behavioral Sciences				
Biochemistry				
Biology				
Biology/				
Calculus				
College				
College				
Comput	DATA NOT COLLECTED			
Humani				
Organic				
Physics				
Psycholo				
Social Sc				
Physical Science				
Biological Science				

Financial Information

	Residents	Non-residents
Total Cost of Attendance	n/r	n/r
Tuition and Fees	$17,920	n/r

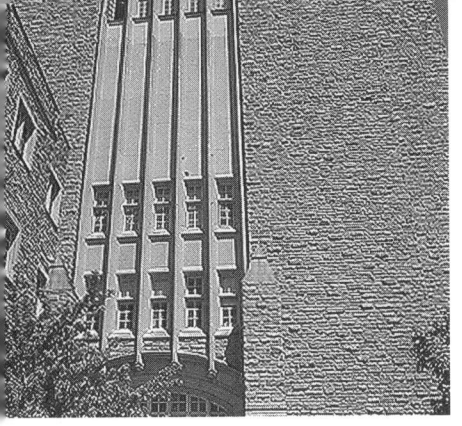

The University of Western Ontario, Schulich School of Medicine & Dentistry

London, Ontario

Admissions & Student Affairs
Schulich School of Medicine & Dentistry
The University of Western Ontario
London, Ontario
Canada, N6A 5C1
T 519 661 3744   F 519 850 2958

Contact: Pamela Bere, Manager, Admissions & Student Affairs
Admissions www.schulich.uwo.ca/education/admissions/medicine
Main www.schulich.uwo.ca
Financial n/a
E-mail admissions.medicine@schulich.uwo.ca

General Information

The Schulich School of Medicine & Dentistry at The University of Western Ontario has a long tradition of excellence, beginning with the founding of the medical school in 1881. Home to more than 1,800 faculty and 2,700 students in medicine, dentistry, medical sciences, graduate and postgraduate training, Western is one of Canada's oldest post-secondary institutions and is committed to providing the best student experience among Canada's leading research-intensive universities.

Mission Statement

The Schulich School of Medicine & Dentistry provides outstanding education within a research-intensive environment where tomorrow's physicians, dentists, and health researchers learn to be socially responsible leaders in the advancement of human health.

Curricular Highlights

Community Service Requirement: Optional.
Research/Thesis Requirement: Optional.

Programs of Study: The Doctor of Medicine program is offered from two sites - London and Windsor, Ontario. A section of each year's class will complete all of their academic studies on the campus of the University of Windsor and graduate from The University of Western Ontario. Curriculum and clinical training will be equivalent at both sites. The undergraduate curriculum is patient-centered in content and student-centered in delivery. It is designed to provide students with an opportunity to acquire the knowledge, skills, and attitudes required to advance to postgraduate training leading to clinical practice, research, or other medical careers. The format is a blend of lectures, laboratory experience, small-group learning sessions, and supervised clinical experiences. The curriculum in first and second year provides students with solid grounding in the basic and clinical sciences. System-based courses include: Introduction to Medicine, Blood, Digestive System & Nutrition, Emergency Care, Endocrine & Metabolism, Heart & Circulation, Infection & Immunity, the Musculoskeletal System, Respiration & Airways, Neurosciences, Eye & Ear, Psychiatry & Behavioral Sciences,and Reproductive & Urinary Systems. Students are also introduced to Community Health and have numerous oppor-

tunities for community involvement. The Clinical Methods courses span two years. During the first year, students participate in patient contact emphasizing a patient-centered approach. During third-year Clerkships, students become active members of clinical care teams in family medicine, medicine, obstetrics and gynecology, pediatrics, psychiatry, and surgery. Under faculty and senior resident supervision, clerks are given graded responsibility in the diagnosis, investigation, and management of patients in hospital, clinic, and outpatient settings. All third-year students are required to complete a community Clinical Clerkship in a region outside London or Windsor for a minimum of four weeks through Schulich's Southwestern Ontario Medical Education Network, to ensure students at all levels gain an understanding and experience of the practice of medicine from both a rural/regional and a tertiary care/urban perspective. Fourth-year Clinical Electives are arranged entirely by the student in any area of medicine. After completion of the Clinical Electives, students return in the Winter term for the Transition Period to complete advanced intergrative basic and clinical science topics.

Selection Factors

Admission consideration is based on academic achievement, MCAT scores, and a personal interview score. Only those applicants deemed competitive will be selected for an interview.

Financial Aid

The Schulich School of Medicine & Dentistry makes financial assistance for students in need a top priority.

Information About Diversity Programs

Schulich Medicine has designated three seats in each entering class for First Nations, Metis, and Inuit students who provide proof of Indigenous status or ancestral Indigenous origin.

Special Features

The Schulich School of Medicine & Dentistry is one of Canada's top centers for medical research and education, with more than $140 million annually in research funding and 49 accredited postgraduate specialty programs.

Application & Acceptance Policies

Filing of Application:
Earliest filing date: July 2010 (via OMSAS)
Latest filing date: September 2010
Secondary Application Required?: No
Fee: No   **Waiver available:** No

MCAT® required?: Yes

Interview Format: One physician, one community person, one senior medical student. Regional interviews are not available.

Acceptance Notice:
Earliest date: May 2011
Latest date: Until class is full

Applicant's response to offer:
Maximum time: Two weeks

Deposit to Hold Place in Class: Yes, $1,000

Start Month/Year: September 2011

International Applicants Accepted: No

Criminal background check: Required

2009–2010 First Year Class

	Residents	Non-residents	International
Applicants	2263	n/r	n/a
Interviewed	463	n/r	n/a
Matriculated	159	n/r	n/a

Total Matriculants: n/r   **Total Enrollment:** 591

Premedical Coursework

Course	Req.	Rec.	Lab.	Sems.
Inorganic Chemistry				
Behavioral Sciences				
Biochemistry				
Biology				
Biology/Zoology				
Calculus				
College English				
College Mathematics				
Genetics				
Humanities				
Organic Chemistry				
Physics				
Psychology				
Social Sciences				

Financial Information

	Residents	Non-residents
Total Cost of Attendance	n/r	n/r
Tuition and Fees	$17,040	$17,040

Université Laval
Faculty of Medicine
Quebec, Quebec

Admissions Committee
Universite Laval Faculty of Medicine
1050 Avenue de la Médecine, Local 4770
Quebec, Quebec
Canada, G1V 0A6
T 418 656 2131 x2492   **F** 418 656 2733

Contact: Evens Villeneuve, Admission Committee Chairman
Admissions www.reg.ulaval.ca/p4.html
Main www.fmed.ulaval.ca
Financial www.bbaf.ulaval.ca/bbaf/entree.htm
E-mail admission@fmed.ulaval.ca

General Information

Universite Laval was established by a Royal Charter in 1852 granted by Queen Victoria. It was named after Monseigneur de Laval, first bishop of Quebec. For more than 150 years, the medical school has been dedicated to the formation of health professionals through high standard teaching programs and research activities. Research opportunities are provided in all the basic sciences and in many fields of clinical investigation. The clinical teaching is provided through a network of affiliated health institutions. Residence accommodations are provided for many students. There is a University Health Service for students, as well as vocational guidance, and counseling services.

Mission Statement

The overall goal of the program is to assure a theoretical and clinical formation which prepares students for practicing medicine competently in a contemporary health system, with emphasis on an approach which is scientific, ethical, global, and humanistic. In addition, the program strives to prepare students for a lifetime of continued learning.

Curricular Highlights

Community Service Requirement: Optional.
Research/Thesis Requirement: Optional.

The curriculum aims to prepare students to undertake any career in medicine. During the first two years, the program provides early introduction to clinical problems and interdepartmental teaching by both basic science and clinical faculty. This part of the curriculum is designed to be flexible and can be spread over three calendar years. The basic clinical clerkships are given in the fourth and fifth years and provide a basic exposure to each major clinical discipline, including family medicine. Both faculty and students monitor the curriculum.

Selection Factors

Preference is given to applicants from the province of Quebec. Admission requirements for application from Quebec colleges (CEGEP) and universities include a standardized autobiographical note and Multiple Mini Interviews which is a subjective structured admission tool with 12 short-interview stations. This test eval-

uates different personal characteristics of the candidates. A few outstanding French-speaking candidates are admitted from other Canadian provinces and the United States. These candidates are selected on the basis of different parameters: scholastic achievement, interview, and curriculum vitae. Sex, race, religion, age, and socioeconomic status are not considered in the selection process.

Financial Aid

Financial aid is available to Quebec residents through the Bursaries Division of the Provincial Ministry of Education. Summer scholarships of $4,200 to $5,000 are also available to students who wish to devote their vacation period to research. There is no financial assistance for foreign applicants.

Information About Diversity Programs

Laval University School of Medicine, associated with other Quebec medical schools, has a program focused on integrating more aboriginal students with four dedicated seats each year. They are supported all along their medical formation.

Setting

The medical school is located in Quebec, a city famous for its walled old city center. Public transportation is widely available and makes travel very easy. Quebec is a lively French city with abundant cultural activities. There are several public parks, cultural institutions, cinemas, shopping areas, and natural areas. The city is surrounded by lakes, rivers, and mountains and enjoys four distinct seasons. Water and snow activities are easily accessible.

Special Features

The medical school has a international exchange program for talented students. Laval has reciprocity agreements with several countries, including Cuba, Peru, Nicaragua, India, Mali, Senegal, and China. The program has two stages: first, five to six weeks of observation and second, three months of medical training.

Application & Acceptance Policies

Filing of Application:
Earliest filing date: November 15, 2010
Latest filing date: March 1, 2011 (Quebec colleges), February 1, 2011 (all others)
Secondary Application Required?: No
Fee: No   **Waiver available:** No

MCAT® required?: No

Interview Format: Multiple Mini Interview (MMI). Twelve OSCE-style stations.

Acceptance Notice:
Earliest date: May 7, 2011
Latest date: Until class is full

Applicant's response to offer:
Maximum time: 10 days after the offer

Deposit to Hold Place in Class: No

Start Month/Year: September 2011

International Applicants Accepted: Yes

Criminal background check: Not required

2009–2010 First Year Class

	Residents	Non-residents	International
Applicants	1780	74	88
Interviewed	500	12	4
Matriculated	214	3	1

Total Matriculants: 218   **Total Enrollment: 218**

Premedical Coursework

Course	Req.	Rec.	Lab.	Hrs.
Inorganic Chemistry	•		•	1
Behavioral Sciences				
Biochemistry	•			1
Biology	•		•	2
Biology/Zoology			•	
Calculus	•			
College English				
College Mathematics	•			2
Computer Science				
Genetics				
Humanities				
Organic Chemistry	•		•	1
Physics	•		•	3
Psychology				
Social Sciences				
Other				

Financial Information

	Residents	Non-residents
Total Cost of Attendance	$5,000	$16,000
Tuition and Fees	$1,800	$12,000

McGill University Faculty of Medicine
Montréal, Quebec

Admissions Office
McGill University Faculty of Medicine
3708 Peel Street
Montréal, Quebec
Canada, H3A 1W9
T 514 398 3517 F 514 398 4631

Contact: Michel Dansereau, Admissions Officer
Admissions www.mcgill.ca/medicine/admissions/
Main www.mcgill.ca/medicine/
Financial www.mcgill.ca/studentaid/
E-mail admissions.med@mcgill.ca

General Information
McGill lies at the foundation, and stands at the avant-garde, of medicine and medical education in Canada. The Faculty of Medicine offers an extensive teaching hospital network, specialized centres and research units. American graduates of our program may return to the U.S. for residency.

Mission Statement
McGill's mission is the advancement of learning through teaching, scholarship, and service to society by offering the best education available; carrying out internationally-recognized scholarly activities; and providing service to society in those ways for which we are well-suited by virtue of our academic strengths. The Faculty of Medicine aims to pursue internationally significant scholarship and provide programs of the highest academic quality so that we may contribute to the well-being of humankind.

Curricular Highlights
Community Service Requirement: Optional.
Research/Thesis Requirement: Optional.
Our curriculum prepares students to meet the highest standards of medical practice and professionalism, cultivating career-long excellence in whole-person care. Graduates function responsibly, in a supervised clinical setting, at the level of "undifferentiated" physicians. Basic sciences and scientific methodology are emphasized as pillars of medical knowledge. Students experience traditional lectures, small group learning, lab- and computer-based teaching. There are 5 components to the curriculum. Basis of Medicine: a system-based, integrated approach to normal/abnormal functions of the body, providing students extensive opportunities for hands-on lab and patient contact sessions. Physicianship and Physician Apprenticeship: small group meetings throughout the 4-year program; focus on the roles of the physician as professional and healer, and on the knowledge, skills, attitudes and behaviours required to fulfil those roles. Introduction to Clinical Medicine: clinical experience (both in-patient and ambulatory) at the Medical Simulation Centre. Core and Senior Clerkships: these last two components involve rotations in urban and rural environments, and opportunities for electives.

Selection Factors
Pre-selection is based on academic achievement (GPA, MCAT, Science GPA), personal characteristics and accomplishments as evidenced in an autobiographical sketch, C.V. and references. All candidates are reviewed without regard to gender, age, ethnic, religious, linguistic, or socio-cultural/economic backgrounds. In general, successful applicants have an overall undergraduate degree GPA of 3.5+ and an MCAT total of 30+. Only pre-selected applicants are interviewed. Admission decisions are final and are not subject to appeal.

Financial Aid
McGill's Student Aid Office assists students with the financial resources necessary to help cover educational costs. For information on government aid programs, McGill scholarship funding, loans, bursaries, debt management, individualized budget counseling, and the Work-Study program: *http://www.mcgill.ca/studentaid/*

Information About Diversity Programs
The Faculty of Medicine is committed to pursuing its mission of social accountability, including the diversity of its student body and equity for under-represented groups, while maintaining its tradition of selecting students most apt for the challenges of medicine in the 21st century. The Faculty of Medicine welcomes applications from students from diverse backgrounds, including students from underrepresented ethnic, cultural and racial groups as well as from all economic backgrounds. Attempts to widen participation of members of under-represented groups are currently underway, through community information sessions, targeted recruitment activities, and contact with high schools, colleges, and various interest groups. Residents of Quebec who self-identify as belonging to the Inuit, Cree, and Naskapi First Nations cultural groups may apply under the aegis of the special program for First Nations and Inuit applicants.

Special Features
McGill's teaching hospital network is an integral part of the Faculty's research, teaching and clinical activities. It consists of the McGill University Health Centre (of 6 teaching hospitals), plus other affiliated urban and rural hospitals. The Medical Simulation Centre is another state of the art teaching facility.

Application & Acceptance Policies

Filing of Application:
Earliest date: September 1, 2010
Latest date: November 15, 2010 - non-residents; January 15, 2011 - residents
Secondary Application Required?: No
Fee: Yes, $85   **Waiver available:** No

MCAT® required?: Yes

Interview Format: Multiple mini-interview (MMI) format, on-site. Regional interviews are not available.

Acceptance Notice:
Earliest date: Early March 2011
Latest date: Until Class is Full

Applicant's response to offer:
Maximum time: two weeks

Deposit to Hold Place in Class: Yes

Start Month/Year: Mid-August 2011

International Applicants Accepted: Yes

Criminal background check: Not required

2009–2010 First Year Class

	Residents	Non-residents	International
Applicants	840	563	93
Interviewed	378	62	38
Matriculated	159	10	7

Total Matriculants: 176   **Total Enrollment: 699**

Premedical Coursework

Course	Req.	Rec.	Lab.	Hrs.
Inorganic Chemistry	•		•	6
Behavioral Sciences				
Biochemistry		•		
Biology	•		•	6
Biology/Zoology				
Calculus				
College English				
College Mathematics				
Computer Science				
Genetics				
Humanities				
Organic Chemistry	•		•	3
Physics	•		•	6
Psychology				
Social Sciences				
Cell/Molecular Biology		•		
Statistics		•		

Financial Information

	Residents	Non-residents
Total Cost of Attendance	$ 29,140	$ 52,678
Tuition and Fees	$ 6,422	$ 24,617

Université de Montréal School of Medicine

Montréal, Quebec

Comité d'admission - études médicales de 1er cycle
Université de Montréal
Faculté de médecine
C.P. Box 6128, Succursale Centre-Ville
Montréal Quebec H3C 3J7
T 514 343 6265   **F** 514 343 6629

Contact: Jean Paradis, President, Admissions Committee
Admissions www.med.umontreal.ca/etudes/programme_formation/doctorate_medicine/admission.html
Main www.med.umontreal.ca
E-mail admission-md@umontreal.ca

General Information

The Faculty of Medicine of the Université de Montréal can be traced back to a school first established in Montréal in 1843 and incorporated in 1845 under the name of École de Médecine et de Chirurgie de Montréal. In 1891 the school merged with the Faculté de Médecine of the Montréal branch of Laval University, which had been founded in 1877. In 1920, by an act of the Quebec legislature, the Montréal branch of Laval University was granted its independence, and the school of medicine became known by its present name. All instruction is in French, and clinical instruction is carried out at 15 affiliated teaching hospitals and research centers.

Mission Statement

The Faculty of Medicine of the Université de Montréal seeks through its undergraduate medical program to provide medical knowledge, clinical skills and professional attitudes so that students will be able to enter postgraduate training in family medicine or medical specialization, or fields related to research, teaching, or health care management.

Curricular Highlights

Community Service Requirement: Optional.
Research/Thesis Requirement: Optional.

In September 1993, a new four-year curriculum came into effect. It consists of two years (70 weeks) of problem-based learning during which students are exposed to biomedical and psychosocial sciences basic to medicine. Courses are interdisciplinary and system-based. Early introduction to clinical skills takes place in a continuous fashion throughout those two preclinical years. Clinical exposure begins with Year 1. Forty-five hours of electives are mandatory during each of the first two years. The third and fourth years consist of an 80-week clerkship. In the new curriculum, formal lecturing is reduced to a minimum and replaced by active methods, especially problem-based learning and small-group discussion. A premedical year devoted to basic biological and behavioral sciences is restricted to students having just graduated from the provincial colleges of general and professional education (CEGEP). Students who have completed one to three years at the university level in others than biomedical fields are also eligible for the premedical year. Residency training in the teaching hospitals is under the responsibility of the Faculty of Medicine. Various courses and symposia are organized by the continuing medical education division.

Selection Factors

Candidates accepted must be either Canadian citizens or landed immigrants, but due consideration is given to French-speaking applicants from other provinces of Canada. Selection of candidates is competitive and based on a global score derived from scholastic records and interviews. Interviews (Multiple Mini-Interviews), conducted on the site of the medical school, are granted to about one-third of the applicants on the basis of their scholastic records. This interview can be eliminatory. For candidates holding a Ph.D. degree, performance in research may constitute an important selection factor. No consideration is given to race, sex, creed, or age.

Financial Aid

Financial aid is available to students through the Bursaries Division of the Department of Education, the Kellogg Foundation Loan Fund, the Scholarships and Loan Committee of the university, and the Jean Frappier Fund. Summer scholarships are also available.

Information About Diversity Programs

Since 2008, a yearly total of four positions are reserved for Quebec aboriginal students (First Nations and Inuit)in the Faculties of Medicine of Quebec.

Satellite Campuses/Facilities

Since 2004, there is a regional campus in the city of Trois-Rivières, located 125 kilometers east of Montréal. Each year, thirty-two students start medical school on Trois-Rivières campus, most of them at the pre-medical level. The curriculums at the Montréal campus and Trois-Rivières campus are identical. Clinical training is completed at community hospitals in the Mauricie region. A medical student can complete his entire undergraduate instruction at this decentralized rural campus.

Application & Acceptance Policies

Filing of Application:
Earliest filing date: December 1, 2010
Latest filing date: January 15, 2011 (March 1, 2010 for Quebec CEGEP students)
Secondary Application Required?: No
Fee: No   **Waiver available:** No

MCAT® required?: No

Interview Format: Multiple Mini-Interviews (MMI). Regional interviews are not available.

Acceptance Notice:
Earliest date: May 15, 2011
Latest date: Until class is full

Applicant's response to offer:
Maximum time: Two weeks

Deposit to Hold Place in Class: Yes, $200

Start Month/Year: August 2011

International Applicants Accepted: Yes

Criminal background check: Not required

2009–2010 First Year Class

	Residents	Non-residents	International
Applicants	2101	44	156
Interviewed	795	8	3
Matriculated	267	3	1

Total Matriculants: 271	Total Enrollment: 1,267

Premedical Coursework

Course	Req.	Rec.	Lab.	Sems.
Inorganic Chemistry	•			2
Behavioral Sciences				
Biochemistry				
Biology	•			2
Biology/Zoology				
Calculus	•			2
College English				
College Mathematics				
Computer Science				
Genetics				
Humanities				
Organic Chemistry	•			1
Physics	•			3
Psychology				
Social Sciences				

Financial Information

	Residents	Non-residents
Total Cost of Attendance	n/r	n/r
Tuition and Fees	$5,000	$26,500

University of Sherbrooke Faculty of Medicine

Sherbrooke, Quebec

Admission Office, University of Sherbrooke
Faculty of Medicine and Health Sciences
3001, 12e Avenue Nord
Sherbrooke, Quebec
Canada, J1H 5N4
T 819 564 5208   **F** 819 820 6809

Contact: Daniel J. Cote, Chair, Admissions Committee
Admissions www.usherbrooke.ca/
doctorat_medecine
Main www.usherbrooke.ca
Financial www.usherbrooke.ca
E-mail admission-med@usherbrooke.ca

General Information

Officially founded in February 1961, the Faculty of Medicine and Health sciences at the University of Sherbrooke is a Franch-spaking institution. It admitted its first students in September 1966. The program has always and is recognized for its innovations and its engagement towards responding to the needs of commmunities it serses. The Faculty opened two outside campuses in September 2006: Saguenay (the central city of a Quebec peripheral region, 500 km from Sherbrooke) and Moncton (the central French-speaking city in the neighbor province of New Brunswick, 1000 km from Sherbrooke). Students complete the program either in the central campus in Sherbrooke (144-148 admitted students), or in Moncton (24 students), or in Saguenay (32 students).

Mission Statement

Improved health and well-being of people and populations through education, research, clinical services, and knowledge transfer.

Curricular Highlights

Community Service Requirement: Optional.
Research/Thesis Requirement: Optional.

The MD degree is granted after successful completion of the four-year program. Learning occurs through small-group problem-based learning in an integrated and system-based curriculum. IT facilities, seminars, small-group discussions, panels, field work, and case studies are used extensively. Learning of clinical skills starts during the first month of the program and goes through a continuous and integrated program throughout the preclinical years. The program is offered in thress different sites: Moncton (New-Brunswick), Saguenay and Sherbrooke (Quebec). Community-based education is a major characteristic of the 18 months duration clerkship. Clinical training starts with the winter trimester of the third year. Clerkship rotations are offered in a network of primary to tertiary health care institutions located in urban, suburban, peripheral, rural and remote areas in the Province of Québec and New-Brunswick offering complementary experience to the students. Each student must spend at least 1/3 of its clerkship in community-based settings. Postgraduate programs are available in most clinical disciplines including community health. MD/MSc and MD/PhD programs are offered to form scientific physicians who could pursue a career in research.

Selection Factors

The first selection step is based on cognitive ability and premedical achievement, as demonstrated by students academic records. The second selection step aims at assessing non-cognitive skills, through the TAAMUS (paper and pencil personality test) and MMI. Approximatily one-hundred and seventy (170) places are reserved for applicants from the province of Quebec. Three positions may be filled by French speaking students coming from Western Canadian provinces and Territories. In addition, twenty-four (24) places are reserved for applicants from New Brunswick, one (1) place is available for an applicant from Prince Edward Island and three (3) places are available for applicants from Nova Scotia. One (1) to six (6) places are available for Canadian Forces candidates. One (1) to four (4) places are available for applicants from First Nations and Inuits from Quebec and one (1) place is available for a qualified foreign applicant with a student visa. In 2009, 196 students entered into the program. Approximately 204 students should enter the program next year. Applicants must be fluent in both written and spoken French language.

Financial Aid

Financial aid is available to students through the Bursaries Division of the Provincial Ministry of Education, the Scholarships and Loans Committee of the university, and a few private foundations.

Satellite Campuses/Facilities

The Saguenay satellite campus is located at the Université du Québec à Chicoutimi and at the Chicoutimi regional Hospital. The Moncton satellite campus is located at the Université de Moncton and partners with Hospital Georges L. Dumont, the French speaking regional hospital in Moncton.

Application & Acceptance Policies

Filing of Application:
Earliest filing date: November 1, 2010
Latest filing date: Candidates must return their admission form before January 15, 2011, except for Quebec College students with no (0) university credit who can return their admission form until March 1, 2011.
Secondary Application Required?: No
Fee: Yes, $70   **Waiver available:** No

MCAT® required?: No

Interview Format: Multiple Mini Interview (MMI). Ten OSCE-style stations.

Acceptance Notice:
Earliest date: May 2011
Latest date: Until class is full.

Applicant's response to offer:
Maximum time: Three hours to 10 days, depending on when the acceptance notice is sent.

Deposit to Hold Place in Class: Yes, $200

Start Month/Year: August 2011

International Applicants Accepted: Yes

Criminal background check: Not required

2009–2010 First Year Class

	Residents	Non-residents	International
Applicants	1746	101	85
Interviewed	746	73	1
Matriculated	166	30	0

Total Matriculants: 196   **Total Enrollment: 796**

Premedical Coursework

Course	Req.	Rec.	Lab.	Sems.
Inorganic Chemistry				
Behavioral Sciences				
Biochemistry				
Biology	•		•	2
Biology/Zoology				
Calculus				
College English				
College Mathematics	•		•	2
Computer Science				
Genetics				
Humanities				
Organic Chemistry	•		•	3
Physics	•		•	3
Psychology				
Social Sciences				
Other				

Financial Information

	Residents	Non-residents
Total Cost of Attendance	$10,330	$17,600-31,000
Tuition and Fees	$4,960	$11,600-25,000

University of Saskatchewan College of Medicine

Saskatoon, Saskatchewan

Admissions
University of Saskatchewan College of Medicine
A204 Health Sciences Bld, 107 Wiggins Rd
Saskatoon, Saskatchewan
Canada, S7N 5E5
T 306 966 8554   **F** 306 966 2601

Contact: Heather Mandeville, Administrative Coordinator, Admissions & Student Affairs
Admissions www.medicine.usask.ca/admissions
Main www.medicine.usask.ca
Financial www.usask.ca/calendar/scholarships
E-mail med.admissions@usask.ca

General Information

The University of Saskatchewan began teaching medical students in a two-year medical sciences program in 1926. The present college was introduced in 1953, with a four-year curriculum leading to the M.D. degree. In 1968, the curriculum changed to five years with a one-year premedical university requirement. The curriculum reverted to a four-year program in 1988 with a minimum two-year premedical requirement. Clinical teaching is based at the Royal University, St. Paul's, and Saskatoon City Hospitals in Saskatoon, and the Plains Health Centre and General Hospital in Regina. Students also complete rotations in Saskatchewan Health Regions. The class size is 84 students with future possible expansions to 100 students.

Mission Statement

The College of Medicine is a departmentalized collegial unit of the University of Saskatchewan. The mission is to improve health through excellence in education, research, and clinical care.

Curricular Highlights

Community Service Requirement: Optional.
Research/Thesis Requirement: Optional.

The College of Medicine provides a curriculum leading to the general professional education of the physician; graduates may select careers in family medicine, specialty practice, or research. The current curriculum was launched in the fall of 1997. Phase A (31 weeks) provides students with an overview of the basic science disciplines appropriate to the study of medicine, as well as an introduction to professional skills (including primary clinical skills) within the context of developing the patient-doctor relationship. This phase includes a two-week clinical experience done in one of the Saskatchewan Health Districts. Phase B (33 weeks) enables students to acquire specific knowledge in those subjects bridging the basic and clinical sciences and to enhance basic clinical skills. Phase C (15 weeks), enables learning of the principles and methods in core clinical knowledge and linking courses. Phase D (64 weeks) of clinical clerkships provides an opportunity to apply the knowledge, skills, and attitudes students have acquired to

the management of patients. Provision is made for clinical electives. Learning in the basic and clinical sciences has been organized by body systems with a problem-solving emphasis.

Selection Factors

The Admissions Committee considers academic ability and personal qualities assessed through scholastic records, letters of recommendation, and results of an interview. All eligible candidates are interviewed during a weekend in March.

Financial Aid

Various loan funds and scholarships are available. A limited number of bursaries enable students to engage in research between the end of one academic year and the beginning of another.

Information About Diversity Programs

There is an Aboriginal Access Program for Canadian residents of Aboriginal ancestry. For more information, contact the Admissions office.

Setting

Our medical school is situated on 755 hectares of land, in the heart of the city of Saskatoon on the scenic bank of the South Saskatchewan River. Much of the original architecture remains from the University's opening in 1909, and greystone buildings ornamented with garrets and turrets are a monument of fine craftsmanship. The University of Saskatchewan has the largest collection of health sciences in Canada.

Satellite Campuses/Facilities

The University of Saskatchewan College of Medicine has a distributive learning environment in which a number of clinical educational experiences take place in a number of Saskatchewan Health Regions and teaching hospitals. Students will be assigned to a core set of rotations centered either in the Saskatoon Health Region or in the Regina/Qu'Appelle Health Region.

Application & Acceptance Policies

Filing of Application:
Earliest filing date: July 1, 2010
Latest filing date: October 29, 2010
Secondary Application Required?: No
Fee: No   **Waiver available:** No

MCAT® required?: Yes

Interview Format: Multiple Mini Interview. Regional Interviews are not available.

Acceptance Notice:
Earliest date: May 15, 2011
Latest date: Until Class is Full

Applicant's response to offer:
Maximum time: Two weeks

Deposit to Hold Place in Class: Yes, $500

Start Month/Year: August 2011

International Applicants Accepted: No

Criminal background check: Not required

2009–2010 First Year Class

	Residents	Non-residents	International
Applicants	379	510	n/a
Interviewed	277	47	n/a
Matriculated	84	n/a	n/a
Total Matriculants: 218		**Total Enrollment: 296**	

Premedical Coursework

Course	Req.	Rec.	Lab.	Hrs.
Inorganic Chemistry	•		•	3
Behavioral Sciences				
Biochemistry	•			6
Biology	•		•	6
Biology/Zoology				
Calculus				
College English	•			6
College Mathematics				
Computer Science				
Genetics				
Humanities	•			
Organic Chemistry	•		•	3
Physics	•		•	6
Psychology				
Social Sciences	•			6
Other				

Financial Information

	Residents	Non-residents
Total Cost of Attendance	n/r	n/r
Tuition and Fees	$12,056	n/r

Resources for Other Health Careers

1. **American Academy of Physician Assistants**
950 North Washington Street
Alexandria, VA 22314-1552
(703) 836-2272; (703) 684-1924
www.aapa.org

2. **American Association of Colleges of Osteopathic Medicine**
5550 Friendship Boulevard, Suite 310
Chevy Chase, MD 20815-7231
(301) 968-4100; *www.aacom.org*

3. **American Association of Colleges of Pharmacy**
1727 King Street
Alexandria, VA 22314-2815
(703) 739-2330; *www.aacp.org*

4. **American Association of Colleges of Podiatric Medicine**
15850 Crabbs Branch Way, Suite 320
Rockville, MD 20855-4307
(800) 922-9266; (301) 948-9760
info@aacpm.org; *www.aacpm.org*

5. **American Association of Colleges of Nursing**
One Dupont Circle, N.W., Suite 530
Washington, D.C. 20036
(202) 463-6930; (202) 785-8320
www.aacn.nche.edu

6. **American Association of Dental Schools**
1400 K Street, N.W., Suite 1100
Washington, D.C. 20005
(202) 289-7201; *www.adea.org*

7. **Association of American Veterinary Medical Colleges**
1101 Vermont Avenue, N.W., Suite 301
Washington, D.C. 20005-3521
(202) 371-9195; *www.aavmc.org*

8. **Association of Schools and Colleges of Optometry**
6110 Executive Boulevard, Suite 420
Rockville, MD 20852
(301) 231-5944
admini@opted.org; *www.opted.org*

9. **Association of Schools of Public Health**
1101 15th Street, N.W., Suite 910
Washington, D.C., 20005
(202) 296-1099
info@asph.org; *www.asph.org*

10. **Roman Explore Health Careers**
www.explorehealthcareers.org

Publications for the Health Professions

1. **300 Ways to Put Your Talent to Work in the Health Field**

   Single copy, $15 member,
   $18.00 non-member
   National Health Council
   1730 M Street, N.W., Suite 500
   Washington, D.C. 20036
   (202) 785-3910;
   *www.nationalhealthcouncil.org/
   pubs/pubs_index.htm*

2. **Autsin, L., What's Holding You Back? 8 Critical Choices for Women's Success**

   $14.00
   Basic Books, 2000
   *www.perseusbooksgroup.com/basic/
   home.jsp*

3. **Bickel, J., Women in Medicine: Getting In, Growing & Advancing**

   $38.95
   Sage, 2000
   (805) 499-9774; *www.sagepub.com*

4. **Educational Survival Skills Study Guide**

   Free
   Office of Statewide Health
   Planning and Development
   Health Professions Career
   Opportunity Program
   400 R Street, Suite 330
   Sacramento, CA 95811-6213
   *www.oshpd.ca.gov/HWDD/pdfs/
   StudySkills.pdf*

5. **Financial Advice and Health Careers Resources Directory for Students**

   Free
   Office of Statewide Health
   Planning and Development
   Health Professions Careers
   Opportunity Program
   400 R Street, Suite 330
   Sacramento, CA 95811-6213
   *www.oshpd.ca.gov/HWDD/pdfs/
   FinancialAdvice.pdf*

6. **The Journal for Minority Medical Students**

   $5.00, published quarterly
   Spectrum Unlimited
   1194A Buckhead Crossing
   Woodstock, GA 30189
   (770) 852-2671, (504) 433-5040

7. **Kaltreider, Nancy B., Dilemmas of a Double Life, Women Balancing Careers and Relationship**

   $49.95
   Jason Aronson, Inc., 1997
   (800) 462-6420;
   www.rowmanlittlefield.com/Catalog/

8. **Minorities in Medicine: A Guide for Premedical Students**

   Free
   Office of Statewide Health Planning
   and Development
   Health Professions Career
   Opportunity Program
   400 R Street, Suite 330
   Sacramento, CA 95811-6213
   *www.oshpd.ca.gov/HWDD/pdfs/
   MinoritiesMedicine.pdf*

9. **Minority Student Opportunities in United States Medical Schools**

   $15.00, published bi-annually
   Association of American
   Medical Colleges
   2450 N Street, N.W.
   Washington, D.C. 20037
   (202) 828-0416;
   www.aamc.org/publications

10. **More, E.S., Restoring the Balance: Women Physicians and the Profession of Medicine, 1850–1995.**

    $69.00 hardcover, $33.00 paperback
    Harvard University Press, 2000
    www.hup.harvard.edu

11. **Need a Lift? College Financial Aid Handbook**

    $3.00, plus shipping
    The American Legion
    P.O. Box 36460
    Indianapolis, IN 46236
    888-453-4466;
    www.emblem.legion.org

12. **The Student Guide**

    U.S. Department of Education Federal
    Student Aid Information Center
    P.O. Box 84
    Washington, D.C. 20044-0084
    (800) 4-FED-AID, (800) 433-3243
    *http://studentaid.ed.gov/students/
    attachments/siteresources/Funding
    EduBeyondHighSchool_0809.pdf*

13. **Time Management for Students**

    Free
    Office of Statewide Health
    Planning and Development
    Health Professions Career
    Opportunity Program
    400 R Street, Suite 330
    Sacramento, CA 95811-6213
    *www.oshpd.ca.gov/HWDD/pdfs/
    TimeManagement.pdf*

14. **Wear, D. (Ed), Women in Medical Education: An Anthology of Experience**

    $22.50 hardcover, $21.95 paperback
    SUNY Press, 1996
    *www.sunypress.edu/details.
    asp?id=53512*

15. **The Young Scientist: A Career Guide for Underrepresented Science Graduates**

    $5.00, published annually
    Spectrum Unlimited
    1194A Buckhead Crossing
    Woodstock, GA 30189
    (770) 852-2671, (504) 433-5040

You can change the face of medicine.

From left: Romeu Azevedo, M.D., Candelaria Martin, M.D., Kahlil Johnson, M.D., Claudine Morcos, M.D.

If you really want to make a difference in people's lives, consider a career in medicine. Too many African Americans, Latinos/as, and Native Americans don't get the care they need. Help us change this reality. Log on to **AspiringDocs.org™**, a new resource from the Association of American Medical Colleges, to learn more.

AAMC
Tomorrow's Doctors, Tomorrow's Cures®

© 2010 AAMC

MCAT | **AAMC**
Medical College
Admission Test

Available Now . . .
"The Official Guide to the MCAT Exam"

Inside You Will Find....

- Passages and questions from actual MCAT exams

- Detailed analyses of both the correct and incorrect answers

- Tips to help you come up with the right solutions

- An analysis of the types of questions you'll find on the exam

- Sample essays and scoring analyses

- The "difficulty levels" of questions, revealing what percentages of examinees answered correctly in the real-life test

- Data that show you how your scores compare to those who apply to medical school

- Data to help determine how likely you are to increase or decrease your scores upon a retake, and by how many points

- A look at how MCAT scores factor into the admissions decision, with insights from a former associate dean of admissions

- Data that show what percentage of applicants were admitted to medical school, based on MCAT scores and GPAs combined

- *and much more!*

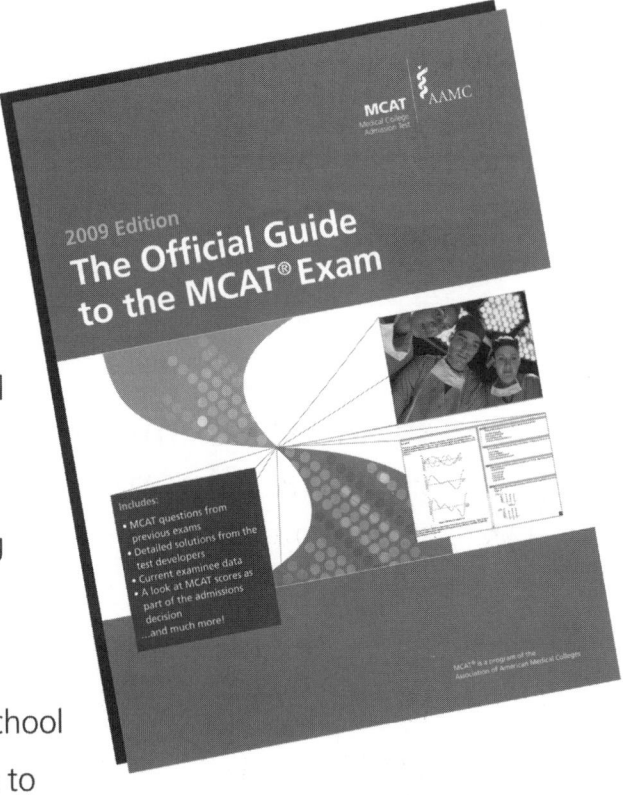

For pricing and ordering information, please visit www.aamc.org/officialmcatguide

MCAT® is a program of the
Association of American Medical Colleges

Questions about Financing Your Medical School Education?
We've got answers: www.aamc.org/first

Applicants - see the library of FIRST Fact Sheets for information on:

- Cost of Applying to Med School
- Financial Aid Process
- Borrowing 101: Intro to Credit
- Budgeting Basics/Interactive Worksheet
- Credit Card Debt
- And numerous other topics

Most US Medical School financial aid offices use AAMC FIRST Fact Sheets as a resource. Shouldn't you?

FIRST *for Medical Education*

Make sure you know the basics. Financial Literacy 101 has quick modules on crucial information for medical students. Invest a few minutes to learn more at

http://aamc.financialliteracy101.org/welcome.cfm

Association of
American Medical Colleges

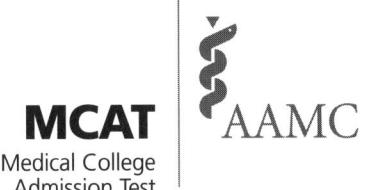
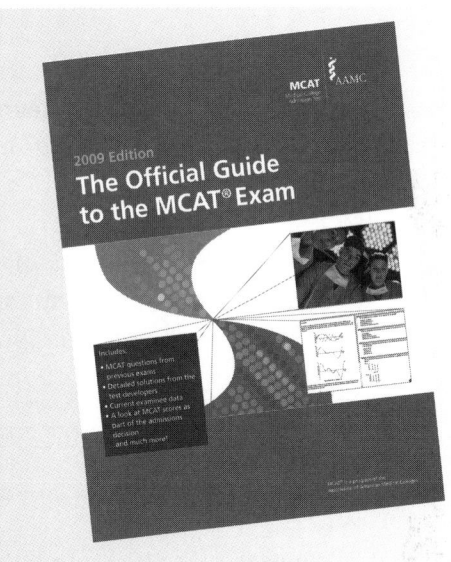
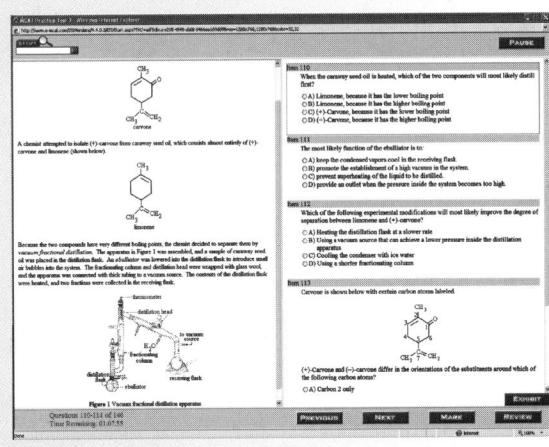

MCAT
Medical College
Admission Test

AAMC

Financial Assistance for MCAT Accommodations

The MCAT Program is pleased to offer a new financial assistance program for MCAT examinees who were previously diagnosed with a disability or medical condition but need updated, current documentation to apply for test accommodations.

To apply:

- If you haven't already, you must receive approval for the AAMC Fee Assistance Program (FAP) before applying for MCAT financial assistance. For details about other FAP benefits and application information, please visit www.aamc.org/fap.

- Apply for the financial assistance early!

- Up to $500 value.

Visit our website for more information, including eligibility details, the application, and technical assistance.

www.aamc.org/mcat/accomodations

MCAT® is a program of the
Association of American Medical Colleges